JOHN J. BAXEVANIS

THE WINE REGIONS OF AMERICA

GEOGRAPHICAL REFLECTIONS AND APPRAISALS

VINIFERA WINE GROWERS JOURNAL
Stroudsburg, Pennsylvania

Library of Congress Catalogue-in-Publication Data

Baxevanis, John J., 1938-
The Wine Regions of America; Geographical Reflections and Appraisals
ISBN 0-922983-51-8
1. Wine and winemaking--United States. 2. Geography--United States
Bibliography
Includes Index.
"Library of Congress Catalog Card Number" 92-60540

Printed in the United States of America

Cover: The Stags Leap District, Shafer Vineyards, used with permission, Shafer Vineyards, 6154 Silverado Trail, Napa, CA 94558, with much appreciation.

Author: Dr. John J. Baxevanis, a graduate of the City University of New York, Indiana University, and the University of North Carolina, teaches geography in one of the State Universities of Pennsylvania. He has published several books on Greece, geography, and is currently editor of the Vinifera Wine Growers Journal. He has written extensively in the field of viticulture and enology, and is also the author of *The Wines of Bordeaux and Western France*, and *The Wines of Champagne, Burgundy, Eastern and Southern France*. Please direct all inquiries to the above address.

FOR MAGDA

For Patience and Endurance

and to

RUSSELL

For Loyalty

FOREWORD

On an average day in America, 7 million cows are milked, and 480 million cups of coffee, 5.2 billion ounces of soft drinks, and 720,000 gallons of grape wine are consumed. This translates to about .7 ounces of wine (out of approximately 64 total liquid ounces) for every citizen and foreign visitor. This book is the story of this small economic activity and associated human behavior pattern in America. Its anthological purpose is to guide the ordinary wine lover through the bewildering array of wines currently on the market, a bit of history, a geographical understanding, a description of the major appellations, a critical review of past and contemporary consumption patterns along with the vast changes that have influenced the present viticultural spatial patterns.

What makes America different is that serious wine-making is a relatively recent business, unlike portions of Europe and the Middle East where its history transcends many millenniums. Pommard, for example, has been continuously cultivated in vineyards since 1005, but in America the premier Vinifera grape growing regions east of the Rocky Mountains--Lubbock, Texas, and eastern Long Island, were both first planted in commercial vineland in the early 1970s. Therefore, the unfolding of American viticulture from the initial settlement by Europeans is a rich and colorful chapter in American history. While American wines were never taken seriously until recently, they have assumed a major, more exalted position since 1970. The days when France was considered the leader in the production of quality dry, red and white table and sparkling wines have long past. America, despite the lack of history, pageantry and a sophisticated cuisine, has quickly bridged the gap as its wine industry has evolved into the most impressive and progressive in the world.

A few words about statistics and data presented. Winery addresses refer to US postal location; planted vine acreage figures (furnished by winery principals and or public relations individuals) include land owned by the owner, partners, winery, and leased land. As a result, figures vary widely as they are subject to change. It is estimated that more than two-thirds of all American wineries purchase wine grapes, and because the source varies, wine quality and consistency of the final product is highly variable. Detailed description of wines, therefore, becomes unnecessary and misleading. Winery founding date can refer to any of the following: bonding date, purchase of property, vineyard development, first crush, winery building date, or first wine release. Production in cases should never be related to acreage because it is common practice for wineries to buy wine from each other and sell it under their own label. Not included are approximately 200 additional wine labels produced by individuals and corporations through custom crush and negociants.

All statistical information is taken from the U.S. Census, Department of Agriculture, and other Federal Departments and Agencies, State Crop Reporting Agencies, County Agricultural Agents, Grape Grower Associations, The Wine Institute, other similar organizations and corporations, and personal interview and survey. Statistics concerning consumption are taken from national organizations headquartered in Washington, D.C., and The Wine Institute. The author has personally visited more than 1,300 wineries, and communicated with more than 1,400 to double check information either verbally or in writing.

In general, historical statistical data (particularly 19th century census material) in the text, tables and graphs, contain minute to significant margins of error. For most of the nineteenth century, and a good deal of the twentieth century, nobody knew exactly how many acres of vines were to be found in each state, and how much wine was produced. The figures contained in agricultural censuses were the product of guess work, both at the county, state and federal level. The first agricultural census was taken in 1840 as part of the sixth decennial census of population, but the degree of standardization was highly erratic. A separate mid-decade census of agriculture was conducted in 1925, 1935, and 1945. From 1954 and 1974, a census of agriculture was taken for the years ending in 4 and 9. Special census occurred in 1978 and 1982, and in theory, at least, after 1982 the agricultural census reverted to a 5-year cycle ending in 2 and 7. U.S. wine production, usually measured by the total amount of standard wine removed from fermenters, including distilled material and increases after fermentation (by amelioration, sweetening, and addition of wine spirits), tax-paid and tax-free withdrawals, is not reliable, but represents the most "official" of all federal statistics. Wine shipments minus imports is just as accurate a statistic. It is obvious, therefore, that due to a lack of reliability and consistency there is also a lack of historical continuity.

Finally, this labor of love could not have been possible without the assistance of many individuals of which the following deserve public and humble acknowledgement: my wife Magda for whom this book is dedicated for her patience and support; the Sonoma County Library, Santa Rosa; The Wine Institute, San Francisco; Hank Wetzel of Alexander Valley Vineyards; Rick Theis of the Sonoma Wine Growers Association; Stanley Miles of Oregon State University; Professor Gerhard Spieler, County historian, Beaufort County, South Carolina; Mr. and Mrs. S.P. Laire of Concord, Massachusetts; Richard Peterson, Napa Valley; Walter Clore, retired agricultural specialist, University of Washington; Barry Lawrence, of Eagle Ridge Winery; Dr. Garth A. Cahoon, Ohio Agricultural Research and Development Center, Wooster; Charles Richard, of Bellerose Winery, Sonoma; Leon E. Sobon, of Shenandoah Vineyards, Sierra Foothills; and Donald G. Holtgrieve, of the Geography Department, California State University, Hayward.

TABLE OF CONTENTS

I

THE WINE REGIONS OF AMERICA

Somewhat more than 21 million acres of the earth's surface are planted in grape vines, of which 815,000, or 3.8 percent, are located in America. It is meaningful that if we add 8,000 growers, 1,519 wineries, and a total grape output of 6 million tons to the economic landscape of continental America, grape-growing and winemaking assume the complexion of a formidable industry. The United States ranks seventh in total world vine acreage, twelfth in wine grape acreage, sixth in wine production, and thirtieth in per capita consumption. With 3.8 per-cent of the world's grape acreage, America produces 5.5 percent of all wine, 17 percent of all table grapes, and 42 percent of all raisins--statistics that articulate a high degree of efficiency. Throughout the decade of the 1980s, Italy produced 22 percent of total world wine, followed by France (21%), Spain (11%), Russia (11%), and Argentina (6.5%). America is also, after France and Italy, the world's third largest wine market.

Table 1.1

WORLD GRAPE ACREAGE (In Thousand Acres)			
Country	1969	1975	1987	Percent
Spain	3,877	4,300	3,798	16.7
Russia	2,597	2,973	2,871	12.6
Italy	3,715	3,460	2,609	11.5
France	3,220	3,262	2,553	11.2
Turkey	2,011	2,088	1,962	8.6
Portugal	835	885	959	4.2
United States	463	751	895	4.0
Romania	819	818	744	3.3
Argentina	706	274	680	3.0
Yugoslavia	651	610	566	2.5
Iran	193	334	460	2.0
Greece	530	492	408	1.8
Hungary	560	509	358	1.6
Bulgaria	481	462	346	1.5
Algeria	734	274	316	1.4
Chile	274	287	277	1.2
Syria	206	198	262	1.1
Germany	205	247	250	1.1
South Africa	238	279	247	1.1
India		215	227	1.0
Brazil	163	166	148	
Mexico	44	86	146	
Austria	114	124	143	
Australia	130	175	141	
Japan	56	72	69	
Other	725	2,100	1,284	
World Total	23,547	25,531	22,719	

Source: Office International de la Vigne et du Vin, Paris, France.

Among the 21 major crops grown in America, grapes, ranking fourth in production and seventh in value, are surpassed only by corn, soybeans, wheat, oats, hay, and tobacco. The number of grape wineries rose rapidly over the past three decades from 300 in 1960, 441 in 1970 (34 states), 700 in 1975, 884 in 1982, to more than 1,519 in 1992 distributed in 41 states, their size varying from small "mom and pop" enterprises to the world's largest. Although the attrition rate is high, newcomers to this fascinating economic endeavor are greater than those failing. Of the 1,519 wineries listed in this book, about 85 percent

were founded after 1970, while fewer than 5 percent, or less than 100, were in existence before 1950. This phenomenal growth is not only related to recent increases in consumption, but to farm winery legislation (Pennsylvania was the first state to enact a farm winery bill in 1968, and since then nearly all states have passed similar laws). About 55 percent of America's wineries are located in California, a state that is responsible for 90 percent of the nation's total output of wine. In terms of consumption, about 73 percent of total in 1991 originated from California, 15 percent from other states, and 12 percent from foreign countries.

Table 1.2

WORLD GRAPE PRODUCTION (In Thousand Tons)			
Country	1965	1975	1987	Percent
Italy	11,767	11,856	12,812	18.3
France	9,823	9,631	10,089	14.4
Russia	4,076	5,952	7,153	10.2
Spain	4,824	5,733	6,828	9.8
United States	4,350	4,366	5,264	7.5
Argentina	2,581	3,246	4,402	6.3
Turkey	3,693	3,609	4,124	5.9
Portugal	2,437	1,200	1,745	2.5
Greece	1,636	1,693	1,672	2.4
Romania	992	1,303	1,569	2.2
Yugoslavia	1,235	1,135	1,460	2.1
South Africa	756	896	1,087	1.6
Chile	606	747	1,016	1.5
Iran	276	882	990	1.4
Germany	711	1,198	986	1.4
Bulgaria	1,470	818	913	1.3
Australia	761	804	863	1.2
Mexico	99	265	717	1.0
Brazil	607	678	644	
Hungary	471	896	565	
Afghanistan	209	408	472	
Syria	227	310	428	
Egypt	99	248	379	
Japan	248	343	338	
World Total	57,819	62,013	69,939	

Source: Office International de la Vigne et du Vin, Paris, France.

Because the North American continent was settled after 1492 by Europeans along the Atlantic and Gulf Coast regions, first attempts at growing native American vines and winemaking were associated with their early settlement. The first attempt to make wine, and perhaps cultivate the vine in Colonial America, was as early as 1564 in northern Florida, 43 years before the Colony of Jamestown was founded. These first attempts along the east coast, important as they were in the viticultural history of America, were not the earliest from a sustained perspective.

While wine was said to have been made in Central America by Spaniards from native grapes in 1518, Vinifera grapes were introduced in Mexico by Cortez in 1524. The vine was cultivated in Mexico City in 1531, in Oaxaca in 1544, and more vineyards were established and wine made from Vinifera grapes in Parras and Coahuila in 1593, and Delicia in 1606. Although the Edict of 1503 made the wine trade a Royal monopoly, wine shortages and production inefficiencies in Spain, and transportation problems could not supply Spanish Colonies in the New World with adequate quantities of wine to meet religious and personal consumption. Consequently, artificial expense and inferior quality led to the first attempts of producing wine in the New World, particularly in Mexico, Chile, Peru, Brazil, Venezuela, and other regions.

Table 1.3

WORLD WINE PRODUCTION (In Million Gallons)				
Country	1938	1968	1980	1989
France	1,274	1,720.3	1,828.2	1,606.7
Italy	1,050	1,723.4	2,286.3	1,579.8
Spain	552	631.4	1,114.9	764.9
Russia	99	489.1	845.4	559.5
Argentina	205	518.4	615.6	536.8
United States	59	182.4	475.5	411.4
Germany	73	159.7	122.4	346.2
Romania	218	150.3	200.8	264.2
South Africa	36	130.1	219.8	251.4
Portugal	239	315.6	268.7	203.7
Algeria	492	271.0	79.5	26.4
Other	855	1,074.3	1,253.1	889.0
World Total	5,152	7,366.0	9,253.1	7,440.0
Source: Office International de la Vigne et du Vin, Paris, France.				

Cortez made a condition to all new land grant holders of Mexico to plant vines, and further attempted to force Indians to grow grapes as well. Surprisingly, early Spanish viticultural attempts in the West Indies and Mexico in the middle of the sixteenth century were so successful Spain banned new vine plantings and the replacement of old vines in Peru in 1569, and in 1595 banned the planting of new and the renewal of old vineyards (by invoking the basic principles of mercantilism) throughout the New World to protect her home export industry. As a consequence, Spanish Colonies began to discover and eventually manufacture alternative alcoholic beverages. Nevertheless, along the fringes of Spanish colonization illicit grape plantings continued; in 1662 Franciscan priests established the Ysleta Mission in present-day Texas, and planted grapes soon after. Although coastal California had been sited as early as 1542, initial Spanish settlement did not begin until 1769. Throughout the southwest, the earliest settlements were mission stations and military outposts, with only the former exhibiting viticultural endeavors, mainly by Franciscan priests.

France in the sixteenth century seriously pondered the possibilities of establishing vineyards in Florida and the lower Mississippi, but initial plantings suffered from disease, and mercantile political and economic suppression. French law encouraged grain production and limited vine acreage (by allocating two-thirds of land for grain) resulting in higher wine prices and a good supply of grain. Spanish and French mercantile policies proved such formidable restraints on wine production that the English began to develop an incipient wine industry along the Atlantic coast. Because England was unable to produce wine

at home, the encouragement of vine plantings and wine production did not constitute a violation of prevailing mercantile policy. Colonial wine production, it was felt, would fill this important economic shortcoming and improve the balance of payments through exports. Unfortunately, this was not to be despite more than 200 years of continuous undertakings.

Figure 1.1

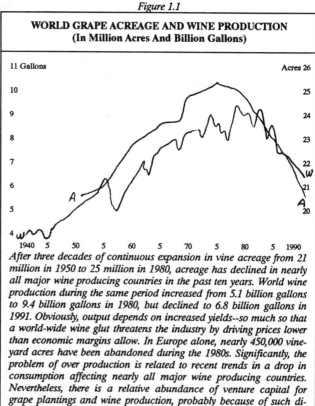

WORLD GRAPE ACREAGE AND WINE PRODUCTION
(In Million Acres And Billion Gallons)

After three decades of continuous expansion in vine acreage from 21 million in 1950 to 25 million in 1980, acreage has declined in nearly all major wine producing countries in the past ten years. World wine production during the same period increased from 5.1 billion gallons to 9.4 billion gallons in 1980, but declined to 6.8 billion gallons in 1991. Obviously, output depends on increased yields--so much so that a world-wide wine glut threatens the industry by driving prices lower than economic margins allow. In Europe alone, nearly 450,000 vineyard acres have been abandoned during the 1980s. Significantly, the problem of over production is related to recent trends in a drop in consumption affecting nearly all major wine producing countries. Nevertheless, there is a relative abundance of venture capital for grape plantings and wine production, probably because of such diverse factors as the mystique of making fine wines and the tax shelters afforded by investments characterized by large infusions of capital and long, uncertain years to profitability. In this kind of climate, it is advisable for wineries to have healthy capital resources.
Source: Office International de la Vigne et du Vin, Paris, France.

From the beginning in the northeastern portion of the nation the geographic diffusion of the grapevine was simple in its distribution as it followed settlement patterns. It was planted along the warmest areas of the Great Lakes, coastal regions, and river valleys. The distribution of native vines was so widespread that the first settlers in practically every Colony, and later in every state in both the United States and Canada, made wine from them, but few, even the indefatigable and dogmatic Thomas Jefferson, could successfully grow Vinifera grapes. Wine made from native grapes was fruity, but subject to a strange "foxy" flavor and high acid content. Because the population along the east coast had a "European" affinity to the types of wines consumed, American-based wines were toyed with, but with time they became the subject of scorn and eventually relegated a secondary position in the pantheon of wine production. Along the Atlantic coast south of New Jersey, however, the spread of Vinifera and Labrusca vines came to an abrupt halt as Pierce's Disease and a host of humidity-related diseases decimated commercial cultivation for these two types of grapes. Even worse, the Spanish element was lacking because, in addition to the grapevine, two associated Mediterranean foods--wheat and olive--could not be grown successfully in the humid subtropical environment of southeastern America. Consequently, the Spanish avoided the Atlantic coastal plain and the Gulf Coast, and were replaced by an English population that preferred beer and distilled beverages to wine.

The grape vine (Vitis vinifera) was first domesticated during the Mesolithic period in the area of present-day eastern Turkey, southern Caucasus, and the foothill region of the Tigris-Euphrates area. The diffusion of winegrowing proceeded very rapidly with the westward spread of sedentary human settlement and reached nearly all areas bordering the eastern Mediterranean by 2,000 B.C. The diffusion process did not spread to the north, south, and east due to the dominance of nomadic people. The Greeks diffused grapegrowing and winemaking throughout the Mediterranean, southwestern Europe, coastal Ukraine, and the Crimea. Vase paintings show grape cultivation, harvesting, and winemaking as common activities among the early Greeks. Pliny in the first century A.D. described nearly 100 different varieties of grapes, the existence of 50 different wines, and gave a detailed account of vine training methods. By 1492, three different types of grapes were cultivated: wine grapes, table grapes, and raisin grapes. Largely for religious reasons, wine grapes were cultivated by Christian communities, and table and raisin grapes by Moslems, the latter mainly in the Iberian and Balkan peninsulas, north Africa, and the Middle East. Because European settlement proceeded in a westward direction from the initial point of settlement along the Atlantic Ocean, early settlers encountered a profusion of native grapes. Once made into wine, Europeans did not like the "foxy" flavor or aroma, and immediately began to import Vinifera vines to America. It is reported that Lord Delaware in 1619 was the first American to cultivate, with little success, Vinifera vines.

Despite the physical and cultural obstacles, minor quantities of wine were made and reported for the first time in the 1810 census figures, published in Philadelphia in 1814. At this time, America produced but 11,755 gallons of wine, of which 9,230 gallons were made from currants and 2,525 from grapes. Of the total quantity reported, 4,875 gallons were made in Rhode Island, 4,480 in Pennsylvania, and 2,400 in Indiana. The report mentions that the Moravian community of Bethlehem, Pennsylvania made wine principally from currants. Although the Census did not enumerate detailed figures on domestic winemaking output, it is significant to note that after 200 years of effective and sustained European settlement in America, commercial grape wine production was less than 3,000 gallons.

The Census of 1840 lists total wine production as 124,734 gallons, a figure that also included non-grape wine. Of the 24 states and the District of Columbia, North Carolina, with 28,752 gallons, or 22 percent of the nation's total output, was the leading state, followed by Pennsylvania, Virginia, Ohio, Indiana, and New Jersey. Orange County, North Carolina, with 8,109 gallons, was the leading county in the nation in terms of production. Highly surprising is the fact that half the nation's wine was made in the humid southeast, and that Connecticut, Rhode Island, and Maine all made more wine than Massachusetts, the latter the most heavily populated state in New England. Ten years later, the Federal Census reported, for the first time, statistics for both wine production and grape acreage. It showed that the largest wine producing states were: California with 58,055 gallons, Ohio with 48,207 gallons, and Pennsylvania with 25,590 gallons.

Table 1.4

WINE PRODUCTION BY STATE AND SELECTED COUNTIES: 1840 CENSUS

State	Gallons	Counties Where Wine Was Produced
Alabama	177	Madison 100; Washington 75
Connecticut	2,666	Fairfield 884; Hartford 762; New Hampshire 682
Delaware	322	Sussex 317
Georgia	8,647	Taliaferro 820; Putnam 1,397; Carroll 1,477; Campbell 1,433
Illinois	474	Madison 450
Indiana	10,265	Sullivan 8,054; Miami 304
Kentucky	2,209	Livingston 300; Greene 1,140
Louisiana	2,884	Livingston 2,884
Maine	2,236	York 1,118
Maryland	7,585	Baltimore 2,419; Dorchester 2,982; Washington 942; Montgomery 524
Massachusetts	193	
Mississippi	12	
Missouri	22	St. Charles 22
New Hampshire	94	
New Jersey	9,416	Warren 7,000; Somerset 265; Bergen 626; Essex 306; Burlington 843; Hudson 129; Monmouth 111
New York	6,799	Jefferson 3,230; Tomkins 1,600; Suffolk 1,026; Westchester 227; Queens 168; Osego 98; Monroe 105
North Carolina	28,752	Orange 8,109; Washington 4,075; Beaufort 1,170; Cumberland 785; Granville 1,700; Haywood 1,108; Wayne 582; Wilkes 1,075; Tyrrell 1,825; Robeson 707; Randolph 310; Pitt 439; Nash 1,073; Martin 1,258
Ohio	11,524	Hamilton 1,627; Miami 955; Richland 7,724
Pennsylvania	14,328	Berks 2,882; Bucks 441; Chester 640; Cumberland 397; Dauphin 172; Franklin 1,434; Monroe 1,713; Montgomery 866; Philadelphia 377; York 155; Beaver 3,270; Indiana 341; Allegheny 885
Rhode Island	803	Providence 405
South Carolina	643	Chesterfield 200; Horry 156; Marion 146
Tennessee	653	Wilson 170; Sumner 150; Rutherford 225
Vermont	94	
Virginia	13,911	Albemarle 960; Carolina 622; Fauquier 1,226; Hanover 1,148; Sussex 625; Stafford 353; Orange 567; Southampton 625; Loudon 470; Prince George 245; Prince Edward 496; Rockingham 697; Clarke 339; Rockbridge 981; Frederick 660; Harrison 400
Washington D.C.	25	
Total, U.S.	124,734	

Source: U.S. Census.

By 1860, out of a total 1.5 million gallons, Ohio became the premier wine producer with 568,617 gallons, followed by California with 246,518 gallons, and New York with 179,848 gallons. Although all three censuses were subject to considerable error they do show that the American government thought the industry important enough to be included with more formidable crops such as cotton and tobacco. The Department of Agriculture considers this as the certifiable date of the birth of the modern American wine industry. The decade of the 1860s is distinguished for many substantial viticultural developments along Lake Erie, the Hudson, Ohio, and Missouri rivers, and the Sierra Foothill region of California. Whereas Missouri in 1870 became the nations leading wine producer, a combination of national overproduction and financial speculation caused prices to decline, and, as a consequence, vineyard abandonment and winery failures accelerated. Yet, by the end of the decade, heavy European migration revived the industry so that between 1881 and 1888 vineyard acreage increased nearly fivefold, and by 1895 California alone was producing more than 20 million gallons of wine annually.

Table 1.5

WINE PRODUCED BY STATE AND SELECTED COUNTIES, 1860 CENSUS		
State	Gallons	Counties Were Wine Was Produced
Alabama	18,267	Dallas 2,398; Sumpter 1,124; Tuscaloosa 1,341;
Washington		2,311; 42 counties made wine.
Arkansas	1,004	Union 565; Phillips 196; 11 counties made wine.
California	246,518	Los Angeles 162,980; Santa Barbara 10,550; Napa 8,745; Sonoma 1,990; Tuolumne 5,825; Yuba 2,180; Solano 3,095; Santa Clara 3,721; Sacramento 4,550; San Bernardino 8,520; Mariposa 10,700; El Dorado 6,464; Contra Costa 2,527; Butte 2,300; Alameda 8,040; 24 counties made wine.
Connecticut	46,783	Fairfield 16,599; New Haven 12,048; Hartford 6,905; 8 counties made wine.
Delaware	683	New Castle 530; Kent 153.
Florida	336	
Georgia	27,646	Wilkes 3,038; Warren 1,517; Monroe 1,400; 45 counties made wine.
Illinois	50,690	
Indiana	102,895	Vanderburgh 10,396; Wayne 1,476; Switzerland 4,314; Posey 1,499; Ohio 2,051; Morgan 1,661; 34 counties made wine.
Iowa	3,369	Mills 519; Muscatine 375; Van Buren 286; 13 counties made wine.
Kansas	583	Franklin 242; Atchison 100; 11 counties made wine.
Kentucky	9,994	Thirty counties made wine.
Louisiana	2,912	St. Martins 2,100; 7 counties made wine.
Maine	3,164	15 counties made wine.
Maryland	3,222	Washington 935; Prince George's 2,100; 7 counties made wine.
Massachusetts	20,915	Worcester 10,464; Middlesex 3,459; 12 counties made wine.
Michigan	14,427	Oakland 3,362; Berrien 1,236; Calhoon 1,195; 30 counties made wine.
Minnesota	412	Five counties made wine.
Mississippi	7,262	Thirty-four counties made wine.
Missouri	27,827	Warren 1,801; Ste. Genevieve 2,580; St. Charles 774; 26 counties made wine.
Nebraska	671	
New Hampshire	9,401	Ten counties made wine.
New Jersey	21,083	Burlington 6,672; Hunterdon 4,328; Somerset 2,205; 20 counties made wine.
New Mexico	8,260	Socorro 4,140; Bernallilo 2,630.
New York	179,848	Orange 25,238, Ontario 3,090; Monroe 5,485; Dutchess 23,302; Yates 1,130; Westchester 1,829; Washington 1,342; Ulster 11,597; Suffolk 1,303; Seneca 1,545; 56 counties made wine.
North Carolina	54,064	Bladen 5,787; Chowan 2,250; Columbus 5,103; Edgecombe 2,320; Halifax 2,788; Hartford 2,199; more than 60 counties made wine.
Ohio	568,617	Montgomery 224,005; Warren 123,541; Scioto 83,685; 33 counties made wine.
Oregon	2,603	Washington 790; 9 counties made wine.
Pennsylvania	38,621	Lancaster 6,842; Allegheny 3,148; Beaver 3,298; Berks 2,488; Chester 1,744; Lehigh 2,566; Montgomery 2,452; 26 counties made wine.
Rhode Island	507	Providence 284; 4 counties made wine.
South Carolina	24,964	Barnwell 5,619; Abbeville 2,437; Anderson 2,553; Edgefield, 245; Marion 2,635; 12 counties made wine.
Tennessee	13,566	Sixteen counties made wine.
Texas	14,199	Victoria 4,491; 11 counties made wine.
Utah	60	
Vermont	2,923	
Virginia	40,808	Greenville 5,036; Chesterfield 4,763; 22 counties made wine.
Wisconsin	6,278	
Washington	179	
Washington, D.C.	118	
Total, U.S.	1,575,679	Does not include 9,288 for territories.

Source: U.S. Census.

It is intriguing to note that while all this excitement was part of the contemporary, dynamic and exciting viticultural history, California was but a minor grape growing and wine producing state. It grew the mediocre Mission grape, made poor wine, and hardly exported any to other states. In 1860 California was producing 250,000 gallons of wine. But while the American economy of the 1870s

had suffered a major industrial and agricultural depression, wine production in California continued to grow faster than consumption. Due to increased immigration after the discovery of gold, acreage grew rapidly and by 1880 there were more than 130,000 grape acres in the entire state. Then, as phylloxera spread rapidly in France reducing production by half and wine exports to America dropped precipitously, California wine prices rose which further encouraged new plantings and production facilities to be built. The period between 1878 and 1885 saw the entire Bay area south of San Francisco overtaken by wine fever. Many vineyards were established, many wineries founded, the population steadily grew to new levels, and in 1881 the Santa Clara Viticultural Society was founded by Charles Wetmore. Throughout these rapid, if not tumultuous years, the relative share of "eastern states" began to decline precipitously, and has since stabilized at less than 10 percent of both total acreage and total wine production, as percent of national aggregates.

Table 1.6

1880 CENSUS SHOWING VINE ACREAGE, WINE PRODUCTION, AND VALUE		
State	Acreage In Vines	Wine Gallons	Value
Alabama	1,111	422,672	$399,765
Arkansas	893	72,750	112,401
California	32,368	13,557,155	4,046,865
Connecticut	64	5,336	6,076
Delaware	125	4,050	4,050
Florida	83	11,180	15,415
Georgia	2,991	903,244	1,335,521
Illinois	3,810	1,047,875	809,547
Indiana	3,851	99,566	91,719
Iowa	1,470	334,970	346,398
Kansas	3,542	226,249	190,330
Kentucky	1,850	81,170	80,908
Maine	71	1,500	2,850
Maryland	699	21,405	19,151
Massachusetts	227	6,338	10,050
Michigan	2,266	62,831	75,617
Minnesota	63	2,831	2,446
Mississippi	432	209,845	310,532
Missouri	7,376	1,824,297	1,320,050
Nebraska	280	5,767	8,982
New Jersey	1,967	215,122	223,866
New Mexico	3,150	908,500	980,250
New York	12,646	584,148	387,308
North Carolina	2,639	334,701	268,819
Ohio	9.973	1,632,073	1,627,926
Oregon	126	16,900	9,240
Pennsylvania	1,944	114,535	128.097
Rhode Island	55	262	516
South Carolina	193	16,988	22,356
Tennessee	1,128	64,797	90,796
Texas	850	35,528	44,704
Utah	658	114,975	175,825
Virginia	2,999	232,479	200,045
West Virginia	466	71,026	61,461
Wisconsin	217	10,968	15,559
Total	181,583	23,453,827	$13,426,174

Note: Figures are questionable. Nevertheless, this attempt gives a good indication of the dimensions of the American wine industry in 1880.
Source: Bureau of the Census.

The 1880 Agricultural Census (the first in which a special grape report was appended) gives an interesting picture of viticulture in the United States. A little more than 110 years ago America was a nation of 50 million, cultivating 181,583 acres, and producing 23.4 million gallons of wine. Of the 35 states growing grapes and producing wine, California ranked first (32,368 acres, 32%), followed by New York (12,646 acres, 12%), Ohio (9,973

Table 1.7

NUMBER OF GRAPE GROWERS AND VINE ACRES, 1890		
State and County	Number of Growers	Acres
CALIFORNIA		
Alameda	161	6,826
Amador	15	204
Butte	781	
Calaveras	36	404
Colusa	26	443
Contra Costa	177	3,142
El Dorado	41	1,512
Fresno	2,053	49,800
Ynyo	24	53
Kern	300	5,895
Lake	12	175
Marin	13	502
Mendocino	20	204
Merced	64	1,846
Monterey	10	65
Napa	707	18,229
Nevada	18	220
Orange	6	144
Placer	135	2,285
Sacramento	321	4,630
San Benito	3	175
San Bernardino	375	3,615
San Diego	203	4,627
San Joaquin	88	1,246
San Luis Obispo	34	471
San Mateo	30	789
Santa Barbara	44	270
Santa Clara	724	11,523
Santa Cruz	148	1,684
Shasta	199	468
Solano	134	3,527
Sonoma	851	22,683
Stanislaus	9	619
Sutter	46	370
Tehama	30	4,012
Tulare	380	9,919
Tuolumne	53	320
Yolo	57	3,700
Yuba	32	693
ALABAMA	18	43
ARKANSAS	37	341(?)
COLORADO	4	5
NORTH & SOUTH DAKOTA	6	9
WASHINGTON, D.C.	1	2
FLORIDA	26	241
GEORGIA	102	409
ILLINOIS	183	689
INDIANA	70	101
IOWA	38	204
KANSAS	36	38
KENTUCKY	105	134
LOUISIANA	20	18
MARYLAND	7	94
MASSACHUSETTS	39	41
MICHIGAN	55	194
MINNESOTA	17	16
MISSISSIPPI	27	19
MISSOURI	201	791
NEW MEXICO	4	8
OTHER, NEW ENGLAND	2	6
NEW JERSEY	165	348
NEW YORK	800	4,692
OHIO	497	2,145(?)
NORTH CAROLINA	102	1,204
PENNSYLVANIA	58	629
RHODE ISLAND	8	7
SOUTH CAROLINA	79	393
TENNESSEE	102	1,204
TEXAS	74	159
VIRGINIA	160	1,240
WEST VIRGINIA	5	14
WISCONSIN	3	8
TOTAL, U.S.	11,208	182,736

Note: *Estimated total wine production in 1880 was 23,453,827 gallons. In 1890, 80 percent of all grapes in the eastern region were for table use.*
Source: *US Department of Agriculture.*

acres, 9.8%), Missouri (7,376 acres, 7%), the remaining 39 percent being distributed among 31 other states. This is a significant departure from the present picture where most of the states east of the Rocky Mountains have experienced radical declines, while Oregon and Washington have become major grape and quality wine producers.

As the frontier expanded westward and the nation's population continued to grow, grape acreage increased. If the 1890 Agricultural Census figures are to be believed, grape acreage during the 1880s increased to 401,261, nearly 23 percent of the total grown east of the Rocky Mountains, of which half the acreage was concentrated in New York and Pennsylvania mainly for table grape production. With three-quarters of total national acreage concentrated in California, the dominance of that state in the vinicultural affairs of America has never been questioned. Increased vine acreage produced overproduction and a glut of grapes, wine, and brandy. A severe agricultural depression gripped the nation during 1891-1892, and a major industrial depression the following year prompted the formation of the California Winemakers Corporation that competed with the "wine ring," a small group of wholesalers, or the California Wine Association. A related discomfort for portions of California was a phylloxera outbreak, particularly in coastal counties. Nevertheless, the national economy, as well as the wine industry, revived only to create another boom period around the turn of the century.

In 1899 the largest grape producing states were California (approximately 55.5 percent of the national crop), followed by New York, Ohio, Pennsylvania, and Michigan. Over the next two decades, and continuing to the present, the implosion of commercial grape production consolidated from 1,992 counties in 1879 to 877 counties in 1909, and the dominance of California becomes apparent. Three major areas of grape production came to dominate grape growing at the beginning of the century: California (coastal counties north of San Francisco, the delta region, south and east of Modesto), Southwestern Michigan, and the Chautauqua area of New York. The Finger Lakes region and the lower Hudson River region of New York, coastal North Carolina, and the highly diffusive area of the present-day Corn Belt were minor grape growing regions. Interestingly, the 1914 Statistical Atlas of the U.S. published by the Bureau of the Census does not indicate any appreciable production for Texas, New Mexico, or Arizona for the year 1909. The concentration of acreage for California represents 77 percent of the national total. New York, the nation's second largest producer, was followed by Michigan. Production of grapes decreased between 1899 and 1909 in every area of the country except California, and, to a minor degree, portions of the mid-Atlantic states, the midwest, the Rocky Mountain states, and North Carolina. During this intercensus period wine production increased from 8,246,000 gallons to 18,636,000 gallons, with California alone producing more than 16 million gallons, nearly three times as much as 10 years earlier. While grape production was experiencing major geographic readjustments, wine production had to struggle with the cacophony of prohibitionist groups.

The Census of 1900 reports the distribution of grape vines, pounds of grapes produced, and value of product for twelve states that reported more than 2 million vines (3,500 acres). Of the total, the Census Office reports that eighteen counties had more than 93% of all vines. In order, the most important in California were Fresno, Sonoma, Santa Clara, Napa, King, and Sacramento, that collectively represented two-thirds of the planted acreage. In New York, Chautauqua, Yates, Steuben, Ulster, Ontario, and Erie counties collectively had 80 percent of all vines. Cuyahoga, Ottowa, Lake, Erie, Lorain, and Ashtabula, with two-thirds of total vines, were the most important in Ohio. Unlike contemporary features, two of the six California counties were located on the coast, all New York counties were located in the Finger Lakes and Lake Erie regions, and all Ohio counties were sited along Lake Erie.

Figure 1.2

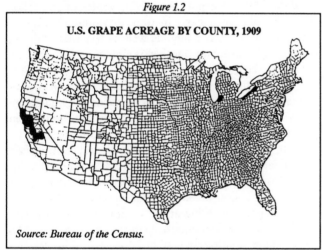

U.S. GRAPE ACREAGE BY COUNTY, 1909

Source: Bureau of the Census.

Between 1895 and the advent of World War I, wine production advanced very strongly, and came to an abrupt halt with the passage of the Eighteenth Amendment of October eighteenth, 1919. Popularly known as the Volstead Act, it was an unusual piece of legislation that forbade "the manufacture, sale, or transportation of intoxicating liquors." Its passage was followed by increased grape acreage and a significant increase in the per capita consumption of alcoholic beverages, including wine. The effect of Repeal was that home-made wine at first remained at Prohibition levels (35 million gallons), in sharp contrast to the negligible quantities before Volstead. Commercially produced wine increased from 38 million gallons in 1934 to just under 100 million gallons in 1939. Of the 64 million gallons of American-produced wine in 1938, California made 55 million, or 86 percent, the remainder being made in other states, primarily New York. Over the next 30 years, the percentage of consumption originating in California declined by 5 percent, while the rest of the nation maintained market share, the remainder absorbed by rising imports.

The Eighteenth Amendment, which virtually destroyed all the advancements of the past 100 years, marked the death of the American wine industry, and Repeal, fourteen years later, its rebirth. Prohibition forced the closing of more than 1,000 wineries, increased vine acreage of inferior grapes, increased the production of poor "basement" wine, and poor wine turned the American consumer away from domestic table wines to fortified wines and distilled beverages. The "noble experiment" also precipitated an avalanche of demand for grapes for home winemaking as well as large scale illegal wine output. The severe grape shortage led to the planting of 300,000 new vine acres during the 1920-1926 period, mostly inferior, thick-skinned grapes. Just as quickly, demand dried up leaving the industry with overproduction, declining prices, and quality deficient grapes that could not produce fine wines and recover the lost market during the fourteen year hiatus. Prohibition was followed by a labyrinth of state regulations that discouraged wine sales, consumption, and made it easier for the average American to consume imported wine. Wine consumption, 67 million gallons in 1938, steadily rose to 213.7 million gallons over the next 30 years. Yet, while this figure is impressive, consumption barely kept pace with population growth.

Table 1.8

VITICULTURAL FEATURES BY SELECTED STATE, 1913			
State	No. of Vines	Pounds of Grapes	Value
California	90,686,458	721,433,400	$5,622,825
New York	29,636,216	247,698,056	2,763,711
Ohio	13,772,800	79,173,873	992,745
Pennsylvania	4,711,039	47,125,437	639,518
Michigan	5,232,450	41,530,369	503,268
Illinois	3,008,888	20,009,400	383,169
Indiana	2,570,579	18,651,380	350,304
Kansas	5,762,700	15,786,019	296,649
Missouri	3,546,319	13,783,656	314,807
Georgia	2,376,904	8,330,485	170,603
Iowa	2,072,101	7,403,900	166,360
Oklahoma	3,542,034	6,111,000	128,500

Source: Bureau of the Census, 13th Census, 1909-1910, published in 1913.

While the combined and cumulative affects of Repeal, recovery from the Great Depression in the late 1930s, the onset of World War II, and the post-World War II economic boom period did much to resurrect the American wine industry, growth was slow, particularly the conversion of the product mix from sweet, fortified wines to varietal table wines. Throughout the recovery, overdue and tedious in the beginning of the 1960s, the wine industry exhibited steady and diligent growth patterns in the second half of the decade. Since then, the growth of the American wine industry has been remarkable. Estimated wine expenditures grew from $1 billion in 1967 to nearly $8 billion in 1983. Between 1968 and 1972, consumption rose from 213 million gallons in 1968 to 337 million gallons, and wine grape acreage exploded from 125,000 in

1968 to 296,000 in 1973 (more than 114,000 acres were planted in that year alone). This optimistic spirit even motivated President Lyndon Johnson to activate a "drink American wine" campaign in the White House. Les Amis du Vin was founded in Washington D.C. in 1964, and thirteen years later the Society of Wine Educators. In 1969, for the first time since Prohibition, table wines outsold dessert wines. That same year wine shipments totaled 172 million gallons, or five times greater than in 1935. Since then, acreage has grown to 815,000, and consumption to more than 550 million gallons.

Table 1.9

U.S. WINERY DISTRIBUTION					
State	1936	1974	1985	1991	Percent
California	723	311	676	820	54.0
Oregon	16		46	96	6.3
New York	131	42	755	95	6.3
Washington	25	7		91	6.0
Virginia			44	48	3.2
Pennsylvania	4	51	47	47	3.1
Ohio	112	29	48	43	2.8
Missouri				28	1.8
Texas				27	1.8
New Mexico				20	1.3
Michigan	14	11	31	19	1.3
New Jersey	57	17	18	19	1.3
Tennessee				14	.9
Indiana				12	.9
Maryland				12	.9
Connecticut				10	.7
Idaho				10	.7
Iowa				10	.7
West Virginia				9	
Massachusetts				8	
Georgia				7	
Illinois		9	6	7	
Wisconsin				7	
Arkansas				6	
Arizona				6	
Colorado				6	
North Carolina				6	
Alabama				5	
Florida				5	
South Carolina				5	
Rhode Island				4	
Minnesota				4	
Mississippi				4	
Kansas				2	
Utah				2	
Hawaii				1	
Montana				1	
Nevada				1	
Oklahoma				1	
New Hampshire				1	
United States	1,245	544	1,289	1,519	

Source: U.S. Department of Agriculture

The number of wineries for selected years have increased as follows: 1970, 193; 1976, 585; 1977, 619; 1978, 676; 1979, 724; 1980, 822; 1981, 934; 1982, 1,028; 1983, 1,114; 1984, 1206; 1985, 1,289; and 1992, 1,519. In 1991 41 states made grape wine, while in 1970 only 22 states made wine. Of the 1,519 wineries in America, there were fewer than 200 in 1970. California, the nation's largest wine producing state, increased the number of wineries from 100 in 1970 to 700 in 1991. An analysis of founding dates illustrates the fact that twice as many wineries were created during the 1980s than during the 1970s, and in that decade twice as many wineries were created than had existed during the previous 200 years. Along the west coast many have been inspired by wealthy individuals wishing to produce fine, world-class wines, and many foreign interests. In the rest of the nation, the proliferation of wineries depended on changing state legislation, primarily the passage of farm winery laws that make financial solvency possible. Most important, the level of quality wines produced during the past 21 years advanced almost exponentially. Because American consumers became more knowledgeable and, consequently, more particular about wines in the 1960s, the industry responded in kind with higher quality grape varieties, less blending in the production of generic wines, vintage dating, estate production, and a greater awareness of viticultural areas.

The euphoria began to stumble in the following decade when more than 200,000 acres of grapes were planted leading to another bust in the continuous "grape and wine" economic cycle. The overplanting that occurred in the 1920s and 1970s had much in common, the former foolishly mistaking the durability of demand, and the latter mistaking the magnitude and depth of the new demand for varietal wines. In both cases, too many grapes were planted in a country that did not sustain similar consumption rates. While the upward trend of the 1970-1983 period has reversed itself, it is debatable whether current market conditions are an indication of long term factors.

With the progressive sophistication of winemaking techniques, American consumers became exposed to an ever increasing number of quality American wines than had previously been available. Throughout the 1960s and 1970s, magazine and newsletter foundings exploded, wine appreciation clubs proliferated, and college wine courses offered for credit became commonplace everywhere in America. Suddenly winegrowing became a glamorous occupation with some winemakers assuming the status of a national celebrity. Within the span of one generation, grape production and winemaking quickly spread to hitherto unheard of places: Wenatchee, Middleburg, North Fork, Traverse City, Lubbock, Asheville, and Truth or Consequences. And while the overwhelming amount of wine continues to emanate from California, just as it did for the past 100 years, the community of grape-growers and winemakers has spread like *flor* to nearly every state in the nation. Today grapes are commercially produced and wine commercially made in 41 states, a remarkable achievement considering the fact that farming was a major economic endeavor in the area north of 125th Street in Manhattan, New York City, 100 years ago.

The unprecedented growth in the number of wineries since 1970 underscores an intensified interest in this industry. Along with growth, the wine industry has also experienced explosive structural changes. With the increase in wine demand in the 1970s, there was a boom in the number of firms, foreign and domestic, that acquired an interest in wineries. Firms with primary investments as diverse as tobacco, real estate, pharmaceuticals, and food processing have found the industry tantalizing, if not always profitable. Therefore, many investors have entered and quickly departed: large corporations have bought and sold wineries, grape growers have purchased wineries, and many wineries have purchased vineyards.

Many explanations have been put forth in explaining recent increases in the production of grapes and wine, and the consumption of wine. One major factor has been a change in the population make-up of the US. The number of adults aged 21 and over began to increase in the mid-1960s and is expected to continue throughout the 1990s, so that by the year 2000 adults between 40 and 60 years of age will constitute about 56 percent of the total population. This age group is associated with higher levels of consumption. Another reason has been large scale travel to the wine producing regions of Europe. This high level exposure and its association with food, wine parties, wine festivals, and the dramatic increase of wine courses have nurtured and sustained interest. The growing demand of wine-related literature has sparked a phenomenal increase in wine writers, wine journals and other publications. The wine industry has also sustained many successful promotional campaigns, and the popularity of winery visitations has further added a new dimension to wine consumption. Other factors propelling the explosive growth in the structure and character of the American wine industry have been the French-American grape revolution after World War II; increased wine awareness; the rise of the eastern wine industry, in part stimulated by the enactment of farm wine legislation; and the successful introduction of new fungicides, pesticides, and vineyard practices enabling the cultivation of Vinifera grapes. Consequently, farm wineries across the nation have grown dramatically in number over the past generation while building local pride and reducing prohibition barriers.

The above simply cannot fuel per capita consumption without a sustained increase in disposable income. Americans over the past two generations have been buying more wine and have been willing to pay higher prices for both domestic and imported wines. In recent years, the fine wine market has behaved in an inelastic fashion. Related are the rapid improvements in wine production, a dramatic increase of women purchasing wine, promulgation of farm winery legislation, and, for the first time in America's history, the successful production of quality Vinifera wines east of the Continental Divide. Consequently, the American wine industry is expected to become a $20 billion market by 2005.

HISTORICAL MILESTONES

986: Bjame Heyulfsen was the first European to land in the New World. Leif, son of Erik the Red, lands in the New World in 1001

(somewhere between Labrador and New England), sees native grapes, and names his discovery "Vinland."

1493: Columbus introduces sugarcane, the first major Old World agricultural commodity, to the Virgin Islands.

1513: Juan Ponce de Leon claims Florida for Spain.

1519: Hernando Cortez makes a beer-type beverage from Agave.

1521: Francisco Gordillo y Quexos is first European to explore South Carolina.

1524: Hernando Cortez brings the Vinifera grape to Mexico (presumably planted that same year), and 257 years later it is introduced to southern California. Giovanni da Verrazano reported off the coast of the Carolinas the profusion of native grapes, and the possibility of a grape and wine industry.

1539: Hernando de Soto explores southeastern North America.

1542: Although coastal California had been sited in 1542, effective Spanish settlement did not occur until after 1769, and wine not made until the early 1780s.

1564: French Huguenots establish a colony near Jacksonville, Florida and make wine from wild Rotundifolia grapes. Many historians claim that 1562 and 1565 to be just as accurate.

1585: Sir Walter Raleigh establishes first of two colonies at Roanoke Island, North Carolina. Scuppernong vines planted.

1606: King James I grants a charter to colonize America, and ever since the first settlement (1607) beer was incorporated into nearly every household becoming a dietary staple. Almost immediately, it became the most popular alcoholic beverage. Captain John Smith reported that wine was made in Virginia. Wine was made in Jamestown in 1608-1609. As tobacco proved a lucrative commercial crop, viticultural endeavors never seriously challenged colonial beer. In an effort to introduce new crops to the New World, Colonial Governors repeatedly attempted to encourage the cultivation of native and Vinifera vines and the making of wine. Prizes were offered and many European viticulturists were brought over to nurture the fledgling industry, but without success until after national independence. Some historians maintain that 1610 is a more accurate date for the first winemaking efforts in Virginia. This may also be considered the first of a series of wine boom and collapse historical periods. While the intensity of the up and down momentums are relative, the American wine industry as a whole and by state has fluctuated dramatically, and perhaps more so than any other.

1623: It is reported that Pilgrims fermented wild grapes to celebrate their first Thanksgiving. The Virginia Colonial Assembly passed legislation requiring each farmer to plant 10 vine plants.

1634: The Massachusetts Bay Colony gave John Winthrop exclusive use of an island in Boston Harbor for a vineyard. The vineyard failed, and ever since eastern America, until the second half of the 20th century, all but abandoned efforts to grow Vinifera. It took more than 300 years for technological efforts to overcome nematodes and fungi, thus making the cultivation of Vinifera possible.

1650: Throughout the second half of the century French Huguenots made wine from native grapes, and attempted unsuccessfully to grow and make wine from Vinifera throughout eastern America. Their efforts were not any better in the 18th century.

1657: Rum is produced commercially in Massachusetts. In tidewater America rum was the preferred distilled alcoholic beverage throughout the 18th century,

1663: King Charles II grants the entire Carolina territory to eight lord proprietors. Vineyards were attempted, but failed.

1678: English establish first permanent settlement at Albemarle Point, South Carolina. By the end of the century, apple cider is distilled into "apple jack" throughout colonial America except the extreme southern colonies. In the 1730s, Governor James Oglethorpe and the London trustees of Georgia banned the use of distilled beverages in Georgia. Vineyards were attempted, but failed.

1733: General James Oglethorpe establishes first English Colony at Savannah, Georgia. Vineyards were attempted, but failed.

1769: French settlers made wine from native vines in Kaskaskia, Illinois.

1774: Anthony Benezet, a Philadelphia Quaker, published *The Mighty Destroyer Displayed*, the first full-scale assault on American drinking habits.

1776: More than 99 percent of wine consumed in the newly established nation was imported, most of it sweet and fortified (mainly Madeira,

Canary, and Sherry); table wines were mainly from Bordeaux. As the nation's territorial boundaries were extended westward, native and Vinifera vines were planted, the former being more successful than the latter. All things French become popular including beverage consumption and food.

1783: The Treaty of Paris expanded the political boundaries of the United States to the Mississippi River.

1789: Elijah Craig produces Bourbon in Bourbon County, Kentucky.

1791: America establishes the first federal tax on whiskey. Annual per capita consumption for an average American over 15 years of age is just under six gallons of absolute alcohol, a figure four times higher than in 1991.

1793: America's first commercial winery, The Pennsylvania Vine Company, in what is now Philadelphia, is founded. It made wine from the Alexander grape, a locally produced hybrid.

1800: There is no evidence that wine was produced in any appreciable commercial quantities until 1800. Tea was more popular than coffee.

1802: Congress made grants on the Ohio River in Indiana to John J. Dufour, a Swiss immigrant, who experimented and established a vineyard near Lexington, Kentucky, and represented a colony of Swiss immigrants. The colony settled in Switzerland (now Vevay, Indiana), and by 1810 had 8 planted acres making 2,400 gallons of grape wine.

1803: Louisiana Purchase expanded the political boundaries of the nation to the Continental Divide, not including Texas. The westward flow of settlement is still slow.

1808: The Union Temperance Society is formed in Moreau, New York.

1810: The U.S. Government reports, for the first time, figures on American wine production. These figures, compiled by Tench Coxe and published in Philadelphia in 1814, indicate that 11,755 gallons of wine were made, of which 9,230 were made from currants, and 2,525 from grapes.

1819: John Adlum "discovers" the Catawba grape at an inn in Clarksburg, Maryland, secures cuttings, propagates, and in 1820 implores Congress to appropriate public land in the District of Columbia for an experimental vineyard, a request that was refused. Until the development of the Concord in the middle of the century, Catawba was the leading grape variety in the east. John Adlum is widely recognized as the first American to seriously grow grapes along the Atlantic coast, and, therefore, represents the first "new era in grape history."

1825: First major successful attempt of large-scale wine production occurs in 1823 in Cincinnati, Ohio when Nicholas Longworth established a vineyard and winery. Although he experimented with vines obtained from John J. Dufour in Vevay, Indiana, it was the Catawba vine that John Adlum sent to him in 1825 that started a successful wine venture. The completion of the Erie Canal, the first all water route from the Atlantic Ocean to the Great Lakes system, acts as the primary medium for the settlement of the midwest and western America.

1830: The most successful wine grape in America was the Scuppernong, soon to be replaced by the Catawba, and then Concord. W.R. Prince, in his treatise on the vine, lists 85 American varieties, a number that rose beyond 1,100 by 1890.

1840: Vineyard culture in America is firmly established, but as a minor crop. Most vineyards were smaller than 2 acres, and wine was relegated the status of a cottage industry. This pattern worsened as German immigrants firmly established breweries throughout America. Not only was the nation non-wine-drinking, but anti-wine-drinking with its consumption considered effete and degenerate. When compared with beer and whiskey, it was said to be "bad for you," and "European bellywash."

1847: The first vine enters western Oregon in 1847, and the Isabella is planted in 1848.

1850: Wine production in America stood at 250,000 gallons, with California producing 21 percent of the total.

1851: The governor of Maine signed into law a bill prohibiting the sale of alcoholic beverages.

1860: Federal Census reports 32 wineries capitalized at $306,300 whose total wages amount to $48,208. Value of wine products is given as $400,791. Considered a landmark year in that it marks the birth of the American wine industry, America produced more than 1.5 million gallons in 33 states. The most popular grape varieties were: Catawba, Delaware, Herbemont, Norton's Seedling, Schuylkill, and Isabella, the first two still popular in the northeast and midwest.

1869: US Department of Agriculture reports that Concord was the most popular grape east of the Rocky Mountains. Other grapes include: Catawba, Delaware, Herbemont, Scuppernong, Iona, Hartford Prolific, Isabella, Diana, Clinton, Creveling, Ives, Salem, Diana, Adirondack, Rebecca, Roger's No. #15, Lenoir, Norton's Virginia, Cynthiana, Maury, Pauline, Iona, Maxatawny, Cuyahoga, Allen's Hybrid, Hamburg, and Warren.

1870: Number of wineries rose to 398, capitalization to $2,334,394, and wages paid to $230,650. Approximate number working in wineries is given by the U.S. Census as 1,486. Value of wine products is given as $2,225,238. More than 50 percent of all wine consumed in America was imported.

1870-1875: California vine acreage expands rapidly only to crash in the second half of the decade. Number of wineries declined from 139 in 1870 to 45 in 1880. This is considered the first of a series of major grape/wine "boom and bust" economic cycles. The industry revived due to heavy European migration.

1880: California becomes the nation's leading grape and wine producer, a position that has never been relinquished. Kansas becomes a "dry" state. The University of California establishes a Department for Viticultural Research and Instruction.

1881-1888: Vineyard acreage increased fourfold, and by 1895 California produced more than 20 million gallons of wine annually.

1900: U.S. Census lists 359 wineries, capitalized at $9,838,015, with $446,055 expended to 1,163 wage earners. Value of wine products is given as $6,547,310. Nearly 83 percent of wine made in America is produced by California.

1901: With an output of 39.6 million gallons, or less than .1 percent of total output, America ranks 14th in the world for wine production.

1914: Per capita wine consumption is .6 gallons. Thirty-three states are "dry." References to alcohol and wine are expunged from school texts in many states. Secretary of the Navy, Josephus Daniels, on June 1 issued General Order 99 ending the officers' wine mess, a move that heralded nation-wide prohibition six years later.

1920: Volstead National Prohibition Act, as the law of the land, was responsible for the closing of 700 commercial wineries. Moreover, Section 29 of the Act allowed a citizen to produce 200 gallons of wine, thus shifting acreage from low-yielding hillside vineyards in California to the flat, productive Central Valley planted in inferior grapes. In the final analysis, Prohibition fostered corruption, and illegal alcohol consumption increased as it didn't reduce nor terminate consumption. Interestingly, during the period 1920-1933, more than 500,000 people were arrested, 1.5 million stills were seized and destroyed, and 45,000 vehicles and 1,300 boats were confiscated. The agricultural sector lost 1 million jobs and more than $20 million during the years 1920-1924. Corn syrup sales increased sixfold, over 150,000 pounds of hops were sold as "spice," 15,000 Americans suffered serious injuries or death from illegal liquor, and the federal government lost an estimated $500 million in taxes.

1933: The 21st Amendment (Repeal) becomes effective. Nineteen thirty-four proved to be a fairly prosperous year, but the bumper crop of 1935 depressed prices. As part of Repeal, the Enology-Viticulture Bureau in the Department of Agriculture was disbanded, one of the most unsung evils of Prohibition.

1935: The four largest distillers--Seagram's & Sons, Schenley, National Distillers, and Hiram Walker entered the California wine industry and by 1943 controlled 25 percent of the nation's total storage capacity. After World War II, a number sold their wineries only to reenter after the mid-1950s, and to exit once again in the 1970s and 1980s.

1936: One thousand three hundred wineries operated in 16 states.

1938: In an effort to stabilize prices and divert excess grapes to brandy production, the Grape Prorate Program was established.

1947: Wine prices collapse; 271 wineries remain in 20 states.

1949: The Federal Raisin Marketing Agreement, diverting surplus raisins into export and other non-ordinary channels, is considered the most effective grape surplus program regulating grape prices.

1950-1990: Increased demand of table wines created sustained plantings of premium grapes in nearly every state in the nation. During this period, there was a profound shift in the popularity of selected Vinifera and French-American varieties, and a decline of native grapes.

1957: The Alcohol Tax Unit allowed flavored wines to be produced, hence the subsequent profusion of flavored, low-alcohol, refreshment wines from grapes, apples, and other fruits and berries. Italy replaces

France as the world's largest wine producer. Italy for the next generation is responsible for more than 50 percent of foreign imports by volume.

1962: The national pattern of grape production began to change when Dr. Konstantin Frank successfully demonstrated that Vinifera vines could be commercially grown east of the Continental Divide. Since then, more than 8,000 acres of Vinifera vines have been planted in eastern America, commanding the highest wine grape prices, and producing the finest wines.

1968-1985: Legislation, primarily in southern New England, New York, New Jersey, Pennsylvania, Tennessee, Maryland, and Virginia, promulgated limited farm winery laws that generated nearly 200 wineries in these states alone. With production varying between 3,000 and 25,000 cases, this is the most rapidly expanding segment of the winery population.

1964: Founding of Les Amis du Vin in Washington, D.C. Per capita wine consumption rises to .9 gallons.

1965: The perennial problems of too many grapes, too much wine, and low wine prices are reversed. With only minor regional and national market corrections, the American wine industry has since enjoyed a historic prosperity like no other.

1966: David Lett of The Eyrie Vineyards planted the first Pinot Noir grapevine in the Dundee Hills region of the Willamette Valley. The United States had 419 bonded wineries, of which 191 were located outside California.

1967: Wine prices decreased relative to most commodities, food, and the cost of living index. Wine industry employs more than 110,000 people. More dry than sweet was produced for the first time in American history.

1968: Founding of the American Wine Society. Table wine consumption exceeds dessert wine consumption. Imported sparkling wine sales triple. Top selling imports in America were Spanish Sangria, Lancers, and Mateus.

1970: There are only 22 wine producing states.

1970s: A decisive national trend for lighter alcoholic beverages be they distilled, malted, fermented, or soft drinks, a movement also in step with lighter food.

1972: American wine market consumes 340 million gallons, four times the volume of 1940. Per capita wine consumption doubled. Winery consolidations, foreign investment, and foreign winery ownership begins and intensifies at record levels by 1991.

1973-1975: Economic recession and French wine scandals combine to slow the demand for wine, the price of wine is also adversely affected by increased grape output.

1974: Despite the above, 51 wine books were published in America. The recession proves to be short lived, and the wine boom continues.

1975: Beginning of the white wine boom.

1976: More dry white wine was sold than red for the first time in American history. For the first time table wine shipments accounted for more than 60% of the total wine market.

1977: Founding of the Society of Wine Educators.

1979: American wine market consumes 400 million gallons. Per capita wine intake is 2.1 gallons. The Founding of the New Hampshire Wine Society in Merrimack. Although the "Granite" state is not known for grape wine production, there was enough interest to form this august body and to sample the following wines: Almaden Blanc de Blanc, Foppiano Cabernet Sauvignon (1974), Mirassou Petite Sirah (1975), Chianti Castello Di Gabbiano (1975), Montevina Late Harvest Zinfandel (1975), Firestone Chardonnay (1976), Burgess Sonoma Zinfandel (1976), and San Martin Chardonnay (1977). After reviewing this tasting the progress made in American viticulture is truly amazing.

1979-1983: National economic uncertainty takes a heavy toll on the American wine industry: winery closings and bankruptcies intensify, high level of excess capacity, and low profit margins plague the industry.

1980: Liquor shipments fell behind wine for the first time in American history.

1981: American wine market consumes 500 million gallons.

1982: Beginning of the Cooler craze; by 1987 coolers accounted for 122 million cases, or more than one-fifth of wine sold in America.

1984: The depressed grape market east of the Continental Divide sparks several determined efforts to improve table wine output. As the demand for dessert wine declined and competition with California and foreign wine intensified, American grape acreage declined, quality French-American grapes (primarily Seyval, Vidal Blanc, Vignoles, Chambourcin, and Chancellor) increased in importance, and quality Vinifera grapes (primarily Chardonnay, Riesling, Sauvignon Blanc, Merlot, and Cabernet Sauvignon) rose to record levels. Due to economic recession and rising $US, the Lambrusco craze altered the American market. Wine imports capture 34 percent of the American market. New Temperance movement attempts to stop wine advertising. Per capita wine consumption reaches 2.4 gallons, a figure that steadily declined to 2 gallons in 1991, exhibiting the most recent downturn of the grape/wine cycle.

1985: Beginning of the Seagram's Alcohol Equivalency campaign.

1987: Sales of California varietal wine exceeded imported wines for the first time.

1989: BATF requires health warning labels on all wine products.

1990: The proposed California Environmental Protection Act of 1990, called "Big Green," would ban sulfur on wine, raisin, and table grapes. Despite recent sluggishness, the American wine market during the 1980s grew from 460 million gallons to 582 million gallons in 1990.

1991: The number of grape wine producing states increases to 41. Per capita wine consumption drops to 2 gallons. American wine exports reach a high of 41 million gallons, worth $160 million. Wine imports drop to 15 percent of total consumption. A comprehensive grape breeding program will intensify. Major breakthroughs are expected in the use of biotechnology to genetically engineer varieties equivalent to the spectacular results of the green revolution of the 1960s. The instant creation of specific genotypes is within grasp.

Table 1.10

LEADING GRAPE PRODUCING STATES (In Thousand Tons)				
State	1919	1934	1962	1975	1990
California	1,345	1,544	3,889	2,928	4,960
Washington			52		220
New York	76	49	107	153	150
Michigan	57	61	68	55	58
Pennsylvania		21	18	48	53
Arizona			12	12	26
Oregon					7
Ohio	20	22	17	14	7
Arkansas	1	16	8	10	5
Virginia					4
Missouri	5	7	4	2	3
North Carolina	3				2
Georgia	2		2		3
South Carolina			3	1	.3
New Jersey			1		
Other States			47	54	161
Total, U.S.	1,575	1,775	3,239	4,300	5,659
Source: New York Agricultural Statistical Service.					

THE GEOGRAPHY OF GRAPE AND WINE PRODUCTION

Not only is America home to more than 50 percent of the world's known species of vine, but nearly every state grows grapes. However, the geography of grape and wine production is lopsided. California grows more and makes more than 90 percent of grapes and wine, and has more than half the nation's wineries. Surprisingly, the grape, with 815,000 acres, is the dominant fruit in America, both in acreage and value of production. The percentage of farms having vineyards is lowest in the arid west (with California and Washington the notable exceptions), the humid south, and the Great Plains; and highest in California, New York, Michigan, Virginia, and Pennsylvania. Of the total, more than 450,000 acres, or 55 percent, are wine grapes that collectively produce more than 5 million tons annually.

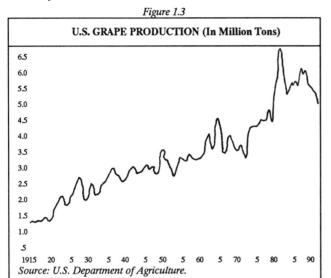

Figure 1.3

U.S. GRAPE PRODUCTION (In Million Tons)

Source: U.S. Department of Agriculture.

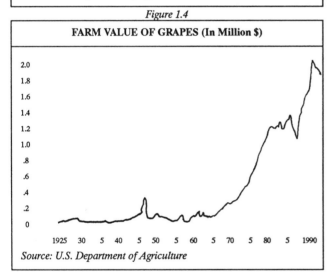

Figure 1.4

FARM VALUE OF GRAPES (In Million $)

Source: U.S. Department of Agriculture

American grape production varies between 4 and 6 million tons with California accounting for more than 90 percent of the total. Washington, with 3 percent, is in second place, followed by New York, Pennsylvania, and Michigan. All other states account for less than 2 percent. For the nation, about 55 percent of all grapes were used for wine, 27 percent for raisins, 11 percent for table use, 5 percent crushed for juice, and 1 percent canned (percentages vary widely by state). Raisin grapes in California, for example, account for 50 percent of the state's total grape production, wine varieties 40 percent, and table grapes for about 7 percent of total output. Raisin grapes are also used for making wine, brandy, and for table use. Table grapes, primarily Thompson Seedless, were also used for raisin and wine making. In New York, the nation's second largest wine producer, Concord grapes represented approximately 70 percent of total production,

and 55 percent of Washington's total output. The farm value of American grapes used for wine totaled about $750 million in 1990. While the amount of total grapes crushed for wine production for the nation as a whole increased throughout the decade of the 1970s, the upward momentum remained somewhat flat in the 1980s. The value of wine produced in the United States approaches $5 billion F.O.B., and the wholesale value exceeds $6 billion. The multiplier from vineyard to retail bottle is estimated to be tenfold, or higher than any other agricultural crop save that of the flowers for perfume.

Table 1.11

PRODUCTION OF GRAPES USED FOR WINE (In Thousand Tons)					
State	1986	1987	1988	1989	1990
California	2,795	2,496	2,852	2,726	2,583
New York	70	95	62	57	55
Washington	29	41	46	43	38
Other States	14	16	22	24	22
United States	2,908	2,648	2,982	2,850	2,698
VALUE OF GRAPE USED FOR WINE (Million $)					
State	1986	1987	1988	1989	1990
California	511	547	722	810	713
New York	15	22	14	15	14
Washington	15	18	17	19	18
Other States	3	3	7	11	10
United States	544	590	760	855	755
GRAPES CRUSHED FOR WINE: PERCENT OF TOTAL GRAPE PRODUCTION					
State 1986	1987	1988	1989	1990	
California 58	53	52	51	56	
New York 43	53	39	38	38	
Washington 18	16	25	19	21	
Other States 18	9	13	15	05	
United States 56	50	49	48	45	

Source: United States Department of Agriculture

From a historical perspective, the 50 leading counties in the production of grapes, number of vines, and acreage for the years 1939, 1969, 1974, and 1982 are presented in Table 1.12. From a geographic perspective for the year 1982 (the most recent year for the compilation of figures by the Department of Agriculture), the leading state was California with 27 counties, followed by New York with 9, Washington 5, Michigan 3, Arizona 3, and Pennsylvania and Ohio each with 1 county. Fig. 1.5 portrays a highly concentrated pattern of grape production in California, the Columbia Plateau, the Willamette Valley, Arizona, and the Great Lakes. While there has been considerable shifting in vine acreage and production in several other states and regions since 1982, the general pattern of production has been largely unaltered since 1939. It is interesting that in this pre-World War II year, California had 26 of the nation's leading 50 grape producing counties, followed by 11 in New York, 5 in Ohio, 3 in Michigan, 2 in Washington and Arkansas, and 1 in Pennsylvania. One of the more remarkable features of the table lies in the consistency of twelve California counties (mostly in the

Central Valley) to maintain their ranking during the past 50 years, and the relative and absolute decline of several historic native grape producing counties in New York, Ohio, New Jersey, Illinois, South Carolina, and Kansas.

of grapes highly durable across the viticultural landscape of America. The southern, non-bunch grape is represented by Vitis rotundifolia, native to the humid southeastern portion of the country.

Table 1.12

GRAPE PRODUCTION: FIFTY LEADING COUNTIES (In Thousand Pounds)				
County	1939	1969	1974	1982
1. Fresno, CA	530	2,566	2,510	3,580
2. Kern, CA	190	568	848	1,495
3. Madera, CA	177	550	652	1,179
4. Tulare, CA	594	794	956	1,059
5. San Joaquin, CA	625	657	714	744
6. Stanislaus, CA	172	249	305	307
7. Sonoma, CA	58	71	123	284
8. Merced, CA	136	149	150	267
9. Napa, CA	52	83	154	251
10. Monterey, CA		25	39	211
11. Riverside, CA	15	85	122	153
12. Chautauqua, NY	42	91	163	149
13. Yakima, WA	7	76	73	131
14. Erie, PA	23	45	100	90
15. Benton, WA	2	40	53	89
16. Mendocino, CA	43	31	64	87
17. Kings, CA	104	53	63	82
18. Yates, NY	14	32	54	61
19. Berrien, MI	31	27	33	50
20. San Bernardino, CA	120	89	78	50
21. Van Buren, MI	23	30	41	35
22. San Luis Obispo, CA	2	11	5	32
23. San Benito, CA	4	15	29	30
24. Santa Barbara, CA			12	29
25. Walla Walla, WA				9
26. Lake, CA		3	2	25
27. Steuben, CA	7	20	26	23
28. Erie, NY	5	16	18	20
29. Franklin, WA	.3	4	3	18
30. Sacramento, CA	63		5	5
31. Schuyler, NY	4	10	16	15
32. Maricopa, AZ		35	21	14
33. Niagara, NY	8	9	14	13
34. Alameda, CA	8	10	10	13
35. Yolo, CA	4		6	13
36. Yuma, AZ	.8	3	6	5
37. Glenn, CA			2	1
38. Santa Clara, CA	25	14	10	8
39. Ashtabula, OH	9	7	13	7
40. Amador, CA			3	7
41. Solano, CA	5	6	13	7
42. Washington, AR	8	10	6	6
43. Ontario, NY	5	9	12	6
44. Seneca, NY	2	2		6
45. Los Angeles, CA		8	13	
46. Kalamazoo, MI	4	3	6	5
47. Cattaraugus, NY	1	2	6	4
48. Benton, AR	1	4	4	4
49. Grant, WA				4
50. San Diego, CA	8	1		4

Source: U.S. Department of Commerce, Agriculture Division

Of the more than 10,000 individual varieties of grape that exist in the world about 100 are widely recognized as making above-average wine, 30 make excellent wine, and fewer than 20 are considered proficient in making "classic" wine. While only America grows all three types of grapes commercially (American, French-American, and Vinifera), native American grapes are divided into two major categories: the cold-hardy bunch grapes, and the Pierce's Disease-resistant Rotundifolia. The native American bunch-type enjoys a more widely diffused geography than Vinifera as its natural habitat ranges from the Canadian border to the higher elevations bordering the humid southeast. Of the several thousand varieties, fewer than 50 are commercially grown, the Concord, Catawba, Niagara, and Delaware being the most important. While the quality of wine produced (especially dry table wines) does not compare favorably with Vinifera, the ability to produce flavorful sweet wines and survive in areas where Vinifera does not, has made this widely divergent group

Figure 1.5

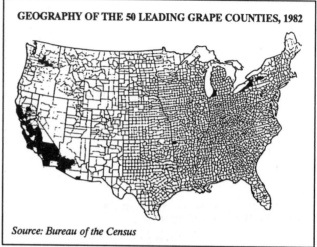

GEOGRAPHY OF THE 50 LEADING GRAPE COUNTIES, 1982

Source: Bureau of the Census

Vinifera, or "Old World" grape, is a thin-skinned, cold and humidity-sensitive vine that was historically concentrated in California and nowhere else in the country. Due to recent innovations in the propagation of vines and the development of fungicides, insecticides, nematocides, herbicides, and soil fumigants, the commercial range of cultivation of Vitis vinifera has been diffused to the Pacific northwest, northern Michigan, southern New England, the Great Lakes, and the borders of the humid south. Without question, Vinifera grapes produce America's finest wines, and dominate the industry. Somewhere between these two extremes are a group of grapes called "French-American" that have increased the number of options available to the grape grower east of the Rocky Mountains.

The distribution of winegrowing, as presented in this book, is divided into nine viticultural regions:

1. New England. This northern, cold, windy, heavily glaciated, and humid region contains but 800 vine acres, more than half of which are non-Vinifera. Historically a major wine import region, only the warmer, southern portion close to warm water is important in the production of grape wine; the colder northern region is an important fruit and berry wine producing area. Because the United States was settled from east to west, it was here (stretching south to Florida) that grapes were first planted by non-Latin Europeans. New England, in terms of farm acreage and percent of total labor force engaged in agriculture, is the least agricultural region in the country.

2. New York. Surrounded by New England to the northeast and east, the Great Lakes on the west, and Appalachian and portions of the Coastal Atlantic Plain to the south, New York has been the nation's second largest wine producer for the past 100 years. Historically known for native Labrusca-based wines, New York today is a highly eclectic viticultural region that produces Vinifera, native, and French American wines in four major regions.

3. The Mid-Atlantic States (Pennsylvania, New Jersey, Maryland, Delaware, and Virginia), a highly diffusive region, is currently switching from native grapes to French-American and Vinifera-based wines.

4. The Midwest. This large, highly diverse region of 12 states is encum-

bered by an interior location that favors the largest spectrum of native grape production. Within the region there are many historic viticultural areas, as well as several newly emerging non-native producing areas, some of which have the ability to produce unusual quality wines. There are about 50 wineries along the lake margins, and another 70 located in the states of Iowa, Missouri, Arkansas, Tennessee, and West Virginia. The midwest contains more cropland than any other geographic region in the nation.

5. The South. This region is best suited for the cultivation of Rotundifolia, grapes that have a natural resistance to Pierce's Disease, year-round humidity, high temperatures, root rot, fungus diseases, nematode parasites, and various insect pests. Vinifera and French-America grapes are killed outright, and even Labrusca-type varieties succumb to the subtropical climate.

6. The Great Plains. This relatively flat, featureless grassland region, located in the center of the nation, experiences the largest seasonal variations of temperature in the nation. Without any protective barrier from cold arctic air in winter, and humid, hot air in summer, the Great Plains are influenced by a climatic regime commonly referred to as "continentality." While only the hardiest grape varieties are able to grow in these extreme climatic conditions, protected areas within incised river valleys offer moderating conditions that can support commercial vineyards.

7. The Northwest. This tri-state, rapidly growing viticultural region is currently becoming one of the most important quality Vinifera grape-growing areas of the nation capable of producing excellent to extraordinary wines.

8. California. Responsible for nearly all the nation's table, raisin, and wine grape production, this state is the envy of the world in its ability to consistently produce quality fruit and wine.

9. The Southwest. This area, widely considered the oldest viticultural region of America, consists of the arid portions of Arizona, New Mexico, and Texas. Although there are minor exceptions, the premier wine grape producing areas are located in either the High Plains or the mountainous interior.

THE AMERICAN GRAPE CROP

U.S. Grape Utilization for 1988: Fresh, 796,420 tons; Juice, 350,070 tons; Wine, 2,860,660 tons; and Other (dried and canned) 1,737,000 tons.

Value of utilized grape crop for 1989: California 90.2%; Washington 4%; New York 2.3%; Arizona 1.1%; Pennsylvania 1%; Michigan .7%; others .7%.

In 1991 the U.S. grape crop was 5,390,000 tons. Of the total, California produced 4,830,000, of which 2.3 million were wine grapes, 1.9 million raisin grapes, and .580 table grapes. New York produced 190,000 tons, Washington 187,000 tons, Pennsylvania 75,000 tons, Michigan 46,000 tons, Arizona 25,000 tons, and other states 33,000 tons.

The geography of wine production presents a pattern that is almost, but not identical with grape production. While California is the nation's leading wine producing state, New York, with slightly more vine acreage than Washington, produces seven times more wine than the latter due to the importation of non-native grapes and must from other states. South Carolina and Washington each produce about 1 percent of total output, but it must be noted that wine production in South Carolina is overwhelmingly the product of Rotundifolia subject to maximum amelioration. And while production for both states is similar in gallonage, there is no comparison in terms of quality and value (both qualitative features favoring the Pacific state). Likewise, Virginia ranked fifth in wine production for the year 1989 because of the production of wine based on imported juice, a situation not too dissimi-

lar in Illinois, New Jersey, Michigan, Georgia, and other "eastern" states. At present only Alaska, North Dakota, South Dakota, Maine, Vermont, Louisiana, Nebraska, and Wyoming do not produce commercial grape wine. While some "old" wine producing states, such as Ohio, Michigan, and New Jersey, have recently shown signs of revitalization, Virginia, Connecticut, Texas, Georgia, Florida, and New Mexico exhibit renewed vigor and vitality. The fastest wine producing growth in recent years has occurred in the southwest, northwest, and Virginia.

Table 1.13

WINE PRODUCTION BY PRINCIPAL STATE (In Thousand Gallons)					
State	1935	1945	1955	1965	1990
Alabama	-	1	-	-	2
Arizona					20
Arkansas	176	587	111	492	157
California	86,904	89,369	109,837	167,522	385,800
Colorado	-	59	1	-	21
Connecticut	12	195	93	-	28
Florida	45	59	12	85	359
Georgia	-	894	228	759	1,515
Idaho	-	2	-	-	288
Illinois	20	535	2,813	3,007	15
Iowa	17	68	7	-	38
Indiana	-	-	-	-	36
Kentucky	-	1	-	-	-
Louisiana	601	39	20	12	-
Maryland	1	116	12	8	43
Massachusetts	9	-	-	-	51
Michigan	526	1,419	2,327	2,526	276
Minnesota		53	-	-	4
Mississippi	-	-	-	-	15
Missouri	141	27	11	196	153
Nebraska	-	-	-	-	-
Nevada	2	-	-	-	-
New Jersey	290	951	3,448	4,027	114
New Mexico	3	12	21	13	127
New York	2,194	7,980	7,992	13,430	27,069
North Carolina	1	461	2	23	134
Ohio	592	1,615	636	837	709
Oregon	31	603	245	75	711
Pennsylvania	3	98	4	1	303
Rhode Island	8	-	-	-	5
South Carolina	-	17	67	102	4,353
Tennessee	-	-	-	-	54
Texas	9	138	2	2	521
Virginia	-	387	1,386	2,091	305
Washington	74	2,624	1,406	2,009	3,671
West Virginia	-	-	-	-	10
Wisconsin	2	1	4	16	62
Other States	51	13	9	100	177
Total	91,712	108,323	130,691	197,321	427,100

Source: Wine Institute.

The above geographic adjustments reflect significant post-World War II changes in American wine consumption patterns. From Repeal until the late 1960s the consumption of dessert wine exceeded table wine in the United States by a significant degree. But within a short period, table wine consumption accelerated and now accounts for more than 75 percent of total consumption. The combined effect of increased wine consumption and table wine in particular, plus the rise of new wine producing regions and the implementation of farm winery legislation in many eastern states has led to many momentous changes in the national grape and wine industries, of which the proliferation in the number of wineries during the past 20 years is most illuminating. The surging number, coupled with increased wine production, has stimulated greater awareness by the public at large through the phenomenal growth of winery visitations.

Figure 1.6

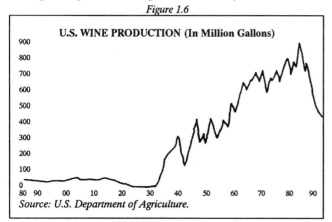

Source: U.S. Department of Agriculture.

Figure 1.7

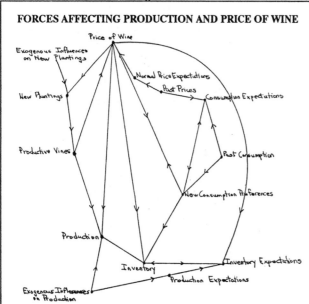

The winegrowing industry is cyclical. Wine grape production varies with the amount of acreage planted, the vagaries of weather, grape prices, and a host of socio-political-economic issues. Because grapevines require from 1 to 2 years of ground preparation and take four years from the time they are planted to become fully productive, vines planted in response to high prices are sometimes unwanted when they begin producing. The supply of wine grapes, wine inventories, international policies, currency fluctuations, etc., create a highly complicated picture.

ECONOMIC SIGNIFICANCE AND STRUCTURE OF THE WINE INDUSTRY

The grape industry, unlike other agricultural commodities, is different. The industry combines the traditional farming activity of raising a crop with the industrial process of making wine, and the commercial activities associ-

ated with sophisticated marketing strategy. While it is possible to make a living as a farmer growing grapes, the livelihood is precariously subject to weather and market fluctuations in product price, as is farm income derived from any other crop. Grapes also differ from most other crops in their historic association with processing into a high value product--wine, a commodity that exhibits peculiar cultural and economic characteristics. The grape industry also displays cyclical patterns not usually associated with other agricultural products. In this regard, the factors affecting the price of wine are shown in Fig. 1.7.

Figure 1.8

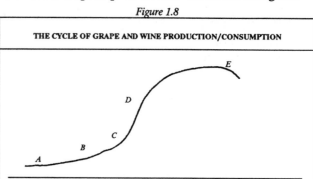

The cyclical nature of the grape/wine business is illustrated by the "S" curve. Stage A shows no or little growth, or the stage of a "traditional market." Stages B, C, and D indicate an acceleration of events, such as the introduction of a new grape variety, a new fungicide, etc., that makes cultivation possible, cultural fashion, increased demand, and grape plantings, etc. Investment per acre, while non-existent in A, increases rapidly to D. The momentum generated in stages B-D creates an irresistible climate for growers to plant more grapes, thus leading to overproduction, and a disruption of the market thus leading to inevitable decline until the next cycle. Since 1840 there have been about twelve periods of major price escalations, all followed by ruthless price declines. E is a negative stage and should be avoided.

As an industry, viticulture has grown to significant proportions in recent years. With a value of $1.7 billion (or 2.2 percent of the nation's total crop value) grapes rank seventh in value among the top fifteen principal crops, surpassed only by corn, soybeans, hay, wheat, cotton, and tobacco, and are ahead of such commodities as rice and sorghum. Grape-growing (for table, raisin, processing, and wine use) is the nation's largest fruit industry; the value of grapes is 50 percent higher than apples, and four times more valuable than the nation's peach crop. The wine industry as a whole has grown beyond $30 billion, a significant increase from $95 million in 1880. In a study conducted by Steve L. Barsby & Associates in 1989 for The National Wine Coalition, the retail value of wine exceeded $12 billion, and in the process the wine industry paid $3.1 billion in wages to 250,000 employees, purchased more than $6 billion in goods and services from other industries, and paid over $1.5 billion in taxes. In addition, it is estimated that for every dollar spent by the wine industry to purchase goods and services it generated an additional $2.11 income elsewhere in the economy.

Another 280,000 jobs were created in secondary industries, such as agriculture and bottle manufacturing, and together the 530,000 jobs created directly and indirectly by the wine industry produced more than $8 billion in wages. Excise, license, sales, and other wine-related levies paid by the wine industry to local and state governments reached $989 million in 1987. The economic activity generated by the wine industry provided local and state governments with an additional $1.7 billion in income, property, and other tax revenues for a combined total industry tax contribution of $2.6 billion. Obviously, the industry's impact was highest in California where the industry created over 119,000 jobs, paid $2.1 billion in wages, and contributed about $9 billion to the state's economy. Ranking after California in total economic contributions were New York, Texas, Illinois, New Jersey, Florida, Pennsylvania, Ohio, and Michigan, in that order.

Table 1.14

ECONOMIC CONTRIBUTION OF THE WINE INDUSTRY, 1987

State	Employment	Wages	State & Local Taxes	Total Business Activity
Alabama	4,700	$65,310,000	$26,930,000	$241,480,000
Alaska	1,100	39,720,000	5,170,000	156,740,000
Arizona	5,330	72,660,000	44,000,000	245,540,000
Arkansas	1,880	27,450,000	5,890,000	109,070,000
California	119,480	2,051,270,000	534,930,000	9,148,480,000
Colorado	6,640	91,420,000	34,830,000	344,300,000
Connecticut	7,980	110,940,000	47,550,000	386,540,000
Delaware	1,520	32,080,0009	280,000	112,250,000
Dist. of Columbia	2,070	38,590,000	17,040,000	139,600,000
Florida	28,740	381,160,000	231,310,000	1,283,340,000
Georgia	8,430	120,360,000	70,020,000	451,060,000
Hawaii	1,520	18,970,000	16,030,000	62,590,000
Idaho	1,630	20,320,000	9,330,000	81,810,000
Illinois	23,620	365,670,000	111,050,000	1,386,270,000
Indiana	8,940	131,150,000	25,910,000	519,150,000
Iowa	5,820	65,880,000	19,190,000	267,280,000
Kansas	3,030	42,660,000	10,580,000	179,100,000
Kentucky	4,340	68,750,000	24,460,000	258,400,000
Louisiana	5,170	77,040,000	17,590,000	320,490,000
Maine	2,020	27,910,000	12,820,000	78,770,000
Maryland	8,100	114,120,000	37,860,000	422,430,000
Massachusetts	14,320	193,730,000	62,190,000	679,170,000
Michigan	20,110	300,140,000	70,000,000	1,139,800,000
Minnesota	7,910	104,110,000	36,700,000	389,580,000
Mississippi	2,290	31,590,000	11,190,000	125,160,000
Missouri	8,720	118,720,000	28,220,000	444,550,000
Montana	1,490	20,430,000	6,430,000	81,820,000
Nebraska	2,470	30,900,000	8,480,000	131,220,000
Nevada	2,910	42,690,000	26,820,000	151,960,000
New Hampshire	1,950	24,280,000	15,850,000	79,830,000
New Jersey	21,650	342,310,000	98,380,000	1,323,380,000
New Mexico	2,300	28,500,000	13,870,000	108,860,000
New York	44,340	821,010,000	288,360,000	2,912,570,000
North Carolina	9,140	122,770,000	50,970,000	447,670,000
North Dakota	810	9,460,000	3,400,000	43,050,000
Ohio	22,680	317,370,000	61,520,000	1,270,580,000
Oklahoma	3,080	48,590,000	15,340,000	205,700,000
Oregon	8,630	109,090,000	24,460,000	404,890,000
Pennsylvania	20,890	319,440,000	121,510,000	1,313,680,000
Rhode Island	2,350	30,900,000	13,020,000	111,160,000
South Carolina	4,350	60,170,000	27,070,000	222,580,000
South Dakota	1,040	11,760,000	4,940,000	45,950,000
Tennessee	5,500	76,090,000	33,920,000	298,200,000
Texas	24,550	372,530,000	104,810,000	1,496,880,000
Utah	2,180	26,510,000	13,830,000	104,910,000
Vermont	1,350	15,930,000	5,920,000	53,240,000
Virginia	9,220	129,030,000	49,930,000	492,030,000
Washington	16,690	237,020,000	92,180,000	890,170,000
West Virginia	1,590	26,450,000	5,540,000	111,140,000
Wisconsin	12,770	149,480,000	34,250,000	565,590,000
Wyoming	720	10,880,000	4,240,000	49,560,000
Total	530,060	$8,095,310,000	$2,645,110,000	$31,889,570,000

Source: Steve L. Barsby & Associates, Inc., Prepared For The National Wine Coalition, 1989.

While there may be many variations and even more interpretations, the following is presented as the author's view of the evolution of a "new wine country--America:"

1. A period of indifference is characterized by low consumption, and the production of inexpensive bulk wine, a large percentage of which is dessert wine. There is little if any regional specialization, and a combination of poor grape varieties planted in unsuitable climates and soils, and high yields produce poor wine.

2. The concomitant developments of industrialization and urbanization induce sustained growth in consumption among various groups: inexpensive, semi-sweet, and sweet wines for the "youth market;" expensive imported wines for the serious "upscale" wine consumer.

3. With increased sophistication and higher disposable incomes there is a rapid increase in the quality of table wines, and a decline in dessert wines. A more cosmopolitan clientele dominates the dry table wine market, and slowly restructures the wine industry to a higher plane. This stage is characterized by rapid growth and turbulent changes. The rank, relative position of the top 20 wineries, is in constant flux from year to year.

4. Although the wine industry remains oligopolistic, boutique wineries grow in number and improve the quality of product offered for sale. There is a more discriminating effort to properly match grape varieties with micro-climates and soil conditions.

5. Production of "estate" bottling, and the rise of appellations increases in intensity.

6. Increased specialization of one or two wines, and a reduction of the "full-line" syndrome follows.

7. Maturity is defined with a significant number of Americans consuming wine with meals, and an increase in international investment. The significance of the former factor is important because it involves the dominance of American-produced quality premium wine, a development of the post-1975 period. The deluge of foreign investment within the past 20 years is considered a sign that the American wine industry, and, in particular, California, has reached the maturity stage. An increased emphasis on family ownership and familial continuity, specialized food or beverage-related corporate ownership are good omens. Another sign of "maturity" is the recent establishment of wineries east of the Continental Divide, wineries that, in large part, are regional in character. Since wine consumption increases in areas that grow grapes and produce wine, this may very well be the answer to America's low wine consumption in comparison to European countries.

Structure of the Wine Industry

There exists a great size range in American wineries-- from E. & J. Gallo, the mega-giant of the industry (with a storage capacity of 330 million gallons), to cottage-type operations that make fewer than 1,000 cases. For the sake of convenience, seven major size divisions are recognized:

1. **The part-time**, or cottage-type, usually operate from basement, garage, rented space, or have someone custom-crush, or bottle their wine. The owners usually depend on off-winery employment for primary sources of income. The entire enterprise, a hobby gone commercial, is on the margin of economic solvency (unless the owner is independently wealthy). However, there are many variations on this theme: some contain state-of-the-art equipment with the wine made by a prominent winemaker engaged full-time in another winery, while others are managed by weekend physicians, mechanics, teachers, or farmers. Production rarely exceeds 3,500 cases, and the enterprise may or may not own vineland. Mainly a product of farm winery legislation, they have grown in number to 600, most located east of the Rocky Mountains. The legislation, remarkably similar in most states, removed establishment barriers simplifying the fermentation of grapes grown by farmers and the marketing of wine at the retail level. The major benefits are the reduction of license fees, and the right to sell retail at the winery and in

various other outlets, but they are frequently restricted by their output--usually 50,000 to 100,000 gallons. In most states wineries can sell related grape products, such as grape juice, jellies, and even non-grape products. While the rate of business failures is high, their number is expected to increase in the coming decades. These small wineries with limited distribution have been helped by several important events in recent years: a steady enhancement in wine quality, farm winery legislation, improved viticultural practices, replacement of French-American by Vinifera grapes, and the emergence of American cuisine that emphasizes regional ingredients and traditional recipes.

2. The small, full-time winery that is self-contained may or may not own vineland, and produces between 3,500 and 10,000 cases. This group varies widely in quality of wine produced--from less than $5 to more than $25 the bottle, and enjoys a local or even national reputation. Depending on the economic viability there will generally be at least one full-time, non-family employee. There are 700 such wineries, with the Pacific Coast having the largest concentration. The number of these wineries is expected to increase in the coming decades.

In 1970, small and medium-sized wineries produced about .7% of all wine, major premium 10%, coops 11%, and the largest 78%. In the early 1970s, the most important premium wineries were: Beringer, Wente, Mondavi, Martini, Korbel, Beaulieu, Simi, Pedroncelli, Freemark Abbey, and Heitz. In 1980, small wineries produced 10%, coops about 6%, large wineries 25%, and the three largest 59% of the national total. By 1991, small to medium-sized wineries produced about 18%, coops 2%, large wineries 28%, and the three largest 52%.

---

3. The medium-sized winery, between 10,000 and 30,000 cases, essentially has the same general characteristics as the small, full-time winery, but usually boasts at least two full-time, non-family employees and vineland. There are about 150 such wineries, with the highest concentration in California. It is important to note that while wine consumption has been sluggish since 1985, small to medium-sized premium wineries have grown in number.

4. The large size winery produces between 30,000 and 100,000 cases. There are about 100 such wineries, mostly in California, with expected increases in the coming decades. Most of these wineries are premium producers, and several elements make them different from those that follow: they are extremely capital intensive; inventory intensive; no single winery has a major market share, thus suggesting fierce competition; they emphasize quality because the serious consumer is willing to pay a premium price. Excessive marketing expenditures for these capital intensive firms and cash flow constraints hurt profitability. Also, they have superior management and technological capabilities, above the average for the industry. Business failures (rare) are the product of excessive optimism and radical business fluctuations.

5. The extra-large wineries, between 100,000 and 500,000 cases, numbering about 50, are mainly located in California. Their number is expected to increase in the coming decades.

6. The super-large winery, between 500,000 and 10,000,000 cases, is one with an economic ability to take advantage of vertical integration. There are about 20 such wineries, and their number is expected to remain the same in the coming decades. While grape growing and winemaking in America dates from to the sixteenth century, large-scale, commercial wine establishments are, with the establishment of Garrett & Company, a phenomenon of the twentieth century.

7. Mega-winery--in the United States and the entire free world there is only one--E. & J. Gallo, of Modesto, California. There is total vertical integration in terms of performing all major levels of production except advertising. This, as well as those wineries listed under numbers five and six, are, or can be, self-capitalizing. It is obvious, therefore, that the American wine industry represents oligopolistic features (a market dominated by only a few firms). The ten largest wineries produce 70 percent, and another 20 are collectively responsible for more than 85 percent of American wine made. These giants have multiple facilities, produce a complete line of wines, market under multiple labels, concentrate on the production of jug wines, advertise heavily, and are mainly confined to the Central Valley of California, and the Finger Lakes district of New York. Several sell to other wineries and do not bottle under their own label. Their success, other than managerial or personality acumen, is based on the advantages of economies of scale. As the cost of fixed equipment, cooperage, physical facilities, and technical expertise exhibit economies of scale, the price of a gallon of wine decreases dramatically with size, hence a decided advantage to large producers. Over the past ten years all but three of the top ten wineries have been purchased, sold, and repurchased by other corporations. As a result, volatility at the top is fierce: as recently as 1986, the largest seven wineries were Gallo, Seagram, Canandaigua, California Cooler, Almaden, Heublein, and the Wine Group, but by 1990 most of the Seagram properties had been sold to Vintners International, Canandaigua declined by more than four million cases, California Cooler sales were reduced by more than 60 percent, and Almaden is now part of the Heublein group. One year later, the fortunes of some of the above as well as other mergers and acquisitions changed the picture again. Throughout these vicissitudes, the dominance of E. & J. Gallo is formidable: in 1987 it experienced an absolute growth of fifteen million gallons, a figure that is bigger than the second largest California winery.

While the top ten wineries are mainly large corporations (or part of holding companies), medium to extra-large wineries are family operations whose reputations rest not with jug but with smaller bottle, varietal wines. Commonly referred to as premium wine producers, the largest advertise in trendy journals, with some becoming extremely successful in recent years. In California, Oregon, and Washington, but particularly in Sonoma, Napa, Mendocino, and Central Coast California counties, medium-sized wineries are the products of very wealthy individuals and corporations replete with resplendent landscaped homes and elaborate tasting room facilities. They offer a much smaller product line, employ prestigious winemakers, invariably produce higher-priced wines, have second labels, and captivate nearly all the critical acclaim of wine writers and magazine articles. In recent years this group of wineries, in combination with smaller farm wineries, has eroded the position of the ten largest wineries, and is expected to further improve its market share position in the future. As the American consumer shifted from jug wines to more expensive "fifth bottles," Vintner's International, Canandaigua, Heublein, and the Wine Group have all experienced declining sales.

FARM WINERY LEGISLATION

Farm Winery legislation, first enacted in Pennsylvania in 1968, permits small wineries to operate under more favorable conditions than large wineries. These laws, currently in force by at least half the states in the union, vary considerably. In Georgia, retail sales are permitted at the winery and at five additional locations in the state if the wine is made from at least 40 percent Georgia-grown fruit. The law also allows the winery to act as wholesaler if no other licensed wholesaler wishes to sell the wine. The annual license fee is $50, and production cannot exceed 24,000 gallons. While the state tax on table wine is $.11 per liter, tax on out-of-state wine is $.40.
In Virginia, 51% of the fruit must come from land owned or leased by the winery; no more than 25% of the fruit used may be imported from other states (exemptions are frequent).

These premium wine producers are characterized by several features that set them apart from the rest of the industry. They are highly capital and inventory intensive, and none have managed to dominate market share in any wine category. While the costs of capital and inventory magnifies, and excessive marketing expenditures lower profitability, the consistent high level quality of production has produced over the long term, a reliable and loyal consumer following. The product line is targeted toward an affluent, middle aged, heavy user consumer that is a consistent purchaser of premium wine. While producing a fraction of 1 percent of all wine, this select group of premium wineries, particularly in California, is responsible for about 5 percent of wine sales by value.

Centralization of productive assets has continued unabated. In 1960, 50 percent of the nation's corporate assets were controlled by small and medium-sized businesses. While less than five percent of all wineries controlled 88 percent of winery assets in 1981, by 1991 less than 2 percent of all wineries controlled more than 90

percent. While the above industry structure has exhibited considerable corporate instability and the number of firms has more than tripled, geographic concentration has not diminished. Despite the rise of Oregon, Washington, Virginia, Texas, and other states since 1960, California has continued to maintain its share of national wine production. The historic spatial patterns of the past 100 years have not decentralized. The above oligarchic picture is likely to continue and segmentation of the market among the many small, specialized wineries will intensify. And while they will not become "national," their posture will become more conspicuous at the local and regional levels.

Table 1.15

AMERICA'S TEN LARGEST WINERIES FOR SELECTED YEARS (By Storage Capacity in Thousand Gallons)		
Company	Capacity	No. of Plants
E & J Gallo	330,000	4
Grand Metropolitan[1]	113,400	5
Vintners International[2]	84,500	5
Canandaigua Wine Co.[3]	55,000	7
ERLY Foods[4]	52,000	2
Vie-Del Co.	51,000	2
The Wine Group[5]	42,800	3
Delicato Vineyards	39,500	1
JFJ Bronco Winery	37,700	1
Guild Wineries[6]	37,000	4

[1]Includes Heublein, Inglenook, Christian Brothers, Beaulieu.
[2]Includes Taylor, Great Western, Paul Masson.
[3]Includes Tenner, Batavia, Widmer's, etc.
[4]Includes Sierra Wines, Beverage Source.
[5]Includes Corbett Canyon.
[6]Includes Cribari, Guild Central Cellars, Bear Creek, Mendocino Vineyards.
Note: Canandaigua has acquired Guild, and, as a result, it now (1992) ranks as the third largest winery in the nation.
Source: Wines & Vines, July, 1991.

While American grape growing ventures are mainly in the hands of 9,000 growers, winemaking and marketing are concentrated by a small number of firms, features that are widely divergent from most European countries. There, grape and wine production is in the hands of many small producers and several cooperatives, with a part of the wine output of small producers being assembled and marketed by negociants.

If there is a compelling criticism of the American wine industry, it lies mainly with a lack of historical continuity and tradition. While one generation may be resourceful and energetic to enter the profession, the next generation, for the most part, exhibits "historical indigence." Unlike his European counterpart where family traditions go back for centuries, there are few American wineries, other than the Mirassou's, that go back five generations. According to the author's calculations, of the 1,519 wineries only 194 had previous family winemaking traditions, 45 exhibit a two-generation tradition, and only eight wineries have been in continuous family operation for three generations. By this measure alone, the American wine industry is young. From a cultural vantage point it is also important to note that among the eight oldest winemaking California families-Mirassou, Wente, Seghesio, Mondavi, Pedroncelli, Martini, Sebastiani, and Foppiano, six are of Italian heritage, and one each French and German.

In recent years viticulture has been influenced by several types of winery/vineyard investors: foreign, corporations already involved in the wine/food/beverage business, financial investors, and comparatively small/family investors. Although not new, foreign ownership (particularly in California) of wineries and vineland has increased significantly in recent years. Beginning with the Nestle purchase of Beringer in 1971, there have been at least 164 other major foreign winery/vineyard investments whose equity capital is estimated to exceed $1 billion. Foreign equity in the spirits industry is estimated at 60 percent (more than $17 billion), and 38 percent in the wine industry, a percentage that is expected to grow in the future. Close to 100 wineries are now owned by foreign interests. The United Kingdom, in particular, controls more than one-third of the spirits and 14 percent of the domestic wine market. Since America is the biggest and most prosperous alcohol beverage market (the U.S. accounts for one-third of all alcohol consumption) in the western world, it seems logical for international firms to have a strong interest in the United States. It is also interesting to note that fourteen important California sparkling wine producers are owned by non-Americans. The principal foreign players are Japan, West Germany, the United Kingdom, France, Canada, and Spain.

The second type of investor is the individual or corporation with a wine affiliation history. These firms become players in the wine trade as market conditions dictated favorable economic returns throughout the century, but have shown a willingness in recent years to become major participants in the acquisition of undervalued properties with the prospect of future market maturity. The recent acquisition of Clos du Bois by Hiram Walker is one such example of a specific winery, but the purchase of valuable vineland, particularly in the coastal counties of California, and, to a smaller extent, prime vineland in Oregon and Washington is a more recent and new direction of horizontal integration by large wineries and other related corporations requiring an excellent source of prime grapes from a prestigious appellation. Aggressive accountants maintain that in todays economic climate, successful national marketing efforts begin with a minimum of 200,000 cases. In recent years Acacia, Firestone, Franciscan, Hiram Walker, Chateau Ste. Michelle, Mondavi, Heublein, Wine World, and United Vintners have all branched out to control other wineries. More winery

mergers and divestitures will occur over the coming years and there will be more new entrants into the wine industry. Profitable operations will continue to expand, and unprofitable wineries will be sold or will cut back on unprofitable lines of business. Still, investor interest and increasingly sophisticated operations will continue to foster keen competition in the industry.

The third group of investors, a new addition to the list of prime vinicultural players, are the financial investors who view the wine industry as any other type of investment. Often institutional investors with an eye on the long haul, these players buy equity and long-term debt, and with the fourth group are considered positive elements. Because throughout the past 20 years the return on equity in the viticultural industry has been three times the industry norm of 12 percent, it is no wonder that winegrowing has attracted new venture capital. It is expected that in the years to come, this type of investor will increase in importance. Winery consolidations will accelerate almost as fast as the founding of new wineries.

The fourth group is a small version of the third, but the aggregate impact of its players may be more substantial to the industry as a whole. This group is composed of a few individual investors who launch or buy an existing winery (with or without vineland). Here, the level of competence can often be high, the motivation infectious, and the productivity of the owners beyond industry standards in an effort to produce a wine bottle label of consequence. In general, these four players are, in concert, instituting changes based not in the production of bulk but quality wine that has not been equaled since Repeal.

There can be little doubt that the American wine industry is the most progressive in the world: American winemakers have developed the finest, state-of-the-art technology, and innovators are continuously improving equipment and methods. They have the most advanced winemaking techniques and know more about viticultural practices than most countries. Consequently, common, everyday American wines are not only considerably better, but consistently better than the average *vin ordinaire* that the rest of the world consumes. Of course, American premium wines now rival, and often outdistance foreign competition. Despite the foregoing, and quite inexplicably, American wines command little respect among foreign aficionados. America, it is said, has not come of age due to a combination of a lack of sophistication, consumer drinking patterns, and an indifferent governmental bureaucracy.

II
THE GEOGRAPHIC FOUNDATIONS OF GRAPE PRODUCTION

One of the maiden accounts on the relative importance of various physical and cultural practices influencing wine quality was given by one Villa Maior in 1884. In an attempt to quantify wine quality in Bordeaux, he points out that of 20 qualitative points possible, vine variety contributed 5, annual temperature 5, soil 4, type of cultivation and pruning 3, vine care 2, and exposure 1. Interestingly, climate is principally reflected by exposure and temperature whose combined weight is less than one-third of the total. On the other hand, Dr. Richard Peterson, one of the most successful winemakers in America, believes that at least 80 percent, maybe as much as 95 percent, of wine quality is influenced by climate, and that soil is only a relatively minor factor. The foregoing may be expressed by the following formula: $V = f(c, s, r, o, t)$, where: V = plant performance; f = function of; c = climate; s = edaphic conditions such as soil characteristics; r = relief and exposure; o = biota, or cultural practices; t = time, or the age of the vine. For the Porto region, in the "registration of property" legislation promulgated in 1948, authorities assigned values in the following manner: low yield (21%), altitude (21%), nature of land (14%), locality (13%), training of vines (6%), grape varieties (6%), degree of slope (4%), exposure (3%), spacing of vines (2%), type of soil (2%), age of vines (1%), and shelter (1%). These formulae not only categorize our thinking but hopefully point out the prospect of a qualitative and quantitative expressions of plant performance.

Figure 2.1

THE WINEGROWING REGIONS OF AMERICA

The grape producing regions of America are highly localized in the Central Valley and coastal counties of California, the Columbia Plateau and the Yakima Valley of Washington, The Willamette Valley of Oregon, southern Arizona, western Texas, southwestern Michigan, the south shore of Lake Erie, the Finger Lakes region of New York, eastern Long Island, and northern Virginia. Collectively, these areas contain nearly 99 percent of all vineland. Nevertheless, the areas shown are exaggerated in area.
Source: Permission granted by Raisz Landform Maps.

An extremely hardy plant, the vine, while responsive to temperature, precipitation and soils, has, by its very amorphous character, diversified into many thousands of varieties. This does not mean that it can flourish with the same intensity everywhere. It is only a narrow climatic band in both hemispheres that is able to produce grapes for the commercial production of palatable wine. However, climate clearly limits commercial grape growing to temperate zones where microclimates severely circumscribe specific varieties. Grapes, native to the earth's warm temperature zones, are most successful between 30° and 50° north and south latitudes. Areas that have a prolonged dormant season and an abbreviated growing season, or a growing season without low temperatures inducing dormancy, are able to grow grapes, but do not produce commercial quantities of fruit. Nevertheless, the distribution of commercial vineyards in a domain of 1,200 miles of latitude and more than 3,000 miles of longitude is shown in Fig. 2.1. It is important to note the anthological nature of variables influencing this unusual pattern: : severity of winter temperatures, the length of growing season, the amount of annual and seasonal moisture, average temperature of the growing season, latitude as determining the length of day, altitude as affecting exposure and all climatic elements normally associated with altitude, the amount of sunshine and degree of luminosity, and the physical, chemical character of the soil, and the human element. Of significance is the fact that the distribution of grapes is not congruent with the sea-level growing season. The minimum length of growing season (the period between the last spring frost and the first autumnal frost) for most grape varieties is 140 days, although the range under unusual circumstances can vary between 90 days to as many as 300 days. Within these broad generalizations, vineyard sites are highly localized within these latitudinal belts among six major climatic groups in 41 states.

CLIMATIC CONTROLS

The factors that cause climatic regimes are known as climatic controls, of which air masses, latitude, sources and type of moisture, wind, elevation, and ocean currents and bodies of water are the most important.

1. Air Masses And Resulting Wind Patterns

Fig. 2.2-3 indicate the dominant air masses of the North American continent for winter and summer. Maritime polar is a relatively mild, moist, but unstable air mass that induces heavy precipitation along the windward slopes, but is less wet after it descends to the east-facing slopes of the Rockies. Highly seasonal, this air mass has an ability to generate Chinook effects. In the eastern portions of the country this air mass is able to generate heavy accumulations of snow and foggy conditions as it flows over a cold surface. Maritime tropical is a relatively stable air mass originating over the colder California Current that generates precipitation as it flows over colder land. Another maritime tropical air mass, originating over the Caribbean and Gulf of Mexico areas of America, dominates the weather patterns of the eastern one third of the nation year round. It encourages high levels of humidity, temperature, precipitation, and, historically, is the bane of viticulturalists.

The most important, along with general characteristics, during winter is: continental arctic, most prevalent in the northcentral portion of the continent extending as far south as the southern Great Plains. This air mass produces long periods of clear, cold, dry weather, and dominates a good deal of the weather patterns of the continent during this season, thus setting the northern limits for viticulture in the northcentral and northeastern portions of the country. In general, the western third of the nation is characterized by high local relief and highly variable weather patterns, but the rest of the nation, not subject to significant topographic obstacles, is open to incursions of both cold, dry air moving southward from Canada, and warm, moist air moving northward from the Gulf of Mexico. Cold air outbursts are caused by a northerly outbreak of continental polar air that in winter regularly penetrates deep into the central and eastern portions of the nation, and often as far south as the Gulf Coast injuring many cold-sensitive plants. These cold waves are defined as a temperature drop of at least 20F in 24 hours, and in the middle of winter are usually below 0F. As limiting as these cold outbursts are to successful viticulture, hot, humid maritime air is just as pervasive during the period of March through November. Flowing north-northeastward, this air mass had contributed much to restricting commercial viticultural activities until recently.

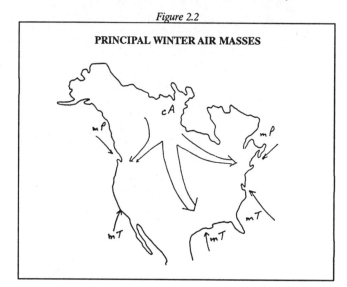

Figure 2.2

PRINCIPAL WINTER AIR MASSES

The summer pattern is significantly different as all major air masses shift northward. Continental polar air masses are less cold and do not penetrate Texas and a good portion of the southeast; the Pacific maritime air masses shift further north, and, as the prevailing winds blow from the colder California Current onto the hot California mainland, they induce aridity. The southwest is dominated by dry, hot continental tropical air, but the central and eastern portion of the country is overwhelmed by six months of hot and humid maritime tropical air.

Figure 2.3

PRINCIPAL SUMMER AIR MASSES

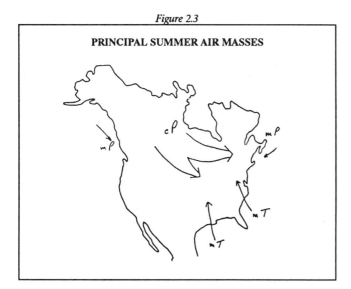

2. Latitude

Latitude determines winter and summer sun angle, the length of day, and the amount of solar insolation or heat that reaches the earth's surface. Of all the major climatic elements temperature appears to be the most meaningful factor affecting the number of days necessary to mature fruit. The temperature of a specific location is chiefly determined by latitude, altitude, and proximity to large bodies of water. Along the same latitude, length of growing season is influenced by elevation, proximity to water, and the slope of the land. The important temperatures (although there are some variations) are 50F for vine growth to begin, and 63F-68F for flowering to occur. Cool weather generally means a higher acid content and sour grapes, while hotter weather produces lower acidity and higher sugar levels.

Figure 2.4

INTENSITY OF SOLAR RADIATION

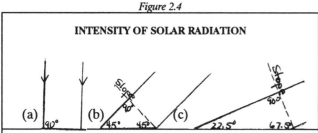

1. The intensity of solar radiation varies with latitude. 2. Solar radiation at the equator is most intense when the sun is directly overhead (a). 3. With increasing latitude, the solar radiation received at the earth's surface is less effective because: (a) it spreads over a larger area; (b) covers more atmosphere; and (c) is less direct, hence, less effective. 4. One way to ameliorate this condition in mid to high latitude regions is for vineyards to be planted on south-facing slopes, thus making solar radiation more effective (c).

For mid-latitude regions, sun angle and length of day are of paramount interest (Fig. 2.4). Sun angle determines the effectiveness of solar radiation, the amount of air penetrated, and the amount of ground covered. The total

cumulative effect in mid-latitude areas is mitigated by slope. For example, the sun penetrates (a) more effectively than (b) and (c) because it covers less land and penetrates less atmosphere. Duration of sunshine will increase color intensity of red wine grapes, and vineyards facing west will ripen earlier than those facing east as the elevation or sun angle is more direct.

Fig. 2.5 shows the significant effect of latitude on the amount of hours of daylight and darkness between Washington and California, where an increase of 14^0s produces nearly three extra hours of daylight. Fig. 2.6 illustrates the incidence of sunshine, and the reduction of annual sunshine in an irregular pattern from the zone of maximum sunshine in southern Arizona to the lowest incidence in the coastal areas of the northwest and the northeast. There is an extraordinary difference between sunshine in the Central Valley with more than 90 percent vs. the south shore of Lake Erie with less than 44 percent.

Figure 2.5

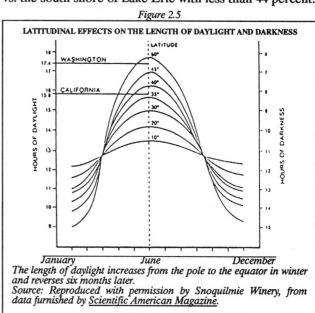

LATITUDINAL EFFECTS ON THE LENGTH OF DAYLIGHT AND DARKNESS

The length of daylight increases from the pole to the equator in winter and reverses six months later.
Source: Reproduced with permission by Snoquilmie Winery, from data furnished by Scientific American Magazine.

Bright sunlight is not used very effectively by a grapevine because a canopy has many layers of leaves with only a relatively few directly exposed to full sunlight during the entire day. Field experimentation has shown that the optimum temperature for photosynthesis by leaves is between 77F and 86F, that it declines rapidly above 86F, and falls to near zero at 113F. In the final analysis, average temperatures below 77F are considered better than those above. Diurnal temperature fluctuations are also important in that sugar gain and loss is a function of average temperature. While this is an obvious advantage for those areas with maximum sunshine by producing sugar during the day, sugar is lost during night respiration.

Another important element influencing air temperature, particularly at the local level, is albedo, or the ability of an object to reflect solar energy. Snow and ice have a greater albedo than bare ground; light colored rocks rather than dark; and water vs. land. Fresh snow reflects 80 to 90% of solar radiation, thus lowering temperatures more intensely than areas along the same latitude without snow, as in the midwest vs. Pacific and Atlantic coastal areas. Ultimately, the significance of solar radiation is the irregular distribution of air temperature.

Figure 2.6

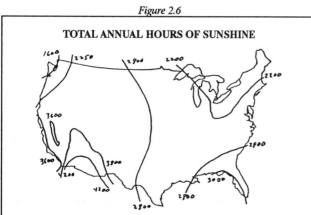

TOTAL ANNUAL HOURS OF SUNSHINE

Average annual sunshine decreases in an irregular pattern from the area of maximum sunshine in the southwest to the mid-Atlantic states and the area to the north The least sunny region in the nation is Puget Sound, Washington. However, the number of clear days in the northwest and the upper Great Lakes is 80; in New England, 120; in central Missouri, 130; and in southern Arizona, 314.
Source: U.S. Weather Bureau

Fig. 2.8 shows the distribution of the frost-free season, or the continuous number of frost-free days per year during the growing season. Frost is the term used to designate the deposit of minute ice crystals on the ground and on exposed surfaces whose temperatures have fallen below 32F. Contrary to current thinking, grapevines will tolerate very heavy winter frosts while dormant, but temperatures below 28F will damage new shoots and buds in the spring, thus reducing yields. Timing of bud burst varies by about four weeks between varieties, so where late frosts are likely, late budding varieties should be selected. For example, the threat of killing frosts to young shoots and buds is 90 percent throughout the Ohio River region up to April 30, and there is a 50 percent chance in the upper Great Lakes region up to June 4th. While unreasonable autumn frosts defoliate vines, they will not, unlike spring frosts, cause crop losses. Moreover, the significance of frost is not just the number of days the temperature falls below 32F, but the number of days whose temperatures fluctuate above and below 32F during the critical winter and spring seasons. While for much of the nation desirable sites are those where the mean date for frost occurrence is prior to April 15, there are many other sites where this date is as late as early June.

Frost deposition involves the principle of heat transfer, which is to say that whenever two adjacent or different portions of the same object have unequal tempera-

tures, the colder always gains heat at the expense of the warmer. This interchange of heat produces radiation and advective frost. Radiation frost is produced by the cooling of the earth's surface by radiation, nearly always occurring on clear nights when the air is dry, at a sub-zero dew point, and in the absence of wind activity. Radiation frost only affects a thin layer of air above the soil, and rarely at heights greater than ten feet. While fairly common in the hilly and mountainous areas of the far west, in the more cloudy eastern portions of the nation, due the greenhouse effect, this type very rarely produces frost activity of the same intensity. Advective frost is produced by the influx of Arctic air masses, and, as a consequence, is associated with thick layers of exceptionally cold air that resist uplift or displacement. It is associated with constantly increasing air pressure, gradually decreasing clouds, falling temperatures, and strong desiccating winds. While radiation frost occurs throughout all mid-latitude regions during spring and fall, advective frost is particularly dangerous throughout the northern tier of the nation east of the Rocky Mountains, and vast tracks of the Great Plains during the winter season as well. Factors promoting frost activity are: cold winds; calm and cloudless nights; bare ground; dry soils (sandy or stony); the absence of large bodies of water; and low lying areas subject to temperature inversions. Therefore, because frost activity is highly site selective, proximity to water (lakes, rivers, oceans, etc.) and hillside locations are desirable. Low lying areas where cold air collects are usually avoided.

Over the years man has devised many different ways to combat and reduce, if not eliminate, frost damage: (1) proper site selection; (2) although not universally successful, growth regulators that, when used properly, delay leafing out; (3) increasing soil moisture; (4) mechanical devices such as overhead sprinklers, heaters, blowers, helicopters, and plastic covering to break up temperature inversions or otherwise protect vines from cold air (5) careful selection of specific varieties; and (6) proper vineyard practices such as growing vegetation between rows; training vines higher from the ground level; delaying spring pruning; selecting late budding vines; and the removal of obstacles in the path of air movement to prevent "frost holes."

In the poleward portion of the middle latitudes, grape growing is limited by a short growing season and severe winter cold. Several days of -10F (or colder) temperatures are likely to kill most dormant Vinifera vines (some parts even damage at 30F). The extreme winter temperatures, although somewhat minimized by the Great Lakes, have been the bane of midwestern growers since early settlement. The southern portion of the nation suffers little from winter kill except for sensitive Vinifera in the higher elevations of the southwest. The northern limits are generally defined by the length of the growing season: one with fewer than 100 days precludes the commercial production of grapes; one between 100 and 140 days (depending on location) is marginal for American and French-American varieties, while Vinifera grapes require more than 160 days for acceptable commercial production. Unlike California where the shortest recorded growing season measured 144 days (Ukiah in Mendocino County), all eastern vineyards, except the humid southeast portions of Texas and Arkansas, have experienced, at varying levels of frequency, growing seasons below 130 days, thus being unable to mature most grapes. Planting of any type of grape in an area with less than 120 frost-free days not only involves risk, but is not to be found in any quality wine producing area in America.

Figure 2.7

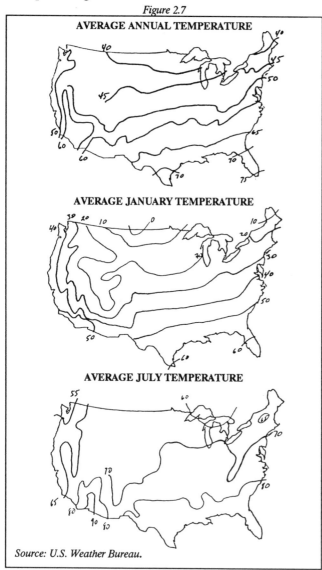

AVERAGE ANNUAL TEMPERATURE

AVERAGE JANUARY TEMPERATURE

AVERAGE JULY TEMPERATURE

Source: U.S. Weather Bureau.

The other extreme is an area with high temperatures. The major viticultural climatic problems in the southeast are prolonged bouts of heat and humidity that in combination induce mildew, black rot, and insect damage; in the southwest the lack of moisture induces desiccation. Generally, temperatures of 105F or higher damage grape quality. Prolonged unseasonable warm spells during the dormant season may cause premature sprouting followed by frost danger. The normal mild winters of northern Virginia are also detrimental to vines as this combination encourages insects and fungi diseases. Higher humidity can be tolerated in a cool region, but very rarely in association with high temperatures. In warmer climes grapes ripen earlier, have lower acids, higher pH, and lower color intensity.

Figure 2.8

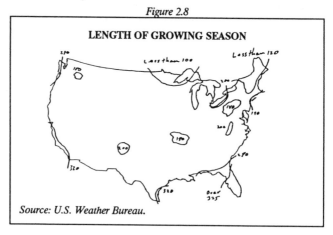

LENGTH OF GROWING SEASON

Source: U.S. Weather Bureau.

Figure 2.9

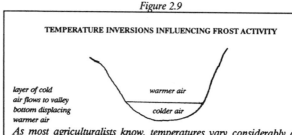

TEMPERATURE INVERSIONS INFLUENCING FROST ACTIVITY

layer of cold air flows to valley bottom displacing warmer air

warmer air

colder air

As most agriculturalists know, temperatures vary considerably over the average farm, and widely over a county area. On clear calm nights temperatures are lower in valleys than on the slopes. Because cool air is more dense (heavier) than warm air, it flows to the lowest spots much as water seeks the lowest levels. During the course of a night in late spring and early fall, cold air can build up to a depth of several hundred feet as a result of air drainage into a valley. Under optimum conditions, temperatures may be 8 to 15 degrees or more lower on the floor of a small valley than on the upper slopes. Undrained valleys represent the worst so-called "frost pockets." The northern slopes, also, will be colder than those exposed to the south since they receive less sunshine during the day and enter into evening shadow conditions earlier. The fact that the air "sits" on the ground for a prolonged period aggravates the danger of frost. As a consequence, vineyards and orchards are located above the inversion layer.

Heat summation is a crude empirical tool developed and applied with success in California for evaluating the grape growing climate in any particular locality. It is the sum of the mean daily temperature above 50F for the growing period of the vine, this temperature being that at which the sap starts to move. This system was developed by Winkler and Amerine who decided that temperature was the basis for segregating the grape producing areas of

California into five climatic regions. For their classification purposes, they used 50F as a base temperature applied specifically to the seven month grape growing season from April through October. Thus, if the average daily temperature is 65F, there would be 15 "heat" units, or degree days. It is also important to note that this 65F day with 15 heat units is equivalent to 15 days with an average temperature of 51F. It is thought that the minimum number of heat units is 1800 for early ripening varieties, and more than 3,000 for some late ripening varieties. According to Winkler and Amerine the five degree day climatic types are: Region I, less than 2,500; Region II, 2,501 to 3,000 ; Region III, 3,001 to 3,500; Region IV, 3,501 to 4,000; and Region V, 4,001+.

Figure 2.10

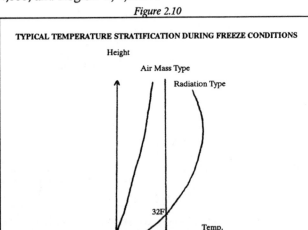

TYPICAL TEMPERATURE STRATIFICATION DURING FREEZE CONDITIONS

Height

Air Mass Type

Radiation Type

32F

Temp.

Air mass freeze occurs when a large mass of cold air invades and covers the area, resulting in low day and night temperatures. Radiation freeze, occurs when a large mass of air remains over the area for several days. Calm wind and clear skies produce higher day temperatures, but night temperatures close to the ground fall below freezing while the air above is warmer.

Despite its apparent notoriety in California, this system has several critics. The base of 50F, first promulgated by the botanist Alphonse de Candolle in 1855, is considered too low, and that the 65F base would be better. Degree days is supposed to give a good impression of the effectiveness of photosynthesis necessary to raise Brix levels, a notion that is quite misleading in semi-desertic and desertic climatic regions. In addition, degree summation is one dimensional as it does not relate with other climatic elements. The inapplicability of the Davis heat summation system in eastern America is best explained by a singular example. The Central Delaware Valley has a Region III 3000 degree day summation, yet it is in no way similar to Calistoga that is also Region III. While the basic requirements for a dormant season and a growing season long enough to ripen grapes exists in both areas, everything else is different. When all the possible physical permutations are taken into consideration and accurately evaluated, the Winkler Heat Summation system is no-

thing but a simple guide. It fails to consider day length and duration of maximum and minimum annual and diurnal temperatures, the albedo of the ground, precipitation characteristics, character of atmospheric humidity, and the amount of heat during grape ripening versus the amount of heat received during the vegetative period, among others. As a consequence, the date of harvest, quality of fruit, type and quality of wines made, and types of grape variety grown cannot accurately be determined by the Winkler-Amerine heat summation system uniformly throughout the world. The system also does not apply to geographically contiguous areas, thus the mouth of a valley facing the direction of ocean breezes can be Region I, while its upper portions may be higher.

Table 2.1

SELECTED TEMPERATURE SUMMATIONS

Location	Day Degrees Above 50F	Winkler Region
Bakersfield, California	5030	V
Altus, Arkansas	5000	V
Edenton, North Carolina	4600	V
Modesto, California	4010	V
Clarksburg, California	3860	IV
Augusta, Missouri	3800	IV
Lodi, California	3680	IV
Vevay, Indiana	3600	IV
Suisun, California	3530	IV
Florence, Italy	3530	IV
Middleburg, Virginia	3500	IV
Cloverdale, California	3430	III
Vienne, France	3430	III
Pinnacles, California	3330	III
Livermore, California	3260	III
St. Helena, California	3170	III
Catchogue, New York	3150	III
Paso Robles, California	3135	III
Catoctin, Maryland	3100	III
Catawba Island, Ohio	3034	III
The Dalles, Oregon	3014	III
Asheville, North Carolina	3000	III
Egg Harbor, New Jersey	3000	III
Placerville, California	2980	II
Ukiah, California	2970	II
Sonoma, California	2950	II
Fennville, Michigan	2,943	II
Conneaut, Ohio	2900	II
Napa, California	2880	II
Santa Barbara, California	2830	II
Central Douro, Portugal	2765	II
Grants Pass, Oregon	2740	II
San Luis Obispo, California	2620	II
Paw Paw, Michigan	2600	II
Clearwater, Idaho	2600	II
Yakima, Washington	2600	II
San Jose, California	2590	II
Bordeaux, France	2519	II
North East, Pennsylvania	2450	I
Geneva, New York	2400	I
Sunnyside, Washington	2397	I
Ben Lomond, California	2390	I
Roseburg, Oregon	2381	I
Traverse City, Michigan	2,356	I
Yakima, Washington	2,279	I
Edna Valley, California	2225	I
Forest Grove, Oregon	2200	I
Santa Maria Valley, California	2200	I
Salinas, California	2144	I
Epernay, France	2060	I
McMinnville, Oregon	1979	I
Lompoc, California	1970	I
Rheingau, Germany	1709	I
Bellingham, Washington	1,321	

Therefore, while it is possible to have many stations

with similar degree summations, the actual climate may be different, as in the case of Calistoga; eastern Long Island; the northern Rhone; Paso Robles; Catoctin, Maryland; Catawba Island, Ohio; The Dalles, Oregon; Asheville, North Carolina; and Egg Harbor, New Jersey. Calistoga is dry during the summer and wet during the winter; eastern Long Island (located in the western Atlantic) has a humid year-round climate that is quite dissimilar to Bordeaux (that lies along the eastern Atlantic Ocean), and The Dalles is dry during the summer and bitterly cold during the winter. The system is only useful when the climate is fairly uniform among the stations being compared, especially hot, dry climates. A more eclectic system should also take into account the following: mean temperature of the warmest month; the difference between mean temperatures of the warmest and coldest months; frequency and duration of temperature fluctuations; base 32F during the months of December-March; total sunshine hours; relative humidity; total precipitation; precipitation during the growing season; and number of cloudy hours during the growing season. It should also be noted that empirical observation indicates that there are no successful viticultural areas with fewer than 1700 heat-summation units. In addition to the Winkler summation system, another guide is called Latitude-Temperature Index, defined as the mean temperature of the warmest month x latitude, that is supposed to be a better correlation between grape growing conditions and climate. Intriguing in theory, empirical observations, however, do not exhibit such a perfect correlation as evidenced by the Yakima Valley vs. the Rhone Valley, two areas with similar LTI's, but a highly divergent grape mix.

While the heat summation debate rages, there is no interlocution over the relationship of certain grape varieties and their proclivity for a minimum number of degree-days for proper grape maturity. Early ripening varieties are mostly white in color, yield less, and are invariably associated with cooler climates, of which Chardonnay, Pinot Gris, Pinot Noir, Riesling, Chenin Blanc, and Gewurztraminer are the most important. Late maturing varieties tend to be red in color and more vigorous, of which Cabernet Sauvignon, Zinfandel, and Grenache are typical examples. Among American varieties the most hardy are Beta, Kay Gray, and La Crosse (all grown in Minnesota), followed by Clinton, Brighton, Concord, Fredonia, and Worden. Among French-American grapes, Seibel 1000 and Marechal Foch appear to be the hardiest, but not more so than the leading American varieties.

3. Type of Precipitation and Sources of Moisture.

Average annual and seasonal precipitation patterns are shown below. While rainfall follows a more regular and predicable pattern in the Great Lakes region, it varies widely along the east coast due to the more widely varying pattern of the jet stream and hurricane movements along the Atlantic coast. Heavy precipitation in the critical months of September-October is relatively low on average, but sudden, aberrant conditions often make the harvest season particularly rainy, spoiling the harvest in both quantity and quality (mold and rot are endemic and often disastrous). Atmospheric humidity is a major problem when it is uniformly high throughout the year, but particularly during the growing season. Since botrytis requires a 24-hour period of a 93 percent humidity level, it thrives in the humid southeast and Gulf Coast regions. In sharp contrast, California, the southwestern portions of the country, and the lee slopes of the Cascades are relatively free of humidity and precipitation during the growing season.

L.M. Mawby Winery, Suttons Bay, northern Michigan
Extreme winter temperatures reduce yields or may even kill more sensitive varieties and old vines. Frosts are particularly devastating in spring when they can kill young shoots and thus reduce yields to disastrous levels. The vine likes a mild, moist spring with a gradual increase in temperature, and moderate amounts of rain during the growing season but not excessive amounts as individual berries swell thus diluting the must, a situation that produces a watery wine with weak color, reduced extract and tannin, and an unstable aging future. An ideal June heralds an abundance of bloom and a good grape set. A wet August brings out a host of parasites and diseases. Most critical during the growing season are the last 15 days in the maturation of the vine: sunny and dry days are ideal for proper maturation prior to picking. A sunny September and October results in a high sugar content and increased concentration, and thick skinned grapes deep in color, tannin, and fruit. It is said that spring makes the quantity and September the quality. Three important physiological processes occur during the fall season: the vine must mature its fruit; mature the wood to allow overwintering; and store carbohydrates to sustain proper bud growth in the spring.

In grape growing it is not only the total annual precipitation figures that are important, but the frequency, duration, intensity, and seasonal patterns. As an example, Fig. 2.11 illustrates the three types of precipitation patterns: convectional, cyclonic, and orographic. Convectional precipitation is characterized by short duration and high intensity, and mainly occurs during the period of high sun. Cyclonic, or frontal precipitation, confined to mid-latitude regions, is noted for cold and warm front rainfall, the former producing short duration and high intensity fea-

clement weather noted for its low intensity and prolonged duration. Orographic precipitation occurs when an air mass encounters a topographic obstacle and as it rises produces precipitation of high intensity, and often of prolonged duration. As a result of these patterns, Miami's annual 60 inch rainfall total, at first glance, sounds pretty wet, but Syracuse, New York, with only about two-thirds the total rainfall, actually has rain twice as often as Miami. Similarly, New Orleans has nearly half again as much rain as Portland, Oregon, but it rains twice as often in Portland as in New Orleans. (Hence, the notion that "how often it rains is more meaningful than how much.")

Figure 2.11

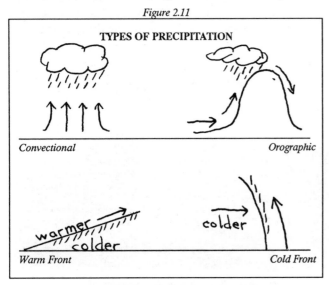

In terms of how much of the time moisture is actually falling, Portland has measurable rain for more than 1,000 hours in an average year. New Orleans, in sharp contrast, receives less than half that, with rain falling just over 450 hours. What is interesting is that Portland's total annual water collection is exceeded by several cities, including Miami, Boston, Atlanta, and Memphis, but in terms of hours when rain is falling Portland is first followed by Syracuse and Buffalo. Portland's 1,009 hours of precipitation means that it rains or snows there 11.5 percent of the time. From Texas to southern California, less than 4 percent (350 hours) of the year has measurable precipitation. Las Vegas and Phoenix have 79 and 109 hours of measurable precipitation respectively. Areas with the most frequent precipitation include the Appalachians, the Great Lakes, New England, and the Pacific northwest. Another interesting, but no less critical precipitation measurement, is growing season rainfall: eastern Long Island has 28;" Bordeaux, 17;" Prosser, Washington 3;" St. Helena 5;" and McMinnville 9." Usually grapes can be dry-farmed with as little as 15 inches of rainfall.

The foregoing have important implications as rain affects every phase of the grape growing effort: heavy late winter rains can delay pruning and budbreak causing a late harvest during a rainy season; rainfall during harvest upsets the grape's sugar/acid balance and promotes mold and rot problems; a cold, waterlogged soil makes vines susceptible to mildew; an absence of summer rainfall, especially during the harvest season, is a favorable factor provided irrigation water is available or winter rains are plentiful; in the southeastern portion of the nation, the timing of summer rains, amount of rainfall, and the length of time before dry conditions return is most critical to the grower; rain during the bloom period may cause a poor berry set resulting in a light crop; quality grape production occurs when there is a dry period just prior to the harvest, a condition that favors the western portion of the nation, particularly California, Oregon, Washington, and portions of the southwest.

Figure 2.12

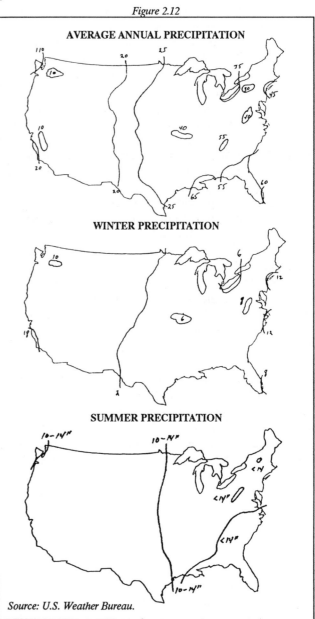

Source: U.S. Weather Bureau.

Precipitation in suspension, commonly referred to as fog, is shown in Fig. 2.13. Fog cools vineyards and shrinks grapes, and works as a natural retentive to keep fruit on the vine longer, thus increasing fruit intensity. In four season climatic regions such as the midwest and northeast, an increase in cloudiness means lower heat summation, an abbreviated growing season, low sugar content, low pH, high acidity, and reduced color intensity. In this area, rainfall during the season is at least 50 percent of the annual total, and erratic in duration and intensity. However, along coastal California, fog promotes a significantly longer, less hot, growing season producing superior grapes than the hot, interior valleys.

Figure 2.13

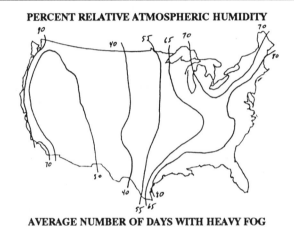

PERCENT RELATIVE ATMOSPHERIC HUMIDITY

AVERAGE NUMBER OF DAYS WITH HEAVY FOG

Cape Disappointment, Washington, at the mouth of the Columbia River, averages 2,552 hours (equal to 106 complete days) of heavy fog annually. Normally foggiest during the period August-September, the fog burns off in late morning and returns late afternoon. Along the east coast, coastal Maine averages 1,480 hours annually of heavy fog; Nantucket Island, in southern Massachusetts, averages 85 days of fog. In the high elevations of West Virginia fog is recorded over 100 days a year.
Source: U.S. Weather Bureau.

Whenever sharp water-land temperatures exist, as in the case of California, dense fog activity is the result. Fog has the ability of creating a mantle that reduces the total amount of solar penetration, thus reducing average daily temperatures. Discounting the effects of elevation, the cooler temperatures are invariably associated with the cold California Current along coastal areas. Fog moderates climate by decreasing light intensity, and acts as a source of moisture for plant life, particularly in certain coastal arid regions. Highly significant is the fact that for many stations located near water, frost is a rare occurrence.

The Deutz Winery, San Luis Obispo, Coastal California
The effect of fog in coastal California: 1. delays the daily maximum temperature by 2 to 4 hours, hence lower average temperature by as much as 20F. 2. High temperatures are maintained only for a shorter period. 3. It is highly localized on the coast and only penetrates interior areas where there is a break in the Coastal Range. 4. Due to the presence of cold coastal water, the West Coast and coastal New England north of Rhode Island have the highest incidence of fog. 5. Approximately one-sixth of the calendar year is shrouded in dense fog along the western coastal margins.

The foregoing suggests peculiar water flow and evapotranspiration patterns as vines exhibit xerophytic and phreatophytic characteristics. To avoid the dangers of drought vines have both lateral roots close to the surface and a long tap root to seek water deep below ground surface. Without water the vine will cease the production of new green shoots and leaves, and acclimate to the stressful condition (reduced water), a desired scenario the last three to four weeks prior to maturity in order to prevent the over enlargement of clusters and berries. If the supply of water is extreme, the vine keeps on producing foliage at the expense of ripening fruit.

Evapotranspiration refers to the movement of water between a vine's roots and the transpiration of moisture through the leaves, the former occurs through the plants root system, and the latter through microscopic holes (called stomata) located in the underside of leaves. Stomata can regulate the transpiration of moisture (by opening or closing) depending upon the general environmental conditions. On cloudy days stomata are closed, and on sunny days, under moist soil conditions, stomata will open to transpire moisture. When it gets excessively hot (or when water is not available to plant roots) and the rate of evaporation is high, stomata will close to conserve moisture. A delicate balance is necessary in a situation where water is not available and the stomata are closed because photosynthesis is impaired leading to lower sugar production. Potential evapotranspiration, or PET, is used to compare the water loss potential of different regions. PET is expressed in inches of water per unit of time and is a measure of how much evapotranspiration should occur from a moist surface. Evapotranspiration rates for vineyards will vary according to the development of the vine canopy, presence or absence of ground cover, cultivation, and atmospheric conditions. In the San Joaquin Valley, Thompson Seedless requires 3.5 to 4.5 inches per month; mature vines between 24-36 inches of water per season. In Charlottesville, Virginia, during June, July and August, there is a deficit of 4.5 inches although annual precipitation approaches 50 inches. Moreover, annual amounts of precipitation do not provide a measure of frequency, and even monthly precipitation averages can give a misleading impression of moisture availability. Summer precipitation in Virginia results from high intensity thunderstorms, usually restricted to small areas and of short duration, resulting in a low rate of absorption. Therefore, drought is usually the norm, not the exception.

4. Local Wind.

Local winds are produced by the same forces that invoke large scale winds--the occurrence of temperature variations due to unequal heating of the earth's surface, and partly by friction. Wind is of importance because it influences temperature, increases evapotranspiration and consequent water needs that enhance or delay grape maturation. In excess, wind results in physical damage reducing shoot length, leaf size, stomatal density, and further disrupts spray schedules. In addition to influencing rainfall patterns at higher elevations, wind has the effect of lowering temperatures on the windward side of mountains and raising temperatures on the leeward side. There is a strong propensity to also lower temperatures (though the related incidence of fog) where air blows over cold water and then over warmer land (California). But in the Gulf Coast and southeastern America, sharp temperature variations between water and land are lacking as there is constant humidity and higher than normal temperatures.

There are four local or regional winds that affect viticulture: sea breeze, mountain valley wind, katabatic wind, and chinook, or foehn wind. All major rivers, lakes and coastal regions can induce localized wind activity. Along Lake Erie, the lake often is cooler than the surrounding land, and the breeze blows onshore and gives welcome relief from heat to the people living within 10 miles of the lake. At night the lake is warmer than the land, and the direction of the breeze changes and blows offshore. These effects cause downdrafts of air over the lake during the day that tend to disperse the clouds and give the lake about an hour more of sunlight each day than the surrounding land. In winter the lake is the cause of lake-effect snowfalls caused by northwest winds blowing across the lake. The temperature of these winds is much colder than that of the lake, and the water that evaporates from the lake's surface is soon condensed into snow. This

Figure 2.14

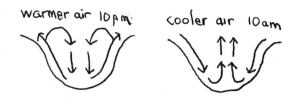

LAND AND SEA, AND MOUNTAIN AND VALLEY BREEZES

Onshore breeze   Offshore breeze

Land and sea breezes: The day to night reversal of wind is a consequence of the different rates of heating and cooling of land and water. Land areas near a large body of water have greater immunity to frosts than do inland locations. Under similar conditions, land warms and cools about five times as rapidly as water. During the winter months the temperature of the water is lowered to such a point that seas and large lakes remain comparatively cool throughout the spring and exert a two-fold influence on the air temperature for a distance inland: (1) the cold air from the water tends to retard vegetation until the period of spring frosts has passed; (2) during the period of spring frosts, it tends to hold the temperature of the air over adjacent lands, particularly at night, above the danger point. Coastal regions are also cooler than interior areas. Therefore, the acid content of coastal grown grapes is twice that emanating from the Central Valley near Fresno.

The part of California that lies along the Pacific Ocean has a different climate from the rest of the state because weather patterns along the coast are caused by winds that blow in from the cold California Current producing fog. Moisture condenses when it reaches a band of cold water that lies about 20 miles offshore. During the summer, as fog progresses inland it gradually dissipates, but in the process it reduces the incidence of sunlight, and, hence, average temperatures. Carneros, the southernmost region in both Napa and Sonoma counties, is a classic example of the significance of a coastal location. Winds are activated nearly every afternoon around 2 p.m., and along with fog, lower average daily temperatures 10F to 15F from areas like Calistoga, 30 miles to the north. The region is also warmer in the winter, has a longer growing season, and bud break is three weeks earlier than the northern Napa Valley.

Upslope breeze   Downslope breeze

Mountain and valley breezes: the reversal of wind is the consequence of the differential heating of mountains during the day and their cooling at night. The poleward limit of the vine is pushed northward and upward by planting vineyards on south-facing slopes, along terraces, on stony soil, and adjacent to lakes and rivers. Radiated and reflected heat from the rocks, walls, and water raise temperatures, a necessary condition in the production of sugar in the juice of the grape.

snowfall on the south shore areas, especially between Cleveland and Buffalo, can amount to more than 100 inches greater than on the north shore. As important as the land-water differences are in interior lake margins, those along oceans are more dramatic because the sea is a greater reservoir of heat. Therefore, average temperature along sea coasts is higher in winter and lower in summer than at interior locations. This is clearly illustrated by the length of the growing season between the coastal margins of southern New England-Long Island, and the southern margins of the Great Lakes.

Mountain and valley winds occur because along mountain slopes there is a thermal circulation that has a diurnal cycle. Due to the differential cooling and heating of the various aspects, wind either moves upslope or downslope. The latter condition occurs during the early morning hours, because the upper, more exposed areas of a hill or mountain cool faster, and the colder air, being heavier than warmer air, begins to flow down slope. This process is reversed in the evening because the upper slopes have warmed up faster than the valley, and, as a consequence, heavier, colder air begins to be pulled upslope by the rising, warmer, more buoyant air. The intensity of the flow and its direction at any point depends on the degree of slope and the configuration of the valley.

One of the most persistent and notable of all winds is the chinook, a wind that is particularly warm and dry, and not caused by the drainage of dense air. Of marine origin, this air mass loses its moisture when directed to a mountain side because of cooling (windward side). As this air then begins to descend along the leeward slope it is warmed at a constant rate (dry adiabatic lapse rate). Chinook winds are always warmer (at comparable altitudes) on the windward side, and significantly drier. Most common along the hilly and mountainous west, the onset of the chinook produces temperatures well above seasonal normals (temperature increases of 40F have been observed within a four hour span.) so that snow is often melted rapidly, hence the use of the Indian word chinook meaning "snow eater."

When a mass of cold air over an elevated area begins to be pulled downward by gravity, it is referred to as a katabatic wind. This "drainage" wind, colder and significantly denser than surrounding air, is only of viticultural importance when it moves through a restricted area causing channeling, or an increase in velocity. Called *mistral* in the Rhone and *bora* in the Adriatic and Aegean, no generic name has surfaced in America. The Santa Ana winds of Southern California can be subjected to strong southerly to easterly winds that descend from the interior plateau of the Mojave Desert when high pressure prevails there and low pressure lies along the coastal plain. This wind surges through the mountain passes to the Pacific Ocean throughout the five southernmost California counties. These winds, originally cool and dry, are heated by gravity as they descend the Coastal Ranges and arrive near the coast as hot, desiccating winds that dehydrate

and strip vines, and, unfortunately, these winds are almost invariably associated with disastrous fires. These downslope winds are to be found throughout southern California, as well as the intermontane region of the Rocky Mountains. In all of the above circumstances, whenever a barrier is placed in the path of wind movement, minor or significant turbulence effects are created.

5. Elevation.

Altitude affects climate because, in general, temperature declines 3F for each 1,000 feet of elevation, producing greater amounts of precipitation than locations along the same latitude but lower altitudes. It follows that a station at a high altitude may sometimes be more suitable for viticulture than one at a low altitude that is further away from the equator. In general, the nearer one gets to the equator, the higher the "grape line," and in the southwestern portion of America, the "grape line" lies more than 5,000 feet above sea level (especially in Arizona and New Mexico), the highest vine altitude in America. Often, an elevation of 1000 feet above the surrounding land can be roughly equivalent to 200 miles of latitude from a climatic sense. Throughout the nation, the direction of the mountain ranges and distance from the sea exert a profound influence upon this limit.

Figure 2.15

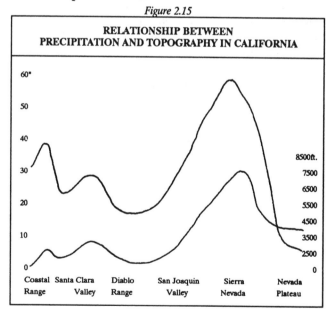

The significance of the above rests in the fact that where mountain ranges stretch for hundreds of miles they act as a friction force to prevailing air masses, and, as a consequence, create diverse climates. The Rocky Mountains, encompassing more than one-quarter of continental America, have in large measure induced the creation of large stretches of desert and semi-desertic climates on the lee side, and more humid conditions along the windward side. The effect of the Coast Ranges and the Sierras upon precipitation is well documented, and the effects upon human settlement and agricultural activities are most evident on the landscape.

6. Oceanic Currents and Bodies of Water.

By cooling and heating more slowly than land, water raises air temperatures in the winter and lowers them in summer. The moderating influence of water is due to its high specific heat, which is to say that water takes up a relatively large quantity of heat for every degree it rises in temperature, and gives off a relatively large amount when its temperature drops. The water thus acts as a regulating reservoir of heat by retaining heat more efficiently than soil, cooling the air in spring, and warming it in autumn. This climatic control is most obvious along coastal areas where there is either cold or warm water, and large bodies of water (including rivers) located in interior locations. The combined effect of areas adjacent to water is to mitigate "continentality," and, as a consequence, coastal regions or small islands may have climates markedly different from interior locations along the same latitude. Not only are they prone to daily sea or lake breezes, but average temperatures are less extreme by being warmer in winter and cooler in summer. Areas with the most pronounced coastal effect are Great and Finger Lakes, the warm Japanese Current region of the northwest, the cold California and Labrador Current regions of California and New England, and the warm water areas of the Gulf Coast and Gulf Stream. In the northeast, maritime influences are limited by the fact that prevailing winds are westerly, so the temperature regime, except for the narrowest of bands along the coast, is continental.

Figure 2.16

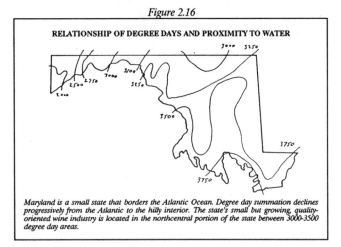

RELATIONSHIP OF DEGREE DAYS AND PROXIMITY TO WATER

Maryland is a small state that borders the Atlantic Ocean. Degree day summation declines progressively from the Atlantic to the hilly interior. The state's small but growing, quality-oriented wine industry is located in the northcentral portion of the state between 3000-3500 degree day areas.

The opposite effect of water as a moderating element of air temperature is called continentality, a condition that makes possible the largest annual variations in temperature in the center of the North American continent. It is estimated that this climatic control affects three-quarters of the nation, but comparable areas along the

Pacific and Atlantic Oceans along the same latitude do not experience similar seasonal extremes. Continental climates are so extreme that without the moderating influence of nearby bodies of water, such as rivers and lakes, grape growing would be next to impossible. Not only is the center of the nation either too warm or cold, but the entire region is subject to frequent changes in weather.

PRINCIPAL GRAPE-RELATED CLIMATES

Given the fact that continental America covers more than 25⁰s of latitude and 65⁰s of longitude, the interaction of the climatic controls discussed above create a complex mosaic of climates across America. The principal determining factors influencing climatic classification are temperature and precipitation among four combinations: hot and dry; cold and dry; cold and wet; and hot and wet, all of which have produced four commonly recognized climates according to the Koppen classification, three of which are important to grape production. The important six stages in the annual cycle of the bud break, flowering or blooming, berry set, ripening, maturity, and wood hardening are subject to wide fluctuations among the principal climatic regions (as well as principal grape variety) encountered in America.

1. Desertic Climates

This climate is characterized by several unique features: it consistently records the highest sunshine levels, the largest diurnal temperature fluctuations, highest temperatures, and the lowest levels of precipitation and relative humidity. The high incidence of sunshine and temperatures combine to produce a series of profound physiological effects: photosynthesis declines rapidly above 86F and falls to nearly zero at 113F. High temperatures reduce photosynthesis through thermal instability of enzymes, tissue desiccation, and closure of stomata, developments that do not yield high quality wine grapes. Another distinguishing feature of this climate is excessive evaporation, or a condition representing a significant mass and energy transfer from the ground to the atmosphere. While a cool mountain valley, for example, may lose 12 inches of moisture through evapotranspiration, an irrigated dessert loses more than 75 inches. Evaporation is much more than the reverse of rainfall or the return of moisture to the atmosphere from a meteorological point of view; but from the world of the living vine, it means that xerophytic features must be accommodated by the physical properties of soil and bedrock, and the degree of transpiration (total loss of water by the plant) of moisture by the vine.

Transpiration is a function of many variables of which climatic factors, type of soil, soil moisture content, wind, topography, aspect, and vineyard practices are the most important. Although there is no specific boundary, rainfall in desertic areas normally is less than 10 inches. In many portions of the southwest, extreme aridity and poor soil drainage combine to produce salt encrustation, a condition that reduces vine growth, crop yield, and quality. In extreme cases, water stress is compounded by toxicity leading to death. These regions, mainly California and Arizona, contain more than 100,000 acres of vineland, most of which are planted in raisin and table grapes. The bulk of wine grape acreage in New Mexico and Colorado occurs at higher elevations where there are significantly higher accumulations of rainfall. No matter what the location, nearly all grape growing activities throughout this climatic regime occur under irrigation.

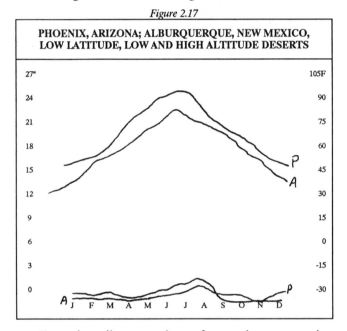

Figure 2.17

PHOENIX, ARIZONA; ALBURQUERQUE, NEW MEXICO, LOW LATITUDE, LOW AND HIGH ALTITUDE DESERTS

Desertic soils, a product of excessive evaporation over incoming precipitation, are described as "mineralized" due to the fact that their organic content is nearly non-existent. The limited profile is well above the water table and there is very little water available for leaching. The dominance of calcium, magnesium and potassium carbonates are a positive viticultural attribute.

2. Low and Middle-Latitude Semiarid Climates

Commonly referred to as steppe, these low latitude and middle latitude semiarid grasslands have more precipitation than desertic climates (between 10 and 24 inches depending on location and altitude), and are characterized by several unique features, of which climatic unpredictability is a key distinguishable feature. Semiarid does not imply half wet and half dry, but from an agricultural perspective some years are very wet, other years extremely dry, and in still other years they are wet and dry at the wrong times. Another feature is the decided continental character of this broad region, especially the northern

portion. Removed from major sources of water, annual and seasonal fluctuations of temperatures are wide for all altitudinal positions relative to similar stations situated along the Pacific and Atlantic.

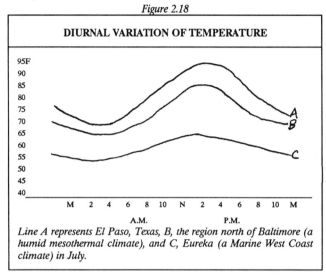

Figure 2.18

DIURNAL VARIATION OF TEMPERATURE

Line A represents El Paso, Texas, B, the region north of Baltimore (a humid mesothermal climate), and C, Eureka (a Marine West Coast climate) in July.

Low-latitude arid and semi-arid climates are characterized by between 10 and 24 inches of erratic precipitation, high but exceptionally variable mean annual, seasonal, and daily temperatures, and a near year-round growing season. Low-lying areas are characterized by such high summer temperatures that only table and raisin grapes are possible, fine table wine grapes being severely limited to higher elevations. Except for minor areas in Texas, New Mexico, Arizona, and California, where wine grapes are site-sensitive, these areas have limited possibilities despite the preeminence of portions of the Central Valley.

Mid-latitude semi-arid and arid regions lie to the north of the low latitude region and are characterized by similar precipitation patterns, but more effective rainfall due to lower annual and seasonal temperatures. Due to increased continentality, these areas experience extreme variations in temperatures between winter and summer, thus making site selection more critical than in low latitude regions due to the fact that the growing season varies between 130 and 180 days. Cold winter temperatures and a short, unpredictable season severely limit grape production in much of the Missouri tributary system in the northern Great Plains, and a good deal of the Intermontane Basin. However, the very conditions that limit the cultivation of grapes in most of this region also provide those critical elements that are able to produce good acid-sugar ratios, color, and excellent fruit aroma and flavors in selected locations. These areas of quality wine grape production are enormous throughout the intermontane region and the Great Plains, but particularly in the Columbia Plateau and portions of Idaho.

Figure 2.19

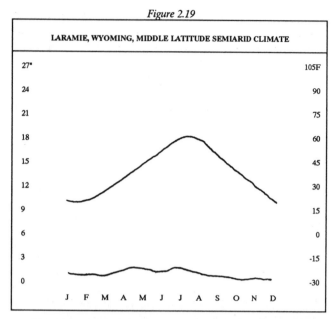

These climatic features are a function of three major air masses: cold Arctic air from the north, cold/warm and dry/humid westerly air, and moist, warm air from the Gulf of Mexico, the latter only affecting the southern portion. For most of the region, the bulk of precipitation falls during May through July. While the High Texas Plains region receives more than twice the rainfall of southwestern Arizona, high temperatures make a good portion ineffective in contrast to areas further north, especially in the Columbia Plateau. Nevertheless, most viticultural endeavors in Oregon, Washington, and the High Plains region of Texas occur under irrigated conditions.

Typical winter conditions in the upper and central Great Plains are characterized by alternating clear, dry, moderate temperatures, cold waves, rising temperatures in the 50sF, and heavy snowfall, often accompanied by driving winds. In late winter and early spring, along the lee side of the Rockies, Chinook winds raise the temperature to as much as 60F within a matter of hours (often evaporating as much as 12 inches of snow in a few hours), only to be followed by subfreezing temperatures several days later.

The climate in eastern Oregon-Washington, at first glance, would appear highly discouraging for viticultural pursuits. It is characterized by low winter and high summer temperatures; low rates of precipitation and high rates of evaporation; desiccating winds; and annual ranges in temperature that are among the highest in the nation. Further to the south, particularly around the Lubbock region of Texas, temperature fluctuations during fall, winter and spring can often be extreme, as was the case during February 12, 1990 when temperatures rose to 80F only to fall to below freezing several days later.

The soils of this climate are formed by calcification, a

process that requires evaporation to exceed precipitation during one season, and the reverse in another. This produces a basic reacting soil with considerable concentrations of calcium and magnesium carbonate, both of which are excellent for grape growing. The soils are well-drained and not leached. Due to the dominance of grass, the soil horizon contains a dark-colored humic horizon.

Figure 2.20

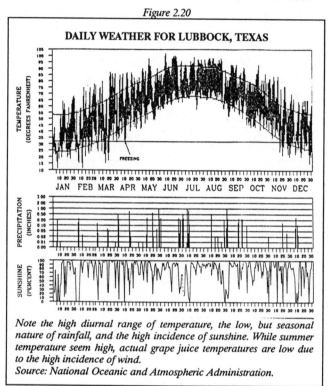

Note the high diurnal range of temperature, the low, but seasonal nature of rainfall, and the high incidence of sunshine. While summer temperature seem high, actual grape juice temperatures are low due to the high incidence of wind.
Source: National Oceanic and Atmospheric Administration.

3. Mediterranean Climate

There is an assured simplicity about Mediterranean climates. The unconventional feature of this climate is its winter rains and summer drought--essentially a two season climate that is only to be found in southwestern United States, central Chile, the southern tip of South Africa, land areas bordering the Mediterranean Sea, and the two southern tips of Australia (all areas of significant grape production). Of all the major mid-latitude climatic subdivisions in the world, this is the only one where winter is dominated by rainfall and summer by aridity.

Located on the western portion of the continent, this unusual climate lies in a transitional area between the desertic climate of northern Mexico and the cool, rainy climate of the higher mid latitudes. Thus, as one proceeds northward from Baja California to the Alaska panhandle, the amount of summer rain increases and the length of the summer drought period decreases. The climatograph illustrates this extraordinary two-season climate clearly, especially when compared with other climatic regions. Also significant is the fact that the winter period, though comprising one-fourth of the year, provides more than three-quarters of the annual precipitation total. Everywhere precipitation is directly proportional to windward, upland elevations, with significantly less rainfall on the leeward side of mountains. Therefore, this climate in its purest form is characterized by a long, hot, dry, sunny summer, and a mild winter with periodic bouts of rain and overcast conditions. Vinifera grapes, requiring long, warm to hot summers and cool winters for optimum development, are native to this climatic--hence the overwhelming concentration in California.

Figure 2.21

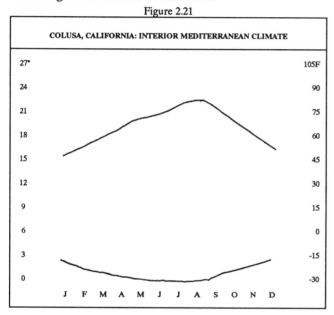

The dry period, coincident with high summer temperatures, incurs a large water deficiency during the summer months, whereas winter rains produce a moisture surplus by early spring. Given the fact that total precipitation is relatively low and highly variable, the amount of winter precipitation is highly critical to plant growth in order to survive the droughty summer. The xerophytic vegetation is characterized by hardleaf evergreen trees and shrubs with a natural proclivity to survive through four rainless summer months. Soils, reddish-chestnut and reddish-brown, and typical of semiarid climates, are remarkably mineralized, and when irrigated highly fertile. The effect of this climatic region in the economic geography of the nation is profound as irrigation has made possible the most productive agricultural landscape.

4. Marine West Coast Climate

This climate is found in only one area of contiguous America--in the western portions of northern California, Oregon, and Washington. The Marine West Coast climate is one devoid of extremes: the warmest month averages below 71.6F and the coldest month averages above 32F. Influenced by maritime polar air masses, the relatively warm Alaska Current, and the flow of the prevailing westerly winds, it is the only area of contiguous America where continental polar air masses do not significantly influence this high latitude region. Because of their tendency to move eastward, severe dry-cold conditions rarely alternate with tropical maritime air masses as in the midwest and northeast. Along the windward margins cooler air temperatures reduce the rate of evaporation and produce a very damp, humid climate with much cloud cover. While southern California enjoys 330 sunny days, Seattle has the pleasure of fewer than 100. Further, proximity to the Pacific Ocean produces a small annual temperature range. Moreover, winters, severely cold at the same latitudes in the midsection of the nation, are, by contrast, surprisingly mild along these Pacific margins. The orographic influences of precipitation along the windward coastal mountains are significant with equally dramatic effects along the leeward exposures. Along the windward margins, strongly leached podzol soil, supports evergreen forests, while the lee sides are essentially covered with grasses and deciduous forest along river courses.

Figure 2.22

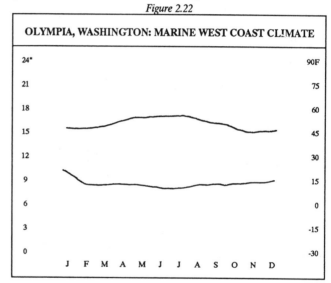

Just as viticulture is discouraged in similar climatic regions in northwest Europe and southern Chile, it does make inroads in the interior areas of western Europe, and along the lee slopes of the Coastal Ranges of Oregon where the climate is modified by less precipitation and more sunshine. In western Washington viticulture is overwhelmingly oriented toward those American and French-American varieties capable of withstanding inclement weather. The protected Nakoosa Valley in northern Washington, just 20 miles from maritime air, is an exception and able to grow Vinifera vines.

This is, therefore, the most temperate mid-latitude climate in the nation, sharply contrasting with the continental type in the center of the continent. Winters are cloudy, and despite their mildness, often dreary. Rainfall, heavy in winter, and abundant in spring and fall, is often inadequate during the summer season. These temperate features are further ameliorated by the "greenhouse effect," a term used to describe the process that allows sunlight to penetrate the earth's atmosphere easily, but releases that heat back into space with great difficulty. Because of the greenhouse effect, the atmosphere retains considerably more heat, and thus the temperature of the earth's surface is higher than otherwise.

Nevertheless, hazardous weather does occur. For the second year in a row and the third time since 1972, Oregon vineyards were hit by a severe freeze in 1990-91 when temperatures dropped to -12F along the Columbia River in eastern Oregon, and -4F in Medford just north of the California border. For the latitude, this is a minor problem when compared with low temperatures in the northeast and midwest. However, while these stations are located in more continental areas, the most significant weather feature injurious to grapes, besides spring frost, is early autumnal precipitation. This metereological phenomena is most distressing and the most critical element in determining highly variable vintage characteristics.

Figure 2.23

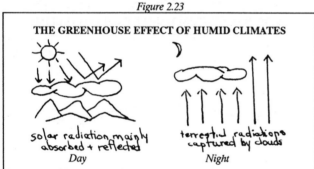

THE GREENHOUSE EFFECT OF HUMID CLIMATES

solar radiation mainly absorbed + reflected
Day

terrestrial radiation captured by clouds
Night

By intercepting short wave insolation, clouds produce lower daytime temperatures, and by trapping long wave terrestrial radiation, clouds raise night time temperatures, thus reducing diurnal temperature ranges. As a result, the largest diurnal temperature ranges are found in semi-arid and desertic regions, and are significantly lower in cloudy areas such as Marine West Coast climates.

4. Humid Mesothermal Climate

Located in the southeastern and Gulf Coast portions of the nation (a narrow belt extends as far north as New York), the humid mesothermal climate is influenced by maritime tropical air masses throughout the year, and, as a consequence, is characterized by hot, humid summers, and equally humid, but cool to warm winters. Precipitation varies from 35 inches to 80 inches (along coastal Louisiana-Mississippi-Alabama, and the southern Appalachians, an area that averages the highest summer rainfall in the nation). Summer is long, hot and humid, with the warmest month averaging over 71.6F. Winters are mild and less wet, with the coldest month averaging above 32F, but less than 64.6F. Tropical maritime air, invariably unstable, initiates relentless thunderstorms, but these downpours merely punctuate long periods of incessant sunshine. It also produces the highest incidence of 7 a.m. temperatures beyond 72F, a feature that clearly affects the distribution of commercial viticulture.

Figure 2.24

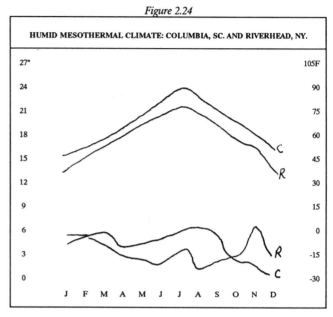

HUMID MESOTHERMAL CLIMATE: COLUMBIA, SC. AND RIVERHEAD, NY.

Tropical disturbances move eastward across the Atlantic with considerable frequency in August and September bathing not only the entire Caribbean and Gulf Coast regions but all of southeastern America, as well as contributing to a high incidence of hurricane activity. Although most of this storm activity is characterized by low pressure disturbances with heavy precipitation and wind velocities considerably below hurricane force, the fact that the storm track occurs over the warmest water on earth during the latter portion of the growing season overlapping with the harvest makes this area of the country marginal in the production of grapes other than those that are acclimated to atmospheric humidity and Pierce's Disease. When high pressure systems weaken in the north-central portion of the nation, these tropical disturbances flow northward, and although more pronounced along the Atlantic coast, they also affect large areas in the midwest as far north as the Great Lakes. This negative condition follows a large list of similar, less than desirable climatic features: a mild but damp winter, and a spring replete with unpredictable frost activity. The humid mesothermal climate is also known for high intensity/short duration precipitation, a condition that is particularly destructive to bunch grapes. New Orleans, Miami, Memphis, and Atlanta have all recorded more than 48 inches of rainfall over a period of 434 to 519 hours. This situation becomes progressively less intense as one proceeds north, northwest and west from the southeastern area of the country.

Despite the pleasant nature of both spring and fall, these seasons are simply not long enough to counterbalance the physical enervation that must be endured to promote successful viticulture in this climatic region. In the final analysis, the high temperature/humidity character of the southeastern portion of the nation generally precludes the commercial cultivation of bunch grapes except those that have resistance to Pierce's Disease. This means that within a seven year period, all Vinifera, Labrusca, and French-American vines will usually die at elevations below 700 feet in elevation. In the northern and upland extremities of this climatic type, bunch grape cultivation is successful throughout Tennessee, North Carolina, Virginia, Maryland, Pennsylvania, and the coastal regions of New Jersey and New York. Only Rotundifolia varieties and bunch grapes (Stover, Blanc du Bois, and a few others) manage to successfully survive the assault of Pierce's Disease and the universality of fungus diseases.

Figure 2.25

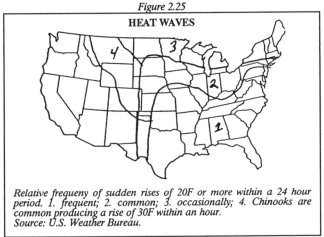

HEAT WAVES

Relative frequeny of sudden rises of 20F or more within a 24 hour period. 1. frequent; 2. common; 3. occasionally; 4. Chinooks are common producing a rise of 30F within an hour. Source: U.S. Weather Bureau.

Another problem is that the winter dormant period is not deep enough to harden wood, particularly in Vinifera. This condition is further compounded by the fact that the Bermuda High inhales maritime tropical air from the Caribbean raising temperatures, and vines begin to lose hardiness and are killed with the passage of the next high pressure front. However, there are instances when the marginal location of the northern producing regions becomes an advantage. Late winter frosts occur on average early in April in Virginia, late March in Napa, and the middle of May in the Finger Lakes region of New York state, hence, the most severe winter in the northeast since 1871 did very little damage south of Virginia in 1981, whereas areas to the north were crippled with a host of winter-kill problems. Nevertheless, the remarkable progress in the development of chemical sprays and new grape varieties has allowed viticultural endeavors to achieve several spectacular breakthroughs in Florida, eastern Texas, Georgia, and other minor areas.

5. Continental Microthermal Climates

The microthermal climatic regimes of the central and northeastern portion of the nation are characterized by four distinct seasons, year-round humidity, sharp seasonal

variations of unpredictable temperatures (including severe spring frost snaps), and precipitation fluctuations. They are distinguished by their colder winter weather, a condition that gets progressively more acute with increased latitude and distance from oceanic water. Not only do the northeastern and midwestern portions of the nation experience lower winter temperatures, but greater annual variability between mean monthly low and high temperatures than all other viticultural areas in the nation.

Figure 2.26

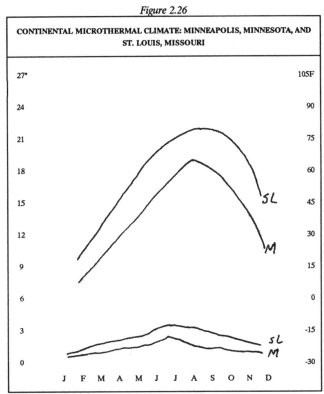

CONTINENTAL MICROTHERMAL CLIMATE: MINNEAPOLIS, MINNESOTA, AND ST. LOUIS, MISSOURI

While this vast region is in no way homogeneous, climatic regimes are subdivided into humid continental--warm summer in which the warmest month averages over 71.6F; a humid continental--cool summer in which the warmest month averages below 71.6F; and a long winter continental where there are four months whose average temperatures are less than 50F. Depending on location, precipitation varies between 25 and 60 inches. Except for lake margins, the annual temperature variations exceed the diurnal variations. These features, distributed over a four-season year, have one extraordinary meteorological feature in common--unpredictability, with disastrous consequences for all grapes, but primarily Vinifera. Mean measurements for any season is nearly always a meaningless reading because the grower's dream of an average to ideal harvest can be intercepted at any season without warning, unlike any other major grape growing American region. Excessive winter temperature fluctuations are not only uncertain but may be totally absent for several years before a particularly bad winter destroys an entire crop;

tion may unleash disease organisms that decimate a crop to the point where the cost of harvest exceeds income; and fall can be wrought with a large assortment of untimely weather conditions--excessive humidity, heavy precipitation, or an early fall frost. Other than weather, it is commonly said that the only other more dangerous circumstance for the eastern grower is politics.

The location of this vast region is intermediate between the source region of polar continental air masses on the north and maritime or continental tropical air masses on the south and southeast. Therefore, this region is a meeting ground for cyclonic and anticyclonic activity. The low pressure (cyclonic) storms usually move across the country in a northeasterly direction where they meet high pressure (anticyclonic) air masses resulting in a three to seven day pattern of clear and inclement weather activity. While the region is not a climatically homogeneous unit, there is considerable variation from lake margins, incised river valleys, interior locations, and higher elevations. Three types of air masses affect this broad region: (1) cold, dry air moving down from subarctic North America; (2) warm, moist air masses streaming northward along the Atlantic Coast, and from the Gulf of Mexico through the Ohio Valley; and (3) cool, damp air moving in from the North Atlantic. Depending on location each air mass will affect the midwest somewhat differently. For example, the extreme northern portion along the Great Lakes is mainly affected by Arctic and Gulf air; New England by cool, moist air from the Atlantic, and warm and moist air moving northward along the Atlantic; the southern extremities are mainly affected by Gulf air for half the year, and polar air in the winter; and the mid-Atlantic regions by a combination of the first two air masses.

One of the most common features of this climate is intense winter cold waves. The extremes in cold weather are a function of polar outbursts flowing south from Canada. Rapidly falling temperatures, driving winds, and blizzard conditions are influenced by the jet stream, a system of migrating upper level winds influencing the movement and alteration of low and high pressure systems in an easterly direction across America. Despite the absence of accurate recording devices until the second half of the nineteenth century, extremely low winter temperature readings occurred with some regularity every fifteen years. The Great Arctic outbreak of 1889 plunged temperatures to -2F in Tallahassee, Florida, and 6.8F in New Orleans. In the midwest, an area unprotected from Arctic cold air, cold waves with temperatures below 0F are fairly common for at least 20 days during the three winter months. Even along the Atlantic coastline unusually low temperatures seem to occur every generation. In one such cold outburst in February 1934, the average temperatures for the entire month averaged close to 0F

from Michigan to New York. This cold wave was repeated again in January 1978 and 1982, and in December of 1989. Although prolonged cold waves are a rarity along the Atlantic margins between Virginia and central coastal Maine, places along the same latitude in the central portion of the country, due to rapid heat loss, experience as many as 176 days of below 32F temperatures (as in Langdon, North Dakota during the period October 17, 1935-April 10, 1936).

This is clearly illustrated by the length of snow cover over two stations along the same latitude. Snow cover, lasting but 20 days in Cape Cod, increases to more than 100 days just 80 miles inland, a condition that is enhanced by the albedo (reflectivity) of snow. Temperatures along the Atlantic Coast are 10F to 20F higher than areas a few miles inland, the difference being greater as one increases latitude. Moreover, the moderating effect of the Atlantic is most evident in determining the length of the growing season. Similarly, excessive cloud cover over the Marine West Coast climatic region and a good portion of the humid northeast are affected by the more moderating greenhouse effect, thus minimizing diurnal temperature ranges. Similarly, during July and August in Lake Erie almost clear skies (less than 20 percent sky cover) prevail for 40 percent of the time, and each day averages more than 10 hours of sunshine. In winter heavy cloud cover prevails 70 percent of the time, with an average of less than three hours of sunshine per day. There are about 190 days free from frost along the south shore, and 130 along the north shore. The frost-free days decrease noticeably away from the shoreline, being as few as 140 in some places within 30 miles of the lake.

Another feature is abnormally hot, humid weather continuing over an extended number of days several times during the summer. The frequency and duration of these "heat waves" (excessive heat as far north as New York, with temperatures in the 90sF for several days in the middle of April not unusual), low and short early in the season, gradually increasing and lengthening by late August (and reenforced by hurricane activity along eastern margins), increase the probability of disease and otherwise interfere with the proper production and maturation of grapes. Not only does a duration greater than five days produce significant human psychological, physiological, and economic effects, but the affect on vines is equally important as fungus and viral disorders multiply necessitating nearly weekly spraying. Only the lee sides of the Great Lakes, isolated areas of the Appalachians, and most of New England escape 95F temperatures. Needless to say, heat wave activity intensifies in a southerly direction to the Gulf Coast and Florida, two areas of the nation that often exhibit six or more months of hot, humid weather. Less severe in terms of grape damage is the penetration of continental heat waves (they are less humid) along the western margins of the microthermal climates.

Therefore, this region, located in the center of the continent, is an area of meteorological extremes. During the winter of 1984-1985 in Missouri, the temperature plummeted from the mid 60sF to -27F causing severe damage not only to French-American varieties, but to American vines as well. Ten years later, the state endured the hottest summer of the previous 60 years. Precipitation is equally erratic throughout the region with the harvest period invariably threatened by untimely rainfall. In September 1986, the record rainfall of 8.23 inches in southwest Michigan is very revealing. The amount was 5.1 inches above normal, 80 percent falling during the harvest. With only one clear day in a 17-day period, cloud level during this time was 90-100 percent, and temperatures were 10F higher than normal promoting the growth of rot. In the previous year, 6.36 inches fell in September, raining for 13 days in a row beginning on September 11. Then the summer of 1988 was the hottest summer in nearly two generations.

Figure 2.27

MINNESOTA: CLIMATIC PATTERNS

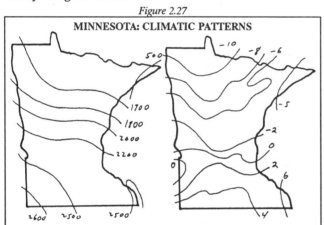

Degree Days   *Mean Minimum January Temperature*
While Minnesota lies along the same latitude as France, the continental character of its location makes grape-growing a precarious endeavor. With temperatures of -30F and below in January, Minnesota is considered the coldest wine growing site in the nation. As a consequence, this state has become the pioneer in cold-weather grape research and the development of such hardy grapes as Beta, Kay Gray, LaCrosse, St. Croix, etc.
Source: U.S. Weather Bureau.

In addition, due to location away from significant oceanic bodies of water, the central portion of the country also experiences the highest degree of continental climatic conditions. This explains why the summer temperature of central Massachusetts can be 60F and 102F in Kansas, while in January they can be 40F and -30F respectively. Although December is characterized as the month containing the shortest day and the most extreme temperature fluctuations (the deepest snows and the coldest temperatures have come during this month), if November is abnormally cold, December can often be warm and

muddy (this month can also be the stormiest month nearly everywhere in the nation). Nevertheless, the concentration of depth of frozen soil, duration of snow, and, date when mean daily temperature normally rises to 35F in the northern portion of the nation, is proof of extreme continentality in this portion of the nation.

Figure 2.28

EXAMPLES OF CONTINENTALITY

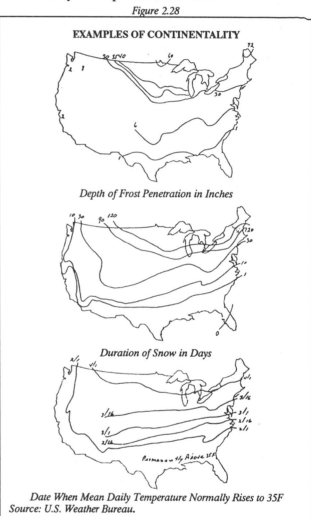

Depth of Frost Penetration in Inches

Duration of Snow in Days

Date When Mean Daily Temperature Normally Rises to 35F
Source: U.S. Weather Bureau.

An interesting feature of this cool climatic region is that ripening is a problem, hence grapes are acidic and low in sugar. For Cabernet Sauvignon grown in a cool climate the smell of bell pepper is quite prevalent due to the presence of 2-Methoxy, 3-Isobutyl Pyrazine, or MIP. It appears that these chemicals are less concentrated in grapes from warmer climates than those emanating from cooler climates. On the other hand, fruit flavors are more pronounced from cooler regions than hot areas, but fungus diseases necessitate early harvesting. In addition, grapes grown in cold climates make the yeast more efficient producing higher alcohol levels than hot region grapes picked at similar Brix levels. On the other hand, because the fruit is usually not ripe, malic acid dominates.

Soils in this climatic zone are podzolic, meaning that

they were formed under conditions of high humidity, low temperatures, and relatively poor drainage. Although the glacial debris does vary, the soils are characterized by well-marked horizons with limited fertility. The A horizon is heavily leached, and the B horizon is heavily impregnated with clay forming impermeable hardpans that impede the vertical flow of water. The natural reaction is acidity, a feature not normally conducive to grape cultivation, particularly Vinifera grapes. In the final analysis, because of the foregoing, successful cultivation of grapes is restricted to well-protected sites (south-facing slopes, and lake and river margins).

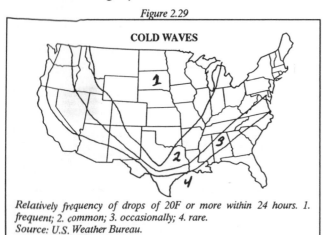

Figure 2.29

COLD WAVES

Relatively frequency of drops of 20F or more within 24 hours. 1. frequent; 2. common; 3. occasionally; 4. rare.
Source: U.S. Weather Bureau.

Given the fact that consumers prefer the taste and flavor of Vinifera-based wines, there is a feverish attempt to cultivate these vines throughout the northeast and midwest. The concerns and overwhelming problems are the survival of buds, canes and trunks from cold injury, fluctuating temperatures, and a damp atmosphere. The northeast and midwest, unlike the cold regions of the Columbia Plateau and western Europe, suffer from this negative environmental trilogy at a higher frequency than the other two. The Rhine and its many tributaries rarely, if ever, experience temperatures below 0F, winter temperatures rarely fluctuate 40F to 60F within days, and summers are decidedly drier. While the Columbia Plateau experiences lower winter temperatures, once they drop in early winter the tendency is for them to remain low without the characteristic "January thaw;" and summers, by contrast, are not only devoid of appreciable precipitation, atmospheric humidity is extremely low. Moreover, the usual host of diseases, like mildews, rot and phylloxera, are absent. The region east of the Rockies north of the 35th parallel is exposed to the vagaries of a highly irregular jet stream that extends the range of polar air masses further southward in winter, thus bathing the entire region in sudden bursts of -0F temperatures. As the jet stream swings further north of Chicago, tropical maritime air penetrates the entire region raising temperatures

rapidly within days, and often hours. For eight months of the year, particularly the critical swing seasons of spring and fall, and throughout the summer, tropical maritime air masses aggravate humidity-related problems. Spring and fall, longer along the southern margins and significantly shorter near the Canadian border, are characterized by unpredictability. Spring can arrive early or late, with or without rain, and the last killing frost may vary by as much as six weeks from year to year. Fall, equally unpredictable, arrives early or late, with or without rain during the critical four weeks prior to harvest (as well as during the harvest), and the severity of early winter depends upon the capricious "Indian summer."

Although found in nearly all viticultural regions, Crown Gall, a nasty, virulent, bacteria-induced disease, is particularly serious in the midwest and northeast. First described in France in 1853, it was scientifically defined in America in 1907. While grasses are immune, more than 640 dicotyledenous species, grapes included, are not. This disease, especially deadly to young vines, is associated with abundant soil moisture and freezing temperatures, especially early in the season, with sudden drops in temperature particularly serious. The disease is characterized by galls or overgrowths that form on roots, trunk, and arms of grapevines. The bacterium, *Argobacterium tumefaciens*, is carried in dormant grape cuttings used in the propagation of plants. Bacterium-free vines, wood hardening before winter, better site selection, better vineyard practices, and no wounding of vines during planting and cultivation reduce the incidence of Crown Gall. In addition, Black Rot, powdery and downy mildew, Japanese Beetles, and bird and deer damage are also serious throughout this region. However devastating these diseases and pests may be, the successful cultivation of grapes, particularly Vinifera, is mainly attributed to better insecticides, pesticides, fungicides, superior rootstocks, and better vineyard practices.

For most of the northeast and midwest the growing season is short, the soils rocky and poorly drained, the winters (the longest season) cold, and, as a consequence, nearly all vines are either American or French-American, with only a small fraction constituting the more expensive and sought-after Vinifera. The eastern grower, therefore, faces a basic troublesome dilemma in this highly unpredictable climate: native grapes grow well, but produce wines that the general market rejects; and, to a lesser degree, the same can be said for French-American varieties although their range does not extend to the more extreme interior continental areas. On the other hand, Vinifera vines, in great demand and at higher prices, suffer from the environmental constraints mentioned above. In the final analysis, the crucial growing problems of Vinifera varieties are essentially two fold: careful varietal selection to be grown in a specific locality; and field practices inducing better physiological wood maturity. Historic disease problems have been largely eliminated through modern chemical sprays, and better rootstocks.

What Is A Cold Climate?

The major problems with a microthermal climate is its ability to both kill grape vines and not provide enough heat to fully ripen grapes. A cold climate is one where grapes will not ripen in some years, and, as a result, it is a relative term as each specific grape variety has adapted over time to different environmental extremes. While there is no standard definition, it is widely defined as when the winter average temperature is below 30F, the average summer temperature is below 66F, and the mean annual temperature is below 48F. In general, cold climates have low winter temperatures, winter thaws, and early killing frosts. In western Washington, cool climate grape growing is defined as the growing of grapes in the coolest possible climate in which they will consistently ripen. This climate is defined regionally as one in which the average daily summer high temperature falls between 74F and 82F, or an area that accumulates annually between 1500 and 2200 warm crop agricultural heat units.

There is considerable confusion in the expression "cold (or cool) climate" by Americans when comparisons are made between the northeastern and midwestern portions of the nation with those of western Europe (especially with the northern limits of vine cultivation in France and Germany) and other areas with Marine West Coast climates (such as western Washington). There simply is no similarity. French and German growers merely use the term in a relative not absolute sense. Average winter and summer temperatures in north and north-central America are appreciably lower and higher respectively than northern France and Germany. In America, cold climate vine-growing and the expression "winter kill" are never just a matter of absolute winter low or even average low temperatures, but also of duration, and the frequency of winter temperature fluctuations. It is important to note that grapes cannot respond nor adapt to sudden 40F-50F declines and increases in temperature within a 72 hour period, a condition that is fairly common throughout the midwest and northeast. Moreover, the expressions infer growing conditions so short or inclement that sugar content is low, acids high, and that there will be a winter vine mortality rate greater than 10 percent. The latter condition need not occur every year, but over a period of ten years the economic costs encumbered by a grower will be sufficiently high to discourage further plantings of Vinifera, French-American, and, to a lesser degree, American vines.

Cold injury need not only occur in winter, and need not involve the formation of ice. In the main, there are four major ways that injury can occur in response to low temperature: membrane injury, starvation, formation or release of toxic substances, and the breakdown of proteins. Membrane injury occurs when its ability to control the flow of substances into and out of the cell is interfered with. Starvation refers to a shortage of carbohydrates in the storage areas of the plant to carry it through periods when there is no or reduced photosynthesis. This is most critical during the winter and spring, especially with the initial stages of bud break, and may lead to serious plant injury as the growing season progresses. The breakdown of proteins is usually related to all of the above as proteins are both structural and metabolic in character. The breakdown leads to the accumulation of toxic substances or an inability to produce the necessary nutrients to keep the cells functioning at optimum levels. All of the foregoing is further aggravated by freezing injury, the lethal destruction of plant cells, or plant stress through dehydration. It is interesting to note that the hardiest American grape vines (Beta, etc.) in the coldest commercial viticultural region of the nation (Minnesota), have some of the highest percentage of bud survival. Among French-American varietals, Seyval exhibits high bud survival. In addition to overall vine health and outright "winter kill," cold climates affect yields, and the chemical characteristics of the must (invariably lower pH, high acids, and lower sugar content).

One way of protecting vines from cold winter weather in the midwest and northeast is to "hill-up" or bury the vines in the soil in late fall in order to protect them from desiccating effects of bitterly cold winter air and wind. While this is costly and rare in the northeast, it remains in the colder interior midwestern portion of the nation. Not only do low temperatures desiccate grape vines, but the problem is aggravated when winter rainfall is reduced. Specific rootstocks not only provide protection against soil-borne deterrents to growth such as phylloxera and nematodes, but also influence the size of the vine and its fruiting characteristics. Most important, rootstocks influence the cold hardiness of the scions they support. Without question, grafted Vinifera on native rootstock have survived much better than ungrafted vines, or even French-American varieties on their own roots. Recent experimentation with exotic rootstock and hybridization with extremely winter-tolerant grapes has raised hopes in the northeast and midwest.

Vitis amurensis, named after the Amur River in east Russia and indigenous to a wide area of eastern Russia and northern China eastward to the Korean Peninsula, offers interesting genetic resources for the creation of new varieties tolerant of a wide range of climatic conditions. The Amur grape, and, to a smaller extent, Vitis silvestris, tolerates winter temperatures below -40F, high winds, and frozen soil as deep as 6 feet. It crosses easily with Vinifera and American grapes and transmits its cold-hardiness to its offspring. Amurensis vines are not tolerant to phylloxera and fungus diseases, but exhibit extreme tolerance for wide winter temperatures, and a short growing season with fewer than 90 frost-free days. While the summer season in northcentral Asia can be hot, humid and extremely short, winter temperatures remain below -0F for more than 80 days, often reaching temperatures as low as -70F for days at a stretch. Because of this environmental tolerance, and the fact that the taste of the fruit and wine is free of "foxy" flavors and fragrances, there is now feverish experimentation to produce superior rootstock and acceptable hybrids. There are now several interspecific varieties offering tremendous resistance to both low temperatures and fungus that are virtually indistinguishable from the indigenous Asian vines that are grown in Germany, the Soviet Union, Hungary, Romania, and Nova Scotia, Canada (two varieties--Michurinets and Severnyy are currently cultivated in experimental plots). Also of significance is a Missouri winery that cultivates a Vinifera vine (St. Vincent) that is resistant to phylloxera, suffers no winter damage, is resistant to most diseases, and produces wine with a clear, clean flavor, and good acid balance. Perhaps in the not-to-distant future, a winter-hardy and disease-resistant wine grape will be developed to meet the needs of the eastern table wine consumer.

The foregoing lead to the following conclusions:

1. Weather influences the rates of change in the chemical constituents during the growing season, and the chemical composition of the grapes at maturity. Under relatively cool conditions, grape maturation proceeds slowly producing excellent table wines in terms of higher acid, lower pH, good color, and intense aroma and flavor. As the climate becomes hotter, varietal aroma and flavor become less intense, acid and alcohol levels decline, and the pH increases producing coarse, less delicate and refined wines. Cultural factors, such as certain vineyard practices and site selections, in addition to weather conditions, can effect the above-mentioned chemical elements.

2. Seasonal variations in average temperature, wind, humidity, rainfall, etc. affect the chemical constituents of the mature grape berry at harvest time, hence the significance of "vintage years." Therefore, it is possible to make better than average wine in a cool growing region during a warmer than average summer, and better than average wine in a hot region during a cooler summer.

3. Cold injury is related to reserve carbohydrates. Grapevine growth is indeterminate, that is, it does not set terminal buds in the summer, but continues to grow into the fall. This growth is detrimental as it interferes with the accumulation of reserves. Plant tissue that is sufficiently desiccated ("hard") can withstand lower temperatures. While freezing water can cause major damage, it is the inability of cell size to shrink during the period of falling temperatures that is the main cause of bud kill.

4. Narrow spacing, and the protection of the graft union will reduce the incidence of winter kill.

5. A fall season with constantly declining temperatures without a major hot spell will reduce the danger of winter kill. After 8 to 10 weeks of dormancy, buds become highly responsive to temperatures above 50F. Roots are activated at 40F, and as root pressure rises the vine becomes highly vulnerable to rapidly declining temperatures. Most important are the rates of cooling and thawing in cell survival, a condition that is particularly destructive throughout the northeast and midwest. Daytime temperatures below 40F, for prolonged periods, are less injurious than so called "mild winter temperatures." When winter temperatures rise beyond 50F carbohydrates are drained, and the vine is weakened.

6. Any major insect infestation and fungus disease reduces effective leaf surface in late summer and early fall promoting winter kill.

7. Site selection is highly important in the northwest, midwest, and the northeastern portions of the nation. All low lying areas should be avoided, as well as hillsides with a tendency to "pond." In addition, soils should be well-drained with a minimum of clay, and no hard pans in the upper ten feet. Non-fertile soils are best, while rich, organic soils will hinder wood maturity. These physical site considerations will not eliminate cold damage, but will mitigate the more extreme physical dangers.

8. Potassium deficiency inhibits winter hardiness, reduces resistance to phylloxera, increases pH, and reduces fruit size and color development.

9. Proper rootstock selection and their compatibility to specific grape varieties and soil conditions is mandatory. Those that produce large vines, excessive vigor, and are late maturing should be avoided.

10. Controlling vigor and high yields will minimize cold injury and an open canopy will minimize cold injury. Growth should be encouraged along a vertical plane, not a lateral direction (thus encouraging air circulation), and it is recommended that no unnecessary leaf layering be present.

11. Proper pruning to limit the fruit crop is essential. Late and double pruning is recommended. Long cane pruning is preferred, and leaf thinning in autumn prior to harvest exposing grapes to low-angle sunlight is imperative to improve color, and varietal flavor intensity.

12. Multiple trunk training would allow the replacement of winter injured trunks. Promote the development of a healthy, deep root system. Avoid a late harvest. Avoid cultivation, nitrogen fertilization, excessive irrigation, and pruning late in the season.

13. Grapes grown in cold climates make the yeast more efficient producing higher alcohol levels than hot region grapes picked at similar Brix levels.

The Geography of Grapes

What determines the range of vine cultivation and what are the optimum conditions for the production of quality wine? While grapes can be grown anywhere, the important wine grape elements of acidity, sugar content, tannin, and overall quality of consistent production are a function of climate, soil, site, intensity of cultivation, variety of grapes grown, and other cultural practices.

Subgenera and Species of the Genus VITIS

Genus VITIS

subgenus MUSCADINIAE		Subgenus EUVITIS
(North American Species)	Eurasian Species	North American Species
Munsoniana	Amurensis	Aestivalis
Popenoei	Armata	Argentifolia
Rotundifolia	Betulifolia	Arizonica
	Coignetiae	Berlandieri
	Davidii	Californica
	Embergeri	Champini
	Ficifolia	Rupestris
	Vinifera	Labrusca
Scuppernong	Cabernet Sauvignon	Catawba
	Chardonnay	Concord
	Pinot Noir	Niagara

Source: Taken from Harm J. de Blij, Wine; A Geographic Appreciation, p. 10.

While the grape, the most widely planted fruit crop in the world, encompasses an area of approximately 21 million acres, its geographic distribution is anything but uniform. What then determines the phenology, or the relationship of climate and the biological activity of the vine in the production of wine in general and quality wine in particular? In the absence of a universal agreement on the relative importance of these factors there is no comparable point system in effect anywhere that is immune from academic controversy, and while appellation legislation regulates grape varieties, viticultural practices, and geographic borders based on physical elements, the imbroglio of unrivaled distinctive enological attributes are not easily proven.

The grape, an extremely hardy and adaptable fruit, is by its very nature one of the most diversified of all in the botanic kingdom. It has diversified into thousands of varieties and is distributed throughout the world except in polar and tropical climates. The grape genus Vitis consists of approximately 52 species (many writers estimate the number to be 60) native to mid-latitudes, of which half are indigenous to North America. Fossilized grape leaves, stems and seeds have been discovered and dated back to Miocene and Tertiary deposits, thus exhibiting a long existence and a considerable geographic distribution pattern. Today, there are about 10,000 different varieties, and from a geographical point of view it would seem that grapes grow everywhere in the temperate and subtropical dry regions of the world, being the most common horticultural crop worldwide. If one were only content with a "fermented" product, the wine of any grape vine would assure success, but a *satisfying* wine is significantly more elusive depending on the right variety, a near perfect microclimate, and timely, expert winemaking skills.

Native American Vines

No matter how distasteful to Old World purists, American grapes have dominated the viticultural landscape east of the Rocky Mountains from the earliest European settlement. While California has, since the 1870s, become the premier vineyard in terms of total planted acreage and superior wine output, acreage east of the Continental Divide is the domain of native grapes. It is estimated that at least 23 species of grapes are native to North America.

Native American vines, cultivated east of the Cascade Range, the Sierra Nevada Mountains, and the Imperial Valley of southern California, are important to the wine industry because of their resistance to disease and tolerance of cold winters and humid summers. Although Vitis labrusca and Vitis rotundifolia are the two most important species of wine grapes, Vitis rupestris, Vitis aestivalis, Vitis riparia, Vitis candicans, Vitis cinerea, Vitis berlandieri, Vitis monticola, and Vitis cordifolia are eight additional species that have left a significant legacy in America's viticultural history as all are used extensively for root grafts. As a group, American grapes have tougher skins, resist phylloxera, exhibit a pronounced odor and flavor not encountered by Old World grapes, and have a layer of sweet juice between the skin and pulp. Their overwhelming use is for juice and processing, followed by wine pro-

duction, while minute amounts are for table use, and none for raisin production. Although interspecific hybridization occurred on a hit and miss basis throughout America's history, few grape varieties have emerged capable of producing major breakthroughs in wine quality. It is also important to note that there are more than 2,400 non-commercial American varieties, few of which are entirely free of Vinifera parentage.

Vitis labruscana (also known as the *northern Muscadine*, *fox* and *skunk* grape), is the most important of all American grapes (there are about 2,000 pure and hybrid varieties) in terms of acreage and the production of wine. At present, between 70 and 80 percent of non-European vines are Concord, followed by Catawba and Niagara. Labrusca grapes are commonly called *fox* and *slip skin*, the former referring to the presence of *methyl anthranilate* (imparts a bubble gum aroma and flavor), and the latter due to the fact that the skin rarely adheres to the pulp. When compared with Vinifera, Labrusca contain lower sugar and higher acid levels. Labrusca's are relatively winter hardy and are geographically distributed from central New England southward to Georgia and throughout the midwest. The core region is an irregular area that hugs the southern margins of the Great Lakes region south to northern Virginia, and westward to western Arkansas, all areas having significant humidity during the growing season. The only major exception to this pattern is central Washington, the site of the largest contiguous acreage of Concord grapes in the nation. Other varieties with important Labrusca parentage are Isabella, Noah, Worden, Steuben, Fredonia, Ives, Diamond, and Campbell. The most successful commercial varieties are Concord, Niagara, and Catawba. While Labrusca varieties are resistant to fungus diseases, they are highly susceptible to black rot, Pierce's Disease, lime chlorosis, and moderately susceptible to powdery mildew, downy mildew, and excessive winter cold. Although Labrusca grapes will produce acceptable crops with a relatively short growing season of 135 days, they are also grown in a 365-day growing season in the southwest.

Vitis riparia (also known as Vitis vulpina, *riverbank* or *frost* grape), the most widely distributed of all North American species, ranges from the St. Lawrence River westward to the Rocky Mountains, south to eastern New Mexico, and eastward to the Atlantic Ocean (its main venue, lies north of Iowa to Canada). Because of its remarkable adaptation for all manner of climate (especially in its resistance to low temperatures) and soil, it has been the object of considerable hybridization efforts and is particularly valuable for rootstock. The vine produces low yields, acidic fruit, low soluble solids, and poorly flavored fruit. While it has limited use as a processing grape, its winemaking abilities are circumscribed. Riparia-based varieties include Elvira, Noah, Clinton, Bacchus, and Beta, the latter quite popular as a wine grape in the colder margins of Minnesota. **Vitis aestivalis** (referred to in the south as the *summer* grape, and in the north as the *pigeon* and *winter* grape), is indigenous to an area extending from the Mississippi River eastward to the Atlantic, and from the upper midwest to the Gulf of Mexico. Due to small berry size, an overpowering spicy flavor, low yields, and the dark color of its juice, (and except for two worthy varieties--Norton and Cynthiana), this species of grape has not been prominent in winemaking, although Herbemont and Lenoir have played a limited historic role. Due to excellent disease resistant capabilities, considerable use is made for rootstock purposes.

Figure 2.30

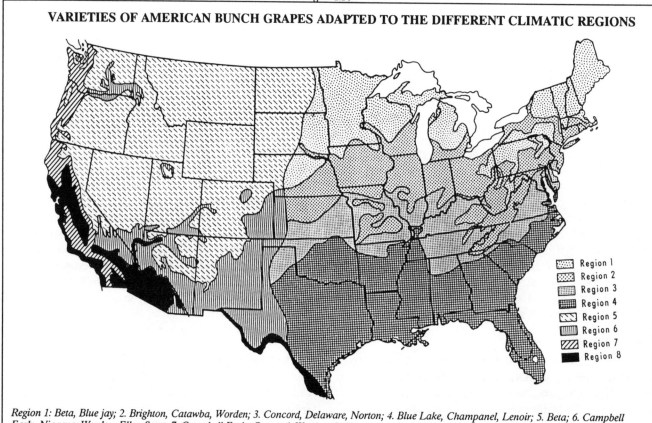

VARIETIES OF AMERICAN BUNCH GRAPES ADAPTED TO THE DIFFERENT CLIMATIC REGIONS

Region 1: *Beta, Blue jay; 2. Brighton, Catawba, Worden; 3. Concord, Delaware, Norton; 4. Blue Lake, Champanel, Lenoir; 5. Beta; 6. Campbell Early, Niagara, Worden, Ellen Scott; 7. Campbell Early, Concord, Worden; 8. Concord, Niabell. Note: there is considerable overlap.*
Source: *Growing American Bunch Grapes, U.S.D.A., Farmers' Bulletin No. 2123, 1973.*

Vitis rupestris (*rock, July, sand, sugar, bush,* and *mountain* grape), exhibits a much more circumscribed growing area than other American varieties. The native habitat extends northeastward from the Mexican border in Texas to central Missouri and eastward to central Tennessee. Because it is highly resistant to phylloxera, its primary use is for rootstock. The vine is sensitive to excessive soil moisture, but adapts well to dry, stony soils. **Vitis lincecumii** (*post-oak, pinewood,* and *turkey* grape), is native to an irregular region of eastern Texas, western Louisiana, Oklahoma, Arkansas, and southern Missouri. Varieties containing Lincecumii parentage are now rare, but the species is still used for rootstock purposes. **Vitis champini** is geographically confined to central Texas where its main function is for rootstock production. Highly vigorous, it roots easily, is tolerant of highly calcareous soils, and resistant to nematodes and other pests.

Three specific grape varieties with Champini parentage are the Nitodal, Champanel, and Lomanto.

Vitis berlandieri (*Spanish* grape), geographically confined to northern Mexico and Texas because it tolerates calcareous soils and is resistant to phylloxera, was a significant grape used by Seibel in breeding French-American varieties. **Vitis cordifolia** (*winter* or *frost* grape), is a highly diffusive variety that ripens late, producing wine with a highly pungent aroma and flavor. **Vitis longii** (also Vitis solonis), commonly referred to as the *bush* or *panhandle* grape, is an early ripening grape well-adapted to calcareous soils and widely used for rootstock. **Vitis candicans** (also known as the *Mustang* grape), indigenous to Texas, this interesting but tough-skinned grape is resistant to Pierce's Disease and produces a bitter tasting wine. It is mostly grown by home enthusiasts. **Vitis monticola** (*sweet mountain* grape), a small clustered grape, is indigenous to the dry, calcareous soils of Texas. Other species of grape used mainly for rootstock purposes are: **Vitis doaniana, Vitis bourguiniana, Vitis simpsoni, Vitis bicolor,** and **Vitis cinerea.**

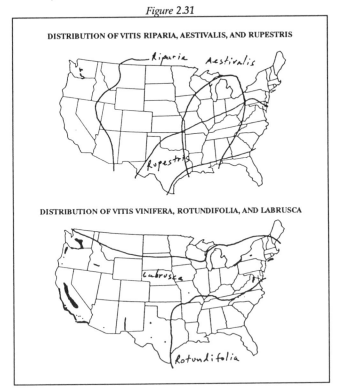

Figure 2.31

DISTRIBUTION OF VITIS RIPARIA, AESTIVALIS, AND RUPESTRIS

DISTRIBUTION OF VITIS VINIFERA, ROTUNDIFOLIA, AND LABRUSCA

Vitis rotundifolia (*Muscadine, Bullit, Bull, Bullace,* or *southern fox* grape) is found in abundance on sandy soils from coastal Virginia to Texas and throughout the humid portion of southeastern America. It consists of more than 400 different varieties, none of which are found anywhere else. First "discovered" by Giovanni da Verrazano in 1524, Rotundifolia berries have a tough skin, are twice the size of Vinifera, and grow in clusters of three to eight instead of bunches. The vine has excellent vigor, is resistant to phylloxera, humidity, root infection, and Pierce's Disease (the vines are so resistant most growers do not use insecticides and fungicides). However, the vine is highly sensitive to limy soils. An unusual feature is that Rotundifolia grapes ripen one berry at a time (and fall to the ground when fully ripe), and in spite of their thick skin are quite fragile and cannot withstand shipment or storage for any length of time. As a result, Rotundifolia have limited commercial use, but do offer excellent hybridization opportunities because they grow fairly well under hot, humid conditions

The most celebrated Rotundifolia from a winemaking perspective is the *white* Scuppernong, named after a river in Tyrrell County, North Carolina where it was "discovered" in 1755. The name is derived from the Algonquin "at or in the country of the askupo" (a Magnolia tree). It

is also called the *big white* grape, and *Roanoke*. The oldest planted Scuppernong is located on or near Sir Walter Raleigh's Lost Colony on Roanoke Island. The vine spread quickly after Vinifera vines failed throughout the humid south, particularly rapid was the diffusion between 1811 and 1840 when it was extensively planted in the Carolina's and Georgia. The Scuppernong became the most popular wine in the country prior to Prohibition under the Virginia Dare label. Historians, especially those of the south, maintain that it is America's oldest cultivated wine grape.

In their wild state various grape species have adapted to a large diversity of soils and climatic conditions, but under domesticated conditions specific grape varieties are somewhat restricted to specific regions. Frequently, one variety will succeed in one area but not in another, and it is a long term, trial and error system that ultimately determines the best site for a specific variety. However, this is mitigated by rootstock selection and vineyard practices. Rootstock is one of the most significant elements in the regulation of vigor; and since most Vinifera vines are grafted to American rootstock, the proper selection thereof is a major consideration. Rootstocks will respond differently to a host of diverse physical characteristics including soils, nature of the bedrock, soil pH, climate, elevation, and various diseases, etc. Today, due to various advances in the treatment of disease-free rootstock, the tendency is to select a medium vigor rootstock, apply the desired clone of a specific grape variety, and adapt the entire package to the appropriate vineyard practices necessary in a specific microclimatic region. This means that not only will growers select the appropriate rootstock and clone for a dry, well-drained soil vs. a wet, poorly drained soil, but that vine spacing, and regulating the trellis system, as well as a host of other factors, are rapidly becoming a major specialty in the industry.

Vitis munsoniana ("*bird* or *everbearing* grape), indigenous to the Gulf Coast, produces high yields, but, as yet, there are no named, commercial varieties used for winemaking. The grape has a delicious sweet, musky, fruit-flavored juice, but unfortunately for those more accustomed to Vinifera wine, the grape yields a musty flavor and aroma (commonly referred to as "wild") and is best when made into a sweet wine than for table use.

Interestingly, California has only two indigenous species of grape--Vitis california and Vitis girdiana, both of which remain unproductive either as rootstock or for quality fruit. California yields a purple grape with hardly any juice, and Girdiana, also called the *desert* grape because it grows in the arid region of the Tehachapi Mountains, is a thick-skinned black grape yielding unpleasant sour juice. So unpleasant were they that the state's history lacks any evidence of domestication attempts.

French-American Varieties

French-American grapes (also referred to as "direct producers," or "hybrids") are the products of interspecific hybridization of American and Vinifera grapes originally developed (mainly during the period 1880-1960) to overcome the phylloxera problem, cold winters, and specific American diseases associated with humid weather not native to Europe. Most French-American varieties are the product of French hybridizers, the most important of whom are: M. Baco, G. Couderc, F. Burdin, A. Galibert, B. Seyve, E. Kuhlmann, P. Landot, J.-F.Ravat, A. Seibel, and V. Villard. As recently as 1955, more than one-third of total acreage in France was planted in these crosses. They are genetically distinguished from others by the presence of diglucoside, a chemical not found in Vinifera grapes. The use of French-American grapes began during the 1930s, and now comprises about 10-15 percent of the eastern vineyard. The largest concentrations, as percent of total plantings, occur in the mid-Atlantic states and the midwest. Considered an improvement over native grapes for wine production, they are, however, not as winter hardy, nor immune to the many Vinifera diseases.

Despite their wide range, the finest French-American wines are made along colder margins in the northeast and midwest. When their range is extended south along a line from northern Missouri to Virginia, pH rises to dangerous levels, and the wines are less good. While the goal is to produce tolerable wine from a climate-tolerant vine, French-American vines were regarded as the long-term alternative to American and Vinifera grapes. Although these grapes have enjoyed a good deal of notoriety within the past 20 years, they continue to be the source of controversy with Vinifera proponents insisting that French-American varietals are unable to produce world-class wines. However, judging by the current price structure of the market place, quality differences are diminished at lower levels than at premium price levels.

Vitis Vinifera

Ever since the grape was domesticated during the Mesolithic Revolution in the mountainous valleys east and north of the Tigris and Euphrates, Vitis vinifera supplied the commercial grapes grown by man. These are the "Old World" grapes identified by the character of their pigments (monoglucosides) whose various varieties produce juice, table, raisin, and wine. Vinifera grapes are native to the region between the eastern Mediterranean Sea and the Caspian Sea, but over the course of many thousands of years Vinifera vines have become "acclimated" to specific regions, and thus exhibit many different physical features. T.V. Munson, maintaining for decades that Vinifera could not be successfully grown north of 35 latitude, and Mendall, while pushing the northern limits to 40 degrees, were both wrong.

Although there are an estimated 5,000 varieties of Vitis vinifera, only about 550 are used commercially for the production of wine. Thin skinned, delicate in constitution, Vinifera are sensitive to low (and fluctuating) winter temperatures, high summer humidity, phylloxera, black rot, and powdery and downy mildew. The culture requires a relatively long growing season, relatively high summer temperatures, low relative humidity, a harvest season free from rain, and relatively mild winter temperatures. Consequently, their distribution overwhelmingly corresponds with Mediterranean, desertic, and protected pockets in microthermal climates. Vinifera vines are overwhelmingly confined to the Mediterranean climate of California, the lee side of the Coast Ranges of Oregon, and the lee side of the Cascade Mountains. Although there are several other minor areas of Vinifera grape cultivation, it is these three regions that consistently provide America with the finest wines, and California offers the finest raisins and table grapes as well--all from Vinifera vines. In the east and midwest, winter kill, low yields, and the uncertainties of viral and bacterial diseases make the commercial cultivation of Vinifera an expensive proposition.

Only recently, due to the introduction of new chemicals, rootstock improvements, and vineyard practices, have Vinifera managed to succeed east of the Rocky Mountains, and cool to cold high latitude desertic and semi-desertic climatic regions. As a consequence of these technological innovations, there have been many spectacular successes in the commercial cultivation of Vinifera wine grapes, most notably in Lubbock and the Hill Section of Texas; the Fenn Valley and Leelanau Peninsula of western Michigan; the Finger Lakes region; eastern Long Island; northcentral Maryland; and northern Virginia. Except for the higher elevations of the Carolinas and Georgia, Vinifera vines are a rarity in the humid southeast and Gulf Coast regions of America. Because throughout all of the above-mentioned areas, the net return on investment, and net present value is greater for Vinifera vines than for French-American and American varieties, it is estimated that Vinifera acreage will expand in the coming years. When proper precautions are taken, Vinifera, for the first time in America's history east of the Continental Divide, have survived winter temperatures as low as -23F.

Grapes are classified according to use: as wine, raisin, table, juice, and processing. When the berry is fully mature, it will be fermented, dried, eaten fresh, or processed into jelly, juice or canned. Only a limited number are able to produce good to fine wine. Three varieties account for most of the commercial raisins, fewer than 20 varieties are grown for commercial table use, less than one dozen produce acceptable juice, only a handful are used for canning, and fewer than 50 are able to produce good to fine wine. Depending upon the type of table wine to be made, winemakers require grapes that are high in acid content and moderate in sugar content. Sparkling wines are usually made from grapes that contain above average acidity.

Raisin grapes are those that yield palatable dried fruit--seedless, pleasing flavor, soft texture, and without inclination to stickiness. In this regard, only the Thompson Seedless, Muscat of Alexandria, and Black Corinth varieties meet most of these requirements. Due to the presence of excessive atmospheric humidity, eastern America does not produce raisin grapes. Grape varieties for table use are chosen for their pleasing appearance, pleasant flavor, and high sugar content. Because they have to be shipped to distant markets (often more than 3,000 miles), firmness of pulp, thick skin and resistance to

---

**MAIN DIFFERENCES
BETWEEN OLD AND NEW WORLD GRAPES**

OLD

1. Can be used for wine, table, and raisin production
2. Higher in sugar, it produces wine with higher alcohol levels
3. Less acidic, it requires the addition of acid and/or unripened grapes
4. More solids in the pulp
5. Good keeping qualities
6. Wines are delicately flavored
7. Wines are less astringent
8. Wines are mainly dry
9. Bunches and berries are larger
10. Higher yields per acre
11. Skin is not irritating to the lips and mouth
12. Taste is less objectionable when consumed as a table grape
13. Pulp separates more easily from pips
14. Berries have a soft and delicate skin
15. The finest wines improve with some bottle aging
16. Wood aging of wine is a common practice
17. Grapes can be dried easily
18. Vines are more compact in their growth habit
19. Vines are less vigorous in growth habit
20. Roots are fleshier and more fibrous
21. More adaptable to different soils and climates
22. Easily propagated
23. Highly susceptible to phylloxera
24. Highly susceptible to black rot, downy and powdery mildew
25. Less tolerant to frost and low temperatures
26. Easily domesticated
27. Less tolerant of hot, humid summers and highly susceptible to Pierce's Disease
28. More tolerant of calcareous/limy soils
29. Thicker shoots with shorter and more prominent internodes
30. Larger buds
31. Leaves are rough and dull in appearance
32. Tartaric acid dominates
33. Intolerant of acidic soils (under 5.7 pH)
34. In general, grapes mature late in the season
35. In general, vines need to be planted in less fertile soils
36. In general, most varieties have an upright growth pattern

NEW

1. Better for juice and jelly than for wine, table, and raisin use
2. Lower in sugar producing lower alcohol levels
3. More acidic requiring the addition of water and sugar
4. More watery, but higher in pectin
5. Poor keeping qualities
6. Flavor is single dimensional highlighted by the distinct "foxy" flavor and aroma
7. Wines are more astringent and bitter on the palate
8. Wines are mainly sweet, not dry
9. Bunches and berries are smaller
10. Lower yields
11. Skin is usually irritating to lips and mouth
12. Taste is objectionable under most circumstances
13. Pulp does not easily separate from pips
14. Berries have a tough skin requiring more pressing pressure to release juice
15. Little improvement with bottle aging
16. Little if any wood aging of wine
17. Difficult to dehydrate
18. More diffusive in growth habit
19. More vigorous in growth habit
20. Roots are less fleshy and fibrous
21. Less adaptable to varied soils and climates
22. More difficult to propagate
23. Phylloxera resistant
24. More resistant to black rot, downy and powdery mildew
25. More tolerant to frost, prolonged bouts of low temperatures, false springs, and sudden temperature fluctuations
26. Domestication relatively difficult
27. More tolerant of hot, humid summers
28. Less tolerant of calcareous/limy soils
29. Thinner shoots with longer but less prominent internodes
30. Smaller buds
31. Leaves are smooth, metallic, and shiny in appearance
32. Malic acid dominates
33. Very tolerant of acidic soils (under 5.7 pH)
34. In general, grapes are early maturing
35. In general, they need to be planted in more fertile soils
36. In general, vines lack an upright growth habit

---

desiccation are important transportation considerations. The above qualities in varying degrees are possessed by Tokay, Ribier, Emperor, Malaga, Red Malaga, Almeira,

Cardinal, and Thompson Seedless--all of which are grown in California and Arizona. The vast region east of the Rocky Mountains has yet to produce an acceptable table grape with commercial success. In the United States, the premier table grape has been Thompson Seedless, known as the "three-way grape" because it can be dried and vinified as well. Juice grapes are from varieties that produce an acceptable beverage when its taste and color can be preserved by pasteurization, filtration and freezing. Nearly all Vinifera grapes suffer from some or all of the above preserving processes, therefore, Concord, and a few other native grapes account for the bulk of all grape juice. Concord, due to its pronounced flavor and deep color, is also the dominant ingredient in jams, and jellies. In Europe, particularly in Switzerland, France, Germany, and Italy, Chasselas, often mixed with Labrusca grape juice, constitutes the principal juice grape. Grapes for canning are all seedless, white in color and mainly used in combination with other fruits, especially in "fruit cocktail."

Facts About Climate and Grapes

1. While precipitation and temperature are the most prominent weather elements affecting the production of grapes, the most outstanding limiting element is temperature as it is directly related to length of growing season, spring frosts, low winter temperature, and total heat units during the growing season. Average annual and seasonal temperatures do not correspond with latitude. The annual range in temperature is small in the southeastern and Gulf Coast regions of the nation, and greater in the northcentral and arid portion of the country. Temperature and other climatic features vary by altitude.
2. Windward areas of a mountain are more rainy and the vegetation more verdant than the lee sides.
3. Grapes are grown commercially in six distinct climates ranging from low latitude desert (at 6,000 feet in elevation), to Mediterranean climates, Marine West Coast climates, interior microthermal climates, middle-latitude steppe climates, and subtropical humid climates, all of which exhibit an east-west dimension of more than 3,000 miles and a north-south dimension of nearly 2,000 miles.
4. The northernmost quality wine producing region in America lies at a similar latitude as southern Labrador, Canada.
5. The southernmost winery in the country is located in southern Florida (on the border of a tropical Savanna and subtropical humid climate); the westernmost winery in Hawaii (located in a tropical rain forest/monsoon climate); the northernmost in Washington State (located in a modified Marine West Coast climate); and the easternmost in Massachusetts (in a modified middle-latitude microthermal climate).
6. Rainfall variability from year to year is greatest in arid climates. Rainfall generally follows the sun, i.e., is greatest in the high-sun season, but not in the Mediterranean climatic region of southwest U.S.
7. Weather patterns in the central portion of the nation move in an easterly direction producing rapid changes, often within 24 hours.
8. Washington and Idaho have the longest, sunniest summer days of any American grape-growing region.
9. The midwest and northeast have the most unpredictable climatic patterns of any major American viticultural region.
10. California and the Columbia Plateau region of Washington state enjoy the most predictable climatic patterns of any American viticultural region.
11. Temperatures immediately above the ground are partly the result of albedo of various objects. The albedo of a forest varies between 4-6 percent, bare ground 10-20 percent, and fresh snow 87 percent. The sandy soils of Long Island reflect a much higher percentage of solar radiation than the dark volcanic soils of the Yakima Valley.
12. Average July temperatures along coastal southern California are

lower than those of northern Michigan, 1,500 miles further north in latitude.

13. Successful commercial viticulture is limited to areas having 1700 or more heat-summation units during the growing season, a distinct and continuous dormant season without major temperature fluctuations, and no excessive humidity.

14. Areas totally unsuitable for grape cultivation are: desertic areas without irrigation, locations with a growing season of fewer than 130 days, locations with extremely severe winter temperatures, and regions of extremely high temperatures and humidity.

15. Cool weather produces high grape acidity, a low pH and good color. Warm days and cool nights enhance optimum aroma development and flavor. In warm to hot climates, grapes are less delicate in aroma, and the wines are less well-balanced. High temperatures raise sugar and pH, and lower acid levels. In the final analysis, cool climatic regions have an ability to produce table wines of considerable distinction with a high degree of vintage variability. Seasonal climatic variations are crucial in the production of above-average grapes and wines. In cool climates, better wine is usually made during a growing season marked by above-average temperatures; and the reverse in hotter climates. The longer grapes hang on the vine, the more flavor they possess at maturity.

17. Sugar level, while partially related to heat units, is not the same as ripeness.

18. Red wines require more summertime warmth than white grapes. In Monterey County, Chardonnay, Pinot Blanc, and Grey Riesling often produce better wines in the upper (northeast) end of Salinas Valley. Red grapes, on the other hand, are at their best in the lower (southern) portion. This pattern is also true for the rest of the nation.

19. Sudden freezing can be more harmful than gradual cooling. Injury to the vine also increases as the length of exposure to lower temperature increases.

20. A winegrowing climate that ripens the grapes rapidly, early, and easily is also a climate that plunders the grapes of their complex flavors and aromatics.

VINE PATHOLOGY

Infirmities affecting grape vines fall into three major categories: (a) environmental events and non-parasitic disorders; (b) diseases of parasitic origin; and (c) human environmental intervention.

A. Environmental Events and Non-parasitic Disorders

(1) Frost. In most grape growing regions of the world (especially along the poleward margins) frost is the most important environmental danger as it reduces the yield to unprofitable levels. Although most vineyards are so situated that frosts will have a minimal effect, periodically those that do occur can be particularly devastating.

(2) Winter Temperature Fluctuations. Along the poleward margins, and especially in those areas where continental climates dominate, there may be recurring bouts of rapidly rising and falling temperatures two to five times during the winter months. This environmental hazard severely limits the cultivation of Vinifera grapes.

(3) Heat. When temperatures exceed 100F for a prolonged period of time grape vines are unable to produce good to excellent quality wine. A combination of excessive heat and wind aggravates the condition promoting desiccation and raisination of grape berries.

(4) Hail. Although fairly uncommon in most grape producing regions, large pieces of solid precipitation have a tendency to scar and remove leaves, damage grapes, weaken the vine, promote disease, and lower the yield.

(5) Wind. Although beneficial in many places by lowering high temperatures, if prolonged in arid areas at sustained velocities exceeding 20 miles per hour, wind has a tendency to dehydrate and wither leaves, and break off or crack shoots and grape berries. Under conditions of persistent wind vines assume a stunted appearance.

(6) Excessive Soil Moisture. Defined as an inability for water to drain properly for a sustained period (about 10 weeks), the vine usually drowns (due to a lack of oxygen) and is unable to recover.

(7) Drought. If prolonged, drought leads to degeneration and eventual death. Stressed plants are small, and their grape clusters are loose with small berries.

(8) Chlorosis. Easily corrected, this ailment occurs when there is an excess of calcium in the soil resulting in iron deficiency with the leaves usually turning yellow.

(9) Trace Element Deficiency. Although there are many, the most important trace elements are boron, iron, potassium, manganese, and zinc, all of which vary in their concentrations by the type of soil parent material and climate. Major nutritional disorders are nitrogen, phosphorus, potassium, magnesium, and calcium.

(10). Couloure. This refers to improper berry development caused by bad weather during flowering. Couloure invariably leads to "shot berries," or small, incomplete grape bunches where the individual berries remain green, hard, and do not mature properly or completely.

(11) Soil Toxicity. The most common is usually salt encrustation, most commonly associated in regions having an excess of evaporation over incoming precipitation. In coastal regions it is possible for grapes to exhibit chloride toxicity.

B. Diseases of Parasitic Origin

(1) Infectious Degeneration or *Fanleaf*. This slowly spreading viral disease first appeared after the phylloxera outbreak in the second half of the nineteenth century. The virus lives in the soil where it weakens the vine and increases mortality. There is no known treatment.

(2) Pierce's Disease. This bacterium disease is universal along the coastal plain of southeastern and Gulf Coast America where it successfully limits the culture of all grapes except Rotundifolia. It is also found in scattered areas in southern California. Only Rotundifolia and a few native grapes (most notably Champanel, Lenoir, and Herbemont) are immune. There is no known cure.

(3) Downy Mildew (*Plasmopara viticola*). Of American origin, this debilitating fungus disease attacks the green portions of the vine before berries turn color. It is only found in areas where there are relatively high humidity levels, and since it spreads by wind action, it spreads quickly.

Figure 2.32

DISTRIBUTION OF PIERCE'S DISEASE

The geography of Pierce's Disease is almost congruent with Rotundifolia, the only specie of grape not affected by this deadly disease. Rotundifolia grapes are indigenous only to America and adapted only to the southern, humid portion of the nation.

(4) Powdery Mildew (*Uncinula necator*). Also known as oidium, this disease thrives on grapes under conditions of high humidity, and unlike other fungus diseases, does not require "free water" for germination of its spores. For certain varieties, this is by far the most destructive fungus disease. All green parts of the vine are affected causing a white powdery growth on the undersides of the leaves, tendrils, etc. If left untreated, it will kill the vine.

(5) Black Rot (*Guignardia bidwellii*). The most widespread disease in the northeast and midwest, it is associated with high humidity, and particularly deadly when temperatures rise beyond 70F. All Vinifera and French-American varieties are highly susceptible, and while many native grapes exhibit some resistance, the following are considered the most resistant: Beta, Norton, Missouri Riesling, Campbell Early, and Elvira, which explains why they became popular in the midwest and portions of the northeast. Although the disease shrivels grape berries and turns them a dark brown, treatment is fairly easy and cost effective when caught in time. Interestingly, the disease was first observed in a Kentucky vineyard in 1804.

(6) Phylloxera. This aphid of American origin saps all life from vines not indigenous to America. The ailment leads to death and there is no cure. Phylloxera has a complicated seven-stage life cycle and can easily be prevented by using resistant American rootstock. Phylloxera is not endemic to sandy soils and, historically, isolated regions west of the Rockies, but at least 28 California counties are affected. The only major quality wine producing regions that are largely immune to phylloxera are portions of Oregon, Washington, and Idaho.

(7) Crown Gall. A bacterial pathogen that attacks more than 600 species of vegetation as a plant cancer, it is particularly deadly to grape vines. It is associated with early freezing, and in order for infection to occur low temperatures, abundant soil moisture, and weeds are usually present. It is most prevalent in early winter and affects young

as well as old plants. The disease, characterized by overgrowth in roots, trunks, and arms, is caused by *Agrobacterium tumefaciens*, a bacterium that survives systematically and is carried in dormant grape cuttings used in propagation. Bacterium-free vines, wood hardening before winter, better site selection, better vineyard practices, and avoiding trunk injury during planting and cultivation reduce the incidence. Although found in all grape growing regions of America, Crown Gall is particularly serious in the northeast and midwest.

(8) Cotton (or Texas) Root Rot. Also called *Phymatotrichum Root Rot*, this fungus disease occurs in areas of high temperature, abundant moisture, and highly alkaline soils, thus is confined to irrigated lands from Texas westward to Arizona. Once the disease becomes established it spreads easily, and is difficult to eliminate.

(9) Eutypa Dieback. Also known as *dying arm*, this unusual fungus disease is associated with areas having more than 24 inches of precipitation, but not in areas having less than 10 inches. Particularly destructive, it is also associated with severe cold winter temperatures, rarely affects vines before their eighth birthday, and is highly virulent in the northeast and midwest.

(10) Botrytis. This particularly troublesome disease is caused by *Botrytis cinerea* affecting varieties with tight clusters under high humid conditions toward the end of the growing season when sugar levels rise. Careful and timely spraying schedules are effective safeguards. While it is often confused with black rot, Botrytis is different, and often beneficial in the production of quality sweet wine.

Other diseases include: Botrytis Bunch Rot, Bitter Rot, Ripe Rot, Macrophoma Rot, Angular Leaf Spot, Root-Knot Nematodes, Dagger and Needle Nematodes, and Lesion Nematodes.

C. Human Environmental Intervention

(1) Burning. This occurs when air pollution, insecticides, and chemical fertilizers damage the vine. One of the most virulent herbicides, 2,4-D, associated with corn and wheat production in the midwest and Great Plains, has made it nearly impossible for any grape to be cultivated in nearby locations. Ozone, hydrogen fluoride and sulfur dioxide emissions are particularly deadly.

(2) Browning. This is a condition of improper vineyard management where inept pruning and overproduction damage the vine. Although browning, if left unattended will eventually kill the vine, the remedy is simple and relatively inexpensive.

THE INFLUENCE OF
SOILS ON GRAPE PRODUCTION

The word soil is derived from the Latin word *solum*, meaning "floor," and refers to the upper level of the earth that supports vegetative growth, or the environment in which vine roots exist. Commonly referred to as *regolith*, the most important soil properties are water availability, nutrients, solar heat, texture, structure, water and air permeability, pH, and seasonal and diurnal variations in temperature. While grape vines can adapt to a wide range of soil fertility, texture and structure, among many other physical attributes, there are certain soils that should be avoided such as those that contain excessive amounts of clay, salts, boron, and other toxic substances.

Because soils are products of rock weathering, organic matter accumulation, geologic time, and method of deposition, the number of permutations capable of producing distinct soils appears to be almost infinite. In addition to the generalized scheme presented in Fig. 2.34, parent material, topography, vegetation, climate and time do much to increase the number of distinctive soil patterns found. While the number of possible distinct soils exceeds 100,000, several thousand soil series have been identified and mapped in America as being above-average for commercial viticulture. Of all the major soils illustrated the most common is alluvial, a fresh water deposited material that is most prevalent in California, Oregon, and large portions of eastern America.

Figure 2.33

A GEOGRAPHICAL CLASSIFICATION SOILS

Transportation Agency	Classification	Examples
Water	Marine	Coastal Areas
	Lacustrine	Lake margins, Great Lakes, Finger Lakes
	Alluvial	Hillsides, most common along the Appalachians and Rockies
Wind	Loess	Everywhere in the arid west, Great Plains, and midwest
Ice	Glacial	Primarily in the northern portions of the country east of the Rockies
Gravity	Colluvial	Along foothills
Weathered in Place	Residual	In isolated areas in western America

Wind blown material called *aeolian*, or *loess* deposits, is a buff to grey, fine-grained material that is also highly permeable (and hence resists erosion), well-mineralized, and extremely fertile. Its depth can vary from several inches to tens of feet. *Glacial* material refers to coarse-textured, bedded and sorted deposits found along the poleward and colder portions of the nation. It includes outwash debris, morainic detritus, and till, all in various forms of stratification that contain clay, and are highly acidic in reaction. Although it can be well-drained, as a rule it is not unless there are large accumulations of sand, gravel, and stone. By comparison, fresh water *alluvium* material is overwhelmingly stratified, well-drained, and fertile. *Lacustrine* material is highly fertile, rich in organic material, and usually poorly drained. *Marine* material is

found only in small, and minor areas, mainly in the east, of which eastern Long Island is the most important. *Colluvial* and residual material are mainly found in the more arid areas in the west, and, when not found in overly hilly locations, are excellent viticultural soils. These soils (referred to as embryonic, lithosol, or entisol) are very shallow, stony, contain little organic matter, and lack a well-developed soil profile. In addition to the dominance of parent material, they may also contain loess. The above, in combination with time and climate, have created three physical attributes that distinguish one soil from another: **a profile, texture, and structure.**

Soil Fumigation in the Dry Creek Region, Sonoma. Baxevanis

If a vertical cut is dug into the soil, several layers or horizons become evident. This differentiation of horizons is the result of many soil forming processes, the most important being physical weathering, the chemical and mechanical removal of material, accumulation or removal of organic matter, and the possible formation of dense or compact layers in the subsoil. Some of these processes take place in all soils, but the number and intensity vary from one soil to another. Since climate is one of the key elements in soil formations it is important to note that all soils reflect this important feature. The soil profile, a characteristic common to all soils, is a "fingerprint" that reveals a history of development expressed by distinct layers from the surface downward. A vertical exposure of a particular soil, usually divided into three sections, is called a "profile." The A horizon, the surface portion, is usually the thinnest, and in humid areas subject to both mechanical and chemical weathering. This layer, often called the zone of eluviation, tends to have the bulk of organic material (hence, darker in color), and the least amount of clay. The A horizon, more exposed to the weathering action of precipitation, sun, wind, ice, and temperature fluctuations, is subjected to physical and chemical disintegration. The B horizon, or subsoil, often referred to as the zone of illuviation (or deposition), is lighter in color, and the recipient of most of the clay removed from the uppermost layer. The C horizon is the weathered parent material. Although there are many soils that do not display all three horizons, this abbreviated treatment does apply to all grape growing regions except desertic soils. The upper horizons of a soil normally are more leached of bases and silicate clays than are lower layers.

Soil texture refers to the size of soil particles, the most common fractions being sand, silt and clay, the latter the smallest, and least desirable in the vineyard. The presence of stone and gravel is usually referred to as a "phase" in association with sand, silt and clay. Soils with a high percentage of sand and a low percentage of clay are frequently low in fertility and water-holding capacity, well-aerated, absorb water readily, and, in general, excellent for wine grape production. Clay soils, on the other hand, are richer in fertility, more moist, and not desirable for wine grape production due to their high water holding capacity. These "heavy" soils hold large amounts of water and promote excessive vine growth that often continues well past *veraison* and harvest. They also exhibit low levels of aeration (reduced oxygen levels), reduced root penetration, and often lead to droughty conditions because of the limited area of root penetration, and limited water-holding capacity at the surface. "Light" soils, with relatively higher proportions of sand, gravel and stone, hold less water and are better drained resulting in less vigor and a cessation of growth much earlier in the season.

The above is highly relevant to soil structure, or the arrangement of soil particles. Rarely does sand, clay, and silt occur as separate units, but combine into aggregates held together by the binding forces of clay and organic matter. The size and form of aggregation is known structure, important as it promotes the absorption of water and the circulation of air in all soil horizons. Their size varies from a fraction of an inch to several in diameter: *massive* (the soil clings together due to clay and organic matter, but does not exhibit sharp lines of cleavage); *blocky* (most common in the midwest prairie region, the soil aggregate exhibits equal vertical and horizontal dimensions); *prismatic*, or columnar (most common in arid regions), refers to the vertical character of soil aggregates, and, hence, has good drainage; *platy* refers to a soil that is overwhelmingly composed of clay, and where the horizontal dimensions are greater than the vertical dimensions; *granular* refers to a rounded shape, and, as a result, the surface area in relation to its mass is high, hence, it is a well-drained soil especially desirable when the granular composition contains gravel and stone. The foregoing soils are also described in terms of their cohesion and adhesion between soil particles as brittle, compact, firm, fluffy, fluid, friable, hard, loose, plastic, and sticky. It should also be noted that parent rock has a tendency to weather into different textures and structures. Granite, for example, has a tendency to be sandy; sand-

stone is less sandy; schist and shale weather into loam; and basalt, limestone, and marl yield heavy accumulations of clay.

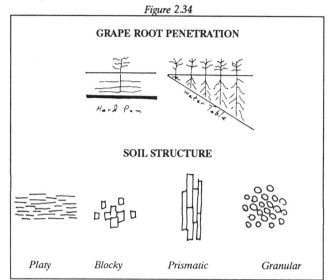

Figure 2.34

In recent years, a lively discussion has ensued concerning the issue of soil imparting definitive flavors and aromas to wine. On the one hand, American academicians favor the "California" school which states that soil drainage along with a favorable microclimate accounts for fine wine quality. The "French" school, particularly those who are members of the Union de Grand Crus de Bordeaux, are of the opinion that the chemical composition as well as drainage and microclimate are not only important in the production of fine wine, but that the mineral component of the soil is responsible for above-average aromatic and flavor characteristics. No doubt the imbroglio will continue in America as UC-Davis, after repeated experimentation, has failed to confirm claims that specific soil minerals impart distinctive wine flavor and aroma. Contemporary opinion now supports the notion that soil structure and its ability to facilitate the downward movement of water is the key element in the production of quality wine. It follows, therefore, that if certain physical impediments of bottomland soils can be overcome, grape and wine quality in comparison with mountain or hillside soils ought to be the same.

Nevertheless, soils are extremely variable and do not lend to easy generalization, and while climate, grape varieties and winemaking techniques are considered the primary factors in determining suitable grape growing regions, there are many who maintain that too much emphasis has been paid to these factors and not enough on site and soil. This is quite understandable given the fact that within a given climate, soil variation can influence the production of different wines from the same grape variety. In the main, the character of the parent material, structure and texture, the amount of water available, mineral matter, depth, and drainage are the most important soil elements contributing to the uniqueness of a particular vineyard.

Soils of moderate to low fertility usually produce higher quality grapes than deep fertile soils that support large vines with heavy yields. Soils that are high in organic matter, rich in natural fertility, and abundantly moist produce high yields that diminish wine quality by reducing extract, color, bouquet, and flavor. Proper drainage is important as vines are intolerant of water logged soil, but are not likely to be killed by excess water unless under very severe conditions. However, even the occasional wet winter can adversely affect vine development as it might not exhibit negative physical manifestations until late spring or summer. With too much moisture vines absorb an excess of water diluting must concentration and delay ripening, thus producing wines that are thin, poor in color, low in tannin and acid, and high in pH. Invariably, these wines lack structure, complexity, depth, and are nothing but single dimensional quaffing wines exhibiting little character. On the other extreme, with too little moisture vines may suffer from dehydration and thus yield a reduced crop of small clusters and berries producing wine that is high in tannin, astringent, bitter, and coarse.

These rounded, water-deposited "Greenfield potatoes" are characteristic debris widely scattered in the Arroyo Seco region. "Arroyo," Spanish word for water course, a creek or its bed, is commonly associated with the word "seco" meaning dry. Gravelly and coarse soils have greater porosity and permeability, and are well-drained. Clayey and fine-textured soils retain the largest amount of moisture.

Although grapes are adapted to a wide range of soils, certain species and varieties exhibit a certain preference for peculiar types of soil characteristics. For example, Vinifera, as deep-rooted vines, prefer pedocal (basic), deep, well-drained soils without a hardpan or clay. They thrive on calcium-rich soils of moderate fertility that are subjected to little or no summer rains, but with sufficient subsurface water necessary for summer growth. In sharp contrast, American vines, indigenous to either colder or warmer but humid climates are not as deeply rooted and more tolerant of the wetter and much shallower pedalfer (acidic) soils. Moreover, they require a higher degree of fertility, are sensitive to calcium, and highly sensitive to alkali salts. The following generalizations are quite germane in understanding the relationship between soil and grape growing. Calcium impregnated soils are good for the production of quality white table and sparkling wines as they impart fragrance, flavor, and ameliorate grape acidity, a primary consideration in short season areas. Although it is said that no correlation exists between the mineral content of soils and the ability to grow good grape vines, a high mineral content does enhance wine quality. Iron and potassium, in particular, exhibit an important quality in the production of red wines as evidenced by the iron-impregnated soils of the Cote d'Or, the Medoc, the Willamette Valley, the Columbia Plateau, the High Texas Plains, and portions of North Coast California counties. Certain varieties also exhibit an affinity with distinct types of soils: Pinot Gris and Riesling do well on volcanic and schistous soils; and while Chardonnay does well when cultivated on carbonate-derived regolith, it lacks adaptability to schistous soils.

The following generalizations are of interest to the grower:

1. Heavy soils increase the vigor of the vines and alter potassium flow, often leading to high pH and lower sugar levels. Heavy soils do not enhance a long, slow process of ripening, and produce grapes that are low in color and flavor.

2. In terms of soil acidity, the nation is divided into two zones: east of the 97th Meridian soils are referred to as *pedalfers*, or leached acidic soils formed under conditions exceeding 25 inches of rainfall; and to the west, *pedocals* or basic soils. Acidic soils have a pH value less than 7.0, and alkaline soils, due to the presence of carbonates of calcium, magnesium and potassium are higher than 7.0.

3. Nitrogen aids vigor, but lowers the quality of wine; excess animal manure enhances vegetative growth, but produces off flavors, and diluted wines.

4. A critical soil condition is temperature, the latter a function of latitude, altitude, exposure, cloudiness, humidity, wind velocity, density and color of the dominant rock, soil moisture, and vegetation cover. Soil temperature is usually measured at 1.5 foot depths, and in California, Mesic varies between 47-59F (only along coastal areas), Thermic varies between 59-72F (in cooler areas of the Central Valley), and Hyperthermic involves temperatures above 72F. Cooler soil temperatures produce higher acids and the fruit ripens in a more timely manner. For all soil temperature groups, cool roots produce a slower vine metabolism and smaller vines/berries having a more concentrated flavor.

5. Hydromorphic (water-logged), clay, and salt encrusted soils are to be avoided. Excessive moisture limits the availability of oxygen, breeds bacterial growth, causes berries to swell and dilute flavors, and inhibits the energy release reaction necessary for root growth. Toxic chemicals (such as salt) will kill the roots through dehydration. Nevertheless, grapes are adapted to a wide range of soil types. Almost any soil will do as long as it is not excessively dry or wet, or contains high concentrations of boron and other toxic substances. Surface crusts restrict plant growth by reducing the supply of oxygen for proper root growth.

6. Internal drainage is very important and soil depth should be more than 10 feet, preferably 25.

7. Factors affecting water-holding capacity of soils are texture, structure, and organic matter, the latter having the capacity to hold water equivalent to an amount several times its weight. Because water loss

from a vine is related to the amount available in the soil, future progress in the management of vineyard soils will rely on "water balance analysis."

8. Bottomland soils are the richest in fertility and the least expensive to farm. When the organic content in the soil is below 20 percent, the soil is described as mineralized. Higher yields emanate from deep alluvial soils in irrigated desertic areas, and lower from skeletal hillside soils. Under irrigated conditions, it has been observed that water available at harvest time increases yields but lowers the quality of wine. When irrigated water is shut off during *veraison* yields decrease but wine quality increases. Bottomland vineyards receive more than 90 percent of precipitation that falls, while sloping sites may lose as much as 10 to 40 percent of all rainfall due to surface runoff.

9. Grape varieties differ in their adaptation to acidic or alkaline soils, but the proper selection of rootstocks can offset the inherent proclivities of the grape variety.

10. The issue of plant nutrients travelling through the plant and imparting a distinctive taste in the wine is highly debated and thought to be false by most American experts.

11. The vine likes soil that is stony, highly mineralized, low in organic matter, retains warmth, and allows for the easy removal of water around the base of the vine and fine rootlets. Clay is not a desired item in large quantities because when fully saturated, it inhibits the vertical percolation of water.

The soils of a large portion of northcentral Texas, especially near Lubbock, contain <u>caliche</u>, a layer of soil cemented by the deposition of calcium carbonate. These excellent, mineralized, well-drained, and basic-reacting soils are the complete antithesis of podsol soils found in the northeast and midwest. Baxevanis

SITE SELECTION (ASPECT AND TOPOGRAPHY)

Because the earth's surface is a highly irregular patchwork of plain, rolling terrain, hill, and mountain (while climatic effects are regional, those of landforms are local), site selection (microclimate) and associated vineyard practices, after climate and soil, are important elements in the successful production of quality wine grapes. In general terms, the site must not be encumbered by any environmental constraints such as a proclivity for severe winter damage, spring frosts, excessive summer heat, or a high incidence of precipitation during the harvest season. The soils must be conducive for the planted grape variety, while the aspect should enhance all important physical characteristics of the site. Some of the more significant site-selective considerations are: (1) exposure in terms of wind, direction, velocity, and seasonal and diurnal flows;

(2) the nature of surface and sub-surface water flow; (3) surface and sub-surface soil features; (4) the nature of the soil microclimate; (5) diurnal and seasonal variations in humidity; (6) elevation; (7) exposure in terms of sunlight, including sun angle and reflection from water bodies; (8) degree of slope influencing water and air flow; (9) proximity to water bodies, including salt air; and (10) the albedo of surface soil material. Other non-physical site considerations are: the proximity of a convenient market; areas free of water and air pollution, especially areas with excessive ozone, fluoride, sulfur dioxide, and other pollutants; areas that are free of 2,4-D.

In the cooler regions of the northwest, midwest, and northeast, the most desirable vineyard sites are those with a southern exposure (maximum sunlight), and good air drainage. In warmer climates, the tendency is to seek out sites that offer more shade to mitigate otherwise high temperatures detrimental to good grape maturation. In the desertic southwest, desirable sites are above 4,000 feet in order to take advantage of cooler, upland temperatures. Due to temperature inversions low-lying areas are plagued by frost and poor quality fruit, and, as a consequence, hilly, south-facing exposures on well-drained soils are much preferred than northern exposures. Although steep slopes often provide excellent fruit, the threat of soil erosion and the high cost of cultivation makes these areas unprofitable sites in America (it takes more than 800 man hours to cultivate one such acre). Vineyards with an eastern exposure receive the early morning sun and warm up early, while those with a western exposure appear to be more moist until they receive the hotter, afternoon sun. Another important element in site selection is choosing an appropriate variety for that locality. Of the many considerations, vine characteristics, hardiness, resistance and tolerance of certain diseases and insects, and desirable fruit features are the most important. In sharp contrast, the grower in the southwest, including California, seeks the coolest sites for the production of quality wine grapes, but not for table or raisin grapes.

Putting the issue of clearing land, feasibility of mechanization and associated costs aside, most, if not all, viticultural experts are of the opinion that hillsides are superior to bottomland in practically all latitudes and climatic regions for many reasons: (1) poor soil; (2) better drained soil; (3) surface water is limited forcing vines to send roots deeper in the soil profile; (4) solar radiation is more direct and, hence, more effective; (5) superior diurnal air circulation with fewer associated fungus and mildew diseases; (6) larger diurnal, seasonal and annual temperature fluctuations; (7) greater sunlight penetration of soil and the base of the vine, thus warming the soil earlier in the season, and maintaining higher soil temperatures later in the season; (8) sharp vertical temperatures (because hillside vineyards contain more bare ground and little water, the dry soil is a poor conductor of heat with only the surface warming up during the day, and that small amount of heat is quickly dissipated at night) (9) smaller grape clusters and berries, and lower yields; and (10) the combination of the above increases color and fruit intensity, tannin, and flavor complexity. Moreover, hillside vineyards are thought to exhibit diminished vegetal flavors and aromas. Therefore, it is no accident that in recent years the most highly capitalized premium vineyards have sought hillside sites nearly everywhere in the nation. While all the foregoing constitutes a comparatively recent phenomenon, the matching of specific grape varieties with aspect and altitude, unlike many mountainous regions of Europe, has yet to be carefully examined. Equally important is the fact that recent experiments have shown that vineyard canopy is equally, if not more, important than low yields in determining wine quality, a theory that is currently revolutionizing vineyard management practices. Although experimentation has not produced conclusive results, there are those who maintain that the low yield/high quality wine theory is more germane to cold climates and less so in warmer to hotter climates. While the imbroglio continues unabated, the mountain, low yield school of thought appears to have the upper hand.

The importance of sloping land locations in mid-latitude regions is directly related to aspect, as the greatest amount of energy per unit area is delivered when solar radiation is perpendicular to the surface. Rays reaching the surface at an acute angle penetrate more atmosphere, experience a larger diffusion rate, and cover more land area, hence, deliver less solar energy per unit area. This hillside condition also favorably affects the phototropism character (the ability of a plant to turn or bend in a certain direction) of the vine, thus maximizing photosynthesis. In addition, hillside sites contain more surface rock, stone or gravel, thus affecting both the absorption and radiation of heat relative to low-lying areas. Due to well-drained features, hillside soils also tend to have lower heat capacity near the surface thus warming earlier in the spring, and have greater diurnal temperature variations than low-lying areas that are less well drained and more heat retaining. Also of significance is the fact that the transmission of temperature oscillations throughout the soil horizon is more varied on hilly sites.

Many enologists maintain that wine quality is lowered when vine yields are high. While the concept of restricted yields per acre is one of the most scrupulous elements of the various European appellations, there is no hard data concerning specific yields for specific grape varieties. The variables are simply too many. High yielding vines, for example, located on rich bottomland may be stressed to reduce yields, and thus raise quality. After all, some of the finest vineyards in the world are not located on excessively steep or equally high elevations. While Americans

and French experts fail to arrive at specific figures, the Italians mention that the ideal yield is 3.3 tons per acre for red grapes, and 3.5 tons to the acre for white grapes. Even the French, while limiting yields in all AOC regions, periodically are at a loss to explain those unusual historical vintages where high quality and high yields coincide.

What Is A Microclimate?

A *microclimate* is a local weather and climatic departure from surrounding areas brought about by wind activity, topographic irregularity, the presence of water, type of soil, character of ground cover, humidity, etc., that collectively combine to display an astonishing array of variations from the general regional climate. "Terrain climatology," "plant climate," or "topoclimate" are three similar expressions. Although more than 10,000 distinct varieties of grape are found in all but the highest latitudes and altitudes of the major climatic zones, specific and ideal climatic circumcision is a major element in the selection of specific vineyard location. While the commercial cultivation of wine grapes is limited to an ill-defined belt between 30° and 50° latitude in both the Northern and Southern Hemispheres, vineyard sites are highly localized within these latitudinal belts because the climatic conditions common over large tracts of continental proportions do not remain constant, hence the need to describe climatic conditions at microclimatic levels.

GROUND MICROCLIMATE

Because many vineyard practices take place above and below the 12-inch ground level, there is special interest in the climate next to the ground. This layer, immediately above the ground surface, is a complex region that exhibits tremendous variation from one elevation to another and from one horizontal location to another. Moreover, air movement and air temperature vary widely both above and below the ground surface. Because the atmosphere is largely transparent to incoming solar radiation, most sunlight heats the ground, not the air. How hot the ground gets is a factor of albedo, sun angle, and how much is conducted into the ground is influenced by the nature of the soil. If the soil or surface rocks are dark in color, and conduct heat poorly, surface temperature can be high. After the ground gets hot, the air in contact with the ground begins to warm by conduction.

While many European countries for centuries recognized above-average sites for quality grape production, the tendency in America, particularly in California and other western states, has been to seek rich, flat land that is able to produce grapes in abundance without regard to quality. It is no wonder, therefore, that the highest yields are found in the Central Valley, the host region for the bulk of common table and dessert wines. Moreover, in many European countries vineyards are commonly restricted to one or two principal grape varieties chosen because of their suitability to the local microclimate. The choice of these varieties is based on long experience, but in America, despite the plethora of published data on the physical requirements of vine growth, there seems to be little, if any, detailed information on the influence of specific microclimates and soils on both the physiography of vine growth and ability to produce specific wines. As a consequence, American appellations do not restrict grape varieties, and are not based on specific soil composition, although there are several exceptions concerning the latter criterion. While we can expect, therefore, a continuous display of controlled and joyous anarchy of grape varieties considered fashionably "in" and the types of wines produced in the future, American growers are paying increased attention to the matching of specific grape varieties to microclimatic and soil conditions.

While climate clearly limits grape growing to temperate zones, specific microclimates severely limit varieties within this broad climatic region. Microclimatic features are characterized by the following:

1. The range of temperature and humidity variations of the air near the ground is much greater than in the free atmosphere and region.
2. Due to increased friction, air movement near the ground is reduced to nearly zero despite the disparate pressure gradients.
3. Soil temperatures exhibit high diurnal variations.
4. Local topographic features are critical. Surfaces having different aspect and exposure have different solar regimes. When one slope is bathed in sunlight, the other is in shade. When north (*ubec*) vs south (*adret*) mid-latitude sites are compared: the former has significantly lower temperatures, more coniferous vegetation, and wetter and higher acid soils, while the latter has higher average temperatures, a longer day, more alkaline soils, and more deciduous vegetation. Furthermore, because aspect affects sun angle, air and soil temperatures vary widely within a short distance. Hilly vs. low lying valley locations influence air movement, temperature, surface runoff of water, evaporation, and relative humidity. Well-drained soils are generally warmer, while clayey soils, due to their water holding capacity, are colder.
5. Different soils have different microclimates.
6. Ground cover alters the character of a microclimate.
7. Irrigated soils create different microclimates.
8. A trellis system too close to the ground in a cold climate will raise humidity, and lead to fungus problems.
9. When forested and open areas are compared: the former experience higher mean winter temperatures, and higher relative humidity throughout the entire year; and the latter has a much warmer mean summer temperature, and higher wind velocities.
10. When valley and hillside locations are compared: the former location experiences more fog and frost, while the latter location experiences higher daytime temperatures.
11. When east-facing and west-facing locations are compared: the former receives morning sun that reduces the incidence of fungus, and has lower average temperatures, while the latter site gets the significantly warmer afternoon sun.

The above *homoclime* descriptions are defined in terms of broad elements common to each of the six climates. The homoclime or agro-climatic analogue concept is based upon a considerable volume of crop data of pure varieties or clones by climate, latitude and altitude. While the homoclime approach has been found to be a commercially rational approach in all manner of more common food and industrial agricultural crops, it has yet to be applied to viticulture, partly because of cost, but partly because homoclime areas and their specific analogues have not been accurately formulated to offer scientific comparisons. It must also be remembered that viticulture is a relatively recent introduction in America. American growers lack long-term experiences with most "Old World" varieties. The overwhelming attention devoted to temperature and precipitation is simply inadequate. As a minimum the following are equally important, all of which clearly and accurately delineate a microclimate: the mean, maximum, and minimum monthly and diurnal temperatures, as well as the seasonal and annual temperatures; the duration of the frost-free period; the average monthly, seasonal, and annual precipitation; the average monthly, seasonal, and annual relative humidity; the characteristics of the length of day; the nature of wind, duration, seasonality, and velocity; the incidence of fog; the incidence of cloudiness; the nature and cause of frost, etc.

Current Trends in Vineyard Management

One way of overcoming climatic limitations is to introduce several vineyard practices that overcome physical environmental constraints. One obvious starting point is to plant grapes according to the individual requirements of the variety, clone, rootstock, soil, and microclimate of the area. Historically, American growers planted the wrong grape variety in the wrong climate and soil. Recently, the vineyard manger has, by fine tuning cultural practices, achieved the status of celebrity with improved vineyard management techniques that led to significant changes in wine quality. Various canopy management practices regulate yield, extend the growing season, improve efficiency, lower the pH of grapes, and reduce the number and severity of diseases.

A dense canopy with reduced light penetration will produce higher potassium levels, lower sugar levels, and when planted in wide rows, sunlight falling on bare soil is wasted. Moreover, the shaded interior will remain wetter longer after rainfall, and the higher humidity will not only promote disease, but will also delay fruit ripening. In addition, if light passes through two layers of leaves the intensity of light reaching the third layer of leaves would theoretically be where the rate of photosynthesis just equals the rate of respiration, and a vine would neither gain nor lose weight. Exposing fruit to air and sun, and increasing air circulation are two general principles in canopy management that reduce fungus disorders and vigor allowing canopies to produce better wine grapes. Under such a management system, malic acids, pH, and potassium levels are lower, there is less bunch rot, better color, phenols, flavor, and usually higher sugar levels. In general, there is better acid balance that helps SO2 efficiency and fights the negative action of bacteria that do not thrive in acidity. Hence, wines with higher acid levels are less vulnerable and better protected. One of the most revolutionary developments in recent years has been the Dyson goblet method of vine training in the Hudson Valley, just north of New York City. Based on a simple principle, the goblet aims to create a more vertical growth pattern for the canes with a single level of fruit that hangs side by side on adjacent wires below the leaf canopy (the system has been patented). The canopy forms a "Y" from support arms that extend outward from the posts and is fastened to them by a cross brace. The system performs extremely well in cold climates as it makes more competent use of the canopy. There is more efficient photosynthesis, less shading, and reduced vigor. A similar, but somewhat less cumbersome system, is the modified gable trellis used in the Yakima Valley.

In most areas of California canopy management is based on the theory that increased sunlight reduces malic, pH, and potassium, increases the level of soluble solids, increases phenolic concentration, and improves the color of both red and white grapes. This goal has spread throughout the rest of the nation because it has been discovered that a high pH affects biological activity, color, and the organoleptic character of the wine. Although it can be adjusted by ion exchange, resin technology, and by various other means, it is felt that it is better done naturally in the vineyard. Low must pH produces better fla-

vored wine, and produces a fruitier and fresher wine than that which has a pH higher than 3.4. In addition, low pH renders wine more microbiologically stable, promotes better coloration, and inhibits oxidation. Another serious innovation is high density plantings (3x5' instead of 8x12'), decreasing production per vine but not the acre. In colder climates this practice has the added bonus of inducing increased winter hardiness.

Among the long list of emerging technologies, genetic engineering, enhancement of photosynthetic efficiency, plant growth regulators, plant disease and nematode control, and organic farming are most promising. Clonal and genetic selection will increase in the future because the industry wishes to avoid the genetic variability (and drift) that results through seed propagation. Finally, the development of methods to regenerate entire plants from cultured grapevine cells in order to genetically modify existing grapevine varieties and to improve their resistance to specific pests, diseases, and environmental stresses, and to alter flavor and fermentation properties will accelerate in future decades.

Dry-farmed Zinfandel Vine in the Dry-Creek Region of Sonoma. Baxevanis

III
THE POLITICS OF WINE

Legislation to administer or prohibit the manufacture, sale, and transportation of wine as well as other alcoholic beverages is of ancient origin. Taxes, duties, and tariffs of various kinds, and social, religious, and economic motives are also used to combat the "evils" of alcoholism, and promote public health welfare and public order. In addition to America, Russia, Sweden, Norway, Finland, Iceland, and Estonia, and a host of other countries experimented with various forms of alcoholic beverage control and prohibition. The strictest legislation takes place in Scandinavian and Moslem countries. Interestingly, legislative measures in southern Europe regulating the production, distribution, and sale of wine (the area with the highest wine production, highest per capita consumption, and extremely low rates of alcoholism) are non-existent. Three specific methods are used to legislate the manufacture, distribution, and sale of wine: regulation of geographic origins and wine nomenclature, licensing mechanisms, and prohibition restrictions.

Labels

All wines sold or offered for sale in interstate commerce must have a certificate of label approval issued by BATF. Mandatory label requirements include the following: brand name, class type (sparkling, table, light, dessert, etc.), alcohol content, name and address of the bottler or packer, net contents, declaration of coloring material, sulfites, and warning statements. Although the above-mentioned, minimum mandatory items are widely accepted, states are in a position to modify federal standards and regulations. For example, Oregon adopted stringent new consumer-oriented labeling and product regulations in 1977 for its grape wines. All wines bearing the "Oregon" appellation must be made entirely of grapes grown within the state, and no Oregon wines are permitted to carry European geographic names such as Burgundy or Rhone. All varietal wines must contain at least 90 percent of the stated variety with the lone exception being Cabernet Sauvignon, a wine that must contain at least 75 percent only if the other 25 percent consists of the traditional Bordeaux blending varieties. A listing of all varieties in the blend must appear on the label, and only names approved by the Oregon Liquor Control Commission are authorized for use.

Vintage Date: A minimum of 95 percent of the wine with a vintage year on the label must be made from grapes harvested, crushed, and fermented during the named year, in contrast to non-vintaged wines that are blends of grapes grown in various years. All vintage wine must carry an appellation of origin, and comply with the stated requirements of that appellation. Some states require that 100 percent of the grapes used in the crush and the making of the wine be of the stated year.

Generic: These are wines made with a variable blend of grapes and labelled according to the type or style of wine rather than the predominant type of grape used. Equally important is the fact that there is no specific method of production implied in a generic wine. Usually marketed under European names such as Chianti, Chablis, Rhine, Bordeaux, Burgundy, etc., generics vary enormously by producer because a good deal of the grapes and wine are purchased on the spot market and made/or blended differently. Although generic wine can be vintage-labeled, it rarely is, and it is also important to note that a good deal of American and "eastern" generics are a blend of low acid and high acid wines. These wines rarely, if ever, resemble their European counterparts, but since the immigrant wine consuming population came from these areas, it was easy to understand why American winemakers imitated easily recognizable names (American consumers also understand and use such names as Irish stew, English toffee and muffins, Dutch ovens, Swiss cheese, Danish pastry, French dressing, etc.). The *Institute National d'Appellation d'Origine* in Paris and similar organizations in other foreign countries wishing to preserve the geographic authenticity of their names have filed legal suits. As a consequence, all American sparkling wine in order to carry the name Champagne must be preceded by "American," "New York," etc. In a recent test case, the French have won a Caribbean case against the use of "Chablis" to describe American white wine. Frank Schoonmaker is given credit as the first post-Prohibition American to advocate a departure from the misleading use of European names. His advise was to name wines after the dominant grape variety, and after 50 years nearly all of America's finest wines are so named. The number of names currently under review by BATF exceeds 5,400, of which 2,113 are considered distinctively geographic, the rest being "semi-generic." For the European and other selected foreign markets, the above "generic" wine names are not permitted, hence, the wines are simply called "American Red Wine" or "California White Wine," etc.

Proprietary: These names are neither generic nor varietal designations but a product of the proprietor's imagination, be it "Barefoot Bernie," or "Sweet Alice." Common names such as "John's Vineyard," and "American Winery" do not necessarily mean that the wine was made from grapes grown in the stated vineyard or made in a winery. The name merely identifies the seller--nothing more, and there are no regulations governing what grape varieties may or may not be in a proprietary wine, or how a particular type of wine be made. Although the majority of proprietary labels are nothing more than "jug" wine, a small but growing number represent a new level of sophistication on the part of American winemakers. Doing away with the generic and varietal labels (the latter often replete with a bewildering amount of useless information such as Brix readings, time and date the grapes were picked, etc.), the upscale, elite, and ultra-perspicacious proprietary label does away with the minimum varietal requirement because the wine is usually a blend of two or more different grapes or de-emphasizes the grape variety as in the case of the outstanding *Etude*. In this regard, not only does the name of the winemaker become the consumer's assurance of quality, but the brand name. Brands with geographical names cannot be used unless the grapes and wine fulfill appellation requirements. If the wine does not originate in the appellation, the word "brand" must appear after the name of the bottler as well as the geographical origin of the wine.

Varietal Designation: This implies that a minimum percentage (75 percent) of the stated variety is present in the bottle. Multi-varietal labeling is allowed but only if both the name and the percentage of each grape variety in the blend is listed. Furthermore, every bottle of varietal wine is required to list an appellation of origin on the label. The appellation must be either a state, county, or approved viticultural area, the latter requiring that 95 percent originate from the area named if the bottle is vintaged. Increased from 51 percent in 1983, the much higher minimum figure takes much of the winemakers flexibility in the production of blends. For example, the 75 percent minimum regulation as it pertains to Cabernet Sauvignon has come under attack because many producers are prohibited from using that name when blended with other "traditional" varieties whose collective percentage exceeds 25 percent.

BATF is currently reviewing varietal designations in an effort to accommodate consumer concerns. It proposes to do away with such items as "White Zinfandel" and "White Pinot Noir," to alter the name French Colombard to Colombard, eliminate Blanc from Seyval, change Black Muscat to Muscat Hamburg, and even attempt to resolve the nomenclature of Gamay Beaujolais, Napa Beaujolais, and Pinot Noir, among others. Vitis labrusca and other American grapes are generally limited to 51 percent due to their strong flavor and odor concentrations. In reality, this figure, because of amelioration, is often significantly lower than the 51 percent legal minimum. Moreover, BATF can lower this percentage if it finds a specific variety to be "too strongly flavored." In the final analysis, the varietal designation is important because some grapes are preferred over others.

Bottler-Producer. The label must show a company name (not always identical with the brand name) and a business location. **Proprietor or Vintner Grown** are two

expressions that refer to a winery that controls or owns 100 percent of the vineyards, but did not perform all winemaking processes. **Grown, Produced and Bottled By,** a highly important designation, indicates that grapes used in the wine were grown by the bottler and the wine was made in a winery owned by the bottler. **Produced and Bottled By,** less reliable than the former, refers to the fact that at least 75 percent of the grapes were crushed and fermented by the bottler. The grapes must have been grown within the area specified but not necessarily by the bottler. This and the following two designations refer to the use of purchased grapes and or wine stocks in order to increase output for a variety of reasons. **Made and Bottled By,** is a designation referring to the fact that not less than 10 percent of the wine was made by the bottler. **Cellared and Bottled By, Prepared and Bottled By, Selected By, Blended and Bottled By,** etc., refer to the fact that 100 percent of the wine was produced by someone else and finished and bottled by the bottler. Your only assurance is the reputation of the bottler.

Prestige, Specific Character, and Quality Designations, such as Reserve, Private Reserve, Special Private Reserve, Night Harvest, Proprietor's Reserve, Mountain Grown, Private Stock, Special Cask, and Special Selection, etc., are wine designations that the vintner confers on rare and exceptional wines. These names are not regulated by law, and your only guarantee of quality is the reputation of the winery. In addition, several terms may be used to describe winemaking and wine character such as Barrel Fermented Chardonnay, Late Harvest Riesling, Dry Sherry, Ruby Port, residual sugar, total acid, pH, etc. It should also be emphasized that the designation "mountain" is a meaningless, unregulated expression with no legal significance whether applied to generic or varietal wines.

Organically Grown In Accordance With The California Organic Foods Act of 1990, has been approved by BATF to be used on a wine label. Faced with a host of health issues, governmental regulations, and consumer resistance to a thirty-fold increase in pesticide use since 1945, the wine industry, like many other branches of agriculture, is currently fascinated by the concept of organic farming. While there is no agreement on a simple definition (each state has defined the concept differently), in essence, the basic idea is to use only naturally occurring substances in the cultivation of vines. That is to say, no synthetically derived chemical pesticides, herbicides, fertilizers, or growth regulators. It also means that the winemaker will not add anything to the grape must before fermentation, during fermentation, and minimize both the processing and manipulation of the wine. Certification, enforcement authority, and marketing and labeling are not standardized, but BATF approval is based on California regulations.

Foreign Names, such as Chablis, Auslese, Bordeaux, Burgundy, etc., may be used, but not in every state. **Bottle Size**: the most common bottle sizes are: 3 liter; 1.50 liter; .750 liter; .500 liter; and .375 liter. **Sugar Content**: There are no federal regulations defining the words *dry* or *sweet*. Anything less than 2% residual sugar can be defined as dry, which to most people is not dry. However, .5% or less residual sugar is usually accepted as dry, .5%-1.5% is widely accepted as semi-dry, 1.5%-2.5% as semi-sweet, and anything above 2.5% as sweet. *Late harvest* is an unregulated expression referring to a wine made from higher than normal sugar levels. It is usually richer in flavor, sweeter, higher in alcohol, and more expensive.

Appellation Designations

Prior to the late 1960s, wine was bought by the barrel and bottled in jugs, and as long as it tasted good geographic origins and other ancestry characteristics (other than California, Napa, Sonoma, and the Finger Lakes) were of no importance to most Americans. Appellation legislation was promulgated by BATF in the early 1980s in order to satisfy EEC regulations and to offer an assurance of geographic origin to an ever increasing number of hitherto European wine-drinking consumers. Since then, the origin of grapes has become as important, and, to many, more compelling than the kind of grapes used.

American refers to blended wine made from grapes grown in America or two or more states (75 percent minimum), and fully finished and bottled in another. Grapes grown in one state and finished in another are presently not entitled to the appellation of the state of origin. Due to dramatic improvements in the transportation of grapes, must, and wine, an enormous amount of wine is shipped from the three western states (but primarily California) to areas east of the Rocky Mountains (as well as Arizona and New Mexico). As long as "eastern" states continue to allow significant "amelioration," the "American" *ava* will become more prominent in the future. It should be pointed out that there are important and significant differences in the labeling of wine that is intended for intrastate vs. interstate consumption. In addition, BATF has determined that a winery in one state should not be subject to another state's laws and regulations in multi-state *ava* designations. **Multi-state** *ava* of origin can be used (so far very rarely) only when two or more states are contiguous. If state requirements conflict so that the wine can't conform with the laws and regulations from all the states involved, then multi-state *ava's* of origin cannot be used. While the order of the states listed on the label is not regulated, the sequence should not mislead the consumer. The state with the highest percentage of grapes grown is listed first, followed by the state name with the next highest grape percentage, etc. A "Pacific Coast" *ava* (California, Oregon, and Washington)

is currently being considered.

State designation refers to the fact that a varying percentage (the actual amount varies widely by state) of the grapes were grown in the state mentioned on the label (as of this writing, only California, Oregon, and Washington require that 100% of the grapes be grown in that state). Due to the young age of the vines and the precarious character of weather in the rest of the country, states allow as much as 70 percent "imported" grapes/must, or wine to be added to the blend, and still call the wine after the name of the state. In Michigan and Virginia, for example, at least 75 percent of the grapes must be grown in the state. **County** designation refers to a minimum of 75 percent of the grapes be grown in the named county. The winery must be located in the state, but not necessarily in the named county. When two or more counties in the same state are designated on the label, 95 percent or more of all the grapes must be grown in the counties displayed on the label, and the wine fully finished in one of the counties with plus or minus 2 percent tolerance.

Approved Viticultural Area refers to a wine growing region whose geography and boundaries are recognized and strictly defined by BATF. When the Approved Viticultural Area name is used on the label, a minimum of 85 percent of the grapes must originate from the stated *ava*, and the wine must be fully finished within the state. When vintaged, 95 percent of the wine must come from grapes grown in the year stated on the label. It is felt that in this manner the winemaker would have sufficient maneuverability to produce the best possible wine through judicious blending while maintaining the basic character attributed to the viticultural area stated on the label.

Vineyard Designation is a name for a specific vineyard where a minimum of 95 percent of the grapes stated on the label originate. This defines the smallest officially accepted boundary in which grapes are grown within an *ava*. This notion is based on the fact that specific, microclimatic/soil conditions dictate wine styles, and are worthy of specific mention. Historically, such labels were rare, but since the promulgation of new labeling regulations in 1983, the number of vineyard-designated wines has increased nationally beyond 300, a figure that is increasing rapidly. Most vineyard names are overwhelmingly associated with a small number of key varietals, such as Chardonnay, Cabernet Sauvignon, Pinot Noir, Merlot, and Zinfandel. Curiously, vineyard designations for Sauvignon Blanc, Riesling, Chenin Blanc, and other varieties are rare. Geographically, vineyard designations are more common in California, Oregon, and Washington, and rare for areas east of the Continental Divide.

The consumer usually pays a premium for this wine, that tends (but not always) to be above average in quality, and more consistent in style than non-vineyard designated wines. As a consequence, the use of vineyard designated wines will increase in the future to bewildering proportions; it is estimated that there are 340 individual vineyard names used, a figure that will rise to more than 1,000 over the next ten years. If and when these vineyards are recognized for the production of above-average and distinctive wine over a long period of time, then it is possible to classify these vineyards in the manner of a "Grand Cru System." While there are many who advocate such a system, the bulk of the industry maintains that it is too early to spawn such a classification. The later position is based on the unfamiliarity of American toponyms, and, hence, meaningless to most Americans.

Estate Bottled, refers to the fact that the winery and the vineyard which are the source of the grapes stated on the label must be located in the same *ava*. In addition, the "approved viticultural area" name must be used on the label, and the winery either own or "control" (in most cases the winery leases the vineyard) the vineyards (in the vicinity of the winery), and all winemaking processes from crushing to bottling be done at that single winery facility. At no time must the wine leave the premises of the bottling winery during the various processing stages. One hundred percent of the grapes used in estate bottled wine must come from the designated *ava* and vineyard, and the wine casks can only be topped with conforming wine from the same *ava*.

Very important is the BATF definition of "controlled" in reference to the origin of the grapes from specific vineyards. Controlled refers to the bottling winery performing all the acts common to viticulture under the terms of at least three years duration whether the vineyard is owned or leased by the bottling winery. Since control includes leased land or that owned by relatives or related corporations (hence, subject to inconsistencies), and its vicinity can be as much as 50 miles away, this is pretty much a meaningless expression unless regulations are administered more rigidly by BATF. Because of the above, the number of wines currently available on the market with "estate" designations are few in view of the number of regulations allowing its use. No term other than "estate bottled" may be used on the label to indicate combined growing and bottling conditions. This expression, therefore, without guaranteeing quality, does sell at a premium, and is confined to the finest varietals. Although this is as close as America comes to "chateau" production in the Bordeaux manner, the concept, given the large size of many approved viticultural areas, can be vague and subject to abuse.

Finally, it should be mentioned that exemption to BATF label approval is granted if the wine will be sold in its home state only and no interstate commerce is involved, the wine complies with the IRS Code, all label information is correct and not misleading, and the bottling winery applies for and receives a certificate of exemption from BATF.

Warning Labels and Ingredient Labeling

As of 1989, when the alcohol content is greater than .5% the following health warnings must appear on the label: *"Government Warning: (1) According to the Surgeon General, women should not drink alcoholic beverages during pregnancy because of the risk of birth defects. (2) Consumption of alcoholic beverages impairs your ability to drive a car or operate machinery and may cause health problems."* This warning, as stern and ruthless as it is, is about to be modified to larger type, with warnings as to the addictive nature of alcohol, and an 800 telephone number for consumers to seek help and/or information.

Although there is no known scientific evidence that wine is a public hazard, wine labels now are mandated to warn the public of "implied" health dangers. Neo-Prohibition tendencies have recently generated enough pressure upon state and federal authorities for legislation requiring health warnings on alcoholic beverage containers. What makes this issue ludicrous is the fact that BATF at present has approved "as safe" more than 200 wine additives, the most recent being aspartame, a sugar substitute in wine coolers. Nevertheless, the cacophony has increased in recent years with the promulgation of the Sensible Advertising and Family Education (SAFE) Act, introduced by Representative Joseph Kennedy, and considered by the House Subcommittee on Transportation and Hazardous Materials. This piece of convoluted reasoning would require the rotation of specific health warnings on all types of alcoholic beverage advertising, including print, radio, television, billboards, and direct mail. Moreover, warning labels are not applied in a uniform manner on all products. While the dangers of smoking are applied to cigarettes, cigars and pipe tobacco are not required to carry warning labels. In the final analysis, warning labels are dangerous to the industry because they stress the negative aspects by the word "use" not "abuse." The immediate danger is the spawning of product liability law suits, a new trend in America where people wish to shift blame from themselves to someone else. The above notwithstanding, one positive element in 1991 was BATF's approval of the Mondavi Mission Label, that reads: *"Wine has been with us since the beginning of civilization. It is a temperate, civilized, romantic, mealtime beverage. Wine has been praised for centuries by statesmen, philosophers, poets and scholars. Wine in moderation is an integral part of our family's culture, heritage and the gracious way of life."*

Of the 500 substances found naturally in wine, there are a host of additives that are added by winemakers to facilitate the winemaking process, of which yeast, sugar, dried skim milk, diatomacious clay, and others are added for a variety of reasons such as raising alcohol or reducing acid levels, regulating color and fragrance, etc. In almost all instances, these "additives" are never found in the final product. Various clays, skim milk, gelatin, and egg white are used to "fine" the wine, and are removed prior to bottling. Mineral oil, for example, is used to remove unwanted odor, but after its addition and a brief agitation, the oil rises to the surface and is removed. Unlike beer, made under continuous, mass-produced processes where a number of stabilizing additives are used to extend life and preserve freshness, wine is made once a year from fresh grapes, and because it's alcohol content is twice that of beer it is more stable. Over the past ten years, enzyme use in the wine industry have become common to substantially increase color intensity, increase the amount of free-run juice, and change the color as well, with no apparent harm to the public.

In California, Proposition 65 placed all alcoholic beverages on the list of "hazardous substances" (among which are cancer-causing products), thus requiring warning labels as of July 1, 1989. The warnings carry a provision that alcohol is a carcinogen only when associated with alcohol abuse. What is particularly disturbing about Proposition 65 is that animal studies fail to support a causal relationship between alcohol and cancer, hence the (apparent) link between alcohol and cancer remains an unproven hypothesis. It is estimated that under Proposition 65 interpretations more than 15,000 products may require warnings. Wishing to eliminate the potentially explosive issue of the carcinogenic solvent urethane from Sherry, brandy, and wine, the industry has spent significant financial resources attempting to reduce urethane levels below 15 ppb in table wines and 60 ppb in dessert wines before 1995. Canadian regulations ban any table wine that exceeds 30 ppb and any dessert wine that has more than 100 ppb. Urethane is produced during winemaking and is found in various concentrations by type of wine. Because the concentrations vary in extremely small amounts (between 0.0090 percent and 0.0000004 percent), the issue is more of an annoyance than anything else.

"Contains Sulfites," is a statement indicating that SO2 is present in the wine. It is estimated that roughly 5 percent of the American population suffers from asthma, and of that total less than 5 percent is allergic to sulfites. In order to warn this sulfite-sensitive group, all wines bear the statement "contains sulfites" if they meet or exceed a threshold of 10 ppm. SO2 is a byproduct of fermentation, and an additive that acts as an antioxidant agent. The concentration varies because when S02 is added it reacts with acetaldehyde to form 1-hydroxeyethane sulfonate--a chemical compound that is not a sulfite. No chemical substitute for this additive exists anywhere in the world at the present time, although Ascorbyl decanoate (a preservative, antioxidant, and bacterial agent) can be used reducing added S02 by 80 percent.

Specifically, S02 protects fermenting juice and new wine from oxidation, browning, microbial contamination, and preserves the wine's natural flavor, among other important functions. Occurring in both free and bound forms, it is a natural wine ingredient. When artificially removed, the wine loses its ability to age (even for a brief period of time), it changes color quickly, surrenders its fruity aroma, and rapidly becomes unpalatable. In fact, wines made with added SO2 are better in taste, color, and stability than those made without it. It occurs in a range between 15 and 50 ppm, but can be as much as 100 ppm with some yeasts used to ferment wine. Current federal regulations permit up to 350 parts per million of sulfites in wine. Despite its continual use for more than 2,000 years, there is no evidence that the modest S02 concentrations contained in wines has ever produced adverse health effects.

Health-related S02 sensitivity is mainly confined to steroid-dependent and severe asthmatic people on medication--collectively only a minute portion of the American population. The S02 abuses are solely confined to solid food, particularly salad bars (where S02 concentrations are as high as 15,000 ppm in a free state), and not wine where it occurs in a bound state. Sulfites are also widely used in preserving seafood, dried fruits, fruit juices, maple syrup, processed potatoes and vegetables, sugar, fruit jellies and preserves, and a host of baked goods. The misuse of S02 by the food industry has produced a "sulfite scare," and BATF in conjunction with FDA has forced the wine industry to indicate the phrase "Contains Sulfites" on the label if commercial wine contains more than 10 ppm. In order to comprehend "parts per million" consider the following: 1 part per million compares to 1 inch in 16 miles; 1 part per billion compares with 1 inch in 16,000 miles; 1 part per trillion compares with 1 inch in 16 million miles. In the final analysis, critics, unfortunately, disregard the fact that the human body both produces and metabolizes sulfur. About 90 percent of the dietary sulfur emerges in the tissue as sulfur dioxide, that dissolves in water as sulfite, the same chemical used in the production of wine. On the basis of a normal diet of 70 grams of protein a day, an adult consumes between 0.7 and 3.5 grams of sulfur amino acids per day, amounts much lower than that ingested from wine under normal conditions.

Even more disturbing than health warnings is the recent absurd notion of "ingredient labeling." The potential for harm is so great that it might be worse than Prohibition, but fortunately this legislation has yet to pass and reek havoc. In essence, few wine additives remain in the final product, so that the notion, while fairly easily adopted and verified in the food industry, becomes unenforceable and potentially life-threatening to the wine industry. Not only is the domestic industry opposed (estimated costs range as high as $600 million), but the EEC and the International Wine Federation have also voiced strong opposition. If such a law were to be enacted, America would be the only country burdened with such legislation, and the impact on imported wines, and small producers (both foreign and domestic) catastrophic. Wines that claim to be "light," may, in the future, be required to state the caloric count on their labels. The wine industry views the words "light" and "lite" to mean low alcohol wines, while public interest groups wish to impose a mandatory calorie-content labeling.

Legally defined wines must have an alcohol content by volume that ranges between .5% and 24%. BATF regulations state that alcohol content must be stated for wines over 14% alcohol content, and optional for wines under 14%. "Table" or "Light" names may be used instead of alcohol content. Tolerance range for alcohol content is 1% + or - for over 14%, 1.5% + or - for under 14%. In general, table wines vary between 10% and 14%, and for light wines it is 7%. Sparkling wines are between 10%-14%. The limits for appetizer and dessert vary between 14%-24%. Red table wine has a spread of 10.5% minimum and 14% maximum; for white table wine it is 10%-14%. Also the minimum volatile acidity in grams, minimum titratable fixed acidity, and minimum extract will vary by state.

Although there is no evidence that lead capsules have ever posed a health hazard to the consumer, the potential threat that even a hint of possible contamination has recently induced many wineries to switch to aluminum and tin. While plastic capsules are quite common on inexpensive bottles, the public usually associates lead capsules with above average quality wines, hence a predisposition for lead capsule preference. The problem is that tin, the preferred alternative, costs significantly more than lead, thus raising the cost of dressing bottles.

Fetal Alcohol Syndrome was first described by a group of physicians in Seattle, Washington as a constellation of symptoms occurring in the offspring of some women who have consumed large amounts of alcohol during pregnancy. The syndrome involved mental retardation, small head size, small stature, and a number of other more subtle skeletal and facial abnormalities such as wide-set eyes. A related syndrome named fetal alcohol effect is a condition that is less severe than FAS, but vague in definition, highly subjective as a concept, and difficult to measure. The problem is that there has never been a case of FAS from a mother using wine in moderate amounts, and certainly it has never been observed in southern European wine-drinking countries. The Seattle group studied a group of women who consumed prodigious amounts of alcohol during pregnancy, primarily inexpensive distilled beverages, and occasionally beer. These women were not normal consumers, but individuals with flagrantly distorted lifestyles. Curiously, not all children of heavy drinking mothers suffer FAS. While no

one denies the existence of FAS, a combination of related lifestyle distortions, such as heavy smoking, poor nutrition, and other related elements, combine to produce FAS.

Little is said of the beneficial elements of wine consumption, and the wine industry has been slow to react to neo-Prohibitionism by emphasizing the health benefits in its moderate use. Wine is not identical to distilled beverages and beer as it is composed of 300 congoners, sugars, pigments, carbohydrates, vitamins, minerals, acids, etc., all of which occur naturally, some simple and some immeasurably complex. When consumed in moderation, wine aids in the digestion of food (as it stimulates the flow of saliva, gastric juices, and hydrochloric acid), prevents, or at least slows down, the accumulation of harmful cholesterol (the daily consumption of wine lowers stroke risk by 33 percent), and raises good cholesterol levels. The Journal of Applied Cardiology states that red wine increases the level of high density lipoproteins (HDL) in the blood, which has been shown to reduce the risk of heart disease, harmful bacterial count of the colon, and is perhaps the most innocent of sedatives. It contains practically no salt, is easily metabolized by the body, enhances and compliments food, promotes sobriety, and is an excellent counter measure to anorexia. Recently, medical findings have come to the conclusion that moderate alcohol consumption is linked to better health in the aged. According to a Surgeon General's workshop on health promotion and aging, low to moderate consumption of alcohol by an aging population may curb some diseases. According to the summary of the workshop issued by the U.S. Department of Health and Human Services' Center for Disease Control, possible beneficial effects include improved eating behavior, mood, sleeping patterns, and social functioning. During the period 1970-1990, as the incidence of Cirrhosis mortality declined from 14.8 to 10.1 per 100,000 population, distilled spirits consumption declined from 1.98 gallons to 1.81 gallons per capita, beer increased from 20.7 to 24.4 gallons per capita, and wine increased from 1.63 to 2.2 gallons per capita. This is dramatic as the percent of wine increase was more than double that of beer.

It is also important to note that Quercetin, an anticarcinogen, found in onions, broccoli, squash, and red grapes, is also found in red wine. Ischemic heart disease (I.H.D.) mortality rates for men are lowest in such countries as Greece (1,991), France (2,145), Spain (1,838), Italy (3,020), and highest in such areas as Scotland (8,841), Ireland (6,683), Norway (6,066), Finland (10,748), and England (7,041, per million of population). Apparently, it matters not that many other common foods, such as meat, coffee, mustard, parsley, basil, celery, and peanut butter, contain carcinogens. The above is particularly important when one inspects the medical and social history of major wine producing districts in Mediterranean Europe. Alcoholism in the wine producing districts of Portugal, France, Greece, Spain, Italy, and Cyprus is practically non-existent without the benefit of restrictive national legislation. The lowest incidence of alcoholic behavior is observed in the following cultures: in grape growing regions, where wine is considered a food and usually consumed with food; where parents set a constant example of moderate drinking; where wine drinking is viewed as a socially responsible activity; and where abstinence is socially acceptable. Not only is excessive drinking not tolerated, stylish, or comical, but social activities are never centered on alcohol, and there are clear ground rules for drinking. In the final analysis, throughout the wine producing regions of Europe, and especially southern Europe, wine has had little or no measurable role as a cause of anti-social or criminal behavior.

Figure 3.1

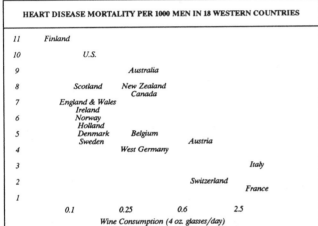

HEART DISEASE MORTALITY PER 1000 MEN IN 18 WESTERN COUNTRIES

11	Finland			
10	U.S.			
9		Australia		
8	Scotland	New Zealand		
7	England & Wales	Canada		
	Ireland			
6	Norway			
	Holland			
5	Denmark	Belgium		
	Sweden		Austria	
4		West Germany		
3				Italy
2		Switzerland		
1				France
	0.1	0.25	0.6	2.5

Wine Consumption (4 oz. glasses/day)

There is a significant difference in the risk of mortality by heart attack among different regions of Europe that cannot be scientifically explained by corresponding differences in the main risk factors of high blood pressure, a high level of cholesterol in the blood, and smoking. Comparative studies of fruit, vegetable, bread, and red wine consumption appear to be more significant. The above data contrasts heart disease rates for eighteen different western countries. The U.S. was rated in a group that drank the least wine and suffered the most deaths from heart disease.
Source: St. Leger, The Lancet, May 12, 1979.

Although considered an essential part of life, very rarely, if ever, is wine considered synonymous with alcohol. The population at large does not consider wine the product of the devil, governmental officials do not denounce wine as physiologically bad, and, unlike the Subcommittee on Transportation and Hazardous Materials in Washington, D.C., have never placed wine in the "hazardous" category. Unlike America, nearly all children in Mediterranean countries drink wine in social gatherings prior to the age of ten. Less than 1% drink before and after meals and hardly ever without food. Mediterranean eating habits tend to be monotonous and regular, unlike the sporadic eating habits of America that promote alcohol abuse. Moreover, throughout the wine producing

Mediterranean regions, it is common knowledge that "the way you drink is extremely important, when to drink is important, where to drink is important, but that the choosing of the right companions is even more important." Solitary, addictive, pathological drinking behavior does not occur to any significant extent in traditional wine producing regions. Wine is usually not a problem in a cultural group unless it is defined as such. These societies define wine as a food, and rarely does it result in disruptive or antisocial behavior. In sharp contrast, problem drinkers have the following in common: they drink quickly and often drink without food, it makes them feel superior by releasing inhibitions, and drunkenness is implicitly and explicitly approved. One thing is certain: alcoholism is not due to the availability of alcohol.

APPROVED VITICULTURAL AREAS

January 1, 1983, BATF-adopted regulations concerning appellation of origin (grape growing regions) on wine labels. The regulations allow the establishment of American viticultural areas and permit the name of an approved viticultural area (*ava*) to be used on an appellation of origin on wine labels, and in all advertising. In its most general form, an *ava* is defined as a delimited grape growing region with geographical features that set it apart from all surrounding areas in terms of historic name, climate, and geographical characteristics (topography, soils, etc.). There are, unlike France and other countries, no limitations on yields, type of grape(s) to be grown, or vineyard and enological practices. Once indicated on the label, at least 85 percent of all grapes used to make the wine must emanate from the stated region. As in all other appellation systems, the appellation name is no guarantee of quality.

Approved viticultural areas are officially established by BATF with the input of consumers, industry officials, grape growers, and others. The first step is a petition by the interested party(ies) that carries the following mandatory information, and, then after lengthy public reviews, a Treasury Decision (TD) is issued establishing the *ava*:

1. Evidence that the name of the viticultural area is locally and/or nationally known as referring to the area specified in the boundaries. Given the recent history of America, this is not necessarily a major impediment to the petitioner except when two or more areas have the same name.
2. Historic or current evidence that the boundaries of the viticultural area exist as specified in the petition. This may be a troublesome issue if boundaries do not conform to clearly delineated geologic and meteorological features.
3. Evidence relating to the geographic features such as climate, soil, elevation, physical features, etc., which set the proposed viticultural area apart from surrounding areas. In the main, this segment is usually either too broad (as in Napa Valley that includes the entire county), or too narrow (as in Cole Ranch).
4. A copy of the appropriate U.S. Geological Survey map with boundaries properly marked. This is a major flaw in the *ava* system as most *ava's* are not delimited by completely uniform geological features.

BATF has three specific objectives in establishing

viticultural areas: (1) to give the consumer more specific information on the label to induce a more informed consumer choice; (2) to allow the wineries to better designate where the grapes are grown; and (3) to obtain more credibility for the American appellation of origin designations throughout the world.

AMERICAN VITICULTURAL AREAS
America has 117 *ava's* distributed in 25 states. The largest, *Texas Hill Country*, spans an area of 15,000 square miles, and is larger than the state of Massachusetts. The smallest is *Cole Ranch* (CA), less than a quarter square mile. California, with 64 *ava's*, leads the nation, followed by New York and Ohio (6), Virginia and Oregon (5), and Texas, Michigan, and Pennsylvania with 4.
The largest concentration are located in Sonoma County (12). *Ohio River* is the only *ava* that is located across four states (Indiana, Kentucky, West Virginia, and Ohio). There are 12 multi-state *ava's* (Central Delaware, Columbia Valley, Cumberland Valley, Kanawha River, Lake Erie, Mesilla Valley, Mississippi Delta, Ohio River, Ozark Mountain, Shenandoah Valley, Southeastern New England, and Walla Walla). *Augusta*, MO, was the nation's first (1980) *ava*.

For centuries, particularly in Europe, people wanted to know the birthplace of particular wines. This detail was so important that a good deal of official concern was applied to guarantee a wine's place of origin, which is another way of protecting the growers of a specific region and not the consumer. In France, these laws, the object of national passion for centuries, have necessitated the promulgation of an immense amount of legal definition often leading to sectional friction and the defense of national and regional dignity. Because the United States is so new a nation with but a scattering of viticultural history, these *appellations de origine* laws were of little consequence until 1983 when BATF first began their legislation. The application of European appellation legislation in America is difficult because: of a short, incomplete history; most wineries buy grapes (are not estate wineries); a lack of continuity from one generation to another, and from one decade to another in terms of types of wines made (American winemaking is in constant flux); and a lack of a distinct history of specific grape varieties growing in particular areas. American approved viticultural areas, as defined above, differ from the European appellation system in several important ways: their size is not limited; there is no historical evidence of specific grape varieties grown in specific soil and microclimatic areas to produce distinctive wine; and boundaries are not guided by viticultural and winemaking practices.

The issue of size and geography are particularly germane and potentially troublesome. The appellation criteria as outlined by BATF include no size limits, and thus it is possible to find *ava's* that are significantly larger than counties, and, in some instances, much larger than states. Cole Ranch, on the other hand, is a microscopic one-quarter of a square mile in Mendocino County. Both *ava's* are defined by the same BATF criteria regardless of

size variations. Moreover, one *ava* may include many other approved delimited areas within its boundaries, as in the North Coast *ava*, and more specifically within Sonoma County, a feature that is not that dissimilar from the general Bordeaux appellation in southwestern France. Thirty additional states contain all or part of at least one *ava*, and their number is increasing rapidly with more than 32 at the "in process" stage. The lack of geographic homogeneity in the larger (and even in the smaller appellation) is an area of some concern. The ten county Finger Lakes region, the multi-state Lake Erie, and even the North Coast *ava* in California, with the sole exception of name, lack physical homogeneity in soils, topography, climate, and could, in the future, develop marketing problems. The geographically approved viticultural areas, as of mid-1992, are described in some measure in their appropriate places in the text. Although appellations have been a prominent element in the world of wine for several thousand years, their sudden appearance in America has generated a heated imbroglio of considerable consequence.

Pro Position:
1. The American system is premature in terms of history, but necessary given the trend away from generic to varietal and estate designations.
2. A governmental sponsored appellation system is necessary if we are to export to the EEC, and other countries requiring wine origin guarantees.
3. Wine is the end product of the total immediate environment--soil, climate, grape variety characteristics, and cultural and winemaking traditions. Therefore, grape growing areas that are geographically distinctive should be delineated and their names protected, including BATF-approved specific vineyard sites.
4. Unlike the rigid nature of the European appellation system, the American is better because the market place decides what grapes will be planted; the European alternative is too inflexible as law determines what vines are planted where. The flexible nature of the American appellation system is its main strength, a consideration that should be maintained. To the credit of BATF, there have been, since 1980, more than ten *ava* boundary modifications. This does not imply that controversies do not arise and questionable decisions made, but, unlike the rigid unyielding European legislation, changes do occur.
5. New names enhance and promote regional awareness and distinctiveness, positive elements to be encouraged.
6. Appellation legislation will protect the growers within the region by eliminating *sous marques*, firms that have a post office address in a prestigious region but who buy grapes and wine from other areas. Napa growers, in particular, are beginning to come to grips with this issue at present. It is perhaps the only way to eliminate or, at best, mitigate against the abusive use of names. Since the promulgation of *ava* designations, at least one dozen law suits have been filled, all of which have upheld the integrity of the geographic designation. Every historic wine producing region in the "Old World" has devised a system to protect its name, so America cannot postpone the inevitable. Never mind that the delineation precedes reputation, the protection of the geographic name is foremost in importance.
7. Appellation legislation, in theory at least, will raise quality and prices. Although there are no guarantees that all winemakers will produce quality wine and show distinction from neighboring appellations, they are honest with a stake in preserving and furthering their appellation name.

Con Position:
1. Does the American system classify wines by type or by region? The critics raise an interesting question. For decades after Prohibition, the consumer purchased domestic wines by sugar content marketed under

foreign names such as Tokay, Madeira, Sherry, etc., then under varietal designations, now under varietal *ava* designations, and increasingly under vineyard name designations. Retailers and restaurateurs, in particular, resent the proliferation of new names. Instead of imitating European appellation characteristics, critics maintain that American wines ought to emphasize proprietary names.

2. The American *ava* system has proceeded too rapidly in too short a time. The number of delimited areas should be limited to several a year. The American wine industry is too crude, unsophisticated, and riddled with inconsistencies. Moreover, BATF is far removed from California, overworked, lacks the staff and capacity to accurately delineate appellations.

3. Delimitation, except for a few minor areas, is not that specific. BATF is not consistent in defining parameters, and usually accommodates industry wishes. The North Coast *ava* has few similarities, its climatic pattern varying from Region I to IV. If this is not enough, the Napa Valley *ava* includes areas that lie outside the Napa Valley drainage system. For the eastern portion of the country, *ava* delimitation becomes a non-issue due to the fact that water and non-estate wine can legally be added, further reducing geographic distinctiveness. Although appellations, in theory, are to be delimited by geographic criteria, reality uses streets, county lines, highways, and other non-environmental, man-made boundaries. The critics maintain that benefits of appellation association accrue to the worst winery, not necessarily the best.

4. America is a recently settled nation without a protracted winegrowing history, and hence, the absence of geographical standards. America simply does not know what grape varieties are ideally suited to specific soils and microclimates. Moreover, BATF requires no minimum acreage figures, thus we find small appellations with one vineyard of 12 acres and one winery in one *ava*, and more than 33,000 acres and 220 wineries in another. Moreover, BATF requires no minimum vine density within an *ava*, thus we find a high figure on Isle St. George and a low figure in southern New England. On Isle St. George, grapes are the dominant agricultural commodity, but not in more than 95 percent of all other *ava's*, either by percent of total land area devoted to grapes or by value.

5. *Ava's* are nothing but a marketing device to sell wine. The address influences the price of the grapes and wine, and magnifies the prestige of the producer. Napa Valley, Howell Mountain, and Dry Creek certainly exhibit a different cache than Lancaster, Pennsylvania.

6. The above differs from the French appellation system of *vin de pays*, VDQS, and AOC. The latter is the more restrictive in terms of specific vine varieties, yields, viticultural practices, and other regulated factors. In America, the critics say, *ava* designations are essentially an arbitrary geographical region without such restrictions and present no distinctiveness over its neighbors. Critics usually highlight the fact that delimited areas are not that distinctive for all or some grape varieties grown.

7. Due to the absence of size limitations, the issue of homogeneity of soil and climate become moot issues. If the delimited region is not geographically homogeneous, then it lacks the ability (according to many) to produce wines distinctive from other neighboring regions. This does not imply that the smallest appellation is the finest wine producing area, only that homogeneity and distinctiveness is directly related. The other alternative, that of a highly physically diverse appellation, requires considerable blending, and, hence, a loss of distinctiveness. Due to percentage and vintage requirements, the present system affords sufficient flexibility, an important consideration if we consider the fact that the winemaker and/or brand name is the most important consideration.

8. In many *ava's* a good portion of the included land area is state or national park--land that is not potentially exploitable, but supposedly included for prestige reasons.

9. Winemaking styles are more important than geographic delimitation. The critics charge that many wineries consistently make better wine than others without the benefit of a prestigious address. While critics stress the importance of soil, they maintain that technology is more important. Critics point out that irrigation has altered traditional patterns of grape growing. While the French appellation system is based on dry farming principles forcing growers to one of several grape varieties, irrigation makes it possible for Riesling, Chardonnay, Sauvignon Blanc, and Chenin Blanc to be grown 20 feet away from Zinfandel and Cabernet Sauvignon. Due to improved vineyard practices and winemaking

techniques, the geography of a place has diminished in importance as two neighboring winemakers within the same appellation can and often do make widely differing wines--without significant distinctive features as to the uniformity of appellation standards.

10. Appellations that require 100 percent of the grapes to originate within their boundaries are confined to Oregon, California, Washington, and several other states. For most quality-oriented appellations (especially county) the figure is 85 percent, and for many states east of the Rocky Mountains the figure is often 40 percent.

PROHIBITION

Prohibition, or the suppression of the production, distribution, sale, and consumption of alcoholic beverages, has been a utopic goal unsuccessfully attempted in many societies throughout history. One of the first such ventures codified into law was set up by Hammurabi, King of Babylon around 2225 B.C. Another was initiated by the Geto-Dacian ruler, Burebista, who ordered the destruction of vineyards in the first century A.D. because of excessive drinking. The Roman Emperor Domitian in 81 A.D. ordered the destruction of half the vineyards and prohibited new vine plantings. The Chinese Emperor Tci-Tsung in 781 A.D. decreed that in all districts of his domain the places allowed to sell alcoholic beverages should be limited by number and license. Also in the eighth century, Ine, King of Wessex in Anglo-Saxon England, regulated beer and the number of outlets. The Act of 1436 in Scotland ordered the closing of taverns, wine shops, and other places serving alcoholic beverages at 9 p.m. Public intoxication was made a criminal offense in England in 1606.

Reflecting the times, the oldest item in the wine library at the University of California-Davis is a proclamation issued in 1535 at Strasbourg (Alsace) regulating the purchase/sale of wine. The single largest religious prohibition originated with Mohammed in the sixth century and quickly spread throughout half the world's ecumene. A 1606 Parliamentary statute, authorizing the courts to fine persons found guilty of drunkenness, served as the model for Colonial legislation for nearly 200 years. More recently, alcoholic prohibition attempted in Russia, Finland, and even in Scotland failed dismally in every instance. The word Prohibition, has forever become associated with the "Great American Ignoble Experiment." This amazing event, the product of congressional action, lasted fourteen years, and ended in social, economic, and political disaster. Although part of our recent folklore, it continues to hover around every corner, and lurks in every shadow. Its a wonder that wine moves nationally given the prodigious amount of governmental red tape, taxes, and the veritable maze of other regulations.

Although, in terms of chronology, the temperance movement began in the middle of the eighteenth century with the "Great Awakening," the first effort at alcoholic regulation in America dates from 1791 (the Prohibition movement in America has a history almost as old as winemaking) when the newly formed republic levied a tax on whiskey distilled in all thirteen states. Within three years, a full fledged "whiskey rebellion" took place in western Pennsylvania led by one Albert Gallating. Over the next 200 years, the federal government implemented a bureaucratic network of regulations and legislation, of which revenue collection is the most important, followed by attempts at protecting the public from adulterated and misbranded goods, and, to a smaller degree, supervising fair trade practices. The basic issues of alcohol consumption and abuse were slowly and steadily taken up by zealous activists who transformed a tax issue into a prohibition movement. The singular most important feature of this movement is its ability to wax and wane with the times: it has emerged and disappeared in an endless series of cycles for more than 200 years.

The first "dry law," enacted in Indiana in 1816, prohibited Sunday alcohol sales (temperance groups also tried to ban coffee). In the 1840s towns, cities, and counties across America began voting dry: Iowa, New Hampshire, Georgia, New York, Michigan, Maine, and Ohio being the most prominent. In 1847 the Supreme Court upheld the constitutionality of the first "local option law," although it proved ineffective as long as neighboring communities did not pass similar legislation. The Washington movement, founded by six Baltimore alcoholics in 1840, was a group dedicated for the reform of other drinkers who called themselves the Washington Temperance Society. Members had to pledge total abstinence, and their message spread throughout the northeast, having 600,000 members by 1848. However, unlike more inflammatory organizations, the Society was dedicated to saving alcoholics, and not general social reform.

In the 1850s Prohibitionist sentiment became popular and thirteen states outlawed alcoholic beverages, only to repeal them in short order. Between 1858 and 1871, throughout the midwest, there were many "pray-ins" in saloons disrupting business and encouraging patrons to abstain, and force saloons to operate only under reduced hours. In 1872, James Black tallied 5,608 votes as the first Prohibitionist candidate. In 1876, Senator Henry Blair of New Hampshire offered Congress the first National Prohibition Amendment to the Constitution. In 1880, the entire state of Kansas went dry, followed by Iowa, and soon after by an additional seven states. Despite a number of minor reversals, the movement continued unbated: following the establishment of the Prohibition Party in 1869, the militant Women's Christian Temperance Union was founded in Evanston, Illinois in 1874; and the Anti-Saloon League in 1893, the latter, a political movement to support any political candidate who would support prohibition. The movement advocated local option and, hence, began to dry up a good portion of the midwest.

According to the provisions of the 1890 Wilson Act,

all alcoholic beverages became subject to the laws of the state as though the beverage was made in that state. In the space of a few years, states imposed all manner of barriers for the importation, distribution, and sale of alcoholic beverages. As a consequence, many states had widely differing mark ups on profit margins, license fees, taxes, registration fees, etc., very similar to the contemporary scene. Arkansas, Florida, New Mexico, Washington, Georgia, and Michigan had historically erected a protective tax that would artificially protect their wine industries. Prohibitionist sentiment re-emerged and by 1896 eight states adopted Prohibitionist legislation, only to have them repealed by 1900, the very year that Carry Nation, the most militant prohibitionist with a bible in one hand and an axe in the other, wrecked three Kansas bars with rocks, bricks, and bottles, rekindling the prohibitionist movement. By 1903 one-third of the nation lived under some type of prohibition, and 1906 marked a high water mark for Prohibitionists before a counter movement set in reversing prohibition in many states. By 1907 only Maine, Kansas, and North Dakota were dry, but the number of dry counties in the entire nation outnumbered the wet. In 1908 the District of Columbia and Indian reservations were dry. Spearheaded by the Anti-Saloon League, prohibition once again became a popular force, and by 1910 eight states enacted Prohibition legislation. The year 1913 saw the passage of the Webb-Kenyon Act that banned the shipment of liquor from wet to dry states, and directly or indirectly about 50 percent of the nation was legally dry.

AMENDMENT XVIII (1919)
Section 1. After one year from the ratification of this article the manufacture, sale, or transportation of intoxicating liquors within, the importation thereof into, or the exportation thereof from the United States and all territory subject to the jurisdiction thereof for beverage purposes is hereby prohibited.
Section 2. The Congress and the several States shall have concurrent power to enforce this article by appropriate legislation.
Section 3. This article shall be inoperative unless it shall have been ratified as an amendment to the Constitution by the legislatures of the several States, as provided in the Constitution, within seven years from the date of the submission hereof to the States by the Congress.
AMENDMENT XXI (1933)
Section 1. The eighteenth article of amendment to the Constitution of the United is hereby repealed.
Section 2. The transportation or importation into any State, Territory, or possession of the United States for delivery of use therein of intoxicating liquors, in violation of the laws thereof, is hereby prohibited.
Section 3. This article shall be inoperative unless it shall have been ratified as an amendment to the Constitution by conventions in the several States, as provided in the Constitution, within seven years from the date of the submission hereof to the States by the Congress.

World War I heightened public prohibitionist sentiment, and by 1918 prohibitionist states increased to 42, the very year that Congress outlawed the manufacture of potable alcohol (except for export) until the conclusion of the war and subsequent demobilization. By January, 1919, the Eighteenth Amendment was ratified by three-quarters of the states, and had legal application as federal law for all states one year later. While all states later ratified,

Connecticut and Rhode Island did not. In October 1919, Congress passed the Volstead Prohibition Act (bringing into effect the Eighteenth Amendment). This extraordinary piece of legislation passed the Senate after only 30 hours of debate, and the House within a day. It passed despite opposition from President Woodrow Wilson who wanted to exclude wine from the final draft (Prohibitionists considered all alcoholic beverages the same: "booze"). The act prohibited the production, transportation, and sale of alcoholic beverages above half of one percent alcohol. On December 5, 1933, Congress repealed the Eighteenth Amendment, and passed the Twenty-first, that restored state's rights to control all alcoholic beverages. During this fourteen year period, the Volstead Prohibition Act was subject to evasion, corruption, loss of state and federal revenues, and cloaked in a mantle of drunkenness, criminality, terrorism, and gangsterism. Prohibition did not eliminate the availability of alcoholic beverages, but merely made it troublesome to get anything but beer, bad whiskey, and nearly impossible to get any kind of wine unless the individual made it himself. Most significant is the fact that Prohibition illustrated the futility of attempting to legislate social custom by law. In 1966, Mississippi, the last "dry" state since Repeal of Prohibition, voted to go "wet."

Although theoretically "dry," in reality America was "wet" as the legislation was obviously ignored for its fourteen-year tenure. Doctors could prescribe wine "for medicinal use," druggists concocted a myriad of "tonics," rabbis made, purchased, and sold large quantities of wine for "religious use," and the federal government allowed a head of household to make as much as 200 gallons a year for personal use (equivalent to 1,000 bottles). For the industry as a whole, Prohibition was a disaster. In California, 600 of the 700 wineries closed, grape prices leaped, and vineland prices rose from $100 an acre to more than $1,000. Moreover, grape acreage increased from 300,000 in 1919, to 400,000 in 1923, to 650,000 acres in 1928 when a big grape glut developed and 18,000 acres remained unharvested. In many places, as much as 700 gallons of wine were made from one ton of Alicante Bouschet, and, if one pressed heavily, added sugar, water, raisins, and concentrate, as much as 1,500 gallons could be made. As the grape market remained unstable while Prohibition continued, the solution, it was thought, was the production of large quantities of grape concentrate to help equalize demand.

Repeal was followed with a bewildering Byzantine patchwork of state regulations that do nothing but stagger the imagination, restrict trade, and limit distribution. The net effect is that the domestic national distribution pattern is, in effect, an interstate system of 51 (including the District of Columbia) different countries, each with distinct laws and regulations inhibiting the mechanisms of a free market. In fourteen states, for example, wine cannot be sold in food stores; in many states advertisements cannot infer or use the words "bargain" or "sale;" in Rhode Island (with the exception of Newport) wine cannot be sold in towns with fewer than 10,000 people. Varying archaic, restrictive state laws and regulations combine to reduce consumption. In states where wine is sold in food stores, per capita consumption is substantially higher (by at least 1.3 gallons). Furthermore, this intentional governmental influence is one of the political causal factors affecting the geography of agriculture in America. In California, Washington, Virginia, and New York, where viticulture is encouraged, the industry is thriving, but in states like Kentucky, West Virginia, and others, the economic geographical landscape does not reflect rational returns from competing systems of land utilization.

Today, the neo-Prohibitionist movement is alive, well, and, because tactics have changed, the movement is as dangerous as it was two generations ago. The Woman's Temperance Union today has 150,000 members in America and another 350,000 abroad. The movement no longer marches, breaks windows, pounds bibles, but is part of multifaceted social/political coalitions. It holds annual meetings, publishes books, pamphlets, and videos, and exercises very effective lobbying efforts both at the local, state, and national fronts.

> *In North Carolina, each county, and each city within each county, was given the right to vote on whether to allow the sale of beverage alcohol, and to establish an agency to regulate the process. The state Alcoholic Beverage Control Commission was established in 1936 to oversee local operations and handle all purchases of spirits from supplier companies. At present, 152 counties and cities have their own ABC boards, and, in 1990, 3.4 million cases of spirits were sold in the state.*

The Effects of Prohibition

During Prohibition legal wine production was reduced to medicinal and sacramental uses, but illegal and homemade wine output rose to record, pre-Prohibition levels, grape production increased fivefold, and grape prices skyrocketed with many producers making more money selling grapes to home winemakers than previously when they made wine. The industry was in ruins: fine wine was no longer legally made; quality winemaking techniques quickly disappeared; inexpensive fortified wines dominated production; the wrong grape vines were being planted; quality wine consumption remained at very low levels; and immediately after Repeal, the country was left with 48 sets of state laws (plus the District of Columbia) regulating alcoholic beverages (since then two more were added). The resulting Byzantine legal arrangements of state legislation and regulations confronting the industry produced a myriad of discriminating medieval protective agencies. The end result has been to deny the average American consumer a national outlet. The wine "market," unlike any other agricultural commodity, is governed by burdensome antiquated regulations by 50 states and more than 3,000 counties.

Among the many significant consequences of Prohibition are the following:

1. Section 29 of the Volstead Act allowed each head of household to make 200 gallons of wine annually. By 1930, 140 million gallons of "homemade wine" was made, or twice the amount that domestic grape production would have produced. The sudden unprecedented, and unpredictable demand for grapes necessary to make home-made wine led to the planting of 300,000 new acres between 1920 and 1928. At the height of Prohibition, approximately 70,000 rail cars of grapes were shipped from California to eastern markets for home winemaking. Unfortunately, poor quality (thick-skinned for better shipment) grapes replaced the good. However, as suddenly and unpredictably, the demand for these grapes subsided after Repeal, and grapes went unpicked across the nation when foreign imports flooded the American market. Another generation had to pass before favorable economic conditions reversed the imbalance for quality grapes.

2. Productive capacity was inadequate to meet the demand for commercial wine once Repeal was enacted. Production of sweet sacramental and medicinal use wine amounted to 6.3 million gallons during 1928-1931, and 18.7 million gallons for 1932. Once the 21st Amendment passed, the industry was unable to meet the upsurge in demand of upwards 100 million gallons.

3. Wine quality dropped to low levels; it was not properly made, aged, nor procured from good wine grapes. Moreover, a good deal of the wine was made by inexperienced winemakers. The production of poor, unstable, non-commercial wine during Prohibition further weakened the palate of the not-so-sophisticated consumer.

4. The industry soon turned from one of under production to under consumption due to the poor quality of the post-Repeal product. America emerged from Prohibition as a "sweet" wine nation producing more fortified sweet wine than any other nation, including Spain, France, Portugal, and Italy. Table wines, too frequently the product of the wrong grapes and usually flawed, were inexpensive, not subject to quality control, and acquired a negative ethnic image. America embarked upon an orgy of cocktail consumption and wine assumed a third-rate position in the production of inexpensive Burgundy, Claret, Hock, Sauterne, Porto, Chablis, Sherry, Madeira, and other generic wines. The market place was governed by volume, cheap wine, and high yielding grape varieties. As recently as 1950, 89 percent of all red wine acreage consisted of two third-rate grapes--Alicante Bouschet and Carignane.

5. After Prohibition, increased wine taxation by most states, continued Prohibition in ten other states, and laws unfavorable to wine sales in another ten states created and perpetuated anarchy and confusion at the national level. The industry remained paralyzed by disorganization, adulteration, mislabeling, and inadequate distribution.

6. Never in the history of America was any law so flagrantly violated as the 18th Amendment. On December 5, 1933 Prohibition was "Repealed." What it ended was a 14 year period of public hypocrisy, profiteering, and the criminalization of a significant segment of American society.

7. America practiced de-facto censorship of the First Amendment. Production of wine was rarely mentioned in printed matter, including Greek and Roman classics, or even the Bible. One printed source had Christ serving grape juice at Cana.

8. Considered a separate industry from distilled spirits prior to Prohibition, wine was now included as an alcoholic beverage along with beer and spirits. Moreover, unlike all other major European countries, American wine production does not fall under the jurisdiction of the Department of Agriculture. More disturbing is the current effort by the Center of Science in the Public Interest and others to make wine part of the Food & Drug Administration.

9. Because of an interpretation of the 21st amendment, alcoholic beverages have been almost entirely deprived of the protection of the Commerce Clause of the 5th and 14th Amendments. It is important to note that no other American business attracts capital investment under conditions where restraint is encouraged by the U.S. Constitution, legislated by 50 states, and sees favored status in the domestic market

given to foreign producers. Indeed, no other agricultural product is so restrictive in interstate shipment as wine. Wine sales, in violation of the freedom of transportation act, are prohibited from being transported across state lines without license, unlike any other food item. It is also interesting to note that the Post Office will not knowingly accept wine for shipment although they will ship guns and ammunition. Exemption of wine from the commerce clause has led to very differing state laws and regulations that, over the decades since Repeal, foster interstate squabbles, and hamper free trade policies. Several years ago California placed a tax on Colorado beef, and the latter state promptly retaliated with higher taxes on wine shipped from California. Similar unconstitutional measures have sprung up since Repeal, all of which violate the spirit of cooperation between states. In 1984 a federal district court judge ruled that a New York State law permitting the sale of New York wine coolers in grocery stores was economic protectionism, and disallowed. In recent years a significant crack has emerged in this historic shibboleth. At present it is illegal to ship, personally transport, or by any other means move a bottle of wine from one state to another, including the US mail, even in states where other forms of delivery are legal. The principle of interstate reciprocity is currently exercised by California (the first state to allow), Colorado, Missouri, New Mexico, Oregon, Wisconsin, Washington, and Illinois. In the remaining 42 states, it remains illegal to ship wine across state lines without a license. Until 1987 every state in the nation had import restrictions that banned private citizens from receiving a personal shipment of wine from another state.

10. Lingering Prohibition persists at the highest official levels. To this day, the United States Department of Agriculture Research Center in Maryland is prohibited from engaging in grape research.

11. One of the "political trade-offs" of Repeal was that the legal responsibility for the regulation of the production, distribution, and sale of alcoholic beverages be a function of state government. Over the years, the following types of state control have emerged: *open license states*, in which private enterprise is allowed to make both on-premise and off-premise sales of alcoholic beverages; *monopoly states*, that monopolize the sale of alcoholic beverages; and *controlled states*, that separate the monopoly of distilled spirits, wine, and beer. Unlike open license states, controlled and monopoly states are essentially in the alcohol business, the only business not subject to the federal interstate trade laws. As a consequence, the wine industry has been faced with a plethora of regulations that restrict the availability and sale of wine. Many control states have a philosophy that alcoholic beverages should be available, but not easy to obtain. Wine, considered the alcoholic beverage of "winos" and college students, was treated with a negative social connotation. Fine and expensive imported wines were considered "elitist," the privilege of the rich and powerful, and not "popular" for the general population. Most important is the fact that some states, acting as a separate "sovereign" government, imposed discriminatory taxes on wine sold in that state but produced elsewhere.

As a measure of the dimensions of the Byzantine character of state regulations consider the challenges, confusions, and complications involved for a single winery marketing wine in all 50 states: (1) the posting a bond in six states, registering with the secretary of state in six states, and the payment of fees (from $500 to $11,000) to stay current each year; (2) the possession of one or more licenses in each of 38 states; (3) giving advance notice (from 10 to 60 days) of pricing changes in 18 states; (4) the registration of all brands (often annually) in 35 states, many of which require samples and/or laboratory analyses; and (5) the remittance of invoices and/or monthly reports to 37 states.

The position favoring state monopolistic control is based on the puritanical notion that state owned stores would not institute tactics to increase alcohol consumption thereby leading to increased alcoholism; state stores would enforce minimum age laws more efficiently thus preventing youthful corruption; revenue enhancement; and a state system would minimize the sleaze factor from the alcohol industry. Since the majority of states are open license, a comparison between the two extremes reveals many interesting elements. Both in this country and especially in Mediterranean Europe there is no correlation between the availability of alcoholic beverages and aberrant behavior of any type. Indeed, there is no evidence to support the thesis that crime of any type is positively related to wine consumption. There is also no evidence to suggest that alcoholism is a product of wine advertising or availability, but a function of genetic and psychological impairment. Further, as the bulk of wines sold in monopoly state stores are the least expensive, the privatization of this segment of the economy would not in any way make the situation worse. Nor is there evidence to suggest that state revenues from the sale of alcoholic beverages would decline should the sector be privatized. Moreover, there is no evidence to suggest that the owner of a liquor store would jeopardize the source of his livelihood by flagrantly breaking the law on a consistent basis by selling to the underage or feeble minded.

Until recently, the minimum drinking age was not standardized among states, nor anything concerning acceptance of credit cards or checks, selling of snack foods and other non-liquor items, nor places of sale such as food stores, drug stores, grocery stores, etc. In addition, states have unfairly taxed non-state wine at higher levels than state-produced wines. In the final analysis, the consumption of wine in controlled states is appreciably lower than in non-controlled states. Where states have deregulated, consumption rises initially by as much as 40 percent in the first two years, and then drops back by one-quarter. It is estimated that if all states deregulated, wine sales for the nation as a whole would increase by as much as $450 million.

Why then do state monopolies persist? Among the many reasons are: revenue enhancement; bureaucratic survival; a good source of political patronage; and the lack of focused opposition. While privatization would bring more revenues, major stumbling blocks for divestiture are patronage and the employee's union. It is estimated that at least 25 percent of all alcoholic beverages in controlled states are purchased elsewhere, and privatization would enhance revenues for the state if purchases were made in-state. Whenever a state changed from a monopoly to a regulated enterprise system, everyone benefited. Consumers benefit from greater convenience through a larger number of retail outlets, a larger selection, and often more attractive prices. One stop convenience shopping when groceries and supermarkets are licensed increases sales and state revenues. In 1973, when the counties of Mobile, Jefferson, and Tuscaloosa in Alabama were permitted to sell non-fortified wines, sales increased by 34 percent. When similar legislation occurred throughout the state of Washington, wine sales increased sixfold during the 1968-1979 period.

In the final analysis, the rates of alcoholism among all age and sex cohorts, and drunken driving offenses are not lower in control states. What is more important, control states are not a consumer's dream because they pay more for liquor and wine than in states with a free enterprise system. Stores are not conveniently located, attractive, nor responsive to local demands, business hours are limited, and there are fewer stores per 10,000 population. In Pennsylvania, there is one store for every 16,000 people, while neighboring New York has one store for every 4,000 people. Moreover, state law places restrictions on what information and recommendations store clerks may provide. Finally, state stores have a limited and standardized inventory so that specialty items are difficult to find, and prices are considered high due to the absence of competitive pricing.

PAST AND PRESENT WINE LEGISLATION PECULIARITIES

1. Prohibition was not repealed in Kansas until 1948; Oklahoma in 1959; and Mississippi until 1966 (the last state in the nation to do so). About 500 of the nation's 3,078 counties are still dry. As recently as 1980: 28 of Alabama's 67 counties were dry; 44 of 75 in Arkansas; 7 of 67 in Florida; 66 of 159 in Georgia; 7 of 105 in Kansas; 84 of 120 in Kentucky; 3 of 64 in Louisiana; 36 of 82 in Mississippi; 1 of 93 in Nebraska; 8 of 100 in North Carolina; 2 of 67 in South Dakota; 59 of 95 in Tennessee; 91 of 254 in Texas; 14 of 95 in Virginia; and 3 of 55 in West Virginia.

2. Until recently, a North Carolina statute made the possession of more than 20 liters of wine in one's private home *prima facie* evidence that the owner was in the business of selling wine without a license.

3. In 1981 California's Governor Brown signed a bill making it legal for a diner to remove the bottle of wine he bought in a restaurant but didn't finish. The bottle, once opened and removed, must ride in the trunk of the car out of reach of the riders. In many states it is illegal for patrons to bring wine (brown bagging) to a restaurant that does not have a liquor license. In many states it is illegal to buy or sell wine in a restaurant, but you can bring your own. In New Jersey restaurants with liquor licenses are barred from allowing patrons to bring their own wine, and in those without a license only wine and beer are permitted. In licensed restaurants in Connecticut, the owner has discretion over what alcoholic beverage patrons may bring, while in unlicensed establishments customers may bring any type of alcohol.

4. In many states a restaurant alcohol license is denied if the premise is within 200 feet of an existing licensed establishment, or house of worship.

5. Many states prohibit the sale of wine in food stores. Throughout wine producing Europe wine is sold in food stores, the site for more than 50 percent of all sales. It in interesting to note that in these countries, this practice has not diminished the importance or sales in fine, privately owned wine/liquor establishments. In 32 of the 50 states, table wine (less than 14 percent alcohol by volume) is allowed in grocery stores. In 12 states consumers can only obtain table wine in state operated stores or state licensed package stores where other alcoholic beverages are sold. In the remaining 6 states and the District of Columbia, the availability of table wines is impeded by many obstacles.

6. Many states allow the sale of wine in drug stores.

7. Nearly all states prohibit the public auction of wine. In practically all states it is illegal for individuals to sell their wine cellars.

8. State taxes on wine vary greatly by state. In 1986, Iowa had a tax of $9.80, Illinois $1.05, and New York $.96 for a bottle of Champagne retailing for $21.00.

9. Most states prohibit the use of credit cards. In those states where they are allowed, credit card sales may account for as much as 70 percent of total store sales. Total store sales have risen by as much as 35 percent when credit card use was allowed.

10. State support (especially from the governor's mansion) of the wine industry varies enormously. While the governor of Virginia is a rabid supporter of the states fledgling wine industry, the governor of West

Virginia offers no support whatever.
11. Federal regulations forbid the use of children's musical tunes to be used in wine advertisements.
12. Some states require that the owners and shareholders of a winery be state residents for a minimum of two or more years.
13. In Alabama it is illegal to buy wine by telephone. In South Carolina wine cannot be advertised on billboards. In Rhode Island wine advertisements cannot list prices. In Missouri it is illegal to sell wine by the glass on Sunday unless it is New Year's Eve.
14. In some states local option applies to urban neighborhoods, thus banning wine sales on one side of the street but not on the other.
15. In Natchez, Mississippi, it is illegal to serve beer to an elephant; in Chicago illegal to give it to a dog; in San Francisco you may not ride your horse to a bar; in Cushing, Oklahoma it is illegal to drink in public in your underwear; in Kentucky is it unlawful to drink in your home; in St. Louis, unlawful to sit on a sidewalk and drink beer from a bucket; one could be jailed for simulating intoxication in Iowa; and in Sausalito, California you may get drunk only after receiving permission from the "Board of Supervisors."

Neo-Prohibition Tendencies

In recent years, for a variety of reasons, the nation as a whole seems to have developed a new attitude toward alcohol consumption. Lawsuits abound on third party liability, drunk driving accidents, health concerns, and the raising of the minimum drinking age in all states to 21 are but a small fraction of the anti-alcohol manifestations targeting all alcoholic beverages. A recent Gallop Poll shows that 25 percent of Americans favor total alcohol prohibition, and another 41 percent prefer a total ban on beer and wine advertising. Anti-drinking campaigns seem to be gathering momentum unparalleled since the end of Prohibition more than half a century ago. The disturbing element common to all these issues is the fact that wine is included (unlike most major wine producing nations) in the same category as distilled spirits. All the historic ground rules are currently in a state of flux, and changing beyond the new awareness of the dangers of excessive drinking. The fact that distilled spirit consumption is down and the social benefits of the two martini lunch a thing of the past is a good, positive element, creating a once in a lifetime opportunity for the wine industry in particular. Wine, unlike beer and distilled spirits, is the beverage of moderation taken with a meal and not the usual alcoholic beverage associated with solitary drinking. In this respect, the "Code of Advertising Standards," promulgated and adhered to by the Wine Institute in 1985, is a highly responsible initiative. Unlike the beer and distilled spirits industry, the code illustrates an unflinching service for the public good.

America is in the throes of a "health consciousness movement," and the wine industry must exploit this awareness. Contemporary America is more aware of the dangers of excessive smoking, nitrates and nitrites, the benefits of moderate exercise, the link between excessive salt and high blood pressure, and so forth. We, as a nation, have reduced in recent decades our intake of nicotine, increased per capita consumption of yogurt and tofu, and dramatically reduced our per capita consumption of distilled spirits. However, a large, broadly based coalition (commonly referred to as the "new drys"), ranging from

the Department of Health and Human Services, Remove Intoxicated Drivers, Mothers Against Drunk Driving, Students Against Driving Drunk, the Center for Science in the Public Interest, Stop Marketing Alcohol on Radio and Television, the National Council on Alcoholism, the National Council on Alcoholism and Drug Dependency, and more, have fueled the emotional energies of the nation to the dangers that any use of alcoholic beverages is inherently dangerous to the health of America. These anti-alcohol organizations have recently been successful in lobbying for warning and ingredient labeling. The most distressing element of all these neo-Prohibitionist tendencies is that it does not distinguish between beer, wine, and spirits. To them, alcohol is alcohol, and nothing but alcohol. Senate hearings on alcohol bans have been recommended by the Surgeon General, and while the effect on the distilled industry is more formidable, the wine industry has been singled out in recent years for similar treatment. These forces have become so powerful that, unless successful opposition is forthcoming, they may succeed in limiting advertising, and ultimately a total ban in the production, distribution, and consumption of alcoholic beverages. They may even begin lobbying efforts against wine columns and wine books! The latest absurdity concerns the Culver City Unified School District officials who banned "Little Red Riding Hood" for first graders due to the fact that the Grimm fairy tale shows a bottle of wine in the picnic basket. The cacophony scares people.

Apparently, it matters not that wine drinkers are the most moderate consumers of alcohol, and that fewer than 4 percent of all intoxicated drivers are impaired by wine consumption. It matters not that alcoholism is practically non existent in the wine producing regions of Mediterranean countries, and that wine drinkers in the culturally Mediterranean departments of southern France have a rate of alcoholism and cirrhosis only one-quarter that of their northern countrymen, the latter primarily a spirit consuming region. The neo-Prohibitionist propaganda, if carried to excess, will carry the wine industry to oblivion as it did two generations ago. Forty percent of all Americans abstain totally from alcohol, and 22 percent from wine is proof enough that the majority of the population does not abuse alcohol. A fanatical, obsessive infrastructure is in place (in southern California, in all major Mormon communities, in scattered areas in the midwest, throughout the Bible Belt, and in affluent pockets of the northeast) across the nation that highlights the harmful effects of wine consumption.

After many silent years, the wine industry has begun to counter-balance neo-Prohibitionist propaganda with the formation of the American Wine Alliance for Research Education, and the National Coalition and Citizens for Moderation. The wine industry not only must become politically active, it needs to solicit the support of such highly respected organizations as the American Council on Science and Health on the subject of the advantages of moderate wine consumption. The movement has even affected the American Congress, a body of legislators that has switched from Bourbon to wine, but is embarrassed to talk about it because of the intimidation tactics of powerful anti-alcohol lobby organizations. Nevertheless, wine is served at all White House state dinners, and there is a wine tasting club on Capitol Hill.

Recently, the high profile and well-financed Century Council has embarked on a broad-based consumer and industry awareness campaign to disseminate and evaluate information about alcohol consumption and its effects. It plans to attack the industry's two worst enemies, the abuse and misuse of alcohol, and thus far has concentrated on drunk driving and underage drinking. If the Council continues to refuse the dissemination of positive information, its pan-industry involvement will disintegrate. In the final analysis, "social and economic progress" is not in the offing until: (1) grape growing and winemaking fall in the jurisdiction of the Department of Agriculture; (2) wine is considered an agricultural product as well as a food beverage; (3) wine is considered a food; and (4) wine be accepted as the beverage of moderation.

Wine in America is considered a luxury product, ethically suspect, drunk too cold and invariably consumed with the wrong food. It is appealing to so few people that it is economically insignificant to nearly three-quarters of the American population. The percentage of disposable income expended on alcoholic beverages in America (.4%) is one of the lowest among developed countries. It is less than half than in France, Italy, Germany, UK, and Czechoslovakia, but significantly above Greece (.1%). Furthermore, it is unimportant in the vocabulary of the majority, treated as a passing fancy (usually after European vacations), or worse, the libation of sissies and snobs. In sharp contrast, throughout the Mediterranean, it is a staple, a significant economic industry, treated as serious business, and protected by all manner of social and political institutions.

In response to an increase in the federal excise tax on distilled spirits in 1985, the Joseph E. Seagram Corporation, one of the largest producers of distilled beverages, wine, and importer of all manner of alcoholic beverages, began an expensive campaign to promote liquor consumption by attempting to convince the public that wine, beer, and spirits affect individuals the same way. The unfounded theory stated that a 12 ounce glass of beer, a 5 ounce glass of wine, and a 1.25 ounce shot of distilled spirits contained the same amount of alcohol--and, therefore, are equally intoxicating. For several years, the lavishly funded campaign caused a lot of controversy and considerable harm to the wine industry by attempting to convince the public and politicians that all alcohol has the same effect. What the distilled industry fails to point out is the fact that in every major wine producing country, wine is considered an agricultural product and a food, while distilled beverages are not.

Over the years, scientific research has repeatedly shown that wine, in reference to distilled spirits (but somewhat less for beer), produces different physiological and psychological effects. Specifically, the chemical composition of all three beverages is different. Although ethanol is the dominant alcohol in all three, there are, in addition, as many as 150 distinct alcoholic compounds in wine not found in the other two. Of significance is the fact that a good deal of these unstable, alcoholic compounds are dissipated harmlessly before and immediately after the initial ingestion, and are metabolized differently once they enter the body. Therefore, distilled spirits consumed in the fasting state result in 33 to 130 percent higher peak blood alcohol levels than equivalent amounts of wine. Moreover, because wine is essentially consumed during meals, peak blood alcohol levels are lower than for the other two. Due to the chemical distinctiveness of wine, even when distilled spirits are diluted to equivalent alcohol wine concentrations, distilled spirits cause a higher peak blood alcohol level than wine. In addition, the physiological and psychological impairment induced by equivalent alcohol amounts from all three beverage sources is greater for distilled spirits, and less for wine.

Finally, the American social ambience influencing alcoholic consumption is dramatically different from other cultures. In Mediterranean wine producing countries wine is mainly a mealtime beverage that is consumed at least twenty times more frequently than distilled spirits. And due to the long duration of the mealtime activity, and the fact that consumption ceases immediately with the completion of the meal, blood alcohol levels rise only slightly, thus reducing the harmful effects of physiological and psychological impairment. The illogical argument of equivalency is not borne out by recent statistics showing the relationship between beer, wine, and distilled spirits and cirrhosis mortality per 100,000 population for the years 1974-1985. While per capita consumption of distilled spirits declined by 11 percent, beer increased by 13 percent, and wine by a strong 47 percent, cirrhosis mortality declined by 34 percent. Moreover, the temperate use of wine is saving many people from insulin attacks (chromium in wine keeps insulin levels in check by making the hormone more efficient), and premature heart disease. Further, there is no evidence whatever to support the contention that wine consumption is positively correlated with family violence, divorce, suicide, and the destructive effects of drunk driving. Amidst political and special interest pressures, it is encouraging to note that many hospitals now allow wine in an effort to enhance food and boost morale.

THE COMMERCE OF AMERICAN WINE

International agricultural trade exceeds $350 billion annually, of which wine represents less than 3 percent of all agricultural exports. This is comparable to the international trade in rubber and cacao, twice as large as citrus fruit, three times larger than tea and bananas, but one-third that of coffee. Tables 3.1-2 reveal an interesting pattern of extreme export and import concentration; more than 85 percent of commercial trade is between Europe and the developed countries along the north Atlantic Ocean. While Italy is said to account for 30-50 percent of all wine exports in terms of volume, France accounts for a similar percentage in terms of value. Annual world movement varies between 1 billion gallons and 1.8 billion gallons, or 14 percent of production, a figure increasing faster than production due to declining per capita wine consumption in the two largest producers--Italy and France. The foregoing is important because America is a net importer of wine with an extremely unfavorable wine trade imbalance; gross exports in 1991 were valued at $145 million, up from $27 million in 1985. In sharp contrast, America imported more than $1 billion in 1987.

Table 3.1

WORLD WINE EXPORTS (Million of Gallons)			
Country	1934-1938	1962	1989
Italy	35.4	65.5	391.3
France	22.0	96.0	349.5
Spain	37.9	56.2	135,1
West Germany	1.2	5.0	77.0
Hungary	7.6	17.6	61.8
Bulgaria	.2	27.6	48.2
Portugal	21.7	61.2	42.9
Greece	11.2	11.8	37.3
Yugoslavia	.6	11.0	24.4
Algeria	340.4	207.0	24.8
Australia		2.3	
United States	.1	.3	22.1
Belgium-Luxembourg	.8	1.8	
South Africa	1.9	4.8	
Morocco	1.2	36.7	
Tunisia	.4	16.2	
Romania	.6	10.6	
Cyprus	1.4	3.9	
Chile	2.3	1.5	
Turkey	.2	1.2	
World Total	520.8	697.6	1,287.0
Source: Office International de la Vigne et du Vin, Paris, France.			

Although America ranks fifth in wine production and fourth in wine imports, it only ranks seventh in wine exports, far behind France, Italy, and Germany. Exports prior to World War II fluctuated around 200,000 gallons, representing a very small portion of total wine shipments (usually between .5 and 1.5 percent of total national production). Total American wine exports in the middle of the 1960s were less than 500,000 gallons. This modest figure grew to 2.5 million gallons by 1977, 5 million gallons in 1978, and 17 million gallons in 1988. In 1990 wine exports exceeded 26 million gallons, a 22 percent increase over 1989, and a 335 percent increase since 1985. Wine exports for 1991 exceeded 40 million gallons with a value approaching $200 million. Wine exports currently account for a small but growing (8%) share of the total domestic production of 460 million gallons. On a dollar value basis, the ratio of U.S. wine imports to exports will move from 37 to 1 ($1.01 billion to $27.6 million) in 1985, to 7 to 1 ($900 million to $140 million) for 1990. With plenty of room for continued growth, this strong performance by U.S. wines is expected to continue as export success fuels new interest among producers in developing foreign markets. It appears that 1979 was the turning point in American wine exports as more and more producers began to cultivate foreign market opportunities more aggressively. At the same time, the international market began to critically recognize American advances in the production of consistent quality. As the American wine industry improved the quality of its grape varieties, produced more varietal wine and fewer generics with European names, vintage-dated most unblended wines, and improved quality, domestic and foreign demand in premium wines increased. Not only is the depressed $US an additional factor increasing America's propensity to export, but foreign markets have finally realized that America is not only capable of producing world class wines, but does so at a lower price and on a more consistent basis than France, Italy, and Germany. As a consequence, wine exports, as percent of total alcoholic beverages, have increased from 11.4% in 1980, 16.7% in 1985, to 38.7% in 1991.

In 1991 the United States exported more wine than the entire previous decade--more than 40 million gallons, with California accounting for 95 percent of the total, a significant amount compared to 1980 when it shipped 30 percent more wine to Pennsylvania than it exported. What is most impressive about American wine exports over the past ten years are the formidable gains made in several foreign markets that can only be described as historically difficult. For 1988, the principal countries collectively responsible for 66 percent of American exports were: Canada, 4.1 million gallons; Japan, 4 million gallons; and the United Kingdom, 3.2 million gallons. Interestingly, Japan led all other countries in value, importing more than $23 million. As a group all Scandinavian countries are becoming a major importing region, with Sweden rising to fourth place for the first time with nearly 800,000 gallons, and Denmark moving to fifth place with 563,000 gallons. Belgium/Luxembourg (400,000 gallons), and Switzerland (300,000 gallons) rank sixth and seventh, and all other countries account for 20 percent of American wine exports. Among the top seven markets, only Canada, historically the largest market for American wines with 4 million gallons, has remained stagnant, but the picture may improve in the coming decade. As of January 1, 1989, all federal tariffs and discriminatory markups by provincial liquor control boards have been reduced drastically. While the American beer industry does not stand to benefit from the bilateral legislation, and the distilled industry gains only a marginal benefit, the American wine segment stands to benefit enormously. The trade agreement calls for a reduction of state markups of 25 percent in each of the first two years, and then a further 10 percent reduction in each of the next five years. American wines, with about 1.4 percent of the Canadian market, are expected to increase market share beyond 10 percent during this period.

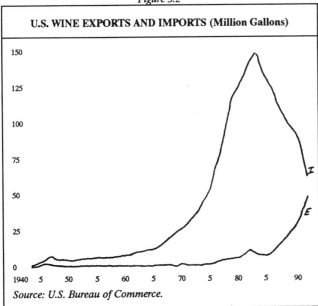

Figure 3.2

U.S. WINE EXPORTS AND IMPORTS (Million Gallons)

Source: U.S. Bureau of Commerce.

American wine exports account for a small but growing 8 percent of total production, and because American wines compete well in major international markets the upward export trend is expected to continue. Historically, wine exports were highly variable in volume, with peculiar geographical destinations. Until recently less than half of all exports went to Canada, most of which was bulk wine used for blending purposes. Approximately one-fifth went to the Caribbean and Central America, and the remainder were exported mainly to areas with large American populations, but very little American wine was shipped to Japan and Europe. Although the falling $US exchange rate has helped improve the trade balance for American wines, the industry's real competitive strength lies in its quality innovations in the vineyard, winery, and final product in the bottle. The elimination of unfair trade barriers, aggressive marketing, and restraint in price increases will propel American exports further, but not without formidable challenges.

The European Economic Community (EEC) is America's foremost competitor. Not only does it account for 47 percent of total world vine acreage, 60 percent of grape production, and 64 percent of all wine, but wine is second among the top five EEC agricultural exports. Moreover, it is the single largest producer of premium, world class wines. Most important is the 25-year trend in wine exports to America. During the late 1960s and 1970s, EEC exporters supplied a rising share of the American wine market, climaxing in a phenomenal one-third share of the domestic market in 1984 when EEC imports peaked. Since then, Spain and Portugal, two countries with an enormous capacity for inexpensive wine production, have joined the trading bloc, raising EEC membership to twelve countries, and augmenting the community's wine lake by one-third.

Table 3.2

WORLD WINE IMPORTS (Millions of Gallons)			
Country	1934-1938	1962	1989
West Germany	24.7	106.5	233.3
United Kingdom	19.6	30.6	177.3
France	351.5	234.4	153.6
United States	3.4	15.3	76.8
Russia		19.7	61.5
Netherlands	2.5	10.2	61.2
Belgium-Luxembourg	9.0	25.1	58.9
East Germany		17.6	53.2
Switzerland	24.8	39.0	53.1
Portuguese Colonies		34.4	48.5
Canada	3.5	4.0	40.4
Austria	5.2		
Denmark	2.1		
Sweden	4.2		
World Total	481.6	595.8	1,249.7

Source: Office International de la Vigne et du Vin, Paris, France.

Since the early 1960s, world wine production has exceeded consumption by at least 2 billion gallons, or one-quarter of world output. More than 80 percent emanates from Europe, principally Italy and France. With Portugal and Spain in the EEC, the wine lake contains a huge surplus of more than 2 billion gallons, and given the propensity for the Portuguese and Spanish governments to subsidize exports, import competition will intensify, but remain an American advantage for many reasons: (a) California enjoys lower transportation costs to the northeast; (b) a better, more consistent product that offsets a 14 percent lower case production cost from Italy, Portugal, and Spain; (c) the $US will not improve dramatically in the near future, thus intensifying the inherent price disparities between American and EEC wine; (d) alcoholic beverage consumption in France, Italy, Spain, and Portugal has shifted from wine to beer; and (e) EEC "jug" wine simply cannot compete with California equivalents. America is in a position to produce higher quality and infinitely more consistent wines at competitive prices to imported generics. Other than brand recognition, what are the advantages of consuming such imported wines as Liebfraumilch, and other regional wines from France and Italy? The importation of non-AOC French wine partly illustrates this case. Between 1970 and 1983, non-AOC

French wine imports increased from 8 percent to a 41 percent share of the French table wine segment, but has since declined to 17 percent as their price competitiveness has been eroded by the depressed $US, and California's ability to produce more consistent wines.

The other expanding market is Japan. One indication of the dimensions of the Japanese market is reflected by the fact that Japan is currently dependent on food imports for approximately 40 percent of its nutritional needs at a cost of more than $25 billion. Of the total, 40 percent, or $10 billion comes from the United States, of which California is responsible for more than $6 billion. This figure represents about 30 percent of all Californian agricultural exports, of which wine represents $20 million, or less than 2 percent of the total. Of significance is the fact that Japanese food imports from California are doubling every seven years.

> *The US exported 1,394,944 gallons of wine in 1911, 957,120 gallons in 1912, 1,075,151 gallons in 1913, and 941,326 gallons in 1914. In 1911 wine exports were valued at $518,536. From 1911 to 1924 wine exports averaged 1 million gallons annually.*

Japan is rapidly emerging as a major American wine market in which taste preferences have slowly evolved from sweet to dry table wines, and per capita consumption has doubled over the past ten years. Japan is affluent, rapidly urbanizing, and eager to import luxuries. The potential is significant as annual per capita consumption is less than .20 gallon, thus presenting a growth potential similar to other American consumer goods. Although 80 percent of the market was firmly in the grasp of French and German exporters, percentage share has slowly given way in favor of American imports at the expense of the other two (since 1982, American share increased from less than 3 percent to more than 16 percent, a remarkable increase when viewed against the formidable, better organized EEC counterparts). Given the fact that Japan and other Asian countries lack a viable domestic industry, the western Pacific-rim countries offer a promising emerging market. The main problems are a lack of understanding of the Japanese market, distribution, and the complex system of duties and taxes. For decades the 21 percent tariff and 50 percent *ad valorem* tax protected domestic producers who bought bulk wine from Third World countries only to blend it with 5 percent Japanese grape juice, and call it "Japanese wine." Ever since Japan was found guilty by GATT in discriminatory liquor tactics, there has been a concerted effort to modify the present system of tariff and tax practices.

What America needs is a strong wine export promotional program, very similar to the French experience. The French over the years built their volume by gaining a reputation for upscale wines in influential high income areas and placing their wines in fine restaurants. American wines have generated international recognition, but

there hasn't been, until recently, a movement to "beat the drums" about the quality of American wines. Rarely do small to medium-sized wineries export more than 10 percent of their production due to the fact that foreign markets were never a major strategic plan of the winery. America has also been hampered by the lack of tradition, not defining foreign tastes, and not making long-term financial commitments. This situation is changing: America is definitely becoming more export-minded, and given the size of the national trade deficit, there is ample evidence that the preoccupation of exporting will magnify in the future. In this regard, the Napa Valley Vintners Association launched in 1991 an Export Program in the United Kingdom. In wine circles, it is widely recognized that wine is a significant international business, and the sooner American wineries enter this growing segment of the market the better, an inevitable development as more American wineries acquire a reputation as world class producers. In this regard, EEC consumers are particularly interested in both Californian as well as "eastern" wines. The lower acid levels, consistent quality, and agreeable prices of the former, and the tantalizing flavor of Labrusca of the latter have made them quite appealing. Moreover, interest lies in both inexpensive as well as premium wines, particularly white, as well as Zinfandel, the latter popular in the United Kingdom.

Because the eastern portion of the country was unable to cultivate and make Vinifera wine, our European ancestors imported European wine from the earliest colonial settlement to the present. Although America imports wine from more than 40 different countries, more than 90 percent originates from France, Italy, Germany, Portugal, and Spain. Fig. 3.2 shows the post-World War II evolution of wine imports. Rising from 4.2 million gallons, or 3.8 percent of total consumption, imports rose to a historic high of 142,411,000 gallons, or 25.6 percent of total consumption in 1984. During this period, the percentage of American wines as share of the domestic market declined from 90 percent to 70 percent in 1985. The steady increase in imports was attributed to the relatively strong $US, more aggressive EEC marketing policies, a steady increase in demand along the northeastern coast (the principal market for quality, expensive French, Portuguese, Spanish, Italian, and German wines), overproduction in France and Italy, and the steady decline in per capita consumption in France and Italy when the reverse was occurring in America. As the $US weakened after a dramatic rise in the early 1980s, wine imports began to fall, reaching a 15-year low of 81 million gallons in 1988. Italy, with 24.2 million gallons, or 42 percent of imports, is the largest exporter followed by France (31 percent). Since 1984, country declines have been as much as 55 percent, and unless foreign currency exchange rates reach an equilibrium, these trends are likely to continue. In particular, French wine imports have declined by more than 40 percent, Italian by 57 percent, German by 63 percent, and Portuguese by 62 percent. In terms of market segment, imports, with more than 50 percent of the premium market, appear to have been reduced markedly in the mid-1980s when the price of the $US relative to most EEC currencies fell.

Imported wine as percent of total consumption has fluctuated widely throughout history. From a high figure of more than 50 percent for most of the nation's colonial history and into the nineteenth century, imports rose from near zero levels after World War II to one-third in the mid-1980s. Several factors, of which a depressed $US and continued improvement of quality wine production, combined to reduce imports to 12 percent in 1991. The percent of wine consumed by origin is shown in Fig. 3.3.

> *In 1990, the 10 leading imported wines were: Riunite (3,925), Bolla (996), Freixenet (980), Canei (800), Folonari (760), Kreusch (675), Martini & Rossi (648), Cella (585), Georges Duboeuf (550), Partager (525), top ten brands 10,444; others 18,438. In 1976 the ten leading imported wine brands were: Riunite (2,000), Mateus (1,400), Yago (1,300), Giacobazzi (900), Blue Nun (825), Bolla (750), Lancer's (700), Cruz Garcia Real (250), Folonari (240), Mouton Cadet (190). (In thousand cases.)*

As imports declined from 108 million gallons in 1986 to 60 million gallons in 1991, and exports increased from 7 million gallons to 40 million gallons for the same years, the ratio of exports to imports declined from 1:15.0 to 1:2.6. Not only has the volume of imports declined but the wine trade deficit has declined by one-third, from nearly $1 billion to slightly over $700 million. Since 1984, the sophisticated image of French wines combined with high prices has contributed to declining sales. French wines, in particular, once considered the "standard" in table wines, traditional, with high profile appellations, chateau labels, sophisticated, upscale, stylish, expensive, and considered intimidating, have had their image tarnished. In contrast, American wines are considered versatile, easy to buy, and offer far better value.

One of the largest recent declines in imported wine is Bordeaux, the most significant imported wine market in terms of $US value (more than 47 percent). The decline in Bordeaux and other French wines was so severe in 1988 (its share of the US wine market declined from 21 to 10 percent during 1984-1991) that French exports to the United Kingdom are now greater than to the United States. The import of 5.7 million cases in 1986-1987 represents a significant decline from the high of 13.2 million cases in 1985, and the first decline since 1974.

Imported table wine has declined from nearly 50 million cases in 1984 to fewer than 27 million cases in 1988. The largest declines have been in light, white, inexpensive blended wines like Liebfraumilch, Sangria, Lambrusco, and various regional and national Italian and French blends. In this wine market segment, the leading brands

are Riunite, Cella, Canei, Folonari, Bolla, Blue Nun, Lancers, Mateus, Giacobazzi, Partager, and others. The ten leading brands (all inexpensive blended wines) account for roughly 55 percent of total sales, and when the next ten brands are added, they account for nearly 75 percent of sales in terms of volume. While the average consumer prefers a familiar name and an uncomplicated product, is it really possible for America, a country that sent man to the moon, not to be able to make similar tasting wines domestically? While wine imports have been declining in recent years, it is significant to note that beer imports have risen from 141.5 million gallons in 1980 to 300 million gallons in 1988.

Figure 3.3

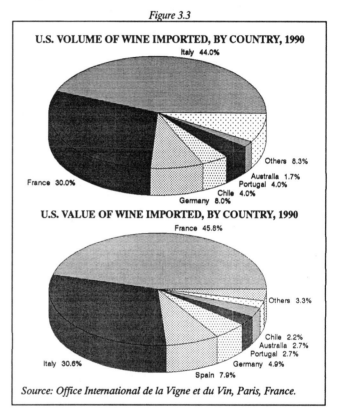

U.S. VOLUME OF WINE IMPORTED, BY COUNTRY, 1990

Italy 44.0%
Others 8.3%
Australia 1.7%
Portugal 4.0%
Chile 4.0%
Germany 8.0%
France 30.0%

U.S. VALUE OF WINE IMPORTED, BY COUNTRY, 1990

France 45.8%
Others 3.3%
Chile 2.2%
Australia 2.7%
Portugal 2.7%
Germany 4.9%
Spain 7.9%
Italy 30.6%

Source: Office International de la Vigne et du Vin, Paris, France.

It is also important to note that while imports have been falling since the mid-1980s, grape concentrate imports are increasing steadily. Although lacking the luster and celebrity of premium imported wine, the grape concentrate business is big business that is a cause of considerable concern. Grape concentrate imports for 1990 totaled 26.7 million gallons, or the equivalent of more than 148,000 tons of grapes. Imported concentrate accounted for 34.3 percent of all concentrate used in California in 1988, ten times the 1982 figure, a considerable erosion. The two major exporting countries are Argentina (75 percent) and Brazil (20 percent), followed by Chile, and Mexico.

It is obvious that throughout the post-World War II period imports were in a steady uptrend, and like many other imports reached critical levels with the wine boom of the late 1970s generating considerable concern among the many industries affected. The United States imports wine from at least 45 countries with a minimum of paperwork and a small duty. American wines, on the other hand, face a bewildering maze of tariffs, duties, paperwork, regulations, special fees, and other impediments. While the American taxpayer generously showered economic assistance to war-ravaged countries after World War II, and introduced highly favorable commercial arrangements in terms of foreign imports, the world economic community began to change rapidly in the 1970s. The open and highly liberal American trade policies over the past 45 years have generated more benefits to the EEC and the western Pacific rimland nations, all of which have instituted more protectionist trading policies. Even after the failure of President Richard Nixon's invocation of the doctrine of fairness in international trade, the wine trade deficit continued to widen rapidly in 1982 when the wine trade deficit was $743 million, or more than 2 percent of the total U.S. trade deficit. The double standard, clearly in Europe's favor, contributes to a wine trade imbalance with Europe that is as much as 110:1, and one reason why America had a wine trade deficit of $1 billion.

Alarmed by the growing deficit, the American wine industry began a lobbying effort to rectify the hiatus between imports and exports in what is commonly referred to as the Wine Equity Act of 1983. Its origins go back to 1970 when California increased total grape acreage by 56 percent, and winegrape acreage by 130 percent during the 1970-1985 period. Europe, on the other hand, experienced increased production and a decline in wine consumption for the same period. The decline, close to 1 percent per year, generated a huge wine lake of unprecedented proportions necessitating subsidies greater than $7 billion to soak up the surplus. In 1983, when the Wine Equity Act was proposed to Congress, the EEC wine surplus stood at 898 million gallons, of which nearly two-thirds was distilled into alcohol at a cost of $1 billion, or twice the cost of the 1983 California grape crop. The 1984 surplus was greater than California's total output as Europe produced twice as much as it consumed. Therefore, if the EEC continues ineffective vineyard and winery subsidies, the dimensions of the "wine lake" will continue to grow and the level of distillation will double by 1997.

This situation was aggravated by several events. Immediately after the 1980 election, the $US appreciated by 33 percent, and with the Mitterand election of 1981, the French Franc collapsed making French wines very affordable in America. As a consequence, imports rose rapidly, so that by 1983, 2.6 percent of the entire American trade deficit could be directly attributed to wine imports (wine is the largest EEC agricultural export to the U.S.). Faced with a $1.2 billion deficit, California wineries saw their

market share decline precipitously and sought relief through legislation. Introduced in the House of Representatives in August of 1983, the bill sought to "harmonize, reduce and eliminate trade barriers in wine on a basis that assures substantially equivalent competitive opportunities for all wine moving in international trade." The most important provision was to assure free trade between wine producing nations, the bill's primary enforcement clause stipulating a trade parity clause. This means that if a wine producing country imposes trade barriers, such as high import taxes on American wines, similar trade barriers would be imposed by the United States on incoming wines produced by that country, and to ban the entry of any foreign wine that is produced with the aid of government subsidies (such as low interest governmental loans to Italian cooperatives). Wine equity would, as the main objective, eliminate the imbalance of foreign governments imposing tariffs that are ten times as high as our tariff. The United States has never really been a wine export-minded nation. It provides no real export incentives such as those that exist in other countries. The Act never passed Congress for a variety of reasons of which its ineffective character, and protectionist features, especially as they failed to engender GATT guidelines, were the most important.

Nevertheless, a trade accord between the United States and the EEC to harmonize wine regulations did create, for the first time, a base for further negotiations. While the accord was ostensibly aimed at lowering non-tariff barriers of American wines to the EEC by providing permanent access to the European market, it is interesting to note that over the next three years European exports accelerated to new records, while American exports to the EEC fell to new lows. Despite the rhetoric, the agreement prevented new uses of European geographic designations, injected a spirit of cooperation in certifying wine labeling standards, and cooperation in international wine fraud investigations. The most important element of the accords was absolutely detrimental to American interests: a more streamlined process for certifying United States wine entry into the EEC did nothing to eliminate high tariff and non-tariff barriers, government monopolies at various levels of government, custom delays, and licensing and regulatory systems. Italy, in particular, has a complicated web of government support programs such as low-cost loans, and direct cash assistance in winery construction that gives an undue advantage to the domestic producer-exporter. One particularly disturbing characteristic of American governmental officials in the past has been their willingness to make unreasonable and often damaging concessions to the EEC without consultation with domestic producers. The basic element of reciprocity as a fair and complete solution to trade inequities has yet to be resolved.

The Wine Equity Act of 1983 was followed by another futile attempt in 1984 entitled The Wine Equity and Export Expansion Act. An interesting departure from the previous 1983 proposal was to include grape growers as part of the industry, and to initiate formidable wine exporting initiatives. As a consequence, in an effort to encourage exports, the US Department of Agriculture has provided support for exports since 1985 under the newly renamed Market Promotion Program (MPP). Administered by the Wine Institute, MPP provides matching funding for category and branded marketing activities involving over 100 California wineries. Under the auspices of the Foreign Agriculture Service, American wines have been placed on exhibit in practically all major world markets of which the Vin Italy exhibition in Verona, was the most important. The effects of the Wine Equity issue seems to have had significant results in many areas. It should be highlighted that as soon as Japan lowered its high tariffs on American wine in 1985, imports to that country leaped by 581,000 gallons. Japan was found guilty of discriminating against imported liquor by GATT in 1987, and has since modified its tariff and importing licensing requirements still further. Similarly, early in 1989, South Korea announced that by 1994 all quotas, bans, and distribution discrimination against American wines will be eliminated. South Korea also reduced the wine tariff from 100 percent in 1987, to 30 percent in 1990. Similar positive developments have occurred in Europe, the most notable in Scandinavia and Germany.

Because the EEC internal market for food is nearly stagnant, current policies actually encourage the production of surplus products, causing stocks of commodities to grow, and, in this respect, the wine industry is no exception. Import pressures are likely to continue given the fact that the EEC wine lake is growing at a time when domestic consumption (with a few nations as exceptions) is declining. Now that Portugal and Spain have joined the community, the wine surplus has increased by 20 percent (with 1.5 million unirrigated vine acres, Spain's entry into the EEC will have a continuing impact on the burgeoning wine lake.). In sharp contrast, American inventories do not exhibit large escalations. The decade of the 1970s averaged 425 million gallons, and the 1980s 750 million gallons. While there is very little that can be done to stem the tide of inexpensive wines, if the $US remains weak and Europe is unable to absorb premium wines from the EEC, parallel importing (or the ability to bypass official agents and thus cut costs) will increase. In addition, a complete economic and monetary union is scheduled to be implemented in 1992, and, as such, the EEC Unified European Market will definitely offer new challenges. As the community standardizes procedures for one market rather than twelve separate (with a combined population of 350 million people) American exporters are likely to face a monolithic policy of value added and excise taxes of historic proportions. Consider the facts: the unified EEC is the world's largest GNP and consumer market, producing more automobiles (an other durable goods) and electricity. Accommodating more than 300 million tourists, the EEC, is also the world's largest tourist region, and if we combine the resident population with the tourist, it is also the world's largest wine producing and consuming area commanding considerable leverage in the international wine market.

The Visitors Center, Wente Winery. Courtesy of Wente Winery

IV
AMERICAN CONSUMPTION PATTERNS

Total per capita beverage consumption has increased from 120 gallons in 1955 to more than 184 in 1987, and it is expected that it will amplify to 225 by 2000. Americans drink more soft drinks than water, more beer than coffee, and more milk than fruit juice. But in 1980, America, for the first time in history, consumed more wine than distilled beverages. Of all beverages consumed in America today, soft drinks account for 51 gallons per capita, followed by water (48), beer (25), milk (18), and coffee (17). While tea ranks about 7 gallons, fruit juice is rising rapidly. Coffee, successfully challenged by the soft-drink and fruit juice segments of the beverage market, has been declining steadily since 1965. Milk, on the decline since 1970, seems to have bottomed out in the mid-1980s.

Table 4.1

PER CAPITA BEVERAGE CONSUMPTION (In Gallons)				
Type	1960	1970	1978	1990
Soft Drinks	12.3	23.1	36.0	51.1
Water	49.6	49.4	47.4	48.8
Beer	15.1	18.7	23.0	25.3
Milk	37.9	31.0	25.0	17.5
Coffee	35.7	32.5	24.0	16.7
Juice	2.7	3.3	4.0	7.8
Tea	5.6	6.9	6.4	6.9
Wine	1.3	1.3	2.0	2.0
Distilled Spirits	1.3	1.8	2.0	1.7

It is estimated that per capita $ expenditures for beverage consumption rose from $116 in 1955, to $950 in 1992.
Source: The Wine Institute.

Soft drink consumption in gallons rose steadily throughout the post World War II period to present levels as the most popular consumed beverage on a per capita basis in America. And despite the aging of the American population, consumption is expected to continue to expand to 60 gallons by the end of this century. Tap water is on the decline being replaced by soft drinks in 1984 as the leading beverage. With sales mushrooming from $237 million in 1977 to nearly $6 billion in 1992, bottled water has grown faster over the past 20 years than any other beverage. The U.S. yearly per capita consumption of bottled water is estimated to be 8 gallons, ahead of tea, fruit juice, distilled spirits, and significantly above wine. With more than 600 domestic brands and more than 50 imported labels, this beverage has developed into a major American beverage mainstay. This growth is not hard to explain. Bottled water contains no calories, caffeine, artificial sweeteners, preservatives, cholesterol, hence, it fits nicely into the contemporary health conscious image of the average consumer. As bottled water competes effectively with soft drinks, its per capita consumption is expected to increase in the future.

Wine competes directly with both beer and distilled spirits, and has shown vitality over the past 25 years by increasing its market share. In the 1970s wine consumption

increased faster than milk, coffee, beer, distilled spirits, and soft drinks. Consumption peaked in 1986, and industry experts state that the industry, faced with a lack of tradition and an ever-increasing non-European population, will be facing an uncertain future. Although per capita wine consumption is a modest 2 gallons, the amount was more than for spirits and cacao, and significantly greater in dollar amount spent than for coffee, tea, cacao, and fruit juice.

Of the nearly $280 billion beverage industry, beer accounts for 28 percent, followed by soft drinks (27%), distilled beverages (15%), wine (12%), milk (6%), fruit juices (6%), and the remaining 6 percent includes coffee, bottled water, tea, and powdered drinks. By far beer represents the largest volume of consumption of alcoholic beverages with a per capita consumption of 25 gallons. What is significant is that imported beer accounts for, unlike the wine and distilled beverage industry, less than 3 percent of beer consumption. Furthermore, during the past 20 years, as distilled spirits have dropped slightly and wine increased by nearly 50 percent, beer has shown the sharpest growth, helped in part by the popularity of light beers.

Table 4.2

PERCENT OF MARKET: US NON-ALCOHOLIC BEVERAGE CONSUMPTION						
Category	1970	1975	1980	1985	1988	1990
Soft Drinks	17.0	20.7	25.8	29.4	31.9	32.1
Water	36.4	34.0	31.4	29.5	29.2	29.3
Milk	16.7	15.8	13.6	13.0	12.8	13.9
Coffee	20.8	18.7	17.0	16.0	14.2	12.8
Fruit Juice/Drinks	4.5	5.4	6.2	6.5	6.8	6.9
Tea	3.6	4.1	4.5	4.1	3.7	3.5
Other	1.0	1.3	1.5	1.4	1.4	1.5

Other includes: powdered breakfast beverage, non-alcoholic cocktail mixes, cocoa/chocolate beverages, herbal tea and infant juices.
Source: The Wine Institute.

First made in the Middle East, beer, an alcoholic beverage made from barley, malt, other grains, hops, yeast and water, is said to be as old as wine. The third leading beverage next to soft drinks and water, beer is a sudsy, cool, refreshing beverage (ubiquitous at picnics, college fraternity parties, bars, and ball parks) that is different from wine in terms of flavor, aroma, cost, and production methods. Although perceived as filling and higher in calories, it has remained the most popular alcoholic beverage in America by a wide margin since the nineteenth century. Since the first commercial brewery was established in 1623, per capita consumption has risen to levels placing America eleventh among the major beer drinking nations, but first in production. Germany, with 39 gallons per capita, leads the list among the world's leading beer consuming nations, followed by Czechoslovakia, Australia, Belgium, Luxembourg, Denmark, New Zealand, Ireland,

England, and Austria. American consumption of more than 6 billion gallons (twelve times greater than wine) represents 85 percent of total alcoholic beverage consumption in America.

The evolution of beer production and consumption on a per capita for the years 1890-1990 is indicated in Fig. 4.1. Although the chronology is abbreviated, it is important to note that in seventeen and eighteen century Colonial America the consumption of beer was less than 1 pint per week. With increased German immigration during the middle of the nineteenth century, production grew to formidable levels, doubling during the period 1860-1870, and by the 1890s beer began to challenge whiskey as the national alcoholic beverage. In recent years, beer has reduced its rapid rate in per capita consumption for the first time since Prohibition. Furthermore, while wine drinkers tend to consume wine with meals, beer consumers drink beer for practically any reason, and at a much lower ounce-per-ounce expense. In terms of sales, beer is expected to rise from $38 billion to $55 billion. Imports, as per cent of total sales, rose from 1 percent of total consumption in 1967 to nearly 7 percent in 1988, but have since declined, very much in the manner of wine. While production has increased from 37 million (31 gallon) barrels in 1934 to more than 200 million in 1990, the number of breweries has declined from 714 to fewer than 50 for the same years.

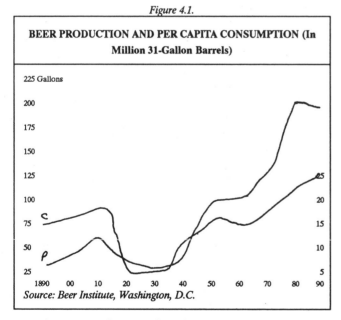

Figure 4.1.

BEER PRODUCTION AND PER CAPITA CONSUMPTION (In Million 31-Gallon Barrels)

Source: Beer Institute, Washington, D.C.

Since 1960, the American brewing industry has faced many geographic changes in production and consumption, one of the most important being the rise of the "sun belt" as the fastest growing beer consuming region in the country. Current growth trends not withstanding, the three states of California, Texas and Wisconsin produce more than one-third of the nation's beer. Surprisingly, the state

with the highest per capita consumption is Nevada (37.7 gallons), followed by New Hampshire (34.7 gallons), and Wisconsin (34.5 gallons). The state with the lowest per capita consumption is Utah (13 gallons), followed by Oklahoma, Kentucky, and Arkansas (19 gallons). Responding to national tastes, non-alcoholic beer increased from 12.6 million gallons in 1984 to more than 24 million gallons by 1990.

Between 1973 and 1988, distilled spirits declined by more than 15 million gallons, while wine consumption rose by more than 29 million, and beer by 12.9 million. Adult consumption of liquor has declined each year since 1975 with distilled spirits declining more precipitously than either wine or beer. Since 1980, distilled spirit consumption has declined by nearly 2 percent each year, a significant sign that America is not only drinking less but lighter. Indeed, total liquor consumption in America declined from 449 million wine gallons in 1981 to 368 million wine gallons in 1989. This is consistent with west European trends as well, where milk, butter, and distilled beverage production have decreased reflecting the tendency toward lighter food and beverage consumption. Brown spirits (Scotch, Bourbon, and Canadian) have declined while Vodka, Rum and Tequila have increased slightly or held a steady course. The consumption of America's premier distilled beverage, Bourbon, has declined by half since 1970, accounting for only 10 percent of the volume of distilled spirits in 1988. Among the main distilled beverage producing nations, America ranks third in production and eleventh in consumption.

Distilled beverages are considered inappropriate as a daytime beverage, and since 1980 "shots," highballs, cocktails, elixirs, and the three martini lunch have declined, a consumer pattern reflected by the fact that wine consumption in 1980, for the first time in American history, surpassed distilled beverage consumption. By a significant margin, wine outsells distilled alcoholic beverages in Arizona, California, Idaho, New Jersey, New Mexico, New York, Oregon, Rhode Island, Washington, and the District of Columbia. The largest geographic markets for distilled beverages on a per capita basis in gallons are: District of Columbia (4.2); Nevada (4.2); New Hampshire (4.1); Alaska (2.4); and Delaware (2.2).

While brown distilled beverages have declined over the past 30 years, California brandy has experienced a significant growth spurt in recent years. During the period 1961-1981, brandy sales have increased from 6.9 million gallons to 21.4 million gallons, with U.S. market share remaining stable between two-thirds to three-quarters of brandy sales. While production is dominated by the large megaliths of the Central Valley, small, highly specialized producers are sprouting everywhere. The most important of this new breed of producers, overwhelmingly concentrated on the west coast, include: Bonny Doon, Clear

Creek, Creekside, Domaine Karakash, Carneros Alambic, and Quady among others. By all measures, an increasing number of wineries throughout America will enter this highly technical, and financially lucrative segment of the wine market.

THE U.S. WINE MARKET

1. Throughout the 1980s, table wine has been the dominant wine in America. It accounted for 63.8% of the total wine market in 1990.
2. Wine cooler sales, approximately 86 million gallons, representing 17% of the wine market, were unknown in 1980.
3. Approximately 36 million gallons of sparkling wines were consumed in America, of which 61% originated in California, 10% from other states, and 29% constituted imports.
4. Dessert and related wines declined from 13% of the U.S. wine market in 1980 to 9.9% in 1990.
5. The American wine market grew 30.3 million gallons in the past ten years, from 479.6 millions gallons in 1980 to 509 million gallons in 1990.
6. American per capita wine consumption is among the lowest of all the beverage groups at 2 gallons. This compares with over 51 gallons for soft drinks and 25 gallons for beer. Furthermore, per capita wine consumption in the U.S. is much below that of most other major wine producing countries. While America ranked sixth in wine production in 1989, after France, Italy, Spain, Russia, and Argentina, its per capita consumption was but one-tenth of both France and Italy.
Source: Wine Institute.

Brandy production has doubled in each of the preceding three decades, and is likely to do the same during the next. While domestic brown, and imported spirits have both shown a significant decline in recent years, domestic brandy production is a major bright spot in the industry. Domestic brandy is lighter, fruitier and more versatile than other distilled spirits, imported brandies, and Cognac. The industry has grown from less than 50,000 gallons after Repeal to present levels exceeding 30 million gallons, a significant growth. The nations largest producer, Gallo, dominates the industry with half of sales followed by Christian Brothers, Korbel, The Beverage Source, and Paul Masson. All others collectively comprise less than 5 percent of total production. California produces more than 95 percent of all domestic brandy, and is responsible for 80 percent of total consumption. The state with the highest per capita consumption is Wisconsin, followed by other Great Lakes states, California, and New England. Because brandy is wine related, most serious, upscale wine drinkers favor it as their spirit drink, and production is expected to increase.

Wine

The product of fermented grapes, wine is considered the oldest fermented beverage and the second most popular alcoholic beverage in America. While America makes a complete spectrum of wine (table, sparkling, and fortified are the most common), subtypes (special flavored, including vermouth and even brandy) number in the dozens with market share constantly in a state of flux depending on consumer preferences. Unlike any other country, America makes wines with the greatest quality and flavor latitudes--from wines lacking in character to highly individualistic libations not found anywhere else. American wines are clean, brilliant in appearance, sanitized, and the most technologically supervised wines in the world. If anything, they are the product of measurement and formula, and not, as the "old world" is fond of saying--"the product of art."

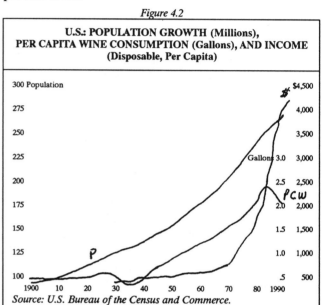

Figure 4.2

U.S.: POPULATION GROWTH (Millions), PER CAPITA WINE CONSUMPTION (Gallons), AND INCOME (Disposable, Per Capita)

Source: U.S. Bureau of the Census and Commerce.

Despite the post-Repeal increase in grape and wine production, and wine consumption, America, among the world's major wine producing countries, is still not a major wine consuming nation. Despite extensive European travel over the past two generations, and exposure to fine dinner and dessert wines, per capita consumption remains sluggish. Moreover, our preoccupation with fads, such as Cold Duck, Pop Wines, and the like, does little to amplify consumption over the long run, and does much harm in the short run. Consumption since 1935 rose from .30 gallons to 1.3 gallons in 1970, to 2.3 gallons in 1982, but declined to 2 gallons since then. Not only did per capita consumption increase since Prohibition, but consumers shifted from sweet to dry table wine. By 1982, table wine constituted 77.5 percent of all wine compared to 29.4 percent in 1955. And while the upward trend will not continue to 2000, total sales rose from $8 billion to $13 billion (or one-quarter of the beer market). World-wide, wine producing nations are experiencing declining per capita wine consumption, and affluent, non-wine producing countries are increasing per capita consumption. Italy, the world's largest wine producer, reduced consumption from 29 gallons in 1965 to 20 gallons in 1988.

World wine consumption falls into three broad groups of countries: high, medium, and low consumers.

The countries with a considerable intake, namely Italy, France, Spain, Portugal, Luxembourg, and Argentina (consistently ranking as the top ten), consume between 15 and 22 gallons per capita annually. With less than 5 percent of the world's population, they consume more than 50 percent of the world's total wine output, a remarkable exploit. Second are countries with medium per capita consumption, that vary, for simplicity purposes, between 7 and 14 gallons per capita. This group includes Germany, Greece, Cyprus, Belgium, Austria, Switzerland, Russia, Chile, South Africa, and Australia, and with 12 percent of the world's population, consume 32 percent of the total world output. The the third group includes those countries that consume fewer than 7 gallons of wine annually. The United States, with but 2 gallons per capita, ranks among the likes of Iceland, Poland, Finland, and the United Kingdom, countries with small populations and no winemaking potential. With a low per capita wine consumption, the American market is considered "young" when compared to the "mature" French and Italian markets. Since 1986, U.S. consumption of wine has declined by more than 15 percent, a development largely attributed to dietary changes and the effects of the anti-alcohol movement. During this period, the only wine category to buck this downward trend has been premium wine--white and red premium table wine in particular. Nevertheless, adult per capita consumption of wine has increased from .49 gallons in 1960, to 3.0 in 1991, a pattern of movement that exhibits a steady, long term increase with few fluctuations. Given the high standard of living, the average American consumes relatively low amounts in comparison to many European nations.

Figure 4.3

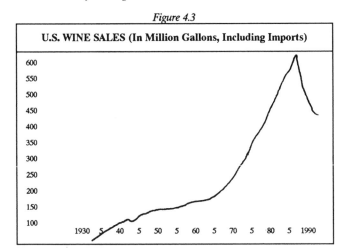

U.S. WINE SALES (In Million Gallons, Including Imports)

Total wine consumption since 1934 is presented in Fig. 4.3. In 1918 wine consumption in the U.S. was a mere 5.1 million gallons, of which 3 million was imported. Most of it was inexpensive bulk wine consumed in American cities by foreign-born German and Mediterranean immigrants. By 1928, wine consumption had increased to 16.4

million gallons, a surprising threefold jump. Wine consumption in America has grown steadily since Repeal, from 34 million gallons in 1934, 95 million gallons in 1937, to 110 million gallons in 1940 (three-quarters of which was fortified wine). Since then, consumption rose steadily peaking in 1985 (nearly 650 million gallons), but has since declined to less than 500 million gallons.

Table 4.3

WINE ENTERING DISTRIBUTION CHANNELS (In Thousand Gallons)
By Selected Year and Per Capita

State	1938	P/C	1973	P/C	1990	P/C
Alabama	335	.1	1,846	.5	4,566	1.0
Alaska			685	2.0	1,466	2.0
Arizona	463	.9	3,580	1.7	8,668	2.2
Arkansas	349	.1	1,367	.7	1,875	.6
California	20,107	3.0	73,625	3.5	105,397	3.5
Colorado	1,051	.9	4,956	2.0	6,263	1.9
Connecticut	704	.4	5,586	1.8	9,197	2.8
Delaware	40	.5	795	1.4	1,552	2.3
District of Columbia	419	.6	3,630	4.9	3,050	5.1
Florida	1,174	.6	14,260	1.8	32,145	2.5
Georgia	402	.1	3,971	.8	11,618	1.8
Hawaii			1,377	1.6	2,753	2.5
Idaho	211	.4	1,010	1.3	1,939	2.0
Illinois	3,612	.4	18,401	1.6	25,954	2.3
Indiana	291	.1	4,211	.8	6,829	1.2
Iowa	151	.1	1,286	.4	3,107	1.1
Kansas			1,263	.5	2,003	.8
Kentucky	148	.1	1,712	.5	2,676	.7
Louisiana	3,502	1.5	3,959	1.1	5,897	1.4
Maine	84	.1	1,235	1.2	2,586	2.1
Maryland	389	.2	6,418	1.6	10,079	2.1
Massachusetts	1,810	.4	11,391	2.0	17,298	2.9
Michigan	1,084	.2	12,826	-1.4	16,128	1.7
Minnesota	360	.1	3,937	1.0	7,202	1.6
Mississippi			1,216	.5	1,420	.5
Missouri	1,232	.3	4,930	1.0	7,080	1.4
Montana	143	.3	636	.9	1,415	1.8
Nebraska	161	.1	1,144	.7	1,927	1.2
Nevada	159	1.5	2,212	4.0	5,179	4.3
New Hampshire	59	.1	1,607	2.0	3,356	3.0
New Jersey	3,609	.9	15,642	2.1	23,712	3.1
New Mexico	514	1.0	1,798	1.6	2,506	1.7
New York	9,822	.7	43,275	2.4	46,719	2.6
North Carolina	269	.1	5,646	1.1	11,407	1.7
North Dakota	167	.3	482	.8	658	1.0
Ohio	3,000	.5	10,961	1.0	14,476	1.3
Oklahoma			2,368	.9	2,603	.8
Oregon	1,032	.9	5,719	2.8	8,200	2.9
Pennsylvania	2,150	.2	13,365	1.1	14,085	1.2
Rhode Island	383	.5	2,162	2.2	2,802	2.8
South Carolina	160	.1	2,751	1.0	5,493	1.6
South Dakota	84	.1	561	.8	739	1.1
Tennessee			2,486	.6	4,418	.9
Texas	1,565	.2	12,143	1.0	27,045	1.6
Utah	369	.7	869	.8	1,170	.7
Vermont	91	.2	1,090	2.3	1,687	3.0
Virginia	1,376	.5	6,433	1.3	11,716	1.9
Washington	1,658	.9	7,684	2.2	15,124	3.1
West Virginia	184	.1	884	.5	1,185	.6
Wisconsin	1,093	.3	6,042	1.3	9,148	1.9
Wyoming	57	.2	359	1.0	598	1.3
U.S. Total	66,023	.5	337,792	1.6	516,116	2.1

Source: Wine Institute

American wine consumption exhibits various interesting geographical, social, regional and institutional patterns. Not only does per capita consumption differ widely by state, but the geography of this consumption is localized along the Pacific rimland and the northeastern portion of the country. The states with the highest per capita consumption were the District of Columbia, Nevada, California, Washington, New Jersey, Vermont, and New

Hampshire. The District of Columbia, and its 5 million metropolitan area inhabitants, is the center of the nation's highest per capita wine intake. Spacious in appearance, cosmopolitan and affluent in its ambience, the District contains more lobbyists, foreign embassy personnel, first class restaurants, and parks per square mile than any other American city. The District of Columbia leads the nation with 5.1 gallons, Nevada is second with 4.3 gallons, and California is third with 3.5 gallons. The other leading states are: Oregon (2.9), Massachusetts (2.9), Rhode Island (2.8), Connecticut (2.8), New York (2.6), Florida (2.5), and Hawaii (2.5). The states with the lowest consumption are Mississippi, West Virginia, Arkansas, Kentucky, Utah, Oklahoma, Kansas, and Tennessee (low consumption rates are due to religious reasons and strong distilled alcohol bias). For the nation as a whole, per capita wine consumption varies because: state taxes and sale restrictions by type of outlet (package stores, super markets, restaurants, etc.), exorbitant license fees and red tape preventing farmers from switching to wine production, the perpetuation of dry counties, and days of sale.

While averages do indicate broad national patterns, the geography of a particular beverage may be a function of residence. Red and white, dry and sweet, and table or dessert wines are not consumed evenly across America, but exhibit specific geographic patterns. Similarly, malt beverages show the lowest levels of consumption in the Bible Belt, Canadian whiskey and brandy are most popular in the northern Plains and northwest, and Bourbon in the Bible Belt.

Regional geographical differences are dramatic: the south leads the nation in total beverage consumption (40%); the northcentral portion of the nation consumes more alcoholic beverages than any other, followed by the south, northeast, and far west; the south consumes more distilled beverages and beer than any other; and the north-central portion of the country consumes more coolers than any other.

In terms of gross consumption by state, the six leading wine markets were (with 31% of total population): California, New York, Florida, Texas, Illinois, and New Jersey, collectively accounting for nearly 300 million gallons, or 54 percent of the entire American market. It is also interesting to note that one out of eight Americans lives in California, and one in five in two states--California and New York, the two states responsible for nearly one-third of total wine consumption. Thirty-four other states had a combined consumption of 130 million gallons, or 22 percent of the national market.

The western wine region, composed of ten states--California, Washington, Oregon, Arizona, Hawaii, Idaho, Utah, New Mexico, Nevada, and Alaska, is a high per capita wine region. In 1991 this area consumed more than 155 million gallons (30% of the national total) and had a per capita consumption of nearly 3 gallons (with more than 41 million people, 37,000 restaurants, and 33,000 retail outlets, it ranks as the nation's premier wine market). In comparison, the northeast, an area of nine states, consumed 120 million gallons, had a per capita consumption

of just 2.4. Significantly, the bulk of all wine sold in New Hampshire, the District of Columbia, Florida, and Nevada, is consumed by non-residents, whereas California is the nation's leading state in resident per capita wine consumption. Two non-wine producing areas--the District of Columbia and Nevada, with abnormal per capital consumption levels, are unusual due to the presence of foreign embassies in the former, and tourism in both.

In terms of market penetration, the three western states of Washington, Oregon and California have more than 54 percent of all households purchasing wine at least once during a 12 month period in comparison with 39 percent for the nation as a whole. It is estimated that 10 percent of households purchased more than 55 percent of all wine, and that 20 percent of households accounted for 66 percent of all wine purchases. Highly significant is the fact that not only are metropolitan areas the largest volume and per capita consumers of wine, but they tend to consume the largest variety of wine products. Rural, and, to a lesser extent, rural non-farm areas in the south and midwest are more homogeneous in their wine preferences.

Table 4.4

US WINE CONSUMPTION BY SELECTED STATE (As Percent of Total)					
State	1944	1948	1970	1986	1990
California	20.2	16.3	22.6	22.3	20.4
New York	14.2	18.3	9.8	9.6	9.1
Florida	1.5	1.1	6.0	5.5	6.2
Texas	3.2	2.7	5.1	5.1	5.2
Illinois	6.9	6.5	4.7	4.7	5.0
New Jersey	4.6	5.2	5.0	4.7	4.6
Source: The Wine Institute					

Another interesting geographical phenomenon is the correlation of wine consumption with urban and suburban lifestyles. The ten largest metropolitan areas (Los Angeles, New York, San Francisco, Chicago, Boston, Philadelphia, Detroit, Washington, San Diego, and Miami) account for 28 percent of all wine sales, and the top 50 urban areas more than 60 percent of the nation's entire wine intake. If one enlarges the geography of metropolitan areas to include Standard Metropolitan Statistical Areas, more than 90 percent of all wine in the nation is consumed in these geographical units. The above not withstanding, there are a number of significant regional, racial, educational, and economic differences: Virginians, Oregonians, Washingtonians, and Texans are very loyal to their state wines; the northeast megalopolis (an area that stretches from Boston to Virginia) consumes more imported wine than any other region in the nation; Afro-Americans in the northeast and portions of the midwest consume a disproportionate amount of sweet, often fortified wine; the ethnic markets of the northeast and midwest consume an ample amount of imported wine; the humid southeastern and humid portion of the nation prefers sweet wines; and California is the nations largest sparkling wine market.

Figure 4.4

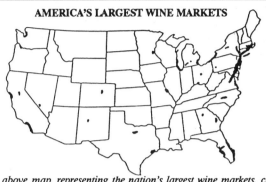

AMERICA'S LARGEST WINE MARKETS

The above map, representing the nation's largest wine markets, contains more than 170 million people. Collectively, these metropolitan areas rank first in the consumption of quality products, include more than 74% of all families with incomes above $95,000, encompass more than 80% of the nation's 100 largest corporations, and more than 70% of wine sales. The importance of urban concentration is clearly illustrated by the residence of members of the Society of Wine Educators shown below, 1988, used with permission.

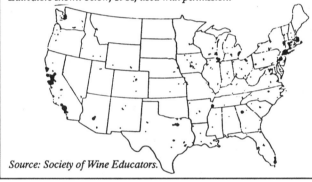

Source: Society of Wine Educators.

There are significant differences among consumers on a regional basis regarding feelings about wine and other beverages. New York, for example, accounts for one-fifth of all vermouth, followed by Chicago; Philadelphia is a major consuming area for imported dessert wines; and brandy is most common in California, Nevada, and the northern tier of states bordering the Canadian border. Places that imbibe the largest volume of alcoholic spirits also tend to consume the largest variety. The larger the metropolitan area and the more culturally diversified, the higher the per capita consumption of wine.

Consumer Characteristics

America since 1960 has gone through its greatest wine boom in history. Over the past 30 years consumption rose from 163.3 million gallons to 587 million gallons, and per capita consumption leaped from .91 to 2. Is this just a passing fancy? Is the current slump a momentary aberration, or will the upward momentum continue? Will the estimated 110 million Americans who abstain from wine be persuaded to consume in the future? Besides the marketing ploys of audience identification, production and packaging innovations, the important elements condi-

tioning wine consumption are more complicated and long term in their formation.

Table 4.5

ADULT PER CAPITA CONSUMPTION BY TYPE OF BEVERAGE						
Type	1970	1975	1980	1981	1982	1983	1990
Beer	30.7	34.7	36.8	36.8	36.2	35.8	35.1
Wine	2.2	2.7	3.3	3.4	3.5	3.3	3.2
Spirits	3.1	3.3	3.0	2.8	2.7	2.6	2.2

Source: The Wine Institute.

Increased American wine consumption during the period 1960-1980 has been influenced by a host of elements of which the following are considered the most important: favorable wine prices as percent of disposable income, changes in diet, an expanding population, increased domestic table wine production, increased advertising, better distribution, and a reduction of controlled states, as well as a relaxation of restrictions on the sale of wine. The above is the complete antithesis of post-Repeal snobbery that emphasized imports and not domestic wines. Slowly but steadily, Americans have turned to drier table wines, at first imports, but as time marched forward, from domestic mass-produced versions to premium labels. By the early 1970s, Americans discovered that table wine is not only good and wholesome, but also not a monopoly of the European winemaker and the privilege of the European aristocrat.

Although wine consumption is the product of many elements, the author is of the opinion that the following are the most important:
1. Per capita consumption is directly related to areas of production, hence the high consumption figures of California, Washington, Oregon, Texas, and New York.
2. Per capita consumption is directly related to availability and facility to purchase, particularly food store sales. The number of states allowing wine to be sold through food outlets is increasing. At present 27 states have enacted such legislation. States like Idaho, Maine, Washington, Alabama, Iowa, and Montana have experienced a phenomenal boom in wine sales when wine was made available in food outlets.
3. Per capita consumption is directly related to diet quality. It appears that as diet becomes more eclectic, and as the quality and quantity of bread consumption increases (among other characteristics), the quantity, quality and variety of wines consumed rises.
4. Per capita consumption is directly related to cultural traditions that promote full course family dinners in which wine is ever-present on the table. The author has found that this is not only a highly significant factor influencing wine consumption, but along with diet and life style, one of the elements contributing to the long-term stability of the wine market. It is estimated that more than half of table wine is consumed with meals, and that less than 22% of all wine is consumed away from home.
5. Per capita consumption is directly related to disposable income. Combined with an ability to travel, this factor enables the storage and consumption of more expensive wines, hence the high per capita wine consumption levels of Nevada, Massachusetts, New Jersey, Maryland, and Connecticut.
6. Wine consumption is directly related to consistency and quality of product. America has been on the cutting edge of technological innovation for the past 50 years and will continue to provide technical leadership. Clonal selection, genetic design of yeast and rootstock, as well as vineyard and fermentation innovations, will accelerate in the future.

By moderate estimates there have been more than 30 major consumer behavior surveys conducted on the subject of wine over the past 50 years. While even a radical abridgement would fill up most of the pages of this volume, suffice it to say that the following (among many more) summarize their findings of the serious wine drinking profile: personal and family income is above average, the majority are college educated, better read, well travelled, professional, urban oriented, family migrated from a wine producing country or area, and live within a two-hour drive from a wine producing region.

One of the oldest of the consumer surveys is the 1946 Wine Consumer Survey prepared for the Wine Advisory Board, by the Wine Institute and the J. Walter Thompson Company. The report summarizes consumer preferences and characteristics in 86 cities across America, and gives a fascinating glimpse into the wine consuming habits of the average American citizen. A more authoritative consumer report, *The U.S. Wine Market*, by Raymond J. Folwell and John L. Baritelle, published by the U.S. Department of Agriculture in 1978, is a large, objective, well-researched and documented survey of America's wine drinking habits. Although too large in scale to summarize, suffice it to say that sex, age, marital status, education, race, family size, employment, income, and market size as variables are analyzed in detail.

Over the past four years, the author conducted his own survey in the states of Pennsylvania, New Jersey, Connecticut, and New York, and has come to the following conclusions: more than 75 percent of all wine is consumed during dinner; 57 percent of all wine consumers do not wish to be educated in matters relating to wine (of those who drink wine on a daily basis, more than 85 percent subscribe to a wine journal and want to be more educated in wine history); 96 percent of all consumers were influenced by habit and advertising in choosing their wine; only 24 percent of all customers consume wine once a month; 75 percent drink wine at home, 70 percent prefer to drink after 5 pm, fewer than 20 percent drink wine as a snack item, and of those that do, about 70 percent fall within the ages of 21-30.

Who is the consumer? The Baxevanis survey found that 64 percent of all families do not buy wine on a regular basis (fewer than three bottles annually); 20 percent consume 34 percent; next 10 percent consume 30 percent; the remaining 6 percent consume 36 percent. Ten percent of all wine is purchased as a gift, and less than 1 percent for cooking. In terms of age cohort: the under 24-year-old population consumes--32% of all soft drinks, 3% of all spirits, 30% of all beer, and 2.1% of all wine; 25-40 year-olds buy 27% soft drinks, 39% spirits, 40% beer, and 26% wine; and the 40 and older age group drink 20% soft drinks, 48% spirits, 24% beer, and 60% wine. Wine, therefore, is the preferred alcoholic beverage of the 40 and over age cohort, while beer and wine coolers attract the youthful portion of the population. For the 55 and over age group, nearly all consume wine on a regular to frequent basis, but only 51% consume beer, 41% consume whiskey, 76% consume brandy, and 85% consume sparkling wine.

The Baxevanis survey identified two diverse types of consumers: 5 percent of the population accounts for about 34 percent of total wine volume and 75 percent of the sales dollar, while the remaining 95 percent of the population accounts for only one-quarter of sales. This high income cohort consumes more than 90 percent of the premium and nearly all the ultra-premium wine segments. For the high income group (the most wine intensive), premium wine is inelastic while for the lower income groups the price of inexpensive wine is quite a barrier for repeat purchases, hence the preference of beer and cheap whiskey in satisfying the need for alcohol, and as alcohol alternatives. In addition, the high income cohort is less fickle in choosing and less of a faddist. In terms of ethnic and racial characteristics, the most rapidly growing minority segments of the population--Asiatics, Hispanics, and blacks, are not major table wine consumers, and are not likely to be in the near future. The most wine-oriented ethnic groups (but not in terms of gross sales) are Greeks, Italians, Portuguese, and Yugoslavs. While the 35-65 age cohort consumes more than 80 percent of all table wine, the 45-65 age cohort consumes a similar percentage of the more expensive fortified wines such as Porto and Sherry-type wines. Eighty-two percent of all college graduates with a Master's Degree or better drink wine, while only 22 percent of all consumers with an educational attainment of a High School Degree or less drink wine. Premium wine drinkers, above average in education and income: pay more per bottle than any other group; purchase wine year-round; consume wine before, during and after dinner; have a gluttonous appetite for wine information; require a high degree of information; purchase many different wines from many countries; buy nearly all the wine books, and subscribe to at least one wine magazine or newsletter. This type of consumer has displaced the older, ethnic wine consumer of pre and post-Prohibition. On the other hand, those that buy the largest volume pay the lowest price; they buy their wine in supermarkets or in liquor stores, not in wineries or retail outlets specializing in wine; purchases tend to be more sporadic and unpredictable; and wine is rarely consumed with meals.

The Baxevanis survey also revealed the following: 34 percent of the population never consumed wine (total abstainers); 26 percent consumed wine once a month or less often (sporadic drinkers); 20 percent consumed wine twice a month (occasional drinkers); 15 percent consumed wine once a week (regular wine drinkers); and 5 percent consumed wine two or more times a week (compelling wine drinkers). While women drink and purchase wine more often than men, the latter still purchase the more expensive, "serious" wines.

> *What is needed to increase the wine consuming base? If a person consumed 6 ounces of wine with dinner every night, he would be consuming 17 gallons annually.*

The survey concluded that wine is a highly differentiated product. Table wines range from inexpensive jug wines to fine varietals, and the pattern in recent years has been for the latter to increase faster than the former. Estimates for the next decade range from fractions of a percentage point increases per annum for jug wines to more than 3 percent for premium table wines. After two decades of steady advances there has been a substantial slowing in the growth of the overall wine market in America. Consumption of all wines declined 20 percent since 1986. It was also found that wine purchases show distinct seasonal patterns, with more than 60 percent of total $ expenditures occurring in the months of November-December. Moreover, less than 1 percent consume wine before lunch; 4 percent with lunch; 17 percent before dinner, 76 percent with dinner, and the remainder after dinner and late evening. Forty-four percent of winery tourists purchase wine. In terms of sex, 58 percent of all wine is consumed by women.

The results of the *International Wine Review* October/November (1988) Reader Survey revealed the following: the most popular wines were Cabernet Sauvignon, Chardonnay, Red Bordeaux, Red Burgundy, Pinot Noir, Merlot, White Burgundy, Sauvignon Blanc, Champagne, Zinfandel, and Rhone wines; 90 percent are male; average cellar exceeds 88 cases; monthly expenditures on wine is $323; average household income is $150,000; and 64 percent are not related to the food and wine industry. The *Wine Spectator* November 30, 1989 Reader Survey revealed the following for Spectator subscribers: they drink wine on average 5.4 days a week, with 35 percent drinking wine several days a week; average consumption is two glasses daily; 37 percent of purchased bottles were in the $10-15 price range; 40 percent had household incomes of $100,000, and 12 percent over $200,000; 53 percent attended graduate school with 23 percent holding a postgraduate degree; 89 percent are male, the median age is 42, and 76 percent are married; 85 percent have a "wine cellar" with an average size of 19 cases; and 71 percent also drink distilled spirits.

In sharp contrast to the above, it is remarkable to note how little the American consumer profile has changed over the past two generations. *The Wine Advisory Report*, published in 1946 concluded: of the 32,550,000 families only 16.7 million consumed wine. In 1946, the number of families increased to 37,616,000, but the number of wine using families increased to 20.5 million, of which 97% consumed coffee; 96% consumed milk; 88% consumed tea; 82% consumed carbonated beverages; 55%

consumed beer; 54% consumed wine and whiskey; and 24% consumed brandy. In 1946, 68% of all wine was purchased by men although women consumed 52% of all wine. Wine consumption by type, however, was different. Ninety-six percent of all families consumed dessert wines; 55% table wines; and 24% consumed sparkling wines. The most popular wines were Port and Sherry, followed by Sauterne, Muscatel, and Burgundy. Also of significance is the fact that 69% of the sample had never consumed table wines.

Why America Will Never Become A Major Wine Consuming Nation

The Problem Stated: With more than 815,000 acres of grapes and a European dominated population, America is not a major wine consuming country.

1. Despite the nutritional value of grapes, America consumes few grape products. In terms of acreage, raisin grapes (mainly for export) have dominated until recently; per capita consumption is but .11 oz, vs. 40 pounds for Turkey, a country of 60 million people and nearly 2 million acres. Per capita wine consumption is 2 gallons vs. 19 gallons for Italy, a country of 2.6 million acres and 55 million people. Table grapes (mainly for domestic consumption) is but 1.5 lbs, vs. 95 pounds for Turkey.

2. The American character, according to Vance Packard (a noted author of the "American scene," is not conducive to wine consumption. According to Packard, America is a nation of "strangers, exhibiting a continual historical pattern of internal migration, very responsive to advertising, and extremely wasteful."

3. According to the Baxevanis geographical hypothesis, America, as the wealthiest country in the world, has low per capita rates of wine consumption because:

(a) America is a new country: the lack of castles, medieval monasteries, and ancient place names do not produce the "European ambience" necessary to draw attention, legitimize the *raison d'etre* of a rural aristocracy, and induce national authority to categorize wine a "food." Americans are preoccupied with foreign names, places, accents, etc., and also feel inadequate in matters of "culture," and, as a consequence, defer these matters to European "experts." In point of fact, few people realize that America produces both better *vin ordinaire*, and outperforms, in terms of consistency, the finest wines of France.

(b) America is a distinct and unique political unit: highly diverse in terms of history, political divisions, and qualifications for public office. In this respect, America is not the usual "ethnic state," state boundaries are entirely artificial (we first created political boundaries and then arranged for human settlements to take place); and we lack standardization of everything except our measuring system (America is a nation of 51 governments with a similar number of legal and thousands of educational systems).

(c) Dionysian vs. Apollonian American cultural characteristics. We are a nation of extremes not moderation; we are a nation lacking consensus; it has been said that the only constant in America is change.

(d) Since 1776, the agricultural population has declined from 97.5 percent to less than 1.5 percent, a rate of decline unequaled anywhere. Contrary to popular opinion, the American population has imploded not diffused over the past two centuries, and by the end of this century more than 85 percent of the nation's population will be residing in megalopoli and ecumenopoli. Unlike European wine producing nations, the non-urban population did not consume wine, and, as a result, was unable to transfer a wine tradition to urban areas. It is interesting to note that Americans are the most mobile population on earth. During the period 1955-1980, one-fifth of Americans had changed their residence annually, with the average citizen moving about 14 times in the course of a lifetime, a sharp contrast to the Japanese who move just twice.

(e) America's food habits. Anthropologists insist that people's food habits change very slowly, yet if our Colonial ancestors spent a day eating with us, they would be wide-eyed and shocked. Without question, the American diet is very different from the traditional diet common in 1600, 1700, 1800, and 1900. In many ways, it is better and in as many ways, worse. The present diet includes many traditional foods such as milk, honey, and potatoes, but it also includes enormous quantities of soft drinks, frozen foods, fast processed foods, and many other foods of the industrial, mass food processing age. Unfortunately, few of these foods compliment the intake of wine. Factors that contributed to our nation's dramatic, unprecedented dietary changes are:

*The new technologies of freezing, dehydration, flavor enhancement, food additives, meat and vegetable bullion, and flavor extracts have had an inverse impact on wine consumption.

*Federal food programs, both food stamps and subsidized school lunches have reduced quality food intake. The youth of America has been conditioned to indulge in snack foods, most commonly those that are overly salty or sweet, and invariably heightened by intense, artificial flavors and exotic textures.

*In more than 70 percent of households, mothers hold a full-time job, and, hence there is a tendency to serve dinner from packaged convenience foods. Given the fact that families are smaller with the absence of grandparents in the same house, the dilution of traditional meal preparation has accelerated.

*The rise of fast foods and restaurant sales. Restaurant meals are increasing at a rate greater than 2 percent annually. Two of three meals are consumed away from home each day, and a similar number do not take longer than 30 minutes. Today's families eat in "shifts" with the television in the "on" position, with little conversation, and not in a leisurely manner discussing daily family affairs.

*An urban population consumes less food and certainly less fat and other "energy" foods. This tends to depress wine sales, along with other alcoholic beverages. Most important is the disturbing pattern of a decrease in complex carbohydrates and an increase in sweetener consumption. The former has been reduced by half over the past fifteen years, and the latter supplies more than 20 percent of all calories, double the 1960 figure. Perhaps the most disturbing elements of our contemporary diet is the poor quality of our bread, the exploding consumption of soft drinks, and the near absence of water on the dinner table. Due to the high intake of acid-rich foods and drinks, America spends nearly $3 billion in antacid medications.

*Contrary to popular notions, wine is not a major part of America's "cultural baggage," and, as a result, it is not the subject of history and education, and commanding no respect. Very puzzling as most Christian churches have never placed wine on the long list of "taboos."

What of the Future?

The case for optimism is fairly simple: wine consumption varies for many reasons, of which acculturation, tradition, religion, diet, and disposable income are among the most important. As these elements grow and become more stable, consumption both in absolute and per capita amounts will grow.

1. The US is among the lowest per capita wine consuming nations (two-thirds of the American adult population consumes less than .3 gallons of wine annually), and, as a consequence, consumption has nowhere to go but up. The fact that wine comprises less than 1% of the beverage total consumed in America is another hopeful sign of future expectation. In addition, the average American consumed 1.2 gallons of absolute alcohol in 1990 (five times less than 200 years ago), but four gallons less than France. America has more total abstainers of wine than any major European wine producing country. The annual expenditure of about $60 a year on wine represents a pitifully low percentage of total income, and significantly less than that expended on soft drinks, beer, distilled spirits, and coffee. Given the fact that 5% of the American population is responsible for more than 75% of all wine sales implies that there is an enormous potential for the rest of the population to increase their consumption of wine.

2. The American wine and spirits market is one of the wealthiest in the world. With millions of consumers spending the smallest percentage of disposable income for food than any other country there is an enormous financial reservoir of latent purchasing power. In addition, the

protagonists for increased growth maintain that since 1955 disposable incomes have risen faster than per capita wine consumption: wine is less expensive today than two generations ago, a condition that provides an incredible growth potential.

3. The American diet will continue to improve, and as it does it will provide an excellent vehicle for increased wine consumption. Once wine is part of the evening meal, and understood and de-mystified, the upscale, snob image of the libation is eliminated. The fact that America is becoming more health conscious will, over the long run, help to increase wine sales.

4. Wine consumption will increase as the economy improves, the population of the 45-65 year old age group increases, states relax their regulation of alcohol sales, and industry marketing campaigns influence consumers to drink more wine. As proof, we are drinking more premium wines than ever before. This segment is increasing rapidly. Wine by the glass and wine bars are new to America, and there is no indication that this trend will not continue. Sparkling wine consumption is increasing. Hard-core wine drinkers are increasing their consumption. Urban, upper-income, educated individuals likewise. Chardonnay has become the standard for dry, white wine.

5. Wine tourism will become big business. Winery visitations are expected to increase from 10 million in 1991 to more than 25 in million 2005. Casual tours of winery facilities will increase wine knowledge and sales are expected to increase. As a consequence, the industry is beginning to focus on historic regions and American place names.

6. Along with fresh vegetables and fruit, wine is an "under-marketed" industry. Solid organizations and promotional budgets are insufficient to propel the industry to new heights. Given the fact that half of the world's advertising occurs in this country, it is strange to find such a small fraction of the industry so under advertised. The ad budget for the industry as a whole is less than 1% of total revenues. Most important, these comments do not necessarily relate to brand identification, but to regional wine names. New marketing strategies will be the key to persuading consumers to increase their consumption of wine. Given the fact that the American palate has improved dramatically over the past 20 years, this may not be a difficult project.

7. Two significant trends in American demographics that will have a profound effect on consumption patterns are the aging character and rising family incomes. As an economically maturing country, America's population has been radically altered over the past two generations. The most significant transformation has been the reduction of the youthful segment and a similar rise in the number classified as "aged." This cohort (over 65 years of age) increased from 12 million , or 8 percent of the total population, to 32 million in 1991, or 12 percent of the population. It is expected that by 2000, the number of Americans 65 and older will grow to 37 million. When the 35-64 year-old population, the so-called "middle aged," is added, it accounts for another 50 percent, responsible for more than 94 percent of all wine consumed. The second is higher disposable incomes augmented by the two-income family. The fact that 80 percent of all married women will be full-time workers by 2005 is expected to alter American lifestyles still further. This population cohort will be less "trendy," more "quality conscious," more sophisticated and selective, better informed, and more prone to be loyal to a specific "brand."

8. On-premise wine consumption will increase. The on-premise market for beverage alcohol sales in 1990 was $44.3 billion, up 70% from 1980. The on-premise business is big business broken down in the following manner--$44.3 billion: beer $21.5 (48.5%), wine 17.6 (39.7%), and spirits 5.2 (11.8%). For off-premise: $43.5 billion: beer $23.5 (54%), wine 12.6 (29%), and spirits 7.4 (17%). The above is in sharp contrast to the on-premise market for food sales (full service restaurants, bars-taverns, and lodging places) that was $134 billion, up 64% since 1980. Given the fact the combined total is $178 billion from 300,000 total on-premise licensees, and the low level of wine consumption in all, the possibility for market penetration is exceptional. Among the many untapped in-premise areas are sporting facilities, hotels, neighborhood pubs and taverns, and fast food outlets.

9. As more states legalize wine sales in food stores, wine consumption will increase. At present 27 states allow wine sales in food stores. In 13 other states all alcoholic beverages must be purchased from state-operated stores or specialty licensed package stores. In the remaining states there are various legal obstacles to buying wine with groceries. There is

an overwhelming amount of evidence that wine sales increase when sale of wine in food stores is permitted. For example, in 1970 per capita consumption of wine was only 0.4 gallons in Idaho. In 1971 the state permitted the sale of alcohol in food stores and by 1972 per capita consumption more than tripled to 1.38 gallons. Four other states have had similar experiences--Maine, Montana, Iowa, and West Virginia. Average per capita wine consumption in states where wine can be bought in food stores is 2.35 gallons per year, while in states with no wine sales in food stores the per capita consumption is 1.4 gallons. Those states with some legal obstacles to obtaining wine in food stores show a per capita average consumption of 1.7 gallons.

10. Wine education is the answer to declining consumption: it helps increase consumption; elitism is reduced, as well as intimidation of consumers in both retail establishments and restaurants. The wine market's future success depends upon removing the mystique surrounding that beverage and bringing it further into the mainstream of American beverage marketing. In addition, wine marketers will have to continue their product segmentation in response to today's new dynamic, and ever-changing consumer.

11. It seems that recent events are about to reverse long-standing American-European wine consumption patterns: (1) French wines will no longer dominate the fine wine market, and the premium French wine market share of the fine wine market segment will decline and not approach 1982-1984 levels; (2) the fine wine segment, long dominated by France, will now be shared with Italy, Spain, Portugal, Chile, South Africa, and Australia; (3) an ever increasing market share of the fine wine market will be absorbed by California, the northwest, New York, and the mid-Atlantic states; (4) increasingly, the language of fine wine will become more American, rather than European; (5) increasingly, wine standards will reflect American technological initiatives.

The voices of pessimism are equally impressive:

1. Because America has an abbreviated history, customs and traditions are not well established. Of all our major holidays, Sunday is the most common, New Years Eve, nearly universal, Thanksgiving, Labor Day, and the Fourth of July (the most secular and American), and Easter and Christmas the most religious. All lack a tradition of wine consumption except Christmas, the most complex, the rest being opportunities for outdoor grilling, football, and other outdoor activities.

2. Unlike other wine producing countries, wine in America is a fashion-sensitive commodity and viewed as belonging to a specific "life-style." Unless this attitude diminishes and is radically altered, wine consumption will not rise beyond modest levels. America will remain a nation of fads as no other nation responds to new situations more quickly. In America, consumer tastes change without warning or explanation. Recent history has shown that tastes changed from Portuguese roses, to Cold Duck, Sangria, apple wine, flavored wines, coolers, and White Zinfandel. Basic to the notion of the American ethos is the fact that people are fascinated by a specific trend: once established, people grasp it, exploit it, and eventually kill it. No one can predict the future, but fads there will be--if its not peach-flavored libations (the 1980s have been referred to as the decade of the peach) it will be something else. The post-World War II period has been characterized by the "flavor business," and there is reason to believe that, given the state of technology in extracting, intensifying, and preserving flavors, the tendency to constantly produce more "flavored" beverages will continue. "Food wine," a euphemism for wine that goes with food--a typical California innovation, was designed to attract attention to wines that are pleasant in taste (low acid/tannin/extract, with some residual sugar, the opposite of lean and tart wines) and aroma, not too high in alcohol, and a catchword for balance and consistency. Historically, the big red and white wines, clumsy, overly ripe and alcoholic that often overpowered even grilled steak, are now libations of bygone days. As America in the future becomes less homogeneous and more diverse, eventually becoming a truly pluralistic society, it will become increasingly difficult to accurately identify future fads.

Fashion in wine is nearly as long as viticultural history. The Crusaders retreating from the eastern Mediterranean brought the taste for rich, sweet wines, such as Malmsey, Commandaria, etc., back to western Europe. Sherry, for many centuries, was a favorite in England only to fall from grace in the 1890s, become popular after World War I, and again fall from grace in recent years. Anjou was more popular in the 17th and 18th centuries than in the 19th. Before the Franco-Prussian War (1870), Alsatian wines were very popular in Paris, but after the defeat of the French for the next 50 years they disappeared from the national French market, the wines being made differently for German consumption. Champagne, very popular during the Belle Epoch period and the 1920s, suffered a sharp decline in America after World War II, only to reappear in popularity in the mid-1970s. As incredible as it sounds, Scotch was little known in England in the 1880s, and, in fact, considered vulgar. Tanqueray and Jack Daniels Tennessee Sour Mash were unknown in the US until popularized by a well-known entertainer in the 1960s. Lambrusco was unknown in America until the mid-1960s. Sangria came and went quickly, and Boone's Farm apple wine even quicker. Today, we like our beverages very cold and carbonated.

> America is likely to remain a "faddist" country, and in this respect "milk wine" may get its turn in the spotlight. Professor Frank V. Kosikowski of Cornell University has found a way to eliminate a "whey lake," the chronic surpluses of cheese making in the dairy regions of America, by developing a technique that makes a brilliantly clear yellow, tart, and dry wine with a subdued aroma. It's versatility is illustrated by the fact that the wine, if baked at 150F for several weeks, develops into a rich "Sherry"-type libation with an amber color and a mellow bouquet. The professor also maintains that it can be distilled.

3. Pessimists have long felt that the so-called enormous wine drinking potential of America is a myth. How can a nation possibly bring itself to accommodate wine when it loves fast foods, ice-cold, semi-sweet beverages, and reacts to every conceivable fad that comes its way? Moreover, we don't have a tradition of lingering over our food, to engage in leisurely conversation, and even entertain formally. While wine consumption has certainly increased dramatically in the last 30 years, so have beer, soft drinks, pop wines, and junk food. In the final analysis, the pessimists maintain it is improbable to think that America, a beer-drinking-producing country, will ever completely accommodate wine into its daily habits. We live in an age of instant gratification, and, as such, wine consumption is not part of the *genre*.

4. While all agree of the need to increase the wine-consuming base, this base, the pessimists maintain, is not readily available. Wine was not, historically, offered as value, and this did not encourage consumption. While this myopic condition appears to be changing, the growth in per capita consumption will not exceed the population growth rate in the near future.

5. Wine advertising has exploited the innocence, ignorance, and naivete of the American consumer. The most critical abuse, and one requiring excessive legislation to correct, is the use of European names, foreign accents, and foreign architecture. Indeed, wine standards to the average American are uniquely "foreign" in matters of wine. Little is done to promote appellation names, and attract a population to these regions. Even less is the proper matching of regional wine with regional food.

6. Although wine is a national food with a long rich history, in the U.S. it is considered nothing more than ordinary alcohol, not allowed to be sold in food stores in many states, and tightly regulated by overlapping federal and state authorities. Moreover, the average American perceives, in order, fruit juice, whole milk, tap water, tea, coffee, and soft drinks to be superior to wine, an alcoholic beverage that is just marginally better than beer and distilled spirits. Interestingly, of the most common beverages, only wine is consumed at room temperature, and the most rapidly growing wine segments in the 1980s--coolers and white wine are consumed cold.

7. It is questionable whether changing food habits will accommodate wine as a daily beverage. It is highly unlikely that the combination of new technologies (such as freezing, dehydration, dried soup mixes, imitation eggs, etc.), government food programs, and the contemporary preoccupation with all sorts of health concerns will help increase wine consumption. Also troublesome is a decrease in the consumption of complex carbohydrates and the increase in artificial sweeteners. Moreover, while America remains a multi-ethnic nation with countless national restaurants, the palates of the average American have not become globalized. And although our diet has changed in recent years

(we eat 30% less beef than in 1960; half as much butter, one-third as much coffee, four times more frozen food, fifteen times more yogurt, and 25 percent more fish), women cook less, with half of all family meals taken away from home, mainly in fast food restaurants, a condition that hardly promotes wine consumption. The pessimists make a compelling case by citing the fact that among all developed countries, Americans spend more on antacids--nearly $3 billion, annually. Today we like our beverages very cold and to drink them with cigarettes, fast foods loaded with flavor enhancers, and to eat quickly, and, more often in a car.

8. Consumers are reducing their intake of alcoholic beverages including wine. In the 1980s the American consumer abandoned distilled beverages, and "brown" spirits in particular; beer declined slightly, but is currently resuming its historic upward momentum; and wine consumption patterns have declined annually since 1985. The pessimists maintain that while wine consumption may stabilize and even exceed mid-1980 historic levels, wine will never become a dominant element in the drinking habits of the average American for the following reasons: less than 20 percent of all wine consumers consider wine to be their preferred alcoholic beverage; less than 10 percent of all wine drinkers are interested in wine history and its social and economic background; on-premise wine-related educational and promotional literature is read by fewer than 5% of all wine consumers; more than 90% of all wine consumers feel intimidated by wine, especially in public; for the average American, wine and food are not directly related; and wine drinkers are reducing their total consumption of alcoholic beverages.

9. America is not a major wine drinking nation. In America in 1950, the most common food beverage was water, followed by milk, soft drinks, and beer. This changed slightly in 1975, and again in the late 1980s. After more than 200 years of statehood, America still lacks a tradition that would permit us to take for granted wine on the dinner table. In sharp contrast, most Europeans treat wine as a common, everyday beverage, and it is curious to note that in the primary wine producing regions of Mediterranean Europe, there are no wine writers, and little snobbishness. Many believe that psychologically, Americans are insecure about drinking wine, and hence their compulsive response to wine writers. France consumes 13 times, Portugal 12 times, Spain 10 times, Greece 5 times, West Germany 4 times, and even Uruguay consumes 4 times more wine than we do. Highly significant is the fact that while wine consumption in Europe is both a rural and urban beverage, in America, wine is essentially a function of urban and suburban existence.

10. The pessimists maintain that wine consumption will not continue to increase because of favorable demographics and increased disposable income. An ever increasing portion of the population is non-wine consuming, as are Asiatics, Hispanics, and blacks, these, the most common immigrants, are the largest growing segments of the population.

11. Where is the business heading? "No Business"--no calories, no alcohol, etc., contemporary features that the pessimists maintain are not good for the industry. Moreover, the pessimists maintain that the American market is cluttered by a large number of similar wines, and that this "sameness" is a mirror of contemporary America, a situation that promotes boredom.

National leadership has much to do with forming, conditioning, and creating a national economic, social and political ambience. Rutherford Hayes banned alcoholic drinks from the White House. Eisenhower enjoyed German wines, Nixon preferred Bordeaux, Ford drank distilled beverages as did Johnson, Carter disliked the latter but accepted light white wines. Reagan entered the Presidency with a California palate, and once installed in the White House quickly began to stock the nation's premier cellar.

---

12. The American wine industry will remain in flux in for the foreseeable future as changes in taste of type of wine occur frequently. Consumer demand is elastic with respect to price; disposable income is directly related to consumption; and demand for domestic wine is inversely related to rising prices of imported wines.

The author has concluded that the following trends in the American wine industry are compelling and worthy of consideration:

1. The trend to lightness in beer, wine, food, and whiskey, will abate and/or become less compulsive. While we have shifted from Guiness Stout, Bock Beer, and Bourbon to light distilled beverages, watered down beer, white wine, and Perrier water, this trend will diminish.

2. Refrigerated wine cartons will gain in popularity as every-day libations.

3. The luxury market for table, sparkling, and specialty wines will intensify. By 2000 the ultra-premium wine market will triple in size. Estate wineries will increase in number, their character divided by their respective markets: local and regional, and national/international.

4. While the number of small, boutique wineries will continue to increase in number, economies of scale will favor consolidation and expansion of the larger wineries, as the capital intensive element of winemaking favors the large producer. It must be emphasized that wine production requires technical knowledge, specialized equipment, large sums of capital, and vine acreage. In the future, not only will wineries "integrate" vertically, but horizontally as well. The contemporary scene exhibits both oligopsonistic and monopolistic tendencies. This does not imply that the number of players will decrease as more premium wineries will enter the industry. Estimated number of wineries by 2025 will be about 2,770, and average winery capacity is expected to triple over the next generation.

5. High quality French/Italian/German/Portuguese/and Spanish imports will continue to decline, partly due to a weak $US, and to the continued improvement in the quality of American wines.

6. Regional specialization will be emphasized and wineries will decrease their product line.

7. Wine education, already a big business, will become bigger in the coming years. Wine education programs will increase in number and intensify in content and degree of specialization. At present, one American in 100 feels "knowledgeable" about wine, a condition that will improve. Wine education will accelerate in intensity with more college continuing education courses, as well as private, associational, and industry seminars. There are more than 200,000 students in more than 1,000 colleges and universities in America enrolled in wine appreciation classes. Wine education not only helps increase consumption, but it promotes a more sober, responsible consumer who drinks wine essentially with meals.

8. The number of negociant concerns will increase and become a much more important element in the American wine industry.

9. The present day trend of dry white table wine elitism will diminish in both scope and intensity. Sweet wines will once again become popular and their share of total consumption will increase. Red table wines will return in favor, and by 2010, more red wine will be made and sold than white. Although certain geographic regions will remain primarily white wine specialists, the white wine revolution will decline in intensity in favor of red table wine.

10. State liquor monopolies will decline in number. A larger percentage of America will become "wet." Federal, state, and control state legislation will liberalize the availability of wine to the consumer. If gasoline, airlines and banking institutions have been deregulated, the wine business cannot be far behind. Also, interstate wine shipments will be commonplace in the decades ahead. A compromise on the loss of state taxes might be the use of a value added federal tax on all sales.

11. Wine advertising, historically conservative and prone to follow social and marketing trends, will emphasize "American" cultural features and not foreign, especially French and Italian. The emphasis will highlight educational, historical, nutritional, and health elements in a positive, responsible manner. Advertising expenditures for wine, about one-fifteenth of beer and distilled beverages, will increase. "Tomorrow's" wineries will be advertising more, be more innovative in the creation of new products and marketing, and be more stable through hands-on family ownership.

12. The "three tier" marketing system (producers/wholesalers/retailers) will be modified, as direct buying by retailers from producers and importers intensifies. Historically, this system has provided limited competition and guaranteed significant markups. As a consequent, "Direct selling" (already common in the Farm Wineries of eastern America) will become more common in the rest of the nation. Winemakers will be able to stay economically viable by making as few as 2,000 cases annually.

13. Vine acreage will increase in response to consumption demands. For each additional gallon increase per capita, 100,000 acres will have

to be planted.

14. America will establish standards and styles for special occasion, Sunday, and *vin ordinaire* wines, and foreign imports will not achieve their historic market share heights of the middle 1980s. American wine produced at reasonable prices will offer excellent value over imported wines in each category. Classical, fine, ultra-premium wines will grow rapidly in terms of percentage and gross output; their quality will increase; their price will increase; and acceptance by the rest of world will become an unequivocal fact establishing an important international position, equal or surpassing French wines in terms of quality consistency. As a consequence, American wine exports will continue to grow becoming a significant element in Canada, the United Kingdom, Germany, Scandinavia, and western Pacific rimland.

15. A significant "wine war" will take place between America and a new, unified European Economic Community.

16. The celebrity status of winemakers and winery owners will increase. An American President will one day, like Thomas Jefferson, own his own winery, and vacation there.

17. Americans are changing their attitudes toward beverages containing alcohol. Over the course of the next generation, distilled beverages, relative to wine will, continue to decline, beer will rise slightly to perhaps 35 gallons per capita, and wine will resume its upward momentum after the pause in the middle and late 1980s. After an erratic growth period in the first half of the century, America, since the early 1960s, has experienced 20 consecutive years of increased wine consumption. Grape growing, winemaking and increased wine consumption is not a passing fancy. Although America will continue to be a beer and soda-pop drinking nation, wine as a mealtime beverage will increase in importance for the middle class. The public's perception of wine in general, the winemaker and the wine salesman (historically looked upon with suspicion), is also changing. The future is optimistic as the number of wine-intelligent people is increasing, along with disposable income and an improved diet.

18. There will be radical changes in nomenclature. BATF is currently considering doing away with terms like "White Zinfandel," "White Pinot Noir," and "White Cabernet." The post-World War II period has been characterized as one in which wine names, wine types, etc., have proliferated beyond the grasp of the average American consumer. Sheer numbers have constipated the industry, and there will be a tendency to reduce the numbers in order to facilitate sales. Brand name recognition will be more important in the future. Standardization of grape varieties will also become more common. BATF is currently considering a name change in French Colombard to "Colombard." Gamay Beaujolais, Pinot Noir, and Napa Gamay are all under discussion for revision. Not only will there be a more careful screening process concerning varietal identification, but clonal selections will dominate the interest and planting programs of growers.

19. Airlines, that spend more than $1.6 billion on food and wine each year, will expand their budget. The present 1.1 million people who travel daily on American airlines will double over the next generation.

20. Organic wineries, currently a minor entity and a curiosity, will increase in number. As the alcoholic industry comes under attack, fertilizer/herbicide/pesticide-free wine may very well become something more than a fad.

21. Although some successful wineries are directed by a consortium of fathers, mothers, sons and daughters, the American wine scene has not been one of dedication and dynasty building. The future will be different, with a much larger percentage of the offspring electing to enter the wine-related profession. When "dynastic" elements create and perpetuate a historic/physical ambience, the small and middle-sized boutique winery has one distinct advantage not available to distilled spirits and beer manufacturers. While the latter have to sell their product three times (by the producer, distributor, and retailer), the winery can sell direct--a formidable advantage.

22. Most wine (by volume) will be sold in food stores by 2010. This has not led to mass drunkenness in Europe where it has been standard practice for centuries. Moreover, package store wine sales have not suffered by this healthful competition.

23. Although producers have largely stopped making them and distributors don't like to carry them, half bottles will become more popular. Although more expensive per ounce, they are reasonable values at restaurants, picnics, and with the smaller household more economical

as there is less waste.

24. Winery-owned vine acreage is increasing, as is the tendency for more "estate-produced" wine, both of which are good, positive elements. In Napa, for example, three-quarters of all acreage was independently owned, and now it is less than 30 percent.

25. Wine competitions will increase in frequency and number, and in the process confuse the American public even more than now. Confusion and distortion of results are inevitable consequences because not every winery enters each competition, and the judges, venue, and conditions of the tastings change.

26. The jug wine market will not disappear. As the American wine palate becomes more sophisticated it will demand good everyday drinking wine. The number of brands will decline and the quality will improve. While jug wines remain a major element in the market place, their share of all wines sold will decline to 35 percent.

27. The fast pace of foreign ownership of the American wine business will not diminish as American real estate costs are significantly lower than in France, Germany, and Italy. Foreign ownership of American wineries and vineyards will intensify if present exchange rates continue. Prime vineland costs more than $200,000 the acre in Japan, and more than $400,000 the acre in Bordeaux, Burgundy, the Mosel, and Rheingau. There will also be many more joint American-foreign ventures.

28. Vineyard preservation efforts such as those promulgated in the Livermore and Napa valleys will be extended to other regions such as eastern Long Island, Leelanau Peninsula, and Temecula.

29. Bottled Vinifera grape juice and Vinifera grape products (primarily Muscats) will become important. A good deal of the juice will be sold fresh and in the refrigerated section of the food market.

30. Regional, non-California wines will increase in appeal, as well as the number of wineries, vine acreage, and amount of wine produced. As more wine producing regions overcome local, regional and political obstacles, California's share of national production and consumption will decline by as much as 10 percent. The new areas of quality production are Washington, Oregon, Texas, isolated areas of the humid southeast, Virginia, Michigan, and eastern Long Island.

31. The number of wine writers will increase, and a code of ethics will evolve slowly promoting greater awareness as well as simplifying issues and topics. In the past, wine writers--too judgmental, serious, nearly always rating wines, and esoteric in their character, will become responsible disseminators of information, not just opinion. Given the low American per capita consumption of wine, America is inundated with wine writers. Unlike Europe, where people do not need writers to tell them what to drink, America is awash in a sea of opinionated wine writers. This press is quite influential, and will become more important in the coming years. As of this writing both the American Wine Society and the Society of Wine Educators conduct programs and certify vinicultural expertise.

32. The number of wine investors and collectors will multiply. Wine in part, especially among the small coterie of fine wines, is a blend of fashion and indulgence. The industry will continue to attract independently wealthy individuals. According to a recent survey, physicians, airline pilots, engineers, and industry executives account for more than 80 percent of the large, trendy, boutique wineries since 1975.

33. Wine will partially replace beer as a "snacking" beverage.

34. Financial assistance leading to the production of winter-hardy vines for the northeast and midwestern portions of the nation will intensify, as will genetically produced vines that will be disease and pest resistant. The process of plant breeding requires at least 25 years from start to finish, thus requiring determination, patience, and luck.

35. As grape storage technology improves, urban wineries in Seattle, Detroit, New York, Philadelphia, Chicago, San Diego, Los Angeles, and more will increase in number.

36. There will be a revival of American grape wines. Not only will they make a serious comeback in popularity, but Alden, Isabella, and Cynthiana will increase in acreage and become "cult" wines by 2010.

37. Auctions and wine as "collectible" objects will increase. While America lacks the European tradition and track record of a small number of wineries, as American boutique wineries get older, and thus establish a record for longevity and consistency, interest will certainly rise to new, unparalleled levels. In recent years, the level of appreciation of many California wines has been greater than Bordeaux first growths, a development that has not gone unnoticed in the international wine

market. Price escalation has prompted the proliferation of small, boutique wineries to concentrate their efforts in the production of even better wine. Wine auctions will intensify in number and frequency, and rival the London market. Wine accoutrement (cork screws, old empty bottles, labels, books, etc.) collecting will increase.

38. Group buying, futures buying, investment portfolios, and buying by telephone, mail order, and credit card will be major marketing strategies in the next century.

39. Fruit and berry wines will increase in production, becoming a major wine segment in the industry. While the media for the most part ignores fruit and berry wines as trivial pursuits, the technology has progressed to the point that fruity flavors and lower alcoholic levels are particularly appealing to the consumer.

CONSUMPTION BY TYPE OF WINE

The nomenclature of American wines is not standardized. Wine types for 149 years since independence until the promulgation of the Federal Alcohol Administration Act of 1925, and in association with the Treasury Department, defined four types of wines: varietal, generic, semi-generic, and non-generic. While there have been many subsequent modifications, governmental regulations mainly classify wines by alcohol content. Since World War II, the dominance of varietal and table wine consumption and production is the industry's major achievement. Dessert wines, once the dominant wine type in America for more than a generation, have experienced a downward course in total sales since 1960. Dessert wines represent a market share of 3 percent in 1991 (in 1976 it was 16%). Sales figures declined from 98 million gallons in 1950 to fewer than 19 million gallons in 1991. Interestingly, as American-produced dessert wine sales declined, imported dessert wines increased market share from 1% in 1960 to 4% in 1976, the latter, declining in half by 1991. Equally important is the fact that while domestic dessert wines are considered "inexpensive" wines, most imported dessert wines are thought to be "premium" products.

Table 4.6

SHARE OF MARKET TREND BY TYPE OF WINE

Type	1970	1975	1976	1977	1978	1980	1985	1991
Table	50	58	61	66	71	76	71	80
Dessert	28	18	16	14	12	10	8	3
Vermouth	4	3	3	2	2	2	1	1
Sparkling	8	6	6	6	6	5	5	7
Special Natural	10	15	14	11	9	7	15	9

Source: The Wine Institute

Over the past 30 years, consumer tastes have changed. Research has confirmed the fact that the consumer wants a lighter, mellower, more supple wine, not one that is high in alcohol, nor astringent, but one that should exhibit high quality, and be relatively full-bodied. Consumers wish to imbibe something that is easy to sip, to enjoy, and fill the void for "a cut above pop wines," elements that helped popularize the white wine and "blush" revolution in recent times. Between 1970 and 1991, white

wine rose from 25 percent of total consumption to 64 percent. In 1967 more dry wine was sold than sweet for the first time in a generation, and in 1976, more dry white wine was sold than red.

Figure 4.5

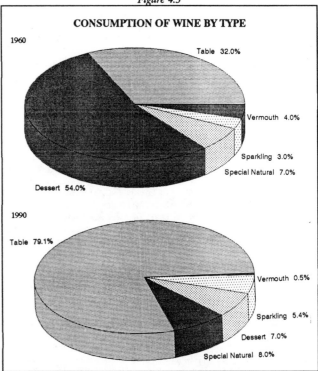

For most of the enological history of the wine drinking world, red wines were more popular than whites due to their suitability with hearty meals at a time when agriculture and hard physical labor dominated employment. Since World War II, white wines have increased thirty-four times, mainly as a result of: changing lifestyles, a drastic reduction in agricultural employment, a rise in tertiary economic activities, central air conditioning, a major shift in our dietary habits from heavy red meat diets to lighter (white meat, fish, and vegetable-dominated) meals, and a preference for lighter-bodied wines. As a result, America has become a white wine drinking country with shipments of red wine declining every year since 1974 despite a slight reversal in 1988-1991. In California the ratio of four white to one red is a much changed position over the course of the past three generations as red wine outnumbered white wine by a similar margin just prior to Prohibition. In 1970, almost half the wine produced was red while the balance was evenly divided between white and rose. By 1984, red wines shrunk to 15 percent while rose stood at 18 percent, and white soared to 67 percent. During this period, while California wine production tripled, red wines actually fell as percent of total output. Reflecting this change, 60 percent of imports are now white instead of the more traditional red table wine.

This recent trend in the popularity of white wine has occurred for several significant reasons: it is significantly cheaper to make; it is more palatable to the beginner; it is usually less expensive; it is the most popular color for women (nine to one); it is consumed chilled; it is lighter than red wine and, hence, versatile with light foods and diets (the thirty-four-fold increase in white since 1960 has occurred as chicken and fish consumption also rose, and the demand of red meat declined); and it is the logical alternative for the consumer who views spirits as heavy and dangerous, and beer filling and weight inducing. While a good deal of white wine is varietal, the overwhelming amount is sold as generic, cooler, and/or white Zinfandel/blush. In general, when white table wine is classified as everyday, Sunday and premium, it exhibits profound variation. The first is bland, low in acid, flavor and scent, and prominent in residual sugar; the Sunday wine is considerably better, contains less residual sugar, is better balanced, more flavorful, and usually offers excellent value. Premium wines offer a wide spectrum of price, flavor/scent, complexity, and value. The very best will be dry, but in recent years, the insidious habit of leaving high sugar levels in the finished wine at the higher end of the price spectrum has hurt the industry.

Although white wine overpowers wine sales and dominates the less expensive portion of market share, the consumer is willing to pay more for red wines. Many experts, therefore, are of the opinion that the white wine dominance is assured to be short-lived because as the American becomes more European in his eating patterns, he will integrate red wine with dinner and not emphasize white. Red wine exhibits the same quality variation, except that there appears to be greater value afforded in the Sunday and Premium price levels than white wine equivalents. With only one exception, red wines dominate the highest price ranges in the premium category and for good reason: they generate the notoriety for longevity and complexity when compared with the finest white wines. Throughout the decade of the 1980s, the tendency was for red wine to be lighter in body and alcohol, to be less astringent on the palate, and to contain less tannin. This trend, the author believes, will diminish in the future. In the final analysis, there are many compelling reasons why red wine will increase in the future: it is the principal and most satisfying food wine with the meat course; beef sales after a prolonged slump are expected to increase in the coming decades; per capita consumption of red wine bottomed in 1988; and as the population grows older it will drink more red wine.

Blush Wines, a recent fad referring to light colored red wines, are also called rose, Blanc de Noir, pink, Oeil de Perdrix, and "white" as in White Zinfandel. Although theoretically they can be made out of any red grape, the most common from California is Zinfandel followed by Grenache and Cabernet Sauvignon. In the strictest definition, blush wines are generic with no statement of varietal content. When the grape variety is stated, it must conform to the 75% minimum regulation. Nationwide, more than 900 producers in 1991 made "Blush" wine, a type that the industry refers to a "blush rush," a very important development at a time when many segments of the wine industry experienced little or no growth.

The increase of the "blush" market has been phenomenal. From 2 million cases in 1984, to 5 million in 1985, to 30 million in 1991. Generally, they are lighter in color than conventional rose's, slightly sweet, fruity, do not receive wood aging, and a good number are fresh and lively, thus very appealing and very drinkable to the average consumer. In addition, they are more versatile, and are consumed with or without food; have a very appealing color and are inexpensive; appeal to all ages, racial and ethnic groups; they taste well chilled; are the beneficiaries of a national health campaign for lighter, alcoholic beverages. One of the major reasons for their recent success, particularly since 1975, has been the apparent improvement in quality--at levels equal to white and red wines. As a result, the varietal blush market has mushroomed from near zero to more than half the California, and one-third the eastern market. The blush market share in 1971 was 26 percent, dropped to 16 percent in 1981, and has since increased to 20 percent in 1990. In 1985, 2 million cases were sold by California wineries, a figure that has since risen to more than 11 million cases for the entire state. It is usually made in two styles--a less expensive range with residual sugar, and a more full bodied wine with good acidity and a bit of tannin. Other imitators such as Barbera, Cabernet Sauvignon, Pinot Noir, and Merlot have made an appearance but have not captivated the market place. Today, there may be as many as 250 White Zinfandel wines on the market. Due to recent price escalations, producers are reducing the Zinfandel content and substituting other white and red grapes, of which Grenache Noir, Chenin Blanc, Riesling, Colombard, and Muscat, are most common.

Behind an ever growing enthusiasm for "varietal nomenclature," is the belief that the name of the grape on the label will assure quality. Americans had exhibited a passion for this at least since 1965. Simply put, whenever a certain grape variety meets minimum qualifications, the name of the wine on the label is nothing but a testament of the type of grape the wine was made from, and nothing else. While unique to America, the habit is rarely used in Europe (Alsace is a major exception), where the identifying name on the label is geographic. It is estimated that for the nation as a whole, varietal wines constitute a market that exceeds 45 million cases, worth more than $3 billion. More significantly, it is a market segment that is growing rapidly in an overall sluggish wine market. Interestingly, California varietals account for more than 40 percent of all wine sold in America, up from 20 percent in 1987.

In 1986 California varietals outsold imports for the first time in that state's history. For 1987, the following were the most popular produced California varietals collectively outselling all jug generic wines in American history for the first time: Zinfandel (8 million cases, by far the most popular, most of it sold as White Zinfandel), Chardonnay (6 million cases), Cabernet Sauvignon (more than 4 million cases), Chenin Blanc, Sauvignon Blanc, Riesling, Pinot Noir, and Merlot. White Zinfandel represents 28 percent of all sales, and is second in dollar sales; Chardonnay, ranking second in production, is the most profitable varietal in dollar sales. Among red varietals, Cabernet Sauvignon led the list with 60 percent of total red wine varietal sales. Of interest is the dominance of Vinifera varietals from California, and the poor showing of American and French-American varietals. For the nation, share of varietal sales for 1991 is shown below.

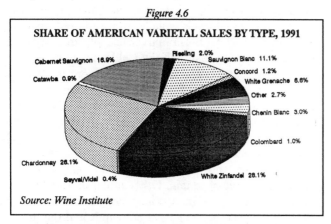

Figure 4.6

SHARE OF AMERICAN VARIETAL SALES BY TYPE, 1991

Cabernet Sauvignon 16.9%
Catawba 0.9%
Chardonnay 28.1%
Seyval/Vidal 0.4%
Riesling 2.0%
Sauvignon Blanc 11.1%
Concord 1.2%
White Grenache 6.6%
Other 2.7%
Chenin Blanc 3.0%
Colombard 1.0%
White Zinfandel 28.1%

Source: Wine Institute

Low Alcohol and No-Alcohol Wines are a recent innovation by the industry. Over the past generation America has produced a decisive trend for lighter alcoholic beverages be they distilled, fermented or malted, a movement also in step with lighter food. The beer industry was the first to capitalize on the trend toward lightness, but soon after all beverages have produced "light" versions in terms of calories, the latter translated into lower alcohol content. When "light," or "lite" is used to indicate reduced calories, calories per 100 ml must be stated on the label.

Soft, light, or low alcohol wines (7% alcohol content), said to have been made first by the San Martin Winery in 1975, became a fashion, but after an initial burst of enthusiasm, low alcohol wines never performed to industry expectations, and thus are considered a short-lived factor in America's drinking habits. The principle behind this initial burst of enthusiasm was that low alcohol wine emphasized fruit and fragrance, especially from such cool growing delicate and aromatic grapes like Chenin Blanc, Riesling, and Gewurztraminer. Low alcohol also makes them more accessible to the market place, thus reducing costs. "Soft" wines, often slightly carbonated, differ marginally from "light" wines because of their lower alcohol content, extra sweetness, and fruitier flavor. Some light wines are now called diet wines with advertisements mentioning the fact that they contain 50% fewer calories and 70% less alcohol than regular wine. For a short time these wines competed with Labrusca for the same audience, but as yet their time has not arrived to make a significant impact. Meanwhile, 22 percent of beer and 19 percent of the soft drink market is "light," in sympathy with light yogurt, salad dressing, bread, milk, cheese, sour cream, etc.

Light wines as a category rose quickly in popularity when they were first introduced, but because they failed to capture the consumer palate, declined rapidly to insignificance within ten years. This whole category of wines peaked at 3.4 million cases, or 2 percent of the market in 1982, but has steadily declined to fewer than 400,000 cases today. One of the major reasons for the demise of this category of wine has been industry's inability to differentiate between the "pop," low-priced, and premium labels, thus confusing the consumer. Another is the legal battle over the definition of "light" wine as one with reduced caloric content, lower alcohol, and light taste. Another factor is that no industry standard developed in terms of production (light wines were made by arrested fermentation, removal of alcohol, and blending high alcohol with low alcohol wines), hence the resulting product varied widely with producer. The fact the east coast and midwest, with their abbreviated growing seasons, did not endeavor to capture a good share of this market remains a mystery.

Along with coolers and low alcohol table wines, there is a new type of wine that may become a major factor in the wine business, and even a whole new generation of wines: "de-alcoholized," "non-alcoholic," "alcohol--free," or "ethanol-free" wine, made by a reverse osmosis (or cryo-extraction), a process whereby water, alcohol, acetaldehyde, and other elements are separated, enabling the winemaker to adjust alcohol and sugar, and concentrate flavor and aroma components. This process is capable of separating out of wine all molecules with a molecular weight of 200. The process holds particular promise for "eastern" wines not only because fragrance, sugar and flavor are enhanced, but 17-18 Brix grapes are equivalent to 22 Brix grapes.

First introduced by J. Lohr Winery and Ariel Vineyards, initial attempts at producing a no-alcohol wine (less than .5 percent alcohol) meant sales of about 300 cases in 1986. After winning a gold medal in a field of standard alcoholic wines, sales began to soar rapidly to more than 400,000 cases by 1990. Although they are called de-alcoholized, federal regulations allow no more than one half of one percent alcohol in sharp contrast to the usual 11 to 14 percent alcohol content of normal table wine. What makes this type of wine distinctive is the fact that the beverage looks, smells and tastes like real wine--with only traces of alcohol. This market segment, led by Ariel Vineyards, is growing by more than 7% annually, and if it continues to grow at these rates it will certainly become a major wine market segment. Because one-fifth of the west European wine market is composed of non-alcoholic wines, the potential for America is sizeable, once, and if, the product proves popular.

Coolers, nothing more than a blend of wine (usually white wine, citric acid, carbonated water, fruit juices, and/or flavorings), created a new beverage category in the 1980s. Their alcoholic content is 6 percent or half the amount of normal table wine. Beginning with just one brand--California Cooler in 1980, there were more than 100 brands on the market in 1987. The growth of this pioneering company has been anything short of phenomenal, rising from 700 cases in 1981 to more than 13.3 million cases in 1985, with retail sales of $334 million, or 5 percent of all wine sales. The company grew so rapidly, it ranked as the fourth largest winery in 1984 with about half of the nation's cooler market. For the market segment as a whole, production grew to 42 million cases in 1985, only to peak at 70 million cases in 1986, or 20 percent of total wine consumption in America. By 1991, cooler production declined to about 37 million cases, and the market has consolidated significantly. Between 1987 and 1991, more than 100 labels have been discontinued, California Cooler lost three-quarters of its market share, and Bartles & Jaymes and Seagrams now control more than 80 percent of the market. Coolers today are part of a national trend toward lighter alcohol beverages, offer a new option at sport arenas, and a refreshing alternative in country clubs, race tracks, museums, and airport bars. It is important to note that coolers adversely affected the beer and soda pop market as no wine in America's history, not to mention the fact that it is the only wine that can be directly consumed from the bottle. While it appears that the geographic market penetration is complete, there are still endless opportunities that need to be exploited.

Because coolers are consumed at bars and social gatherings and not at the dinner table, it is assumed that it will be a passing fancy. Nevertheless, while sales are declining in America, the trend seems to have caught on in Europe where growth has expanded from fewer than 2 million cases in 1984 to more than 28 million cases in 1988. Although there are many who maintain that coolers are merely a fad and will disappear like Cold Duck, there are others who take an opposing view. Citing brand loyalty, strength in the 21-35 year-old market, and that more

than 55 percent of all consumers are women, experts are of the opinion that this market segment will continue, but at significantly lower consumption levels.

Jug/Generic Wines, long the staple product of California wineries, have recently experienced declines. Throughout the 1960s and 1970s, 80 percent of the wine boom was "jug wines/generic" libations packaged in large bottles and labeled after famous European wine producing districts, such as Burgundy, Rhine, Chianti, etc., or what the Italians call *"vino da tavola,"* and the French, *"vin ordinaire."* Convenient in size and inexpensive in price, the "wine boom" was fueled by the daily, monthly, and yearly increases in output, largely from the Central Valley of California. In addition to the obvious advantage of low price, these wines bequeath clean, simple flavors, often with considerable sugar, and are made to appeal to the widest audience. Jug wines, since 1984, have experienced declining sales and are not expected to reach their 1970s high in market dominance. A combination of a bad image that cheap is bad, generic names are no longer "in," and the fact that "jugs" appeal to "ethnics" and people who eat hot dogs and drink beer straight from the can while watching football has hurt sales in an era of varietal wine consumption by an upscale wine consumer. The fact remains that quality has improved markedly and jug wines, and California jug wines in particular, offer exceptional value over imported "plonk" at $15 the bottle. In the final analysis, jug wine is "affordable quality." The fact that imported jug wines sell as well as they do constitutes one of the more perplexing elements of the contemporary American market most often defined and least understood by Madison Avenue.

Historically, this segment of the wine market was, and still is, dominated by large firms, but ever since profit margins and sales began to decline in the late 1970s, many firms have sold their operations to others. In addition, over the past ten years the size of the jug has been reduced from the gallon to the 1.5 liter bottle, the latter now accounting for 40 percent of the "jug" market. In nearly all instances, quality has improved, and in some cases the screw closure has been replaced by a cork to upgrade the image. The tendency of many firms is to change their image by using varietal designations and adding appellation names. More than 44 percent of the 200 million-case jug market is dominated by Gallo, followed by Almaden, Inglenook, Canandaigua, Paul Masson, and Taylor California Cellars. For the entire decade of the 1980s, jug wines are estimated to have declined by 21 percent, a trend that is expected to continue. This market segment is also highly concentrated in the hands of large Central Valley producers, with Gallo commanding a 44 percent market share, and supplying more than 60 percent of all restaurant wine.

Over the past 20 years, California winemakers have

come to realize that not only can they make good to outstanding premium table wine, but excellent jug wines. While the premium varietal wines emanate from the cooler coastal counties, the Central Valley with its admirable climate and productive soils is able to produce huge quantities of first-rate everyday table wines--like no other region in the world. If a jug is defined as an everyday, inexpensive wine of good quality that one can pour, drink, and enjoy with every meal day after day, than California meets these specifications ably.

Interestingly, *Impact*, a trade publication, reported in 1985 that of the 20 largest selling brands in the United States ten were jug wines, five were coolers, two were specialty wines, one was a sparkling libation, one was a line of dessert wines, and only one (ranked last in cases sold) was a line of varietal wines. Seven of the 20 brands were produced by the world's largest privately-owned winery--Gallo. While varietal jug wines sell better than generics, the latter offers excellent relative value. While premium varietal and proprietary wines are more "visible" and dominate the image of the industry, most people drink "jug" wines with their meals. Over the past 20 years, however, the percentage of jug wines relative to "other" has declined by half.

Fortified Wines consist of a bewildering number such as Porto, Sherry, Madeira, Angelica, Marsala, Malaga, etc., and a host of "flavored" wines that contain between 14 and 24 percent alcohol. While they transcend the complete spectrum in terms of sweetness, the majority are sweet, and made in a large number of bewildering styles. The three most important "serious" fortified wines are Porto, Sherry, and Madeira, all three of which are named after specific appellations in Portugal and Spain. It should be emphasized that American fortified wines, with rare exceptions, have little if any resemblance to European equivalents. In practically all instances, climate, soil, grape varieties, and winemaking techniques all vary to the same remarkable degree as wine styles, and while there may be a flavor and olfactory resemblance, the wines are rarely similar. This does not mean that American versions are inferior, just different, and, in many instances, superior to the European counterparts. However, there are fundamental differences between west coast and eastern fortified wines, the former from Vinifera grapes, and the latter from American and French-American varieties.

Historically, sweet, fortified wine had an extremely negative connotation in America as it was associated with alcoholism. In addition to the poor image, fortified sweet wines fell out of favor after the middle 1950s as the consumer preference changed to "dry" table wines. While the pre-Prohibition period still maintained a small segment of American society with sweet wine traditions, half of total wine consumption was represented by inexpensive fortified wines. After Prohibition, these inexpensive fortified wines became the least expensive alcoholic beverage, and constituted three quarters of total wine consumption in America. Muscatel, the most notorious fortified wine at the time, was considered the wine of "winos," the libation that would give the "cheapest drunk." Fortunately for the industry, little Muscatel has been made during the past ten years. Nevertheless, the negative image of sweet fortified wines continues as the preferred wine of winos, the aged, and the "masses."

The fortified sweet wine market, dominated by Porto, appears to be significantly larger than late harvest sweet wines. There is a strong element of incongruity in the small size of the contemporary fortified wine market given the fact of the nation's enormous consumption of sweet soft drinks, other sweet drinks, and the inertia of the pre-1970 sweet wine market. Until a generation ago, these wines constituted more than half of California's total output, and more than two-thirds of total American wine production. At the time of America's founding, Madeira and other sweet wines were the preferred alcoholic libations of Colonial America, a consumption pattern that lasted until the 1920s primarily in tidewater Virginia, the Carolinas, and Georgia.

Production grew from virtually nothing after Repeal to more than 120 million gallons in the mid-1950s, and then slowly declined to 55 million gallons in 1988. Of interest is the fact that in 1938, sweet fortified and unfortified wines accounted for 80 percent of the American market. California fortified wines rose from near zero at the end of Repeal to nearly 100 million gallons in the middle 1950s, only to fall dramatically to less than 30 million gallons by 1989, or less than 7 percent of the wine market. At present, the market has declined to historic low levels, and, as a such, it offers enormous opportunity for growth. Fortified wines are now described as entertainment wines because they are generally not accompanied by food. Fortified wines have had a highly recalcitrant history, and it appears that it will remain that way although new techniques in the enhancement of color, flavor and aroma have revolutionized this market segment.

The two most prized fortified wines are Porto and Sherry, both of which deserve mention. Porto is not only made from Zinfandel, but from Petite Sirah, Cabernet Sauvignon, and other red grapes. Authentic Portuguese varieties--Souzao, Alvarelhao, Tinta Madeira, etc. are now being planted, and, consequently, quality and quantity are expected to increase in the near future. Since the 1975 vintage, Portuguese Porto has become more popular and increasingly expensive (imports rose to more than 109,000 cases in 1986). This unexpected (Sherry in sharp contrast has experienced declining sales) interest has prompted an ever-increasing number of American producers to make Porto-type wines from a large number of grapes (from Concord to Zinfandel), including authentic Portuguese varieties.

Sherry in America has been an elusive quality and market conscious commodity. Lacking the necessary soils, Sherry making has lacked a dedicated following, and, unlike Europe, the range in styles is not based on flavor, but on color and degree of sweetness. The fact that "eastern" Sherries are based on Labrusca grapes has not helped the wine's image. There are three types of Sherries--*flor* (named after specific yeasts that develop on the surface of the wine flavoring it); baking (raising temperatures to impart flavor); and aging in wood without flor or baking to impart flavor. Although there are dramatic quality differences between all three, Sherry-type wines are surprisingly good and steadily improving. Unfortunately, this type of wine is currently out of favor, a surprising development given the fact that in 1953 more than 34 million gallons of Sherry-type wines were produced.

Among the other lesser known fortified wines, vermouth, both dry and sweet, has declined significantly over the past 20 years along with the Martini and Manhattan. Aleatico is rarely encountered or made at all. At one time it was called Red Muscatel, and also used to make a table wine of the same name. Tokay in no way resembles the authentic version from Hungary. Angelica, one of the historic wines of California (first made in the 1860s), was a classic *mistelle* (unfermented grape juice with added brandy), but with time it became an inexpensive sweet wine made from fermented grapes and marketed both as a fortified and unfortified wine. It was made from the Mission grape; its sweetness varied by producer; and in time the name became a generic name for an inexpensive sweet wine. Although the market has shown an interest in recent years, Angelica is made by fewer than ten producers. It is said to derive its name from the city of Los Angeles. Marsala, Malaga, and, to a lesser extent, Madeira have all become practically extinct.

Unfortified sweet and flavored wines are fashion-sensitive, and, as such, their names, production, and popularity have fluctuated widely in this century. These wines consist of a bewildering number and type, a good deal of which are non-grape in origin. Dessert wines go beyond Porto and Sherry, and more and more producers have shifted their attention to producing non-fortified sweet wines, usually late harvest Riesling, Gewurztraminer, Vignoles, and a variety of Muscats. Sangria, kosher, fruit, and specialty flavored wines have enjoyed a momentary period of heady sales, only to plateau, decline, and stabilize at much lower levels than their peak sale period. Moreover, there is a fundamental difference between a sweet wine, and one that is simply "late harvest" and/or botrytized. Most American sweet wines are the result of arrested fermentation, and/or addition of sugar, and as such are appreciably cheaper in price and inferior in quality to the finest from Europe. In recent years there has been a resurgence of quality sweet wines characterized by lightness and delicacy, and production is expected to increase. In the future, quality sweet wines by freezing grapes before pressing to enrich the must with sugar and fruit flavors will make this market segment much more important.

In both fortified and unfortified sweet wines, the sweet taste is due to the presence of glucose and fructose, alcohol and glycerol. Because all vary dramatically (fructose, for example, is much sweeter than glucose) by type of wine and producer, sensitivity to sweetness, smoothness, and overall flavor sensations are highly diverse. Late harvest wines, especially from California, also refer to red wines, particularly Zinfandel, as well as Chardonnay. Although most Americans maintain a "sweet tooth," there has been a slow acceptance of late harvest American wines. In 1969 Wente produced a *spatlese*, and in 1973 an *auslese*. In the same year, Freemark Abbey produced *Edelwein*.

Late harvest wines acquire their unctuous flavor and aroma by extended "hang time" on the vine, thus raising sugar levels to concentrations beyond 40 percent. If associated botrytis infection occurs, all the better. *Botrytis cinerea* (noble rot) generally attacks thinner skinned grapes and dehydrates them, reducing water and elevating sugar levels, thus producing exquisitely flavored and scented wine. Due to low yields and extra care, these wines are rarely inexpensive, and usually sold in half bottles. *Botrytis* is common everywhere in the northeast and midwest, but in California it is naturally limited to the coastal valleys and the Sierra Foothills. In the northwest, Washington has recently made a large number of late harvest wines that herald a bright future. Late harvest wines are generally heavier, fuller in body, and although they are often sweeter, excessive sweetness is not a general feature. Although white wines are the norm, red wines can be made in this fashion. Despite the fact the market for botrytized and late harvest wines is limited to dedicated aficionados, their popularity is expected to continue.

Among the more popular grape varieties for the production of unfortified sweet wines are Riesling, Gewurztraminer, Semillon/Sauvignon Blanc, and the highly neglected group of Muscat varieties, a good number of which have the ability to produce some of the most memorable and distinctive wines. Of the many varieties currently under cultivation, Orange Muscat, Muscat Blanc, and Muscat Hamburg show the most promise. While Labrusca grapes and Rotundifolia have long made sweet wines in eastern America, in recent years, Vignoles and Vidal Blanc have produced many stunning, highly successful libations.

In recent years sweet fruit and berry wines, principally from cooler areas in the nation (Oregon, Washington, Wisconsin, Minnesota, Michigan, and New England states), have expanded their production. Invariably made with considerable sugar, they are characterized by unique fruit and berry flavors (blueberry, raspberry, and cranberry are popular), and with enough acidity and comparatively low alcohol levels that output has become significant in recent years. These wines, in many instances, mirror the parochial patriotism of handcrafted wine and local history that is blossoming in every corner of the nation. It is estimated that there are 100 fruit and berry wineries in the nation, and more than 5,000 home winemakers flirting with the glories of local fruit and berry produce. Therefore, there is every indication that fruit and berry wine production will increase in the future.

Sparkling Wine was first made nearly 150 years ago in Ohio by Nicholas Longworth when he produced his sparkling Catawba in 1847 (more than 10,000 cases in 1850, a remarkable figure for the times). In California the first sparkling wine was made by Benjamin Wilson in 1855, in Missouri in 1957, and in the Finger Lakes region of New York in 1863. Agoston Haraszthy made sparkling wine in Sonoma in the late 1850s, and while his initial efforts proved unsuccessful, his son, Arpad, produced the first above-average Champagne method wine in the late 1870s. Called "Eclipse," the wine was made from Zinfandel, and caused a major sensation. Cook's Imperial, one of the most popular throughout the midwest and south, was produced in the 1860s in St. Louis. Whatever the history of sparkling wine production in America, its use, until recently, was mainly confined among connoisseurs who consumed it as an aperitif, at New Year's celebrations, and the ubiquitous wedding toast. Until recently consumption of both domestic and imported versions was pitifully low. Today, sparkling wine is produced by more than 186 wineries in 29 states, a dramatic increase from 75 producers in 1982. California, with 73 producers, leads the list, followed by New York (26), Washington (14), Ohio (11), Oregon (9), Michigan (9), Missouri (7), Pennsylvania (9), and New Jersey (5). Twenty-three other sparkling wine producers are scattered in 20 other states. Total American consumption of sparkling wines remained less than 2.4 million cases from 1934 to 1963, but with the growth of the wine boom consumption increased from 3.3 million cases in 1965 to nearly 18 million cases in 1988, thus making America one of the largest sparkling markets in the world. Imports, historically low, increased from 400,000 cases in 1975 to more than 5.6 million cases in 1988, capturing nearly 30 percent of the American market. However, the origin of imports, over the past 30 years has changed radically as French market share declined from 71 percent in 1960 to 17 percent in 1991. The importation of Spanish sparkling wine increased from nearly zero to 39 percent of imports for the same years.

For a generation after Repeal sparkling wine consumption exhibited only modest gains, but with the growth of Cold Duck in the 1960s and early 1970s sparkling wine has shown a sharp upturn (a fivefold increase during the period 1960-1971). A good portion of the growth of this category was imported sparkling wine (that exhibited double-digit growth during the period 1975-1985), and inexpensive domestic. As a category within the wine market spectrum, sparkling wines account for between 5 and 8 percent of all wine sales, or more than 40 million gallons. Less than 2 percent of all wine consumers purchase sparkling wine at a frequency greater than once a month, and except for special occasions few consume the product in the same manner as most other table or fortified wines. Interestingly, since 1970 premium sparkling wine had risen in volume from 515,000 cases to 3.8 million cases, while the mid-priced and low-priced sparkling wines increased their volume by 45 and 40 percent respectively. An interesting element in the production of domestic sparkling wine is the obvious advantage of the larger producers over the small, especially in the production of inexpensive wine. Due to high fixed costs, the only way that American producers can reduce costs is through the savings of economies of scale--an economic reality that favors the industry giants. Small producers, can only stay in business by producing quality sparkling wine and not competing with the largest firms in the production of large quantities of inexpensive Charmat process wines.

American sparkling wine, after decades of relative stability, grew rapidly in the 1980s, shedding its image of a "major event" wine. Champagne is no longer considered *the* symbol of elegance, and the "preferred" libation of festive occasions. The tendency today is to view sparkling wine as a beverage that goes with everything--not just elegant dinners with formal attire. As a consequence, production in America has increased significantly since 1975 because it is a logical extension of the white wine boom, as well as appealing to the image conscious consumer. It enjoys immense popularity for the large 35-60 age cohort segment of the population. Not only has it become popular, but it comes in all manner of style, price range, method of production, and dominant grape flavors. The southeast makes sparkling Rotundifolia, Ohio makes sparkling Catawba, Michigan Cold Duck, New York sparkling Concord and Riesling, and the midwest a bewildering array of American, French-America and Vinifera. The heavy, overly alcoholic versions of yesteryear have largely been abandoned, and character of the wines is less sour, softer on the palate, and consistently good. Alcohol varies between 10 to 14 percent, sweetness from nearly zero to 6 percent, and the color from near straw yellow to dark red. Although the tendency is for quality producers not to label sparkling wine "Champagne," the continuous use of the expression will hurt the industry over time, especially when Americans wish to export sparkling wines in markets that prohibit the name (as in Europe, Bermuda, and other areas in the Caribbean and Asia). The very best is made from Vinifera grapes, particularly Chardonnay, Pinot Noir (the two usually in combination), Pinot Meunier, Pinot Blanc, and Riesling; with Gewurztraminer, Chenin Blanc, and various Muscats (it is expected that sparkling Muscat wines, competing with Asti Spumante, will become more popular in the future). In the final analysis, sparkling wine complements contemporary lifestyles nicely: it is white (generally), is carbonated, consumed cold, and considered a fun beverage.

Sparkling wine is made by the following processes: *Champagne method* (capturing carbon dioxide in solution during a secondary fermentation by the addition of sugar and yeast in a bottle); the *transfer method* (the transfer of the wine from the bottle to a pressurized tank, and the wine filtered prior to bottling), *Charmat or bulk process* (secondary fermentation takes place in a tank rather than a bottle), and *simple carbonation* (or the artificial addition of carbon dioxide to still wine). The leading producers of the Charmat process are E & J Gallo, Guild, Canandaigua, Heublein, Weibel, The Wine Group, Sutter Home, Bronco, and the Christian Brothers. The main transfer process producers are Taylor (New York), Almaden, and Paul Masson, and the main Champagne method producers are Korbel, Domaine Chandon, Kornell, Piper Sonoma, Schramsberg, Chateau St. Jean, Wente, Mumm, Corbett Canyon, Gloria Ferrer, Mirassou, and Sebastiani. Of the 17 million cases of sparkling wine made in America, 13 million are made by the Charmat Process, 1.3 million are made by the transfer method, 3 million by the Champagne method, and only miniscule quantities as carbonated wine.

Table 4.7

U.S. SPARKLING WINES BY TYPE AND PERCENTAGE					
Type	1970	1975	1983	1985	1990
Charmat	72.4	75	76	77.1	73
Transfer	26.5	21	14	12.4	10
Champenoise	1.1	3	9	11.5	17
Source: Wine Institute					

Despite the production of sparkling Catawba by Longworth in Cincinnati in the first half of the nineteenth century, both its production and consumption are relatively new to America. Prior to 1900 consumption was less than 200,000 gallons, a figure that doubled by 1934, rose to nearly 1 million gallons by 1945, and to 1.5 million gallons by 1950. From this base level of under 2 million gallons, the consumption of sparkling wine rose quickly to 4 million gallons by 1960, 7.5 million gallons by 1965, and to 22 million gallons by 1970, a figure that remained static

until the 1980s when consumption again resumed its upward momentum reaching the all-time record of 47 million gallons in 1984. Since then, consumption and production has reflected the downward trend of the wine industry in general. Until the late 1960s, California and eastern states each produced 40% of market share (20% were imports), but since then, good, reliable Charmat processed sparkling wines began to dominate market share, reducing eastern sparkling wine production, and especially New York, to less than 9% of market share. It is important to note that during this historical period, significant structural elements in terms of geographic origin were at work. Before Prohibition, more than 50 percent of total consumption was composed of imported wine. After World War II, imports and domestic sources were relatively the same, with New York the largest producing state. As the wine boom accelerated during the 1960s, New York's share of the sparkling wine segment declined drastically with California producing more than 70 percent, and imports falling to just 10 percent of total consumption. Thanks to the success of the Charmat process, California inexpensively-priced sparkling wine gained in popularity until a strong $US enabled imports to capture more than 30 percent of the American market by 1984.

The price of sparkling wine is a function of process, quality of grapes, and handling; hence, the most expensive is made by the Champagne method, from Pinot Noir, Chardonnay, and Pinot Meunier grapes, and bottled after at least twelve months of *lees* aging. Medium-priced sparkling wines are commonly made by the transfer method, and made from the same grape varieties plus less expensive grapes such as Colombard, Chenin Blanc and Thompson Seedless. The least expensive are Charmat and carbonated wines, usually made from inexpensive grapes, and do not receive any lees aging. As a result, excellent, not just good or acceptable sparkling wine, will always be expensive due to the cost of expensive premium grapes and extensive care.

Although California versions are hardly identical to authentic wines, they are remarkably consistent and characterized by fruitiness and suppleness, and less tart, less dry, and softer on the palate. California sparkling wine rarely acquires the "yeasty/chalky" flavor of true "Champagne," and rarely is it as dry and "sour." While Champagne producers emphasize the importance of cuvee and the base wine used, California producers have yet to master the technique of preventing the dominance of varietal aroma and flavor, and the consistency of aged stocks used to form the foundation of the house blend. Consequently, clearly defined styles have yet to develop. Generally, American sparkling wines are made from sweeter and fruitier grapes than in Champagne (although eastern grapes are acidic). Major criticisms usually hinge on the lack of style and nomenclature (there is no standard definition for Brut, Extra Dry, etc.), excessive fruit (a condition brought about by the lack of chalky soil and overly ripe grapes), less yeast aging, fewer reserve blending stocks, and little or no brandy in the *dosage*. In addition, the critics maintain that not only are American sparkling wines fruitier, but that fruit is a primary consideration, and that subtlety, depth of flavor, and complexity are secondary elements. Recently, American quality levels have improved to the point that the finest American wines offer better value than imports.

California sparkling wine production has been in the forefront of major technological innovations that have steadily resulted in product improvement. Total output is impressive: 1.9 million gallons in 1960; 10.2 million gallons in 1965; 19.1 million gallons in 1979, and more than 40 million gallons in recent years. By origin, California supplies 70 percent of the American market, followed by Spain (9%), Italy (7%), France (6%), and New York (6%). Currently minor, but expanding states are Oregon, Washington, Michigan, and Ohio. While the bulk of domestic wines are made by the Charmat process, nearly three-quarters of the value of sparkling sales is dominated by Champagne method wines. Andre (Gallo), with more than 70 percent of total market share dominates the inexpensive sparkling wine segment, and Korbel is the giant among the Champagne method producers. Nationally, California supplies more than 94 percent of the under $5 segment, France, with more than 97 percent of market share, stands alone in sparkling wines priced above $30.

Besides the bulk producers of the Central Valley, quality sparkling wine production is overwhelmingly concentrated along the cooler coastal counties of California. Until the 1970s, "premium" producers were located in the Napa Valley, of which Schramsberg, Kornell, Beaulieu, and the Christian Brothers were the most notable. Within the past 20 years, Sonoma, especially the Russian River Valley and the Carneros region, has become the leading area in the production of the finest sparkling wines in the state. The leading houses are: Domaine Chandon, Iron Horse, St. Jean, Piper-Sonoma, Korbel, and Domaine Carneros. The trend here is to imitate classic Champagne by blending Pinot Noir with Chardonnay in order to produce expensive, refined, and often elegant Champagne method libations. Other emerging sparkling regions in California are the cooler areas of Monterey, Mendocino, Livermore, Santa Barbara, and Temecula. Recently, sparkling wine production has received a good dose of encouragement by serious foreign investment, especially French. Faced with an expanding market and limited vineyard areas in the three primary quality producing regions of Champagne, at least ten French Champagne concerns have started operations, of which Moet Chandon is the largest, followed by Mumm, Deutz, Piper, Roederer, Taittinger, Pommery, Michael Tribaut, a smattering of Japanese, Spanish, Swiss, and other lesser known interests. Today, this historically neglected industry has become "big business" and it appears that it will remain so in the immediate future.

To create awareness that their product merits increased acceptance with the world's finest sparkling wines, a small, but select group of California *methode champenoise* sparkling wine producers have formed the CM/CV Society ("Classic Methods/Classic Varieties"). Membership is limited to California sparkling wine producers using only the classic *methode champenoise* to produce wines from the classic grape varieties: Pinot Noir, Chardonnay, Pinot Blanc, and Pinot Meunier. The standards the members are to adhere to include: limitations of grape sources to the three coolest UC-Davis growing areas; specification of permitted production equipment, especially presses suited to the gentlest extraction of juice, without stemming or crushing the fruit; maximum yield of 160 gallons per ton (roughly equivalent to the volume of free-run juice per ton in top quality still wine production); minimum aging on the yeast (*en tirage*) of one year; definition of dosage parameters in terms of grams/liter of sugar so that consumers will know with confidence just what sweetness level is represented by the terms *Natural, Brut, Extra Dry, Sec,* and *Demi Sec*; guidelines for varietal composition of *Blanc de Blanc* and *Blanc de Noir* wines. Highly significant is the fact that members are discouraged to call their wines Champagne.

V
THE WINES OF EASTERN AMERICA

The scenograph of the New World was a strange place to the English settlers who landed in Jamestown to found the first permanent settlement in Colonial America. The Indian population, engaged mainly in hunting and gathering activities, produced no large sedentary settlements; surfaced roads were absent, as were domesticated animals, and practically all agricultural crops currently grown. Because European settlement in America occurred from east to west, grapes were cultivated and wine first made in the "east"--a section of the country that, for the sake of convenience, refers to all areas east of the Rocky Mountains and the non-desertic portions of Texas. With 65,000 acres of grapes and 465 wineries, eastern America has 7 percent of America's grape acreage, 30 percent of all wineries, and makes more than 25 million gallons of wine, or less than 7 percent of the national total. Within its boundaries are about half of the known species of grapes, and a greater variety of commercially grown grapes than any other area in the world.

Eastern America, in comparison with Washington, Oregon, and California, is an area characterized by distinct histories, disparate climates, and unusual grape varieties grown and wines made. This is the largest area in the world growing three types of wine grapes: American, French-American, and Vinifera. Indeed, between the Atlantic and Rocky Mountains more species of grapevine are grown than in the rest of the world. Called "Vinland" by the early Norsemen, native vines stretched everywhere along the coastal margins of maritime Canada to the Mexican border. What makes the region different from the west coast is the element of early European history, first attempts at making wine, a climate that discourages the cultivation of Vinifera grapes in most places, the dominance of native and French-American grapes, early hybridization efforts to produce an acceptable wine grape, and the character of wines made. Indeed, few plants inhabit such a wide variety of geographic topography and climate. Nowhere else in the world but in eastern America can one find blends of Merlot-DeChaunac, Chardonnay-Cayuga, Catawba-Magnolia, and Seyval-Cranberry, among other similarly strange combinations. There is no such thing as an "eastern" wine except to say that more than 85 percent are made from American grapes, 14 percent from French-American, and the remainder from Vinifera grapes. The overwhelming number are blended, proprietary, and white in color. While progress has been rapid in recent years, only a small fraction of eastern wine is considered premium by the marketplace.

One of the principal reasons for the failure to establish a sustained, premium, commercial wine industry in eastern America from the early Colonial period to the 1950s was the incorrect assumption that Vinifera grapes could grow in America because native American grapes flourished. However, the grape species that evolved on the two continents bordering the Atlantic, metamorphosed under quite different physical environments and thus produced different grapes and wines. Vinifera grapes, lacking resistance to American diseases, humidity, and low winter temperatures, did not become established in eastern America despite repeated attempts. The major reason was the inability to counter the ruinous effects of black rot, powdery and downy mildew, Pierce's Disease, phylloxera, and inappropriate cultural practices necessary to counter low and widely fluctuating winter temperatures. Once tried and disliked, native grapes were ignored and neglected until almost all hopes of establishing Vinifera grapes had failed. Once a more or less acceptable native grape was found, tried, and yielded to domestication, the winegrowing industry became vested. By the middle of nineteenth century Catawba and Concord wines became widely available, but with the emergence of California in the 1870s native grapes were once again disparaged, denounced as inferior, and denigrated to an insignificant position in the pantheon of quality wine grapes.

Today, despite the historic poor image of most wines, the eastern portion of the nation is an area of rapid and dramatic growth: in 1975 there were fewer than 100 wineries east of the Rockies, but today the figure exceeds 465. This recent growth is directly related to the various farm winery laws passed in nearly all states during the past three decades. Consequently, more than 90 percent of all wineries are cottage-type operations, small (less than 8,000-cases), family-owned, catering to a local and regional market, and overwhelmingly oriented to American, and French-American wine production. With few but notable exceptions, the owner and family members do nearly all the work as most wineries are undercapitalized with tight budgets and low profit margins.

While winemaking east of the Continental Divide, although widely distributed in nearly all states, is highly localized in a small number of areas, the historical pattern of viticulture based on Vinifera grapes was confined to a small and highly unstable region of what is now western Texas and portions of New Mexico. Native grape cultivation and wine production was highly localized in the Hudson River, the coastal areas of New England, the coastal and mountainous areas of the mid-Atlantic states, and isolated areas throughout the humid southeast and Gulf Coast region. With the successful crossing of the Appalachians and the march of civilization westward, the Finger Lakes of New York, the south shore of Lake Erie, the southeastern shore of Lake Michigan, the Ohio and the Missouri rivers became significant grape-growing and winemaking regions. During the first three centuries of effective American settlement, commercial grape production was introduced in practically every county in the country, but with little success. In the post-World War I period, northwest Arkansas and the Rosati region of Missouri became minor areas of grape production. Collectively, these regions are generally described as the "old producing areas" of eastern America. While French-American varietals have replaced a large segment of native grapes in the mid-Atlantic states, New York, and portions of the midwest, the geography of viticulture, with only minor exceptions, has not expanded significantly during the past 140 years. However, over the past 20 years the following have emerged as "new producing areas:" eastern Long Island, New York; southern New England; Hunterdon County, New Jersey; southeastern Pennsylvania; northern Virginia; central and eastern Tennessee; northern Georgia; central and northern Florida; the Leelanau Peninsula of Michigan; The Rio Grande area of New Mexico; and central and western Texas.

History

Early settlers throughout the eastern seaboard and later in the midwestern portion of the nation found a large profusion of indigenous vines, but to their dismay they were not the same as the Old World Vinifera. Although many were domesticated early and rather easily, their growing habits, fruit and winemaking character were totally different from what Europeans had been used to. It is estimated that over the past 400 years, more than 2,000 varieties have been described, nearly all of which have become extinct. Indeed, many an ampelographer has maintained that America is the largest fossil grape region in the world.

Parris Island, North Carolina represents the site of the first vineyard, and St. Augustine, Florida the site of the very first wine made along the Atlantic Coast. Since the quality of wine made was not altogether to the settlers gustatory delight, attempts at hybridizing native grapes and growing Vinifera vines began almost immediately. By 1616 settlers began to import Vinifera vines; John Winthrop, governor of the Massachusetts Bay Colony, tried growing Vinifera in 1630; William Penn was among the first to make the attempt; Lord Delaware imported Vinifera vines from France; the French Huguenot immigrants made countless efforts throughout the Atlantic seaboard; many a slaver ship brought vine cuttings from Portugal and the Madeira Islands; and Jean Dufour brought Vinifera cuttings to the Ohio Valley from his native Switzerland.

In all cases, the Vinifera vines suffered from a combination of factors mentioned previously and, as a consequence, those interested in making wine began to improve American vines by crossing them with other varieties both native and Vinifera, of which the Alexander, Catawba, Missouri Riesling, Concord, Delaware, Dutchess, Elvira, Herbemont, Niagara, and Steuben are important. But it was not until French-American vines were growing in large numbers in France during 1890-1930 that Philip Wagner, an amateur winemaker working for the Baltimore Sun, began to take an active interest in growing these vines as a solution to the "foxy" American vines, and the cold and humid climatic conditions of northeastern and midwestern America. These varieties over the past two generations have offered considerable advantages over native grapes, especially in the production of dry table wines. However, while white wines have proven to be particularly successful, red varietals are not able to compete with the finer Vinifera vines. The latter, successfully grown first by Konstantin Frank in the 1950s in the Finger Lakes region of New York, have since scattered in a widely diffused pattern throughout the country east of the Continental Divide.

> *What were the reasons for the relatively late development of the wine industry in America when it had long held an important position in Europe? One reason for the delay was the dominance of beer, rum, and whiskey as the preeminent alcoholic beverages.*

Dr. Konstantin Frank, a Russian-born German agriculturalist instrumental in establishing state-run Vinifera vineyards in the Ukraine, came to the United States and planted the first commercial plantings of Riesling and Chardonnay for Gold Seal along the hillsides overlooking Lake Keuka in 1953. In 1960 it was estimated that there were fewer than 150 Vinifera acres east of the Rocky Mountains, a figure that rose slightly to 200 acres in 1970, and to more than 6,000 acres in 1990. Still, for all eastern states, the dominant grapes are American varieties despite the fact that many French-American grapes have seriously eroded their historic dominance. For the mid-Atlantic states, French-American varieties have become the "bread and butter" grapes, and are increasingly becoming important in the midwest and portions of the humid south.

Despite continued viticultural and winemaking advances, prejudice against "eastern" wines, whether from native or French-American varietals, is not hard to find. From the very beginning, American history has been closely linked with European events. While European immigrants brought to America a widely divergent mix of languages, skills, and lifestyles, wine preferences were decidedly Vinifera, and they have remained so for nearly three hundred years. As a consequence, America seems to have always deferred to European standards, with many things American considered suspect, and native wines deemed unacceptable to wine aficionados. Another meaningful problem is California's ability to consistently produce low cost Vinifera wine. After the Civil War, California began to compete with wine producers east of the Rocky Mountains, and over the next generation there was such fierce competition that in 1894 the Pure Wine Law was passed legalizing the use of sugar in winemaking east of the Rockies. This apparent attempt to equalize wine-making costs between the two regions institutionalized the insidious habit of "amelioration."

> *Gallization and Petiotized Wines are two archaic expressions applied to "eastern wines." When sugar is low and acid high, it is best to dilute the must to lower acidity, and then add sugar to raise alcohol levels. This is called Gallization after Dr. Gall. Petiotized wines are made from pomace to which sugar is added and allowed to ferment. Excessive total acidity in the east is not subject to easy remedy. It is legally done by adding 35% water in order to dilute and reduce high acid levels. Sugar is also added to increase alcohol. Both "amelioration" methods reduce the strong "foxy" flavors and odors of Labrusca-based grapes.*

The most common method to reduce acidity (and to also correct for sugar deficiency) is by amelioration (the addition of dry sugar, liquid sugar, water, corn syrup, concentrate, etc.). Although federal regulations limit the level of amelioration so that the volume of the wine does not increase by more than 35 percent, or the total acidity not be lowered below .5 percent, the process often exceeds established limits because abuses are difficult to detect. Amelioration not only adjusts sugar deficiencies, it also mutes unpleasant "foxy" aroma and flavor, and stretches the yield per acre. Acidity is also reduced by: ion exchange, a process that adversely affects wine quality; calcium carbonate, a simple and reliable process, but one that usually affects acid balance by leaving high levels of malic acid and the maintenance of tartrate instability; and blending with low acid wine--very common, and usually in combination with the other, aforementioned processes. As a consequence, it is estimated that more than two-thirds of eastern wine is labeled "American," an obvious reference to low acid California wine used in amelioration.

The main beneficiaries of amelioration are Labrusca and Rotundofolia. In addition, Labrusca varieties, high in acid and low in sugar, have been subjected to "hot press-ing" (heat extraction or thermovinification), a well-established practice whereby grapes are heated to 140F-175F in order to extract color, flavor, and mute the foxy flavor and odor of American grapes that so many find objectionable. Labrusca grapes, particularly Concord, respond well and are the mainstay of the kosher and Labrusca-based fortified market in the east. Recently, excellent results have been achieved by carbonic maceration, a process that seems to produce fruity, light-bodied, eminently fresh wines, hitherto unheard of. Carbonic maceration is also of immense benefit to French-American varietals, particularly DeChaunac.

Therefore, it is not surprising to explain the relatively low position of eastern wines in the pantheon of wine quality. After Repeal, the small winemaker in the east, midwest, and south could not compete with inexpensive California wine, and was essentially driven out of business. Those that survived were inexpensive, fortified, or specialty wines. The consumer turned to Europe for fine wine, and California for a quick "alcohol fix" from sweet fortified wines and inexpensive Central Valley jug table wine. In addition, high taxes, burdensome license fees and bonds, lingering Prohibition (particularly in the south and border states), competition with distilled spirit interests (particularly in the midwest and border states like Kentucky and Tennessee) did much to ruin the industry.

A major problem with the "east" is the fact that it has failed to take advantage of consumer preferences since World War II. As table wines increased market share from 32 percent in 1960 to 75 percent by 1985, the eastern market continued to produce sweet wines, Cold Duck, Sparkling Burgundy, and flavored wines. As a consequence, market share fell from 22 percent to 12 percent, and has yet to recover to post-World War II high's. Until the recent introduction of Vinifera and a small number of quality French-American varietals, the only unique wines have been sweet Labrusca and Rotundifolia--wines that are decidedly out of favor with most consumers. These wines are generally not consumed outside the producing region, are limited to "specialty" markets, and, as such, are true American *vins de pays* libations, definitely not consumed by those with a "European taste." What is objectionable to the latter group is not the color or degree of sweetness, but their strong flavor and aroma, and their incompatibility with most foods. The above notwithstanding, fruit and color extraction technologies have recently improved to the point that the quality of both American and French-American flavor and aromatic wine components have benefited immensely. As a consequence, the adverse affects of oxidation have been minimized, and freshness and fruitiness brought to new heights.

The future lies in building large volumes of proprietary labels capable of competing with large, cost-efficient California producers on the one hand, and small, prestigious European and American wineries on the other. The task is not easy, but the recent popularity of quality Vinifera and French-American wines at competitive prices by Virginia, mid-Atlantic, and eastern Long Island wineries has seriously altered the buying strategies of the eastern consumer. The eastern winemaker is beginning to realize that in order to increase market share in a stable and growing market one must meet local demand, maintain quality, and offer value. After several centuries of dismal failure, a new crop of professional and dedicated wine-makers is meeting this challenge and taking advantage of lower real estate costs.

CHRONOLOGY OF EASTERN WINEMAKING

Circa 1000: Leif Erikson discovered wild grape vines along the northeastern American coast.

1492: Christopher Columbus discovers Hispanola.

1524: Giovanni da Verrazano, an Italian explorer, was the first to observe Rotundifolia grapes off the coast of North Carolina south to northern Florida.

1534: Jacques Cartier, a French explorer, observed native grapes in the St. Lawrence region, calling the area "Bacchus Island."

1564: first mention of winemaking from native grapes in the New World by Captain John Hawkins near St. Augustine, Florida by a group of French Huguenots. Historians give 1565 as an alternate date.

1568: Spanish settlement at Parris Island, South Carolina attempts to grow Vinifera and native grapes, America's first attempt at growing grapes under domesticated conditions.

1584: Amadas and Barlow, who visited Roanoke Island, North Carolina, reported a land "so full of grapes as the very beating and surge of the sea overflowed them.....In all the world the like abundance is not to be found." Sir Walter Raleigh establishes a colony on Roanoke Island, North Carolina. Scuppernong vines planted, one from the historic "Mother Vineyard" remains.

1600s: In their quest for economic diversification, the prevailing Mercantilist ideology encouraged the production of agricultural commodities in Colonial America that would supplement the English economy. The most important crops were tobacco, indigo, rice, silk, olives, and grapes. The Virginia Company, and later English Kings, preferred to encourage French emigration to both instruct the English, as well as establish their own private agricultural pursuits. There were two major periods of such French settlement: the era of the Virginia Company (1606-1624), and the period of French Huguenot emigration (1680-1732). Highly significant is the fact that America was and remains a net wine import nation from the earliest settlement to the present. Colonial use of wine occupied a minor consumption pattern. Throughout the 1660s the primary trading ports were Boston, New York, and Philadelphia, and the most popular imported wines were from the Canary and Madeira islands. During the 18th century to 1776, Colonial trade was largely confined to Virginia and the Carolinas, and despite the poor quality, a combination of English law, geographical location of the islands, and reciprocal trade made Madeira an important source of wine for the Atlantic colonies.

1600-1605: After 1600 three missions were established near Jemez Pueblo and one north of the present-day Santa Ana Pueblo in New Mexico. In 1605 a mission was built at San Felipe Pueblo and soon after another at Sandia Pueblo near Albuquerque, nearly all having a small mission vineyard for sacramental and local use.

1607-1620: First permanent English settlement in Jamestown, Virginia, and the site of the first significant wine making efforts in Anglo America. As the first vines failed, the Colony relied heavily upon Frenchmen to cultivate vines. However noble, all viticultural efforts failed after a varying length of time--from the mid-Atlantic states to coastal Georgia.

1616: Lord Delaware brings the first recorded Vinifera vines to the Atlantic coast, a development widely considered as representing the first commercial attempt at growing Vinifera grapes in Colonial America. In 1616 he wrote to the London Company suggesting that the northeast was ideal for viticulture. Despite the failure of his efforts, Colonial governors and English Kings encouraged emigration by offering favorable terms to all emigrants who could establish new industries. In 1619 the London Company sent several French "vine-dressers" and a collection of French grape varieties. The Virginia Assembly compelled every household to plant ten cuttings and to protect them from injury.

1619-1705: During the Stuart Era England encouraged viticulture in Colonial America (most notably during 1619-1622, 1628-1632, 1638-1639, 1642, 1662-1667, 1679-1690, and 1705), but with no memorable success. The accessibility of inexpensive imports, better economic returns from other crops, and the inability to grow Vinifera vines precluded successful viticulture. While viticultural efforts continued for the next 200 years, the zeal and excitement for wine production began to wane. With each passing year, viticultural efforts became secondary to the most important cash crop in the mid-Atlantic states--tobacco. As the cyclical tobacco prices proved disruptive to the economy, there were periodic interests in viticulture to diversify the mid-Atlantic economy, but these efforts were never sustained, and the attempts failed miserably. Vinifera vines were shipped and planted in Virginia in 1619.

1621: Wine served at the first Thanksgiving Day feast in Plymouth, Massachusetts is widely mentioned in folklore, but there is no historical evidence of local winemaking efforts.

1630: Vinifera grapes were planted by the Massachusetts Colony by Governor John Winthrop.

1643: Queen Christina of Sweden commanded the New Sweden Colony to plant vines and produce wine.

1648: Wine was made from wild grapes in the northern portion of Chesapeake Bay by French Huguenots.

1662: Lord Baltimore, during one of the many periodic tobacco gluts, planted 300 acres with vines. Although the vines survived, the effort proved commercially untenable and was soon abandoned.

1662-1670: Chasselas and Black Hamburg are introduced by French Huguenots in Boston. Later Muscats are grown in greenhouses.

1663: King Charles II grants the entire Carolina Territory to eight lord proprietors. A concentrated program to introduce silk culture, viticulture, and olive production failed.

1664: Nicolls, the first English governor of New York, granted Paul Richards "a monopoly of the industry for the colony" stipulating that he could make and sell wines free of impost and gave him the right to tax any person planting vines in the colony five shillings per acre. Richard's vineyard was just east of Queens, Long Island. This date is considered to be the first date for commercially grown grapes in the State of New York.

1681-1718: William Penn considered viticulture an important agricultural activity. Despite his avid interest, his vineyard failed, not because of environmental factors, but his prolonged absences from the colony, and the suspension of his proprietary rights. By 1722 an ordinance was passed encouraging beer production. Interestingly, Pennsylvania's Great Seal displays grape vines.

1682: Vinifera grapes were planted in Charleston, South Carolina.

1685: Revocation of the Edict of Nantes made possible large scale immigration of French Huguenots to Colonial America, and the establishment of vineyards in Pennsylvania, New York, North and South Carolina, and Rhode Island (the site of one of the earliest vineyards is Narraganset County in 1692). It is about this time that Colonial America shifted from French table wine imports to those from Madeira and Canary Islands.

1740: Thomas Penn's gardener, James Alexander, discovers a wild vine, later named Alexander, one of the most widely distributed grapes in Colonial America. The short lived success of this grape redirected American viticulture toward indigenous grapes, and soon after the Isabella and Catawba became more important.

1750: Wine grapes were cultivated in Flushing, a section in the Borough of Queens, New York City. About 400 acres of grapes planted in the middle Rio Grande Valley of New Mexico.

1769: Virginia Assembly passes a bill providing money and land at Williamsburg for a Frenchman by the name of Estave to carry out experiments in growing and winemaking. In 1773 he concluded that Vinifera vines would never succeed and that the industry would have to be based on native grapes.

1772: M. St. Pierre petitioned the Board of Trade for 20,000 acres of land in Georgia for grapes. The Lords of the Treasury awarded him 5,000 acres in South Carolina.

1773: Thomas Jefferson as ambassador to France cultivated a taste for fine wine. Dr. Filippo Mazzei plants Vinifera grapes at Monticello, Virginia. By this time it had become obvious that Colonial America was a region of two distinct cultures and economies. The north was rapidly becoming a plural and industrialized society, the site of most European immigrants, and the area most active in extending the frontier westward. In sharp contrast, the southern portion of Colonial America retained and fostered an aristocratic, socially divisive society with few opportunities for economic, political, and social mobility. The economy was highly dependent upon a handful of agricultural crops for export. The failure of viticultural pursuits in Colonial America was the result of many factors: physical environmental elements such as disease, and, equally important, English fiscal economic problems and colonial economic conditions. Because attempts to establish Vinifera vineyards failed, there were many feverish efforts made to hybridize (or improve through domestication) American grapes, of which the more important were Isabella, Ives, Concord, Catawba, Niagara, and Delaware.

1783: Great Britain agreed to a proposal that granted to America an area that extended from the Atlantic to the Mississippi and from the Great Lakes to within miles of the Gulf of Mexico. While most Americans lived east of the Appalachians, the Treaty of Paris quadrupled the nation's land area, and created a rich heartland for potential settlement. This region, practically unpopulated, and nearly devoid of indigenous permanent sedentary settlement, contained few potential native agricultural crops. As American penetration was slow and gradual through the various water and wind gaps, effective settlement did not occur until the 1820s with the completion of the Erie Canal, the major conduit for settlement of the midwest.

1793: First commercial American vineyard established in Spring Hill, north of Philadelphia by Pierre Legaux. Wine was made from the Alexander grape. It is widely assumed that the Alexander grape was the first commercial grape in America. The geographic division of American ampelography is established: Labrusca dominates in the north and Rotundifolia in the south.

1796: John James Dufour, a Swiss grape grower and winemaker, came to America to seek a suitable region for the cultivation of vineyards and the making of wine. After visiting all the existing grape growing regions of eastern America, he settled in central Kentucky where he established a vineyard in 1799. The vineyard failed in 1802 and he established another vineyard at Vevay, Indiana, which also failed. His *Treatise on the Cultivation of the Vine* was published in 1826, the year before his death.

1801: T.V. Munson noted that the Catawba was found wild in a forest near the Catawba River, North Carolina.

1803: Colonel George Morgan planted 3,500 Vinifera vines in Washington County southeast of Pittsburgh, the first cultivated vines west of the Allegheny Mountains. The religious-socialist Harmonists, founded in Germany, settled near Pittsburgh, Pennsylvania, and planted ten acres of Vinifera grapes.

1811: A Rotundifolia grape was given the name Scuppernong after the name of a river in Tyrrell County, North Carolina. First European discoverer is unknown, but it is reported by Sir Walter Raleigh's Lost Colony. The "modern" date of discovery is 1755. The vine spread quickly, and between 1811 and 1840 it was planted extensively in the Carolina's and Georgia. The Scuppernong became the most popular wine in the country prior to Prohibition under the Virginia Dare label.

1818: Deacon Elija Fay becomes the first grape grower in the Chautauqua region of New York State.

1823: Publication of the first American book on American grapes: *A Memoir on the Cultivation of the Vine in America, and the Best Mode of Making Wine*, by John Adlum. Adlum is considered responsible in popularizing Catawba, the first American wine grape in general use in eastern America.

1826: Publication of the second major work, *Vine Dresser's Guide*, on American viticulture by one James Dufour in Cincinnati, Ohio.

1827: Commercial viticultural history of the lower Hudson River Valley begins with one W.A. Underhill, who planted a vineyard of Catawba and Isabella grapes at Croton Point. With time, his 75-acre vineyard became the largest in the state under his son Dr. Robert Underhill. Over the next 30 years, this region became known as the "birthplace" of American viticulture as it contained the highest density of vineyards and wineries on the east coast.

1828: The Maryland Society for Promoting the Culture of the Wine was incorporated by the State Legislature to promote Vinifera grape growing and winemaking. It is apparent that throughout the Atlantic coast, Old World vines were repeatedly tried, but time and again they failed.

1829-1830: Rev. William Bostwick becomes the first grape grower in Hammondsport, New York, in the Finger Lakes region. His influence precipitated an avalanche of growers, so that by 1880 the Finger Lakes region of New York became the largest winegrowing region in the state with Lake Keuka the site of the largest wineries in the east.

1830: C. S. Rafinesque in his *American Manual of the Grape Vines*, gives an account of 41 species of native grapes. Although his botanical

studies have largely been discredited by others, he gives the first estimate of vine acreage in America for the years 1825 and 1830. His assessment for 1825 was a modest 600 acres, and for 1830 his estimate was 5,000 acres. Several historians consider his unpublished monograph the first written work on American grapes. Catawba and Isabella grapes replace the Alexander as the most popular commercial American grapes. Nicholas Longworth of Cincinnati, Ohio experimenting with Vinifera grapes for 30 years, becomes most successful with Catawba.

1835: Dr. D.N. Norton of Richmond, Virginia propagates an indigenous, non-foxy, blue grape that eventually bore his name. The production of this grape introduces a further division of American grapes--the Midwest with Vitis aestivalis (Norton), and Vitis riparia (Clinton). As the American frontier moves progressively westward, the number of American species increases.

1843: The seed of a wild grape is planted in the fall of 1843 by E. W. Bull in Concord, Massachusetts. In 1849 it bore fruit and cross-pollinated with at least one other Labrusca grape. In 1852, the Concord grape was exhibited before the Massachusetts Horticultural Society. The Concord was offered for sale in 1853, and in short order replaced Catawba as the most popular commercial grape throughout the east and midwest. The pace of American hybridization increases, but, in the main, fails to produce a quality table wine grape.

1845: Dr. Robert Valk was the first American to succeed in making a deliberate cross of a native grape (Isabella) and Vinifera (Black Hamburg) that was named Ada.

1850: Pennsylvania ranked third in grape production.

1850s: Edward S. Rogers of Massachusetts was an active breeder of Vitis labrusca and Vitis vinifera. Although not overly successful (one Agawam still survives), he did illustrate the utility of Vinifera grapes in imparting fruit character to hybrid offspring.

1853-1880: The Concord grape proves a huge success, and highlights the most successful period of sustained viticultural growth in eastern America.

1855: Originated in the garden of Paul Provost of Frenchtown, New Jersey, the Delaware grape variety was commercially released by A. Thompson of Delaware, Ohio.

1859: Ohio becomes the largest wine producing state in the nation. It produced 570,000 gallons, or about 30 percent of the national total, and more than twice the amount produced in California. E.M. Erskine, Secretary of the British Legation in Washington, D.C., reports between 1,500-2,000 acres of grapes near Cincinnati along the Ohio River, and 100 acres at Cleveland, Ohio. According to his estimates, Ohio led the nation with 3,000 acres. Kentucky had 500 planted grape acres; 1,000 in Indiana; 500 in Missouri; 500 in Illinois; 100 in Georgia; 300 in North Carolina; 200 in South Carolina. He states that 22 of the nation's 32 states cultivated grape vines, collectively producing 2 million gallons of wine. Erskine reports 6,500 acres for the nation, while others estimate the figure to be larger.

1860: The Pleasant Valley Wine Company was founded in Hammondsport, New York in the Finger Lakes region.

1860-1864: Civil War disrupted and depressed the southern economy, and, to a minor degree, wine producing regions along the border states. As a consequence, southern states could not support another labor-intensive industry, thus making the growing of grapes and the making of wine a "backyard affair" until recently.

1865-1960-: New York emerges as the largest producer of sparkling wines in America. New York at one time produced more than 75 percent of the nation's total production.

1871: With an output of more than 500,000 gallons, The Golden Eagle Winery, located on Middle Bass Island in Lake Erie, becomes the largest winery in America.

1873: A bottle of Great Western Winery sparkling wine from the Finger Lakes region wins a gold medal at the Vienna Exposition.

1879: The Urbana Wine Company in the Finger Lakes region wins two gold medals for its sparkling wines at the Paris Exposition.

1880: California grape and wine production become formidable competitors to eastern viticulture; eastern grape prices fell, and new plantings were curtailed. Vine acreage in New York and Pennsylvania stood at 14,590; in Ohio, Indiana, and Illinois 17,634 acres; 10,918 acres in Kansas and Missouri; and 10,707 acres in Kentucky, Tennessee, Virginia, North Carolina, and Georgia. The most widely planted varieties are Concord, Catawba, Delaware, and Niagara. The 1880 Census reports that New Mexico ranked fifth in wine production with 905,000 gallons from 3,150 acres.

1900: Concord dominates acreage and production. The south shore of Lake Erie produced 192 million pounds, more than nine-tenths of which were Concord. This region is also the second most important grape producing region east of the Central Valley.

1920: Prohibition. A small number of wineries survive Prohibition by selling grape juice, "medicinal tonics," and sacramental wine. Among the more notable survivors were: Renault Wine Company (Egg Harbor, New Jersey, founded in 1868); The Brotherhood Wine Company (Washingtonville, New York, founded in 1839); The Pleasant Valley Wine Company (Hammondsport, New York, founded in 1860); Taylor Wine Company (Hammondsport, New York, founded in 1880); Gold Seal Vineyards (Hammondsport, New York, founded in 1865); Widmer's Wine Cellars (Naples, New York, founded in 1888).

1928-1988: Dr. Robert T. Dunstan of North Carolina and Florida, a major, unrecognized hybridizer, successfully crosses Euvitis with Rotundifolia. Over the years he developed many varieties, of which Suwanee, Rijote, Carolina Blackrose, and Aurelia survive commercially.

1934: Charles Fournier left his winemaker position at Veuve Clicquot Ponsardin in France to become production manager at Gold Seal, in Hammondsport, New York. Until his retirement as president in 1967, he experimented with French-American varietals, and produced Chardonnay and Pinot Noir varietal wine in 1960.

1937: Philip Wagner, an amateur winemaker and a lifelong enthusiast for French-American varietals in the northeast and the midwest, began experimental French-American plantings. He established his Boordy Vineyards Winery in Maryland in 1945.

1952: High Tor Vineyards, founded by Everett Crosby in the lower Hudson River Valley, did much to revitalize interest in the region.

1968: First farm winery legislation promulgated in Pennsylvania, an event that spread to at least 20 other states, and revitalized the wine industry. The Pennsylvania Limited Winery Act, one of the most generous in the nation, allows a winery to produce 200,000 gallons and have five retail outlets.

1973: The founding of Hargrave Vineyards as the first all-Vinifera winery on Long Island revolutionizes winegrowing along the east coast.

1980: The beginning of a significant decline in domestic jug wine sales, and the start of premium wine escalation.

1982-1984: A peak in the importation of European wines, particularly French Bordeaux, brought about mainly by the strength of the $US. As international exchange rates reversed themselves, expensive French imports have been steadily declining.

Grapes and Wines

Due to the climatic differences described previously, the wines of eastern America were historically the product of native grapes, followed by French-American, and more recently by Vinifera grapes. The regional variation of grape varieties is due to a patchwork of factors, the most important of which is climate (susceptibility to low winter temperatures), disease (Pierce's Disease in the humid south), cultural preferences (Concord-based kosher wines in the northeast and midwest), and 2,4 D in the midwest (only a handful of grape varieties, most notably Baco Noir, Chancellor, Chelois, DeChaunac, and a few others exhibit any tolerance to this deadly herbicide).

Crop variation is significantly higher in the east than in California. A combination of spring freezes, drought, severe winter kill, disease, and other factors cause partial to total crop failure. There is a general tendency for vines to bear heavier every other year since the best buds are generally produced after a light crop. Throughout the northeast and midwest, Crown Gall and bird damage are

major problems. In general, the geographic distribution of the three principal grape types is influenced by the variability of winter and spring temperatures, and the concomitance of humidity and high temperatures. Hardy native grapes dominate the Great Plains and the coldest portions of the midwest; Labrusca-type grapes are positioned in warmer regions; French-American grapes comingle with Labrusca, but only along warmer margins (not in excessively humid areas); Rotundofolia and related grapes are found only along the warm to hot humid margin in the southeast and Gulf of Mexico; and Vinifera vines are found only in those temperate areas where the growing season exceeds 160 days. Yields for Vinifera vary between 1-3 tons per acre, for French-American varietals 3-5, and for American, 4-7. Harvest begins in the middle of July and continues until the end of October, and sometimes into December.

Until recently, most, if not all, of the extension work associated with state agricultural experiment stations dealt with American grape varieties. The emphasis has changed in such states as Virginia, New York, Michigan, Texas, Ohio, Missouri, Georgia, North and South Carolina, and Florida, which have made determined efforts to energize the industry with new grape varieties, field training systems, and other cultural practices. "Dyson's Goblet Trellis" has been well received in the lower Hudson River region, and new field grafting techniques have enabled farmers to change from one variety to another rapidly and economically. Site selection is improving (with growers making fewer mistakes), and the development of new rootstocks and clones are increasing the range of the Vinifera and French-American varieties. In this regard, proper variety and site selection are imperative in order to minimize the problem of excess vigor. In relatively cool growing areas, such as the Great Lakes and the northeast, grape maturation, even in the hardiest, long-growing season variations, is a problem. One way to achieve greater maturation is to choose sites with southern exposures, good air and water drainage, and crop control measures such as heavy cluster thinning and pruning.

While the most important American, French-American, and Vinifera varieties are listed below, the following Vinifera exhibit promise: Ehrenfelser, Ortega, Lemberger, Muller-Thurgau, Muscat Ottonel, Scheurebe, Sereksia, Mariafeld (a Pinot Noir clone of Swiss origin, and Gewurztraminer. The future may also be kind to a host of new white East European grapes such as: Mtsvane, Furmint, Harslevelu, Feteasca Alba, Rkatsiteli, and Grasa de Cotnari. Red wine grapes with a future include: Saperavi, Babeasca Neagra, and Buket.

Although there are exceptions, eastern America is white wine country as far as table wines are concerned. Leading the list are Seyval and Vidal Blanc, followed by Chardonnay, and other minor Vinifera grapes. However, eastern America is still searching for the elusive red table wine grape. Native grapes have been discarded long ago (although Cynthiana and Norton offer possibilities), and all French-American varieties exhibit serious problems in terms of yield maintenance, susceptibility to disease, sugar levels, winter hardiness, color retention, ability to age, and palatability. A red grape variety to everyone's liking does not exist. Only in select locations does one find small quantities of Cabernet Sauvignon, Merlot, and Cabernet Franc. The problem for the grower and winemaker in recent years is to meet the demand for non-American, non-French-American wines, which means they have to uproot the old and replant finicky, shy-yielding vines--a very expensive proposition. Ever since 1978, when the Taylor Wine Company canceled contracts, prices for "traditional" grapes fell, growers went out of business, and many wineries closed their doors. Whatever the personal misfortunes happen to be, the eastern winemaker must come to grips with the contemporary market place.

In this respect, the price structure of eastern grapes reveals many surprises. The highest prices paid to growers are for Vinifera (between $800 and $1,400), namely Chardonnay, Pinot Noir, Cabernet Sauvignon, Merlot, Gewurztraminer, and Riesling. Although the lowest prices are for American grapes, especially Concord and similar varieties, the most expensive native grape is the obscure Norton/Cynthiana, currently being offered at more than $1,400 the ton. The most expensive French-American varietal is Vignoles at $600, followed by Seyval at $500, and Vidal Blanc, Marechal Foch, and Chancellor at $450. All prices vary significantly with vintage and region, especially Vinifera varieties, Norton/Cynthiana, and Vignoles.

Nearly all American wines are blended, with special dispensation from BATF allowing eastern producers to ameliorate beyond the 25 percent varietal designation (for native and French-American varietals only). One hundred percent Labrusca, as in the case of Niagara, Concord, and others, is overpowering in flavor and odor intensity, prompting many to describe these features as *gout sauvage*. It is estimated that more than half of production contains between 3 to 5 percent residual sugar; 25 percent contains between 1 to 3 percent sugar; and the remaining 20 percent are dry, crisp wines with less than 1 percent sugar. It is this type of wine that is enabling the eastern vineyard to establish a foothold in the table wine segment. Therefore, quality winemaking is shifting from kosher, sweet (both of which are usually blended with non-eastern wine), and inexpensive wines to more distinct, dry, medium to full-bodied white and red table wines; dry, crisp, fresh and fruity white wines; off-dry, fruity, medium-bodied, "casual" wines; and dry sparkling wines, the latter particularly promising due to their high acid content and pronounced flavor. As yet untapped, the pro-

duction of late harvest wines also appears to offer excellent potential. Nouveau wines, the product of carbonic maceration, are a recent and interesting innovation expected to increase in importance. In the final analysis, American grape wines since initial European settlement, have not held an important national position. The wines, due to their distinct flavor and odor, are quite different from Vinifera, and their demand has proven to be painstakingly limited to regional, non-urban markets. Furthermore, the historic emphasis has been to meet the demands of the processing and table portion of the market. Most important, wine output has concentrated in the production of sweet, not dry table wines.

Figure 5.1

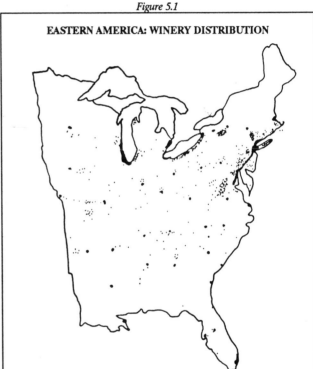

EASTERN AMERICA: WINERY DISTRIBUTION

Large dots and dark areas indicate major urban units. The majority of wineries are associated with urban and tourist areas; the northern tier is devoid of winemaking as is the Coastal Plain and the Gulf region. The recent viticultural resurgence in Appalachia is encouraging.

However, the east, particularly the northern sections, is in an enviable position to produce excellent late harvest Riesling, Gewurztraminer, and Vignoles. The recent successes of Vinifera wine production in the Leelanau Peninsula, eastern Long Island, southeastern Pennsylvania, Maryland, Virginia, and Texas are highly encouraging. Other important considerations favoring future winemaking possibilities in the east are improved vineyard and winemaking practices, growing state support, proximity to market, and increased wine sales in food stores. Moreover, the second generation, post-Konstantin Frank winemakers are revolutionizing the Vinifera industry. Further, the wine revolution in the humid south, an area that was historically beer and whiskey country, is steadily expanding.

The geographic distribution of wineries, presented in Fig. 5.1, illustrates two distinct patterns: a rural orientation and a market orientation, the latter, increasingly becoming more important. The former location, defined in terms of significant distance from a major metropolitan center, can only survive economically when it offers a unique product based on distinctive physical growing conditions. Given the fact that there are precious few such areas, the tendency for economic viability is, as a consequence, a market association. This market linkage is a recent phenomenon, and offers the following advantages: 1. greater access to the print, audio, and visual media. Historically, eastern wines were treated as non-entities, relatively unknown in major cities, unproven and rejected as the bulk of quality wine consumption was imported. The preferable image was, and continues to be, France, Italy, Germany, Portugal, Spain, and California, not Pennsylvania, Rhode Island, Vermont, or West Virginia. 2. greater access to the consumer; most eastern wineries are within a 50 minute automobile ride from major urban areas. By increasing winery visitations, the consumer becomes more familiar with the product; and the winery, by selling on site, bypasses the distributor, thus increasing profit margins. Moreover, by strategically locating within a large metropolitan area, distribution costs are decreased. For those wineries producing fewer than 5,000 cases, the bulk of sales occur at the winery. The strategy is not to talk about appellations, but types and styles of regional wines to entice the consumer to taste and eventually buy. As a result, the elements of convenience, pandering, local history and pride appear to have made significant inroads in the wine drinking habits of many eastern areas. 3. specific market orientation: (a) large metropolitan areas, such as New York (hence the wine producing regions of southern and Hunterdon County, New Jersey, western and southern Connecticut, the lower Hudson River region, and eastern Long Island); Washington, D.C. (more than 80 wineries have been established over the past 30 years, north, west and south of the nation's capitol); southeastern (Philadelphia) and southwestern (Pittsburgh) Pennsylvania; Tennessee (nearly all wineries are located within a 60-minute driving distance from Memphis, Nashville, and Knoxville); etc. (b) tourist attractions: Monticello, Virginia; Branson, Missouri; western Michigan, the Finger Lakes region of New York, etc. (c) college and university towns: State College, Pennsylvania; Bloomington, Indiana, etc. (d) restored towns: Williamsburg, Virginia; St. Charles, Missouri, etc.

American Varieties

From the first European settlement, the eastern grape wine industry has been based on American varieties, nearly all of which are hybrids of the native species found growing wild throughout eastern North America. American vines can be tall and slender climbers, bush-like, dwarf-like, low or high yielding, difficult or easy to grow, and of varying longevity. While most can be domesticated, easily hybridized (it is estimated that more than 1,000 varieties exist), and, by nature, prolific, by wide margin the most successful, in terms of acreage, has been Vitis labrusca, of which Concord, Catawba, Niagara, Delaware, and Dutchess have been the most important. The most expensive commercial nursery vines are Worden, Norton, Cynthiana, and Valiant.

One of the first grape breeders to practice inter-specific hybridization between Vinifera and American grapes was Edward S. Rogers of Massachusetts, an active hybridizer and a contemporary of Ephraim Bull. He produced more than ten of which Agawam still remains. His general contributions were not the commercial varieties developed but that valuable hybridization could contribute to good fruit quality. Another breeder, George W. Campbell of Ohio, was the originator of Campbell Early, a variety still commercially active. Twentieth Century contributors have been Charles Arnold of Canada who clearly demonstrated the use of the riverbank grape-Riparia as an important strain leading to cold hardiness. Louis Saulter, a more successful breeder from Minnesota, developed the Beta. Among many others, M.J. Dorsey, A.N. Wilcox, N.E. Hansen, and R.P. Peterson have all made considerable contributions in the production of cold-hardy grapes.

> It is estimated that there are 45,000 acres of Concord, 6,000 acres of Catawba, and 5,000 acres of Niagara in the east. While Concord, Catawba, Fredonia, Niagara, Aurore, DeChaunac, Baco Noir are declining in acreage, Seyval, Vidal Blanc, Chambourcin, Rotundifolia, Riesling, Pinot Noir, Cabernet Sauvignon, and Merlot are increasing in acreage.

Of all American species of vine, Vitis labrusca is, by far, the most important in terms of historical development, acreage, and total impact on the American economy. While its commercial geography is the most extensive of any native grape, the area of concentration is east of the Great Plain states, and north of the 35th parallel. Labrusca produces intensely grapey, well-flavored wines that are dramatically different from Vitis vinifera. Rich in flavor, fruity, and primarily marketed as kosher, Sherry-type, Porto-type, and other fortified sweet wines, Labrusca grapes have dominated the northeastern-midwestern section of the United States to the near exclusion of all other grapes. Their aroma and flavor are a product of *menthyl anthranilate*, or bubble gum flavor, often called "foxy" (wet dog), and perfume (floral). By some accounts, Beauchamp Plantagenet, in his account of New Albion (a portion of present day Delaware), used the word "fox" for intoxicate.

Nevertheless, there are many differing explanations

of the origin of the word "foxy," most notably from: (1) wild vines; (2) foxy as in to intoxicate; (3) a distortion of the French *faux*, to indicate a false grape, or one that is not similar to Vinifera; (4) its appearance, in that the leaves from several varieties resemble the print of a fox's paw; and (5) from the "fox connection," namely that foxes liked to eat them, that the odor attracts small animals (including foxes), and that the grapes smell of the fox. In the final analysis, there is no concise definition nor origin, but there is widespread support for the notion that the peculiar "wild" musky odor and aroma of the grape reminded the early settlers of the "wild," whatever that might have been along Atlantic America. In addition, Labrusca, as well as other native grapes, has a pronounced woody, stemmy, musty aroma and flavor, a combination leading to what is commonly referred to as "palate fatigue." As a result, American grapes, unlike the more delicate Vinifera varieties, have limited raisin and table use appeal.

T.B. Welch, the man who made the Concord grape the most popular variety east of the Continental Divide, produced the first "unfermented" wine in America. Courtesy of Welch Foods, Communications Department, Westfield, NY.

When made as dry table wines their intense grapey, foxy flavor, bitterness, predilection for poor color, poor aging potential and rapid oxidation have proven to be major disadvantages when compared with Vinifera and French-American varieties. While Labrusca wine has never been accepted by those with "a classical European taste," the economics of production, and the persistency of demand by a small segment of the population makes the cultivation of many Labrusca grapes and winemaking economically viable both at the cottage and large winery levels possible. Under no circumstances should American wines be compared with Vinifera, although some comparisons can be made with French-American varietals. After 300 years of attempting to produce palatable native wines in the east, and after 150 years of competition with California, the east has not increased its market share beyond 10 percent for any significant period. Moreover, the native grape wine market is limited to the producing regions. Red table wine, in particular, is high in acid, foxy in flavor, low in sugar, tart, often very bitter, and, in general, inferior to white Labrusca, and certainly to French-American and Vinifera alternatives. The number of acceptable (even passable) red Labrusca grapes suitable for table wine production remains elusive. Historically, the only way to make red wine palatable was to reduce its foxy aroma and flavor, add sugar and neutral Vinifera wine from California. It is estimated that more than 80 percent of eastern wineries make and depend on native wine for their sustenance.

The important white varieties are:

Diamond (Moore's), first developed in 1870 in Brighton, New York from a cross of Concord and Iona, is a vigorous, hardy variety almost exclusively grown in the Finger Lakes region of New York State. More popular in the past than now, it was made as a varietal by the Widmer Winery in Naples, New York. Because of its resistance to browning and high acid levels, this variety is judiciously used in Finger Lakes sparkling wine production because of its pungent, green, dry, and austere character. Despite its limited distribution, acreage has given way to Seyval, Vidal Blanc, and other less foxy varieties.

Dutchess, is a variety that can no longer compete with hardier white grapes in the production of table, sparkling, and sweet wines. The grape, more sensitive to winter cold and disease than other varieties, is usually confined to the warmer portions of the northeast, particularly in the Hudson Valley, and Finger Lakes district of New York. Acreage, as a consequence, has declined to fewer than 250 acres, mostly in Pennsylvania and New York. Similar, but considered less fine than Delaware, it browns easily, and the finest contains considerable residual sugar.

Elvira (Riparia/Labrusca), developed in Missouri by Jacob Rommel in 1869-1880, is mainly confined to the southern portion of America's heartland. Its main advantages are hardiness and ability to withstand rapid temperature fluctuations, but its overly foxy character, musky flavor, and inability to compete with other grapes has reduced its former importance. Its parentage is strongly influenced by Vitis riparia, and, hence, this is a productive, winter-hardy, and disease-resistant grape. Although acreage is decreasing, Elvira is the most widely cultivated grape in the Niagara Peninsula of New York State.

Missouri Riesling, supposedly developed by Nicholas Grime in Hermann, Missouri in the 1850s, became one of the most widely cultivated wine grapes in the midwest, mainly in the second half of the 19th century. A Labrusca-Riparia cross, it is confined only to Missouri and Arkansas, and with fewer than 50 acres, declining in importance.

Niagara (Labrusca/Vinifera), is a good, all-purpose, highly flavored grape that is economically sound for many growers and winemakers throughout the northeast. It is vigorous, but only moderately hardy, and somewhat susceptible to downy and powdery mildew. With a strong Labrusca flavor and aroma, it can be stretched by amelioration, and improve neutral tasting wine through blending. Because of its intense flavor, and the fact that it is invariably made as a sweet wine, Niagara is the most widely planted white Labrusca in America. First propagated by C.L. Hoag and B.W. Clark in 1878 in Niagara County, New York, by 1886 there were more than 1,200 planted acres in the Chautauqua region. Despite considerable inroads by French-American and Vinifera vines, this widely accepted grape is increasing its acreage in many areas from Pennsylvania to the midwest. Planted acreage is estimated at 4,000. Niagara is also the most important grape for the production of white grape juice.

Ventura, a cross of Elvira and Chelois first released in 1974, is an extremely winter-hardy vine that makes a musty flavored and scented wine. With fewer than 50 acres in the United States, only one Finger Lakes winery makes it as a varietal wine. Canada, its place of origin, has more than 500 planted acres. Other white grapes include: **Ontario**, a difficult grape that is best known for sweet wine production; **Portland**, difficult to grow and practically extinct, is mainly used for sweet wine production; **Edelweiss**, one of the many Elmer Swenson varieties, is mainly planted in the northern portion of the midwest; and **Brocton**, an obscure Geneva Agricultural Experiment Station variety with limited acreage. It is estimated that an additional 500 varieties are planted, mainly in experimental plots and home gardens.

The red grape varieties are:

Agawam (Labrusca/Vinifera), although rarely encountered in the United States, this obscure grape is still grown in Canada. **Alexander** (Labrusca/Vinifera?), one of the first native grapes to be domesticated, this hardy, foxy grape dominated grape acreage in the east until the domestication of Catawba. Although widely distributed, the shorter growing season north of Pennsylvania restricted this variety to the mid-Atlantic states and the southern portion of the midwest. **Beta**, (Riparia-Concord) developed by Louis Suelter, a Missouri hybridizer in the late 1880s, withstands temperatures as low as -40F, but, unfortunately, the foxy, high-acid wine has limited appeal. **Campbell Early**, a Labrusca-Vinifera variety, was a highly praised grape vine when it was introduced in the last decade of the 19th century. Due to its highly finicky soil requirements, the vine is nearly extinct.

Catawba (Labrusca/Vinifera), named after a river in North Carolina where the grape was first discovered in 1801, is mainly planted along the south shore of Lake Erie, and the Finger Lakes region. It is a vigorous, productive, winter-hardy, late ripening vine, well-adapted to a wide variety of soils. Catawba is much superior to Concord in the production of wine, nearly all for sweet and sparkling wine. Because it ripens late and is susceptible to fungus diseases, its geographic distribution is more circumscribed than the ubiquitous Concord to the sandy, clay, and gravelly soils of the Finger Lakes region, Lake Erie, and scattered areas in Missouri. This interesting grape, considered American and indigenous to the Carolina's, does, however, exhibit several Vinifera features that question its true origins. It produces well-flavored wines, particularly sparkling, and was, until the introduction of the Concord, the most widely planted vine in the nation. One of the oldest "premium" native grapes in the east with a fascinating history, it made its debut in the garden of one John Adlum in the District of Columbia in 1823, and was planted near Hammondsport, New York by the Rev. William Bostwick in 1830. It was introduced by Longworth in Cincinnati in 1825, and for a short time it became the leading variety in southern Ohio.

Clinton (Riparia/Labrusca), widely assumed to be the first important Riparia variety, this vine enjoyed considerable prominence in the early stages of American viticulture due to its hardiness and vigor, but due to its high sensibility to calcareous soils, its distribution has always been limited. Clinton is a black, acidic grape grown in scattered areas in the northeast and midwest since 1819.

Concord (Labrusca/Vinifera?), developed by Ephraim Bull (a gold beater) in Concord, Massachusetts in 1843, proved so popular it became the leading American grape by 1860, and was referred to as "the grape for millions" by Horace Greeley. Concord is grown on a greater variety of soils and under a wider range of climatic conditions than any other commercial American grape. Winter hardy to -20F, the high yielding Concord has become, over the past 150 years, the premier commercial eastern grape. Easily grafted, this disease resistant vine does particularly well in the volcanic-rich soils of Washington State, as well as the high-acid, podzolic soils of the humid northeast and midwest. Concord, with more than 45,000 acres (or half the acreage in eastern America), is the most commonly planted grape east of the Rocky Mountains. The high versatility of the fruit for many commercial purposes gives it a large market outlet. Total Concord production in America varies between 325,000 and 475,000 tons.

During a five year period, Ephraim Bull tried 22,000 seedlings, propagated 125 vines, and on September 10, 1849 picked a bunch of grapes that henceforth became the present Concord. In 1853, the Concord seedlings were exhibited before the Massachusetts Horticultural Society, and the following year he placed the grape on the market named after the town of Concord where he lived. Vines were sold at the unheard of price of $5.00, but unfortunately, Ephraim Bull never reaped financial gain, dying a poor recluse in 1895. Within seven years of its commercial introduction, the Concord spread beyond the Mississippi River. Over the past 140 years, it has become the most famous of all American grapes, eventually playing a historic role in the vine growing and winemaking fortunes of the northeast and midwest, as well as forming the base for the grape juice and jelly industry of the entire nation. Extremely hardy, adaptable, disease resistant, and early maturing, this high yielding vine (more than ten tons to the acre) is low in sugar, high in acid, and highly flavorful. It is the most common grape for juice and jelly, a prime ingredient in eastern bulk wine production, and the key ingredient in the making of eastern coolers, sweet table, fortified, and flavored wines. Prior to 1960, it was also the prime grape in the production of "eastern Dago red," and continues to be the key ingredient in the production of "kosher" wines. Concord should not be confused with Concord Seedless, a low yielding variety, and the White Concord, both of which enjoy limited commercial success. As important as this variety has been since its development, little acreage exists in the rest of the world, with Canada, with, and, to a smaller degree, Brazil the only major exceptions.

Table 5.1

CONCORD GRAPE PRODUCTION, 1988		
State	Tons	Percent
Arkansas	4,300	1.2
Michigan	45,500	12.8
Missouri	1,200	.3
New York	111,000	31.1
Ohio	7,300	2.1
Pennsylvania	51,000	14.3
Washington	136,000	38.1
Other States	220	.1
U.S.	356,520	100.0

Aggregate figure represents 5.9 percent of total US grape output. Concord production in 1987 was 454,970, in 1986 it was 333,730. Percent of national grape production varies between 5 and 8%. Source: U.S. Department of Agriculture.

Today more than 400,000 tons of Concord grapes are harvested from nearly 70,000 acres, the latter highly localized in five specific geographic regions. Production accounts for 5 to 7 percent of the total national harvest, with more than three-quarters of the output confined to Washington and New York. (The largest is the Yakima Valley and portions of the Columbia Plateau of Washington.) Historically the most important in the nation is the south shore of Lake Erie stretching from south of Buffalo, New York, through Erie County, Pennsylvania, and into Ohio as west as Toledo. The third most important region is southwestern Michigan, the fourth is the Finger Lakes region of New York, and the fifth, and smallest, is the Springdale region of Arkansas and central Missouri. The rest of the nation contains fewer than 3,000 acres.

It is estimated that in 1975, the Concord grape was responsible for 10 percent of the American wine market. In addition to the processing industry, the Concord had been the historic mainstay of the kosher, dessert, and sparkling segments of the wine industry in the midwest and northeast. The Concord received a major boost with the popularity of Cold Duck and Sparkling Burgundy in the 1960s, but soon plummeted when demand for kosher, dessert, and flavored sparkling wines began to decline precipitously. In addition, grape juice sales for the period 1961-1985 increased by 1.3 percent annually, much less than other juices (principally orange), and the processing industry was unable to absorb the excess Concord grape crop. Another major problem was formidable competition from Washington (less expensive), and by 1984 the bottom fell out of the Concord market with grapes remaining unpicked and vineyards either bulldozed or sold. As a consequence, Concord acreage declined in the midwest and northeast by more than 20,000 acres during the period 1982-1986.

The history of the Concord grape is inextricably related to the Welch Foods Co., a corporation that has $400 million in sales, nearly all of which are directly related to the processing of Concord grapes. This corporation, one of the largest food processors in the nation, handled 164,000 tons of Concord grapes from 1,554 growers cultivating 37,430 acres. Dr. Thomas Bramwell Welch and his son made the first commercial Concord grape juice in 1869 in Vineland, New Jersey for sacramental purposes in the local Methodist Church. The new and distinct flavor of Concord juice was so well received that he began to produce it commercially, turning the business over to his son, Charles, in 1872. In 1896 he moved his operations from New Jersey to Watkins Glen, New York, and the following year he moved the company again to Westfield, New York in the Chautauqua area. The initial successes made the pasteurized Concord bottled juice America's favorite for three generations. It was particularly popular during the Woodrow Wilson administration, and the Prohibition years. It was served at diplomatic dinners in the White House, and Josephus Daniels, Secretary of the Navy, substituted Welch's Grape Juice for the sailor's monthly ration of rum. Today, the Welch Food Co. operates processing facilities in Westfield, New York; North East, Pennsylvania; Lawton, Michigan; and Kennewick and Grandview, Washington.

Site of Bull's Original Concord Vine
Although the original Concord grape vine, developed over many years by Ephraim Wales Bull, perished decades ago, a replacement grows on the original site on his home, "Grapevine Cottage" in Concord. According to Bull: "I looked about to see what I could find among our wildings. The next thing to do was to find the best and earliest grape for seed. This I found in an accidental seedling at the foot of the hill. The crop was almost abundant, ripe in August, and of very good quality for a wild grape. I sowed the seed in autumn of 1843; among them the Concord was the only one worth saving." Baxevanis

Cynthiana (Labrusca/Aestivalis, and possibly Vinifera), also known as "Red River," is indigenous to Arkansas, and has practically disappeared in the east except for 50 commercial acres in Arkansas and Missouri. Often confused with Norton, it is the only American variety that makes above-average to excellent, dark, spicy, often complex red wine without even a hint of foxiness. Unfortunately, a difficult culture and low yields limit its appeal to growers. As incredible as it reads, this is the most expensive non-Vinifera grape in the east. Among those in the know in Missouri, Cynthiana is considered superior to Norton. The grape was described in New York City in the middle of the 19th century at the same time that it was "discovered" in Missouri (1858). Many wineries and growers in Arkansas and Missouri maintain that Cynthiana is a true Aestivalis, and considered different and superior to Norton.

Delaware (Labrusca/Bourquiniana/Vinifera), historically one of the most popular grapes in the east because of its tolerance to black rot and its good table character, has declined to near extinction in recent years due to its high sensitivity to mildews, fastidiousness about soil conditions, the small size of its berries, its popularity with birds, and inability to compete with other grapes for contemporary white wine production. Nevertheless, with a clean, fresh, fruity and spicy flavor, it is not only a fair table grape, but was widely made into good table and sparkling wines. After Catawba, it is the second most popular red fruited native grape producing white wine. Delaware is one of the few native grapes that develops excellent sugar levels, but its main disadvantages--low yields, poor vigor, susceptibility to mildew, a pronounced foxy flavor, and a propensity to oxidize have reduced acreage. For a short time in the 19th century it was the most widely planted Labrusca grape in the nation. The single largest concentration is in the Finger Lakes region of New York State, and isolated portions of the northeast. Originating in Frenchtown, New Jersey in 1849 along the Delaware River, it was introduced to the Ohio River in the 1850s where it spread throughout the midwest, and for a time was regarded as the finest native variety producing white wine (it sold for $6 the gallon in the 1850s in Missouri). The origin, commonly thought by many to have been Ohio, is particularly interesting and controversial.

Fredonia, developed by the Geneva Agricultural Experiment Station in 1927, was historically used in the production of fortified wines and in processing. Acreage has been declining recently, and it is thought that there are fewer than 150 acres remaining. **Herbemont** (Bourquiniana), a vigorous and productive vine very sensitive to low temperatures, is a Pierce's Disease-resistant variety whose now limited acreage stretches throughout the humid Gulf Coast, but is mainly confined to eastern and southern Texas. This once popular grape is also known as Warren, Warrenton, and Herbemont's Madeira. For more than a century, Herbemont enjoyed the same relative rank as Concord in the northeast and midwest. **Isabella**, one of the earliest and most successful Labrusca grapes (developed in Flushing, New York in 1815, and named after Mrs. Isabella Gibbs of Brooklyn), is known for good winter hardiness, a strong foxy flavor, and little else. It, like most other early Labrusca grapes, has had its acreage decline below 150 acres. While at one time this Labrusca/Vinifera? grape was one of the most widespread in the nation, it remains widely diffused outside America-- from the Fiji Islands, the Balkans, and the Madeira Islands. **Ives**, one of the older American varieties (developed in Cincinnati in 1840), is known for deep, rich color, and because it is stemmy and heavy in tannins, it was widely used in the past as an important blending grape for full-bodied, robust red wines. Because it lacks vigor, and is difficult to grow (it is highly ozone-sensitive), acreage has declined to less than 100. Historically, it was the most important quality red wine grape in the Finger Lakes region. **Lenoir** (Bourquiniana/Vinifera), similar to Herbemont, this Pierce's Disease resistant variety is a minor entity only in the humid portions of the Gulf Coast, particularly Texas. As proof of its widespread geographic distribution of yesteryear, the variety has at least 42 synonyms of which Jacques and Black Spanish are the most common.

Muench, developed in the late 1880s by Thomas V. Munson, this obscure variety, found only in scattered backyard vineyards, is commercially made into wine (for blending) by Mount Pleasant Vineyards in Missouri, as well as several others in the midwest. **New York Muscat**, a cross between Muscat Hamburg and Ontario, this variety, more popular in Ontario, Canada, spills over into New York to produce minor quantities of dessert wines. Historically more important, it is estimated that there are fewer than 50 acres left in production in America. **Norton, Norton's Virginia, or Norton's Seedling** (Aestivalis/Labrusca), developed in Virginia in the 1820s, it slowly made its way to Hermann, Missouri in 1845-1850 creating the never ending controversy about the distinctiveness between it and Cynthiana. While the distinguishing features between Norton and Cynthiana are nearly impossible to all but the professional, the debate on whether they are two distinct and separate varieties continues. It appears that Norton is more adaptable to rich alluvial soil, more vigorous, and given to higher yields than Cynthiana. Norton, like Cynthiana, produces a rich, dark wine that ages well. **Steuben**, developed by the Geneva Agricultural Experiment Station in 1947, this variety, after a long period of neglect, has received renewed interest in the making of a light, yet uncomplicated, fruity rose with some considerable flavor appeal. The acreage of this Labrusca/Vinifera variety is expected to increase. **Valiant**, an obscure blue/black grape developed by the University of South Dakota that ripens three weeks earlier than Concord, is thought to be as winter hardy as Beta, but considerably better as a wine grape, and should be more widely planted in the cold northern regions of America. **Worden** (Labrusca), the most expensive nursery vine of any American variety, is an obscure blue/black grape that ripens three weeks earlier than the Concord. Although resistant to both mildews, it is not as hardy as other native grapes, and because the fruit cracks easily, it is not widely planted. For a time, it was considered superior to Concord.

Other red varieties include **Bacchus** (grown since the 1870s), a glassy black grape with deep red juice and a pronounced foxy odor; **Eumelian** (grown since 1847), at one time widely planted in the Finger Lakes region, has practically disappeared; **Diana**, related to Catawba, unpredictable in yield and inconsistent in winemaking, is nearly extinct; **Iona**, developed in 1855 on Iona Island in the Hudson River, is a highly aromatic variant of Diana, and nearly extinct; **Noah** (Riparia/Labrusca/Vinifera), an obscure and highly foxy grape first grown in Nauvoo, Illinois in 1869, is produced commercially only in a few isolated areas in Missouri and Arkansas.; **Vergennes**, first grown in Vermont, has a few minor commercial pockets in the Finger Lakes region, but otherwise is extinct; **Carman**, an obscure variety found in the humid portions of Texas and the Gulf Coast, is presently not commercially grown. **Champanel**, an obscure wine and table grape, is grown only in northcentral Texas. **Stark-Star** (Labrusca/Vinifera/Aestivalis), a most unusual variety, originated in Arkansas in the 1890s, and, although obscure and unimportant in terms of acreage, has received a certain celebrity in the production of sweet, fortified wine. This rare variety is overwhelmingly concentrated in the warmer areas of Missouri and Arkansas, and it appears that the recent interest in its popularity is genuine. In addition to the above-mentioned varieties, it is estimated that nearly 1,000 more American grapes are planted, mostly in experimental plots and home gardens. Although the above list is comparatively short and many varieties appear exotic, it is important to note that many eastern nurseries maintain nursery stock for hundreds of grape varieties that have long been considered extinct or commercially useless. Some of the more popular include: Agawam, Elvira, Fredonia, Rosette, Valiant, Worden, Yates, Canadice, Einset, Lakemont, Remaily, Vanessa, and Venus.

AVERAGE DATE OF GRAPE HARVEST IN THE FINGER LAKES REGION OF NEW YORK STATE			
Variety	Date	Variety	Date
Aurora	9/9	Fredonia	9/16
Diamond	9/18	Buffalo	9/21
Verdelet	9/24	Seyval	9/24
Niagara	9/26	Marechal Foch	9/26
Cameo	9/26	Delaware	9/29
Cascade Noir	9/28	Chelois Noir	9/28
Baco Noir	9/30	Elvira	9/30
Rougeon Noir	9/30	Colobel Noir	9/30
Dutchess	10/4	Rosette Noir	10/6
Ives Noir	10/6	Ives Noir	10/6
Chardonnay	10/8	Vignoles	10/8
Chancellor	10/10	Steuben	10/11
Isabella	10/12	Pinot Noir	10/15
Concord	10/15	Cabernet Sauvignon	10/15
Catawba	10/15	Riesling	10/20

Vitis Rotundifolia

Until recently this specie of vine, part of the subgenus *Muscadiniae*, was second in importance to Labrusca. Rotundifolia (as well as the unimportant Munsoniana and Popenoei), native to the Gulf of Mexico, the coastal plain and the lower Piedmont areas of the southeast, were domesticated early and grown in backyards for nearly 400 years. These interesting grapes grow in this portion of America and nowhere else, and while the total pool of available varieties is 700, only a handful exhibit commercial possibilities, of which the Scuppernong (historically the most important variety, is named after a stream in North Carolina, and considered the oldest native commercial grape in the nation), Noble, Carlos, Conquistador, Magnolia, and Higgins are the most important. They have a tough skin to protect against the ravages of prolonged humidity and insects, grow in clusters like cherries, ripen early, and the yield can vary enormously. Furthermore, they are not susceptible to the rapacious Pierce's Disease. Also of significance, Rotundofolia are highly susceptible to drought and low temperatures.

These grapes have a rich scent, and produce a sweet wine with a flavor that, to the traditional purist, must be acquired. Its flavor is even penetrating enough to mask a Concord and Niagara, no insignificant feat. But despite its obvious physical attributes the rest of the nation finds the resulting wine disagreeable. The fame of Rotundifolia skyrocketed, for a brief period, through the efforts of the energetic Paul Garrett, who named the wine after the first child born of English parents in America--Virginia Dare.

Rotundifolia acreage has varied widely throughout recorded history, but, in general, acreage has declined significantly since 1975, although there are several pockets of growth. For example, while acreage has declined in Virginia, North and South Carolina, and Texas, it has grown in Georgia and Mississippi. Because the flavor improves dramatically when blended with other fruits, and the fruit is processed in much the same way as Labrusca grapes, Rotundifolia are not expected to disappear entirely from the southeast in the near future. In fact, recent technological improvements in the winery have produced a fresher, less musky product that for the first time allows the production of quality *mistelle*, dry and sparkling wines.

SELECTED LIST OF AMERICAN GRAPES

Grape/Species, Date of Discovery and/or Introduction, And State of Origin

Scuppernong (Rotundifolia)	1525	FL
Alexander (Labrusca/Vinifera?)	1740	PA
Herbemont (Bourquiniana)	1774?	GA
Catawba (Labrusca/Vinifera)	1801	SC
Sage (Labrusca)	1811	CT
Cunningham (Bourquiniana)	1812	VA
Devereaux (Bourquiniana)	1815	GA
Isabella (Labrusca/Vinifera)	1816	NY
Clinton (Riparia/Labrusca)	1819	NY
Lenoir (Bourquiniana)	1820	SC
Norton (Aestivalis/Labrusca)	1825	VA
Perkins (Labrusca/Vinifera)	1830	MA
To-Kalon (Labrusca/Vinifera)	1830	NY
Ohio I (Bourquiniana)	1834	OH
Diana (Labrusca/Vinifera/Aestivalis)	1834	MA
Ives (Labrusca/Aestivalis)	1840	OH
Taylor (Riparia/Labrusca)	1840	KY
Union Village (Labrusca/Vinifera)	1840	OH
Maxatawney (Labrusca/Vinifera)	1843	PA
Allen's Hybrid (Labrusca/Vinifera)	1843-1844	MA

Concord (Labrusca)	1844	MA	Brighton (Labrusca/Vinifera)	1870	NY
Cynthiana (Aestivalis/Labrusca)	1843	AR	Diamond (Labrusca/Vinifera)	1870	NY
Eumelian (Labrusca/Vinifera/Aestivalis)	1847	NY	Moore Early (Labrusca)	1870	MA
Hartford (Labrusca/Vinifera?)	1849	CT	Peabody (Riparia/Labrusca/Vinifera)	1870	NY
Delaware (Labrusca/Bourquiniana/Vinifera)	1849	NJ/OH	Pocklington (Labrusca)	1870	NY
Telegraph (Labrusca/Aestivalis)	1850	PA	Rockwood (Labrusca)	1870	MA
Walter (Vinifera/Labrusca/Bourquiniana)	1850	NY	Early Victor (Labrusca/Bourquiniana)	1871	KS
Winchell (Vinifera/Labrusca/Aestivalis)	1850	VT	Ideal (Labrusca/Vinifera/Bourquiniana)	1871	KS
Adirondack (Labrusca/Vinifera?)	1852	NY	Oneida (Vinifera/Labrusca)	1871	NY
Northern Muscadine (Labrusca)	1852	NY	Victoria (Labrusca/Vinifera)	1871	NJ
Rebecca (Labrusca/Vinifera)	1852	NY	Advance (Riparia/Labrusca/Vinifera)	1872	NY
Marion I (Riparia/Labrusca)	1853	OH	Hayes (Labrusca/Vinifera)	1872	MA
Eureka I (Labrusca)	1854	NY	Ironclad (Riparia/Labrusca)	1873	PA
Dracut Amber (Labrusca)	1855	MA	Prentiss (Labrusca/Vinifera)	1873	NY
Iona (Labrusca/Vinifera)	1855	NY	Jewel (Labrusca/Bourquiniana/Vinifera)	1874	KS
Clevener (Labrusca/Riparia/Aestivalis)	1855?	NJ	Geneva (Vinifera/Labrusca)	1874	NY
Marion II (Labrusca/Vinifera)	1855	OH	Jefferson (Labrusca/Vinifera)	1874	NY
Creveling (Labrusca/Vinifera)	1857	PA	Black Pearl (Riparia/Labrusca)	1874	OH
Goethe (Vinifera/Labrusca)	1858	MA	Early Daisy (Labrusca)	1874	PA
Janesville (Labrusca/Riparia)	1858	WI	Lady Washington (Labrusca/Vinifera)	1874	MA
Wilder (Labrusca/Vinifera)	1858	MA	Standard (Labrusca/Vinifera/Bourquiniana)	1874	KS
Merrimac (Labrusca/Vinifera)	1859	MA	Vergennes (Labrusca)	1874	VT
Othello (Vinifera/Riparia/Labrusca)	1859	CA	Woodruff (Labrusca/Vinifera?)	1874	MI
Autuchon (Riparia/Labrusca/Vinifera)	1859	CAN	Centennial (Labrusca/Aestivelis/Vinifera)	1875	NY
Massasoit (Labrusca/Vinifera)	1859	MA	Hosford (Labrusca)	1876	MI
Salem (Labrusca/Vinifera)	1859	MA	Poughkeepsie (Bourquiniana/Labrusca/Vinifera)	1880	NY
Oporto (Riparia/Labrusca)	1860	NY	Antoinette (Labrusca)	1877	NJ
Challenge (Labrusca/Vinifera?)	1860	NY	Beauty (Labrusca/Vinifera/Bourquiniana?)	1877	MO
Diana Hamburg (Vinifera/Labrusca/Aestivalis)	1860	MA	Bertrand (Bourquiniana)	1878	GA
Hermann (Aestivalis/Labrusca)	1860	MO	Grein Golden (Riparia/Labrusca)	1878	MO
Lindley (Labrusca/Vinifera)	1860	MA	Naomi (Vinifera/Riparia/Labrusca)	1879	NY
Louisiana (Bourquiniana)	1860	LA	Bacchus (Riparia/Labrusca)	1879	NY
Requa (Labrusca/Vinifera)	1860	MA	Montefiore (Riparia/Labrusca)	1879	MO
Triumph (Labrusca/Vinifera)	1860	OH	Empire State (Riparia/Labrusca/Vinifera)	1879	NY
Agawam (Labrusca/Vinifera)	1861	MA	Early Dawn (Labrusca/Vinifera/Aestivalis)	1879	NY
August Giant (Labrusca/Vinifera)	1861	MA	Etta (Riparia/Labrusca)	1879	MO
Wyoming (Labrusca)	1861	PA	Regal (Labrusca/Vinifera)	1879	IL
Elsinburgh (Vinifera/Aestivalis)	1862	NJ	Ulster (Labrusca/Vinifera)	1879	NY
Essex (Labrusca/Vinifera)	1862	MA	Norwood (Vinifera/Labrusca)	1880	MA
Lady (Labrusca/Vinifera)	1862	OH	Delawba (Labrusca/Vinifera/Bourquiniana)	1880	NY
Bryant (Riparia/Labrusca/Vinifera)	1863	CAN	Eclipse II (Labrusca/Vinifera)	1880	KS
Senasqua (Labrusca/Vinifera)	1863	NY	Colerain (Labrusca)	1880	OH
Worden (Labrusca)	1863	NY	Eureka II (Bourquiniana/Labrusca/Vinifera)	1880	NY
Gaertner (Vinifera/Labrusca)	1864	MA	Excelsior (Vinifera/Labrusca)	1880	MA
Norfolk (Labrusca/Vinifera)	1864	MA	Shelby (Labrusca/Riparia)	1880	NY
Aminia (Labrusca/Vinifera)	1865	NY	Superb (Labrusca/Vinifera/Aestivalis)	1880	GA
Herbert (Labrusca/Vinifera)	1865	MA	White Imperial (Vinifera/Labrusca/Bourquiniana)	1880	KS
Downing (Vinifera/Aestivalis/Labrusca)	1865	NY	Bell (Riparia/Labrusca/Bourquiniana/Vinifera)	1881	TX
Croton (Vinifera/Labrusca/Bourquiniana)	1865	NY	Faith (Riparia/Labrusca)	1881	MO
Black Defiance (Labrusca/Vinifera)	1866	NY	Eaton (Labrusca)	1882	MA
Black Eagle (Labrusca/Vinifera)	1866	NY	Early Ohio (Labrusca)	1882	OH
Monroe (Labrusca/Bourquiniana?)	1867	NY	Nectar (Labrusca/Bourquiniana/Vinifera)	1883	NY
Rochester (Labrusca/Vinifera)	1867	NY	Brilliant (Labrusca/Vinifera/Bourquiniana)	1883	TX
Secretary (Vinifera/Riparia/Labrusca)	1867	NY	Gold Coin (Aestivalis/Labrusca)	1883	TX
Martha (Labrusca/Vinifera?)	1868	PA	Alexander Winter (Labrusca/Vinifera?)	1884	OH
Highland (Vinifera/Labrusca)	1868	NY	Ambrosia (Labrusca/Vinifera)	1884	NY
Berckmans (Riparia/Labrusca/Bourquiniana)	1868	SC	Alice II (Labrusca/Aestivalis/Vinifera?)	1884	NY
Dutchess (Vinifera/Labrusca/Bourq.?/Aest.?)	1868-1880	NY	Florence (Labrusca/Vinifera/Bourquiniana)	1884	NY
Niagara (Labrusca/Vinifera)	1868	NY	Ozark (Aestivalis/Labrusca)	1885	MO
Barry (Labrusca/Vinifera)	1869	MA	Columbian Imperial (Labrusca/Riparia)	1885	OH
Golden Drop (Labrusca/Vinifera/Bourquiniana)	1869	VT	Fern Munson (Lincecumii/Vinifera/Labrusca)	1885	TX
Cottage (Labrusca)	1869	MA	Goff (Labrusca/Vinifera/Aestivalis)	1885	NY
Elvira (Riparia/Labrusca)	1869	MO	Lutie (Labrusca)	1885	TN
Imperial (Vinifera/Labrusca)	1869	NY	Rommel (Labrusca/Riparia/Vinifera)	1885	TX
Noah (Riparia/Labrusca)	1869	IL	Hercules (Labrusca/Vinifera)	1886	IL
Mills (Labrusca/Vinifera)	1870	CAN	Green Early (Labrusca/Vinifera?)	1887	NY
Jessica (Labrusca/Vinifera)	1870	CAN	Bailey (Lincecumii/Labrusca/Vinifera)	1887	TX
Kensington (Vinifera/Riparia/Labrusca)	1870	CAN	R.W. Munson (Lincecumii/Labrusca/Vinifera)	1887	TX
Missouri Riesling (Riparia/Labrusca)	1870	MO	Beacon (Lincecumii/Labrusca)	1887	TX
Champion (Labrusca)	1870	NY	Ohio II (Labrusca)	1888	OH
Eldorado (Labrusca/Vinifera)	1870	NY	Red Eagle (Labrusca/Vinifera)	1888	TX
Amber Queen (Vinifera/Riparia/Labrusca)	1870	MA	Ester (Labrusca)	1889	MA

Isabella Seedling (Labrusca/Vinifera)	1889	NY
Glenfeld (Labrusca)	1889	NY
Alice I (Labrusca)	1890	NY
James (Rotundifolia)	1890	NC
Jaeger (Lincecumii/Bourquiniana)	1890	TX
Lucile (Labrusca)	1890	NY
Eclipse I (Labrusca)	1890	IL
Chautauqua (Labrusca)	1890	NY
Perfection (Labrusca/Bourquiniana/Vinifera)	1890	KS
McPike (Labrusca)	1891	KS
America (Lincecumii/Rupestris)	1892	AR
Campbell Early (Labrusca/Vinifera)	1892	OH
King (Labrusca?)	1892	MI
Carman (Lincecumii/Vinifera/Labrusca)	1892	TX
Brown (Labrusca/Vinifera)	1892	NY
Elvicand (Candicans/Riparia/Labrusca)	1893	TX
Headlight (Vinifera/Labrusca/Bourquiniana)	1895	TX
Hidalgo (Vinifera/Labrusca/Bourquiniana)	1895	TX
St. Louis (Labrusca)	1897	MO
Amethyst (Labrusca/Vinifera/Bourquiniana)	1898	TX
Hicks (Labrusca)	1898	MO
Banner (Labrusca/Vinifera/Bourquiniana?)	1898	AR
Wapanuka (Labrusca/Riparia/Vinifera/Bourquiniana)	1898	TX
Cloeta (Lincecumii/Rupestris/Labrusca/Vinifera)	1902	TX
Canandaigua (Labrusca/Vinifera)	1906	NY

French-American Varieties

French-American varieties, the progeny of Vinifera and non-Vinifera vines, were first developed as a solution to eastern environmental problems in America, and to phylloxera in Europe, the latter significantly more successful in the production of modern, successful commercial varieties. As the phylloxera epidemic spread quickly in Europe in the second half of the nineteenth century, many new proposals were put forth as solutions to a pest that was decimating vineyards by the thousands of acres each year. One solution promulgated was the production of American-Vinifera crosses to produce a phylloxera-resistant vine. Over the course of the next two generations since the outbreak of phylloxera in Europe in 1868, French hybridizers (Francois Baco, J.F. Ravat, J.L. Vidal, Albert Seibel, Bertelle Seyve, Eugene Kuhlmann, Victor Villard, and Pierre Landot, among others) produced thousands of crosses with varying degrees of success. By 1952, more than 1 million acres were planted in France. In eastern America the problems from the beginning have been three-fold--to make them winter resistant, to eliminate the foxy flavor and scent, and to produce a vine that would yield a distinctive wine with character. Although the phylloxera problem was solved by grafting Vinifera vines to phylloxera-resistant American rootstock, the objective of developing the "perfect" grape for the cold climates of America continues to this day. Nevertheless, French-American varieties have, since the mid-1970s, become the second most important type of grape in eastern America.

French-American vines, arriving in the United States in the late 1930s, were thought to be a panacea by Philip Wagner, newspaper publisher and owner of Boordy Vineyard in Maryland. Although there is considerable varia-

tion among all French-American varieties, they are not as tolerant as native grapes to cold, humidity, and widely fluctuating winter and spring temperatures. The main advantage, particularly among the most successful white varieties (Vidal Blanc and Seyval are said to account for more than 50 percent of French-American acreage), is the absence of a pronounced foxy flavor and aroma. They have higher sugar levels, and most have acid levels similar to American grapes. As varietal wines, they are not as fruity, have more pronounced musky odors and flavors, but blend and produce different wines. There is a growing trend to blend Vinifera wine with French-America wines with some measure of success. The the most popular varietals are Seyval, Vidal Blanc, Vignoles, Chambourcin, Aurore, and Chancellor, the first four yielding the highest financial returns.

The white varieties are:

Aurore (Seibel 5279), is a flavorful, spicy, grapey variety used for blending purposes, and in the production of sparkling wines. Due to its ability to adapt to most soils, this vigorous, hardy, and dependable yielder, is one of the most widely cultivated French-American varieties. Because it buds early, it is widely grown in areas with a short growing season, but due to black and bunch rot, it has limited possibilities in the more humid and hotter southern portions of the nation. It makes pleasant, fruity wine, and is particularly good when made sweet. Until 1980 it was the most widely planted French-American variety in New York. It is one of the few white varieties whose flavor and aroma improves with wood aging. Developed in the late 1880s, the vine is also spelled Aurora. **Baco Blanc** (Baco 22A), although an approved A.O.C. grape in France, this variety, the product of Folle Blanche and Noah, has fewer than 10 acres in America. **Rayon d'Or** (Seibel 4986), is a hardy and productive variety that cannot compete with Seyval, Vidal Blanc, and Vignoles. **Cayuga** (Geneva White #3), developed by the Geneva Experiment Station, and named after one of the Finger Lakes, is a vine producing full-flavored wine with considerable body and substance. It is a cross between Seyve-Villard and Schuyler (a cross of Zinfandel and Ontario). Although the cross was made in 1945 and the fruit first described in 1952, the variety was rather rapidly diffused throughout the Finger Lakes region, the Hudson River Valley, Lake Erie, and in scattered areas throughout the midwest. In the mid-Atlantic region its introduction and eventual adoption did not occur until recently. Best made with low alcohol levels and some residual sugar, the wine is fresh on the palate, appealing, and not overly foxy. To date it has been unsuccessful in competing with both Seyval and Vidal Blanc.

Seyval (Seyve-Villard 5276), commonly referred to as the "Chenin Blanc of the east," is a winter hardy vine that produces consistently high yields, tolerates a broad range of soils (even wet soils), and is considered by many to be superior to Vidal Blanc in the production of quality white table wine. Despite its often criticized bitter and astringent character, it has the ability to vary its flavor and aroma components with growing conditions. It is made in three distinct styles: stainless steel with some residual sugar, stainless steel and dry; or wood-aged and dry. The latter, most commonly made from riper grapes in the mid-Atlantic states and Virginia, is fuller, rounder, and exhibits impressive bottle improvement. The stainless steel styles have higher acid levels, are fresher, fruitier, and their character dominated by more pronounced apple and green-fruit flavors. Wine quality improves dramatically when blended with fruit and berry wines, Chardonnay, Riesling, and Sauvignon Blanc.

Seyval, although widely distributed, is mainly confined to the mid-Atlantic states, Connecticut, New York, and the warmer and more protected areas of the midwest where it matures comparatively early. It is the most widely planted white French-American grape in the east. It is interesting to note that the first commercial Seyval grape was grown by G. Hamilton Mowbray in Westminster, Maryland in 1955. At present, Seyval and Vidal Blanc are the two most successful white French-American varieties for the production of quality white table wine. While growers in the mid-Atlantic states and portions of New York consider this grape to be more reliable than Vidal Blanc, its acreage is surprisingly low given its potential as a quality French-American variety.

Verdelet (Seibel 9110), is a variety that is able to produce fair quality dry wine, but since it is not winter hardy, it has limited appeal in the colder portions of the east. One bright spot for future potential lies in the fact that it resists oxidation, thus maintaining good color. The wines contain a measure of delicacy, particularly when made with some residual sugar.

Vidal Blanc (Vidal 256), is widely grown in the mid-Atlantic states, and to a lesser extent in the Great Lakes region. Containing no pronounced Labrusca flavor (it is a cross of Rayon d'Or and Ugni Blanc), it is disease resistant, easy to grow, and gives high yields primarily in the mid-Atlantic states, where it is considered the premier "economic" grape. Vidal Blanc has a tough, thick skin that resists most diseases, is able to "hang" until Christmas, and can, due to a wide spectrum of flavors and aromas, be made into many different styles. Growing particularly well in southeast Pennsylvania, the vine produces a wine with a pronounced bouquet and elegance. The search for the best growing area continues as the character of the grape changes dramatically with growing conditions. It is becoming quite popular because of its geographical adaptability, its ability to produce above-average quality dry table to sweet late harvest wine, and improve other French-American wines. Its acreage, therefore, is likely to grow in the near future.

Vignoles (Ravat 51), is considered a rising star due to its ability to mature with abnormally high sugar and acid levels, producing excellent, well-balanced sweet wine. Although Aurore and Niagara compete, it is Vignoles that produces the finest sweet wine (bitterness and astringency are major flaws when made into a dry, table wine) in the entire northeast and midwest among French-American and American varieties. Despite low yields, a tendency for fungus diseases and somewhat limited aging potential, its high acid levels, intense flavor, and penetrating aroma make it one of the finest grapes in the northeast, particularly in the cooler portions. Acreage has increased dramatically from fewer than 50 in 1960 to more than 500, mostly in New York, Michigan, Pennsylvania, and Ohio. It is a mid-season, thin-skinned, golden-colored grape with good potential. **Villard Blanc (Seyve-Villard 12375)**, is a minor, late ripening grape used for sweet wine production in the central portion of the east where the growing season is longer, but not excessively humid.

The red varieties are:

Baco Noir (Baco No. 1), first introduced in the Finger Lakes region in 1949, is one of the most popular French-American red varieties. A cross of Folle Blanche and Riparia, its main advantage is that it ripens early in a short season, hence, its popularity in cooler areas. Because it will grow on poor glacial soils and ripen one month earlier than Concord, it is often made into a varietal in the cooler regions of the east, especially in the Great Lakes region where it does best. Its more common use is as a blending grape in New England, New York, and nearly everywhere in the midwest. Extremely vigorous, it unfortunately is susceptible to late spring frosts, and will succumb to trunk damage and fungus diseases. Although it maintains good color, has a good spicy flavor and aroma, it does not age, and its quality varies widely with the growing area. **Cascade (Seibel 13053)**, is an obscure, blue-black, early ripening variety that produces light, fruity, rose-type wines. Historically important in the Finger Lakes region of New York, fewer than 10 acres remain.

Chambourcin (Seyve 26-205). Although Joannes Seyve is given credit as the hybridizer, there is controversy as to its true origins because it is a monoglucocite. Although it looks and tastes like a French-American hybrid, its genetic make-up is Vinifera. Nevertheless, it is becoming the most important French-American red variety in the east, and is, after Cynthiana/Norton, the most expensive non-Vinifera, red wine grape. In France, it is the second most widely planted red French-American variety, where its acreage increased rapidly from 158 acres in 1958 to more than 8,000 acres in 1979. Recent experimentation in Australia has proven favorable for commercial plantings in the Hastings Valley. Although introduced in the east in the early 1960s, acreage did not expand until the mid 1970s when an Ohio winery made it as a varietal in 1973. Since then, acreage has expanded to 700 acres, and is

growing. It is one of the few red French-American varieties whose wine improves with wood aging and enjoys a good and expanding position, particularly in the mid-Atlantic states. Considered by many to be superior to Chancellor, the vine is easy to grow, a predictable high yielder, and quite hardy in its ability to withstand wide winter temperature fluctuations (but not prolonged low temperatures as in the Finger Lakes region of New York), and because it ripens late, it produces one of the highest sugar levels of any French-American variety. Adaptable to different soils and not overly prone to the destructive effects of false springs, it is susceptible to black rot and powdery mildew. It produces a dark, highly stained wine, but because it ripens late, it often has green, vegetative flavors, hence, is highly restricted to the warmer mid-Atlantic states, and scattered portions of the midwest such as southeastern Pennsylvania, Maryland, Virginia, Arkansas, and Missouri. However, its spicy, peppery flavors and color intensity decline rapidly as the summer season is extended, as in North and South Carolina.

Chancellor (Seibel 7053), an excellent grape in the Hudson River Valley in terms of flavor, dark color, body, longevity, and reduced foxiness, is essentially a blending grape throughout the rest of the northeast. Due to the fact that this vigorous, high yielding variety is susceptible to downy and powdery mildew, and only moderately winter hardy, its geographic distribution is highly localized in those areas where considerable protection exists. When properly made and carefully wood-aged, Chancellor is one of the finest French-American varietals.

Chelois (Seibel 10878), one of the older varieties, has a good berry flavor and aroma, and while used as a blending grape in the northeast, it is often seen, despite noticeable green, vegetal and Labrusca flavors, as a varietal in the Great Lakes and Finger Lakes regions. While this vigorous variety yields well, it is susceptible to bunch rot and eutypa, thus limiting its geographic distribution. Historically more popular, this fairly hardy variety is not as popular as Chambourcin and Chancellor, hence, declining in acreage. While it is, perhaps, best for rose wine production, Chelois improves significantly when blended with Cabernet Sauvignon.

DeChaunac (Seibel 9549), often referred to as the "Zinfandel" of the east, was a highly overrated and overplanted grape in the 1960-1980 period. For a time it was considered a shining star and a panacea in the search for the ideal red eastern grape. The vine offered many distinct advantages, the most important of which were its ability to grow profusely, withstand rapid drops in temperature without major damage to the trunk and buds, and resistance to fungus diseases. Although it is easy to grow, its vigorous bushy canopy, unpredictable but generously high yields, and propensity to produce wine devoid of delicacy have quickly scared its early successes. The major disadvantages are that the wine doesn't age well, and its rough, vegetal and herbal flavor is all to often dull, tired, and unexciting. Because high pH levels preclude an inability to retain color, it is best used in the making of blush wines by carbonic maceration. It is often said by disappointed winemakers that not only is it incapable of making good wine, but birds even refuse to eat it. Although a true Seibel, it has been unofficially baptized DeChaunac after Adehmar de Chaunac (1896-1972), a Bordeaux-born Canadian who worked as a chemist for Brights Winery, and who imported and introduced the vine from France.

Landot Noir (Landot Noir 4511), a rather recent arrival in the east, is rapidly being taken seriously due to its high yields and ability to improve with barrel aging. With fewer than 100 acres throughout the northeast and the mid-Atlantic states, acreage is expected to increase substantially in the near future. The variety is resistant to mildews, but because it is sensitive to low temperatures, its future lies in the warmer areas of the east. This variety should not be confused with Landot 4511, a good winter hardy vine, but a less desirable wine grape. **Leon Millot (Kuhlmann 194-2)**, a product of a black Riparia and Rupestris, among others, is a little known, early maturing, high yielding variety more widely grown in the upper midwest than in the northeast. This variety is responsible for herbaceous and grassy flavored wines not too dissimilar from Marechal Foch. **Marechal Foch (Kuhlmann 188-2)**, a cross between Vitis Riparia/Rupestris, Gamay Beaujolais, and Pinot Noir, is an early maturing, winter hardy, and vigorous producer that is resistant to downy mildew. The vine, widely planted throughout the cooler portions of the northeast and midwest, produces good sugar levels, and a wine that can be exceptionally fruity. The berry-flavored wine, however, has poor color, is often bitter, lacks tannin, has a grassy and/or herbaceous aroma, and a tendency to oxidize. Despite its geographic diversity, it enjoys an element of celebrity only in selected fringe areas along the Great Lakes. Strangely, it produces a surprisingly good and expensive wine in the Willamette Valley of Oregon. **Rougeon Noir (Seibel 5898)**, is a high yielding variety that matures late, but because it is moderately susceptible to both downy and powdery mildew, it has limited potential in areas where it competes with Concord despite the fact that it has good color, and a muted foxy nose and flavor.

Other French-American varieties include **Sovereign Opal**, a cross between Marechal Foch and Golden Muscat first released by the Agricultural Research Station in Summerland, British Columbia. Similar to Riesling with a hint of Muscat, it is considered good for the northeast and midwest; **Colobel**, a *teinturier* used for blending purposes, is otherwise undistinguished; **Florental**, a Gamay hybrid, is not only difficult to grow, but produces tart, undistinguished wine as well; **Castel 19-637**, a vigorous, winter-hardy variety, makes dark-colored, but musty flavored wine with limited appeal. Other minor varieties include Bellandais, Couderc, Landal, Ravat Noir, Rosette, and Villard Noir.

Vinifera Varieties

When native grapes proved to be wine disappointments, legendary attempts were made to import and grow Vinifera varieties throughout eastern America. Planted repeatedly for hundreds of years, commercial Vinifera plantings failed, due to a combination of winter kill, fungus diseases induced by high heat and humidity, phylloxera, poor vineyard practices, the dominance of acidic soils, and, until recently, an absence of effective chemicals to combat disease. Still, enough evidence has been collected over the past 30 years to suggest that Vinifera can survive north of latitude 35 degrees if properly planted on sites that are protected from cold northerly winds, and sound vineyard practices are followed. This means that crop reduction is imperative as this cultural practice hardens wood faster and alleviates the danger of winter injury; that only the hardiest clones and the finest rootstocks be selected; and a rigid vineyard management system be adopted using higher vine densities per acre, as well as the most effective fungicides.

The problem with Vinifera vines is that they are unable to weather the sudden variations and low winter temperatures of the northeast and midwest. Every eight to ten years, a severe cold winter will kill a large number of vines, and frustrated growers will not replant. However, new grafting techniques, superior clones, and better vineyard practices in recent years have markedly improved the marginal growing habits of most Vinifera vines. Despite the dramatic strides made with Vinifera grapes during the past 30 years, the number of "Vinifera-only" wineries is limited to fewer than 50, nearly all located in New York, Virginia, Texas, and Maryland. Nevertheless, the growth of Vinifera plantings since 1960 has been nothing short of spectacular, rising from fewer than 50 acres to more than 6,000 planted mainly in New York, southern New England, the mid-Atlantic states, Virginia, Michigan, and Texas. In cold interior locations where climatic conditions are marginal, growers are reluctant to plant Vinifera vines because of low yields, and the fact that the vines do not come into bearing as quickly as American and French-American varieties. As quality Vinifera (Chardonnay, Pinot Noir, Cabernet Sauvignon, Merlot, Sauvignon Blanc, Gewurztraminer, Semillon, and Riesling) are currently fetching prices ranging from $600 to $1,400 the ton, a 10 acre vineyard, in sharp contrast to native and French-American varieties, has become a lucrative economic proposition.

The two mainstays of the white eastern Vinifera grapes are Riesling and Chardonnay, followed by Gewurztraminer, the latter, a distant third but showing some demand stability. Others include Rkatsiteli, Pinot Blanc, Sereskia, Aligote, Semillon, and Sauvignon Blanc. Riesling produces a tight cluster of small-berried fruit, is subject to winter injury, and susceptible to disease, especially black rot. There are many clones, and the fruit is fragile, ripening unevenly in most vintages. While one of the hardiest Vinifera, the wines, unfortunately, are highly variable, ranging from true varietal character to thin, watery, nondescript wines. At its best, Riesling offers incredible range of style from dry to sweet, all being clean, crisp, and absolutely first class in ability to refresh the palate with delicate fruit and flower flavors. At the moment, its popularity is handicapped by a poor image, inappropriate food affinities, and the high cost of production relative to Chardonnay, a more easily marketed variety.

Chardonnay, the most prestigious white Vinifera vine in the nation, encompasses 2,000 acres in the east, of which Texas, New York, the mid-Atlantic states, and Virginia account for more than 90 percent of the acreage. Although it was first grown in the Finger Lakes region, there are fewer than 900 acres in New York, 350 acres in Virginia, 100 acres along the fringes of the Great Lakes, and 800 acres in Texas. Each major producing region generally exhibits distinct characteristics: Chardonnay from Long Island is fruity, delicate, and fresh; from the Finger Lakes region it is fruity, austere on the palate, and highly acidic; from southeastern Pennsylvania it is austere and bitter on the palate; from Virginia, the wine is rich, round, full-bodied and satisfying; and from Texas, the wine is austere, alcoholic, and lean. Because Chardonnay suffers from early bud break, and therefore susceptible to frost damage, it does best in the maritime portions of eastern Long Island and mid-Atlantic states. Despite these regional variations, all eastern Chardonnay, due to higher acids, is generally more French in style than Californian. Gewurztraminer is an underrated wine, particularly in the production of late harvest and sparkling wine production. It does best in western Michigan, eastern Long Island, and the Finger Lakes. Sauvignon Blanc, less winter-hardy than Pinot Blanc, but significantly more vigorous than Merlot, is mainly grown in eastern Long Island where it produces excellent, dry, well-balanced wines.

Among red Vinifera varieties, the most important, with an estimated 1,500 acres, is Cabernet Sauvignon, a grape that, due to greater cold sensitivity, enjoys a more limited geographic distribution pattern than white Vinifera varieties, particularly Riesling. It is, therefore, mainly confined to eastern Long Island, the mid-Atlantic states, and Texas, although there are several excellent producers in the Lake Erie portion of Ohio, Lake Keuka, southeastern Pennsylvania, and the Hudson River Valley. First grown in the Finger Lakes region in the 1950s, there are now more than 65 wineries producing wine from what is generally acknowledged to be the finest red grape. Although temperamental, the vine does much better than its arch-rival--Pinot Noir, a vine that ripens unevenly, is less winter hardy, and makes light-bodied, flavorless wine. Merlot, less winter-hardy than Pinot Noir and Cabernet Sauvignon, is the second most popular red Vinifera varietal. It generally produces a soft, well-flavored and balanced wine that is the equal of Cabernet Sauvignon, primarily in eastern Long Island and northern Virginia. In the final analysis, all Vinifera varieties, when allowed to ripen fully, have a capacity to produce well-balanced, complex and fruity wines. The very best currently compete favorably with west coast equivalents.

NEW ENGLAND

Never regarded as a significant wine producing region, New England, over the course of the past 20 years, has quietly experienced an impressive viticultural revolution. From just one winery and fewer than 20 commercial acres in 1971, the six-state region now contains 22 grape wineries (11 of which were established in the decade of the 1980s), about 35 vineyards, and nearly 800 acres of grapes. The region also contains many thriving commercial fruit and berry wine producers. While New England has been historically littered by several unimpressive vineyards and wineries, the success rate has been so remarkable in recent years that the industry trend is expected to continue its upward momentum.

The main climatic features may be described as follows: (1) even distribution of precipitation among the four seasons; (2) large ranges and fluctuations of temperature, both daily and seasonal; (3) significant differences in temperature in the same season or month of different years; and (4) considerable diversity in the weather over short periods of time. The procession of contrasting air masses and the relatively frequent passage of storms bring about a roughly twice weekly alternation from fair to cloudy or storm conditions, usually attended by abrupt changes in temperature, moisture, sunshine, and wind directions. There is no regular or persistent rhythm to this sequence. Weather is better known for its day to day variability rather than monotony.

Figure 5.2

WINERY DISTRIBUTION AND APPELLATIONS

1. Western Connecticut Highland, 2. Martha's Vineyard, 3. Southern New England.

Climate is a function of elevation, exposure, shifting prevailing westerlies through the St. Lawrence Lowland, the cold Labrador Current bathing coastal areas as far south as Boston, and the Gulf Stream extending the growing season by at least 30 days in southern Massachusetts. As a result, the growing season, in all but the southern facing margins of Massachusetts, Connecticut, and Rhode Island, ranges between 100 and 145 days. However, along the southern margins of Massachusetts, Rhode Island, Connecticut, and the offshore islands of Massachusetts and Rhode Island, the growing season extends to 190, and often to 200 days. In addition, the abbreviated growing season and the persistency of false springs, a high incidence of cloudiness, a clay-dominated subsoil, and the dominance of a cold, relentless winter have limited French-American production to protected sites, and Vinifera plantings only to localities where the growing season extends to at least 180 days. While precipitation varies from 30 inches in the south to 45 inches in the north (most of which falls during the growing season), it is the variable character of temperature unpredictability that is most unfavorable to viticulture.

A distinctive physical and cultural region, New England, with 7 percent of the nation's population and 2 percent of the land area, manages to produce 3 percent of the nation's agricultural wealth. An area of highly concentrated population, and large areas of depopulated and abandoned hill areas, New England is the keeper of about 12 percent of the nation's total demand deposits forming one of the most concentrated pockets of high disposable income in the country. Because dairying, the leading agricultural activity, is on the decline, viticulture, in scattered, well-chosen locations, competes well with other crops.

New England, consisting of Maine, Vermont, New Hampshire, Massachusetts, Rhode Island, and Connecticut, is one of the most readily identifiable geographic regions of America. The region consists of a series of north-south glaciated hills, low mountains, and river valleys with a marginal climate for American, and a forbidding climate for Vinifera and French-American grape production. Unlike the southern section of the Appalachians, the glacial character New England formed during the Pleistocene is most pronounced and dominates the physiography and soils of the entire region. New England is also less humid, colder, and has few minerals, particularly fossil fuels, than hilly regions further south. Soils are characterized by glacial drift and alluvial material, especially in coastal areas and river valleys. While devoid of calcareous material, the preponderance of crystalline rocks has resulted in thin, highly acidic regolith littered with stone and boulder. The sequence of deposition of outwash glacial material throughout the warmer portions of the southern section has produced many locations where well-drained sand, silt, and gravel provide good viticultural opportunities.

Figure 5.3

NEW ENGLAND: CLIMATIC PATTERNS

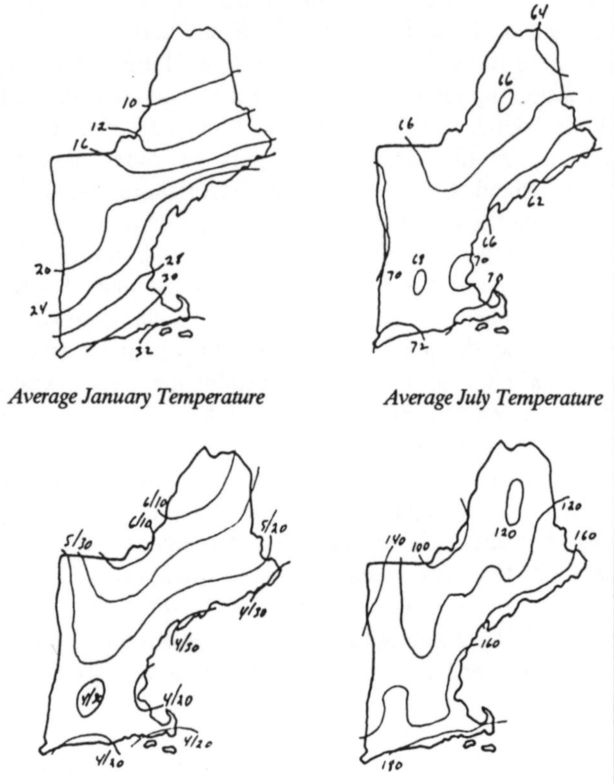

Average January Temperature   *Average July Temperature*

Last Spring Killing Frost   *Length of Growing Season*
The distribution of grapes in New England is a function of winter temperatures, last spring frost date of April 30, and a 160-day growing season. Consequently, winegrowing is concentrated along the southern margins. The lack of vineyards in coastal Massachusetts north of Boston is restricted by urbanization.
Source: U.S. Weather Bureau.

History and Viticultural Areas

Long before California's Napa, Sonoma and Central Valley's wine districts were producing wine, it is reported that the Mayflower Pilgrims attempted to ferment wine from wild grapes in 1621. While that noble experiment has been questioned by historians, wine was made by the Massachusetts Bay Colony in 1632, and soon, backyard vineyards were being planted along the Atlantic Ocean, many river valleys, and along Long Island Sound. However, while there were many attempts throughout the colonial period to grow vines commercially, all attempts at making good wine resulted in failure, including the valiant effort by Governor John Winthrop to grow grapes and make wine in Boston Harbor (Conant's Island) in 1632. Given the fact that these first attempts resulted in ruin, it is no wonder that New England has long been known for its beer, hard cider, rum, and whiskey consumption. Wines consisted of locally produced apple and various berry libations. One interesting innovation, particularly in Massachusetts and Rhode Island, was the production of grape wine from greenhouse grown fruit, but that too did not last long. While a few "cottage" wineries pressed grapes along the Charles River in the middle of the nineteenth century, New England's mark in the enological history of eastern America did not occur until the development of the Concord grape.

In 1843 Ephraim Bull developed the Concord grape in Concord, Massachusetts, and while hardy and adaptable, it failed to influence the wine drinking habits of the region. Until recently, the commercial cultivation of vines proved impossible, but in 1964, Lucille and John Canepa of White Mountain Vineyards created the first bonded winery in New Hampshire producing wine from French-American varieties. Today, the three northern states of Maine, New Hampshire, and Vermont make nothing but fruit and berry wines (with only one exception in New Hampshire). The principal fruit wineries are: Bartlett Maine Estate Winery (Gouldsboro, Maine, 1983, Apple, Blueberry, Mead, Pear, Raspberry, Strawberry), Bishop Farms Winery (Cheshire, Connecticut, 1987, Apple, Pear, Cranberry), Joseph Cerniglia (Proctorsville, Vermont, 1986, Apple, Pear, Raspberry), Down East Country Wines (Trenton, Maine, 1984, Blueberry, Apple), Nashoba Valley Winery (Bolton, Massachusetts, 1980, Apple, Pear, Blueberry, Plum, Peach, Strawberry, Raspberry), North River Winery (Jacksonville, Vermont, 1985, Apple), and West County Winery (Colrain, Massachusetts, 1984, Apple, Raspberry, Peach). With one winery in New Hampshire the only exception, only the three southern New England states of Massachusetts, Rhode Island, and Connecticut produce grape wine.

Rural New England, described as "rock-ribbed, thin-soiled, acidic, and unfriendly," has long been plagued by land abandonment in favor of more lucrative electronics, defense-oriented, and commercial pursuits. Yet, over the past fifteen years, this region, known for baked beans and fish, but not wine, has tripled its vine acreage and number of wineries. Although all are small (the largest only makes 27,000 cases) and family owned, they are the product of farm winery legislation. Wineries are found only in the extreme southern margins of New England, especially in Connecticut, a state that has more than 50 percent of the regional total. It is an area with some optimism, with new capital, and young, innovative winemakers. Not only is vine acreage highly concentrated in Connecticut, but it is also the state with the greatest potential because it lies in a transition zone between the humid subtropical climate to the south and the humid continental climate to the north. The state contains at least 2,000 potentially suitable acres of vineland and a growing season greater than 185 days. Unfortunately, the finest grape producing regions of New England--Martha's Vineyard and Nantucket Island, have limited future potential due to high land costs. In 1981, with eleven wineries, New Englanders met and formed a regional association of wineries and grape growers. Of considerable importance is the presence (mostly in the three northern states of Vermont, New Hampshire, and Maine) of at least seven additional wineries that make nothing but fruit and berry wines. Although historically the wines of new England were relegated to the status of *vin de pays*, quality has been markedly improved in recent years, and the wines are now distributed outside the northeast. The winemaking future of New England bodes well for two good reasons: the region contains a highly urbane, affluent, and sophisticated population, and per capita wine consumption is rising.

Grape acreage of less than 800 acres for the entire region supports 23 wineries that collectively produce fewer than 150,000 cases. What is interesting about this hitherto unknown vineyard is the fact that more than half of the acreage is devoted to Vinifera vines, mostly Chardonnay, Riesling, Pinot Noir, Cabernet Sauvignon, Merlot, and Sauvignon Blanc. While the amount of acreage is small, the combined Vinifera acreage is that which exists in the midwest, but one-fifth that found in eastern Long Island, and one-quarter of existing Vinifera acreage in Virginia. Among French-American varieties, the most common are Vidal Blanc, Seyval, Cayuga, Chancellor, and Baco Noir. Despite the historic importance of Concord, the region produces few commercial American grapes. Although there are wide variations in style and type, the character and quality of New England wines is influenced by a long growing season, and cool summer temperatures (July temperature for Long Island Sound-Rhode Island averages 70F) that collectively produce fruit that is high in acid. Grapes are picked with a low pH, and the resulting wines are exceptionally fruity, fragrant, and

delicate. The finest areas for future vineyard expansion lie on carefully selected sites along Long Island Sound, and the fragmented, deep water coast and islands of Rhode Island and Massachusetts. The only winery in the northern portion of the region is The New Hampshire Winery (Henniker, 1969), formerly White Mountain Vineyard, and Lakes Region Winery (located in Lakonia), a 1,500-case winery that makes Marechal Foch and a blended French-American (Aurore, Edelweiss, Seyval, Marechal Foch, and DeChaunac), proprietary, various varietal Vinifera wines (from California must), fruit wines, and also bottles spring water.

There are three *ava's* in New England: *Martha's Vineyard (1985)*, *Western Connecticut Highlands (1988)*, and the much larger *Southeastern New England (1984)*, the latter, encompassing 2,450 square miles of coastal land adjoining the Long Island Sound region of southern Connecticut, Rhode Island, and Massachusetts south of Boston. This *ava* hugs the coast and only extends eleven miles inland to Stonington in eastern Connecticut. Due to its coastal location, the climate is a patchwork of microclimates, more temperate than interior locations, with highly variable glacial soils changing every ten feet.

Massachusetts And Rhode Island

Although Massachusetts is not the largest state, it does contain nearly half of the region's population (more than 6 million people), the largest metropolitan city, and the largest wine market. It is densely populated and highly irregular in shape, with most of the population residing in metropolitan Boston, an area containing seven of the state's largest fifteen cities. Like its sister states to the south, 80 percent of the land area lies at elevations below 1,500 feet. It was first explored by Bartholomew Gosnold, and became the first area to accommodate English settlement in 1620 at Plymouth. Boston was settled in 1630, and Harvard the first college, was established in 1636.

Ever since Massachusetts passed a Limited Winery Law in 1977, first proposed by Chicama Vineyards, seven other wineries have been founded, and another three are expected to open by 1993. There are 325 acres, half of which are planted in Vinifera vines, mostly in Dudley and South Dartmouth. The only *ava* entirely within state borders is *Martha's Vineyard*, a 100 square mile area with only one winery--Chicama Vineyards. Its *raison d'etre* is its glacial morainic soils, and a 210-day growing season, the longest in the state. While the long growing season delays frost damage, strong and persistent salty oceanic winds not only destroy leaves, but ruin proper flower set. Interestingly, while American vines are indigenous to the island there are no large scale commercial plantings of American grapes. With the demise of Commonwealth Winery in 1988, the state's largest, Massachusetts has only eight remaining grape wineries, all superbly sited to attract the tourist.

They are: **Chicama Vineyards** (Martha's Vineyard, 1971), is an 18-acre, 6,500-case winery that makes Chenin Blanc, Chardonnay, Sauvignon Blanc, Gewurztraminer, Cabernet Sauvignon, Pinot Noir, Zinfandel, Merlot, and sparkling wines mostly from purchased fruit. **Huntington Cellars** (Huntington, 1983), is a 1,500-case grape, fruit and berry winery, all from purchased fruit. **Inn Wines** (Hatfield, 1985), is a tiny, 1-acre, 300-case, cottage activity that makes blended grape, fruit, and berry wines. **Mellea Farm Vineyards** (West Dudley, 1988), is a 3-acre, 1,000-case winery that makes Seyval and Vidal Blanc, and fruit and berry wines. **Nantucket Vineyard** (Nantucket Island, 1986), is a 7-acre, 3,000-case winery that makes Chardonnay, Riesling, Sauvignon Blanc, Pinot Blanc, Pinot Noir, Merlot, and Cabernet Sauvignon blends. **Plymouth Colony Winery** (Plymouth, 1983), located in the middle of a cranberry bog, this 4,500-case winery makes above-average, soft, supple, well-flavored Vinifera, French-American, fruit and berry (especially cranberry) wines from purchased fruit. **Via della Chiesa Vineyards** (Raynham, 1990), is an impressive, 10-acre, 4,000-case winery that makes Cayuga, a Cayuga/Muscat blend, and cranberry blends. **Westport Rivers Vineyard and Winery** (Westport, 1989), is a 40-acre, 7,000-case winery that makes above average Chardonnay, Riesling, sparkling, and proprietary wines.

Chicama Vineyards, Martha's Vineyard
Legend has it that Captain Bartholomew Gosnold, who sited the island on May 21, 1602, named it after his five-year-old daughter. Two other explanations state that the island is a corruption of Martin Wyngaard, and for the profusion of native grape vines. Chicama Vineyards, lying entirely on glacial sand, is the easternmost winery in America. Baxevanis

As the smallest state in the union (37 miles wide and 48 miles long), and surrounded by higher elevations toward the north and west, Rhode Island has always looked toward the sea for its sustenance (the state is sometimes referred to as the "Ocean State"). It contains one million people, most of whom reside in metropolitan Providence. Lacking good agricultural soil, the population from early colonial days (Providence was founded in 1636 by Roger Williams) exhibited an independent spirit (it was the first colony to proclaim independence from the King of England), and engaged in maritime commerce. Rhode Island was instrumental in developing the triangular trade in rum, slaves and sugar, and to this day it mainly consumes

imported, not domestic wines. The combination of high income and a stylish tourist industry has recently spawned a revival in grape growing and wine making. After many mistakes were made by planting grapes in unprotected, windswept, interior locations, the industry has localized in the southern extremities of the state, and as the caliber of vineyard practices and winemaking have improved, the state is currently producing above-average to excellent wines.

As remarkable as the state's economic progress has been, agricultural activities in general, and viticultural activities in particular, parallel those of its sister states. French Huguenots planted grapes and made wine in the late 1820s with little success. Native grapes dominated acreage and production, and because of the poor quality of the final product, the population has long remained partial to beer, distilled beverages, and imported wine. At present there are 100 vine acres, but the economic contribution of wine to the state's economy is quite formidable given its small size and population. It is reported that directly and indirectly, the wine industry generates over $111 million to the state's economy.

There are four wineries: **Diamond Hill Vineyards** (Cumberland, 1979), is a 5-acre, 3,500-case winery specializing in Pinot Noir, fruit and berry winery. **Prudence Island Vineyards** (Prudence Island, 1973), is a 15-acre, 2,500-case winery that makes Chardonnay and Pinot Noir. **Sakonnet Vineyards** (Little Compton, 1975), is an excellent, 44-acre, 27,000-case winery that makes stylish, reliable Vinifera and French-American wines of which Chardonnay, Gewurztraminer, Pinot Noir, Vidal Blanc, and Seyval are the finest. The bulk of the wines are proprietary blends. This excellent winery, the largest in the state and New England, is in the throes of a major expansion. The wines are sold throughout New England and as far south as Florida, an unusual feature for a regional New England winery. **Vinland Wine Cellars** (Middletown, 1988), is an aggressive, 17-acre, 14,000-case winery, the newest in the state, that makes Vinifera and French-American wines of which Chardonnay, Riesling, Vidal Blanc, Seyval, and Marechal Foch are the most interesting. The winery is located on Aquidneck Island just to the north of Newport.

Connecticut

Connecticut (called the "Nutmeg State" because the spice was used as currency in colonial days), the southernmost New England state, was first claimed by one Adriaen Block for the Netherlands in 1614. The state, occupying the southwestern portion of the region, extends for 90 miles in an east-west direction and 75 miles from north to south. It is a small state of 5,018 square miles whose rivers flow southward to Long Island Sound, and, while the highest elevation does not exceed 3,000 feet, two-thirds of the total land area lies under 600 feet. The highly urbanized population of 3.4 million is overwhelmingly localized in the Connecticut Valley, and along the western portion of Long Island Sound adjoining the New York metropolitan area. While the population exhibits aging features and a low rate of growth, it is highly affluent and sophisticated exhibiting rising wine consumption patterns.

Primarily a dairy, egg, and specialized crop producer,

the state's agricultural acreage has been, like most other states in the northeast, declining in recent decades. Although grapes garnish the official seal of the state since 1647, grapes have never been a major crop in Connecticut. With the subsequent passage of the farm winery bill in 1978, vine acreage increased from fewer than 20 acres to 325 by 1991, and the number of farm wineries grew from one to eight for the same period. Although vine acreage is pitifully small (grapes and wine collectively contribute less than .4 percent of the gross state product) by west coast standards, it has increased sufficiently in recent years to earn more money than apple production. The recent viticultural interest is also reflected by the fact that total wine output has increased from fewer than 3,000 cases in 1977, to more than 85,000 cases in 1991, in the process playing an important role in state's economy. Directly and indirectly, the thousands of jobs and millions of dollars in wages and taxes it generates add over $386 million to the economic activity of Connecticut. Despite the state's central location in the northern portion of the northeast megalopolis, more than 75 percent of the states total land area is devoted to forest, and the 10 percent that is currently devoted to commercial agriculture exhibits at least an additional 2,000 acres of good quality land with viticultural potential. Vine acreage and the number of wineries are expected to increase in the coming decades due to a combination of positive elements: rising income, state encouragement, an auspicious tourist climate, and increased per capita wine consumption.

In 1987, a Farm Winery Development Council was formed, and along with an active Grape Growers Association have energized the industry in recent years. Unable to supply all their winemaking needs, most wineries purchase fruit (estimated to be 50 percent of the crush) from neighboring states. Although a distinct style has yet to be defined, the wines, characterized by sharp acidity, fullness and depth of flavor, are consistently good. About 65 percent of the total vine acreage is planted in French-American, 30 percent in Vinifera, and the remaining 5 percent in American varieties.

In addition to a small portion of the Southern New England *ava* that is located in eastern Connecticut, the state contains one other approved *ava--Western Connecticut Highland*, a 1,570 square mile region located along the New York border, but entirely within the state. The Western Highlands are an extension of the Green Mountain Range with elevations ranging between 200 to 2,000 feet above sea level, and are colder in terms of winter temperatures than the Long Island Sound region. It encompasses all or portions of three counties, and the soils are described as gravelly with limestone accumulations in the subsoil. Climatic and soil conditions are such that white wine varieties (of which Seyval is particularly good) are better suited than red. Although Vignoles, a late ripening

variety, is able to produce excellent wine, it is difficult to grow, and is highly susceptible to many diseases. This *ava* contains fewer than 120 acres of vineland, and three wineries. The wineries are:

Chamard Vineyards (Clinton, 1988), is a 20-acre, 4,000-case winery owned by the Chairman of Tiffany's. Initial production of Chardonnay, Pinot Noir, and Cabernet Sauvignon blends (Merlot and Cabernet Franc) indicates considerable potential. **Crosswoods Vineyards** (North Stonington, 1983), is a 32-acre, 9,000-case winery that makes above-average to excellent Chardonnay, Riesling, Gewurztraminer, Pinot Noir, Merlot, and Gamay from estate and Long Island grapes. This well-managed 433-acre property is considered the leading Vinifera winery in the state, and by many the finest winery in New England. **DiGrazia Vineyards** (Brookfield Center, 1984), is a 56-acre, 5,000-case, meticulous and serious winery located in the southwestern corner of the state that makes above-average wines from French-American vines, principally Seyval, Vidal Blanc, Vignoles, Marechal Foch, Chancellor, and Leon Millot under a large list of proprietary labels. **Haight Vineyard** (Litchfield, 1978), the first vineyard to be licensed after the passage of the Farm Winery Law, is a 50-acre vineyard producing 8,500 cases of French-American and Vinifera table and sparkling wine. It is located on the hilly (vineyards are sited above 1,100 feet) portion of central Connecticut in a microclimate producing average temperatures 7F higher than the surrounding countryside. In addition to generic red, white, and sparkling wines (the first in the state), Riesling, Chardonnay, and Marechal Foch are produced as varietals. **Hamlet Hill Vineyards** (Pomfret, 1980), the largest winery in the state, is a well-managed and aggressive, 68-acre, 22,000-case winery that produces French-American and Vinifera wines of which Seyval, Gewurztraminer, Riesling, and Chardonnay are considered the finest. The beautiful winery, sited on top of a drumlin, is one of the more interesting in the northeast. **Hopkins Vineyard** (New Preston, 1979), is a 20-acre, 7,000-case winery that makes good, sound generic, sparkling, and varietals, of which Seyval, Vignoles, and Chardonnay are the most interesting. The vineyard is well-sited 400 feet above Lake Waramaug in northwestern Connecticut. **McLaughlin Vineyards** (Sandy Hook, 1988), is a 15-acre, 2,000-case winery that makes Chardonnay, Riesling, Cayuga White, Marechal Foch, and Leon Millot. **Nutmeg Vineyard** (Andover, 1982), is a 6-acre, 2,000-case winery that makes Labrusca, French-American, fruit and berry wines. Seyval and Vidal Blanc are particularly good. **St. Hilary's Vineyard** (North Grosverondale, 1978), is a 7-acre, 500-case winery that makes French-American, fruit and berry wines. This was the pioneering winery that drafted the passage of the state's Farm Winery Act. **Stonington Vineyards & Winery** (Stonington, 1979), formerly the Clarke Vineyard, is an immaculate, well-tended, 10-acre, 4,000-case winery that makes above-average to excellent Chardonnay, Riesling, Pinot Noir, and French-American blends, offering excellent value.

Crosswoods Vineyards and the stone fences so common throughout New England. Baxevanis

NEW YORK

Since the repeal of Prohibition, New York ranks second (after California) in grape acreage and wine output, and third (after California and Washington) in grape production. It makes more than 25 million gallons of wine, fourteen times less than California, and three times greater than Washington, the nation's third largest producer. Directly and indirectly the state's wine industry contributes $2.9 billion to the state economy, second only to California. The state makes all manner of wine, small amounts of brandy, and approximately 5 percent of the nation's sparkling wine.

Table 5.2

VITICULTURAL AREAS OF NEW YORK				
AVA	Sq. Miles	Vine Acres	Wineries	Growing Season
Lake Erie	3,495	19,500	8	180
Finger Lakes	4,000	14,000	42	150
Cayuga Lake	N/A	460	8	155
Hudson River	3,500	1,000	20	160
North Fork, L.I.	159	1,200	14	220
The Hamptons, L.I.	213	79	2	215

Nearly 33,000 vineyard acres yield between 130,000 and 200,000 tons of grapes, with a retail wine value of $350 million. Employing a labor force of 20,000 people, the state contains 1,095 growers, 97 wineries, 10 juice manufacturers, and 25 table grape brokers. Within the fruit sector, grapes rank second only to apples in crop value. As is the case with other Concord grape producing states, approximately 60 percent of the harvest grape crop is used in the processing of juice and jellies, 38 percent is made into wine, and 2 percent is for table use or sold to out of state processors. Although there has been a slight improvement since 1970 in grape utilization in favor of wine (New York is the nation's largest grape juice producer), the difference is only relative given the fact that few American grapes and juice are shipped out of the state.

New York, "the Empire State," represents the northern extension of Appalachia and stretches from Lakes Erie and Ontario to the Atlantic. The state, therefore, is too large to be treated as a homogeneous climatic entity, and viticulture (as in other areas of the northeast and midwest) conforms to its proximity to large bodies of water assuring a longer than normal growing season for the latitude. All interior highland and mountainous regions of the state, such as the northern extension of the Appalachian plateau and the Adirondack Mountains, are totally devoid of commercial viticultural activities as the growing season is less than 140 days. Fig. 5.5 illustrate the importance of water bodies, June-January mean temperatures, first and last killing frost, length of growing season, and average precipitation as dominant controlling elements in the distribution of vines in the four principal regions. Although the four major grape growing areas show remarkable similarities, it is obvious that eastern Long Island is the most temperate grape growing region in the state. The difference between this area and the climatically marginal three other regions is illustrated by the type of grapes grown. In the final analysis, despite its dominance as the major wine producing state in the east, there is no justification to think that New York has overwhelming natural advantages over other grape producing regions east of the Continental Divide.

Figure 5.4

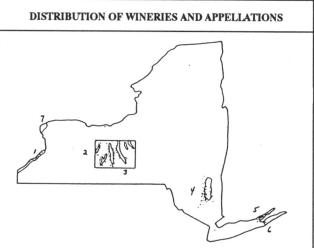

DISTRIBUTION OF WINERIES AND APPELLATIONS

1. Lake Erie, 2. Finger Lakes, 3. Cayuga Lake, 4. Hudson River, 5. North Fork, 6. The Hamptons, 7. Niagara, once a very important grape-growing region, has declined recently.
Source: New York Agricultural Statistics Service.

While the effects of a short growing season have been outlined in Chapter 2, it is important to note that two of the four grape producing regions are plagued by severe winter temperature fluctuations, false springs, and comparatively short growing seasons. In the final analysis, due to the severity of the winter season, and, hence, an abbreviated growing season, New York is essentially, with more than 85 percent of total output, a white wine producing state.

Of the 25 counties producing grapes, the leading in terms of acreage are: Chautauqua, Yates, Steuben, Erie, Schuyler, Suffolk, Niagara, Seneca, and Ontario. Placed on a map, the grape/wine pattern exhibits four non-contiguous geographic regions. The Chautauqua region, by far the largest, contains 61 percent of the state's planted acreage, followed by Finger Lakes (32%), Long Island (4%), and the Hudson River region (2%). Although total acreage has been declining steadily over the past 20 years, there has been significant redistribution in acreage and types of vines planted within the four principal regions. While acreage during this time has declined by more than 7,000 acres for the state as a whole, nearly the entire decline has occurred in the Chautauqua, Niagara, and Finger Lakes regions, with significant gains only in eastern

Long Island, and a mild resurgence in the Hudson River region. Although two of New York's 97 wineries rank among the nation's largest, half are nothing more than cottage-type firms that produce fewer than 6,000 cases of wine annually. Eight wineries are located in Chautauqua, 47 in the Finger Lakes, 24 in the Hudson River region, 16 in Long Island, and 1 in New York City. While the geography of wineries exhibits one pattern, the spatial origins of wine reveal a totally different picture: approximately 85 percent of all wine is made in the Finger Lakes, 7 percent in Chautauqua, 4 percent in the Hudson River, and the remainder in eastern Long Island.

Figure 5.5.

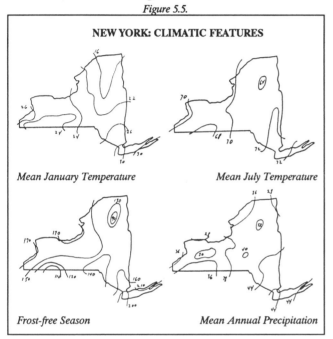

NEW YORK: CLIMATIC FEATURES

Mean January Temperature

Mean July Temperature

Frost-free Season

Mean Annual Precipitation

In terms of vine acreage, the Chautauqua region, the eastern extension of what is the largest vineyard east of the Continental Divide, is the most important. Although it contains the bulk of the regional acreage, it is home to only eight wineries as more than 80 percent of grapes are used for processing and not winemaking. The Finger Lakes region, lying in the midst of the northern extension of the Appalachians, is a windswept, agriculturally poor area, and one of the main regions of farm abandonment in the state. With approximately 11,000 acres and 47 wineries, it is the principal winemaking region in the state producing 85 percent of the state's total wine output. Ever since the establishment of the Taylor Wine Company in 1880, this region has remained the center for the industry in terms of volume of wine produced, and as the site of the largest wineries.

Southeast of the Finger Lakes is the lower Hudson River, a region containing 1,000 acres of vineland, 24 wineries, and currently in the midst of a renaissance. The fourth, and fastest growing region in terms of absolute

and percentage increases is the extreme eastern tip of Long Island in Suffolk County. Blessed with proximity to an affluent population, well-drained glacial soils, and the longest and most temperate growing season in the state, this region has become, with 1,300 acres and sixteen wineries, the premier Vinifera growing region east of Pacific America. Niagara County, historically the state's third most important grape growing region, has declined in recent years. Straddling Lake Erie and Lake Ontario north and northeast of Buffalo, this 30-mile wide peninsula, heavily planted in Elvira and other Labrusca grapes, enjoys a rather temperate climate, yet despite a comparatively long viticultural history it has never generated a wine industry. The state has six approved *ava's*: *Lake Erie* (1983, shared with Pennsylvania and Ohio); *Finger Lakes* (1982); *Lake Cayuga* (1988); *Hudson River* (1982); *North Fork of Long Island* (1986); and *The Hamptons, Long Island* (1985); the first is described in the Ohio section, and the remainder are described in this chapter.

Table 5.3

LEADING GRAPE COUNTIES (In Acres)					
County	1966	1970	1980	1985	1990
Chautauqua	16,210	18,717	19,644	19,339	16,476
Yates	4,814	5,688	7,707	7,844	5,577
Steuben	2,668	2,935	3,085	1,970	2,205
Erie	2,376	2,217	2,214	2,032	1,881
Schuyler	1,429	1,570	2,075	2,112	1,253
Niagara	1,559	1,811	2,778	1,733	1,173
Suffolk		59	110	935	1,279
Seneca	292	276	1,115	1,209	899
Ontario	1,616	1,700	1,202	1,052	713
Cattaraugus	551	471		607	
Other	1,740	1,435	2,049	647	1,390
Total	33,255	36,879	41,979	39,480	32,846
Source: New York State Agricultural Statistics Service					

History

One of the first in colonial America to grow grapes and produce wine, viticultural activities in New York began in what is now the Borough of Manhattan in the middle of the seventeenth century. Viticulture diffused to portions of Long Island, the lower Hudson River, and eventually to the Finger Lakes and Lake Erie. The Reverend William Bostwick, rector of St. James Episcopal Church in Hammondsport, is credited with the first introduction of the Isabella and Catawba grape in his garden in 1829, but it was not until 1853 that one Andrew Reisinger began the first commercial, 2-acre vineyard in nearby Pulteney. Still, the honor for the state's first commercial winery, and the nation's oldest operating winery is Brotherhood, the product of an interesting social experiment that first made wine in 1839 in the lower Hudson River. It is also interesting to note that Lake Erie, the eastern terminus of the Mohawk Gap, accommodated many foreign immigrants prompting vine plantings and winemaking efforts early in the 1820s.

Large scale commercial production, did not begin

until 1860 with the founding of the Hammondsport and Pleasant Valley Winery (becoming U.S. Bonded Winery No. 1, and later Great Western Winery). Success encouraged the founding of Urbana Wine Company in 1865, Eagle Crest Vineyards in 1872, the Taylor Wine Company in 1880, and Widmer's Cellars in 1888. After a prolonged hiatus from winemaking, the Hudson Valley Wine Company was founded in 1907 in Highland along the Hudson River. In 1881, the first of the French sparkling wine producers arrived--one Jules Crance, from Moet & Chandon, who made sparkling wine for the Urbana Wine Company. In 1934, Charles Fournier of Veuve Clicquot arrived and revolutionized the production of sparkling wine, and in the 1950s another immigrant, Dr. Konstantin Frank, successfully introduced Vinifera vines in the Finger Lakes region.

CHRONOLOGY OF VITICULTURAL EVENTS IN NEW YORK
Taken in part from the New York Wine & Grape Foundation's *The New York Wine Course and Reference.*

1647-1664: Grapes planted on Manhattan Island by the Dutch.

1667: First grapes planted by French Huguenot settlers in Ulster County. Vinifera vines fail and they begin cultivating American varieties.

1737: Robert Prince establishes the Linnaean Gardens in Flushing, New York City.

1816: Obtained from a garden in South Carolina by a Mrs. Isabella Gibbs, the Isabella grape is introduced to the northeast by William Prince of Linnaean Gardens.

1818: Elijah Fay plants first vineyard in Chautauqua County.

1827: First commercial vineyard and winery in the Hudson Valley planted by Richard Underhill on Croton Point on the Hudson River.

1829: Reverend William Bostwick plants first vineyard in the Finger Lakes in his rectory garden in Hammondsport, New York.

1839: Jean Jacques opens Blooming Grove, later to be named Brotherhood Winery.

1840: First grapes grown in the Niagara district.

1848: Edward McKay plants the first vineyard on Canandaigua Lake.

1850: Andrew Reisinger, a "vine dresser" from Germany, plants a vineyard and introduces pruning and training to the Finger Lakes. William Kniffin, a Hudson Valley stonemason from Clintondale, develops the pruning system that bears his name.

1853: Ephraim Bull introduces the Concord grape, a grape that became the most widely planted variety in the state and the northeast by 1870.

1859: Elijah Fay's son, Joseph, opens the first winery in Chautauqua County in Brocton.

1860: Charles D. Champlin and several partners establish the Pleasant Valley Winery, and hired sparkling wine makers from the Ohio Valley.

1865: Urbana Wine Company founded, later to be known as Gold Seal Vineyards.

1867: Andrew Caywood develops the Dutchess grape in Ulster County.

1872: Niagara grape developed in Lockport, New York by Hoag and Clark.

1873: Great Western Champagne takes the first gold medal ever won by an American wine in foreign competition in Vienna.

1880: Master cooper, Walter Taylor, arrives in Hammondsport to build barrels for the growing wine industry, and shortly thereafter establishes a vineyard and winery.

1882: New York Agricultural Experiment Station founded.

1888: Widmer's Wine Cellars established in Naples.

1920-1933: Prohibition. Many New York wineries survive by making sacramental wines, grape juice and by providing grapes to home winemakers.

1934: Charles Fournier joins Urbana Wine Company (Gold Seal) as winemaker. Born in Rheims, where he became production manager of Veuve Clicquot, he arrived in the United States just as Prohibition ended to make sparkling wine for the Urbana Wine Company. He introduced French-American grape varieties (1936), and later, along with Konstantin Frank, began to plant Vinifera varieties (especially Chardonnay and Riesling), and produced the first successful Vinifera wines.

1941: Widmer's Wine Cellars begins labeling their wines with varietal names.

1945: Kosher wines aggressively marketed, and for a brief period are among the most popular.

1950: Gold Seal's Charles Fournier New York State Champagne Brut wins the only gold medal awarded at the California State Fair. Fair officials subsequently bar non-California wines from the competition.

1953: Gold Seal hires Konstantin Frank as a consultant to begin production of Vinifera varieties. Experimental plantings of several varieties and rootstocks begin.

1961: First commercial Vinifera wines produced at Gold Seal. Taylor Wine Company buys the Pleasant Valley Wine Company.

1962: The founding of the first all-Vinifera winery east of the Continental Divide--Dr. Frank's Vinifera Wine Cellars, on Lake Keuka, the Finger Lakes district. Dr. Konstantin Frank, a Russian-born German, was the first to successfully produce Vinifera wine in the Finger Lakes region. A highly opinionated and resourceful man who scorned Labrusca and French-American grapes, his Vinifera vines survived because his early maturing rootstocks enabled them to survive -20F temperatures. Arriving penniless in New York City in 1951, Frank spent the next several years earning a living doing menial work totally unrelated to viticulture. In 1953 he was invited by Charles Fournier of Gold Seal to begin a nursery of Vinifera grapes at Urbana on the western edge of Lake Keuka. His success at Urbana and the founding of his own winery several years later revolutionized recent viticultural history. Today the winery is owned and operated by his son, Willy. Konstantin Frank's granddaughter is assistant winemaker, while a grandson manages the Banfi vineyard on Long Island.

1964: Taylor subsidiary, Great Western, introduces the first French-American hybrid varietal wines.

1973: Alex and Louisa Hargrave plant first commercial Vinifera vineyard in eastern Long Island, and establish a winery.

1976: Governor Hugh Carey signs the Farm Winery Act.

1977: Coca Cola of Atlanta buys the Taylor Wine Company. **1979:** Seagram Wine Company acquires Gold Seal Vineyards. **1983:** Coca Cola sells Taylor and Great Western to the Seagram Wine Company. **1987:** Taylor, Great Western, and Gold Seal are sold as part of a package to Vintners International.

1991: Grapes are second to apples in value among all fruit grown in the state. Grape production is 190,000 tons, one of the largest on record.

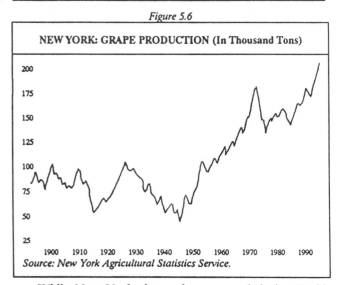

Figure 5.6

NEW YORK: GRAPE PRODUCTION (In Thousand Tons)

Source: New York Agricultural Statistics Service.

While New York vineyards prospered during Prohibition by selling grapes to home winemakers, the grape market collapsed after Repeal as Vinifera-based wine competition, high winery license fees, and taxes proved to be unbearable. Growers switched to other crops and for a long time the industry concentrated on inexpensive, sweet wine production. After World War II winemaking mirrored events in agricultural state-wide trends. Although New York is the second most populous state, its agricultural importance in the nation has diminished considerably over the past quarter century. It ranks 24th in the number of farms and total farm receipts, and 35th in land and farms. New York, primarily a dairy state, ranks second in tart cherry production, third in corn for silage, apple, and grape production, and fourth in the production of pears. Over the past ten years, the number of farms has declined by 8,000, from 49,000 in 1981 to 41,000 in 1987, farm assets have declined, and farm income has not kept pace with the rate of inflation. Farm land has been declining by more than 1 percent each year since 1973. In terms of farm cash receipts, livestock and products account for 71 percent, field crops 9 percent, vegetable crops 9 percent, fruit crops 5 percent (of which grapes comprise but 1.3 percent), and other crops 7 percent. The value of the grape crop, varying between $25 to $52 million, or 45 percent of the total value of fruit production, has along with all other fruit crops declined from nearly 9 percent to less than 5 percent of the total value of farm output within the past ten years.

Fig. 5.7 shows the historical evolution of wine-making in New York. From rather modest, but sustainable production levels prior to 1945, real growth in production has been the result of post-World War II Jewish immigration, black migration, and a demand in the northeast for inexpensive sweet wine. As a result, production increased from fewer than 3 million gallons in 1945 to nearly 40 million gallons in 1982. While annual wine production continued to climb unabated for nearly 30 years, the structural weakness of the state's wine industry became apparent after 1975. Throughout this period New York wine production as percent of national output in the nation fluctuated between 5 and 8 percent. Vine acreage, increasing more gradually than wine production, peaked in the early 1980s (42,000), and has since declined by nearly 10,000 acres to just over 32,000 acres, or less than the 1933 figure, a rather significant turn of events during the past three generations.

Given the fact that the national wine industry has grown substantially during this period, the state's performance is less than exemplary. More important is the fact that industry officials are not optimistic about the relative competitiveness of the state in comparison to other major grape growing regions. By the year 2010, it is estimated that the number of growers will decline by more than 40 percent to 945, and acreage drop to the 27,000 level, or 15,000 fewer acres than 1982. If we consider the fact that

the cost of producing grapes per acre is more than most other major grape growing regions in the country, yields will have to rise by at least 50 percent for New York to remain competitive.

Figure 5.7

NEW YORK: WINE PRODUCTION (In Million Gallons)

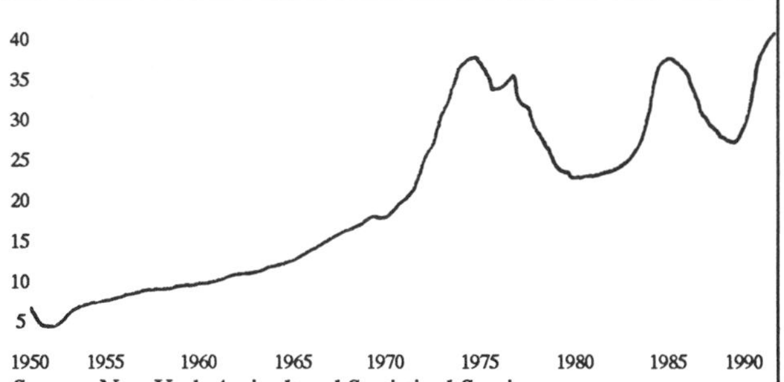

Source: New York Agricultural Statistical Service.

Table 5.4

NEW YORK GRAPE ACRES BY VARIETY

Variety	1966	1975	1990	Percentage
Concord	26,881	27,568	21,006	64.0
Catawba	1,399	3,477	2,102	6.4
Niagara	1,255	2,355	2,055	6.3
Aurora	1,805	1,727	1,389	4.2
Chardonnay	9	107	983	3.0
Delaware	1,248	2,051	841	2.5
Elvira	301	538	466	1.4
Seyval	87	187	441	1.3
Riesling	5	123	404	1.2
DeChaunac		899	353	1.1
Baco Noir	65	643	348	1.0
Pinot Noir		0	196	.6
Cayuga		0	192	.6
Cabernet Sauvignon		0	160	.5
Merlot		0	152	.5
Vidal Blanc	0	35	152	.5
Dutchess	41	345	131	.4
Ventura			113	.3
Gewurztraminer		1	103	
Rougeon		225	98	
Vignoles		46	87	
Colobel		97	85	
Marechal Foch	25	276	79	
Cabernet Franc		0	73	
Moores Diamond	7	130	68	
Fredonia	22	166	59	
Ives	10	596	45	
Sauvignon Blanc		0	40	
Chelois	4	156	38	
Isabella	15	87	37	
Chancellor	3	75	35	
Cascade		183	32	
Rosette		95	28	
Other	73	465	455	
Total	33,255	42,653	32,846	

Source: New York Agricultural Statistics Service

In the middle of the 1980s, the industry was locked in the throes of a devastating depression brought about by a combination of elements that were brewing for at least fifteen years. Throughout the preceding two decades New York failed to take advantage of the burgeoning wine boom: sales lagged, there were lower grape juice prices, and consumers preferred dry table wine rather than sweet, Labrusca-based wines. Equally important was the fact that New York failed to compete with California and foreign imports both in quality and value. At a time of major increases in per capita wine consumption, it is estimated that throughout the 1970s New York wineries lost as much as half of their national market share. During this time and into the early 1980s, grape production costs rose and grape prices fell setting the stage for a major catastrophe. The market crash occurred with the bumper crop of 1984 that prompted the Taylor Wine Company to cut grape purchases by 92 percent (from 15,000 tons in 1984 to 1,800 tons in 1985). Seven of the fourteen principal varieties were to be cut off completely--Baco Noir, DeChaunac, Dutchess, Elvira, Rougeon, Ives, and Diamond. The state government responded with legislation creating the New York Wine & Grape Foundation, an industry organization that emphasized the strengthening of the market for Concord, the grape variety accounting for nearly two-thirds of the state's total grape output.

The foundation now has a membership of 350 grape growers, grape juice producers, table grape marketers, wineries, wine retailers and wholesalers, restaurants, other associated businesses, and consumers. The Foundation, extremely successful since its inception, has produced many worthy publications, encouraged tourism, and with its close association with Cornell University and the New York Agricultural Experiment Station in Geneva many research projects concerning vineyard productivity, vine diseases, variety selection, and wine quality have been promulgated.

As Concord prices plunged by more than $100 the ton, grapes remained unpicked as vineyards were bulldozed, abandoned, or foreclosed, and wineries ceased operating. During the decade of 1975-1985, farms declined from 2,153 to 1,524, and vineland by 4,000 acres. This sad state of affairs, it must be clearly stated, only affected the American and Labrusca portion of the market, not the expanding Vinifera and French-American boutique wineries. The grape depression remained in place until the state legislature allowed grocery store sales of wine coolers that dried up the surplus wine and firmed prices. At the same time, there was a swift shift in grape varieties planted, the dollar strengthened, new, more experienced winemaking talent entered the industry, and the rise of eastern Long Island as the premium wine area of the state did much to repair the state's poor image.

The wine industry received a major impetus with the passage of the Farm Winery Act in 1976, an event that increased the number of wineries from 16 in 1975 to 97 by 1990, with an additional 15 expected by 2005. While these new, mostly small (less than 10,000 cases), family-operated wineries account for only a small portion of total production, their impact is impressive by extending the premium market to a more sophisticated consumer. The Farm Winery Act, in particular, has reduced license fees,

permits direct sales at the winery, and, unlike other states with similar legislation, New York farm wineries are allowed a maximum production of 150,000 gallons. It is interesting to note that while the number of new farm wineries has nearly ceased in most eastern states since 1987, the industry has enjoyed unparalleled promotion and success in New York. Fueled by financial success and consumer acceptance, most notably in the Finger Lakes and Long Island regions, and 1 million wine-related tourists, the number of farm wineries is expected to increase in number.

The picturesque Finger lakes region, hilly, less humid than areas to the south, and the site of many of the state's oldest wineries, also contains many charming waterfalls. Baxevanis

Of the 72 wineries opening during the 1976-1990 period, 38 are to be found in the Finger Lakes, 15 in the Hudson River, 4 in the Lake Erie region, and 15 in Long Island. Collectively they produced more than 500,000 gallons in 1985 from 2,500 acres, or 6 percent of the state's total acreage. Most significant is the fact that they are the source of nearly all the best Vinifera and French-American grapes, and quality wine produced. One major reason for the recent upsurge in new wineries is the relatively lower "start-up" costs in comparison to California. Although the industry has a long way to go to reach its true potential, the significant progress of these small wineries over the past ten years is truly remarkable. Not only have they been on the forefront of quality improvement, but have consistently been the most exciting and innovative group in the industry. They have switched from American, to French-American and Vinifera grapes; from red to white grapes; from sweet to dry table wine production; and have offered, for the first time in recent memory, quality wines that the consumer actually likes.

Because of the foregoing, New York since 1985 has experienced an economic turnaround to the point where industry growth and confidence have replaced declining prices and pessimism. While all fruit crops showed a decline in 1987, only the grape harvest rose in value, and New York grape growers are estimating that within the next 20 years the number of wineries will number 120. Moreover, the grape/wine industry, whose gross sales were valued at $300 million in 1987, is expected to double by 2010. The firming of grape prices and the expansion in the number of new wineries, however, are not state-wide events. The most dramatic growth in recent years has been in eastern Long Island, along with a new infusion of capital in the Hudson River and Finger Lakes regions. Production is still dominated by Canandaigua, Vintners International, and Kedem, all huge in volume and name recognition, but low in quality--their wines overwhelmingly based on American and French-American grapes. The recent revitalization of the Brotherhood Winery by a group of investors in the production of "upscale" Vinifera-based wines is an encouraging note for the Hudson River region.

The Grapes And Wines Of New York

New York makes five broad categories of wine--table, dessert, fortified, sparkling, special, and vermouth. Table 5.5 indicates the recent evolution of all types for the years 1950 and 1990. The growth in table wines from 7 to 43 percent of total production is encouraging, particularly when one considers that one-quarter of the total is the product of Vinifera grapes. Equally impressive are the steady gains in sparkling wine production, especially the excellent Riesling from Hermann Wiemer, and the sparkling wines of Chateau Frank and Pindar. These wines are made primarily by large wineries in the Finger Lakes region, and to a smaller extent along Lake Erie and Long Island. The dramatic rise of the "special" category is due to the popularity of coolers, but this trend of the early 1980s quickly declined by 1990. The dessert (sweet) and fortified category (nearly all made from American grapes), long the staple for inexpensive and poorly made wines, has been reduced from 81 percent in 1950 to half that amount by 1990. White table wines fall into three broad categories: poor quality American and French-American-based wines; slightly better French-American-based wines (the best of which are Vidal Blanc and Seyval); and the finest from Vinifera vines, primarily from

eastern Long Island and the Finger Lakes region (Chardonnay, Riesling, and Gewurztraminer). Quality red American and French-American wines are virtually non-existent; quality red Vinifera are limited to Merlot and Cabernet Sauvignon, a near monopoly of eastern Long Island. While the finest sweet white French-American wine is confined to Vignoles, quality sweet Vinifera wines include Riesling and Gewurztraminer.

Table 5.5

NEW YORK: WINE PRODUCTION BY TYPE					
Year	Table	Dessert	Sparkling	Vermouth	Other
1950	6.8	81.2	6.4	4.0	1.6
1960	17.6	61.4	10.2	6.3	4.5
1970	22.0	55.6	17.6	3.1	1.7
1980	28.6	48.1	19.5	1.7	2.1
1990	42.9	38.5	8.0	1.2	9.4

Source: New York, Department of Agriculture and Markets.

The New York wine industry is based on American, French-American, and Vinifera varieties whose annual production fluctuates between 150,000 and 200,000 tons, 95 percent of which are American and French-American. Although not as important as a generation ago, American varieties (Concord, Catawba, Niagara, Delaware, Dutchess, and Elvira) are mainly for juice and jelly, with smaller amounts for inexpensive generic and fortified wine production. Acreage devoted and the proportion used for wine has been steadily declining in the past 20 years, a trend that is expected to continue. It is important to note that of the state's 32,000 vine acres, American grapes, overwhelmingly concentrated in the Chautauqua, Niagara, Finger Lakes, and the Hudson River regions, in that order, cover 26,000 acres (Concord, the mainstay of the processing and sweet wine industry, accounts for 21,000 acres). The second most important group of grapes are the French-American varietals, of which the following dominate: Aurore, Seyval, Vidal Blanc, DeChaunac, Baco Noir, Rougeon, and Marechal Foch. The largest concentrations of French-American varietals are located in the Finger Lakes, Chautauqua, and Hudson River areas, with only traces in eastern Long Island and the Niagara Peninsula. With fewer than 2,400 acres, Vinifera varietals, overwhelmingly confined to eastern Long Island and the Finger Lakes region, are mainly white, of which Chardonnay and Riesling are the most important, followed by Gewurztraminer and Sauvignon Blanc. Red Vinifera are dominated by Cabernet Sauvignon, Merlot, and Pinot Noir.

Table 5.6 indicates the geographic evolution since 1955 of American, French-American, and Vinifera planted acreage. It is interesting to note that all American grapes, particularly Concord, Catawba, Niagara, Delaware, Dutchess, and Elvira, have declined in all regions except eastern Long Island where they were not historically planted in large numbers. Since 1975, more than

5,000 acres have been uprooted and replaced with French-American and Vinifera vines, a rather significant transformation of the historic New York grape picture. Moreover, the trend over the next generation is for American varieties to decline; white French-American varietals to increase vineyard share with red varieties declining in importance; and for Vinifera acreage to increase beyond 6,000 acres, primarily in eastern Long Island, and in selected areas in the Finger Lakes, Lake Erie, and Hudson River regions. As far as acreage is concerned, the biggest increase at the expense of American vines has been the emergence of French-American grapes, particularly white varieties. At present there is no favorite as each variety exhibits some affinity for its selective area. When French-American red varieties are compared with Vinifera equivalents, growers make a concise statement on the subject: "French-American are cheaper to grow but much harder to sell;" and that Vinifera vines are "more costly and more difficult to grow, but easier to sell." Everyone agrees that American vines are the cheapest and easiest to grow, but impossible to sell--unless they are ameliorated.

NEW YORK GRAPE CROP: 1973 and 1990
The 1973 New York grape crop of 126,000 tons consisted of the following varieties: Concord, 95,660 tons; Catawba, 7,130; Niagara, 7,100; Delaware, 5,000; French hybrids, 6,800, and others, 4,320.
The 141,000 ton, 1990 crop consisted of the following varieties: Concord, 97,551; Catawba, 9,855; Niagara, 9,188; Delaware, 2,741; Elvira, 3,662; Aurore, 6,754; DeChaunac, 2,010; Baco Noir, 1,141; Vinifera, 2,064, and others, 6,034.

At best, French-American varieties provide the New York grower with the means to make something better than from American grapes. In 1960, representing less than 2 percent of the 20.3 thousand ton crush, there were fewer than 600 tons of French-American grapes delivered to wineries in New York State. By 1975, the figure rose to more than 13,000 tons, or 16 percent of the 1975 81,000 ton crush. Yet, in the mad dash to plant French-American varietals 20 years ago, many mistakes were made necessitating costly remedies. The mistakes invariably involved red varieties, principally DeChaunac, Chelois, Marechal Foch, Baco Noir, and Chambourcin. A good deal of DeChaunac, for example, has been uprooted, or budded over.

The main problems with red French-American varietals are their inability to age due to a low tannin content, and their tendency to become bitter, lose color, and develop off odors and flavors with age. White French-American varietals, on the other hand, particularly Seyval, Vidal Blanc, and Vignoles, have made surprisingly good wine in recent years. Having a far more muted foxy aroma and flavor, when properly made and aged they can be made into a large number of different styles. Seyval, one of the most impressive, appears to do well in the Fin-

ger Lakes and Hudson River regions; Cayuga, unheard of fifteen years ago, now accounts for nearly 200 acres and is expected to increase acreage share in the future, particularly in the Finger Lakes and Chautauqua regions; Vignoles, a popular and serious grape for the production of quality sweet wines, sells at prices that rival the finest late harvest wines of California. Contributing more than 50 percent of total varietal wine output, French-American varieties have become the mainstay of all but the most prestigious farm wineries.

Table 5.6

NEW YORK: GRAPE PLANTINGS BY TYPE (As Percent of Total)						
Grape Type	1955	1970	1975	1980	1985	1990
American	**99.9**	**95.7**	**91.0**	**91.4**	**90.1**	**83.3**
Catawba	3.1	5.6	7.0	7.0	5.6	6.4
Concord	89.4	77.0	70.6	72.0	74.9	64.0
Niagara	2.1	4.8	5.0	5.4	4.0	6.3
Delaware	2.0	3.9	4.5	2.9	1.9	2.6
Dutchess	.3	.2	.6	.6	.4	.4
Elvira	1.4	1.7	1.3	1.6	1.8	1.4
Ives	.8	1.5	1.1	.7		.1
French-American	**.1**	**4.2**	**8.8**	**8.1**	**8.6**	**10.0**
Aurore						4.2
Baco Noir						1.1
DeChaunac						1.1
Seyval						1.3
Vidal Blanc						.5
Vinifera		**.3**	**.2**	**.5**	**1.3**	**6.7**
Cabernet Sauvignon						.5
Chardonnay						3.0
Merlot						.5
Pinot Noir						.6
Riesling						1.2
Total	100.0	100.0	100.0	100.0	100.0	100.0
Source: New York Statistics Service.						

Table 5.7

GRAPE UTILIZATION BY SELECTED YEAR (As Percent Of Total)			
Year	1956	1970	1990
Juice/Processing	84	66	60
Wine	15	31	38
Fresh	1	3	2
Source: New York Statistics Service.			

The real success story in the past fifteen years is the tremendous growth of Vinifera acreage, increased from 324 in 1980 to 2,300 in 1990. Grape utilization as percent leaped from .8 percent in 1977, to 2 percent in 1981, to 3.9 percent by 1990, the year that Vinifera grape production increased 6 percent while total state tonnage declined by 5 percent. While they are less hardy and more temperamental in the colder regions of the state, they have found a welcome environment in eastern Long Island, a vineyard that houses more than 60 percent of the state's total Vinifera acreage. The Finger Lakes region has one-third of the acreage, while the remainder is found along Lake Erie and the Hudson River regions. The principal Vinifera variety, with an estimated share of nearly 50 percent of all acreage, is Chardonnay, with more than 45 wineries producing it. While it is made in a hard, steely, austere style in the cooler portions of the state, the finer versions from Long Island are excellent to outstanding. Other Vinifera varietals, in decreasing importance in terms of acreage, are Riesling, Gewurztraminer, and Sauvignon Blanc. Among red Vinifera the shining stars are Cabernet Sauvignon and Merlot. The group as a whole ranks number one in all prestigious farm wineries, second in importance for the second tier of farm wineries, and least important for all large wineries with an output greater than 100,000 cases. In the final analysis, Vinifera grapes have a bright future primarily because their value per acre is more than ten times that of corn and seventeen times that of hay. While only two wineries produced Vinifera varietal wine in 1965, the number in the past fifteen years has increased to 47.

Contemporary Issues

The problem with the aforementioned is that while the state ranks second in total wine production, and is home to two of the nation's largest wineries, no one considers the state a "serious" wine producing area in terms of quality wine production. There are many reasons for this mindset:

1. New York suffers from seven formidable competitors: California for wine grapes and quality wine at low cost; Washington for high Concord yields and quality Vinifera wines at low cost; Michigan for high Concord yields and quality French-American wines; Virginia for quality Vinifera and French-American wine production at lower cost; Oregon for the production of quality Vinifera wine; Bordeaux as the symbol of foreign imports and the east coast standard of what table wine should be like; and the tropical world for the production of sugar used to ameliorate New York wine. Most important, New York has failed to respond to market pressures and consumer tastes over the past two generations. Since Prohibition, New York's wine market had been in the kosher, dessert, and sparkling segments of the market. It is estimated that between Repeal and 1975 more than 85 percent of the state's domestic market was composed of these three types of wine. In 1960, for example, dessert wines composed over 55 percent of market share, but have since declined to less than 15 percent by 1989. Likewise, the demand for sweet, kosher-type, and Cold Duck-type wines has diminished to record low levels. Although the product line has shifted rather dramatically since 1971, the competitive position of the state in reference to all abovementioned areas (except for quality Vinifera table wine production from Long Island) is overwhelmingly oriented toward the lower portion of the price spectrum and borders on thin economic margins. As a consequence, New York's share of the American wine market has fallen from 14 percent in the late 1960s to less than 6 percent.

2. New York suffers from the stigma and poor reputation of American (the state is commonly referred to as a three-grape producing region due to the historic dominance of Concord, Catawba, and Niagara), and French-American wines, a peculiar situation compounded by the fact that the "serious" wine-drinking population of the northeast and mid-Atlantic states has for centuries been more closely allied with the Vinifera flavor of European wines. Here, the major problem is the lack of acceptance of the foxy flavor and aroma of American and French-American grapes. In an effort to mitigate against this flavor, New York wineries have lobbied state representatives to legislate provisions that are anathema to wine purists. Depending on how one interprets the law, a winemaker can add between 25 and 53 percent water and/or sugar (or corn syrup), and as much as 25 percent wine or must from other states (usually California). Furthermore, an additional 10 percent water is allowed if the wine is fortified with alcohol. It must also be emphasized that while the New York grape output amounts to 3 percent of the national crop, wine production as percent of national total is at least twice that amount. Nearly all large and some medium-sized wineries use bulk tank-car wines shipped from other states. The fact that more than half of all table wine, nearly all dessert and fortified wine, and all vermouth and coolers are based on American grapes is regrettable. Although this negative perception harms the industry, the fact remains that New York-based wineries produce only 14 percent of the wine sold in New York state--proof positive that the consumer has rejected the type of wines produced in the state despite the fact that the wines are perceptibly less foxy than years past. This allegation is further supported by the fact that New Yorkers consume eleven times more imported wine than New York-produced wine.

A related problem is the inability of American and French-American red wines, both notoriously low in tannin, to age. As a result, consumers in the sophisticated, Bordeaux-oriented northeast Megalopolis market have consistently rejected table wine made from these types of grape. Be that as it may, the consumer continues to be wary and harbors preconceived notions about the ability of these grapes to produce quality wine comparable to that offered by western Europe--and for good reason. Vinifera acreage remains small, and only grown in selected areas. There are only six Vinifera-only wineries in the Finger Lakes region: Chateau Frank, Dr. Konstantin Frank Vinifera Cellars, Hermann Wiemer, King Ferry Winery, NewLand Vineyard, and Fox Run Winery. The fact that wineries offer some Vinifera wine from purchased fruit does not alleviate the structural weakness of the industry: an inability to compete (in terms of quality, taste, and price) with California, Oregon, and Washington. The retrenchment from sweet, American-based and French-American wines is not fast enough to generate a new, favorable image with the vast majority of consumers despite recent and dramatic viticultural developments.

In the final analysis, it is important to note that the historic emphasis in American grapes is still very much alive in the contemporary grape/wine industry mix, with a significant portion of the non-Vinifera, non-French-American grapes used both for processing as well as winemaking. New York ranks as the nation's largest producer of grape juice, a market segment that requisitions more than 50 percent of the entire grape crop. Of the sixteen juice processors (seven in Chautauqua County, eight in the Finger Lakes area, and one in the Hudson River region) four are wineries, and twelve strictly fruit processors. Eighty percent of the total is Concord, while the remainder is composed of other American grapes. The above notwithstanding, more than a dozen wineries have recently begun making above-average to outstanding late harvest (and related) wines that merit considerable attention. Consecrated with excellent acidity and sugar levels, Riesling, Gewurztraminer, Vignoles, and Vidal are the leading varieties, and equal to many imported wines in quality.

3. The use of generic names, such as Moselle, Rhine, Chablis, Porto and Sherry-type, Burgundy, etc., has not improved New York's image of low quality, blended, mass-produced wines. Unlike New York, California is a more consistent producer of both jug and premium wines.

4. The production of fortified, Sherry/Porto-type, and kosher wine production has not helped the state's image of sweet, inexpensive wines. For example, New York, with an annual production of 400,000 gallons, is the nation's second largest Sherry-type wine producer, nearly all sweet, inexpensive, and mainly the product of American grapes. Historically one of the mainstays of the wine industry, fortified wines are made almost exclusively by the largest wineries: Taylor, Canandaigua, Widmer's, and Royal Kedem. Another problem is the state's association with kosher wine production, historically sweet wines from Concord and other native grapes. Invariably, kosher wines to most consumers represent high alcohol, a syrupy consistency (one producer historically described the wines as "the wine you can almost cut with a knife"), and foxy flavors whose general quality has been less than spectacular. Although popular with the large Jewish and Afro-American communities throughout the northeast and portions of the midwest, kosher wines lack an element of celebrity and sophistication among serious table wine consumers. Fortified and kosher wines are usually the product of a "hot pressing" to extract as much color as possible. While production has been reduced by half since 1950, this segment of the market accounts for approximately 40 percent of total production.

5. Although sparkling wine was first made in the Finger Lakes in 1860, New York has not taken advantage of its inherent ability to increase production of quality sparkling wine despite the fact that a Great Western blend of Delaware and Catawba wine won a gold medal at the Vienna Exposition of 1873 (as well as other cities). New York was the nation's leading sparkling wine producer from Repeal until 1964 when it was surpassed by California. This leading position (as recently as 1952 New York made 75 percent of all sparkling wines) slowly deteriorated: its share of national output declining to 23 percent in 1970, and to less than 6 percent in 1990. It is important to note that while sales of sparkling wine fell from 700,000 cases to fewer than 350,000 cases during the period 1968-1984, they have since rebounded to 1.1 million cases.

A welcome sign on Lake Keuka, an area that produced more than 50 percent of the nation's sparkling wine as recently as 40 years ago.
Baxevanis

Dating back to the second half of the nineteenth century, the potential for sparkling wine production is extraordinary: the combination of a cool climate producing acid-rich, highly flavorful grapes places the entire state in a envious position. Of the now several producers that make sparkling wine by the Champagne Method, Bully Hill (Seyval Blanc), Hermann Wiemer (Riesling), Chateau Frank (Pinot Blanc, Chardonnay, Pinot Noir, and Pinot Meunier), McGregor (Chardonnay and Pinot Noir), Glenora (Chardonnay blended with other white grapes), and Pindar (Chardonnay, Pinot Meunier, and Pinot Noir) are considered the finest. Historically, the most popular grapes were Catawba, Aurore, Delaware, Dutchess, and, recently, Vidal Blanc and Seyval among French-American, and Chardonnay, Riesling, and Pinot Noir among Vinifera grapes. Aurore, Dutchess, Delaware, and Catawba were the historic grapes because of their high acid levels and pronounced flavors, especially when made in a sweet style, until recently the preferred type. Sparkling wines have lately improved dramatically because it has been discovered that when American and French-American grapes are picked early, "foxy" flavors are muted, while yeast flavors and aroma are accentuated. Because aging intensifies Labrusca flavors, sparkling wines, made from American grapes (unlike those from California) are not made by *methode champenoise*.

In recent years the sparkling segment of the industry has been energized by a small cadre of astute, discriminating, and perceptive winemakers that have produced a string of superb wines, most notably Chateau Frank, Hermann Wiemer, and Pindar Vineyards. Although New York lacks the magnetism of California, one Champagne firm, A. Charbaut of Epernay, France, has shown interest in the production of quality sparkling wine in the lower Hudson River Valley, as are several on Long Island, including the Banfi Corporation. As of 1992, there were 25 sparkling wine producers.

6. Although Labrusca grapes are particularly suitable for the production of brandy, New York makes little to nothing. This sad state of affairs, in part, was due to the high $21,000 license fee until it was reduced to $100 in 1975. Bully Hill is considered the largest producer of brandy among the smaller wineries.

7. There is a lack of industry leadership. The New York wine industry has been dominated by a small number of large wineries--a profile that exhibits conditions of both oligopoly and oligopsony. Canandaigua, Vintners International, Kedem, and Mogen David collectively account for 90 percent of the state's total wine output, and are commonly referred to as "commercial" in sharp contrast to the vast sea of "farm wineries," the latter making fewer than 10,000 cases annually, primarily from their own grapes with only minor purchases (of the 97 wineries in the state, 4 make more than 100,000 cases, 5 produce between 50,000 and 100,000 cases, 10 between 25,000 and 50,000 cases, and 78 less than 20,000 cases). The typical farm winery operates 20 acres, grows 5 different grape varieties, makes 7 different wines, and produces about 6,000 cases annually. Although total "farm winery" production was but 10 percent of the state total in 1990, it represents a dramatic increase from .5 percent in 1975. Their volume of wine produced has leaped from 75,000 cases in 1975 to more than 900,000 cases in 1991. Most important, the entry of new farm wineries exceeds their exit by a factor of at least 4 to 1--a clear indication that the farm winery legislation first promulgated in 1976 has been a success. Another significant element of the recent proliferation of farm wineries is the not insignificant fact that they produce a far lower percentage of American wine than "commercial" wineries.

Nearly all independent growers sell grapes to the five largest wineries. Historically, as long as competition for the low-end of the wine market was not too severe, the largest wineries were able, thanks to the magic of amelioration, to make a handsome profit. The industry, until recently, felt safe and secure, and did little to modernize,

encourage growers to plant better grapes, or make better wine without the benefit of amelioration. As competition increased in the past 20 years, more than 20 wineries have gone out of business, and all but the two largest wineries have gone through rigorous buy-outs and restructurings. During the same period more than 1,000 growers have gone out of business. In 1985, of the 1,524 farms, only 11 were larger than 200 acres, 44 cultivated between 11 and 199 acres, and 137 farmed between 50 and 99 acres. Another 296 growers cultivated fewer than 5 acres. Well over 1,000 growers, or 68 percent of all, cultivated fewer than 50 acres, a figure that is not considered economically viable.

8. With minor exceptions, New York has not improved its wines as rapidly as other states. Given the fact that production costs are high, labor expensive, and the grape yield per acre low, New York must emphasize quality, and not attempt to compete with the California, low-end price portion of the market, particularly with dry table, fortified, and generic wines.

9. Domestic wine production has not kept pace with imported wines. While total wine production has steadily increased from 9 million gallons in 1956 to 40 million gallons in 1982, this figure represents but one-fifth of the state's total consumption. When compared with the rest of the nation, the percentage of wine produced by New York has fluctuated between 6 and 9.5 percent over the past 35 years. Equally significant is the fact that the state produces 3.2 percent of the nation's grapes, a percentage that has fallen slightly over the past ten years.

10. Although New York was one of the first states to grow grapes and produce wine, it has been unable to develop, throughout its formidable history, a strong wine industry lobbying organization similar to The Wine Institute in California. In an effort to encourage research, marketing, and promotion of state grapes and wine, the New York Wine and Grape Foundation was created with state financial support in 1985. Since its founding, this organization has emerged as a highly potent lobbying body with several significant achievements, but its real challenge has yet to come. Estimates from official and unofficial sources indicate that over the next generation, total grape production will stabilize between 175,000 and 250,000 tons, yields will increase by close to 50 percent, the number of growers to decline by 25 percent, and the price of American and French-American grapes to decline relative to Vinifera grapes. If this scenario appears realistic, New York wines must emphasize the higher priced Vinifera varietal libations in order to increase the quality of its wines, maintain market share, diffuse adverse publicity, and prevent winery closings by providing much needed assistance. During the wine slump of the early 1980s, the Governor and a broad coalition of state legislators forged a comprehensive, market-oriented public framework that has catalyzed

a fundamental economic turnaround. The program, unfortunately, emphasized the strengthening of the Concord market, the grape variety accounting for nearly two-thirds of the state's total grape output.

GRAPE VARIETIES INTRODUCED BY THE NEW YORK STATE AGRICULTURAL EXPERIMENT STATION BY YEAR

Alden (Red, 1926), Ontario and Gros Guillaume.
Athens (Red, 1925), Hubbard and Portland.
Bath (Red, 1937), Fredonia and New York 10805.
Buffalo (Red, 1921), Herbert and Watkins.
Canada Muscat (White, 1928), Muscat Hamburg and Hubbard.
Canadice (White, 1954), Bath and Himrod.
Eden (Red, 1923), Ontario and New York 10085.
Einset Seedless (Red, 1963), Fredonia and Canner.
Erie (Red, 1930), Goff and Worden X Worden.
Glenora (Red, 1952), Ontario and Russian Seedless.
Hanover (Red, 1924), Brighton and Niagara.
Hector (Red, 1923), Chasselas Rose and Brocton.
Horizon (White, 1945), Seyval and Schuyler.
Kendaia (Red, 1925), Portland and Hubbard.
Melody (White, 1965), Pinot Blanc and Ontario.
Naples (Red, 1928), Delaware and New York 8042.
Ruby (Red, 1930), Keuka and Ontario.
Schuyler (Red, 1926), Zinfandel and Ontario.
Steuben (Red, 1925), Wayne and Sheridan.
Van Buren (Red, 1936), Fredonia and Worden.
Watkins (Red, 1930), Mills and Ontario.
Westfield (Red, 1930), Herbert and Concord Seedless.
Yates (Red, 1923), Mills and Ontario.
Bronx Seedless (Red, 1925), N Y 8536 and Thompson Seedless.
Concord Seedless (Red, 1921), a rare Concord mutant.
The above is a selected listing; three dozen additional grapes have also been introduced.

---

11. The New York wine industry has lacked support from the Agricultural Extension Service at Geneva (its primary interest has involved American and recently French-American research, not Vinifera grapes). Nevertheless, the Agricultural Station has introduced more than 100 new varieties of fruit, of which nearly 50 have been grapes. Closely allied with the large American grape producers and processors, its main accomplishments have been a new Sherry-type process that accelerated production, the development of new varieties, wine fermentation processes, and extension services to growers. Of the many grape varieties developed, only two, Cayuga and Steuben, has shown a moderate degree of commercial success. Melody, named in 1985, and presently commercially made into wine by only one winery, also appears to have commercial possibilities as it yields a delicate and spicy wine of good acid balance without exhibiting foxy flavors and fragrance. Another variety, Horizon, lacks Labrusca flavor and aroma, and makes an appealing neutral wine, but Glenora and others have not been commercially successful. In 1990 the Station named a Seyval x Chardonnay cross, originally tested as GW9, Chardonel. It appears moderately winter hardy, slightly susceptible to mildews and botrytis bunch rot, but as yet the quality of the wine is inconclusive. Recombinant DNA techniques on grape

cells to make Vinifera vines more resistant to disease is a recent exciting chapter in the history of this 100-year institution.
12. A lack of export initiatives. While there is a limited future for Labrusca-based wines in America, the market possibilities in the export sector are formidable. The problem is that few producers have bothered with overseas promotion primarily in Latin America, tropical Africa, and southeast Asia.

Erie-Chautauqua

The *Erie-Chautauqua* (1983) viticultural district of western New York, with 3,495 square miles, 19,500 acres, 700 growers, and eight wineries, is the single most important vineyard in the state, and along with the Niagara Peninsula constitutes the largest segment of the eastern "Concord Belt." It borders the south shore of Lake Erie and extends, in an almost unbroken stretch, south from Buffalo to Pennsylvania and into Ohio where it continues to the Lake Erie Islands. The producing region, less than 40 miles long, and usually less than three miles wide, represents the largest contiguous stretch of vineland east of California. Paralleling the narrow lake plain and rising some 70 feet above is the Allegheny escarpment, the northern terminus of the Appalachians that separates the grape/fruit producing region from dairying activities. This region has more than half of the state's vine acreage, but produces less than 10 percent of the state's total wine output because it is mainly planted in Concord and Catawba vines used in the juice and jelly industry. The region contains three important cities: Westfield, Portland, and Fredonia--all architecturally and viticulturally important. Fredonia, the most prominent, has two interesting claims to fame in addition to being the center for the cultivation of Concord grapes. It is said that the street gas lamp was first placed here, and it was the headquarters of the Women's Christian Temperance Union.

Chautauqua (synonymous with Concord, Niagara, and Catawba) produces grape juice, jelly, concentrate, inexpensive wine, and is general purveyor of frozen grapes and juice to the kosher wine industry. Although small, non-kosher/sweet wineries have always reared their heads over the past 100 years, all but two of the eight wineries now in existence were founded prior to 1976. Despite the small number of wineries, total wine output exceeds 1 million gallons annually. To the north of the Erie-Chautauqua grape belt, 1,500 acres of additional vineland are found along the Niagara Peninsula and the south shore of Lake Ontario. It was here that the Niagara variety, often called White Concord, was created by crossing Concord with an obscure variety called Cassidy.

What makes this comparatively small geographic region favorable for fruit cultivation, and the Concord grape in particular, is its position to Lake Erie and topographic aspects. Its low latitude location (in comparison to the other lakes) along the southeastern shore is coincident with prevailing lake winds, while the deepest portion of the lake basin delays flowering in the spring until the threat of frost danger has passed. The lake allows for a long and gentle growing season, enabling the grapes to develop higher than normal sugar levels for the latitude. The vines are not encumbered by excessive heat and prodigious moisture, nor is there a need to irrigate due to drought. The frost-free season varies between 170 and 185 days, and periodically as many as 195 days, or more than one month longer than the upper fringes of the Finger Lakes area.

Labrusca Grapes South of Buffalo. Baxevanis

Summer temperatures, unlike many other interior areas, rarely exceed 95F. The site is unique because nowhere else is the lake plain so narrow and as steeply inclined towards the lake. The proximity of deep water, a narrow plain, and a high escarpment results in better air drainage and an intense air circulation system, both of which, in unison, produce a longer growing season and a near fungus-free environment. Another major climatic advantage (also applying to the Finger Lakes region) is the absence of hurricane-related activity in late summer and early fall. Equally important is the site of the mile-wide beach ridge extending between the flat lake plain and the Allegheny escarpment. These excellent, well-drained, 30-foot deep soils, beautifully positioned between the poorly-drained lacustrine lake plain and the steep, clay-

dominated escarpment soils, contain more than 90 percent of grape acreage. Despite the comparatively cold winter and the northerly latitude of the region, the area receives 2,500 degree days, a figure that is significantly higher than Champagne, Chablis, and the Moselle vineyards.

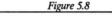

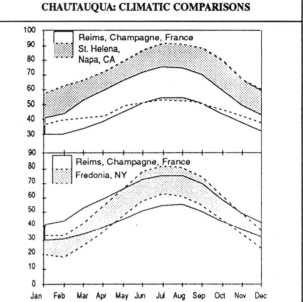

Mean daily temperature range (F) for each month for Reims, France, St. Helena, Napa Valley, and Fredonia, New York.
Source: 1989 New York Sparkling Wine Symposium: Champagne Comes to Chautauqua, State University of New York College at Fredonia, p. 2.

The first native vines were planted in 1818 by a Baptist Deacon, one Elija Fay, who later replaced them with Isabella and Catawba in 1824, and made wine as a hobby until his death in 1860. Forty-one years later, his son built the first winery in Brocton in 1859, and with steady population growth throughout the second half of the nineteenth century, many vineyards were established. Almost coincidentally with the rise of viticulture, the temperance movement was born in Saratoga County, and by 1835 the society was advocating total abstinence from alcohol. It comes as no surprise, therefore, that the region developed into a "dry" grape area with such ardent Prohibitionists as Charles and Thomas Welch. As a result, for nearly 150 years, the region has remained the nation's largest producer of processing grapes instead of a major winegrowing area.

By 1900, more than 2 million gallons of wine were made between Fredonia and Westfield. The wine industry was first based on two grapes--the Concord and Isabella, and while other varieties were gradually introduced, it was the Concord that survived the severe winter of 1872-1873. While all other grapes either matured late, lacked vigor, succumbed to rot, or were insufficiently productive, the hardy Concord triumphed. Unlike any other American grape, the Concord is ideally suited to the region, and its success is truly remarkable. Therefore, throughout this region, American and Labrusca grapes were planted in the first half of the nineteenth century as the frontier moved progressively westward, but it was after the Civil War that plantings increased as the pace of immigration and urban growth accelerated. Vine acreage grew at a spectacular rate, particularly after 1880 with the introduction of refrigerated cars, and especially after the establishment in 1897 of the Welch Grape Juice Company in Westfield.

As the success of the grape juice and jelly industry proved spectacular, acreage and grape production accelerated to unheard-of levels. It is estimated that of the more than 27,000 acres, 98 percent were Concord. This represented not only a rare monoculture scenograph in the northeast, but as much as 80 percent of all arable land in some townships was devoted to grape cultivation. This region (including the rest of the Lake Erie south shore) was, for a short time, the second largest concentration of grapes in the nation (the Fresno area being first). If California is excluded, the south shore of Lake Erie represented, as recently as 1955, more than 50 percent of the nation's remaining grape acreage. Grown by more than 2,000 individual farms, production immediately after World War II reached 90,000 tons. Unfortunately, rising costs encumbered throughout the period after 1955 made the Chautauqua region less competitive than both Michigan and Washington, the latter particularly better suited to the production of Concord. The end result was the 1984-1985 crash in Concord prices. Although the region never fully recovered its winemaking potential after Prohibition, the 1960s are important for two notable events: the establishment of Mogen David and the Johnson Estate Winery, the latter, the first of many small wineries.

Curiously, the grape mix has not altered appreciably in recent years, and there are indications that Concord, Catawba, Niagara, and Delaware acreage has actually gained at the expense of other, less desirable varieties. What has changed is total grape acreage: more than 6,000 acres of climatically and/or productively marginal land has been uprooted, but Concord and Catawba still dominate planted acreage for processing needs. Still, there is an active attempt to increase French-American and Vinifera acreage for the production of wine. Currently in the making is an interesting plan by a syndicate to plant 600 acres of Chardonnay by 1993. Should this project come to fruition, it will be the largest single planting of Chardonnay in the nation east of California.

With a growing season that is a month longer than the Finger Lakes area and a low incidence of fungus diseases, the ability to compete with the Finger Lakes in the production of quality white table and sparkling wines (from Seyval, Chardonnay, and Riesling) is within the realm of the possible given the propensity of this region to produce quality, well-balanced, flavorful, and scented grapes. Equally important is the fact that Vinifera vines do not suffer from winter kill to the same extent as the Finger Lakes and Hudson River region. Chautauqua, therefore, has a marvelous potential for Riesling, Gewurztraminer, Chardonnay, and Pinot Noir production, the latter, particularly suited for sparkling wine output. What the region requires is massive capital infusion, more wineries, and more dry table wine production. Most of all, this highly underrated region suffers from insufficient credibility.

In the final analysis, it is amazing how this region survived given the number and rapidity of turbulent and uncertain economic cycles that it has endured over the past 100 years: grapes were first used commercially by local wineries; later it won regional acclaim as a table grape producer; with the advent of the Welch Company it became known primarily as a juice producing region; during Prohibition it supplied home winemakers with enormous amounts of fresh grapes and juice; the processing grape industry crashed several times after 1950 because of over-production, and competition from Washington, Michigan, and, to a smaller extent, Missouri and Arkansas; more recently, the consuming public has switched from grape juice to other juices, further placing structural stresses on the industry. However, given the presence of inexpensive vineland, favorable soils and climatic conditions relative to the Finger Lakes and lower Hudson River region, this area has a bright future in the production of quality grapes, and particularly in the production of white table and sparkling wines.

The wineries are: **Chadwick Bay Wine Company** (Fredonia, 1980), a grape growing concern until 1980, the winery now buys all fruit and makes 15,000 cases of generic red, rose, and white wines from American and French-American grapes. **Johnson Estate Wines** (Westfield, 1961), is a 120-acre, 20,000-case winery that makes a large selection of varietal and proprietary wines, of which Aurore, Seyval, Ives, Chancellor, and Liebestroepfchen (a semi-sweet Delaware-Chancellor-Seyval blend) are interesting. **Merritt Estate Wines** (Forestville, 1976), is a fourth-generation grape growing family that has long provided grapes to both the fresh market and the processing industry. In 1976 it began producing a large selection of wines (10,000 cases) from 100 acres--mostly proprietary blends of Aurore, Seyval, Vidal Blanc, Niagara, Delaware, DeChaunac, Baco Noir, and Marechal Foch. **Mogen David Wine Corporation** (Westfield, 1967), part of the Wine Group of San Francisco, is a 300,000-case winery that functions as a primary source for kosher and fortified wine production from purchased grapes, must and juice. **Roberian Vineyards Ltd.** (Sheridan, 1988), is a 15-acre, 2,000-case winery that makes American, French-American, and Vinifera wines, of which Vidal Blanc, Chardonnay, and Riesling are considered the finest. **Schloss Doepkin Winery** (Ripley, 1980), located on the site of the Brocton Wine Company, is a 60-acre, 2,500-case winery that makes American, French-American, and Vinifera wines, of which Chardonnay, Riesling, and Gewurztraminer are the finest. **Vetter Vineyards** (Westfield, 1987), is a 21-acre, 3,500-case winery that makes a large selection of French-American and Vinifera wines, of which Vidal Blanc, Seyval, Chardonnay, Riesling, and Gewurztraminer are the finest. **Woodbury Vineyards** (Dunkirk, 1979), is an aggressive and rapidly expanding, 128-acre, 32,000-case winery operated by a three-generation vinegrowing family that produces high quality grapes from a vineyard located on a glacial ridge. Most wines are made from Vinifera grapes first planted in 1971, of which Riesling and Chardonnay (one of the finest in the state) are the most important. In recent years, the improving sparkling wines have done much to enhance the reputation of this winery, and, as a result, production has increased dramatically. The winery also makes an interesting Nouveau from Gamay grapes. The acreage owned by this winery represents the single largest Vinifera planting in the Chautauqua region. As one of two premier wineries located along Lake Erie, the vineyard practices in this innovative winery are impeccable.

The Finger Lakes Region

While commercial grape growing and winemaking in New York dates back to the second decade of the nineteenth century, the Finger Lakes region has been the center of the state's wine industry since the Civil War, and the largest and best established wine industry east of the Continental Divide. This is not surprising as settlement by a European population has produced many toponyms like Venice, Dresden, Odessa, Orleans, Delphi, Ithaca, etc. The Finger Lakes region, located in the west-central portion of the state, marks the border between the northern terminus of the depressed and depopulated Appalachian plateau and the southern margin of the Lake Ontario drainage basin. The northern extensions of the lakes are shallow and framed by flat terrain; the southern ends, much deeper, are bounded by 1,200-foot high hills. This once heavily forested region has been markedly modified by human activity over the past 150 years, and as recently as the second half of the last century more than half of the acreage has been altered to arable and grazing land. Most of the dairy farms have since disappeared and much of the land abandoned. Amidst this negative agricultural picture, the Finger Lakes region is an area of legendary beauty, captivating geology, spectacular waterfalls, small historic towns, outstanding glacial remains, and rolling hills. Peppering the entire region, the remaining and best vineyards rest on hillsides that overlook the lake water.

This region is comprised of two *ava's*: *Finger Lakes* and *Cayuga Lake*. The latter, the smaller of the two, is an enclave encompassing portions of three counties (Seneca, Tompkins, and Cayuga), has 600 acres of vineland, 18 vineyards, and 10 wineries. Due to a slightly lower altitude and deep lake water, the hillside microclimate adjacent to Lake Cayuga is moderated thus lengthening the growing season to 170 days, or more than two weeks than surrounding counties. More important, the persistency of air movement lowers the possibility of disastrous frost in early spring. The glacial soils are mainly derived from shale, limestone, and slate. The much broader *Finger Lakes ava* refers to a cluster of eleven narrow, north-south, glacial lakes that include ten counties--Steuben, Ontario, Livingston, Monroe, Tompkins, Yates, Wayne, Schuyler, Seneca, and Cayuga. The entire region encompasses 4,000 square miles, contains 2.5 million acres (14,000 of which are planted in vines), 350 individual vine-

yards, and 47 of the states 97 wineries, two of which rank among the nation's 10 largest. With but 38 percent of the state's vine acreage, the region produces 95 percent of its wine. Historically the two most important lakes were Keuka and Canandaigua, but recently Lakes Cayuga (the largest) and Seneca (the deepest) have attracted significant interest. For the entire region, acreage has declined by more than 25 percent since 1980, and vineland is being consolidated by fewer and fewer growers.

Figure 5.9

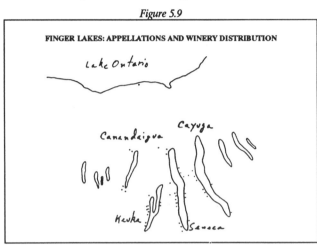

FINGER LAKES: APPELLATIONS AND WINERY DISTRIBUTION

Lake Ontario

Canandaigua Cayuga

Keuka Seneca

Although not the largest vineyard in the state, the Finger Lakes have historically received most of the viticultural acclaim ever since the Reverend William Bostwick planted Isabella and Catawba vines in his Hammondsport garden in 1829. Since then the Finger Lakes produced some of the nation's largest and most colorful wineries. The first commercial winery established in 1860 was the Pleasant Valley Wine Company, later baptized Great Western Winery. Gold Seal Vineyards, just north of Hammondsport, was founded as the Urbana Wine Company in 1865, and has specialized since its inception in the production of sparkling wines. The Taylor Wine Company was founded in 1880 by Walter Taylor, a cooper by trade, and a major proponent (as well as his son and grandson) of French-American varietals. This winery was purchased by Great Western in 1961, only to be acquired by Coca Cola of Atlanta in 1977, the Seagram Corporation in 1983, and by United Vintners of New York in 1987. John Widmer founded a winery in Naples in 1888 five years after his arrival from Switzerland. The last of the big wineries in the Finger Lakes is the Canandaigua Wine Company, a publicly traded company that ranks as the nation's third largest. This huge holding company owns wineries in three states, and makes everything from inexpensive Scuppernong to table, kosher, sparkling, and cooler wines.

The first vine plantings by Reverend William Bostwick established a pattern that endured for 120 years. Finger Lakes vinegrowing was based on hardy American vines, overwhelmingly Concord, Catawba, Isabella, Dutchess, Ives, Delaware, Niagara, Noah, and a host of other lesser known varieties. After 1960, French-American grapes gradually increased their acreage, and since 1973 Vinifera varieties. Nevertheless, 80 percent of the planted area remains in American varieties (Concord, Catawba, Niagara, and Delaware); 18 percent are French-American; and the remainder Vinifera. As long as the dominant wines remain sweet, fortified, and sparkling, American and French-American vines will dominate. Among French-American varietals, the most important, and those with the most promise, are Seyval, Vidal Blanc, Cayuga, and Vignoles--all white grapes. With more than 500 acres, the most popular is Seyval, a hardy, moderately vigorous, disease resistant grape that produces a rather lengthy assortment of clean, fresh, fruity, and often complex wines. However, red French-American varietals continue to elude the thirst for good, sound, reliable red table wine. Likewise, red Vinifera varietals, particularly Cabernet Sauvignon, Merlot, and Pinot Noir, take a back seat to the better whites, particularly Chardonnay, Rkatsiteli, Riesling, and Gewurztraminer.

One of the major problems with the Finger Lakes is the high cost of producing grapes. In the 1950s the average price of New York grapes was twice that of the Great Lakes, and significantly higher than California, a condition that has also not improved with the nation's largest producer of Concord grapes--Washington. Costs per ton are now 40 percent higher than Lake Erie and 60 percent higher than Washington State. Amelioration and the importation of neutral, less expensive California Central Valley bulk wines make the blending of wine a common practice among the largest producers. Acreage has declined by more than 3,000 acres since 1950 despite the fact that 89 new wineries have been constructed during this time period. The number of growers has declined from 700 to 350 between 1982 and 1988, and of this total fewer than 90 can be considered "serious" in terms of size and capitalization. In addition, upscale restaurants and New Yorkers, especially those with expensive cellars, have not (except the wines of Long island) accepted the wines from this region. While all the "new boys" of Long Island get prominent mention on retail shelves and restaurant lists, only Glenora, Wagner, Dr. Konstantin Frank, and Hermann Wiemer from the Finger Lakes, Woodbury in Lake Erie, and Millbrook and West Park from the Hudson River region compete in the premium wine market.

Therefore, to compensate for the high cost of local grapes, industry growth over the past ten years has been based on the importation of west coast and eastern Long Island Vinifera grapes and juice. While the above hardly paints a favorable picture, this remote region (in relation to the state's principle wine market) presents many advantages and seems to have a bright future. Among the more notable items are: firm wine grape prices since 1986; a rising tourist flow; increased Vinifera acreage; new and expanding winery construction; better vineyard and winery practices; and significant state-related help and encouragement. The region also has two interesting museums: the Greyton H. Taylor, located at Bully Hill, and another in Hammondsport. The former, the first vineyard museum, is highly unusual in terms of depth of items on display, while the latter offers a clear and concise reflection of the area's colorful history.

East-facing vineyards, Lake Seneca. There is a major controversy as to which aspect of the lakes is better for grapes--east or west. Baxevanis

The Finger Lakes have a moderately humid continental climate. The flow of air, from the west and north, results in cold, dry weather, while short periodic bouts of southerly winds bring humid, unstable weather. Summers are hot and short; winters, long, cold and dry; spring, short and unpredictable; and fall, long, cool and relatively dry. While seasonal temperature extremes are noticeable, precipitation is not, there being no well-defined wet or dry season. Interestingly, in each year there is a 70 percent chance that the months of December-February will have at least three days when temperatures will fall below -20F (in sharp contrast, the lowest temperature in the Rheingau is -9F), and during the months of January and February there will be at least fifteen days when the temperature will fall below 0F. It is not uncommon for exposed sites to experience sudden temperature drops to -10F leading to trunk shatter with roots freezing and breaking, thus killing vines outright, particularly the more tender Vinifera. Average precipitation is 32 inches, anything less than 24 inches being considered a drought. Each month receives more than six days with at least .10 inches of rain. However, August and September can be excessively wet, interfering with a successful vintage one out of every three years. There are 60 snow days: occasionally heavy, both in terms of individual storms and monthly amounts, and there is at least one storm each winter depositing 12 inches or more. Monthly totals of 20 inches or more, common in December, January, February, and March, are considered a positive element in preventing severe winter kill. The snow season begins early in November and continues until the first half of April.

Figure 5.10

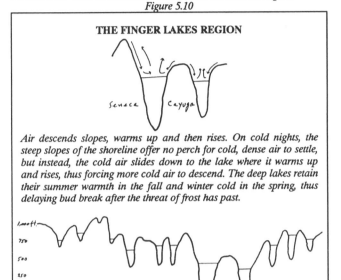

THE FINGER LAKES REGION

Air descends slopes, warms up and then rises. On cold nights, the steep slopes of the shoreline offer no perch for cold, dense air to settle, but instead, the cold air slides down to the lake where it warms up and rises, thus forcing more cold air to descend. The deep lakes retain their summer warmth in the fall and winter cold in the spring, thus delaying bud break after the threat of frost has past.

*Cross-section of the Finger Lakes Region.
Most vineyards are located between Keuka and Cayuga.*

Historically, it was thought that the four principle lakes had a microclimate that was unique to the northernmost extension of the Appalachian plateau: the combination of glacial till, dry summer weather, and thick fog during spring and fall ameliorated an otherwise brutal climate making grape growing possible and business ventures profitable. Indeed, because water heats and cools more slowly than land, it has the ability to retard vegetal growth in the spring, lower diurnal temperature variations, lengthen the growing season, and hinder the onslaught of the first fall frost. The hillsides, also, slope gently thus allowing for good air drainage inhibiting both frost and disease. In summer the cooling effect of the lakes tends to reduce daytime heating and thereby reduce the incidence of thunderstorms. Likewise, cooling at night is also reduced, and for this reason the frost-free growing season is inversely proportional to distance from lake margins. This is excellent choreography for the vine-grower; the colder lake water in the spring lowers atmospheric temperatures slowing the production of bud break on the vine until after the threat of frost has diminished. In the fall, the process is reversed; higher than normal ambient water temperatures over the lakes prevent early frost damage to the ripening grapes. To the grape grower, correct exposure of his vineyards allows for a longer

growing season that is limited to the intermediate shoreline, while the surrounding, more exposed areas some distance from lake water are faced by a rather precarious climatic regime of colder winters, and spring and fall frosts.

The foregoing are presented as favorable viticultural conditions as long as vineyards are planted near lake margins to benefit from wind movement and the moderating effects of lake water. The influence of the Finger Lakes is particularly marked in connection with the length of the growing season as delimited by the last and first killing frosts. May fourth is the date of the last killing frost, and October tenth is the first one in the fall, giving a growing season of 135-150 days, or one that is shorter than eastern Long Island, the lower Hudson River, and Lake Erie. Average heat degree day summation for April-October is less than 1,700, among the lowest in the nation. However, more than 80 percent of the present planted acreage is located on the higher interfluves out of sight of lake water whose growing season is reduced to fewer than 140 days (it is interesting to note that New York City has a 190-day growing season; Buffalo, 175; Columbus, Ohio, 160; and Riverhead, on eastern Long Island, 215). While lake valleys do indeed exhibit a climatic pattern different from dry valleys, the difference is limited to elevations within 500 feet from lake water, and does not offer significant advantages above that elevation. In the final analysis, all of the above implies that the bulk of the Finger Lakes viticultural region is unsuited to the production of quality wine grapes; meteorological evidence does not substantiate a regional climatic superiority for the area. Only the hardiest native American grapes can consistently weather the annual climatic battle; French-American, less hardy, must be grown in more sheltered locations; and Vinifera, the most tender of the three, prevail only through extraordinary vineyard practices.

The soils are of glacial origin, with uplands having considerable amounts of glacial till; bed rock is limestone, sandstone, and shale, usually deep, but often through glacial action, discontinuous. Glacial and lacustrine soils are intermingled with drumlin features--long, low hills with well-drained soils, all excellent for grape growing. While drumlins are cold, windswept and often droughty, the lacustrine soils of depressions lying between drumlins are poorly drained, have a perched water table, and subject to temperature inversions.

Distinct soil associations number in the hundreds, and because they are intermingled, vineland rarely exhibits a uniform picture on the landscape. The best vineyards are planted on slopes facing the lakes on shale-limestone-derived soil, rich in minerals that are said to be responsible for much of the acidity in the wine. The soil is porous, permitting vine roots to penetrate deeply into the subsoil and find a permanent source of water thus protecting vine roots in extreme cold weather as well as in periods of reduced summer precipitation. In winter the heavy snow blanket protects roots close to the surface and leaves sufficient moisture for spring growth. The growing season is characterized as hot and dry with evenings sufficiently cold to produce pronounced dew-falls.

Bully Hill Vineyards. Author's wine class on tour. Baxevanis

Another aspect of the microclimate is the orientation of the vineyards. Most are planted facing east and southeast in order to receive the first burst of solar radiation early in the morning. Throughout the region it appears reasonable that these considerations, plus a well protected site from westerly and northerly winds would dominate sites, but these are not universal axioms. Most vineyards have an eastern exposure for one additional and critical reason: because lakes lie in the center of the west-to-east cyclonic storm pattern, and as vineyard exposure is on the lee side of this storm track, the incidence of sunshine is increased annually by 8 percent, and in the critical month of May by nearly 15 percent in comparison to New York City. Hence, east-facing slopes warm up faster than west-facing slopes during spring, thus lengthening the growing season. This easterly exposure also assures less dew and fewer fungus diseases.

The Finger Lakes Wineries

Of the five westernmost Finger Lakes, Conesus, Hemlock, and Canandaigua are the most important. Lake Canandaigua ("chosen place" in Indian), commonly referred to as the "American Rhine," is the most tourist-intensive of the Finger Lakes, home to the state's largest winery, and the site of the largest vineyard. Lake Hemlock, lying to the west of Lake Canandaigua in the westernmost portion of the Finger Lakes *ava*, has but one winery, Eagle Crest Vineyards. The entire region contains seven wineries:

Arbor Hill Grapery (Naples, 1988), is a 17-acre, 1,500-case winery that makes interesting Chardonnay, Riesling, and Pinot Noir under the Lake Boat label, as well as proprietary French-American wines. The winery also makes small quantities of sparkling wine.

Batavia Wine Cellars (Batavia, 1940), with an annual output of more than 250,000 cases, this historically much larger, bulk producing winery now makes low-priced, bulk American and French-American table, sparkling, and vermouth wines under the *Capri, Imperator*, and *Royal Seal* labels. It is owned by the Canandaigua Wine Company.

Canandaigua Wine Co. (Canandaigua, 1945), growing very rapidly as a publicly traded company in the last 20 years, became the third largest American winery in 1991. It makes a large number of low-priced, highly variable and undistinguished wines. The main brands are Virginia Dare, Richard's Wild Irish Rose, Ch. Martin Vermouth, J. Roget sparkling wine, Manischewitz, and Sun-Country Cooler. New York-produced wine is less than 1 million cases, more than half of which are considered dessert and fortified wines. Sales rose dramatically from $150,000 in 1946 to more than $140 million in 1986. Canandaigua operates wineries in South Carolina, California, and New York (the Petersburg, Virginia winery was closed in 1989). The company formed Richard's Wild Rose (two-thirds of sales) in 1951; purchased the Mother Vineyard Winery in Manteo, North Carolina in 1956; Tenner Brothers Wine Co. in Patrick, South Carolina in 1965; the Hammondsport Wine Co. in 1969; acquired the rights to the Virginia Dare label in 1973; purchased the Bisceglia Brothers Wine Co. in Madera, California in 1976; Robin Fils in New York in 1984; Widmer's Wine Cellars in 1986; the Monarch Wine Co. in 1987; Kassers Distillers in Philadelphia in 1989; and in 1991, Guild Wineries and Distilleries. Despite these acquisitions, declining sales have recently forced several plant closings and the sale of certain company divisions. Recently the winery has introduced a Brazilian White Zinfandel. Total production from all divisions and brands is estimated to be more than 10 million cases.

Eagle Crest Vineyards (Conesus, 1872), originally established as O-Neh-Da Vineyard to produce sacramental wine, is an 8-acre, 20,000-case proprietary (from American and French-American grapes) winery that markets wines under the Barry, O-Neh-Da (for sacramental wines), and Eagle Crest labels. The winery was founded by the Roman Catholic bishop of Rochester, repurchased by the Society of the Divine World in 1924, the Cribari family in 1968, and by the present owners in 1982. Historically, it was known for the production of Missouri Riesling, Delaware, and Cream Sherry wines, but now makes and uses Chancellor, Cayuga, Vidal Blanc, Vignoles, and Niagara, among others.

Widmer's Wine Cellars (Naples, 1888), founded by a Swiss immigrant, this steadily growing winery now produces more than two dozen different wines, of which Sherry and Porto-type wines are popular. Output exceeds 700,000 cases from 250 acres of mainly American and French-American grapes. The winery has recently introduced a new line of Chardonnay, Cabernet Sauvignon, and Sauvignon Blanc wines made from purchased fruit, must, and wine. Other wines include Seyval and a line of proprietary wines. The winery, part of the Canandaigua Wine Co., is the site for Manischewitz wine production as well.

North of Lake Canandaigua, on the southern outskirts of Rochester, lie two other wineries: **Casa Larga Vineyards** (Fairport, 1978), is a well-sited, 35-acre, 10,000-case winery that makes excellent, estate-produced wines with restrained alcohol from French-American varietals, generic, and sparkling wines. Quality production rests with Riesling, Chardonnay, Gewurztraminer, and Cabernet Sauvignon. **Thorpe Vineyard** (Wolcott, 1980), formally Staubling Vineyards, is a 3-acre, 600-case winery that makes Chardonnay, Pinot Noir and proprietary wines.

Also referred to as the "the American Rhine," Lake Keuka, the most spectacular of the Finger Lakes (22 miles long, fork-shaped, with steep hills rising 1,000-feet from the lake water), is historically the most important of the Finger Lakes in terms of vine acreage and amount of wine made. Today the lake is home to the second largest winery in the state, the site of Hammondsport (the original site of grape vine plantings), the origins of Walter Taylor Winery, and 10 wineries:

Bully Hill Vineyard (Hammondsport, 1970). The son and grandson of the founder of Taylor Winery established a winery on the original property owned by Walter Taylor in 1880. All wines are estate produced without the addition of water, additives, or bulk wines. While the mainstay of total output is blended generic white, rose, and red wine, Seyval, Aurore, and Baco Noir, among others, are made as varietals (the list often exceeds 20 different wines, including sparkling). Of the 500 acres, 150 are planted in vines (25 different varieties), mostly French-American. Annual production exceeds 100,000 cases. This very unusual and controversial winery maintains a loyal following and is the only one in the region that makes brandy. The present owner is a man who has led a personal crusade against the adulteration of New York State-produced wine through elaborate and sophisticated amelioration efforts. He is one of the most unforgettable and accomplished personalities in the east, and judging by the sad state of affairs of the larger wineries in the state, his prognostications about "ameliorated" wine have all come true. In the east, it is widely assumed that the Taylor family, for three generations, has been growing grapes and making wines longer than anyone else.

Cana Vineyards (Hammondsport, 1984), one of the smallest wineries in the Finger Lakes region, this 900-case facility makes Chardonnay, Riesling, Gewurztraminer, Seyval, Cayuga, and Vignoles from purchased fruit.

Chateau Frank (Hammondsport, 1986), is a 28-acre, 4,000-case winery that makes nothing but sparkling wine from Chardonnay, Pinot Blanc, Pinot Noir, and Pinot Meunier grapes. The initial wines (aged for three years) exhibit extraordinary fragrance, structure, finesse, elegance, and a mousse that is absolutely outstanding--wines that simply should not be missed as they are the finest thus far from the entire state. In the formative stages is an interesting blend of Riesling, Pinot Blanc, and Gewurztraminer. Located next to Vinifera Wine Cellars, it is owned by Willy Frank.

Dr. Frank's Vinifera Wine Cellars (Hammondsport, 1962), is a 70-acre, 8,000-case winery founded by Dr. Konstantin Frank. Now operated by his son, Willy Frank, the winery is one of several quality producers in the Finger Lakes region. The wines, consistent to a fault since 1984, are: Chardonnay, Rkatsiteli, dry and late harvest Riesling, dry and sweet Muscat Ottonel, sweet Sereksia, Gewurztraminer, Cabernet Sauvignon, and Pinot Noir. The late harvest Muscat Ottonel and Sereksia are outstanding, memorable, and not to be missed. Always distinctive and long-lived, the wines from this immaculate, expertly managed property always offer exceptional value and should not be missed. The fact that this was the first all-Vinifera winery in New York is significant.

Heron Hill Vineyards (Hammondsport, 1977), is a 50-acre, 22,000-case, white wine winery whose reputation rests on Riesling, and, to a smaller extent, on Chardonnay, Cayuga, Seyval, Aurore, Cabernet Sauvignon, fruit, and proprietary blends. Other labels: *Otter Spring, Little Heron*.

Hunt Country Vineyards (Branchport, 1987), is a 70-acre, 5,500-case winery that emerged as an independent entity after the merger of Finger Lakes Wine Cellars with Glenora. It makes estate Seyval, Chardonnay, Cayuga, Vignoles, Riesling, Vidal Blanc Ice Wine, and proprietary blends, all offering good value.

HUNT COUNTRY
Vidal Ice Wine
Finger Lakes Table Wine
1987 Estate Bottled

Keuka Spring Vineyards (Penn Yan, 1985), is a 7-acre, 1,000-case winery that makes good, sound Riesling, Chardonnay, Vignoles, Seyval, and proprietary wines.

McGregor Vineyard Winery (Dundee, 1980), is a well-sited, 23-acre, 9,000-case, quality-oriented winery that makes Chardonnay, Gewurztraminer, Saparavi, Rkatsiteli, Riesling, Pinot Noir, sweet Muscat Ottonel, Sereksia, Pinot Noir, Vignoles, sparkling, and proprietary wines, all consistently well-made.

St. Walter de Bully Wine Co. (Hammondsport, 1984), owned by Walter Taylor of Bully Hill Vineyards, is a 15-acre, 1,000-case winery that produces "Claret" made from 13 different grape varieties.

The Taylor-Great Western-Gold Seal Winery (Hammondsport, 1880), was, until recently, the largest winery in the state producing a large assortment of wines. The winery (consisting of 28 buildings and 400 acres) is now part of Vintners International, and is the central administrative center for Taylor, Gold Seal, and Great Western Winery label operations (producing 1 million cases). More than 50 labels represent a bewildering variety of wine from light table to sparkling and fortified wines. The finest wines from all three labels are the dry Vinifera-based sparkling and table wines. Interesting is an Isabella rose, Seyval, and a smooth Cream Sherry. Due to declining sales, the winery, labels, and acreage are for sale. **Gold Seal** (Hammondsport, 1865) was founded

Willy Frank, of Chateau Frank and Dr. Frank's Vinifera Wine Cellars. Two consumer friendly wineries that makes superb wines. Baxevanis

originally along the western shore of Lake Keuka as the Urbana Wine Co. After 1960 it entered into a period of rapid expansion eventually producing a "complete line" of wines, of which the "Charles Fournier" label was considered the finest. In 1961 Gold Seal marketed the first Chardonnay and Riesling from Lake Keuka vineyards, a revolutionary step for the times. As of 1984 all production facilities have been transferred to the Taylor Wine Co., and the historic winery sold. **Great Western Winery** (Hammondsport, 1860), known historically as the Pleasant Valley Wine Co., continues as a label for sparkling wines and small amounts of ice wine, the latter distinctive, deserving attention. For a period of nearly 35 years after Prohibition, this winery's sparkling wine was the most popular in the nation. Founded in 1860, it was the first winery in the Finger Lakes region, and is now listed in the National Register of Historic Places.

Seneca Lake, the second largest of the Finger Lakes, lies between Cayuga and Keuka, and is home to fourteen wineries, all of which were founded after the passage of the Farm Winery Act in 1976. Known by the Indian word "Seneca," meaning "place of the stone," it is, with a depth of 640 feet, the deepest of the Finger Lakes, one of the most rapidly growing areas for new vineyard plantings, and the site of several of the finest wineries in the region. It is also the only lake that rarely freezes. Of the nineteen wineries founded after 1975, more than half were established since 1985:

Amberg Wine Cellars (Clifton Springs, 1989), is a 10-acre, 3,500-case winery that is sited on an 19th century vineyard. The winery makes Chardonnay, Riesling, Pinot Noir, and proprietary French-American blends. The winery also runs a thriving nursery.

Anthony Road Wine Company (Penn Yan, 1989), is a 30-acre, 2,500-case winery that makes Chardonnay, Seyval, Vignoles, and late harvest Vignoles.

Barrington Champagne Cellars (Dundee, 1986), is a tiny, 600-case winery that only makes sparkling wines (Blanc de Blanc, Cremant, Reserve, and Blanc de Noir).

Castel Grisch Winery (Watkins Glen, 1987), is a 23-acre, 5,000-case winery that makes clean, crisp Chardonnay, Riesling, Gewurztraminer, Seyval, Catawba, Baco Noir, and proprietary wines.

Chateau LaFayette Reneau (Hector, 1985), is a 35-acre, 6,500-case winery that consistently makes a large selection of which Chardonnay, Riesling, Pinot Noir, Seyval, Niagara, and proprietary wines are above average.

Four Chimney's Farm Winery (Himrod, 1980), is a 50-acre, 5,500-case, "organic-farm" winery that makes a large number of varietal (Seyval, Chardonnay, Riesling, Cayuga, Delaware), sparkling, proprietary, fruit and berry wines from American, French-American, and Vinifera grapes, most of which are sweet.

Fox Run Winery (Penn Yan, 1989), is a 20-acre, 2,500-case, all-Vinifera winery that makes Chardonnay, Riesling, Gewurztraminer, and sparkling wine from Pinot Noir and Chardonnay.

Fulkerson Wine Cellars (Dundee, 1988), is a 70-acre, 2,500-case winery that makes Delaware, Seyval, Riesling, Cayuga, Diamond, late harvest Vignoles, dessert, and proprietary wines. Producing fruit and grapes has been an ongoing activity by this family since 1805, and this may well be the oldest continuing grape producing farm in the region.

Giasi Winery (Rock Stream, 1979), is a 20-acre, 3,000-case winery that makes good, sound Chardonnay, Cayuga, Seyval, Riesling (dry and late harvest), Canadice, cherry, and proprietary wines. The emphasis lies in well-aged red table wines, Pinot Noir, and French-American blends (one of which uses the unusual Himrod).

Glenora Wine Cellars (Dundee, 1976), this aggressive, 5-acre, 40,000-case, tourist-oriented winery is known for its large selection of Chardonnay, Riesling (dry and late harvest), Cayuga, Gewurztraminer, Seyval, sparkling (Brut Reserve is excellent), small quantities of Himrod and Glenora, Cabernet Sauvignon, and proprietary wines. The reserve wines tend to be more consistent, and significantly better in quality.

Hazlitt 1852 Vineyards (Hector, 1985), is a 46-acre, 6,500-case winery that makes American, French-American, and Vinifera wine, of which the most interesting are Riesling, Chardonnay, Cayuga, Vidal Blanc, Seyval, Aurora, Pinot Noir, Baco Noir, and L'Ambertille (the product of an obscure French-American variety). The name is derived from the fact that Hazlitt family has been in the grape growing business since 1852.

Hermann J. Wiemer Vineyard (Dundee, 1979), one of the finest wineries in the Finger Lakes region, this 65-acre, 14,000-case winery specializes in dry and late harvest Riesling, Chardonnay, Gewurztraminer, Pinot Noir, and sparkling wines. Expertly made, the wines are sold by subscription and in fine restaurants. The winery is owned by a native of Bernkastel Kues, Germany, who is an avid spokesman for Vinifera-based wines. The vineyard is expertly managed, and the wines, carefully and tediously made from low yielding vines, are always distinctive and among the finest made in the Finger Lakes, especially Chardonnay, dry and late harvest Riesling, and Riesling-based sparkling wines. The winery also maintains one of the largest Vinifera nurseries in the northeast. A partnership has produced another label: *Chateau Neckermann*, a Chardonnay for the German market.

Hermann J. Wiemer, proprietor of another consumer friendly winery, makes outstanding wines. Baxevanis

Lakewood Vineyards (Watkins Glen, 1988), is a 60-acre, 4,000-case winery that makes Chardonnay, Riesling, Vignoles, Delaware, Niagara, Cayuga, Catawba, and proprietary wines.

Lamoreaux Landing Wine Cellars (Lodi, 1990), is a large 130-acre, 3,000-case winery that makes Chardonnay, Riesling, Pinot Noir, Merlot, and a blend of Cabernet Sauvignon-Cabernet Franc.

NewLand Vineyard (Geneva, 1987), is an all-Vinifera, 10-acre, 1,200-case winery that makes Chardonnay, Gewurztraminer, Riesling, Sauvignon Blanc, Merlot, and Pinot Noir.

Poplar Ridge Vineyards (Valois, 1981), is a 24-acre, 6,500-case winery that makes sound varietal American, French-American, Vinifera and proprietary wines, of which Chardonnay, Cayuga, Vignoles, Riesling, Seyval, and sparkling wines are the finest.

Prejean Winery (Penn Yan, 1985), one of the top Finger Lakes wineries, is an outstanding, 40-acre, 6,500-case winery that makes above-average to excellent Chardonnay, Gewurztraminer, Riesling, Cayuga, Seyval, Vignoles, Merlot, and Marechal Foch.

Rolling Vineyards Farm Winery (Hector, 1981), is an 85-acre, 3,000-case winery that makes interesting, flavorful American, French-American, and Vinifera wines, of which Chardonnay, Gewurztraminer, Seyval, Vignoles, Vidal Blanc, and Riesling offer good value.

Squaw Point Winery (Dundee, 1986), is an 8-acre, 4,500-case winery that makes Chardonnay, Riesling, Seyval, Vignoles, sparkling, and proprietary wines.

Wagner Vineyards (Lodi, 1978), is a well regarded, 300-acre, 50,000-case winery that makes a large selection (more than 20) of American, French-American, and Vinifera wines, of which the Vignoles, Vidal, Gewurztraminer, Riesling, Chardonnay, late harvest, and sparkling wines are considered the finest. The winery was also the first to make Melody, a new French-American variety developed by the New York Experiment Station.

Stretching from Seneca Falls in the north to Ithaca in the south, the western shore of Lake Cayuga (this lake is the longest in the system) is the rising star of the Finger Lakes as vine acreage has grown to nearly 600, and all nine wineries founded after 1980, a rather remarkable achievement at a time when economic conditions have been depressed. While the high lime, high pH soils are mainly planted in French-American varieties, Vinifera vines enjoy the highest percentage of the planted area than any of the other Finger Lakes. The wineries are:

Americana Vineyards Estate Winery (Interlaken, 1981), is a 10-acre, 1,500-case winery that makes Riesling, Cayuga, Seyval, Niagara, Aurore, Baco Noir, and proprietary wines. **Cayuga Ridge Estate Vineyards** (Ovid, 1980), formerly Plane's Cayuga Vineyard, is a 34-acre, 9,500-case, well-managed winery that specializes, unlike most Finger Lakes wineries, in the production of dry Cayuga, Chardonnay, Riesling, Vignoles, Pinot Noir, Chancellor, and proprietary wines. **Frontenac Point Vineyard** (Trumansburg, 1982), is a 24-acre, 3,000-case, estate winery that specializes in well-oaked Chardonnay, Riesling, Seyval, and proprietary wines from French-American grapes. **Hosmer Winery** (Ovid, 1985), is a 40-acre, 3,000-case winery that makes Cayuga, Seyval, Riesling, Chardonnay, and proprietary blends. **King Ferry Winery** (King Ferry, 1988), located on the east shore, is a 24-acre, 2,500-case, all-Vinifera winery that makes excellent Chardonnay (distinctive, ranking as one of the finest in the state), Riesling, Gewurztraminer, and Pinot Noir. The well made estate wines are marketed under the *Treleaven* label. **Knapp Vineyards** (Romulus, 1982), is a 75-acre, 8,000-case winery that makes interesting Chardonnay, Riesling, Seyval, late harvest Vignoles, Cabernet Sauvignon, Pinot Noir, proprietary blends, and sparkling wines. **Lakeshore Winery** (Romulus, 1982), is a 3-acre, 2,000-case winery that makes Chardonnay, Riesling, Gewurztraminer, Cabernet Sauvignon, Baco Noir, sparkling, and proprietary wines. **Lucas Vineyards** (Interlaken, 1980), is a 21-acre, 4,000-case winery that makes above-average Chardonnay, Riesling, Cayuga, late harvest Vignoles, sparkling (100% Cayuga), and proprietary wines (under the *Tug Boat* label). **Six Mile Creek Vineyard** (Ithaca, 1987), is a serious, 7-acre, 2,500-case winery that makes Cayuga, Vignoles, Seyval, Chardonnay, Riesling, Baco Noir, Marechal Foch, De Chaunac, Chancellor, Chelois, and proprietary blends. **Swedish Hill Vineyard** (Romulus, 1985), is a 30-acre, 35,500-case winery that makes well-flavored, mainly proprietary wines. It is the only American winery to makes large quantities of Ventura, a new Canadian grape, as a varietal. Also made are Chardonnay, Riesling, Cayuga, Pinot Blanc, Chancellor, Marechal Foch, Porto-type, sparkling, and proprietary wines from American and French-American wines. The late harvest Vignoles is interesting.

Hudson River Region

Long referred to as the "cradle" of the state's wine industry, the lower Hudson River region, a rapidly urbanizing area of more than 6 million people, encompasses nine counties immediately to the north of New York City, of which Ulster and Columbia counties are the two dominant grape-growing areas in the region. Less than 6 percent of the land area is used for agriculture (mostly for fruit, dairy, and horticultural specialties). While urban encroachment is a detriment to vineyard expansion, winemakers see the increased population growth as a major new market just waiting to be tapped. Few areas in the nation contain such a high density of large suburban estates, stately mansions, several state parks, and small, historic towns. Among the more notable sites are Philipsburg Manor, a colonial estate of 90,000 acres, the "Legend of Sleepy Hollow," Van Cortland Manor, Hyde Park, and the palatial homes of several "robber barons."

Because the middle and lower section of the Hudson River is well protected from cold northerly winds, it has long been a major horticultural region, ranking third in the nation as an apple producer. Of the four principal wine producing regions in the state, the Hudson River has been producing wines the longest, and is considered the oldest continuously planted *ava* in the New World (over 300 years) with portions of the historic High Tor Vineyard (granted to the Van Orden family by King George III) continuously planted for more than 200 years. This vineyard and winery, resurrected by Everett Crosby in the early 1950s, had several owners with financial problems, and is now a housing development.

Vines were cultivated throughout the lower Hudson River region in early colonial history (as early as 1624)--from the southernmost portions of Westchester County to the protected fluvial niches just south of Kingston. While first attempts proved to be nothing more than interesting backyard affairs, the settlement of French Huguenots in New Paltz in 1678 added a more serious note as the newly arrived immigrants from western France possessed both the necessary skills and the palate for fine wine. Huguenot settlement was particularly heavy along the left bank between Haverstraw and New Paltz, the latter, containing the oldest street in America where the original houses still stand. Due to their inability to accommodate the flavor of the native grapes and to successfully cultivate Vinifera vines, they abandoned production, preferring instead to import the more familiar European wines.

The first commercial winery was not established until 1827 on Croton Point in Westchester County by Dr. Richard T. Underhill, nearly 150 years after the first winemaking attempt. Brotherhood, the oldest operating winery in the nation located in Washingtonville, was established in 1839 by a charismatic, utopian religious group that subsequently moved to Brocton, New York (on Lake Erie), and then to Sonoma County, California. One of the pioneers, and an expert viticulturist in the town of Marlboro, was Andrew Jackson Caywood who developed the Dutchess grape. While the Hudson Valley attained a certain viticultural importance prior to Prohibition, wine-making efforts declined until the middle 1950s with the establishment of High Tor and Benmarl. Although the Hudson Valley is said to be the oldest wine growing region in Anglo-America, it has been very slow in developing a large, strong, economically viable wine industry. The reasons are not hard to find: the sophisticated regional market was overwhelmingly oriented toward Vinifera imports and California wines, both of which were significantly more delicate and drier in flavor than the sweetish, strongly-flavored American wines. As growers switched from American to French-American grapes in the late 1960s, and with the passage of the Farm Winery Act of 1976, the number of wineries increased from 4 in 1975 to 24 by 1992.

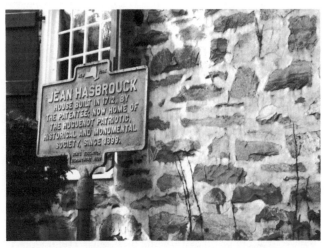

The Jean Hasbrouck Memorial House (1692-1712), an excellent example in America of medieval Flemish stone architecture, and Huguenot Street in the old section of New Paltz, New York. The French Huguenots were highly instrumental in diffusing viticulture throughout Colonial America.
Baxevanis

Because American grapes are indigenous to the region, "traditional" American wines have been made since colonial times. However, this small, but recently rejuvenated region has shifted, since 1954, to French-American and Vinifera vines, and at a time when the Lake Erie and Finger Lakes regions are having trouble selling their wines, the Hudson River viticultural region, despite its geographically diverse character, is growing as evidenced by the recent swell in new wineries and a surprisingly large cadre of home winemakers. Although all but seven wineries are located along the west bank of the Hudson, new emerging areas along the east bank, such as Millbrook, are expected to increase in the near future. With Kedem, Winery at Rivendell, and Brotherhood the only exceptions, most wineries are family affairs that produce

between 2,000 and 10,000 cases annually, three are bona-fide estate wineries, and only two specialize in the production of Vinifera wines only. Wine quality, especially from farm wineries, has improved markedly in recent years. Finally, it is strange to find that in this historic and economically affluent region, the wine industry should have remained so neglected and undercapitalized.

While both banks of the Hudson River contain vineyards, it is the left bank, an area primarily shrouded by the scenic Catskill and Shawangunk Mountains, that is home to 24 wineries. Historically a resort area of small towns and large estates, the primary agricultural activity has been, due to the protected and moderating element of the Hudson River, orchards, particularly apples. The largest single area for winery concentration is the small town of Marlboro, 60 miles north of Manhattan. Of all wineries, Brotherhood is the oldest, three were founded prior to 1960, and the remaining were all established after 1975. Over the past fifteen years, the area has attracted many accomplished individuals (stockbrokers, industrialists, pharmaceutical executives, etc.), and the area appears to be on the verge of a major renaissance.

Of the four major viticultural districts in New York, the Hudson River area contains the highest percentage of French-American varietals. Over the past generation, growers and boutique wineries have switched from Concord, Catawba, Dutches, and Niagara, to Seyval, Vidal Blanc, Cayuga, Vignoles, Chambourcin, Baco Noir, Chelois, Chancellor, and Marechal Foch. Seyval, Vidal Blanc, and Vignoles are three grapes that do particularly well in the Hudson Valley. Acreage in Vinifera varietals in the past ten years has increased from fewer than 10 acres to 129, of which Riesling and Chardonnay are the most widely planted.

There is one *ava--Hudson River Region*, a large area that includes all of Columbia, Dutchess, and Putnam counties, the eastern portions of Ulster and Sullivan, nearly all of Orange County, and the northern portions of Rockland and Westchester counties. It consists of 3,500 square miles, 1,000 acres of vineyards (90 percent of which are located in Columbia and Ulster counties), and 24 wineries, 7 of which are located in the hilly region east of the Hudson River (Amberleaf, Eaton, Cascade, Clinton, Millbrook, Northeast, and North Salem). Bounded by 2,500-foot mountains on the west and hills to the north, the left bank of the Hudson River is well-protected from northern and westerly cold winds. Moreover, the Hudson River is widest at this section, so that the combination of estuary and maritime conditions extends the growing season to 180 days. It is slightly warmer than the Finger Lakes region, but far colder than the Lake Erie and eastern Long Island *ava's*. Although the river is a major conduit for maritime air, temperature inversions and false springs are common, and often quite severe. Soils, variable in their composition of limestone, shale, slate, and schist, are derived from glacial activity.

The entire *ava* is not homogeneous in any physical element except its proximity to a large, affluent urban population. It consists of four distinct physiographic regions: the Hudson River lowlands, the northern extension of the Ridge and Valley Province, the Triassic Lowlands, and the Taconic Mountains. The Hudson River plain, highly irregular in its elevation, width, and soil composition, is the least important of the four as a grape growing region due to its ability to attract frost and temperature inversions. Between Newburgh and Kingston along the Hudson, and extending southwestward into Pennsylvania, is the northern extension of the Ridge and Valley Province, a narrow valley that contains a complex of hills and terraces underlain by folded sedimentary rocks, littered with glacial drift, and drained by the Wallkill River, from which the valley takes its name. The valley is framed by the steep Shawangunk Mountains, an important physical obstacle to the southerly flowing cold air masses. In the extreme southern portion of the *ava* is the Triassic Lowland, a low, rolling area underlain by shales, soft limestone, and lava. On the right bank of the Hudson, the river plain is much narrower, and bordered by the high and rugged Taconic Mountains, a mass of crystalline rock that provides the basis of much of the regions grape acreage. The principal wineries are:

Adair Vineyards (New Paltz, 1987), is a 10-acre, 2,800-case winery that makes Seyval, Chardonnay, Vignoles, Baco Noir, and proprietary wines.

Amberleaf Vineyards (Wappingers Falls, 1987), is a tiny, 4-acre, 800-case, estate winery that makes minute quantities of Chardonnay, Riesling, Seyval, Vidal Blanc, Cabernet Sauvignon, Merlot, Chancellor, and Chambourcin.

Baldwin Vineyards (Pine Bush, 1982), is a 15-acre, 7,000-case winery that makes a wide assortment of Vinifera, French-American, fruit and berry wines. Although inconsistent, this young winery often offers excellent value as Strawberry, Riesling, and Landot Noir are particularly good.

Beaunois Wine Cellars (Marlboro, 1987), owned by an excellent winemaker, is a 15-acre, 1,000-case winery that only makes Chardonnay and Pinot Noir.

Benmarl Wine Company (Marlboro, 1971), is a unique vineyard of 72-acres (from individually owned vines by members of the "Societe des Vignerons") that makes 10,000 cases. The vineyard is planted in French-American and Vinifera vines, primarily Seyval, Vignoles, Vidal Blanc, Marechal Foch, Chelois, Baco Noir, and small quantities of Chardonnay, Pinot Noir, Riesling, and Cabernet Sauvignon. It is reported that in 1885 the Dutchess grape was developed by Andrew Jackson Caywood on this site. Sparkling wines are also made.

Brimstone Hill Vineyards (Pine Bush, 1979), is a 7-acre, 800-case, farm winery that makes mainly Seyval, Chardonnay, and red, rose, and white proprietary wines from French-American grapes.

Brotherhood Winery (Washingtonville, 1839), with an output of 25,000 cases, this is considered the oldest winery (a National Landmark) in continuous operation in the United States. Named after the utopian "Brotherhood of the New Life," this historic winery was sold to a group of investors in 1987. More aggressive and tourist-oriented, it historically produced a complete line of uninspiring, American-based wines, but recent ownership changes will emphasize Vinifera wines from purchased grapes, mainly Chardonnay, Cabernet Sauvignon, Riesling, and sparkling wines. Originally named Blooming Cove, the winery was named The Brotherhood of New Life in 1886 when it was acquired by

Jesse Emerson, a wine merchant. It was renamed once again in 1894 as the Brotherhood Wine Company.

Cagnasso Winery (Marlboro, 1977), is a 10-acre, 2,500-case winery that makes proprietary wines from American and French-American grapes.

Cascade Mountain Winery (Amenia, 1977), is a 14-acre, 6,000-case winery that makes above-average to excellent, wood-aged, French-American wines sold mainly through subscription or at the winery. The owner is related to Charles Wetmore who planted the original Cresta Blanca Vineyard in California in the 19th century. Vignoles and Seyval are both excellent.

Clinton Vineyards (Clinton Corners, 1977), is a 15-acre, 3,500-case winery that makes Seyval, and small quantities of Riesling and sparkling wines, all offering excellent value.

Cottage Vineyards (Marlboro, 1981), is an 8-acre, 800-case winery (partly located on the original Andrew Caywood farm) that makes interesting, fresh, fruity Seyval offering good value. The winery has recently closed but there are plans to resurrect.

Eaton Vineyards (Pine Plains, 1981), is a 10-acre, 2,000-case winery sited on a 200-acre estate in the Taconic Mountains along the east bank of the Hudson River near the Connecticut border. The owner, an expert horticulturist and former director of Duke Gardens, makes above-average, crisp Seyval.

El Paso Winery (Ulster Park, 1978), founded by a Uruguayian winemaker, this small, 2,000-case winery makes interesting, full-bodied and flavored wines from French-American grapes.

Hudson Valley Wine Co. (Highland, 1907), is a 5-acre, 9,000-case winery purchased in 1972 by a New York wine importer from the estate of the founder, an Italian investment banker. The winery is currently making a wide and poor assortment of American (Delaware and Iona grapes dominate), French-American, proprietary, sparkling, coolers, and fruit wines, under many labels, of which the *Regent Champagne Cellars* label is the most important.

Magnanini Farm Winery (Wallkill, 1983), is a 11-acre, 2,000-case winery that makes respectable Seyval, DeChaunac, and various blends from American and French-American grapes.

Northeast Vineyard (Millerton, 1975), is a 2-acre, 500-case winery that makes Aurore and Marechal Foch.

North Salem Vineyard (North Salem, 1979), is an 18-acre, 2,000-case winery specializing in the production of above-average Seyval, Chancellor, DeChaunac, and Marechal Foch.

Royal Wine Corporation (Milton, 1948), is the corporate name for "Kedem Wines," a kosher winery with Czechoslovakian origins. Located in Milton since 1958, this winery (the largest in the region) makes 30 different wines, from coolers, dry table, sweet kosher, sparkling, to flavored, nearly all of which are below average in quality. Production exceeds 300,000 cases, of which a good portion is sold in bulk. In addition to local supplies, the firm buys grapes and must from California, the Finger Lakes region, and other places. The firm owns 170 acres of vineland, mostly Aurore, Riesling, Seyval, Baco Noir, Concord, and Catawba.

The Winery at Rivendell (New Paltz, 1978), is an aggressive and highly innovative, market-oriented, 55-acre, 25,000-case winery that ranks as one of the finest in the Hudson River region. Historically known as the Gardiner Winery, and then as Chateau Georges Winery, the latest name is part of a large-scale upgrading of facilities. The winery is known for proprietary, French-American, and Vinifera varietals, of which Chardonnay (from Long Island), Riesling, Seyval, Vidal, and Merlot are the finest.

Veraison Wine Cellars (Millbrook, 1987), is a 45-acre, 8,000-case, Vinifera-only winery (one of two in the region) founded by a New York industrialist and ex-chairman of the State Power Authority. The owner, a principal author of the 1976 Farm Winery Act, produces above-average to excellent Chardonnay, Riesling, Pinot Noir, Cabernet Sauvignon (blended with Merlot and Cabernet Franc), and sparkling wines (from Chardonnay and Pinot Noir), bottled under the *Millbrook* label. Nebbiolo and Sangiovese are planted but have yet to be made commercially. The vineyard, a superb collection of many experimental vines, is also responsible for many developmental trellising systems. The owner also owns substantial vineland in the Chianti district of Italy, and the Mistral Vineyard in California. Other label: Hunt Country.

Walker Valley Vineyards (Walker Valley, 1978), owned by a college professor, is a 9-acre, 3,500-case winery that makes good, sound, and attractively priced French-American, Vinifera, and fruit wines offering good value.

West Park Wine Cellars (West Park, 1983), is a 5-acre, 3,000-case winery solely devoted to the production of well-made, fresh, lightly oaked, and attractively priced Chardonnay.

Windsor Vineyards (Marlboro, 1980), formerly Great River Winery, is a 25,000-case negociant concern with Sonoma County, California connections that blends California/New York wines, primarily sparkling.

Woodstock Winery (West Shokan, 1983), is a 1,000-case, white wine winery that makes good, sound Seyval, Chardonnay, and late harvest Vignoles from local and Finger Lakes grapes. It also makes apple wine.

Long Island

Long Island, the largest island adjoining America proper, extends for nearly 120 miles east of the mouth of the Hudson River. It contains two of New York City's Boroughs, two important suburban counties--Nassau and Suffolk, and nearly 10 million people. The island is one huge terminal moraine compounded by boulder, gravel and silt deposited and stratified by continental glacial activity. Long Island is composed of low plateaus on the north side, and gently sloping plains to the south of a series of moraines running through the central portion of the island. The state's newest and most promising premium wine region, nearly entirely in the eastern portion of Suffolk County, is surprisingly the state's leading agricultural county as well. While grapes do not occupy more land than truck crops, they compete unexpectedly well with other, more traditional crops in terms of $ returns per acre. The 1,300 acres of grapes amount to 4 percent of the country's total farm land, and are, after potatoes, other vegetables and grain, the fourth most widely planted crop. It is also interesting to note that while potato acreage has declined from 60,000 acres to less than 14,000 acres between 1946 and 1989, vineland is expected to triple within the next fifteen years.

While eastern Long Island produces less than 2 percent of the state's total wine output, it accounts for more than 90 percent of the state's premium wine sales (average price of a bottle of wine is $10.50, perhaps higher than any other American viticultural region). Long Island, producing no bulk, sweet, fortified, or kosher wines, has found its niche by providing the most expensive varietal wines at the upper end of the price range in New York. Given the status of the $US in overseas markets, and the cost of producing premium wine in California, Long Island is the only area in the east that offers formidable competition to all other major wine producing regions--including France, Germany, and Italy.

Although historical accounts indicate that vinegrowing and winemaking had occurred since the 1600s when one Moses Fournier pioneered viticulture, and William Prince established a vineyard in what is now Flushing, Queens (one of the boroughs of New York City) in 1750, it was John Wicham (whose family settled in Cutchogue on the North Fork in 1697) who decided to plant grapes

on his truck farm (for table use). Yet, it wasn't until 1973 with the founding of Hargrave Vineyard that major plantings were established. At present there are sixteen wineries, all but two of which are small. The high cost of real estate not withstanding, the area has increased its vine acreage from zero in 1970 to more than 1,300 in 1992. Continuing improvement of wines, proximity to a wealthy and sophisticated wine consuming clientele, fashionable summer resorts, and a sizeable tourist activity are favorable reasons for optimism. Indeed, Long Island currently produces 300,000 cases of wine, and with a potential acreage of 7,000 (along the middle section of the North Fork) has the ability to produce more than 1.5 million cases of premium wine. Favorable estimates indicate that over the next 20 years more than $500 million will be invested in new vineyard development, construction, and equipment by at least 20 additional wineries.

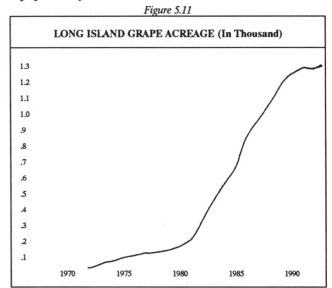

Figure 5.11

Given the remarkable history of the last two decades, this scenario is not that all unlikely. At present the eastern Long Island region contains 49 individual vineyards, 40 of which are located on the North Fork. Potato land prices, $3,000 the acre in 1973, increased to $20,000 in 1990, and are expected to surpass $30,000 the acre for grape growing over the next decade, thus establishing eastern Long Island as the premier wine producing region (based on land prices) east of the Napa Valley. With Le Reve, Pindar, and Bidwell as exceptions, the majority of wineries make fewer than 15,000 cases. Like many areas in coastal California, there is a great deal of interest by wineries and growers to preserve agricultural land from urban encroachment. County government now disallows the sale of development rights, thus preserving land for agricultural use.

What makes eastern Long Island an exciting wine producing region is the fact that it has the longest, coolest growing season of any vineyard in the northeast; it receives as much sunlight as the Napa Valley; contains good, well-drained, friable soils; and the harvest is usually not marred by untimely precipitation. Moreover, due to the presence of a persistent land and sea breeze, even in times when relative humidity exceeds 90 percent for prolonged periods of time, black rot, powdery and downy mildew, with a proper spray schedule, are not major problems. The eastern New York vineyard, therefore, is overwhelmingly planted in Vinifera vines to the near exclusion of others. While Vinifera vines can be successfully grown in the Finger Lakes with considerable struggle, Vinifera vines are able to ripen in eastern Long Island each and every year with little effort.

Figure 5.12

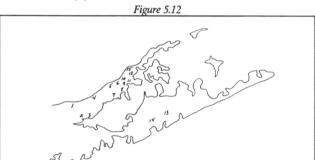

Long Island, surrounded by Long Island Sound on the north and the Atlantic Ocean to the south, has, for the latitude, a very temperate climate of mild winters and a long growing season. Because the water does not heat as rapidly in the spring, vines are slow in their development, and bud break is delayed until the threat of frost has passed. In the fall, the warmer oceanic waters extend the growing season by an additional 30 days well into late November, and often into December. This has allowed the cultivation of cabbage, potatoes, cauliflower, and unlike interior areas just 100 miles to the west, the successful cultivation of "tender" Vinifera varieties. 1. Palmer, 2. Paumanok, 3. North House, 4. Mattituck, 5. Hargrave, 6. Bidwell, 7. Gristina, 8. Peconic, 9. Pugliese, 10. Bedell, 11. Pindar, 12. Lenz, 13. Bridgehampton, 14. Sauvage. 15. Soundview. Banfi is off the map to the west.

Surrounded by water on three sides (inducing daily sea breezes, thus lowering summer and raising winter temperatures), this area experiences a 210-day growing season, and a microclimate that rarely allows winter temperatures to reach 0F, a sharp contrast to the 150-day Finger Lakes growing season. Average temperature is 50F with winter temperatures rarely going below 0F, and summer temperatures beyond 90F. It is the sunniest portion of the state, and since winters are so mild, winter kill, the bane of northeastern and midwestern grape growers, is non-existent. The glacially-derived clay loam soils, interlaced with sand (Riverhead Haven is the most common), are well-drained and warm up easily in the spring. Due to the length of the growing season, eastern Long Island is the only area north of the Maryland/Virginia region that is able to ripen Vinifera grapes with any degree of consistency. Annual precipitation ranges between 30 and 36 inches, half of which falls between April 1 through October 30th, with only a minute fraction during the harvest. Average daytime summer temperature is below 77F while evening temperatures drop to 60F. The area receives one-third more hours (2,800) of sunshine than the Finger Lakes region, and is classified as a Region II. However, unlike the Napa Valley where grapes bake under 100F temperatures, summer heat in eastern Long Island is rarely intense or persistent (with 13 days above 90F, July, 1987 was an exception). Due to the proximity of the warmer temperatures of the Gulf Stream, grapes planted in the South Fork mature after those of the North Fork, a major distinguishable feature between the two *ava's*. The flowering occurs early in June, and the yields vary between 2.5 and 4 tons to the acre. Bird damage is painful each fall, and while the threat of hurricane injury is a possibility, it rarely materializes.

Because of the foregoing, this small vineyard has the largest single concentration of Vinifera vines east of Lubbock, Texas. About 47 percent of the planted acreage is Chardonnay, followed by Cabernet Sauvignon (15%), Merlot (12%), Riesling (9%), Pinot Noir (4%), Gewurztraminer (4%), and Sauvignon Blanc (3%). Over the past five years the combined acreage of Petit Verdot, Cabernet Franc and other minor varietals amounted to only 4 percent of the total acreage. The most expensive Chardonnay, Cabernet Sauvignon, Pinot Noir, Gewurztraminer, Merlot, and Sauvignon Blanc east of the Pacific west coast come from eastern Long Island. There is no commercial American grape variety acreage, and only one winery grows and makes Seyval wine. Due to the fact that the local wineries are unable to process the entire harvest, it is estimated that approximately 10 percent of the grape crop is sold to other New York, Connecticut, New Jersey, and Pennsylvania wineries. Of interest is the fact that eastern Long Island produces the most expensive grapes in the northeast--more than $1,400 the ton.

The wines, due to the young age of the vines, are steadily improving. More than three-quarters of production is white wine, all significantly softer than the hard, acidic wines produced in other areas of the state. While the emphasis is on Chardonnay and Riesling, Sauvignon Blanc and Gewurztraminer are also above-average. They exhibit true varietal odor and flavor, are well-balanced, and, thus far, have not shown dramatic vintage variability. Although Gewurztraminer is not overly popular, Long Island versions (grossly underrated) may be the finest in the nation. Red wines, primarily Cabernet Sauvignon and Merlot, are well-colored and scented, but suffer from grassy and vegetal bitterness, a condition that is related to the age of the vines and former potato fertilizer residue in the soil. Nevertheless, their quality, characterized by elements of depth of flavor, penetrating fragrance, finesse, and delicacy, is superior to all others in the state, and when compared with similar varieties from California are less "fat," lower in alcohol, and often better-balanced.

Although the red wines of Long Island resemble similar libations from the Gironde in terms of restrained alcohol and somewhat higher acid levels, there is absolutely no resemblance (contrary to recent protestations by area wineries) to the Medoc in either soil composition or climate. Although Pinot Noir is used in the production of sparkling wine, it has yet to make a credible varietal libation equivalent to the Willamette Valley. While Long Island grapes are the most expensive in the northeastern portion of the nation, all wines are competitively priced and sell quickly. Nevertheless, the four unique marketing features of proximity to a large, wealthy clientele, consistently high wine quality, price competitiveness, and the prospects of increased production in coming decades should be of concern to premium California wine producers. While the island's current production of 300,000 cases (nearly all priced over $10 the bottle) is but a drop in the sea of California wine, it does mean that California will export that much less to the lucrative New York market.

In the final analysis, the proximity of the region to the huge greater New York Metropolitan population offers an incredible opportunity for eastern Long Island to become the premier wine producing region east of the Rockies. The New York Metropolitan area, the center of a $10 billion American and import market, and the epicenter of the American ecumene, is not a focal area for New York State wines (or for other eastern American and French-American-based wines), but Vinifera-based wines. Due to the presence of a large affluent market, and a diverse ethnic population (it is the nation's single largest market for French, Israeli, Spanish, Hungarian, Greek, German, Italian, Romanian, and Yugoslav wines), New York is the nation's single largest metropolitan area for the consumption of imported wines. While these libations range from the most prestigious single vineyard Burgundian luxuries to Retzina, the proximity and ability of the eastern tip of Long Island to offer quality Vinifera-based wines to this market cannot but help propel this region to the forefront of quality wine production in the coming decades. Interestingly, Manhattan, adjacent to Long Island contains one winery: **Schapiro's Wine Company** (Manhattan, 1899), a 100,000 case, Labrusca-based table, sparkling, fruit, berry, and mead winery.

There are two *ava's* on Long Island: *North Fork of Long Island*, and the *The Hamptons, Long Island*. The latter is a 213 square mile region of 136,448 acres (with fewer than 200 vine acres) that measures 54 by 2 miles. Encompassing the South Fork of eastern Long Island, it is bounded by the Atlantic Ocean to the south and east, and Peconic Bay on the north. This region differs markedly from the northern portion in that it is flatter, contains more silt and dune sand, retains water better, and enjoys higher winter and lower summer temperatures than the North Fork. Because of its proximity to the Atlantic

Ocean, the *ava* also has a shorter growing season (195 days), and 400 fewer degree days (Region I and II), and, as a consequence, the grapes have a higher acidity and lower pH, producing wines with a slightly higher flavor intensity and scent, particularly for Chardonnay, Gewurztraminer, and Sauvignon Blanc. Although the cooler and windier weather often precludes the successful ripening of Cabernet Sauvignon, Merlot is frequently the most distinguished red grape, and the one with a bright future. While fog is practically absent on the North Fork, it is common in the South Fork, a condition that promises excellent botrytized grapes.

The *North Fork of Long Island ava*, a 159 square mile region of 101,440 acres, is bounded by Long Island Sound to the north and the Great Peconic Bay in the south. The *ava*, less than 5 miles wide in most places, begins east of Riverhead and extends eastward for 35 miles. Historically a fishing and truck crop region, it contains the bulk of the island's acreage and all but three of the wineries. This *ava* has a 210-day growing season (it often rises to 230) with at least 2,800 hours of sunshine, 3,000 degree days (same as Napa), mild winters, and summers, although not hot, do receive half of the year's total precipitation. Long Island is the only area in the state that has a climate mild enough and long enough to ripen red and white Vinifera grapes consistently. Although bud break arrives in mid May vs. March in the Napa Valley, most grapes are harvested only two weeks later, a clear indication on how efficient photosynthesis is on Long Island. As a consequence, chaptalization and acidification are both infrequent. Sudden declines in winter temperatures, such as the one that affected the Finger Lakes in December 1982, are a rarity, and sudden temperature spikes are not common, hence, the maintenance of high acid levels. Equally important are the ravages of false springs--a condition that affects the state's three other viticultural districts. The sandy soils tend to magnesium deficiency, and the grapes, unlike those from the Finger Lakes region, have higher pH, two conditions that are easily corrected. However, overcropping is a serious problem, as are canopy management, and a chronic bird problem. The wineries are:

Banfi Vintners (Old Brookville, 1986), is a 70-acre, 7,500-case winery that makes well-flavored and scented, round Chardonnay under the *Old Brookville* label. Minor quantities of sparkling Chardonnay and Pinot Noir are also being produced. The splendid 127-acre estate and 60-room English mansion serve as corporate headquarters for the Banfi Corporation.

Bedell Cellars Winery (Cutchogue, 1985), is a 26-acre, 4,000-case, underrated winery that makes excellent to outstanding, full-flavored, crisp, often complex Chardonnay (the reserve is superb), Riesling, Gewurztraminer (a Gewurztraminer blend is called *Cygnet*), and supple, complex, mouth-filling Merlot and Cabernet Sauvignon, all offering excellent value. The Merlot reserve is outstanding.

Bidwell Winery (Cutchogue, 1986), is an outstanding 36-acre, 18,000-case winery that makes well-structured, full-bodied Chardonnay, Riesling, Sauvignon Blanc, Pinot Blanc, Merlot, and Cabernet Sauvignon. Consistent to a fault, this young winery has become one of the premier producers on the Island whose wines should not be overlooked.

Gristina Vineyards (Cutchogue, 1988), is a 30-acre, 4,500-case, quality-oriented winery specializing in Chardonnay, Cabernet Sauvignon, and Merlot (with Cabernet Franc blended).

1982

Hargrave Vineyard
North Fork
Long Island   New York
Cabernet Sauvignon

Grown, Produced & Bottled By Hargrave Vineyard
Cutchogue, N.Y. 11.7% Alcohol By Volume

Hargrave Vineyard (Cutchogue, 1973), the first in eastern Long Island, is a substantial 50-acre, 10,000-case winery that makes above-average and stylish Pinot Blanc, Chardonnay, Sauvignon Blanc, Pinot Noir, Cabernet Sauvignon, Merlot, and proprietary wines. The wines are made in a Burgundian style (barrel-aged and dry), but are quite variable; however, when good the wines are often second to none. The winery leases an additional 60 acres.

Lenz Winery (Peconic, 1983), is an emerging, well-managed, stylish, 52-acre, 12,000-case winery that makes Gewurztraminer, Chardonnay, Merlot, Cabernet Sauvignon, and sparkling wines, all of which are above-average in quality, particularly the reserve wines. The property has recently been sold, acquired the talents of a superb winemaker, and a significant elevation in wine quality is envisioned in the coming years.

Mattituck Hills Winery (Mattituck, 1987), is a 40-acre, 4,000-case winery that makes above-average Chardonnay, Riesling, Cabernet Sauvignon, Merlot, and Pinot Noir.

North House Vineyards, Inc. (Jamesport, 1985), formerly North Fork Winery and Jamesport Vineyards, is a 40-acre, 5,000-case winery that makes Chardonnay, Sauvignon Blanc, Gamay, Merlot, Cabernet Sauvignon, and sparkling wine under the *Jamesport Vineyards* and *North Fork Winery* labels.

Palmer Vineyards (Aquebogue, 1983), is an immaculate, well-organized, 55-acre, 10,000-case winery that makes rich, opulent Riesling, Chardonnay, Gewurztraminer, Merlot, Cabernet Sauvignon, Cabernet Franc, and Pinot Noir, all of which are well-made and supple, offering good value. Chardonnay is outstanding, but all other white wines often lack varietal character; red wines are consistently good, well-colored and flavored, fruity, smooth, and intensely scented.

Paumanok Vineyards (Aquebogue, 1989), is an expanding, 77-acre, 5,000-case winery that historically sold grapes to neighboring wineries, but as of 1989 has begun to make Chardonnay (outstanding), Sauvignon Blanc, and Merlot (blended with Cabernet Franc and Cabernet

Sauvignon). The winery is named after the Indian word for Long Island.

Palmer Vineyards, known for soft, yet well-structured white and red wines.
Baxevanis

Peconic Bay Vineyards (Cutchogue, 1984), is a 25-acre, 5,000-case winery that makes Chardonnay, Riesling, Cabernet Sauvignon, Merlot, and a late harvest Riesling labeled "Vin de l'Ile."

Pindar Vineyards (Peconic, 1979), with 265 acres (Chardonnay, Riesling, Gewurztraminer, Cabernet Sauvignon, Pinot Noir, Merlot, and Cabernet Franc are the most important), and a total output of 45,000 cases, this is the largest winery and vineyard on eastern Long Island. Named after the ancient Greek poet, this aggressive, highly successful and innovative winery conducts a lively tourist trade out of a 200 year-old potato barn. The reserve Chardonnay, Merlot, and Cabernet Sauvignon are considered the finest. Proprietary wines are above-average, offering good value. While sparkling wine is variable, the "Cuvee Rare" (100% Pinot Meunier) is excellent. A Meritage-type wine (Cabernet Sauvignon, Merlot, Cabernet Franc, and Petit Verdot), called "Mythology," has been introduced and has set a new, super premium standard for the island's wine industry. Also made is a good, robust Porto-type libation. Although expensive, it ranks among the finest available from Washington and California, and is a must for the serious collector.

Pugliese Vineyards (Cutchogue, 1987), is a 21-acre, 2,000-case, estate winery that makes Chardonnay, Merlot, Cabernet Sauvignon, and sparkling wines.

Sauvage Vineyards (Water Mill, 1986), one of the largest and most impressive wineries in eastern Long Island, is a 160-acre, 30,000-case, ultra-modern facility that makes three types of wines under the Le Reve label: Long Island Series (Chardonnay, Riesling, Pinot Noir, Cabernet Sauvignon); American Series (from grapes and must from other states: Chardonnay, Sauvignon Blanc, Pinot Noir, and Merlot); and sparkling wines. First bottlings have been quite variable, but improving. Chardonnay is full-bodied along classic lines, and the Riesling is fruity and well-flavored. The winery has suffered serious financial problems, and production is expected to decrease.

Soundview Vineyards (Peconic, 1987), is a 20-acre vineyard whose 9,000 cases of wine are made at a neighboring winery. What is most unusual about this property is that it makes only fresh, crisp, eminently quaffable, dry, semi-dry, and blush Seyval.

The Bridgehampton Winery (Bridgehampton, 1982), is a 27-acre, 10,000-case, trendy South Fork winery that makes superb, full-flavored and complex Sauvignon Blanc, Chardonnay, and late harvest Riesling, Gewurztraminer, Merlot, and Cabernet Sauvignon. The wines, consistently good to a fault, offer excellent value and should not be missed. Other label: *Hampton Cellars*.

The Bridgehampton Winery, located on sandy soils, known for excellent Sauvignon Blanc. Baxevanis

MIDDLE ATLANTIC STATES

This region, extending from Pennsylvania to the Great Valley and coastal Virginia, is a buffer area between a much colder glaciated physical environment to the north, and the subtropical maritime climate of the humid southeasterly-Gulf Coast region to the south. Proceeding as a narrow belt in the north and widening in the south, it includes four specific physiographic regions: (a) a fragmented sandy coast of estuaries and bays with a width of as much as 100 miles; (b) an intermediate hilly region that is rather narrow in the north, widening further south in Virginia; (c) the Ridge and Valley portion of the Appalachians, (d) and the Allegheny Plateau in the westernmost portion of the area. Although comparatively small in area, there are considerable physical distinctions between coastal cities, and interior valleys and highlands. Modern agriculture is limited to hardy fruit, vegetables, and dairy products.

This rapidly expanding viticultural region, offering incredible grape growing and winemaking potential, includes five states (New Jersey, Pennsylvania, Maryland, Delaware, and Virginia), has 12,000 acres of planted vines, and produces more than 1 million gallons of wine. Approximately three-quarters of the planted acreage is located in the Lake Erie Concord belt of northwest Pennsylvania, an area not historically known for quality wine production. These states are the central and southern focus of the largest megalopolis in the nation--collectively possessing an affluent, urbane, knowledgeable, and sophisticated wine-drinking population. Not only does it contain the nation's capital, the site of the largest per capita wine consumption, but each state in the region exhibits above average wine consumption patterns.

From Morris, Pennsylvania to the historic Charlottesville region of north central Virginia, scores of new wineries have mushroomed since the early 1970s to begin a new chapter in eastern winemaking. Beginning with a clean slate, an infusion of capital, Vinifera and French-American vines, and infectious enthusiasm by a small cadre of dedicated winemakers, these mid-Atlantic states are producing above-average to excellent quality wines. As a consequence, this region has recently emerged as a serious wine producing region, particularly from well-capitalized wineries in Virginia and Maryland.

Nearly all wineries are creatures of farm winery legislation and, by California standards, small in size. Wines that have captivated recent attention have been Chardonnay, Gewurztraminer, Riesling, Sauvignon Blanc, Cabernet Sauvignon, Merlot, and Cabernet Franc among Vinifera, and Seyval, Vidal Blanc, Vignoles, and Chambourcin among French-American varieties, the latter exhibiting a dramatic improvement in recent years. Three-quarters of vine acreage is devoted to American varieties, principally Concord, Catawba, and Niagara, all of which are declining in both acreage and winemaking importance. Agriculture throughout this region is diversified with no single type accounting for more than 40 percent of production. However, fruit and other related horticultural crops, previously just 2.3 percent of the regional agricultural economy, have recently increased their share to 7.8 percent of the agricultural product.

Fig. 5.13 indicates an interesting pattern of winery location. The majority are located in the protected pockets of hilly areas in the Ridge and Valley, and Allegheny Plateau. Although many wineries and vineyards were initially located in inappropriate areas, the tendency today is to select far more ideal soil and microclimatic regions. Because of the prevalence of greater local reliefs and running water in the Ridge and Valley physiographic province, most wineries and vineyards are located in this area and not in the Plateau region. While rocks vary from pre-Cambrian gneisses, schists, slates, and quartzites, the preferred vineyard locations are limestone, and well-drained glacial deposits. The second largest area of winery concentration is along the coastal plain and in the immediate foothills of the Appalachians. This includes all the wineries of New Jersey and Maryland, and nearly 20 percent of those in Virginia. Here the preferred sites are south facing, well-drained locations, and sandy areas that have good air drainage. The Lake Erie region, the most important in terms of grape acreage, is a minor area in the production of wine. Its circumscribed wine output notwithstanding, this region contains one of the most favorable microclimates and soils for grape growing and wine making despite recent regional declines. The remarkable viticultural possibilities, especially in the production of quality sparkling wines, are destined to resurrect the viticultural fortunes of this area in the coming decades.

For the region as a whole, mean temperature varies from a low of 50F in the north to 59F in the south. Along the coast, where the ocean moderates temperature extremes, the frost-free period varies from 230 days in coastal Virginia to 200 days in southeastern New Jersey. Inland, the frost-free period ranges from 135 to 175 days. Annual precipitation over the entire region varies from 32 to 50 inches with the heaviest amounts falling along the coast and the higher interior elevations. While a good deal of the southern portion is located in Region II and III, highly variable winter temperatures make Vinifera growing a precarious activity. Most important, wildly fluctuating winter temperatures, excessive summer precipitation, high growing temperatures and humidity are major problems that have not been completely overcome.

Figure 5.13

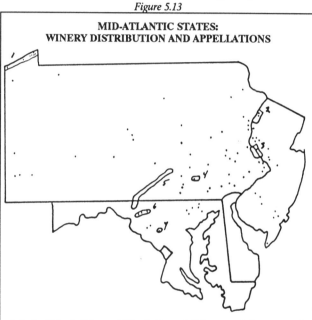

**MID-ATLANTIC STATES:
WINERY DISTRIBUTION AND APPELLATIONS**

1. Lake Erie; 2. Warren Hills; 3. Central Delaware; 4. Lancaster; 5. Cumberland Valley; 6. Catoctin; 7. Linganore. With few exceptions, nearly all wineries are associated with urban centers, tourist sites, and college towns.

Given the above climatic patterns and the inertia of past and current history, grape acreage is dominated by American varieties (mainly in the Lake Erie region of Pennsylvania), principally by two red varieties-Concord and Catawba, and three white grapes--Naigara, Delaware, and Noah. As in most areas of the east, the most popular French-American varieties are white, mainly Aurore, Seyval, Vidal Blanc, Rayon d'Or, Villard Blanc, and Vignoles. Red varieties are mostly Chambourcin, DeChaunac, Chancellor, Baco, Chelois, Marechal Foch, Landot, and Leon Millot. The dominant white Vinifera varietal, by a wide margin, is Chardonnay, followed by Riesling, Sauvignon Blanc, Gewurztraminer, with Rkatsiteli a dis-

tant fifth. The most popular red varieties are Cabernet Sauvignon, Merlot, Cabernet Franc, and Pinot Noir.

New Jersey

New Jersey is a small state with eight million residents that lies almost entirely along the coastal Atlantic plain. As the most urbanized state in the nation, it is the fulcrum of the northeast megalopolis and a major wine market. Although New Jersey, first settled by the Dutch in 1660, was the first state to produce the celluloid, flexible photographic film, phonograph, submarine, synthetic vitamin B-1, motion picture, log cabin, condensed soup, cultivated blueberries, saltwater taffy, transistors, the first brewery (Hoboken), and Thomas Welch's "invention" of unfermented wine in Vineland, New Jersey, it has never ranked as a primary grape and wine producer despite its high per capita income and significant wine consumption. New Jersey ranks sixth among states in wine entering distribution channels (more than 23 million cases), and per capita (3.1 gallons) consumption. The wine industry contributes $1.3 billion to the state's economy, and employs more than 21,000 people. In spite of its high population density and its reputation as a "bedroom state" for Philadelphia and New York City, New Jersey ranks among the top five states in fruit, vegetable, and purebred horses, but with 115,000 wine gallons annually, twentieth in wine production.

One of the first commercial vineyards in the nation was established by Edward Antill at Raritan Landing in 1764, and three years later a New Jersey wine received a medal from the London Royal Society of Arts. One of the most notable post-colonial achievements was the work of Paul Prevost, a fugitive from the French Revolution who experimented with both Vinifera and American vines. The Delaware grape, developed by him, was named by settlers who moved from the Delaware River region in New Jersey-Pennsylvania to Delaware, Ohio. Backyard and minor farm plantings of both Vinifera and native grapes occurred throughout this early period, but the industry remained relatively dormant until one Louis Nicholas Renault opened New Jersey's first commercial winery at Egg Harbor in 1864. Representing a Champagne house, native grapes were planted, and by 1870 it was the largest sparkling winery in America with Egg Harbor acquiring the name "wine city." Nevertheless, the industry failed to stimulate additional major plantings and was virtually eliminated during Prohibition. It did resurface again as a processor of California-based grapes with its wines serving the east coast, particularly the New York and Philadelphia metropolitan areas. Vinegrowing received a noticeable boost in the late 1860s due to the pioneering efforts of Thomas Welch, but black rot in the 1880s and an inadequate supply of grapes forced the thriving juice company to move to Westfield, New York in 1897. While vine acreage declined throughout the first half of this century, the state by 1940 had 28 wineries, and ranked fourth nationally in the production of finished wine.

Although the large, bulk producers of tank-car California wine have long disappeared, the state now boasts 650 acres of vines and nineteen wineries. Nearly all are farm wineries established since the passage of the Farm Winery Act of 1981, a bill that enlarged the scale of such establishments from 5,000 to 50,000 gallons annually. Prior to that time the state was burdened by an antiquated law that limited licenses to seven, one for each million residents. A subsequent amendment in 1984 provided for the creation of the New Jersey Wine Industry Advisory Council to advise the Department of Agriculture on the development of this expanding agricultural industry. As a consequence, the number of wineries more than doubled from seven in 1980 to eighteen in 1992, with more in prospect. Acreage has increased from 120 to 650, of which 450 are planted in French-American varieties, 100 in Vinifera, and the remainder in American. The wines, particularly those from Hunterdon County, are mostly white, soft, well-scented and flavored, and sell well throughout the state.

Despite limitations posed by high real estate prices and taxes (New Jersey ranks first in the nation in average value of farmland and buildings per acre), the possibility for further growth is quite bright in this small, affluent, and heavily urbanized state (less than .5 percent of the population is engaged in agriculture), which not only has the nation's highest population density, but produces less than 1 percent of the wine it consumes. With increased capitalization, areas with considerable potential are the southern sandy soil regions (historically devoted to truck farming, hence the name "garden state"), and Hunterdon County, the latter, a rural region of protected, rolling, well-ventilated hills, the center of the largest vineyard concentration in the state. This county, with 400 acres and eight vineyards, has seven wineries, all established after 1981.

New Jersey has two *ava's*-- *Warren Hills (1988)*, and *Central Delaware Valley (1984)*. The *Central Delaware Valley*, the oldest *ava* (shared with Pennsylvania), covers a 150 square mile region on both sides of the Delaware River from Phillipsburg to Washington's Crossing just north of Trenton. With 200 acres, there are nine commercial vineyards, and three wineries with one more in the planning stage. A hilly terrain, excellent air drainage, and proximity to the Delaware region are the main geographic elements distinguishing the region from the surrounding countryside. Although American, French-American, and Vinifera varieties are currently planted, the latter accounts for at least 23 percent of plantings, of which Ries-

ling and Chardonnay are the finest. Similar in size to the Central Delaware Valley *ava*, the only *ava* that is entirely located in New Jersey, the *Warren Hills Viticultural Area*, is a 226-square mile section of Warren County. This region, bounded by the Delaware and Musconetcong Rivers, and the smaller Paulins Kill, consists of long, narrow parallel valleys running northeast to southwest containing predominantly limestone soils. The region includes three wineries, and about 80 acres of vineland. The largest area in the state in terms of vine acreage and number of wineries--Hunterdon County, is scheduled to be the next *ava*.

The wineries are:

A. Cataldi Winery (Penns Grove, 1987), is a 5,000-case winery that makes unusual Sauvignon Blanc, Chardonnay, Muscat Blanc, and proprietary wines from California concentrate, offering good value.

Alba Vineyard (Milford, 1983), with 35 acres and an output of 7,500 cases, is the largest and one of the better wineries in the state. It makes a large number of French-American and Vinifera wines, of which Seyval, Riesling, Chardonnay, Cabernet Sauvignon, Cayuga, Gewurztraminer, and Primavera (a blend of Riesling, Vidal, and Cayuga) are the finest.

Amalthea Cellars (Atco, 1982), a 12-acre, 4,200-case winery, is one of the better producers in the state best known for a large assortment of unusual, well-made wines: Rkatsiteli, Pinot Blanc, Gewurztraminer, Chardonnay, Aligote, Pinot Noir, Pinot Gris, Cabernet Sauvignon, Chancellor, and several other French-American wines. The Cabernet Sauvignon is particularly good.

Amwell Valley Vineyard (Ringoes, 1982), is a 9-acre, 1,000-case winery that makes a small assortment of American and French-American wines, of which Landot Noir is unusual and spicy on the palate.

Balic Winery (Mays Landing, 1974), one of the oldest in the state, is a 30-acre, 8,000-case winery that makes a wide assortment of inexpensive American, Labrusca, and French-American table and sparkling wines, nearly all sold under proprietary labels. This is one of the few wineries in the mid-Atlantic region that makes wine from such grapes as Ives and Noah.

Cape Winery (Cape May Courthouse, 1989), is a 6-acre, 1,500-case winery that makes Seyval, Diamond, Villard, Chancellor, Chardonnay, and Cabernet Sauvignon.

Cream Ridge Vineyards & Champagne Cellars (Cream Ridge, 1987), is a 6-acre, 1,000-case, Labrusca, French-American, Vinifera, fruit and berry winery.

DelVista Vineyards (Frenchtown, 1982), the first winery to be licensed under the state's farm winery law, is an 11-acre, 2,000-case property located on the site where the Delaware vine was developed by Paul Prevost in the early 1880s. The winery and vineyard, located on well drained red shaley loam on a minor plateau overlooking the Delaware, is planted mainly in French-American and Vinifera grapes. The vineyard maintains the most diverse plantings in the state, and the expertly made wines offer excellent value. Major wines include Aurore, Chardonnay, Riesling, Seyval, Villard Blanc, Delaware, Cabernet Sauvignon, Chelois, and DeChaunac. The rose and Riesling are particularly good. Other label: *Deerhaven Cellars* for a line of sweet wines.

Four Sisters Winery at Matarazzo Farms (Belvedere, 1984), is a 390-acre, fruit and vegetable farm with 17 acres planted in American and French-American vines. The winery makes nearly two dozen different wines (Niagara, Leon Millot, Chancellor, Seyval, Vidal Blanc, Villard, Chardonnay, and Riesling), proprietary, and fruit and berry wines, primarily from purchased fruit. Total output is 6,000 cases.

King Ridge Wine Cellars (Frenchtown, 1990), is a 15-acre, 1,000-case winery that makes Seyval, Vidal Blanc, Chancellor, Chambourcin, Leon Millot, and Baco Noir wines.

King's Road Vineyard & Winery (Asbury, 1980), is an immaculate, 25-acre, 5,000-case winery planted in French-American and Vinifera grapes, of which Chardonnay, Riesling, Pinot Noir, Seyval, Aurore, Sauvignon Blanc, and Villard Blanc are the most important. The name dates back to pre-Revolutionary times when the property was part of a

King's grant. While all the wines are carefully made, the Chardonnay and Riesling are impeccable.

La Follette Vineyard and Winery (Belle Mead, 1985), is a 15-acre, 2,000-case winery that specializes only in dry, crisp, well-flavored Seyval, one of the finest in the northeast.

Poor Richard's Winery (Frenchtown, 1990), is a 15-acre, 1,000-case winery that makes Seyval, Vidal Blanc, Chancellor, Chambourcin, and proprietary wines.

Pride of New Jersey Vineyards (Bordentown, 1938), formerly the Jacob Lee Winery and Buck Country Vineyards and Winery, is a 7-acre, 18,000-case winery that makes a large assortment of American, French-American and Vinifera (Chardonnay, Cabernet Sauvignon), and fruit and berry wines.

Renault Winery (Egg Harbor, 1864), the oldest winery in the state and oldest winery with its own vineyard in continuous operation in the nation, is part of a large 1,400-acre estate on which 144 acres are planted in American, French-American, and Vinifera vines producing more than 26,000 cases. Founded by a French Champagne maker from Reims, the winery became the largest producer of sparkling wine (from Concord grapes) in the nation. The winery remained open during Prohibition under a special Federal permit, and for a short time produced one of the most popular wine "tonics" in the country. Since 1919, it has been owned by the Milza family (except for one short period during the 1970s), and has been recently renovated and enlarged to accommodate more than 130,000 visitors annually. The winery makes a bewildering number of wines, all of which have been recently improved, aggressively marketed, and often offer good value. Sparkling Blueberry, Chablis, May wine, Spumante, and other sparkling wines are better than one suspects.

Sylvin Farms (Germania, 1985), is an unusual, 6-acre, all Vinifera, 1,000-case winery located on a knoll on the eastern shore of the Pine Barrens of Atlantic County. Planted are: Pinot Noir, Chardonnay, Sauvignon Blanc, Gewurztraminer, Pinot Gris, Pinot Blanc, Muscat Ottonel, Rkatsiteli, Cabernet Sauvignon, Merlot, and Gamay Beaujolais, all of which are above-average in quality, offering excellent value. Merlot, Cabernet Sauvignon, and Pinot Noir are particularly good.

Tamuzza Vineyards (Hope, 1985), is a 40-acre, 4,000-case, French-American winery specializing in Marechal Foch, Aurore, Seyval, Leon Millot, Pinot Noir, Vidal Blanc, Vignoles, Cayuga, Chambourcin, Chancellor, DeChaunac, Cabernet Sauvignon, Riesling, Chardonnay, a sweet sparkling, and proprietary wines.

Tewksbury Wine Cellars (Lebanon, 1979), is a 22-acre, 7,000-case winery that makes French-American and Vinifera wines of which Chambourcin, Riesling, and Gewurztraminer are the finest, particularly the latter, one of the best east of the Rockies.

Tomasello Winery (Hammonton, 1933), is a 100-acre, 40,000-case, third generation winery that historically made a large number of American-based wines, but has recently switched to French-American and Vinifera grapes.

Pennsylvania

Pennsylvania, the "Keystone" state, with a population of 12 million, not only lies in the center of the original Atlantic colonies, but because it has so much in common with the rest of the nation, it has been called "a miniature United States." The largest in size and population among the mid-Atlantic states, Pennsylvania stretches from Lake Erie to Delaware Bay, enveloping the bulk of the Allegheny Plateau and the Ridge and Valley physiographical provinces. More than 80 percent of the state is composed of old mountain chains with a humid climate supporting dense vegetation (half of the state's total land is forested, most of it broadleaf deciduous). There are four sharp and distinct seasons, and few broad river valleys.

Among the many "firsts" for the state are: the first oil well, savings bank, insurance company, locomotive, banana split, library (founded by Benjamin Franklin in 1731), and the first paper mill. The state also has an interesting early history: Swedish settlers in 1643 found a colony on Tinicum Island, the Dutch in 1655 attack and conquer this colony; the English in 1664 seize control from the Dutch; and Charles II grants the area of southeastern Pennsylvania to William Penn, who establishes a colony in Philadelphia in 1681.

For the past 100 years three economic poles governed the economic fortunes of the state: anthracite coal in the northeast, diversified manufacturing and financial institutions in Philadelphia in the southeast, and steel and chemicals in Pittsburgh in the southwest. Today the state's economy is rapidly changing from coal and heavy industry to services, pharmaceuticals, and electronic components. Agriculturally, Pennsylvania is primarily a dairy producing state whose modern winemaking industry began to grow rapidly with the passage of a liberal Farm Winery Act in 1967 (the first in the nation). The state ranks first in the nation in mushroom production, third in corn for silage, fourth in peaches, cherries, and fresh sweet corn, and fifth in grapes. Like many other states in the northeast, agriculture is in retreat. While the size of the average farm since 1960 has increased from 116 acres to 151 in 1988, the number of farms has declined from 106,000 to 55,000, and agricultural land dropped from 12.3 million acres to 8.3 million acres.

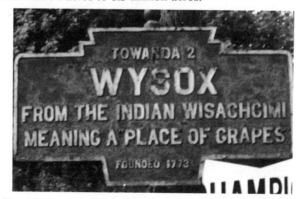

Throughout eastern America historical references to grapes are common. Courtesy of Joseph Castelli.

While agricultural activities are in decline, wine making traditions stretch back to the mid-1600s when Queen Christina of Sweden directed the Governor of New Sweden, John Prinz, to encourage wine production through the importation of Vinifera vines in what is now the southeastern portion of the state extending southward into Delaware. While the effort never fully materialized, it was William Penn who first planted Vinifera vines in 1684 in what is now Fairmount Park in Philadelphia, all of which failed. Despite these early failures, Pennsylvania is given credit as the site of America's first commercial vineyard--the Pennsylvania Vine Company established in 1793 along the Schuylkill River at Spring Mill by Pierre

Legaux (considered the first commercial American wine-grower). Although many Vinifera grapes were planted, after many years of experimentation only the interspecific Alexander grape survived, and the vineyard and winery were abandoned in the late 1820s. The Alexander grape was eventually replaced by Catawba and Isabella, but despite these valiant efforts to grow grapes and produce wine along the Schuykill River in the first three decades of the nineteenth century, the industry slowly withered on the vine. Other notable vineyards were planted in southern Pennsylvania after 1790: Colonel George Morgan started a vineyard in 1793 in the southwestern portion of the state; and in York County in 1818 one Thomas Eichelberger planted the Alexander grape. A large Vinifera vineyard was established in 1803 by Rappists in Harmony, just north of Pittsburgh, and later a Labrusca vineyard near the Ohio River in Allegheny County.

Figure 5.14

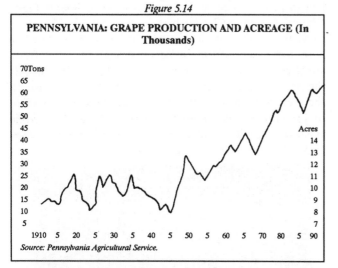

PENNSYLVANIA: GRAPE PRODUCTION AND ACREAGE (In Thousands)

Source: Pennsylvania Agricultural Service.

Lake Erie, the only major area in the state to continue growing grapes without interruption, was first planted in the middle of the nineteenth century soon after the completion of the Erie Canal. Long known for the first stern-wheel steamboat, the home port of the U.S. Brig *Niagara*, the oldest operating forge in the world, and home to the Drake Oil Well Museum, the Lake Erie viticultural region is sandwiched between the New York and Ohio portion of the south shore. The fortunes of this vineyard parallels that of the other neighboring states in terms of its grape composition and its close association with the Welch Grape Juice Company. While winemaking did not begin as early as in neighboring New York and Ohio, the region's first winery was established in North East by one William Griffith in 1863 (South Shore Wine Cellar). While the number of wineries and vineyards grew, with the formation of the national Prohibition Party in 1869, and by the first chapter of the Women's Christian Temperance Union four years later, the enological fortunes of Erie County did not prosper. The character of

the industry after 1880 soon changed to the cultivation of the Concord grape for the production of juice and processing.

One of the most prominent achievements in the viticultural history of Pennsylvania was the development of the Alexander grape (so named after Governor John Penn's gardener) in the 1730s. A hardy and comparatively high yielder, the grape quickly spread (falsely as a Vinifera grape by the Pennsylvania Wine Company) to other colonies and as far west as the Ohio Valley. By the middle of the nineteenth century, the toll from a series of bad winters, virus, fungus, and *phylloxera* reduced the industry to comparative obscurity. However, as the popularity of the Concord expanded, new vine acreage began to increase, so that by 1880 all but ten of the state's 67 counties made wine, and total acreage stood at 2,000. While the center for wine production was the Lake Erie district, wine output ceased to exist with the advent of Prohibition, a condition that continued for an additional 29 years (unlike most other grape growing states) because the state liquor monopoly discouraged wine production. Selling through the state monopoly system, Conestoga Winery in 1963 was the first to open since Prohibition, closely followed by Presque Isle Wine Cellars and Penn Shore Vineyards in 1969. Since then, and largely attributed to the passage of the Farm Winery Act that allowed up to four retail outlets and Sunday sales, wineries have continued to grow: from 2 in 1969 to 47 in 1991. Because there were no wineries prior to 1963, the present picture represents explosive growth second only to Virginia in the northeastern portion of the nation. It is important to note that as this precipitous growth began in 1969, winemaking shifted closer to market concentration from the Lake Erie region to southeastern Pennsylvania, and resulted in small but steady shifts in grape acreage from Lake Erie to other portions of the state. While the southeastern portion of the state is not climatically superior to the Erie region, it does contain more than 50 percent of the state's population and 68 percent of wine consumers. Another 26 percent of consumption takes place in metropolitan Pittsburgh, where consumption levels appear to be 25 percent greater than for the state as a whole. However, vine acreage (but not the total output for the 1977-1985 period) declined by 5,000, and the number of growers by more than 40 percent. Viticultural activities are formidable as the state ranks fifth in the nation in terms of grape production, and contributes $1.3 billion to the state's economy, employes 21,000 people, contributes $319 million in wages, and $121 million in taxes.

Unlike any other mid-Atlantic state, Pennsylvania lies almost entirely within the Piedmont, Ridge and Valley, and the Appalachian Plateau physiographic regions, and, as a consequence, climatic patterns are not only diverse, but highly variable. While it is safe to say that the coldest areas of the state are the northern interior regions, viticulturally favorable climatic patterns are mitigated by the presence of abundant microclimates in the Cumberland Plateau and within the folds of the Ridge and Valley sections. The latter region, for example, is oriented in bands stretching from southwest to northeast across the central portion of the state in a series of successive ridges. These ridges act as a natural barrier to help deplete severe storms originating in the Great Lakes region. As a result, southeastern Pennsylvania has less severe storm activity, less hail, and a slightly drier, less humid climate than the Lake Erie region.

Figure 5.15

PENNSYLVANIA: CLIMATIC PATTERNS

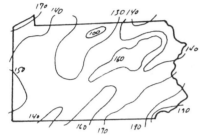

Length of Growing Season

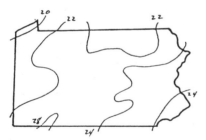

Average Growing Season Precipitation

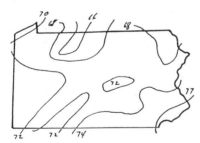

Average July Temperature

Despite the fact that southeastern Pennsylvania has the longest growing season and a milder winter than the Lake Erie region, many maintain that the higher growing season rainfall regime with associated excessive humidity levels precludes the successful cultivation of Vinifera. This notion is discredited because Maryland and northern Virginia are able to grow Vinifera.

Source: U.S. Weather Bureau.

Interestingly, despite the presence of a longer growing season in southeastern Pennsylvania, the bulk of commercial vineland is located along a narrow ribbon between Ohio and New York. Similarly, while Lancaster County consistently registers more days of temperature below 0F, or less than Adams County on the Maryland border, it is an area with increased plantings in recent years. The best soils are sited on the well-drained, limestone-based, narrow Lake Erie plain, the much richer limestone areas of the Ridge and Valley region, and the mica-rich areas of York County. Soil selection, unfortunately, has often been given a secondary position. As a consequence, a good many vineyards had been sited on poorly drained land encouraging Crown Gall, a deadly disease found throughout the state. The only major climatic disadvantage of the southeastern portion of the state in comparison to the Erie region is the unpredictability of rainfall during the growing season--when too much it interferes with the harvest (in late September and early October), or when insufficient it creates drought conditions.

Unlike other mid-Atlantic states, American and Labrusca varieties account for approximately 82 percent of the acreage, French-American varieties 12 percent, the remaining being planted in Vinifera. Although Concord remains the leading grape variety, Catawba is a distant second, while Niagara and Delaware are losing their rank to Seyval and Vidal Blanc as the third and fourth most widely planted varieties. As in many other eastern states, American and Labrusca varieties are slowly giving way to French-American and Vinifera varieties for winemaking. Very revealing is the list of the most popular varietal wines produced in the Commonwealth: Vidal Blanc leads with 80 percent of all wineries making it, followed by Seyval (77%), Riesling (53%), Chambourcin and Chardonnay (both 50%), Concord and Apple (40%), Cayuga (37%), DeChaunac (30%), Cabernet Sauvignon and Catawba (27%), and Vignoles and Delaware (20%). The following are made by fewer than 18 wineries: Strawberry, Chancellor, Marechal Foch, Aurore, Steuben, Cherry, Pinot Noir, Diamond, Raspberry, Pinot Gris, Peach, Baco Noir, Gewurztraminer, Cabernet Franc, Chelois, Landot Noir, Sauvignon Blanc, Rougeon, Rosette, Chardonel, Florental, Fredonia, Blackberry, Blueberry, Cascade, Rayon D'Or, Villard Noir, Petite Syrah, Carmine, Aligote, Dutchess, Gladwin, Isabella, and Alden.

It is also important to note that only 10 percent of the state's grape crop is used for winemaking purposes, a minor improvement over 1969 when only 6 percent of the state's grapes were used for winemaking. Nevertheless, grapes and grape products, that contribute more than $15 million to the state economy, are second in importance to apples as a fruit crop. While the tonnage of grapes harvested over the past 20 years has averaged 50,000 tons, it is important to note that while production has increased rather significantly since 1955, the tonnage used for the making of wine has declined steadily in the 1980s.

At a time when wineries were mushrooming throughout the state, grape acreage during the period 1978-1990 declined from 14,000 acres to 9,000 acres. Grape production rose from 49,000 tons in 1969 to nearly 63,000 tons in 1987, making Pennsylvania the fifth largest wine producing state in the nation. Although not bordering the Atlantic Ocean, Pennsylvania does exhibit a similar spatial distribution pattern in grape growing as its immediate neighbor to the north, New York. The Lake Erie region contains 6 wineries, but 95 percent of the state's acreage, 85 percent of which is used for juice and jelly processing. The center of grape production is North East, located in Erie County. Sandwiched between Ohio and New York, this area is part of the "Concord Grape Belt." For the state as a whole, growers are declining in number rather precipitously--from 474 in 1978 to fewer than 281 in 1989. One encouraging sign is the fact that the average size vineyard has increased from 26 acres to 34 acres during the 1974-1989 period.

Quality Vinifera table wine acreage is highly concentrated in the warmer, northwestern portion of the state in Erie county. In the southeastern portion of the state, York, Berks, Bucks, Lancaster, and Cumberland counties are the main grape growing counties, of which only Bucks County lacks the necessary available space for significant expansion. Adams, Dauphin, Franklin, Lehigh, and Northampton counties, with at least 50,000 acres of potential quality vineland, offer considerable opportunity. Collectively, these counties, along with the rest of the southeastern portion of the state, contain nearly 60 percent of the state's population, and form the largest single wine market. Along with a significant history, this area is also the nucleus of a large and varied tourist industry. It contains the state's largest city and metropolitan area, a significant Colonial history, the home of Pearl S. Buck, and the nation's mushroom capital.

Other counties with viticultural potential include Allegheny, Beaver, and Butler counties in the western portion of the state. Erie County, the most important grape producing county in the state, has enormous possibilities if growers switch from American to French-American and Vinifera varieties. In addition, considerable capital and technical expertise is required to energize an otherwise lackluster industry, very much in the manner as the New York portion of the Lake Erie ava. Although more than two-thirds of the state is forested and sparsely settled and dairy farming declining, with the existence of many suitable sites in the southeastern portion of the state, viticulture is expected to increase in the future. The added advantages of higher grape yields, higher soluble solids, and much lower acid grape levels in southeastern Pennsylvania over the colder interior and Lake Erie region are major considerations in solidifying the future growth of the state's wine industry in that portion of the Commonwealth.

In view of the state's large size and population, it is interesting to note the absence of a single large winery (wineries vary from less than 250 to just under 100,000 gallons, and cultivate a mean acreage of 34). In relationship to other neighboring states, the industry is characterized by under capitalization, with more than half being nothing more than cottage-type operations existing on the margins of economic solvency, and doing little to enhance the winemaking image of the state. For example, of the 47 wineries, 30 produce fewer than 2,500 cases, 6 make more than 8,000 cases, and only one winery, Bucks County, prior to 1991, made more than 100,000 cases. While the economic attrition rate remains high, many more have entered this lucrative profession, and it is estimated that by 1995, 6 more will open their doors.

Unlike a number of small neighboring states, Pennsylvania's wineries exhibit highly effusive features compounded by a lack of state-wide organization and a coherent focus. In this respect, the industry mirrors the highly fragmented, parochial, and regional socioeconomic state patterns. Therefore, its not at all surprising to find 95 percent of all Pennsylvania-made wine sold at the winery, 1 percent out of the state, and only 4 percent through the state monopoly store system. Nevertheless, Pennsylvania has a promising future: a large, affluent population with a rising per capita wine consumption trend, a long growing season without the extremes of the midwest, and a sympathetic state legislature. Late in 1988, the state Liquor Control Board authorized the first of what promises to be a series of "wine only" specialty stores in an effort to stimulate wine sales.

Pennsylvania has four ava's, three of which are shared with neighboring states: Lake Erie, Central Delaware Valley, Cumberland Valley (1985), and Lancaster Valley (1982). Cumberland Valley is an 80-mile long valley that arches from the west bank of the Susquehanna River at Harrisburg to the Potomac River in Washington County, Maryland. The valley is bordered on the southeast by South Mountain (the northernmost extension of the Blue Ridge Mountains), and on the northwest by the Allegheny Mountain complex. It is a 1,200 square mile region located in the rain shadow of both the South and Allegheny Mountains. Being a part of the Great Valley, the soils are primarily derived from limestone. Of the nearly 800,000 acres available only 100 are planted in grapes, supporting three wineries.

The Lancaster Valley ava, located in the Lancaster-Frederick lowland, is a flat limestone depression east of the Susquehanna River, and southeast of Harrisburg. The 12 by 30-mile long valley (roughly 225,000 acres) is the wealthiest agricultural county in the state. The Lancaster depression, 400 feet in elevation, is surrounded by nearly 1,000-foot elevations. It receives 41 inches of rainfall, and with about 3,100 degree days, is a Region III climatic area. The deep, well-drained, water-retaining soils are very fertile and, until recently, were not planted in vines for more than 100 years. The first successful vineyards in Lancaster were planted in 1790 and continued to thrive until the mid-1800s when disease and unusually cold weather eliminated commercial acreage. Modern vine-growing reentered the picture in the 1960s with the establishment of Conestoga Vineyards, and Tucquan Vineyard. Interestingly, it was in this valley that the broad-wheeled Conestoga wagon (the prairie schooner that settled the west) was first built. Today, there are 100 acres of commercially planted grapes, and two wineries.

The York region, known as the "Barrens" in colonial times, is another future *ava*. Protected by the Ridge and Valley section of the Appalachians, the rolling country-side has excellent soils derived from decomposed mica-schist that are friable, and rich in iron and potash. Trending in a southwest to northeast arc, the numerous valleys and low hills receive less precipitation from storm activity coming from the west (southern air masses parallel the hills), and because the upland ridges act as a barrier, there is less humidity, hail, and fungus disease. Although berry maturation is predictable and uniform, the region is located along a line where winter injury is common. In addition to the wineries listed below, three more wineries are expected to open by 1993 in southeastern Pennsylvania.

The wineries are:

Adams County Winery (Orrtanna, 1975), is a 6-acre, 1,000-case winery that makes French-American, Vinifera, and fruit and berry wines, of which Vidal Blanc, Seyval, Siegfried, Chardonnay, and Muscat are the most interesting.

Allegro Vineyards (Brogue, 1980), is a 15-acre, 3,500-case winery located along a protected slope in southern Pennsylvania several miles to the west of the Susquehanna River. It produces several French-American wines, but is best known for superb Cabernet Sauvignon, above-average Chardonnay, Seyval, Vidal Blanc, and berry wines. It also makes "Celeste," a wine made from 25 percent peach and 75 percent Seyval. The vineyard is sited 700 feet above sea level on highly friable, 15 feet-thick, well-drained, red schistous soil. "Cadenza," a proprietary red wine made from Cabernet Sauvignon, Cabernet Franc, and Merlot, is outstanding, one of the finest wines in the northeast.

Brookmere Farm Vineyards (Belleville, 1984), is a 5-acre, 3,000-case winery that makes a large assortment of American, French-American, Vinifera, proprietary, fruit and berry wines, of which Niagara, Riesling, and apple are particularly good. All are well-made and supple on the palate, offering good value.

Buckingham Valley Vineyards (Buckingham, 1972), is an excellent, 20-acre, 12,500-case winery that makes American, French-American, and fruit wines, of which Vidal Blanc, Seyval, Cayuga, and Niagara appear to be the finest, all offering excellent value.

Bucks Country Vineyards and Winery (New Hope, 1973), is a 30,000-case winery affiliated with a sister winery in Bordentown, New Jersey. The wines number more than 15 and are based on American and French-American blends. Fruit and sparkling wines are also made and marketed for the large tourist trade, offering little value.

Calvaresi Winery (Bernville, 1981), is a small, aggressive, 6-acre, 3,500-case, consumer friendly winery that makes American, French-American, Vinifera, fruit and berry wines, of which Cayuga, Seyval, Vidal Blanc, Riesling, Vignoles, Chambourcin, and Steuben are particularly good. Expertly made, all wines represent good value.

Cefalo's Wine Cellars (Pittstown, 1985), is a 1,000-case winery that makes Seyval, Vidal Blanc, DeChaunac, and Baco Noir.

Chaddsford Winery, highly successful and one of the premier wineries in the state. Baxevanis

Chaddsford Winery (Chadds Ford, 1983), the leading winery in the extreme southeastern portion of the state, leases 19 acres of vineland and makes 22,000 cases, all of which are distributed through subscription and three retail outlets in the greater Philadelphia area. Although the emphasis lies on French-American, American-based and proprietary wines, the finest are Chardonnay, Riesling, Cabernet Sauvignon, Cabernet Franc, Pinot Noir, and Steuben. Made by one of the most celebrated Pennsylvanian winemakers, the pricey wines should not be missed. A related firm, The Chaddsford Wine Co., handles non-Pennsylvanian wines.

Cherry Valley Vineyards (Saylorsburg, 1985), is a 14-acre, 4,000-case winery that makes a large selection of American, French-American, and Vinifera (Chardonnay, Vidal Blanc, Cayuga, Niagara, Chancellor, Aurore, Seyval, Marechal Foch, DeChaunac, and Concord), sparkling, proprietary and fruit and berry wines.

Clover Hill Vineyards and Winery (Breinigsville, 1984), is a 25-acre, 6,000-case winery that makes good, sound American, French-American, Vinifera, fruit, and proprietary wines. While Rayon D'Or, Seyval, Riesling, Niagara, DeChaunac, and Chambourcin are consistently good, the surprise is an exquisite and rare Alden, one of the few wineries in the east that makes and vinifies this nearly extinct grape.

Conneaut Cellars Winery (Conneaut Lake, 1982), is a 6,800-case winery that makes a large selection of Vinifera, French-American, and American wines, of which Vidal Blanc, Seyval, Gewurztraminer, Chardonnay, Cabernet Sauvignon, and proprietary wines are considered the finest.

Country Creek Vineyard & Winery (Telford, 1977), is a 10,000-case American, French-American, Vinifera, fruit and berry winery. The most important wines are Vidal Blanc, Concord, Niagara, Marechal Foch, Chelois, and a peach-Nectarine blend.

Fox Meadow Farm (Chester Springs, 1983), is a 4-acre, 1,000-case winery that makes good, sound Seyval, Vidal Blanc, Chancellor, and French-American blended and proprietary wines.

Franklin Hill Vineyards (Bangor, 1982), just south of the Delaware Gap, is a 13-acre, 5,000-case French-American winery, of which Cayuga, and Vignoles are the finest.

Gobbler's Knob Vineyard (Honesdale, 1991), is a 6-acre, 1,000-case winery that makes Aurore, Chardonnay, Marechal Foch, and Chancellor wines.

Heritage Wine Cellars (North East, 1977), is a 10,000-case American, French-American, and fruit winery that makes more than 30 different wines--from generic, spiced, proprietary, to varietal. Most common varietals include: Concord, Niagara, Isabella, Delaware, Dutchess, Vidal

Blanc, Catawba, DeChaunac, and Seyval. The winery also produces the only "Gladwin 113," an unnamed variety developed by the Geneva Experiment Station.

Hillcrest Winery, Ltd. (Greensburg, 1982), is a 7-acre, 800-case winery that makes small quantities of Chambourcin, Chardonnay, Cabernet Sauvignon, Seyval, Vidal Blanc, and Riesling.

Hunters Valley Winery (Liverpool, 1986), is a 2-acre, 900-case winery that makes Vidal Blanc, Seyval, Chardonnay, Delaware, Concord, Niagara, and Chancellor.

In and Out Vineyards (Newtown, 1985), is a 2-acre, 3,000-case winery that makes French-American varietal wines marketed under private labels.

Kolln Vineyards (Bellefonte, 1978), is a 6-acre, 2,000-case vineyard located just north of State College that makes above-average wines from American and French-American grapes. Interestingly, Bellefonte is home to six governors.

Lancaster County Winery (Willow Street, 1979), formerly Pequea Valley Vineyard and Winery, is a 10-acre, 4,000-case French-American, estate-bottled winery, of which Chancellor, Seyval, and Vidal Blanc are the finest. Fruit and proprietary wines are also made.

Lapic Winery (New Brighton, 1977), is a 6-acre, 6,300-case winery that makes a large selection of American, French-American, Vinifera, proprietary, and fruit and berry wines.

Laurel Heights Winery (Landenburg, 1987), is an ambitious, 4-acre, 1,800-case winery that makes above-average Vidal Blanc, Seyval, Baco Noir, Castel, Cabernet Sauvignon, Pinot Noir, Chardonnay, Riesling, Gewurztraminer, and proprietary wines.

Lembo Vineyards and Winery (Lewistown, 1972), is a 7-acre, 6,000-case American and French-American winery.

Mazza Vineyards (North East, 1972), is a 3-acre, 13,500-case American, French-American, Vinifera, and fruit and berry winery that makes a large selection, of which Niagara, Catawba, Concord, Seyval, Cayuga, Gewurztraminer, Vidal Blanc, and Riesling are considered the finest. The recently improved wines offer considerable value and should not be overlooked.

Mount Hope Estate & Winery (Cornwall, 1980), is a 10-acre, 25,000-case winery with an impressive 32-room Victorian mansion surrounded by 87 rolling acres. Although a limited number of Vinifera wines are produced, an overwhelming proportion of output is based on American, French-American (of which Vignoles, Seyval, and Vidal Blanc are the finest), and fruit wines.

Mount Nittany Vineyard & Winery (Centre Hall, 1980), is a typical University town winery that buys and makes wines from purchased grapes, total output being 2,000 cases. In addition to the following proprietary wines--"Tears of the Lion," "Laugh of the Lion," "Heart of the Lion," and "Apple of the Lion's Eye," Seyval, Vidal Blanc, Chancellor, DeChaunac, and Marechal Foch are made as varietals.

Richard Naylor, an accomplished vineyardist and one of the better winemakers in the state. Baxevanis

Naylor Wine Cellars (Stewartstown, 1978), is a 27-acre, 12,000-case winery that makes more than 20 different American, French-American, Vinifera, and fruit and berry wines. Owned by one of the most knowledgeable and practical winemakers in the east, he is convinced of the commercial merits of Seyval, Vidal Blanc, Vignoles, and Chambourcin (his finest wines) for southeast Pennsylvania, and not Vinifera cultivation. The wines from this excellent winery are consistent, offering good value.

Nissley Vineyards (Bainbridge, 1976), is an immaculate, well-organized, 52-acre, 20,000-case winery that makes a large selection of estate-bottled American, French-American, and fruit wines. This conscientious winery, one of the finest in the state, sits on an old limekiln. There are few other wineries with the talent to produce American and French-American wines as good as this one.

Oak Springs Winery (Altoona, 1987), is a 3-acre, 4,000-case American, French-American, and fruit and berry winery best known for Steuben, Vidal Blanc, Chambourcin, and Cayuga.

Oregon Hill Wine Company (Morris, 1983), is a small, conscientious, 2,000-case winery that makes above-average Gewurztraminer, Chardonnay, Gamay Beaujolais, Pinot Noir, Cabernet Sauvignon, Colombard, Riesling, Vidal Blanc, Seyval, American, and fruit wines marketed under the *Wenden Villa Cellars* label. This northernmost winery (and one of the most isolated) in central Pennsylvania buys nearly all the grapes locally.

Peace Valley Winery (Chalfont, 1984), is an expanding, 28-acre, 4,000-case American, French-American, Vinifera, sparkling, fruit, and proprietary winery. Seyval, Vidal Blanc, Niagara, Fredonia, and Spumante from red Muscat are particularly good. Output of Vinifera wines, primarily Chardonnay, Gewurztraminer, Pinot Noir, Merlot, and Riesling, is increasing.

Penn Shore Vineyards (North East, 1969), is a 10,000-case winery that makes a large assortment of American, French-American, sparkling, and proprietary wines, of which Vidal, Vignoles, Seyval, and Chancellor are considered the finest.

Preate Winery (Old Forge, 1985), formerly known as Capri Winery, with 2.5 acres and an annual production of 20,000 cases, is the largest winery in northeastern Pennsylvania. In addition to proprietary wines, it makes Chardonnay, Seyval, and Vidal Blanc. Marechal Foch, aged for two years in wood, and berry wines are interesting.

Presque Isle Wine Cellars (North East, 1969), is a distinctive, 160-acre, 2,000-case winery, wine supply house, and grape and juice purveyor. It grows and makes an interesting assortment of grapes/wines: Riesling, Chardonnay, Aligote, Vignoles, Gewurztraminer, Pinot Gris, Vidal Blanc, Seyval, Cayuga, Cabernet Sauvignon, Cabernet Franc, Petite Syrah, Marechal Foch, Chancellor, Chambourcin, Dutchess, Catawba, Steuben, Carmine, and Delaware.

Ripepi Winery & Vineyards (Monongahela, 1989), is a 10-acre, 2,000-case winery that makes Niagara, Diamond, Cayuga, Chancellor, DeChaunac, Marechal Foch, proprietary, and three unusual varietal apple wines (Jonathan, Golden Delicious, and McIntosh).

Sand Castle Winery (Erwinna, 1987), is a 40-acre, 6,000-case winery that makes dry and sweet Riesling, Chardonnay, Pinot Noir, Cabernet Sauvignon, and proprietary wines. Well situated above the Delaware River, this handsome estate, the largest all-Vinifera winery in the Commonwealth, is currently producing excellent (but expensive) wines, all of which should not be missed. The muscular Riesling and the equally big, well-structured Pinot Noir are often outstanding. This is one of the few wineries in the east that buries the vines to prevent winter injury.

Sara Coyne Winery (Erie, 1986), is a 10-acre, 1,700-case winery that makes above-average Seyval and Vidal Blanc, as well as smaller quantities of Cayuga, Dutchess, and Chambourcin.

Shuster Cellars (Irwin, 1984), is a 3-acre, 13,000-case American and French-American winery that makes varietal Diamond, Concord, Catawba, Vidal Blanc, Seyval, Marechal Foch, Chelois, sparkling, fruit, and proprietary wines, of which Volksvine is the most popular.

Slate Quarry Winery (Nazareth, 1988), is a 13-acre, 1,000-case winery that makes good, sound, blended libations from Vidal Blanc, Seyval, Chardonel, Vignoles, Chardonnay, Sauvignon Blanc, Chambourcin, Florental, and other less common varieties. The serious, innovative wines that should not be overlooked, are made by an engaging college professor.

Susquehanna Valley Winery (Danville, 1987), is a 4-acre, 400-case winery that makes traditional eastern libations: Concord, Baco Noir, Niagara, Catawba, Vidal Blanc, and Aurore.

Sweet Williams Mountain Winery (Wilcox, 1987), is a 1,000-case winery that makes Riesling, Gewurztraminer, Vidal Blanc, Catawba, Steuben, Concord, Chancellor, and Chambourcin.

Trach Cellars (Wescosville, 1984), is a 250-case winery that makes dry Seyval, DeChaunac, and Marechal Foch.

Twin Brook Winery (Gap, 1989), is a superb, 16-acre, 6,000-case winery that makes outstanding Seyval, Cayuga, Vignoles, Chambourcin, Chancellor, and proprietary wines. All are eminently fruity, well-crafted and balanced, offering excellent value. In the final analysis, this winery is writing the final chapter in the production of exquisite French-American wines.

Victorian Wine Cellars (Rohrerstown, 1983), is a 1,400-case American, French-American, fruit and berry winery.

Vynecrest Winery (Breinigsville, 1988), is a 3-acre, 500-case winery that makes good, sound Vidal Blanc, Seyval, Cayuga, Baco Noir, and Chambourcin.

Windgate Vineyards (Smicksburg, 1986), is a 15-acre, 2,400-case winery that makes good, sound French-American (primarily Seyval, Vidal Blanc, Marechal Foch, DeChaunac), and smaller quantities of Cabernet Franc, Riesling, and Chardonnay.

Maryland And Delaware

As the nation's fourth smallest state, Maryland exhibits fascinating contrasts: it's first colony was founded on religious tolerance, and it was the first state with a commercial railroad, a Linotype machine, a telegraph line, a friction match, and a dental college. The fact that it is a major center for thoroughbred racing belies a refined elegance, a rich history, and a rural, aristocratic ambience. For a small state, Maryland stretches for more than 240 miles from the Blue Ridge Mountains to the Atlantic Ocean, and has a longer coast line than New Jersey and Delaware combined. Historically, tobacco was the state's most valuable crop, but today tertiary activities and commerce dominate economic fortunes. The state contains 5 million people, three-quarters of which reside in metropolitan Baltimore.

As in all other mid-Atlantic states, winemaking in Maryland began in the middle of the seventeenth century when one Tenis Palee made wine in 1648 from wild American grapes, but due to the pronounced and strange flavor and aroma of the native grapes, the early colonists attempted domestication and hybridization. When these efforts failed to improve the quality of the wines, Vinifera vines were imported as the final solution. The first such attempt by Lord Baltimore in the early 1660s ended in failure as cold winter weather and summer diseases killed the tender Old World vines, not unlike other areas along the northeast coast. By 1665 Governor Charles Calvert planted 340 acres (some were Vinifera) along St. Mary's River, all of which failed by 1672.

In the second half of the eighteenth century the only vine with commercial possibilities was the Alexander, although it, too, failed by 1785. Nearly every colonist with financial resources attempted vinegrowing and winemaking with little success until John Adlum moved from

Pennsylvania to Havre de Grace and created a short-lived reputation first by cultivating the Alexander and later the superior, hardy, adaptable Catawba. Both grapes diffused quickly, so that by 1829 the "Maryland Society For Promoting The Culture of The Vine" was founded. Unfortunately, fungus diseases destroyed all commercial vineyards by the middle of the nineteenth century, and the industry did not resurface until a century later when Philip Wagner began to experiment with French-American grapes in the 1930s. His Boordy Winery was established in 1945, and he did much to encourage winegrowing in the state. Despite the state's notorious history for restrictive legislation (county-wide legislation, among others), Maryland has promulgated "Limited Wineries Legislation" so far reaching that eleven of the twelve wineries currently in existence have been founded after 1976, the year the bill was passed. Interestingly, Maryland has the highest density of wineries to square miles of vineland of any state in the Union.

Because Maryland is highly urbanized, affluent, the site of an expanding tourist flow, and has a climate that is similar to that of neighboring Virginia, the state offers interesting possibilities for Vinifera plantings. For all but the highest elevations, the mean temperature is 54F, and summers are hot but seldom above 95F in both the hilly interior and coastal areas. Annual precipitation varies between 40 and 45 inches, sudden thunderstorms are frequent throughout the growing season, and fungus diseases common. Winters are mild, snowfall light, bitterly low temperatures rare, but warm spells followed by freezing temperatures are frequent. Within this generalized pattern, there are two areas with considerable possibilities for vinegrowing: the sandy coastal region, and the hilly interior, particularly the well-drained, iron-rich soils of the Catoctin Valley. The former area, more temperate than interior areas, resembles eastern Long Island, except that spring arrives about three weeks earlier and fall two weeks later. The Catoctin Valley yields complex, well-balanced, unusually rich, intensely-flavored and scented Cabernet Sauvignon and Chardonnay wines.

Reflecting a positive regional awareness, acreage has increased from 70 in 1978, to 344 in 1989 (the largest vineyard contains 35 acres), and the number of wineries has jumped from four to twelve for the same period. Of the estimated 45 different varieties grown in the state, three (Seyval, Chardonnay, and Cabernet Sauvignon) account for nearly 58 percent of the total vine acreage. About 51 percent of the total acreage is planted in French-American varieties, the highest such percentage among all states in the nation. Forty-eight percent is planted in Vinifera, and 1 percent in American vines, the lowest percentage in any state in the northeast and midwest. Given the recent successes in Virginia, the percentage of Vinifera, particularly Pinot Noir, Cabernet Sauvignon, Merlot, Cabernet Franc, Chardonnay, and Riesling, as percent of total acreage, will increase. Three other promising varieties are Sauvignon Blanc, Gewurztraminer, and Vignoles, the latter for the production of sweet wine. Vine acreage is highly concentrated in Baltimore, Frederick, Montgomery, and Washington counties. Two-thirds of the total state output is white wine, nearly all fresh, zesty, and well-made. The finest is Chardonnay, followed by Sauvignon Blanc, Riesling, and the two dominant French-American varieties--Seyval and Vidal Blanc. The finest red wine, Cabernet Sauvignon, especially when mixed with Merlot and Cabernet Franc, can often be outstanding to memorable.

Given the state's central location along the northeast Megalopolis, its high disposable income, and a sophisticated clientele, the steadily improving wines are of high quality, offering excellent growth potential. Although the twelve wineries are not large by California standards, all but three lack the cottage-type ambience of other eastern states. Unlike Pennsylvania and New Jersey to the north, the average price of the wines, particularly Vinifera varietais, is similar to the finer wines of eastern Long Island. Despite declines in vine acreage over the past 20 years, wine production since 1977 has increased fivefold to more than 45,000 cases.

Maryland has three *ava's*, two of which lie solely within state boundaries: *Cumberland Valley, Linganore (1983),* and *Catoctin (1983). Linganore,* located in the center of the state has fewer than 60 acres of vineland and contains only one winery. Just north of Hagerstown, and framed by the Catoctin, South Mountains and the Potomac River, *Catoctin,* a 22-mile long valley rich in Colonial history, encompasses 170,000 acres, 70 acres of vineland and two wineries. The *Cumberland Valley ava,* mentioned above, contains only one winery.

Surprisingly, Delaware, the only state in the mid-Atlantic region that lacks farm winery legislation, contains two small commercial vineyards near the Pennsylvania border, but no wineries. Small and narrow, Delaware, bounded by the Atlantic, New Jersey, Pennsylvania, and Maryland, is called the "Diamond State" because its economic value is disproportionate to its size. It is mainly composed of small farms, busy cities and resorts, and devoid of winemaking activities despite a comparatively high per capita wine consumption.

The wineries are:

Basignani Winery (Sparks, 1986), one of the finest in the state, is a superb, 8-acre, 1,400-case winery that makes Cabernet Sauvignon, Merlot, Chardonnay, Riesling, less good French-American varietals (Seyval, and Vidal), and blends. The Chardonnay, in particular, is often outstanding, and should not be missed.

Berrywine Plantations/Linganore Wine Cellars (Mount Airy, 1976), is a 35-acre, 4,500-case winery that makes a large assortment of French-American (Seyval, Vidal Blanc, Cayuga White, Melody), and fruit and berry wines. The finest, estate-bottled and vintage-dated, are labeled *Linganore Wine Cellars*; fruit and berry wines are under the *Berrywine* label, all others are under the *Plantation* label.

Boordy Vineyards (Hydes, 1945), Maryland's oldest and second largest winery, is a 16-acre, 8,500-case property sold in 1980 by the founders. Now part of a 350-acre farm, output is still dominated by French-American varieties, of which Seyval, Vidal Blanc, Chambourcin, and Villard Noir are the finest. The emphasis has recently switched to Vinifera, of which Chardonnay, Riesling, Cabernet Sauvignon, and Cabernet Franc are the finest. Sparkling wines are also made.

Byrd Vineyards and Winery (Myersville, 1976) is an impressive, 25-acre, 6,000-case winery specializing in quality Vinifera-based wines. It is one of the better producers in the mid-Atlantic states area, especially for full-bodied, flavorful Gewurztraminer, Chardonnay, Sauvignon Blanc, Riesling, and Cabernet Sauvignon.

Catoctin Vineyards and Winery (Brookeville, 1983), is an 33-acre, 4,500-case winery that makes excellent Cabernet Sauvignon (full-bodied, well-structured, and complex), Riesling (dry and aromatic), Chardonnay (full-bodied and elegant), and Seyval (dry, clean, and crisp). Consistently good, the wines are expertly made, sensibly priced, and offer excellent value.

Elk Run Vineyards & Winery (Mount Airy, 1983), is a 4-acre, 3,000-case, Vinifera and proprietary winery, of which Chardonnay, Riesling, Sauvignon Blanc, and Cabernet Sauvignon are the finest. Estate wines, marketed under the *Liberty Tavern* label, offer good value.

Fiore Winery (Pylesville, 1986), is an 8-acre, 1,500-case French-American (Vidal Blanc, Seyval, Chancellor, and Chambourcin) winery. In the future are Cabernet Sauvignon, Chardonnay, Merlot, and Gewurztraminer.

Loew Vineyards (Mount Airy, 1985), is a 6-acre, 1,000-case winery that makes Seyval, Chardonnay, Riesling, Cabernet Sauvignon, and French-American proprietary wines.

Montbray Wine Cellars (Westminster, 1979), one of the better wineries in the state, is an innovative (it is the world's first vineyard cloned by somatic embryogenesis), 20-acre, 3,000-case winery that makes above-average Seyval, Chardonnay, Riesling, Cabernet Sauvignon, and Cabernet Franc, offering good value. This was the first American winery to produce a varietal Seyval. The future seems uncertain as the winery has recently been sold.

Whitemarsh (Hampstead, 1984), is an 18-acre, 2,500-case winery specializing in sparkling wines (mainly from Seyval, Chardonnay, and Riesling) under the *Aspen Run* label.

Woodhall Vineyards & Wine Cellars (Sparks, 1983), is a 5-acre, 1,200-case, French-American and Vinifera winery, of which Seyval, Vidal Blanc, Chambourcin, and Cabernet Sauvignon are the finest.

Ziem Vineyards (Downsville, 1977), the westernmost of Maryland's wineries, is an 8-acre, 1,000-case winery offering above-average, carefully made French-American wines, the best of which are Aurore, Vignoles, Seyval, Marechal Foch, and Chancellor.

Virginia

With 45 wineries, 154 commercial vineyards, and nearly 1,600 acres, Virginia ranks approximately eighth in the nation among winegrowing states. One of the most historical corners in America, Virginia (Old Dominion to purists) has long altered its indolent Civil War plantation image. In recent years the state has rapidly increased its urban population to nearly 7 million (half of whom reside within 100 miles of Washington, D.C.), and while it boasts the largest shipyard and single-unit textile mill on earth, its agricultural economy is still dominated by tobacco, its oldest cash crop. Since World War II, apples around Winchester, beef cattle in the southwestern portion of the state, and peanuts, poultry, eggs and dairy products have made considerable inroads in diversifying this economic sector. However, the most dramatic growth in agriculture since 1970 has been grape growing and winemaking.

Virginia, an unlikely state for an emerging winemaking industry, departs from the New York-mid-Atlantic pattern of vinegrowing and winemaking in many ways: three-quarters of the planted area is in Vinifera vines; it produces expensive wines (Vinifera varietal wines are as expensive as the finest from Long Island and the Finger Lakes); and it produces no bulk or jug wines, preferring instead to market white wines (primarily Chardonnay and Riesling), and red wines (primarily Cabernet Sauvignon and Merlot) under their varietal names. Virginia also differs significantly from its neighbors to the south: it has no significant Scuppernong acreage, its wines are comparatively dry, and the degree of capitalization per acre is remarkably high. The combination of large infusions of capital, excellent winemakers, and stylish medium-sized wineries producing high quality wines make Virginia a fascinating and exciting vineyard. There is also a tendency for wineries to concentrate on relatively few wines, and not, like states to the north and the midwest, on a large number of highly diverse, and often confusing names and styles. In this regard, it is interesting to note that more than 80 percent of the acreage is planted in six varieties-- Chardonnay, Riesling, Cabernet Sauvignon, Seyval, Vidal Blanc, and Merlot. Equally important is the fact that the state legislature is highly supportive of grower and winery needs, and there are a host of interest groups that obsessively support the industry: the former liberally funds the Virginia Wine Marketing Office, and the governor-appointed Virginia Winegrowers Advisory Board; among the latter are the Virginia Foothills Association, the Jeffersonian Wine & Grape Growers Society, the Virginia Vineyards Association, the Virginia Wineries Association, and the Vinifera Wine Growers Association. State-wide, there are more than 50 wine-related public events. As a consequence, farm wineries have encountered little difficulty in consumer acceptance despite the relatively high prices and lack of historic celebrity.

Named after the Virgin queen, Elizabeth I, Virginia, in less than twenty years, has established herself as one of the seven leading states in the nation for quality wine production, and is second to New York in the east for Vinifera acreage and wine production. With 45 wineries and 204 growers, Virginia has increased acreage from fewer than 50 in 1972, and 963 in 1983, to 1,600 in 1992. Until the closing of the Richard's Wine Cellars facility in Petersburg in 1989 (this was, since 1951, the state's largest winery making inexpensive, fortified, Scuppernong-based wines under a large number of labels), Virginia ranked third in volume for wine production with nearly 3 million gallons, sixth in the number of wineries, and tenth in grape acreage. The sale of farm winery wine now approaches 300,000 gallons, and vineyard and winery investment stands at $24 and $75 million respectively. The number of wineries has increased from just 6 in 1979, to 45 in 1992, with an additional 8 planned by 1995. Reflect-

ing national patterns of industry consolidation, the 5 largest wineries produce more than 47 percent of all wine, and the top 10, more than 70 percent. The wine industry, directly and indirectly, contributes nearly $500 million and employs more than 9,000 people. Highly significant is the fact that since 1984, the annual per capita consumption of wine has increased by more than 10 percent.

Figure 5.16

VIRGINIA: DISTRIBUTION OF WINERIES AND APPELLATIONS

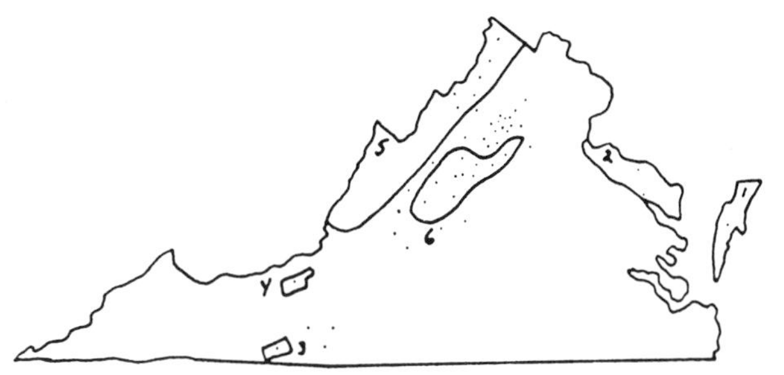

1. Virginia's Eastern Shore (includes the southern portion of the Delmarva Peninsula), 2. Northern Neck George Washington Birthplace (a historic region, and one of the oldest settled areas in the nation), 3. Rocky Knob, 4. North Fork of Roanoke, 5. Shenandoah Valley, 6. Monticello.
More than 50% of total grape acreage is located in Fauquier, Albermarle, Madison, Orange, and Shenandoah counties, all located in the northern portion of the state.
One third of the planted area is Chardonnay, followed by Riesling, Seyval, Vidal Blanc, Cabernet Sauvignon, Villard Blanc, Chambourcin, Pinot Noir, and Gewurztraminer. Source: Virginia department of Agriculture.

One of the most interesting aspects of Virginia winemaking is its recent ascendency among winemaking states. A good deal of this spectacular growth is due to highly aggressive and progressive state initiatives: it spends more than $1 million annually on promotion (third in the nation); created three full time wine related jobs--a marketing specialist, viticulturist, and an enologist; and promulgated one of the most liberal farm winery laws (1980) in the nation that enabled winemakers to sell through food and pharmacy stores, slashed license fees, and eliminated state taxes. Although a Virginia farm winery must produce 51 percent of its wine from fruit grown on land that the winery owns or leases, a commercial winery can bottle wine without this restriction and can use juice from fruit grown anywhere. The state has also been instrumental in establishing and encouraging the formation of a Winegrowers Advisory Board with the objective of making the state the leading quality winemaking state in the east. At present, Virginia is selling more wine than it produces, and although this might at first appear to be a positive element, inventories, as percent of sales, are the lowest in the nation. This imbalance is not expected to reverse itself until the end of the decade. Although a few wineries have failed financially, the attrition rate is one of the lowest in the nation. The exciting growth since 1975 is similar to that of Washington and Oregon.

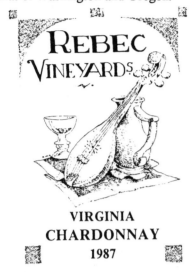

VIRGINIA
CHARDONNAY
1987

While wine occupied a significant position among the landed aristocracy in colonial America, the story of colonial viticulture in Virginia was based on many conscientious attempts, but unfortunately, very little wine. The Spanish constructed a short-lived mission on the York River in 1570, but there are no historical documents supporting the notion that they made wine. The first organized viticultural attempt began when John Smith landed in 1607 in Virginia and saw abundant wild grapes. His Jamestown colonists, the first in the country to make commercial wine out of those grapes, were also the first to apply the expression "foxy" to the taste of native grapes. It is reported that a few bottles of non-commercial Scuppernong wine, made in Lynnhaven Roads in 1607-1609 by French immigrants, were shipped to London, thus making Virginia the first colony to export wine to Europe. Not liking the scent or flavor of these strange grapes, Vinifera cuttings were imported in 1619, and soon after one of the first acts of the Virginia Assembly in 1623 required that for every four men in the colony a garden should be laid off, a part of which was to be planted in vines, but unfortunately, all failed. The census of 1625 reported that one George Dandys cultivated a 2-acre vineyard, and William Brocas made wine from grapes grown on the banks of the Rappahannock. In 1657 the Virginia Assembly offered a prize of 10,000 pounds of tobacco to the first person who made two tons of wine from colony produced grapes (the prize remained unclaimed). When King Louis XIV revoked the Edict of Nantes (1685) denying French Protestants the right to practice their religion in public, French Protestants, known as Huguenots, emigrated overseas in large numbers. Many settled in Virginia and the Carolina's where they established formidable colonies, particularly in South Carolina. In 1699, 800 French Huguenots produced wine 20 miles from Richmond, but in general, all Vinifera winemaking efforts failed. Therefore, while the profusion of wild vines along the Atlantic gave hope (eight distinct species of the genus *Vitis* grow wild in the state), and attempts at Jamestown and other areas represented Protestant zeal and determination, fungus diseases, phylloxera, and inexpensive West Indian rum meant eventual failure.

In yet another attempt to grow Vinifera vines early in the eighteenth century, Governor Alexander Spottswood encouraged many German vignerons from the Rhine to settle along the Rapidan River in 1710. Although vines were cultivated and wine made at Germanna, little came of the venture. The final major colonial winemaking attempt occurred in 1769 when the General Assembly in Williamsburg promulgated "An Act for the Encouragement of the Making of Wine." This interesting piece of legislation provided for the funding of 100 acres, a French winemaker, and a work force in establishing an experimental vineyard and winery. Seven years later, the project was abandoned and York County declared "unfit" for viticulture. Despite climatic adversity, Vinifera winemaking, in the final analysis, failed because of its inability to compete with tobacco production, a more lucrative economic activity under prevailing mercantile English economic policies (for a short time Virginia tobacco represented between one-fourth and one-half of total exports from North America). The landed aristocracy preferred the importation of expensive European wines (Madeira, Porto), and brandy; the small middle class, rum and other spirits; and the working class, beer, fortified Rotundifolia, fruit and berry wines.

Thomas Jefferson, one of the most celebrated men in American history, was a prime mover of the American Revolution, the author of the Declaration of Independence, diplomat, Secretary of State, and two-term President. He made the Louisiana Purchase possible, and his love for the soil and scientific inquiry led him to major non-political accomplishments. While Ambassador to France from 1785 to 1789, Thomas Jefferson undertook a three-month wine tour throughout France. Though not the founder of American viticulture, he was an avid proponent of viticulture who unsuccessfully tried to grow Vinifera grapes and make wine at Monticello. The first attempt to plant a Vinifera vineyard at Monticello was in 1771, ten years before vines were planted at Mission San Juan Capistrano in California. In 1774 Jefferson entered into a partnership with Philip Mazzei (an Italian, to manage vineyard operations and winemaking), but met with little success. By 1809, Jefferson had relinquished his dream of producing Vinifera wine in Monticello, and began to recommend the cultivation of native grapes. In 1987, a small portion of the original vineyard was replanted. Interestingly, he advocated the unrestricted importation of wine to America. George Washington was another unsuccessful Virginian who attempted to grow Vinifera vines and make wine.

While all these futile endeavors ended in tragic disappointments, Dr. D.N. Norton of Richmond developed the first "non-foxy" grape in 1835 (named after himself), and in the second half of the nineteenth century one Colonel T. Bland is given credit for another new grape called Bland's Madeira. Armed with the Norton grape and a desire to diversify the rural economy, farmers began to establish vineyards at a heady pace after the Civil War. Vine acreage increased from less than 100 to more than 3,000 by 1869. The principal variety was the Norton, followed by Catawba, Alexander, Clinton, and Ives--all for table wine production, while Delaware and Concord varieties were planted for dessert wine output. Then, as now, the Charlottesville region was designated the "Capital of the Wine Belt of Virginia." In 1878 Virginia's "Norton Claret" was awarded a medal at the Paris Exposition as America's best wine, and by 1880 the state ranked as the eleventh largest wine producer in the nation. As fungus, black rot, phylloxera, and other "New World" ailments took their toll, Vinifera and American grape winemaking soon disappeared after 1890.

Prince Michel Vineyard, stylish, the largest in the state, and the site of supple, well-flavored wines. Baxevanis

Although winemaking attempts persisted on a small non-commercial scale, the frustrated Virginian eventually turned to fruit and berry wines, beer and whiskey. By the time Prohibition was repealed all winemaking facilities were closed. In 1933, the Monticello Grape Growers Cooperative attempted to revive the industry, but failed. One John Lewis, an Afro-American farmer, produced sweet American-based wines near the North Carolina border after Prohibition, but the winery ceased production after his death. By 1969 there were only 50 acres of vineland,

nearly all Concord and Scuppernong. Winemaking was practically non-existent until the establishment of the Richard's Wine Cellars in 1951. But it was the success of a few Virginia wine pioneers in the early 1970s that spurred the rebirth of the state's wine industry. Serious Vinifera and French-American experimental plantings began with Charles Raney of Farfelu, Archie Smith of Meredyth, and Carl F. Flemer of Ingleside, all in the 1960s. The turning point occurred in 1973 when Mrs. Thomas Furness created the first all-Vinifera winery in Middleburg, and Dr. W.R. Guth, a Hamburg surgeon, decided to reestablish Vinifera vines along the Rapidan in 1976. Soon after, under the able guidance of a small band of dedicated Virginians, the Farm Winery Act was passed in 1980, a truly momentous occasion that sparked a major agricultural revolution. By 1982 Vinifera acreage surpassed hybrids and American grapes for the first time in the state's history.

Although five viticultural regions are recognized (northern, central, eastern, the Shenandoah Valley, and the southwest), the overwhelming majority of Virginia's wineries and vineyards are located on the east-facing Blue-Ridge foothills, regions that collectively contain many of the highest elevations in the Appalachian Mountain chain. More than two-thirds of the planted vine acreage is concentrated within a 70-mile radius of Charlottesville, and three-quarters of all wineries are located in the north central portion of the state bounded by Lynchburg in the south, the Great Valley in the west, and the Blue Ridge foothills in the east. This region, with its profusion of favorable microclimates, is also permeated by a large collection of 200 year-old colonial and post colonial towns that do much to inflate tourist interest, and hence, promote the wine industry. Eastern Virginia contains three wineries, and the extreme southern portion another three. Affording excellent opportunities, the hilly margins of the Shenandoah Valley contain five wineries. With several minor exceptions, the area between Charlottesville and Middleburg, with nearly two-thirds of all wineries and more than three-quarters of total acreage, is the center of the state's quality wine production. Of the 154 commercial vineyards diffused throughout the state in 43 counties, about 40, or 25 percent of the total, are found in Fauquier County, and another 53 percent in the neighboring counties of Albemarle, Madison, Orange, and Rappahannock. Most vineyards are planted on hilly terrain in order to maximize local microclimatic characteristics favorable to growth (good soil and air drainage), and to avoid dangerous low winter temperatures and false springs.

Virginia, lying south of the brutally cold winters of the northeast and midwest, and north of the deadly Pierce's Disease of the humid southeast, exhibits an interesting and, as yet, untapped reservoir for future grape plantings. Measuring 200 miles north-south, and 430 miles east-west, Virginia, with more than 40,000 square miles, is a triangular-shaped state with a large number of climatic, topographic, and soil disparities. Proceeding from east to west, Virginia is composed of a coastal plain (one-quarter of the state), or "tidewater" region; the Piedmont Plateau (half of the state); and between the Blue Ridge and the Allegheny Plateau, is the Great, or "Shenandoah" Valley. Degree days fluctuate between Region I and V, precipitation between 34 and 55 inches, and for a good deal of the state "hard" frosts are relatively unknown, although false springs are rather frequent in the northern portion. As a result, the grape harvest season extends over a period of two months--first in the Tidewater region, and much later in the higher and cooler Blue Ridge area. It has been estimated that as many as 50,000 acres are suitable to Vinifera, and as many as 200,000 acres for French-American and American varieties.

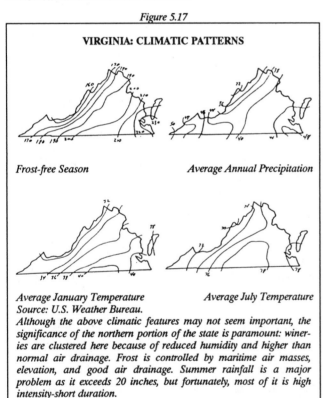

Figure 5.17

VIRGINIA: CLIMATIC PATTERNS

Frost-free Season   *Average Annual Precipitation*

Average January Temperature   *Average July Temperature*
Source: U.S. Weather Bureau.
Although the above climatic features may not seem important, the significance of the northern portion of the state is paramount: wineries are clustered here because of reduced humidity and higher than normal air drainage. Frost is controlled by maritime air masses, elevation, and good air drainage. Summer rainfall is a major problem as it exceeds 20 inches, but fortunately, most of it is high intensity-short duration.

Fig. 5.17 give a good impression of the basic reasons why grape growing is highly concentrated along the Blue Ridge foothills between Charlottesville and Winchester. It is the only inland region with a 200+-day growing season, a variety of small microclimates, excellent air drainage and well-drained soils, particularly those with a high incidence of iron-bearing and quartz elements. The area is moderate in terms of rainfall (40 inches), and air humidity levels are substantially below areas to the east. False springs are common, and there are large spring and win-

ter temperature fluctuations, the latter particularly troublesome as temperatures may vary 70F thus causing widespread bud and trunk damage. In higher elevations precipitation is unpredictable and often heavy. However, for many grape growing regions in the state, torrential, hurricane-induced precipitation with associated high humidity rates appears to be the most significant environmental hazard. It is interesting to note, however, that all Vinifera vines planted since the mid-1970s are still in existence, and despite the persistency of Japanese Beetles, black rot, crown gall, and other fungus disorders, modern vineyard practices have kept the most destructive elements at bay. Nearly all vineyard sites have a minimum of 3,200 degree days, but due to microclimatic variations, the harvest season extends over a period of two months. While the geographic distribution of vineyards is surprisingly widespread, more than half of the acreage is localized in northern Virginia.

The most common Vinifera vines are Chardonnay, Riesling, Cabernet Sauvignon, Merlot, Gewurztraminer, and Semillon. The most popular French-American varieties are Seyval, Vidal Blanc, Chancellor, Chambourcin, DeChaunac, Baco Noir, and Chelois. In fact, east of the continental divide, Virginia is third to Lubbock, Texas, and Long Island, New York in Vinifera acreage, particularly Cabernet Sauvignon and Chardonnay. Cabernet Sauvignon, in particular, is a vine with a future ever since a new clone, that resists disease stress and lives longer, was introduced in the mid-1970s. It is interesting to note that Virginia's Vinifera varieties, particularly Chardonnay, Merlot, and Cabernet Sauvignon, are second to Long Island in price in eastern America. Of the 1,600 acres, 1,072 are planted in Vinifera (69%), 423 in French-American (27%), and 64 in American vines (4%), most being Concord, Delaware, Niagara, and Catawba. Char-donnay, Riesling, and Cabernet Sauvignon lead the list of the most commonly planted Vinifera grapes, followed by Seyval and Vidal Blanc for French-American. The dominance of Vinifera varieties is rather surprising because state agricultural officials historically encouraged the planting of French-American grapes, a posture not too dissimilar from other states in the northeast and midwest. But unlike all other states, Virginia, very early in its recent viticultural resurgence, elected to persevere with Vinifera grape varieties, and, as a result, has the highest percent of Vinifera acreage of any state east of the 95th Meridian. Ninety-five percent of the grapes grown in the state are used in winemaking and 5 percent are for table and juice; the former figure is generally considered the highest percentage for wine use in eastern America.

There are six *ava's*, five within the state and one shared with West Virginia: *Shenandoah Valley (1983), Monticello (1984), Rocky Knob (1983), Northern Neck George Washington Birthplace (1987), North Fork of Roa-*

noke (1983), and Virginia's Eastern Shore (1991). Shared with West Virginia, *Shenandoah Valley* (the northern portion of the Great Valley), a well-defined valley between the Blue Ridge Mountains in the east and the Allegheny Mountains to the west, is drained by the Potomac at Harpers Ferry, West Virginia, and the Shenandoah. Although there are more than 2.4 million acres within the established boundaries of ten counties in Virginia and two in West Virginia, the five wineries and 315 vine acres are mainly located in the northern portion. While general climatic features appear to be relatively constant throughout the valley, both microclimatic patterns and soils vary to significant degrees by altitude, exposure, and aspect. The best soils appear to be associated with rocky (limestone and sandstone), east-facing slopes.

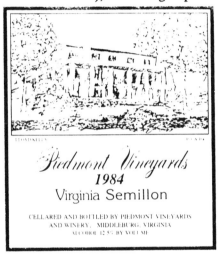

Piedmont Vineyards
1984
Virginia Semillon

CELLARED AND BOTTLED BY PIEDMONT VINEYARDS
AND WINERY, MIDDLEBURG, VIRGINIA
ALCOHOL 12.5% BY VOLUME

The *Monticello ava*, a small region of hills stretching north and south of Charlottesville, and encompassing portions of Albemarle, Orange, Nelson, and Greene counties, is named after Monticello, home of Thomas Jefferson. Although the Monticello Grape Growers Cooperative Association produced less than 3,000 gallons of wine when formed in 1934, the fledgling industry withered to insignificance until Vinifera vines were successfully cultivated in 1974 on the La Abra farm in Lovington. The *ava* is 1,250 square miles, contains 14 wineries, and more than 500 acres, or one-quarter of the state's total vineland. The area does not enjoy a microclimate that is that distinctive from the Shenandoah and North Fork of Roanoke areas, but its iron-rich, quartz-dominated soils do make it different. *Rocky Knob*, a tiny *ava* located in the Rocky Knob Recreational Area, enjoys a slightly longer growing season than surrounding areas. It contains 60 acres of vines and one winery. This small *ava* is distinguished from surrounding areas by a relatively high elevation, gravelly soils, and good air drainage. The *North Fork of Roanoke ava*, the southernmost delimited area in the Ridge and Valley portion of the Appalachians, is located on the Atlantic portion of the mountain range. It is distinguished

from surrounding areas by hilly terrain, a drier climate (less humid and rainy with far fewer destructive thunderstorms), and well-drained limestone and sandstone soils. *Virginia's Eastern Shore*, consisting of Accomack and Northampton counties, lies on the southern portion of the Delmarva Peninsula. The large *ava* of more than 436,000 acres, excludes coastal islands and coastal marshy regions. Although the sandy soils are rich in truck farming, there are but 35 acres of wine grapes, one winery and three vineyards.

Northern Neck George Washington Birthplace, carved into its shorelines by the Potomac and Rappahannock rivers, is situated in the tidewater region east of Fredericksburg that encompasses five counties--Westmoreland, King George, Richmond, Northumberland, and Lancaster. This region, centered on the birthplace of George Washington, consists of 922 square miles, 146 acres of grapes, 16 vineyards, and three wineries. Although the *ava* contains well-drained alluvial soils, and its climate is moderated by surrounding water bodies, there are significant variations of both as one proceeds from water margins inland. "neckland" soils, found mainly along river flats, are inferior to "upland" soils found along the interfluves at elevations ranging from 50 to 190 feet above sea level. The *ava*, due to the location of Stratford Hall Plantation, Washington's birthplace, Fredericksburg, and the proximity of Colonial Williamsburg, Jamestown (England's first permanent foothold in the New World), and Washington D.C., offers excellent winemaking opportunities due to intense tourist activity. The historic nature of this region reflects the name and ambience of the various wineries that are emerging in this area.

There are two additional *ava's* currently waiting approval. The proposed *Montpellier* viticultural region, lying adjacent and partially overlapping the *Monticello ava*, encompasses the lush rolling hills of Culpeper, Madison, and Orange counties. It is the site of James Madison's home, and along the Rapidan River, the 1710 Germanna settlement, one of the original vinegrowing communities in the state. The *Northern Virginia* viticultural region, lying east of the Shenandoah and north of the Monticello viticultural area, will include the important Prince Michel and Virginia Wine Cooperative, eight other wineries, and all, or portions of ten counties (Arlington, Culpeper, Fairfax, Fauquier, Greene, Loudoun, Madison, Orange, Prince William, and Rappahannock). Appomatox Plateau includes Appomatox, Charlotte, and Prince Edward counties, two wineries, and several vineyards; and Fauquier County, with its five excellent wineries, horse farms, stone fences, historic antebellum houses, and large estates, may in the future, become two additional *ava's*.

The wineries are:
Accomack Vineyards (Painter, 1986), the first winery to be located in the southern portion of the Delmarva Peninsula, is a 2-acre, 1,000-case winery that makes Chardonnay, Riesling, Cabernet Sauvignon, Merlot,

and proprietary wines.

Afton Mountain Vineyards (Afton, 1978), formerly Bacchanal Vineyards, is a 10-acre, 2,200-case winery that makes Chardonnay, Riesling, Semillon, Zinfandel, and Cabernet Sauvignon. Present owners (1990) are currently expanding acreage and winery operations to include Chenin Blanc, Gewurztraminer, and Pinot Noir.

Autumn Hill Vineyards (Stanardsville, 1979), is a 7-acre, 1,700-case winery that makes Chardonnay, Riesling, and Cabernet Sauvignon.

Barboursville Vineyards (Barboursville, 1978), is a 50-acre, 12,000-case winery that makes a large number of wines of which Chardonnay, Riesling, Gewurztraminer, Merlot, Sauvignon Blanc, and Cabernet Sauvignon are consistently above-average, and improving. The firm represents the first sizeable investment by a foreign company—Zonin of Italy. The winery, a registered Virginia Historic Landmark, lies on a plantation owned by former Governor James Barbour. The planted area, part of an 830-acre estate, will expand further in the near future.

Blenheim Wine Cellars (Charlottesville, 1983), is a 10-acre, 2,000-case winery that only makes Chardonnay. Dark in color, well-aged, full-bodied, and well-flavored, it is one of the finest in the state offering excellent value. A national historic site, the main house, built in 1745, is the third oldest in the Charlottesville area.

Burnley Vineyard and Winery (Barboursville, 1984), is a 16-acre, 5,000-case winery specializing in Riesling, Chardonnay, and Cabernet Sauvignon, all offering good value. Also made are a blush from Chambourcin, and a dry and sweet Vidal Blanc. A consumer friendly winery where the enthusiasm is infectious, this family winery consistently makes above-average wine offering good value. Other label: *Rivanna*, for a line of sweeter wines.

Chateau Morrisette Winery (Meadows of Dan, 1983), is a 60-acre, 8,000-case winery that makes Riesling, Chardonnay, Vidal Blanc, a Cabernet Sauvignon blend, sweet Niagara, Merlot (American *ava*), and several proprietary wines. Other label: *Woolwine Winery.*

Chateau Naturel Vineyard (Rocky Mount, 1983), is an 8-acre, 1,000-case winery that makes blended French-American and berry wines.

Chermont Winery (Esmont, 1981), is a 13-acre, 3,000-case winery with an excellent reputation for Chardonnay, Cabernet Sauvignon, and Riesling. The wines are hard to find, but well worth the effort.

Deer Meadow Vineyard (Winchester, 1987), is an 8-acre, 1,200-case winery that makes Chardonnay, Cabernet Sauvignon, Seyval, Chambourcin, Marechal Foch, an interesting Steuben, and proprietary wines.

Domaine de Gignoux (Ivy, 1981), is a 4-acre, 900-case Chardonnay, Merlot, Cabernet Sauvignon, and Cabernet Franc winery.

Farfelu Vineyard (Flint Hill, 1975), is a 7-acre, 2,000-case winery that makes proprietary blends, Cayuga White, Chardonnay, and Cabernet Sauvignon.

Fruit of the Bloom Farm Winery (Salem, 1983), is a 5-acre, 1,000-case winery that makes fruit, berry, Concord, and Niagara wines.

Guilford Ridge Vineyard (Luray, 1983), is a 4-acre, 950-case winery that makes blended white and red wines from Chelois, Marechal Foch, Seyval, and Rayon d'Or, of which *Page Valley Red* is the finest.

Hartwood Winery (Fredericksburg, 1989), is a 9-acre, 1,500-case winery that makes Chardonnay, Riesling, Vidal Blanc, Seyval, Cabernet Sauvignon, and proprietary wines.

Horton Vineyards (Charlottesville, 1977), formerly Montdomaine Cellars, is a 55-acre, 14,000-case winery that consistently makes above-average Chardonnay (crisp, full-bodied, with a pleasant bitterness), Cabernet Sauvignon (dark, full-bodied, complex), Merlot (soft, yet complex, dark and smooth), and *Heritage*, a Meritage-type wine, all under the *Montdomaine Cellars* label. The winery maintains the largest Vinifera vineyard and, as vines age, the improving wines offer excellent value. Many changes are in the making as the winery has been acquired by an energetic vineyard owner. One major departure for the winery is the planting of Viognier, Mourvedre, Syrah, and Marsanne. The winery also has 8 acres of Norton, a very unusual development for the state. Other label: *Monticello Wine Company* for the production of Porto-type wine.

Ingleside Plantation Vineyards (Oak Grove, 1980), is a 58-acre, 20,000-case winery that often makes average to excellent, well-flavored and balanced Chardonnay, Cabernet Sauvignon, and sparkling wines. The winery, part of a 2,500-acre estate, is also the site of the largest nursery in the state.

Lake Anna Winery (Spotsylvania, 1989), is a 12-acre, 2,500-case winery that makes excellent Chardonnay, Seyval, Merlot, Cabernet Sauvignon, and proprietary white and blush wines.

Linden Vineyards (Linden, 1987), is a 12-acre, 3,000-case winery that makes above-average to excellent Chardonnay, Sauvignon Blanc, Riesling/Vidal Blanc blend, Seyval, and Cabernet Sauvignon.

Locust Hill Vineyard (Rectortown, 1983), is a 5-acre, 1,000-case winery planted in Cabernet Sauvignon, Chardonnay, Seyval, and Riesling, all above-average.

Loudoun Valley Vineyards/Schloss Tucker-Ellis (Waterford, 1988), the northernmost winery in the state, is a 22-acre, 2,500-case winery that makes Chardonnay, Riesling, Cabernet Sauvignon, Zinfandel (with small infusions of Cabernet Sauvignon and Chambourcin), and proprietary wines.

Meredyth Vineyards (Middleburg, 1975), is a pioneering, 59-acre, 15,000-case winery managed by one of the most astute and meticulous winemakers in the northeast. The historic emphasis is on French-American vines (Seyval is particularly good), but the trend is to increase Vinifera output, particularly Chardonnay, Riesling, Sauvignon Blanc, Cabernet Sauvignon, and Merlot.

Misty Mountain Vineyard (Madison, 1986), is a serious, 20-acre, 5,500-case winery that makes above-average to excellent Chardonnay, Riesling, Seyval, Gewurztraminer, Merlot, Cabernet Sauvignon, and proprietary wines.

Mount Hermon Vineyard (Basye, 1988), is a 5-acre, 1,000-case winery that makes Riesling, Chardonnay, Cabernet Sauvignon, and Pinot Noir.

Mountain Cove Vineyard (Lovingston, 1973), is a 12-acre, 2,000-case winery that makes French-American, proprietary blends, and fruit wines. Other label: *Elk Hill Vineyard.*

Naked Mountain Vineyards (Markham, 1981), is a 13-acre, 3,500-case winery that specializes in the production of Vinifera wines, of which Claret (from a Cabernet Sauvignon, Merlot and Cabernet Franc blend), Riesling, Sauvignon Blanc, and Chardonnay (more than 80% of output) are the most important. The meticulously made wines—robust and flavorful, are moderately priced offering excellent value.

North Mountain Vineyard & Winery (Edinburg, 1990), is a 10-acre, 1,500-case winery that makes good, sound Chardonnay, apple, and proprietary wines that belong in every serious cellar.

Oakencroft Vineyard & Winery (Charlottesville, 1983), is a 17-acre, 4,000-case winery that specializes in Seyval, and smaller quantities of Chardonnay, Cabernet Sauvignon, Merlot, and proprietary wines.

Oasis Winery (Hume, 1977), the second largest winery in the state in terms of capacity, is a substantial, 45-acre, 11,000-case winery that has established a reputation for well-made, outstanding Chardonnay, Riesling, Cabernet Sauvignon, Merlot, Chelois, and sparkling wines. The winery also cultivates on an experimental basis 14 additional varieties, of which Gewurztraminer and Sauvignon Blanc are the most interesting. The sparkling wine is outstanding, offering superb value.

Piedmont Vineyards (Middleburg, 1973), is a recently expanded, 60-acre (half is leased), 7,000-case winery widely considered one of the finest in the state. The emphasis is on three white wines—Chardonnay, Semillon, and Seyval, of which the first two (particularly the Semillon) are the finest. It is considered the first Vinifera winery in the state, and the first, in modern times, to market wine outside the state. This is a winery worth watching as it has exhibited an ability to consistently produce world class wines. Chardonnay and Semillon are often outstanding and the equal to any from California. Although the winery was historically only known for white wines, it will be producing well-aged Bordeaux-type blends shortly. The house is a registered Historical Landmark.

Prince Michel Vineyard (Leon, 1983), with more than 130 acres and an annual output of 70,000 cases, is the largest winery in the state. This aggressive, technical and innovative winery (it maintains the highest density vine plantings per acre in the state) makes many varietal and blended wines, but is particularly known for Riesling, Chardonnay (Barrel Select is particularly good), Cabernet Sauvignon, Merlot, and sparkling wines. Recently, the winery has released a super premium, Meritage-type wine (with an American *ava*) called "Le Ducq," the most expensive east of the Continental Divide. Both Prince Michel and Rapidan are owned by VaVin (a name chosen in honor of the son of the exiled king of Poland, an acquaintance of one of the shareholders), a holding company. The winery also owns a 24-acre vineyard in St. Helena, Napa Valley.

Rapidan River Vineyards (Culpeper, 1978), is a 55-acre, 12,000-case vineyard owned by Prince Michel that specializes in "German" style (with some residual sugar) white wines. Quite naturally, Gewurztraminer, Riesling, and Chardonnay dominate output; and while Cabernet Sauvignon, Merlot, and Pinot Noir have recently been planted, the mainstay is an excellent Riesling. The wines are made at Prince Michel.
Rebec Vineyards (Amherst, 1988), is a 5-acre, 600-case winery that makes good, sound Chardonnay, Riesling, Cabernet Sauvignon, and proprietary wines. Rebec is a medieval stringed instrument introduced to Spain by the Moors.
Rose River Vineyards (Syria, 1976), is a 6-acre, 800-case winery that makes Cabernet Sauvignon, Chardonnay, blended proprietary, fruit, and mead wines.
Shenandoah Vineyards (Edingburg, 1976), is a 55-acre, 10,000-case winery that makes Chardonnay, Vignoles, Riesling, Vidal Blanc, Seyval, among others. The well-made wines tend to be light-bodied with Chardonnay and Seyval considered the finest, offering good value. Other label: *Stoney Creek.*
Simeon Vineyards (Charlottesville, 1986), is a 14-acre, 2,000-case winery that makes above average, distinctive Chardonnay, Riesling, Cabernet Sauvignon, Pinot Noir, a rare Chenin Blanc, and generic wines.
Stonewall Vineyards (Concord, 1983), is a 10-acre, 3,500-case winery that makes Cayuga, Vidal Blanc, Chambourcin, proprietary, and a mead wine called *Pyment.*
Swedenburg Winery (Middleburg, 1987), is a 15-acre, 3,000-case winery (part of the 200-acre, Valley View Farm, dating back to 1762) that makes Riesling, Chardonnay, Sauvignon Blanc, Seyval, Cabernet Sauvignon, and proprietary wines.
Tarara Vineyards (Leesburg, 1989), is a serious, well-managed, 36-acre, 3,000-case winery that makes Chardonnay, Cabernet Sauvignon, and proprietary wines. The winery is also a hub of activity for experimental grape varieties not common to Virginia, and several rootstocks.
The Rose Bower Vineyard & Winery (Hamden-Sydney, 1979), is a 10-acre, 2,000-case winery that makes Chardonnay, Riesling, Cabernet Sauvignon (blended with Cabernet Franc), Vidal Blanc, Seyval, fruit, and proprietary wines, of which the Rose O'Grady is an unusual semi-sweet Chelois and Vidal blend.
The Williamsburg Vineyard Winery (Williamsburg, 1987), is a stylish, 300-acre farm and winery that overlooks College Creek and the James River. At present 58 acres of vines produce 30,000 cases of good, sound, above-average Chardonnay, Merlot, Cabernet Sauvignon, and proprietary wines. The aggressive winery has planted vines at Montpelier, home of President James Madison, and will soon be marketing wine under that label. Other label: *Acte 12.*

The Williamsburg Winery. Courtesy of The Williamsburg Winery
Tomahawk Mill Winery (Chatham, 1989), is a 2-acre, 250-case, Chardonnay only winery.
Totier Creek Vineyard (Charlottesville, 1992), is a 20-acre, 2,000-case winery that makes good, sound, well-structured Chardonnay, Riesling, and Merlot, Pinot Noir, and Cabernet Sauvignon.
Virginia Winery Cooperative (Culpeper, 1986), is a 19-member, 58-acre, 12,500-case winery that makes first class, blended Cabernet Sauvignon, Chardonnay, Riesling, (both off-dry and semi-sweet are outstanding), and others under the *Dominion Wine Cellars* label.
Willowcroft Farm Vineyards (Leesburg, 1984), is a 3-acre, 1,200-case winery that makes Riesling, Chardonnay, Seyval, Cabernet Sauvignon, Cabernet Franc, and Merlot, all offering good value.
Winchester Winery (Winchester, 1984), is a friendly, 18-acre, 3,500-case

winery that makes Riesling, Seyval, Vidal Blanc, Chambourcin (dark and well-flavored), and proprietary wines.

THE MIDWEST

The American midwest, the vast heartland of the nation, extends from the Appalachian Plateau to the eastern edge of the Great Plains. Although there is no standard definition of what constitutes "the midwest," the following states will comprise the region in this book: Minnesota, Wisconsin, Iowa, Michigan, Illinois, Indiana, Ohio, Missouri, Arkansas, Kentucky, Tennessee, and West Virginia. It is a vast area of 1.2 million square miles, 68 million people, 18,000 acres of vineland producing 8 million gallons of wine, and 157 wineries. The northern portion is dominated by the cooler and glaciated Great Lakes, and the southern section by hilly terrain and a warmer, more humid climate. The entire region is highly diverse in terms of climate, soils, urban concentrations and agricultural land use. The latter, characterized by large, highly productive Corn Belt and dairying functions, supports one of the largest and most prosperous rural populations where, with few exceptions, monoculture based on specialty crops is rare and not important for the region as a whole. Historically, midwestern agriculture stood in sharp contrast to the plantation economy of the south, and the extensive (grazing and grain) and intensive (irrigated specialty crops) agricultural economies of the west.

The image of the "midwest" conjures up notions of what the "typical farm" is like--high productivity, diversified production, and neat, orderly fields with well-constructed farm houses. With more than 50 percent of the nation's corn and a larger percentage of dairy products than any other comparable region, the midwest also represents the historic center for lumber, industrial rubber, steel, chemicals, and surface transportation vehicles. This area is also the home of the second largest megalopolitan urban region, a near unbroken stretch of cities from Milwaukee, Wisconsin to Buffalo, New York, along the south shore Great Lakes margins.

This twelve state region is a highly fragmented, totally unorthodox wine producing area. It ranges from progressive, high volume producers, imprudent state legislatures compelling growers to struggle for a living, to a population that is largely content to consume jelly, grape juice and fruit and berry, rather than grape table wine. While there has been progress over the past 20 years in doubling the number of wineries, increasing wine output, and augmenting the percentage of French-American and Vinifera vines, grape acreage has declined by more than 6,000 acres since 1960 over the entire region, and the Concord, Catawba and other American varieties still account for more than 80 percent of the entire acreage (French-American vines account for 19 percent, and Vinifera varieties less than 1 percent). The principal white French-American varieties are Vidal Blanc, Vignoles, and Seyval, while the more popular grape varieties are Chelois, DeChaunac, Baco Noir, Marechal Foch, Chancellor, and Chambourcin. Generally speaking, the hardiest varieties (like the Beta, Monitor, and Suelter) are located in the colder, northern portions, and the more tender varieties along the southern areas. It is estimated that for the entire region, more than three-quarters of all wine made is white in color.

The climate of this interior region is of a type generally described as continental, referring to the fact that weather conditions are not strongly affected by maritime influences. Success in growing grape vines rests largely upon two physical considerations: a growing season delayed by lake influences until the danger of frost has past, and proximity of hilly land that causes favorable air circulation. Therefore, viticulture is highly confined to lake margins, protected river valleys, isolated portions of the Ozarks, the Cumberland Plateau, and the Ridge and Valley sections of the Appalachians. The first type of vineyard lies on glacial hill and dune, primarily along southwestern Michigan and Lake Erie; the second on the Ozark Plateau and along the Ohio, Missouri and Arkansas rivers; and the third in scattered mountain and hilly sites in West Virginia, Ohio, and Tennessee. The geographic distribution of the viticultural pattern is a direct reflection of continental location characterized by extremes in temperature. While the midwest lies adjacent to the geographical center of North America, it is the prime meeting ground for cyclonic circulation in which cold polar air masses meet the warmer and more humid westerly and maritime tropical air masses thus producing highly variable weather. Extreme seasonal variations in temperature are, unlike the humid south and Mediterranean California, the rule, not the exception. Hot summers and cold winters, prominent elements of a continental climate, produce a short growing season for most of the area. Along the southern margins the climate is hotter and more humid; along the northern fringes it is colder, drier and the growing season shorter; in the western portion, continentality increases and precipitation declines to precarious levels; and in the eastern sections increased topographic irregularity produces a profusion of protected valleys against the onslaught of cold polar air.

The biggest problem is the persistency of very low temperatures of long duration followed by sharp increases in temperature, with equally sudden drops during the months of November through April. Average annual precipitation ranges between 28 inches to 36 inches over most of the region but increases to 45 inches along the Ohio River, and 55 inches along the southern extremities of Arkansas and Tennessee. The freeze-free season varies between 115 and 170 days, except in narrow belts adjacent to the Great Lakes where it is as long as 200 days. The central portion, more favorable to agriculture, is mainly devoted to dairy and Corn Belt activities, while the northern portions, with 20 to 30 inches of precipitation, a shorter growing season, far poorer soils, and vast tracts of bog and swamp, are mainly forested.

The northern portion of the midwest is dominated by the Great Lakes, a maritime world in the heart of the North American continent consisting of five inland seas that collectively hold at least 20 percent of the earth's fresh surface water. Forming a chain whose sheer size staggers the imagination (they stretch for nearly 1,000 miles), these sweet water seas hold more than six quadrillion gallons of fresh water or 95 percent of all the surface water in continental United States, a figure that is absolutely crucial in explaining the presence of viticultural activities in a region that is otherwise too cold for proper grape maturation. The lakes outline 8,000 miles of shoreline, cover an area larger than Michigan and Illinois combined, and the immediate bordering land areas encompass at least 40 million people, or 15 percent of all Americans. The inland areas surrounding the lakes are rich in forest, agricultural, and industrial creativity.

The Great Lakes lie midway between the equator and the North Pole in an open corridor by which frigid Arctic air from the north and mild subtropical air from the south meet and travel from west to east--a phenomena that is not duplicated anywhere else on earth with such consequences. Of the six major lakes, Lake Michigan, Lake Erie, and Lake Ontario are the most important viticulturally. Their latitudinal extent is equivalent to a distance from the Florida/Georgia border to North Carolina, and their longitudinal extent is equivalent to a distance from Philadelphia to Indianapolis. Across this vast region of land and water, climatic conditions and microclimatic variations, in response to water and land relationships, prevailing air masses, depth of water, land exposure, and soils, are highly variable and significant. The latitudinal differences of eight degrees within the Great Lakes Basin insure the existence of significant contrasts of climate between northern and southern lakes. The varying depths of the lakes influence the heating and cooling rates of the water, their capacities to interact with moving air, and the probability of ice formation.

Grapes are grown mainly along the southern lake margins and islands of Lake Erie, and the eastern portion of Lake Michigan, all of which enjoy the longest growing season in the Great Lakes region. And it is along these areas with 180-day growing seasons that we find, after the California Valleys and Florida, the nation's third largest fruit region. A good example of microclimatic location is the lake portion of Michigan where the deeper waters of Lake Michigan rarely freeze over and, consequently, yield heat in winter to the prevailing westerly winds, bringing about heavy snow accumulation, in sharp contrast to the bitterly low temperatures of interior areas. In spring, cold wind retards the budding stage of vine growth, usually until all danger of killing frosts has passed. In combination, there is a tendency to extend the growing season to 200 days as far as Ludington to the north. The Berrien, Van Buren, and Allegan counties have an unusual warm mesothermal climate where the January mean is 27F and the late July mean is under 72F. The only other portion of the state with a favorable climate is southeastern Michigan, but due to the urban sprawl of Detroit towards Toledo, there is little room for large scale vine growing. The northern part of the state not located within the windward path of the prevailing westerlies, is classified as mid-latitude microthermal, and has markedly lower temperatures--13F in winter and 64F in summer.

Figure 5.18

THE CLIMATIC "LAKE EFFECT"

The more climatically temperate "eastern lake shores" are influenced by the northwesterly flow of continental polar air masses. As these cold air masses blow over the warmer waters they generate fog along the western lake margins, evaporate a good deal of moisture, and when confronted with cooler land along the leeward margins, deliver copious precipitation, a good deal of which is snow during the winter months. Deep snow acts as an excellent insulating cover for vines during the prolonged, cold winter. During spring, the colder lake waters prevent budding until the passage of the last spring frost. During the summer and fall, westerly wind movement is warmer than that found over the Great Lakes thus producing a more temperate climate. As a consequence, only western Michigan, the southern margins of Lake Erie, and portions of the Niagara Peninsula are able to support commercial vineland. The "lake effect" increases the number of degree days by more than 200.

While Lake Superior is the largest, deepest and coldest, lakes Michigan and Erie are much shallower and warmer. Prevailing winds are from the west and north, and, as a consequence, vineyards are located on eastern and southern shore locations, the latter clearly illustrated by Lake Erie. Lining the south shore of Lake Erie are lake plains and beach ridges formed by higher lake waters during glacial times. The height and width of these ridges and their proximity to the highlands of the Appalachian

Plateau affect the intensity and duration of the land and lake breezes. Hardly ever are vineyards encountered 5 to 10 miles inland or on low-lying margins, but nearly always on gradual rises to facilitate air drainage. Another factor is the nature of the soil: vineland soil is nearly always well-drained, composed of sand and glacial till, and devoid of significant clay pans.

Minnesota And Wisconsin

Minnesota and Wisconsin have a continental climate characterized by chronic outbursts of polar air throughout the year. While there are occasional periods of prolonged heat during the summer, particularly in the southern portion when warm air moves northward from the Gulf of Mexico, winter is the longest season. Climatically, both states are noted for cold winters and cool, humid summers. In winter, days are short, shadows long, snow cover deep, and the absence of high mountains ascribes the dominance of cold Arctic air for much of the year. In Wisconsin, only the southeast corner of the state has a growing season that begins before May 25, and in Minnesota only a small area in the southeastern portion of the state begins before June 1. For more than 60 percent of the land area in both states, the growing season begins after June 5.

The soils in Minnesota and Wisconsin are too wet, acidic, and when coupled with a devastatingly short growing season, grapes are nearly impossible to mature except in the extreme southeastern portion of Minnesota and southern Wisconsin. As in New England, Michigan and Ohio, there is a good deal of fruit (primarily cherry and apple) and berry (cranberry) wine, and precious little grape wine. With fewer than 400 acres of commercial grape acreage in both states, eleven wineries (seven of which are in Wisconsin) produce fewer than 30,000 cases of grape wine between them, or less than five times the output of fruit and berry wine. The economic impact of wine production (including fruit and berry) and the retail wine industry is rather formidable for both states: $389 million for Minnesota, and $565 million for Wisconsin.

Minnesota is a large state of 84,402 square miles and 4.5 million people. Known as the "North Star" state, it is relatively flat, highly glaciated, and littered with thousands of lakes, with Lake Itasca the source of the Missouri River. It is interesting to note that wine was made on both the Atlantic and Pacific coasts before Minnesota was settled. While the first permanent settlement was Fort St. Anthony, later renamed Fort Snelling in 1819, large scale settlement began in 1853 when the Mendota and Traverse des Sioux Treaties were signed. In fact, Ohio was producing more than 550,000 gallons of wine when Minnesota became a state in 1859. North Europeans, mostly Germans, Swedes and Norwegians, but the former, in particular, with a strong wine producing tradition, introduced grape growing and winemaking. By 1875, wine was made in St. Peter, La Crescent, Excelsior, Fair Bault, St. Paul, and other early settlements. By 1900 annual grape production was 50,000 cases, or double current levels.

It is reported that vineyards were first planted at Lake Minnetonka west of Minneapolis in 1855. In time, the majority were to be found in the southeastern portion of the state near the Mississippi River. No matter what the inclination of the early settlers, two elements doomed the industry: cold temperatures and a population with a preference for beer and distilled beverages (Wisconsin is the nation's leader in the per capita consumption of brandy). Today, grape acreage is located south of the Twin Cities region, with only minor plantings in Aitkin (in the north), St. Cloud (south-central), and Redwood Falls (in the southwest). The most popular grape variety is Seyval followed by Marechal Foch and Leon Millot, and then by a host of exotic Swenson hybrids and other varieties such as LaCrosse, Kay Gray, St. Croix, Bluebell, St. Pepin, Edelweiss, and Canadice, all of which account for more than one-third of the planted state acreage. As important as these varieties are, more than 50 percent are French-American and Labrusca.

Despite environmental shortcomings, Minnesota is not without winegrowing achievements: dissatisfied with non-hardy grapes, settlers in the second half of the nineteenth century began experimenting with alternatives, of which Beta (a hardy cross of Riparia and Labrusca grapes, was first developed and named by one Louis Suelter) is a major accomplishment. Officially recommended in 1905 by the state's Horticultural Society, production of Beta wine rose from 5,000 cases in 1920 to 60,000 cases by 1929, only to fluctuate between 5,000 and 20,000 cases for the next 30 years, all of which was made sweet. Needless to say, this early ripening, hardy, vigorous, and productive black grape had replaced, just prior to Prohibition, a good deal of the Labrusca acreage, and was considered by many to be the leading variety in the state. Beta, however, is not without controversy with opinion evenly divided as to its true origins. Today, its well-flavored character is insufficient for serious commercial production given its tartness, low yields, and deficient sugar content. On the decline for all but the "purist" home winemaker, it has lost its competitive edge to other varieties and now accounts for less than 5 percent of planted acreage. Another interesting but less popular variety is Dakota, a grape similar to Beta but one that produces sweeter fruit and matures two weeks earlier. Other similar grapes include Alpha, Suelter, Hungarian, Monitor, and Janesville.

In the late 1960s, Elmer Swenson, "the Dean of Grapes," and one of the most prodigious grape breeders, found the Minnesota #78, a Rupestris-Labrusca cross that outperformed all others. Over the years, he has used Vitis riparia, a very adaptable grape, as the basis of his

hybridization efforts, developing in the process many new varieties of which Swenson Red, Edelweiss, St. Croix, Kay Gray, St. Pepin, Espirit, and La Crosse are the most important. He developed many other grapes, none of which reached commercial expectations. Two other, but less celebrated hybridizers of cold-hardy grapes are J. M. Dorsey and A. N. Wilcox, and in neighboring South Dakota, N. E Hansen and R. M. Peterson. Notwithstanding the introduction of more than 500 "winter hardy," "hybrid" grapes, the "miracle" wine grape able to produce good table wine has yet to be discovered. Despite the small scale character of vine growing and winemaking, the Minnesota Grape Growers Association was founded in 1975, and in 1984 a wine cooperative was founded. Also, the state, in an effort to stimulate vine acreage and winemaking, adopted a Farm Winery Law in 1980.

The wineries are: **Alexis Bailly Vineyards** (Hastings, 1973), a 12-acre, 2,000-case winery, is the first in the state to make wine from 100 percent Minnesota-grown grapes. The well-made wines consist of French-American varietals and an unusual dessert wine (Hastings Reserve) made from Rupestris grapes. **Chateau Devenois** (Rice, 1988), is a 4-acre, 1,500-case winery that makes blended Vinifera (from Washington grapes), and French-American wines, most of which are sold through the family restaurant. **Northern Vineyards Winery** (Stillwater, 1983), a cooperative of 13 members cultivating 25 acres, produces 2,000-cases of Seyval, Vidal Blanc, Marechal Foch, and proprietary blends. **Scenic Valley Winery** (Lanesboro, 1984), is a 4,000-case fruit and berry winery that also makes small quantities of grape wine from wild American grapes.

With one notable exception, the viticultural and winemaking history of the "Badger" state, Wisconsin, a state without a farm winery law, is even less spectacular. Its only claim to fame lies with the founder of Sauk City--Count Agoston Haraszthy, and his legacy to Wisconsin--the Wollersheim Winery. As the leading beer producing state in the nation, Wisconsin is, because of its dominant German population, synonymous with beer and not wine.

The principal wineries are: **Christina Wine Cellars** (LaCrosse, 1979), part of the three Lawler wineries in the midwest, this 10,000-case winery makes a large selection of table, sparkling, and fruit and berry wines from purchased fruit. **Door-Peninsula Wine Inc.** (Sturgeon Bay,

1974), is a 10,000-case winery that makes mostly fruit and berry wines, and only miniscule amounts of Concord-based grape wine. **Spurgeon Vineyards and Winery** (Highland, 1981), is a 15-acre, 2,000-case winery that makes American and French-American wines; a sister winery, **Beautiful Harvest,** makes fruit and berry wines. **Stone Mill Winery** (Cedarburg, 1971), is a 7,000-case winery that makes American, French-American, fruit and berry wines from purchased fruit. **Wisconsin Winery** (Lake Geneva, 1979), is a 3,000-case, American, fruit and berry winery producing from purchased fruit. **Wollersheim Winery** (Prairie du Sac, 1847), is a 27-acre, 6,000-case winery located on a southwest bluff above the Wisconsin River. A National Historical Site, the property was once owned by Agoston Haraszthy. The well-made Seyval, Vignoles, Riesling, Marechal Foch, Leon Millot, and sparkling wines have a peculiar smokey flavor and aroma offering good value.

Michigan

Michigan, a medium-sized state of nearly 10 million people, surrounded by four of the five Great Lakes (it leads the nation with 3,200 miles of freshwater shoreline), is the largest fruit producer in the midwest with the southwestern portion of the state ranking as one of the largest fruit producing areas in America. Although the "Wolverine" state is considered a major dairy producer, it ranks first nationally in the output of tart cherries, potted geraniums, cucumbers for pickles, and navy, black and cranberry beans. It ranks second in the production of prunes, plums, apples, bedding plants, gladioli, and potted Easter lilies. With 10,800 acres, Michigan ranks sixth among grape producing states in the nation (1 percent of national production), and, with an output of about 700,000 gallons, ninth in terms of wine production. Grapes rank as the third most important fruit in the state after apples and cherries. Automobile assembly, tourism, and dairying are the state's most important industries. Interestingly, Michigan, in 1908, was the first state in the nation to build a concrete highway.

Figure 5.19

DISTRIBUTION OF WINERIES AND APPELLATIONS

1. Leelanau Peninsula (second largest fruit growing region), 2. Old Mission Peninsula, 3. Lake Michigan Shore, 4. Fennville (the largest and most important fruit growing region).

Viticulture in Michigan is wholly influenced by climatic forces. The following figures illustrate the rather extraordinary differences between western Michigan along Lake Michigan and the rest of the state in terms of

average and seasonal temperature, precipitation, and length of the frost-free season. These climatic features are dominated by prevailing westerly, southern, and northern winds that are unencumbered by significant topographic features and the moderating effect of the Lake Michigan. It is obvious, therefore, that the combined influence of climate has exerted a profound concentration of grape growing in seven counties, of which Van Buren, Berrien, Cass, Allegan, and Kalamazoo, all located in the southwestern portion of the state, are the most important. Several hundred acres of vineland are widely distributed in the center and eastern portions of the state, but it is the northwestern area that is rapidly becoming a major quality-oriented wine producing region for Vinifera and French-American varieties. While Concord represents more than 90 percent of the total acreage, French-American and Vinifera vines have increased from fewer than 50 acres in 1970 to 1,200 acres in 1992, or approximately 35 percent of the "wine utilized" grape crop. Of the more than 50,000 tons of grapes produced, more than 48,000 are destined for jelly and juice processing, Michigan being, as a consequence, the third largest, after Washington and New York, processor of Concord grapes.

Although Count de Pontchantrain described wild Grapes in the Detroit Post region in 1686, and French traders encountered dried grapes for human consumption in 1691, commercial grape growing did not occur for nearly 200 years when the Welch Grape Juice Company began buying Michigan grapes in the 1870s. By 1880 Michigan had 2,266 acres, nearly all confined to southwestern Michigan, with a wine output of 62,000 gallons. Major Concord plantings began in 1905, and accelerated when Welch's constructed a processing facility in Paw Paw (southwestern Michigan), an area that has dominated grape production for the past 100 years. Grape acreage and production has fluctuated widely over the past 100 years: acreage rose steadily throughout the first decade of the century, accelerated rapidly during the early Prohibition years, peaked at nearly 50,000 acres in 1929, and has since fallen to fewer than 11,000 acres in 1992.

Grape production rose steeply from 4,000 tons in 1889 to 60,000 in 1909, continued its upward momentum during Prohibition, declined to an average output of 25,000 tons during the period 1935-1960, and has since doubled output from fewer than 11,000 acres. The peak production of 77,000 tons in 1932 has not been achieved since. The small wineries in existence prior to Prohibition closed their doors, but acreage did not suffer due to demand from home winemakers. With the collapse of grape prices after Repeal, Michigan passed legislation protecting wineries by a legal maneuver that kept a dozen, inefficient firms from improving a poor product, usually a sweet, high alcohol wine, until 1982 when the protective features of the law were abrogated. Combined with increased competition in the production of Concord grapes from Washington, viticulture and winemaking languished since 1945. Also of significance is the fact that the percentage of Concord acreage has declined from 95 percent in 1974 to 85 percent of the total planted acreage in 1992. Given the economics of Concord production east of the Yakima Valley, it appears that further declines in acreage are inevitable.

Figure 5.20

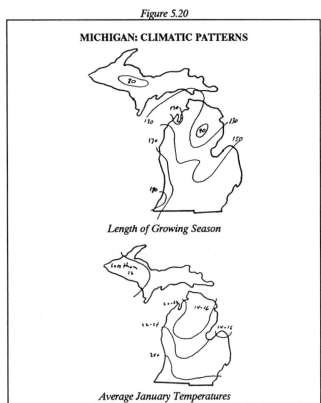

MICHIGAN: CLIMATIC PATTERNS

Length of Growing Season

Average January Temperatures
The congruency of Lake Michigan extending the length of the growing season and raising winter temperatures along western Michigan is obvious. Nearly all grape acreage is located along Lake Michigan; about 95% of the total is sited in the 5 southwestern counties, the warmest area of the state.
In Leelanau, Aurore is the first grape to mature in mid-September, followed by DeChaunac and Seyval in late September, Vignoles in mid-October, and Riesling in November. Grape maturity in the Fenn Valley occurs one to two weeks earlier, and two to four weeks earlier in central Missouri.

As wine consumption tripled during the decade of the 1970s, the number of wineries increased from three to seventeen during the years 1961-1981, nearly all located in the western portion of the state, an unusual condition as the greater Detroit metropolitan region contains half the states population, and serves as the largest wine market. Interestingly, Michigan contains a large number of comparatively old wineries, some of which originated in Canada during Prohibition. The recent resurgence in quality wine production is the consequence of several events that should not be underrated. The Michigan Grape Society, founded in 1978 by a group of growers and wineries, the

Michigan Grape Research Council, and the establishment of the Michigan Grape and Wine Industry Council within the state's Department of Agriculture have all done much to transform the once cottage industry into an economically viable entity. The outcome has been a huge upsurge in the direct and indirect economic impact of the wine industry: from less than $300 million in 1965 to more than $1.1 billion in 1988.

Figure 5.21

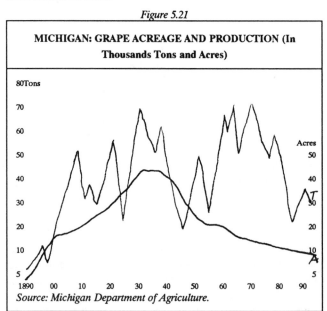

MICHIGAN: GRAPE ACREAGE AND PRODUCTION (In Thousands Tons and Acres)

Source: Michigan Department of Agriculture.

Michigan, despite its formidable acreage and production, suffers from a poor quality table wine image. Historically, the wines lacked style, a certain cachet, and, all too often were among the most expensive on store shelves sold within the state; unable to compete outside the state, Michigan wines were rarely tasted by the rest of the nation. Like New York, Pennsylvania, Missouri, and Ohio, the "Concord image" is not easily discarded given the fact that of the 11,000 acres of grapes, only 2,000 are used for the making of wine, and of that portion 1,000 are French-American, and fewer than 200 are Vinifera, the latter, representing a rather dramatic improvement over 1960 when fewer than 20 acres of French-American and Vinifera vines were planted in the state. Because the value of Concord grapes is one-fifth that of Vinifera and one-third of French-American varieties, non-native grape acreage is expected to increase in the coming decade.

However long a bastion of Concord juice and jelly production, sweet and fortified wines, Michigan is now showing a viticultural renewal. Although Concord still accounts for the overwhelming proportion of acreage, there are many large wineries and growers that are seriously planting French-American and Vinifera vines, of which Riesling, Gewurztraminer, Chardonnay, Seyval, Vignoles, Pinot Gris, Chambourcin, DeChaunac, Baco Noir, and Chancellor are the most important and show the greatest potential. The vineyard management mistakes of the 1960s and 1970s have largely been corrected, and the recent infusion of new capital and winemaking techniques have done much to improve both the final product and the state's image.

Table 5.8

MICHIGAN: GRAPE ACREAGE						
	1978		1982		1986	
Variety	Acres	Percent	Acres	Percent	Acres	Percent
American						
Cayuga			17	.1	17	.1
Concord	13,112	88.6	10,981	86.6	9,840	84.8
Delaware	1,051	7.1	705	5.6	885	7.6
Niagara	1,051	7.1	705	5.6	885	7.6
French-American						
Aurore	40	.3	54	.4	30	.3
Baco Noir	65	.4	84	.7	40	.3
Chelois			41	.3	15	.1
DeChaunac	49	.3	52	.4	50	.4
Marechal Foch			58	.5	40	.3
Seyval			87	.7	95	.8
Vidal Blanc			142	1.1	165	1.4
Vignoles			79	.6	65	.6
Vinifera						
Chardonnay					40	.3
Riesling					65	.6
Others	329	2.2	260	2.1	160	1.4
Total	14,806	100.0	12,676	100.0	11,600	100.0

Another encouraging sign is the recent increase in per capita wine consumption. The present figure of 1.7 gallons is nearly a threefold increase from the .54 gallon figure in 1965, a formidable augmentation given the fact that the state's population rose from 8.3 to 9.5 million during the same period. During this time, total gallons consumed jumped from 4.4 to 19 million gallons, and the percentage of Michigan-produced wine declined from 82 percent of total consumption to less than one-third. Furthermore, the state's moderately active research efforts have improved vineyard practices, and have led to renewed optimism. Given the fact that a sustained wine industry is a product of long, steady efforts, the quantum leap of the state's wine program in relation to the mediocre performance of neighboring states is rather remarkable. Another encouraging sign for the wine industry is the steady rise of tourism. With 3,200 miles of shoreline along the four Great Lakes, and 11,000 inland lakes, tourism (20 million annually, of which 350,000 visit wineries) has become a major industry offering enormous opportunities to the 20 wineries, nearly all favorably situated.

The Michigan grape harvest in 1990 was 43,000 tons, of which 93.5% was used for processing, 4.8% was used for wine production, and 1.7% consumed fresh.

Michigan has four *ava's*: *Leelanau Peninsula (1982)*, *Old Mission Peninsula (1987)*, *Lake Michigan Shore (1983)*, and *Fennville (1981)*, all located along the warmer, and windier eastern shore of Lake Michigan. On average, the prevailing westerly air masses flowing over the lake raise January temperatures along the eastern

shore between 5F and 10F, and, most importantly, lengthen the growing season between 40 and 50 days. Equally important, the lake effect lowers the incidence of summer thunderstorm activity, hence, the incidence of rot, and results in fewer than five dense-fog days, one of the lowest such coastal readings in the country.

Fenn Valley

1985
Lake Michigan Shore
VIGNOLES
Premium dry dinner wine
ESTATE BOTTLED

Encompassing Berrien and Van Buren counties, and portions of Allegan, Kalamazoo and Cass counties, *Lake Michigan Shore*, the largest *ava*, is a shoreline region that extends from central Michigan to northern Indiana. It contains more than 96 percent of the states acreage, 1,000 growers, and at least eight wineries. Located on the northwestern portion of Michigan, the *Leelanau Peninsula*, the center of the state's sour cherry production, is a low Region I on the Davis scale with a 160-170 day growing season. A picturesque hilly region, its indented coastline contains Leland, a charming fishing village, Northport and Traverse City, the latter, the hub of the Grand Traverse region, and a major tourist attraction. Weather is appreciably modified by both Lake Michigan and Grand Traverse Bay. Despite the northern latitude, the region is several degrees warmer than southeastern and central Michigan, benefits from good air drainage, and enjoys 2,100 degree days, that along with the Old Mission Peninsula *ava* is the highest such number in the Great Lakes at that latitude. A hilly promontory surrounded by water on three sides, soils are gravelly, sandy loam with clay, but well drained. Exposure is on south-facing glacial ridges that accentuate the effect of sunlight. The area receives between 140-180 inches of snowfall between November and April. Commonly referred to as the "little finger" area, it contains 200 acres of Vinifera, American, and French-American vines and four wineries, all of which have generated a good deal of attention in recent years.

Old Mission Peninsula, a long finger-like peninsula surrounded by the waters of the Grand Traverse Bay, and connected on the south at Traverse City, is the most recent *ava*. The *ava*, 19 miles in length and no more than 3 miles wide, is approximately 30 square miles. Including Marion and Bassett islands, it is located in Grand Traverse County, and enjoys a warm microclimate well-protected from cold weather affording a comparatively long growing season as it is double-tempered by both Lake Michigan and Grand Traverse Bay. The region experiences about 2,100 degree days, and despite the high latitude, killing frosts are virtually non-existent. The soils in this hilly, cherry-tree studded area are glacial in origin, and well-drained. Although additional acreage is scheduled for planting, there are only 80 producing vine acres at present, and one winery. The *Fennville ava*, the state's first approved viticultural area, is a 60 square mile, triangular region planted in orchards since the mid-1800s. Bounded by Lake Michigan on the west, the Kalamazoo River on the north, and the Middle Fork of the Black River on the south, it is a meeting point for a glacial moraine and outwash plain. The resulting soil is sandy, light, well-drained, and supports the largest concentration of fruit farms in the state. It also contains Holland, the largest tulip producer in the midwest. Lake Michigan moderates the climate to such a degree that average winter temperatures are at least two degrees higher, and summer temperatures lower than surrounding areas. Fennville is planted in American (mainly Concord), French-American (Aurore, Seyval, Vidal Blanc, Baco Noir, Chelois, Marechal Foch, and Vignoles), and Vinifera (Riesling and Gewurztraminer), and the wines tend to be fruitier and more delicate than all others in the state.

The wineries are:

Berrien Vintners (Harbert, 1933), also known as Lakeside Vineyard, is a 4-acre, 18,000-case winery that makes a large assortment of table, dessert, sparkling, fruit and berry wines from purchased fruit. Other labels: *Lakeside, Berrien Cellars, Molly Pitcher.*

Bernard C. Rink of Boskydel, a former librarian, makes what may very well be the finest French-American wine in America. Baxevanis

Boskydel Vineyard (Lake Leelanau, 1975), is a 35-acre, 5,000-case winery well sited on a southwest-facing slope overlooking Lake Leelanau. This well regarded winery makes impeccable, flawless, French-American and Vinifera wines, of which Riesling, Chardonnay, Pinot Noir, Seyval, Aurore, DeChaunac (outstanding, perhaps the finest in the nation), and Vignoles are particularly good offering excellent value. Under the proprietary name of "Soleil Blanc," the winery makes a superb Seibel 10868, the only such wine in the state.

Chateau Grand Traverse (Traverse City, 1974), is a 50-acre, 25,000-case, Vinifera-only winery that makes above-average quality estate Riesling, Chardonnay, Gewurztraminer, Merlot, Gamay Beaujolais, Pinot Noir, Zinfandel, and sparkling wines. Other labels: *O'Keefe Cellars, Vintners Selection.*

Fenn Valley Vineyards (Fennville, 1973), is a 52-acre, 10,000-case winery considered one of the finest in the state. It makes more than 12 different wines of which Riesling, Gewurztraminer, Vidal Blanc, Seyval, Chancellor, sparkling, and berry wines are the finest. It also crushes for several other wineries and restaurants.

Fenn Valley Wines of Rockford (Rockford, 1979), is a tiny, 150-case winery that makes Vignoles, Vidal Blanc, and cherry wines from purchased fruit.

Good Harbor Vineyards (Lake Leelanau, 1980), operated by a farming family dating back to 1773, is a 14-acre, 5,000-case winery located on the Leelanau Peninsula. In addition to fruit, the principal grape wines are Seyval, Vignoles, Vidal Blanc, Chardonnay, Riesling, Marechal Foch, and Baco Noir.

Leelanau Wine Cellars (Omena, 1975), is a 43-acre, 16,000-case winery that makes a large assortment of wines of which Riesling, Chardonnay, Vignoles, Aurore, Pinot Noir, Baco Noir, cherry, peach, and sparkling are considered the finest. French-American varietals were historically emphasized, but in recent years Vinifera acreage has been enlarged, and will soon dominate production.

L. Mawby Vineyards Winery (Suttons Bay, 1978), is a 9-acre, 2,500-case winery known for excellent, dry Vignoles, Pinot Gris, Seyval, Marechal Foch, and sparkling among others. The wines, expertly made, intensely flavored and scented, and consistently above midwestern standards, offer outstanding value and should not be missed.

Lemon Creek Vineyards (Berrien Springs, 1984), is a 40-acre, 3,000-case winery that makes estate dry and sweet Vidal Blanc and Riesling, and Baco Noir, all offering good value.

Loaf and Mug Restaurant and Winery (Saugatuck, 1985), is a 1,500-case winery that makes table, sparkling, and proprietary wines.

Peterson & Sons Winery (Kalamazoo, 1983), is a 4,000-case winery that makes a large assortment of fruit, berry, American and French-American grape wines sold under the *Naturally Old Fashioned Wines* label.

Rogue Winery (Rockford, 1988), is a 150-case winery that makes Vignoles, Vidal Blanc, Baco Noir, and cherry wines.

St. Julian Wine Co. (Paw Paw, 1921), originating in Ontario, Canada, the winery moved to Detroit in 1933, and again to its present location in 1936. The state's largest winery with an output of more than 150,000 cases, it is best known for bulk, proprietary, sparkling, fortified Sherry-type, Seyval, Vidal Blanc, Vignoles, Riesling, Chardonnay, Niagara, Chan-cellor, and Chambourcin wines from purchased fruit, must and concentrate. The Sherry is, by far, their finest wine.

Sharon Mills Winery (Manchester, 1989), is a 1,000-case, all-Vinifera winery that makes Chardonnay, Riesling, sparkling, and proprietary wines.

Tabor Hill Vineyards (Buchanan, 1970), is an aggressive, 46-acre, 28,000-case winery that makes a large selection of table, dessert, sparkling, and proprietary wines. Increasingly, Vinifera varietals have come to dominate output, of which Chardonnay, Riesling (dry and sweet), Gewurztraminer, Scheurebe, and Merlot are the most important.

Tartan Hill Winery (New Era, 1985), is an 8-acre, 400-case winery that makes Seyval and proprietary wines.

The Seven Lakes Vineyard (Fenton, 1983), is a 30-acre, 2,800-case, estate winery that makes blended red, rose, and white proprietary wines, as well as Vignoles, Seyval and Vidal Blanc.

Warner Vineyards (Paw Paw, 1938), the second largest winery, is a 100-acre, 35,000-case firm that makes a large assortment of wine, but mainly American and French-American wines. Historically the fourth largest grape juice producer in the nation with more than 120,000 gal-

Ions, the winery has recently reduced this amount to 10,000 gallons, and now concentrates in wine production. This winery also custom crushes for others, and ships in wine from Santa Barbara for blending purposes. Although the winery produces more than two dozen different wines (most of which are proprietary), Niagara, Chardonnay, Riesling, Sauvignon Blanc, Vidal Blanc, Seyval, Chancellor, Pinot Noir, and Zinfandel are the most important varietals. Sparkling wines are also made. Other labels: *Cask, Grape Valley, Paw Paw.*

Winegrow Inc. (Buchanan, 1986), formerly known as Eschner's Vinifera Vineyards, is a 22-acre, 3,000-case, Vinifera-only winery that makes well-balanced, flavored and scented, estate Riesling, Chardonnay, Gewurztraminer, and Pinot Noir under the *Madron Lake Hills Estate Wines* label. This immaculate and serious winery, located on two drumlins, also maintains experimental plots of 32 additional varieties of which Pinot Gris, Gamay, Carmine, Cabernet Sauvignon, Cabernet Franc, Barbera, and Scheurebe are the most prominent offering good potential. This highly aggressive, quality-oriented winery will soon expand to 27 acres with new ambitious plantings of Cabernet Sauvignon and Merlot. The vineyard is located within the extension of the Valparaiso Moraine near the Indiana border. Other label: *Heartland Vineyards.*

Madron Lake Hills Estate, superbly located on a drumlin, makes excellent wines. Courtesy of Madron Lake Hills Estate

Ohio

Ohio is a medium-sized, compact, heavily populated state of 11 million people and 41,330 square miles. With a heavy Germanic population, it is the site of an impressive viticultural history, and the birth in 1874 of the Women's Christian Temperance Union in Cleveland. As a major midwestern industrial state, Ohio has long been known for its steel and chemical industries, and inventors. Wilbur and Orville Wright built their first flying machine in Dayton, a city that also fathered the auto ignition system and the modern cash register. Ohio has also been responsible for the storage battery, automated bottle factories, bicycles, rubber, and a host of other transportation-related commodities. Not only is Ohio second to Virginia in the genesis of Presidents, but was responsible for the first interracial, co-educational college, the first professional baseball team, and enacted the first law regulating the working hours of women and children. Despite its industrial achievements and overwhelming urban character, Ohio is also a major agricultural state that ranks high in wool, dairy, and fruit products.

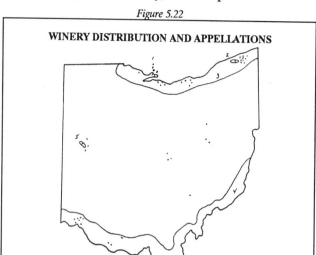

Figure 5.22

WINERY DISTRIBUTION AND APPELLATIONS

1. Isle St. George (North Bass Island), 2. Grand River (follows a portion of the Grand River in Lake, Ashtabula, and Geauga counties), 3. Lake Erie (extends from an area east of Toledo to New York State), 4. Ohio River Valley (extends from Wheeling, West Virginia to Evansville, Indiana), 5. Loramie Creek.

The geographic distribution of wineries exhibits a highly localized structure. Of the 43 wineries, 26 are located along the fringes of Lake Erie, 10 are sited north and east of Cincinnati, and the remainder are widely scattered throughout the rest of the state. Grape acreage is even more concentrated: just under 2,000 acres of vineland are found in four counties: Ashtabula and Lorain (collectively contain 55 percent of all vineland in the state), followed by Lake and Ottawa. Fewer than 250 acres are to be found in the rest of the state. This concentration in acreage reflects the advantage of lake location: it is drier by fewer than ten inches of precipitation than all other areas in the state; has lower relative humidity; and has well drained soils, particularly the sandstone and shale ridges of Ashtabula County. Most vineyards are located not on lacustrine soils (dominated by organic and clay matter, lake deposited, nutritionally rich, and poorly drained), but on glacial ridges 500 to 1,000 feet in elevation that contain greater accumulations of silt loam.

The leading quality wine producing districts are the Lake Erie islands (also known as the "wine islands"), and the south shore of Lake Erie. The former consists of four lake islands: North Bass Island (Isle St. George), Middle Bass Island (Isle des Fleurs), South Bass Island (Put-in-Bay), and Kelleys Island, all of which have a rich nineteenth century viticultural history. One acre of grapes was first planted on Kelleys Island in 1842, and the first winery established in 1850. German and American settlers came to South Bass Island in 1850 and by the end of the decade

North Bass, as well as the other two were transformed into thriving vineyards. By the 1890s, the lake islands had nearly 6,000 acres of planted vines, the highest square mile vine density vineyard in the nation. The biggest winery, Lonz, was built on Middle Bass in 1884. Today, of the 600 acres planted, half are found in North Bass Island, Middle Bass has fewer than 20 acres, South Bass, 200 acres, and Kelleys Island fewer than 50 acres. Historically planted in Labrusca varietals such as Concord, Catawba, Niagara, Delaware, and others, the trend in recent years is for French-American and Vinifera varieties to increase their share of the planted area. The continued success of the islands is based on a long growing season (the longest in the northeast at that latitude) due to the moderating effects of Lake Erie. Interestingly, irrigation is often necessary due to the presence of well-drained, limestone soils. Winter kill, still a perennial problem, necessitates the practice of partially burying vines (Vinifera) for protection in a few areas. Artificial snow is also being attempted to further insure a safe winter.

Figure 5.23

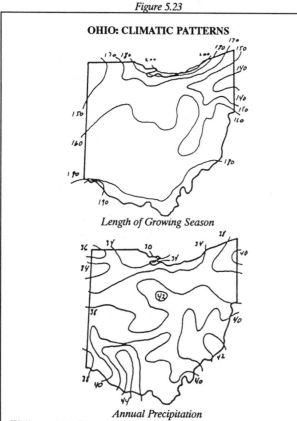

OHIO: CLIMATIC PATTERNS

Length of Growing Season

Annual Precipitation

While the Ohio River region was the first area for major winegrowing endeavors, disease eliminated nearly all such efforts and transferred the industry to Lake Erie. The reasons are not hard to find: the Lake Erie region has a longer growing season, a more temperate climate, higher incidence of sunshine, and less rainfall during the growing season.

Source: U.S. Weather Bureau

The history of grape growing and experimental

winemaking in Ohio begins with Elijah Fay along Lake Erie in 1818, and Moravian missionaries who first settled in the Gallipolis and Marietta areas of southeastern Ohio several years later. Winemaking as a viable commercial economic activity first surfaced in southern Ohio along the banks of the Ohio River in the 1820s when Nicholas Longworth (the "little man from Cincinnati") realized the full potential of the hardy Catawba grape, the most popular variety in Ohio at the time. Discovered in North Carolina in 1801, Catawba was propagated by Major John Adlum in Georgetown, D.C. who sent cuttings to Longworth in 1825. The vine became so popular along the Ohio River that by 1850 more than 95 percent of all grape varieties in the Cincinnati region were Catawba.

Figure 5.24

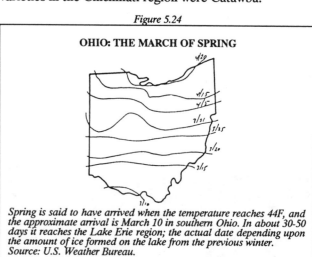

OHIO: THE MARCH OF SPRING

Spring is said to have arrived when the temperature reaches 44F, and the approximate arrival is March 10 in southern Ohio. In about 30-50 days it reaches the Lake Erie region; the actual date depending upon the amount of ice formed on the lake from the previous winter. Source: U.S. Weather Bureau.

Once fully established, vine acreage grew rapidly from 350 acres in 1845 to 3,000 acres in 1859, the year Ohio led all other states in wine production with an output of 568,617 gallons, or 35 percent of the national output. Of the total, Hamilton County (Cincinnati) contributed nearly two-thirds of the state's total. This rather phenomenal growth was sustained by a large and steady stream of German immigrants from the Rhine Valley. It is also significant to note that Ohio was also in the center of significant grape hybridization efforts. It is estimated that during the period 1820-1895, more than 200 new grape varieties were developed, of which Union Village (by the Shakers), Ives, Black Pearl, and Campbell Early were the most important.

Although Nicholas Longworth in 1845 said that "The day is not distant when the Ohio River will rival the Rhine in the quality and quantity of this wine....It rivals the best Hock and makes a superior Champagne," there is little to indicate that the next 150 years have been accurately prophesied. Although Longworth founded and dominated the Ohio wine industry for 30 years and made it the premier wine producing state in the nation, today the state's wine industry is characterized by one huge wine holding company that makes more than 85 percent of the state's wine, and, by last count, 43 small, cottage-type wineries, nearly all of which produce typical midwestern sweet to semi-sweet, grapey-flavored, American-based wines. Except for Markko Vineyards, Chateau Debonne, Harpersfield Vineyard, Wyandotte Wine Cellar, and a few others, most wineries lack dedication, expertise, and the necessary capital to become viable commercial entities necessary to engender a reputation beyond a local following.

Winemaking in Ohio was big business in the nineteenth century. In 1860, Ohio led the nation in wine production, and not only did it possess the largest winery in the nation in 1871, it was the first and leading state in the nation for the production of sparkling wine. Ohio was also the home to many ambitious viticultural historical figures: Nicholas Longworth, the largest vineyard owner in the state who pioneered sparkling wine production (1847); James Taylor and Robert Buchanan, like Longworth were early pioneers; Henry Ives developed the Ives grape; Kaspar Schraidt developed Black Pearl; and Charles Carpenter developed several minor varieties. Winemaking in Ohio, however, after the death of Longworth followed two divergent paths.

Although Lonz Winery, Middle Bass Island, Lake Erie, is no longer making wine, it breathes the history of nineteenth century America.
Baxevanis

Due to black rot and mildew, vineyard abandonment became common during the Civil War, and by 1870 winemaking became a thing of the past throughout the Ohio River. But along the southern shores of Lake Erie, an area known for its windy and less humid weather, the lighter, sandier soils lowered operating costs (in comparison to the heavier clay soils of the Ohio River), and "vine fever" gripped the population. Railroads made the area a major transportation corridor and it attracted many am-

bitious men like J. Kirtland, Irad and Datus Kelley, Lewis Harms, Andrew Wehrle, Charles Carpenter, and others.

Although Catawba was the favorite, Concord, Isabella, Ives, Cynthiana, and Clinton were also widely planted. During the 30 year period of 1865 to 1895, several large wineries were established by German immigrants, and grape acreage rose steeply from 5,000 to more than 33,000 acres, most of which occurred on the Erie Islands, and in Lake, Ashtabula and Ottawa counties. By this time, the "old" historic Ohio River vineyard cultivated fewer than 100 acres. Vine acreage at this time stood at sixteen times present levels and grape output (more than 50,000 tons) was five times the output of 1987. Despite the fact that grapes were sold for table use as well as processing, Ohio ranked third as a wine producing state throughout this period. Acreage declined precipitously after 1895 due to a number of disastrous years when Black Rot decimated vineyards throughout the midwest. Yet there was considerable improvement after the Welch Food Co. began to process Ohio Concord grapes for juice production early in this century. Wine production grew from 400,000 gallons in 1904 to 1.5 million gallons by 1908.

Unfortunately, vineyard abandonment became common as Ohio failed to compete with other states, and acreage over the next 20 years declined to 15,000 where it stabilized until 1950 when it once again began to steadily fall to present levels. Grape growing was particularly vulnerable during the 1895-1919 period due to the propagandistic effects of the temperance movement and the cumulative effect of Black rot, mildew, a string of exceptionally cold winters, and low grape prices, all of which severely curtailed wine production by 1920. Like elsewhere, acreage expanded during Prohibition due to home winemaking demands, but the new acreage was mainly confined to Lake Erie near the Pennsylvania border. Of all the grapes grown in northern Ohio, it was the Concord that was most in demand, and as Catawba and other grapes declined, the Concord maintained its supremacy accounting for as much as 85 percent of the planted acreage. After Repeal, the state's wine industry lost its former leading role in sparkling wine production to New York, its *vin ordinaire* to California, and has only been able to maintain a minor foothold in the production of inexpensive sweet wines. As a result, vine acreage and wine production began to decline precipitously between 1940 and 1965, and it was only in the 1970s that it made a mild recovery. A minor turning point occurred in the late 1960s with the introduction of French-American varieties that were not widely accepted by growers as demand then laid steadfastly with American-flavored wines. Despite the recent introduction of Vinifera and French-American varieties and an active program to improve grape quality, total acreage continues to decline.

Figure 5.25

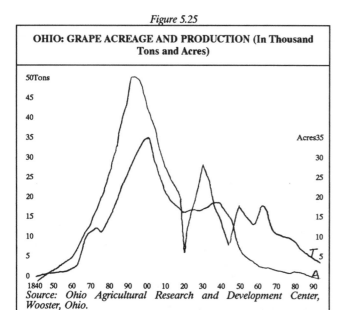

OHIO: GRAPE ACREAGE AND PRODUCTION (In Thousand Tons and Acres)

Source: Ohio Agricultural Research and Development Center, Wooster, Ohio.

Eventually, in an attempt to improve image, flavor, and market share within the state, the wine industry became fragmented into three main branches. Paramount Distillers began to purchase historic wineries (Meier's Wine Cellars, Lonz Winery, Mon Ami, and Manley Vineyards), and make a complete line of wines by using both Ohio and non-Ohio grapes. The second group, consisting of a small number of quality producers (headed by Markko) using Vinifera and/or French-American grapes, make premium wine. The third group, more than 90 percent of all producers, are nothing more than cottage industries who make small amounts of American and, in increasing quantities, French-American-based wines that are substantially below national quality levels. Indeed, of the 43 wineries in the state, 6 make fewer than 1,000 cases, another 7 between 1,000 and 1,500 cases, 11 between 2,000 and 3,000 cases, and 7 between 4,000 and 5,000 cases. Eight wineries make between 6,000 and 23,000 cases, and the largest, outside the Paramount group of wineries, makes 40,000 cases. Today, the "Buckeye State," part of the dairy and corn belt, ranks eleventh in grape production, and eighth in wine output, a significant drop in the national standings when it ranked second or third in all categories at the turn of the century. Within the state, grapes rank third in value after apples and strawberries. Nevertheless, the direct and indirect economic impact of the wine industry for 1988 was $1.2 billion.

Ohio, which ranked as the leading wine producing state in 1859, dropped to third place in 1940, and ninth place by 1980, a year that saw acreage decline to 3,000 acres, down nearly 2,000 acres from 1959. By 1992, vine acreage declined still further to fewer than 1,800. The number of vineyards fell from nearly 400 in 1959 to 242 in 1982, and fewer than 150 by 1992. More significantly, the

number of growers has declined from 394 in 1968 to 150 in 1992, and wine production has not kept pace with consumption. Grape production now averages between 5,000 and 9,000 tons annually, of which only one-third is made into wine. Concord and other Labrusca grapes comprise 84 percent of the planted acreage; French-American varieties account for 15 percent and Vinifera vines account for just over 100 acres. The area east of Cleveland continues to be the historic bastion of Concord, while Erie, Ottawa and Sandusky counties are mainly planted in Catawba, where they are locally known as "Cats." While Concord and Catawba dominate, other popular varieties are Delaware, Niagara and Dutchess. The most common French-American grapes are: Vidal Blanc, Seyval, Vignoles, Cayuga, Chambourcin, Chancellor, DeChaunac, Marechal Foch, and Baco Noir. While the recent resurgence of vinegrowing in the Ohio Valley has a tendency to emphasize French-American varieties, nearly all Vinifera plantings are confined to Riesling, Chardonnay, Pinot Noir, and Cabernet Sauvignon, geographically concentrated on the Lake Erie islands, Ashtabula County, and the Conneaut area. The latest statistics indicate that 65 percent of all grapes are processed, 30 percent are used for winemaking, and 5 percent are grown for table use.

Figure 5.26

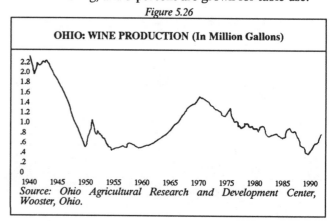

OHIO: WINE PRODUCTION (In Million Gallons)

Source: Ohio Agricultural Research and Development Center, Wooster, Ohio.

More important, improvement of wine quality has not been as rapid as that from Michigan, New York, or the mid-Atlantic states. The industry is still dependent upon sweet Labrusca-based wines (invariably high in alcohol, coarse and blended with inexpensive California wine), and wineries, all to often, are of the opinion that as long as the propensity for inexpensive sweet wine by the large central and east-European population exists, they will continue to meet this demand. So much sweet wine is consumed along Lake Erie that winemakers are fond of saying that "Ohio is closer to Germany than California." A few, and only a few, wineries are consistently making quality table wines from French-American and Vinifera varietals. There is, however, a bright side to the above-mentioned negative viticultural climate. The Ohio Wine Producers Association was organized in 1975, the Ohio

Grape Industries Program in 1981, and, in an effort to reduce the deterioration in the state's wine industry, the Ohio legislature reduced taxes on Ohio-produced wines and increased financial allocation for research and promotion in 1982. Furthermore, there has been a renewed spirit in the Ohio State OARDC at Wooster to improve grape varieties, vineyard practices and wine quality.

Ohio has five *ava's*: *Lake Erie (1983), Isle St. George (1982), Grand River Valley (1983), Loramie Creek (1982),* and *Ohio River Valley (1983)*. The 1 square mile *Isle St. George ava*, one of the smallest in the nation, has the highest grape density. The unique quality of this island lies in the fact that its subsoil is derived from dolomite, unlike the softer limestone on other islands and shale along Lake Erie. No point on the island is higher than fourteen feet from the lake level, and the moderating effect of the surrounding water extends the growing season beyond 200 days. All grapes are forwarded to the mainland for processing as there is no winery on the island. It is interesting to note that the *Ohio River Valley ava*, with 26,000 square miles, contains fewer than 500 vine acres.

The *Lake Erie ava* is a 4,075 square mile region that begins near Toledo in the northwestern portion of the state and continues along the southern shore of the lake into New York State. The alternation of succeeding continental ice movement not only produced the lake, but along the south shoreline layers of shale, limestone and dolomite. It is a narrow belt climatically defined by a 10F-15F difference between lake margins and 15 miles inland. The *ava* contains the bulk of the vineyards and 26 of the 45 wineries, plus another 15 in Pennsylvania and New York. About 26,000 acres of vineland are found between northcentral Ohio and Fredonia, New York, forming the next most important vineyard concentration east of the Rocky Mountains. Eighty-five percent of the acreage is planted in Concords, more than three-quarters of which are used for processing, the remainder for winemaking.

Throughout the entire region, the frost-free season varies between 175 to 185 days, but in a few localities it often extends to 195 days. The lake effect is much broader in Ohio and Pennsylvania, but in New York, due to the proximity of the Allegheny Plateau, the moderating influences of the lake are limited to within 3 miles. What makes Lake Erie an interesting *ava* is the fact that the lake has, by far, with an average depth of only 58 feet and one-thirtieth the volume of Lake Superior against a surface area of nearly 10,000 square miles, the largest surface to volume ratio of any of the Great Lakes. As a result, Lake Erie encounters the greatest annual temperature variation of any of the Great Lakes. Temperatures range from a high of 72F in late August to 30F in January, a month in which the lake contains 90 percent or more ice cover than any other Great Lake. In addition, there are fewer thunderstorms near the lake, more sunlight, and

less fog than any area within 250 miles. Also significant is the fact that while spring frosts are quite common in Ohio (especially the western section), the Chautauqua region of New York suffers very little (the notorious Christmas massacre of 1980 when temperatures fell from 32F to -20F within a six hour period in the Finger lakes region, did not greatly affect this portion of the Lake Erie grape belt).

Markko Vineyard, the premier winery in the state is known for Chardonnay, Cabernet Sauvignon, and Riesling.

The *Grand River Valley ava*, an enclave of the Lake Erie *ava*, follows the path of the Grand River in Lake, Ashtabula and Geauga counties. Supposedly, the improved air drainage within the river valley distinguishes this *ava* from surrounding areas. Bordered by the Loramie and Tuttle Creeks, *Loramie Creek*, a 3,600-acre *ava* located in Shelby County in the western portion of the state, is the only *ava* not sited near a major natural body of water. Although there are two man-made lakes in the region built to furnish water to the Miami Canal, winter temperatures habitually fall to -20F, deadly spring frosts are endemic, the growing season is less than 170 days, and the *ava* lies on the margin where cooler Canadian air meets warmer and much more humid Gulf air creating an unstable climatic pattern. Nevertheless, there are five small wineries in the region, two of which are located within the *ava*. The *Ohio River Valley ava*, one of the largest in the nation in terms of total square miles (30,000), continues for 25 to 30 miles on both banks of the Ohio River from Wheeling, West Virginia to the Illinois border (it includes only portions of Ohio, West Virginia, Indiana, and Kentucky). Despite its immense size, the *ava* contains fewer than 550 vine acres, and fewer than fifteen wineries. It was in Vevay, Indiana that one of the nation's first commercial vineyards was established in 1803. The name is derived from the Iroquois word *Ohyui*, meaning "great river." Needless to say, precipitation, temperature, and soil conditions are highly variable. The wineries are:

Anthony M. Greco (Middletown, 1983), is a 6-acre, 800-case winery that makes good, sound Seyval, Vidal Blanc, Cayuga, and DeChaunac.

Breitenbach Wine Cellars (Dover, 1980), is an 11,000-case, American, French-American, fruit and berry winery with a reputation for Niagara, Delaware, Catawba, and Chancellor from purchased grapes. Other labels: *Charming Nancy, Frost Fire, Dusty Miller*, among others.

Brushcreek Vineyards (Pebbles, 1977), is a 2-acre, 350-case winery that makes Niagara, Catawba, and a Concord/Marechal-Foch blend.

Buccia Vineyards (Conneaut, 1978), is a 4-acre, 800-case winery that makes good, sound Seyval, Vignoles, Baco Noir, and a Steuben blush.

Cantwell's Old Mill Winery (Geneva, 1986), is a 4,000-case winery that makes a large selection, the best of which are Vignoles, Riesling, Chardonnay, Catawba, Cayuga, Gewurztraminer, Vidal Blanc, Niagara, Concord, and Chambourcin. The winery, housed in an old grist mill that dates back to 1864, also makes sparkling wines.

Carl M. Limpert Winery (Westlake, 1934), is a 15-acre, 800-case Concord and Niagara winery.

Chalet Debonne Vineyards (Madison, 1971), is a well-regarded, 70-acre, 40,000-case winery that makes American, French-American and Vinifera wines, of which premium vintage-dated varietals are sold under the *Debevc Vineyards* label (Chardonnay, Riesling, Vignoles, Vidal Blanc, Seyval, and Cabernet Sauvignon are the finest), offering good value.

Colonial Vineyards (Lebanon, 1977), is a 5-acre, 1,500-case winery that makes mostly American grape wine, but Seyval appears to be the finest.

Dankorona Winery (Aurora, 1986), is a 3,000-case winery that makes a large assortment of American, French-American and Vinifera wines (Riesling, Vidal Blanc, Aurore, Niagara, Seyval, and Delaware) from purchased fruit.

Dover Vineyards (Westlake, 1932), originally a cooperative, has functioned as a private winery since 1959. It makes undisclosed quantities of American-based wines (under many labels) blended with imported wine and grape concentrate.

Ferrante Winery and Vineyard (Geneva, 1937), is a 50-acre, 22,000-case winery that makes Chardonnay, Riesling, Seyval, Cayuga, Vidal Blanc, Delaware, Niagara, Catawba, and proprietary wines.

Firelands Wine Company (Sandusky, 1986), is a 30-acre, 80,000-case winery that also processes grapes and must for several related labels. It continues to produce and market wines under the *Mantey* label, as well as a new line of varietal wines under the *Firelands* label. More than 95 percent of all wines are American and French-American-based, mostly sweet, flavored, and overpriced. Sparkling wines are also made. This is not a growers cooperative but the central offices and processing center for four wineries/labels that are part of Paramount Distillers: Lonz Winery (Middle Bass Island, 1875); Mantey Vineyards (Sandusky, 1880); Mon Ami Winery (Port Clinton, 1934); and Meier's Wine Cellars (Silverton, 1895).

Grand River Wine Company (Madison, 1971), is a 20-acre, 4,000-case winery that makes above-average American, French-American, and Vinifera wines, of which Vignoles, Cayuga, Chardonnay, Gewurztraminer, and Chambourcin are the finest.

Hafle Vineyards Winery (Springfield, 1974), is a 2-acre, 2,000-case American and French-American winery.

Harpersfield Vineyard (Geneva, 1986), is a 16-acre, 1,000-case, Vinifera-only winery that makes excellent Chardonnay, Gewurztraminer, Riesling, and sparkling wines (from Chardonnay and Pinot Noir). Representing one of the top four wineries in the state, its impressive assortment of wines should not be overlooked.

Heineman Winery (Put-In-Bay, 1888), is a 50-acre, 18,000-case winery with a spectacular view of Lake Erie that makes a large assortment of American, French-American, and Vinifera wines. Most are sweet, moderately priced, American-based blended wines, offering good value. The Niagara, Riesling, Seyval, and Vidal Blanc are interesting.

Heritage Vineyards (West Milton, 1978), is a 20-acre, 5,500-case American and French-American winery.

Johlin Century Winery (Oregon, 1870), is an old, well-established, 5,000-case winery that makes blended American wine from purchased grapes, and an interesting strawberry wine.

John Christ Winery (Avon Lake, 1947), is an 18-acre, 3,000-case, American, French-American, fruit and berry winery.

Kelley's Island Wine Company (Kelley's Island, 1982), is a 10-acre, 8,000-case label that makes proprietary French-American and limited amounts of Chardonnay and Riesling, partly from purchased grapes.

The dry Vignoles is interesting.

Klinghirn Winery (Avon Lake, 1935), is a 15-acre, 6,000-case winery that makes American, French-American, and fruit wines, of which Vidal Blanc and cherry are particularly good.

Markko Vineyard (Conneaut, 1968), is a superb, 14-acre, 2,500-case winery that makes absolutely marvelous Vinifera-based wines, particularly Chardonnay, Riesling, late harvest Muscat, Cabernet Sauvignon, Pinot Noir, proprietary, and a superb sparkling wine that should not be missed. The expertly-made wines, the finest in the state, exhibit a dark color, are full-bodied, muscular, robust, and well oaked.

Meier's Wine Cellars Inc. (Silverton, 1895), with an annual production of more than 1.1 million cases, this is the largest winery in Ohio. Owned by Paramount Distillers, this firm produces large quantities of Catawba-based sparkling wine, proprietary blends, and dessert wines. Total production for Meier's and all other associated wineries/labels is estimated at 1.2 million cases.

McIntosh's Ohio Valley Wines (Bethel, 1972), is a friendly, reliable and well-regarded, 25-acre, 5,000-case, American, French-American and berry winery, offering good value.

Moyer Vineyards (Manchester, 1973), is a 12-acre, 4,200-case, French-American, Vinifera and berry winery, of which Vidal Blanc, Chambourcin, strawberry, and sparkling wines are the finest.

Old Firehouse Winery (Geneva-on-the-Lake, 1988), is a small negociant concern (distributes Sauvignon Blanc, Vidal Blanc, and coolers) that also makes 1,700 cases of Catawba.

Pompei Winery (Cleveland, 1914), is a 10,000-case, American-based winery/bottler.

Portage Hills Vineyards (Suffield, 1987), is a 17-acre, 4,000-case winery that makes more than one dozen Labrusca, French-American, Vinifera, and berry wines.

Rainbow Hills Vineyard (Newcomerstown, 1988), is a 2-acre, 1,200-case winery that makes blended Labrusca, French-American, mint and sassafrass wines.

Rolling Hills Winery (Conneaut, 1988), is a 3-acre, 1,000-case winery that makes Niagara, Catawba, Concord, Baco Noir, Steuben, and proprietary wines.

Ronsara Winery (Lebanon, 1988), is an 8-acre, 1,500-case winery that makes Vidal Blanc, Seyval, Niagara, Catawba, DeChaunac, Baco Noir, and Concord wines.

Shamrock Vineyard (Waldo, 1084), is a good, 4-acre, 1,500-case, American, French-American, and fruit winery best known for Seyval, Vidal Blanc, Chancellor, and proprietary wines.

Steuk Wine Company (Sandusky, 1855), is a 4-acre, 2,000-case, mainly American, French-American grape, and sparkling winery. It is the only one in the state that makes Black Pearl, an obscure grape that along with Campbell's Early and Ives were developed in Ohio. The winery also grows Beta, Elvira and Montefiore. It is the second oldest winery in the nation still owned and operated by the founding family (Mirassou is older by one year).

One of the more unusual American grapes still in production.

Stillwater Wineries (Troy, 1981), located on a gravel pit, is a 17-acre, 23,000-case winery that makes good, sound Labrusca and French-American wines. Vidal Blanc, Cayuga, and Catawba are particularly good.

Tannery Hill Winery (Ashtabula, 1985), is a 2,500-case, American-based winery producing from purchased must.

The Winery at Wolf Creek (Norton, 1984), is a 14-acre, 2,600-case winery that makes above-average French-American wines.

Troy Winery (Troy, 1988), is a 17-acre, 3,000-case winery that makes interesting Niagara, Cayuga, Vidal Blanc, Delaware, Catawba, Concord, and berry wines.

Valley Vineyards Farm (Morrow, 1969), is a 50-acre, 6,000-case, American and French-American winery that makes good Vidal Blanc, Catawba and Baco Noir. The winery also makes the state's only Blue Eye wine from a grape variety that was first developed in Missouri as a table grape from T.V. Munson varieties.

Vinoklet Winery (Cincinnati, 1987), is a 15-acre, 3,500-case winery that makes Niagara, Vidal Blanc, Catawba, Concord, DeChaunac, and Chardonnay from California grapes.

Wickliffe Winery (Wickliffe, 1911), is a 400-case winery that makes Niagara, Concord, Catawba, and fortified wines.

Willow Hill Vineyards (Johnstown, 1988), is a 7-acre, 2,000-case winery that makes Vidal Blanc, Seyval, and several Labrusca-based wines.

Wyandotte Wine Cellar (Gahanna, 1976), is a 3,000-case winery that makes a large assortment of fruit, berry, and grape wines from purchased grapes. This successful winery has founded a sister winery (**William Greystone Winery**) in Columbus. The facility is housed in the former Schlee Bavarian Brewery, listed in the National Register of Historic Places. Of interest is Chardonnay and raspberry.

Iowa, Illinois And Indiana

These three, flat, agriculturally rich corn belt states (innovators in corn, soybean, and pig production) collectively cultivate 700 acres of vines and produce fewer than 200,000 cases of wine, or one-tenth their 1880 acreage and production figures respectively. Historically, the bitterly cold winters and vast ocean of prairie grass repelled rather than attracted settlers. The thick prairie sod, too tough for ordinary plowshares, was considered worthless until the railroad, reaper and steel plow offered proper conditions for effective agricultural settlement. Although grapes were widely planted along the more humid and hiller southern portions of all three states, a combination of cold winters, politics, and 2, 4-D, a deadly weed killer, finally convinced growers that corn and grapes were neither symbiotic nor profitable. Together, these three states have one of the lowest (except for the greater Chicago area) per capita wine consumption levels, high whiskey consumption levels, and high winery mortality levels in the nation.

Iowa (the "Hawkeye" state), a large state with a declining population of less than 3 million, is the locus of the corn belt economy in the prairie regions of America. Its economy for more than three generations has focused on the production of just four commodities: corn, soybean, beef, and pork. Despite contemporary low levels, 100 years ago Iowa produced more than 300,000 gallons of wine mainly from wild American grapes and rhubarb (or *piestengel* wine) by several Amana Colonies (located in Homestead, Amana, East, Middle, West, South, and High Amana), utopic religious communities of Germanic origin. A good deal of the "colonies wine" was labeled "naturally fermented other than standard wine" that referred to the addition of sugar in order to raise alcohol levels (it

was reported that one resourceful colony even made wine from milk).

However, in corn-growing, whiskey-drinking Iowa, today's output, the product of ten wineries, is 70,000 gallons, most of it sweet fruit and berry wine made from purchased fruit. The principal area for grape production is the small Cedar River Valley near the Illinois border. While sales were historically restricted to 216 stores, as of 1985 Iowa is no longer a "controlled" state. As a consequence of "deregulation" there has been a 41 percent increase in wine sales as the law now allows wine to be sold in groceries, drug stores, service stations, and restaurants.

The most important, quality-oriented winery, and the only one producing nothing but grape table wine, is **Vollbehr Cellars** (Tipton, 1985), an 11-acre, 2,500-case, French-American and Vinifera winery. The only other grape-oriented winery (it also makes fruit and berry wines) is **Christina Wine Cellars** (McGregor, 1974). Part of the Lawler group of family-owned wineries, it makes 3,500-cases of table, dessert, and sparkling wines from purchased fruit. The following are primarily fruit and berry wineries with only a small portion of their output being grape: **Ackerman Winery** (South Amana, 1956, 3,500 cases); **Der Winekeller** (Amana, 1974, 6,500-cases); **Ehrle Bros. Winery** (Homestead, 1934, 2,400 cases); **The Grape Vine Winery** (Amana, 1982, 2 acres, 3,500 cases); **Little Amana Winery** (Amana, 1971, 3,500-cases); **Old Wine Cellar** (Amana, 1961, 3,000 cases); **Private Stock Winery** (Boone, 1977, 8,000 cases, the largest in the state); and **Sandstone Winery** (Amana, 1960, 3,000 cases).

Grapes were first planted in Illinois ("the Crossroads" and "Prairie" state) in 1851 by two German immigrants, and while it produced more than 142,000 gallons of wine from locally grown fruit by 1880, like so many others in middle America, Illinois never recovered after Prohibition. For a time, Nauvoo, a former Mormon stronghold, became the state's wine capital when French Icarian communists planted vines and produced wine. Success, given the instability of the utopian community and competition from other agricultural crops, proved to be a short-lived experience, and the last winery ceased operations in 1986.

In 1977, Illinois ranked third in the production of wine because of the presence of the Mogen David Corporation, headquartered in Chicago that made wine from grapes, must, and wine shipped from other states. With the demise of this company and facilities, Illinois is a state with fewer than 100 vine acres (mostly American and French-American varieties) and seven wineries:

Alto Vineyards, Ltd. (Alto Pass, 1988), is an 8-acre, 2,000-case winery that makes above-average to excellent Concord, Catawba, Vidal Blanc, Villard Blanc and Noir, Vignoles, and Chambourcin, the latter particularly good. **Baxter's Vineyards** (Nauvoo, 1857), formerly Gem City Vineland Company, and the oldest winery in the state, closed during 1986-1988 and reopened under its present name in 1989. It has replanted 42 acres, and expects to make more than 5,000 cases of Concord, Catawba, Delaware, Niagara, and other wines under the *Old Nauvoo Winery* label. **Chateau RA-HA** (Grafton, 1985), located near the Missouri border, makes 450 cases of grape and fruit wines, mainly from purchased American and French-American grapes. **Galena Cellars Winery** (Galena, 1984), part of the Lawler group of wineries, is a 7,500-case fruit, berry, and American/French-American-based table, dessert, and sparkling winery. **Lynfred Winery** (Roselle, 1979), is a successful, highly innovative, 7,000-case winery with a reputation for a large selection of Vinifera, French-American, fruit (apricot is particularly interesting) and berry wines produced from purchased fruit and must from California, Washington, and various areas in the midwest (Chardonnay, Chenin Blanc, Seyval Blanc, Riesling, Sauvignon Blanc, and Cabernet Sauvignon, offering good value). This winery, one of the finest in the midwest, often produces exceptional wines worthy of any disciplined cellar, and should not be overlooked. **Thompson Vineyard and Winery** (Monee, 1964), is an "on again, off again" winery that makes 1,000 cases of sparkling, fruit, berry, and tables wines, mainly French-American from purchased fruit. **Waterloo Winery** (Waterloo, 1985), is a progressive and innovative, 12-acre, 3,000-case winery that makes above-average Riesling, Moore's Diamond, Vignoles, Seyval, Baco Noir, Chambourcin, Villard Noir, Chelois, and New York Muscat. The vineyard, located on reclaimed coal land, contains more than 35 experimental grape vines.

Vevay, Indiana, marks the second vineyard attempt by Jean Jacques Dufour after his failure in Lexington, Kentucky, first planted in 1798 when he established the Kentucky Vineyard Society. Dufour petitioned Congress for land claiming that the Ohio River could furnish the Atlantic States, West Indies, and Canada with wine. Vineyards were again established in 1987, 186 years after the introduction of commercial vinegrowing in southern Indiana. It is also interesting to note that Vevay, Switzerland (pop. 17,000, a suburb of Lausanne), is the corporate headquarters of the Nestle Corporation ($33 billion in sales), owners of Wine World Estates of Napa, California. Today, the above vineyard is owned by the Vevay Switzerland County Foundation, Inc. Baxevanis

Indiana is a medium-sized state with 5.6 million people, of which more than half live in two metropolitan areas: greater Chicago-Gary, and Indianapolis. The state, flat and wind-swept, lacks (except for a small section bordering Lake Michigan and the Ohio River) the necessary hilly, mountainous and water requirements to temper the "arctic express," bitterly cold northern winter winds. As a result, the fledgling 500-acre grape industry is located in the extreme southern portion of the state. Like most states bordering the Ohio River, the "Hoosier" state had a thriving wine industry early in the nineteenth century (one Jean Jacques Dufour, a Swiss, established a vineyard in Vevay, which disappeared in 1830 due to Black Rot), and while the industry suffered the same fate from disease,

Prohibition, and competition from California, it was revived after the passage of the Small Winery Act of 1971. Since then no fewer than eighteen wineries have been established, but, unfortunately, half have ceased operations in recent years. One positive note is the recent planting of nearly eight acres of French-American vines on terraced slopes overlooking the Ohio River in Vevay.

As in the nineteenth century, the hilly, protected areas along the Ohio River still provide the finest sites for a resurgent wine industry. The area enjoys the longest growing season in the state, and well-drained, wind-blown soils deep and rich in mineral matter. With considerable limestone rock, it is a perfect site for the production of quality sparkling wines, hitherto, an unrealized potential. The only *ava's* are the southern extension of the *Lake Michigan Shore* delimited area, and the *Ohio River Valley ava*, both of which were described above. In addition to the non-commercial quantities of wine made by a seminary in Saint Meinad, the principal wineries are:

Brown County Winery (Unionville, 1985), is a 1,500-case winery that makes good, sound Concord, Seyval, Vidal Blanc, Marechal Foch, fruit and berry wines from purchased fruit. **Butler Winery** (Bloomington, 1982), formerly The Bloomington Winery, is a 3,000-case, French-American, sparkling, fruit and berry winery located near Indiana University that makes good, grapey wines. **Chateau Pomije** (New Alsace, 1987), is a young, aggressive, 40-acre, 2,500-case winery that makes good, sound Seyval, Vidal Blanc, Marechal Foch, DeChaunac, and Steuben. **Chateau Thomas Winery** (Indianapolis, 1984), is a 2,000-case winery that makes Chardonnay, Riesling, Sauvignon Blanc, Cabernet Sauvignon, Merlot, and Zinfandel from purchased California grapes. **Easley Enterprises Inc.** (Indianapolis, 1974), is a 20-acre, 2,000-case, French-American winery that uses grapes grown in Cape Sandy along the Ohio River. **Huber Orchard Winery** (Borden, 1978), is a 10-acre, 6,500-case, American, French-American, fruit and berry winery. **Kauffman Winery** (Mt. Vernon, 1988), is 7-acre, 1,000-case winery that makes Seyval, generic and proprietary wines. **Oliver Wine Co.** (Bloomington, 1972), is a 12-acre, 11,000-case, American, French-American, Vinifera (from California fruit), and mead winery. **Possom Trot Vineyards** (Unionville, 1978), is a 3-acre, 1,000-case, French-American and fruit winery. **Scotella Vineyards & Winery** (Madison, 1985), is an aggressive, 11-acre, 7,000-case, French-American winery that makes above-average Vidal Blanc, Aurore, DeChaunac, Baco Noir, Seyval, and Marechal Foch. **The Ridge Winery** (Vevay, 1991), is a 7-acre, 1,000-case winery that makes French-American wines, principally Seyval and Vidal Blanc. **Villa Milan Vineyard** (Milan, 1983), is a 10-acre, 4,000-case winery that grows American and French-American grapes, and makes above-average quality DeChaunac.

Missouri

Missouri, a large state in land area, contains a population that is smaller than neighboring Indiana, more than half of which is concentrated in metropolitan St. Louis. Because of its location and the fact that it is bordered by eight other states, Missouri is often called the "Center State," and, in many ways, it mirrors the rest of the country in terms of geography, history, and demographics. While the Spanish were the first to loosely administer the region, it was the French that established the first settlements, introduced slavery, and were soon followed by Irish, English, and German immigrants. Italians began to arrive in the second half of the nineteenth century, as did other non-Anglo-Saxon Europeans. As a result, nearly all the state's counties are named after prominent American and French names, with a scattering of Indian place names.

Missouri, historically a "border state," lies adjacent to the Corn Belt, the Great Plains, the humid South, and Southwest. The northcentral section of the state is known as "Little Dixie" due to its southern sympathies and politics; the region west of St. Louis is known as "Missouri Rhineland" due to heavy Germanic settlement; a portion of the Ozarks is known as the "Irish Wilderness" due to the poverty of this hilly physiographic province; several counties in northwestern Missouri are known as "Mormon Country" due to the historic presence of a large Mormon population; the central portion of the Missouri River is known as "Boonslick Country" after Daniel Boone, Boonville, and salt production; the eastern and central portions of the state are known as "Hildalgo Country" after a small group of families who received large Spanish Land Grants; and the region of southwest Missouri is known as "Bootheel," due to cotton and soybean production.

Figure 5.27

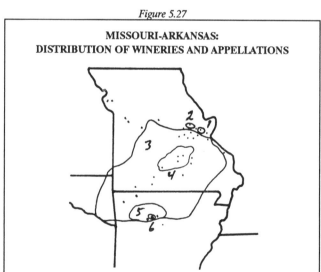

MISSOURI-ARKANSAS:
DISTRIBUTION OF WINERIES AND APPELLATIONS

The most important grape growing counties in Missouri with two-thirds of the planted acreage are: Adair, Crawford, Gasconade, Phelps, Platte, St. Charles, and Wright.

The centrality of Missouri is also highlighted by the fact that for most of its course the Missouri River marks the southern boundary of continental glaciation, and significant climatic boundaries. In many ways, Daniel Boone exhibits the spirit of the frontier; the Missouri River, the gateway to the west; Mark Twain, the restless spirit that attempted to bridge the east with the west; and continental location in the center of the nation represents an inability to overcome viticultural obstacles to successful commercial winegrowing.

Nationally ranking second in number of farms, hay,

beef, and hog production, Missouri is a classic "Corn Belt" state. While it ranks fifteenth in grape production and thirty-second nationally in per capita wine consumption, in the midwest it ranks third in the output of wine, third in vine acreage, and second in grape production. Producing a scant 2,700 tons annually, Missouri accounts for .1 percent of the nation's total grape harvest. Wine output, reflecting the ups and downs of grape production (the state produced 11,200 tons of grapes in 1931 and only 900 tons in 1985) in America's heartland, has stabilized at 170,000 gallons.

Wine was first made from native vines in 1823 by Jesuit priests, but domesticated vines were not planted until 1843 when one Jacob Fugger introduced the Isabella. Cynthiana, Catawba, Concord, and Delaware followed soon after. By 1843, Hermann, a small town on the Missouri River 80 miles west of St. Louis, became a prime vine producing center and major center for the development of new varieties. The Elvira grape was developed by Jacob Rommel, Hermann by F. Langendoerfer, Martha by Samuel Miller, Missouri Riesling and Grein Golden by Nicholas Grein, several by Hermann Jaeger, and Dry Mill Beauty by the Robyns family. It is estimated that during the relatively short period of 1844 and 1885, more than 200 grape varieties were developed in the state.

So important was the grape to this German community that the town of Hermann endorsed grape culture by encouraging any resident to take from one to five vacant "public" lots at a cost of $50 each, to be paid within five years without interest providing the owner grow grapes on them. The largest winery in the state, and one of the most impressive in the nation--Stone Hill Winery--was founded in 1847 (it became the second largest in the nation and the third largest in the world by the turn of the century). For a time, Cook's Imperial Champagne Cellar of St. Louis was a primary sparkling wine producer, and one of the largest wineries in the midwest.

A favorable account of the agricultural wealth of north central Missouri was given by one Baron Von Bock ("Report On A Journey To The Western States Of North America") in 1829, and for the Dutzow area in particular (founded in 1835), which did much to encourage German immigration, primarily during the years 1830-1870. This significant immigration stream brought about a major effort in the cultivation of fruits, especially apples and grapes. A large number of these settlers, who came from the Rhine and laid roots along the Missouri River, were very adept in cultivating vines, and by 1845 there were 300 acres in Hermann alone, a figure that increased to 650 in 1846, 900 acres in 1848, and 1,100 acres by 1849.

The winegrowing success at Hermann led to extensive plantings at Ste. Genevieve, Boonville, Franklin, Warren, and St. Charles counties. By 1856, 100,000 gallons of wine were made in Hermann, and as viticultural efforts progressed, Missouri, on the eve of The Civil War, was responsible for one-third of America's total wine output. The early grapes in Hermann were Isabella, Catawba, and Cynthiana. For a short time St. Louis formed the hub of wine production and distribution in middle America. The Missouri Wine Company, founded in 1832, was acquired by Isaac Cook, who launched the highly celebrated Cook's Imperial Champagne, a wine that was bottled at a rate of 10,000 bottles a day by 1901. Other notable wineries were Cliff Cave Wine Company, Isidor Bush & Co., The Stone Hill Company, and Bardenheier's Wine Cellars.

The importance of viticulture in Missouri in the middle of the nineteenth century is illustrated by the fact that the only American periodical solely devoted to grape culture and winemaking, the *American Grape Culturist*, was published in St. Louis by George Hussmann, one of the most celebrated horticulturists of his day. It was in Missouri that the state entomologist, Charles V. Riley, determined that phylloxera can be contained by grafting Vinifera cuttings onto American rootstock, a discovery that prompted a Swiss immigrant, Hermann Jaeger, to ship seventeen carloads of Ozark rootstocks in the 1870s to combat phylloxera in France. Isadore Bush was also instrumental in the development of St. George Rupestris, a very popular rootstock used throughout America.

An unbiased approach to alcohol beverage preferences.....on the grounds of the Stone Hill Wine Company. Baxevanis

By 1866 Missouri surpassed Ohio as the second largest wine producing state in the nation, but during the years preceding Prohibition, its position dropped to third place despite the presence of more than 100 wineries. In the aftermath of Prohibition, wineries concentrated on the production of sweet wines made from American vines, and growers continued to plant Concord and Catawba to meet processing demands for jelly and juice. The wine industry was not revitalized until 1975 when the Uni-

versity of Missouri began a campaign to increase the percentage of French-American vines in an effort to improve the quality of state produced wine. The passage of the farm winery act in 1978, one of the most liberal in the nation, has helped raise the number of wineries from 11 in 1977 to 28 in 1992. Although more than half are nothing more than cottage-type enterprises, the cumulative effect of modern winemaking technology, better site selection, and superior vineyard management, has significantly raised wine quality levels in recent years. Unlike most other midwestern states, at least 85 percent of the winery's fruit must be grown in the state for the wine be labeled domestic. Despite these recent encouraging developments, the direct and indirect economic wine benefits total $444 million, significantly less than other mid-western states. Whether or not these developments (as well as in Arkansas) will continue is debatable as the Welch's company will close is Concord facility, thus affecting 1,000 acres in both states.

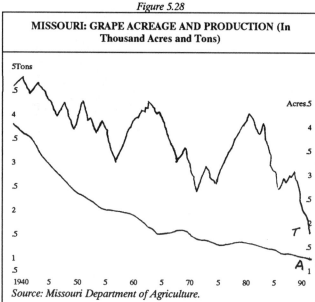

Figure 5.28

MISSOURI: GRAPE ACREAGE AND PRODUCTION (In Thousand Acres and Tons)

Source: Missouri Department of Agriculture.

Although Missouri exhibits minor topographic variations, there are three physiographic divisions of significance: the northern portion of the state is mainly prairie, the south is part of the Ozark Highlands, and the area south of St. Louis is part of the more humid Mississippi River region. The prairie area, flat, featureless, and characterized by deep, friable loess soils, is richly endowed and part of the Corn Belt region of the midwest. The Ozark area, delineated by narrow and deep valleys with limestone, shale and sandstone, is much poorer in fertility, but far better in accommodating the vine. The rich, alluvial soils of the Mississippi, although home to native varieties of vine, are unsuited for commercial viticultural exploitation.

While altitude and local relief are not sufficient to

affect the state's climate in a major way, local physical and cultural peculiarities have played a role in influencing the location of grape production and winery location. Wineries are located near major cities and historic grape producing regions. The tendency in recent years is for new wineries to locate near historic areas such as St. Charles (one of the oldest settlements west of St. Louis), Sainte Genevieve (the state's first settlement), Cape Girardeau (one of the oldest settlements along the Mississippi), and Boone and Gasconade counties (the first because of Daniel Boone, and the latter because of the historic Stone Hill Winery). Vineyards are mainly located along the Missouri River between Jefferson City and Webster, along the Meramec River from St. James to Cuba (both contain half the vine acreage, but produce more than three-fourths of all wine grapes), and in scattered areas such as Washburn, Mountain Grove, Koshkonong, and Sikeston, all near the Arkansas border.

Figure 5.29

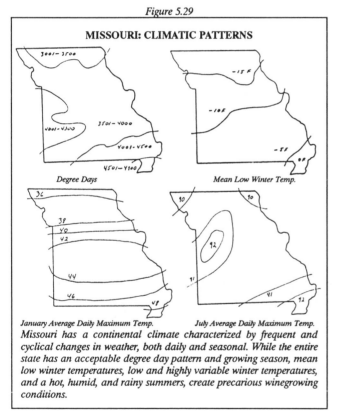

MISSOURI: CLIMATIC PATTERNS

Degree Days   *Mean Low Winter Temp.*

January Average Daily Maximum Temp.   *July Average Daily Maximum Temp.*

Missouri has a continental climate characterized by frequent and cyclical changes in weather, both daily and seasonal. While the entire state has an acceptable degree day pattern and growing season, mean low winter temperatures, low and highly variable winter temperatures, and a hot, humid, and rainy summers, create precarious winegrowing conditions.

Reflecting the state's continental location of wide temperature fluctuations, vineyards are generally planted on well-drained loess sites and hillsides that have a propensity to warm up early in the spring and are protected from heavy frost and cold northerly winds. As a result, 12 of the 28 wineries are located on or near the Missouri River, another 8 within the confines of the Meramec River, 2 others near the Mississippi, and a similar number near a protected valley in the central Ozarks. The latter

region, nearly 40 percent of the state's total land area, is a large plateau mainly composed of dolomite, sandstone, and limestone with a poor, rocky soil, which, when mixed with loess, is particularly good for viticulture. So widespread is the incidence of limestone and sandstone, that Missouri is known as the "Cave" state. Given the excellent site advantages of the Missouri River and the Ozark uplands, the state offers incredible opportunities for a viticultural renaissance despite its reputation for hogs, corn fields, one-story houses, farm houses huddled behind windbreaks, and endless prairie. The aforementioned advantages not withstanding, the attrition rate for wineries is high with at least seven failing since 1983.

Table 5.9

GRAPE ACREAGE IN MISSOURI BY VARIETY (1991)		
Variety	Acres	Percent
White American		
Catawba	258	19.6
Niagara	31	2.4
Delaware	22	1.7
Missouri Riesling	21	1.6
New York Muscat	8	
Elvira	4	
Red American		
Concord	200	15.2
Cynthiana/Norton	46	3.5
Steuben	2	
Alden	1	
Isabella	1	
Muench	1	
White French-American		
Seyval	230	17.5
Vidal Blanc	200	15.2
Vignoles	64	4.9
Villard Blanc	28	2.1
Cayuga	23	1.7
Rayon d'Or	6	
Aurora	5	
Meynieu 6	3	
Red French-American		
Chancellor	30	2.3
Chambourcin	26	2.0
Villard Noir	15	1.1
DeChaunac	14	1.0
Couderc Noir	12	
Baco Noir	11	
Marechal Foch	11	
Rougeon	11	
Chelois	8	
Leon Millot	7	
St. Vincent	5	
Colobel	1	
Landot 4511	1	
Vinifera		
Chardonnay	4	
Cabernet Sauvignon	3	
Riesling	2	
Merlot	1	
Zinfandel	1	
Total	1,317	

Source: Missouri Grape Growers Association.

Missouri has 1,317 acres of vineland, of which 344 acres are planted in white American, 251 in red American, 559 in white French-American, 152 in red French-American, and 11 in Vinifera varieties. While total acreage has steadily decreased since 1978, the mix of planted vines has been altered extensively. Most significantly, the percentage of American varieties has declined from 98 percent in 1975, to 85 percent in 1982, to 70 percent in 1989, a clear reflection of weakness in the juice and processing industry for two key grapes--Catawba and Concord (the latter, approximately 40 percent of the total grape acreage). Among major American varieties, Concord dominates acreage, but Catawba is the more important wine grape especially in the production of sparkling wine, followed by Niagara, Delaware, Missouri Riesling, and Cynthiana, the last two are particularly interesting as they have adapted well.

Developed in Hermann in the 1850s, the Missouri Riesling, (a Labrusca-type grape) is, after a long period of obscurity, becoming popular. Its acreage is increasing as its muted foxy flavor makes it good for blending and the making of sparkling wines. The other historic grape, Cynthiana, responsible for full-bodied, richly-flavored red wine capable of extended cellaring, is mainly planted in the Missouri and Meramec River valleys, and considered the finest red grape variety. Since there is heated discussion on whether or not there are distinct differences between Norton and Cynthiana, state law allows for wineries to use either name on the label. In this regard it is interesting to note from the 1888 Bushberg Grapevine Catalogue that Cynthiana "is a true Aestivalis in all its habits, and resembles Norton's Virginia. The Cynthiana is considered different from and superior to the Norton, and makes our best red wine."

Among French-American varietals (increased from 134 to 335 acres between 1982 and 1989) the most important and preferred grapes for quality white wine production are Vidal Blanc (considered the Chardonnay of French-American grapes) and Seyval (230 acres). Vignoles, regarded by many as the finest French-American variety in Missouri, produces both zesty dry and refined sweet wines. Red French-American varieties are not as successful but the two that consistently outperform the rest are Chancellor and Chambourcin. Vinifera vines, mainly Chardonnay and Riesling, comprise a mere eleven acres for the entire state. It is estimated that more than three-quarters of the state's total wine output is white wine, a good deal of it sweet or semi-sweet.

There are three *ava's* located solely in Missouri: *Augusta (1980)*, *Hermann (1983)*, and *Ozark Highlands (1987)*, and one--*Ozark Mountain (1986)*--that is shared with Arkansas, Oklahoma, and Kansas. *Augusta*, the nation's first *ava*, is located in St. Charles County 30 miles west of St. Louis, and one mile north of the Missouri River. It is distinguished from surrounding areas by bowl-shaped, 400-foot high topographic features that help create a unique microclimate. Augusta, lying on the southernmost bend of the Missouri, has the advantage of reduced frost danger, well-drained soils (they contain iron-rich limestone and are overlain with thick, rich loess), and a longer than normal growing season. Just prior to Prohi-

bition, there were no fewer than thirteen wineries within the immediate vicinity. Along with Hermann and other similar towns bordering this stretch of the Missouri, Augusta is characterized by extraordinary tourist opportunities. Surrounded by ghostly communities marked only by cemeteries, this section of Middle America is a veritable backwater of ironsmiths, one street towns, stately nineteenth century mansions, and a way of life that has not changed appreciably for 100 years (it was once called the "Missouri Rhineland"). Although small towns and the family farm have given way to larger cities with huge discount malls surrounded by interstate highways and huge corporate farms, this small portion along the Missouri River, for whatever the reasons, has managed to preserve the second half of the nineteenth century. The Augusta *ava* includes the small towns of Defiance and Matson, contains 100 vine acres and three wineries. The fact that this, plus the Hermann *ava*, is so close to metropolitan St. Louis with its affluent, 2.4 million population remains a major advantage over all other winemaking regions in the state.

Vineyards sited on the loess bluffs overlooking the Missouri River.
Baxevanis

Hermann, located in the northern portions of Gasconade and Franklin counties, is an 80 square mile *ava* with 300 acres of vineland and seven wineries. Due to excellent air drainage and well-drained, friable soils, vines were first planted in 1843, five years after the first settlers arrived in Hermann in 1838. By 1904 Hermann produced 97 percent of the state's total wine output and was considered the largest wine town in America in terms of volume of wine shipped. The heart of the Hermann *ava* has but 27 inches of rainfall, and nearly 4,000 degree days. It contains limestone overlain by loess soil, with appreciable quantities of iron in the subsoil. The wines have noticeable features when compared with other producing re-

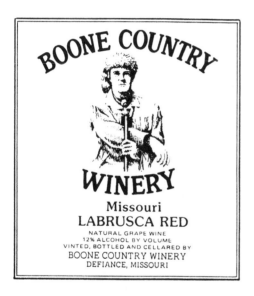

gions in the state and the east--softer white wines, and full-bodied, herbaceous red wines.

The *Ozark Highlands ava* (1987), is an enclave of the much larger Ozark Mountain *ava*. With 400-500 acres of vineland encompassing all or portions of eleven counties, and home to six wineries, it is the largest *ava* in the state. Drained by Big Piney, Bourbeuse, Current, Gasconade, Jack's Fork, and Meramec rivers, it is a flat, irregular basin 1,000 feet above sea level ringed by higher elevations. Although lacking precise boundaries, the *ava* is distinguishable from surrounding areas by a warmer climate, soils, a longer growing season, and air circulation patterns. Grapes have been grown here since 1898 when 1,000 Italians from Bologna, Italy arrived, and, as a consequence, the region has been called the "little Italy of the Ozarks" ever since. By 1929, vine acreage stood at 1,000, rose to nearly 3,000 in the early 1960s, but has since dropped precipitously as the demand for Concord grapes fell.

Boone Country, Labrusca, Missouri, and Defiance, a true American label in the center of the nation.

The *Ozark Mountain ava*, with nearly 3,000 acres of vineland (practically the entire grape acreage of both Missouri and Arkansas) and more than 20 wineries, is a 55,000 square mile region that encompasses the entire Ozark region spread amongst four states (Missouri, Arkansas, Oklahoma and Kansas, collectively larger than the state of New York), but there is no general agreement concerning the boundaries of the Ozarks. The name is derived from the French *aux-Arcs*, meaning "to Arkansas." The region, composed of folded ridges similar to the Appalachians, is heavily forested, and blessed with the pioneering efforts of Daniel Boone. The topography of the Ozarks is one of hills, plateaus, and incised valleys, many with significant local reliefs. Limestone and dolomite are common with much chert, producing many springs, caves,

sinkholes, and collectively one of the most important karst landscapes in the nation. Despite its formidable geographical dimensions, the highest elevation is less than 2,000 feet. Although the *ava* is officially delimited by five major rivers (Mississippi, Missouri, Osage, Neosho, and Arkansas), it is important to note that the Ozark Mountains do not stretch to the Mississippi River. Nevertheless, more than 50 percent of the area is covered by oak-hickory forest that marks the westernmost extension of the great deciduous forest that once covered eastern America. Surrounded by four different climatic regions, this hilly, upland plateau, carved by numerous streams and rivers, has generated many microclimates that serve to isolate and give refuge to regional plant and animal life. Dairy, ranching and forest products industries dominate the economic life of the region, with grapes and fruit crops accounting for less than 1 percent of total farm value.

Due to higher elevation, precipitation rises beyond 40 inches, and annual temperatures become more extreme in terms of variability. Thus the growing season is reduced to less than 170 days, and the dominant grape is Concord, used for processing. Grapes, historically grown by German immigrants along the Missouri, gradually shifted further south, first by Catholic German Swiss (near Altus), and then by Italian immigrants who first cultivated under the leadership of an Italian priest in 1898. Two major areas of grape cultivation are Tontitown in Washington County, Arkansas and Rosati in eastern Phelps County, Missouri. Of the two regions, Tontitown grew from 30 acres in 1900 to more than 6,000 acres by 1935, becoming the largest vinegrowing region in Arkansas. The Rosati region in Missouri had a similar, but less spectacular history. Due to heavy stream and river incision, the entire *ava* is a varied collection of microclimates and soils. The wineries are:

Adam Puchta Winery (Hermann, 1990), is a 7-acre, 3,000-case winery that makes Stark Star, Norton, Seyval, sparkling, and proprietary wines. This winery, founded by the same family in 1855, still maintains the original stone-wheeled grape crusher.

Augusta Winery (Augusta, 1989), is a 6,000-case winery that makes Vidal Blanc, Seyval, Cynthiana, proprietary, and blackberry wines. Other label: *Cedar Ridge*.

Bardenheier's Wine Cellars (St. Louis, 1873), is a 30,000-case winery that makes dessert wines and wine coolers. As recently as 1980 the winery produced more than three-quarters of the state total.

Bias Winery (Berger, 1980), is a 7-acre, 1,500-case winery that makes good, sound, well-flavored American (Catawba), but primarily French-American (Vidal Blanc, DeChaunac, Seyval), fruit, and mead wines.

Blumenhof Vineyards & Winery (Dutzow, 1986), is a meticulous, 14-acre, 2,200-case winery that makes excellent proprietary and varietal French-American wines, of which Vidal Blanc and Seyval are the finest.

Boone County Winery (Defiance, 1985), is a 10-acre, 1,000-case winery that makes well-flavored American, French-American, fruit and berry wines. The name derives from the fact that the winery is located on land once owned by the Daniel Boone family.

Bristle Ridge Vineyard (Knob Noster, 1979), is an interesting, 5-acre, 1,800-case winery that makes American and French-American-based wines, of which Seyval, Vidal Blanc and Villard Noir are the finest.

Bynum Winery (Lone Jack, 1989), is an 800-case winery that makes Vidal Blanc, Seyval, Villard Blanc, Chancellor, and fruit wines.

Ferrigno Vineyards & Winery (St. James, 1982), is an 18-acre, 1,800-case, American and French-American winery that makes soft, restrained, well-flavored wines. The Chelois and Vidal Blanc are particularly good.

Gloria Winery (Mountain Grove, 1989), is an 8-acre, 1,000-case winery that makes red table wine from French-American grapes.

Heinrichshaus Vineyards & Winery (St. James, 1978), is a serious, 10-acre, 2,400-case, American and French-American winery that makes, unlike most other wineries, mostly dry and consistently above-average to excellent wines, of which the red may be the finest in the state. The moderately priced wines offer excellent value, and should not be missed, particularly Cynthiana and Seyval.

Hermannhof Winery (Hermann, 1852), one of the oldest wineries in the nation, is a 50-acre, 22,000-case winery (placed on the National Register of Historic Sites) that makes a large assortment of American, French-American, fruit, and sparkling wines, most of which are sold under proprietary names. Closed during Prohibition, the winery produced nearly 1 million cases of wine in 1984.

Les Bourgeois Winery (Rocheport, 1986), is a 3-acre, 5,000-case winery that makes good, flavorful Seyval, Vidal Blanc, proprietary, plus small quantities of full-bodied Norton.

Mission Creek Winery (Weston, 1987), is a 10-acre, 2,000-case winery that makes good, clean, dry Seyval, Vidal Blanc, Vignoles, Cynthiana, and Baco Noir. Other label: *Sunny Slope* and *Rialto*.

Montelle At Osage Ridge (Augusta, 1976), is an aggressive and rapidly expanding, 30-acre, 8,000-case winery (merged with Osage Ridge Winery in 1987) that makes a wide assortment of American, French-American, fruit and berry wines, of which Cynthiana and Chancellor appear to be the finest under the *Montelle Vineyards* label. Other label: *Osage Ridge*.

Mount Pleasant Wineries Abbey Vineyard (Cuba, 1980), is a 6-acre,

4,000-case winery owned by the Mount Pleasant Winery that made American, French-American, fruit and berry wines, but is now limited exclusively to the production of fruit wines.

Mount Pleasant Winery (Augusta, 1881), was founded by a Lutheran minister that remained dormant from 1920 until it was revived by the present owners in 1968. Considered one of the better wineries in the state, this aggressive, highly innovative, 70-acre, 18,000-case winery is located on 40 feet thick loess soils producing Chardonnay, Missouri Riesling, Rayon d'Or, Seyval, Vidal Blanc, Pinot Noir, all five Bordeaux red varieties, sparkling, ice and proprietary wines. It also makes a Porto-type wine from Stark Star and Contessot grapes. The sparkling wines can often be excellent.

O'Vallon Winery (Washburn, 1987), with 130 acres of prime varietals, this modest winery of 6,000-cases is the single largest vineyard, and one of the finest wineries in the state. It makes excellent, dry, crisp, well-flavored Vidal Blanc, Seyval, Vignoles, and a chewy, fragrant Norton.

Ozark Vineyards (Chestnut Ridge, 1976), is a 2,000-case winery that mainly makes proprietary wines from American and French-American varieties.

Peaceful Bend Vineyard (Steelville, 1972), is a 10-acre, 1,200-case French-American winery known for good, sound, blended, proprietary (*Courtois*, *Whittenburg Creek*, *Meramec River*, *Yadkin Creek*, and *Houzzah*) red, rose and white wines.

Pirtle's Weston Vineyards (Weston, 1978), is a 13-acre, 5,000-case French-American (Seyval, mead, and Catawba are above-average), fruit and berry winery located in a church built in 1867.

Reis Winery (Licking, and Lake Ozark, 1978), is an expanding, 8-acre, 2,000-case winery that makes Seyval, Vidal Blanc, Leon Millot, and proprietary wines.

Robller Vineyard (New Haven, 1990), is a 5-acre, 1,000-case winery that makes good, sound, above-average Vidal Blanc, Steuben, Chancellor, and Cynthiana wines.

Sainte-Genevieve Winery (Ste. Genevieve, 1984), is an 8-acre, 2,000-case winery that makes inexpensive Seyval, Vidal Blanc, Villard Blanc, Concord, and fruit and berry wines. The winery seeks to take advantage of its location in the center of the town's restoration (founded in 1735) efforts.

St. James Winery (St. James, 1970), is a 70-acre, 25,000-case winery that makes more than two dozen American, French-American, sparkling, mead, fruit and berry wines, of which Munson and Cynthiana are the most interesting.

Spring Creek Winery (Blue Springs, 1989), is a 500-case winery that makes Seyval and apple wines.

Stone Hill Wine Company (Hermann, New Florence, and Branson, 1847), operated until Prohibition and reopened in 1965, this designated National Historic site winery cultivates 70 acres and produces 30,000 cases of American, French-American table, dessert, fruit, and sparkling wines. The most important are: Seyval, Vidal Blanc, Vignoles, Missouri Riesling, Catawba, Concord, and Norton, the latter one of the finest wines made in the state. The second largest winery in the nation in 1910, it contains the largest underground vaulted cellars in the midwest. The winery also maintains a newly constructed sparkling wine facility in New Florence. This aggressive, well-managed property, the current showcase of the state's emergent wine industry, consistently makes above-average quality wines that should not be missed. The founder of this winery, one Michael Poeschel, immigrated to America in 1839, and when he retired a wealthy man, his winery was the third largest in the world.

Winery of the Little Hills, in the center of restored St. Charles. Baxevanis
Winery of the Little Hills (St. Charles, 1860), reestablished in 1982, is
an aggressive, 3-acre, 9,000-case winery that makes a large assortment
of American, French-American table, dessert, sparkling, fruit and berry
wines.

As American as Boone Country Winery may be, Blumenhof, Hermannhof,
Heinrichshaus, other ethnic groups (Armenian, French, Italian, etc.),
reflect nineteenth century migration to middle America. Baxevanis

Arkansas

Arkansas is a comparatively large but sparsely populated
state of 2.4 million people that became a territory in 1819
and the twenty-fifth state in 1836. Given the fact that
Hernando de Soto spent nearly a year in Arkansas, Spanish settlement and a subsequent viticultural tradition was
not to be. Although the state has twice the vine acreage as
Missouri directly to the north, it has but one-sixth as
many wineries, and when Wiederkehr and Post, the former a Swiss and the latter a Bavarian, both began making
wine in 1880, it was nearly 60 years after wine was made
in Missouri. The state (named after an Indian clan called
Arkansea), burdened with an unsympathetic state legislature toward wine interests, has seen its vine acreage decline from 6,000 in 1925 to 1,900 in 1991, its wine output
from 2.5 million gallons to less than 800,000, and its
wineries from 40 to 6, for the same period. Forty-three of

the state's 75 counties are dry, Sunday winery sales are
not permitted, and the tax was recently increased from 5
to 75 cents per gallon. Due to poor crops in recent years,
the percentage of wine and juice imported to the state has
increased to 65 percent of grapes processed for wine.

The state has fewer that 50 growers, nearly all of
whom are affiliated with Welch's Foods, of which half are
located in the Tontitown-Springdale (Benton, Washington, and Franklin account for more than 90 percent of
total acreage) region of northwest Arkansas along the
protected slopes of the White River. More than 95 percent of the declining acreage is planted in American varieties for the juice-jelly market. Of the 800 acres of wine
grapes, nearly all are located in Franklin County, while
the extreme northwest corner of the state contains fewer
than 100. Altus, the other, better, but much smaller table
wine producing region, is located on the foothills of the
Boston Mountains along the Arkansas River, and is the
center for four of the five wineries in the state.

Figure 5.30

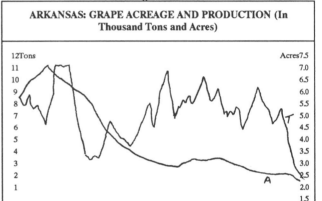

ARKANSAS: GRAPE ACREAGE AND PRODUCTION (In
Thousand Tons and Acres)

Source: Arkansas Agricultural Statistics Service.

Concord grapes accounted for 56 percent of grapes
grown in Arkansas in 1981, or six times the acreage of the
second most popular variety. While French-American varieties have seriously eroded the Concord and Catawba
acreage share in recent years, 50 acres are planted in
Rotundifolia vines (used for both processing and winemaking), and fewer than 15 acres are planted in Vinifera
vines. As a quality grape, Cynthiana (considered by many
growers to be different from Norton and indigenous to
the state) has interesting possibilities. Another interesting
grape is the Stark Star, a cross of Cynthiana and Catawba,
first developed in 1892 in Altus. This hardy vine, resistant
to most diseases and sharp seasonal temperatures, produces fair yields of well-balanced must suitable for Porto-
type wines. Grape yields, low when compared with neighboring states, can be appreciably augmented with irrigation. The state Agricultural Experiment Station has developed four table grapes since 1977, an industry segment

that is considered promising by state officials.

The state has two *ava's* located entirely within the state. The *Arkansas Mountain (1986)*, a 4,500 square mile region south and north of the Arkansas River, is distinguished from neighboring areas to the north, west and south by a combination of microclimates. Because the Ozark and Oichita Mountains trend in a north-east direction, protection from colder northerly winds lengthens the growing season and minimizes winter injury; the mountain barrier also prevents large infusions of warm air and more humid weather from the south to extend the range of Pierce's Disease into the northwestern portion of the state. *Altus (1984)* is centered in the town of the same name, but extends from the Arkansas River benchland to the edge of the Boston Mountains, a distance of 5 miles. This region, with nearly 1,000 acres of vineland and four of the state's six wineries, was settled in the 1880s by Swiss migrants. The Arkansas Mountain and Altus *ava* regions are both enclaves of the much larger Ozark Mountain *ava*, discussed previously.

The principal wineries, all of which produce good, sound wines, are: **Concert Vineyards** (Lakeview, 1989), is an unusual, 20-acre, 2,000-case winery that makes proprietary wines from 200 different American, French-American, and Vinifera. The staples, however, are Chardonnay, Vignoles, Vidal Blanc, Seyval, Cabernet Sauvignon, Chambourcin, and Cynthiana. **Cowie Wine Cellars** (Paris, 1967), is a good, conscientious, consumer-oriented winery of 2,000 cases that makes American, French-American, fruit and berry wines, of which Cynthiana is the finest. **Mount Bethel Winery** (Altus, 1956), is a 15-acre, 4,500-case winery that makes sweet American and Rotundifolia table, fruit and berry wines. **Post Familie Vineyards** (Altus, 1880), is a 125-acre, 80,000-case, fruit, berry, American, Rotundifolia, French-American and Vinifera table, dessert and sparkling winery, of which Aurore, Niagara, Delaware, and Cynthiana are the finest. **The Eureka Springs Winery** (Eureka Springs, 1989), is a 1,000-case winery and restaurant owned by Cowie Wine Cellars that makes interesting Porto-type wines from the Stark Star grape. Also made are fruit and berry, and other specialty wines from American grapes. **Wiederkehr Wine Cellars** (Altus, 1880), admirably located on a sandy plateau, this family-owned winery makes a large assortment of American, Rotundifolia, French-American, and Vinifera table, dessert and sparkling wines, of which Chardonnay, Riesling, and Cabernet Sauvignon are the finest. With 475 acres and an annual output of more than 250,000 cases, this is the state's largest winery.

West Virginia, Kentucky, And Tennessee

West Virginia, Kentucky, and Tennessee, three states with a strong Appalachian imprint and excellent wine potential, are totally divergent in recent viticultural histories. Collectively the three states have 750 acres of vineland and eighteen wineries, none of which produce more than 12,000 cases annually. Unfortunately, the dominance of coal and whiskey in their respective economies, and a historically rural, isolated, and less affluent population than surrounding states, has done much to discourage wine acceptance, and, ultimately, recognition and consumption.

With an unusual shape and a declining population (less than 2 million), West Virginia is a state with small cities and a low standard of living. It is a product of the

Civil War as the western counties of then Virginia refused to secede and remained in the Union, becoming the 35th state in 1863. Coal was discovered in 1742, a commodity that dominates the economy as the state's most important resource. Composed of folded, parallel ridges of the Appalachians in the eastern third of the state, and a maize of hills and hollows of the Appalachian Plateau in the western portion of the state, West Virginia, a state with eight wineries, first enacted Farm Winery legislation in 1981. Since then it has made a valiant effort to produce wine mainly from American and French-American varieties, and to encourage wine sales by permitting their sale in food stores. Although wine was made by early settlers in 1826 (wild grapes were found everywhere, with at least half of the state's counties reporting planted grapes), commercial wine was produced in 1856 by the Friends of Brothers Winery in Dunbar. By 1880, eleven counties made wine, but the industry languished as whiskey, beer, and Prohibition took effect, and no records of winemaking were kept by state authorities during the period 1880-1981. The state offers many advantages for further viticultural expansion, of which inexpensive land costs and an excellent physical base are the most important.

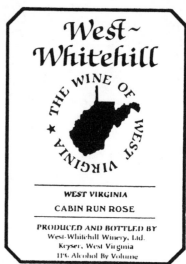

Geographically, the Ridge and Valley portion of the state, located in the east bordering Virginia, offers superb viticultural microclimates. It has three of the state's eight wineries, nearly three-quarters of grape acreage, and contains a combination of high relief, moderate rainfall, outstanding air drainage, and excellent limestone-based soils, all of which make this area of folded parallel ridges an outstanding region for grape growing. The other important area with good viticultural potential is the Ohio River region, historically the most important area in the state.

Today there are 350 acres of vineland, 148 of which are planted in American, 175 in French-American, and the remainder in Vinifera varieties. All wineries are small, family-owned affairs whose owners are fully employed in other businesses, and, unlike neighboring Virginia there is no corporate and foreign investment. The main obstacle to the promulgation of a viable wine industry is, unlike Tennessee and Virginia, weak state support, a rather formidable problem given the fact that the cottage-type industry maintains a poor public image. Not only is the state's economy preoccupied with coal mining and heavy industry (historically, the unemployment problem was solved by exporting people to other states), but the wine industry receives little support from the State University. Furthermore, the state ranks forty-ninth in wine consumption in the nation, and the anti-wine sentiment is about to drive two wineries into neighboring Virginia, where state authorities are more supportive of industry needs. In addition to the ten wineries mentioned below, several more are expected to be licensed in the near future as part of the state's Department of Agriculture Demonstration Vineyard Program. Besides the *Ohio River* and the *Shenandoah Valley ava's*, which West Virginia shares with other states, the only *ava* wholly within state borders (and an enclave of the Ohio River *ava*) is the *Kanawha River Valley (1986)*, a 1,000 square mile region with just nineteen acres of vineland and one winery.

The wineries are: **A.T. Gift Winery** (Harpers Ferry, 1987), is a 2-acre, 1,000-case winery that makes mostly fruit wines, and smaller quantities of Catawba, Concord, Niagara, and Fredonia. **Fisher Ridge Wine Co.** (Liberty, 1977), is a 7-acre, 3,000-case American and French-American winery. **Forks of Cheat Winery** (Morgantown, 1990), is a 5-acre, 1,000-case winery that makes Vidal Blanc, Villard Blanc, Seyval, Niagara, Leon Millot, Baco Noir, Marechal Foch, and an obscure Van Buren. **Laurel Creek Winery** (Brooks, 1985), is an interesting, 5-acre, 650-case winery that makes Seyval, Cascade, Chancellor, Concord, and minute quantities of Chardonnay, Pinot Noir, Cabernet Sauvignon, and fruit and berry wines. **Little Hungary Farm Winery** (Buckhannon, 1985), is an unusual, 8-acre, 2,000-case winery that makes an excellent white and red mead/grape wine blend, offering excellent value. **Robert F. Pliska and Company Winery** (Purgitsville, 1983), is a 14-acre, 1,000-case, French-American winery that makes above-average, often refined Seyval, Aurore, Marechal Foch, Chancellor, fruit, sparkling, and proprietary wines, all offering excellent value. **Schneider's Winery** (Romney, 1987), is a 17-acre, 7,000-case winery that makes Seyval, Niagara, Marechal Foch, Concord, fruit, and proprietary wines. **Tent Church Vineyard** (Colliers, 1983), is a 10-acre, 600-case winery that makes Aurore, Seyval, Concord, and Marechal Foch under the *Vandalia Wines* label. **West-Whitehill Winery** (Keyser, 1981), is an 8-acre, 2,000-case winery known for Aurore, Seyval Blanc, Chardonnay, Vidal Blanc, DeChaunac, and proprietary wines.

Although Kentucky enjoys favorable farm winery legislation, it is very difficult to establish a profitable winery in a state strongly associated with whiskey production. Long known as the "Bourbon" state, the annual consumption of wine is less than three quarts per person annually, one of the lowest in the nation. Ironically, Kentucky had one of the earliest viticultural histories in the nation. In 1796, Jean Jacques Dufour, a French Swiss, first planted vines 25 miles south of Lexington, but subsequently moved to Vevay, Indiana after a phylloxera and Black Rot epidemic combined to decimate his vineyards early in the nineteenth century. Soon after, Trappist monks planted

vines and made wines in 1848, and by 1880 Kentucky had nearly 2,000 acres producing more than 138,000 gallons of wine. Sad to say, despite favorable microclimates and exceptional limestone-based soils, viticulture is in retreat. In recent years the state's three wineries have ceased operations, and total state vine acreage is estimated to be less than 40, highly concentrated in the south-central portion of the state.

CHRONOLOGY OF WINEGROWING IN TENNESSEE

1840s: Vineland, Tennessee, in Van Buren County was settled by German immigrant families. It is presumed the town was named Vineland because the settlers discovered native vines and identified the potential of the location for winegrowing. The settlement is known to have included at least four winemakers. Other pre-Civil War grape-growing counties in Tennessee were Maury (settled by Germans), Grundy and Lewis (both Swiss settlements), Lawrence (home to Alsatians) and Giles.

1880: U.S. Census reports a wine output of 90,000 gallons.

1899: Knox County, with a harvest of 560,495 pounds, was the largest grape producing county in the state. Davidson County followed with a harvest of more than 220,000 pounds. The largest wine producing county was Lawrence County followed by Warren, Knox, Grundy, and Davidson counties. Other active and grape and wine counties at the turn of the century were: Morgan, Meigs, Franklin, Sumner, Henderson, Washington, and Wilson. Altogether, the historical records show that a total of 93 counties in the state of Tennessee were both growing grapes and producing wine at this time.

1919: Prohibition closes all wineries and grape output is reduced to a home cottage industry.

1973: Judge William O. Beach organizes the Tennessee Viticulture & Oenological Society Society in Clarksville.

1977: Judge Beach and the TVOS influence new state grape and wine legislation, reducing fees and taxes, increasing production limits, easing the founding of farm wineries, and re-establishing a commercial wine industry. Only 60 acres of grapes to be found in the state.

1980: Highland manor Vineyard and Winery in Jamestown, becomes the state's first licensed winery since Prohibition. Since then, the number has increased to 15.

1982: Grape acreage increased to 100.

1984: Tennessee commercial grapegrowers and winemakers organize Tennessee Farm Winegrowers Association.

1985: Governor Lamar Alexander appointed the first Viticulture Advisory Board.

1986: Five wineries founded.

1991: Four wineries founded.

Source: Mostly from Tennessee Farm Winegrowers Association.

In sharp contrast to the dismal viticultural condition in neighboring Kentucky, whiskey-drinking Tennessee, a narrow but exceptionally wide state, is currently undergoing a wine revolution of significant proportions. Vine acreage increased from fewer than 40 acres in 1976 to 300 in 1992, and the number of wineries jumped from one to fifteen, all founded after the passage of farm winery legislation in 1977. Eight of the fifteen wineries are located in the Ridge and Valley section of the Appalachians north, west, south and east of Knoxville, four others are sited near Nashville, and the last three are located north and east of Memphis (in addition to the Stroh California Cooler facility). One interesting feature of the state's wine law prohibits anyone who has not lived in the state for at least two years from owning or even holding shares in a Tennessee winery.

Figure 5.31

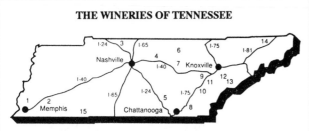

THE WINERIES OF TENNESSEE

The above indicates the distribution of wineries in the Ridge and Valley section vs. the Plateau and Mississippi areas of the state. All wineries are located in tourist sites, a trend common throughout eastern America.
1. Laurel Hill; 2. Cordova; 3. Beachaven; 4. Shangrila; 5. Monteagle; 6. Highland Manor; 7. Stonehaus; 8. Tennessee Mountain View; 9. Tennessee Valley; 10. Orr Mountain; 11. Loudon Valley; 12. Mountain Valley; 13. Smoky Mountain; 14. Countryside; 15. Twin Oaks. Source: Tennessee Farm Winegrowers Association.

Unlike West Virginia and Kentucky, Tennessee (the "Volunteer" state) is not only larger in both territory and population (more than 5 million), but it is a rapidly growing industrial and high-tech state with a sizeable and rapidly rising disposable income. Although Tennessee is primarily known as a whiskey producing state, winemaking is no stranger because as recently as 1880 (31 years after the first settlement in the Watauga Valley) more than 95,000 gallons were produced, a figure similar to current levels. In reality, Tennessee is not one but three states, each with its own history, dominant economy, lifestyle, and regional city. The western third of the state lying next to the Mississippi River--the flattest, hottest, most humid and the one with a growing season that exceeds 230 days, represents the northern portion of the historic Cotton Belt, but is the least important in the production of wine and grapes. The central portion of the state, dominated by the higher elevations of the Cumberland Plateau, is windswept, humid, rainy, and mainly planted in American and French-American vines. The area has retained and cherished the memory of Mark Twain's father as he attempted to cultivate grapes and produce wine on his Jamestown farm. The most important portion, the extreme eastern section, dominated by Knoxville, is higher in elevation, and offers, due to the large number of microclimates, excellent prospects in the production of both French-American and Vinifera vines. However, while wine is made from American, Rotundifolia, French-American, and Vinifera vines, French-American vines dominate, and nearly all wines contain some residual sugar. Of the 294 acres, 174 are French-American, 94 American, and 26 Vinifera. Seyval and Vidal Blanc account for nearly 40 percent of the acreage, followed by Concord, Niagara, and Catawba. According to the Tennessee Viticultural Oenological Society's special demonstration projects in various areas in the state, Vidal

is the most successful French-American grape variety; Chardonnay the finest among Vinifera: and Delaware produces good fruit but poor wine. While no wine was made prior to 1980, the state now produces 100,000 gallons annually.

The wineries are: **Beachaven Vineyards & Winery** (Clarksville, 1986), is an aggressive, 17-acre, 5,500-case winery that ma-kes American, French-American, and Vinifera wines, of which Vignoles, Cayuga, and sparkling wines are the finest. **Countryside Vineyards Winery** (Blountville, 1990), is a 6-acre, 1,000-case winery that makes Golden Muscat, Vidal Blanc, Cayuga, Steuben, Chambourcin, and Concord wines. **Cordova Cellars** (Cordova, 1989), is a 5-acre, 2,500-case winery that makes Chardonnay, Vidal Blanc, Gewurztraminer, Niagara, Vignoles, Cabernet Sauvignon, and proprietary wines. This small, but highly innovative winery (planted are more than 14 different grape varieties) also makes an unusual rose from the obscure Venus table grape. **Highland Manor** (Jamestown, 1980), a 20-acre, 4,500-case winery located on the Cumberland Plateau of northcentral Tennessee, was the state's first licensed winery in this century. This highly regarded winery makes a large and unusual assortment of American, Rotundifolia, French-American, and Vinifera wines, of which Riesling, Niagara, Chardonnay, Catawba, Concord, and sparkling Rotundifolia are particularly good. **Laurel Hill Vineyard** (Memphis, 1984), is an 11-acre, 1,000-case winery whose vineyards are located 175 miles east of Memphis on the Cumberland plateau of Lawrence County. This region, located in "Blue Grass" country, 1,000 feet in elevation between the Tennessee Valley and the east central basin of Tennessee, was settled by Alsatians in the 1800s who planted vines and made wine until Prohibition. Chardonnay, Riesling, Vidal Blanc, and Villard Blanc are particularly good. **Loudon Valley Vineyards** (Loudon, 1987), is a 10-acre, 1,500-case winery that makes American, French-American, and Vinifera wines, of which Sauvignon Blanc, Chambourcin, Catawba, Zinfandel, and Rotundifolia are above-average in quality. **Monteagle Wine Cellars** (Monteagle, 1986), formerly Marlowe Wine Cellars, is an 11,000-case, winery that makes American, French-American, and Vinifera (Riesling, Niagara, Sauvignon Blanc, Seyval, Gewurztraminer, Sewanee, Chancellor, Cabernet Sauvignon, Marechal Foch, and Concord, among others) from purchased grapes. **Mountain Valley Winery** (Pigeon Forge, 1991), with 11 acres and an output of 15,000 cases, this winery, the largest in the state, makes Chardonnay, Niagara, Seyval, Vidal Blanc, Merlot, and Cynthiana. **Orr Mountain Winery** (Madisonville, 1986), is a 16-acre, 2,500-case winery that makes French-American and Vinifera wines. **Shangrila** (Lebanon, 1986), is a 3-acre, 1,800-case winery that makes American and French-American wines. **Smokey Mountain Winery** (Gatlingburg, 1981), is a 5,000-case winery that makes American, French-American, Vinifera, fruit and berry wines from purchased fruit. **Stonehaus Winery** (Crossville, 1990), is an 8,000-case winery that makes Chardonnay, Riesling, and Sauvignon Blanc from Washington State grapes, and proprietary wine from American and French-American varieties. This winery was established by the same person who founded the first winery since Prohibition. **Tennessee Mountain View Winery** (Charleston, 1986), is a 17-acre, 2,500-case winery specializing in American (mainly Concord, Niagara, Catawba, and Riesling) wines. **Tennessee Valley Winery** (Loudon, 1984), is an aggressive, 48-acre, 5,000-case winery that makes good, sound American, French-American, and Vinifera wines (mainly Vidal Blanc, Chardonnay, Aurore, Sauvignon Blanc, DeChaunac, Marechal Foch, and Leon Millot). **Twin Oaks Winery** (Shiloh, 1991), is an 8-acre, 1,000-case winery that makes Vidal Blanc and Chancellor wines.

THE GREAT PLAINS

In the Great Plains, vine growing and winemaking, totally subjugated by wheat, corn and soybean production, grazing land, and poisoned by 2, 4-D, is practically a nonexistent economic activity. Of the eight states included in this region, there are only 100 acres of vineland and 10 wineries (whose total production is less than 7,000 cases, or about the annual output of a small farm winery). Baco Noir, Beta, Buffalo, Delaware, Verdelet, Seyval, Himrod, and Rosette exhibit some tolerance to 2, 4-D, and, hence, are widespread. Less tolerant American and French-American varieties are only grown in physically protected areas, and in regions where 2, 4-D is not common.

The Great Plains forming one-fifth of the land area of the United States, is a "high plains" area extending from the Mackenzie River delta in Arctic Canada in the north to the Rio Grande River in the extreme south. In America, the Great Plains lie between the Central Lowlands and the Gulf Coastal Plain on the east and the Rocky Mountains on the west. They extend for a distance of 1,800 miles as the "crow flies" in a north-south dimension, and their width, in places, exceeds 500 miles. A sparsely populated area of few large cities, the agricultural land use is overwhelmingly given to cereal cultivation with scattered irrigation. While variations exist over this huge land area of more than 586,461 square miles (more than ten times the size of Illinois), the region is treeless, semiarid, and its topography is flat to gently undulating. Although there are minor exceptions, the Great Plains slope downward toward the east from altitudes of nearly one mile in the foothills of the Rocky Mountains to altitudes of 1,800 feet along the eastern margins.

The Great Plains, characterized by short grasses and less than 20 inches of annual precipitation, are underlain by soils in which moisture does not penetrate to the water table. The resulting soils, called pedocals, are often characterized by a limy layer beneath the land surface. Geologically, the Great Plains are underlain by extensive horizontal layers of sandstone, limestone, shale, various conglomerates, the world's largest lignite deposits, and overlain by thick deposits of alluvial and glacial sediments. The severe continental climate is characterized by great extremes of temperature difference between winter and summer. Therefore, while excellent for either winter or spring wheat, the widely fluctuating climatic regimes of the region preclude a commercially viable viticultural industry for all but the most hardy grape varieties. Although North and South Dakota, two wheat producing states, do not have a viticultural history, a 5-acre vineyard of Baco Noir, DeChaunac, and Aurore grapes has recently been planted by two sisters in Wakonda, South Dakota. It is also interesting to note that while Nebraska has no commercially operating winery, the state has enacted farm winery legislation.

Proceeding from north to south, Montana has one winery: **Mission Mountain Winery** (Dayton, 1984), is a 22-acre, 10,000-case winery located on the west side of Flathead Lake that makes Riesling, Chardonnay, Pinot Noir, sparkling, and an interesting proprietary blend of Pinot Noir and Lemberger, partly from Washington state grapes.

Nearly twice the size of Michigan, half the land area of Colorado lies along the eastern portion of the continental divide. As a result, its rivers flow to the east, west and south, and are the source of both the Colorado and the Rio Grande. Its population of 4 million people (extremely youthful with a high rate of in-migration) is highly concentrated between Fort Collins in the north and Pueblo in the south along the High Plains, an area that contains the largest cities in the state. While the entire state lies above 3,000 feet in elevation, about half of the state is higher than 6,000 feet in altitude.

Colorado, a state long known for gold, molybdenum, wheat and cattle, now has, along with high-tech electronic industries, 275 acres of vineland and six wineries (all founded since 1978), two of which are located between Denver and Colorado Springs. Although there are records of vineyard plantings throughout Colorado's history, existing commercial acreage dates back to only the early 1970s. While slow in developing, the recently enacted Colorado Wine Industry Development Act, signed into law in 1990, is a major trend setter in the Great Plains. Among its major objectives, the Act will encourage and promote viticultural and enological research and development, assist in the marketing of wines and grapes, and promote the integration of the fledgling wine industry with the state's lucrative tourist program.

Colorado is a very interesting grape growing and wine producing state because the vineyards and the wineries are located in two different areas much like the state of Washington. Length of the frost-free season ranges from 80 days in the northwest mountains to 160 days in the southwestern and eastern areas, the latter known as the "High Plains." Precipitation is highest in the mountains and lowest in the western deserts and the "steppes" of the High Plains. However, because of widely fluctuating temperatures on the High Plains, suitable vineyard areas are essentially limited to the Grande Valley of the Colorado, the North Fork Valley of the Gunnison, and the area near Canon City (where there is a Grape Creek nearby). All three areas are located above 4,000 feet, but the protected character of the growing regions is quite similar to the Columbia River region of Washington, and makes them suitable for grape growing. The region near Grande Junction, in particular, protected by the Roan Plateau and Book Cliffs, is the only major region in the state that is able to grow peaches.

Colorado has the highest mean elevation (6,800 feet) in the nation, and of North America's 98 mountains with peaks above 14,000 feet, 54 are located in this highly mountainous state. Chinook winds moderate cold winter weather with temperatures rarely falling below -10F for sustained periods of time, and seasonal temperature extremes are rare despite 100F summer temperatures. Due to the semi-desertic climatic nature of the vineyards (less than 16 inches of rainfall), the high altitude, and the high incidence of illumination, evenings are cool (the diurnal variation in temperature can often be 50F), hence, the grapes develop good sugar levels and excellent varietal flavor and aroma. Thus far, Chardonnay, Lemberger, Gewurztraminer, Riesling, and Orange Muscat have done well in experimental plots. Nearly all the vineyards are located along a single road across East Orchard Mesa in western Colorado. The prohibition of Sunday sales restricts marketing severely. The state has one *ava*: *Grande Valley*, located in the Grand Junction area between Palisade and Fruita in the western part of the state, it occupies part of the floor of the Grande Valley of Colorado. The area includes within its boundaries three areas that are locally known as Orchard Mesa, the Redlands, and the Vinelands. The Grande Valley is an area of 50 square miles containing 90 grape acres, 16 vineyards, and 6 wineries.

The wineries are: **Carlson Vineyards** (Palisade, 1988), is a 4-acre, 1,300-case winery that makes flavorful Riesling, Orange Muscat, Zinfandel, Lemberger, and fruit wines. **Colorado Cellars** (Palisade, 1978), formerly Colorado Mountain Vineyards, the largest and oldest, is a 20,000-case winery (sited 4,800 feet in elevation near the Utah border) that makes above-average, zesty Riesling, Chardonnay, Gewurztraminer, Merlot, Lemberger, and fruit and berry wines from purchased fruit. **Grande River Vineyards** (Palisade, 1991), is a 42-acre, 1,500-case winery that makes Chardonnay, and both white and red Meritage-type wines. **Pikes Peak Vineyards** (Colorado Springs, 1983), is a 25-acre, 4,000-case winery that makes Chardonnay, Gewurztraminer, Riesling, Sauvignon Blanc, Seyval, Pinot Noir, and Cabernet Sauvignon. **Plum Creek Cellars** (Larkspur, 1985), is a 12-acre, 1,000-case winery that has generated a reputation for Sauvignon Blanc, Semillon, Napa Gamay, Merlot, and Cabernet Sauvignon. **Vail Valley Vintners** (Palisade, 1992), is a 2,000-case winery that makes Chardonnay and Merlot.

With 7,267 acres and an output of more than 584,000 gallons, Kansas ranked among the top ten states in the nation for wine production in 1880. Indeed, the state ranked in the forefront of grape hybridization as it developed nearly 24 distinct grape varieties. One of the most important was Dr. Joseph Stayman, a physician who developed numerous strawberries, raspberries, apples (the Stayman being the most notable), and grapes, of which White Imperial was the most notable. However important these accomplishments were, a combination of severe winters, Prohibition, 2, 4-D, competition from California wineries, and an unresponsive state legislature reduced the industry to fewer than 20 vine acres in 1960. Nevertheless, Kansas passed a Farm Winery Law in 1983, has recently reduced licensing fees, allows on premise tastings and Sunday sales. As a result, Kansas, that voted Prohibition in 1880, granted its first post-Prohibition winery license in 1988 and quickly followed with two others. There are now 150 grape acres and 20 growers cultivating American and French-American varieties. Other than those associated with wineries, acreage is in scattered vineyards along the protected sites of the Kansas and

Arkansas rivers: however, the eastern portion of the state adjoining Missouri appears to be the area with the highest winemaking potential. It is interesting to note that, due to unpredictable weather, the state allows less than 60 percent Kansas-grown fruit in "Kansas" wine.

The state's two wineries are: **Balkan Winery** (Arma, 1988), is a 12-acre, 1,000-case winery that makes Vidal Blanc, Seyval, Catawba, DeChaunac, and Baco Noir. **Field's of Fair Winery** (St. George, 1988), is a 12-acre, 2,000-case winery that makes Vignoles, Vidal Blanc, Ventura, Concord, a Steuben blend, and fruit wines. It is located in the northeastern portion of the state in the Kav Valley of the Flint Hills.

Of all the Great Plains states, only Oklahoma, Colorado, and Kansas generated any interest in the promulgation of Farm Winery legislation to stimulate acreage and production. In 1986, Oklahoma (a state widely known for wheat fields, cattle, oil wells, and a church on every block) has permitted farm wineries to sell "on the premises," and it is expected that three new wineries, in addition to the one already in existence, will be licensed shortly. Because of aridity and the high incidence of desiccating winds, only the eastern portion of the state (part of the Ozark Mountain *ava*, and commercially associated with Missouri and Arkansas) is favorable to grape cultivation. The only winery, **Cimarron Cellars** (Caney, 1983), is a 40-acre, 12,500-case winery that makes Colombard, Chenin Blanc, Aurora, Seyval, Vidal Blanc, Catawba, Rougeon, Marechal Foch, Petite Sirah, and proprietary wines.

SOUTHEASTERN AMERICA

South of the Mason Dixon line the geographic scenograph changes to a more humid climate, smaller farms, smaller towns, and fewer cities. Stretching from North Carolina to Louisiana, the southern American vineyard, the core of Rotundifolia grape production, is a region of large, widely dispersed cities, specialized manufacturing and agricultural crop production. Geographically, more than half of the area is on low-lying unconsolidated material along the coast, with the foothills and low mountains of the Appalachians stretching for more than 200 miles in the interior. The product of long disintegration, the residual soils, derived from gneiss, granite, and schist, are low in humus and fertility, and, hence, heavily fertilized. Climatically, this portion of America is surrounded by warm water with year-round humid air currents, and monotonously high, uniform temperatures.

As recently as 1938 the south depended upon cotton and tobacco for two-thirds of its cash income (more than half of its farmers depended upon cotton alone). As the nation's major economically depressed region, the south ranks (with Florida the exception) last in terms of income, quality of housing, and educational attainment. While it is an area of poor farmland and chronic out-migration, its predominantly native-born Protestant population has produced an aristocratic tradition, and a distinct regional diet. Nevertheless, the south contains half of the nation's forested land, produces 40 percent of the nation's poultry, is the leading area for kraft paper production, and its rapidly growing cities have recently attracted significant technologically advanced industries.

The southern vineyard includes the states of North and South Carolina, Georgia, Florida, Alabama, Mississippi, and Louisiana, and shares with the southern tier of mid-Atlantic states an early history of viticultural experimentation. It contains 3,700 acres of vineland, 29 wineries, and many unique viticultural enological elements: it is the last remaining region of the nation with strong Prohibitionist tendencies; the first place in Colonial America where wine was made; and the only area in the nation growing four types of grapes--American, French-American, Vinifera, and Rotundifolia. It is a region whose per capita wine consumption is increasing faster than elsewhere in the nation, has unlimited amount of inexpensive vineland, and table grapes have the potential of competing with citrus fruit in Florida and the Gulf Coast.

Table 5.10

U.S. SOUTH: GRAPE ACREAGE AND WINE PRODUCTION				
	Acres			
State	1970	1990	Gallons	Wineries
Alabama	50	50	14,000	5
Florida	40	580	336,000	4
Georgia	50	1,200	850,000	6
Mississippi	0	1,000	65,000	3
North Carolina	3,000	500	390,000	6
South Carolina	539	400	3,500,000	5
Total	3,679	3,730	2,800,000	29
Source: Compiled from State Agricultural Departments.				

Under no circumstances, however, can grape growing and winemaking be described as significant in a region whose diet is characterized by hush puppies, "white meat," fat back, black eye peas, yams, and collard greens. Professor Harm de Blij, a geographer of some repute, recently wrote: "Even knowledgeable oenophiles have a blind spot for Dixie on their mental maps. Subtropical environments, ignoble native grapes, and lingering Prohibition conjure up an image of syrupy, musky wines." Indeed, the five largest selling wines are either fortified or fruit wines, such as Richard's Wild Irish Rose, MD 20/20, Thunderbird, Night Train, and Boone's Farm, among others.

Nevertheless, this hitherto bastion of whiskey, beer, inexpensive fortified wines, mayonnaise, and ice tea has recently exhibited considerable interest in winegrowing. While planted acreage has remained the same from 1970 to 1992, the number of wineries leaped from 3 to 29, and the amount of wine jumped from 1.9 million to 2.8 million gallons. Most important, the distribution of vine acreage has shifted from North and South Carolina, to Florida, Georgia, and Mississippi, and the quality of the wines improved immensely (the percentage of inexpensive fortified wines from Monarch and Tenner Brothers, sold as Wild Irish Rose, has declined). Throughout the region, per

capita consumption has tripled since 1960, Rotundifolia-based juice is rapidly becoming a major industry, and the demand for southern-made specialty foods has created a demand for southern wines.

Although the humid southern portion of America was the center of important agricultural exports (cotton, peanuts, tobacco, rice, and indigo prior to 1860), was a stronghold of English aristocracy, had early Spanish settlement and a significant French cultural influence in Louisiana, winemaking never made important inroads in the economic and cultural life of the south. Yet, this area boasts an interesting early history: the discovery of Rotundifolia grapes occurred in 1524 by Giovanni da Verrazano, the Florentine navigator who explored the Cape Fear River Valley of North Carolina for the French; the first efforts at winemaking occurred in St. Augustine, Florida from native Rotundifolia vines in 1564 (Sir John Hawkins, at Fort Caroline found 20 hogheads of Rotundifolia wine after taking the fort from the French); and the first vineyards were established in coastal South Carolina on Parris Island between 1566 and 1568, and soon after on Roanoke Island, North Carolina.

Over the next two centuries concerted attempts to attract winemaking European immigrants to the Carolina's and Georgia were interminable, but futile. After the first attempts of Rotundifolia winemaking proved less than desirable, Vinifera vines were imported, but died soon thereafter, and nothing further came of these noble experiments. Although Savannah, Georgia was a major site for grape cultivation in the early 1700s, disease and more lucrative cotton endeavors doomed the fledgling industry. Dr. Andre Turnbull envisioned a New World utopia in New Smyrna, Florida in the 1770s, but vinegrowing, silk culture, and weaving did not materialize. Another failure was New Bordeaux, South Carolina, founded by French Huguenots who were granted 30,000 acres by the English government for a wine industry in the southern part of the state.

Interest in fermenting Rotundifolia grapes after the Civil War accelerated, and by 1880, 7,457 vine-acres were being cultivated in the six southern states, of which 2,999 acres were located in Georgia, and 2,639 acres in North Carolina. It was reported in 1883 that the single largest vineyard (the Tokay Vineyard Winery) east of the Rocky Mountains was located 3 miles north of Fayetteville, North Carolina on an undulating tableland overlooking the Cape Fear River. Wines from 20 Mississippi counties were exhibited in 1885 at the World Industrial and Cotton Exposition in New Orleans, and prior to the enactment of the Volstead Act Mississippi had 32 producing wineries. Prohibition wiped the industry out in all southern states, and winemaking was not considered a viable southern activity until recently. As the rural-to-urban migration accelerated after 1950 and major cities grew to metropolitan status, interest in wine brought forth many initiatives to produce wine in southern states. Of the 29 wineries in existence in 1992, two were founded immediately after Repeal, one in 1968, 8 or 9 between 1972 and 1979, and 15 between 1981 and 1992. Responding to regional wine demand, vine acreage in some states increased rapidly over the past 20 years: more than 1,000 acres in Mississippi, 1,200 acres in Georgia, and 580 acres in Florida. Impressive as these figures appear to be, lingering Prohibition tendencies (as evidenced by the number of "dry counties"), and a regional diet that does not encourage wine consumption are major constraints to future growth. It is important to note that the region contains a disproportionate amount of dry states and counties, whose main objective is to not encourage consumption but "control" it.

The climate of the southern vineyard is determined by the presence of tropical water in the Gulf of Mexico, the Caribbean, and the Atlantic Ocean; the lack of cyclonic patterns for most of the year; and the absence of strong westerly wind movement. As a consequence, weather is characterized by a constant year-round high air humidity, a pronounced summer wet season (for most of the area, the rainy season, June through September, receives more than half of the annual total), uniformly high temperatures, and the absence of a pronounced dormant season. In addition, precipitation is characterized by high intensity and short duration, and the effect is compounded by infertile, droughty soils. Climatically, the southeast falls within Region IV and V, and the frost-free period, abbreviated to below 170 days in the extreme higher elevations of the Appalachians, is greater than 280 days through the coastal areas and a good deal of the interior foothills.

This climate offers a number of constraints to successful vine cultivation. The presence of Pierce's Disease, rapacious insects, and bacterial and viral diseases mandate a regular, unwavering spray schedule that is outrageously expensive. The dominant environmental elements determining choice of grape variety planted are nematode problems, humidity and the proclivity toward fungus diseases, hence the tendency to raise Rotundifolia and not Vinifera or French-American varieties. Excessive precipitation and the persistent atmospheric and soil humidity, at this moment, preclude large-scale cultivation of Vinifera, and, to a lesser degree, French-American grapes. Indeed, Vinifera vines are mainly grown in the Pierce's Disease-free, higher elevations of North Carolina and Georgia, and, to a smaller extent, in one vineyard in Mississippi. Equally significant is the fact that the cost of producing Vinifera grapes in the south is more than twice that of California, not including land costs. It is also important to note that the commercial cultivation of Rotundifolia is only marginal, at best, in comparison with other agricultural crops.

One of the biggest problems with grape growing throughout humid, southeastern America is Pierce's Disease (also known as degeneration, die-back, or decline), an incurable infection whereby bacterium clogs the xylem (water conducting elements of the vine) causing leaf yellowing, uneven wood maturity, delayed budbreak, a decline in vigor and production, and eventual death after five to seven years. This rapacious disease, spread by leafhopper vectors, is endemic to the hotter, coastal, southeastern portion of the nation (it generally does not affect elevations above 800 feet), and is absolutely deadly to all Vinifera, American, and French-American vines. Rotundifolia vines, due to centuries of adaptation, are apparently the only family of vines that are immune. Recently, developed interspecific American and Rotundifolia hybrids are also immune to Pierce's Disease (a minor, but manageable problem in central and southern California, and several isolated areas in Arizona, New Mexico, and Texas).

As a result, the dominant grape is Vitis rotundifolia and its dominant subclass: the Scuppernong, described as "God's gift to the sunny south." Scuppernong is the name given to various varieties (it is also the name of a specific variety) that produce white juice, while others are referred to as Muscadine (the subgenus name) that give a natural pink juice. Rotundifolia grapes grow well in the hot, humid climate of the Gulf Coast and southeastern America, which is to say, in areas where winter temperatures rarely fall below 10F, although hardy varieties extend northward to tidewater Virginia and westward to the Piedmont. Site selection is mainly in areas where there is good air and soil drainage. Curiously, grape clusters and individual berries ripen unevenly because night temperatures can be as hot as daytime (it requires at least 10 degrees difference to ripen berries evenly). Therefore, while the cooler areas account for higher quality wines, larger diurnal temperature extremes during the last 30 days of maturation is a more important element in the production of quality wines.

Rotundifolia, low in total acidity, sugar, and soluble solids, are strongly flavored and scented grapes. Yields are much larger than American varieties in the northeast and midwest with most grape varieties yielding between 5 and 12 tons to the acre, whereas French-American varieties rarely produce above 5 tons to the acre. A significant industry just waiting development is the excellent juice of the Scuppernong grape, considered by many superior to any other because of its versatile character. Of the estimated 3,500 vine acres, 79 percent are true Rotundifolia, 15 percent hybrid bunch grapes, 5 percent French-American, and less than 1 percent Vinifera, the later mainly confined to North Carolina and Georgia. The overwhelming number of growers, however, "proudly" cultivate Rotundifolia that are made into a wide assortment of jellies, juice, and a bewildering number of table, flavored, and sparkling wines. Scuppernong Mistelle, in particular, can be outstanding. As popular as it is, Scuppernong is rapidly being replaced throughout the southeast by more consonant, less musky flavored and scented varieties.

Rotundifolia varieties with good winemaking potential are Carlos, Scuppernong, Dixie, Magnolia, Noble, Roanoke, Welder, Sterling, Tarheel, Regale, and Doreen. Bunch grapes with an excellent future include Blanc Du Bois, MissBlue, MissBlanc, Stover, Lake Emerald, Suwanee, and Conquistador. The four popular white Rotundifolia are Carlos, Magnolia, Sterling, and Scuppernong; the three popular red are Creek, Noble, and Jumbo, the latter, with a very large berry, as the name implies, gives high yields but is relatively low in sugar. There are many important distinctions between these grapes: bunch grapes in the extreme southern portion ripen late in July, while Rotundifolia ripen between mid-August and late-September. In terms of general characteristics, Rotundifolia are relatively high in tannin, and extremely aromatic and flavorful, the latter based on 2-phenyl-ethanol. Due to color instability in red varieties, "white" Rotundifolia are more important in the production of wine. In the final analysis, the taste and flavor appeal of Rotundifolia grapes in the south is legendary; because of high fiber, calcium, iron, potassium, magnesium, and a low sodium content, these grapes are recommended by nutritionists as an important dietary supplement.

Southern wines, dominated by the peculiar flavor of Rotundifolia grapes, are invariably ameliorated, hence, high in sugar and alcohol levels, and inexpensive, conditions that do not favor an easy transition to dry table wines. Most are different in flavor and scent, but not all that distinct from Madeira and other fortified wines that were long the bastion of southern plantation aristocracy. The Madeira of old, along with the social rituals associated with rural and small town living, has yet to be transformed into cosmopolitan lifestyles. As a consequence, although there is increasing interest in dry table Vinifera wines, the southeast, as a general rule, has a beer/whiskey drinking population, and Rotundifolia wine has been relegated a role for the lower half of the working population, while California and imported wines remain the preferred libations of the more affluent. The future lies in widening the market for the unusual taste and flavor of the drier versions of Rotundifolia and bunch grape table and sparkling wines. The very best wines display the variety and species on the label, but the overwhelming majority of wine is blended and sold under proprietary labels.

North And South Carolina

The "Tarheel" state, known for its long stretches of beach, first class universities, tobacco farms, oysters, Christmas trees, and scenic mountains, has had a long and varied viticultural history. Despite its association with the Bible Belt and its dominant Baptist religious group, North Carolina is the home of the nation's first cultivated wine grape (Scuppernong) and the notorious Catawba, and the place of discovery of two unusual and lesser known grapes--Meisch and Flowers. While the wild Rotundifolia vines were everywhere along the coastal areas south of Cape Fear and throughout the eastern margins of the Piedmont section, North Carolina claims to be the state that originally domesticated the Scuppernong, or as the early settlers called it--"the big white grape." One of the most remarkable aftermaths of Sir Walter Raleigh's Colony on Roanoke Island is the presence of an original Scuppernong vine still living 400 years after it was planted.

This rapidly growing state (7 million), one of the wealthiest in the south, is nearly 500 miles broad--stretching across three major physiographic provinces--the Appalachians, Piedmont, and Coastal Plain. Viticultural pursuits have been part of the agricultural history of the state for more than 400 years, first as a home cottage industry, and for the past 100 years by larger commercial wineries. Wine was made by German Swiss settlers in the early 1700s, and by 1809 there were several extensive plantings, some as large as 600 acres. It is reported that in 1810, 1,368 gallons of Scuppernong wine was made in Washington County and at least in 14 other counties. The state's first commercial vineyard, 12 acres of black Rotundifolia was founded in 1835 by Sidney Weller in Halifax County. The state had 25 wineries in the 1850s, but after the Civil War the southern population was prohibited from legally producing alcoholic beverages, and all wineries closed. In 1880 North Carolina had 2,639 acres of planted vines, ranking among the nation's top ten states. Some began production after laws were amended, but an unresponsive state legislature and Prohibition put many out of business.

The celebrated wine personality, Paul Garrett, born in Edgecombe County in 1863, was not only the state's most famous winemaker, but was responsible for marketing the nation's most successful wine brand--"Virginia Dare" (named after the first child born of English parents in America). This brand was, for 20 years after Prohibition, the most widely sold wine in America--an extraordinary achievement as well as a reflection of contemporary tastes. The Scuppernong-based, non-vintaged, blended wine was made in five different wineries in North Carolina, and, for a brief period, popularized the fame of this native grape. Beginning as a salesman for his father and uncle (they purchased the famous Medoc Vineyard, North Carolina in 1865), Paul Garrett was no outsider to the wine industry. He quickly recognized the economic potential of blended Rotundifolia, purchased the family business in 1905, and by 1919, on the eve of Prohibition, had built the largest wine empire in the nation with seventeen wineries (with a total capacity of 10 million gallons) located in North Carolina, Ohio, Virginia, Missouri, and New York. He died of pneumonia in 1940 at the age of 76, and since he had no heirs his wine empire was dissolved, and with his demise the state's wine industry lay dormant until the mid-1960s.

Figure 5.32

NORTH CAROLINA: CLIMATIC PATTERNS

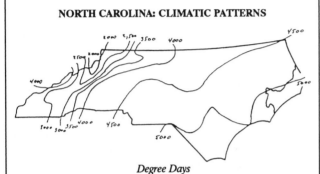

Degree Days
The area bounded by the 5000-degree-day isoline is planted primarily in Rotundifolia; regions fewer than 4000 degree days are planted in bunch grapes; only the higher elevations of the Piedmont and Appalachians are planted in Vinifera.

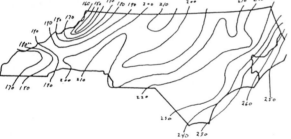

Average Length of Frost-free Season. The region with fewer than 200 frost-free days exhibits Vinifera potential. The area surrounding Asheville, the site of the state's largest Vinifera acreage, is, with 60 inches, one of the wettest areas in the state.

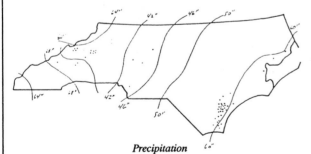

Precipitation
The distribution of grapes are not affected by precipitation patterns. Each dot represents 10 acres.
Source: U.S. Weather Bureau.

Other historic wineries were Niagara Vineyard located in Southern Pines, and Tokay Vineyard Winery near Fayetteville, the latter making nearly 50,000 cases in 1885. Much larger (100,000) cases, but less elegant, was the Castle Hayne Vineyard Co. of Wilmington. By 1906 there

were more than 20 wineries in 14 counties producing Rotundifolia-based wines. In 1909, the wine industry came to an abrupt halt when state-wide prohibition was adopted. Grape production dropped steadily until Prohibition, when demand by home winemakers stimulated production until Repeal. Total grape output dropped from a high of 7,300 tons in 1934 to 800 tons in 1957, the smallest harvest of the century. Grape production for the years 1955-1957 averaged but 1,000 tons, and grape acreage declined to 180, the lowest in nearly 100 years. It is interesting to note that despite the state's rather formidable historical importance, insignificant quantities of wine were made after Repeal, and it was only after the formation of Duplin Wine Cellars in 1976 that large-scale wine production began. Prior to 1976, grapes were shipped to wineries in Virginia and South Carolina. Today, North Carolina makes fewer than 200,000 cases of wine, the bulk of the grape must (mostly Rotundifolia) is shipped to out of state wineries for blending purposes.

In the depth's of the economic depression afflicting Rotundifolia production, the first post-Prohibition vineyard (25 acres) was established in 1955 by Raymond Hartfield in Onslow County on the Coastal Plain. In the 1960s, as in many other states, there was renewed interest in the commercial possibilities of Rotundifolia grapes for wine production, and during the ensuing years grape acreage and wineries began to increase. In 1961 Richard Wine Cellars in Virginia offered growers a five-year contract at guaranteed prices to establish vineyards. By 1962 there were over 250 acres, and by 1976 it was estimated that there were 2,494 acres of commercial vineland, a figure that has since declined to fewer than 500 acres, in part because of a disastrous hard freeze in 1985. Grape prices rose from $130 the ton in 1959 to $333 the ton in 1973, a figure only to be exceeded by the $341 per ton price established in 1984. Despite the apparent grape boom, three wineries ceased operations in the 1980s, and wine production has declined since 1984.

Unfortunately, the vineyard explosion of the 1960s and 1970s, impressive as it was, was overwhelmingly confined to six southern coastal plain counties, and cultivated vines were dominated by Rotundifolia varieties. The biggest buyers were Richard's Wine Cellars of Petersburg, Virginia, and Tenner Brothers of Patrick, South Carolina, both of which began to reduce grape purchases throughout the 1980s, and totally ceased to purchase North Carolina grapes in 1988.

There are fewer than 25 growers producing less than 4,000 tons from 500 acres of vineland, of which 275 are planted in Rotundifolia, 200 in Vinifera (grown mainly by two wineries), and about 25 in French-American and American varieties. Climate, more than soil and topographic factors, limits the cultivation of all four types of grapes. Vinifera are located either on the Blue Ridge or the upper elevations of the Piedmont, both of which contain fewer than 3,000 degree days, and are relatively free of Pierce's Disease. Rotundifolia grapes are overwhelmingly concentrated in the southeastern portion of the state in and around Clear Lake, an area that has almost 5,000 degree days, and a growing season of nearly 300 days. The minor plantings of American and French-American varieties are widely distributed throughout the state, but mainly in the Piedmont.

This Scuppernong vine, part of the historic "Mother Vineyard," is located on the south side of Roanoke Island, 2 miles south of Fort Raleigh. The present vine, sited on private property, is all that remains of a much larger Scuppernong vineyard that might have predated English settlement. More than 400 years old, some maintain that it may the oldest man-planted biotic matter still alive in the New World. It measures about eight feet at the base. Baxevanis

Today North Carolina ranks extremely low in the nation for wine production, grape acreage, and total economic contribution to the state economy, but, unlike Virginia to the north, the state remained viticulturally undeveloped throughout the post-World War II period, due, in large part, to an unsympathetic state legislature. Nevertheless, in an effort to stimulate grape and wine production, the North Carolina State legislature in 1972 reduced the annual winery fee from $1,000 to $100, and cut the state tax from .60 to .05 cents per gallon. Although this gesture proved to be too little too late, per capita con-

sumption in the past fifteen years has doubled, and the success of Biltmore Estate Wine Co., Duplin Wine Cellars, and West Bend Winery is cause for some optimism. Meanwhile, a breeding program at North Carolina State University has produced no fewer than eleven new varieties, Carlos, Magnolia, and Noble being the most important (others include Albemarle, Chowan, Pamlico, Roanoke, Dixie, Regale, Sterling, and Doreen). One of the most notable viticulturists of the southeast was Dr. Robert T. Dunstan, an academician who successfully demonstrated that crosses of Euvitis and Muscadiniae were possible. Although a linguist in the foreign language department at Greensboro College, he cultivated, bred and crossed Rotundifolia with considerable acumen. He successfully demonstrated that new varieties could be bred to possess the most desirable features of both Euvitis and Muscadiniae.

Figure 5.33

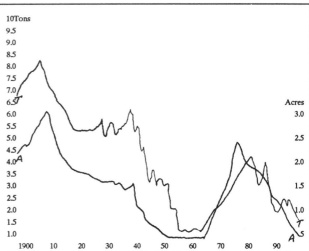

NORTH CAROLINA: GRAPE PRODUCTION AND ACREAGE
(In Thousand Tons and Acres)

The viticultural fortunes of North Carolina (as well as its immediate neighbor to the south) have fluctuated with the production of inexpensive fortified wine and one large winery located in South Carolina. Vine acreage historically had been confined to the Coastal Plain. The most important grape growing counties are: Sampson, Lenoir, Washington, Pender, Brunswick, and Cleveland. Due to the dominance of Rotundifolia grapes, all but Cleveland County are located along the Coastal Plain. Carlos, Magnolia, Scuppernong, and Fry are the most important varieties.
Source: North Carolina Department of Agriculture.

The six wineries are: **Biltmore Estate Wine Company** (Asheville, 1977), is a magnificent, 172-acre, 40,000-case winery located 2,400 feet above sea level in the extreme western portion of the state. It produces a limited line of highly variable Vinifera wines under two labels: *Biltmore Estate* for blended white, red, and rose; and *Chateau Biltmore* for classic white and red varietals, and sparkling wines. The most important are Chardonnay, Sauvignon Blanc, and Cabernet Sauvignon. The wines are sold in selected outlets in the state and at the 8,000-acre estate that draws more than 500,000 tourists annually. **Duplin Wine Cellars** (Rose Hill, 1975), is a 100,000-case winery that makes a large assortment of Rotundifolia-based brandy, table, and sparkling wines. The winery crushes nearly the entire state's Rotundifolia crop. **LaRocca**

Wine Co. (Fayetteville, 1968), is a 2,500-case Rotundifolia winery that makes only dry white and red wine from purchased grapes under the *Carolina Pines* label. The well-made, flavored and scented wines, made from Hunts, Carlos, and Magnolia, offer good value. **Southland Estate Winery** (Selma, 1985), is a 7-acre, 52,000-case winery (made at Duplin Wine Cellars) that offers a large assortment of sparkling, fortified, and table wines from Rotundifolia grapes. **Villar Vintners of Valdese** (Valdese, 1989), is a 1,500-case winery that makes blended proprietary white, blush, and red wines, mostly from French-American grapes. **West Bend Winery** (Lewisville, 1988), is a 25-acre, 3,000-case winery currently growing the finest Vinifera grapes (mostly Chardonnay, Cabernet Sauvignon, Riesling, Merlot, Gamay Beaujolais), with minor plantings of French-American vines. The vineyard (southwest of Winston-Salem) has been selling grapes for the past ten years to Virginia wineries. The wines, crisp, fruity, and expertly made, rival those from the Biltmore Estate.

Raymond Hartfield harvesting Scuppernong near Clear lake on the Coastal Plain. Baxevanis

While South Carolina resembles Virginia and North Carolina in terms of culture and historic traditions, it has a much smaller population of 3.7 million, a land area that is nearly half the size of North Carolina, and a per capita wine consumption figure that is half that of its immediate neighbors. For all its viticultural shortcomings, the state has had a rich history that goes back to 1521 when one Francisco Gordillo y Quexos became the first European to explore the coast. In 1663 King Charles II granted the entire Carolina Territory to eight lord proprietors, and in 1678, the English established the first permanent settlement at Albemarle Point. For the next two centuries South Carolina represented a true feudal aristocracy whose economic prosperity was based on indigo, cotton, tobacco, and rice, and its social customs were modeled after those prevailing in England and France. By 1768 South Carolina was responsible for one-fifth of the colo-

nial exports to England. Rice was so important a commodity it was used as currency, and by 1820 the state produced one-third of the nation's cotton crop. A good indication of the preeminence of Charleston as one of the most prosperous cities in the country were its two golf courses in 1791.

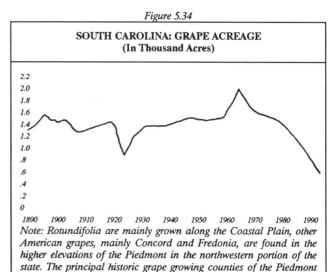

Figure 5.34

SOUTH CAROLINA: GRAPE ACREAGE
(In Thousand Acres)

Note: Rotundifolia are mainly grown along the Coastal Plain, other American grapes, mainly Concord and Fredonia, are found in the higher elevations of the Piedmont in the northwestern portion of the state. The principal historic grape growing counties of the Piedmont are: Spartanburg, Chesterfield, Lexington, Greenville, and Laurens. Florence, Williamsburg, and Horry are the most important along the Coastal Plain.
Source: South Carolina Crop Reporting Service, and personal interview. The state stopped the taking of grape statistics in 1959.

While South Carolina, the "Palmetto" state, lacks the historical significance of a Paul Garrett, its viticultural history is long, varied, and quite similar to that of North Carolina. It is here that the Isabella is thought to have originated in 1816, the Herbemont was grown commercially by Nicholas Herbemont of Columbia in the early 1820s, and Lenoir in 1829. Viticulture, though insignificant at present, goes back 400 years to early Spanish exploration in the second half of the sixteenth century, and a French Huguenot settlement in 1562 near present-day Parris Island near Beaufort. The Spanish made wine along the coast from Parris Island to St. Augustine in the 1560s, and the French Huguenots attempted cultivation and made wine in at least five different settlements: Charleston, Goose Creek, Orange Quarter, St. Johns, and Jamestown. One additional group of Huguenots, coming from Bordeaux, adept at silk production as well as grape growing, settled near the Savannah River and actually called their town "New Bordeaux." Despite their energetic character, they were not successful in cultivating either the grape or the silkworm. Along with other minor vineyards in Aiken and other places, a 300-acre vineyard was established by Louis de Saint Pierre in 1772, and by 1784 two vines dominated production--Blue French and Brown French--known today as Lenoir (widely planted along the Gulf Coast states and eastern Texas), and Herbemont (an old grape dating back to colonial days whose virtues were promulgated by Nicholas Herbemont). With time, South Carolina made fewer attempts at growing grapes and making wine, preferring instead to import the famed Madeira (particularly for the Madeira Club of Savannah) and other fortified wines from Spain and Portugal. By 1880 South Carolina had 193 acres of Rotundifolia vines under cultivation and produced but 16,988 gallons of wine.

One hundred years later the Farm Winery Act was passed, and the state had 1,406 acres, 51 vineyards, and three licensed wineries (one of which has since closed). In that same year, the state legislature substantially lowered the tax on state grown wine with less than 14 percent alcohol. South Carolina, as well as its sister state to the north, in an effort to diversify production from traditional crops such as tobacco, cotton, peanuts, and forest products, is slowly but seriously aiding viticulture, but not enough to stem the tide of vine acreage reduction. In 1988, of the 418 acres of grapes in existence, 251 were various Rotundifolia, 79 Concord, and the remainder a large assortment of other bunch grapes, mostly French-American varieties. Despite declining acreage, the varietal mix and types of grapes grown have shown improvement since 1967 when 57 percent of the planted acreage was Concord, 32 percent Rotundifolia, and the remainder native bunch grapes, of which Catawba, Fredonia, and Niagara were the most prominent. Although acreage is spread over five coastal counties, Spartanburg, with more than 200 acres, is the most important. Given the fact that the state beverage is "iced tea," wine production and viticulture, in general, are not about to expand significantly.

The state's five wineries are: **Foxwood Wine Cellars** (Woodruff, 1979), is a 300-acre, 70,000-case winery that makes various types of table wines, but the mainstay are fortified wines selling under the *Ramblin' Rose* and *Dealers Choice* labels. **Cruse Vineyards** (Chester, 1986), is a 5-acre, 1,200-case winery that makes Chardonnay, Riesling, Villard Blanc, Seyval, Vidal Blanc, Burdin (#8753, a rare Gamay hybrid), Chancellor, and Pinot Noir. **Montmorenci Vineyards** (Aiken, 1989), is a superb, 16-acre, 2,500-case winery that makes excellent

Cayuga, Seyval, Vidal Blanc, Chardonnay, Suwannee, Blanc de Bois, Vignoles, Melody, and Chambourcin. **Tenner Brothers Winery** (Patrick, 1935), is a 1.6 million-case winery owned by the Canandaigua Wine Co. that makes fortified Rotundifolia-based wines for the *Richard's Wild Irish Rose* label. Although this is the largest winery in the southeast, the final product is made through the importation of juice and concentrate from other states, primarily California. **Truluck Vineyards** (Lake City, 1976), founded by a dedicated dentist, this 53-acre, 15,500-case winery is the state's premier winery, and one of the finest in the entire south in terms of quality and commitment. Three hundred different varieties of grape (most of them in experimental plots) produce a large number of blended and varietal American, Rotundifolia, French-American, and Vinifera wines, of which Chambourcin (the Blanc is particularly good), Villard Blanc, Vignoles, Cayuga, Vidal Blanc, Cabernet Sauvignon, and an unusual Munson are considered above-average. Small quantities of sparkling wine are also made. This venerable winery, the largest quality producer in the state, has recently closed, but may reopen.

Georgia And Alabama

As one of the largest states of southeastern America, Georgia has rarely exhibited the usual southern stereotype. Unlike its neighbors to the north, its large population of 7 million is highly concentrated in the Piedmont, and total wine economic contributions to the state's economy is similar to that of Virginia. Moreover, Georgia was the first state to send a woman to the Senate, to grant women full property rights, to franchise eighteen year-olds, and to develop since 1945 an economy that has grown at twice the national average. Although Georgia ranks near the bottom in per capita wine consumption, in 1880 it was the sixth largest wine-producing state (2,999 acres and 903,000 gallons) whose production was double that of New York. For 44 years until 1980, this peanut, cotton, and pecan producing state had but one winery, the large Monarch firm in Atlanta. But beginning with the first (1980) of what appear to be annual farm winery bills, the wine industry has began to experience a revival of considerable proportions. Acreage since 1950 increased from 200 to over 1,200, and over the past six years four new wineries have been constructed. Seventy percent of the acreage is planted in Rotundifolia (mainly in the southern Coastal Plain around Albany), American (10 percent), French-American (15 percent), and Vinifera (5 percent) whose acreage is confined in a triangular area between Gainesville-Covington-Athens. Eison, a red Rotundifolia recently developed by a nursery, appears to have solved the color retention problem, and is being planted by several growers. Should it prove successful, the palatable red wine problem may yet be solved in the southeast.

The state's seven wineries are: **Cavender Castle Winery** (Dahlonega, 1989), is a 6-acre, 2,000-case winery that makes Sauvignon Blanc, Seyval, Vidal Blanc, DeChaunac, and proprietary wines. **Chateau Elan** (Hoschton, 1984), is a 200-acre, 35,000-case winery that makes average quality Chardonnay, Sauvignon Blanc, Riesling, Chenin Blanc, Cabernet Sauvignon, Merlot, Rotundifolia, and French-American wines. The winery, part of a 1,000-acre estate containing a stable of recreational facilities (more than 250,000 visitors annually), is expected to produce 200,000 cases by 1998 from estate grown and purchased grapes. **Chestnut Mountain Winery** (Braselton, 1988), is an interesting, aggressive and innovative, 10-acre, 3,500-case, all-Vinifera winery that makes Chardonnay, Chenin Blanc, Cabernet Sauvignon, Nebbiolo, and Merlot wines. **Fox Vineyards Winery** (Social Circle, 1987), is a 15-acre, 5,500-case winery that makes Cabernet Sauvignon, Sauvignon Blanc, Chenin Blanc, Orange Muscat, Seyval, Vidal Blanc, and proprietary wines, all offering good value. **Georgia Wines** (Chickamauga, 1983), is a 15-acre, 1,600-case winery located just south of Chattanooga that makes a large assortment of berry, fruit, sparkling, and table wine from American, French-American, and Vinifera grapes most of which are purchased. **Habersham Vineyards Winery** (Baldwin, 1983), is a 32-acre, 15,000-case winery that makes more than 15 different wines, of which Seyval, Chardonnay, Riesling, Chancellor, Cabernet Franc, and Cabernet Sauvignon appear to be the finest. Other label: *Etowah Ridges*. **Monarch Wine Company of Georgia** (Atlanta, 1936), was the only winery in the state until 1980. With an annual production exceeding 300,000 cases (plus bulk sales) of vermouth, table, fruit, berry, and fortified wines, this is the largest winery in the state selling under the *Bojangles, King Cotton, Red Rooster, Roho Sangria, Deuce Juice, Square Johnson*, and other labels.

Despite the fact that Alabama was first explored by Hernando de Soto in 1540, the first permanent white settlement was established in Mobile by the French in 1711. Viticultural endeavors were first introduced in 1813. Notwithstanding the fact that there are fewer than 35 acres of commercial vineland, five wineries, and 9,000 cases of wine made in Alabama, unofficial estimates are said to be much higher due to an active underground network of state-licensed wineries making more than five gallons of wine. Besides Rotundifolia, the most important and highest yielding variety is Concord.

The wineries are: **Alistair Vineyards** (New Market, 1988), is a 4-acre, 1,500-case winery that makes Vidal Blanc, Villard Blanc, and Chancellor wines. **Braswell's Winery** (Dora, 1984), is an aggressive, 207-acre (planted in fruit, berry and grapes), 5,000-case winery that makes 16 different wines. Besides unusual berry and fruit (it makes an excellent persimmon) wines, the firm makes various Rotundifolia, Fredonia, Concord, Catawba, Villard Blanc, and Niagara wines. Highly unusual is the fact that the vineyards are not sprayed and the vines have never been affected by Pierce's Disease. **Bryant Vineyard** (Talladega, 1985), is a 6-acre, 250-case winery that makes Rotundifolia wine. **Peacock Valley Winery** (Perdido, 1979), is a 3-acre, 3,000-case winery that makes Noble, Magnolia, Villard Blanc, fruit, and proprietary wines. **Pinecroft Winery** (DeArmanville, 1985), is a .5-acre, 100-gallon, licensed, but non-commercial winery that is owned by a physician engaged in the production of experimental vines (Chardonnay, Cabernet Sauvignon, and Villard Blanc, the latter the most successful), and the production of minute quantities of wine.

Mississippi

Unlike other Gulf Coast states, Mississippi, the "Magnolia" state, boasted many vineyards and wineries in the nineteenth century. The Viticultural Census of 1880 records 432 acres of vineland in nine counties, and in 1919, on the eve of Prohibition, there were 31 commercial wineries in the state. Acreage, reduced to non-commercial home plantings after Repeal, began to grow steadily in the late 1970s to more than 60 acres in 1980. This figure increased rapidly to 200 in 1984, and by 1994 it is estimated that there will be more than 1,000 acres of planted vines--in the very state that repealed Prohibition as recently as 1966 (the last state in the Union to do so). While Rotundifolia dominate commercial acreage, Catawba, Isabella, Concord, Ives, Delaware, and such ob-

scure varieties as Herbemont, Tuloka, Iona, and Hartford, among others, are also planted by amateur winemakers. It is estimated that over the past several years, more than 700 acres of Rotundifolia varieties have been planted in Mississippi to supply the demands of the energetic Southeastern Specialty Foods Company located in Ellisville. When this acreage is fully bearing by 1993, Mississippi will have more than half of the commercial Rotundifolia in the southeast, a rather remarkable achievement.

Almarla

Cream Scuppernong
of Mississippi
A SWEET WHITE WINE
PRODUCED AND BOTTLED BY
ALMARLA VINEYARDS
MATHERVILLE, MISSISSIPPI

Six years after Prohibition was repealed in the state, the Bureau of Alcohol, Tobacco and Firearms granted a permit for the making of experimental wine on the campus of Mississippi State University, and, as a result, viticulture, under the guidance of Dr. Richard Vine at Mississippi State University, has undergone a minor renaissance in recent years. Not only does the University grant degrees in enology and viticulture, but the curriculum has produced a good number of southern winemakers, and maintains experimental plots of Vinifera, American, and Rotundifolia vines. In 1976, the "Native Wine Law" by the state legislature was enacted making it possible once again for wineries to legally make wine 43 years after federal repeal. Even more revealing about the "winds of change" in this traditional southern state is the fact that in 1988 the state repealed the ban on wine advertising.

Mississippi contains one *ava, Mississippi Delta (1984)*, a 180-mile long, 65-mile wide, flat, alluvial plain that coincides perfectly with the topography of the Yazoo Basin, the former Mississippi flood plain. This huge 6,000 square mile area is bounded on the east by 100-foot high loess bluffs (of wind-blown soil), and the Mississippi River on the west. It extends from the southern margins of Memphis, Tennessee to Vicksburg, Mississippi. The *ava* contains the state's vine acreage, and its four wineries, all of which have generated good, local reputations.

The wineries are: **Almarla Vineyards** (Matherville, 1979), with 42 acres and an output of nearly 20,000 cases, is the largest winery in the state. The owner, a former BATF chemist, is a conscientious, capable winemaker and viticulturist with a keen sense of what can be accomplished in the humid Gulf Coast. In addition to generic and flavored wines, the specialty is Rotundifolia. **Clairborne Vineyards** (Indianola, 1984), is a 5-acre, 2,000-case winery that makes a small assortment of Vinifera and French-American wines, of which Seyval is particularly good. **Old South Winery** (Natchez, 1979), is a conscientious, 7,000-case, Rotundifolia winery with a good reputation for semi-sweet Carlos. **The Winery Rushing** (Merigold, 1977), the first winery in Mississippi since Prohibition, is a 22-acre, 10,000-case winery that makes good, sound Noble, Magnolia, and Carlos.

The neighboring state of Louisiana discourages wine-growing by imposing a $1,000 winery license fee and other impediments. As significant as recent events have been, the state ranks 23rd in the nation in terms of total economic contribution by the wine industry. The fact that it has a relatively small (3 million), youthful population does little to improve both the image and consumption of fine wine.

Florida

Florida, the "Sunshine" state, is a large state in both area and population. It is 367 miles across its northern boundary, and more than 500 miles long. Even more surprising is the fact that its northern boundary is 100 miles further south than the southern boundary of California. Miami is located further west than Buffalo, New York, and most of the state lies due south of Ohio and Indiana. Florida is also a relatively new state as far as population is concerned. As recently as 1890, Key West, with a population of only 18,000 was the state's largest city; but in 1925, due to railroad construction, more than 2.5 million people entered Florida over the next ten years. The population grew from 1.5 million in 1930 to nearly 13 million in 1990, and the fact that the state accommodates more than 35 million tourists annually is a remarkable achievement by any standard. That it is the only state in the Union without an area above 600 feet is equally significant.

Of all the southern states Florida exhibits the most favorable economic climate for future viticultural development. With a rapidly growing wine-drinking population, and a large tourist population, the state ranks, with more than 30 million gallons of wine, as the third largest wine market. The cities of Gainesville, Miami, West Palm Beach, Sarasota, Ft. Meyers-Naples, and Orlando individually consume more wine than the national city average, and while the national per capita consumption level has been declining since 1984, this state's wine consumption has been increasing. Of the 50 largest wine consuming metropolitan areas, six are in Florida: Tampa, Miami, West Palm Beach, Jacksonville, Orlando, and Ft. Lauderdale.

While Juan Ponce de Leon claimed Florida for Spain and Hernando de Soto explored a good deal of the peninsula in 1539, it has been reported that wine was first made by French Huguenot settlers in Florida in 1564 near the Georgia border. Despite this early endeavor, wine grow-

ing never propagated enthusiasm for more than 300 years. Vitis labrusca grapes were introduced in the early 1880s, and by 1894, 500 acres were planted in Orange County. While Concord dominated acreage, Niagara, Ives, and Worden were widely planted in the northern panhandle. However, by 1900 the vines began to die, and by 1907 all commercial Labrusca vineland ended in failure. The most notable personality at that time was one Emile Dubois who came to Tallahassee in 1882, planted grapes near the seventeenth century Spanish mission San Luis, and made wine, an endeavor that eventually won him a gold and silver medal at the Paris Exposition of 1900. Although many different American, French-American, and Rotundifolia varieties were grown on an experimental basis by the United States Department of Agriculture, none but Rotundifolia varieties proved hardy enough to warrant recommendations for commercial cultivation. In the early 1920s, several T.V. Munson grape varieties, particularly Extra, were introduced, and by 1928 there were nearly 4,000 acres (primarily Munson varieties) under cultivation. Unfortunately, the vines succumbed to degeneration, and by 1938 grape acreage declined to fewer than ten acres, none of which were commercial. Today the state's 580 grape acres (with a value of less than $1 million) are dwarfed by citrus fruit, the state's most valuable agricultural crop.

Figure 5.35

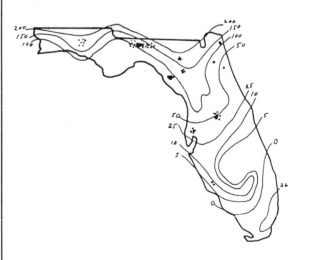

FLORIDA: GRAPE AND WINERY DISTRIBUTION

Each dot represents 10 acres. Lines indicate number of hours per year below 24F. No commercial grape vines are to be found south of Alva, the site of the southernmost winery in America.
Source: U.S. Weather Bureau; Florida Agricultural Statistics Service.

Although Florida produces fewer than 200,000 cases of wine, it is the center of a four-decade breeding effort by state university agencies that is producing many disease resistant vines and new, improved vineyard management practices. The combination of a sympathetic state legislature (Florida has one of the most liberal farm winery laws in the nation, and maintains no state taxes on wine made from Florida grapes), the infusion of new capital and a small number of dedicated growers have helped to raise acreage from 70 acres in 1972 to 580 acres in 1992 (and according to the Florida Grape Growers Association, acreage is expected to double by 2000), 60 percent of which are Rotundifolia, and the remainder bunch grapes--both of which have shown rapid growth in recent years due to the explosive popularity of wine coolers. Except for minor test plantings, no Vinifera or French-American grapes are commercially grown, although, with proper vineyard management and modern insecticides and pesticides, it is conceivable that environmental burdens will be overcome. It is important to note that after centuries of experimentation, by 1950 only Scuppernong and Black Spanish remained in Florida. All Vinifera and French-American varieties died from Pierces's Disease, and excessive heat and humidity. In recent years, a dynamic breeding program has been underway to produce new bunch varieties that are not only disease resistant and capable of sustained high yields, but also efficacious in the production of table wine with good flavor intensity. The introduction of Stover, Suwannee, and Blanc Du Bois during the period 1954-1987, all of which are Pierce's Disease-resistant and capable of above-average wine production, has laid the groundwork for a successful wine industry. The most important red Rotundifolia grapes are Noble, Regale, and Tarheel, and the best white are Welder, Dixie, and Doreen. Slightly less than half of total acreage is planted in Rotundofolia, of which the following are the most important: Noble, Carlos, Welder, Dixie, Higgins, Magnolia, Cowart, Jumbo, Southland, Scuppernong, Granny Val, and Dixie Red. While considerable wine is made from the above grapes, acreage is declining relative to bunch grapes due to lower yields and inferior wine quality.

Florida has the potential of growing the earliest table grapes of the season and at a lower cost than California. Further, grapes do not suffer from cold weather; and central and northern Florida contain thousands of acres of very favorable microclimates suitable for large-scale winegrowing. The majority of future vine acreage will be in central Florida, in former citrus producing areas, and along the northern panhandle. Although 35 counties across the state will have some commercial acreage, more than 50 percent of the total acreage will be located in Leon, Lake, Walton, Gadsden, Jefferson, Alachua, and Pasco counties.

Commercial production of bunch grapes is limited to those cultivars that exhibit resistance to Pierce's Disease. Interest in vinegrowing dates back to 1933 when the Florida Grape Growers Association, a state agency that

began to develop disease-resistant grapes, developed the Watermelon Field Laboratory in Leesburg as a vine research facility. After a long period of inactivity, it has developed since 1944 many new grape varieties of which the following are the most important: Lake Emerald, first developed in 1944, is a white bunch grape with small berries that produces highly flavored and scented wines that are among the most expensive in the south. This variety produces both high sugar and acid levels with relatively low pH. Although the must and wine is easily oxidized, when well-made it has, unlike all other Rotundifolia and interspecific varieties, a pronounced floral aroma and scent. It is a cross of Pixiola (a native form of Vitis simpsoni) and Golden Muscat. Lake Emerald, in addition to its high yields, is highly resistant to Pierce's Disease, as well as other diseases. After four decades of obscurity, this vine is now being grown in many areas, but particularly in the fossilized limestone soils of the Caloosa Basin at Alva. Blanc Du Bois, the first major grape developed by the Institute of Food and Agricultural Sciences at Leesburg, is resistant to Pierce's Disease, and able to produce one of the finest wines in the south. Named after Emile du Bois, an immigrant French grape grower who made wine in Tallahassee in the 1880s, it is a cross of several bunch grapes, Golden Muscat, and several Vinifera. It grows on its own roots, maintains high yields, ripens early, is easy and economically grown, and makes a delicious, spicy white wine, very similar to Sauvignon Blanc. Stover, named after the scientist who bred it at Leesburg in 1968, makes a good, clean, assertive table and sparkling wine with some merit, although it will never approach the delicacy of Blanc Du Bois. Although it can exhibit pronounced rough edges, and be slightly coarse, when well-made, it is above-average in quality, and a good seafood partner. Released in 1968, Stover is the product of an unusual cross between Mantey and Roucaneuf, the latter, an obscure Seyve-Villard 12-309. Highly flavorful and reliable as a yielder, its acreage is expected to grow. Conquistador, a red, Pierce's Disease-resistant grape with Concord parentage, is not sensitive to frost, maintains high yields, and is above-average as a table, juice, and wine grape. Suwannee is a white, Pierce's Disease-resistant, table and wine grape with slight Muscat flavor that is above-average in quality.

Other grapes include: Blue Lake (a red grape with very high yields); MissBlanc (developed in 1987, this premium white grape, best suited to sandy soils, is highly disease-resistant, and makes crisp, fruity wine); MidSouth (a table and juice grape); MissBlue (a table and juice grape); Orlando Seedless (a good table grape); Tampa (an excellent rootstock); Daytona (a table and juice grape); Liberty (a table and juice grape); and Norris (a table and juice grape). The energetic Research and Educational Center in Leesburg has developed approximately

24 additional table, juice, and wine grapes (nearing release), of which Fla. CA4-72, Fla. DC1-56, Fla. DN16-59, Fla. CN2-100, Fla. CN10-62, and Fla. DN18-47 appear to be the most promising for the production of wine.

Whereas until 1972 Florida had one grape winery and several fruit and berry wineries, there are now five economically viable wineries with several more expected to open by 1995. Despite the fact that an overwhelming portion of Florida wine is sold as cooler (74 percent), followed by fortified and flavored, table wines represent less than 5 percent of total output, but the trend for further growth is quite favorable given the existence of a significant tourist and luxury wine market.

The wineries are: **Chautauqua Winery & Vineyards** (De Funiak Springs, 1989), is a state-of-the-art, well-financed, 89-acre, 40,000-case winery that makes Carlos, Welder, Noble, sparkling, and proprietary wines. **Eden Vineyards** (Alva, 1986), the southernmost winery in continental America, is an expanding and highly aggressive, 14-acre, 10,000-case winery specializing in hand crafted, dry white table wines made from the Lake Emerald grape, and two proprietary wines--*Coral Bell* and *Alva White*, both of which are blended with Vinifera. **Lafayette Vineyards & Winery** (Tallahassee, 1983), is a 38-acre, 15,000-case winery that makes excellent table and sparkling wine from Welder, Magnolia, Sterling, Blanc Du Bois, Stover, and Suwannee. **Lakeridge Winery** (Clermont, 1989), is a 33-acre, 32,000-case winery that makes Blanc Du Bois, Suwannee, MissBlanc, Stover, and proprietary wines. This and Lafayette are owned by the same person. **The House of Midula** (Tampa, 1972), founded as Fruit Wines of Florida, this is, with 60 acres and an output of 70,000 cases, the state's oldest and largest winery. It makes a large selection of fruit, berry, citrus, and grape wines, of which Orange, Conquistador, and Stover are the most important.

The Biltmore Estate Winery, Asheville, North Carolina. Courtesy of The Biltmore Estate Winery

VI
THE WINES OF THE SOUTHWEST

The southwestern vineyard consists of Arizona, New Mexico, and Texas. Although there are several exceptions, this large region of high mountains, countless valleys and many plateaus, receives little rain, and has few people for an area its size. Due to the paucity of rainfall, this is historically a land of wide distances, of pasture not farms, of vast arid distances, clear skies, denuded landscapes, and of lariat not plow. About one-fifth of the area is bolson, or "filled-basin" country, regions of interior drainage, with many salt flats, and considerable alluvial and talus (gravity) slopes. Highly concentrated around state capitals and several industrial cities, the population density throughout the tri-state region is less than twelve persons per square mile, one of the lowest in the nation. This is also the only area with a pronounced ethnic imprint; all three states, historically part of Mexico, were settled by Spaniards before California was settled, and are the oldest section of the country with an effective Spanish cultural imprint. The area is replete with Spanish toponyms, the Spanish language, and the Roman Catholic Church. Yet, since Spanish exploration and settlement hinged on the ill-fated Coronado expedition for the "seven cities of gold," Spanish political dominion of this vast region failed. Nevertheless, Spanish influence in architecture, food (cumin has invaded German cuisine in central Texas), and music is endemic. Another major cultural imprint is the large Indian population relative to other areas in the nation, and the numerous reservations that create an ambience that belies a former hunting and gathering society. Nevertheless, although Mexicans speak Spanish in a grocery store, and Indians one of the many tongues on the reservation, the economy of the southwest is dominated by national corporations engaged in large-scale agribusiness irrigation, mineral exploitation, and specialized manufacturing.

The cultural imprint notwithstanding, this portion of America is important because winemaking goes back to the second half of the seventeenth century when Franciscan friars established missions and introduced the Mission grape in all three states at least 130 years before similar developments occurred in California, making the Nogales area of Arizona, the Mesilla Valley of New Mexico, and the El Paso del Norte Valley of Texas the oldest grapegrowing regions in America. Despite a 400-year winemaking tradition, these states represent an emerging winegrowing region that holds much promise. Collectively, the region has nearly 19,000 acres of vineland, and 55 wineries that produce 500,000 cases annually. Although Arizona, among the three, is mainly a raisin and table grape producer and the least important in terms of wine production, New Mexico and Texas have nearly all the

wineries and account for nearly the entire wine output.

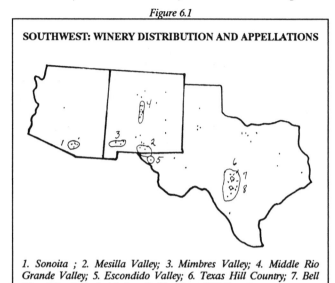

Figure 6.1

SOUTHWEST: WINERY DISTRIBUTION AND APPELLATIONS

1. Sonoita ; 2. Mesilla Valley; 3. Mimbres Valley; 4. Middle Rio Grande Valley; 5. Escondido Valley; 6. Texas Hill Country; 7. Bell Mountain; 8. Fredericksburg In The Texas Hill Country.

The geography of the southwest is conducive to viticulture because the region has an arid climate characterized by sufficient heat to ripen grapes, abundant sunshine, and cool nights providing conditions necessary to produce grapes of excellent quality. Furthermore, while a good portion of the southwest is further south in latitude than California and nearly all other major grape-growing states, the region's higher altitude more than compensates for this latitudinal difference. The southern portion of the Rocky Mountains stretches from the north through the southern portions of New Mexico and Arizona. The higher altitudes, between 4,000 and 5,500 feet above sea level, result in cooler nights and unique microclimates that are ideal for growing varietal grapes and making good wine.

In all three states, the wines are clean, true to their varietal character, and above-average in quality. For the region as a whole, two-thirds of wine output is white in color, an increasing portion of which is made sparkling. While few significant state or regional distinctions have emerged, as the vines mature and the winemaking skills improve, more definitive white and red regions will emerge. The financial problems of wineries in the southwest aside, there are several obstacles in making the industry economically viable. An important issue confronting existing wineries is the production of an image and reliable style consistent with a reputation for excellence, and lingering Prohibitionist tendencies. Mediocre wine simply cannot compete with beer in the southwest, no matter how inexpensive it may be. Being an area with significant Spanish and Indian cultural influence, it is difficult to increase wine sales when the cuisine is pickled okra, tamales, beef brisket, Jalapeno peppers, and salsa "galore," hence wine takes a backseat to beer and whiskey. Yet in recent years grapes have become particularly tempting to farmers because they require less than half the irrigated water of most other crops, and the return per acre is significantly greater than for cattle grazing and cotton. It bears noting, that despite the early history of winegrowing, commercial grape-growing has never been a major crop in the economies of these three states. In the final analysis, all three states face the same problems: Texas Root Rot, Pierce's Disease, an unstable wine market, a credible image, low population densities and vast distances, unresponsive state legislatures, and a lack of interstate legislation allowing personal shipments of wine from one state to another. If the future fails to meet these challenges, winery failures, already high (nearly one-quarter of all wineries established within the past ten years have failed), will intensify.

Climate, Soils, and Grape Varieties

The southwest is an area of great contrasts: there are mountains of all ages, shapes and origins, high plateaus, broad open fertile valleys, and subtropical coastlines. Climatic variations produce deserts with less than three inches of rainfall to forests receiving fifteen times that amount. While climatically diverse, the three states, for purposes of generalization, are divided into three distinct regions: the humid portion of eastern and southern Texas, the arid interior, and the cooler uplands. The humid area of eastern Texas and the western extension of the humid subtropical climatic region of the Gulf Coast have a long growing season, heavy precipitation, prolonged bouts of humidity, and mild winters. The growing season exceeds 220 days, and the presence of Pierce's Disease precludes all but Rotundifolia grapes from successful cultivation.

The arid interior (areas receiving less than ten inches of rainfall) is characterized by long, hot, daytime temperatures (90F-115F), cool evenings (45F-70F), low relative humidity (usually less than 40 percent), unpredictable rainfall, high wind velocities, and a large diurnal range in temperature. Aridity increases in intensity away from the Gulf Coast, and is maximized in the southern Rocky Mountains, as in Arizona, a state that lies on the same latitude as Georgia and the Carolinas. Summer temperatures, in particular, can be unbearably hot and monotonous in lowland areas, but are ameliorated with elevation. Although the growing season under irrigated conditions exceeds 190 days, the interval between bud break and harvesting is less than 155 days (mid-March to late July), thus placing many desertic regions of the southwest not in Region V, but in Regions II-IV. The annual temperature of the upland areas (55F to 65F) is similar to the Sierra Foothills region and a good deal of coastal Califor-

nia, therefore, good for premium Vinifera vines. These upland areas, particularly in Arizona and New Mexico, are sufficiently cool and thus able to raise acid levels and heighten varietal character. In all but the highest elevations, the harvest season in Texas, New Mexico, and Arizona is over two months before it begins in California's north coast counties. Nevertheless, the hot, desertic climate, common in Arizona, is excellent for table and raisin grape production.

Due to the cloudless climatic patterns of these arid areas, heat summation ranges from 2,300 to more than 5,000. Average harvest dates in Arizona are the third week of August to the middle of September, although for several varieties the harvest can begin as early as the third week of July. On the other hand, bud break west of Austin, Texas is late March with the harvest by the end of July. In terms of degree days, the growing season between these two benchmarks is not Region I, but Region V if we extend the growing period by California standards to October. Once spring arrives in the southwest, the growing season accelerates rapidly. Due to the near absence of rainfall, irrigation is an absolute necessity, the vines requiring five to nine gallons of water a day in the more arid regions of the southwest during the growing season. Desiccating winds can be troublesome, as is hail, particularly in the north central and western portions of Texas, and the higher elevations of New Mexico and Arizona. More important are the erratic temperature patterns of north and central Texas during the winter months when 50F temperature fluctuations are experienced within 72 hours. Often Vinifera vines do not harden off sufficiently and are damaged by early blasts of cold air; even more damaging are mid-winter thaws followed by below freezing temperatures.

Upland regions, areas higher than 4000 feet in elevation, particularly in New Mexico and Arizona, offer interesting possibilities for viticulture as the higher elevations provide intense solar radiation, lower temperatures, and well-drained soils. Three formidable problems are a lack of water, unpredictable winter temperatures, and spring freezes, all combining to either kill the vine or reduce crop yields (as in 1987/1988). In addition, precipitation, rarely exceeding 30 inches during the year, is highly erratic, and often disastrous in the production of severe flooding. Rainfall comes in two "rainy" seasons: during the winter precipitation arrives as widespread, gentle storms during the months of December to March; summer thunderstorms, producing more than two-thirds of the annual rainfall total, occur during July through August, usually in heavy down pours washing away a good deal of the surface soil. As disastrous as summer thunderstorms are, the periodic bouts of drought are more troublesome in areas without sufficient irrigation water.

Both extreme winter and summer weather affects the

limits of grape cultivation. Severe low winter temperatures in the higher elevations limit the successful commercial cultivation of Vinifera vines, as well as preclude Rotundifolia in all three states. Abnormally heavy summer rains and humidity stimulate several fruit and leaf diseases that significantly place limits in the eastern boundary for Vinifera and French-American varieties. Major diseases are Pierce's Disease and Texas Root Rot. Although first recognized as a virus in Anaheim, California in 1894, Pierce's Disease, native to the humid climates of the Gulf Coast and southeast America, is caused by a bacterium. Pierce's Disease limits commercial production of most wine grapes, particularly Vinifera varieties, to central and west Texas, and nearly all areas of New Mexico and Arizona. The disease is transmitted by man through grafting, and by leafhopper insects, often some distance from primary infestation. There is no control method other than careful selection of tolerant varieties. Mainly confined to the alkaline soils of Arizona, New Mexico, and Texas, Texas Root Rot (or Cotton Root Rot), a fungus, is a deadly disease that affects deciduous fruit trees, ornamental plants, and vines, severely affecting and limiting grape cultivation at elevations below 5,000 feet. Vitis rupestris, Vinifera, and Baileyana are highly susceptible, whereas Champini, Candicans, and Berlandieri are tolerant, all others being moderately susceptible.

Soils, basic in reaction, are the product of calcification producing caliche features. Most are calcareous in origin with considerable loess accumulations (especially in Texas), heavily impregnated with minerals, and usually provide excellent root penetration. The combination of high temperatures and maximum sunshine, mineralized soils, irrigation, and a hot growing season means high yields, rarely below five tons to the acre.

Texas

The name Texas is thought to have originated from the Indian word *Teyas* for "friend," first recorded by Spaniards in 1541. By 1683 other Indians conveyed the idea of a great fictional kingdom, and the Spaniards applied the name Texas to the vast region east of New Mexico. Nomenclature aside, Texas is considered the "crossroads of North American geology." Within the state's boundaries four great physiographic subdivisions of the North American Continent combine (the Coastal Plain, the lower portion of the Great Plains, the High Plains, and the Rocky Mountain region) to produce a huge amphitheater that slopes toward the Gulf of Mexico. As the nation's third most populous state (17 million and growing by more than 100,000 annually), Texas exhibits youthful demographics. More than 50 percent of the population resides in the metropolitan areas of Dallas, Houston, and San Antonio.

The state also is proud of its early history: Alonso Al-

varez de Pineda first claimed Texas for Spain in 1519; in 1541 Francisco Vasquez de Coronado explored western Texas, while Hernando de Soto explored eastern and central Texas the following year; and in 1682 Spaniards established the first permanent settlement at Ysleta near El Paso. Independence came to Texas before statehood, and has played an important part in the formation of regional character. Whether in the northern plains, the Spanish west, or the cotton lands of the east, life throughout the state is lived in the presence of the past: everyone, it seems, cherishes history as few other Americans. Consequently, Texans, who identify first with the region, then the state, and finally with the nation, are diverse in terms of race, ethnic background, and alcohol tolerance. Pride as Texans is expressed as independence, self-assurance, strength, and a host of superlatives. Not only was Texas the largest state in the union before 1959 (it accounts for one-twelfth of the land area of continental America), but it boasts the deepest oil well, the largest farm, and the highest production of rice, beef, sheep, goats, wool, cotton, sorghum, and pecans. It also flaunts the presence of more grassland pasture and more idle cropland than any other state. Because of its immense size (roughly 800 miles north-south, and east-west), Texas is home to 100 different varieties of cactus, 570 different kinds of grasses, and more than 5,000 different wild flowers. But in the world of viticulture, it is the home to more species of grape than any other comparable land area in the world (Bailey's Cyclopedia of Horticulture lists 36 species, of which 15 are native to Texas).

Texas is the home of three premier American viticulturists: U.A. Randolph, E. Mortensen, and T.V. Munson (1843-1913), the latter, the most famous, is widely considered the father of the state's wine industry. A remarkable man, he began crossing native varieties with Vinifera in 1876 in Denison, Texas, eventually producing more than 300 different hybrid varieties (115 are still in existence), only one of which, carries his name, Vitis munsonia. He has been credited, along with others, in shipping phylloxera-resistant root-stock to France (the entire Cognac vineyard is grafted on Munson-developed Texas rootstock), and was awarded the title "Chevalier du Merite Agricole" for his efforts. Over a period of 30 years Munson travelled to 40 states collecting and classifying nearly every specie of American grape.

In the 1500s when Spanish explorers were anxious to discover large numbers of Indians and precious metal, there were accounts of expeditions passing through the area of El Paso, but no permanent settlements were made until 1682 (circa) when the Pueblo revolt in New Mexico forced missionaries south toward Mexico and portions of what is today the state of Texas. Franciscan priests brought the Mission grape from Mexico and founded a mission at Ysleta, the oldest settlement in Texas. Despite these beginnings, winemaking never captivated the attention of dedicated winegrowers although the area was favorable for viticultural activities. A combination of low population, Spanish preoccupation with precious metals and exploration, and early European indifference (until

German and French migration in the middle of the nineteenth century) are the main reasons for meager vine plantings. With statehood and increased northwestern European settlement, interest in viticultural pursuits intensified so that by 1895 1,800 acres in vineyards dotted the Texan landscape.

The largest single planting of Vinifera grapes at Fort Stockton, owned by the University of Texas and managed by Cordier. Baxevanis

For more than 100 years the largest and oldest wine producing region of Texas was the El Paso Rio Grande area. It 1847 it was reported that, besides brandy, 200,000 gallons of wine was made, and by the turn of the century El Paso had some of the largest and most profitable vineyards in the state. As in many other areas, a series of floods and succeeding droughts damaged the vines and many died of disease. Prohibition 20 years later finished the industry, and when Prohibition was repealed, cattle, cotton, and other crops were so firmly entrenched that no one considered planting grapes on a commercial scale until 1975. On the eve of Prohibition, there were 21 wineries in Texas, of which all closed after the passage of the Eighteenth Amendment. The recent interest in winemaking has increased vine acreage from 90 acres in 1970 to nearly 5,000 acres in 1992, a figure that is expected to double again by the end of this century. Similarly, wine production increased from less than 2,000 gallons in 1975 to more than 800,000 gallons in 1991, two-thirds of which is made by three firms--Cordier Estates, Llano Estacado, and Teysha Cellars. While grape acreage and wine production have soared to unprecedented levels in recent years, the projected rise of grape acreage from 3,000 in 1982 to 9,000 in 1990 by Texas A&M University has not transpired, and is a further indication of the state's erratic

enological history. Nevertheless, wine is said to be, in the land of cotton, cattle, and oil, the discovery of the 1980s.

Geographically, Texas is both southern and western. Lying between the lower Rockies and the Mississippi River Valley, Texas embraces 267,339 square miles of which 3,826 square miles are water. It measures 801 miles north-south, and 773 miles east-west; elevations range from sea level to 8,751 feet atop Guadalupe Peak east of El Paso. Sandwiched between the warm waters of the Gulf of Mexico and the high plateaus and mountain ranges of the western interior, the state exhibits a disparate range of climatic conditions: mountain, continental, and marine, the latter modified by periodic bouts of continental air. The High Plains, separated from the Lower Plains by the Cap Rock Escarpment, lie in a cool temperate zone, and except for a small region in the extreme western portion of the state, the remainder of the state lies in a warm temperate subtropical zone.

The Ysleta Mission in west Texas,
one of the earliest areas for winegrowing in the nation. Baxevanis

Proximity to the Gulf of Mexico allows the easy penetration of a southerly and southeasterly flow of tropical maritime air. Therefore, precipitation patterns show several irregular bands stretching in a general east-west direction, and each area gets progressively drier as one travels westward. Rainfall averages range from 56 inches in the east to less than 8 inches in the west. Annual and seasonal temperature patterns lie somewhere between the extremes of maritime tropical, desertic and continental climates. The growing season ranges from 329 days in the lower portion of the Rio Grande to 178 days in the northern portion of the High Plains. Nevertheless, while climatic variations across the state are considerable, they are gradual with no natural boundary to separate the moist east from the dry west, and the cooler northern portion.

Figure 6.2

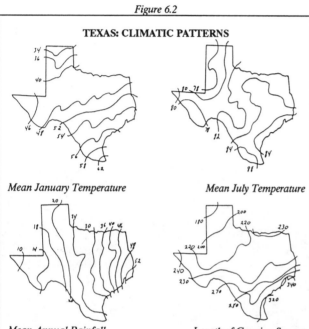

TEXAS: CLIMATIC PATTERNS

Mean January Temperature   *Mean July Temperature*

Mean Annual Rainfall   *Length of Growing Season*

Most areas in Texas contain more than 4000 degree days. The High Plains and the Trans-Pecos regions are the coolest; the Hill Country exhibits lower heat units than surrounding areas. Before 1950, the leading grape producing areas of the state were the Red River Valley, south central Texas, and the lower Rio Grande Valley. In recent years, the Lubbock, Hill Country, and Fort Stockton regions have become the leading producers. The Lubbock region, for example, increased vine acreage from 5 acres in 1973 to 2,000 acres in 1991. The western portion of the state augmented vine acreage from 20 acres to 1,500, and the Hill Country from 10 to 700 for the same years.
Source: Texas Agricultural Experiment Station, College Station.

Because of the strong imprint of Baptist and Methodist congregations, prohibitionist tendencies have been strong in Texas. In 1870 the United Friends of Temperance was founded, only to be reenforced the following decade by the Women's Christian Temperance Union. In combination with other sympathetic groups such as the Grange, and the Greenback Party, the cacophony against alcohol consumption proved absolutely devastating to the industry, prompting amendments to enact state-wide prohibition as early as 1887. Although it failed, the Texas Local Option Association was organized in 1903, and four years later the Anti-Saloon League entered the struggle against alcohol consumption. Despite these persistent prohibitionist pressures, Texas had 25 wineries and 3,000 acres of wine grapes, mainly in Montague, Tarrant,

Grayson, and El Paso counties. By 1915, the Texas Woman's Anti-Vice Committee was successful in passing a state law whereby the sale of liquor within ten miles of any place where troops were quartered was prohibited. National prohibition in 1920 totally obliterated the industry by forcing all wineries to close thus reducing wine grape acreage to near zero. After Prohibition several wineries reestablished, but only Val Verde Winery in Del Rio survived the post-Prohibition period.

Figure 6.3

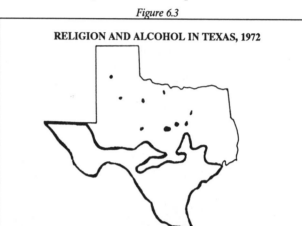

RELIGION AND ALCOHOL IN TEXAS, 1972

Lightly shaded areas are primarily Baptist and Methodist regions; blank areas are Catholic (Spanish) and Lutheran. The distribution of religion and alcohol sales show a spatial correlation. Catholic and Lutheran areas generally choose to be "wet," while Baptist-Methodist areas retain prohibition.
While the southwestern portion of the state was settled by Spaniards, viticultural activities in the central, eastern, and northern sections of the state had to wait for European settlers in the middle of the 19th century when French, Alsatians, and Germans began making wine. With time, the fundamentalist elements gained strength and wine-making endeavors disappeared. In this regard, it is interesting to view the state not as one political entity but as two separate and distinct regions--the wine/alcohol consuming Spanish-speaking population dominate the southwestern region bordering Mexico, while the wine/alcohol abstaining "Bible Belt" prevails in the eastern and northern portion of the state.
Source: 38th Annual Report of the Texas Alcoholic Beverage Commission, Austin, 1972, p. 49; and Churches and Church Membership in the United States: 1971, National Council of the Churches of Christ in the U.S.A., 1974. Taken from p. 213, The Human Mozaic; A Thematic Introduction to Cultural Geography, Terry G. Jordan and Lester Rowntree, New York, Harper & Row, 1990.

Today the state is in the midst of a wine revolution. Besides the Val Verde Winery that was founded in 1883, all other wineries date from 1975, and of the 27 existing wineries 20 were founded after 1982. One of the key elements in the recent resurgence in wine interest is the University of Texas. Having both land and money, it decided to enter, after a brief flirtation with kiwi fruit, almond and olive production, into the wine business having found that wine grapes give the highest return per acre in west Texas. The University owns 2 million acres, mainly in Culberson and Pecos counties, and is the single largest vineyard owner in the state (more than 1,000 irrigated acres in west Texas near Fort Stockton). The potential for growth is enormous. Texas is the fourth largest alcohol market in the nation, and while 43 gallons of beer are consumed annually by each person, a paltry 1.6 gallons of wine are consumed, a figure that is only slightly better than bottled water. Between 1970 and 1980, Texas went from the fourth most populous state to third, and per capita wine consumption increased faster than the national average making it the fourth largest wine consuming state in the nation. Besides a large and growing population, an accommodating climate and inexpensive land (less than $2,000 the acre vs. more than $50,000 in the Napa Valley), the state has the necessary technology and money to unleash latent productive forces capable of propelling the industry further. Equally important is the strong political support given to the industry by two of the nation's most influential politicians--Senator Lloyd Bentsen and Representative E. Kika de la Garza.

Dallas, one of the emerging wine markets of America. Baxevanis

It is also important to note that the Grape Growers Association was formed in 1976, and a Farm Winery Bill passed in 1977; and while all this was happening wine consumption increased from .78 gallons in 1970, to 1.3 in 1980, 1.4 in 1984, and by 1991 it had approached the national average. Equally significant is that Texans are very loyal to their wineries provided they maintain high standards. Local affection, exhibiting infectious characteristics, can expand the industry further since only 1 percent of wine consumption is produced in the state. It is an understatement to say that much has happened since the "Chateau Bubba" wisecrack was applied to Texas wine in the mid-1970s. Nevertheless, the industry still has several hurdles to overcome, one of the most formidable being lingering prohibitionist tendencies. A peculiar aspect of state law holds that while wineries may exist state-wide, it is illegal for any to serve or sell in a dry county (as of 1986, half of the 254 counties were dry). Another interesting piece of legislation in the "Lone Star" state holds

that 51 percent of the winery ownership must be Texan. Perhaps the most significant stumbling block is the maintenance of a sustained and effective demand. The inability of many wineries in the state to maintain consistency, to produce large quantities of everyday table wine, to upgrade the image, and, therefore, compete with the finer wines of California appear to be major obstacles.

The T.V. Munson Viticulture and Enology Center, Denison, Texas. T.V. Munson's contributions to the world of viticulture included: a reclassification of the Vitis species; authoring <u>Foundations of American Culture</u> (1909); developing over 300 hybrid grapes between 1890 and 1913; and combating phylloxera in France. In 1988, the T.V. Munson Viticulture and Enology Center was founded. It not only houses historic memorabilia and a library, but offers an Associate of Science Degree in Enology. The Center also maintains 65 of Munson's varieties. Baxevanis

Over the past 20 years, commercial grape-growing has developed in the following four areas:

1. The South Plains/Lubbock region, with approximately 2,000 acres, was historically a French-American variety producing area, but ever since Pheasant Ridge pioneered the successful cultivation of Vinifera varieties vine acreage is dominated by Chenin Blanc, Chardonnay, Cabernet Sauvignon, Merlot, and Cabernet Franc. Extending into New Mexico, the region (roughly 200 by 200 miles), known as "Llano Estacado" (a future *ava*), was named after a 1540-1542 Spanish Expedition by the explorer Francisco Vasquez de Coronado when he drove stakes as markers higher than the native Buffalo grass in order to find his way back from his search for gold. The Llano Estacado is a bare, flat, featureless, upland plain. This (predominantly limestone) upland, one of the most monotonously level areas on the continent, is bounded by the Mescalero Escarpment on the west overlooking the Pecos Plains and Pecos River Valley, and by the Cap Rock Escarpment on the east overlooking the Osage Plains of the Central Lowlands. Therefore, this part of the High Plains is somewhat distinctly marked off from surrounding regions. Lubbock, once the headquarters for

trail drivers and buffalo hunters, today is the center of a thriving cotton, oil, and cattle region. It lies in the center of this flat agricultural area, and dominates an incredible sea of cotton (more than three million acres), followed by sugar beets, and sorghum. The entire region is located between 3,000 and 4,000 feet in elevation, and receives less than 20 inches of rainfall. The calcium-rich soils (high pH) are deep, iron deficient, nitrogen-rich, and excellent for wine grape production.

What makes this an interesting *ava* with considerable potential (it is the state's finest grape-growing region) is the interplay of physical aspects that bestow several unique elements: the mean temperature is but 59F; degree days between bud break and harvest are but 2,400; and winter temperatures rarely plunge below 0F causing minimal winter injury. Also, while July temperatures often exceed 100F, the high elevation and the persistence of wind reduce grape temperatures by 20F, making this region cooler than most areas along a similar line of latitude. It is considered one of the best areas for grape-growing because of the presence of the Ogalala Aquifer for irrigation water; low relative humidity eliminating Pierce's Disease, mold, fungi, and mildew; and a regional deer, bird, rabbit-free environment. Because most rain falls in the months of May, June, and July, it is possible to reduce, or eliminate irrigation in August and September during the harvest season. Soil-borne diseases are absent and the well-drained calcareous soils produce excellent grapes as the combination of hot, dry summers and cool nights produce high sugar with sufficient acidity necessary for good balance. The enviable and consistently good weather patterns usually assure a good harvest, rarely requiring amelioration.

Table 6.1

CLIMATIC CONDITIONS FOR THE TEXAS AGRICULTURAL EXPERIMENT STATION, LUBBOCK

Variable	1985	1987	1988
Rainfall, total	23.39"	19.46"	13.31"
May-July	10.87	11.16	7.20
August-September	6.58	3.92	2.90
Irrigation	3.1"	1.8"	4.3"
Degree Days	4,154	3,958	3,982
Bloom to Harvest	3,092	2,419	2,336
Minimum Temperature			
Preceding the Crop Year	2F, 2/2/86	12F, 1/22/87	12F, 2/12/88
Last Freeze	3/26/86	4/3/87	4/12/88
Hail	None	None	6/29/88

Interestingly, since 1911 annual rainfall fluctuated between 8.3" to 30;" August rainfall has varied from .05" to 8.85."
Source: Texas Agricultural Experiment Station, Lubbock

2. West Texas, with approximately 1,500 acres, is the second largest area of vine plantings, mainly in Fort Stockton, Bakersfield, Fort Davis, Valentine, Van Horn, Del City, Midland, and El Paso. Due to its vast size and topographic irregularity, this region defies easy generalizations. While most of the area is characterized by Region V features, there are many pockets that resemble Region

III and IV. And while most vineyards tend to be small and widely scattered, the largest concentration is to be found near Fort Stockton, a former military outpost that is now a significant cattle and oil producing region. Chardonnay, Chenin Blanc, Sauvignon Blanc, and Colombard are the most important white varieties, while Cabernet Sauvignon and Merlot are the dominant red grapes. A combination of high altitude, a drier and more variable climate, well-drained soils, good yields, and inexpensive real estate prices have stimulated new plantings, but acreage is not expected to increase as rapidly as the Lubbock and Hill Country areas. The area has one *ava--Escondido Valley (1992)*, a 50 square mile region that contains 250 acres and one winery.

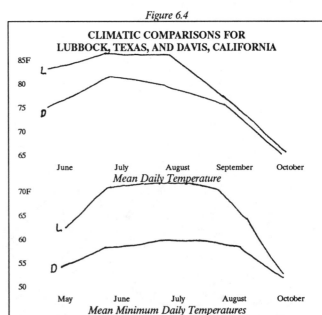

Figure 6.4

CLIMATIC COMPARISONS FOR LUBBOCK, TEXAS, AND DAVIS, CALIFORNIA

Mean Daily Temperature

Mean Minimum Daily Temperatures

Interestingly, mean daily temperatures for Davis are decidedly lower than Lubbock for the critical months of June-August. More consequential are the minimum daily temperatures for the two stations. While one would expect Lubbock to produce grapes with a lower acid content, the reverse is true. Due to the higher altitude and the presence of persistent winds, the microclimate produces better balanced fruit than the region surrounding Davis. The harvest for Chardonnay, Chenin Blanc, Sauvignon Blanc, and Cabernet Sauvignon occurs during the period of late July-early September, similar to Davis, CA.
Source: "Influence of Temperature and Pierce's Disease on Texas Grape Culture, by Ronald L. Perry, Texas Agricultural Experiment Station, College Station, Texas, 1975, paper given to a professional organization.

3. The Northcentral Texas (or the West Cross Timbers region), with 500 acres, principally in Springtown, Weatherford, Denison, Montague, Arlington, Granbury, and Ivanhoe, is an area that cultivates American, French-American, and Vinifera grapes. Part of the Red River Valley, this historically important region was a major laboratory for T.V. Munson. Microclimates and soils are highly variable, and acreage is growing as the area is within a short driving distance from the state's largest ur-

ban metropolitan center--Ft. Worth-Dallas.

4. The "Hill Country," the southern extension of the "High Plains" south of Lubbock, is bounded by the Pecos River in the west, and the flatlands of the Gulf Coast to the south and east. Although seemingly flat, the Edwards Plateau, a region of hills, gulches, and rocks sprinkled with grass and bushes, was historically occupied by sheep, goat and cattle. A poor, dry, desolate area with a very low population density, it is said that the cattle ate the best grass, the sheep the weeds, and the goats (nearly half the nation's goats are located here) ate the bushes. The Texas Hill Country, never clearly delimited, refers to the more humid, eastern portion of the Edwards Plateau north of San Antonio to the area west of Waco. This expanding viticultural region contains 700 acres of grapes, and there is some evidence that wine was made here as early as 1716.

Bobby Cox, proprietor of Pheasant Ridge Winery, one of the finest winemakers in the state. Baxevanis

Most of the soils in the Hill Country of the northern portion of the Edwards Plateau are derived from limestone and are heavily impregnated with iron oxide and flintstone, hence the Spanish name "Pedernal." The deep limestone soils (5 to 30 feet) are replaced by sandstone, and below 50 to 160 feet, by granite. In hilly areas where all three strata are exposed, it is possible to plant and maintain a wide array of grape varieties. Climatically the region is a transition zone between the higher and more arid west, the colder and higher northern plains, and the warmer and more humid Gulf Coast and eastern section of the state. Although it escapes the colder winter temperatures of the Llano Estacado, the Hill Country, with a 220-day growing season, is more humid, and lies on the

border of Pierce's Disease, and due to higher temperatures is supplemented by drip irrigation.

Under the auspices of the Society for the Protection of German Immigrants in Texas, the Hill Country was settled in 1845 by idealistic pioneers from Germany (Adelsverein colonists). It is no wonder that the names of the many settlements belie central European origins such as New Braunfels and Fredericksburg, the latter settlement deriving its name from Prince Frederick of Prussia who was the highest ranking member of the Adelsverein. Settling within the confines of the Pedernales, Colorado, San Antonio, and Guadalupe Rivers, these early settlers began making wine from wild grapevines, principally Mustang, and eventually founded a wine industry that disappeared during Prohibition. The *ava*, as well as the surrounding areas, due to the notoriety of the Pedernales River, L.B. Johnson Ranch, historic towns, many lakes, abundant water, and a pleasant climate, offer excellent possibilities for vineyard expansion. The region, blessed with excellent limestone soil and sprinkled by many springs, is also the site of the finest eclectic cuisine in the state. It is estimated that the tourist flow will increase from more than 1 million to 6 million over the next ten years.

The portion of the Hill Country west of Austin has emerged as the second most promising grape-growing area in the state, and has been delimited into three *ava's*: *Fredericksburg In The Texas Hill Country (1989)*, *Bell Mountain (1986)*, and *Texas Hill Country (1991)*, the latter, a large, irregular, 15,000 square mile area (bounded by San Antonio, Austin, Lampasas, Brady, Junction, and Uvalde) with ten wineries, 40 vineyards, and nearly 700 acres of vineland. This large region contains all and some parts of 23 counties, and contains within its borders the two smaller *ava's* of Fredericksburg In The Texas Hill Country and Bell Mountain.

Located 80 miles west of Austin, and entirely within Gillespie County, the *Fredericksburg ava* has approximately 110 square miles, more than 500 acres, and eight wineries within and immediately outside the *ava*. Lying to the north of the Pedernales River, the delimited, "bowl-shaped" region, including the town of Fredericksburg, has steep terraces that the Spanish christened "Los Balcones" (or balconies), and a fertile interior containing most vineland. The area is a collection of limestone hills with periodic rosy granite domes, and the continent's first step upward on its way to the Rocky Mountains. The Hill Country also separates the coastal plain of the southeast from the 2,500-foot high plateau on the west, and enjoys a unique climatic regime. It is said that in this "geographical heart" of Texas, spring arrives early and stays late.

Bell Mountain Vineyard, a single vineyard *ava* simply called *Bell Mountain*, is one of the finest areas for the production of Vinifera vines (particularly Cabernet Sauvignon). Owned by the Oberhellmann Winery, this is a 55-acre vineyard located 2,000 feet in elevation on the southeast slope of Bell Mountain. The soil is granite, gravelled clay-loam with considerable iron oxide and excellent drainage. Growing season temperatures range from the mid-90sF during the day to the low 50sF at night. Annual rainfall is less than twelve inches. The grape variety that has generated a reputation is Cabernet Sauvignon--usually dark in color, well-balanced, lush, and rich in character.

Eastern Texas exhibits a strong imprint of the southern plantation aristocratic society whose economy was historically based on cotton. Acting as a definite limiting factor for Vinifera and French-American varieties, Pierce's Disease, excess humidity and high temperatures combine to form a deadly combination throughout eastern Texas stretching along the Gulf Coast to the Mexican border. Yet, 100 acres of Rotundifolia are grown near the Louisiana border, and an unknown number along the Gulf Coast to the Mexican border. It is expected that Van Zandt County, the site of considerable Rotundifolia acreage, will become a prospective *ava*.

Figure 6.5

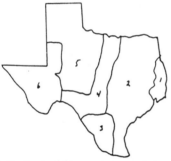

DISTRIBUTION OF GRAPE VARIETIES

1. Rotundifolia; 2. American and Rotundifolia; 3. American; 4. French-American varietals; 5. Vinifera, French-American, American; 6. Vinifera, French-American.
The distribution of Vinifera, American, and French-American grapes is a function of climate and the incidence of Pierce's Disease, Black Rot, Downy Mildew, and Bunch Rot. For Vinifera varieties, unpredictable low temperatures, unseasonable high summer temperatures and precipitation, and Pierce's Disease are the most inhibiting elements.
Source: Texas Agricultural Experiment Station, Lubbock.

Grapes grow naturally in Texas as half of the world's known species of grapes grow in the state, most of them between San Antonio and the Red River. As recently as 1940, 44 counties reported grape production of more than ten tons (nearly all non-commercial), a rather remarkable accomplishment for a state not generally known for its grape output. Due to its large size Texas is able to grow, like the entire southeast, Rotundifolia, other American, French-American, and Vinifera grapes. Vinifera grapes grow best in the western part of the state; French-American in the north central portion; Rotundifolia in the east-

ern portion; and native American throughout the entire state, but mainly confined to the central and eastern areas. Despite the highly generalized picture, one of the biggest problems in the state's grape industry is knowing what grapes to grow where. American grape varieties, well adapted to the north-central and southcentral areas of the state, exhibit the widest adaptability range of any grape type in the state. In general, Texas planted Lenoir and Herbemont prior to 1970, French-American grapes during the period 1970-1980, most notably Chambourcin and Vidal Blanc, and during the decade of the 1980s a complete litany of Vinifera, the most important being Chardonnay, Riesling, Chenin Blanc, Sauvignon Blanc, Cabernet Sauvignon, and Merlot.

The principal American grapes, from a historic perspective, are Lenoir (red), Herbemont (white), Champanel (red), Favorite (red), Mustang (red), Fredonia (red), Carman (red), Ellen Scott (red), Beacon (red), and Golden Muscat (white). Lenoir, or "Black Spanish," a vigorous and productive vine that tolerates extreme heat and cold, is resistant to Pierce's Disease, and, historically, very important in southcentral Texas. The vine, producing a small black grape with large, tight clusters, is unusual in that it can be grown throughout the state, and is used mainly for the production of juice, jelly, and home wine production. Carman, the most widely grown vine in north Texas until recently, is not only resistant to insects and fungal disorders, but is the most productive commercial native grape. Herbemont, a vigorous, productive, and highly adaptive grape to both heat and cold, is both resistant to Pierce's Disease and humidity, hence, it is one of the more important grapes of south and east Texas. Historically popular and long considered the favorite wine grape, this variety produces must much sweeter than most other American grapes.

Champanel, a vigorous vine tolerant of heat and drought, grows well in alkaline and prairie soils, thus is well-adapted to all areas of Texas except the extreme easternmost area of the state. Its versatility is further enhanced because it is excellent for arbor culture as well as for root stock. Despite its historic advantages, today this large, red grape is mainly used for rootstock, home processing, and decoration. Favorite, first discovered in Brenham, Texas, is similar to Lenoir, but considered superior as a wine grape. Fredonia, early maturing, hardy and vigorous, is similar to Concord, and while one of the oldest American black grapes grown in Texas its popularity has declined. Golden Muscat, very productive in north central Texas, is mainly grown as a table grape. Ellen Scott and Beacon are two obscure grapes found mainly in the central portion of the state. While fewer than 80 commercial acres are said to exist in the state, non-commercial American "backyard" acreage is estimated to exceed 650 acres. It should also be emphasized that until the University of Texas planted 1,000 acres of Vinifera vines, Herbemont and Lenoir were the two largest commercial grape varieties, and the mainstay of the state's wine industry.

THE WILD MUSTANG GRAPE

The geographical distribution of Vitis mustangenis (or Mustang) extends eastward from the 100 Meridian across the borders of Texas into Oklahoma, Arkansas, western Louisiana, and southward into Mexico. This extraordinarily vigorous, disease resistant (it has few natural enemies) grape does particularly well along the alluvial flood plains of three rivers: Colorado, San Antonio, and Guadalupe. Not only will the Mustang endure abnormal bouts of drought and heat, but its skin is tough and almost impossible to eat as it is bitter, and irritates the mouth and lips. While not commercially cultivated, the vine can be seen growing wild by enveloping deciduous trees along and near river banks. Easily recognized by its saucer-shaped leaf, and its white/grey felt underside, it was the first wine made by German settlers in the early 1840s.

In the eastern portion of the state the principal Rotundifolia varieties are: Regale, Fry, Sugargate, Magnolia, Carlos, Higgins, Cowart, Hunt, and Summit, all exhibiting relatively high sugar and low pH levels. Other bunch grape varieties currently receiving consideration are: MissBlue, MissBlanc, Stover, Lake Emerald, and Blue Lake. For optimum growth a well-drained soil and a hillside location for proper air drainage are mandatory site selection criteria. Although disease resistant in the humid eastern and Gulf Coast portions of the state, Rotundifolia vines are restricted from the central and western portions of the state due to the presence of alkaline soils and cold winter temperatures. Commercial acreage is estimated to be below 100 acres, and along with French-American varieties, they are not expected to increase their acreage in the future. From a historical perspective French-American varieties particularly adaptive to north central Texas are: Verdelet, Himrod, and Villard Blanc, all of which have been replaced in recent years by Chancellor Noir, Vidal Blanc, Chambourcin, and Seyval Blanc. The declining commercial acreage of French-American grapes is estimated to be less than 300.

As recently as 1984 Texas grew more than 40 different Vinifera varieties of which Chenin Blanc, Colombard, Sauvignon Blanc, Riesling, Emerald Riesling, Barbera, Chardonnay, Thompson Seedless, Carnelian, Ruby Cabernet, Cabernet Sauvignon, and Zinfandel were the most important. Over the past several years growers have found that Chenin Blanc, Sauvignon Blanc, Chardonnay, Cabernet Sauvignon, Merlot, and Cabernet Franc produce the better wines, and, as a consequence, they are expected to increase their acreage. Approximately 80 percent are white, of which Chenin Blanc, Sauvignon Blanc, and Chardonnay dominate (harvested acreage for 1991 consisted of Chenin Blanc, 26%; Sauvignon Blanc, 18%; Chardonnay, 16%; Cabernet Sauvignon, 15%; and all others, 25%). Although Vinifera varieties occupy a commanding position throughout the west, High Plains, and the Hill regions, site selection is most important as winter injury, humidity, and excessively nitrogen-rich soils limit the potential of these areas. Nevertheless, the recent successes of the state's wine industry are due, in part to the excellent pedocal soils, early harvest, and good cultural practices. The wineries are:

Cordier Estates, the largest winery in the state. Baxevanis

Alamo Farms Winery & Vineyard (Adkins, 1988), is a 3-acre, 1,500-case winery that makes Emerald Riesling, Colombard, Sauvignon Blanc, Malvasia Bianca, Shiraz, and proprietary wines.

Bieganowski Cellars (El Paso, 1988), is a 250-acre, 40,000-case, aggressive and rapidly expanding winery that also owns La Vina Winery in New Mexico. The leading wines are: Chardonnay, Sauvignon Blanc, Cabernet Sauvignon, Zinfandel, several proprietary blends, a dry sparkling, and semi-sweet sparkling Muscat Blanc.

Cordier Estates (Fort Stockton, 1984), with 1,018 acres and an annual output of 200,000 cases, is the largest winery in the state. While the vineyard is planted with more than fifteen different grape varieties, the most important are Chardonnay, Sauvignon Blanc, Colombard, Chenin Blanc, Barbera, Ruby Cabernet, Merlot, and Cabernet Sauvignon, sold under the *Ste. Genevieve* (the patron saint of Paris) label. The well-made wines (also includes sparkling) are all fresh and fruity, but rarely rise to the lofty levels of the better producers. Located between the Old Spanish Trail in San Antonio and the Chihuahua Trail to Mexico, this large facility is a Texan anomaly: it is a $15 million state-of-the-art winery located in a desolate region far removed from any significant settlement, and with 1,018 acres of vineyard owned by the University of Texas, this huge facility is managed and operated by Domaine Cordier, a French concern. Other label: *Domaine Cordier*, very popular in France.

Fall Creek Vineyards (Tow, 1979), is an 80-acre, 16,000-case winery that makes above-average to excellent, firm, well-flavored Chardonnay, Sauvignon Blanc (also a Semillon blend), Emerald Riesling, Chenin Blanc, Cabernet Sauvignon (blended with other "Bordeaux" varieties), Carnelian, Zinfandel, and proprietary wines. This is one of the most consistent of the state's premium wineries in terms of quality, and certainly one of the friendliest.

Grape Creek Vineyards (Stonewall, 1989), is a 16-acre, 3,500-case winery that makes Chardonnay, Sauvignon Blanc, and Cabernet Sauvignon.

Guadalupe Valley Winery (Gruene, 1975), the second oldest bonded winery in the state, is a 1,500-case facility that makes Aurore, Lenoir, and Ruby Cabernet.

Hill Country Cellars (Cedar Park, 1990), is a 5-acre, 9,500-case winery that makes Chardonnay, Sauvignon Blanc, dry and semi-sweet Riesling, Cabernet Sauvignon, and *It'za Spritza Premium Wine Spritzers.*

Fall Creek Vineyards, stylish and consistent to a fault. Baxevanis

Homestead Vineyard & Winery (Ivanhoe, 1989), is a 9-acre, 3,000-case winery that makes Chardonnay, Chenin Blanc, Cabernet Sauvignon, and proprietary wines.

La Buena Vida Vineyards (Springtown, 1978), is an 18-acre, 9,000-case winery that makes blended proprietary table, sparkling, and Porto-type wines from Vinifera and French-American grapes, usually offering good value. Other label: *Springtown.*

La Escarbada XIT Vineyard & Winery (Amarillo, 1985), is a 65-acre, 4,000-case winery that makes Riesling, Chardonnay, Cabernet Sauvignon, and proprietary wines.

Llano Estacado Winery (Lubbock, 1976), is a 13-acre, 85,000-case, rapidly expanding winery that makes average to excellent Chardonnay, Sauvignon Blanc, Riesling, Gewurztraminer, Pinot Noir, sparkling, proprietary, and superb Chenin Blanc, Cabernet Sauvignon, and Merlot. *Cellar Select* wines are particularly good. The winery, the first to open after Prohibition, buys grapes from 400 neighboring acres.

Messina Hof Wine Cellars & Vineyard (Bryan, 1983), the easternmost Vinifera winery in the state, is a rapidly expanding, 40-acre, 25,000-case firm that makes above-average Chardonnay, Sauvignon Blanc, Chenin Blanc, Riesling (table and late harvest), Zinfandel, proprietary, and Porto-type wines.

Moyer Champagne Co. (New Braunfels, 1980), is a 17,000-case, sparkling wine facility owned by the French Richter Wine Group. Three types of sparkling wines are made: Brut Naturel, Texas Brut, and Brut Especial from Chenin Blanc and Chardonnay grapes. It is expected that, in the future, the winery will be producing its own grapes. The firm also makes coolers and distributes California wines.

Bell Mountain Oberhellmann Vineyards (Fredericksburg, 1983), is a 55-acre, 8,000-case, estate winery that makes above-average Chardonnay, Gewurztraminer, Riesling, Sauvignon Blanc, Semillon, Pinot Noir, Cabernet Sauvignon, and Carmine. The unusual iron and calcium oxide soils provide an excellent base for well-flavored and scented wines, all offering good value. Other labels: *Bell Mountain, Oberhof.*

Pedernales Vineyard (Fredericksburg, 1986), is an aggressive, 20-acre, 2,500-case, estate winery that makes excellent, firm, well-structured Sauvignon Blanc and Cabernet Sauvignon, both of which should not be missed.

Pheasant Ridge Winery (Lubbock, 1982), the first, all Vinifera winery in the state, is a 48-acre, 16,000-case firm that makes rich, opulent Chardonnay, Chenin Blanc, Sauvignon Blanc, Semillon, Cabernet Franc, Merlot, Petit Verdot, Cabernet Sauvignon (full-bodied, flavorful, and complex), and proprietary wines. These wines are not to be missed as the winery ranks, along with Llano Estacado, as the "top banana" in the state.

Piney Woods Country Wines (Orange, 1985), is a 3-acre, 800-case Rotundifolia and blackberry winery.

Preston Trail Winery (Gunter, 1986), is a 50-acre, 5,000-case winery that makes good, sound Colombard, Sauvignon Blanc, Pinot Noir, Merlot, Cabernet Sauvignon, and proprietary wines.

St. Lawrence Winery (Garden City, 1987), is a 27-acre, 5,000-case winery that makes good, sound Chardonnay, Sauvignon Blanc, Riesling, Cabernet Sauvignon, and proprietary wines, all offering good value.

Sanchez Creek Vineyards (Weatherford, 1980), is an 8-acre, 3,000-case winery that makes above-average Chardonnay, Chambourcin, Cabernet Sauvignon, Merlot, and Zinfandel.

Schoppaul Hill Winery At Ivanhoe (Ivanhoe, 1988), formerly Texas Vineyard, is a 12-acre, 9,000-case winery that makes above-average to excellent Colombard, Riesling, Chardonnay, Gewurztraminer, Sauvignon Blanc, Chenin Blanc, Muscat Blanc, Cabernet Sauvignon, and Zinfandel.

Sister Creek Vineyards (Sisterdale, 1988), is a 5-acre, 1,500-case winery that makes Chardonnay, Pinot Noir, and Cabernet Sauvignon.

Slaughter-Leftwich Vineyards (Austin, 1988), is a 50-acre, 10,000-case winery that makes good, sound, flavorful Chardonnay, Sauvignon Blanc, Cabernet Sauvignon, and proprietary blush.

Tejas Vineyard & Winery (Mesquite, 1984), is a 5-acre, 3,000-case winery that makes good, sound Chardonnay, Sauvignon Blanc, Riesling, Chenin Blanc, Cabernet Sauvignon, fruit, and berry wines, all offering good value. Other labels: *Tejas, Frankenhaus.*

Teysha Cellars (Lubbock, 1988), is a stylish, state-of-the-art, 110-acre, 22,000-case winery that makes Chardonnay, Riesling, Gewurztraminer, Chenin Blanc, Sauvignon Blanc, Cabernet Sauvignon, white and red Meritage-type wines, and proprietary wines.

Teysha Cellars, traditional in appearance, makes soft wines. Baxevanis

Val Verde Winery (Del Rio, 1883), the oldest winery in the state, is a 30-acre, 3,000-case firm that makes estate and proprietary wines from Lenoir and Herbemont, as well as Riesling and Cabernet Sauvignon from purchased grapes.

Wimberly Valley Winery (Driftwood, 1983), is a 5,000-case winery that makes Chardonnay, Chenin Blanc, Riesling, Cabernet Sauvignon, Ruby Cabernet, and sparkling wines from purchased grapes.

Llano Estacado Winery, one of the top five wineries in the state.
Baxevanis

New Mexico

New Mexico is a state of 2 million people nearly all residing in a narrow ribbon along the Rio Grande, and its rapidly growing, youthful population resides at elevations higher than 3,500 feet. The nation's fifth largest state in area became Spanish in 1598 with the construction of the first Roman Catholic Church at San Juan Pueblo near Santa Fe, one of the oldest cities in America. The region was first explored by Marcos de Niza in 1539, by Francisco Vasquez de Coronado in 1548, and Pedro de Peralta who founded Santa Fe in 1610. During 1601-1604 three missions were established near Jemez Pueblo and one north of the present day Santa Ana Pueblo. In 1605 a mission was built at San Felipe Pueblo, and soon after another at Sandia near Albuquerque, but it is debatable whether the missions grew grapes and produced sacramental wine. It is widely assumed that wine was first made in New Mexico at Senecu, the site of San Antonio de Padua Mission, in 1632-1633, but others maintain that the year 1662 is more accurate. In either case, after the Atlantic Colonial coastline, New Mexico is not only the second oldest winemaking region in America, but the oldest *commercial* wine growing region in the nation. This is rather remarkable because the territory remained a marginal frontier region until the Santa Fe Trail was established in 1821, and became the 47th state in 1912.

If the earlier date is accepted, this frontier winery operated for 40 years when in 1675 Apaches attacked and destroyed the mission and its vineyards. Although by 1680 the Spanish were driven from New Mexico, the reconquest began in 1693, and by 1776 vineyards (400 acres is a common estimate by several historians) were established in Santa Cruz, Sandia, and Albuquerque. Winemaking on a small scale continued throughout the nineteenth century (General Stephen Kearny, when he proclaimed New Mexico a territory in 1846, reported commercial winemaking), and by the 1850s about 10,000 gallons were made along the Rio Grande south of Albuquerque. Population growth with the advent of the railroad sparked a minor wine boom, output rising to 905,000 gallons (from the Mission grape) in 1880, placing New Mexico fifth in wine production in the nation. The 1880 census reported 3,150 acres, or twice the cultivated vine acreage of New York. Severe competition from less expensive and better California wine reduced output to less than 300,000 gallons by 1890, and 34,000 gallons by 1900. After a series of destructive floods, first in 1897 (followed by a series of droughts), and then again in 1904, wine production declined to a miserly 1,684 gallons by 1910, and by 1914 only eight acres were reported in the entire state. Prohibition closed the industry down completely until the recent resurgence in wine interest.

Unlike most states, the climatic, and associated vegetation and soil patterns are directly related to elevation, and, as a result, the state exhibits a high degree of diversity. While elevation in the state ranges from 5,500 feet above sea level in the northwest to 3,000 feet in the southeast, 85 percent of the state has an altitude over 4,000 feet. The highest peaks are above 13,100 feet in elevation, most of which run in a north-south pattern. The various landforms are complex because they include parts of the Rocky Mountains and the Great Plains in addition to innumerable plateau, bolsons, and minor, lower ranges. Agriculture is mainly confined to alluvial basins and not to rivers since nearly all are confined to well-entrenched canyons. The Rio Grande is not only the largest river, but the site of the largest alluvial basin formed by regolith washed down over a long period of time. This thin sliver of greenery is the very center of population, industry, agriculture, and viticulture. It is dominated by Albuquerque, the largest urban unit and the largest wine market in the state.

Like Arizona, aridity is the chief feature of the landscape. Indicative of this is the fact that only 155 square miles of the state's total of almost 122,000 square miles is water. Generally, temperature and precipitation are both functions of altitude: the higher you go, the cooler the temperatures become, an increase in precipitation more likely, and a significantly higher risk of dangerous frost activity. This latter meteorological condition is endemic:

even during the winter rainy season, the state receives more than 75 percent of the maximum possible. Summer temperatures range from the 90sF during the day to the low 60sF at night, and the fairly long winter restricts the growing season to less than 200 days in most places, with winter kill severe in most higher elevations. The 1987-1988 winter was particularly damaging as it affected 1,400 acres. As a consequence, virtually all vineyard practices in northern New Mexico are oriented toward cold problems and not high temperatures. Not surprising, one of the largest plantings of vineland is in the Deming-Lordsburg area of southwestern New Mexico, with the longest frost-free season--220 days, a region that is just barely longer by ten days than eastern Long Island, the latter lying 10F further north in latitude.

Figure 6.6

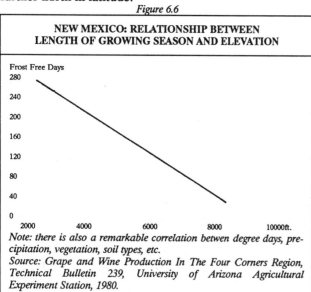

NEW MEXICO: RELATIONSHIP BETWEEN LENGTH OF GROWING SEASON AND ELEVATION

Frost Free Days

Note: there is also a remarkable correlation betwen degree days, precipitation, vegetation, soil types, etc.
Source: Grape and Wine Production In The Four Corners Region, Technical Bulletin 239, University of Arizona Agricultural Experiment Station, 1980.

While the average annual precipitation in New Mexico is 15 inches, rainfall increases significantly with elevation, particularly along the Rocky Mountains, an area that often receives 60 inches. Most inland, sheltered locations receive less than 10 inches as they are removed from the source of moisture, the Gulf of Mexico and the Pacific Ocean. Whatever the amount, precipitation usually occurs during the months of June through September, and is characterized by high intensity, short duration storm activity, little of which is absorbed by the hard, barren soil. Because the winter season is normally dry, the combination of low temperatures and winter drought presents a deadly scenario of dehydration as well as winter kill. This is not at all surprising because, due to the protective nature of the high mountains that dominate the state, New Mexico has the lowest average humidity of any state in the nation.

The soils of the Rio Grande are alluvial in origin (mainly silt and clay), but the finest vineland soils are to be found on former benchland and on higher sites having

colluvial material. Mineral-rich and well-drained, the lime-based soils can suffer from chlorosis, but are otherwise excellent for grape production.

Figure 6.7

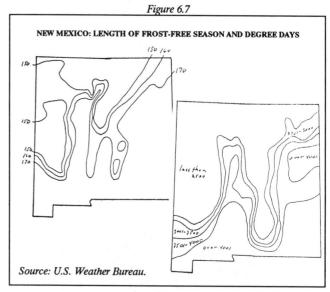

NEW MEXICO: LENGTH OF FROST-FREE SEASON AND DEGREE DAYS

Source: U.S. Weather Bureau.

Agriculture in New Mexico is overwhelmingly confined to animal, grain, and field crops, with fruit and nut operations largely composed of pecan, apple, and grape. Of the latter three crops, pecan acreage, production, and value lead grapes and apples by a wide margin. Grapes rank third to pecans and apples. Nearly all agricultural activity is confined to the Rio Grande, one of the longest in the nation, and the lifeline in a state that is mainly desertic. As the river flows in a southerly direction from Colorado, it snakes (and divides) the state nearly into two equal portions creating innumerable fertile, alluvial valleys along its banks; and as it meanders, it provides and sustains the state's diverse agricultural economy. Grapes are considered the future "agribusiness" of the state, easily supplanting such traditional crops as cotton, onions, and pecans in terms of returns per acre.

Table 6.2

NEW MEXICO: CLIMATIC PATTERNS				
Station	Elevation	Average Length of Growing Season	Mean Rainfall	1986
Albuquerque	5,326	194	8.15"	12.98"
Lordsburg	4,250	195	10.45"	18.22"
Deming	4,305	193	8.61"	22.01"
Cuba	7,045	105	12.87"	26.61"
Santa Fe	7,200	158	13.78"	19.28"
Elephant Butte	4,576	227	8.88"	16.94"
Socorro	4,585	185	8.77"	14.39"
Las Lunas	4,840	161	8.17"	14.87"
Source: New Mexico Department of Agriculture.				

In the 1970s the state's Economic Development and Tourism Department (as well as the Four Corners Regional Commission) made several exaggerated claims concerning the future potential of grape-growing in the "land of enchantment," and, as a result, many vineyards and wineries were established. At the time, it was estimated that the state had the potential of more than 30,000 vineland acres by 1988; and while these claims proved to have been unfounded, there was considerable speculation by Europeans in vineland south and north of Albuquerque. Several investment companies have made as many as 86,000 acres of potential vineland available to prospective European interests. One of the largest of the many failures was Zanchi & Sons, a French corporation that purchased 21,000 acres near Truth or Consequences in 1980, and planted 200 acres, with the venture abandoned several years later. Nevertheless, at least seven of the 20 wineries are foreign owned with a significant number engaged in the production of sparkling wines. Another significant consequence of the state's projected grape-growing potential was the indiscriminate planting of more than 40 different grape varieties, a good percentage of which were planted in unsuitable areas. Furthermore, heavy taxes and a myriad of state regulations make it virtually impossible for small wineries to operate and become viable economic enterprises, critical considerations for the rather high winery attrition rate.

The above notwithstanding, the state's wine industry has grown rapidly during this past decade. Acreage prior to 1980 stood at 85 acres, but with the passage of the state's farm winery legislation, planted area rose sharply to 165 in 1981, 540 in 1982, 1,450 in 1983, and 4,150 in 1985, but declined to 2,750 acres in 1989. Recent declines are largely attributed to cotton root rot (considerable acreage was planted on former cotton land), and two disastrous winters in 1987 and 1988. Nevertheless, wine production, increased from 190 gallons in 1983 to 200,000 gallons in 1987, and the number of wineries from four in 1981 to 20 by 1992. Despite recent climatic problems, there are few compelling reasons why the industry does not flourish: the state has a good climate and soils, vineland is comparatively inexpensive, and the quality of the wines above-average. Furthermore, because a significant percentage of the state is comprised of Indian reservations, vinegrowing is particularly lucrative for the American Indian as he has access to water rights.

Planted vine acreage is overwhelmingly concentrated in Hidalgo, Luna, Sierra, and Socorro counties, all located in the central and southwestern portions of the state. Nearly all vineyards and the state's 20 wineries are located in the Rio Grande Valley, or close to it. Expanding vinegrowing areas are Truth or Consequences, the region north of Albuquerque, and the Lordsburg-Deming region due to the presence of a major aquifer. The four principal weather stations in each county are located between 4,250 and 4,585 feet in elevation, and have a growing season that varies between 185 and 227 days. Precipitation varies between 8 and 12 inches, but the brilliance of sunshine

(due to high elevation, and a lack of cloud cover during the growing season), and low evening temperatures increase the sugar making potential of the grapes. Over the past ten years, grasshoppers, frost, cotton root rot, poor vineyard practices, and water shortages have ruined many a vineyard in New Mexico. Most of the wineries are located in a corridor from the northeastern quarter of the state, south along the Rio Grande, down the center of New Mexico to the Texas line, and then west to the Arizona line. The two smallest wineries are located in the northeastern corner near Las Vegas; the two largest wineries in the southwestern corner of the state; Rio Grande del Centro has six wineries; the Mesilla Valley has three wineries; and the Mimbres Valley has one, the state's largest.

Table 6.3

NEW MEXICO: GRAPE ACREAGE BY VARIETY, 1989		
Variety	Acreage	Percent
Chardonnay	440	14.2
Pinot Noir	235	7.6
Riesling	230	7.4
Cabernet Sauvignon	185	6.0
Sauvignon Blanc	180	5.8
Ruby Cabernet	180	5.8
Zinfandel	170	5.5
Chenin Blanc	160	5.2
Colombard	130	4.2
Barbera	90	2.9
Vidal Blanc	90	2.9
Merlot	60	1.9
Muscat Blanc	40	1.3
Seyval	40	1.3
Baco Noir	10	.2
Other	863	27.8
Total	3,103	

Note: *Grape acreage in 1987 stood at 3,700, but due to a disastrous freeze the following winter (temperatures fell to -10F in most areas) more than 500 acres were lost. The state had but 400 grape acres in 1982.*
Source: *New Mexico Department of Agriculture.*

Vinifera vines are better adapted to the warmer southern portion, while American, and more frequently French-American vines are more widely planted in the colder northern regions. The French-American-based wines of New Mexico are different from those emanating from the northeast and midwest. In fact, the northern portion of the state makes some of the finest French-American wines in the nation. Both red and white wines are generally soft, fruity, delicately scented, and are very pleasant on the palate. Among the red varietals, Baco Noir produces big, powerful wines, and Seyval and Vidal Blanc make excellent, well-scented, balanced wines. Approximately three-quarters of the entire acreage is planted in Vinifera grapes, of which Chardonnay, Chenin Blanc, Colombard, Sauvignon Blanc, Riesling, Zinfandel, Ruby Cabernet, and Cabernet Sauvignon are the most important. Unlike California, wines contain modest alcohol levels, rarely exceeding 13 percent.

New Mexico has three *ava's. Mesilla Valley (1985)*, located along the Rio Grande north of Las Cruces to El

Paso, contains 23 growers, 3 wineries, and 284,000 irrigated acres most of which are located between 3,700 and 4,200 feet in elevation. The *ava* takes its name from one of the most historic settlements in America--Mesilla, a small Spanish city built around a Plaza Mayor, and the site of Billy the Kid's conviction of murder. In 1854 Mesilla, with the signing of the Gadsden Purchase, became the capital of the Arizona Territory. One of the principal grape varieties is Colombard, a grape with higher than average acid levels that is used mainly for blending and in the production of sparkling wines. The second most popular grape, Ruby Cabernet, a high yielder, makes tannin-rich, astringent, and herbaceous wine that ages well. The *Mimbres Valley (1985) ava*, grows most of the Chenin Blanc, a grape that produces fruity, fresh, light wines. The valley, a large 636,000-acre region, contains twelve growers, 1,500 acres of vineland, but only one winery. Located in Luna and Grant counties, it is named after the river of the same name. Deming, the principal city, lies in the center of this highly intensive irrigated valley. Middle Rio Grande *V*alley (1988) is a narrow, nineteen-mile wide valley that extends just north of Albuquerque southward for 106 miles to San Antonio. The *ava* includes portions of four counties (Sandoval, Bernallilo, Valencia, and Socorro), and contains six wineries with three additional planned by 1992. The *ava* consists of approximately 278,400 irrigated acres, of which fewer than 500 are planted in grapes between 4,800 and 5,200 feet in elevation. The wineries are:

Alamosa Cellars (Elephant Butte, 1987), is a 100-acre, 6,000-case winery that makes clean, fresh, Riesling, Sauvignon Blanc, Chardonnay, Zinfandel, and sparkling wines under the *Domaine Mont-Jallon* label.

Anderson Valley Vineyards (Albuquerque, 1984), is a 125-acre, 18,000-case winery that makes Chenin Blanc, Chardonnay, Muscat Blanc, Sauvignon Blanc, Ruby Cabernet, Cabernet Sauvignon, and proprietary wines mainly from purchased grapes. This state of the art winery, one of the largest in the state, was founded by the world-famous balloonist Maxie Anderson.

Balagna Winery (Los Alamos, 1986), is an interesting, 1,000-case winery that makes, under the *San Ysidro Vineyards* label, Chardonnay, Vidal Blanc, Seyval, Riesling, Barbera, Zinfandel, Pinot Noir, Chancellor Noir, and proprietary wines.

Chateau Sassenage (Elephant Butte, 1989), formerly Elephant Butte Wine Company, is a rapidly expanding, 125-acre, 30,000-case winery that makes Chardonnay, Sauvignon Blanc, Muscat Blanc, Cabernet Sauvignon, and Merlot. This 4,800-feet high winery is in the center of a large resort area.

Devalmont Vineyards (Albuquerque, 1987), is a 10-acre, 12,000-case, excellent winery that only makes rich, well scented and flavored sparkling wines from Chardonnay and Pinot Noir grapes marketed under the *Gruet* label.

Domaine Cheurlin (Truth or Consequences, 1985), is a 100-acre, 30,000-case winery that makes Chardonnay, and Brut and Extra Dry sparkling wines, all moderately priced offering good value.

Hurst Vineyards (Bosque, 1986), is a 5-acre, 500-case winery that makes Vidal Blanc, Seyval, Villard Noir, and Villard Blanc.

Joe P. Estrada Winery (Mesilla, 1955), the oldest winery in the state, is a 2-acre, 1,000-case facility that makes only table wine from the Mission grape.

La Chiripada Winery (Dixon, 1981), is a 10-acre, 2,500-case winery that makes an excellent Vidal Blanc, Riesling, a Porto-type wine, and a large collection of blended wines mainly from Zinfandel, Ruby Caber-

net, Baco Noir, Leon Millot, Villard Blanc, Cayuga, and Aurore. Located 6,000 feet in elevation, this may very well be the highest winery in the nation.

La Vina Winery (Chamberino, 1977), is a 20-acre, 10,000-case winery that makes a wide assortment of Vinifera varietal and proprietary blends. The winery, recently purchased by Bieganowski Cellars of El Paso, will increase production to 39,000 cases and concentrate on Chardonnay, Sauvignon Blanc, Cabernet Sauvignon, Zinfandel, and sparkling wines.

Las Nutrias Winery & Vineyard (Corrales, 1985), is a 60-acre, 2,000-case winery that makes Riesling, Pinot Noir, Chancellor, and a white proprietary wine.

Madison Vineyard (Ribera, 1985), is a 4-acre, 1,000-case winery that makes Aurore, Seyval, Vidal Blanc, DeChaunac, Baco Noir, and proprietary wines.

Mountain Vista Vineyards & Winery (Albuquerque, 1988), is a 20-acre, 1,000-case winery owned by the New Mexico Winegrowers Cooperative that makes proprietary wines from French-American grapes.

New Mexico Wineries (Lordsburg, 1985), formerly Blue Teal Vineyards, is a large, 280-acre, 70,000-case winery owned by a European syndicate that makes Chardonnay, Sauvignon Blanc, Riesling, Muscat Blanc, Zinfandel, Cabernet Sauvignon, Merlot, and proprietary wines. Other labels: *Blue Teal* and *Mademoiselle de Santa Fe*.

St. Clair Vineyards (Deming, 1984), with 625 acres and an output of 85,000 cases this was the largest and most modern winery in the state until it was sold at auction in 1989. It is now owned by a Texan who will resume the production of Sauvignon Blanc, Chardonnay, Cabernet Sauvignon, and excellent sparkling Muscat Blanc.

Sandia Shadows Vineyard & Winery (Albuquerque, 1984), is a 14-acre, 3,800-case winery that makes Chardonnay, Seyval, Chancellor Noir, and red and white proprietary wines, all offering good value.

Sandia Shadows Vineyard & Winery The vineyards of New Mexico and Arizona occupy the highest elevations in the nation. Baxevanis

Santa Fe Vineyards (Espanola, 1984), is a 4-acre, 2,500-case winery that makes Vidal Blanc, Chardonnay, Riesling, Chancellor Noir, Cabernet Sauvignon, Zinfandel, and proprietary wines, all offering good value.

Sun Wines (Las Cruces, 1987), is an 87-acre, 9,000-case winery that makes Chardonnay, Chenin Blanc, Riesling, Cabernet Sauvignon, Merlot, and Barbera.

Tularosa Vineyards (Tularosa, 1989), is a 4-acre, 1,000-case winery that makes Chenin Blanc, Sauvignon Blanc, Muscat Blanc, Chardonnay, Mission, Zinfandel, Merlot, and Grenache Noir wines.

Vina Madre Winery (Dexter, 1977), is a 35-acre, 2,000-case winery that makes Chardonnay, Riesling, Zinfandel, and Cabernet Sauvignon.

Arizona

Arizona, the "Grand Canyon" state, was historically a forbidding desertic region where sun and space were formidable obstacles to early Spanish settlement. After the first initial Spanish expedition in 1539 proved fruitless, the region remained neglected for 300 years as an unyielding wilderness. By 1850 only one wagon road crossed the entire territory, and even gold and silver discoveries in the post-Civil War period failed to attract many Americans. The state had but 9,658 inhabitants in 1870, 122,931 in 1900, and only modest growth over the next 40 years when the population rose to nearly 500,000 by 1940. Since then, sun and space have become major assets attracting millions of Americans from the northeast and midwest, and, as a consequence, the population rose to nearly 4 million in 1990, one of the most significant population increases encountered by any state in the nation. Phoenix, a small city of 106,000 in 1950, has grown to nearly 2 million by 1990. Nearly the entire population of 4 million reside in metropolitan Phoenix and Tucson.

Economically and culturally, Arizona has had an unusual history from its immediate neighbors. Its economy, based on mineral resources, irrigated crops (the state produces more cotton than Georgia and Alabama combined), and grazing land has been dominated by powerful mining and railroad interests rather than by farmers. Approximately one-quarter of the resident population is Hispanic while another 5 percent is Indian, and although the total Indian population of Arizona is half the number residing in New Mexico, Arizona contains the largest reservation land in the nation comprising about 20 percent of the state's total land area. It is also significant that 10 percent of the total land area is national forest, and another 5 percent officially classified as national park, monument, or wild refuge area.

The nation's sixth largest state, more than twice the size of New York state, Arizona is either too hot, too cold, or too dry (you know its dry because the state flower is the white blossom of the saguaro cactus) for viticulture. Environmental constraints rule out nearly the entire state except those areas where soil temperatures (the most critical physical quality factor for wine grapes) vary between 47F and 72F at elevations between 4,000 and 5,000 feet above sea level. Consequently, production is within the southeastern portion of the state in what is a basin and range geographic zone, on soils commonly referred to as *Terra Rossa*, or those rich in iron and calcium carbonate.

While Texas and New Mexico have all but six of the region's total number of wineries, Arizona has, with 12,000 acres (ranking fourth in the nation), more than half the grape acreage. Of the total, 400 are planted in wine gra-pes located mostly in the high elevations of Cochise and Santa Cruz counties south and east of Tucson. Eight thousand are planted in raisin grapes, and another 3,500 in table grapes. While valley locations give higher yields, only upland areas (mesothermic soil areas) have the ability to produce premium wine. While many historians maintain that grapes were grown and wine made as early as the 1650s at the Guevavi Mission near Nogales, an equal number suggest a date similar to those missions located in New Mexico and Texas.

Arizona, unlike neighboring New Mexico, has had a significant Mormon population that passed in 1913 a prohibition for much stricter legislation than the Eighteenth Amendment. From 1913 until 1980, no wine was made in Arizona--until R.W. Webb established his winery. As a consequence, until recently, grape acreage has been used for table and raisin grape production. Despite religious obstacles to winemaking, the state passed a farm winery bill in 1980, and by 1984 there were four wineries. The legislation permits the production of as much as 75,000 gallons, winery sales, a wine tasting room, and in order for the wine to carry a state appellation, 75 percent of the fruit must be home-grown. Since 1980 wine grape acreage has grown from less than 26 acres to more than 350 by 1992.

The state has one approved *ava, Sonoita (1984)*, the name and settlement both dating back to 1691. With fewer than 200 acres of vineland and one winery, this 325 square-mile region is bounded by the Santa Rita, Huachuca, and Whetstone Mountain ranges whose elevations vary from 2,500 to 4,500 feet above sea level. It is the largest area in the state planted in wine grapes. The region is arid with only desert grassland and scattered shrub. The principal wine grapes are Colombard, Chenin Blanc, Riesling, Sauvignon Blanc, Ruby Cabernet, Petite Sirah, and Cabernet Sauvignon. Approximately 70 additional acres are planted in French-American varieties, and although most of the wine is white, red wines have generated a much better reputation in recent years.

The wineries are: **Arizona Vineyards** (Nogales, 1983), is an excellent, 5,000-case winery that makes a large assortment of proprietary Vinifera-based wines (*Dessert Dust, Rattlesnake Red, Apache Red*, etc.). Highly unusual is the use of chestnut barrels. **Callaghan Vineyards** (Elgin, 1991), is an 18-acre, 1,000-case winery that makes Sauvignon Blanc, Chardonnay, Merlot, Cabernet Sauvignon, and proprietary wines. **R.W. Webb Winery** (Vail, 1980), is a 20-acre, 7,000-case winery that makes Colombard, Riesling, Sauvignon Blanc, Cabernet Sauvignon, Petite Sirah, Zinfandel, Porto and Sherry-type, fruit, and proprietary wines. **San Dominique Winery** (Camp Verde, 1981), is a 5-acre, 5,000-case winery that makes Sauvignon Blanc, Riesling, Cabernet Sauvignon, fortified, and proprietary wines. **Santa Cruz Winery** (Elgin, 1992), is a 23-acre, 2,000-case winery that makes Sauvignon Blanc, Chardonnay, Cabernet Sauvignon, Pinot Noir, and sparkling wines. Other label: *Naveh Vineyards* for kosher wines. **Sonoita Vineyards** (Elgin, 1983), is a 40-acre, 4,000-case, estate winery that makes Sauvignon Blanc, Colombard, Pinot Noir, Cabernet Sauvignon, sparkling, and proprietary wines.

VII
THE WINES OF THE NORTHWEST

The northwest, consisting of the three states of Washington, Idaho, and Oregon, collectively represents the northernmost viticultural area in the nation (vineyards in Washington are in fact closer to the north pole than the equator). Despite the facility of modern communications, many people still conceive this large region as virtually a frontier wilderness. This image is largely derived from frontier fiction, and its peripheral location to the historic centers of American settlement. While the northwest remained largely unexplored as recently as 100 years ago, it is now one of the most rapid economically developing areas in the nation, its population growing from 3.4 million in 1940 to nearly 10 million in 1991, a sharp contrast to the census of 1850 when the European population of Washington and Oregon was 1,201 and 12,093 respectively. Interestingly, while the collective land area of Oregon and Idaho is two-thirds larger than Washington, the latter has more than 50 percent more people.

While Aldous Huxley once remarked that in "Europe one travels in the fourth dimension-the dimension of time," in the northwest, travel is through space. A region of bold and varied natural resources, it is a titanic domain of mountains, broad plateaus, and narrow ribbons of rich, irrigated agricultural land. From west to east, the Pacific northwest is an area of coastal mountains, the north-south Puget Sound-Willamette lowlands, the Cascades, and a series of large and small plateaus and river valleys, all of which are, in contrast to the humid and verdant western portion, semi-arid. The entire region displays an incongruous array of snow-capped volcanoes, moss-clad rain forests, seemingly unlimited grasslands, sunbaked lava, and broad vistas that stimulate and captivate the imagination. While climate, topography, and natural vegetation tend to dissect the northwest into many dissimilar geographical units, the Columbia River Basin, providing drainage for more than two-thirds of the region, is a major unifying element.

As with California, Spain was also the pioneer in discovering the northwest when Bartolome Ferrelo sailed along the Oregon coast in 1543, as did Francis Drake a generation later. In 1602-1603 Martin de Aguilar discovered the mouth of the Columbia River, and in 1775 Bruno Heceta became the first white man to set foot in what is now the state of Washington. In spite of the frantic search for the Northwest Passage, effective European settlement was prevented by the cold, rainy environment. American claims to the region date from Robert Gray's second voyage for a group of Boston merchants when he named the Columbia River after his ship. The northwest region was approached by land by the Hudson Bay Company in 1670 (circa), but due to distances encountered from existing settlements there was little interest until the 1803-1806 Lewis and Clark Expedition opened the northwest to settlement. It is surprising to note that grapes are not indigenous to the northwest as the first grapes (type and variety unknown) were planted around 1825 at Fort Vancouver on the Columbia River, the first Vinifera grapes planted in the 1860s in eastern Washington at the Tampico area near Union Gap, and the Worden variety planted on Stretch Island in 1872.

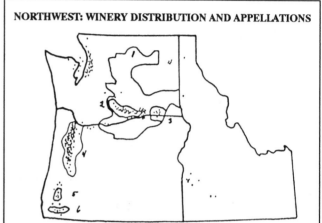

Figure 7.1

NORTHWEST: WINERY DISTRIBUTION AND APPELLATIONS

The northwest contains six ava's: (1) Columbia Valley (1984), (2) Yakima Valley (1983), (3) Walla Walla (1984), (4) Willamette Valley (1984), (5) Umpqua Valley (1984), and (6) Rogue Valley (1991).

The economy of the northwest, due to its low population density and peripheral location to the American industrial core, has historically been based on natural resource exploitation. While forest products have long dominated the economic life of the humid, western margins, and the eastern semi-arid regions have emphasized extensive grazing and wheat production--it is only with the construction of large hydroelectric dams that associated irrigated agriculture, and aluminum and aircraft manufacturing have changed the historic look of this vast region. Gold fever brought settlers when this precious metal was discovered in British Columbia in 1858 and two years later at Oro Fino Creek in Idaho. Prospectors rushed to the Salmon River, Boise Basin and the Owyhee region when silver was discovered several years later. While the towns of The Dalles, Walla Walla, and Lewiston competed for trade along the Columbia River drainage area, Portland emerged as the major city in the northern portion of the Willamette Valley. Later, Seattle, Tacoma, and Portland, the three largest cities west of the Cascades served as the western terminus of the Great Northern, Northern Pacific, and Union Pacific railroads, respectively. While forest products (at least 40 percent of the national total), and extensive agricultural activities have long dominated the economy of the northwest, the area experienced many economic growth periods: a major mineral cycle during the period 1850-1880; shipbuilding in the late 1890s; lumbering during the period 1910-1940; fishing during 1900-1950; and aluminum and aircraft manufacturing since World War II. Agriculturally, only 10 percent of the total land in the region is classed as cropland, the largest contiguous areas being the Willamette Valley, the Columbia Basin, northeastern Oregon, southeastern Washington, and the Snake River region of Idaho. With the exception of portions of the Willamette Valley and Puget Sound region, all other cropland regions are irrigated. The dominant activity in terms of land use is ranching, followed by wheat, with harvested cropland representing less than 17 percent of total land in farms.

No major quality viticultural area of the nation has grown as rapidly over the past 30 years as the northwest. From fewer than 500 acres in 1967, the three states of Washington, Oregon, and Idaho cultivate as of 1990 more than 42,500 acres, of which 35,500 are located in Washington, 6,100 acres in Oregon, and nearly 1,000 acres in Idaho. Table wine production for the same period has risen from less than 90 thousand to more than 3 million cases. This spectacular, meteoric explosion of vineland is equally matched by the quality of its premium wines, particularly Pinot Noir, Cabernet Sauvignon, Merlot, Riesling, Gewurztraminer, Chardonnay, Chenin Blanc, Sauvignon Blanc, and Muller-Thurgau. Because there is a strong element of regional cooperation, in 1976 the Northwest Regional Commission authorized a tri-state grape research project with experimental vineyards to determine which Vinifera vines would do best, and explore vineyard practices best suited to each climatic area. In a remarkable short span of time the northwest has produced many world class wines that have offered justification to the pioneering efforts of the early founders. The desire to prove that the three state region is capable of producing excellent wine has been demonstrated beyond doubt: Oregon is producing excellent Pinot Noir; Washington outstanding Merlot, Cabernet Sauvignon, Riesling, Chenin Blanc, Muscat Blanc, and Chardonnay; and Idaho superb Riesling, Chenin Blanc, and sparkling wines. The above varieties grow with relatively high yields, inexpensively, and so perfectly, that they, by any measurement, demonstrate that the northwest is a far more versatile viticultural region than most, thus offering excellent competition to such established wine producing areas as California, Germany, and France.

Although nearly 23,000 vine acres are planted in Concord, French-American varietals, and other American vines, table wine production (unlike New York, the nation's second largest wine producer) is the product of Vinifera grapes. In addition, the three states, particularly Washington and Oregon with more than 200,000 cases

(all of which are above-average in quality), are the nation's leading fruit and berry wine producers. The leading wines are strawberry, raspberry, boysenberry, blackberry, loganberry, apple, pear, peach, and cherry. Small fruit and berry wines are surely to grow because the quality of the intensely flavored fruit is high, the application of state of the art techniques, the intensification of research, and the number of producers entering this highly rewarding field is increasing. There is also now a growing interest in producing sparkling wines, the first efforts of which have been highly promising.

In spite of the relatively recent history of winemaking in the northwest, the three states have managed to produce wines with clearly identifiable characteristics: clean, fruity, lean (almost austere), well-balanced libations that set themselves apart from the nation's leader--California (offering excellent value). With less than 4 percent of the nation's total vine acreage, the northwest produces 14 percent of the premium wines of America, a remarkable achievement given the young age of the industry. Given the fact that the regional population exhibits the highest per capita consumption of domestic wines in the nation, and is a young, sophisticated consumer that is loyal and spends heavily on premium wine production, the possibilities of further growth appear to be substantial. Without question, the undiscovered wines of the northwest have been discovered--to the delight of everyone.

While viticulture began with some of the original settlers in the second half of the nineteenth century, the growth of the industry started in the early 1970s. From just one commercial winery in 1963, the industry exploded to more than 190 by 1992. Obviously, until recently, the wines of the northwest were little known outside the region, and production was only miniscule by California standards as it did not even meet the demands of local markets. Because prime, abeyant viticultural land in the three states varies between 300,000 and 500,000 acres, the potential for future growth is extraordinary. Therefore, the northwest is the sleeping giant of American viticulture and with good reason: it has excellent and varied microclimates, relatively inexpensive vineland, a moderately insect and disease-free environment, and an enormous reserve of capital to finance winemaking. Acreage is overwhelmingly concentrated in the Columbia Plateau, Yakima Valley, the Willamette Valley of Oregon, and five other minor areas--Puget Sound, Snake River, Walla Walla Valley, the Spokane region, and southern Oregon. It is noteworthy that while an overwhelming portion of the acreage and wineries in Oregon are located between the Coastal Ranges and the Cascades, Washington exhibits a more complicated pattern in which vine acreage is mainly confined to the semi-arid interior plateau regions, with 40 percent of all wineries found in the Puget Sound region.

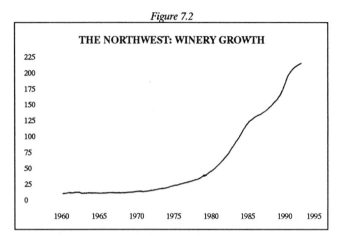

Figure 7.2

THE NORTHWEST: WINERY GROWTH

winds, and the Cascade Range, a 700-mile stretch of volcanic cones, of which Mt. Rainier (14,410 feet in elevation) is the highest. With 26 live glaciers on its slopes, this is also the single largest tourist attraction in the northwest.

In the final analysis, the entire northwest is an unlikely area for quality wine production because it lacks a large sophisticated market with a wine tradition. A permanent American settler, a farmer-pioneer, did not arrive in the northwest until the 1840s. Oregon attained statehood in 1859, Washington in 1889, and Idaho in 1890. In 1880 there were but 175,000 people in Oregon and just 75,000 in Washington. The region boasts one of the lowest population densities in the nation, and has only three major cities, the largest of which, Seattle, has but 2.5 million people ranking eighteenth among the top 100 metropolitan areas in the nation. Metropolitan Portland, with 1.3 million people, is second, followed by Spokane, a distant third with 500,000 people. Regionally, with less than 10 percent of the combined total area being used for agricultural purposes, vineland constitutes less than 1 percent of total cropland, yet grapes generate one of the highest returns per acre, thus becoming one of the most lucrative crops in the entire northwest. In addition, the northwest contains 42,500 grape acres (of which 19,500 are Vinifera), produces more than 3 million cases of wine, and makes much of the finest premium Chardonnay, Cabernet Sauvignon, Merlot, Pinot Noir, Riesling, Semillon, Gewurztraminer, Chenin Blanc, and Sauvignon Blanc in the nation.

The Geographical Base For Quality Wine Production

Collectively, Oregon and Washington extend for 500 miles in a north-south dimension, and more than 650 miles from the Pacific Ocean to the eastern Idaho border. Throughout this large area differences in elevation and distance from the Pacific Ocean provoke significant variations in climate, one of the most important being the distinctions between windward and leeward exposures. Therefore, within this huge block of 248,730 square miles are a multitude of mountains and interior basins combining to produce a multi-varigated pattern of distinctive climatic patterns. The three main climatic influencing elements are the Pacific Ocean, the prevailing westerly

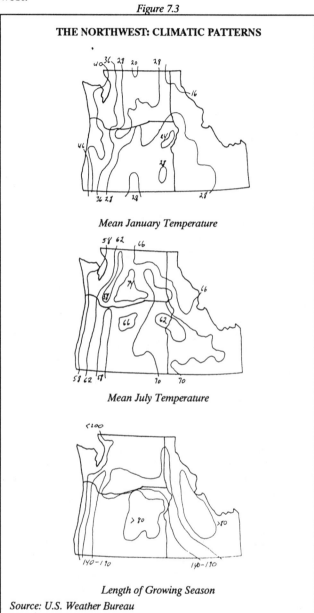

Figure 7.3

THE NORTHWEST: CLIMATIC PATTERNS

Mean January Temperature

Mean July Temperature

Length of Growing Season

Source: U.S. Weather Bureau

To some people the Cascade Range of the Pacific northwest is a series of mountains, a skiing paradise, a laboratory of geological marvels, and a mineral and lumber treasure. To a vinegrower it is a barrier that keeps the moist-laden prevailing westerlies out, and, hence, makes excellent viticultural pursuits possible along the leeward margins of the Cascades. Almost everyone agrees, that no matter what the climate, with sufficient water, everything seems to grow with abundance. The Cascade Range runs north-south through Washington and Oregon and divides the climate of the northwest into two distinct regions, each with different climates based on precipitation and temperature. Areas to the west, due to the presence of the Pacific Ocean, have more rainfall, a narrower annual temperature range, and fewer seasonal extremes.

The area between the Alaska panhandle and southern Oregon is similar to the Marine West Coast climate of western Europe in which a good deal of the precipitation of coastal and windward areas is the result of the frequent movement of cyclonic storms (a steady succession of cold and warm fronts), pushed along by humid, water-laden prevailing westerlies. The intensity of precipitation is generally determined by proximity to the ocean and altitude, a feature known as *orographic precipitation*, as air, forced to rise along mountains, cools, producing copious amounts of rain. (The Olympic Mountains are the wettest spot in continental America; Los Angeles has 35 rainy days, San Francisco 54, and Seattle has 163.) While the windward, west-facing slopes are bathed in rainfall, descending air on the leeward slopes produces not only little rainfall, but promotes aridity as well. Therefore, the combination of a major source of moisture, prevailing winds, and a formidable topographic barrier produces one of the most astonishing climatic divides in America: a sharp and dramatic transition from the Pacific humid and windward margins to the mid-latitude, semi-desert.

important consideration that explains the distribution of Vinifera grapes along the leeward sections of the Coastal Range. Because daylight is the key element in ripening grapes (and not necessarily temperature), the long daylight hours of the growing season set this area apart from the more cloudy Puget Sound region. Therefore, while the growing season is longer by more than two months in nearly the entire Puget Sound region, the high incidence of cloud cover, heavy precipitation and cooler temperatures prevent large-scale, commercial viticultural endeavors from taking place. In sharp contrast, because of greater seasonal climatic variation, the Willamette Valley is adversely affected by untimely spring frosts and untimely harvest-time precipitation promoting mildew, and other diseases. Poor vintages, defined as wet and cloudy (and invariably below average in total heat), occur every four years. An excellent year, 1987 was characterized by a warm spring with early bud break, a warm and dry summer, with September and October the driest in history. The harvest was three weeks earlier than usual, producing low pH and richly colored wines. In general, Pinot Noir, Pinot Gris, Chardonnay, and Riesling, the principal quality grapes of the Willamette Valley, ripen slowly and evenly producing wines known for their fragrance, flavor, and complexity.

Figure 7.4

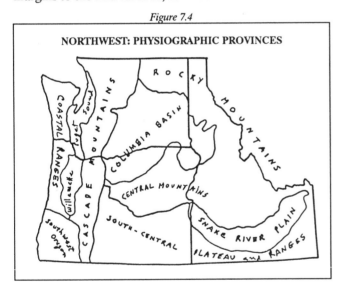

NORTHWEST: PHYSIOGRAPHIC PROVINCES

Figure 7.5

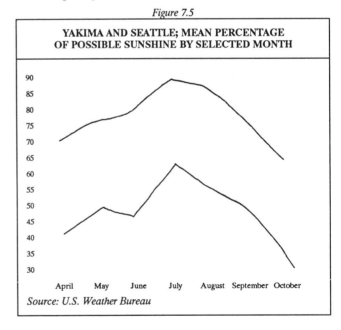

YAKIMA AND SEATTLE; MEAN PERCENTAGE OF POSSIBLE SUNSHINE BY SELECTED MONTH

Source: U.S. Weather Bureau

West of the Cascades there are significant regional climatic variations. Due to the breaks in the Coastal Ranges, maritime weather influences penetrate much of the interior lowlands. As a consequence, for nine months Marine West Coast influences give rise to overcast skies, moisture-laden winds, and copious winter rainfall. Summer winds, however, are often heated by the land producing relatively dry summers. Precipitation, which varies from 50 to 180 inches along the coast and Olympic Ranges, is sharply reduced in the Oregon lowlands, a very

1. The Pacific Coast Range, formed by folding and volcanic intrusions, is a north-south mountainous and heavily forested region 30 to 50 miles wide that separates the Pacific Ocean from the Willamette Valley. The coastal region of both Washington and Oregon is dominated by forested west-facing slopes. Annual precipitation averages 60 to 100 inches, most of which falls during the winter season. Marine influence dominates: the frost-free season varies between 210 and 250 days; except for higher elevations, snow is rare; temperatures are moderate for the latitude; and soils wet and acidic. The cool, moist environment favors heavy coniferous vegetation and inhibits most agricultural crops

except dairying and specialty items such as cranberries and flowering bulbs. Except for minor acreage of American grape varieties and an occasional wine tasting room and winery, this region is nearly devoid of grape-growing endeavors.

2. The Puget Sound-Willamette Lowlands consist of relatively narrow and irregular glacial-influenced low lying areas that stretch from Canada to central Oregon. A favorable combination of water, climate, forests, soils, and water transportation accessibility have fostered the development of this most densely settled region in the entire northwest. Both the Puget Sound and the Willamette Valley are located along the leeward side of the Coastal Range, and, as a consequence, are decidedly drier than windward areas. The Puget Sound, a deep, inland arm of the Pacific Ocean, contains many excellent harbors, hundreds of islands, and the much of the state's industry and population. As a result, the bulk of the wineries are found north, east and south of Seattle, nearly all of which purchase grapes from the central and eastern section of the state. Those wineries that are located on lee exposures (highly localized, site-specific), as part of the mainland or on islands, are mainly engaged in fruit, berry, and non-Vinifera production. Although the number of accumulated heat units (between 1300 and 1700) appear to be within tolerable limits similar to those found in the Mosel and Rhine, high humidity levels and mildew are major obstacles in the production of Vinifera grapes. The Willamette Valley, without an access to the Pacific Ocean, is warmer, drier, and exhibits a more evenly and closely spaced settlement pattern than the Puget Sound. It is the only quality grape producing region west of the Cascades, and with only a small number of exceptions, nearly all the vine acreage and wineries are located on the east-facing slopes of the Coastal Range along the left bank of the Willamette River. Due to the northerly position of this valley, site selection is particularly important: usually south-facing hillsides, 400 to 1,000 feet in elevation, with deep, friable, humus-poor soils. When the soil is shallow and contains iron and calcareous material, it is exceptionally good for Pinot Noir and Chardonnay. This valley is the heartland of Oregon with more than 50 percent of all farms and industrial activity, and more than two-thirds of the total and urban population. While more than three-quarters of the total land area of this well-watered valley is devoted to pasture and field crops, it also is the main region for the production of fruit, hazelnuts, mint, and other crops.

3. The Cascade Mountains rise abruptly 60 to 100 miles from the Pacific Ocean sharply dividing Washington and Oregon into a cool and humid western section, and a drier, more continental interior (including Idaho). The Cascades intercept east-moving, rain-bearing westerly winds, with the western slopes often receiving more than 100 inches of rainfall producing dense stands of evergreen vegetation that support a dynamic wood products industry.

4. The continental interior lies entirely within the rain shadow of the Cascades, and includes many important agricultural regions. This irregular, and geographically diverse region differs from the windward portions of the Cascades in terms of a greater annual range in temperature, less precipitation, and a shorter but warmer frost-free season. Not only is the leeward side of the Cascades relatively free of vine pests and diseases, but the low humidity and low winter temperatures minimize fungal diseases (but not birds and coyotes, both of which are serious problems). Two to four sulfur applications are generally enough to contain powdery mildew in the Yakima Valley, a sharp contrast to the more than 14 applications in the mid-Atlantic states and the midwest. In addition, the soils are light-textured, silt loams varying in depth from several inches to more than four feet, overlain with heavy accumulations of loess resting on volcanic rock. They are high in carbonate with pH values between 7 and 8.5. Soils heat up rapidly in the spring, allow for good root penetration, are highly permeable, and well-adapted to Vinifera varieties. While higher elevations are either forested or denuded of vegetation, and plateaus are mainly planted in wheat, irrigated valleys are broad or thin slivers of significant agricultural productivity. Vineyards are invariably located on the hilly margins of these irrigated areas to take advantage of air drainage and to increase sunlight effectiveness. The most important of these interior irrigated valleys is the Yakima, Columbia, Walla Walla, Snake, and Wenatchee.

5. The Southwestern portion of Oregon is dominated by the Rogue and Umpqua Rivers. Unlike the Willamette Valley to the north, this is a region with rugged topography and heavily forested upland areas. Due to its relatively high elevation and southerly location, the climate is dry, summers warm to hot, and winters are moist with considerable snow accumulations in the higher elevations. There are a number of interior basins that experience considerable continental features of more sunshine, a shorter frost-free season, reduced precipitation, and greater variability in annual temperature fluctuations. Settlements, characterized by small cities and towns, are grouped into four areas: Bear Creek Valley (the most important, with Medford and Ashland, the largest cities); Coos Bay; Coquille Valley; and the Middle Rogue Valley (with Grants Pass as the regional city). Mining, wood processing industries, and extensive ranching have long dominated the economic life of this region, but recently tourism and a growing viticultural interest have instilled new life into the growing economy.

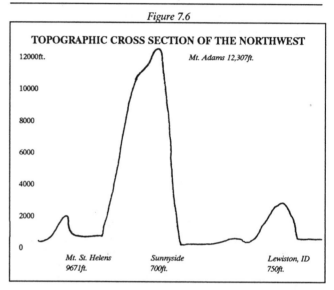

Figure 7.6

TOPOGRAPHIC CROSS SECTION OF THE NORTHWEST

It is apparent from the accompanying figures that the influence of the Pacific Ocean is particularly effective in restricting annual temperature fluctuations along the windward coast, and the increased effect of continentality is reflected by the greater range between winter and summer east of the Cascades. The frost-free season varies considerably by altitude and proximity to the Pacific Ocean: it is 300 days along the Pacific margins in Oregon/Washington; 240 days in portions of the Puget Sound; between 160 and 200 in the Willamette Valley and areas to the south; 200 days in Walla Walla and portions of the Columbia Valley in Oregon; between 160 to 200 days in the Snake and Clearwater areas of Idaho; and less than 180 days in the Yakima Valley. Generally, all stations east of the Cascades above 2,500 feet have a frost-free season below 140 days totally prohibiting grape cultivation. East of the Cascades the frost-free season supporting grape cultivation is not homogeneous but appears as tiny, discontinuous slivers of heat traps. Areas east of the Cascade Mountains are characterized by: a shorter but warmer frost-free season; less rainfall; lower atmospheric humidity; greater diurnal temperature ranges; a greater propensity for dry, almost desiccating winds; greater annual ranges in temperature; a greater danger from frost; and lower winter temperatures than stations located west of the Cascade Mountains.

Throughout the entire region east of the Cascades, as well as the north central region of Oregon, low winter temperatures are a major environmental problem. Although the risk of growing grapes is less than for most other agricultural crops, winter temperatures can drop by more than 50 degrees in less than 24 hours, as in January of 1979. The winter of 1991, particularly in Yakima, will also be remembered as exceptionally severe, resulting in significant injury. Still, weather during the growing and harvest season can only be described, relative to most other grape-growing areas, as consistently good bordering on perfection.

Figure 7.7

CLIMATIC DIFFERENCES OF YAKIMA AND SNOQUALMIE

Yakima (Y), located on the lee side of the Cascades at 1,061 ft., has 7.3" of rainfall, and a mean annual temperature of 51.6F.

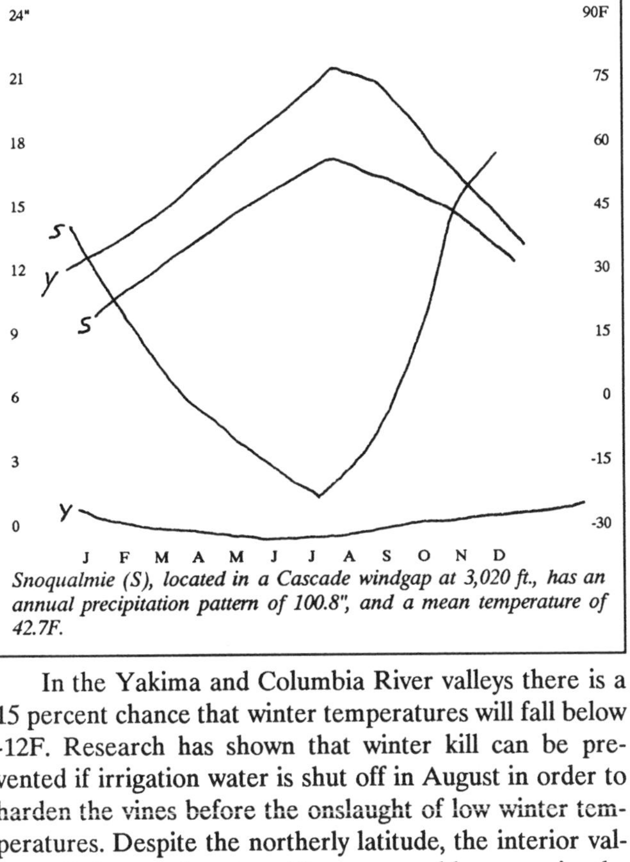

Snoqualmie (S), located in a Cascade windgap at 3,020 ft., has an annual precipitation pattern of 100.8", and a mean temperature of 42.7F.

In the Yakima and Columbia River valleys there is a 15 percent chance that winter temperatures will fall below -12F. Research has shown that winter kill can be prevented if irrigation water is shut off in August in order to harden the vines before the onslaught of low winter temperatures. Despite the northerly latitude, the interior valleys of the northwest, unlike comparable areas in the midwest and northeast, experience an uninterrupted winter (without high-low temperature fluctuations), and, hence, a long dormant period. Moreover, in spring and fall, the sun is not very intense due to the low angle above the horizon thus preventing false spring problems. In the final analysis, the area enjoys unparalleled advantages over most other regions in America: longer and cooler summers with less intense heat, but abundant sunshine; diurnal temperatures are wide and quite conducive to the

production of excellent grape acidity and higher sugar levels; excellent soils; and a near-absence of phylloxera and other vineyard pests. In Washington and Idaho, the harvest begins in mid-September and continues to November. In the Willamette Valley, it is very much abbreviated between early September when Pinot Noir and Chardonnay mature, and mid-October when the last grape, Riesling, ripens.

The annual and seasonal patterns of precipitation are shown in Fig. 7.7. Interestingly, while summer is drier than winter, there is much more summer rainfall in the Puget Sound-Willamette trough than in areas east of the Cascades. Furthermore, humidity, not shown on the climatic figures, is continuously greater than 50 percent for all seasons. As a result, the combination of greater annual precipitation and higher humidity produces a narrow range of annual temperatures. East of the Cascades the intermontane regions of plateau and valley are characterized by higher summer-winter temperature ranges, and a pronounced summer drought requiring irrigation. These areas are virtually deserts with less than twelve inches of precipitation, and often with less than six. Here the natural vegetation is grassland, and because of the latitude, with up to 17 1/2 hours of sunlight during the month of June, the growing season is more effective. Intensity of sunlight and degree day variation (from 1,300 in the Willamette Valley, to more than 3,500 in the Columbia Valley), account for the sharp differences in style between Oregon and Washington/Idaho wines. Rieslings, for example, are more delicate and Mosel-like in the Willamette, but rounder, fuller, better-balanced, and capable of bottle improvement from grapes emanating from the other side of the Cascades. Summer is characterized by cool nights and dry, crisp sunlight days producing high acid grapes with intense varietal flavor and scent. This condition is dramatically different from Napa and Sonoma, two premium areas whose much higher heat summations produce lower acid/higher alcohol levels. When properly grown east of the Cascades, Vinifera vines have generally shown excellent winter survival when temperatures have fallen to -12F, especially Gewurztraminer, Riesling, and Chardonnay. Almost as successful are Muscat Blanc, Merlot, and Chenin Blanc. The least winter hardy varieties are Cabernet Sauvignon, Grenache Noir, Semillon, Sauvignon Blanc, and Pinot Noir. In general, Riesling and Chenin Blanc are the most cold hardy and last to be picked; Chardonnay, usually planted on warmer, west-facing slopes in the Yakima, is a mid-season variety; and throughout the northwest Gewurztraminer is one of the first grapes to be picked.

Reflecting the climatic patterns of the Pacific northwest, soils west of the Cascades are wet, acidic, and dominated by clay throughout the coastal and bay areas. They vary from poorly drained, glaciated material in the

Puget Sound, to slightly better, but still poorly drained re-golith in the Willamette Valley, to excellent, iron-rich, well-drained soils in the hilly western margins of the Willamette, an area that represents the finest viticultural region west of the Cascades. On the lee side, the better vineland soils are an unusual blend of volcanic, alluvial, and lava with a heavy deposit of loess, or wind-blown material. They are heavily mineralized, and extremely fertile when fertilized and irrigated.

Figure 7.8

WASHINGTON: CLIMATIC PATTERNS

Mean Annual Rainfall
The rainshadow effect of the Cascades is obvious with amazing results for the production of irrigated fruit and vegetables in the interior valleys.

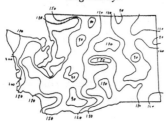

Degree Days

Growing Season
Note the location of the state's largest grape producing region amidst extreme minimum temperatures of -20F, a most annual feature for Vinifera grapes. The longest growing season area, by at least 50 days, is coastal Washington. Upper, interior elevations have a growing season of less than 90 days. However, those valleys with elevations under 1200 feet, enjoy an ideal growing season that varies between 160-190 days.

With degree days varying between 1,300 and 3,500, and a climatic pattern that ranges from cool and humid to the west of the Cascades, to cool/hot and dry on the lee side, grape varieties are generally selected for their adaptation to these extremes. While cool climate varieties have received preference, in recent years Cabernet Sauvignon, Merlot, several Muscats, and Semillon have enjoyed a faster rate of growth. While more than 35 grape varieties are commercially grown, the most important Vinifera varieties in terms of acreage are: Riesling, Chenin

Blanc, Pinot Noir, Chardonnay, Gewurztraminer, Cabernet Sauvignon, Merlot, Sauvignon Blanc, and Semillon. Of the 20,000 Vinifera acres, 6,000, or 25 percent, are red.

Regional grape variety adaptation is rather striking. The Willamette Valley, due to cooler growing conditions than California, is a land of early ripening, cold-adapted vines, such as: Pinot Noir, Riesling, Chardonnay, Gewurztraminer, Pinot Gris, and Chenin Blanc. The dominant red grape, considered the finest in the nation, is Pinot Noir. The favorite white grape, with more than 1,400 acres, or one-quarter of the acreage, is Chardonnay, followed by Riesling and Gewurztraminer. In the drier, summer-hot, winter-cold regions east of the Cascade Ranges, the most successful white grape varieties consist of Riesling, Chardonnay, Sauvignon Blanc, Semillon, Chenin Blanc, and Gewurztraminer, all intensely varietal and well-balanced. Nevertheless, white grapes are rapidly losing ground to red grapes, the most important of which are Cabernet Sauvignon and Merlot, both of which are typically full-bodied, complex, equal to, and often exceeding the complexity and balance of North Coast California equivalents. Due to the cool summer weather, high rate of humidity, and wet, acidic soils, the historic grape varieties of the Puget Sound region have been native American and French-American grapes.

NORTHWEST VINTAGES
Washington vintages: 1983, outstanding, tannic rich, and thick; 1987, excellent to outstanding; 1988, excellent; 1989, outstanding, rich, silky, dark, round, and well-balanced; 1991, the product of low yields due to unusually low winter temperatures and an early harvest, has produced exceptionally rich, fruity wines. Note: Washington vintages are known for their consistency as there are no "poor" vintages in recent memory. For Oregon vintage variation is more common, but 1983, 1985, and 1989 were outstanding.

Riesling, historically a highly profitable variety, is the dominant grape for the entire tri-state region. However, its percentage of total grape acreage has fallen in recent years as emphasis has gradually shifted to premium red grapes and Chardonnay. Its relative decline not with-standing, Riesling, characterized by low pH and sugar, and naturally high malic acid, is an excellent base for sparkling wines, as well as superb table and dessert wines. So prized are its inherent qualities that northwest grapes and juice have been shipped to New York and other "eastern" states for years, and in ever increasing quantities to California. At its best, Riesling can age, has intense flavor and aroma, and is, perhaps, the closest to high quality German versions. Chardonnay, increasingly becoming the favorite white grape, is usually dry, lightly oaked, rich, and very satisfying. While it exhibits a wide range in style and character, it appears to be much softer in the Willamette Valley, a sharp contrast to the more austere, acidic, but fuller versions of central and eastern Washington. Gewurztraminer is spicy, well-scented and mellow. Among the many grape varieties exhibiting promise are: Auxerrois, Ehrensfelser, Lemberger, Scheurebe, Muller-Thurgau, and Ortega.

Although the wines of the northwest historically lacked national recognition, make no mistake about the dramatic quality advances of recent years. The wines are above-average for industry standards and getting progressively better. Currently little known outside the northwest, they are rapidly gaining recognition for their reliability and high standard, and they will, by the end of this century, be as widely known and as prestigious as any from California. Because few wineries have more than a dozen years experience, appellation styles have yet to evolve into easy generalizations. Pinot Noir, Oregon's premier wine, although good to outstanding, and widely acclaimed as America's best, exhibits great diversity. Washington and Idaho have produced outstanding Chenin Blanc, Cabernet Sauvignon, Chardonnay, Sauvignon Blanc, Merlot, Riesling, and Gewurztraminer, but a general style has yet to take hold, and no winery claims to set the standard. In general, both white and red wines are tightly structured, crisp, acidic, well-balanced, and concentrated in fruit and fragrance. The high acid and low pH concentrations mean that northwest wines are not only age worthy, but better than average when made sparkling, the latter a market segment that has expanded rapidly in recent years. While the entire tri-state region cultivates two-thirds the Vinifera vine acreage of Napa, the quality of the finest fruit and wines can only be described in superlatives. However, due to the northerly location of the region, vintage variation in all three states is significantly greater than in California.

Washington

While Washington had fewer than 1 million people as recently as 1940, European exploration was comparatively early. Bruno Heceta and Juan Francisco Bodega y Quadra landed in what is now coastal Washington in 1575; James Cook, in search of the northwest passage, arrived in 1778; Lewis and Clark entered the lower margins of the Columbia River in 1805; the first Protestant mission was established in Walla Walla in 1836; territorial status was achieved in 1853; and statehood was attained in 1889. Today, Washington, with nearly 70,000 sq. miles and more than 5 million people, is the dominant state in the northwest. Except for Spokane in the eastern portion, more than 85 percent of the population resides west of the Cascades in the Puget Sound trough, with more than half residing in metropolitan Seattle.

Although grapes were first said to have been planted in Walla Walla in the early 1860s, with wine made for sale by one Frank Orselli in 1865 (another alternative date is 1876), Washington's grape industry was founded on Stretch Island in 1870 when one Lambert Evans first

planted grapes. Due to the relatively high rainfall and humidity, the vineyard was mainly (as well as those that followed later) confined to native American and French-American varieties. As grape-growing increased steadily after statehood, the wine industry grew to 42 wineries by 1917 but was insignificant in terms of total volume. Wineries were overwhelmingly cottage-type in structure and made inexpensive fruit, berry and dessert wines, the latter based on Concord and other Labrusca and American grapes. The quality was poor, consumption levels low, and quality imported wines scarce. Nevertheless, due to the small size of part-time producers, the majority survived the ravages of Prohibition, and subsisted with state protection after Repeal only to suffer from intensive California competition in the 1950s.

Walter J. Clore, Research Horticulturist, Washington State University Emeritus, was born in 1911 in Oklahoma. He received his Ph.D. in Pomology from Washington State University in 1947, and until his retirement worked for the State University System. He has published over 200 scientific papers and articles, travelled extensively to all major wine producing countries, and has been a consultant to many foreign governments, states, and vineyards/wineries.

The modern phase dates back to 1960 when Professor Walter Clore undertook a number of what proved to be highly optimistic feasibility studies, and along with Charles Nagel and Mohammed Ahmdullah pioneered Vinifera research. As a result, Vinifera acreage increased prompting the founding of the state's largest winery-- Chateau Ste. Michelle in 1967. Since then, the number of wineries exploded from 6 in 1975 to 17 in 1980, to 88 in 1992. Fortunately, the growth of Vinifera plantings coincided with favorable state alcoholic legislation, an increase in table wine consumption, and an avid interest in state production of Vinifera wine. In 1969 the state abrogated the post-Repeal domestic price advantages, and the historic fruit, berry and Concord wine industry was faced with aggressive competition from California. Almost immediately Washington turned away from Labrusca to

Vinifera grapes in a significant way. The leading factors influencing the recent growth are: lower land costs, high yields, slight winter loss due to better management practices, strong state support, and the near absence of phylloxera (the aphid has infected several vineyards, but to date the disease has been contained), and other vineyard pests.

WASHINGTON: HISTORICAL HIGHLIGHTS

1870: Lambert Evans settles on Stretch Island, and two years later plants Labrusca grapes.
1871: German immigrants plant Vinifera grapes in the Yakima Valley.
1902: Modern irrigation arrives to Sunnyside in the Yakima Valley and spurs a major agricultural renaissance.
1934: The Yakima Valley Grape Growers Association is founded.
1937: American and Vinifera grape research started.
1950: Concord research projects started.
1964: Vinifera and wine projects started.
1967: Chateau Ste. Michelle releases its first wine.
1982: Yakima Valley granted appellation status.
1983: Walla Walla Valley granted appellation status.
1984: Columbia Valley granted appellation status.
1987: The Washington Wine Commission was created to promote Washington State wine.
1991: Over the past 20 years Vinifera grape acreage increased from 1,300 acres to 12,000, the number of wineries rose from 3 to 88, and wine production from 43,000 to 8,000,000 gallons. Washington is second to California in the production of premium Vinifera wines. The state produces seventeen varietal wines, and a growing number of dessert wines.

Ever since the average American discovered table wines in the early 1960s, winemaking has become a major agricultural growth industry contributing significantly to economic development, tourism, and the agricultural base of the local producing region. Washington is a prime example of this newly discovered agricultural activity. With 88 wineries and 35,000 acres of vineyards, Washington has become the second largest producer of premium wine in America, the third largest grape producer, and the largest producer of Concord grapes in the nation. Grapes now rank as the twelfth largest agricultural product in the state in terms of value of output. The state produces more than six million gallons of wine annually, capital investment in vineyards and wineries stands at $450 million, and the product value exceeds $170 million annually. The state is, with total economic contributions of nearly $900 million (both direct and indirect), the eighth largest American wine market, and the fourth highest in per capita wine consumption. Moreover, while national wine sales have declined slightly in recent years, Washington's gross sales have enjoyed sustained double digit increases, particularly in national and international markets. From four wineries in 1972 and 18,221 acres (of which only 1,155 were Vinifera), Washington's wine industry has grown rapidly in recent years. Vinifera acreage, in particular, has shown dramatic growth, increasing from fewer than 1,000 in 1970, to 4,000 acres in 1982, to more than 12,000 in 1992.

Wine grape production rose from 6,650 tons in 1976 to more than 45,000 tons in 1987. American and French-American varietals account for another 23,000 acres, but total land devoted to these varieties (mostly Concord) is remaining stable. Wine production leaped from fewer than 400,000 gallons in 1940 (mostly fruit and berry wines) to nearly seven million gallons in 1990.

Given the fact that state-produced wine accounts for only 12 percent of consumption, Washington offers enormous potential for expansion because there are as many as 400,000 additional acres suitable for grape-growing in the Yakima, Columbia Valley, Walla Walla, and Spokane regions. This seemingly unlimited amount of prime viticultural land, currently selling at less than $2,000 the acre (the least expensive in the nation), places Washington in the enviable position of producing the lowest cost premium grapes in the country. In the final analysis, and in the words of Dickens--Washington represents "magnificent expectations."

Figure 7.9

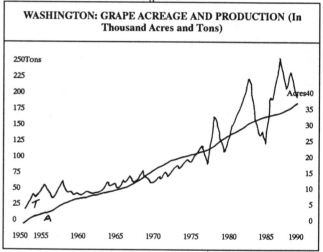

WASHINGTON: GRAPE ACREAGE AND PRODUCTION (In Thousand Acres and Tons)

The industry is well capitalized, the winemakers dedicated and expert, and the physical plant is state of the art technology. The industry's future lies in enlarging fermenting and storage capacity, exporting to the large midwestern and eastern markets, and the maintenance of quality, particularly of Riesling, Chenin Blanc, Gewurztraminer, Chardonnay, Cabernet Sauvignon, and Merlot. Many consider the above list too long, and that it lacks definition and identity burdening the consumer with many divergent styles and individual grape varieties to remember. However, while incipient regional distinctions have emerged in recent years, the wines have generated a reputation for consistency and value.

Grape production earns more than $55 million and ranks twelfth among the top 40 agricultural commodities in the state, a rather significant figure because viticulture in 1960 ranked 57th. Since 1985, Washington grapes averaged the highest prices in the nation at $455 the ton compared with the national average of $209 the ton. Grapes constitute only 6 percent of the value of fruit and nut production, apples (with 71 percent of total value) are the leading fruit (Washington produces one-third of all apples grown in America, and over half of all apples eaten fresh), followed by pears and cherries. Among all states, Washington ranks first in hop, spearmint, sweet cherry, apple, carrot, and red raspberry production; second in asparagus, pear, prune, fall potatoes, and peppermint oil; and third in grape production. Agriculture in the state is an $8.5 billion industry--bigger than forest products and aerospace, and growing faster than both.

Figure 7.10

WASHINGTON: WINE PRODUCTION (In Thousand Gallons)

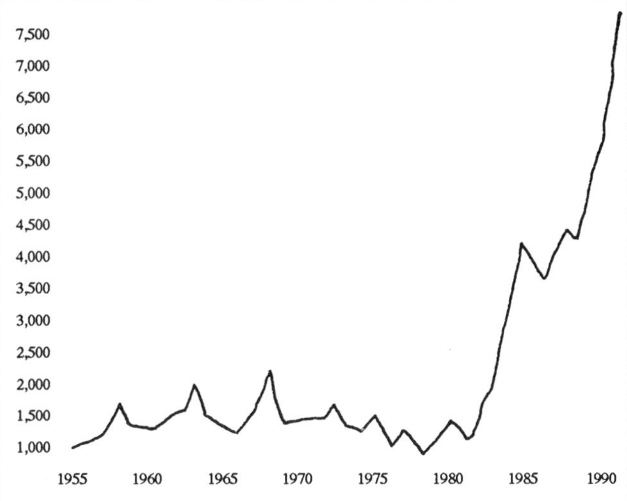

It is interesting to note that vinegrowing was historically concentrated in the Puget Sound region, but after the completion of the Yakima irrigation and reclamation project in 1906, there was renewed interest in growing grapes east of the Cascade Mountains. Since that time grapes have been largely confined to the Yakima Valley, but over the past ten years production has shifted to the much larger Columbia Valley. Unlike a good deal of California, and certainly the northeast and midwest, vineyards are rather extensive in size, a rather sharp departure from times past when vine growing was considered a secondary activity in multi-crop enterprises. While grapes often remain an important part in apple and asparagus operations, they have supplanted sugar beets and are now second in importance to hops as a cash crop in the Yakima Valley, particularly in Sunnyside, Grandview, Prosser, and Pennon City. Of the 88 wineries, approximately 45 produce less than 10,000 cases. The eight largest, with more than 95 percent of total production, are: Chateau Ste. Michelle, Snoqualmie Winery, Columbia Winery, Coventry Vale, Staton Hills Vineyard & Winery, Cascade Crest Estates Winery, Preston Wine

Cellars, and The Hogue Cellars.

Viticulture in Washington state is divided between two dissimilar climatic regions. While nearly all grape acreage is concentrated east of the Cascades, the bulk of population and one-third of all wineries are located west of the Cascades, primarily the area bordering the Puget Sound region, the industrial and urban core of the state. Called Pugetopolis (a 100-mile region from Bellingham to Olympia), this narrow strip contains 85 percent of the state's population. It is very humid, cloudy, and much rainier than areas located along the rain shadow of the Cascades where dense pine and deciduous forests give way to grassland, rolling farmland and mid-latitude semi-deserts. With more than half the state's total grape acreage Yakima county ranks first, followed by Benton, Franklin, Grant, Kitititas, Klickitat, and Walla Walla, all of which are located in the Columbia Plateau region.

It is here, in sagebrush country, where temperatures are hot in summer and bitterly cold in winter, that Washington's grape acreage is located. To harden the wood, vines are not irrigated after August, and no longer buried in soil as was done prior to 1974. This is an area of extremes: temperature varies from -20F to 110F, and diurnal variations exceeding 45F are common for at least four months during the year; less than ten inches of rainfall; pronounced atmospheric aridity; and a high incidence of wind. During the past 56 years, in one year in three, winter temperatures have been -7F or colder, and in one year in eight, temperatures have ranged from -12F to -20F. Nevertheless, the following red varieties exhibit minimal damage and do particularly well: Cabernet Sauvignon, Lemberger, Pinot Noir, Pinot Meunier, and Merlot. White varieties with a good track record for winter survival are: Chardonnay, Chenin Blanc, Riesling, Gewurztraminer, Colombard, Muller-Thurgau, Muscat Ottonel, and Pinot Blanc. Due to the near absence of phylloxera, the majority of the vineyards are planted on ungrafted stock. Displaying exceptional flavor and acid balance, the resulting wines sell exceptionally well both in and outside the state, defying recent national trends.

The state contains three *ava's--Yakima Valley, Columbia Valley,* and *Walla Walla Valley,* the latter two are shared with Oregon. The largest area of vineyard concentration is the historic fruit growing region of the Yakima Valley, followed by the greater Puget Sound region, the tri-state region of the Columbia Valley, and the Walla Walla Valley. Vine acreage is currently being expanded in the Snake River, Wenatchee Valley, as well as in many other minor river valleys. While grape acreage exhibits a strong concentration in the Yakima Valley, the geography of winery location is more diffusive: 32 in the Puget Sound region; 22 in the Columbia Valley *ava*; 23 in the Yakima Valley; 6 in the Walla Walla *ava*; and 5 in the greater Spokane region. When compared with its neighbor to the south, Washington has more than twice the Vinifera acreage of Oregon, and produces nearly four times as much wine. Washington has higher yields, lower production costs, grows a much larger selection of wine grapes, has larger wineries, is better organized, and has a much larger potential for future expansion. In terms of wine quality, Washington State Vinifera, French-American, and native grapes have a higher sugar-acid ratio than do those from eastern, southern, and southwestern grapes. For native and French-American grapes, this means that the must is sweeter and the Labrusca flavor and scent much milder than similar vines planted east of the Continental Divide.

Grapes and Wines

The evolution of principal grape varieties for the years 1968, 1972, and 1990 are presented in Table 7.1. Over the past five years, Cabernet Sauvignon, Chardonnay, Merlot, Chenin Blanc, and Sauvignon Blanc have shown rapid growth, while Gewurztraminer and Riesling have declined. While French-American varieties declined to fewer than 100 acres from more than 600 in 1982, Concord acreage has expanded by more than 2,000 acres over the past three years. The table highlights the important trends in the state's ability to improve wine quality, particularly in reference to the nation's second largest wine producer, New York. Whereas Concord grape production in New York fell dramatically since the early 1980s (its share of total grape acreage has remained surprisingly stable between 71 and 75 percent), the percentage of Concord grapes in Washington has dropped from 91 percent in 1967 to 65 percent in 1990. As Concord acreage has remained relatively constant, other American and French-American varieties have declined both in absolute and relative terms compared with Vinifera acreage. Growing from a mere 431 acres in 1967, to 12,140 acres in 1990, many state experts believe that Vinifera acreage will surpass Concord acreage over the next 20 years. French-American varieties comprise fewer than 20 acres, the most important of which are Baco Noir, Marechal Foch, Cascade, Aurore, and several Seibels.

HARVEST DATES FOR SELECTED VARIETIES	
Variety	Projected Harvest Dates
Chardonnay	September 30-October 25
Chenin Blanc	October 25-November 9
Gewurztraminer	September 20-October 15
Muscat Blanc	September 15-October 10
Sauvignon Blanc	September 10-October 10
Semillon	October 15-November 10
Riesling	October 15-November 10
Cabernet Sauvignon	October 10-October 15
Merlot	September 25-October 25
Pinot Noir	September 15-October 15

It is interesting to note the dramatic progress made in planted grape varieties since the mid-1960s when Dr. W.J. Clore described the state's grape variety composition. Of

the 10,500 acres of grapes in 1966, all but 800 were Concord, mainly grown in the lower Yakima Valley for juice and processing. The next largest variety, with 150 acres, was Island Belle, overwhelmingly planted in the Puget Sound area for table and home winemaking use. Other home-use varieties were: Seneca, Delaware, Niagara, Fredonia, Ontario, Buffalo, Schuyler, Interlaken Seedless, Catawba, Moore's Diamond, Van Buren, Worden, and Portland, among others, most of which were hardy northeastern and midwestern grapes that collectively amounted to 450 acres. The remaining 200 acres were a collection of 30 different Vinifera varieties, of which Thompson Seedless, Riesling, Muscat of Alexandria, and Zinfandel dominated.

Table 7.1

WASHINGTON: PRINCIPAL GRAPE VARIETIES					
Variety	1968	1972	Percent	1990	Percent
Concord	9,458	16,440	90.2	22,689	64.8
Campbell Early	297	360	2.0		
Niagara	203	11			
Diamond	173	173	.9		
Other American	217				
Riesling	138			2,577	7.4
Sauvignon Blanc	21			1,084	3.1
Chenin Blanc	59			1,141	3.3
Gewurztraminer	60			520	1.5
Semillon	50			996	2.8
Muscat Blanc				229	
Chardonnay		127	.7	1,994	5.7
Cabernet Sauvignon		48		1,711	4.9
Merlot	44			1,233	3.5
Pinot Noir	74			270	
Other Vinifera	431				
French-American		19			
Others	595	1,052		581	
Total	11,820	18,230		35,025	

Source: Washington State University Cooperative Extension, Grandview Station.

Riesling, with 21 percent of the planted wine grape acreage, is the most widely planted wine grape in Washington due to its high yield, consistent quality, hardiness, and versatility. Generally favoring southern exposures, it grew rapidly from 519 acres in 1980, to 2,679 acres in 1984, but it has since declined in both absolute and relative terms. Riesling, the mainstay of the Washington vineyard, is a grape that does particularly well throughout all producing districts east of the Cascades, ripening with infallibly and producing excellent fruity wine. Despite its formidable acreage, Riesling is considered a third-rate vine, and along with Chenin Blanc and Gewurztraminer, it has yet to make its mark in the pantheon of fine, noble grapes in the state. The vine, however, is extremely versatile, its very character changing with the venue. Its style can vary from fruity, low to high acid, crisp and floral, and whether it is made as a dry table, sweet, late harvest or ice wine, Washington Riesling is generally considered the finest in the nation. While chaptalization is universal in Germany often producing flabby wines, and acidification is endemic in California, Washington Riesling yields eminently balanced wines that are well-flavored and scented, and remarkably refreshing on the palate.

Chardonnay, with more than 15 percent of total Vinifera planted acreage, is the second most popular wine variety. Although many wineries make it in a fresh, lively style with little barrel aging, the finer, more expensive versions are invariably wood-aged (often barrel fermented), full-bodied, clean, flavorful, and rarely bottled with discernable residual sugar. Chardonnay is usually given considerable skin contact, and both low temperature and long fermentation emphasize the intensity of flavor and aroma. Chardonnay is mainly grown along west-facing slopes, and is one of the last grapes to be picked. When overcropped, Chardonnay is winter hardy to -12F. Chenin Blanc is the third most widely planted wine grape, its acreage increasing despite consumer resistance to the wine when sold as a varietal. Chenin Blanc is fresh, lively, fruity, well-flavored, often aggressive on the palate, high in acid, and competes with Riesling for the same market. When made dry, it exhibits a strong, steely flavor with a touch of bitterness, not unpleasant, but different, and certainly mouth filling; when semi-sweet, it emits a strong floral flavor; and when made as a sweet, late harvest wine, it is at its best in the grand Vouvray tradition. Although it is a high yielder (often as high as thirteen tons to the acre), and an easy wine to make, acreage in the future is not expected to increase, but decline slightly due to low demand.

> The 1991 vintage produced 26,000 tons of Vinifera grapes. Riesling, with an output of 10,150 tons or 39% of the harvest, ranked first, followed by Chardonnay (4,550 tons), Cabernet Sauvignon (2,400 tons), Sauvignon Blanc (1,950 tons), Merlot (1,450 tons), Chenin Blanc (1,400 tons), Semillon (1,350 tons), and Gewurztraminer (1,150 tons).

As Riesling, Chenin Blanc, and Gewurztraminer are declining in acreage, Sauvignon Blanc and Semillon are increasing. Sauvignon Blanc, a highly vigorous vine, produces crisp, well-scented and flavored wines, often eclipsing the grassy and herbaceous versions of California. When well-made and aged in wood, Washington Sauvignon Blanc offers a classic "peacock tail," in terms of depth and roundness, not usually encountered by similar wines from other producing regions, and because it is priced sensibly the wine offers excellent value. Acreage has more than doubled since 1983 to more than 1,084, and there is every indication that its popularity will continue. Semillon, with 996 acres, may very well be the most underrated variety in the state. Although more difficult to grow than Sauvignon Blanc, it is invariably rich in glycerine, maintains a beautiful color, is well-balanced, and able to age with little browning. Semillon is usually made dry, and is much fruitier and austere in flavor than similar bottles from Napa and Sonoma. Picked in early October in Yakima, it is often handicapped by a pronounced grassy flavor, but the finest, wood-aged blends with Sauvignon Blanc, are round, complex, well-balanced, and magnificently flavored. In recent years, the popularity of sweet wines, primarily Riesling, Muscat Blanc, Chenin Blanc, Semillon, and Gewurztraminer, has intensified.

While Gewurztraminer fails to achieve true varietal character in the northeast and midwest, and is flat and dull in most areas of California, it reaches new heights of perfection in Washington and Idaho where it is crisp and fruity. A finicky grape that oxidizes easily, it must be picked at optimum sugar-acid ratios to produce fragrant and well-balanced wine. When low in acid and high in sugar, as is usually the case in California, the wine is bitter. In Washington, acid levels are high, the wine balanced, and the aroma and flavor superb, especially in the Yakima Valley where it is outstanding, being one of the hardiest, early maturing grapes that survives cold weather well. Unfortunately, Gewurztraminer suffers, like Chenin Blanc, from a poor table wine image despite the fact it consistently makes one of the finest dry and sweet wines in the nation.

Table 7.2

GRAPE ACREAGE BY TYPE						
Type	1967	1972	1978	1981	1990	Percent
Concord	9,458	16,440	19,015	20,571	22,689	64.7
Other American	491	560	1,067	711	181	.5
French-American					57	.1
Vinifera	466	1,230	2,686	6,625	12,155	34.7
Total	10,415	18,230	22,768	27,907	35,025	100.0

Source: Washington Agricultural Experiment Station, College of Agriculture, Washington State University.

Other minor white varieties include: Muscat Blanc Muscat Canelli), the principal Muscat variety, is used in blending and as a sweet, well-balanced dessert wine. A grape with some potential is Aligote, a high yielding grape that when judiciously used in blending may provide a good base for inexpensive white table wine. Morio Muscat, a cross of Sylvaner and Pinot Blanc, has also shown promise. Four Vinifera varieties found in the humid Puget Sound region are: Madeleine Angevine (an obscure Loire Valley grape), Madeleine Sylvaner (less good than Madeleine Angevine and used for blending), Muller-Thurgau (never as good as Riesling, Chenin Blanc, and Gewurztraminer, is used for blending), and Okanogan Riesling (an obscure grape that was imported from Canada). Whereas Sylvaner does particularly well in the cool Yakima Valley, its acreage is not expected to increase as it is unable to compete with other white grapes for market share.

Although white grapes and white wines have dominated the state's wine industry, the most exciting wines in recent years have been superbly balanced Cabernet Sauvignon and Merlot, two red varieties surrounded by a sea of white vines. Unlike the high alcohol styles of Napa and Sonoma, these two varieties are less fruity, leaner, darker in color, lower in alcohol, and more austere on the palate.

Resembling the structure of fine Bordeaux, they offer complexity and an ability to improve with age as few other "Bordeaux-type" California wines. Both varieties produce intensely flavored, complex, full-bodied wines, and as they are grossly ignored by the rest of the country, they offer outstanding value.

No matter how good Cabernet Sauvignon is, Merlot, adapted well in the Yakima, Columbia Valley and Walla Walla *ava's*, makes big, opulent, tightly-structured wines, and is slowly generating a reputation as the best red wine grape in the state. Indeed, many wineries are de-emphasizing the Cabernet Sauvignon name on the label, preferring to label it as proprietary or as a Merlot varietal with added Cabernet Sauvignon. The finest versions are not only outstanding, but often better than classified St. Emilion properties, as well as the more prominent wineries of Pomerol. For the Yakima and Walla Walla regions, it is the red grape variety with enormous potential, and, as a consequence, the present acreage of 1,200 is expected to increase beyond 10,000 over the next fifteen years. Due to its popularity, it is envisioned that Washington will become the nation's largest producer of this variety. Although Cabernet Sauvignon is considered by many to be the state's finest red wine grape, its cultural habits and predisposition for high pH make it difficult for growers and winemakers when compared with Merlot, hence, its future growth may not be as important as the last ten years. Curiously, Pinot Noir, so successful in the Willamette Valley, is the one Vinifera grape that does not do well in all the producing regions of the state. This, despite the fact that Sunnyside (in the Yakima Valley) has 2,397 degree days compared to 2,400 in Beaune, France. Nevertheless, there are signs of improvement, and there have been encouraging signs that Cabernet Franc and Petit Verdot will be equally successful as Cabernet Sauvignon and Merlot.

Two minor, but unusual, and thoroughly provincial red grapes are Island Belle and Lemberger. Island Belle, an obscure red variety found only in the northwest, produces light to medium-bodied, fruity, easily quaffable wine not encumbered by powerful "foxy" flavors. Although fewer than 50 acres are planted, it is estimated that plantings will increase in importance in the near future. Without question, this is the most revered and sentimental of all varieties because it marks the founding of the Washington grape industry by one Lambert Evans, a Civil War veteran who settled on Stretch Island (also called the "Isle of Grapes") in 1870 and two years later planted Labrusca vines, of which Campbell Early was one of the most important. It appears that Campbell Early mutated rather easily, and there are some who maintain that Evans developed Island Belle. Another settler, Adam Eckert arrived sixteen years later, planted a fruit nursery in 1888, and after purchasing a portion of Evans' vine-

yard, began crossing Campbell Early, eventually creating a prolific survivor that he also named Island Belle early in the 1930s. With time, acreage devoted to this new variety spread to the lee side of the Cascades, only to give way to the higher yielding Concord. Apparently not all Island Belle vines are identical, and, as such, it is another in a long list of "mysterious" American vines. The imbroglio becomes heated if one believes (and there is every indication that this is true) that the original Campbell Early variety was not developed until 1892 in Delaware, Ohio. In Washington the controversy is both heated and entertaining.

Lemberger (also Limberger), popular in eastern Europe and in the Danubian Basin, is considered the Zinfandel of Washington. Although susceptible to 2, 4-D and mildew, it is comparatively easy to grow once established, yields six to eight tons to the acre, and withstands large seasonal temperature changes. Because it matures in late September before Cabernet Sauvignon and Merlot, has relatively low pH, is well-flavored, has good color, and can be made both in a heavy and Beaujolais style (there is even a white Lemberger), it has a viable future in the state. This easy to like, low tannin wine, that ages well in American oak, may very well be the next cult wine. There are now eight wineries that make it (and sell out almost immediately upon release), with more awaiting acreage to come in production. Despite the disadvantages of marketing a little known grape variety, acreage is expected to increase in the near future from 80 to 150 acres.

A road sign on the approach to Stretch Island. Also known as the "Isle of Grapes," this interesting little island is the site of the state's first major vineyard and first bonded commercial winery (St. Charles Winery). Not only are there hamlets called "Grapeview" and "Grapetown," and a post office called "Detroit," but as recently as 60 years ago there were as many as 410 acres of grape, three wineries, and two grape juice plants on the island. Baxevanis

There are several other minor grape varieties of which Grenache Noir and other Rhone varieties are receiving much attention in the southern portion of the state. It is estimated that there are fewer than ten acres of

Grenache Noir, a grape that makes interesting, spicy, strong, and distinctive rose. It is highly sensitive to cold, and does well only on protected sites in the lower Columbia River where it produces higher acid levels than in California. Two other similar Rhone varieties are Syrah and Mourvedre.

With more than 23,000 acres, Washington is, since 1977 when it displaced New York, the nation's leading producer of Concord grapes. Acreage rose rapidly from fewer than 3,000 acres in 1964 to 16,440 acres in 1972, to present levels in 1992. Overwhelmingly concentrated in the lower Yakima Valley (as a supplementary cash crop by most farmers) and the Columbia Plateau, the state offers many advantages to both the grower and the consumer. Not only is the yield significantly higher (over 10 tons to the acre), but Washington state Concords contain a higher sugar-acid ratio than do eastern grapes from Missouri, Arkansas, Michigan, Pennsylvania, and New York. Not only sweeter, the grapes have a milder Labrusca flavor thus making them more appealing to the process industry, especially for juice purposes. After a slight decline due to the depressed market in the mid-1980s, acreage has recently expanded as Concord prices firmed in recent years. It is expected that as long as demand for Concord grapes continues, Washington will remain the nation's leading producing state. Other American and French-American varietals, with less than .5 percent of planted acreage, have steadily declined over the past ten years. The most popular white variety is Niagara (used primarily for the white juice market), and the most widely planted red variety is Marechal Foch, both of which are rarely made as varietals, but used for blending with other neutral flavored wines.

The Puget Sound Region

Puget Sound is an irregular, highly fragmented, glacier-deepened, and drowned arm of the Pacific Ocean with significant maritime influences. It stretches from the Canadian border in the north to the Columbia River in the south. With more than 85 percent of the state's population, this area contains the main cities, the bulk of industrial production, and all major harbors. Seattle, the largest city in the northwest is also a major port, and its airport provides the shortest route to Japan. Bathed by perpetual viridity, sprinkled with irresistible intimate neighborhoods, and clothed by an element of sophistication, this dominant metropolis of the northwest is both clean, orderly, and without the bustle of New York. Sited between two mountain ranges and surrounded by water "the emerald city" is named after an Indian leader replacing its baptismal name of "Duwamps." Because every pore of its being breathes elements of charm, spectacular beauty and affluency, it is one of the nation's most rapidly growing cities, attracting more than 60,000 people annu-

ally to its already 2 million inhabitants, a rather formidable increase from the 3,000 residents enumerated in the 1880 Census.

What distinguished western Washington from the rest of the state is a high incidence of cloudiness, a mild year-round maritime climate, dense evergreen forest (hence the name "Evergreen" state), industry, high population density, many cities, and liberal politics. This is also the area that possesses 30 wineries, but less than 1 percent of the grape acreage. If there was ever a market oriented wine industry--it is to be found here, a business decision to bring winery access to the consuming public, more than 100 miles to the west from vineyards located east of the Cascades. In sharp contrast, areas east of the Cascades are characterized by aridity, little industry, dams for irrigation and the production of electricity, a low population density, few cities, and conservative politics.

The Puget Sound and the Willamette Valley to the south, with their adequate rainfall, fertile soils and comparatively long growing season, are well adapted to mixed farming, and, as a result, have attracted the bulk of the regional population. Large diversified cities with aerospace, electronic, timber, fishing, and port-oriented economic activities dominate this 300-mile, north-south region. While mineral discoveries, the opening of the Panama Canal, and the transcontinental railroads helped the economy prior to World War I, post-Depression events supported by new maritime connections to the Orient, the aerospace industry, irrigation projects east of the Cascades, and huge hydroelectric facilities all helped propel this region to unprecedented levels of economic development.

The Seattle skyline in August. Seattle may not be considered the rainiest city in the Pacific northwest, but it seems that way. There are 163 precipitation days annually, in comparison to 54 days in San Francisco and 35 days in Los Angeles. Seattle, with a metropolitan area of more than 2 million people, is the largest urban agglomeration in the northwest. It was founded by five families in 1852. Baxevanis

The Puget Sound, a lowland region of hundreds of islands, is sandwiched between Vancouver Island (Canada), Coastal Range (Washington), and the Cascades. Because the Coastal Range are one-seventh as high as the Cascades, the lee exposures are more affected by rain shadow conditions along the Willamette, and much less in the Puget Sound as there is a break in the coastal chain thus allowing maritime influences to penetrate and bathe the area north and south of Seattle. As a result, a good deal of the Puget Sound region receives (depending upon elevation and exposure) more than twice the precipitation of the Willamette, lower summer temperatures, more humidity, and a higher incidence of cloudiness, thus promoting severe mildew and other fungus disorders. In general, rainfall progressively rises with latitude from the southern Willamette to the Canadian border just north of Bellingham. In addition, the glaciated soils, highly acidic, wet, sandy or gravely near the surface with thick clay pans in the subsoil, are totally unacceptable for all but the hardiest varieties, such as American and French-American, all of which produce thin, acidic, and unappealing wines.

If the Puget Sound area is too cold, cloudy, and rainy for Vinifera vines, it is the home base of the state's historic fruit and berry wines, the site of a local hybrid grape called "Island Belle," and some of the largest wineries in the state. This large, discontinuous viticultural region contains fewer than 300 vine acres, but no *ava*. Because the leeward portion of the Olympic Peninsula is significantly drier, there are possibilities for several minor appellations, of which the historic Stretch Island is a prime candidate. However, two areas with a decidedly drier climate, and, hence, regions with a bright viticultural future are the La Center region and the Nooksak Valley.

Mount Baker Winery, the northernmost winery in America, located in the beautiful Nooksak Valley, makes excellent and unusual wines. Baxevanis

While California winemakers seek cooler areas, those in the Puget Sound ferret out dry, warm areas. One such area is the Nooksak Valley, a unique microclimatic area measuring only 5 by 12 miles that is totally surrounded by mountains and water-bearing clouds, offering considerable viticultural possibilities. Called the "hole in the smoke" by the Indians, the Nooksak Valley enjoys milder, sunnier weather with a near total absence of frost than surrounding areas, and is particularly good for the production of white grapes. The second major area with viticultural potential is the La Center region, just north of Portland. While the area currently contains but two wineries, the future is considered bright. Three other grape-growing areas are the Puyallup and Carbon River Valleys, and Bainbridge Island in Puget Sound.

Although the number of accumulated heat units, between 1300 and 1700, appear to be within tolerable limits similar to those of northern Germany, high humidity levels and mildew are major environmental obstacles in the production of Vinifera grapes. Quite naturally, the dominant Vinifera vines are all early maturing (Madeleine Sylvaner, Madeleine Angevine, Okanagan Riesling, Muller-Thurgau, and Gewurztraminer), and with rare exceptions hardly produce anything above-average in quality. American and French-American varieties, such as Concord, Leon Millot, Marechal Foch, Cascade, Aurore, and DeChaunac, all produce thin, acidic, low sugar, and unappealing wines. The wineries are:

Andrew Will Winery (Seattle, 1989), is a 600-case winery that makes excellent, full-bodied, well-structured, yet supple Merlot and Cabernet Sauvignon under the *Andrew Will* label.

Bainbridge Island Winery (Bainbridge Island, 1982), owned by a climatologist/geographer, is an excellent, 5-acre, 3,400-case winery that makes German-style (comparatively low alcohol, soft, yet well-balanced, slightly sweet) Muller-Thurgau, Riesling, Sylvaner, and outstanding late harvest Chardonnay, Gewurztraminer, Madeleine Angevine, Siegerrebe, Strawberry, and proprietary wines. The moderately priced wines from this little-known property offer remarkable value.

Cavatappi Winery (Kirkland, 1985), is a tiny restaurant winery (with 1 acre planted in Nebbiolo) that makes 1,000 cases of Sauvignon Blanc, Nebbiolo, and Cabernet Sauvignon.

Chateau Ste. Michelle (Woodinville, 1934), with more than 2,000 planted acres (one-sixth of the state Vinifera total) and an annual output of more than 800,000 cases (more than half of which is premium varietal wine), is the largest winery in the state (one of the top 25 in the nation), and a pioneer winery in the production of Vinifera wine. It makes estate and non-estate, varietal, proprietary, and sparkling wines whose quality is highly variable. The firm operates three wineries: in Woodinville, Grandview (winemaking began in this facility in 1937 when the National Wine Company purchased the Cement Block Warehouse; red wine production under the Chateau Ste. Michelle label began in 1967), and Paterson, the latter, making wine under the Columbia Crest label, is a state-of-the-art facility offering outstanding value. Chardonnay, Semillon, Gewurztraminer, Riesling, Chenin Blanc, and Sauvignon Blanc appear to be the best of the white wines, Merlot and Cabernet Sauvignon are the better reds (especially from the Cold Creek Vineyard), while sparkling wines have shown steady improvement. The firm, owned by Stimson Lane Wine and Spirits, accounts for nearly two-thirds of the state's total wine production and 90 percent of out of state sales. It is the nation's largest producer of Riesling. The winery is currently developing a 700-acre vineyard at Canoe Ridge, along the Columbia River. The parent company also owns Conn Creek and Villa Mt. Eden in the Napa Valley. Other labels: *F.W. Langguth,* and *Saddle Mountain Winery.*

Columbia Winery (Woodinville, 1962), one of the pioneering wineries of the state was known until 1984 as Associated Vintners. This highly respected and well-managed winery has recently purchased and moved from Bellevue into the former Haviland Winery facility. Annual output exceeds 100,000 cases, most of which consist of Chardonnay, Riesling, Gewurztraminer, Chenin Blanc, Semillon, Syrah, Merlot, and Cabernet Sauvignon, all of which are round, well-flavored, balanced, and well above industry standards. The *Red Willow, Otis,* and *Sagemoor* vineyard's Merlot and Cabernet Sauvignon, and the *Wyckoff* vineyard Chardonnay are particularly good. Pinot Noir and Chardonnay are produced under the upscale label of *Woodburne,* and the David Lake Signature Series wines are excellent. Ranking among the top ten wineries in the northwest, Columbia wines consistently offer good value, and should not be missed.

Coolen Cellars (Port Orchard, 1986), is a tiny, 1-acre, 400-case winery that makes Cremant from an unusual combination of Madeleine Angevine, Siegerrebe, Muller-Thurgau, Merlot, Pinot Noir, and others, all sulfite-free, low in tannin, mild, and supple.

Domaine Whittlesey Mark Winery (Seattle, 1983), is a 2,500-case winery that specializes in sparkling wines (Brut, Brut de Noir, Blanc de Blanc) from Oregon Chardonnay and Pinot Noir, and Chardonnay, Sauvignon Blanc, and Cabernet Sauvignon from eastern Washington grapes under the *DiStefano* label. The winery is in the process of moving to Bainbridge Island.

E.B. Foote (Seattle, 1978), is a 2,000-case winery that makes dry, lean Gewurztraminer, Riesling, Chardonnay, Pinot Noir, Cabernet Sauvignon, and late harvest Riesling.

Facelli Winery (Redmond, 1988), is an excellent, 3,000-case winery that makes dry Riesling, Semillon, Sauvignon Blanc, Chardonnay, Merlot, and Cabernet Sauvignon. The well-structured, acidic wines usually offer excellent value.

Fidalgo Island Winery (Anacortes, 1986), is an interesting, 3,500-case winery that makes sulfite-free Chardonnay, Riesling, and Cabernet Sauvignon from purchased grapes.

French Creek Wine Cellars (Woodinville, 1983), is a 10,000-case winery that makes Gewurztraminer, Chardonnay, Riesling, Muscat Blanc, Pinot Noir, and late harvest wines.

Hedges Cellars (Issaquah, 1990), is a 20-acre, 30,000-case winery that makes a Cabernet Sauvignon/Merlot blend.

Hoodsport Winery (Hoodsport, 1979), is a 5-acre, 18,000-case (two-thirds fruit and berry wines) winery that makes Chardonnay, Riesling, Chenin Blanc, Gewurztraminer, Lemberger, Merlot, and is the largest producer of Island Belle. The raspberry wine is outstanding.

Johnson Creek Winery (Tenino, 1984), is a 3-acre, 2,000-case winery that makes Riesling, Chardonnay, Chenin Blanc, Muller-Thurgau, Cabernet Sauvignon, Merlot, and Pinot Noir from purchased grapes.

Lopez Island Vineyards (Lopez Island, 1991), is a 40-acre, 2,000-case winery that makes interesting, good, sound, and highly fragrant and flavored Madeleine Angevine, Siegerrebe, Chardonnay, and Cabernet Sauvignon. The island, located on the lee side of the Olympic Peninsula has an unusual dry climate and an eight month growing season, features that may attract other wineries and an unusual *ava.*

Lost Mountain Winery (Sequim, 1981), is a small, 550-case winery that makes sulfite-free, full-bodied, well-flavored Muscat Alexandria, Cabernet Sauvignon, Merlot, and Pinot Noir from purchased grapes.

Manfred Vierthaler Winery (Sumner, 1976), is a 5-acre, 18,500-case winery known for a large number of wines (table, fortified, and proprietary), of which Muller-Thurgau is considered the finest. Using California must, a large proportion of output is labeled "American."

McCrea Cellars (Lake Stevens, 1988), is a tiny, 700-case winery that makes hand-crafted, full-bodied, barrel-fermented Chardonnay, Grenache Noir, and exciting proprietary wines with a Rhone-style emphasis.

Mount Baker Vineyards (Deming, 1983), the northernmost winery in the nation, is a 25-acre, 12,000-case winery located 500 feet from the floor of the Nooksak Valley. It makes highly distinctive German-style wines from several unusual grapes: Okanogan Riesling, Madeleine Angevine, Precoce de Malingre, and Leon Millot. It also produces the more familiar Gewurztraminer, Muller-Thurgau, Chardonnay, Pinot Noir, Cabernet Sauvignon, and Merlot, as well as a delicious plum wine.

Neuharth Winery (Sequim, 1979), with several acres of experimental vines, is a small, 2,300-case winery that makes first class, distinctive Riesling, Chardonnay, Cabernet Sauvignon, Merlot, and proprietary wines, all offering outstanding value.

Pacific Crest Wine Cellars (Marysville, 1985), is a 1,000-case winery that makes light to medium-bodied, fruity, supple Riesling, late harvest Gewurztraminer, and big, opulent Chardonnay.

Paul Thomas Winery (Bellevue, 1979), is a rapidly expanding winery of 25,000 cases that makes highly distinctive, handcrafted wines, of which more than 50 percent are fruit wines (the rhubarb, raspberry, and pear are sensational). The Riesling, Chardonnay, Muscat Blanc, Sauvignon Blanc, Chenin Blanc, Cabernet Sauvignon, and Merlot are all outstanding in terms of balance and depth of flavor, offering exceptional value. The reserve wines are extraordinary. Other label: *Rushcutter Bay Wines*

Quilceda Creek Vintners (Snohomish, 1978), is the only winery in the state that specializes in the production of only one wine: a superb, full-bodied, highly complex, unfiltered, and unblended Cabernet Sauvignon that is a must for every serious cellar as the wine ages well. Production is limited to less than 2,000 cases, making it one of the most sought-after wines on the west coast.

Rich Passage Winery (Bainbridge Island, 1989), is a 500-case winery that makes Chardonnay, Sauvignon Blanc, and Pinot Noir.

Salishan Vineyards (La Center, 1976), is a 12-acre, 4,500-case winery located 30 miles southwest of Mount St. Helens. The expertly made Riesling, Chardonnay, Cabernet Sauvignon, Merlot, and Pinot Noir are all above-average, cleanly made, and well-flavored.

Salmon Bay (Woodinville, 1982), formerly known as Vernier Winery, is a 5,400-case winery that makes good, sound Riesling, Chardonnay, Sauvignon Blanc, Cabernet Sauvignon, and Merlot, all offering good value.

Silver Lake (Bothell, 1988), is a 8,500-case winery that makes Riesling (dry and ice wine), Chardonnay, Sauvignon Blanc, Cabernet Sauvignon, Merlot, and an alcoholic sparkling cider.

Snoqualmie Winery (Snoqualmie, 1983), is an aggressive, state-of-the art, 110,000-case winery that makes fresh, fruity, and delicate Semillon, Riesling, Gewurztraminer, Muscat Blanc, Chenin Blanc, Sauvignon Blanc, Chardonnay, Lemberger, Cabernet Sauvignon, Merlot, and late harvest wines. The name refers to a waterfall, the site of an Indian meeting ground that has become the second largest tourist attraction in the state. The winery is currently developing the 60-acre "Winery Ridge" complex, replete with a lodge, microbrewery, restaurant, and other tourist-oriented facilities. A huge debt rendered the winery subject to Chapter 11 issues in 1990, and it has since been acquired by Stimson Lane in 1991, owner of the states largest winery.

Soos Creek Wine Cellars (Renton, 1991), is a 600-case, Cabernet Sauvignon-only winery.

Tagaris Winery (Snoqualmie, 1987), is a 120-acre, 15,000-case winery that makes good, sound Riesling, Chenin Blanc, Sauvignon Blanc, Chardonnay, Pinot Noir, Cabernet Sauvignon, and blended proprietary wines, all offering good value. The Taggares family own the world's largest Concord vineyard.

Vashon Winery (Vashon Island, 1987), is an interesting, 1,500-case (Chardonnay, Semillon, and Cabernet Sauvignon) winery owned by two of Chalone Vineyard's original investors. All wines are full-bodied and well-structured, offering good value.

Whidbeys (Greenbank, 1984), with the nation's single largest planting of loganberrys, is a 40-acre, 14,500-case winery that specializes in loganberry liqueur and wine, and vintage Porto, the latter made mainly from Cabernet Sauvignon. This unusual property is owned by Stimson Lane.

Columbia Valley

The *Columbia Valley* is Washington's largest *ava,* encompassing both the Yakima Valley and Walla Walla *ava's.* The Columbia River (the nation's second largest river system) defines much of the Washington/Oregon border (the Columbia River drains eastern Washington and northern Oregon), encompasses at least one-third of the state's total land area, and irrigates much of its semi-arid landscape. Throughout most of its 1,210-mile length, more than 20 dams and 137 hydroelectric projects provide the cheapest electricity in the nation, and when the latest Grand Coulee project is finished, it will become the largest installed power facility in the world. It has twice the flow of the mighty Nile, and ten times the volume of the Colorado for most of its course. Yet, for all the celebrity that the river has brought upon Washington and Oregon, its vast interfluves remain largely wheat and grazing country. However, irrigated areas the size of small eastern states (Yakima, Wenatchee, Snake, and Columbia are the most important) provide an endless variety of crops for distant markets. Nearly the entire length of the Columbia River, protected from coastal inclement weather by the Cascade Mountains, is warmed by long sunny days during the growing season, and with only the northern portions as an exception, the main vine growing areas do not suffer from prolonged frost actively. A small portion of the *ava* spills over into northern Oregon, an area with good potential, but as yet few planted vine acres. The climate of the Columbia River Valley, along with its two subsidiary *ava's*, is unique in that the short growing season (it varies between 150 and 205 days, is characterized by a high incidence of sunshine (there are more than two additional hours of sunlight than Napa), low evening and high daytime temperatures, all of which produce extremely ripe grapes and full-bodied, intensely flavored and scented wines. Except near rivers, the land is nearly treeless, degree days range from Region I to IV, with the best sites located on Region I and II. Rain during the harvest is rare.

The rich soils, formed by a combination of lake and wind deposition, are light in texture, and range from loamy sands to silt loams. Their depth varies from several inches to more than three feet with basalt being the parent rock material underlying nearly the entire plateau. In practically all instances, soils, due to the scant 6-8 inch rainfall in most areas, are high in carbonate (1-8 percent), and pH varies between 7.0 and 8.5. The area between Vancouver to tri-cities, particularly Bingen, Prosser, and Paterson, is the primary area of recent interest. There are 5,000 irrigated acres of planted vineland, most near the tri-cities region, producing the complete spectrum of Vinifera vines.

It is obvious, therefore, that in this vast region, only a miniscule portion of the *Columbia Valley ava* has been planted in vines. Covering nearly one-third of the state's land area, it is second to California in the production of premium Vinifera wine grapes, and, as yet, there is no regional character to distinguish the wines from the Yakima Valley and Walla Walla. While nearly all white grapes do well, Semillon, Riesling, Chenin Blanc, Muscat Blanc, Gewurztraminer, and Chardonnay are particularly good. Cabernet Sauvignon and Merlot, the finest red grapes,

often produce, when properly planted on the warmer sites and on excellent exposures, dark, full-bodied, and intensely flavored wines. Pinot Noir, successful only in the more humid western portion of the *ava*, is best represented by Salishan Vineyards. The *ava*, also including 23,000 acres of Concord grapes, is the nation's premier juice producing region. This large *ava* contains more than 90 percent of the state's total vine acreage (nearly all Concord), and two-thirds of the state's 86 wineries. The *ava* received an element of interest and speculation in 1990 when Chalone Wine Group, a quality oriented wine holding company, acquired a 50 percent interest in the 200-acre Canoe Ridge Vineyard (94 acres of which are planted in Cabernet Sauvignon, Merlot, and Chardonnay). Under terms of the agreement Chalone will manage the vineyard and construct a 25,000-case winery on the property before the 1993 vintage. It appears that this California investment is only the beginning of an avalanche of future expansionary moves in this hitherto ignored viticultural state. The wineries are:

Badger Mountain Vineyard (Kennewick, 1987), is a successful, 80-acre, 20,000-case, organic winery that makes moderately-priced Chardonnay, Chenin Blanc, Riesling, Semillon, and Gewurztraminer. This unusual, white wine-only winery also custom crushes for others.

Barnard Griffin (Kennewick, 1983), owned by one of the most accomplished winemakers in the state, this 2,000-case winery makes well-oaked Riesling, Chardonnay, Sauvignon Blanc, Semillon, Cabernet Sau-vignon, and Merlot, all offering excellent value. In the future, small quantities of Merlot-based Porto-type wines will also be made.

Bookwalter Winery (Pasco, 1983), is a 6,500-case winery known for distinctive, full-bodied, robust, well-flavored, yet accessible Riesling, Chenin Blanc, Chardonnay, Sauvignon Blanc, Muscat Blanc, Cabernet Sauvignon, late harvest Riesling, and sparkling wines.

Caroway Vineyards (Kennewick, 1983), is a 40-acre, 1,600-case winery known for above-average quality Semillon, Riesling, and Chardonnay, the latter, full-bodied, balanced and round, offering good value.

Cascade Crest Estates Winery (Sunnyside, 1987), with an output exceeding 125,000 cases, and a partnership controlled 246-acre vineyard, is one of the newest, and third largest winery in the state. It makes a wide assortment of wines (Riesling, Semillon, Chenin Blanc, Gewurztraminer, Chardonnay, Sauvignon Blanc, Muscat Blanc, and Cabernet Sauvignon) of varying, but improving quality.

Cascade Mountain Cellars (Ellensburg, 1987), is a 4,000-case winery that makes soft, supple Chardonnay, Chenin Blanc, Riesling, Muller-Thurgau, Merlot, Lemberger, and sparkling wines, offering good value.

Champs de Brionne Winery (Quincy, 1983), is a magnificently sited, 140-acre, 35,000-case winery that makes distinctive Chardonnay, Riesling, Gewurztraminer, Semillon, Chenin Blanc, Sauvignon Blanc, Pinot Noir, Cabernet Sauvignon, and Merlot.

Charles Hooper Family Winery (Husum, 1985), is a 6-acre, 1,200-case winery that makes Riesling, Chardonnay, Gewurztraminer, and small quantities of Pinot Noir. Not only is the emphasis on white wines very much in the German manner, but it is also the only winery in the state that trains the vines on individual stakes.

Chateau Gallant Winery (Pasco, 1987), is a 25-acre, 2,000-case winery that makes Chardonnay, Sauvignon Blanc, and Riesling.

Columbia Crest (Paterson, 1985), is a 2,000-acre, 500,000-case winery that is owned by Stimson Lane. The wines, mainly Chardonnay, Riesling, Semillon, Sauvignon Blanc, Merlot, and Cabernet Sauvignon, are consistently above-average, offering outstanding value. Other labels: *Allison Combs, Farron Ridge*.

Coventry Vale Winery (Grandview, 1983), is a 600-acre, 400,000-case winery that makes Chardonnay, Riesling, Chenin Blanc, Cabernet Sauvignon, Merlot, sparkling (the bulk of production under its own label), and proprietary wines. Its major function is to custom-crush for other wineries.

Gordon Brothers Cellars (Pasco, 1983), is a 85-acre, 3,500-case winery best known for Chardonnay, Merlot, Cabernet Sauvignon, and smaller quantities of Sauvignon Blanc and Chenin Blanc.

Hunter Hill Vineyards (Othello, 1984), is a 28-acre, 7,000-case winery that makes full-bodied, robust and zesty Chardonnay, Chenin Blanc, four styles of Riesling, Cabernet Sauvignon, Merlot, and fruit wines.

Mercer Ranch Vineyards (Alderdale, 1985), is a 131-acre, 4,000-case winery that makes excellent, estate Lemberger, Cabernet Sauvignon, Muscat Blanc, and several proprietary wines, all offering good value. Despite the address, the winery is located on a superb site (considered one of the finest Cabernet vineyards in the state) in the Columbia *ava*.

Mont Elise Vineyards (Bingen, 1975), formerly Bingen Wine Cellars, is a 35-acre, 6,000-case winery that makes good, sound Riesling, Chenin Blanc, Gewurztraminer, Sauvignon Blanc, Pinot Noir, Gamay Beaujolais, and sparkling wines. Before becoming a winery the property was the first to grow Vinifera vines in the Bingen region in 1965.

Neely & Son Winery (Kennewick, 1988), is a 10-acre, 2,000-case winery that makes several styles of Riesling.

Powers Winery (Kennewick, 1987), is an 80-acre, 25,000-case winery that makes good, sound, moderately-priced Chardonnay, Riesling, Gewurztraminer, Semillon, Chenin Blanc, and Cabernet Franc. The property is the only certified organic vineyard in the state.

Preston Wine Cellars (Pasco, 1972), is a large, pioneering, 190-acre, 60,000 case winery specializing in white wine production, particularly Riesling, Chardonnay, Sauvignon Blanc, Chenin Blanc, Gewurztraminer, Muscat Blanc, with smaller quantities of Cabernet Sauvignon, Merlot, Pinot Noir (all full-bodied, robust, astringent, and flavorful), and proprietary wines. The unusual and meticulous vineyard cultural practices are considered outstanding, and the modest pricing policy makes the wines an excellent value. Other label: *Columbia River Cellars*.

Quarry Lake Vintners (Pasco, 1986), is a 110-acre, 31,000-case winery (part of a large agricultural enterprise) that makes excellent, medium-bodied, supple Riesling, Sauvignon Blanc, Chenin Blanc, Semillon, Chardonnay, Merlot, and Cabernet Sauvignon (the last three are full-bodied and well-structured), all impeccably made, offering superb value.

Redford Cellars (Alderdale, 1978), is a 1,000 case label of a former winemaker at Mercer Ranch Vineyards. The excellent, smooth, often refined Cabernet Sauvignon, and a Cabernet/Merlot blend made from Washington and Oregon fruit, should not be missed.

Wenatchee Valley Vineyards (East Wenatchee, 1986), is an 18-acre, 11,500-case winery that makes Chardonnay, Riesling, Sauvignon Blanc, Merlot, Cabernet Sauvignon, and Pinot Noir, all offering good value. The winery custom crushes an additional 20,000 cases. This is the pioneering winery in the cool Wenatchee Valley, north of Yakima.

White Heron Cellars (George, 1986), is a small, but interesting, 5-acre (planted in Syrah, Roussane, and a few more Rhone grapes), 1,600-case winery that makes a unique Riesling (dry and the product of malolactic fermentation), Pinot Noir, and a Cabernet/Merlot blend.

Yakima Valley

The *Yakima Valley ava*, bounded by a series of east-west basaltic uplifts, is hot and arid in summer and bitterly cold in winter. Forming a distinct geographical region, it is defined by four intriguing landmarks: Rattlesnake Mountains, Horse Haven Hills, the Cascade foothills, and Ahtanum Ridge. Named after an Indian tribe, the economic center of this *ava* is the medium-sized (200,000 people) city of Yakima, a rather remarkable urban unit in terms of sophistication and excellent urban planning. Yakima, with 300 sunny days and a 195-day growing season, is one of the most distinctive and important agricultural regions of the northwest whose productivity is made possible by huge irrigation projects. Its wealth is

based on the production of sugar beets, fruit, hops, and other crops, ranking first among all American counties in the production of apples, mint, and hops, and fourth in value of all fruits. With a value exceeding $245 million, grapes and wines have become the third most important agricultural products in Yakima after cattle and apples (one acre in 120 is planted in grapes).

Figure 7.11

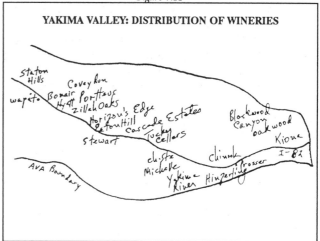

An enclave of the much larger Columbia Valley *ava*, this intensely cultivated region is nearly 75 miles long and 22 miles at its widest. The entire basin, encompassing nearly 3,000 square miles (of which nearly 400,000 acres are irrigated), is drained by the Yakima flowing for more than 120 miles until it reaches the Columbia near Pasco. Much of the Yakima Valley was covered with native grasses and sagebrush, but ever since irrigation was introduced in 1906 the valley has become one of the premier agricultural areas of the northwest. Soils in the Yakima Valley, a varying mixture of silt, sand, calcium carbonate, volcanic ash, and loess, are deep, light in color, well-drained, and extremely fertile when irrigated. Of the thirteen major associations, Warden-Shano and Scootenay-Starbuck dominate vineyard location. The finest of the two, Warden-Shano, found on hillsides, is moderately deep and lies atop basalt bedrock; the latter, a rich, deeper alluvium found only next to the Yakima River, is largely confined to Concord production. Annual precipitation varies between 6 and 9 inches. The principal cities and towns, such as Yakima, Zillah, Granger, Sunnyside, Grandview, Prosser, and Benton City, will one day become as familiar as Margaux and Napa to enophiles.

The Yakima Valley, with more than 24,000 acres of vineland and more than half of the premium Vinifera grapes, became Washington's first *ava* in 1983. While dry-farmed Vinifera vines were planted near Union Gap in the 1880s (and died within several years), modern commercial plantings consisted of Island Belle, introduced in the early 1900s. Large-scale holdings of Concord grapes were planted during the post-Repeal period (Yakima today, with 16,000 acres, is the center of the states Concord juice industry). It was only in the early 1950s that Vinifera grapes began to be planted in earnest (and successfully) along southern exposures on the north bank of the Yakima River by Dr. Lloyd Woodburne and his associates at the University of Washington at Seattle. Throughout the 1960s vine acreage increased, but the more dramatic new plantings and wineries were established after 1979. Today the Yakima Valley is primarily a white wine region (Riesling, Chenin Blanc, Gewurztraminer, Semillon, Sauvignon Blanc, and Chardonnay). However, the inroads of Merlot and Cabernet Sauvignon are beginning to change the complexion of the state's most important *ava*. Of the two, Merlot, in recent years, has produced extraordinary wines that have led many to pronounce the Yakima Valley as the premier Merlot/Cabernet Sauvignon producing area in the nation. The wine, dark in color and well-balanced, offers an unusual array of soft tannins, flavors, and fragrances, and should be taken seriously. When compared with California versions, Cabernet/Merlot wines are lower in alcohol, less fruity, more austere, higher in natural acidity, lower in pH, hardly ever over-oaked, and considerably rounder with greater depth of flavor. Both Merlot and Cabernet Sauvignon are consistently well-made and of superior quality, often surpassing the finest from California and Bordeaux. Red Mountain contains some of the finest vineyards in the valley. Due to recent successes in both the quality of fruit and wine produced, vine acreage speculation has recently become fashionable. Sapporo in a joint venture purchased the Snipes Vineyard in the Yakima Valley to supply Chardonnay and Riesling grapes to St. Clement Vineyard in St. Helena. The Chalone group has also recently purchased an interest in a well-regarded vineyard in the Columbia Plateau.

Vinifera grape acreage and wine output has been rapid in recent years, and as of 1986 there were eighteen major wineries contributing two-thirds of Vinifera vine acreage and a near similar percentage of the state's wine output. It is interesting to note that as recently as 1978 there were only two wineries in the valley. Although the area is Region II (2,360 degree days), it is marginally cooler (several exposed areas experience fewer than 1,500 degree days) than major portions of the Columbia and Walla Walla *ava's*. Yakima is on the same latitude as the area north of Baden, Germany, but the climatic regime is not at all similar as summers are longer, hotter and drier, and winters colder. Although the valley is characterized by sharp seasonal, continental features (over the past 30 years heat units have varied from 1744 to 2400), winter temperatures as low as -14F adversely affect only young vines, and those not properly hardened. While spring frosts are a problem only on poor sites (grapes are extremely site sensitive), water availability appears to be the

biggest environmental problem. The harvest usually begins in the middle of September and can last through mid-November, as in 1987, a very hot, but excellent year for red wine production. Yields are good and the quality of wine excellent, particularly for the production of Cabernet Sauvignon and Merlot. Intensely flavored and scented, white wines, such as Chardonnay, Riesling, Sauvignon Blanc, Semillon, and Gewurztraminer, are beginning to set a standard for the entire northwest region. Sweet white wines are not only good, but often exceptional, their recent successes prompting the Yakima Valley Winegrowers Association in 1987 to adopt a new labeling classification. Recent viticultural progress has been so spectacular that the grape-growing possibilities of Yakima appear to be limitless. The *ava* contains 25,000 acres of grapes, of which more than 8,000 are Vinifera.

YAKIMA VALLEY LATE HARVEST WHITE WINES
(Minimum Standards)

No Designation: Dry table wines, consistent with half of a Kabinett style wine based on minimum 1971 German wine law standards. Minimum sugar is 17-24 degrees Brix with residual sugar after fermentation of less than 4% by weight.

Late Harvest: White wine grapes picked in an over-ripe condition with some incidence of botrytis. Minimum sugar is 24 degrees Brix with residual sugar after fermentation of a minimum of 4% and not more than 10% by weight.

Select Cluster or Select Late Harvest: Picked only from grapes infected with beneficial mold, botrytis, and having a minimum sugar level at harvest of 27.5 degrees Brix. Residual sugar after fermentation is less than 15% by weight.

Individual Bunch Select (with or without late harvest): Picked clusters must be completely infected by the beneficial mold, botrytis. Minimum sugar standards are 32 degrees Brix with residual sugar after fermentation between 15% and 19.9% by weight.

Dry Berry Selection or Individual Dry Berry Selection (with or without late harvest): Picked berries are either partially or completely raisined and have been infected by the beneficial mold, botrytis. Minimum sugar standards are 38 degrees Brix. Residual sugar after fermentation is greater than 20% by weight.

Ice Wine: Grapes must be hard frozen on vines at time of harvest. Berries must be partially infected by the beneficial mold, botrytis. Minimum sugar standards are 35 degrees Brix. Residual sugar after fermentation is greater than 18% by weight.

Source: Yakima Valley Wine Growers Association.

The principal wineries are:

Blackwood Canyon Vintners (Benton City, 1982), is a 50-acre vineyard located along the southern slopes of Red Mountain in the eastern portion of the Yakima Valley. Output consists of 36,000 cases of big, round, complex Chardonnay, Semillon, Riesling, Cabernet Sauvignon, Merlot, Pinot Noir, and late harvest wines, some of which, such as *Penultimate* (a Gewurztraminer ice wine), and *Pinnacle* (a 100% botrytized Riesling), can be extraordinary. While red wines are well-structured monsters, white wines are unusual because varietal flavors are often secondary to the winemakers ability to introduce new flavors and aromas, making them some of the most distinctive in the nation. The unusual array of wines are not for everyone, but mandatory for the serious enophile. Other labels: *Phynex* and *Windy River*.

Bonair Winery (Zillah, 1985), is a small, 5-acre, 3,500-case winery that makes distinctive, round, complex Chardonnay, Riesling, Riesling/Cabernet Sauvignon blush, Cabernet Sauvignon, and proprietary wines.

Cascade Estates Winery (Sunnyside, 1987), is an aggressive and market-oriented, 246-acre, 128,000-case winery that makes Riesling, Semillon, Chenin Blanc, Sauvignon Blanc, Chardonnay, and proprietary wines, all offering excellent value. Initial offerings have thus far been above-average in quality.

Chinook Wines (Prosser, 1983), is a small, impeccable winery of 5,500 cases that makes absolutely first class Chardonnay, Sauvignon Blanc, a blend of Semillon and Sauvignon Blanc called *Topaz*, Merlot, and a rare, flavorful sparkling Riesling, all offering excellent value.

M. Taylor Moore, proprietor of Blackwood Canyon Vintners. In a nutshell, The unconventional wines are nearly always extraordinary, and often memorable. Baxevanis

Covey Run Vintners (Zillah, 1982), formerly known as Quail Run, is a 200-acre, 45,000-case, predominantly white wine producer that makes Riesling, Chardonnay, Sauvignon Blanc, Chenin Blanc, Gewurztraminer, Morio-Muskat, Aligote, a blend of Semillon/Sauvignon Blanc, Lemberger, Merlot, Cabernet Sauvignon, and ice wine, all impeccably made, offering outstanding value. The Riesling ice wine can often be stunning. Sparkling wine is made in a satellite facility in Kirkland.

Eaton Hill Winery (Granger, 1986), is a 7-acre, 1,000-case winery that makes Semillon and Riesling.

Hinzerling Vineyards (Prosser, 1975), one of the oldest wineries in the state, is a 30-acre, 7,000-case vineyard specializing in estate Chardonnay, Gewurztraminer, late harvest Riesling and Gewurztraminer, Merlot, and Cabernet Sauvignon, the latter tannin-rich and flavorful. The finest red wines (also blended with Malbec) are big and age-worthy. The winery has also experimented with Porto-type wines, a rare feature in the northwest. Other label: *Prosser Falls*.

Horizons's Edge Winery (Zillah, 1985), is a 20-acre, 3,000-case winery that makes robust, zesty Chardonnay, Muscat Blanc, Cabernet Sauvignon, Pinot Noir, and sparkling wine made from Pinot Noir and Chardonnay, all offering good value. The winery is known for a large number of vineyard-designated Chardonnay, some of which are memorable. The winery is also affiliated and makes the wines for Mission Mountain in Montana.

Hyatt Vineyards Winery (Zillah, 1987), is an 80-acre, 9,500-case winery that makes excellent Chardonnay, Chenin Blanc, Riesling, Sauvignon Blanc, and Merlot. Sweet wines, under the *Thurston-Wolfe* label, consist of Black Muscat, late harvest Sauvignon Blanc called *Sweet Rebecca*, late harvest Riesling, and Zinfandel Porto-type wine. The Thurston-Wolfe label is scheduled to become a separate winery soon.

Kiona Vineyards Winery (Benton City, 1979), is a 30-acre, 20,000-case, serious winery that makes distinctive, handcrafted Chardonnay, Riesling, Chenin Blanc, Merlot, Cabernet Sauvignon, and Lemberger, all

offering exceptional value. The Merlot, Cabernet Sauvignon, and Lemberger, in particular, are all luscious, ripe, fruity, and complex. The Chenin Blanc ice wine is outstanding.

Kiona Winery, one of the finest in the northwest. Baxevanis

Oakwood Cellars (Benton City, 1986), is a 3-acre, 3,500-case, innovative winery that makes Chardonnay, Semillon, Riesling, Cabernet Sauvignon, Merlot, and Lemberger, the latter particularly good.

Pontin Del Roza (Prosser, 1984), is a 15-acre, 8,500-case winery that makes delicate, fruity Riesling, Chardonnay, Sauvignon Blanc, Chenin Blanc, Semillon, Cabernet Sauvignon, Merlot, and proprietary wines, all offering good value. The Cabernet Sauvignon is particularly good.

Portteus Vineyard (Zillah, 1987), is a serious, 47-acre, 3,500-case winery that makes rich, complex Chardonnay, Semillon, Cabernet Sauvignon, and Zinfandel, all well-made and flavorful. The Cabernet Sauvignon, one of the finest in the nation, is not to be missed.

Seth Ryan (Benton City, 1985), is a 65-acre, 3,000-case winery that makes several Rieslings, Gewurztraminer, Chardonnay, Cabernet Sauvignon, Merlot, and Cabernet Franc.

Staton Hills Winery, northern portion of the Yakima Valley. Spectacular vistas, excellent wines, and inexpensive vineland, all spell continued success. Father Charles Pandosy, a missionary, introduced agriculture and encouraged sedentary agriculture to the Indian tribe, the Eyakima, or "well-fed" people. Baxevanis

Staton Hills Vineyard & Winery (Wapato, 1984), is a rapidly expanding and well-managed, 16-acre (with 300 additional acres under lease), 60,000-case winery known for spicy Gewurztraminer, fruity Riesling (a "pink" Riesling is also made), Chenin Blanc, Sauvignon Blanc, Semillon, Muscat Blanc, Merlot, Cabernet Sauvignon, Pinot Noir, and sparkling wines. Also made is an unusual Porto-type wine from Cabernet Sauvignon, and a fortified Muscat Blanc. The Jokuriku Coca-Cola Bottling Co. of Japan has recently acquired a majority interest with plans to expand acreage, facilities and production. This is one of the few wineries in the nation that exports more than 35 percent of output. Other labels: *Status, Titon,* and *Ridgemont Vineyard and Winery,* the latter, for red wines made from California grapes.

Stewart Vineyards (Granger, 1983), is a 50-acre, 9,000-case winery with grapes planted both in the Columbia and Yakima River valleys. Estate wines include *Wahluke Slope* from the former area and *Sunnyside Vineyard* in the latter. Gewurztraminer (the late harvest is excellent), Chardonnay, Sauvignon Blanc, Riesling (one of the finest in the state), Muscat Blanc, and Cabernet Sauvignon are particularly good, offering outstanding value.

Tefft Cellars (Outlook, 1991), is 2-acre, 1,500-case winery that makes excellent Gewurztraminer, Merlot, Cabernet Sauvignon, Black Muscat ice wine, late harvest Chardonnay and Sauvignon Blanc, and sparkling wines. Other label: *Penguin.*

The Hogue Cellars (Prosser, 1982), is part of a large, 1,300-acre farming operation that also produces hops, asparagus, and Scotch spearmint. This rapidly expanding, well-managed winery of 700 acres (400 in Concord) makes 200,000 cases of Semillon, Chardonnay, Sauvignon Blanc, Chenin Blanc, Riesling (Markin and Schwartzman vineyards are particularly good), Merlot, Cabernet Sauvignon, and sparkling wines, all outstanding, offering excellent value. Reserve Merlot and Cabernet Sauvignon are usually excellent. Meticulous to a fault, this winery has grown from fewer than 2,500 cases in 1982 to present levels without a decline in quality.

Tucker Cellars (Sunnyside, 1981), is a 75-acre, 10,500-case winery whose owners were pioneer grape growers for more than 50 years. The moderately priced, well-made wines consist of Riesling, Muscat Blanc, Chardonnay, Gewurztraminer, Chenin Blanc, Pinot Noir, Cabernet Sauvignon, late harvest, and proprietary wines.

Vin de L'ouest Winery (Toppenish, 1990), is a 3,000-case winery that makes Chardonnay, Riesling, Gewurztraminer, Chenin Blanc, Muscat Blanc, Pinot Noir, and Cabernet Sauvignon.

Washington Hills Cellar (Sunnyside, 1988), is an expanding, 100,000-case winery that makes Chardonnay, Riesling, Chenin Blanc, Gewurztraminer, Sauvignon Blanc, Merlot, Cabernet Sauvignon, and proprietary wines. The winery also makes excellent Chardonnay, Merlot, Cabernet Sauvignon, Montage (a white Bordeaux-type blend), and late harvest Riesling under the *Apex* label.

Yakima River Winery (Prosser, 1978), is a 25,500-case winery that makes Cabernet Sauvignon, Merlot, Pinot Noir, late harvest and ice wine, blended proprietary, and an unusual Porto-type wine made from Merlot. Red wines are often big, powerful, and tannin-rich.

Zillah Oakes Winery (Zillah, 1987), is a 10,000-case winery that makes Aligote, Riesling, Chenin Blanc, Grenache Noir, and several proprietary wines, all offering good value.

Walla Walla Valley

The emerging *Walla Walla ava*, overlapping into Oregon, contains an enormous potential for quality wine production. The city (the largest in Washington between 1865-1875) is named after an Indian tribal name recorded in the Lewis and Clark journals for "little swift water," a small river that originates in Oregon. Slowly, but steadily as the Concord acreage has been reduced and Vinifera plantings increased, the quality of the region's wineries is excellent, with many described only by superlatives. The delimited area consists of 178,560 acres, 315 acres of vineland and seven wineries, one of which is located in Oregon. Its rough triangular shape is defined by three important physical features: the Horse Haven Ridge, the Blue Mountains (4,900 feet), and the Touchet Slope.

The valley is located in an inland basin completely sheltered from the westerly movement of moist Pacific air, while the higher Rocky Mountains of the north shield the valley from cold Arctic air masses moving south. Although there is some summer precipitation, most rain falls during the winter months, but unlike the rest of the Columbia Plateau and the Yakima Valley, annual precipitation varies between 10 and 25 inches, while the Blue Mountains to the east and southeast receive as much as 45 inches. Interestingly, mean monthly high and low temperatures vary between 66F and 39F, with a growing season that varies between 190 and 220 days. Surprisingly, the southern portion of the *ava* has the same number of heat units as St. Helena in the Napa Valley. As Walla Walla is slightly warmer and wetter than Yakima, Cabernet Sauvignon, Merlot, and Chardonnay do exceptionally well. Soils are heavily mineralized, covered with loess and are somewhat droughty. While the entire valley is known for wheat production, green peas, and sweet onions, grapes and wineries now have become the glamorous economic activities. As strange as it might sound, the name Walla Walla may very well become one of the more revered *ava's* in the nation. The wineries are:

The name may be uncommon to the stranger, but the name Walla Walla may one day be as famous as Pauillac. Downtown area is friendly, clean, gracious, capacious, yet homey. Baxevanis

Biscuit Ridge Winery (Waitsburg, 1987), in a unique microclimate, is a 15-acre, 2,000-case winery that makes dry, crisp, flavorful Gewurztraminer, and small quantities of Pinot Noir, offering excellent value.

Leonetti Cellar (Walla Walla, 1977), is a small, but superlative, 2,500-case winery that makes big, well-structured, flavored and scented Chardonnay, Cabernet Sauvignon, and Merlot. The tannin-rich and dense wines are distinctive, expensive, equal to any from California, and a must for any serious cellar.

Lowden Schoolhouse Corp. (Lowden, 1983), is a 3,000-case winery that makes powerful, massive, well-structured Chenin Blanc, Semillon, and Merlot with a capacity to age, offering excellent value. This is one of the better small wineries in the state that deserves wider recognition. The finer wines are marketed under the *L'Ecole No 41* label, and a small line of moderately-priced wines under the *Walla Voila* label.

Patrick M. Paul Vineyards (Walla Walla, 1988), a 5-acre, 700-case winery that makes Cabernet Franc, is one of the few wineries to make a dark, meaty, sweet Concord.

Waterbrook Winery (Lowden, 1984), is a 32-acre, 7,000-case winery with a good reputation for Sauvignon Blanc, Chardonnay, Cabernet Sauvignon, and Merlot, all supple, finely textured, fragrant, and flavorful. This underrated and deceptively small winery is part of a large agribusiness operation. The serious wines belong in every cellar.

Woodward Canyon Winery (Lowden, 1981), is a 10-acre, 3,800-case winery that makes solid, dense, complex, multi-layered, peppery Cabernet Sauvignon and Chardonnay wines that should not be missed. The finest Chardonnay comes from the Roza Vineyard, and the stunning *Charbonneau* (a blend of 70% Merlot and 30% Cabernet Sauvignon) emanates from a low-yielding vineyard of the same name. Equally good, but infrequently made, are Merlot (outstanding) and Riesling. Meticulous to a fault, this is one of the most distinctive wineries in the country, its Chardonnay and *Charbonneau* ranking among the top 10 wines in the world. The winery uses 100 percent new French oak each year. Along with the Chalone Wine Group, it is currently developing Canoe Ridge, a 100-acre vineyard considered one of the finest in the state.

Woodward Canyon Winery--small, unassuming, but home to spectacular, captivating, world-class wines. Baxevanis

The Spokane Viticultural Region

Spokane, the second largest, right-of-center, conservative city (often called the "Lilac City"), is the locus of what is called the "Inland Empire," the economic nexus for eastern Washington, parts of Idaho and Montana. Wheat, cattle, deciduous fruit from the Palouse region, minerals from Coeur d'Alene, and timber and hydroelectric power from the higher elevations--all contribute to the wealth and importance of Spokane. Recently, two other commodities have made their mark in this interesting region--grapes and wine. The wineries are:

Arbor Crest Wine Cellars (Spokane, 1982), is owned by a 19th century farming family that pioneered orchard development in eastern Washington. Today it cultivates 100 acres and produces more than 40,000 cases of impressive to outstanding Chardonnay, Sauvignon Blanc, Riesling (dry, semi-sweet, and late harvest), Muscat Blanc, late harvest Gewurztraminer, Cabernet Sauvignon, Merlot, and proprietary, all of which are consistent in quality, full-flavored, complex, and well-scented, offering excellent value. The Sauvignon Blanc, one of the finest in the nation, should not be missed.

Latah Creek Wine Cellars (Spokane, 1982), is a 16,000-case winery that makes light-bodied, fresh, zesty, fruity, and quaffable Chenin Blanc, Riesling, and limited amounts of Merlot and Muscat Blanc, all offering excellent value. Cabernet Sauvignon and Merlot, full-bodied, spicy and complex, often rival the finest in the state.

Mountain Dome Winery (Spokane, 1986), is a 1-acre, 1,400-case winery that specializes in the production of well-aged sparkling wine made from Pinot Noir and Chardonnay.

Steven Thomas Livingstone Winery (Spokane, 1988), is a 5,000-case winery that makes Chardonnay, Sauvignon Blanc, Riesling, Merlot, and Cabernet Sauvignon.

Worden's Washington Winery (Spokane, 1979), the oldest of the five Spokane wineries, makes 18,000 cases of above-average wine, the mainstay of which are Riesling and Cabernet Sauvignon/Merlot, followed by Chardonnay, Chenin Blanc, Gewurztraminer, and proprietary wines. Other label: *Suncrest* for Riesling, Gewurztraminer, and Muller-Thurgau, all organically produced.

Oregon

Oregon, a comparatively large state of nearly 97,000 square miles, contains approximately 4 million people, a homogeneous, predominantly white, Protestant population with midwestern roots. More than two-thirds of the state's total land area lies at elevations above 3,000 feet and a similar percentage of the total land area is east of the Cascades (an area that contains less than 15 percent of the entire population). The only areas below this elevation are small portions of the Columbia River and the Willamette Valley. As a consequence, cropland is concentrated along these two areas except for wheat and related "dry-farmed" cereals in the eastern portion of the state. Oregon east of the Cascades is generally too high, cold, and dry for conventional agriculture, and along the Pacific margins too rainy and cloudy. Because more than 55 percent of the total land area is owned by the state (there are more than 200 state parks) and federal government, geographic diversity in topography, climate, vegetation, settlement, and economic history make this state one of the most fascinating in the nation (the state animal is the earthworm and the state bird is the mosquito).

Over 85 percent of the state's population, and nearly all its intensely cultivated cropland, is located in the Willamette Valley, a rich heartland composed of alluvial and volcanic soils. Southern Oregon, the Columbia and Snake River Basins, and south central portions of the state are, due to low rainfall and high elevations, given to extensive livestock, wheat, and scattered irrigated potato, sugar beet, and fruit production. Oregon, ranking as the nation's top producer of lumber products and the leader in the production of plywood (invented in Oregon in 1905), is a land of countless acres of magnificent Douglas fir, Ponderosa pine, hemlock, aspen, and cottonwood whose products have long dominated the state's economy. Agriculture consists of more than 100 different crop and livestock enterprises, of which the leading ten commodities are cattle and calves, wheat, dairy products, nursery crops, potatoes, hay, rye grass seed, onions, pears, and Christmas trees. The total value of agricultural production now exceeds $2 billion, a figure that has doubled within the past ten years, but is thirty times smaller than that of California. Nevertheless, farms are large, well-capitalized, and productive. Nationally, Oregon ranks first in peppermint, hazelnut, prune, and plum; second in snap beans, cauliflower, onion, and hops; and while Vinifera wine grape acreage ranks third in the nation, grapes rank 10th in value among fruit and nut production. State-wide, livestock contributes one-third of all agricultural commodities, followed by wheat, greenhouse nursery products, and milk. With more than 6,000 acres of vineland, grapes are the fourth most important fruit crop in the state after pears, cherries and apples, and although berry acreage exceeds 17,000 acres, grapes rank higher in terms of value. Grouped together, Oregon has more than 75,000 acres of nuts and fruits under commercial cultivation.

Although the Hudson Bay Company established a vineyard at Fort Vancouver in the 1820s, Oregon's viticultural history is fairly recent for several good reasons. Oregon's first permanent settlement (Astoria) was established in 1811, the territory became a state in 1859, and only joined the rest of the nation in 1880 when the Pacific Railroad was completed. Despite the "frontier" image, recent settlement, and Oregon's neoteric history, viticulture began when the first European settlers brought vine cuttings, mostly on an experimental basis, over the Oregon Trail in the middle of the last century. It is reported that the first grape vine planted was the Isabella, part of the Henderson Lewelling collection brought across the Great Plains in 1847 and planted in 1848. Writing in 1892, A.R. Shipley recommends "Delaware, Concord, Hartford, and Isabella, and perhaps Herbert and Worden." Writing in the same year, J.H. Reese recommends Concord, Delaware, Coloma, Eumelian, Pocklington, Salem, and Miles as varieties succeeding in the vicinity of Newberg.

The first winery was built by Peter Britt in the 1850s (there is now a Peter Britt festival), and in 1904 one Ernst Reuter of Forest Grove won a silver medal at the St. Louis Exhibition. Over the course of the next 20 years, there were many attempts in establishing vineyards, but the wine industry remained overly preoccupied with the fermentation of berries and fruits, not grapes. Yet despite this early introduction, winemaking did not become a significant agricultural industry until the late 1960s. The first agricultural census of 1860 reports wine production as 2,603 gallons, a figure that reached 15,000 gallons in 1880 and held steady until it exceeded 2 million gallons in 1988 (including non-grape wines). In 1933, the first post-Prohibition wine license was granted to Louis Herbolt, and between 1933 and 1938 28 wineries were licensed. After a peak of 1 million gallons of wine was produced in 1938, output steadily declined until the late 1960s when Oregon began to emerge from obscurity to take advantage of the change in consumer taste from dessert to table wine con-

sumption.

While the growth of the wine industry was slow, provincial, and obscured by California's preeminence, it is important to note that after Repeal wine output was mainly the product of fruits and berries, and that grape wine was dominated by non-Vinifera varieties. The post-World II wine renaissance began in 1961 when Richard Sommer, a University of California (Davis) graduate, first planted grapes and founded Hillcrest Winery in the Umpqua Valley two years later. He was followed by David Lett (often referred to as the "father of Pinot Noir") of The Eyrie Vineyards in 1966, and David Erath and Carl Knudsen in 1968. These pioneers realized early in their careers that Oregon could grow grapes and make wine just like California, and, perhaps, better Pinot Noir, Riesling, Pinot Gris, and Gewurztraminer than most states.

This encouragement was largely the result of a report on the potential of the state's wine industry undertaken by the Economic Development Division of the Oregon State Department of Commerce. The optimistic report urged viticultural, enological, and marketing assistance to the developing industry. This prompted the planting of new varieties in research centers located in Corvallis, Medford, and Aurora. Commercial winemaking, therefore, is a relatively new industry in Oregon, and a wide departure from the historic fruit and berry production of yesteryear. Acreage nearly tripled during the decade of the 1980s, and the potential for 20,000 additional acres by the year 2,010 is not far fetched given the fact that acreage is one-quarter the cost of comparable land in the Napa Valley, and the demand for Pinot Noir sempiternal. Grape acreage in 1989 stood at 5,400, distributed in 15 counties, and farmed by 194 growers, half of whom culti-vate fewer than 10 acres, and only 29 more than 30 acres. Annual wine production, approaching 2 million gallons, is growing rapidly as more vine acreage becomes bearing.

Figure 7.12

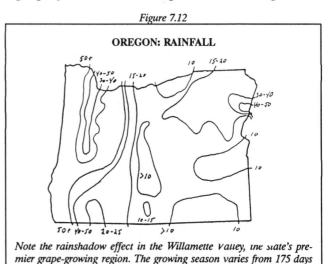

OREGON: RAINFALL

Note the rainshadow effect in the Willamette Valley, the state's premier grape-growing region. The growing season varies from 175 days in Forest Grove in the north to 207 days in Eugene in the south.

Without the presence of fastidious baronial mansions, $20 million wineries, extensive acreage, and financially-healed oil magnates, Oregon lacks the up-scale, glamour-infested wine industry image of Napa Valley. The democratization of the Oregon wine industry is expressed by small, family-owned, rustic, and low-key enterprises operated by dedicated winemakers and their families. Nevertheless, despite its small size, the Oregon wine industry has shown rapid growth since 1963. Acreage leaped from fewer than 35 acres to more than 6,000, and the number of grape wineries from 3 in 1970 to 92 in 1992. The value of grape production increased from less than $250,000 in 1966, to $7 million in 1980, and more than $35 million in 1988. Wine production jumped from 2,000 cases of Vinifera-based wine in the mid-1960s to 200,000 cases in 1984. By 1991 output leaped to 700,000 cases (150,000 cases of fruit and berry wines were also produced), and it is expected that it will triple by 1995 when additional vineland becomes bearing. Of the 92 wineries, only 7 produce more than 20,000 gallons (collectively one-third of the annual total), while the overwhelming number--38 wineries--make fewer than 5,000 cases each year. While, the typical Oregon winery is a small, undercapitalized, family operated business with an annual gross of $250,000, Oregon over the past 20 years has established an enviable record for fine, world class wines. By any conservative measurement, the future looks bright. As many as 100,00 acres are available for additional planting, and as wine quality improves still further, increased capitalization is inevitable in order to expand winery capacity and encourage out-of-state exports. Directly and indirectly, the wine industry contributes more than $400 million to the state's economy.

Table 7.3

OREGON: PRINCIPAL GRAPE VARIETIES				
Variety	1981	Percent	1991	Percent
Pinot Noir	404	32.6	1,984	34.9
Chardonnay	272	22.0	1,367	24.1
Riesling	266	21.5	836	14.8
Pinot Gris	29	2.3	292	5.1
Cabernet Sauvignon	63	5.1	291	5.1
Gewurztraminer	94	7.6	246	4.4
Muller-Thurgau	12	1.0	155	2.7
Sauvignon Blanc			153	2.7
Semillon			51	.8
Zinfandel			31	.5
Others	81	6.5	276	4.9
Total	1,238	100.0	5,682	100.0

Pinot Noir, Chardonnay, Pinot Gris, Cabernet Sauvignon, and Gewurztraminer are growing rapidly in acreage. Oregon grape harvest varies between 9,000 and 16,000 tons. There are 320 growers.
Source: Oregon Wine Growers Association, Portland.

Because the young wine industry has performed well in the maintenance of the quality of its staple wines--Pinot Noir, Chardonnay, Riesling, Cabernet Sauvignon, and Pinot Gris--Oregon has recently attracted considerable foreign and non-resident financing for the production of both vineyard development and winery creation. Well-known writers and California wineries (Girard Winery and Stag's Leap) have recently acquired 1,900 acres near Monroe, and plan to plant Pinot Noir, Merlot, Chardonnay, and Pinot Gris. The William Hill Winery purchased 400 acres near Amity in the Eola Hills, and a Burgundian shipper (Maison Joseph Drouhin) made a commitment in 1987 primarily for the production of Pinot Noir. In 1989 Laurent-Perrier, a major Champagne producer, purchased 80 acres in the Dundee Hills to give a boost to the infant, but expanding sparkling wine industry. For the French, faced with expensive vineyard real estate in Bordeaux, Champagne, and Burgundy (additional prime vineland is not available), the seemingly unlimited acreage (inexpensive and, in most areas, phylloxera-free) is a veritable bargain ripe for further development. For the American winemaker and entrepreneur the prospect of buying first class vineland for the production of the elusive Pinot Noir, Chardonnay, and sparkling wine is too much of a temptation, and, as a consequence, many out-state wineries not only purchase Oregon grapes and/or must, but are beginning to invest in vineland as well. In this connection, it is interesting to note that 25 percent of all grapes are utilized for estate purposes, 62 percent utilized within Oregon, and the remainder used by other states.

Figure 7.13

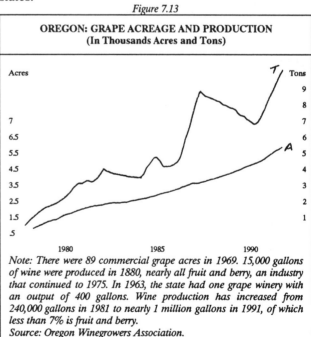

Note: There were 89 commercial grape acres in 1969. 15,000 gallons of wine were produced in 1880, nearly all fruit and berry, an industry that continued to 1975. In 1963, the state had one grape winery with an output of 400 gallons. Wine production has increased from 240,000 gallons in 1981 to nearly 1 million gallons in 1991, of which less than 7% is fruit and berry.
Source: Oregon Winegrowers Association.

Despite the apparent "cottage-type" character of the state's wineries (not one winery makes more than 70,000 cases), winemaking standards in Oregon are high, and wine quality above national levels. If the industry finds itself burdened with a problem it is that of success. Oregon is a state that produces fine wines, not everyday "jugs," and since 90 percent of total production is consumed within the state, there is precious little available for the rest of the country. Oregon has also promulgated the most consumer-oriented labeling laws in America--far ahead of federal minimum standards. State regulations require that varietal wines include a minimum of 90 percent of the stated grape. Equally important, an appellation name must be used, and the grapes of that wine must originate entirely from the stated region. It is illegal to use names such as Chablis, Champagne, Burgundy, Bordeaux, Rhine, and other foreign place names, and even Johannesburg Riesling is known as Riesling. Another important element contributing to high quality wine standards is the practice of high density plantings, particularly for Pinot Noir. Since 1970, only virus-free vine cuttings can be imported, and pesticides and fungicides are highly restricted. Birds appear to be the biggest environment problem. A rare problem, but one that occurred in 1988, was a drought-induced, boron deficiency reducing the crop (as much as 80 percent in some places) in areas where there was no rainfall for as many as 81 days (primarily the Willamette Valley).

OREGON GRAPE STATISTICS, 1991

Total Acres: 6,072.
Acreage by Principal Counties: Yamhill (1,476); Washington (898); Columbia River region (884); Polk (820).
Tons Harvested by Region: Total for state, 9,600 tons. Yamhill (3,800); Polk (2,200); Washington (1,749); Columbia River Region (100).
Total Acres by Variety: Pinot Noir (2,130); Chardonnay (1,430); Riesling (800); Cabernet Sauvignon (350); Gewurztraminer (286); Pinot Gris (398).
Tons Harvested by Variety: Pinot Noir (3,073); Chardonnay (2,500); Riesling (1,819); Muller-Thurgau (478); Cabernet Sauvignon (442).
Crop Value in $Million (1990): Pinot Noir ($1.9); Chardonnay ($1.8); Riesling ($.6); Cabernet Sauvignon ($.3). Total crop value in 1991 was $8.2 million.
Percent Market Share by Tons: Chardonnay (26); Pinot Noir (31.5); Riesling (18.8); Pinot Gris (5); Muller-Thurgau (4.4); Cabernet Sauvignon (4.3); Gewurztraminer (2.9); Others (7.6).
Percent Market Share by Value: Pinot Noir (36); Chardonnay (31); Riesling (13); Pinot Gris (5.3); Cabernet Sauvignon (4); Muller-Thurgau (2.6); Gewurztraminer (2); Others (5.9).
Price Per Ton in $: Pinot Noir ($1,018); Chardonnay (950); Pinot Gris (945); Cabernet Sauvignon (780); Merlot (785); Sauvignon Blanc (650); Riesling (500).
Price Per Ton in $ (Average): 1987 (570); 1988 (620); 1989 (745); 1990 (780); 1991 (860).
Tons Lost to Frost: Riesling (1,100); Chardonnay (640); Pinot Noir (410); Cabernet Sauvignon (230); Others (400).
Disposition of Grapes: Purchased by Oregon wineries (66%); Estate (26%); Washington (4%); California (4%).
Source: Oregon Winegrowers Association.

With nearly three-fourths of total acreage, the principal grape varieties of Pinot Noir, Chardonnay, and Riesling are commonly referred to as the "big three." They are followed by Pinot Gris, Cabernet Sauvignon, Gewurztraminer, and Muller-Thurgau. While Cabernet Sauvignon, Sauvignon Blanc, Gewurztraminer, Pinot Gris, and Muller-Thurgau are the fastest growing varieties (in terms of percentage), Pinot Noir and Chardonnay account for much larger absolute annual acreage increases, and for

more than 52 percent of total market share by value. Among the many minor varieties are Concord, mainly for juice production, and Marechal Foch, a ubiquitous French-American eastern variety that makes an interesting wine commanding prices of $12.50 the bottle. Five counties collectively account for 80 percent of all vine acreage, of which Yamhill, Washington, and Polk are the most important. Although more than 95 percent of all wines carry a varietal name, excitement abounds about the state's ability to produce quality sparkling wine primarily from Pinot Noir and Chardonnay. Output is less than 25,000 cases, all excellent--crisp, fruity and yeasty, yet refined, well-balanced and complex.

The Geography of Wine Production

While there are five distinct grape-growing areas, the state has three *ava's* wholly within the state, *Willamette Valley, Umpqua Valley*, and *Rogue Valley*, and two that are shared with Washington--the southern portions of Columbia River and Walla Walla. The principal area of grape and wine production, the beautiful *Willamette Valley ava*, is the southern extension of the Puget Sound trough, an area bounded by the Columbia River, Coast Range Mountains, Calapooya Mountains, and the Cascade Mountains. The delimited area consists of 5,200 square miles, nearly 6,000 acres of vineland, and more than 60 wineries. The principal areas for vine acreage and number of wineries are Yamhill, Washington, and Polk counties. Collectively, they contain more than 4,000 acres, and 39 wineries. It further contains 80 percent of the state's population, all major cities, the capital, and 40 percent of the agricultural product. The entire valley is dominated by Portland, the largest city, the locus for secondary and tertiary activities, and a metropolitan area that encompasses more than half of the state's population. Minute in scale when compared with Portland, Eugene and Salem are the next two largest cities, with no other settlements above 34,000 in population east of the Cascades.

This "heartland" is a north-south alluvial plain that stretches for 180 miles, and is 60 miles broad west of Portland, tapering gently to less than 10 miles in the south. It is agriculturally diverse (one of the most fertile valleys in the nation), and the source for more than three-fourths of vine acreage and wineries. In this fertile, verdant valley, vineyards are dispersed amongst the recumbent landscape of strawberry patches, nut groves, orchards, and dairy herds. While there are exceptions, most vineyards are located on south-facing volcanic slopes 300 to 950 feet in elevation where evening maritime breezes lower temperatures developing moderately high acid levels and intense fruit flavors. Higher slopes are too cool and humid, and valley bottoms are prone to frost, the latter condition aggravated by the presence of heavy clay soils. Many vineyards, perhaps more than any other group in the nation, plant at far larger grape vine densities. Curiously, the Geneva Double Curtain training system is very popular, as are many other systems.

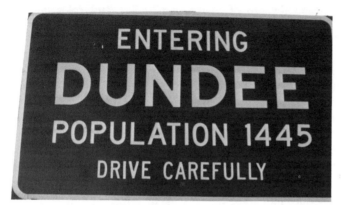

One day this hitherto insignificant town may be as famous as Beaune.
Baxevanis

The Willamette Valley is sheltered from the cool maritime air masses by the Coastal Range, and from the extremes of continental temperatures by the Cascades on the east. Rainfall, rather high at 50 inches, falls mainly between the months of October to April, with July and August being relatively dry, although five to ten inches falls during the summer. Summer temperatures are relatively warm to cool with fewer than ten days above 90F, but autumn weather is characterized as humid, moderately cool, and lingering. Degree day heat units average 2,150, with lows of 1,600 and high's of 2,700, a fairly wide range, hence the wide variability of vintage years (unlike the lee side of the Cascade Range, and most areas of California). The above is highly significant because the Napa Valley experiences a much narrower range of between 2,700 and 3,400 degree days. The northern Willamette is warmer than the Rheingau (1,700), but slightly cooler than the Cote d'Or (2,400). While low winter temperatures (as low as -5F) are rarely a problem in the Willamette and as far south as the Grants Pass region, temperatures as low as -20F along portions of the Columbia River are disastrous, as was the case during the 1988-1989 winter. Spring frosts, considered more serious, are common only in valley bottomland and in the Grants Pass area. Precipitation, however, is a major problem during the harvest as mildew and flavor dilution are major concerns. Generally, the northern portion of the Willamette, in contrast to the Umpqua and Rogue valleys, receives more precipitation and is significantly cooler. Umpqua receives ten inches less rainfall and is about 5F

warmer, while the Rogue Valley, further south, is the driest with fewer than 20 inches of precipitation and, at 1,400 feet in elevation, is the warmest with temperatures frequently rising to 100F.

In the northern portion are several local variations in microclimate and soils: The Tualatin Valley, the "Red Hills" of Dundee, and the Eola Hills all exhibit significant physical elements to make their wines somewhat distinct. Tualatin, for example, is a small valley drained by the meandering Tualatin River, a tributary of the Willamette. The best sites (grey-white soils with little iron), located between 200-450 feet from the valley floor, are blessed by good air drainage that hardly ever endangers the vine to frost. While more than 90% of Oregon grapes are planted on their own roots, phylloxera has been spotted in the Willamette Valley, however as the vineyards are not contiguous, its spread is not expected to be rapid.

The "Red Hills" of Dundee, called Oregon's Cotes de Beaune, are the largest contiguous concentration of vineyards in the state. Dundee, located in Yamhill County, is the site of 40 percent of the state's total vine acreage, and 90 percent of the nation's total hazelnuts as well. The area receives an element of celebrity because of its volcanic, iron-rich soil, the best of which is called Jory (Laurelwood and Cornelius are also good), particularly between the triangular area of Yamhill, Newberg, and McMinnville. The region contains more volcanic rock than the Tyee region near Corvallis, and its irregular intrusions of sandstones, limestone, and grey shale combine to produce one of the better sites (south-facing slopes 400 to 900 feet in elevation) in the Willamette area. It is here that Pinot Noir dominates and gives new meaning to excellent Pinot Noir wine production. The wines are full-bodied, spicy, complex, and much darker than those from California, and marginally more consistent than equivalent versions from the famed Cote d'Or. The northern Willamette region differs in several dramatic ways as far as Pinot Noir is concerned. Rainfall, for example, is heavier in winter than Carneros and Burgundy, and more substantial in summer than Carneros. While rot is an occasional problem in the Willamette and Carneros, it becomes a perennial consequence in Burgundy where precipitation is more evenly distributed throughout the year. That there are fewer degree days in the Willamette than in the Cote d'Or is another important distinction.

In addition to Pinot Noir, Chardonnay, Riesling, and Gewurztraminer are also planted, followed by minor but rising acreage of Pinot Blanc, Pinot Gris, and Pinot Meunier, the latter thought to be a future staple in the production of sparkling wine. In the Yamhill area, Muller-Thurgau does exceptionally well on Woodburn Series, moderately well-drained soils that are located on terraces with up to 20 percent slope. On the other hand, Riesling does particularly well on Willakenzie soils that are characterized by well-drained (20 to 40 inches deep) soils, sited on low hills with slopes of 2 to 15 percent. Immediately to the south, the Eola Hills region, a small chain of hills (basaltic outcrops) rising from the valley, contains 700 acres of prime vineland, and fourteen wineries. Due to their position in the middle of the Willamette Valley, "the hills" are bathed in wind (the name is derived from the Greek "Eolian" for windy) that not only lowers surrounding temperatures, but dries the vineyards during the harvest. This area overlaps several counties and produces above-average Pinot Noir from a soil similar to that found in Dundee. South of Corvallis, vineyards are mainly located on thick beds of bluish-grey to grey sandstone rock that produce firm, compact soils.

The Grapes of the Willamette Valley

Due to the cool growing season, grape varieties are limited to those that ripen early. The state's signature grape variety, Pinot Noir, with 2,000 acres, accounts for 40 percent of the state's planted acreage, nearly 90 percent of which is found in the Willamette Valley. Although ·Pinot Noir is grown in the wrong places (in terms of deep, fertile soils, level land, poor aspects, and subjected to excessive nitrogen fertilization), this grape, at its best, is able to produce well-balanced and delicate wine with a pronounced aroma and flavor that is second to none in the nation. Oregon Pinot Noir is more austere and less fat, better structured, and lacks the flabby, low-acid, raisin-flavored elements that appear endemic to nearly all California versions. While it is grown by nearly all wineries, its primary area of concentration is the cool, hilly region of the northern Willamette Valley. Although style variations do exist, nearly all are aged in oak to develop complexity, and the very best is well-balanced, round, supple, with ripe, multilayered cherry and berry flavors.

Pinot Noir, it appears, has found its home in the Willamette Valley, without question the most successful area in the nation for its production. One possible explanation for the apparent success of this grape variety might lie in the fact that the most popular clone is the Pommard (Wadenswil, Gamay, and Hatcher are also good), considered the favorite because of its excellent tannin levels, thus assuring structure and longevity while producing a creamy, rich wine with a dose of refinement. Pinot Noir is planted on sites known for their cool, marginal growing habits so that the grape berries do not overly ripen, and spaced much closer together thus producing a more even ripening necessary for the production of intense varietal flavor concentration. Over the years growers and winemakers have discovered that total heat units are only part of the story in determining wine quality; more important is the time grapes hang on the vine, a feature that improves color, flavor and scent--major constituents in that elusive term "wine quality." As a consequence, Pinot Noir

is not only much higher in total acid and significantly lower in both pH and alcohol, but it can be in perfect harmony with extract, color, and flavor. If the growing season is short and subjected to higher temperatures, grapes are characterized by lower acid levels, higher pH, harsh, hot, often raisiny flavors, and poor coloring. Therefore, both Pinot Noir and Riesling, requiring a long hang time for proper maturation, flavor, and color development, are picked after October 15.

As the vines have aged since large plantings took place in the 1970s, winemakers have perfected fermentation techniques that extract the most from this fragile and quality-evasive grape. Generally, there are two types of Pinot Noir wines: low acid wine from young vines made in a style to appeal to contemporary tastes; and, by far the better wine, a spicy, fruit-laden, highly complex, dark, full-bodied libation that is able to compete with the very best from the Cote d'Or. The best recent vintages for Pinot Noir have been 1979, 1980 (small crop, outstanding), 1983 (outstanding), 1985 (excellent, ripe, and fruity), 1986 (excellent, well-structured, aging better than 1985), 1987 (excellent and well-structured), and 1988 (small crop, intense, concentrated wines). It should also be noted that while the explosion of wineries and young vineyards has produced a string of highly variable wines in recent years, the region's capability for quality Pinot Noir production remains undisputed. If Oregon Pinot Noir is to become nationally and internationally famous, sloppy winemaking, replete with shortcuts, increased yields, and the persistency of lax, "take for granted" attitudes of a large number of wineries must give way to greater consumer responsibility.

Chardonnay, not necessarily considered the mainstay of the Willamette grower despite its formidable acreage, has been much improved over the past ten years. It is usually crisp, well-flavored, intensely scented, and not at all soft and supple as in California. Having about 1 percent less alcohol, it is not acidified, and invariably is allowed to complete malolactic fermentation in order to mitigate excess acidity. In the past, Chardonnay was described as the "Achilles heal" due to its inconsistency in terms of roundness and complexity because growers were using California clones suited to California climates. Recently Chardonnay has become quite elegant, fruity, and blessed with a lingering smooth, satisfying finish. Because no distinct style has emerged, Chardonnay varies from light to full-bodied. Riesling, historically the state's leading variety (Richard Sommer of Hillcrest Vineyards is given credit for its introduction to Oregon in 1961), has recently slipped to third place in terms of acreage despite its profitability and meteoric rise in acreage from 379 acres in 1980 to 836 in 1990. While it has the ability to produce a crisp, acidic, well-scented wine unequaled anywhere in the nation (Washington and Idaho being notable exceptions) for its balance and aging potential, it fails to captivate the attention of the national market, but is very popular within the state. If and when alcohol levels decline and the wines become more delicate and refined, the popularity of Riesling will increase.

Pinot Gris, an obscure, early ripening and mildew resistant variety (introduced along with Pinot Noir to Oregon by David Lett), is rapidly becoming a serious grape in the Willamette Valley as it produces a full and well-flavored, acidic wine with moderate alcohol and a mild, delicate bouquet that is a superb match for fowl, pork, seafood, and grilled chicken (when paired with salmon Pinot Gris assumes the image of a cult wine in Oregon). The vine requires an exacting physical environment as its roots have a tendency to penetrate deeply. The fact that it ripens before Riesling and Gewurztraminer, thus avoiding fall rain, is another appealing factor contributing to its recent popularity. With nearly 300 acres of commercial Pinot Gris available (acreage has doubled during the period 1987-1990), this much sought-after wine may become another successful Pinot Noir story (despite its caricature as the poor man's Chardonnay). Because of its meager yield per acre there is much speculation as to its future marketing requirements, but, in the meantime, a good deal of Riesling and Gewurztraminer is being budded over to this, hitherto, equivocal variety. As its popularity intensifies, it is expected that the number of Pinot Gris styles will proliferate. Interestingly, in recent years this grape variety has become the most expensive grape in Oregon.

Cabernet Sauvignon, the fifth most popular grape variety, is mainly grown in the drier and warmer Columbia River region, and in the warmer regions south of the Willamette Valley near the California border. It appears that the cool, wet, spring season in the northern Willamette region interferes with berry set. While quality and yields are less spectacular than those emanating from Washington, recent advances have produced spectacular wines worthy of serious recognition, particularly from the state's Walla Walla *ava*. Ranking sixth in total acreage, the low yielding Gewurztraminer produces a flowery, spicy wine that is nearly always made dry. This variety is particularly troublesome as it is difficult to prune, control vigor, and only yields above-average wine once every three years. However, due to its balance, fragrance, and superb spicy flavor, it is well worth the effort, and usually affords outstanding value. Sauvignon Blanc is increasingly becoming popular as reflected in new plantings (second to Merlot in percent of new plantings since 1982), and despite stylistic variations, most of it is made in a dry, crisp, steely manner very much in the Graves style. Muller-Thurgau, an early ripening variety, is known to give one of the highest yields and produces a rather neutral wine widely used for blending. Originally planted for its high

yields and ability to ripen before the autumnal rains, the variety has not lived up to expectations, and, as a result, it is slowly being replaced by more popular varieties. An unusual grape variety that is causing much excitement is Marechal Foch, a French-American variety known to produce nothing but average wine in the northeast and midwest. In Oregon, a consistent producer of 6 tons to the acre, it is produced as a varietal, used to add color to Pinot Noir, and fetches a surprisingly high price.

The wineries of the Willamette Valley are:

Adams Vineyard Winery (Portland, 1981), is a 13-acre, 4,000-case, underrated winery located amidst an industrial district in Portland. Chardonnay, Sauvignon Blanc, and Pinot Noir are all full-bodied, complex, and distinctive, offering good value.

Adelsheim Vineyard (Newberg, 1978), is a highly regarded, 50-acre, 20,000-case winery with excellent exposure on the south-facing slopes of the Chehalem Mountains that makes Riesling, Pinot Noir, Pinot Gris, Chardonnay, and Merlot. *Elizabeth's Reserve* Pinot Noir is excellent. Other label: *Wallace Brook Cellars*.

Airlie Winery (Monmouth, 1986), is an aggressive and successful, 35-acre, 6,000-case winery that makes light-bodied, easy-drinking Gewurztraminer (dry and late harvest), Riesling, Muller-Thurgau, Marechal Foch, Pinot Noir, and proprietary wines.

Alpine Vineyards (Alpine, 1980), located on the foothills of the Coastal Range, is a 30-acre, 10,000-case winery that makes estate-bottled Chardonnay, Pinot Gris, Gewurztraminer, Riesling, Pinot Noir, and Cabernet Sauvignon, all consistently well-made, offering good value.

Amity Vineyards (Amity, 1976), is a 15-acre, 10,000-case, underrated winery with a reputation for delicate, supple, and expertly made Chardonnay, Gewurztraminer, Riesling, Pinot Noir, Gamay Noir a Jus Blanc (the first in the nation), and proprietary wines. The reserve Pinot Noir is outstanding.

Ankeny Vineyards (Salem, 1985), is a 22-acre, 2,500-case winery that makes impressive, barrel-fermented Chardonnay, Pinot Noir, Cabernet Sauvignon, and fresh, zesty Riesling and Gewurztraminer.

Argyle, Dundee Wine Co., (Dundee, 1987), represents the first, large scale, serious attempt in the production of sparkling wine in Oregon. The company leases a 35-acre vineyard, purchases grapes and will make 21,000 cases of sparkling wine, primarily from Pinot Noir and Chardonnay. Initial attempts have been encouraging, as the Brut wine is rich, full bodied, yeasty on the nose, and expensive. The winery, formerly known as Crochard Company and The Dundee Wine Company, also makes small quantities of Riesling and Chardonnay. While the principal shareholder is an adventurous Australian, the Knudsen Erath Winery is also a principal.

Arterberry Winery (McMinnville, 1979), is a 6,500-case winery that makes good, sound Chardonnay, Sauvignon Blanc, Gewurztraminer, Riesling, Pinot Noir, and two fresh, zesty, well-balanced sparkling wines from purchased grapes (this was Oregon's first commercial sparkling wine in 1982). The winery also makes a superb cider.

Autumn Wind Vineyard (Newberg, 1987), is a 15-acre, 3,000-case, consumer-friendly winery that makes excellent Chardonnay, Sauvignon Blanc, Muller-Thurgau, and Pinot Noir.

Bellfountain Cellars (Corvallis, 1989), is an expanding, 10-acre (35 acres by 1994), 3,000-case, estate winery that makes Chardonnay, Pinot Gris, Sauvignon Blanc, Riesling, Gewurztraminer, Pinot Noir, Cabernet Sauvignon, and Gamay.

Bethel Heights (Salem, 1984), is a 51-acre, 7,000-case winery located on the rim of an ancient volcano in the historic Eola Hills region. The well-made wines consist of Chardonnay, Gewurztraminer, Riesling, Chenin Blanc, and Pinot Noir, the last two particularly good.

Broadley Vineyards (Monroe, 1986), is a 15-acre, 2,500-case winery that makes good, sound, well-flavored, age-worthy, distinctive Pinot Noir and Chardonnay.

Cameron Winery (Dundee, 1984), is a serious, 5-acre, 3,500-case winery that makes excellent, often refined, opulent, complex, barrel-fermented Chardonnay, Pinot Noir, and Pinot Blanc, all offering good value. Although rich and full-bodied, the winery departs from its neighbors with higher than normal acid levels.

Chateau Benoit (Carlton, 1979), is a highly regarded, quality-oriented, and rapidly expanding, 22-acre, 20,000-case winery that makes good estate and non-estate-bottled Gewurztraminer, Pinot Gris, Muller-Thurgau, Sauvignon Blanc, Riesling, Chardonnay, Cabernet Sauvignon, Merlot, and Pinot Noir. Impressive sparkling wine is also made. Other label: *Crystal Creek*.

Chateau Bianca (Dallas, 1991), is an aggressive, 50-acre, 4,000-case winery that makes Riesling, Gewurztraminer, Chardonnay, and Pinot Noir.

Cooper Mountain Vineyards Winery (Beaverton, 1987), is a 72-acre, 2,000-case winery that makes above-average to excellent Pinot Noir, Chardonnay, and Pinot Gris.

New plantings at Domaine Drouhin. Baxevanis

Domaine Drouhin Oregon (Dundee, 1988), is an 179-acre property (35 planted in vines) owned by one of the most prestigious negociant houses of Burgundy. Initial crush at a neighboring winery produced 3,000 cases of Pinot Noir in 1988, but with the completion of the new winery production is expected to rise to 12,000 cases by 1994, all estate-produced.

Duck Pond Cellars (Dundee, 1989), is a 200-acre (the largest vineyard in the area), 3,000-case winery that makes Chardonnay, Pinot Noir, and Cabernet Sauvignon.

Edgefield Winery (Troutdale, 1990), is 17-acre, 4,000-case winery that makes Chardonnay, Riesling, Pinot Gris, Pinot Noir, Cabernet Sauvignon, and proprietary wines. The projected facility, located on Portland's historic poor farm, calls for a 100-room hotel, restaurant, bakery, brewery, and pub.

Elk Cove Vineyards (Gaston, 1977), is a 46-acre, 13,000-case, underrated winery that makes excellent, full-bodied and complex Chardonnay, Pinot Gris, Gewurztraminer, Riesling (dry and late harvest), Pinot Noir, and Cabernet Sauvignon, all offering excellent value. Other label: *La Boheme Vineyard*, for an upscale line of Chardonnay and Pinot Noir, two of the most expensive wines in the state.

Ellendale Vineyards (Dallas, 1982), is an 16-acre, 8,000-case winery that makes a large selection of fruit, berry and grape wines, the latter consisting of Riesling, Chardonnay, Cabernet Sauvignon, Pinot Noir, Merlot, and sparkling wine under the *Crystal Mist* label, as well as unusual Niagara and Mead.

Eola Hills Wine Cellars (Rickreall, 1986), is a 67-acre, 10,000-case, conscientious estate winery that makes well-structured Chardonnay, Sauvignon Blanc, Chenin Blanc, Pinot Noir, and Cabernet Sauvignon, most of which offer good value.

Evesham Wood Vineyard & Winery (West Salem, 1986), is a 12-acre, 2,500-case winery that makes excellent, full-bodied, big, well-flavored Chardonnay and Pinot Noir by one of the states most accomplished winemakers. This underrated winery also makes small quantities of

Gewurztraminer and Pinot Gris, the latter particularly rich and flavorful.

Forgeron Vineyard (Elmira, 1978), is a 20-acre, 10,000-case winery that makes average quality Chardonnay, Riesling, Pinot Noir, and Pinot Gris.

Flynn Vineyards (Rickreall, 1985), is an aggressive, 83-acre, 8,000-case winery that makes sparkling wine (85% of output), and smaller quantities of Chardonnay and Pinot Noir.

Hidden Springs Winery (Amity, 1980), is a 20-acre, 4,400-case winery located high in the Eola Hills overlooking the Willamette Valley and the Cascade Mountains that makes above-average quality Pinot Gris, Chardonnay, Riesling (dry and sweet), Pinot Noir, Cabernet Sauvignon, and proprietary wines.

Hinman Vineyards (Eugene, 1979), is a 50-acre, 35,000-case winery that makes good, affordable Gewurztraminer, Riesling, Chardonnay, Cabernet Sauvignon, and Pinot Noir. This rapidly expanding winery is one of the few that crushes grapes from eastern Oregon and sells most of its wines at less than premium prices. Very innovative, the winery markets a good deal of its output to restaurants under many labels and proprietary names. Significant changes are unfolding as the winery has recently been sold.

Honeywood Winery (Salem, 1933), the oldest continuously operating winery in the state, is a 14,000-case facility that was mainly a fruit producer until 1981 when it began to make varietal grape wines, mainly Chardonnay, Gewurztraminer, Riesling, Muller-Thurgau, Pinot Noir, and proprietary wines, one of the best being *Twin Harvest*, a blend of 98 percent Riesling and 2 percent fruit juice.

Houston Vineyards (Eugene, 1983), is a 5-acre, 1,400-case Chardonnay (fruity and non-oaky) label that usually offers good value. Curiously, the custom crush occurs in a Yakima Valley winery.

Knudsen Erath Winery (Dundee, 1972), with 65 acres and an annual output of 25,000 cases, this large winery makes superb Pinot Noir, crisp Chardonnay, Gewurztraminer, Riesling (dry and sweet), Cabernet Sauvignon, and sparkling wines that rank among the top in the state. The meticulously made wines often offer outstanding value, and should be part of any serious cellar. This winery is the largest producer of Pinot Noir in the state. The Vintage Select Pinot Noir and Chardonnay are outstanding.

Kramer Vineyards (Gaston, 1989), is an 12-acre, 2,400-case winery that makes Chardonnay, Riesling, Muller-Thurgau, Gewurztraminer, Pinot Gris, Pinot Noir, and berry wines.

Kristin Hill Winery (Amity, 1990), is a 14-acre, 3,000-case winery that makes Chardonnay, Gewurztraminer, Pinot Gris, Pinot Noir, and sparkling wines.

Lange Winery (Dundee, 1987), is a 6-acre, 3,000-case winery that makes full-bodied Pinot Noir and excellent barrel-fermented Chardonnay, Sauvignon Blanc, and Pinot Gris, the latter unusual in that it is barrel fermented and oak aged.

Laurel Ridge Winery (Forest Grove, 1986), is an 85-acre, 10,000-case winery located on a site that once housed a 19th century winery, Reuter's Hill (1883). The unusual winery makes good, sound, attractively-priced Pinot Noir, Sauvignon Blanc, Gewurztraminer, a sparkling Riesling, and a 100 percent Pinot Noir sparkling wine, the latter two dominating production.

McKinlay Vineyards (Newberg, 1987), is a young, aggressive, 11-acre, 2,500-case winery that makes barrel fermented Chardonnay, Pinot Gris, and supple Pinot Noir.

Marquam Hill Vineyards (Mollala, 1988), is a 23-acre, 2,500-case winery that makes Pinot Noir, Chardonnay, Alsatian style Riesling, Muller-Thurgau, and Gewurztraminer.

Mirassou Cellars of Oregon (Salem, 1985), is a 45-acre, 12,500-case winery that makes good, but often inconsistent Gewurztraminer, Chardonnay, Riesling, Pinot Noir, and Cabernet Sauvignon under the *Pellier* label. Many changes are occurring as the new owners are specializing in Chardonnay, Pinot Noir, and Pinot Gris.

Montinore Vineyards (Forest Grove, 1987), with 475 planted acres and an output of more than 80,000 cases, this classy, aggressive, state-of-the-art winery (the largest in the state), well sited and lavishly financed, is expected to set the trend for future winery developments in Oregon. The well-made, intensely-flavored wines (Muller-Thurgau, Riesling, Chardonnay, Pinot Gris, Gewurztraminer, Sauvignon Blanc, Chenin Blanc, Pinot Meunier, Cascade, Marechal Foch, Pinot Noir, and sparkling) are fruity and well balanced offering good value. The late harvest and ice wines are interesting. It is expected that more than 75 percent of future wine output will be sold outside the state.

Mulhausen Winery (Newberg, 1979), is a 30-acre, 9,000-case, bankrupt winery that lay dormant for several years. It has recently been sold, and is now in the process of being resurrected.

Nehalem Bay Winery (Nehalem, 1973), located along the Pacific coast, is a 8,000-case winery mainly known for its fruit wines, but also offers modest amounts of grape wines (Niagara, Chardonnay, Riesling, and Pinot Noir) from purchased grapes.

Oak Grove Orchards Winery (Rickreall, 1987), is a 7-acre, 1,000-case winery that makes Golden Muscat, Concord, and fruit wines.

Oak Knoll Winery (Hillsboro, 1970), is a 30,000-case winery that makes Pinot Noir, Chardonnay, Gewurztraminer, Riesling, Muller-Thurgau, Cabernet Sauvignon, and Pinot Noir from purchased grapes. The firm also makes a rare Niagara, as well as berry wines.

Orchard Heights Winery (Salem, 1982), formerly Glen Creek Winery, is a small, aggressive, 20-acre, 5,500-case winery that makes good, sound Gewurztraminer, Chardonnay, Sauvignon Blanc, Pinot Noir, and fruit and berry wines. Under new ownership, this winery is currently revamping winemaking methods and product line.

Oregon Cellars Winery (Cheshire, 1988), is a serious, 20-acre, 1,500-case winery that makes Chardonnay, Riesling, and Pinot Noir under the *Rainsong* label, and sparkling wines from Pinot Noir, Pinot Meunier, and Chardonnay under the *Northern Silk* label.

Oregon Estates Winery (Eugene, 1989), is a 19-acre, 1,500-case winery that makes Chardonnay, Sauvignon Blanc, Riesling, Gewurztraminer, Pinot Noir, Cabernet Sauvignon, and small quantities of sparkling wines.

Panther Creek Winery (McMinnville, 1986), is a 3,000-case winery that only makes lush, fruity, dark, well-textured and distinctive Pinot Noir, and an unusual, barrel fermented, yeasty Melon, both of which should not be missed.

Ponderosa Vineyards (Lebanon, 1987), is a 12-acre, 1,500-case winery that makes sulfite-free Chardonnay, Sauvignon Blanc, and Pinot Noir.

Ponzi Vineyards (Beaverton, 1969), is an aggressive, 22-acre, 10,000-case winery that makes average to excellent, soft, supple Riesling, Chardonnay, Pinot Gris, Pinot Noir, and proprietary wines. The Pinot Noir and Chardonnay reserve are particularly good.

Redhawk Winery (Salem, 1990), is 5-acre, 1,600-case winery under construction that makes excellent Chardonnay, Pinot Gris, and Pinot Noir.

Red Hills Vineyard (Dundee, 1987), is a highly regarded 50-acre vineyard that makes 1,000 cases of excellent Pinot Noir and Chardonnay wines under the *Marsh Hill Vineyard* label.

Rex Hill. While design is ultra modern, the wines are very traditional.
Baxevanis

Rex Hill (Newberg, 1982), is an aggressive, 75-acre (also manages an additional 150 acres), 14,000-case winery that makes above-average to excellent, well-aged Pinot Noir and Chardonnay, as well as fresh, Sauvignon Blanc, Riesling, Pinot Gris, and Symphony. Although inconsistent in the past, this winery now offers good to excellent value, especially for the Medici, Maresh, and Archibald Vineyard's Pinot Noir. This is one of the few wineries that uses a high trellis system to mature grapes three weeks before the fall rains. The winery has recently purchased an interest in Sokol Blosser. Other label: *Kings Ridge*.

St. Innocent Winery (Salem, 1988), is a 2,500-case, serious winery that makes crisp Chardonnay, supple Pinot Noir, and sparkling wines.

St. Josef's Weinkeller (Canby, 1983), one of the few wineries along the right bank of the Willamette River, is a 10-acre, 5,500-case winery that makes distinctive Cabernet Sauvignon and less successful Chardonnay, Gewurztraminer, Zinfandel, Riesling, and Pinot Noir.

Saga Vineyards (Colton, 1989), is a 3-acre, 2,000-case winery that makes barrel-fermented and aged Chardonnay, Riesling, and Pinot Noir.

Schwarzenberg Vineyards (Dallas, 1987), is an aggressive 50-acre, 20,000-case winery that makes fresh, supple, low alcohol, non-woody Chardonnay (excellent), Riesling, and Pinot Noir, all offering good value.

Secret House Vineyard Winery (Veneta, 1989), is an aggressive and rapidly growing 32-acre, 3,500-case, Riesling, Chardonnay, Cabernet Sauvignon, and Pinot Noir winery.

Serendipity Cellars Winery (Monmouth, 1981), is an innovative 2,500-case winery that makes distinctive Marechal Foch, a spicy Muller-Thurgau, a "truffled" Chardonnay, Chenin Blanc, Cabernet Sauvignon, and Zinfandel. The Marechal Foch, highly unusual for the Willamette Valley, is outstanding.

Shafer Vineyard Cellars (Forest Grove, 1978), is a 28-acre, 9,000-case winery that makes distinctive Sauvignon Blanc, Chardonnay, Gewurztraminer, Riesling, and Pinot Noir, all intensely flavored, full-bodied, and firm on the palate. The wines are meticulously made, offer excellent value, and rank among the finest in the state.

Shallon Winery (Astoria, 1978), located in the oldest settlement in the northwest, is a tiny, but unusual 1,200-case winery that makes fruit and berry (Salal, similar to a Huckleberry, is interesting) wines, a Muscat of Alexandria, and Whey wine (for those that really haven't tried the ultimate).

Silver Falls Winery (Sublimity, 1983), is an 18-acre, 4,000-case winery that makes improving, light-bodied, supple, fruity Chardonnay, Pinot Gris, Riesling, and Pinot Noir.

Sokol Blosser (Dundee, 1977), is a 161-acre, 26,000-case winery known for average to above-average Riesling, Gewurztraminer, Chardonnay, Muller-Thurgau, Sauvignon Blanc, and Pinot Noir, all soft with some residual sugar, and moderately priced.

Springhill Cellars (Albany, 1988), formerly Meridian Vintners, is a 15-acre, 1,500-case winery that makes excellent, full bodied Chardonnay, Riesling, Muller-Thurgau, and Pinot Noir, all moderately priced, offering good value.

Starr and Brown (Portland, 1991), is a classic urban winery that makes 1,500 cases of above-average Chardonnay, Riesling, Pinot Gris, and Pinot Noir under the *Starr* label.

Tempest Vineyards (Newberg, 1988), is a 3,000-case winery whose delicate and supple wines, Gewurztraminer, Chardonnay, Pinot Gris, Early Muscat, Muscat Ottonel, Gamay Noir, Pinot Noir, and Cabernet Sauvignon, are made in a neighboring winery.

The Eyrie Vineyards (McMinnville, 1970), the second oldest winery in the state and the first all-Vinifera firm since Repeal, is a 54-acre, 8,000-case winery. The owners pioneered Vinifera grapes in the Willamette Valley, and have established a reputation for Pinot Noir (often superb), Chardonnay, Muscat Ottonel, Pinot Gris, Pinot Blanc, and Pinot Meunier.

Tualatin Vineyards (Forest Grove, 1973), overlooking the Tualatin Valley (pronounced Tu-wai-a-tin, Indian for "gentle and easy flowing"), is an 85-acre, 34,000-case winery that makes above-average to excellent, estate-bottled Riesling, Gewurztraminer, Muller-Thurgau, Sauvignon Blanc, Flora, Chardonnay, Pinot Noir (all rich, full on the palate, robust, and well-balanced), and proprietary wines. The flawlessly made wines are known for flavor and fragrance, offering excellent value.

Tyee Wine Cellars (Corvallis, 1985), is a 6-acre, 3,500-case, much improved winery that makes Gewurztraminer, Chardonnay, Pinot Gris, Pinot Blanc, and Pinot Noir.

Van Duzer Winery (Willamette Valley, 1989), is a 900-acre property (an undisclosed number are currently in the planting stage), 20,000-case label that makes Chardonnay, Riesling, and Pinot Noir (the first two in the Napa Valley, and the latter in a neighboring winery in the Willamette Valley). The property and label is owned by William Hill and partners of Napa County. A winery is planned for the 1994 crush.

Veritas Vineyard (Newberg, 1983), is a 26-acre, 6,500-case winery with an emphasis on estate-produced Chardonnay, Muller-Thurgau, Pinot Gris, Riesling, and Pinot Noir, all impeccably made, offering good value.

Viento Wines (Rickreall, 1986), is a 1,600-case label that makes Riesling, Coteaux de Viento (a white table wine made from Pinot Noir and Chardonnay), and sparkling wines: Cuvee R, an Extra Dry Riesling, and Viento Brut, made from Pinot Noir and Chardonnay.

Willamette Valley Vineyards (Turner, 1989), is a new, 25-acre, 16,000-case, publicly traded corporation that makes Chardonnay, Riesling, Gewurztraminer, Pinot Noir, and Cabernet Sauvignon.

Windy Ridge (Tigard, 1988), with an output of more than 50,000 cases (one of the largest in the state) it makes Riesling and Cabernet Sauvignon, and large quantities of sparkling wine under the *Northwest Cuvee* label. Half of total output is custom crushed for other wineries and labels. The winery was sold in 1990, and is in the process of being relocated in a joint venture with a microbrewery. Other label: *Alder Creek*.

Witness Tree Vineyards (Salem, 1987), is a 35-acre, 4,000-case winery that makes yeasty, well flavored Chardonnay and Pinot Noir.

Placing support stakes at Yamhill Valley Vineyards. Baxevanis

Yamhill Valley Vineyards (McMinnville, 1983), is a stylish and aggressive, 100-acre, 15,000-case winery with an emphasis on estate-bottled Riesling, Muller-Thurgau, Pinot Gris, Chardonnay, and Pinot Noir (big and well-structured, it is one of the finest in the state), all offering good value.

The Columbia River Region

The Oregon portion of the *Columbia Valley ava*, located on the lee side of the Cascades, stretches east from Hood River to Boardman, and includes the important Hood River fruit producing region, and the nation's leading wind surfing area. This remarkable stretch of 160 miles contains a vast array of stunning topographic features rarely matched. While the Willamette Valley is verdant and naturally productive, Oregon's Columbia River region is hotter by day, cooler by night, considerably drier, and the vineyards are found in river valleys that cut through semi-desertic country and must be irrigated. The dense, dark grey, fine-grained basalt rocks overlain by potassium-rich soils, the higher elevation, increased illumination, large diurnal temperature swings, and higher yields make this region a major future growth area for the state. Although there are only six wineries in this portion of the *ava*, the potential for large-scale grape production has not gone unnoticed. Boardman Farms, a large 8,500-acre ranch, cultivates 450 acres of grapes (nearly 10 percent of the states total), mainly in Riesling, Chardonnay, Merlot, Cabernet Sauvignon, Chenin Blanc, and Pinot Noir. This semi-arid region produces excellent quality grapes, particularly the hitherto-underrated Cabernet Sauvignon. It is interesting to note that a good deal of the present stock (including Zinfandel) dates back to 1917 when the Sam Hill family (of the Great Northern Railway) planted a vineyard.

The five wineries are: **Hood River Vineyards** (Hood River, 1981), is a 12-acre, 4,000-case winery that makes average to excellent Gewurztraminer, Riesling, Chardonnay, Sauvignon Blanc, Pinot Noir, Cabernet Sauvignon, a rare Zinfandel, proprietary, and fruit and berry wines. **La Casa de Vin** (Boardman, 1982), is a 9-acre, 2,100-case winery that makes good, sound Riesling, Zinfandel, Chardonnay, Cabernet Sauvignon, Pinot Noir, and raspberry wines. The winery closed in 1989, but there are signs that it might be resurrected. **Rivercrest Farms** (Boardman, 1990), is the winery for the states largest vineyard (Boardman Farms), a 450-acre, 30,000-case, capacity bulk wine facility. **Seven Hills Winery** (Milton-Freewater, 1988), located just south of Walla Walla in Washington, but within the *ava*, is a 30-acre, 2,500-case winery that makes excellent Chardonnay, Sauvignon Blanc, Merlot, and Cabernet Sauvignon, all offering good value. **Three Rivers Winery** (Hood River, 1986), is a 5-acre, 4,500-case winery that makes Gewurztraminer, Riesling, Chardonnay, and Pinot Noir. **Wasson Brothers Winery** (Sandy, 1982), located on the slopes of Mt. Hood, is an excellent, 13-acre, 4,000-case winery that makes fresh and distinctive Pinot Noir, Gewurztraminer, Muscat Blanc, Riesling, as well as fruit and berry wines.

The Umpqua Valley

Interrupting Oregon's Coastal Ranges are several minor valley lowlands drained by small streams that empty into the Pacific Ocean. Because of their east-west direction, they are known as "cross valleys," of which the Umpqua and Rogue are the most important. The *Umpqua Valley ava* (1984), with 768,000 agricultural acres, 500 acres of vineland and nine wineries, is a highly promising viticultural region. Centered around the city of Roseboro are the "Hundred Valleys" of the Umpqua Valley (due to the meandering nature of the North and South Umpqua), a comparatively humid region where Riesling, Gewurztraminer, Sauvignon Blanc, Semillon, Cabernet Sauvignon, and Merlot are the mainstays, and not Pinot Noir--a rare occurrence in a state where Pinot Noir reigns supreme.

This divergent pattern is due entirely to climate. While summer temperatures are higher, spring weather is much cooler, and fall is significantly drier than the Willamette Valley to the north. The growing season is 217 days and the area enjoys one of the lowest wind velocities anywhere in the nation. The Umpqua Valley is composed of the lowlands of Douglas County sandwiched between the Cascade and Coastal Ranges, and the Klamath Mountains. Within this sparsely populated, scenic and tranquil county the value of grape and wine production ranks third after forest products and nursery output. The best sites contain soils derived from volcanic and sedimentary rocks located on hillsides often as high as 1,000 feet in elevation. Winemaking dates back to the early 1880s when two German brothers planted vines and made wine.

The principal wineries are: **Callahan Ridge Winery** (Roseboro, 1987), located on the original site of Garden Valley Winery, is an aggressive, 5-acre, 7,000-case winery that makes distinctive Chardonnay, Gewurztraminer (dry and sweet), Sauvignon Blanc/Semillon, Cabernet Sauvignon, Zinfandel, Pinot Noir, and Riesling (dry, sweet, and a superb individual select berry wine called *Vinum Aureolum*). **Davidson Winery** (Tenmile, 1969), formerly Bjelland Vineyards, is an 8-acre, 3,000-case winery that makes Riesling, , Chardonnay, Cabernet Sauvignon, and Pinot Noir. **Girardet Wine Cellars** (Roseburg, 1983), is a well-managed, 19-acre, 8,000-case winery that makes outstanding, distinctive, and highly complex Riesling, Gewurztraminer, Chardonnay, Pinot Noir, Sauvignon Blanc, Cabernet Sauvignon, and proprietary wines (an interesting mixture of Vinifera and French-American varietals), all supple and affordable. **Hillcrest Vineyard** (Roseburg, 1963), the oldest and one of the largest wineries of southern Oregon, is a 35-acre, 18,500-case winery that makes above-average quality Riesling (both dry and sweet), Gewurztraminer, Chardonnay, Semillon, Sauvignon Blanc, Pinot Noir, Zinfandel, Cabernet Sauvignon, and proprietary wines. **La Garza Cellars** (Roseburg, 1975), formerly Jonicole Vineyards, is a 16-acre, 4,500-case winery that makes Chardonnay and Cabernet Sauvignon. **Lookingglass Winery** (Looking Glass, 1988), is a rapidly expanding, 8-acre, 2,800-case winery that makes supple, low alcohol Riesling, Sauvignon Blanc, Pinot Noir, and Cabernet Sauvignon. **S.C.S. Cellars** (Roseburg, 1985), is a small winery that makes 2,000 cases of cooler wine under the *Bachelor* label mainly from California grapes and wine. **Scott Henry's Winery** (Umpqua, 1978), is a 31-acre, 12,500-case winery that makes average quality Gewurztraminer, Riesling, Chardonnay, Muller-Thurgau, Cabernet Sauvignon, Pinot Noir, sparkling, and proprietary wines under the *Henry Estate Winery* label. The reserve Chardonnay is excellent. **Umpqua River Vineyards** (Roseburg, 1988), is an unusual, 20-acre, 4,500-case winery that makes only wood-aged Cabernet Sauvignon, Cabernet Franc, and supple, fresh Semillon, Gewurztraminer, and Sauvignon Blanc.

Medford-Grants Pass Region

The Medford-Grants Pass area, of which the Applegate, Bear Creek, and Illinois River valleys are the most important, is the southernmost and smallest of Oregon's viticultural regions. These broad glacial valleys, green with extensive grazing, and warmer than the Willamette Valley to the north, have long supported orchards, particularly for pear production. With less than 15 inches of precipitation, irrigation is routinely practiced and grape varieties are mainly red, not white, unlike the rest of the state. The soils in all three river valleys, a mixture of glacial and alluvial origins, consist of thick beds of rock and gravel (the Illinois Valley in particular). It is also interesting to note that winegrowing is an old activity dating back to the middle of the nineteenth century. Ashland, for example, grew and shipped Flame Tokay grapes before Lodi, California.

Although Medford is the largest city in southern Oregon, this rapidly growing region is dominated and focused on the beautiful, historic, and tourist-oriented city of Ashland. Founded in 1852, the city contains a disproportionate number of structures on the National Historic Register, recreational parks, Mt. Ashland, and proximity to Crater Lake. The region's seven wineries are strategically located to take advantage of the tourist trade. Long considered "Oregon's outback viticultural region," this area in recent years has produced several excellent wineries, some of which are quite consistent and reliable.

In February of 1991, BATF granted Oregon its latest *ava-Rogue Valley*, an irregular area that straddles Jackson and Josephine counties. Although the *ava* applies to areas as high as 2,800 feet in elevation, the *ava* is the warmest (Region II and III) and the area with more sunshine during the harvest season of any other Oregon *ava*, thus a prime area for the production of Cabernet Sauvignon, Cabernet Franc, and Merlot. The *ava*, with more than 15,000 potential acres, has 500 planted vine acres, and growing.

The wineries are: **Ashland Vineyards and Winery** (Ashland, 1988), located in the extreme southern portion of the state, this 13-acre, 4,500-case winery makes soft, supple, almost flat Chardonnay, Sauvignon Blanc, Muller-Thurgau, Cabernet Sauvignon, and Pinot Noir. **Bridgeview Winery** (Cave Junction, 1986), is one of the newest, largest, and one of the most aggressive and innovative southern Oregon wineries. It has 74 established acres and is expected to make by 1992 more than 40,000 cases of Chardonnay, Riesling, Pinot Gris, Gewurztraminer, Muller-Thurgau, and Pinot Noir. **Foris Vineyards** (Cave Junction, 1986), is an aggressive, 95-acre, 10,500-case winery that makes excellent Gewurztraminer, Chardonnay, Early Muscat, Pinot Noir, Merlot, Cabernet Sauvignon, and proprietary wines, all offering good value. **Rogue River Vineyards** (Grants Pass, 1983), is a 4-acre, 7,500-case winery that makes, in addition to fruit wines, Riesling, Chardonnay, Gewurztraminer, Pinot Noir, Cabernet Sauvignon, and proprietary wines. **Siskiyou Vineyards** (Cave Junction, 1978), located in the scenic Illinois Valley, is a 14-acre, 7,000-case winery that makes Chardonnay, Muller-Thurgau, Riesling, Sauvignon Blanc, Pinot Noir, Zinfandel, Merlot, Cabernet Sauvignon, and proprietary wines. **Valley View Vineyards** (Jacksonville, 1976), is a 26-acre, 10,000-case winery located 1,500-feet high in the fog-free "sunshine Applegate Valley" that makes excellent proprietary, Chardonnay, Sauvignon Blanc, Riesling, Merlot, and Cabernet Sauvignon, the latter two among the finest wines of the northwest. The wines from this underrated winery should not be missed. **Weisinger's of Ashland Winery & Vineyard** (Ashland, 1988), is a 6-acre, 4,000-case winery that makes clean, fresh, excellent Gewurztraminer, Chardonnay, Sauvignon Blanc, Cabernet Sauvignon, Pinot Noir, late harvest Riesling, and proprietary red wine named *Mescolare*. This is the southernmost, and, at an elevation of 2,100 feet, the highest winery in the state.

Idaho

Idaho, the "Gem" state, is unusual among its two northwest neighbors: the first influx of settlers came from the west and not from the east; it produces only two important agricultural crops (potatoes and sugar beets) with a national ranking; its population is less than that of metropolitan Portland; it leads the nation in silver production, is second in lead, and third in zinc output. Because Lewis and Clark crossed the region in 1805, permanent settlement in small, measured amounts did not occur until the late 1850s when several Mormon families began farming in the Snake River with the mistaken belief that they were in Utah. With the discovery of gold in the 1860s, however, miners and subsequent ranchers began to arrive in large numbers, with statehood achieved in 1890. However, large-scale, effective settlement did not arrive until major irrigation systems were introduced and developed after 1950. While most towns contain fewer than 1,000 inhabitants, nearly the whole of the state's 1 million, youthful population lies within a 40-mile stretch from Boise to Pocatello within the Snake River Valley.

The name Idaho is derived from the Indian description of the spectacular sunrise effects when the higher elevations are colored pink and gold while the lower valleys are in darkness, an accurate portrayal of a forbidding, isolated, mountainous country. Devoid of geographic unity, and so inhospitable and prohibitive was this region to the early settlers, it was first known as the "Columbia River Country," was part of the "Oregon Country" after 1820, and after the establishment of the "Oregon Territory" in 1848 Idaho's territorial boundaries were changed five times during the next seventeen years. As a result, Idaho was reduced to its present strange, irrational, nonfunctional configuration.

Lying entirely west of the Continental Divide, Idaho is a mountainous state with extreme local reliefs (the deepest canyon in the nation is found here), mainly semi-arid (with large contiguous stands of forest in high elevations), and highly fragmented, with only a small stretch of the Snake River containing any appreciable amounts of level land, the rest of the state being appallingly hilly and mountainous. Due to the nature of the terrain, climatic change is rather dramatic, every few miles creating an unusual scenograph with abandoned mines, allied ghost towns, and modern, large-scale irrigated farms (10 percent of the total land area).

Embracing rugged mountain ranges, canyons, high grassy valleys, arid plains, and fertile lowlands, Idaho reflects in its topography and vegetation an expansive range of climatic patterns. Although it is located 300 miles from the Pacific Ocean, Idaho is, nevertheless, influenced by westerly maritime air masses. These rain bearing air masses, most frequent in winter, produce greater amounts of precipitation, a higher incidence of cloudiness, and mean temperatures that are above those at the same latitude and altitude further eastward. However, Idaho lies in the rain shadow of the coastal and interior mountain ranges to the west, and, as a result, precipitation in valley locations is less than 15 inches, a dramatic contrast to upland areas that receive more than 40 inches. The highest annual temperature averages are found in the lower elevations of the Clearwater and Little Salmon River Basins, and in portions of the Snake River Valley, including the ancillary valleys of the Boise, Payette, and Weiser Rivers. The Lewiston area in the northern portion of the state, with 200 days, has the longest growing season, while the southern valleys of the Snake, Boise, Payette and Weiser vary between 150 and 190 days. Periodically, however, winter temperatures can plummet to -25F, as in December 1990, and, as a result, the entire state produced fewer than 2,000 gallons of wine the following year.

Idaho offers several advantages for the production of quality wines. As nearly the entire state lies above 3,000 feet in elevation, it has a rarefied, brilliant, and cloudless atmosphere, less than 12 inches of rainfall, sharp diurnal temperature extremes, a near absence of viral and bacterial diseases, excellent air drainage, well-drained, calcific soils, and low vineyard costs. Commercial grape-growing and winemaking began in 1976 with the founding of Ste. Chapelle, the states only winery until 1981 when Weston Winery was founded, and from these ignoble beginnings, the state now has ten wineries. While the industry has a modern frontier flavor, Vinifera grapes were produced throughout the fourth quarter of the nineteenth century only to disappear with Prohibition. The last winery to cease operations was the Gregory Eaves Winery in Lewiston in 1945. Unlike most states, Idaho wineries exhibit a high degree of instability with many financial failures and corporate takeovers.

Grape acreage, standing around 800, is growing by 40 acres annually, all located along the Snake River from Boise to Ontario, Oregon, particularly in a small section called "Treasure Valley" (because of high yields), and, to a smaller extent, the Clearwater Valley in the northern portion of the state. Because there were fewer than 10 acres of Vinifera plantings in 1967, and the first winery did not crush until 1976, this is rather remarkable progress in a state with only 1 million people. Vine acreage is expected to continue increasing despite opposition from the alcohol-abstaining Mormon community because 25 acres of grapes give the same financial return as 200 acres of wheat. Winemakers are projecting wine output to rise from the current 350,000 gallons to more than 2 million gallons by the year 2000.

The two largest vinegrowing regions are the Snake River and the Clearwater area. The Snake River, very similar to the Columbia River, is much higher in elevation

(2,500 feet) and significantly colder, thus the presence of greater annual temperature extremes, and a perennial danger from frost. Despite these environmental dangers, the Snake River region is the center of nearly all grape acreage (Sunny Slope, near Caldwell, contains 600 of the state's 800 acres), a position that will hold for some time. The Clearwater region, lying along the lee side of the Palouse Hills, also appears to be a good vinegrowing area, especially near Lewiston where the Clearwater enters the Snake River (2,600 degree days and an 180-day growing season). Both the Clearwater and Snake rivers have hot summer days and cool nights, a condition that lingers for a particularly long time during the last 50 days of the growing season. What makes these regions remarkable is their microclimate: from April to October average temperature is higher than any other *ava* in California except Fresno and Cucamonga. Not only are temperatures ideal, but direct sunshine is especially high assuring perfect grape ripening with good sugar/acid levels. In the face of these interesting and favorable physical features, it might just be possible for Idaho grapes, in the future, to generate a reputation equal to the famous potato.

Due to the cool climate Idaho is white wine country. The three principal grape varieties with consistent track records are Riesling, Chardonnay, and Chenin Blanc, all crisp, intensely flavored and scented, and often elegant. Although quality levels are reliably high, weather variability can interfere with ripening, and acid and sugar levels are less than ideal when compared with those of neighboring Washington. Chardonnay, in particular, is known for its crisp but austere flavor, the latter not necessarily considered a negative feature. Riesling and Chenin Blanc, usually made with some residual sugar, are delicately scented, well-flavored, and the equal of any in the nation. Two other grapes with some measure of success are Gewurztraminer (dry and crisp), and Pinot Noir (for use in blush and sparkling wine production). Although Semillon does not enjoy the celebrity of Riesling, Chardonnay, and Chenin Blanc, it is considered above-average as a quality wine grape, and acreage is expected to increase.

In addition to **Seven Sisters**, an apple winery located in Bonners Ferry, the grape wineries are: **Camas Winery** (Moscow, 1983), is an interesting, innovative, 1,600-case winery that makes above-average to excellent, soft Chardonnay, Riesling and Cabernet Sauvignon from purchased Washington State grapes. It also makes an interesting Cabernet Sauvignon/Gewurztraminer blush, and a proprietary *Hog Heaven Red* made from Cabernet Sauvignon and cherry wine. The name of the winery is derived from the Blue Camas bulb, a favorite hog food. **Cana Vineyards** (Wilder, 1990), is a 6-acre, 1,500-case winery that makes Riesling and proprietary wines. **Carmela Winery** (Glenns Ferry, 1990), is a 60-acre, 3,000-case winery that makes above-average, supple, yet well-structured Chardonnay, Muscat Blanc, Merlot, and proprietary wines. **Chapelle USA** (Caldwell, 1976), with 203 acres (sited at 2,500 feet above sea level) and an annual output of more than 120,000 cases, this winery is the largest in the state and the fourth largest in the northwest tri-state region. In the past it made more than 20 different wines, of which more than 90 percent were white. It buys most of its

grape requirements from the Symms Fruit Ranch, manages 500 additional acres in Sunny Slope, and 50 acres in neighboring Washington. Chardonnay, Chenin Blanc, Sauvignon Blanc, Gewurztraminer, Riesling, Merlot, Pinot Noir, Cabernet Sauvignon, late harvest, and proprietary wines are consistently well-made and often offer outstanding value. The winery is also one of the leading producers in the northwest of a large and interesting line of sparkling wines. Reserve wines (Chardonnay and sweet wines) are particularly good. Because the state has a small population and no tradition in the production and consumption of wines, the success of this winery as one of the top 100 American wineries is a remarkable achievement. The wines are marketed under the *Ste. Chapelle Winery* label named after a historic and famous church in Paris, France. **Cocollala Winery** (Athol, 1987), located in the northern portion of the state, is a 2,500-case winery that makes sparkling wine (secondary fermentation and aging occurs in an old abandoned silver mine) from Washington State grapes. Table wines are custom-crushed in a Washington winery. **Hells Canyon Winery** (Caldwell, 1980), formerly Covey Rise, is a consumer friendly, 5-acre, 1,000-case winery that only makes barrel-fermented Chardonnay, offering good value. The winery is named after the deepest canyon in America. **Pintler Cellar** (Nampa, 1988), formerly Desert Sun Winery, is a 19-acre, 6,000-case winery (part of a large 1,600-acre farm) that makes rich, ripe, and complex Chardonnay, Riesling, Chenin Blanc, Semillon (dry and late harvest), Cabernet Sauvignon, Pinot Noir, and proprietary wines. **Valley Vintners** (Hagerman, 1984), is an outstanding, small, but expanding, 35-acre, 10,000-case winery that makes distinctive, well-balanced, meaty Chardonnay, Riesling, Pinot Noir, Cabernet Sauvignon, Merlot, and proprietary wines under the *Rose Creek Vineyards* label. The Cabernet Sauvignon can often be sensational. **Weston Winery** (Caldwell, 1981), is a 14-acre (sited at 2,750 feet above sea level), 5,000-case winery that makes attractively priced Chardonnay (full-bodied, crisp, and well-balanced), Riesling, Sauvignon Blanc, Gewurztraminer, Cabernet Sauvignon, Pinot Noir, and sparkling Riesling. **William Neville Stowe Winery** (Kuna, 1987), is a 18-acre, 5,500-case winery that makes well-balanced Riesling, Chardonnay, Semillon, Chenin Blanc, Pinot Noir, and Cabernet Sauvignon under the *Indian Creek Winery* label. The winery also grows and makes varietal wine from French-American grapes (Chelois and Interlaken).

A superb, well-aged, botrytized Riesling in the Yakima Valley. Baxevanis

VIII
THE WINES OF CALIFORNIA

Say what you will, California is geographically, culturally, and economically disparate in practically every respect from the rest of the world. Even its name is an unusual interpretation of human events. California first appeared in a novel written by Garcia Ordonez de Montalvo, published in Seville, Spain in 1510, and officially appeared in a document dated July 2, 1542 in the diary of Juan Rodriguez Cabrillo, the first Spanish naval explorer of California. Unlike any other, five flags have flown over this remarkable state: Spanish, British, Russian, Mexican, and American. California is a state as well as a country, and its immensity, diversity, and distinctiveness set it apart from the rest of the nation. Although Texans usually exaggerate size and dimension, it is in California that we find the largest continuous mountain range (Sierra Nevada), the tallest and largest trees (Redwood and Sequoia), the deepest valley (Death Valley), highest waterfalls (Yosemite), tallest mountain in coterminous America (Mt. Whitney), and the largest city in terms of land area (Los Angeles). The superlatives abound, and, in many ways, the state expresses the coming events of the next century.

California, a state of 158,786 square miles, is larger than Italy, Japan, the United Kingdom, and three times the size of New York. In a state where history is skin-deep and two-thirds of the population not native-born, California is a remarkable man-made, geographic entity. It boasts the finest of everything--climate, trees, agriculture, bridges, surfboards, motion movies, hot tubs, spa cuisine, and half the nation's backyard swimming pools, among other real and dubious achievements. The state, the third largest in the nation in terms of land area, is the largest in population, value of agricultural product, and grape and wine production. It has been called an unstratified society--one that is highly mobile, uprooted, and unfocused. The state's population, overwhelmingly youthful, grows by 200,000 migrants annually, and is second to New Jersey in the percent of residents urbanized. It ranks first in the nation in economic output, and if California were an independent country, it would rank as the world's fifth largest nation in GNP, and with but 4 percent of its population it produces the same number of goods and services as India.

Viticulture plays a prominent economic role in the state and the nation. With 700,000 acres of vineland, the state produces more than 5 million tons of grapes, or 90 percent of the nation's total output, and a similar percentage of wine whose retail value is estimated to be more than $7 billion. Over the past 20 years California has produced 68-75 percent of all wine consumed in America, with imports accounting for 15-25 percent, the remainder coming from New York and other states. With more than 820 bonded wineries, the state also contains about half the nation's total, including nine of the ten largest. California, with more than 40 million gallons, is the nation's leading exporter of wine. In addition, California is responsible for more than 99 percent of the nation's table grape and raisin output. The dominance in grape and wine production becomes even more significant because nearly all grapes are Vinifera. In a report prepared for The National Wine Coalition, Steve L. Barbsby & Associates reports that the grape and wine industry directly and indirectly contribute nearly 120,000 jobs and more than $9 billion in sales to the state economy. Yet despite its domestic dominance, California produces just 4 percent of the world's total and ranks fifth among principal international wine producers.

CALIFORNIA'S ROLE IN THE U.S. WINE MARKET

1. From 1980 to 1990 California wine production averaged 420 million gallons per year, accounting for slightly more than 90% of wine produced in the United States.

2. California's total share of the U.S. wine market reached 73% in 1990, and averaged 71.8% annually during the past five years. The remainder is nearly equally divided between imports and production from other states.

3. California wine shipments to all markets have grown from 338.7 million gallons in 1980 to 390.4 million gallons in 1990. Nearly all was shipped to the U.S. market; exports are still a minor factor, although 6% of California wine is shipped abroad. In 1990, the value of U.S. wine exports increased to $124.9 million from $29.8 million in 1980. California is the leader in wine exports, providing 90% of wine shipped overseas.

4. The California wine industry continues to exhibit change: (a) Many small wineries have emerged during the past decade. There were just over 470 bonded winery premises in California in 1980, and more than 800 in 1992. (b) The varietal composition of winegrape acreage has undergone a great change, with a much higher percentage of the acreage now consisting of varieties that are most suitable for the production of quality table wines. For example, in 1980 California had 17,000 acres of Chardonnay grapes; in 1990 there were 52,150 acres. For Cabernet Sauvignon, the totals were 22,800 acres in 1980 compared to 33,200 acres in 1990. Chardonnay and Cabernet Sauvignon grapes represented only 14% of the value of grapes crushed in California in 1980; in 1990, the same two varieties accounted for 43% of the total.

5. The estimated retail value of the wines shipped by California wineries in 1990 exceeded $7 billion.
Source: The Wine Institute.

Most important, with distinct viticultural patterns on the economic and cultural landscape, California differs from the rest of the country in many significant ways: (1) a distinct, Mediterranean climate; (2) the largest area of vine acreage and wine production; (3) most viticultural districts are clearly defined; (4) vine density within the viticultural areas is clustered and not diffusive; (5) grape wine dominates unlike other regions where fruit and berry wines compose a much larger share of total wine production; (6) nearly all wine originates within the state, unlike other states that "ameliorate;" (7) due to a combination of environmental factors, grape yields are much higher than most states; (8) high consistency of final product, hence a considerable loyalty for California wine in most national markets; (9) average bottle price is higher due to consistent quality, and (10) the dominance of Vinifera grapes.

HISTORY

The "boom and bust" character of California winemaking began in 1778-1779 when Father Junipero Serra planted grapevines in the first mission established in San Diego. Over the next 54 years an additional 20 missions were constructed as far north as Sonoma, each one making sacramental wine for mass and table wine for the neighboring ranches. The dominant grape planted was the Mission, a grape of undetermined origin, also known as the Los Angeles grape, and thought to be related to Malaga. Winemaking, however, was limited because records indicate that the largest wine producing mission (San Gabriel) was only making 50,000 gallons in 1830. The Franciscan missions, connected by El Camino Real, or the "Kings Highway," also introduced the olive and fig, as well as many more Mediterranean crops.

An American, Joseph Chapman, planted a vineyard in 1824 in Los Angeles, and was soon followed by William Wolfskill. The first commercial, non-Spanish wine was first made in 1837 (in Los Angeles) by a Frenchman, Jean Louis Vignes, an energetic cooper, grower, vintner, and nurseryman who did much to foster winemaking in the Los Angeles area. By the mid-1830s Mexican economic policies could not be sufficiently enforced, secularization expanded, Spanish culture weakened, and the missions were abandoned. As population expanded northward from the San Diego-Los Angeles region, viticulture slowly expanded from the southern portions of the state to the San Francisco Bay counties and the Sierra Foothills during the gold rush. In Sacramento County, the celebrated Captain John Sutter pressed his first vintage in 1841, Henry Thomann established a vineyard in 1852, Jacob Knauth received a prize in 1861, and Jacob Routier planted a 30-acre vineyard about 1864. Wine production grew rapidly from 3,967 gallons in 1860 to 170,369 gallons by 1870, a remarkable achievement for the times in a county whose population was less than 35,000.

Much of the success of Californian viticulture was the result of Count Agoston Haraszthy, one of the most celebrated personalities of the nineteenth century. Coming to the United States in 1840 as a political refugee, he settled in Wisconsin where he founded a town. He subsequently established a steamboat line, a sawmill, a gristmill, and a brickyard. He dealt in livestock, grain, operated a general store, wrote a book, and is credited with the introduction

of sheep and hops to Wisconsin. In 1849 he went to San Diego where he farmed 160 acres, founded a town (now part of San Diego where Haraszthy Street still stands), and was sheriff of San Diego County. Shortly thereafter he became a member of the state legislature. In 1852 he moved to San Francisco where he became a smelter for the United States mint, engaged in land speculation, and in 1856 or 1857 purchased 560 acres in Sonoma Valley. By 1864 his land holdings grew to 6,000 acres, of which 400 were planted in vines. In 1861 he advocated the establishment of a state agricultural school, and in 1868 one was authorized for Berkeley. His crowning achievements were the founding of Buena Vista, the introduction of better wine grape varieties, and the success of his propaganda efforts that stimulated a wine boom affecting half the counties in the state (between 1856 and 1862, the number of vines in the state grew from 1.3 million to 10.5 million).

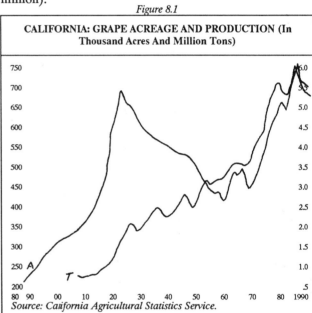

Figure 8.1

CALIFORNIA: GRAPE ACREAGE AND PRODUCTION (In Thousand Acres And Million Tons)

Source: California Agricultural Statistics Service.

Vineland had spread northward from Los Angeles to the Sierra Foothills, the hill portions of the Central Valley, and throughout the Bay county region. North of San Francisco, Haraszthy was preceded by General Mariano Vallejo, one of the more enlightened and egregious Spaniards in northern California. Not only did he purchase the abandoned Sonoma Mission vineyards in 1834, but in the process he maintained viticultural endeavors along the northern fringes of civilized California. The 1850s and 1860s also attracted such venerable personalities as Jacob Gundlach, George Yount, William Hood, Emil Dresel, Isaac De Turk, Charles Krug, Jacob Schram, the Beringer brothers, W. C. Watson, and others.

As Spanish settlement proceeded in a northward direction, it is strange to note that the viticultural landscape as an expression of the expanding ecumene was not widespread. Despite the Spaniards penchant for grape cultivation and winemaking, there are few place names describing grape-growing. There is a *Vina* in Tehama, Leland Stanford's *Vina*, *Las Vinas* in the San Joaquin, *Uvas Valley*, and *Arroyo de la Vina* in Santa Barbara, but little else. With the approach of Anglo-Saxon culture, toponyms associated with grape culture became more numerous, of which *Vineburg* in Sonoma, *Vineyard* in Los Angeles, and *Vine Hill* in Contra Costa County are among the most prominent.

Table 8.1

CALIFORNIA GRAPE ACREAGE, 1887			
County	Total Grapes	Wine	Table	Raisin
Alameda	6,826	6,396	236	194
Amador				
Butte	781	111	66	605
Calaveras	404	404		
Colusa	423	24	28	371
Contra Costa	3,142	2,085	975	82
El Dorado	1,512	1,019	370	123
Fresno	49,500	5,574		43,926
Inyo	53	13	31	9
Kern	1,200			1,200
Lake	1,061	1,046	15	
Los Angeles	4,695	4,632	40	23
Marin	502	477	25	
Mendocino	204	190	14	
Merced	1,846	425		1,421
Monterey				
Napa	18,229	18,177	52	
Nevada	220	190	30	
Orange	144	140		4
Placer	2,285	354	1,431	500
Sacramento	4,630	3,131	1,164	335
San Benito	175	140	35	
San Bernardino	3,615	1,024		2,591
San Diego	4,627	132	40	4,455
San Joaquin	1,246	900	346	
San Luis Obispo	471	437	33	1
San Mateo	789	748	26	15
Santa Barbara	270	260	10	
Santa Clara	11,523	10,294	1,126	103
Santa Cruz	1,684	1,365	319	
Shasta	468	122	104	241
Solano	3,527	1,928	1,167	432
Sonoma	22,683	22,351	332	
Stanislaus	619	82	13	524
Sutter	370	38	47	285
Tehama	4,012	3,705	80	227
Tulare	9,919	70		9,849
Tuolumne				
Ventura	320	100	23	197
Yolo	3,700	1,575	1,000	1,125
Yuba	693	570	123	
Total	168,366	90,228	9,300	68,838

Source: California Department of Agriculture. Enumeration is reported as partial or incomplete.

The wine industry, healthy and vibrant throughout the post-gold rush period, experienced a major boom during 1867-1875 when wine production doubled in an effort to export wine to phylloxera-infested France. Once the dreaded louse came under control, wine exports dropped, and the euphoria of high prices eventually ended with over production and sheer panic as phylloxera also struck California. The wine glut of the 1870s turned to scarcity ten years later as the demand for wine and grape cuttings far exceeded supply. Vine plantings grew rapidly to 50,000 acres in 1880 (70 percent of which were Mission), and by 1890 there were more than 256,000 acres. The number of growers rose to 6,000, wine production to 5 million gallons in 1878, 8 million in 1881, and 18 million by 1886. Some of the pioneers during this period were Leland Stanford, George Hearst, General Henry Nagle, William Bowers, and Elias Baldwin. The planting boom of 1880-

1885 eventually resulted in overproduction so that by 1888-1895 another crisis developed, a condition that prompted a switch from wine to raisin grapes, and a dependency on shipments to other states. Although California wine was shipped to midwestern and eastern markets as early as the 1860s, the momentum began to quicken early in the 1880s, increasing from 31 percent of total production in 1882 to 88 percent of production by 1895.

Table 8.2

CALIFORNIA: VITICULTURAL FEATURES, 1899			
County	Value of Grapes	Number of Vines	Pounds of Grapes	Gallons of Wine
Alameda	145,276	3,549,414	15,750,000	453,094
Amador	13,972	448,502	1,567,800	13,066
Butte	19,435	227,799	1,369,800	5,218
Calaveras	1,196	67,980	154,800	26,680
Colusa	12,146	236,812	1,784,000	700
Contra Costa	150,891	2,400,257	13,622,500	83,621
El Dorado	13,196	704,702	1,767,200	49,597
Fresno	2,007,355	24,904,559	274,233,500	622,576
Glenn	5,046	105,610	411,300	1,816
Humboldt	684	6,780	58,000	935
Inyo	4,478	51,570	252,400	1,151
Kern	10,240	265,537	1,454,600	6,560
Kings	433,216	4,218,824	58,572,800	
Lake	6,397	233,614	1,318,400	14,635
Los Angeles	127,459	2,884,144	18,037,900	93,405
Madera	91,008	1,483,354	15,537,800	240
Marin	10,830	161,806	1,689,500	24,560
Mariposa	1,300	34,660	108,000	2,767
Mendocino	7,767	238,547	1,055,600	23,190
Merced	20,181	429,645	2,687,200	86,093
Modoc	5	42	200	40
Mono	28	1,240	2,000	
Monterey	1,749	81,203	213,600	5,908
Napa	174,451	4,859,490	19,844,200	407,612
Nevada	4,819	155,772	446,100	11,253
Orange	27,736	621,428	3,708,300	31,778
Placer	65,648	816,983	5,746,800	16,631
Riverside	17,899	603,010	2,448,300	2,720
Sacramento	308,799	3,639,513	29,073	11,962
San Benito	7,874	84,246	944,500	2,310
San Bernardino	90,573	1,752,046	12,672,200	69,530
San Diego	73,829	1,420,060	8,251,600	33,850
San Francisco	1,975	37,600	176,300	5,000
San Joaquin	149,172	2,346,061	18,016,300	55,864
San Luis Obispo	7,348	269,902	922,700	5,062
San Mateo	15,396	328,027	2,000,000	79,800
Santa Barbara	7,329	179,840	900,700	38,758
Santa Clara	306,331	7,103,402	36,311,800	975,895
Santa Cruz	60,448	1,385,422	7,063,700	160,843
Shasta	5,509	213,677	556,200	6,832
Siskiyou	747	12,969	91,400	250
Solano	85,077	1,042,477	6,991,200	250
Sonoma	667,844	15,004,458	94,476,900	1,198,716
Stanislaus	14,530	209,306	2,015,600	18,885
Sutter	18,678	148,187	2,186,100	12
Tehama	97,384	1,436,122	12,803,000	802,079
Trinity	3	24	200	
Tulare	200,883	2,473,308	27,174,500	200
Tuolumne	2,902	153,531	303,100	6,465
Ventura	5,442	1,408,196	12,957,800	2,963
Yolo	113,275	1,408,196	12,957,800	2,933
Yuba	7,034	112,570	935,000	1,065
Hupa Valley[1]		185		
Mission[1]	5	5,533	100	
Round Valley[1]		818		

[1]Indian Reservation
Source: California Agricultural Statistics Service

Despite today's grape acreage concentration in the San Joaquin Valley, viticultural endeavors were slow in developing until the latter half of the nineteenth century. Although Captain Charles Weber established the first vineyard, it was George West who created the first commercial vineyard and winery (El Pinal Vineyard near Stockton) in 1852. By 1888, only 4,000 acres devoted to vines were to be found in San Joaquin County. In 1854 George H. Krause established Red Mountain Vineyard in Stanislaus County. In neighboring Fresno County, Francis T. Eisen, the first grower and winemaker, started in 1873 and was making 250,000 gallons by 1885. Robert Barton started a Fresno winery in 1881. By the end of the century the desertic San Joaquin Valley, because of large scale irrigation with consequent high yields and lower relative severity from disease, became the prime grape-growing region.

The industry made a quick recovery after the conclusion of World War I, but suffered a fatal blow with the passage of the Volstead Act in 1919. It wiped out more than 600 wineries, and only a few survived (Almaden, Sebastiani, Beaulieu, and Beringer being among the more prominent) by producing sacramental wine. Although wineries closed their doors, acreage for all grapes (raisin, table, and wine) rose sharply as people created a market for home winemaking. Acreage rose from 361,404 in 1919 to 614,568 in 1928 on the eve of the Great Depression, and then fell sharply by 100,000 acres eight years later in 1936. If anything, Prohibition destroyed the finest vineyards in California as decline in wine quality was brought about by the abandonment of upland vineyards. With production overwhelmingly concentrated in the Central Valley, wine output shifted from table to inexpensive fortified libations. In demand were thick-skinned "juice" grapes, well-colored and able to withstand transcontinental shipping. Consequently, Mission, Alicante Bouschet, Carignane, and Zinfandel dominated acreage. Chicago, St. Louis, Detroit, Cleveland, Cincinnati, Boston, Philadelphia, and New York were the leading markets. Untaxed home made wine increased from 4 million gallons in 1915 to 90 million by 1925. Nearly all the wine was bad, produced by people with limited experience and ability who knew even less about quality grapes. The common varieties planted in the 1920s were not replaced in the Central Valley until the 1970s. Fine wine grapes were either grubbed up or grafted over by poor varieties. The result of this noble experiment was that after Repeal the "fine" wine market was dominated by imports, common grapes dominated acreage, and Americans, who consumed poor table wine during Prohibition, shifted to beer, cocktails, imported wines, and poorly-made domestic sweet wines.

Faced with declining demand, growers uprooted vines and planted prunes, walnuts, and other tree crops. Despite the reduced acreage, wine quality was below industry standards because the wrong varieties were planted, and the failure to harvest early and control fermentation temperatures meant spoiled and unstable wine that inhibited sales. This sad state of affairs continued into the next decade as the post-World War II period saw a dramatic downturn in all acreage, but primarily in wine grapes, as many returning soldiers and a post-War economic recovery created a demand for imported wine, not domestic. While table and raisin acreage has exhibited an erratic pattern since 1955, wine grape acreage, from a low of 125,000 acres in 1958-1959, has staged the most sensational sustained recovery of the three types of grapes,

reaching an all time high of 335,236 acres in 1990, and surpassing raisin grape acreage since 1972. Over the past 30 years, the number of wineries increased from 200 to 800 and wine production from 143 million gallons to 600 million gallons, one of the most spectacular agricultural increases of any commodity. Today California's wine industry is the epicenter of technological perfection making not only world class wines in every category, but the finest, most consistent, and value-laden *vin ordinaire*.

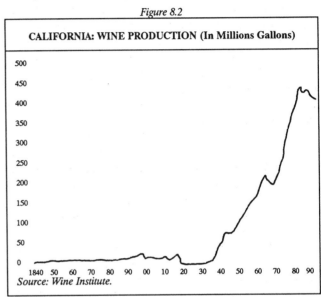

Figure 8.2

CALIFORNIA: WINE PRODUCTION (In Millions Gallons)

Source: Wine Institute.

The post-Repeal period, however, was not without major achievements as many legendary figures, such as the Mondavi brothers, Louis Martini, and August Sebastiani, among many others, began the development of what amounts to dynastic individual accomplishments under adverse conditions north of the Bay area. Amidst a flood of inexpensive jug, table, and fortified wine production, these individuals sensed an incipient demand for quality table wine, and began to fill this hitherto unmet domestic market niche by planting superior grape varieties, improving winemaking techniques, and introducing oakwood aging. Louis Martini built his winery in 1933; Buena Vista was resurrected in 1941; Martin Ray purchased Paul Masson's winery in 1943; the Mondavi family acquired the prostrate Charles Krug Winery in 1943; Souverain and Freemark Abbey were born in 1943; and Hanzell Vineyards revolutionized the boutique image in 1956. While coastal valleys attracted small, family-oriented wineries, the Central Valley was dominated by fewer than ten large wineries, of which the E. & J. Gallo facility at Modesto is the most celebrated. An incredible success story, the two Gallo brothers, Ernest and Julio, began as grape growers, but soon commenced making wine eventually creating a company pattern of internal growth that set industry standards for the next 60 years.

Not only did the post-Repeal period attract many energetic business people, growers and winemakers to the fledgling wine industry, but several governmental efforts offered stability and hope for the future. A 1938 program to distill surplus wine in order to stabilize prices proved a blessing amidst industry chaos and depression. Perhaps the most important development in the 1930s besides Repeal and wine price stabilization efforts was the transfer of the Viticulture and Enology Department from Berkeley to Davis. The Department, founded in 1880, has made over the past 50 years a series of incredible contributions. Not only does it matriculate about 200 students each fall in its degree programs (it also offers more than 1,000 seats in its many wine courses), but its contributions to viticultural practices, fermentation analysis, and development of new wine grape varieties are impossible to calculate. It is not an understatement when one hears that there have been more advances in viticulture and enology in the past 40 years at Davis than in the previous 5,000 years. Reflective of these significant developments, California shipments of wine per capita gradually increased from .26 gallons in 1934 to .67 in 1946, and 3.5 in 1990. Similarly, storage capacity increased threefold during 1934-1950, fourfold during the period 1941-1966, and fivefold during 1970-1990.

Table 8.3 illustrates the evolution of winery location for selected years. Forty-four counties contain wineries, of which more than half are located in Napa, Sonoma, Lake, and Mendocino. Napa County leads the list with 256, followed by Sonoma with 167, both of which account for nearly 50 percent of the total. Collectively they account for a relatively small percentage (10 percent) of the state's total wine output, but more than one-half of the total dollar value. Other counties with a significant number of wineries include San Luis Obispo, Mendocino, Santa Cruz, Santa Barbara, Santa Clara, Monterey, and Amador. Generally, the greatest growth in number of wineries has occurred in the coastal valleys and Sierra Foothill counties. These areas are characterized by many small premium wineries, many of which have developed name recognition for their wine that appeals to a much smaller consumer group than the popular wines produced in the San Joaquin Valley. Significantly, the recent growth of wineries along coastal valleys between Mendocino County and San Diego has not diminished the dominance of the Central Valley in wine production and storage capacity. At the beginning of Repeal, California had approximately 160 wineries with live licenses. By the end of the year the number increased to 500, and by the middle of 1935 the figure rose to 750, many being inoperative and cottage in nature. With one minor exception after World War II, the number of wineries declined to 228 in 1966, and 140 in 1970, but rose steadily thereafter to 314 in 1975, 406 in 1977, 662 in 1985, and 820 by 1992. Measured by total storage capacity, the industry grew as average

winery size increased dramatically from 200,000 gallons to 1.8 million gallons. The number of wineries with a storage capacity greater than 5 million increased from 9 in 1940, to 14 in 1947, 18 in 1965, and 36 in 1977. The greatest decline in absolute winery numbers occurred in coastal California, primarily north and south of San Francisco, particularly Santa Clara, Napa, and Sonoma. These wineries were nearly all involved in small scale production of table wine, and not, as in the case of the Central Valley and Cucamonga, in the production of dessert and inexpensive jug wines. Indeed, while winery failures dotted the peripheral areas of the state, the Central Valley was characterized by increased plant capacities. During the period 1935-1965, crush capacity in the Central Valley increased from 41 percent to 79 percent of state total, and while there was an aggregate reduction of wineries in the state as a whole, wine production increased considerably. Significantly, the number and size of cooperatives, highly important in the post-Repeal era, have declined in recent years.

Table 8.3

GROWTH IN THE NUMBER OF WINERIES					
County	1970	1980	1983	1987	1991
Alameda	9	22	23	20	18
Amador	2	11	15	15	22
Butte	1	0	2	2	2
Calaveras	0	2	2	3	3
Contra Costa	6	4	8	6	1
El Dorado	2	5	9	10	12
Fresno	20	22	21	19	10
Humboldt	0	3	4	6	1
Kern	4	8	9	10	6
Kings	1	0	0	0	0
Lake	0	2	6	7	9
Los Angeles	4	10	11	17	8
Madera	4	8	8	5	7
Marin	2	7	7	8	6
Mariposa	0	1	1	2	3
Mendocino	3	13	30	36	35
Merced	0	1	1	0	0
Monterey	2	9	14	17	23
Napa	36	102	131	184	256
Nevada	0	0	1	2	2
Orange	0	3	4	2	2
Placer	2	1	1	1	1
Riverside	5	8	12	15	13
Sacramento	3	4	4	7	8
San Benito	3	7	7	6	3
San Bernardino	21	15	13	5	4
San Diego	2	4	8	7	6
San Francisco	1	3	5	7	3
San Joaquin	24	21	23	21	23
San Luis Obispo	4	7	21	34	41
San Mateo	3	6	9	11	5
Santa Barbara	3	13	15	20	32
Santa Clara	29	41	46	45	26
Santa Cruz	4	15	20	22	33
Shasta	0	0	1	2	0
Solano	2	3	5	8	4
Sonoma	33	78	120	155	167
Stanislaus	4	4	5	8	7
Trinity	0	0	0	1	1
Tulare	4	2	4	4	2
Tuolumne	0	2	2	3	2
Ventura	0	1	4	5	4
Yolo	0	4	7	11	8
Yuba	0	1	1	1	1
Total	245	470	639	770	820

Note: For several counties there is overlap.
Source: The Wine Institute

Of the 820 wineries in production, fewer than 40 date back to the nineteenth century (none of which reside on original property/buildings or boast continuous operation): Almaden, Paul Masson (1852); Mirassou, Buena Vista (1854); Gundlach-Bunschu (1859); Charles Krug (1861); Schramsberg (1862); Boeger (1870); Sutter Home (1874); Beringer (1876); Alta (1878); Markham, Valley of the Moon, Inglenook (1879); Bisceglia, Burgess, Geyser Peak (1880); Korbel, Chateau Montelena, York Mountain (1882); Concannon, Wente (1883); Kornell, Villa Mt. Eden, Chateau Chevalier (1884); Beaulieu, Far Niente, V. Sattui, Frei Bros. (1885); Freemark Abbey (1886); Trefethen (1886); Martini & Prati (1887); Christian Brothers (1888); Mayacamas (1889); Stag's Leap, Simi, Nichelini, Cribari (1890); and Foppiano (1896).

In the early 1970s infectious optimism surrounded the California wine industry. During the five years that ended in 1972, American wine sales advanced at more than a 7 percent annual rate as the success of new "pop" wines augmented favorable trends in the table and varietal wine market segments. With sales growth outstripping the expansion of grape supplies, sizable new investments in grape plantings (more than 200,000 acres of new vineland were established during the years 1973-1982) and winery capacity grew at unprecedented levels. This boom period came to an abrupt halt during the 1973-1975 recession. Bordeaux and Burgundy were faced with scandal, while wine sales growth slowed markedly in America. With bearing acreage increasing, grape supplies for the wine market could not be absorbed, and grape prices dropped to depression levels with many vineyards replaced by more lucrative crops.

Figure 8.3

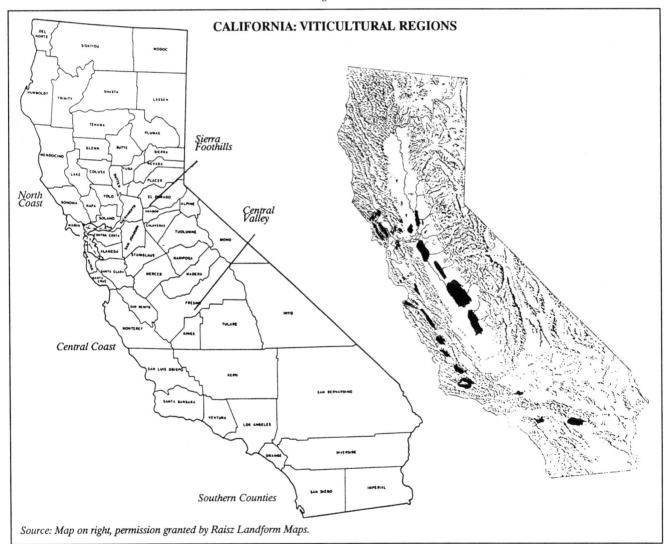

CALIFORNIA: VITICULTURAL REGIONS

Source: Map on right, permission granted by Raisz Landform Maps.

The next eight years showed a relentless increase in wine sales. Sustained growth in American wine consumption, modest additions of bearing grape acreage, and minor increases in winery capacity brought a better supply-demand balance. As Americans increased their per capita consumption, wine sales doubled from just under $3 billion to $5.4 billion in 1983. This formidable wine boom saw many foreign investments pouring in the two principal premium wine producing counties-Sonoma and Napa. Like all industry booms, this one came to an abrupt halt after the highly acclaimed 1982 Bordeaux vintage began arriving in America in 1984. Grape prices escalated to new heights that threatened the "fighting varietal" category. Despite the phenomenal growth of the cooler market segment, the next eight years, although momentous in terms of quality wine production, saw a continuous erosion in gross consumption and a decline in grape prices. By 1989, Zinfandel fetched $350, less than half 1988 prices. Per capita intake dropped from 2.4 gallons to 2.0 by 1992. Nevertheless, the industry is poised again for another "boom." Adult per capita consumption of table wines, tripling since 1960, will once again increase to new heights. California, the "Great Expectation" according to Carey McWilliams, has finally come of age...to stay. Indeed, it is hard to imagine otherwise: what makes California wines so drinkable is their low tannic structure, high level of fruitiness, and low acidity. And should there be a touch of residual sugar, even better for the bulk of Americans.

Over the past seventy years, five major grape-growing and winemaking regions have emerged: (a) The Central Valley, having steadily grown in terms of output and storage capacity, completely dominates the output of dessert, cooler, and less expensive generic bulk wine production. Collectively, the largest ten wineries produce 80 percent of the state's total wine output, the bulk of which is shipped to other states. As consumer tastes changed, the Central Valley has introduced the latest crushing, fermenting and storage technologies to produce a clean, fresh product (especially white wines), reduced the output of dessert wines, and radically altered the mix of grape varieties. It is significant to note that since table wines require half as many grapes per gallon as do dessert wines, the continued decline for dessert wines created a mild oversupply of grapes during the 1978-1983 period, but with the phenomenal growth of coolers since 1984, this excess capacity has been effectively utilized. It is also interesting to note that over the past three generations the percent of total wine made in the Central Valley has remained remarkably constant, 78 percent in 1947, 80 percent in 1957, and 77 percent in 1991.

It should be noted that the picture becomes muddled as a large quantity of the wine bottled by Central Valley wineries is actually made in other areas, and vise versa. Moreover, many wineries lease and/or own vineland outside their winery venue, as in the case of Delicato, E. & J. Gallo, and others. Although these practices allow wineries in all areas to expand their product line, the actual origin of the must venue is uncertain. Nevertheless, the divergence between the Central Valley and coastal wineries will intensify. While coastal wineries will escalate their production of quality premium and super-premium wines, Central Valley wine will remain inexpensive. Part of this divergence is due to the differences in land costs, $10,000 vs. $50,000, but mostly because of the inherent advantages of superior grape-growing land in the coastal regions.

(b) The North Coast embraces the heart of the premium table wine market, and more than half of the state's total winery population. While Napa and Sonoma counties dominate grape acreage, publicity, and celebrity, Lake County, in the northernmost portion of this region, is beginning to produce excellent wines. Along with the Central Coast, more than 80 percent of all wineries have been established since 1970, and, with only several major exceptions, most are small to middle-sized enterprises. This is the center of "boutique" wineries--privately owned and operated, small in production, and mainly in the business of attempting to produce distinctive quality wines. Because many buy grapes, must, and wine, there is no relationship between the number of wineries and crush and storage capacity.

In 1938, the coastal districts produced 70 percent of the state's total table wine and only 17 percent of the state's dessert wines, while the Central Valley produced the opposite. By 1966, the coastal counties produced 34 percent of table wine and less than 2 percent of all dessert wine, but since 1987 the figures have remained virtually unchanged. The coastal counties, due to cooler, maritime microclimates, not only produce the highest percentage of table wine, but nearly all of the premium category, and the finest sparkling and late harvest wines. When compared with the bulk Central Valley producers, small coastal wineries produce a more limited line of small lots of varietal wines. The wineries of 1992, comparatively small, sophisticated, capital intensive and recipients of formidable expertise, differ from the large, bulk producers of olden days. Their names, new and unfamiliar, are associated with new appellation designations (equally unfamiliar). Difficult to acquire nationwide as production is limited, the wines are expensive and are unknown unless the consumer reads wine-related literature. Unlike the pre-1950 producers, these small wineries do not attempt a "complete portfolio" of 30 different wines, but concentrate on either white, red, or a small mixture of Chardonnay, Sauvignon Blanc, Cabernet Sauvignon, and Merlot. They never use foreign names, and their wines are not marketed in bulk. Therefore, the diligence, dedication, personality, sizeable financial investment, and high degree of innovation makes these pioneering efforts forerunners to "chateau-type" Bordeaux properties. Those with the necessary fortitude to continue the family tradition are destined to succeed. Like any other business, many, for a variety of reasons, have closed their doors, but the majority are economically successful, and a small number have now passed the "wine thief" to another generation. Despite recent declines in per capita wine production in America, these are the halcyon days for the small, specialized winery.

Another major departure from olden days, and especially from traditional French "chateau producers," is the nature and character of the winemaker. In France, the significantly older winemaker took a lifetime to learn the trade in an atmosphere of a "traditional vocational education." California winemakers, in sharp contrast, are young, energetic, impatient, and trained by the finest and latest methods in an academic atmosphere that takes the "mystery" out of an occupation often described as "art." This young, sophisticated winemaker works not in a traditional vocation but in a laboratory called California, a frontier, pioneering viticultural region where custom and tradition are subject to continuous assault.

Table 8.4

CALIFORNIA: PERCENT WINE MADE BY GEOGRAPHIC DISTRICT						
Region	1937	1947	1957	1968	1977	1991
Central Valley	88.6	91.2	90.5	80.1	79.6	76.3
North Coast	1.5	1.9	5.4	12.5	13.1	15.2
Central Coast	.7	.8	1.0	5.0	5.2	7.3
Southern Coast	9.2	6.1	3.0	2.3	1.9	.2
Other			.1	.1	.2	1.0

WINE GRAPE ACREAGE BY GEOGRAPHIC REGION				
Region	1890	1939	1973	1990
North Coast	40,718	39,496	47,424	83,494
Central Coast	20,280	18,664	62,501	51,522
Central Valley	10,030	69,219	181,204	188,727
South Coast	5,788	30,002	18,220	3,577

Source: California Agricultural Statistics Service.

(c) The Central Coast, located between San Francisco and Ventura County, is a newly emerging viticultural region. Although highly diffusive in character, two viticultural valleys in Santa Barbara County, and the middle portion of Monterey County have recently carved out many interesting niches. While nearly 100 wineries have been established in Monterey, San Luis Obispo and Santa Barbara counties, the historic viticultural regions just south of San Francisco, particularly Santa Clara, have largely disappeared due to urban encroachment.

(d) The Sierra Foothills, one of the most prominent viticultural regions in the middle of the nineteenth century, declined in importance for more than 100 years. However, during the past 20 years a combination of inexpensive real estate costs, pristine rurality, and a resurgent frontier spirit have attracted more than 100 growers and 35 wineries.

(e) The Southern Coastal Counties, California's nineteenth century historic viticultural regions, have largely disappeared or are in rapid decline. The only bright picture in this sea of unrelenting urbanization is the recent spectacular rise of the Temecula region, located equidistant between Los Angeles and San Diego. The extreme south (excluding Temecula), has declined by more than 80 percent since 1960, especially the Cucamonga district. The decline of this historic area, particularly in the production of jug and dessert wines, is very striking. Southern California since 1920 has lost more than 90 percent of its total acreage and winemaking potential.

CALIFORNIA: HISTORICAL MILESTONES

Historically, the California wine industry, characterized and guided by simplicity and convenience, has evolved rapidly in recent years. Over the past two generations the heuristic nature of knowledge generated has produced viticultural advances of extraordinary proportions. The additive character of information notwithstanding, a short chronology of significant events is presented below.

To 1769: Indian tribes: collectors and gatherers of seeds and shellfish, produced no commercial agricultural activities, no domestication of animal and biotic matter, no sedentary existence, no metal smelting, no wheel, and no written language. The tripod of culture (control of fire, production of tools and the formation of a language) was in a formative state. Indian population is estimated to have been less than 125,000. California is the home of two native grapes—Vitis californica and Vitis girdiana, both of which are unimportant in the production of wine. Vitis californica, found everywhere along river courses, is a strong, vigorous vine that trails along the ground, but unfortunately, not very good as a table, raisin, or wine grape. Vitis arizonica, found in the extreme southeastern portion of the state, is an upright grower that also lacks commercial attributes.

1519-1524: Spain conquered the Aztecs. Hernando Cortez introduces the grapevine to Mexico during the period 1520-1524 (actual date is in dispute). Dictating the establishment of a wine industry in the New World, holders of land grants were to plant 1,000 vines per year for five years for every hundred Indians living on the land. Fearing competition, Spain took steps to restrict colonial wine production. Spaniards grew the Mission grape from seed in Mexico eventually spreading it to Baja California, and after nearly 300 years to "Alta" California. Curiously, this vine is not to be found anywhere else in Europe at this time. Chronologically, the vine was introduced by California missions according to the following approximate dates: San Diego, 1778; San Gabriel, 1779; Los Angeles, 1781; and Santa Barbara, 1786. It is important to note that Spanish mercantile policy neither encouraged nor initiated any economic activities in the New World that would compete with those existing in Spain. Consequently, winemaking was never encouraged except in marginal territories where wine was used for religious purposes. With independence in the 19th century most Spanish speaking countries, climate permitting, began viticultural activities.

1536: Hernando Cortez discovers Baja California. 4 years later, Hernando de Alarcon travels to the northern portion of the Gulf of California, and the Colorado River.

1538: Spanish Mercantile policies inhibit the growth of a commercial wine industry. Garcilaso El Inca in 1538 reported that he could not find in Mexico or Peru grapes like those in Spain. A long list (mostly secret) of directives by Spanish Kings to Viceroys and Governors forbade the planting of new vines and replacing decayed vines. These directives continued in nearly all Spanish territories until independence. While periodic shortages encouraged illegal vine planting, the industry for centuries remained insignificant.

1542: Spanish discovery of coastal California by Juan Rodriguez Cabrillo, the first European to reach California. The site of his landing is now Cabrillo National Monument in San Diego County.

1579: Sir Francis Drake sailed north of San Francisco, and claimed the region he called "Nova Albion" for England.

1603-1769: Period of Spanish neglect of Mexico.

1697: Father Juan Ugarte was Baja California's first wine grower (Mission grape) at Mission San Francisco Xavier.

1769: Father Junipero Serra arrives in San Diego on May 15, and along with another land party there were 50 soldiers, 73 Indian archers, an engineer, several interpreters, cooks, muleteers, laborers, and 700 large animals such as cattle, mules, horses, and donkeys, an event that took place 7 years before the American Revolution. This is considered the beginning of Spanish colonial settlement. Plant and animal introduction included grape, orange, olive, potato, onion, wheat, fig, pepper, horse, cattle, sheep, goat, pig, donkey, and mule; establishment of ranches and gravity flow irrigation; and the introduction of brush and earth dams, clay tile, adobe masonry, and stucco. Spain established a mission in San Diego, the first European settlement in California. Since then, 21 missions were established, each one day apart along the Camino Real as far north as Sonoma. The time between 1769 and 1834 (the year the missions were secularized) is known as the "Mission Period." As the missions spread northward to Sonoma they planted vineyards. The dominant grape planted was the Mission, also known as the Los Angeles grape, a grape of undetermined origin, and said to be related to the Malaga. All but a handful had a vineyard (Santa Cruz, Santa Clara, and San Francisco did not because the Mission grape would not ripen at those sites) and made wine. Grapes were generally acknowledged to have been planted in Mission San Juan Capistrano in San Diego during the period 1778-1781, and the first wine made in 1782. Many historians claim that the first vintage could have taken place in 1783 or 1784. While cereals and alfalfa were widely cultivated, the missions emphasized three important crops--olive, grape and fig. With time, Spaniards introduced more than 100 agricultural crops, many domesticated animals, a host of cultural trappings, and a long list of place names. Thirty counties bear names of Spanish origin and perhaps a quarter of all place names in the state have a similar origin.

1771-1850: The Mission grape, or *cepa creola*, dominated California vine acreage.

1773: The total Spanish population in California was composed of 61 soldiers and eleven priests.

1781: The European population of southern California included only 600 people.

1783: The first secular viticulturist was Governor Pedro Fages, who planted Mission grapes in Monterey.

1797: Vines are planted in Alameda County by Spanish friars.

1812: Russians build a stockade named Rossiya (now known as Ft. Ross) 100 miles north of San Francisco and planted grapes. The settlement was evacuated and sold for $30,000 in 1841.

1821: European population of southern California increased to 3,270. Mexico becomes politically independent with California a province until 1848.

1824: Father Jose Altimira establishes Mission San Francisco Solano in Sonoma, the last and northernmost of the Spanish missions. Joseph Chapman, first American viticulturist, planted 4,000 grape vines in Los Angeles.

1826: First overland party of Americans reach California under Jedediah Smith, the first Anglo-Saxon migrant.

1830s: Los Angeles County region was the largest wine producing area in the state--all wine made from the Mission grape.

1833: Jean Louis Vignes established a 104-acre vineyard in what is now Union Station in Los Angeles, and was the first Californian to import vines from Europe. By 1839 he had more than 40,000 planted vines. 1831 is also given as the date for the establishment of his vineyard, and 1837 for his first vintage.

1834: Commercialization of the wine industry begins with the secularization of the missions with most of the productive land falling into the hands of civil officials. Vineyards and orchards, important sources of mission wealth, were gradually abandoned, an event that marks the beginning of modern grape-growing and winemaking. The wine industry (dominated by altar wine production) languished until the eve of the Civil War when other Vinifera grapes reduced the importance of the Mission; total dominance of non-Mission grapes occurs by 1879.

1836: General Mariano G. Vallejo, last military commandant of Sonoma, assumes control of Sonoma Mission's vineland, and immediately replants and expands the vineyard.

1838: William Wolfskill, along with his brother, acquired the first of many vineyards in Los Angeles, and by 1858 cultivated 145 acres, and 55,000 vines, with a cellar capacity between 60,000 and 100,000 gallons. Next to Jean Louis Vignes he was the second largest grape and wine producer in the state. George Yount established the first vineyard in Napa County.

1839: Grape vines were planted in Cucamonga at the historic Thomas Winery.

1840: John A. Sutter began experimenting with brandy from wild grapes at the fork of the Sacramento and American rivers. 1841 is an alternative date.

1841: The Russians plant 2,000 vines at Fort Ross.

1842: European population less than 6,000.

1846: Dr. John Marsh presses first vintage in Contra Costa County.

1848: Gold is discovered in Coloma, Sierra Foothills, making this region the fastest growing viticultural area in the state. The state's population rises from 15,000 in 1847 to 379,994 in 1860. The gold rush begins in earnest in 1849, and becomes a principal stimulus to commercial viticulture creating a boom period during the decade of the 1850s. It is said that at no time in the 19th century had there been such a high demand for wine. Incipient irrigation enlarges the scope of agricultural possibilities, and, with increasing frequency, an ever-greater portion of the Central Valley succumbs to large-scale hydraulic systems. This is also the beginning of Chinese immigration, a source of inexpensive labor that constructed many of California's early wineries.

1849: European population at the beginning of the year was 26,000; by the end of the year the figure stood at 115,000, fourth-fifths of whom were Americans.

1850: One-third of the state's population resides in San Francisco. California becomes the 31st state, originally with 26 counties (now 58). Two new viticultural areas were established: the counties north of San Francisco and those immediately to the south of the city, principally Santa Clara Valley. Captain Charles Weber founded the city of Stockton and established San Joaquin County's first vineyard. Wine production for the state stood at 58,055 gallons, nearly all of it in Los Angeles. This figure from the U.S. Census is said to be too low; another figure for the year 1847 estimated wine output at 1.6 million gallons, this figure is considered too high. The grape history of California exhibits a marked cyclical pattern of prosperity and adversity, coupled with a long term trend of sustained growth. As viticultural activities grew in importance, the many new grape varieties shipped to California were and became falsely labeled causing great confusion for the next 140 years.

1852: State Census reports El Dorado, with 40,000 residents, to be the largest county, followed by San Francisco with 36,154. Sacramento and Los Angeles counties had but 12,418 and 8,329 residents respectively. Charles LeFranc establishes first commercial non-Mission vineyard and winery (Almaden) in Santa Clara County. The population rises to 224,435, more than half were gold miners.

1854: The establishment of the first of the many major wine companies--Kohler & Frohling, in San Francisco. George Krause planted first vineyard in Stanislaus County. Vines first planted in Lake County.

1854-1856: Introduction of the plum, almond, and beekeeping; commercial winemaking is overwhelmingly concentrated in southern California, primarily in San Diego and Los Angeles.

1855: Vines first planted in Merced County. California wines are exhibited for the first time at California State Fair, an annual entry except during Prohibition and World War II. Production of first sparkling wine.

1855-1872: California wine boom begins in earnest; more than 10,000 acres were planted, mainly in the central portions of the state.

1856: It is estimated that there were 1.5 million vines cultivated in the entire state. A severe drought partly destroys the power of the "golden age of the cattle ranches," and marks the beginning of the end of the unproductive Spanish feudal order in California. Founding of D'Agostini Winery (now Sobon).

1857: Los Angeles Vineyard Society, a cooperative effort founded by Charles Kohler and John Frohling, two leading wine merchants in San Francisco, operated for two years, failed and then reorganized as the Anaheim Colony Vineyards. California produced 385,000 gallons of wine, of which 350,000 gallons were made in Los Angeles, and 20,000 gallons in Santa Clara. Viticultural investment in this area was estimated at $1 million with 600,000 bearing vines; wine output was estimated to be 500,000 gallons in 1858. First shipment of Napa wine to San Francisco. Agoston Haraszthy established Buena Vista in Sonoma. Beyond question, he was the most important single individual in the establishment of the industry at this time, and a key personality with an interest in improving and replacing the Mission grape.

1860: Kohler & Frohling began shipping California wine to eastern America in large quantities. The firm was also the nation's largest exporter of wine. Charles Kohler, "the Longworth of the Pacific Coast," emerges as one of the leading personalities of the state's wine industry. The state's three most important agricultural crops were wheat, barley and grapes. It is estimated that during the period 1860-1864, about 3 million vines were planted each year. Wine production is estimated to be 246,518 gallons. California had 4.5 million grape vines, 2 million of which were in Los Angeles and San Bernardino. By the middle of the decade, acreage in northern California came into production, seriously affecting wine output in the Los Angeles region. However, the 1860 federal Census lists only 202 persons engaged in growing grapes and/or making wine. The list is considered incomplete as many growers and winemakers went unreported.

1860s: Increased Chinese immigration: they cleared land, laid out vineyards, tended the vines, harvested the grapes, built wineries and cellars, and even made wine. By the mid-1880s they composed up to 85 percent of the vineyard workers in the state. Major issues were the continuation of planting inferior Mission grapes, excise taxes, tariff concerns, and the need for a "pure wine law." Sonoma, Anaheim, and Los Angeles were the three most important wine counties in the state. Wine exports to other states increased from less than 1,000 gallons in 1861 to nearly 500,000 gallons in 1869.

1861: California legislature enacts resolution for a commission (State Board of Viticulture) to improve the grape and wine industry; Agoston Haraszthy is dispatched to Europe and returns with 100,000-200,000 Vinifera cuttings that became the foundation for the post-Mission viticultural history of the state.

1861-1862: California wine is shipped to British Columbia, Hawaii, Australia, China, Europe, Mexico, and Peru. Imposition of a high excise tax on wine and brandy severely reduced production. The Department of Agriculture was founded. The California Wine Growers Association is founded in December, one of many such organization to be formed during the next 20 years determined to reduce industry taxes.

1863: Buena Vista Viticultural Society, the state's first cooperative, formed after Agoston Haraszthy sold his property. General Mariano G. Vallejo has a vineyard with 70,000 vines.

1868: California produced 4 million gallons of wine, of which less than one-third was made in Los Angeles. For the first time more wine is produced in central California than southern California.

1868-1876: Viticultural prosperity in California: plantings, exports, and shipments to the rest of the nation increased to record levels.

1869: California becomes the leading wine producing state in the nation. Weibel Winery founded by California's first Governor. George West of Stockton is credited with the production of the first White Zinfandel wine. Leland Stanford begins a long association with grapes and wine by purchasing land in Warm Springs, Alameda County, where 350 acres of vines were planted and a winery constructed. In 1881 he acquires "Vina" in Tehana County, becoming, with nearly 4,000 acres, the largest vineyard in the world. Union Pacific Railroad provided access to eastern and midwestern markets, and by 1875 more wine was shipped by rail than by sea. Sonoma County surpasses Los Angeles County in planted vine acreage, and Southern California ceases to be the center of the wine industry.

1870: Second major viticultural boom period begins. California had 133 wineries distributed in the following counties: 58 in Calaveras; 39 in Los Angeles; 15 in Amador; 8 in Solano; 6 in Santa Barbara; 5 in Sonoma; 1 in Yolo; and 1 in San Francisco. Viticultural investment was estimated to be more than $30 million in gold. The state population rises to 560,247 people.

1872: William Thompson introduces a new grape "Lady de Coverly," now known as Thompson Seedless, in the Sacramento Valley, becoming in time the most widely planted grape in the state.

1873: Introduction of the Naval orange. Phylloxera is discovered in Sonoma, and during the period 1873-1879 more than 400,000 vines were destroyed.

1874: Introduction of the Lisbon lemon.

1875: Sonoma becomes the leading wine producing county in the state. The honor of "father of California wine science" falls on Waldemar Hilgard, Dean of the College of Agriculture in Berkeley. Seventy years before his time, he advocated the planting of better wine grape varieties (between 1880 and 1894 he tested at least 100 different wine grapes), early harvests, low yields, sanitary winemaking, low temperature fermentation, microclimate specialization, the elimination of European nomenclature, and the production of light, fruity wines. This extraordinary individual was born in Germany in 1833, became state geologist in Mississippi, Professor of Chemistry at the University of Mississippi, and Professor of Geology and Natural History at the University of Michigan in 1873. Arriving in California in 1875 he become a major force in viticultural affairs until 1896, publishing 64 major viticultural works. His efforts led to major replanting efforts of better wine, raisin, and table grapes.

1875-1886: This period began and ended with severe depression. Phylloxera created anxiety, and, in combination, these events encouraged the conversion to superior wine grapes. The wine depression was caused by overproduction, reduced demand, and poor wine quality. Although the recession was short lived, it was severe for the wine industry as it resulted in the failure of three-fourths of all wineries, with many marginal vineyards diverting efforts to other crops or replacing by better grapes. Fraudulent wine was common (many wines were flat, overly alcoholic, and "doctored"), and the state's reputation suffered. This prompted the passage of federal legislation heavily taxing imports. Despite higher tariffs, demand shifted to imported wines in the east and midwest. High freight rates further reduced demand from California. Wine prices fell to $.10 the gallon in 1877 prompting major grape acreage reductions. Mission grape declines in importance.

1876: Ice railroad service begins grape and wine shipments to the midwest and east.

1877: California wine production exceeds 4 million gallons, of which 38 percent was shipped to other states.

1878: Leon Chotteau proposed a 10 year trade treaty of low tariffs on imported wine, among many additional features considered injurious to California's wine interests. His proposal was defeated in 1879.

1878-1890: Phylloxera epidemic in Europe increased the demand for California wine; prices and wine exports rose sharply prompting major grape acreage increases.

1879: California produced 7 million gallons of wine.

1879-1919: California, having replaced Missouri as the largest wine producing state, and transformed winemaking from a cottage industry to a capital intensive industry, has dominated national production ever since. The second half of the 19th century was a major milestone in the state's viticultural evolution. It marked the birth of a University viticulture and enology department, the concentration of enormous human resources, and the growth of a dynamic industry.

1880: Napa Valley had 47 wineries; 10 years later the number increases to 166. Juan Gallegos, a Castilian who amassed a fortune in Central America, arrives in California and builds a winery in Alameda County. By the end of the decade he cultivated more than 4,000 acres of grapes and his winery was considered the largest in the world. This underrated Spaniard built a gravity-flow winery, used oak barrels, attempted pasteurization, and planted premium grape varieties. Formation of the State Board of Viticultural Commissioners leads to the establishment of viticultural classes at the College of Agriculture, and the enactment of a Pure Wine Law in an attempt to clarify the use of spirits, brandy, sugar, water, coloring matter, and other substances in winemaking. It also made provisions to combat plant pests and improve vineyard practices. Experimental grape-growing station and courses in viticulture are established at the College of Agriculture of the University of California at Berkeley. Facilities and the establishment of the department of Enology and Viticulture is located at Davis, the site of the nation's largest experimental vineyard and one of the largest related libraries. State vine acreage stood at 56,000, doubling by 1885.

1880s: California produced 10.2 million gallons of wine. Economic prosperity was due in part to phylloxera devastation in Europe. Many new winemakers enter the industry of which Pierre Pellier, Pierre Mirassou, Etienne Thee, Charles Lefranc, Carl Wente, James Concannon, Charles Krug, and Gustav Niebaum were among the most celebrated. California farmers switch from apples to large plantings of plum, peach, prunes, apricots, and pears, and the state emerges as the nations largest deciduous fruit producer.

1880-1895: A combination of rising demand and the devastation of phylloxera caused a significant impetus to increase vine acreage. Leland Stanford alone during 1881-1883 planted more than 1 million vines at his "Vina" Vineyard. The 1880-1885 expansive period was so rapid that vine acreage increased to more than 120,000. Overproduction and the severe depression of 1886 prompted growers to plant superior, high quality grape varieties, and not, for the first time in the state's history, Mission. Immediately after this significant historical phase, the number of medals won by California wines increased rapidly. The industry suffered another of its periodic downward cycles during the panic of 1886 (an economic climate that lasted well into the 1890s) with premium wine selling for less than $.09 cents a gallon, a condition aggravated by claims of adulteration, and high transportation costs. Most wines were sold under European names.

1883: 140,000 acres of vineland in California.

1884: More than 20 New York firms engaging in the large-scale adulteration of California wine created turmoil, and severely reduced the sale of wine.

1885-1894: Among the leading personalities during this time were Graham Fair, George Hearst, and Leland Stanford, whose combined output of wine exceeded 1.7 million gallons and who cultivated more than 7,000 acres of vineland. All three legendary figures represented the state in the U.S. Senate in the 1880s.

1886-1895: Economic depression reduces vine acreage, but wine output increases. Eighty-eight percent of total production is shipped to other states. Anton and Joseph Korbel begin making sparkling wine in Guerneville.

1887: Average grape prices per ton: Cabernet Sauvignon, $25-30; Riesling, $18-20; Mourvedre, $16-18; Zinfandel, $14-16; Charbono, $13-15; Mission, $7-8.

1888: Large-scale commercial shipping of table grapes begins.

1889: Passage of the "Sweet Wine Bill," by which producers of sweet wines were permitted the use of brandy for fortification free of taxation. This gave the California producer a major advantage over east coast wineries, and 97 percent of the sweet wine market before Prohibition. Thirty-five gold, silver and bronze medals are awarded to California wines at the Paris Exposition.

1890: Introduction of the seedless grapefruit. "Vina," Leland Stanford's vineyard, winery, and distillery, produced more grape brandy than any other in the world.

1891: 20,000 cases of sparkling wine are produced, a figure that rose to 6.5 million cases in 1973, 10 million in 1980, and more than 17 million cases in 1990.

1894: Founding of the California Wine Association to stabilize wine prices.

1895: Functions of the State Board of Viticulture are transferred to the University of California College of Agriculture.

1900: Secundo Guasti, arriving in Cucamonga in the late 1880s, acquires 5,000 acres of vineland, considered at that time one of the largest vineyards in the world. California wine wins gold medal at Paris Exposition. 150,000 acres were producing 19 million gallons of wine.

1906: Introduction of the avocado. Founding of the University of California at Davis, which dealt solely with agriculture until 1952 when new faculties were added. Today it matriculates several hundred enology and viticultural majors and grants doctoral degrees. It is now considered the leading academic center for viticultural scholarship and research.

1910: Average price per grape ton was $16; in 1987 $700. Grape acreage was nearly 350,000.

1914: Congress, imposing an excise tax on domestic wines for the first time since the Civil War, caused a reduction in demand.

1916: Internal Revenue Act of 1916 (Pure Food and Drug Act) allowed eastern producers to add sugar and water to unfermented grape juice (up to a maximum of 35 percent). In return, the excise tax was reduced.

1920: The Volstead Act enacted the "Noble Experiment," or Prohibition, for the next fourteen years. Grape prices soared and vineyard acreage grew (more than 200,000 acres were planted during the period 1920-1926) as demand from the 200 gallon or less home wine maker increased. Alicante Bouschet acreage increases due to its red juice, thick skin, and ability to ship well. Legal commercial wine existed for sacramental and medicinal use only, the production of which averaged 6 million gallons; however, two years before Repeal, production rose to more than 20 million gallons, two-thirds of which were dessert wines. Commercially legal, illegal, and home-made wines throughout Prohibition averaged more than 125 million gallons. By 1929 fewer than 300 wineries maintained their bonds, and on the eve of Repeal fewer than

160 remained active.

1933: Prohibition is repealed, and the industry begins a long rebuilding period.

1934: Post-repeal recovery was slow as imports dominated the eastern and midwestern markets. The main product for the next generation was sweet dessert wine sold under generic names. Wine quality was poor due to the use of redwood containers, the shortage of capital and expert help. Although 804 wineries were registered in 1934, only 48 were economically viable. The founding of the Wine Institute, the principal professional organ of the state's wine industry over the past two generations, and, in time, the most effective wine association in the country. Over the years it has been instrumental in the establishment of wine standards, has become the largest source of statistical compilation, and otherwise acts as a spokesman for the industry. Although critics may disagree, the Institute has been instrumental in reducing high state taxes and license fees, and has promulgated an educational program. Membership in the Institute has increased from 40 in 1934 to more than 536 in 1990. Total commercial wine production was 38 million gallons, of which California consumed half.

1935: University of California Davis experimented with more than 150 varieties of wine grapes immediately after Repeal, and again after World War II. While table wine grapes were limited in appeal after Repeal, its efforts and reports prepared the base for the sharp interest in quality grapes in the 1960s. Beginning in the 1930s, Dr. Olmo developed the following varieties: Ruby Cabernet and Emerald Riesling in 1948; Calzin, Flora, Helena, Rubired, and Royalty in 1958; Carnelian in 1973; Centurion and Carmine in 1975; and Symphony in 1982.

1937: California Marketing Act stabilized wine prices, and through aggressive marketing activities California emerged, immediately after Repeal, as the nation's premier wine supplier.

1938: Andre Tchelischeff arrives in the United States from Paris, and for the next 38 years works for Beaulieu Vineyards. He is one of the more important personalities in post-Repeal California history. Overproduction and a slump in demand precipitates a plan (Prorate Order) whereby 10,000 growers and 250 wineries divert 35 percent of the wine grape crop to the production of high-proof brandy, thereby reducing total state wine production by nearly 38 million gallons. Subsequent amendments to the Prorate Order of 1938, referred to as Marketing Orders, continued until 1968.

1940: Schenley Distillers, Inc. acquires the Roma Winery, the first of a series of "spirit" companies buying California wineries. By 1956 spirit companies control nearly one-third of the state's wine output.

1941: Beginning of rapid population growth. The 1941 Colorado River Aqueduct allowed Los Angeles to grow unchecked, and large-scale north to south transfers of water helped to quench agriculture's thirst. World War II induces an atmosphere of scarcity and grape prices rise, only to fall precipitously in 1947. The Korean War promoted the rise of the aircraft industry, which in turn launched the aerospace business, major economic activities that propelled an economic growth boom period for two generations.

1945: Population rises to 9 million. Many distilleries purchased wineries and began production of large quantities of jug and dessert wines. This was followed by economic depression in the wine industry due to a surplus of 39 million gallons.

1946: Introduction of the 100 percent varietal wine. California becomes the first state to ferment in oak.

1950: California produced 3 percent of the world's wine; 20 percent of all table grapes; and 40 percent of all raisins. Wine sales amounted to 132 million gallons, 22 million more gallons than 1940. Founding of the American Society For Enology and Viticulture.

1952: First attempt to harvest grapes mechanically.

1955: "Pop wine" revolution encourages increased consumption of party wines.

1957: The introduction of cold stainless steel fermentation of Chardonnay, and Limousin oak for aging Pinot Noir and Chardonnay in Hanzell Vineyards, as well other wineries. Eventually oak and stainless steel replaced the inferior redwood tanks and barrels, thus changing the flavor and complexion of California wines.

1959: Only 200 acres of Chardonnay planted in the Golden State.

1960: Red wines accounted for 74 percent of table wine output.

1963: California becomes the most populous state in the nation.

1964: Beginning of explosive increase in table wine consumption and the associated decrease in dessert wines.

1965: Williamson Act, a law allowing growers to place vineland into agricultural preserves thus paying taxes on current agricultural use rather than potential non-agricultural value. This has relieved economic pressures and has, most notably in Livermore and the Napa Valley, kept urban sprawl to a minimum. Urbanization encroached Santa Clara and Cucamonga reducing grape acreage, and increased in Mendocino, Lake, Sonoma, and the central and southern coast counties.

1967: Introduction and eventual universal acceptance of field grape harvesters. Table wine outsold sweet dessert wines for the first time since Repeal.

1969: State legislature determines that wine is subject to a one-time inventory tax, thus saving the industry millions of dollars.

1970: Two digit wine growth raised grape prices, and tax inducements enabled grape acreage to rise by 200,000 acres to 457,000 bearing acres of vineland. The price of North Coast Chardonnay was $375 the ton, and $450 the ton for Cabernet Sauvignon. This "boom" precipitated another decline, only to pick up again in the second half of the decade.

1970-1992: New wineries are formed at a rate of 30 per year. The number of wineries grew from 268 in 1970 to 800 in 1992. California attracts, in ever increasing frequency, foreign investment in winegrowing. With the formation of Clos du Val, the acceleration has attracted numerous French, Spanish, Swiss, Italian, Japanese, German, Thai, Canadian, and more, all of whom now control 30 percent of the California wine grape acreage, up from 5 percent in 1975. As of 1991 it is estimated that more than 30 wineries are owned by foreign interests, controlling more than one-third of storage capacity and 40 percent of premium vineland. The consequence of this "new" investment, other than the immediate economic benefit, is a new fresh "international" point of view that has revitalized the industry in practically all producing areas, but primarily along the coastal counties.

1971: Population rises to 20 million. Wine sales amounted to more than 274 million gallons. Creation of the Brandy Advisory Board.

1973: Napa Cabernet Sauvignon wins blind wine tasting over many classic equivalent libations in Paris, France, an event that places an element of celebrity to California. E & J Gallo begins to produce cleaner, lighter wines that appealed to a much larger market.

1973-1974: The wine boom of the 1960s stumbled during the economic recession of 1973-74. Overproduction of both grapes and wine, coupled with a national economic recession, and a series of scandals in France, depressed the wine market. As Cabernet Sauvignon soared from $170 the ton in 1962 to $800 the ton in 1973, it plunged to $350 the ton by 1974-75. Many wineries closed their door, and several large, multi-national corporations sold operations, but by 1976 the industry rebounded, reaching new highs until the slump of the mid 1980s.

1975: A rapid increase in the number of new "boutique" wineries in California.

1976: First year that more white wine was sold than red, signaling the start of the "white wine boom."

1980: Premium table wines comprised only 4 percent of table wine by volume.

1981: Napa Valley Appellation, the first in the state, was awarded on February 27, 1981.

1984: Sixty-two percent of table wine consumed is white.

1986: Governor George Deukmejian signed into law legislation that would permit interstate wine shipments (two cases per month) to and from California on a reciprocal basis with those states adopting similar legislation.

1987: Grapes become the number one cash crop in Sonoma County. Sale of California varietal wines (28.6 million cases) exceeded imported table wines (27.8 million wines).

1988: Value of quality (but undeveloped) Napa and Sonoma Valley vineland reaches $25,000 the acre, plus $15,000 to develop. Agriculture in California is big business, contributing more than $20 billion annually to the state's economy.

1990: California accounts for 91 percent of national wine output: 80 percent of the generic jug market, more than 90 percent of premium wine, 90 percent of coolers, 70 percent of the table wine market, more than 80 percent of sparkling wines, and a similar percentage of all domestic, harvested grapes. California, with an output of 400 million gallons and 700,000 acres, ranks as the 5th largest wine producer, and the 10th largest vineyard in the world. The premium table wine revolution continues; within a 10 year period premium table wines increase volume share from 5 to 25 percent; premium table wine represents 31 percent of shipments and 62 percent of sales (or more than $1.1 billion since 1980). With existing vine acreage selling for more than $80,000 an acre, winemaking becomes a capital intensive industry.

1992: Population rises to 30 million, or nearly eight times the nation's population in 1776. The California wine industry is 214 years old, but it is just emerging from its infancy having had more than its share of disruptions. Some of these were natural like the dreaded phylloxera, while others, like Prohibition, were man made. However, since the repeal of the "noble experiment," viticultural activities have made spectacular strides. UC-Davis matriculates 100 graduates and accommodates more than 1,000 students in its various course offerings.

TOPOGRAPHY

California is a state whose physical diversity staggers the imagination. Its length is about 825 miles (or a comparable distance from Chicago to southern Louisiana), its width 200 miles, and its coastline corresponds to a distance from Massachusetts to South Carolina. The highest elevation, Mt. Whitney, is 14,495 feet, and the lowest point lies 280 feet below sea level. Offering immense variety, nearly the whole of California is a collection of mountains, valleys, and deserts, nearly all of which are considered economically usable, and more than three-quarters (despite the apparent aridity and high forested elevations) extremely rich.

Topography is dominated by a series of Coastal Ranges along the Pacific Ocean, the Central Valley, the deserts of the southeast, and the Sierra Nevada in the east, the latter a continuous block, 400 miles long with more than 50 peaks above 13,000 feet. The principal mountain ranges and smaller complex associations, including the Sierra Nevadas, the Cascades, Coastal Ranges, Tehachapi and Transverse Ranges, are all large-scale features that strongly influence the geography of California. These features, to a large extent, determine the supply of water, and define the agricultural geography of each region. While their size can vary from the large Sacramento Valley to the small "canyon," each and every little physical region has its own special characteristics and ambience. Of the many varied geomorphic regions, only three are important for viticulture: the Coastal Ranges, the Central Valley, and the Sierra Nevadas. The extremely humid northern coastal regions, as well as the colder higher elevations are devoid of viticultural activities. In the extreme south, however, a small number of desertic climatic regions do produce grapes under irrigated conditions, most of which are for raisin and table use, not wine.

The Coastal Ranges

The Coastal Ranges trend southeastward and are interspersed with a series of valleys opening northward to the ocean, and south and north to San Francisco Bay. In the northern portion their elevations range between 3,000 and 4,000 feet, but in the south they are twice as high. They are widest in the north (90 miles) where they merge with the Klamath Mountains and narrowest in the southern extremities where they descend abruptly in the Central Valley. For the most part, because the Coastal Ranges exhibit a distinctive echelon character of ridges and valleys, they form a significant barrier to maritime air flow. Collectively, these mountain masses occupy more than one-third of the state's total land area. Throughout the entire length of coastal California less than 10 percent of the total area is used for agriculture and only a miniscule fraction of the total area (less than 4 percent) accommodates 90 percent of the population--the latter, mainly confined to the greater San Francisco Bay Area and adjoining valleys.

The Coastal Ranges are rarely greater than 50 miles from the coast to the crest of the range. These mountains rise abruptly from the ocean or from the narrow coastal plain north and south of San Francisco to elevations that average between 2,000 and 4,000 feet. The continuity of the coastal trend is interrupted by only one open embayment--San Francisco Bay and several valleys opening up a good portion of central California to the moderating effect of the Pacific Ocean. South of San Francisco the Coastal Ranges are fragmented and composed of at least seven separate ranges, each with their own system of valleys. Small areas of igneous rocks are found, and north of San Francisco volcanic rock is ubiquitous. However, sedimentary rocks of both marine and non-marine origin dominate the western fringes of the Transverse Ranges, particularly the Santa Ynez and neighboring ranges. The numerous alluvial valleys, a geological product of folding, uplifting, faulting, and subsequent erosion, offer the finest vineyard land in the state. More specifically, the finest areas coincide with gravelly and limestone soils, the latter, extremely rare. The largest single cluster of limestone and dolomite occurs east of Salinas, the southern portions of Santa Cruz County, minor areas in San Luis Obispo, and the Santa Ynez Valley.

The complex geology of the Coastal Ranges is one of folded and faulted rocks nearly all of which have been metamorphosed. Some of the ridges are short and others long; some are narrow while others are broad; and while some summits are gently rounded, others are irregular and highly etched by youthful erosion. Valleys, filled with alluvium, contain the bulk of population, agriculture, and settlement. Green with irrigated water, they stand in sharp contrast to the wooded or oak and grass covered ridges. Each valley is a small, separate and distinct agricultural region.

The Coastal Ranges south of Mendocino (the principal quality wine producing region) are defined by winter rain and occasional winter frost. Although precipitation ranges from 15 to 45 inches in most places, summer is a water deficit season with nearly all crops requiring irrigation. The Coastal Ranges, although not excessively high,

are rough with extreme local reliefs. Consequently, the soils are mainly colluvial, and in valley bottoms and hillsides rich, heavily mineralized alluvium. The nature of this alluvium is determined by the source of the sediment from which they were formed. Their depth is a function of slope, type of rock and rock age, that in combination produces a highly variegated pattern of soils that can change every 20 feet.

Between San Luis Obispo County and Los Angeles are a group of mountains known as the Transverse Ranges, the largest of which are the Santa Ynez, San Gabriel, and San Bernardino mountains. Their higher elevation (more than 9,500 feet), east-west orientation, and granitic masses set them apart from the Coastal Ranges to the north. The Los Angeles Basin, the state's principal population concentration, lies in the largest lowland area fronting the Pacific Ocean. South of the Transverse Ranges are a group of granitic mountains known as the Peninsular Ranges. Extending south from San Bernardino to the Mexican border and beyond, they collectively contain fewer than 6,000 acres of vineland.

Along the Coastal Ranges isotherms run north-south, and parallel to the mountain contours, instead of east-west as is common in most parts of the temperate zone. Along the Pacific-facing slopes the climate is dominated by the effects of the cold California Current. Warm winters, cool summers, small daily and seasonal temperature ranges, and high relative humidity are the foremost climatic features. With increasing distance from the ocean the maritime influence decreases. Areas that are well protected from the ocean experience a more continental type of climate with warmer summers, colder winters, greater daily and seasonal temperature ranges, and generally lower relative humidity. Throughout the Coastal Ranges major rivers are rare, and streams are small and intermittent. The two largest coastal rivers are the Russian and Salinas, both of which empty into the Pacific.

The Central Valley

The Central Valley, one of the world's largest intermontane basins and the nation's most productive agricultural region, is a huge alluvial plain bounded by the Sierra Nevadas on the east and the Coastal Ranges on the west. The "Valley" occupies one-fifth of the state's total area, and possesses more than two-thirds of its irrigated farmland. Covering half the size of New York State, this immense valley is a product of the merging of many alluvial fans originating at the mouths of canyons through which tributary streams flow from the surrounding mountains. It is, with the help of irrigation, one of the most productive agricultural regions in the world, and the locus of nearly three-quarters of the state's total vineland. However, despite its dominance in both grape acreage and volume of wine made, the Central Valley has yet to rise to the prestigious quality heights of the coastal counties.

The Central Valley usually gives the impression that it is one large plain with seemingly uniform agriculture and land use. In reality it is highly variable with four significant components. The eastern margins (especially in the San Joaquin section), containing soils derived from granitic rock, coarser and sandier than elsewhere, support more than half of the grape acreage in the entire Central Valley. The soils on the western side of the Central Valley, derived from volcanic, igneous, and metamorphic rocks, are finer in texture, and because they are more arid (they are located on the lee side of the Coastal Ranges) they are highly alkaline. Due to limited leaching, these soils develop appreciable quantities of calcium carbonate and usually exhibit peculiar fertility problems due to the unavailability of such elements as phosphorus and zinc, and, as a consequence, contain few vineyards. The third soil type is an irregular, foothill belt in the northern portion of the Sacramento and San Joaquin rivers. Characterized as old, they have well developed profiles, contain considerable clay accumulation in the "B" horizon, and are generally considered good vineland when well-drained. The fourth, the Sacramento-San Joaquin delta, due to the presence of recently deposited alluvium, is one of the most fertile and intensively cultivated agricultural regions in the state. The combination of recently deposited, well-drained alluvium, and proximity to the moderating effects of San Francisco Bay make this one of the better grape producing regions in the entire valley.

The Sierra Nevada

The physiography and climate of the Sierra Nevada present a dramatic contrast to the other geographic regions mentioned above. It is a single mountain range, nearly as extensive as the Alpine system in Europe, that occupies one-fifth of the total area of the state. More than 430 miles long, and 80 miles wide, the Sierra Nevada, a classic fault-block mountain range, tilts westward and is incised by enormous canyons. Precipitation (often more than 90 inches), increasing with elevation, results in a large annual water surplus. The snow pack, one of the highest in the nation, frequently stores more than 40 inches of water to become the major source of irrigation water for the Central Valley.

Geologically the region is highly diverse, and viticulture is mainly confined to the relatively warmer elevations outside the influence of glaciation. The preferred sites are within the 800-4,000 foot, foothill zone characterized by older, deeper and well-drained, reddish-brown soils. Above the 4,000-foot contour, timber production dominates (with much of the land in state and federal water management zones) as it is cold, rainy, and contains soils that are too shallow and acidic. While the Coastal Ranges produce few significant rivers, the Sierra Nevadas are the source of major rivers and hundreds of small streams that feed the two principal rivers--Sacramento and San Joaquin. Huge amounts of melting snow and orographic-induced precipitation are the genesis of more than three-fourths of all surface water available for residential and agricultural use. The soils are mainly of igneous origin and, with few exceptions, well drained.

CLIMATE

It is rare for people to think of California as a land of climatic contrasts between mountain, desert and coast. It is commonly thought of as a land that is neither too hot or too cold if one does not know that there is an extreme range of nearly 140F in Death Valley to -50F at the higher elevations in the northeastern portions of the state. Annual precipitation at one station exceeds 161 inches, while other stations less than 200 miles away experience less than 2 inches. While there are areas in the state where the growing season is less than 30 days, and vegetation is absent in areas larger than Rhode Island, most of the state, certainly the populated portions, has one of the most temperate of all climates, a feature reflected by the length of the frost-free season. The growing season varies from 365 days in the extreme southern coast to less than 30 days at high elevations. Most coastal valleys and the Central Valley have a frost-free season of 225 to 300 days. However, due to the presence of cold oceanic water and significant topographic irregularity, temperatures and rainfall are a function of coastal orientation and elevation, and not necessarily latitude. The combination of these influences results in pronounced climatic changes within short distances. As a consequence, along the coast and in various inland locations, lower temperatures are not necessarily to the north, nor higher temperatures toward the south. For example, oranges ripen several weeks earlier at Oroville in the north than at Riverside, 400 miles south. Grapes ripen six weeks earlier in Calistoga than at Santa Barbara, 300 miles south.

The foregoing has produced, for a large state, three major climates with one dominating human settlement (Mediterranean), two dominating agriculture (Mediterranean and desert), and a humid upland climate (north of Mendocino County and the High Sierras) characterized by lumbering and tourist activities. Interestingly, less than 1 percent of the world's land area is classified as "Mediterranean," and California is the only state of the nation that contains this climate. As with all Mediterranean climates, there are few navigable rivers, few large natural lakes, a water deficiency during the growing season necessitating irrigation, and non-contiguous tree vegetation.

Three weather elements combine to produce the varied climatic pattern of California: the prevailing westerlies, orographic influence, and the Pacific Ocean. Fig.

8.4 shows that isotherms run north-south rather than east-west, an unusual feature not encountered elsewhere to such a great extent in America. Mean maximum July and mean minimum January temperature ranges show a unique pattern of moderate coastal temperatures and a significantly more extreme interior. While temperature ranges between 50F and 65F along the entire length of the coastline, a few miles inland temperatures rise by more than 20F (in some interior areas, summers have recorded the highest temperatures anywhere in the world). This temperature discrepancy is due to the fact that the Coast Ranges act as an impediment to the cooling effect of the ocean and prevailing wind patterns. January temperatures illustrate the moderating influence of the Pacific Ocean in contrast to the rapid winter cooling of terrestrial space. Consequently, temperatures along the coast vary less than 10F. It is obvious, therefore, that the above collectively lengthen the growing season along the coast rather than interior areas. If ideal temperatures (77F-86F) are maintained and prolonged during the period of maturation, sugar levels rise without a major drop in acid levels, thus producing above-average quality wine. Cooler temperatures increase the "hang time" raising acid levels; and warmer than normal temperatures reduce acid levels.

Figure 8.4

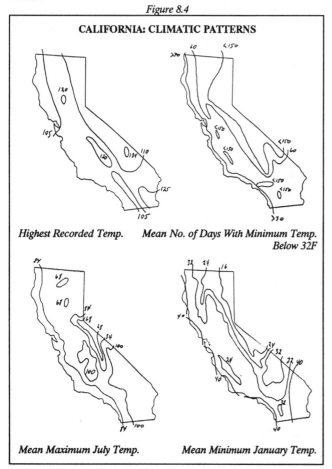

CALIFORNIA: CLIMATIC PATTERNS

Highest Recorded Temp.   Mean No. of Days With Minimum Temp. Below 32F

Mean Maximum July Temp.   Mean Minimum January Temp.

Figure 8.5

CALIFORNIA: CLIMATIC PATTERNS

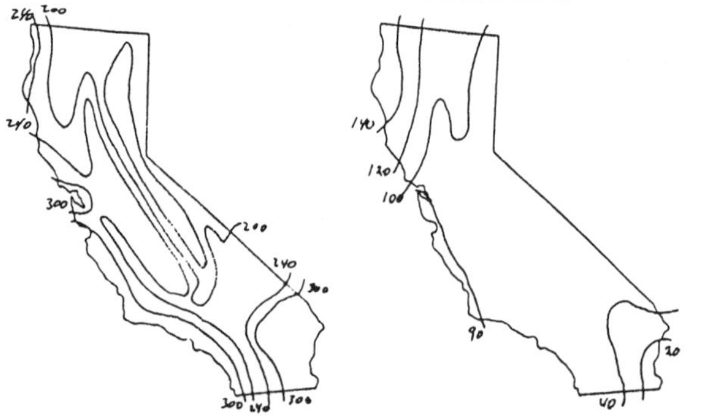

Length of Growing Season   Mean No. of Cloudy Days

Rainfall patterns are unusual in California: there is a reduction from north to south and west to east, an increase with elevation, and heavier along western exposures. Unlike the region east of the continental divide nearly all rainfall arrives in winter, a pattern of seasonal distribution that covers the entire state. Prevailing westerly winds, common throughout the year north of San Francisco, blow over relatively warm water, absorb moisture and bathe coastal areas as far north as central Alaska with copious rainfall--less at sea level but progressively more with increased vertical uplift in the presence of mountains. In general, precipitation decreases from north to south and west to east, increases with altitude, and is greater on the west and south sides of mountains than on the north and east exposures. While this precipitation regime is fairly evenly distributed throughout the year north of California, there is a distinct seasonal pattern for the California coast and a good deal of the interior. Winter winds come from the west, but because they blow over a low pressure area (warmer water), they absorb moisture and, as a result, precipitation occurs only during the winter season. The alteration of cyclonic storm activity is most prevalent in the northern portion, hence, its more pronounced character north of Mendocino County and in the higher elevations of the Sierra Nevadas where rainfall often exceeds 110 inches in the northwest (less than 2 inches in the southeast). Along the coast, latitude and elevation are most important as Eureka receives 40 inches of rainfall, San Francisco 22, Monterey 20, Los Angeles 25, and San Diego 10.

According to the above, more than half of the state falls into a water-deficit region for normal, mid-latitude agriculture. Desertic and semi-desertic areas are characterized by high evaporation rates, diminished precipitation, non-contiguous vegetation, lower rates of atmospheric humidity, high incidence of sunshine, and mineralized soils. It follows that the summer drought favors the growth of xerophytic plants, like oleander, olive, and grape. Given the location of mountain and precipitation patterns, 80 percent of the available water yield for agriculture use originates from the northern and eastern sections of the state. While seasonal and annual temperature fluctuations occur, they are minor to the larger fluctuations in rainfall. In Sonoma, for example, average annual temperature variability was less than 2F during 1980-1983, while mean annual rainfall variability ranged from a low of 25.6" in 1980 to 63.4" in 1983. Rainfall for interior areas under 300 feet in elevation is usually less than 25 inches, and as a consequence, irrigation is necessary for viticulture throughout the state except for selected coastal locations, because the average date when stored soil moisture supply is exhausted is March-April in the southern counties, and by the middle of June along North Coast valleys.

Figure 8.6

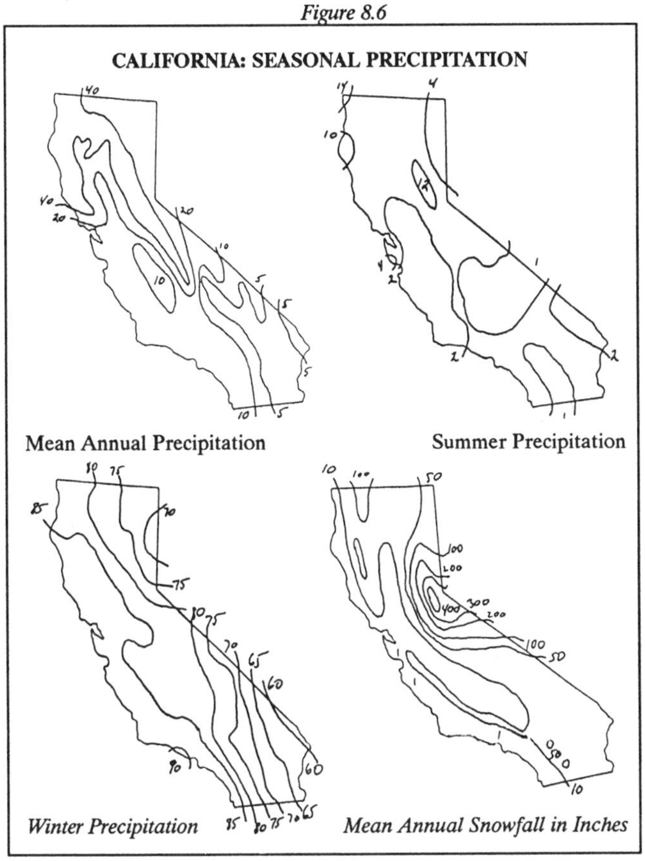

CALIFORNIA: SEASONAL PRECIPITATION

Mean Annual Precipitation   Summer Precipitation

Winter Precipitation   *Mean Annual Snowfall in Inches*

The relationship between topography and amount of precipitation is apparent: the climatic significance of mountains is that they lower temperatures, induce heavier precipitation, and, due to their orientation, produce windward and leeward exposures. Throughout the state the intensity and duration of rainfall is a function of elevation and access to rain bearing winds. Average temperatures are also directly influenced by the location and height of mountain ranges. Significantly, the lowest summer temperatures are along the windward, or west-facing slopes, and the highest along the lee or east-facing side of mountains. With only minor exceptions, climate in the higher elevations is a modified version of the Mediter-

ranean climate of low lying regions. Usually temperatures decrease 3F per 1,000 feet of elevation, and, as a consequence, upland temperatures, in contrast to low lying areas, are significantly lower. Lower temperatures lead to heavier precipitation, a good deal of which is not effective due to higher evaporation rates caused by a more dynamic atmosphere. When rain bearing winds are unable to penetrate interior locations, desertic climates occur, and of the five principal "dry" counties, viticultural pursuits are found mainly in San Bernardino and Riverside, primarily for the production of raisin and table grapes. While the above winter wet, summer dry climatic pattern is ideal for the cultivation of Vinifera grapes (most grapes are produced in areas having less than 25 inches of rainfall), irrigation is a necessary requirement for all but the most humid regions of the state.

Figure 8.7

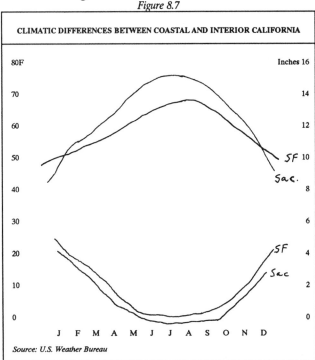

CLIMATIC DIFFERENCES BETWEEN COASTAL AND INTERIOR CALIFORNIA

Source: U.S. Weather Bureau

Because weather is dominated by air masses flowing in an eastern direction, the influence of the cold California Current is most prevalent along the coast and several valleys accessible to the Pacific. Throughout the summer, coastal areas are bathed by *velo* clouds--often as low fog, but most commonly as high fog that overcasts the sky until burned off by the mid-day sun. These clouds moderate heat and retard evaporation. They reach farthest inland in the Sacramento-San Joaquin delta, lower and western Sonoma, Salinas, and throughout southern California. Closer to the ground in coastal valleys, these clouds are commonly called *fog*, especially during the summer, where in places they can be thick and long in duration. To illustrate this unusual condition, Mark Twain allegedly wrote that the coldest winter he ever spent was a summer in San

Francisco. Coastal fog was so thick that Cabrillo, Ferrer, Drake, Gali, Unamuno, and Vizcaino all missed the entrance to San Francisco Bay, the latter having 288 foggy days vs. fewer than 10 for Fresno. Because fog reduces the incidence and effect of a hot, searing sun, coastal areas, cooler than interior areas on the same latitude, produced microclimates that have developed the premier wine producing regions in the state. Above all else, the presence of the cold California current is responsible for lower coastal temperatures than areas immediately inland, the difference being at least three hours in reaching 90F temperatures. For example, Los Angeles International Airport, just 3 miles from the Pacific Ocean, has an average January temperature of 54F, and 69F in July. At San Bernardino, 65 miles inland, average January temperature is 51F, and 78F in July. Where possible, prevailing winds follow natural breaks in the Coastal Ranges (most notably in San Francisco, Monterey, and Santa Barbara), thus substantially lowering average temperatures in inland locations. However, in many coastal locations, excessively low temperatures during the growing season, high wind, and pervasive fog preclude commercial quality grape production.

Figure 8.8

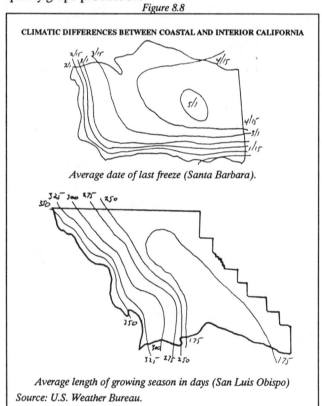

Average date of last freeze (Santa Barbara).

Average length of growing season in days (San Luis Obispo)
Source: U.S. Weather Bureau.

In combination, the three climatic-determining factors of altitude, prevailing winds, and cold, oceanic water produce divergent seasonal temperature and precipitation patterns. While temperatures vary only slightly along the coast, the annual range becomes appreciably greater as

one proceeds inland. In January, inland temperatures tend to be cooler than along the coast due to a combination of elevation and the land's capacity to heat and cool more quickly. July temperatures are much higher than coastal locations because the Coastal Ranges act as a barrier to the cooling effect of the ocean and prevailing winds. This cooling effect is often associated with the phenomena of "upwelling," a process whereby deep, colder water is brought to the surface near the coast, hence the production of fog. The heat summation for Red Bluff, Paso Robles, Ukiah, Livermore, St. Helena, and Santa Maria, presented in Fig. 8.9, from April 1st to October 31st is highly illustrative of this seasonal variation between coastal and interior areas.

Figure 8.9

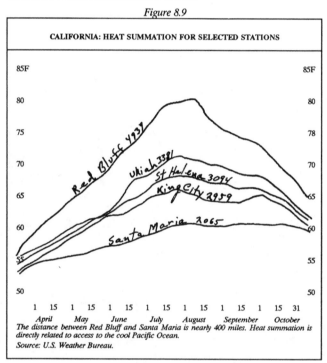

The distance between Red Bluff and Santa Maria is nearly 400 miles. Heat summation is directly related to access to the cool Pacific Ocean.
Source: U.S. Weather Bureau.

The foregoing has produced an unusual climate. Instead of the usual four distinct seasons encountered in the midwest and northeast, the climate of California is divided into wet winter and dry summer seasons for much of the state, and nearly all of the populated areas. Seasonal temperature ranges are generally narrow, winter is mild, spring and fall are of short duration and poorly defined, and summer, the longest season, is dry, ranging from hot to warm. The Mediterranean climate, covering half the state's land area, is characterized by winter rainfall, summer drought, and significant modifications along the coast where fog is a common occurrence. This latter condition, commonly referred to as "Mediterranean heather climate" due to the dominance of this perennial herb, occurs in those areas where the summer fog lowers the mean temperature below 71F for the warmest month. Occurring further in the interior, the "Mediterranean olive climate," the most common and widespread, is dominated by significantly higher temperatures and a vegetation pattern dominated by scattered oaks, short bunch grasses, and chaparral on rugged slopes. While the map indicates a widespread pattern throughout the state, it extends further east in the central portion of the state than elsewhere due to the presence of San Francisco Bay. The Mediterranean climatic regime, however, is not homogeneous; it is divided into three important subtypes: hot summer, warm summer, and cool summer, the latter, a coastal region with more than 30 days of fog. When compared with all other Mediterranean/climate viticultural regions, California's climate is not unusual, as it is nearly identical with Chile and the Capetown region of South Africa. But when compared with the much larger wine producing region bordering the Mediterranean Sea, the presence of the cold California Current does mitigate high temperatures and extremely low humidity rates producing more mesothermal features.

Figure 8.10

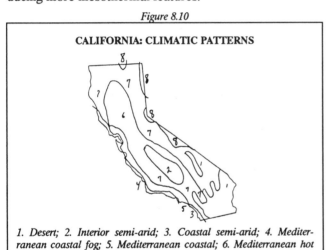

CALIFORNIA: CLIMATIC PATTERNS

1. Desert; 2. Interior semi-arid; 3. Coastal semi-arid; 4. Mediterranean coastal fog; 5. Mediterranean coastal; 6. Mediterranean hot interior; 7. Dry summer upland; 8. Alpine.

In the extreme southern portion of the San Joaquin Valley, and in the interior valleys further south and east of Los Angeles and San Diego, low latitude, hot desert lands dominate the landscape collectively covering perhaps one-fifth of the state's total land area. These areas are characterized by high evaporation rates, diminished precipitation, non-contiguous vegetation, a lack of surface water, mineralized soils, lower rates of humidity than comparable coastal regions, and high incidence of sunshine. Consequently, the long, hot summer requires irrigation, and, like ancient Rome, California is a state of aqueducts, dams, and reservoirs. Although the grapevine is a xerophytic plant, well-adapted to long periods of high evaporation and transpiration rates, current estimates place the percentage of total grape acreage under irrigation to 96 percent. While productivity is extremely high for both grape and other crops, grape acreage is overwhelmingly concentrated for table and raisin use and not

for quality wine production, including fortified wines. Nevertheless, to make good wine in hot climates requires inexhaustible care in growing the right grapes, and titanic skill in their vinification. White wines from the Central Valley, Cucamonga, and other desertic regions are subject to rapid oxidation, and tend to be dull and flat; red wines are astringent, poorly balanced, and have weak color. Both fetch one-seventh to one-third the price of coastal grapes. Therefore, these areas are in decline, a trend that will continue in the future.

Figure 8.11

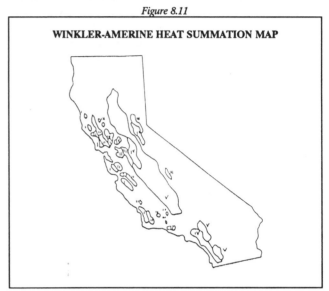

WINKLER-AMERINE HEAT SUMMATION MAP

The foregoing has produced the widely used heat summation system developed by Winkler-Amerine. The heat summation notion is important because it sets reasonable (not absolute) limits to the inherent character of individual grape vines to grow in one area as opposed to another. The warm to hot Napa Valley is ideally suited to Cabernet Sauvignon, and totally unsuitable for Gewurztraminer, Riesling, and Pinot Noir-three grape varieties that demand a cooler growing season. With the past mistakes of planting huge acreages of Cabernet Sauvignon in Monterey not withstanding, the present pattern of grape varieties being matched to specific microclimates has become a refined science, and very much in demand given the huge outlays required in establishing a modern, commercial vineyard. In the final analysis, the finest wine producing regions are associated with the cool, fog-laden coastal hillsides and valleys with scarcely a quality wine producing region (except perhaps portions of the Sierra Foothills) more than 150 miles inland.

In general, the best quality vines are matched with heat summation and geographic region in the following manner:

Region I: Riesling, Pinot Noir, Gewurztraminer, Chenin Blanc, Pinot Blanc, and Chardonnay. Portions of Santa Barbara, Santa Cruz, Monterey, and Sonoma Counties.
Region II: Pinot Blanc, Chardonnay, Riesling, Sauvignon Blanc, Petite

Sirah, Sylvaner, Cabernet Sauvignon, and Chenin Blanc. Portions of Napa, Sonoma, Santa Barbara, and San Luis Obispo counties.
Region III: Sauvignon Blanc, Chenin Blanc, Semillon, Zinfandel, Cabernet Sauvignon, Colombard, Merlot, and Petite Sirah. Portions of the Sierra Foothills, and portions of Napa, Sonoma, San Luis Obispo, and Monterey counties.
Region IV: Ruby Cabernet, Barbera, Palomino, Tinta Madeira, Grenache, Carignane, Mourvedre. Portions of Santa Clara and San Benito counties, and the Central Valley.
Region V: Colombard, Ruby Cabernet, Barbera, Carignane, Palomino, Grenache, and Tinta Madeira. Nearly the entire Central Valley, and Riverside and San Bernardino counties.

In reality, the above oversimplified picture means that certain grape varieties can grow in more than one area, and that many have no business being planted in areas where they presently exist. More often than not, growers plant a specific variety because of demand for reasons other than quality, the production of a specific wine, for high yields (a significant factor), resistance to disease (a significant factor in reducing production costs), and for insurance (as in the Thompson Seedless, a three-way grape that can be sold for raisin, table, or wine use, depending on market conditions). Often a grower will plant a specific grape variety simply because he wants to defy nature and prevailing opinion; to establish a quality reputation; to be singular among a sea of uniformity; etc. As sunny and predictable as the climate is, every year is not a vintage year in California, and often there are unusual and unforeseen disasters, hence, a formidable vintage divergence, as illustrated by several vintages furnished by Simi Winery. In this regard it is interesting to note the harvest dates for Beringer in neighboring Napa during the period 1976-1984: 1976, 9/12-11/2; 1977, 9/28-11/14; 1978, 9/6-10/25; 1979, 9/8-19/29; 980, 9/10-11/3; 1981, 8/24-10/4; 1982, 9/6-10/27; 1983, 9/2-10/23; 8/9-9/26. It is noteworthy, however, that while the vintage date varied by more than 30 days during this nine-year period, the average length of the harvest is a remarkable 47.8 days in duration,

Figure 8.12

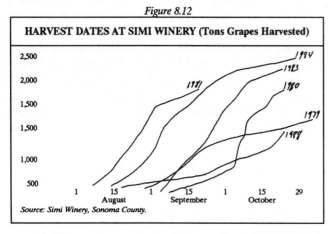

HARVEST DATES AT SIMI WINERY (Tons Grapes Harvested)

Source: Simi Winery, Sonoma County.

Unlike most areas east of the continental divide, California is very fortunate in being nearly disease-free and devoid of major hazards adversely affecting the industry.

The unpredictability of high seasonal variations of temperature and precipitation--serious conditions that plague areas east of the continental divide, are lacking, as are the lethal features of 2 4-D, Root Rot, and Crown Gall. Although phylloxera is periodically injurious, in the main this disease has been confined for over 100 years with no significant economic loses until recently. However, its geographic incidence is widespread afflicting more than 24 counties, otherwise contiguous from Mendocino in the north to Kern in the south, but, strangely, it is not a particularly significant problem in San Benito, Stanislaus, Merced, Mariposa, Calaveras, Amador, and Nevada counties. A recently discovered new type (Biotype-B) seems to be troublesome (it is resistant to 75 percent of existing rootstock), and it appears that it is about to cause serious damage. It is estimated that in Napa and Sonoma counties alone, the spread of phylloxera is doubling each year, and that more than 30,000 acres will have to be replaced by the end of this decade at a cost of more than $450 million.

Pierce's Disease is a minor problem on low lying, poorly drained sites in the southern portion of the state. Phosphorus deficiency is chronic yet manageable, but soil salinity is a deadly problem in those areas that are imperfectly drained. Because most vineyards are removed from industrial complexes, the effects of sulfur and ozone emissions are within controllable limits. However, the capricious nature of earthquake activity can wreak havoc; the April 18, 1906 San Francisco earthquake destroyed 15 million gallons of wine in that city. Over the years, earthquake damage has been substantially reduced, but can be sizeable for many small producers as in Santa Cruz in 1989. Although the threat from terrestrial tremor is statewide, to the author's knowledge, only the Guenoc Winery in Lake County is entirely earthquake-proof. An unusual katabatic wind--El Nino caused $1.1 billion in damages (crops, houses, and roadways) during 1982-1983, with abnormally high precipitation when normal west-moving winds reversed. Although rare, these winds can be extremely destructive to man, animal and agriculture.

NAPA-SONOMA VINTAGES

It is difficult to give an accurate vintage picture of viticultural growing conditions because of the near countless microclimates. Furthermore, exposure, aspect, and altitudinal considerations, grape varieties planted, vineyard practices, and the age of individual grape vines all vary dramatically. Therefore, all vintage charts should be considered as broad guides to a particular year. It becomes extremely difficult to be faithful and precise for the entire appellation or region since particular sites differ substantially from each other. Moreover, the vintage will vary according to grape variety, method of vinification, and aging characteristics. Consequently, the following is nothing but a series of broad generalizations.

Weather is perhaps the most important factor, but averages and such expressions as "perfect growing conditions," and the like are both misleading and inaccurate. One thing is certain, the expression "every year is a vintage year in California" is correct, as all wine grape regions have a growing season above 144 days (the shortest ever recorded), and abundant sunshine. Unlike Bordeaux, Champagne, the midwest, and northeast, growing conditions in the many microclimates of California vary tremendously every year due to the somewhat arbitrary character of the state's dominant climate. While the latter does not exhibit significant variations, all *weather elements* are capricious and highly erratic in a Mediterranean climate, and it is this uncertain feature that adds to the significance of vintage variation. While *controlled* rainfall in the form of measured and carefully applied water has removed a large measure of uncertainty, and most frost activity is subject to mitigation, all other natural weather elements are simply too aberrant. As the number of premium wineries continues to increase, the quality of premium wines escalates, and as the business of prestige wines becomes ever larger, the market place will pay closer attention to vintages than heretofore.

The deviation in ratings refer to regional geographic variations and their effects on individual grape varieties. Gewurztraminer, Pinot Noir, and Chardonnay, three early ripening varieties, differ significantly in their maturing features and overall quality from mid-season and late-season ripening varieties. The finest vintages in recent decades have been 1958, 1968, 1970, 1973, 1974, 1978, 1980, 1984, 1985, 1986, 1987, 1988, and 1991. "Fat" wine styles were most prevalent for the years 1970, 1973, 1974, 1976, 1978, 1980, 1984, and 1986. Early harvests occurred in 1984, 1985, 1986, and 1987.

1991: 16-20 The five-year drought finally came to an abrupt halt with nearly continuous rainfall during the period February-April (20 inches in March). Summer, and early fall, in particular, were exceptionally cool (June was cold) resulting in the latest harvest since 1975. Unseasonable hot weather in late September-early October (90F+ temperatures were common) matured all late-maturing grapes to perfection, and, as a result, Cabernet Sauvignon and Zinfandel are considered exceptional. However, the growing season was characterized by an inconsistent ripening sequence and many varieties ripened out of turn. The vintage is considered better than 1989, marginally better than 1990 (especially for white wines), and one of the finest of the decade.

1990: 12-19 Characterized by cool nights, foggy mornings, and warm days, the long 1990 growing season along coastal California produced intensely flavored wines. Only major drawback was a rainstorm in late May (up to 6 inches is some areas) causing considerable bloom damage in isolated areas, but, unfortunately, not sustained in intensity to alleviate the drought. Although most varieties weathered the storm, Cabernet Sauvignon, Merlot, Pinot Noir, and, to a lesser extent, Chardonnay were somewhat affected by shatter and lower yields. Summer was relatively cool, dry, and the harvest season was even drier (with unseasonably high late September and October temperatures). Quantity was less than 1989, but the quality throughout the state was above-average, particularly in North Coast counties where the wines exhibit concentration, richness, depth, and good balance. Many wineries in Sonoma and Napa have pronounced the vintage as the best ever. Cabernet Sauvignon, in particular, is considered the finest since 1986, but Merlot and Pinot Noir have fared less well. Chardonnay is rich, well-structured, yet supple on the palate. Mid-harvest rain in the Central Coast reduced concentration and richness.

1989: 8-16 A dry winter was followed by copious spring rains and early bud break resulting in the largest crop of the last 3 years. The vintage year began under excellent conditions, and ended, for some regions, with disastrous results. The harvest began in late August under fair weather, but by mid-September unseasonable heavy rain accompanied by hail and fog contributed to the formation of bunch rot and mold, unlike the 1988 harvest that was virtually rain-free and significantly warmer. The quality of grapes and wines was highly variable. Due to the long and cool growing season, late maturing varieties fared much better than early maturing grapes. Chardonnay in both Mendocino and Sonoma counties experienced a 50 percent decline. Although many Chardonnay are of mediocre quality, prices have remained the same or even increased. Vintage conditions were more normal in the Central Valley and along the South Coast, while the Central Coast counties managed to escape inclement weather producing some of the finest wines in the state. Zinfandel was successful in the Sierra Foothills.

1988: 10-18 The vintage season was characterized by a one-third reduction in rainfall after a wet winter (the second dry year in a row), spring frosts (as the dry soils warmed up quickly, the vines budded early re-sulting in widespread shatter), and a summer hampered by low temperatures. There was a heat wave in February, no rain in March, lower temperatures and heavy rain in April and May. The result was an uneven crop, with growers describing the first six months as one of healthy grapes but lousy weather. Excessive summer heat and a lack of water stressed vines and reduced yield, but produced well-structured, highly concentrated wines. Weather conditions throughout the year ranged from wet, hot, cold, dry and hot (100F temperatures in October), but during veraison, fog lowered temperatures, and, in the process, lengthened the growing season. The harvest ended in the middle of November with raised sugar levels and improved color. Despite crop reductions from 15 to 60 percent (particularly bad for Pinot Noir and Sauvignon Blanc), fruit juice flavor in many areas was outstanding. It was a better than average vintage, but not better than 1984, 1985, 1986, and 1987, although there are many dissenters to this opinion. Wines have good balance, and intense flavors. Red wines, particularly Zinfandel and Cabernet Sauvignon, are dark, firm and fleshy, especially from North Coast hillside vineyards. Monterey wines exhibit clean fruit and good flavor intensity; Riesling was particularly good; Cabernet Sauvignon, affected with improper set, produced small clusters and berries, and low yields, but will produce excellent, concentrated wines. The vintage marks the fifth successful vintage of the decade, but due to a small premium North Coast grape crop, prices rose sharply.

1987: 12-19 After a dry winter, bud break and bloom were both ahead of schedule, but a heat wave and strong wind generated problems with berry set, affecting late ripening grapes such as Cabernet Sauvignon, Merlot, and Sauvignon Blanc. This produced an early harvest, a 13 percent reduction of the crop (the smallest since 1983), and some varieties, such as Merlot, by as much as 40 percent in some localities. The weather for the rest of the season was cooler and the harvest two weeks ahead of schedule, but in some areas close to forest fires a brown haze prolonged the harvest season for nearly one month. Generally, the growing season was free from rot and mildew, and a large second crop harvest booted the harvest to acceptable economic levels. A strong demand for premium varietals raised prices, particularly for Cabernet Sauvignon, Merlot, Chardonnay, Pinot Noir, and Zinfandel. Although this was the smallest harvest since 1983, quality, particularly for Cabernet Sauvignon, Zinfandel, Pinot Noir, Chardonnay, and Merlot, was high in terms of concentrated flavor and color intensity; alcohol levels are higher than 1986 and 1985. Red wines have good fruit, are rich in tannin, and loaded with concentrated flavors, but unlike the 1984-1986 vintages, they are uncommonly tight, unyielding, and require considerable cellaring. The overwhelming red grape success of the vintage may very well be Merlot. Chardonnay is well balanced, firm, intensely scented, and well structured. The vintage may turn out to be better than the three previous vintages.

1986: 14-19.5 For the third year in a row, both the growing season and harvest began earlier than normal. Although marred by unusual weather conditions (alternating periods of hot and cool weather) this was the third successful vintage in a row. February was a warm, wet month (with considerable flooding in Napa and Sonoma) with early bud break; March was greeted with unexpected frost in widely divergent areas; and a cool, even growing season produced grapes with good acid balance, good fruit, and widespread mildew. In Sonoma, throughout July and August, chilly, foggy weather prevailed, with some newspapers calling the growing season as the "summer that never was." There were 30 foggy mornings in June and July, and 26 in August. The fog was unusually thick, breaking up only in late afternoon. Although considerable rain fell during September 16-20 and again on 24-27, there was minimal damage as most of the crop was already harvested; a good Indian Summer presented excellent conditions for the Cabernet Sauvignon harvest in early October. One of the coolest years on record, the growing season was longer by at least 30 days leading to slow ripening, good flavor concentration, and excellent color. The vintage, therefore, was characterized by high quality fruit; berry size was small with good, concentrated flavor, and excellent sugar-acid balance. · A combination of higher yields, sugar and acids, and moderate alcohol levels made for a more Bordeaux-type wine than usual for California. Wines are well scented, firmer, less flabby, but 1986 has been called the winemakers vintage because of the wide diversity of wines made. The quality is equal or better than 1985 due to lower alcohol levels, high acidity and more intense flavors. White wines were above-average to excellent in quality, particularly Chardonnay, Sauvignon Blanc, Riesling, and Gewurztraminer. Cabernet Sauvignon, Merlot, and Zinfandel (all above-average to outstanding) are firmer than those of 1985, and will be more durable. Pinot Noir is excellent, as well as late harvest wines, the latter fruity and supple. The white and red wines of Santa Barbara County were excellent, the finest in recent memory. In the final analysis, because this vintage fell between two excellent vintages, it has been easily overlooked, but will receive the acclaim it deserves by patient and discerning aficionados.

1985: 16-20 The 1985 growing season was characterized by a warm, dry spring, early bud break and excellent fruit set. June and July experienced 100F temperatures, but coastal fog and cool weather lowered temperatures into September and the harvest. This unusual, trouble-free, long, cool, growing season and problem-free vintage produced a surprising combination of high acids and adequate sugar levels. Grapes were healthy, and the wines are well-structured, tannin-rich, complex, intense, with good color, and superbly balanced. It was not only a superb vintage, but a large harvest (the third largest in history) of more than 2.8 million tons. This was a remarkable vintage and one of the finest in the last 30 years.

1984: 11-18.5 For some wineries this was the earliest harvest on record. Unlike 1982 and 1983, 1984 was a hot growing season (Napa and Sonoma had 30 days of 100F+ temperatures) producing low acid grapes, higher sugar levels, dark color, and high alcohol levels. One of the driest springs in memory was followed by early bud break, good fruit set, and high temperatures producing small bunches and berries resulting in a reduced crop but above-average vintage, although quality was uneven because many varieties ripened simultaneously (a good portion of which were dehydrated). Depending on location, picking and winemaking skills, wines ranged from early maturing, supple libations to raisiny, high alcohol wines. For example, while Chardonnay was not as good as 1985, it was above-average in Carneros; and while Central Coast wines were higher in acidity, Napa made rich, ripe, generous, and fat Merlot and Cabernet Sauvignon.

1983: 4-15 The growing season began with the wettest winter on record, and climaxed with a rainy harvest. While precipitation totals varied dramatically by region, all areas received too much and at the wrong time causing a loss of 20 percent throughout most of the coastal counties, with losses of 50 percent for some varieties such as Chardonnay, Pinot Blanc, Chenin Blanc, and Riesling. The rain, compounded by excessive heat, interrupted photosynthesis contributing to low Brix levels. As panic picking was common, and rot endemic, the harvest, referred to as the "El Nino Vintage" due to high rainfall and humidity at harvest time, resulted in a significant crop reduction. In reality there were two vintages: those grapes picked before the harvest deluge made excellent, concentrated and well flavored wines; those picked after made diluted, flavorless, weak wines offering little value. However, there were many surprises. Along the north coast, some white wines were well scented, but precipitation and rain-swollen red grapes, particularly Cabernet Sauvignon, were less good (Merlot was more successful), although those that were picked late managed to produce tannin-rich, tightly structured wines. In nearly all areas, grapes had difficulty ripening, and when they did they all ripened at once. Early ripening grapes such as Chardonnay and Pinot Noir are light bodied. This was the smallest crush since 1976.

1982: 5-18 The 1982 vintage has gone down in history as one of the most turbulent and variable, with wine quality ranging from poor to excellent. Record rainfall in January and February, widespread spring frosts, heavy April rainfall, snow and hailstorms, and the coolest June and July temperatures in 50 years presented severe mildew problems as there was abnormal cloudy and rainy weather with fog. Untimely and heavy rainfall, beginning on September 15 with downpours on 23-24, diluted and reduced the crop still further, producing rot in many areas. Harvest season was late, but proceeded rapidly after the September deluge with many grapes being harvested between 16 and 19 percent sugar; selective harvesting was necessary and a major problem. The large harvest was chaotic and quality varied from valley to valley and from grower to grower. In the north coast, a good deal of Chardonnay was lost to rot, but the late maturing Cabernet Sauvignon was saved by a timely Indian Summer.

1981: 11-17 This vintage, characterized by a series of heat waves that matured grapes rapidly, was one of the earliest harvests since 1933, and

a complete reversal of 1980. The growing season was highlighted by a mild winter with low rainfall, a frost-free spring, and a hot June-August summer (there were 110F temperatures in northern Napa for three weeks in June). Lacking the usual coastal fog conditions, grapes ripened early, and all about the same time, abbreviating the harvest period from eight to four weeks. As high sugar levels diluted fruit concentration in white wines, the combination of excessive rain, high temperatures and high humidity failed to develop good pigmentation in red grapes. White wines are good to excellent, but many are flawed by low acid levels. Red wines are very forward, early maturing, flavorless, and lacking good color. Surprisingly, Pinot Noir and late harvest wines were above-average in quality. Monterey, in particular, had a more successful harvest and quality vintage than most other coastal counties.

1980: 12-18 The vintage was characterized by uncommon weather: a long, wet and warm winter followed by early bud break, with temperatures remaining in the low 70sF rather than in the 80sF (with only a few hot spells in July and August). However, this cool spring and summer period ended in September with a major heat wave that lasted two weeks; by harvest, temperatures soared beyond 100F raising sugar levels and dehydrating the vines. Although relatively large in terms of quantity, quality was highly uneven due to microclimatic variability. Some exceptional, rich and fruity wines were made, particularly by those wineries that picked late. In general, red wines were better than white.

1979: 12-19 An uneventful growing season was marred by a two week heat wave before harvest (causing dehydration), followed by copious amounts of rainfall during the harvest producing rot and diluted must concentrations. The vintage was highly variable by region: Napa suffered from pronounced dehydration (temperatures approached 115F) aggravated by high winds, and an October rainstorm affected Cabernet Sauvignon adversely. White grapes picked before the heat wave were of excellent quality, but those picked after were very poor. In Sonoma the heat wave was less pronounced and white and red varieties much better. Mendocino faired better than Napa and Sonoma, but quality was very spotty. Zinfandel in many places produced excellent wines. Monterey was also subjected to the September heat wave and rain damage was extensive. In sharp contrast, the Central Valley enjoyed one of the finest quality vintages in a generation with less heat and rain than normal.

1978: 8-17 Heavy precipitation in the winter lasting into spring caused widespread mildew. The highly variable vintage was characterized by a long, cool growing season that produced many excellent to outstanding, big, intense wines. Monterey, with an early harvest, produced excellent fruity table and late harvest wines, particularly Riesling and Gewurztraminer. The very best from Sonoma-Napa were alcoholic, rich, intensely flavored and scented, particularly Cabernet Sauvignon and Zinfandel.

1977: 12-18 Despite continuing drought conditions, output was marginally larger than 1976. Early budbreak and a cool summer benefited early maturing varieties by producing excellent sugar-acid levels. Cool September weather was followed by seasonal coastal storms slowing the grape maturation of late ripening varieties and producing a below normal crop. This is an underrated year in which many excellent wines were made. Napa made above-average to excellent red wines, and Sonoma and Mendocino equally good white wines. Vintage was above-average in Monterey. Late harvest wines, particularly Sauvignon Blanc, were outstanding.

1976: 9-15 This was a below average year with a difficult harvest as a dry fall and winter were followed by high, erratic temperatures with heavy rain during the harvest. There was considerable sunburning, and early ripening varieties were particularly hard hit, such as Chardonnay and Gewurztraminer whose yields were reduced by at least 25 percent. Grape quality throughout the state was highly spotty: while Monterey made below average Chenin Blanc, Gewurztraminer, Pinot Noir, Riesling, and Cabernet Sauvignon; fruity, intense and well structured Chardonnay, Cabernet Sauvignon and Zinfandel were made north of San Francisco; and concentrated, alcoholic wines were produced in the Central Valley.

1975: 11-17 The growing season was characterized by extremes (spring frosts and late rains) resulting in a small and late harvest (2.15 million tons compared with 3.85 million tons in 1974). An abnormally hot July severely sunburned many grapes causing dehydration; August was cool;

September warm; and on October 4th a frost alarm, followed by 4 inches of rainfall with another deluge in the middle of the month. Many grapes, picked in November, were low in sugar producing fruity, but high acid, early maturing wines. Chardonnay and Sauvignon Blanc were particularly good, but less good was Cabernet Sauvignon. White wines from Mendocino were above-average in quality.

1974: 13-20 Widely hailed as the finest vintage of the decade, the very successful Cabernet Sauvignon has captivated the attention of American enophiles for many years. A long, cool summer, and a warm, dry harvest ripened the grapes producing succulent, ripe, fruity, outstanding red wines, particularly from Napa and Sonoma. As good as the weather patterns were, quality was spotty due to poor vineyard practices such as overcropping. White wines were thin and unsubstantial on the palate (due in part to 100F temperatures in early September and intermittent rain causing bunch rot and mildew), but red wines, particularly Zinfandel and Cabernet Sauvignon, were noted for their body, color, high alcohol and tannin content. Despite historic accolades, not all red wines, made in a big, powerful style, have aged gracefully.

1973: 11-17 This year was known for a record crush, high prices, and average to above-average quality white and red wines, particularly from Napa and Sonoma. A long, cool summer provided ideal growing conditions producing both high sugar and acid levels, and fruity, yet rich Cabernet Sauvignon and Zinfandel, particularly from Mendocino.

1972: 3-11 The vintage was characterized by cool spring weather, high summer temperatures, and record October rains diluting the must and producing thin, watery wines. While Cabernet Sauvignon lacked concentration, Petite Sirah and Zinfandel in Mendocino were ripe and supple.

1971: 6-12 This was a highly uneven vintage with mostly average to below average weak wines. Mendocino and Sonoma fared slightly better than other coastal counties.

1970 11-18 The vintage is best known for severe frost activity, a reduced harvest, high prices, and above-average to excellent Cabernet Sauvignon, and average to above-average Zinfandel and Chardonnay, particularly from Napa and Sonoma.

Older Vintages: Historically, of a superior nature have been: 1936 (despite a severe frost), 1941 (one of the finest on record), 1944, 1946, 1947, 1950, 1951, 1958, 1961, 1965, 1968.

Soils

Based on age and location seven major types of soils are recognized. In terms of extent of area covered, 40 percent are classified as *undifferentiated upland*, soils that are moderately weathered, deep to shallow, most of which are too steep for cultivation, mainly forested, and located at elevations higher than 3,000 feet, principally in the northern and eastern portions of the state. *Lithosols* (20 percent), or rocky hillside soils, are mainly associated with chaparral, shrub, and forest, and are mainly non-commercial. They are shallow, skeletal, and lack moisture-holding capacities. However, when the terrain is modified, they provide excellent vineland, but due to the high cost of development to bring them under commercial production, it is estimated that fewer than 10,000 acres are planted on true lithosolic soils. These soils are the farthest removed from valley floors in terms of both geologic time and elevation. Seventeen percent are classified as *desertic*, most of which are deep, highly mineralized soils that are mainly uncultivated due to the lack of water. When irrigated, these soils are excellent for the production of raisin and table grapes.

The remaining four types are all important in the cultivation of grapes. About 5 percent are described as *valley basin* (or bottomland), mostly slightly weathered, heavy-textured (clay, silt, and organic-rich), alluvial or lacustrine material. The terrain is mainly flat to gently sloping, and the deposits deep, with the soil horizon poorly drained; but when improved, they are highly productive. Twelve percent of the state contains soils that are described as *valley* (first bench). Well drained, these are described as the state's best all-purpose agricultural land, and comprise more than 80 percent of all viticultural land, mainly in the Central Valley. *Terrace soils* (or more elevated bench/foothill), with 6 percent, are extensively weathered alluvium material that lie above the valley soils, accounting for some of the finest vineland in the state. Gently undulating with occasional steep cliffs, *hill-mountain soils*, with a much higher percentage of stone, represent some of the finest vineland in the state. As recent demand for vineland has intensified in several premium coastal counties, vineyards are now being planted at ever higher elevations, and it is expected that more *hill* and *mountain ava* designations and vineyard names will enter the lexicon.

Most of the state's vineyards are planted on valley soils because they are the easiest to develop and the least expensive to farm. Physical differences are a function of elevation, exposure and character of parent material (basic rock), and, as such, there are several major observations: (1) although lacking in most areas, limestone and dolomite deposits occur east of Salinas, and southern portions of Santa Cruz County, San Luis Obispo, and Santa Ynez Valley; (2) the Sierra Nevada Range is mainly composed of granite with some impregnations of iron; (3) the region north of San Francisco is mainly volcanic with rich concentrations of iron-impregnated soils; (4) the Central Coast and the Temecula regions contain granitic rock, isolated pockets of limestone, and flysch (conglomerate), especially in Temecula.

California Agriculture: Grape And Wine Production

Historically, California agriculture has evolved through three distinct stages: the era of extensive livestock ranching, the age of bonanza grain farming, and the period of specialized farming. California's agriculture is not only highly specialized and productive, but capital intensive, and, as it is based on economies of scale, landholdings are huge in dimension. It is the nation's premier agricultural state, ranking first (each year for the past 43 years) in terms of total farm cash receipts. Not only does the state lead the nation in irrigated land, value of crop acre, and farm capitalization, but it ranks first nationally in 58 agricultural commodities, of which walnuts, peaches, strawberries, tomatoes, eggs, lemons, lettuce, cut flowers, almonds, nursery plants, apricots, avocados, and grapes are the most important. California supplies more than 50 percent of the nation's vegetables, fruits and nuts. Reflecting this high degree of specialization, fewer than 5 percent of the states 133,000 farms are "general" farms, the rest are all "specialized" in production exhibiting remarkable centralization by geographic region. Almond production, once widely diffused, is now concentrated in two counties, and a similar picture for nearly all crops exists, including grapes.

The magnitude of the state's agribusiness is expressed by the following statistics: 3 percent of the nation's farmland supplies more than 50 percent of America's fruits, nuts and vegetables, and 30 percent of the nation's table food. Cash farm receipts exceed $18 billion, followed by Texas with $10 billion, and Iowa with $9 billion. Of the ten leading national agricultural counties, eight are located in California. Fresno is the largest agricultural county, and if it were a separate state its farm production would rank higher than 25 other states. Agricultural exports generate nearly $4 billion in total cash receipts, 185,000 jobs, and contribute nearly $14 billion in total economic activity. The success of Californian agriculture is the product of an excellent sunny climate, abundant supplies of irrigation water, superb soils, and a huge midwestern and eastern market with a high purchasing power. The reaction of Californian farmers to these stimuli has been a high degree of spatial specialization in fruit, nut and vegetable farming unmatched by any other comparable sized area in the nation. It is no wonder, therefore, that in a relatively short time span, agriculture became agribusiness and finally big business.

> In 1988, 95.8% of the nation's grape crush was concentrated in California; New York 2.1%; Washington 1.5%; and the other states .6%. The Central Valley was responsible for 84.2%, the North Coast 8.8%, the Central Coast 6.2%, and the rest of the state .7%.
> The 1991 harvest was 5.1 million tons, of which 2.3 were raisin grapes, 2.2 wine grapes, and .6 table grapes.
> Source: California Agricultural Statistical Service.

One remarkable feature of California agriculture is how little space it occupies. Of the 100 million acres of land area, less than one-third is used for agriculture. Because 55 percent of the state's total land area is owned by the state and federal government, cropland occupies less than 8.3 million acres, and grapes, with nearly 700,000 acres, constitute about 8 percent of this amount. The three principal agricultural regions are the Central Valley, the coastal valleys, and the interior desertic regions east and southeast of Los Angeles. With the exception of the large, more diversified Central Valley, the rest of the state seems to specialize in one or two specific crops, be it the mundane iceberg lettuce, or industrial agricultural commodities such as long-staple cotton. The five most important agricultural counties (Fresno, Tulare, Kern, Monterey, and Riverside) are nearly all irrigated. While Fresno, Kern and Tulare rank as the nation's top 3 agricultural counties, another 22 in the state are among the 100 richest agricultural counties nationwide. The superiority of these three areas as the premier agricultural regions in the nation derives mainly from the most extensive development of irrigation in the country. This development has been made possible by the proximity of the Sierra Nevadas to the east of the Central Valley, the Coastal Ranges, and the Colorado River. Consequently, not only are California farms large, but the average value per acre is twice the national average, and second only to Arizona in net income per farm.

> In 1974, wines accounted for 83% of grape crush requirements, 13% for brandy, and the remainder for concentrate and juice. The grape crush of 2.3 million tons consisted of 1.2 million tons of wine varieties, .75 million tons of raisin varieties, and .37 million tons of table grapes. As a percent of type of grape, crush use of wine grapes was 96%, raisin varieties 39%, and table grapes 59%. The crush utilized 58% of California's grape production in 1974.
> Approximate tons of California grapes used for concentrate is about 450,000 tons, up from 350,000 tons in 1985. This figure represents 80% of all concentrate used in America, a figure that is steadily eroding because of imports.
> Canned grape production rose from 2.3 million tons in 1929 to more than 30 million in 1948, but has since declined.

California is one of the world's consummate vineyards. Grapes, one of the five most important agricultural crops, occupy more than 692,595 acres out of 35.5 million acres, or 2 percent of all farmland, and an astounding 8 percent of the state's total cropland. If one excludes cropland that is pastured and cropland not harvested or pastured, then grapes occupy 9.7 percent of all harvested cropland, the highest such state figure in the nation. Over the past 60 years the relative position of grapes among the state's ten leading commodities in terms of value has moved from fifth place in 1930, to third place in 1971, to second place in 1991. The farm value of grapes for the same three years increased from $33.6 million, to $305 million, to $2.8 billion. Grapes also comprise 33.5 percent of the state's total fruit and nut acreage, and are grown in 47 of the state's 58 counties. Wine grapes from coastal counties also enjoy the highest market value per acre (as much as $20,000 in comparison with $5,500 in the Central Valley) than any other crop. Grapes constitute the third largest exportable agricultural commodity in terms of value, and with the amount of potential land that remains, California's true potential is significant. Grapes rank as the number one crop in Fresno, Madera, Sonoma, Napa; second in Kern, Riverside, San Joaquin, and Kern; and among the top six in San Luis Obispo, Tulare, Santa Barbara, and Kings.

Grape acreage and production have followed a definite cyclical but upward trend for the past 100 years. Vineyard acreage grew rapidly from 56,000 acres in 1880, to 112,000 acres in 1885, to 336,000 acres in 1910, to 672,000 acres in 1935, the latter, a figure that has fluctuated significantly since then. Grapes are cultivated from the Pacific Ocean to the Sierra Nevada Mountains, from the Oregon border to Escondido in San Diego County (a distance that includes more than 700 disparate microclimates). California has 10,000 growers, a decline of nearly 5,000 since the mid 1930s. The number of cooperatives and cooperative-produced wine has fallen sharply from more than 50 million gallons to less than 10 million gallons. Many of the state's largest and most historic cooperative wineries, like Allied Grape Growers, Del Rey, Lockeford Winery, St. Helena Cooperative, and Woodbridge Vineyard Association are no more.

CALIFORNIA RAISIN, TABLE, WINE GRAPES

Wine Grapes: Of the state's 700,000 acres of vineyards, just over half are planted with wine grape varieties. Two thirds of that acreage is planted in some 45 "black" varieties, a share that is decreasing because of the popularity of white wine, and one third is planted in about 30 "white" varieties, a share increasing.

Raisin Grapes: The 6 varieties classified as raisin grapes are grown on more than 276,000 acres, or 40 percent of the total under vines. Two varieties-Thompson Seedless (36 percent of all acreage in California) and Muscat of Alexandria-are called "3-way grapes" because they can be picked early for sale as table grapes or for drying to make raisins, or picked later for crushing.

Table Grapes: the other 10 percent of the state's vineyard land grows some 25 varieties either destined for being eaten off the stems or crushed at wineries. The Flame Tokay can be used for table, wine and brandy production.

The 1990 geographic distribution of all raisin, table, and wine grape acreage in California, by county, is presented in table and graphic form below. Of the 692,595 total grape acres, 77 percent are located in the Central Valley, 11 percent in the North Coast, 7.2 percent in the Central Coast, 3.5 percent in the Southern Coast, and .4 percent in the Sierra Foothills region. Indicating a high degree of concentration, 63 percent of all grape acreage is located in just four Central Valley counties: Fresno, Madera, Kern and Tulare, all of which are located in the San Joaquin Valley. Of total acreage, 330,356, or 48 percent, are classified as wine grapes, 276,907, or 40 percent, are raisin grapes, and the remaining 85,332 acres are classified as table grapes. It is important to note that while 30 years ago 55 percent of all table grapes, 40 percent of all raisin grapes, and 90 percent of all wine grapes (10 percent were used for brandy) were crushed for winemaking, the current percentages of table and raisin are now half the pre-1965 figures.

The 1890 grape crop: 213,230 acres of grapes; 280,869 tons: 43,414 tons for table use; 173,037 tons for wine, 41,166 tons for raisins, and 23,252 tons, other uses.

For 1990, grape acreage stood at: 692,595, of which 276,907 were raisins (40%), 85,332 were table (12%), and 330.356 were wine(48%).

Approximately 60% of all raisin grapes are located in Fresno, 15% in Madera, 12% in Tulare, 10% in Kern, and 3% in other counties. 52% of table grapes were evenly divided between Kern and Tulare, 16% in Riverside, 16% in San Joaquin, 10% in Fresno, and 5% in other counties. 24% of all wine grapes were nearly evenly divided between Madera and San Joaquin, 31% nearly evenly divided between Fresno, Napa, and Sonoma, 16% between Monterey and Glenn, and the remaining 29% among 35 other counties.

Of the 276,907 acres devoted to the production of raisin grapes, 97 percent of total are found in four south San Joaquin Valley counties, on irrigated soils producing the highest grape yields in the state. After growing rapidly to 307,000 in 1926, raisin grape acreage has fluctuated between 215,000 and 280,000 acres for many of the past 60 years. Until 1972, when raisin grape acreage was overtaken by wine grape acreage, its share of total acreage was twice that of wine and table grapes. Raisin grapes in recent years have not shown impressive growth patterns, exports are not increasing, and as the demand for jug and generic wines are in decline, raisin grape acreage is not expected to increase. Consequently, the percentage of raisin grapes being crushed for wine production has declined dramatically since 1970 from an average of 951,000 tons (47.8% of the total crush), to 505,000 tons (18.1%) in 1986.

Figure 8.13

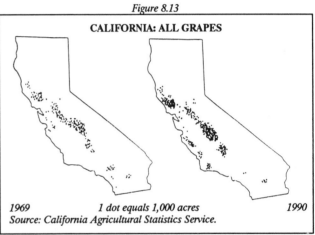

CALIFORNIA: ALL GRAPES

1969   1 dot equals 1,000 acres   1990
Source: California Agricultural Statistics Service.

Thompson Seedless, with 96 percent of total acreage (267,258), is the principal raisin grape, followed by Muscat of Alexandria (5,731), Black Corinth (2,281), and Fiesta (1,254). The significance of raisin grapes in winemaking is reflected by the versatile Thompson Seedless grape, often referred to as the "three-way" grape because it can be made into raisins, wine, or consumed fresh. The ultimate destination is determined by market conditions, and, as such, its percentage in the total wine grape crush varies between 20 and 30 percent, or between 600,000 and 900,000 tons. Although it enjoys a good reputation, the Thompson Seedless grape is a ubiquitous ingredient in most white jug wines, including many prestigious labels. Of all the Central Valley white raisin grapes used in winemaking, the Thompson Seedless resists browning, and blends particularly well with Chenin Blanc. Approximately 98 percent of all Thompson Seedless is grown in the Central Valley, and it represents 38 percent of the state's total grape acreage (in 1966, it accounted for half the acreage). This highly versatile variety, due to cooler demand in the 1980s, experienced unprecedented growth, and, as a result, prices per ton rose by 35 percent between

1982 and 1986. As the cooler market softened in recent years, acreage has not declined as expected, and is above its 1937 figure of 162,084 acres. The leading county is Fresno (165,103), followed by Madera (41,902), Tulare (32,669), and Kern (27,683), collectively about 97 percent of the total.

The geographic distribution of table grape acreage exhibits a picture not too dissimilar from raisin grapes. Reflecting contemporary dietary shifts, table grape acreage more than doubled from 44,936 acres in 1977, to 85,332 in 1990, or approximately 13 percent of all planted grapes, of which more than 96 percent of acreage is located in Fresno, Kern, Riverside, San Joaquin, and Tulare counties. The most popular grapes in terms of acreage are Flame Seedless, followed by Flame Tokay, and Emperor, the three collectively accounting for 50 percent of the total. Approximately 200,000 tons of table grapes are used for winemaking, two-thirds of which are Flame Tokay. Although Thompson Seedless is officially classified as a raisin grape, more than 23 million boxes were shipped in 1990. Total sales hover around $700 million, more than 10 percent of which account for exports. While California production of table grapes is 800,000 tons, it is just 14 percent of world production of 5 million tons. With 1.5 million tons, or 33 percent, Italy ranks first, while California is the world's second largest table grape producer, followed by Chile (13%), Mexico, Greece, Japan, Yugoslavia, Argentina, France, and South Africa. It is estimated that one-third of the 450,000 tons of grapes (primarily table and raisin) produced in Madera, Fresno, Kings, Tulare, and Kern counties is processed into concentrate.

Table 8.5

RAISIN AND TABLE GRAPE ACREAGE BY COUNTY, 1990		
County	Raisin	Table
Fresno	165,103	8,924
Madera	41,902	2,478
Tulare	32,669	22,464
Kern	27,683	22,304
Riverside	4,042	13,841
Kings	2,196	522
Merced	1,826	238
San Joaquin	196	13,386
Other	1,290	1,175
Total	276,907	85,332
Source: California Agricultural Statistics Service.		

The geography of wine grapes exhibits a totally different picture than raisin and table grape distributions. While the latter two grapes are overwhelmingly sited in six counties in the San Joaquin Valley (plus Riverside County), only 57.8 percent of all wine grapes are located in the Central Valley, 24.5 percent in the North Coast, 15.4 percent in the Central Coast, 1.4 percent in the South Coast, and .8 percent in the Sierra Foothills. Despite the notoriety of the coast counties as premium wine produc-

ing regions, it is remarkable to note that within the past ten years the geographic pattern of wine grape acreage has remained stable among the five geographic regions with only the South Coast and Sierra Foothills increasing slightly relative to the other three. However, over the past 30 years, the North Coast counties have evolved from an ancillary role to the large wineries in the Central Valley (known for robust, high alcohol, table and dessert wines), to the premium producing areas for quality table wines. In terms of quality of wine produced and total yields, the Central Valley is responsible for more than three-quarters of the wine grape crush, but for much lower quality wine production. Its winemaking evolution over the past 30 years has progressed from inexpensive, coarse table, and sweet, flat tasting dessert, to crisper, fruitier white and red table, and much improved dessert and sparkling wine production.

Figure 8.14

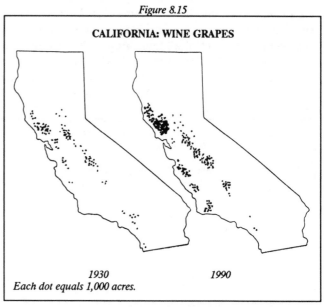

CALIFORNIA: RAISIN AND TABLE GRAPES, 1990

Raisin Grapes   Table Grapes
Each dot equals 1,000 acres.

Figure 8.15

CALIFORNIA: WINE GRAPES

1930   1990
Each dot equals 1,000 acres.

Wine grape acreage has grown significantly over the past 40 years, increasing from 157,000 acres in 1970, to

330,356 acres in 1990. Reflecting the rapid rise in wine grape acreage, grape output rose from 300,000 tons in 1895, to an average of 2.7 million tons during 1949-1953, and 4.5 million tons over the past 15 years. In comparison, deciduous tree fruit has declined slightly over the past 20 years, but citrus fruit, which rose dramatically until the early 1940s and then declined, is now second to grape production. Good reasons for the increase in production are attributed to irrigation, better stock, and the absence of major diseases and pests. With only Washington as a major exception, yields are at least 70 percent higher in California than for the rest of the nation, particularly eastern growers. Seventy-one percent of total wine grape acreage is located in seven counties: Madera (38,596), San Joaquin (37,726), Fresno (34,265), Sonoma (33,317), Napa (33,194), Monterey (28,496), and Kern (27,881), four of which are Central Valley counties. Although U.S. Department of Agriculture projections of wine grape acreage increasing to 498,000 acres by 2000 will not be achieved, total acreage is expected to continue its upward momentum.

The principal red and white wine grape varieties for selected years are presented in the tables below. It is most significant that in 1981 white grapes exceeded red grape acreage for the first time in the state's history. Among white varieties, four--Colombard, Chenin Blanc, Chardonnay, and Sauvignon Blanc--account for 82 percent of total acreage. Varietal concentration among red grapes is less intense with the top six varieties--Zinfandel, Cabernet Sauvignon, Carignane, Barbera, Grenache, and Ruby Cabernet--accounting for only 72 percent of all red wine grapes. Of the top twelve varieties in 1979, more than two thirds were black and not white grapes. Since then the production of red wine grapes has shown a relative decline reflecting consumer preferences. However, while Zinfandel, Cabernet Sauvignon, Pinot Noir, and Merlot have exhibited steady increases, Grenache, Carignane, Barbera, and six others have recorded major declines. The percent of white wines, during the interval 1969-1979, doubled from 16 percent of total plantings. In 1979 the fact that 49 percent of all wine was white indicates that a significant portion of the Thompson Seedless crop was crushed for wine and brandy production. By 1984 the rise of white grape varieties increased dramatically; two specific varieties accounted for 39 percent of the crush--Colombard and Thompson Seedless. For all white varieties harvested in 1984, Colombard accounted for 45 percent of the total--the primary ingredient in white generic wine, and the principal ingredient in cooler production. By 1990, Colombard accounted for one-third of the planted wine grape acreage, followed by Chardonnay (29%), Chenin Blanc (18%), and Sauvignon Blanc (7.5%). All other varieties accounted for less than 3 percent of planted acreage. White grapes, such as Burger,

Palomino, Sauvignon Vert, and Sylvaner, have been replaced by Chardonnay, Sauvignon Blanc, Chenin Blanc, and Riesling.

Table 8.6

WINE GRAPE ACREAGE BY COUNTY						
County	1936	%	1981	%	1990	%
Alameda	3,235	1.9	605	1.0	1,743	.5
Amador	756	.4	1,338		1,775	
Butte	310		97		98	
Calaveras	392		93		189	
Colusa	214		55		1,257	
Contra Costa	5,472	3.2	556	.6	738	
El Dorado	250		333		482	
Fresno	12,137	7.1	28,104	11.2	34,265	10.4
Glenn	97		1,178		1,478	
Humboldt	10					
Imperial	3					
Kern	1,787	1.0	20,397	8.9	27,881	8.4
Kings	524	2.7	754		1,221	
Lake	591		1,995		3,238	.9
Los Angeles	3,131	1.8			24	
Madera	3,092	1.8	29,495	5.5	38,596	11.7
Marin	548		8		8	
Mariposa					34	
Mendocino	7,649	4.5	7,543	3.7	12,346	3.7
Merced	3,958	2.3	11,261	5.2	13,961	4.2
Monterey	147		19,930	3.7	28,496	8.6
Napa	11,027	6.5	18,241	8.2	33,194	10.0
Nevada	145		20		127	
Orange	12					
Placer	2,615	1.5	78		80	
Riverside	2,304	1.3	1,322	.4	2,396	
Sacramento	4,026	2.4	2,191		4,044	1.2
San Benito	1,670	.9	1,696	2.6	1,775	
San Bernardino	20,802	12.2	1,157	6,029		
San Diego	2,493	1.5	51		102	
San Joaquin	34,596	20.3	25,083	14.5	37,726	11.4
San Luis Obispo	868	.5	3,591	.4	8,343	2.5
San Mateo	45		12		45	
Santa Barbara	251		5,270		9,302	2.8
Santa Clara	7,375	4.3	602	1.4	961	
Santa Cruz	1,467	.8	51		111	
Shasta	320		24		36	
Solano	1,539	.8	497	.4	1,233	
Sonoma	20,600		19,067	8.3	33,317	10.0
Stanislaus	9,879	5.8	12,109	8.9	15,675	4.7
Sutter	203					
Tehama	77		122		141	
Trinity			2		6	
Tulare	3,008	1.7	6,857	5.3	10,480	3.2
Ventura	22				8	
Yolo	1,003	.6	636		1,966	
Yuba	65		252		309	
Total	170,715		222,673		335,236	

Source: California Agricultural Statistics Service.

The evolution of red wine grapes in this century is most revealing. Increasing from 43,016 acres in 1915 to 159,445 acres by 1940, the top five red wine grapes were Carignane, Zinfandel, Alicante Bouschet, Mourvedre, and Mission, collectively accounting for 132,596 acres, or 83.2% of the total. Since 1970, with the exception of Zinfandel, Prohibition-popular red wine grapes, such as Carignane, Alicante Bouschet, Mission, and Grenache, have been largely replaced by Cabernet Sauvignon, Merlot, and Pinot Noir. Before 1950, Carignane and Zinfandel were the dominant red grapes followed by Alicante Bouschet--these three accounting for 75 percent of all red grapes. By 1990 the dominant red wine grape was Zinfandel (23%), followed by Cabernet Sauvignon (22%), Grenache (9%), Carignane (7%), Barbera (7%), Pinot

Noir (6%), and Merlot (5%). Collectively, premium grapes now account for about 60 percent of all red wine grapes. The red grapes of the Central Valley have suffered the most because of the demise of the red jug market, and the "red juice" grapes (Royalty, Rubired, Salvador, and Alicante Bouschet) have experienced a similar fate.

wine grape acreage) of UC-Davis-developed "botanical wonder" grapes that were supposed to be prolific, adaptable to the hot climate and rich soils of the Central Valley, and to be the equal of "classic" red and white French grapes.

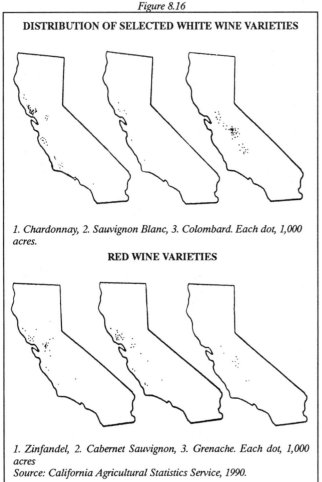

Figure 8.16

DISTRIBUTION OF SELECTED WHITE WINE VARIETIES

1. Chardonnay, 2. Sauvignon Blanc, 3. Colombard. Each dot, 1,000 acres.

RED WINE VARIETIES

1. Zinfandel, 2. Cabernet Sauvignon, 3. Grenache. Each dot, 1,000 acres
Source: California Agricultural Statistics Service, 1990.

Table 8.7

CALIFORNIA: WHITE WINE GRAPES BY ACREAGE AND PERCENT						
Variety	1976	%	1985	%	1990	%
Colombard	23,485	29.7	73,241	37.5	58,888	32.8
Chardonnay	10,869	13.8	27,424	14.0	52,157	29.0
Chenin Blanc	17,338	22.0	41,462	21.2	32,957	18.4
Sauvignon Blanc	3,526	4.5	15,383	7.9	13,433	7.5
Riesling	6,210	7.9	10,046	5.1	4,979	2.8
Burger	1,130	1.4	2,307	1.2	2,302	1.3
Semillon	2,002	2.5	3,039	1.6	2,229	1.2
Malvasia Bianca	655	.8	1,842	.9	2,115	1.2
Gewurztraminer	2,025	2.6	3,983	2.0	1,858	1.0
Pinot Blanc	1,339	1.7	2,265	1.2	1,839	1.0
Emerald Riesling	2,025	2.6	2,928	1.5	1,304	
Palomino	2,425	3.2	2,702	1.4	1,484	
Muscat Blanc	899	1.1	1,657	.8	1,352	
Grey Riesling	1,516	1.9	2,436	1.2	491	
Sylvaner	958	1.2	1,233	.6	193	
Other	2,372	3.0	3,316	1.7	1,969	
Total	78,775	100.0	195,264	100.0	179,550	
Source: California Agricultural Statistics Service.						

CALIFORNIA: RED WINE GRAPES BY ACREAGE AND PERCENT						
Variety	1965	1976	1985	%	1990	%
Zinfandel	16,550	21,672	25,367	17.1	34,163	22.7
Cabernet Sauvignon	1,966	17,395	22,617	15.2	33,206	22.0
Grenache	11,813	12,350	15,701	10.6	13,644	9.0
Carignane	23,076	16,132	16,341	11.1	11,037	7.3
Barbera	1,092	14,615	14,825	10.0	10,666	7.1
Pinot Noir	1,452	7,067	7,816	5.3	9,549	6.3
Merlot	1,742	2,497	2,538	1.7	7,435	4.9
Rubired	2,072	7,271	8,076	5.4	7,136	4.7
Ruby Cabernet	1,326	10,555	10,577	7.2	6,921	4.6
Petite Sirah	3,232	4,733	5,105	3.5	3,072	2.0
Alicante Bouschet	5,806	2,841	3,210	2.2	2,101	1.4
Napa Gamay	1,050	2,342	2,452	1.7	1,541	
Gamay Beaujolais		2,426	2,526	1.7	1,424	
Mission	5,856	2,277	2,314	1.6	1,150	
Carnelian	1,519	1,592	1,638	1.1	1,252	
Other	3,936	5,744	6,689	4.6	6,509	
Total	86,289	130,681	147,792	100.0	150,806	

Although European viticultural patterns show strong regional and local grape wine specialization, California, in 200 years, has just recently begun to develop a regional grape emphasis. While several hundred different wine grape varieties are grown, only 60 are planted in commercial quantities, and of that approximately 20 account for more than 90 percent of the total wine grape acreage. The present distribution pattern indicates a reduction in the degree of variety proliferation within each producing region, and a tendency for the better producing areas to specialize in the cultivation of a smaller number of varieties. The popularity of three premium vines is reflected in the number of wineries making varietal wines: 613 make Chardonnay; 519 make Cabernet Sauvignon; and 316 make Zinfandel. Another interesting development is the relative demise (only accounting for 7 percent of total

Over the past 30 years several regional variety specialization patterns have emerged that clearly reflect a movement by growers and wineries to match specific grapes to local conditions. While the movement is still in its infancy many generalizations are possible: (a) for the first time in the state's history a viticultural region (Temecula) has emerged primarily as a "white wine" producing region; (b) the most expensive grapes are grown along the cooler, coastal margins; (c) within this region incipient specialization is emerging (Chardonnay and Pinot Noir in Carneros and Russian River valleys, Zinfandel in the Dry Creek Valley, etc.); (d) quality wine grape production in the Central Valley is increasingly being concentrated in the cooler regions closest to San Francisco Bay; (e) premium grape varieties increased from 1 percent in 1960 to nearly two-thirds in 1990; (f) premium grape varieties in Sonoma and Napa counties have increased from 7 to 96 percent in 1990; and (g) as information is gathered as to which microclimate/soil combination is best for each variety, it is expected that these premium grapes will be given the best sites. Yet, California, unlike Europe, has yet to match specific varieties with exposure, altitude, and soils.

Changing consumer tastes have dictated that wineries produce higher quality table and sparkling wines, with an emphasis on white wines. These trends are translated to grape growers by prices that wineries are paying for each grape variety. Growers, in turn, plant grapes that command high prices and remove grapes from production that show weak potential. The largest acreage increases appeared in the planting of Chenin Blanc and Colombard, both of which were influenced by the combination of rapid price increases during the late 1970s. The second group of grapes showing rapid increases were Chardonnay and Sauvignon Blanc, the two most important premium white wine grapes.

What makes California an unusual viticultural region is an ideal climate and good soils for the consistent production of three types of grapes: wine, table, and raisin grapes; a propensity for industry inquisitiveness, experimentation and innovation; and promulgation of unfailing quality for common table and premium wine production. Over the past 50 years California has emerged as the epicenter for enological and viticultural experimentation and innovation, and has become the largest single source of academic university enology departments and industry research facilities producing a small army of excellent winemakers. Consequently, the Roman expression *ut vinum habeat colorem, odorem et saporem* ("wine should have color, scent and taste") has become an obsessive winemaking objective.

Most important, California has responded favorably to the wishes of the American consumer. Since the early 1960s, table wine production has increased from 20 million gallons to 71 million gallons in 1968, to more than 200 million gallons in 1990. Sparkling wine production more than tripled between 1957 and 1968, and again by 1990. Flavored wines, including Vermouth, declined to new low levels. In 1990 the breakdown of wines was: 69 percent generic (producing but 38 percent of total revenue), while premium table wines accounted for 31 percent of the total volume, but an impressive 62 percent of the total $7 billion revenue.

Led by White Zinfandel and Chardonnay, varietal wines continue to grow in output to 52% of total production, up from 19% in 1985. Generic wines dropped from 81% to 60% for the same period. These impressive figures reveal the important fact that generic output declined from 86 million cases to 67 million, and varietals increased from 20 million to 45 million, out of a total market of 139 million cases of table wine. Other varietals include Cabernet Sauvignon (10%), Sauvignon Blanc (10%), Grenache (7.5%), Chenin Blanc (5%), Colombard (2%), Riesling (2.4%), and Merlot (2%). A related direction is the recent trend toward white wine production. While red wine production declined from 31 percent in 1977 to 16 percent in 1991, white wine output rose from 44 percent to 67 percent for the same period.

VITICULTURAL PRACTICES BEFORE AND AFTER 1960

Prior to 1960	After 1960
Excessive use of redwood	Oak becomes more popular,
Wineries purchased most of their grapes	Wineries produce a much larger share
Little estate bottling	More estate bottling
Product line very extensive	Product line reduced
Little evidence of regional specialization	More specialization
Less capital intensive	More capital intensive
Quality less consistent	Quality more consistent
Inability to compete with imports	Competition increased
Wines overly alcoholic	Wines less alcoholic
Wines unbalanced	Wines more balanced
Wines overly sweet	Table wines dominate
Use of foreign names	Foreign names reduced sharply
Vineyard practices limited	Vineyard practices expanded and improved
Generic wines dominated	Varietal wines increased

California has three winegrowing histories in this century: before and after Prohibition, and the period after 1960. Before 1920 wine production was dominated by inexpensive (and inconsistent) dessert and table wines. The period immediately after Prohibition was equally defective. California emerged after Repeal with few good grapes, and fewer still grown on ideal locations. Vine pests and diseases were rampant, little irrigation in the quality-producing coastal counties, no frost protection, and no modern vineyard and winery technical equipment. Yet, as the state matured economically and culturally, the seeds of incipient quality grape and wine production became established by a small number of dedicated producers. Problems were clearly identified and scientific solutions began to be implemented. These conditions were altered immediately after World war II, at first slowly, but since the middle 1960s at a rapid rate that defies the imagination. All the above negative conditions were reversed seemingly overnight: better grape varieties planted on ideal sites; frost protection produced more even annual production levels; fewer diseases, as nearly all new plantings since 1975 have been disease-free, thus allowing for better production, higher sugar levels, and better balanced wine. Machine picking allows for cooler pickings at night and shortens the "sit" period; grapes are crushed faster and also crushed in better condition. At the winery level, there are now better trained people, better fermentations due to stainless steel tanks; better presses; and the increased use of small barrel fermentation and aging have broadened wine styles and increased the number of flavor components. Despite spectacular sales growth during the period 1960-1980, the wine industry has seen volatile swings in its economic health during the 1980s. In part, this reflects changing economic conditions, with consumption dropping in recession and rising in recovery.

As impressive as the long list of accomplishments is, the state does face several significant problems. Increased competition from quality varietal Vinifera-based wine from New York, Virginia, New Jersey, Maryland, and Pennsylvania has increased to formidable levels. The total amount now exceeds 500,000 cases, a quantity that is essentially carved out of California's market share, not imports. While increased competition from the "east" is serious enough, that which emanates from Washington, Oregon, Idaho, Texas, and New Mexico appears to be more immediate with serious long-term implications as production now exceeds 3 million cases. Not only does regional production reduce the market for California wines, but the ability of the various non-California viticultural regions to produce premium wines, such as Riesling, Gewurztraminer, Pinot Noir, Semillon, Sauvignon Blanc, Merlot, and Cabernet Sauvignon, has seriously tarnished California's image as the "nations only premium Vinifera wine region." The combined effect of the current 3.5 million case non-California quality Vinifera wine is a major cause of concern for those California winemakers with a sense of direction. The industry, since 1984, has been troubled with declining sales, increased number of bearing vines, and excess fermentation and storage capacity.

A major complaint, often justifiable, lies in the fact that many wineries are producing low-acid, low-extract wine, in part due to excessive fining and filtering, high yields, and high residual sugar. Other minor criticisms that have been placed on the doorstep of Californian producers are: the wines are too dull, bland, and not individualistic enough; wineries tend to "follow the leader;" the wines are expensive, and hence a poor value; the winemaker has been glorified and elevated to the status of an idolized celebrity; wineries are propelled by medalmania; and the profusion of thousands of labels confuses the public. The 820 wineries produce more than 4,000 labels. Among the many major areas of criticism are the continued use of generic wines, European names, the casual definition of approved viticultural areas, the production of large quantities of cheap, fortified wine for the "sleaze" market, and the non-aggressive nature of the industry leaders to tolerate foreign "dumping," and playing a passive role in the heady contemporary neo-prohibition movements. The above notwithstanding, the contemporary wine scene is bright indeed. Winery and vineyard asset values have never been higher, grape prices are exhibiting record increases, and the volume and value of exports have never been higher. Most important, the quality of California wines and the level of technical expertise have improved to new heights. The number of new wineries each year rises by more than fifteen, and foreign interest has never been more intense. Over the past generation the state has responded remarkably well to fickle American taste changes.

In the past California had a need to establish its position in the world, but as it lacked the *cache* of name and history, it was easily snubbed by the "eastern establishment," the nation's leading consuming region of French and other European wines. Post-World War II cultural and technical achievements finally raised quality levels beyond hitherto acceptable levels, and California could no longer be denied as a primary quality wine producing region among the rarified pantheon. Just as American's need not "lard" their beef (as the French do) due to the superior nature of the product, California wine, from the most inexpensive to expensive bottle, can stand on its own and compete with equivalent imports.

California makes all manner of wine and cultivates practically every Vinifera variety known in America. Winemaking, styles of wine, and types are not standardized as in most European viticultural areas. This means that while it is easy to tell the difference between Beaujolais, Bordeaux, Vouvray, and Alsace in terms of authorized grape varieties and winemaking techniques, California represents and clearly expresses a spirit of continuous experimentation. While Burgundy clearly expresses a geographic region, types of white and red wines, and dominant grape varieties, Napa and Monterey do not. Therefore, it becomes perplexing and frustrating to generalize about California appellations and styles of winemaking due to the juxtaposition of all manner of grape variety, physical environmental factors, and winemaking philosophies. Cultural, winemaking, and marketing advances over the past 30 years have been spectacular. Usually changes take place slowly in the world of wine, but the progress in California over the past generation has been both riveting and exciting in its ability to dispel myths by adding a good dose of scientific fact to all facets of the industry. In the absence of hallowed tradition anything and everything goes. It is often said that while France follows tradition, California creates it. Perhaps the most formidable element of contemporary winemaking is the willingness to experiment, and the ability to create new styles.

If anything, California represents continuous change. Unencumbered by traditional and rigid appellation legislation, producers keep changing the way they make wine along the full spectrum of fermentation, aging, and style. One year the wines are light, another full; one year they are aged in Limousin Oak, and the next in Yugoslavian Oak; one year by slow and cool fermentation and the next by a quick, high temperature method. Consistency for many is definitely not the pattern, thus confusing the Bordeaux wine lover. Experimentation is the order of the day, sometimes with the intent of catering to the consumer, but equally as often to please the winemaker. In the vineyard, canopy management has become a refined art, new trellis systems, summer pruning and thinning, higher vine density per acre, and the matching of specific grape varieties with specific soils have achieved new horizons. In the winery, lees contact experimentation, new blending methods, extended maceration, a reduction of the use of sulfur, and a determined effort to examine what conditions promote the extraction of one type of phenol and its interaction with others affecting color, flavor, and longevity have resulted in a continuously improving product.

In contrast to the old-fashioned European winemaker who inherited the job from his father or by a long laborious apprenticeship and who considered the trade "an art" not a science, the contemporary California winemaker is a scientist who feels comfortable with acid levels, Brix readings, cool fermentations, and the like. He is precise, dogmatic, a chemist at heart who is affected by public relations, press releases, and professional tasting evaluations. In the main, there are three types: the first is an older group of individuals with considerable time in the trade and, by implication, individuals who have paid their dues in the industry. Pioneers in post-Prohibition viticulture are Andre Tchelistcheff, Brother Timothy, Hanns Kornell, Louis Martini, E. and J. Gallo, Robert and Peter Mondavi, among a list that numbers many dozens. The second type are retired professionals from all walks of life who exhibit a genuine interest in the field and take pride in producing a quality product. They buy the finest equipment and hire the most professional winemakers. The third type is a young winemaker who is the product of a university viticultural department, full of energy and inquisitiveness daring to question traditional methods. All three driven individuals have two things in common: to outdo the other and to be as competitive as possible.

Although comparisons with Bordeaux are chronic and inevitable, it is debatable that quality California wines, both white and red, will ever be the same or even similar. Higher alcohol content, lower acid levels, and a more pronounced fruit level are the main points of divergence. More important, these features are more compatible to contemporary dietary habits, and, as a result, Americans will reduce the inclination to emulate French winemaking styles. For one, California's reputation as a world class producer of wine rests on quality grapes: fine red wine is based on Cabernet Sauvignon, followed by Merlot and Zinfandel. Recent bottlings of Petit Verdot, Cabernet Franc, Pinot Noir, Charbono, Mourvedre, and Malbec represent encouraging efforts. Equally praiseworthy white wine is based on Chardonnay and Sauvignon Blanc. As percent of total acreage, California has a larger percentage of "noble" grapes planted than France. Furthermore, California, unlike France, has a larger percentage of quality wine grapes grown in cooler areas, and no French-American grape acreage.

One of the most spectacular evolutionary developments has been the rise of the small boutique winery, a forerunner in quality wine production. A combination of capital, immense enthusiasm, and an almost unbelievable acceleration in the art of vinification has elevated wine quality to hitherto new levels. In the process, it appears that the handful of large wineries, historically the leaders in the industry, have been relegated a shorter and less important role since 1960, and, consequently, their relative situation, particularly in the premium wine market, has not grown for the past 30 years. The foregoing has not only produced many prestige wineries, but their position relative to comparable producers in France, the leader in quality wine exports, has improved to unheard of levels. Californian wines, therefore, have bested, in comparative tastings, the finest French Grand Cru in Europe. Quality and comparative foreign exchange rates notwithstanding, the one singular element placing Californian wines in the limelight is their consistency.

Because the historic reputation of California wines was based on inexpensive jug wines, over the past generation the premium wine producers embarked upon a quest for varietal character. Although there are countless arguments about what the "varietal" character of a specific grape variety really should be, a conscientious movement has developed dedicated to promoting wine defined by variety rather than European regional name equivalents. Whatever the merits, varietal wine legally increased from 51 percent to 75 percent varietal, along with a good portion of complimentary wines added for balance and complexity, hence the movement to make Cabernet Sauvignon from all the five primary Bordeaux varieties, not just one or two. The result, nothing short of spectacular, is certain to continue. Indeed, California, in practically every type and price bracket, has closed the gap with France: not only has the quality of all California wine improved significantly, but the state is able to offer superior value in Cabernet Sauvignon, Merlot, Sauvignon Blanc, Chardonnay, and generic jug wines. Only in dry Alsatian-type, Muscadet-type, and northern Rhone wines is California lacking.

One further historical element that both circumscribes and illuminates contemporary varietal favorites is America's restless ethos and its lack of tradition. Consequently, grape varietals come and go producing an endless diary of boom and bust features, not too dissimilar to any other commodity. Cabernet Sauvignon, for example, rocketed to celebrity in the 1960s, declined in the late 1970s and early 1980s, only to rise again after 1983. Red Zinfandel plummeted to insignificance when acreage declined from 40,000 in the mid-1940s, to 14,000 in 1959, only to be resurrected in the 1980s; Petite Sirah, once a formidable varietal in the 1970s, has recently fallen to near extinction. Over the course of the last 100 years, more than a dozen varieties rose and fell from prominence with significant economic consequences. The 1988 color mix of California varietal wines was: White Zinfandel (28%); Chardonnay (18%); Cabernet Sauvignon (14%); Sauvignon Blanc (8%); Chenin Blanc (6%); Riesling (3%); Zinfandel (4%); other reds (5%); other whites (4%).

Today, California winemakers, some young, some old, some immigrant, and almost all technically skilled, try harder. The very best are subject to "winemaker merry-go-round," a tendency to change positions every two years from one prestigious winery to another, making wine as socially desirable as designer labels, a Rolls Royce, and a villa on the Cote de Jure. This creates an element of instability and an inability to rank the top 50 or even 100 wineries for the following reasons: very few wineries have been established for more than 30 years; very few have produced a "consistent style" for more than 10 years; very few have produced a consistent product because the source of the grapes changes every few years; and there are very few, if any, wineries that have not added or dropped wines from their product line.

White Grape Varieties

Colombard (also known as French Colombard), with 58,888 acres, is the most widely planted white wine variety in California, 95 percent of which is produced in 7 Central Valley counties. The largest, with more than 16,000 acres is Madera, followed by Fresno, Kern, Merced, San Joaquin, Stanislaus, Tulare, and Sonoma, the latter, the only county outside the Central Valley with significant acreage (715). While new plantings in recent years have been reduced sharply from the halcyon year, 1982, when 12,017 acres were planted, acreage increased from 28,172 acres in 1976 to present levels, but less than the peak of 73,845 acres in 1983. With production increasing to nearly 700,000 tons (up from 190,000 tons in 1976) it has easily become the dominant white (and red) wine grape in California, effortlessly surpassing the historic favorite, Thompson Seedless. Colombard, with yields above 10 tons to the acre, produces bland, innocuous, but relatively high acid wine that forms the base for generic blends, sparkling, coolers, and brandy. Colombard, therefore, fulfills three essential Central Valley growing requirements: high yields, high acid, and white color. Due to recent technical improvements in its vinification, the wine is much cleaner than formerly, and much improved when Chenin Blanc, and other more aromatic wines are added. Colombard, representing 42 percent of all new white wine grape acreage during 1977-1986, will continue to increase in the foreseeable future should the cooler and generic white wine market sustain momentum. Many, however, predict an uncertain future for this variety as it competes with Chenin Blanc and Thompson Seedless. Although not mentioned frequently, Colombard, Chardonnay, and Sauvignon Blanc, in small quantities, are added to Cabernet Sauvignon and Zinfandel to add an element of piquancy.

Chardonnay, the apotheosis of California white table wine, with 52,157 acres, or 29 percent of all white wine grape acreage, is not only the second most important white wine variety, but the most widely produced varietal, and the most expensive white table wine in the nation. World-wide, it is the most coveted white wine grape. It is almost inconceivable, but in 1960 there were fewer than 150 acres, mostly in Alameda and Napa--a figure that increased to 11,500 acres in 1975, and to more than 54,000 acres by 1992, more than 29,000 of which were planted after 1980 (it is estimated that in 1987-1989 more than 8,000 acres were planted, and another 8,000 grafted, a large number in the region north of Lodi). Similarly, production has increased from 7,300 tons in 1976 to more than 105,000 tons in 1990. This is a remarkable achievement because total Chardonnay acreage is slightly more than that found in France (51,000 acres). With more than 5,000 additional acres in the rest of the nation, the U.S. contains more Chardonnay than any other country.

If present trends continue, it is possible for Chardonnay to outdistance Colombard in acreage by 1993. Interestingly, since 1984 Chardonnay bench grafts have outnumbered all other varieties. Its popularity is reflected in the fact that more than 500 Chardonnay are made in California and nearly 700 in the nation, or by 50 percent of all wineries. It is estimated that in 1990 more than 8.1 million cases of California Chardonnay were sold, a figure that is expected to rise beyond 15 million cases by 1995 when more than 15,000 acres become bearing. Although grape prices have softened in recent years, the present grape "glut" is not expected to diminish the number of brands and consumer interest primarily because Sauvignon Blanc, Chenin Blanc, Riesling, and Gewurztraminer do not have the range of quality table wine capability. While the prestige image has become synonymous with "status," prices range from a modest $5.50 to $45.00. Its popularity is reflected in the escalation of prices per ton in recent years--$856 in 1986, $922 in 1987, and nearly $1,800 in 1991. Often referred to as the "queen of the wine grapes," and the most celebrated white grape for dry table wine, its rapid popularity has also made it the standard for dry, white wine.

Chardonnay acreage is confined to cool, coastal locations, of which Sonoma County (with 11,276 acres), Napa (with 9,6390 acres), and Monterey (with 8,469 acres) are responsible for 56 percent of total acreage. These three are followed by Santa Barbara, San Joaquin, Mendocino, and San Luis Obispo, collectively accounting for another 30 percent of total acreage. Wine quality varies greatly with yield and location. Chardonnay is a shy bearer, susceptible to many diseases, and being very sensitive to high temperatures and excessive sun, "sun scald" is a condition that most growers attempt to avoid. While several dozen clones were planted at different times and in different places, in recent years "clone 108" (the "Wente" clone) has emerged as the preferred Chardonnay among growers. Many winemakers believe that for Chardonnay to be at its best it should be made from several clones grown on different sites. To an appreciable degree, the above mentioned physical imperatives are negated by winemaking techniques such as controlled skin contact, barrel and malolactic fermentation, lees contact, wood aging, and ultrafiltration.

As the hallmark of a good Chardonnay is balance, complexity, and depth of flavor, and the final product is a function of the vine, the immediate physical environment and the winemaker, its stylistic variations are never ending in the quest of the "finest." The most expensive is always made from riper grapes that are fermented in wood and undergo malolactic more often, aged longer (usually in French oak), and are filtered, fined and tampered with less than inexpensive wines. Chardonnay styles range from fruity, fresh, inexpensive wine, to barrel fermented, wood and/or lees-aged, super premium, vintage dated wine. The finest, well-structured and complex in both aroma and depth of flavor, does not tire the palate, is refreshing, fruity, fleshy in texture, and eminently satisfying. Five styles are generally recognized: thin, green, quickly made wines with some residual sugar that sell at popular prices; fruity wines with some measure of varietal flavor and aroma; well made, fruity wines with true varietal flavor and aroma, but more complexity due to barrel aging, and usually with some residual sugar (the most popular of the premium priced versions); the remaining two styles are a combination of hand crafted wines that undergo barrel fermentation, extended lees contact, careful clone selection, ideal sited grapes, older grapes, etc., with only the preponderance of fruit, wood, and balance separating them. These wines, usually selling above all others, comprise less than 5 percent of total output, but capture nearly 100 percent of the favorable publicity. Unfortunately, there are too many look-alike Chardonnay. They are the product of stainless steel, temperature controlled, judicious use of oak, barrel fermentation and malolactic fermentation.

Fresh and lively in youth, Chardonnay between two and five years of bottle aging becomes darker in color and more complex in flavor and scent. Prolonged aging exaggerates flaws, often making the wine virtually undrinkable. The big, alcoholic, overly oaked wines of the 1970s have recently been changed to rounder, lower alcohol, fat, slightly sweet wines that often lack balance. Frequently, Chardonnay is made with perceptible residual sugar and blended with lesser, inexpensive grapes, prompting a series of questions from professional wine tasters. Heavy criticism has been levied on their richness on the palate and their inability to age. More disturbing is the notion that sugar can mask an ever increasing percentage of non-Chardonnay grapes in the blend. The "Chardonnay residual sugar imbroglio" notwithstanding, the thirst for Chardonnay remains unquenchable to the point that production and consumption are commonly described as "Chardomania," with more than 8 million cases produced annually (growing by 150,000 cases each year).

Chenin Blanc, with 32,957 acres, or 18 percent of all white wine grape acreage, was until 1987 the second most important white wine variety when it was displaced by Chardonnay. Up sharply from 430 acres in 1960, the spectacular growth of this white variety reflects the past 20-year momentum of white wine consumption in the America. Although acreage has declined from a high of 43,900 acres in 1983 (4,000 acres removed from production near Lodi), this variety produces an uncomplicated, fruity, pleasantly scented, easy to make, easy to drink wine that is a major ingredient in most generic white wines, especially those emanating from the Central Valley. More than 50 million gallons of Chenin Blanc are made each year, but less than 4 percent are sold by its name (200 wineries), the rest competing with Thompson Seedless and Colombard for blending. Exhibiting a pattern almost identical with Colombard, 78 percent of Chenin Blanc is planted and 85 percent of wine production occurs in seven Central Valley counties: Fresno, Kern, Madera, Merced, San Joaquin, Stanislaus, and Tulare. One area in the Central Valley with a reputation for above-average Chenin Blanc is Clarksburg, in the Sacramento/San Joaquin delta region. However, due to the vine's ability to produce above-average, fragrant, fresh, high acid, and flavorful wine in cooler climates, nearly one-fifth of acreage is found in coastal counties, especially Napa, Sonoma, Monterey, San Luis Obispo, Mendocino, and Santa Barbara. The Charles Krug winery has been given credit for producing the first above-average Chenin Blanc in 1955.

Because Chenin Blanc is a major ingredient in white blends, it exhibits an extremely high stylistic range: dry, off-dry, semi-sweet, sweet, and late harvest under equally diverse vinification and aging procedures (its flavor components range from fruit, lemon, citrus, apple, and flower). With its flexibility and high yield (often as high as 13 tons to the acre), acreage is expected to remain at present levels. The main problem with this variety is that a clear California style has yet to emerge capable of captivating a significant portion of the wine drinking public (even winemakers who love this varietal can't agree on how it should be made). While nearly all of production contains some residual sweetness, an elusive dry style has yet to emerge. However underrated it may be (primarily due to the recent success of Chardonnay and Sauvignon Blanc), it holds much promise in the cooler North Coast counties. It is definitely upscale from Thompson Seedless and Colombard with more than double the price per ton of each. Most surprising is the little known fact that, despite its youthful appeal, Chenin Blanc has a remarkable ability to age. Interestingly, Chenin Blanc was called "White Zinfandel" before Prohibition, and for a short time after Repeal "White Pinot."

Sauvignon Blanc, incorrectly known as Fume Blanc among premium white varieties, has been one of the most rapidly expanding premium grapes since 1970. Acreage grew from the occasional plot before 1960, to 879 acres in 1966, to 13,433 in 1990 (about the same amount as France), and there is every indication that it will continue to increase acreage. Sauvignon Blanc, the grape of Sancerre, Pouilly-Fume, Graves, and Sauternes (where it is a second cousin to Semillon), produces dry, crisp, often grassy, herbaceous, and citrus flavored wine, and like Chenin Blanc is considered a less expensive alternative to Chardonnay. Nearly 450 California wineries, and another 40 in other parts of the nation now produce this grape as a varietal. Inevitably, this groundswell of interest and eventual sales prompted David Stare of Sonoma County and several other winemakers to found the Society of Blancs, or SOBs, a professional group with a sense of humor and a penchant for having fun.

Make no mistake about it, the growth of Sauvignon Blanc not only reflects the recent shift to white wine consumption, but its ability to be made in many different styles (from sweet to dry; light to full bodied; grassy and herbaceous to ripe, round and complex in flavor), and to adapt to many differing soils and microclimates. By any mea-

sure, it is a serious grape variety that makes dignified, and often expensive wine. Although not considered the equal of Chardonnay in terms of complexity and depth of flavor, quality has recently improved as the vines became older and it has judiciously been blended with Semillon, Chenin Blanc, and other varieties to heighten complexity and flavor. Sauvignon Blanc, with enormous variation in style and price, usually offers excellent value as a varietal wine, and is second to Chardonnay as evidenced by the fact that the American market accommodates about 500 labels. While this variety was rarely aged in American oak or subjected to malolactic fermentation, wine making refinements are beginning to transform this well-flavored variety into many subtle and elegant styles. It will never be Chardonnay, but the very best is more than agreeable given its lower price.

When compared with Bordeaux counterparts, California Sauvignon Blanc is fruitier, more supple, and less acidic. With a greater diversity of style than Chardonnay, it is often called the "poor man's Chardonnay." The wine is appealing because it is less expensive than Chardonnay, easier to match with food, and exhibits greater regional variation than Chardonnay. Historically made into a sweet, Sauternes style wine, Sauvignon Blanc today is a product of many different clones exhibiting divergent cultural habits and wine characteristics (flavor and scent varying from fig, melon, asparagus, cheese, herb, and grass, to name a few descriptors). The chamelion-like vine produces wine with few common elements in many states and within California, where it is made into 6 main styles: thin, watery, and unsubstantial on the palate; grassy and acidic; full-bodied, round with added Semillon, often sweet; fruity and light bodied; barrel fermented, big and round; and late harvest.

Until recently all Sauvignon Blanc was the product of cuttings imported from Chateau d'Yquem by Charles Wetmore and Louis Mel in the late 1870s. Extensive experimentation has revealed that there are as many different clones of Sauvignon as there are for Chardonnay and Pinot Noir, of which Sauvignon Musque is considered the authentic Bordeaux. Unlike other clones, Musque prefers cooler sites, and it is expected that the estimated 2,000 acres already planted in this clone will expand. Interestingly, before Chardonnay became popular in the late 1960s, Sauvignon Blanc was the most popular white varietal. While only 260 acres of Sauvignon Blanc were planted in 1960, nearly 3,000 acres were planted in 1981, total acreage doubled between 1976 and 1980, and tonnage leaped from 4,000 tons in 1976 to 65,000 tons in 1986. While it will grow well in Region I, it produces fewer vegetal flavors when grown in Region II and III areas. Despite the predilection for cool weather, the leading county, with nearly 3,000 acres, is Napa, followed by Sonoma (1,627), Monterey (1,489), San Joaquin (1,487), Mendocino (880), Merced (778), San Luis Obispo (702), and Lake (608). While 31 counties produce Sauvignon Blanc, 6 coastal counties contain 8,179 acres, or 61 percent of the planted acreage. Very surprising is the singular fact that Lake County, widely considered one of the finest areas for the production of Sauvignon Blanc, has but 608 acres.

Sauvignon Blanc is grown in 5 major areas in France--Sancerre, Pouilly-Fume, Graves, Quincy, and the Touraine, covering 16,800 acres in 1979, and 15,000 acres in 1989, a figure similar to California. Sauvignon Blanc has larger yields and is easier to grow than Chardonnay. It also grows extremely fast in late spring, ripens slowly in September, and matures about the same time as Semillon. It is an easy to grow but very aggressive vine, prone to excess vigor and heavy yields. Consequently, the most common urge is to emphasize restraint by toning down its herbaceous and grassy disposition. The stress is to produce either clean, crisp, fruity and austere wines, or full-bodied, wood influenced, round, multiple layered libations. Surprisingly, few, if any, American wines resemble the acidic wines of Sancerre and Pouilly-Fume.

Riesling (also known as White, and Johannisberg Riesling), with 4,979 acres, is the fifth most widely planted white wine grape variety. Highly distinctive, it should not be confused with Grey Riesling, Emerald Riesling, Okanogan Riesling, Welschriesling, and Franken Riesling. Interestingly, other states contain 4,500 acres, France 5,426, and Germany 47,641. Despite its versatility and strong varietal character (perhaps the most pronounced and elegant of any other noble grape), it is considered by many in California as a third rate vine (similar to Chenin Blanc), or a wine not to be taken seriously as it is usually made sweet, semi-sweet, soft, inoffensive, and bland for quaffing purposes.

Its current sales slump is promulgated by an unwarranted poor image problem. Along with Gewurztraminer and several other varieties, Riesling has yet to make its imprint in the pantheon of California white wine grapes. Not only does it fail to compete with German wines, but California Riesling also pales to insignificance when compared to Oregon, Washington, Michigan, New York, and Virginia. The vine, however, despite low acid levels, is versatile, its wine character changing significantly with winemaking techniques, and, despite the lack of consumer acceptance, planted area doubled since 1965. Further, Riesling is a major ingredient in adding a fragrant enthusiasm to dull Cabernet Sauvignon, Zinfandel, and other wines.

Riesling, indigenous to the Rhine, is a late ripener, and grows particularly well along the northern limits of grape-growing. At its best, it produces a wine with superb acid balance, aromatic fragrances, and a fullness in the mouth that can only be described by superlatives. Unlike many other white wine grapes, it is a low yielder, and does particularly well on slatey, rocky, and volcanic soils--important considerations as the color and character changes significantly with the venue. While 30 different clones grow in Germany, proper identification and careful selection of California vines is limited. The Research Institute in Neustadt, Germany has recently developed the controversial Clone 90 that is supposed to be extremely intense in both aroma and flavor.

Since it is a cool climate variety, it is particularly successful in coastal counties--all but 135 acres are found along the Pacific coast. Four counties with 4,143 acres, or 83 percent of the state total, dominate acreage. The leading county is Monterey, followed by Santa Barbara, Napa, and Sonoma, a surprising picture as many growers and winemakers believe that Lake County is the finest area in the state for its cultivation. Recently, there is a tendency to produce, with limited success, highly distinctive dry, as well as luscious, honey flavored, late harvest botrytized wines. Its lack of popularity is a puzzle (especially when compared with the large volume of innocuous white Zinfandel) as the wines have never been better, are constantly improving, and offer good value. When compared with Washington State equivalents, however, finesse, intense flavor, a pungent, yet delicate aroma, and perfect acid balance, hallmarks of a good Riesling, are somewhat lacking.

Semillon, an essential variety in the production of Sauternes, and a minor player in the making of dry white Graves wines, has long remained an obscure variety for both blending purposes and as a varietal in California. This highly underrated grape, expanding from 1,560 acres in 1978 to 2,229 acres in 1990, appears as if it will soon emerge as another "super premium" varietal not only in California but in Washington and Virginia. Although it usually produces a fat, dull, and easily oxidized varietal wine, it improves the higher acid Sauvignon Blanc, Chardonnay, Riesling, and Gewurztraminer. It is just beginning to receive the notoriety that it deserves--as a dry table wine, luscious sweet wine, or as a superb blending grape. Susceptible to botrytis with the onset of fall rains, the so-called "noble rot" pierces the skin enabling the evaporation of water, resulting in the concentration of sugar. The finished product is of fine golden color, full bodied, smooth on the palate, and pleasant on the olfactory senses. Semillon does not tolerate a wide variety of climates: when too hot the grape yields a wine with little fruit, matures rapidly, has low acid levels, and inevitably makes a mediocre wine with few memorable attributes. Therefore, because it produces a flabby, nondescript wine in the hotter portions of the Central Valley, future plantings are destined for the cooler areas of Region I and II, and, in particular, Washington State where the potential appears extraordinary. Interestingly, Semillon usually yields more than Sauvignon Blanc, but with lower alcohol levels. Although Semillon is widely planted in 25 counties, the leading county, in terms of acreage, is Monterey (397), followed by Napa (345), Madera (207), Sonoma (195), and Kern (178). In the past, Gross and Petit Semillon were both planted, but it appears that the superior Gros clone will dominate new plantings in the future.

Gewurztraminer, along with the Muscat family, is the most aromatic, assertive, and easily identifiable of all noble grapes. It takes its name from the Traminer that has an extra touch of spice or "gewurz," an intense combination of floral, musky and spicy flavors. It is also one of the most difficult, expensive, early ripening varieties to grow, make, and sell in America. Its former history notwithstanding, it has recently shown several positive signals as consumer demand has increased in recent years. Acreage has expanded from fewer than 400 acres in 1970, to

1,858 in 1990, and there is every indication that acreage will continue to increase in the future. It is also rapidly expanding in the northwest, and minor plantings are to be found in the northeast and Virginia. And while demand is not excessively strong as a dry, semi, and sweet varietal, Gewurztraminer, in ever increasing quantities, is used as a blending grape for many white and red libations lacking flavor, aroma and acidity, particularly Chardonnay, Zinfandel, and sparkling wines. In addition, it fits very nicely in contemporary "food wine" categories such as Chinese, Japanese, Mexican, and Cajun.

Of the nearly 2,000 planted acres, three coastal counties contain 1,449, or 78 percent of the total. Monterey, with 739, is the leading county and, perhaps, the best, followed by Sonoma (433), and Mendocino (277). The preference of a cool climate by the variety is evident as the Central Valley contains fewer than 15 acres, a clear indication that this vast region is unable to produce grapes with high sugar, low pH, and high acids--the three essential ingredients in producing high quality Gewurztraminer. The fact that the grape doesn't attain any character until fully ripe, and it tends to make a flabby, uninteresting wine when it is overly ripe, means that its geographic distribution will be confined to the cooler portions of Washington, Oregon, and the counties of Mendocino, Sonoma, Monterey, Lake, and Santa Barbara. Gewurztraminer ripens early, yields more than Riesling, has a heavy skin making it resistant to the ravages of frost, rain, hail, and bad weather in general. It tends to be resistant to botrytis, and its juice is slow moving and sticky. Among major white wine varieties, Gewurztraminer exhibits the largest variations in flavor and aroma--from sweet spice, honeysuckle, apple and cinnamon, to geranium; and from flat tasting to mouth filling, flavorful acidity that titillates the palate for more. The tendency toward bitterness, in part due to high pH levels, has largely been ameliorated in recent years, and the wine has never been better.

Pinot Blanc is receiving interest because it makes a good base wine for sparkling wines, and a full bodied table wine, often with considerable character. The skin also contains one of the highest tannin contents, a most unusual feature for a white variety making it an ideal blending grape for the low-acid wines of the Central Valley. Although there is a tendency to brown, cold fermentation and careful picking combine to produce good, austere, full bodied, often rich wine, with excellent aging potential. It is not an easy wine to find, but Chalone, the finest producer, is reliable although expensive. The number of actual acres devoted to Pinot Blanc has yet to be determined because the majority is not the authentic vine from eastern France but the Melon (also known as Melon de Bourgogne), both of which are difficult to differentiate in the vineyard. Historically little known, acreage in recent years has expanded from 1,000 acres in 1978 to 1,839 acres in 1990, and it is expected to increase further. Slightly more than half the acreage (1,069) is concentrated in Monterey County, followed by 206 acres in Sonoma, 147 in Napa, 137 in San Benito, and 79 in Santa Barbara, all of which are cool, coastal climate areas.

Burger, grown in Germany and Alsace where it is known as Elbling, this high yielding, low acid, lackluster vine is used for blending in such generic concoctions as Sauternes and Chablis. Until 1960 it was one of the leading white wine grapes in the San Joaquin Valley, and despite its diminished acreage it contributes between 6 and 8 percent of the total white wine grape crush annually. Of the 2,302 acres currently in production, 1,224 are located in San Joaquin County, 387 in Kern, and 199 in Tulare. **Palomino** is a superb Mediterranean grape variety responsible for the finest Spanish Sherries. While it does best on lime-impregnated soils, this high yielding variety exhibits considerable adaptation in California. Of the 1,484 acres, 527 are located in Fresno, 397 in Madera, and 123 in San Joaquin, with the North Coast counties containing fewer than 200 acres. This thick skinned grape with a viscous pulp produces a neutral tasting wine that is unsuitable for table wine production, and, invariably is grown for the domestic Sherry market. Unlike many other grape varieties used for fortified wine production, acreage over the past 10 years has remained steady. For years this variety has also been known as Napa Golden Chasselas. The "other" Sherry grape--Pedro Ximenez, in terms of both planted acreage and wine production, is less important.

The **Muscat** family of grapes, among the oldest and most ubiquitous of grapes, come in all color and shape, of which Muscat Blanc, Muscat of Alexandria, and Muscat Hamburg are the most important in terms of acreage and quality. Muscats are characterized by medium to high yields, high sugar content, and a pronounced flavor and aroma that makes them ideal table grapes provided they are not shipped long distances. Grown in California since the 1850s, it is estimated that more than 12 different varieties were cultivated before 1960. Present acreage for all varieties is 7,267, substantially less than the 60,000 acres reported in 1939, 21,000 in 1961, and 12,000 acres in 1972. Before Prohibition more than 10 percent of all sweet wine was made from Muscats, but during the Prohibition years acreage more than tripled as home winemakers in the east created a demand for these grapes. In 1948 Muscats made up 10 percent of the total crush, but steadily dropped to less than 1.5 percent in 1987. With few exceptions, nearly all require the heat of Region IV and V climates for proper maturation. All Muscats are characterized by unique flavor and scent, but are handicapped by low acid and high pH levels. While intensely flavored, Muscat wines brown easily, and when made in a dry table style, their bitterness precludes formidable competition with the far-better white table wine grapes. The Muscat family of grapes are currently in vogue as four of the top ten sparkling wine brands are made primarily from Muscat grapes. In addition, while wine consumption has declined by more than 15 percent since 1986, Muscat wine has increased by 17 percent. And because many winemakers like to "enhance" the flavor of dull flavored wines by adding minute amounts of Muscat, vine acreage has increased. Similarly, the number of wineries producing Muscat-based wines has increased from fewer than ten in 1975 to more than 80 in 1990. Of the many varieties, Muscat Blanc, Orange Muscat, and the hybrid Symphony appear to make the finest wines.

Muscat Blanc (also known as Muscat Blanc a Petits Grains, Muscat de Frontignan, Muscat Canelli, etc.) plays a major role in the production of sweet white wine throughout the Mediterranean, and is the major white Muscat wine grape in California where it produces excellent, delicately flavored wine. One-sixth of the 1,352 acres is found in Tulare, followed by Madera, San Luis Obispo, Fresno, and Monterey counties, collectively accounting for 80 percent of the planted acreage. Because of the existence of a symbiotic relationship between sugar and flavor/scent, practically all Muscat Blanc grapes enter the sweet or semi-sweet segment (including sparkling wine). The second popular quality Muscat, **Muscat Orange**, is an obscure variety of 52 acres, 50 of which were planted after 1979. This variety produces a beautiful colored wine, with, as its name suggests, a charming, delicate, orange/spice scent and flavor. Madera contains 22 acres, followed by 19 in Amador, 5 in Monterey, and the remainder in four other counties. **Muscat of Alexandria**, with 5,731 acres, is more common, but officially classified as a raisin grape. A good portion of production, however, does enter the wine market mainly in the production of less expensive sweet and sparkling wines. Nearly all acreage is found in Fresno, Kern, Tulare, Kings, and Madera counties, with the first three counties accounting for more than three-quarters of total acreage. For contemporary reasons, Muscat table, sweet, and sparkling wines are having a difficult time finding a niche in the marketplace (perhaps because it was a major ingredient in fortified "Muscatel" wines) despite an inherent ability to produce above-average wines. Muscat Hamburg is listed with red grapes. **Malvasia Bianca**, grown in California for at least 100 years, is a Muscat flavored grape that is decidedly inferior to Muscat Blanc in the production of quality sweet wine. Five counties (Madera, Merced, Monterey, Stanislaus, and Tulare) account for 2,016 of the 2,115 planted acres. Nearly the entire output of this ancient variety is used in the making of sweet fortified dessert wines. Acreage is decreasing.

Emerald Riesling, is a cross of Riesling and Muscadelle, a University of California-Davis variety first released in 1948, and pioneered by Paul Masson Winery. It grows very well in the warmer climate of the Central Valley where yields are comparatively high, but because it oxidizes rapidly, it requires extreme care. It produces a fresh, tart, acidic, and somewhat fragrant wine. Of the 1,304 acres, 78 percent are in Kern County, followed by Fresno, Madera, and Tulare. Despite the optimistic reports of yesteryear, acreage is declining rapidly. **Grey Riesling**, called Chauche Gris in France, was pioneered by Wente Winery 100 years ago, but when it was discovered in the early 1960s that this grape had lowly origins, there was an effort to stop making it as a varietal wine, with few growers adding to acreage. A moderate yielder with a good sugar-acid ratio, it is one of the earliest ripeners, and although currently out of favor as a varietal grape, it is widely used as a blending grape. Today, of the 491 acres in production, 375 are located in Mon-

terey, Alameda, Napa, and Mendocino counties.

Symphony, a cross of Grenache Gris and Muscat of Alexandria, was developed in 1948 at University of California-Davis by Harold Olmo. Because it is able to grow in a variety of soils and climates, it is vigorous and produces more than 12 tons to the acre of highly concentrated Muscat flavors mixed with clove, cinnamon, orange, sweet spice, and a slight, appealing bitterness at the finish. Surprisingly, the vine makes equally good dry, as well as sweet wines, resists oxidation, retains flavor and scent well after bottling, and is a variety with considerable future potential. Most unusual is the fact that it has an ability to bottle age. There are 191 commercial acres, mainly in Madera, Sonoma, San Joaquin, and Yolo counties. **St. Emilion**, known as Trebbiano and Ugni Blanc, is a ubiquitous grape in the Cognac and Tuscan regions, but one that produces a flat, often bland wine in California. The 1,800 acres for Chablis and Sauterne production as well as Vermouth and brandy before 1970, declined to 774 acres by 1990, most of which are confined to Fresno, Tulare, and Kern counties.

BRIEF OUTLINE OF THE DEVELOPMENT OF SYMPHONY

I. 1940 Dr. Harold Olmo hand pollinated Grenache Gris with Muscat of Alexandria.
A. Goals: 1. Eliminate bitterness of the Muscat parent. 2. Create white table wine variety to grow in regions III and IV.
B. Results: 1. Ninety-four seedlings were grown to maturity in a UCD test block--first fruit produced in 1945. 2. Individual bottles were fermented for each vine in 1948 and 1949.
Wines were evaluated and non-satisfactory vines were removed from the block. 3. Row 5--Vine 58 was the Star, producing more fruit and distinct flavor and aroma characteristics even before full fruit maturity: (a) tight clusters with low propensity for rot; (b) short internodes; (c) fruitful basal buds and cluster formation regularly on nodes 2 and 3.
II. 1958 cuttings from the seedling vine were grafted to St. George rootstock and planted in two 12 plant plots at the Oakville Experimental Station to test cool climate performance.
A. Results: 1. Same growth and fruiting characteristics as the selected seedling vines at Davis. 2. Consistently bore six to seven tons per acre on unirrigated soils.
III. 1971 J5-58 cuttings were planted at the Kearney Horticultural Field Station in Fresno to test hot climate performance.
A. Results: 1. Same growth and fruiting characteristics as the selected seedling vines at Davis. 2. Consistently bore seven to nine tons per acre.
IV. Dr. Olmo overheard a U.C. panel member call a J5-58 wine "most befuddling and confusing wine to classify with its wide range of flavors and aromas...rather mixed up like a symphony with something going on here and something going on there, and yet another thing happening elsewhere." So he named it Symphony.
V. During 1960-1967 five gallon lots of experimental wines were made from the Oakville plots.
A. Unexpected Results: 1. Samples over 12 years old retained excellent white wine color. 2. Those same samples also retained the fresh, young Muscat aromas and flavors--unlike the parent Muscat of Alexandria which was known for showing oxidation flaws only after a few years in the cellar.
VI. Symphony, now named, took over ten years to get through the indexing process of the State/UC certification program for virus free stock. Most varieties take two to three years only. Its buds were susceptible to the extreme heat of the process.
VII. U.S. patent was awarded to the Symphony cultivar on March 29, 1983.
Source: Information provided by Chateau De Baun, from data furnished by University of California, Davis.

Sylvaner, or Franken Riesling as defined in California, is a somewhat soft, moderately fragrant and fruity wine with a touch of sweetness. Grown to produce higher acid levels in the Central Valley, it has not been successful in recent years in its ability to compete with better varieties. Of the 193 acres still in production, 138 are located in Monterey, followed by Santa Clara and Santa Barbara counties. Because the wine loses its freshness quickly, demand and acreage have declined.

Green Hungarian, a variety known for the production of flavorless wine, is, with exceptions, a blending wine with limited appeal. Of the 162 acres, 89 are located in Mendocino County, the remainder equally distributed in Kern, Napa, San Joaquin, San Luis Obispo, Solano, and Sonoma counties. **Sauvignon Vert**, rarely bottled as a varietal because of its low acidity and pronounced flavor, is invariably used for blending. Interestingly, despite the obscurity of its origins and name, 102 acres remain, mainly in Sonoma and Napa counties. **Flora**, a cross between Gewurztraminer and Semillon, was developed for the hot Central Valley. The variety is not popular and its 46 acres are now all located in Napa, Mendocino, Monterey, and Solano counties. The grape adds flavor to Central Valley sparkling wine due to its fruitiness and high acid levels, but, in the final analysis, it is less fragrant and not as good as its ancestors.

Other minor varieties include: **Golden Chasselas**, once a popular variety of Sherry-type wines, produces a dull, low-acid table wine devoid of character. Often confused with Palomino, fewer than 10 acres remain. **Folle Blanche**, with 64 acres, is used in blends and brandy making because it has rather high acids and a neutral flavor. **Servant Blanc**, an obscure variety found only in the Livermore Valley, produces a rich, sweet table grape, and a full bodied, well scented wine. **Peverella**, native to the southern Tyrol, makes well balanced wine, but one without much character. Two Rhone varieties with a bright future are **Roussanne** and **Marsanne**, mainly for the production of both complex, wood aged wines, and fresh, crisp, stainless steel styles. **Viognier**, grown in the northern Rhone where it withstands the periodic bouts of drought and the Mistral well, is a shy yielder that produces excellent, full bodied, fragrant wine. Because this tough-skinned variety requires a long growing season, it produces high acid, very flowery, intensely flavored wines. There are 50 acres, but planted area is expected to increase. **Ehrenfelser**, a cross of Riesling and Sylvaner, has fewer than 5 acres planted, but much promise.

Black Grape Varieties

Zinfandel, with 34,163 acres, or 22 percent of red wine grapes, is the most widely planted red wine grape variety in the state. It is also the variety with the most extravagant history, enigmatic legends, and complicated myths. After a lengthy period of neglect it has become popular. Over the past 10 years acreage has increased by nearly 10,000 (along with Cabernet Sauvignon, the largest absolute increase of red wine grapes). The variety exhibits a high degree of concentration in 6 counties (80% of total acreage), of which San Joaquin, with 11,733 acres (38%) is the most important, followed by Sonoma (4,424 acres), Napa (2,110 acres), Monterey (1,981 acres), Mendocino (1,719 acres), and San Luis Obispo (1,268 acres).

Zinfandel, described as the most versatile grape in California, is made in many different styles: fleshy, chewy, thick, high alcohol; dry and off-dry "white;" semi-sweet to sweet rose; "light;" sparkling; fortified; "nouveau," or Beaujolais style; and late harvest, dry or sweet but with a high alcohol content. Growing conditions will produce raspberry, spice, eucalyptus, mint, pepper, raisin, cherry, and cedar flavors. Despite its versatility Zinfandel has always produced a good quaffing wine, a good blush, but has never been the equal of a first class Cabernet Sauvignon or Pinot Noir. Historically, Zinfandel was a staple of the red jug trade, a favorite of the Italian community, and as a supportive base for improving low alcohol and weakly colored red wines. More recently, Zinfandel as a variety became a darling of the North Coast counties in the 1970s when the wine was made in a big, ponderous, high alcohol style. By 1980 demand dropped just as quickly as Pinot Noir, Chardonnay, and Cabernet Sauvignon rose in popularity and many wineries stopped making varietal red Zinfandel. The tendency today is to make it in a lighter, softer style, but unfortunately, faced with declining demand, less varietal red Zinfandel is made than 20 years ago. When well made from old vines in a Cabernet Sauvignon style, the wine ages admirably for six years, assuming extraordinary layers of spicy flavor, fruity fragrance and a distinctive complexity. According to aficionados, the formula for excellent red Zinfandel is simple: well drained hillside soils, old head pruned, and low yielding, stressed vines. Although Zinfandel is easy to grow, uneven ripening and a sensitive thin skin make it finicky.

Further, the quality, ageability, and palatability of Zinfandel are influenced by fermentation techniques, wood, and bottle aging. Surprisingly, above-average temperatures in late August-early September have a tendency to ripen most grapes simultaneously, and, in the process, Zinfandel is picked after Chardonnay and other more prestigious varieties. Accordingly, with abnormally high sugar levels and excessive raisining, it produces high alcohol, unbalanced wines. Another disgruntled note about the seriousness of red Zinfandel is that it rarely improves after the sixth year, thus removing this variety from lofty Cabernet Sauvignon levels. The short-lived fruit, coupled with high alcohol, often exaggerates flaws, thus mitigating complexity and elegance. On the other hand, the very finest can be rich, dense, eminently satisfying, and a most enjoyable experience. Blending with Cabernet Sauvignon and other varieties is common practice, and a positive element. In the final analysis, whether or not it will attain an aristocratic status in the state's pantheon is a matter of conjecture.

REAL AND UNREAL FACTS ABOUT ZINFANDEL

1830: First record of Zinfandel being grown in the U.S. by William Prince on Long Island, New York. He identifies it as a Hungarian variety.
1834: First reported exhibit of Zinfandel by Samuel J. Perkins of Boston.
1839: *Zinfindal* wine wins its first award as part of the Otis Johnson collection on the East Coast.
1840: Agoston Haraszthy settles in Wisconsin after leaving Hungary. Plants vines.
1848: John Fisk Allen of Salem, Massachusetts, publishes description of locally grown *Zinfandal* that closely matches what is now called Zinfandel.
1848: Haraszthy gives up cold winters of Wisconsin and moves to San Diego, plants vines, and is elected sheriff.
1852: The year Haraszthy imported Zinfandel into California, according to his son, Arpad, writing in the 1880s.
1852: Antoine Delmas reportedly imports Black Saint Peter's to California from France. Later believes this to be the Zinfandel everyone is raving about.
1854: General Vallejo plants Black Saint Peter's in Sonoma.
1857: Haraszthy, having moved from San Diego to San Mateo, moves to Sonoma.
1857: Captain Frederick W. Macondray and J. W. Osborne exhibit *Zinfindal* at Mechanics Fair in San Francisco.
1858: Commissioner of Patents lists *Zinfandel* as part of his collection.
1858: A. P. Smith of Sacramento exhibits *Zeinfindall* at State Fair.
1858: Haraszthy publishes *Report on Grapes and Wine*. Fails to mention Zinfandel.
1859: Antoine Delmas wins first prize for his wine, believed to be Zinfandel, at the State Fair.
1860: William Boggs plants Zinfandel in the propagation garden of the Sonoma Horticultural Society. This leads to extensive Zinfandel plantings in the county.
1860: General Vallejo's winemaker, Dr. Victor Laure, advises Sonoma growers to plant all the Zinfandel they can.
1861: Haraszthy takes his famous European grape buying trip. Publishes his catalog of 156 Hungarian vines but fails to mention Zinfandel.
1864: Haraszthy wins first prize from San Francisco Mechanics Institute for a red wine made with grapes purchased from General Vallejo. The grapes are believed to be Black Saint Peter's.
1866: Haraszthy deposed as head of Buena Vista Viticultural Society. Moves to Nicaragua to make rum.
1868: First North Coast award (a silver medal) for a Zinfandel given to Sonoma pioneer winemaker Jacob R. Snyder at the Mechanics Institute Fair.
1869: First successful White Zinfandel made by George West.
1869: Haraszthy disappears, believed eaten by alligators.
1880: Charles A. Wetmore, State Viticultural Commissioner at Large, believes Zinfandel corrupted from the name *Sylvaner-Zierfahndl*.
1885: Noted Sonoma Historian Robert A. Thompson attacks Haraszthy claim. Traces introduction of Zinfandel through California nurserymen with New England backgrounds.
1885: Arpad Haraszthy declares that Zinfandel is a seedling of Pinot Noir from his mother's vineyard in Hungary.
1947: J. Pedroncelli becomes one of the first wineries in the area to bottle its own wines. Labeled "Claret," the red wine is made from Zinfandel grapes.
1967: Dr. Austin Goheen finds the Primitivo grape in Italy to look exactly like Zinfandel. Prompts UC-Davis research to solve the mysterious question of Zinfandel's origin.
1977: Wine writer Sheldon Wasserman reports Primitivo introduced to Italy 40 to 50 years after Zinfandel was growing in California.
1978: California wine historian Charles Sullivan reports extensive research on Zinfandel to California Historical Society. Research strongly supports introduction of Zinfandel from New England nurseries where it was grown in hothouses as a table grape.
1982: UC-Davis librarian John McConnell writes to *Wines and Vines* that what we know as Zinfandel could not possibly be the same as the *Zinfindal* grown on the East Coast in the early 1800s since that was a table grape and not a wine grape. Suggests Zinfandel, like Mission, might be a seedling.
1982: In response to McConnell's letter, *Wines and Vines* editor comments on the origin of Zinfandel, "I am reminded of Rhett Butler's scorning of Scarlett O'Hara: *Frankly my dear, I don't give a damn.*"
1984: Foreign wines labeled Zinfandel banned by BATF.
Note: Some of the names associated with the Zinfandel legend include: *Zinfindal, Zinfardel, Black Zinfandel, Zirfahnl, Cirfandli, Zirafandel, Zirifandler, Zeinfindall, Kadarka, Zierfandel, Black Saint Peter's, Zoldszilvani, Gruner-Zirifandler, Sylvaner-Zierfahndl, Sylvaner Noir, Zinifal, Ziehfadl, Zierfahndler, Plavac Mali, Zingarello, Primitivo de Gioia, Zirfahler, Zinfantler, Primitivo.*
Source: J. Pedroncelli Winery, Geyserville, Sonoma County.

In recent years, white Zinfandel (more than 50 percent of total output), a fresh, zesty, spicy wine with considerable appeal, has become very popular as it contains some residual sugar. It is a wine hard to ignore in California. A prominent American wine writer has described white Zinfandel as a "marketing masterpiece and a monument to American ingenuity." More than 10 million cases of white Zinfandel are made each year, of which 1 million are sold in southern California.

Zinfandel, therefore, has become the nation's most popular premium varietal, with the three best selling varietal brands being white Zinfandel (Sutter Home, Beringer, and Paul Masson). In recent years, White Zinfandel has taken on a new twist: when blended with Chardonnay, it is called Blush Chardonnay. The popularity of white Zinfandel in recent years has helped quadruple Zinfandel grape prices, and prompt the importation of questionable Zinfandel wine from Brazil.

Long considered a "mystery" grape variety, and often said to have been developed independently from seed in California, the origins of Zinfandel continue to captivate audiences and generate considerable discussion. Considered a mutant of several related Adriatic and Danubian European varieties, it was brought to New England in 1832, and grown in greenhouses as a table grape in Massachusetts, where it was known as Black St. Peter's. It subsequently found its way to San Jose in the 1850s, where the cuttings were labeled as Zinfandel. Spreading quickly throughout California between 1860 and 1900, it eventually replaced the Mission as the dominant red wine grape. By 1910 Zinfandel accounted for 90 percent of all planted wine grapes, the remaining amount being Mission, Malvasia, and smaller quantities of other obscure varieties. In the 1920s it was estimated that more than 80,000 acres were devoted to Zinfandel for wine production. It is certain that it was not brought to California by Count Agoston Haraszthy, and it is interesting to note that as of 1985 BATF does not allow the importation of southern Italian Primitivo di Gioa to be marketed as Zinfandel in America. Curiously, Zinfandel is considered the state's first sparkling wine made by Haraszthy's son, Arpad, in 1862 called "Eclipse." Truly American, Zinfandel has no French, German or Italian wine equivalent, and, hence, no specific wine to imitate.

Long described as the "ugly duckling" of red wine varieties, Zinfandel was given the least desirable corner of the vineyard (due to its adaptability), and a cursory interest in the winery (since it always made good, dark, robust wine). Today, this ugly duckling has spread its wings to become one of the more expensive, refined, and distinctive red wines to be found anywhere. More importantly, it is unique to California in terms of history and notoriety. Zinfandel varies considerably in quality and character (spicy throughout the Sierra Foothills, intense and rich in Fiddletown, spicy and well rounded in Paso Robles, berry flavored in Napa, firm in Lake County, big, rich and spicy from the Dry Creek and Sonoma Valley, and baked and raisiny in the Central Valley). The very best comes from the Fiddletown area of Amador County, the hill vineyards of Napa County, the Dry Creek area and Sonoma valley of Sonoma County, and the southern portions of Mendocino and Lake counties.

When cultivated in an area with a long and moderately cool growing season, raisining and uneven ripening are prevented, acid levels are appreciably higher, and fruity flavors are more intense. The very best Zinfandel, especially those with a full bodied style, usually have small amounts of Cabernet Sauvignon, Pinot Noir, Petit Sirah, Carignane, Chardonnay, and Gewurztraminer added for additional color, roundness and flavor intensity. Unfortunately, good Zinfandel is not considered (judged by prevailing prices) a substitute for Cabernet Sauvignon, Merlot, and Pinot Noir, although it usually offers better value than all three. It appears that the consumer is more willing to pay twice as much for equivalent quality Cabernet Sauvignon, than for Zinfandel despite the similarity of production costs for both grapes. Although Zinfandel acreage declined steadily during 1978 through 1985, it is currently expanding due to the popularity of white Zinfandel, and renewed demand for more traditional full bodied styles. Consequently, Zinfandel prices throughout the state, and particularly grapes from older vineyards, have doubled during 1987-1989. Red Zinfandel over the years has acquired the trappings of a cult (often described as Zimphomania): there is a Zinfandel Guild in California, a Zinfandel Club in London, and although there are half as many red Zinfandel producers now as there were 15 years ago, California's love affair with Zinfandel is not about to expire because quality has never been higher, offering excellent value.

Cabernet Sauvignon, in terms of geographic diversity, is the most widely planted quality red table wine grape in the world. In terms of price, number of wineries making it and notoriety, Cabernet Sauvignon is California's most celebrated and consistent premium quality wine variety. Its popularity is reflected by the fact that more than 519 wineries make it as a varietal (in contrast to 289 making Zinfandel, 242 making

Pinot Noir, and 207 making Merlot), media attention is relentless, and acreage continues to steadily increase from 220 in 1944 to more than 33,000 in 1990 (output for the same period jumped from 2 thousand cases to 6 million). Although grown in 36 counties, 6 contain 81 percent of total acreage: Napa 9,131 acres (28%); Sonoma 6,468 acres (20%); Monterey 3,763 acres (11%); San Joaquin 3,151 acres (9%); San Luis Obispo 2,451 acres (7%); and Mendocino 1,314 acres (4%). Another 4,285 acres, or 13 percent, are found in Lake, Kern, Sacramento, and Santa Barbara counties. About 25,505 acres, or 77 percent, are located in the coastal counties, indicating a high degree of concentration. Vine acreage expanded during the period 1968-1975 when UC-Davis developed a new clone that was supposed to be disease-free. Despite the variety's notoriety as the state's premier red wine grape, its tenure in California only goes back to the period immediately after the gold rush. Other states contain about 3,500 acres, and, surprisingly, France has but 56,000 acres, and declining.

Indigenous to the Gironde in southwestern France, Cabernet Sauvignon is responsible for the basic structure of the finest wines of the Medoc. Ideally, it does well only within a narrow climatic zone: it cannot tolerate high temperatures as its varietal character is destroyed, while overly cold regions produce thin, astringent and vegetative wines. When fully ripe the grape produces wine with a distinct depth of flavor and aroma forming a complex and distinctive package that is altogether first rate. It has a pronounced bouquet, a high tannin content, a sweet juice, and with aging produces the characteristic "cigar box" bouquet. In California it produces big, powerful, well structured, flavorful, and intense wines, the finest of which emanate from the Dry Creek, Sonoma, and Alexander valleys of Sonoma County, Napa Valley (particularly the middle portion of the valley, as well as the surrounding hilly uplands), and the warmer, hilly regions of Mendocino and Lake counties.

The wine defies easy generalization because geographic characteristics and style vary so widely (flavors range from herbaceous, eucalyptus, tea, bell pepper, spice, green olive, and cigar box). In addition, more than 50 percent of the planted acreage is composed of young vines less than 15 years old. Although widely grown, Cabernet Sauvignon is sensitive to California's growing conditions: it needs ample heat and sunshine, but without the excessive heat of Region IV and V areas, nor the cooler weather of the upper limits of Region I, the former producing baked flavor, and the latter thin, acidic, herbaceous tasting wine that is often bitter and lacking in body. Historically made in a dark, heavy, high alcohol/tannin fashion, the style in recent years has drifted toward roundness, delicacy, finesse, and softness. The very best wines usually have some Merlot, and perhaps Cabernet Franc, Malbec, and, increasingly, Petit Verdot added to lend complexity to the final blend. These wines are also the product of low yielding, non-vigorous vines planted on hillsides and not rich bottomland. The immense variability in quality (the result of yield, fermentation practices, grape origins, wood aging, etc.) continues to plague this variety.

Thick skinned, hardy, and moderate in yield, Cabernet Sauvignon has a unique taste and aroma. Aged in wood for a variable time period, the wine in recent years not only rivals classic Bordeaux, but routinely outperforms it in flavor, balance, aroma, and is able to age just as well. The major differences tend to be stylistic: while Bordeaux has lower alcohol levels, it is higher in acidity, and more austere on the palate; California Cabernet Sauvignon is more supple, fruitier, and nearly always higher in alcohol. There are usually four types of Cabernet Sauvignon: a normal bottling, a "reserve," vineyard designations, and super premium. Although there can be significant differences between the four, "Reserve" Cabernet Sauvignon, twice the price of a "regular" bottle, is common for most major producers, even for those with secondary labels, while the super premium, three times more expensive, usually offers poor value. In the final analysis, while the Dionysian-Apollonian extremes still prevail--big, bold, overpowering wines vs. flat, dull, nondescript wines, the bulk of Cabernet Sauvignon is supple, fruity, and well-structured offering exceptional value. It definitely is more consistent, year in and year out, than French counterparts. The popularity of Cabernet Sauvignon, among all red wine grape varieties, has exhibited in recent decades a strong, consistent demand.

Over the past 10 years, there is a growing tendency for the establishment of a *Premier Cru* club (Dominus, Insignia, Lyeth, Opus One, and Rubicon, among many) with prices rivaling the asking prices of top tier Bordeaux properties. Equally good, if not better, are wines produced by winemakers under their own names, the most notable being Ric Forman. Nevertheless, California Cabernet Sauvignon is good, some of it exceptional, and for many "life is Cabernet." The "futures" market, a recent innovation in America, hinges around Cabernet Sauvignon and is becoming a major marketing element in the sale of premium wines. Although premium Cabernet Sauvignon has been a monopoly of coastal California, serious competition is surfacing from Washington State; eastern Long Island; northern Virginia; Lubbock, Texas; and Maryland.

In recent years Cabernet Sauvignon has been the subject of four important controversies. The 1st is centered on the polemics of its ability to age in the manner of classic Bordeaux. While there is an environmental tendency for California growing conditions to produce ripe, rich, often opulent wines marked by lower acid levels, there is no evidence to suggest that excessive aging beyond 15 to 20 years is beneficial to most, if any, table wines. By its very character, California Cabernet Sauvignon, with its lush fruit, lower acid, and soft, round flavors, is more accessible than Bordeaux at an early age, and the majority tend to age more gracefully than their counterparts on the eastern side of the Atlantic. Unfortunately, the ageability issue of California Cabernet Sauvignon is usually made when the opponents are a handful of quality oriented properties, and only for selected years. The average American consumer (not to mention wine writers) fails to realize that more than 80 percent of all red Bordeaux is thin and acidic, not aged in wood, and consumed within the first year. The remainder, when allowed to age for an excessive period of time (somewhere between 10 and 25 years depending on the vintage), dry out to the point that only philosophical arm chair discussions can rescue their bygone honor and dignity.

The second major issue is a Cabernet Sauvignon classification, first promulgated by Ronald Kapon in 1982. Because the wine industry is going through a strenuous exercise in adjusting to the realities of a national appellation system, the timing for a "classification" is somewhat premature. Another reason for failure is the fact that of the 500 California producers of Cabernet Sauvignon, fewer than 100 have been making this wine in a consistent fashion for more than 10 years as of this writing. The third controversy is a direct development of the second, and lies in the fact that the wine is the center of the American wine auction, and contemporary "collecting" frenzy. As the quality of American Cabernet Sauvignon continued its steady improvement throughout the past several decades, interest in fashionable auctions, collecting and charitable affairs expanded by exponential rates. As appreciation began to outperform the Dow Jones averages, many private collectors and "investment clubs" began to proliferate throughout the nation further fueling the appeal and seductiveness of this newly discovered social and economic preoccupation. Naturally, price escalation has not altogether been absent from the scene. Critics maintain that large scale "institutionalized" wine auctions and collecting has driven prices beyond reason. Because fewer than 10 wineries in 1960 produced it as a varietal, the enological prominence and commercial gravity of Cabernet Sauvignon since 1974 cannot be denied. For nearly a generation this wine has captivated the imagination and dominated the state's fine wine segment. The source of the fourth (and most interesting) imbroglio is the name "Meritage," a euphemism for a red and white wine made by "traditional" Bordeaux grapes described elsewhere.

Grenache, with 13,644 acres, or 9 percent of all red wine grapes, is the 3rd most important variety. Nearly all is planted in 6 Central Valley counties--Stanislaus, San Joaquin, Merced, Fresno, Kern, and Madera, the last three alone having more than 70 percent of total acreage. Of Spanish origin, Grenache has adopted well in all hot, dry vinegrowing areas, particularly southern France, the Central Valley, Australia, and Argentina. In addition to being used in the production of sweet fortified wines, its main function is to produce high yields (more than 12 tons to the acre) destined for inexpensive blended wines, and, historically, it was the most popular variety for the production of jug rose wine. Contrary to popular opinion, Grenache is a fragile and delicate grape, and recent improvements in vineyard management and vinification techniques have improved quality. Whole cluster fermentation, for example, slows down the fermentation rate and helps retain fresh berry characteristics. When made into a 100 percent varietal table wine, it rarely improves with wood aging, and oxidizes rapidly. However, aging on lees and judicious blending improves body, structure, and retains freshness. Although commonly referred to as a "hot weather" grape,

Grenache will also grow well in coastal counties. Over the past 20 years, acreage has declined from 21,000 to present levels, although there is some cause to think that recent declines in acreage are about to be reversed. In an effort to create "Rhone-type" wines (of which Grenache is a major constituent), hillside (non-irrigated) acreage (along with Mourvedre and Syrah) has recently expanded along the North and Central Coast regions. In the Central Valley growers are also highly optimistic for this variety because Grenache stands to benefit from the white Zinfandel craze. "White Grenache" is not only less expensive than Zinfandel, but in many ways is superior in flavor, as evidenced by the fact that E. & J. Gallo is shipping more than 2.4 million cases.

Carignane, with 11,037 acres, or 7 percent of all red wine grapes, is the 4th most important variety. Although a native of Spain, Carignane, as in the Midi of southern France, is known for exceptionally high yields, and used in the production of robust jug blends, and fortified sweet wine production with little redeeming value in California. While more than 82 percent of acreage is found in the Central Valley, mainly in Madera, San Joaquin, Stanislaus, Merced, Kern, and Fresno counties (where yields in Region IV and V areas surpass 13 tons to the acre), Mendocino and portions of Napa and Sonoma counties contain old vines that are currently producing excellent wine, some of which is produced as varietal. Over the past 50 years acreage has declined to present levels from 31,000 acres in 1940, and is expected to decline further. Because of its excellent shipping qualities, 21,835 acres were planted during the Prohibition years in order to satisfy the demands of the home winemaker.

Barbera, the fifth most popular red wine grape, contains 10,666 acres, or 7 percent of total acreage, nearly all of it grown in the same counties as Grenache. A native of northern Italy, this variety produces dark, robust, full bodied wine very popular with the Italian community because it contains plenty of flavor, and, unlike Grenache, Carignane, and Ruby Cabernet, more acidity and fragrance, thus it is used in the production of blended jug wine. Hailed as the red wine grape of the Central Valley, acreage grew rapidly from 200 in 1960 to more than 20,000 twenty years later. However, coarseness, dullness, and the unbalanced character of its wines, in contrast to Bordeaux varietals, have diminished interest. Despite its adaptability to many soils and climates, Barbera acreage, after a dramatic rise, continues to decline from its peak of nearly 22,000 acres in 1970. Although found in Regions I and II, it apparently does best in the warmer areas of the Central Valley. Ninety-three percent are found in Fresno, Madera, Kern, Merced, and Stanislaus counties, of which the first two account for most of the acreage. Old plantings in Sonoma and Napa, however, manage to make rare, above-average quality varietal wine. With the recent revival of interest in Italian grape varieties, it is possible that this variety will emerge from current obscurity.

Pinot Noir is considered the supreme grape variety in the vinous kingdom, and the grape variety offering the greatest challenge to contemporary winemakers. Although Pinot Noir rarely makes memorable wine, it is a vine that is hard to ignore. Commonly called the "Holy Grail," this "troublesome" vine has distinguished itself in only 6 small regions--the Cote d'Or, the Willamette Valley, the Carneros region, northern Monterey, Santa Barbara, and the Finger Lakes area of New York. With 9,549 acres, or 6 percent of all red wine grapes, American Pinot Noir represents but one-fourth of the planted acreage in France, and 40 percent of that available in the famed Burgundy district. Other American states contain fewer than 4,000 acres. Historically, Pinot Noir nurtured the "bad guy" image in California due to high yields, diminished flavor, color instability, irregular growth patterns, and an inherent ability to produce unacceptable quality wine. Pinot Noir of olden days (varietal wine in measured quantities first began to appear in the late 1970s) had a raisiny aroma and flavor, practically no varietal character, was light in color and made like Cabernet Sauvignon, offering little interest.

Today this vine is the focus of a determined effort to identify clones and adapt them to specific root stocks and microclimates in an effort to produce outstanding Burgundy-style red table wine, and Champagne-style sparkling wines. While Wadenswil and Pommard account for more than 90 percent, UCD 5 is considered the finest clone in the production of dark, intensely flavored wine. Other clones include the Mt. Eden Selection, the Wente Clone, the Martini Clone, and the

UCD 1. It is widely assumed that among premium grape varieties, Pinot Noir is the most finicky in the production of quality wine from specific vineyard sites. As a consequence, yields have declined from 5 to 3 tons the acre as superior clones have been introduced, and new areas of production have surfaced. The markedly improved wines have achieved a good dose of celebrity, and, as a result, prices have risen sharply in recent years. Acreage (7,465, or 78% of total) is overwhelmingly confined to 3 counties on the cooler portions of coastal California: Sonoma (3,130, or one-third of all acreage), Napa (2,719), and Monterey (1,616). It is widely acknowledged, however, that the finest sites are the Russian River area of Sonoma, the Carneros appellation, the cooler areas of Monterey County, and the Santa Maria Valley of Santa Barbara County.

Grown in Burgundy since the 14th century, Pinot Noir is considered the finest (or noble) red wine grape. It is one of the oldest varieties grown in nearly all major wine producing areas. As a red, rose, and sparkling wine, it simply eludes replication outside its area of domestication-the Cote d'Or. While it was introduced in California in the first half of the 19th century, extensive experimentation did not occur until the 1880s in a series of trial plots by the University of California. It is estimated that during the period 1880-1900, no fewer than 15 different Pinot Noir variants were planted and investigated. Due to low yields, and an unstable genetic constitution, Pinot Noir was never considered a "serious" grape, and hence, not recommended. However, its formidable history begins with Martin Ray after World War II in Santa Cruz, and by Hanzell in Sonoma County in the 1950s. Its recent meteoric rise, unlike other "noble" grape varieties, has been anything but stellar (despite its current popularity). The vine is difficult to grow, its yields are meager, its clusters small and compact making a host of diseases possible, and unlike other good red wine grapes, it only begins to produce excellent fruit after its 15th birthday. Pinot Noir demands (but rarely gets) iron rich, slightly alkaline and limestone impregnated soils, cool hilly sites, a long and cool growing season, and must be cultured to produce low yields. It is highly susceptible to rot, high humidity, and late frost. In a warm climate region (particularly one with warm nights), Pinot Noir loses its elegance and finesse, delicacy, aroma, and freshness, conditions aggravated by its low acid, high pH character. Not only is the growing season demanding, but winemaking requirements are equally challenging as the wine's subtleties are easily lost. Unfortunately, in California, as well as the rest of the nation, there is no universal on how to make the ideal Pinot Noir wine. Consequently, method of fermentation, residual sugar, alcohol content, type of yeasts used, malolactic fermentation, degree of filtering and clarification, the addition of other wines, such as Zinfandel, Riesling, Cabernet Sauvignon, Petite Sirah, etc., and more, are part of the contemporary story of Pinot Noir.

The physical elements necessary for excellent berry production are more circumscribed for Pinot Noir than most other red varieties: Pinot Noir has a propensity to mutate, is shy bearing, early ripening, extremely finicky about soil, disease-prone, and, due to its thin skin, very susceptible to high temperatures during the growing season, the latter particularly significant because phenolic compounds oxidize making its color dull and light. Equally important, the sugar-acid ratio is affected and distinctive raisin-like flavors occur, making vineyard cultural and winery practices the critical elements in the final product of above-average Pinot Noir wine. It is estimated that there may be as many as 300 different clones in the state that produce a chamelion-like personality with bewildering variations in foliage, growth habits, fertility, cluster size, and berry weight, collectively producing wide variations in grape quality, fruit color, and eventual wine quality.

Although California Pinot Noir has shown a marked improvement in recent years and is considerably more consistent from vintage to vintage, whenever Americans think of Pinot Noir they talk of the Willamette Valley, and not necessarily California. Equally important is the notion that fine Pinot Noir is associated with limestone soil although no one knows how limestone influences wine quality. In the quest to produce excellent table wine, acreage has increased by one-third since 1980, and it is estimated that over the next decade California's Pinot Noir acreage will exceed the 13,680 acres (1979) found in the Department of Cote-d'Or. Of the 13,000 Pinot Noir acres available in the United States, 9,549 acres are in California, 2,200 in Oregon, and the remainder in other states. If this projection materializes, California will lead the world in Pinot Noir acreage, a most unusual phenomenon in view of the fact that the state had fewer than 1,500 acres in 1965.

Aficionados maintain that Pinot Noir is the wine of the future in California-*the* wine that will propel the state's reputation as the finest wine producing region in the world. The problem, as one prominent wine writer stated, is simply this: "Pinot Noir fanatics are like Mediterranean theologians or New Yorkers giving directions. Everybody has a good idea of the goal (Chambertin, Heaven, and Canarsie), but there are more than a few opinions about how to get there." The central issue, however, rests on the fact that the grape lacks a definitive Pinot Noir taste, thus making the final wine the subject of considerable manipulation either through winemaking processes, or by the addition of other wine to add color, flavor, alcohol, longevity, etc. While it is often gentle, round, subtle, and with an apparent sensation of sweetness, it lacks flavor. Passionate opinions abound, and the lack of a consensus of what the "ideal" Pinot Noir wine ought to be means that there will be continued unbridled experimentation and controversy. In the meantime, there is a rush to isolate the more successful virus-free clones, to pair them with the finest rootstock and soil/microclimate regions, and to increase vine density per acre. In the winery, grapes must contain high acids, natural yeasts be suppressed, and "lees" aging mandatory. The grape is also unpredictable, and the wine undergoes several "cycles" in its bottle evolution. One significant reason why it will always be expensive lies in the fact that Pinot Noir does not lend itself to large-scale winemaking, responding best when made in small batches. Pinot Meunier, an inferior strain of Pinot Noir, is only planted in experimental plots, and is a minor entity in both sparkling and table wine production.

Merlot, one of the most important and expensive red wine grapes has, despite its introduction to California in the late 1880s, only expanded recently: from just 2 acres in 1960, to 7,435 acres in 1990. Its geographic distribution is nearly identical with that of its close partner, Cabernet Sauvignon: 29 percent of acreage is located in Napa, followed by Sonoma, San Joaquin, Monterey, and Sacramento, collectively responsible for 78 percent of all plantings. Present acreage represents nearly 2,000 fewer acres from a high of 4,500 in 1976, a decline that reflects the uprooting of vines planted inappropriately in Monterey, San Luis Obispo, and Santa Barbara counties. Despite acreage decline, Merlot has evolved into a high quality wine (some say it has achieved the status of a cult) as the number of wineries making varietal Merlot has increased from several to more than 190. Merlot serves two important functions; it softens and rounds out the character of the more astringent and tannin rich Cabernet Sauvignon, and increasingly is made as a complex, stylish, multifaceted, well balanced varietal wine that is often better than Cabernet Sauvignon, and far more reliable than Pinot Noir. As Cabernet Sauvignon, Cabernet Franc, Zinfandel, and other grapes are added to give it firmness and structure, Merlot is no longer considered a blending grape but a classic varietal that "satisfies."

Merlot is said to be the vine of the Caesars, as Merulus is "black," Merulator "a wine drinker," and Merulentus, "a drunk." Its nomenclature notwithstanding, acreage (especially when compared with Pinot Noir) devoted to this increasingly popular variety will increase for a many reasons: it is a vigorous and consistent producer of up to 10 tons per acre; disease resistant; easy to grow; can tolerate a much larger range of soils and climates than most red grape varieties; and produces excellent quality, early maturing wine. Moreover, being early budding, early flowering, and early ripening, it usually avoids the first autumnal rains. Rich bottom land soil almost always produces wines with a grassy, herbaceous flavor and odor; but upland, skeletal soils, under conditions of stress, manage to produce rich, plummy, fruity, well structured wines. Low yielding vineyards and the dry benchland and hilly vineyards in Sonoma County are excellent areas for the production of Merlot. However, the vine will not yield good wine in Region III, IV, and V areas, preferring instead cooler but sunny locations in Regions I and II. Heat apparently produces raisined berries, and unpredictable cool weather in the spring results in disastrous berry shatter, often reducing the crop by 50 percent.

Another significant problem lies in the fact that half of all Merlot acreage was improperly located on rich soils that were high in nitrogen-a plant nutrient extremely sensitive to Merlot. Furthermore, low malic acids, and high pH levels, if not properly handled by a competent winemaker, often spell disaster. Like all other "Bordeaux" varieties, demand is currently outstripping supply, thus raising prices and accelerating the planting of additional acres. Because of its pedantic past, growers have only recently recognized the need to identify particular areas and microclimates: of importance are the clay soils of Carneros, the hill regions of southern Sonoma and Napa counties, the hotter, less humid portions of Mendocino and Lake counties, the Placerville region of Amador County, and the lee slopes of the Central Coast counties.

The latest statistics indicate that with 7,435 acres, Merlot is the 4th most widely planted quality red grape in California, ranking behind Zinfandel, Cabernet Sauvignon, and Pinot Noir, among the more prestigious varietals. France has 100,000 acres; Italy 60,000; the Balkans 5,000; and Chile and Argentina more than 7,000. Interestingly, while Merlot has nearly twice the acreage of Cabernet Sauvignon in the Gironde Department (its primary area of cultivation), there is 10 times more Cabernet Sauvignon acreage in California than Merlot. When first planted in large amounts in the 1970s the grape was generally used to enhance the depth of Cabernet Sauvignon (very similar to its role in the Medoc), but beginning in the early 1980s wineries began to offer varietal bottlings, either as 100% Merlot, or blended with small quantities of Cabernet Sauvignon and other Bordeaux varieties, very much in the tradition of Pomerol and St.-Emilion along the north bank of the Gironde estuary. Although many bottles exhibit a tired, fruitless, dull character, the majority from the finest wineries are above-average to outstanding in quality, and as the vines get older wine quality steadily improves. The finest Merlot is singularly supple, rich and readily accessible, although there are producers that make it into a tannin-rich, long-lived wine. It is widely assumed that Louis Martini in 1968, and Sterling Vineyards in 1969 were the first wineries in Napa to produce a varietal Merlot. Merlot producers increased from 23 in 1976 to more than 220 in 1991, and annual output of varietal Merlot now exceeds 1 million cases.

Other Bordeaux Varieties: **Cabernet Franc**, **Petit Verdot**, and **Malbec**, enjoy the same status Merlot had 20 years ago. There are no compelling reasons why these varieties should not experience a similar growth period because each one adds a different and significant dimension to Cabernet Sauvignon and Merlot blends. The single, most important reason why acreage in Merlot, Cabernet Franc, Petit Verdot, and Malbec is so low, is that UC-Davis had historically not recommended the varieties to growers, citing low acid and high pH levels as the major objections.

Cabernet Franc, usually referred to as the "little cousin," is one of 5 quality red grapes of Bordeaux, and the grape of choice in such first rate wines as Chinon and Bourgueil. Historically, the variety has not been a major player in California until recently when it attracted much attention as a varietal and blending grape. Consequently, demand has risen sharply making this variety one of the three most expensive grapes in the state. Of the 1,620 acres, 636 are planted in Napa, 457 in Sonoma, and nearly all of the remaining 527 acres are mainly confined in the warmer pockets of coastal California. The wine, less astringent than Cabernet Sauvignon, has good body, color, a muted bouquet, and ages much sooner than Cabernet Sauvignon. Used to add complexity and roundness to Cabernet Sauvignon and Merlot, production rests almost exclusively with the more prestigious producers. Cabernet Franc does not appear to add, despite protestations to the contrary, a measurable amount of longevity, and it will not improve color stability, fruitiness, and roundness to levels publicized by growers and winemakers. It appears that its qualities have been exaggerated, and a good deal of misplanted acreage will be replaced in the coming years. New areas of production (particularly in the cooler, upland North Coast regions), better cultural practices, and improved winemaking techniques will considerably improve the image and quality of this Bordeaux grape. This grape, very much like Cabernet Sauvignon, is often mistaken for it, and while it rarely reaches the heights of Cabernet Sauvignon, its parentage belies a close affinity.

Petit Verdot, a late ripener, has more promise than any other quality red grape in California due to its dark color, fantastic scent, and uncanny ability to improve all other Bordeaux grapes by reducing the vegetal flavor and aroma commonly found in Cabernet Sauvignon and Merlot. It has excellent color and depth of flavor greater than Cabernet Sauvignon and Merlot combined, adding immense complexity to blends, and lengthening the wine's finish. Moreover, of the four principal Bordeaux varieties, it is Petit Verdot that has the greater future be-

cause it has higher acids--a most important consideration in an area that produces low acid wines. Unlike other "Bordeaux" varieties, Petit Verdot thrives on rich alluvial soils producing wines without a hint of grass-herb odors and flavors. It is also significant to note that Petit Verdot, unlike Merlot, is a wine whose delicacy and fruit does not readily dissipate with time in a glass. While fashion and low pH yields have reduced its importance in the Gironde, there are few compelling reasons why California winemakers should not make better use of this excellent variety. Of the 97 planted acres, 55 are located in Napa, 31 in Sonoma, 5 in Monterey, 2 in Amador, and one each in Lake, Calaveras, Mendocino, and Santa Clara counties.

Malbec, more than any other of Bordeaux's primary grapes, exhibits precocious growing habits along with poor berry set and irregular yields that discourages many growers. There are 122 acres, nearly all in Sonoma, Stanislaus, and Napa counties, but there is nothing to suggest that selected coastal areas cannot produce wines similar to those from Cahors, the region in southwestern France that has made this grape famous. Malbec produces early maturing, dark, rich, spicy wine. Made as a varietal wine by several wineries, it is assumed that the number will increase in the coming years. **St. Macaire** (50 acres), best known for its intense color, good acidity and tannin content, is not as good for blending purposes as the above. Two other minor red grapes are Gros Verdot and Carmenere.

Few would quarrel with the argument that the finest Medoc wines are, and should be, blends of the 5 above-named varieties (in various proportions). Should an American winemaker wish to replicate the formula, what do you name the wine when it isn't 75 percent of one specific grape variety? Wishing to standardize a name that all wineries may use, a 36-member association was formed to solicit suggestion, and after a year's search, the name *Meritage* was selected in 1989. The association will govern the licensing of the trademarked name, and in order to qualify the wine must be made solely from a variable mixture of Cabernet Sauvignon, Merlot, Cabernet Franc, Petit Verdot, Malbec, St. Macaire, Gros Verdot, and Carmenere, be the winery's most expensive wine (there are to be no exceptions to this requirement, such as a higher priced estate bottled wine, or a single vineyard wine), be limited to 25,000 cases, and have an appellation name on the label.

There is also a white "Meritage" whose grape mixture is limited to Sauvignon Blanc, Semillon, and Muscadelle. Unfortunately nothing in the by-laws mentions quality, grape sources, alcohol content, aging features, etc., so that quality and physical wine characteristics are subject to wide diversity. The motivating reasons are sound, and the name, with time, will be successful for both producers and consumers. It is believed that this will be the precursor to a formal "official" classification of Meritage producers by 2000. As of this writing there are nearly 40 members of the Meritage association with only three Meritage producers outside California: Woodward Canyon of Washington, Prince Michel in Virginia, and Pindar Winery in New York. The name, idea and execution of the concept have been criticized as further cannibalization of market segments as the wines are not varietal or regional. The success of the name, however, might become so popular that the enforcement of quality standards may decline as additional wineries join the association.

Forty wineries are making Meritage-type wines, nearly all of which have acquired a good measure of celebrity: Benziger of Glen Ellen (Sonoma, *A Tribute*, red and white); Beringer (Napa, *Nightingale*, white, sweet); Carmenet Vineyard (Sonoma, red and white); Chateau Julien (Monterey, *Platinum*, white); Clos du Bois (Sonoma, *Marlstone*, red); Concannon Vineyard (Livermore, *Assemblage*, white); Cosentino Winery (Napa, *The Poet*, red); De Lorimier Winery (Sonoma, *Spectrum* and *Mosaic* for white and red respectively); Dry Creek Vineyard (Sonoma, red); Estancia (Sonoma, red); Flora Springs Winery (Napa, *Trilogy*, red); Franciscan Vineyards (Napa, *Oakville Estate*, red); Geyser Peak Winery (Sonoma, *Reserve Alexandre*, red); Gold Hill Vineyard (Coloma, red); Guenoc Winery (Lake County, *Langtry*, red and white); The Hess Collection (Napa, red); Inglenook-Napa Valley (Napa, *Reunion* and *Gravion*, red and white respectively); Justin Vineyards (San Luis Obispo, *Reserve*, red); Kendall-Jackson (Lake, *Cardinale*, red); Konocti Winery (Lake, red and white); Lyeth Winery (Sonoma, red and white); Merlion Winery (Napa, white, red, and sweet); Merryvale Vineyards (Napa, red and white); Mt. Veeder Winery (Napa, red); Pahlmeyer Winery (Napa, red); Pindar Vineyards (Long Island, New

York, *Mythology*, red); Prince Michel Vineyards (Virginia, *Le Ducq*, red); Rombauer Vineyards (Napa, *Le Meilleur du Chai*, red); Royce Vineyards (Sonoma, red); Sebastiani Vineyards (Sonoma, *Wildwood*, red); Stonegate Winery (Napa, red); Vichon Winery (Napa, *Chevrignon*, white); Woodward Canyon Winery (Walla Walla, Washington, *Charbonneau*, red). While the member list fluctuates, it is expected that the number of wineries producing Meritage-type wines by the end of this century will increase beyond 75.

Rubired, a cross of Alicante Ganzin and Tinta Cao, is a successful UC-Davis productive variety that was designed to produce blending wine, Porto-type wine, and red juice concentrate in Region IV and V areas. Although acreage initially grew rapidly beyond 10,000 acres, its popularity declined, but acreage has recently increased to 7,136. Fresno, Kern, Madera, and Tulare counties collectively account for 89 percent of total acreage. **Ruby Cabernet**, with 6,921 acres, or 5 percent of all red wine grapes, is the ninth most widely planted variety, nearly all found in 4 Central Valley counties: Fresno, Kern, Merced, and Stanislaus. A cross of Cabernet Sauvignon and Carignane, it was developed by UC-Davis specifically for the hot Central Valley, and has remained the most popular of the crosses developed by H.P. Olmo. Available in 1936 and first planted commercially in 1948, its purpose was to combine the excellent winemaking character of Cabernet Sauvignon with the productive character of Carignane, and, although a high yielder, its main use was for blending purposes. At first, its advantages were formidable: high yields, good color, and high acid levels; the wine, however, never approached the quality levels of Cabernet Sauvignon. As useful as it was in the past as a blending grape, its acreage has declined sharply from a high of 20,000 acres in the early 1970s. Because its future was based on the continued growth of generic jug wines, its demise is understandable as it is no match (it has a peculiar "green olive" flavor and lacks depth of flavor) for the superior Bordeaux-type grape varieties from coastal counties.

Petite Sirah has more tannin, and a more subdued nose and flavor than Zinfandel, good color, moderate acidity, and because of higher glycerin is smooth on the palate. Very popular in the 1960s and early 1970s, its acreage has declined (by 8,000 to 3,072 acres in 1990) proportionally with its reputation as a varietal wine (whether made in a big, ponderous, bold, mouth filling, or in a more supple, lighter style did not matter). Its recent decline is perplexing as it is one of the better blending grapes because of its multitude of flavors (depending on growing conditions), such as pepper, berry, cherry, tea, and plum. Today its current celebrity rests with its ability to improve Zinfandel and generic wines by adding tannin and complexity. It is thought that a good deal of the planted acreage is the lowly Durif. First produced successfully as a varietal by Concannon Winery in 1961, it was quickly made by others, expanding from 4,000 acres in 1970 to 11,778 in 1973 with yields of 6-9 tons to the acre. In 1977 more than 40 wineries were marketing a varietal Petite Sirah, but by 1980 demand began to decline in favor of other red wines. While not currently the center of immense popularity, the wine, particularly from old vines, can be one of the finest in the state. 5 counties, Sonoma, Monterey, Merced, Mendocino, and Madera, collectively account for 70 percent of total acreage.

Alicante Bouschet, a prolific producer with red juice (called the "king of juice grapes"), thick skin, high sugar content, and high yields, is an appealing grape for blending. Originating in France in 1865 from a cross of Grenache and Petite Bouschet, it is a major grape extensively grown in southern France and Algeria. Historically one of the leading grapes used by home winemakers on the east coast (called the "shipping variety") during Prohibition (23,158 acres were planted), today nearly all of it is used for blending purposes, with only two wineries (Papagni and Michael Topolos at Russian River Vineyards) making a varietal wine out of it. Acreage has declined from 29,321 acres in 1940 to 2,101 in 1990. Fresno, the leading county, contains 768 acres (37%), followed by Tulare (477 acres), Kern (281), San Joaquin (194), and Madera (184). Interestingly, the Central Valley and the Sierra Foothills contain all but 130 acres of the total planted area. When made from old, high density vineyards, Alicante Bouschet is able to produce rich, luscious, well flavored, chewy, age worthy wines.

Gamay (Napa), not related to Gamay Beaujolais, is a highly adaptable vine that produces red and rose wine with low pigmentation. Because it ripens fully along the California coast, it is confined to the cooler areas of Sonoma, Mendocino, Napa, Monterey, and Solano.

One-quarter of acreage is found in the cooler regions of Sacramento County. Unlike the more common Gamay Beaujolais, Napa Gamay has proven to be a very successful varietal by a handful of dedicated producers, particularly Duxoup Winery. Newly introduced clones produce wine with excellent acid balance, dark color, and yields that are appreciably higher than Pinot Noir. To some, Gamay, unlike Gamay Beaujolais, is the same variety as that grown in the Beaujolais region of southern Burgundy, and to others it is the more common Valdiguie from southwestern France. Acreage, recently declining to 1,541, is mainly found in Napa (357), Monterey (280), Sonoma (221), and Kern (143). **Gamay Beaujolais**, growing in the warmer portions of the coastal counties and in the Central Valley, is now considered a clone of Pinot Noir (#105), with larger berries, higher yields, and lower sugar levels than Gamay. Although the vine is able to produce good, fresh, and pleasing wine, it is not the equivalent of Napa Gamay, and, consequently, acreage has decreased by more than 2,000 since 1970, to 1,424 in 1990. The principal counties, Mendocino (430), Monterey (385), San Benito (260), and Sonoma (240), collectively contain 88 percent of the planted acreage. Undisclosed acreage assumed to be Pinot Noir is actually Gamay Beaujolais.

Mission (also Criolla, and El Paso in Texas and New Mexico), first planted in the 1770s, is the oldest continuously cultivated grape in California. Because of its historical importance, Mission, unlike Zinfandel, is considered native to the state's wine history, especially when associated with the production of Angelica. This vigorous, high yielding, late ripening vine produces common, coarse, low acid, weak colored/flavored table wine with few redeeming attributes, and, consequently, acreage has declined. Until 1870 it was the state's leading wine grape variety, and in 1880 it is estimated that there were 30,000 acres planted. Of questionable origins, Mission requires hot weather and plenty of sunshine, hence is confined mainly to the Central Valley and southern deserts, particularly in San Joaquin (275), San Bernardino (250), Stanislaus (187), and Fresno (147). Despite its easily oxidized character, it was once the dominant "blending" grape in California, and a major element in the production of dessert wines. Although it is steadfastly adored and respected by a small cadre of aficionados, it is no longer an important factor in winemaking.

Carnelian, a UC-Davis cross of Carignane, Cabernet Sauvignon and Grenache (released in 1973), is an attempt to combine bouquet, productivity, and palatability in a Central Valley red wine grape, but it has only been able to produce light, early maturing wine without much character. Its 1,252 acres are mainly confined to Fresno (534), Kern (490), and Madera (203) counties. Carnelian, which ripens late, is subject to virus and bacterial infection, and lacks high sugar levels. Although mellow and less tart, it lacks Cabernet Sauvignon flavor, and, hence, planted acreage has been declining. **Royalty**, a cross of Alicante Ganzin and Trousseau, this UC-Davis productive variety, used for color enhancement, red juice concentrate, and Porto-type wines, was commercially introduced in 1958. Its 863 acres are confined to 6 Central Valley counties, of which Madera, with 417 acres, is the most important. **Salvador** is a UC-Davis red juice variety that grew rapidly before 1975, but has since declined in importance. Its 749 acres are mainly confined to 4 Central Valley counties, of which Kern, with 642, is the most important. **Centurian**, a vine released by UC-Davis in 1975, has the same parentage as Carnelian but is totally and completely different adapting more readily to the warmer portions of the Central Valley, attaining higher sugar levels, a darker color and a more pronounced flavor. It makes acceptable table, and reasonably good Porto-type wines. Its 591 acres are concentrated in 4 Central Valley counties, of which Fresno, with 580 acres, is the most important.

Valdepenas, from east-central Spain, is a vigorous and productive vine that does well in Region IV and V areas, but due to low acid levels and poor wine character has declined in recent years from 3,000 acres in 1970 to 540 in 1990. Since it is used as a blending grape for the production of jug wines, acreage is expected to decline still further.

In recent years, much interest has been expressed by several wineries to produce Rhone-type wines. This small cadre of winemakers, known as the "Rhone Rangers," has developed a small but loyal following, and is of the opinion that the trend for southern French type wines is not a passing fancy. Given the state's amenable climate and the magnitude of California innovation, this does not appear to be an unreasonable assumption. Among the principal grape varieties (mainly red grapes) that fall into this category are Grenache (by far the most important in terms of acreage), Carignane, and Alicante Bouschet. Smaller in acreage but more expensive are Mourvedre, Syrah, Cinsault, and Charbono. Their increased popularity in recent years has prompted an energetic grafting program.

Mourvedre (also called Mataro) is a variety of Spanish origin widely cultivated in the south of France. In California it does particularly well in Regions II and III, but because of low yields, it is not widely planted. Unfortunately, the vine is cultivated in the wrong areas, and, as such, it yields poor, coarse, heavy wine with little varietal character. At its best, it can be spicy, flavorful and well scented, but rarely smooth and velvety. Although its 272 acres are mainly confined to 6 counties, Contra Costa dominates acreage with 139, followed by Riverside. However, due to a concerted effort to produce "Rhone-type" wines by several wineries, this variety has recently enjoyed a minor renaissance that might continue in the coming decades. Another similar grape, **Syrah**, a major variety in the Cote-Rotie, generally produces wine that is high in tannin, dark in color and harsh in youth, but one that softens considerably with time. There are only 344 acres of this difficult grape, half of which are located in the warmer areas of Mendocino and Sonoma counties where they produce lush, rich, fruity, and full bodied wines. Because demand is relatively high (prices have risen accordingly) for these two grape varieties, planted acreage is expected to increase. The vine, however, is highly sensitive to stress during maturation causing high pH and loss of fruit, and does best on well drained hilly terrain rather than valley floor locations. Syrah, not to be confused with Petite Sirah, is expected to become more important. **Charbono** (Corbeau in French), is an obscure French grape (some maintain it is of Italian ancestry) mainly confined to Napa, Sonoma, and Mendocino counties. It is a low-yielding, finicky vine that makes, when handled correctly, a dark, rich, smooth, well structured wine that is above-average as a varietal, and superb for blending purposes, especially with Zinfandel. Although this variety offers exceptional opportunities, there are only 87 acres, growing at a scant one acre every year.

Minor Italian varieties. Despite the formidable Italian influence in the state's viticultural history, it is highly surprising to find so few Italian red grape varieties in California (and even fewer white Italian varieties). Besides Barbera, the most important varieties are: **Grignolino**, with fewer than 15 acres, is a vine that makes fragrant, light colored wine with limited appeal. **Nebbiolo**, the famous Piedmont grape variety, has fewer than 20 acres planted, mainly in the Central Coast due to the interest of one major winery. Recent plantings in Sonoma and scattered areas offer interesting prospects. The vine produces

grapes with thick skin, robust tannin, high acids, but it suffers from color instability and coarseness. **Refosco**, an obscure northern Italian variety, is made only by Weibel as a fresh, fruity, pleasing varietal wine, especially when served slightly chilled. It is estimated that there are fewer than 15 acres. **Aleatico**, with fewer than 50 acres, is a member of the Muscat family, and best known for Vin Santo. In California it produces thin, low acid, high pH wines unable to compete with other, better varieties. **Sangiovese Grosso**, the venerable red grape responsible for Chianti and Brunello di Montalcino among others, covers fewer than 190 acres. Like Nebbiolo, interest is increasing mostly for blending purposes, but several wineries are also making it as a varietal. **Dolcetto**, a popular red variety producing light to medium-bodied quaffing wines in Piedmont, is currently made as a varietal by at least one winery. Acreage is so small that it is not even listed in the annual grape report published by the state's statistical bureau.

Portuguese Porto varieties, such as **Alvarelhao, Souzao, Touriga, Tinta Cao, Tinta Madeira, Bastardo, Tinta Pinheira**, and others, collectively cover fewer than 250 acres, but will increase in the coming years as demand for quality Porto-type wine continues. While all of the above yield well, produce grapes with good color and high sugar levels, Souzao and Touriga, with high acid and sugar levels, have a bright future. Souzao is a rich, aromatic grape; Tinta Cao is known for delicate flavors; Touriga is full flavored and fragrant; and Tinta Madeira (123 acres) is known for rich, fruity flavors.

Other minor varieties include: **Aramon** (less than 10 acres) is an extremely heavy yielder of poorly colored, low acid wine; **Black Malvoisie**, also known as Cinsault (87 acres, all but 2 located in the Central Valley), is a low acid/high sugar variety historically used for dessert wine production. With the increased popularity of Rhone-type wines, it is envisioned that acreage will increase in the coming decades. **Carmine** (less than 20 acres) is a UC-Davis cross first released in 1946 that has fallen short of expectations; **Early Burgundy**, with 208 acres, more than half located in Monterey, Napa, Solano, and Sonoma counties, is used (because of high acid levels) as a blending grape. **Pinot Meunier** (138 acres), the most important grape in terms of acreage in the production of Champagne, has recently expanded acreage in Sonoma, Mendocino, and Napa for the production of sparkling wine. Acreage is expected to triple by 2000 despite the fact that it is considered an inferior strain to Pinot Noir. **Pinot St. George** (also known as Red Pinot), with no relation to the Pinot family of grapes, has only 84 acres (667 fewer acres than in 1970) cultivated in Napa and Monterey. The grape produces tart, chewy, but otherwise undistinguished wines.

Earthquake Damage in the Livermore Valley. Baxevanis

IX
THE WINE REGIONS OF CALIFORNIA

NORTH COAST COUNTIES

The North Coast counties of California consist of Solano, Mendocino, Lake, Sonoma, Napa, and Marin. With about 83,000 acres of vineland and a total output of nearly 25 million cases annually, they constitute the center of premium wine production in California. The *North Coast ava (1983)* refers to the combined acreage and wine production of these six counties, of which the wines of Sonoma and Napa counties are considered the finest and most celebrated. Although wines from two counties to the north, Mendocino and Lake, are considered less distinguished than the more famous counties to the south, the very best (particularly Riesling, Chardonnay, Sauvignon Blanc, Gewurztraminer, Zinfandel, and Cabernet Sauvignon) can keep company with the finest from the more illustrious. For the sake of convenience, Trinity and Humboldt counties (not part of the North Coast *ava*), located to the far north, are also included in this section.

North and south of San Francisco are the Coastal Ranges. As mountains go, they are modest affairs of two to four thousand feet elevation that serve two important functions--to hold back the cold ocean cloud banks and intercept their moisture. As a consequence, nearly all vineyards are to be found on the lee sides, facing south, west and east, but always protected from the prevailing westerlies. With a few notable exceptions, the microclimates are interfaced with topographic irregularity, soil peculiarities, and exposure generally associated with the north-south orientation of the Coastal Ranges. In general, temperatures are lower and precipitation higher in those river valleys open to maritime air, while temperatures are decidedly higher and precipitation lower in interior valleys protected from maritime air by hills and mountains. In the latter locations, the diurnal variation in temperature is markedly higher, the incidence of fog lower, the incidence of sunshine higher, and average winter temperatures much lower than areas influenced by maritime air. Hence, those areas close to maritime influence are classified as Region I and II, while valleys, removed from the Pacific Ocean, are classified as Region III and IV.

Effective settlement of the North Coast counties did not occur until the last mission, San Francisco de Solano, was established in Sonoma in 1824. To counterbalance Russian influence, Mariano Guadalupe Vallejo was named commander of Sonoma, and soon embarked upon a homesteading effort to attract settlers. After statehood, the North Coast counties played a pivotal role in viticultural matters, particularly in the southern portions near San Francisco Bay, by attracting an above-average number of men with vision, energy, and dedication. Acreage in all counties grew rapidly during the period 1870-1919, but after Repeal acreage in these predominantly "dry table wine" counties declined because consumer demand shifted to inexpensive jug and dessert wines from the Central Valley.

Although there are exceptions, viticulture in terms of vine acreage in the six North Coast counties is localized in valleys, the most prominent of which are in Napa, Sonoma, Mendocino, and Lake counties. Within these broad generalizations, vineland is overwhelmingly concentrated, due to facility in planting and farming, on bottomland. With minor exceptions, bottomland in all four counties is remarkably similar in origin, chemical composition and depth. These bottomland soils, in comparison to those found on hillside and mountain, are decidedly less well drained, more fertile, give the highest yields, and less distinguished wine. Because bottomland soils are less expensive to plant and maintain, few hillside and mountain soil regions have been developed, although there is a tendency in recent years to do just that for several good reasons. One is that quality bottomland in Napa is already planted, and although Sonoma has yet to saturate its potential, vineyards already occupy the best sites. Furthermore, as the demand for high-quality grapes outstrips supply in the years ahead, vineland expansion will occur at higher elevations in all counties.

The higher elevations above the valley floors, terraces (older "benchland"), and mountain soils are more varied in geology, thinner, less fertile, and better drained giving significantly lower yields, and often producing outstanding wines. The best of these soils, derived from volcanic rock, are to be found in Napa, Sonoma, and Lake counties, and only to a small extent in Mendocino County where the rocks are predominantly sedimentary. Because higher elevations, due to their complexity and physical orientation, exhibit greater climatic and soil variability, significant specific wine variety distinctions will emerge between all four counties in the coming decades. In other words, while bottomland-derived wine exhibits a narrow band of quality differences between the four counties, the more important soil and climatic differences of high terrain will significantly set apart each hillside and mountain vineyard from one another. It is widely accepted that grapes from mountain regions ripen more slowly but mature earlier, develop higher acid and sugar levels, lower pH, and possess a more pronounced varietal character than wines emanating from bottomland. Although yields can be significantly lower, the grapes tend to command, along with many excellent valley vineyards, some of the highest grape prices. Throughout this six-county region the selection, purchasing, developing, and selling of prime vineland is now big business. The fact that vineland has grown from fewer than 8,000 acres in 1969, to 21,000 acres in 1978, and 83,000 acres in 1990 is a good reflection of the popularity, productivity, and high quality of the North Coast.

The *North Coast (1983) ava* (Napa, Sonoma, Mendocino, Solano, Lake, and Marin) collectively contains more than 25 percent of the state's wine grape acreage, nearly 60 percent of all wineries, and nearly 90 percent of the state's "premium" wine production. In addition, the six counties account for the bulk of "premium" grapes, such as Chardonnay, Cabernet Sauvignon and Merlot, and command the highest prices per ton in the state. The *ava* contains about 5,000 square miles, or slightly more than 3 million acres, and 32 other *ava's* within the six county region. Due to the celebrity of the nearly three dozen smaller *ava's*, the North Coast *ava* is not as popular today as it was in the past in that the more expensive wines can be sold far easier under more prestigious *ava's* such as Stags Leap and Mt. Veeder.

What exactly constitutes a North Coast grape-growing region is a matter of heated controversy. While marine air definitely affects portions of Napa, Marin, Sonoma, Mendocino and Solano counties, most of the vineland is not subject to maritime air movement as it is located on the lee side of hills and mountains. As a consequence, the difference in the growing season between windward and leeward location, and elevated sites on the same altitude can be more than four weeks.

Table 9.1

GRAPE ACREAGE IN THE NORTH COAST

County	1937	1964	1979	1990	Percent
Sonoma	20,794	9,652	27,251	33,321	39.9
Napa	11,027	8,978	25,363	33,194	39.8
Mendocino	7,646	4,057	10,111	12,349	14.8
Lake	591	64	2,469	3,259	3.9
Solano	1,578	561	1,314	1,233	1.5
Marin	378	1	15	8	
Humboldt	17			80	
Trinity				50	
Total	42,031	23,313	66,523	83,494	

Number of wineries in 1937: Humboldt, 2; Lake, 3; Marin, 2; Mendocino, 10; Napa, 47; Solano, 5; Sonoma, 91.
Source: California Agricultural Statistical Service.

Humboldt And Trinity Counties

These two "fringe" counties, located in the sparsely populated extreme northern mountainous region of the state, reflect the passion of Californians to pursue the noble art of grape-growing and winemaking. Humboldt County is a newly emerging viticultural area of 80 acres that contains five wineries and even has an approved viticultural area-- *Willow Creek (1983)*, a region influenced by both Marine West Coast and Central Valley climatic patterns. In general, the *ava* experiences colder temperatures in winter and hotter temperatures in summer. This rugged, mountainous county, containing fewer than 125,000 people, is

mainly forested, with agriculture, due to a short growing season, exhibiting limited possibilities other than pasture for small-scale dairying. With the largest producers making fewer than 2,000 cases of wine annually, the "cottage" nature of the industry is only at its infancy. With the coastal areas being too cold, foggy and rainy, planted acreage is limited to the drier, warmer interior valleys some distance from the Pacific Ocean. The Willow Creek *ava* follows the Trinity River for about fifteen miles, and contains about 50 acres of vineland. The dominant, cool weather grapes are Riesling, Gewurztraminer, Chardonnay, and Pinot Noir, the latter considered one of the better areas in the state for its production.

The five wineries are: **Alpen Cellars** (Trinity Center, 1984), is a 7-acre, 1,500-case winery that makes Chardonnay, Gewurztraminer, and Riesling. Located in a unique microclimate, this winery, the only one in Trinity County, makes interesting wines which offer good value. Due to its proximity to the Sacramento River, this northernmost winery could also be considered part of the Central Valley. **Briceland Vineyards** (Redway, 1985), is a 1-acre, 1,000-case winery that makes above-average to excellent Sauvignon Blanc, Chardonnay, Gewurztraminer, Riesling, Pinot Noir, and sparkling wines. It is the only winery in the extreme southern portion of Humboldt County. **Ed Oliveira Winery** (Arcata, 1983), is a 2-acre, 650-case winery that makes Chenin Blanc, Petite Sirah, Zinfandel, Cabernet Sauvignon, and Merlot. **Fieldbrook Valley Winery** (Arcata, 1969), is a 1,000-case winery that makes Chenin Blanc, Sauvignon Blanc, Zinfandel, Pinot Noir, Cabernet Sauvignon, Cabernet Franc, Petite Sirah, and sparkling wines. **Willow Creek Vineyard** (McKinleyville, 1975), is a 3-acre, 1,000-case winery that makes Gewurztraminer, Chardonnay, Zinfandel, and Cabernet Sauvignon.

Mendocino And Lake Counties

North of San Francisco lies the "Redwood Empire," a region of beautiful vistas, relatively low population densities, and violent controversy between environmentalists and developers. Ever since Mendocino was founded in 1852 by William Kasten, a German immigrant who was the lone survivor of a shipwreck, these two counties were noted for their boots, plaid shirts, and rustic, laid-back life style. In years past, "boontling" was a local dialect that kept outsiders in the dark, and wine was called "Frattey" after a local winemaker named Frati. Sprinkled with former "draft dodgers, drug dealers, communists, freethinkers, and newly converted Hindu's," these groups, it is said, sought refuge here during the 1960s due to the relative isolation of the region. Historically, this is timber and ranching country with few refined and stately homes, and "hardly any Republicans." The social and political proclivities of the two counties not withstanding, this area represents the northernmost quality wine producing region in the North Coast *ava*. It is an area of 14,000 vine acres, and 44 wineries, nearly all of which are small, family-owned affairs. Only four--Fetzer, Weibel, Kendall-Jackson, and Parducci produce more than 100,000 cases annually. Larger than the state of New Jersey, these two counties are more mountainous, greener, cooler, less known, and more isolated than the exalted, more popular Sonoma and Napa viticultural areas to the south. In the nineteenth and early twentieth centuries both counties were known for Mercury, lumbering, stylish summer resorts, extensive animal grazing, and hop production. Since the Great Depression, the two most important economic activities are lumbering and tourism; agriculture consists of scattered pear (both Mendocino and Lake counties rank as the leading counties in the state), walnut, and occasional ranching. Over the past 20 years, however, grapes have become the most profitable agricultural commodity in both counties.

Long considered the edge of the ecumene, these two counties, lying peripherally to Sonoma and Napa, have long been overlooked as premium wine producing regions, and, as a consequence, were the last to exhibit a post-1960 viticultural renaissance. Lake County, the fastest growing North Coast county, has increased acreage from fewer than 85 acres in 1950, to 264 in 1970, to more than 4,500 by 1990. Mendocino, nearly four times larger than Lake County, has had a similar history: 4,000 acres before 1950, 4,400 acres in 1960, 6,334 in 1969, and more than 12,000 acres in 1989. This is rather remarkable as the arable acreage comprises less than 1.5 percent of the county's total land area. Collectively, these two counties contain wineries with an impressive track record for quality wine production.

Lake County, just north and east of Napa, is much higher in elevation, and shut-off from the cooler maritime winds resulting in higher daytime temperatures than Ukiah to the west. The higher elevation, however, does mean lower evening temperatures, a greater seasonal variation, a greater frost danger, a somewhat shorter growing season, lower relative humidity, and a cooler harvest season than the vine growing regions of Mendocino. The soils of both counties are primarily derived from volcanic rocks.

Although coastal Mendocino was discovered by Juan Rodriguez in 1542, effective Spanish settlement was minimal until a group of missionaries arrived in 1776. Russian penetration from the north, active in the late eighteenth century, did not produce any permanent settlements until 1820 at Fort Ross, the site of the first cultivated vines from Black Sea cuttings. However, commercial winegrowing in Mendocino dates back to 1857 when Samuel Orr established a vineyard north of the town of Ukiah. Twenty-two years later, the first winery was constructed by Louis Finne near the present site of Fetzer Winery, and by 1880 there were 330 planted vine acres. While Lake County had 36 wineries and more than 3,000 vine acres by the end of the century, Mendocino had half as many wineries but nearly twice as much vine acreage. Prohibition soon brought an end to winemaking, but beginning in the middle of the 1960s, the industry was revived with renewed vigor. Today there are more than 30 wineries in Mendocino County, a significant increase

from the three wineries existing in 1970. In recent years, as the amount of bulk wine has come to an abrupt halt, wineries have concentrated on the production of medium and high-priced varietal and sparkling wines. In the two counties fewer than 40,000 acres are available for conventional farming, one-third of which are planted in vineyards. Although illegal Marijuana is considered by many to be the biggest cash crop in remote hill locations, winegrowing is second to commercial lumbering--and growing fast.

Mendocino

For more than 100 years Mendocino County was an agricultural frontier region located on the fringes of San Francisco respectability. Although it still contains unspoiled forests and unmatched spectacular coastal topography, its small nineteenth century population consisted of "lumber jacks and frontier desperados," of which Black Bart was the most prominent. A large, rugged country, Mendocino is fragmented into six wine valleys, all located in the southern portion which contains nearly all the grape acreage.

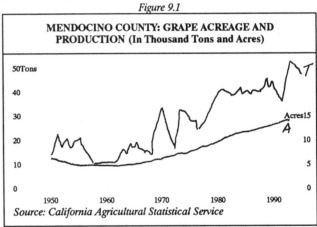

Figure 9.1

MENDOCINO COUNTY: GRAPE ACREAGE AND PRODUCTION (In Thousand Tons and Acres)

Source: California Agricultural Statistical Service

While vinegrowing is not new to the county, the ascendency of farm wineries and white wine production is. The number of wineries grew from 3 in 1970, to 32 in 1989, more than half of which produce quality wine capable of competing with the more prestigious wineries to the south. During Prohibition the tendency was for small growers to plant vines that produced fruit which could withstand rigorous transport to home winemakers, hence the dominance of red wine varieties, particularly Carignane and Zinfandel, followed by Early Burgundy, Sauvignon Vert, Colombard, and Napa Gamay. As recently as 1969, 53 percent of the planted acreage was Colombard and Carignane, a figure that has fallen below 12 percent by 1990. Carignane has declined from 2,445 acres in 1969 to 1,055 acres, Colombard, the principal white variety a generation ago, declined from 1,235 acres in the early 1960s to less than 500 acres by 1990 (replaced as in other

North Coast counties by Chardonnay, by far the most important variety as it dominates the white table as well as the sparkling wine market segment). In the middle of the 1970s, Parducci, Fetzer, Husch, and Edmeades took the initiative and began aggressive replanting efforts to restore the image of the county's wine output. As a consequence, "Prohibition grapes" were gradually replaced by premium wine grape varieties. Not only do Chardonnay, Riesling, Sauvignon Blanc, and Chenin Blanc rank among the finest, but Gewurztraminer, especially from the Anderson Valley, is the most expensive in the state.

Table 9.2

PRINCIPAL GRAPE VARIETIES IN MENDOCINO COUNTY				
Variety	1969	1974	1979	1990
Chardonnay	53	355	831	3,435
Sauvignon Blanc	62	81	310	880
Chenin Blanc	191	156	458	558
Colombard	894	970	613	470
Gewurztraminer	11	63	185	277
Riesling	8	230	231	201
Grey Riesling	119	90	103	39
Semillon	17	17	11	34
Pinot Blanc	32	32	32	26
Viognier				11
Zinfandel	766	1,042	1,090	1,849
Cabernet Sauvignon	288	1,148	845	1,314
Carignane	2,445	2,367	1,201	1,055
Pinot Noir	78	300	429	690
Gamay Beaujolais	104	589	390	378
Petite Sirah	348	454	340	344
Merlot		37	44	266
Syrah			14	112
Cabernet Franc				79
Napa Gamay		140	85	72
Grenache	76	89	25	35
Other	388	421	1,490	224
Total	5,880	8,581	8,727	12,349
Total White	1,475	2,065	2,774	6,091
Total Red	4,405	6,516	5,953	6,258
Source: California Agricultural Statistics Service				

As the demand for premium white grapes rose, the traditional mix changed from 76/24 percent red-white in 1960, to nearly 50/50 in 1990. Even more significant is the fact that grapes now account for about 40 percent of the county's total agricultural value. During the decade of the 1960s and 1970s, most growers sold their grapes to large wineries in Napa, Livermore, and the Central Valley, and over half belonged to Allied Grape Growers Cooperative, their grapes blended with Sonoma County grapes and the wine sold through Italian Swiss Colony. In the early 1970s, only one winery, Parducci, sold bottled Mendocino wine. Mendocino wines were virtually unknown, and for a short time during the decade of the 1960s acreage declined by more than 2,000 acres.

Vineland and winery distribution is highly localized around six principal southern valleys, of which only Anderson has an outlet to the Pacific. The five delimited areas are: *Mendocino (1984), Cole Ranch (1983), McDowell Valley (1982), Potter Valley (1983),* and *Anderson Valley (1983). Mendocino,* the largest and most general of all *ava's,* forms the letter "V," and encompasses all others. *Potter Valley,* the northernmost viticultural region in

Mendocino, is a 27,000-acre valley wedged between the heights of the Ukiah Valley and Lake County that is drained by a small tributary of the Russian River. Although classified as Region III, this is the northernmost and highest viticultural area in terms of altitude in the county. It suffers from late spring and early fall frosts, and, hence, is planted mainly in early varieties such as Gewurztraminer, Chardonnay, Pinot Noir, and Sauvignon Blanc, and is known for exceptional late harvest wines. A combination of well-drained soils and altitude combine to make highly concentrated, fragrant, and well-balanced Riesling.

Figure 9.2

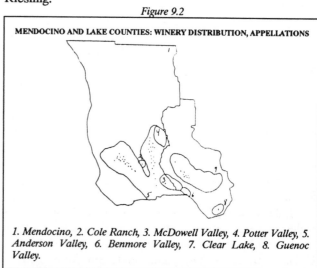

MENDOCINO AND LAKE COUNTIES: WINERY DISTRIBUTION, APPELLATIONS

1. Mendocino, 2. Cole Ranch, 3. McDowell Valley, 4. Potter Valley, 5. Anderson Valley, 6. Benmore Valley, 7. Clear Lake, 8. Guenoc Valley.

Cole Ranch, a postage stamp *ava,* has generated an excellent reputation for full-bodied, flavorful, long-lived Cabernet Sauvignon and delicate Riesling. The appellation is located in a small, narrow mountain valley between the Anderson and Ukiah valleys, most of which is owned by Cole Ranch, the only grape producer. Although the appellation encompasses several thousand acres, fewer than 175 are planted, mainly in Riesling, Chardonnay and Cabernet Sauvignon. *McDowell Valley,* 1 mile wide and 2 miles long, lies 25 miles east of the Pacific Ocean in the southeastern portion of Mendocino County. Although it is higher and cooler than the Sanel Valley, it is a warm region and it too is planted mainly in red grapes, principally Petite Sirah, Zinfandel, Cabernet Sauvignon, and Syrah. There are nearly 1,000 vine acres within the *ava. Anderson Valley,* commonly referred to as the "jewel of Mendocino," was settled in the 1850s and named after Walter Anderson, who settled there in 1851. A small, narrow valley (2 by 25 miles) without a significant flood plain, its "V-shaped" features meander north and west to Philo and Navarro. The center of feverish vinous activity over the past ten years, this historic apple and pear growing valley, extending from Cloverdale along the Navarro River (in northern Sonoma County) to the Pacific Ocean, is the center for nine wineries and more than one-quarter of the county's total acreage. Localized to the west of the Sanel-Ukiah-Redwood complex of valleys, it faces east-west, is cooler (Region I, fewer than 2,500 degree days), wet (higher elevations receive as much as 50 inches of rain), and, hence, significantly better than interior valleys for the production of Riesling, Gewurztraminer, Chardonnay, and Pinot Noir. Fog is a critical climatic element producing lower temperatures due to the influence of the cool Pacific Ocean. Strong winds transport the cool, humid air 20 miles into the interior, lowering daytime temperatures by as much as 15F. Remarkable in its ability to concentrate a small collection of above-average wineries, this valley has about 3,200 vine acres, and because it is one of the coolest vinegrowing regions in the state, more than 50 percent of all grapes are white. Recently, it has become a leading center for the production of sparkling wine, and may become more celebrated in the near future than the Russian River region of Sonoma. However, despite the similarity to Epernay, France in terms of degree days, the two areas are not identical in terms of weather, climate, and soil conditions.

In addition to the above, there are three other prospective appellations. *Redwood Valley*, the northernmost of the string of Russian River valleys, lies 8 miles north of Ukiah and Lake Mendocino on a series of higher terraces. Representing the birthplace of Mendocino winemaking, it is the home of some of the county's largest wineries. With more than 40 percent of the county's acreage, it is the most important of all the producing regions in the two county region. A region II area, it produces above-average quality Zinfandel, Cabernet Sauvignon, Chardonnay, Petite Sirah, and Sauvignon Blanc. One of its elements of celebrity is the considerable quantity of Manzanita soil. The *Ukiah Valley* (the name is taken from the Pomo Indian word "Yokayo") lies north of Hopland and is the center for the county's largest grape acreage (in the Talmage area), containing some of the oldest plantings of Zinfandel, Carignane and Gewurztraminer. It is drained by the Russian River which flows south, is classified as Region III, and is planted in all the major grape varieties, including Carignane and Colombard, two prolific vines that were historically more popular than today. Further south, the *Sanel Valley*, dominated by the town of Hopland, lies near the Sonoma border, and is officially classified as a Region III vinegrowing area (due to rugged terrain, however, climate varies between Region I and IV). Most vineyards, however, are mainly found on bottomland and planted in Carignane, Cabernet Sauvignon, Petite Sirah, and Zinfandel, but in recent years Chardonnay and other white grapes have made inroads in the valley. The wineries are:

Brutocao Cellars (Hopland, 1982), is a 200-acre, 3,500-case winery that makes fresh, fruity, sound, moderately priced Chardonnay, Sauvignon Blanc, Cabernet Sauvignon, Merlot, and Zinfandel.

Christine Woods Winery (Philo, 1982), is a 15-acre, 2,000-case winery that makes Chardonnay, Riesling, Sauvignon Blanc, Merlot, Pinot Noir, and Cabernet Sauvignon.

Claudia Springs Winery (Philo, 1989), is an 1,200-case winery that makes good, sound Chardonnay, and fruity Pinot Noir.

Decanter Corporation (Talmage, 1987), is a 17,000-case winery that makes Chardonnay, Cabernet Sauvignon, Merlot, Meritage-type, and proprietary wines marketed under the *Royce Vineyards* and *Shadow Mountain Vineyard labels*. The Reserve wines are interesting.

Dolan Vineyards (Redwood Valley, 1980), is a 5-acre, 2,000-case winery that makes excellent Cabernet Sauvignon, and big, expansive, well-oaked Chardonnay from purchased grapes.

Domaine Karakash (Ukiah, 1983), is a 4,000-case winery known for full bodied, flavorful, and well balanced Chardonnay and Sauvignon Blanc. The hard-to-find wines are stylish and consistently good, offering good value. Also made is an unusual, 18 percent alcohol Chardonnay laced with brandy labeled *Charbay*.

Domaine Saint Gregory (Ukiah, 1988), is a 2,000-case winery that makes excellent, big, well-structured, and intensely flavored Chardonnay and Pinot Noir, both of which offer good value.

Duncan Peak Vineyards (Hopland, 1985), is a 4-acre, 500-case winery that makes medium bodied, well flavored Cabernet Sauvignon, offering good value.

Edmeades Vineyards (Philo, 1972), one of the oldest, is a 10,000-case winery located in the Anderson Valley that historically produced Gewurztraminer, Chardonnay, Riesling, Cabernet Sauvignon, Zinfandel, and sparkling wines. In the past, unusual Colombard wines have been made, but as the winery has been recently purchased by Kendall-Jackson, a good deal of the 120-acre vineyard is being budded over to Pinot Noir and Chardonnay for the production of *methode champenoise* sparkling wines.

Elizabeth Vineyards (Redwood Valley, 1987), is a 50-acre vineyard whose 700 cases of delicate and fruity Chardonnay, Sauvignon Blanc, and Zinfandel wines are made in a neighboring winery.

Fetzer Vineyards (Redwood Valley, 1968), with more than 2.6 million cases (only 2,000 cases were made in 1968) produced each year, this highly successful, aggressive, innovative and value conscious firm is the largest winery in the two county region, and one of the largest in California. It has more than 1,600 planted vine acres supplying less than one-fifth of the winery's requirements. All wines are quality controlled, expertly made in many styles and carry many different *ava's* offering excellent value. The barrel select and reserve wines (especially Chardonnay and Cabernet Sauvignon) are particularly good. Acreage is divided into three major vineyards whose name often appears on labels: Home (Redwood Valley, planted mainly in Cabernet Sauvignon, Sauvignon Blanc, Zinfandel, Pinot Noir, and Pinot Blanc); Sundial Ranch (Hopland, planted in Chardonnay, Pinot Noir, Chenin Blanc, Colombard, and Riesling); and Valley Oaks Farm (Hopland, planted mainly in Sauvignon Blanc, Chenin Blanc, Chardonnay, Cabernet Sauvignon, and Zinfandel). The winery, with more than 525,000 cases of Chardonnay, is one of the largest producers in the state. It is also, with an output of 150,000 cases, one of the largest producers of premium Gewurztraminer. Originally a red wine producing winery, 80 percent of all sales are now white and blush. A new winery (its storage facility will accommodate 40,000 oak barrels) has just been completed in Hopland for Bel Arbors Vineyards (*American ava*), a label that is responsible for more than 50 percent of production. Always on the cutting edge, the winery has 500 "organically" registered vine acres, and will be producing a line of wines from organically-produced grapes under the *Sanella* label. The winery has been acquired by Brown-Forman.

Frey Vineyards (Redwood Valley, 1980), is a 40-acre, 18,000-case winery that makes Grey Riesling, Sauvignon Blanc, Gewurztraminer, Colombard, Cabernet Sauvignon, Syrah, Zinfandel, Pinot Noir, Petite Sirah, Barbera, Carignane, and proprietary wines. Red wines are above-average in quality, offering excellent value. The grapes are organically grown and there are no sulfites added.

Gabrielli Winery (Redwood Valley, 1991), is a 13-acre, 7,000-case winery that makes distinctive Chardonnay, Zinfandel, proprietary, and *Ascenza*, a barrel-fermented Chenin Blanc-Riesling-Semillon-Chardonnay. The winery has recently planted Sangiovese, Syrah and Viognier.

Greenwood Ridge Vineyards (Philo, 1980), is a 12-acre, 4,000-case, conscientious winery that makes above-average quality Chardonnay, Riesling (the late harvest is sensational), Sauvignon Blanc, Merlot, Zinfandel, Cabernet Sauvignon, and Pinot Noir, offering good value.

Handley Cellars (Philo, 1982), is a 25-acre, 15,000-case winery that makes Chardonnay, Sauvignon Blanc, Gewurztraminer, Pinot Noir, sparkling wines, and proprietary blends.

Hidden Cellars Winery (Ukiah, 1981), is a 12,000-case winery that makes above-average to excellent (under many different vineyard designations) Riesling, Chardonnay, Sauvignon Blanc, also a Meritage-type blended with Semillon called *Alchemy* (one of the finest and most expensive in the state), Zinfandel, late harvest Riesling, an unusual Viognier, and sweet generic wines, offering good value. Other label: *Monte Rosso*, for a line of Italian-type wines, is a joint partnership with Domaine Saint Gregory.

Husch Vineyards (Philo, 1971), the oldest winery in the Anderson Valley, is a 200-acre, 25,000-case winery that makes good, sound, intensely flavored, estate bottled Chardonnay, Sauvignon Blanc, Gewurztraminer, Chenin Blanc, Cabernet Sauvignon, and Pinot Noir. The moderately priced wines are consistent in quality offering excellent value.

Jepson Vineyards (Ukiah, 1985), formerly Baccala Vineyards, is a large 1,240-acre ranch of which 108 acres are planted in vines producing 15,000 cases. The winery only makes estate produced Sauvignon Blanc, Chardonnay (dry, full bodied and robust), sparkling wine, and minute quantities of brandy. Although expensive, all wines are well made, distinctive, and intensely flavored, offering good value.

Konrad Vineyards (Redwood Valley, 1982), formerly Olson Winery, is a conscientious, expanding, 58-acre, 10,000-case, organic winery that makes Sauvignon Blanc, Chardonnay, Petite Sirah, Zinfandel, Merlot, Cabernet Sauvignon, and Porto-type wines, all expertly made offering good value. The estate Chardonnay is outstanding. The winery was recently sold, and changes in acreage, production, and wines made are in the offering. Other label: *Olson Winery.*

Lazy Creek Vineyards

1987
GEWÜRZTRAMINER
Anderson Valley, Mendocino

Lazy Creek Vineyards (Philo, 1973), is a 20-acre, 3,000-case, above-average, quality winery that makes estate bottled Chardonnay, Pinot Noir, and excellent Gewurztraminer.

Lolonis Winery (Redwood Valley, 1982), is a 300-acre, 18,000-case winery that makes excellent, well balanced, supple, and fruity Sauvignon Blanc, Cabernet Sauvignon, Zinfandel, and Chardonnay, the latter exceptionally rich and flavorful. This superb vineyard (since 1920, the oldest grape-growing family in Mendocino) historically sold grapes to the finest North Coast wineries, but has, since 1982, begun to make and bottle under its own name.

McDowell Valley Vineyards (Hopland, 1978), California's only solar powered winery, consists of 350 acres and makes more than 70,000 cases. The well made, moderately priced wines are Grey Riesling, Sauvignon Blanc, Chardonnay, Zinfandel, Cabernet Sauvignon, Grenache, and a true Syrah, one of the finest in the state. Mourvedre, Cinsault, and Viognier are also planted and will be offered under the "Signature Series" designation. All wines are expertly made, distinctive in flavor and offer excellent value.

Mendocino Vineyards (Ukiah, 1946), known as Mendocino Cooperative and Cresta Blanca until 1988, this large winery enjoyed one of the more celebrated reputations in the county. Owned by Guild of Lodi, it mainly crushed, stored, and bottled wines for others, and suffered from a poor image. Although it will continue to perform these functions

(annual production exceeds 300,000 cases), the restructuring under the new label will eliminate all bulk, sparkling, fortified wines, and brandy. Production (about 80,000 cases) will be confined to three generic wines, and four varietals--Chardonnay, Sauvignon Blanc, Zinfandel, and Cabernet Sauvignon, marketed under the *Dunnewood* label.

Milano Winery (Hopland, 1977), is a 60-acre, 2,000-case winery housed in a former hop kiln that makes good, distinctive Chardonnay, Cabernet Sauvignon, and Zinfandel.

Navarro Vineyards (Philo, 1975), is a 910-acre, former sheep ranch that maintains 60 acres in Gewurztraminer, Chardonnay, Riesling, Cabernet Sauvignon, and Pinot Noir, and makes 12,000 cases. The emphasis and reputation rests on excellent, wood aged, dry (Alsatian style), late harvest Gewurztraminer and Riesling. Smaller amounts of equally good Chardonnay, Sauvignon Blanc, Pinot Noir, and sparkling wines are also made. Reserve Chardonnay and late harvest wines are exceptional. Other label: *Indian Creek.*

Obester Winery (Philo, 1989), is a recently replanted, 7-acre, 5,000-case winery that makes Gewurztraminer, Chardonnay, Riesling, Sauvignon Blanc, and Pinot Noir. The winery offers robust, full bodied Zinfandel and Cabernet Sauvignon under the *Gemello* label from Santa Cruz grapes.

Octopus Mountain Cellars (Philo, 1985), is a 25-acre vineyard that markets 1,000 cases of Chardonnay, Sauvignon Blanc, Pinot Noir, and Cabernet Sauvignon.

Pacific Star Winery (Westport, 1987), owned by Star in Napa, is a 3-acre, 1,500-case winery that makes good, clean, fresh Gewurztraminer, Cabernet Sauvignon, Zinfandel, and Charbono.

Parducci Wine Cellars (Ukiah, 1932), with 450 acres and an annual output of 350,000 cases, is the second largest, but oldest winery in Mendocino County. Historically, the winery produced generic wines, and made as many as 24 different wines without much character. In recent years the product line has been reduced (mostly Chardonnay, Sauvignon Blanc, Gewurztraminer, Colombard, Muscat Blanc, Chenin Blanc, Zinfandel, Cabernet Franc, Petite Sirah, Merlot, Gamay Beaujolais, and Cabernet Sauvignon), and the quality has improved dramatically. The *Cellarmaster Selection*--Chardonnay, Sauvignon Blanc, Cabernet/Merlot, Petite Sirah, and Pinot Noir are all above-average; and the *Chateau Marjon* Sauterne, made from 100 percent botrytized Chardonnay and aged in oak, is excellent. Highly underrated, this excellent winery offers outstanding value.

Pepperwood Springs Vineyard (Philo, 1981), is a tiny, but good, 7-acre, 700-case winery that specializes in Chardonnay and Pinot Noir, the latter, well flavored and balanced.

Roederer U.S. (Philo, 1982), is a splendid, stylish, 585-acre (of which 370 will be planted), 33,000-case, sparkling wine facility that is expected to revitalize the obscurity of Mendocino County. This state-of-the-art winery uses equal amounts of Chardonnay and Pinot Noir in its final non-vintage Brut blend, a high acid, rich, savory, austere, non-fruity wine with a fine mousse. Also made are a Brut Rose and a Prestige bottling. This is the only sparkling winery that ferments in wood.

Scharffenberger Cellars (Philo, 1981), is a rapidly expanding, 655-acre (58 planted), 30,000-case winery that specializes in the production of clean, crisp, complex, delicate, and often refined sparkling wines (Brut, Brut Rose, Blanc de Blancs, and Cremant) made entirely from Pinot Noir, Chardonnay, and Pinot Meunier. The winery, recently purchased by Champagne Pommery, will expand vineyard acreage to 250 acres, and output to more than 60,000 cases by 1993 when a new winery will be built.

Tijsserling Vineyards (Ukiah, 1981), is a 250-acre, 40,000-case winery that makes well structured, elegant wines, particularly Chardonnay, Sauvignon Blanc, Cabernet Sauvignon, Petite Sirah, and sparkling wines, offering considerable value. Other label: *Mendocino Estate.*

Tyland Vineyards (Ukiah, 1979), is a 40-acre, 12,000-case winery that served as the original site of the Tijsserling family. Although treated separately, the wines (Chenin Blanc, Chardonnay, Cabernet Sauvignon, Gamay Beaujolais, and Zinfandel) are made along the same style, though less oaky than those at Tijsserling.

Weibel Vineyards (Ukiah, 1945), is a 1,400-acre, 490,000-case winery, originally founded in Fremont, California, that farms, crushes and bottles in Ukiah. Historically, the winery bottled and stored for more than 400 private labels, and produced more than 34 different wines under its own label. Although the bulk of production continues to be inexpensive sparkling wine, the generic and proprietary product lines have been reduced in number. The Fremont facility sits on land originally settled by Franciscan missionaries, and Leland Stanford vineland. Consuming about 10 percent of all grapes, Weibel is a major player in the viticultural fortunes of Mendocino County. Indeed, with the closing of the Santa Clara facility, the winery is expected to increase its grape acreage, and become the largest producer of grapes in the county. Varietals include Chardonnay, Green Hungarian, Chenin Blanc, Gewurztraminer, Sauvignon Blanc, Black Muscat, Pinot Noir, Cabernet Sauvignon, Zinfandel, and sparkling wines (60% of total output, mainly custom labeled). Also made are Porto, Sherry, and *Tangor*, an interesting flavored aperitif. Other labels: *Stanford, Jacques Reynard, Chateau Napoleon, Chateau Lafayette*.

Whaler Vineyard Winery (Ukiah, 1981), is a 23-acre, 1,200-case winery that specializes only in premium red Zinfandel.

Tyland Vineyards in Winter. Courtesy of Tyland Vineyards.

Lake County

Once called "paradise" by the famed Lillie Langtry, Lake, a rapidly growing county of 50,000 people, takes its name from Clear Lake, the largest natural, fresh-water lake in California. Ringed by inactive volcanoes, it is estimated that this lake is approximately 450,000 years old, and possibly the oldest lake in North America: core samples indicate that its shoreline and depth have remained the same for at least 10,000 years. Created in 1861 when it separated from Napa, Lake County, a comparatively little known viticultural region, is currently making exceptional Sauvignon Blanc, Riesling, Chardonnay, Cabernet Sauvignon, Merlot, and Zinfandel. It is also the site of two outstanding wineries: Kendall-Jackson and Konocti. Noted in the

past for its quicksilver, expensive resorts in such places as Nice and Lucerne, it is now the site of the world's largest geothermal steam industry, and the Homestake Gold Mine. Agriculturally it grows superb Bartlett pears (accounting for about 20 percent of the county's total agricultural value), walnuts, almonds, kiwi, and wild rice.

The restored Lillie Langtry house, Guenoc Winery, one of the finest on the North Coast. Baxevanis

Grapes, now the most important agricultural crop, were first planted by one David Voigt in 1872 near Lower Lake (he also built the county's first winery), and within 25 years the county boasted more than 7,000 acres and 36 wineries. While the area attracted many colorful personalities and wine syndicates, it was in 1887 that the county received an element of notoriety when Lillie Langtry purchased a portion of the Guenoc Valley, established "Langtry Farms," and imported a Bordeaux winemaker. However, the combination of relative isolation, poor transportation (there are no railroads), and expensive road tolls discouraged further growth and significant settlement. Moreover, because the region is surrounded by mountains, it was settled comparatively late by Americans, and exhibits little Spanish influence unlike areas further south.

Unable to compete with the grape producing areas of Sonoma and Napa, all wineries ceased operations during Prohibition (3,000 acres were plowed under in the 1920s). By 1950 there were fewer than 100 acres, but with the wine renaissance of the 1960s acreage began to increase steadily to more than 3,200 acres (nearly all ungrafted) by 1990. There were but 532 vine acres in the county when the Konocti Cellars Cooperative was established in 1974. Since then acreage has increased by nearly 200 each year, and of North Coast output they have, since 1975, won more medals per acre than any other viticultural area of California. As a result, this long forgotten corner is now experiencing considerable renewed interest, and unprecedented viticultural prosperity. Recently, Beringer purchased 194 acres, Louis Martini acquired 485, and Geyser Peak Winery more than 1,000 acres (300 to be planted) in the Benmore Valley. Furthermore, Buena Vista purchased 200 acres to be planted in Sauvignon Blanc, and is considering increasing acreage and constructing a separate winery. Considered by the author as the most consistent premium wine producing region in the state, Lake County exhibits unlimited potential, and is a region to watch.

Table 9.3

PRINCIPAL GRAPE ACREAGE IN LAKE COUNTY		
Variety	1979	1990
Sauvignon Blanc		608
Chardonnay	5	553
Riesling	94	88
Chenin Blanc	105	55
Muscat Blanc	-	55
Semillon		26
Cabernet Sauvignon	1,185	1,163
Zinfandel	305	390
Merlot	69	116
Napa Gamay	221	85
Cabernet Franc		56
Gamay Beaujolais	18	12
Syrah		10
Petite Sirah	10	10
Other	47	32
Total	2,059	3,259
Total White	224	1,396
Total Red	1,835	1,863
Source: California Agricultural Statistics Service.		

Lake County, due to its higher elevation, enjoys far lower evening temperatures, and has one of the longest growing seasons in the state. The slow maturation of the fruit is ideal for the production of excellent Sauvignon Blanc, Riesling (perhaps the finest in the state), and Chardonnay. Lake County wines are very fresh, with excellent acid balance, fruity, and utterly captivating. While red grapes are slight favorites, about one-third of the total acreage is planted in Cabernet Sauvignon, followed by Sauvignon Blanc, Chardonnay, Zinfandel, Merlot, and Riesling. While first plantings in the 1960s were almost exclusively in three red grapes (Cabernet Sauvignon, Zinfandel, and Napa Gamay), the emphasis in recent years has been in white varieties, particularly Sauvignon Blanc, Chardonnay, Riesling, and Chenin Blanc. The geography of vine plantings exhibits a marked concentration in three areas: north of Clear Lake along Route 20; south of Clear Lake (by far the largest single concentration) in and around Kelseyville; and the extreme southern portions of the county surrounding the town of Middletown.

Lake County contains three *ava's--Clear Lake (1984), Guenoc Valley (1981),* and *Benmore Valley (1991). Clear Lake* is an area lying between the Mayacamas Mountains

on the southwest and the Mendocino National Forest on the northeast. Rimmed by steep mountains, the *ava* has an average altitude of 1,650 feet, as opposed to an average of 700 feet for Mendocino and 100 feet in Napa. Although the region is climatically described as Region II and III, a number of peculiar weather elements distinguish it from similar areas in northern Napa and Sonoma. Due to the higher elevation, diurnal temperatures are much greater than Mendocino, Sonoma and Napa. Equally important, Clear Lake exerts a strong influence on regional weather by exaggerating mountain and valley breezes, thus there is a near total absence of fog during the growing season, brilliant, intense sunshine, little fluctuation in relative humidity levels, and a sharp reduction of humidity-related diseases. The light textured, volcanically-derived soils are well drained, highly fertile, and well mineralized. These rich soils pose a viticultural anomaly: while they have an ability to produce high yields, proper vineyard practices keep the yields low, and wine quality high.

Figure 9.3

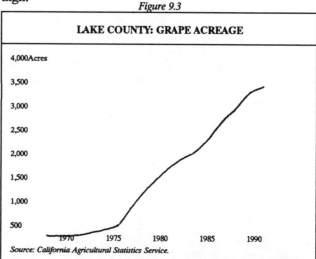

LAKE COUNTY: GRAPE ACREAGE

Source: California Agricultural Statistics Service.

The other *ava, Guenoc Valley,* is bordered by Napa Valley on the south, and Sonoma and Mendocino counties on the west. It takes its name from the Spanish rendering for "lake," and it first appeared in print in an 1844 land grant. Approximately two miles long, .3 miles wide, and 1,000 feet in elevation, it is the only *ava* that is wholly owned by a single vineyard/single proprietor winery-- Guenoc. The crescent-shaped Guenoc Valley, warmer than surrounding areas and filled with volcanic-derived rock and alluvial material, is especially suited to the cultivation of Cabernet Sauvignon, Merlot, Malbec, Petit Verdot, Cabernet Franc, Zinfandel, and Petite Sirah. White grapes include Chardonnay, Chenin Blanc, Sauvignon Blanc, and Semillon. The 1,440-acre *Benmore Valley,* a quality producing region located between Hopland and Cow Mountain near the west county line surrounded by the Mayacamas Mountains, is approximately 2,500 feet above sea level with the lower portion only 90 feet less. Besides the high elevation, excellent air drainage, and soils suitable for viticulture, the other interesting feature of this area is that nearly the entire valley was once owned by the Hare Krishna religious cult. There are fewer than 200 acres of vineyards and no wineries. The wineries are:

Channing Rudd Cellars (Middletown, 1976), located high on a mountain, is a 10-acre, 1,000-case winery that makes robust Chardonnay, Merlot, and Cabernet Sauvignon.

Guenoc Estate, Vineyards & Winery (Middletown, 1981), is an underrated, stunning, state-of-the-art, 320-acre (one-third in Napa County), 110,000-case winery known for expertly made, firm, fruity, well structured Chardonnay, Sauvignon Blanc, Chenin Blanc, Cabernet Sauvignon, Petite Sirah, Petit Verdot, and Zinfandel (all offering excellent value), the best of which are sold under the Reserve Vineyard Designated label (the Genevieve Magoon Vineyard Reserve Chardonnay is extraordinary). The Estate Guenoc Valley wines are impeccable. With an emphasis on Cabernet Sauvignon, Merlot, Malbec, Cabernet Franc, and Petit Verdot, the Meritage-type red wine (outstanding) is marketed under the *Langtry* label. Offering excellent value, premium varietals emanate from North Coast, Napa Valley, and Lake County. This is also the only major winery that aggressively planting the most underrated Bordeaux grape--Petit Verdot, and has meticulously instituted scientific vineyard practices. Amidst a large, 23,000-acre ranch, this consistent, earthquake-proof winery, partially located in Big Basin, a flat region ringed by mountains, is superbly managed by an energetic, retired engineer that has capitalized on the mystery and allure of Lillie Langtry, who owned a home, vineyard and winery on the 5,000-acre property. The restored home has since become, under the present owner, a major tourist attraction. The age worthy wines, improving steadily as the vines mature, are a must for the serious enophile. Other label: *Domaine Breton* for a popular-priced line of wines.

Horne Winery (Middletown, 1988), is a 17-acre, 800-case winery that makes above-average Sauvignon Blanc, Cabernet Sauvignon, and Cabernet Franc.

Kendall-Jackson (Lakeport, 1982), formerly Chateau du Lac, is a splendid, aggressive, and rapidly expanding, 80-acre, 750,000-case winery (made fewer than 25,000 cases in 1983) that consistently makes some of the state's finest wines. It makes (under many *ava's*) well structured, firm, distinctive, fruity Chardonnay (about 400,000 cases), Sauvignon Blanc, late harvest Riesling and Muscat Blanc, Zinfandel, Syrah, Cabernet Sauvignon, and Merlot (among others), offering excellent value and should not be missed. Seventy percent of output is white wine, of which 75 percent is Chardonnay (in all price ranges). The Proprietor's Grand Reserve wines are excellent to outstanding. The winery owns portions of the former Tepusquet Vineyard in Santa Maria where it has recently constructed another premium winery, Cambria. In addition, Kendall-Jackson has recently acquired Edmeades Winery in Mendocino (to become a sparkling wine facility), and the 65-acre, 22,000-case Stonestreet Winery and Vineyard Winery in the Alexander Valley (that will emphasize red wines). The winery purchases grapes from more than 14 different *ava's* and vineyards throughout coastal California, and controls more than 3,500 acres. The winery is in the process of building a winery near Santa Rosa. Collectively, the winery controls 4 wineries with a combined production of 820,000 cases. Other labels: *Northstar* and *Mariposa.*

Konocti Winery (Kelseyville, 1974), located near Clear Lake, the winery is named after Mt. Konocti, a 4,200-foot inactive volcano meaning "slumbering maiden" in Pomo, by the local Indians. Originally it was founded as a cooperative (there are still 18 participating grower members who cultivate more than 400 acres). The Parducci Winery is now a partner and is expected to help increase capacity and production in the years ahead. Although red wine is made (Cabernet Sauvignon, Cabernet Franc, and Merlot are firm, flavorful and above-average), the finest wines (80,000 cases) are white, particularly Sauvignon Blanc, Riesling, Chardonnay, Muscat Blanc, and proprietary wines that should not be missed. Prices for these highly underrated wines are moderate, thus offering outstanding value. The winery is currently being enlarged, refurbished, and, in the future, the production mix will focus on Sauvignon Blanc, Semillon, Cabernet Sauvignon, Merlot, and Cabernet Franc.

Reeves Winery (Middletown, 1992), is a 4-acre, 3,000-case winery that specializes in White Meritage and Barbera.

Roumiguiere Vineyards (Lakeport, 1982), is an 800-acre vineyard whose grapes are sold to other wineries, but maintains a label for small quantities (4,000 cases) of excellent Chardonnay, Sauvignon Blanc, Cabernet Sauvignon, and dry and late harvest Riesling.

Steele Wines (Lower Lake, 1991), is a 4,000-case label owned by the former winemaker of Kendall-Jackson that specializes in premium Chardonnay, Cabernet Sauvignon, and Zinfandel.

Wildhurst Winery (Lower Lake, 1991), is a 170-acre, 10,000-case winery that makes Riesling, Sauvignon Blanc, and Cabernet Sauvignon.

Sonoma County

Sonoma is second to Napa County in number of wineries, and about the same in planted vine acreage. Lying north of Marin and west of Napa counties, it is approximately twice the size (extending 50 miles north to south with a variable width of 30 to 40 miles), and three times more populous than Napa. Geographically the county is highly diverse. In the east, separating Sonoma from Napa and Lake counties, is the complex volcanic Mayacamas Range, an upland area that has been carved into hundreds of small, discontinuous valleys. While the volcanic northern portion is mainly forested, the heavily faulted, highly irregular, and fragmented Pacific coastal plain is verdant, and the least populated. Only in the south-central portion of the county, between Petaluma and Healdsburg, do we find some semblance of urbanization and intense human activity. From Mendocino to San Pablo Bay, the county is a collection of valleys drained by many rivers and creeks, of which the Dry Creek, Petaluma, Sonoma, and Russian are the most important.

Proposed Sonoma County Wine Center, Rohnert Park: replete with small winery, tasting room, and educational facilities. Courtesy of the facility.

Interestingly, as one of the state's original 25 counties, it has the lowest federal, state and local government ownership of land (3.9 percent) of any county in California, and is the only one to have increased in size. The entire county, however, is a collection of quaint towns, planned communities, former Mexican, Spanish, and Russian colonial outposts, historic streets, and a peculiar blend of rural and urban California. Vine growing and winemaking are mainly confined along the Russian River from Cloverdale south to Sebastopol, and west to Guerneville and Sonoma Valley. The main vinegrowing centers are Cloverdale, Healdsburg, Sonoma, Sebastopol, Windsor, Geyserville, and Asti, all but two having either a provocative history or a sizeable population. The largest in size is Sonoma, site of Sebastiani, Vallejo, Haraszthy, San Francisco Solano Mission, and the "Bear Flag Revolt." Further north is Healdsburg, established in 1867 around a Spanish-style *plaza mayor* reflecting one of the few early attempts of California town planning.

Described by Luther Burbank as the "chosen spot of all the earth as far as nature is concerned," Sonoma is the leading agricultural county north of San Francisco, and second only to Solano among the six North Coast counties. However, over the past 26 years the southern portion of the county has changed from a basically rural to an urban bedroom community. County population more than doubled in the past 30 years from 147,000 to nearly 400,000. Santa Rosa, the largest city and the financial, administrative, and commercial center of the county, grew from nearly 9,000 people in 1920 to more than 100,000 in 1988. Like its neighbor to the east, more than two-third's of Sonoma's agricultural income is derived from grapegrowing and winemaking, while dairying, second in importance to grape-growing, is in decline. Wineries, in particular, have increased from fewer than 30 in 1978, to more than 160 in 1992. Sonoma County, with more than 33,000 acres, has more vine acres than any other coastal county in the state, and just 6,000 fewer than Fresno, the state's largest. With but 1 percent of the state's total land area and 10 percent of all winegrape acreage, its vineyards contribute more than 21 percent of the premium grapes. These impressive figures, however, are fairly recent, and do little to indicate the county's long and often obscure viticultural history. Prior to 1960 Sonoma cultivated fewer than 10,000 acres of vineland, was a producer of jug wines, and had fewer than 15 wineries, in sharp contrast to 1919 when the county had nearly 22,000 acres in vines and 256 wineries, the latter figure dropping to fewer than 25 during period of the "noble experiment."

Having labored in the shadow of the Napa Valley since the depression, Sonoma County has emerged in the past 20 years as a premier white, red, and sparkling wine producing region. Sonoma wines were considerably less expensive than those from Napa; and its wineries, less well known and elegant, lacked the element of sophistication and celebrity. However, in the years to come, Sonoma County, being much larger than Napa County in land area and planted vine acreage, stands on the threshold of becoming among the coastal counties the leader in quality wine production. Some even believe that Sonoma has successfully challenged Napa as the leading premium wine producing county in the state (not that far fetched

given the fact that more Napa wineries buy grapes from Sonoma than the other way around). Today, Sonoma County crushes less than 4 percent of all California wine grapes, and is the home of more than 40 percent of the most prestigious wineries.

Buena Vista Vineyards was established in the "Valley of the Moon" in 1832 for the Mission San Francisco Solano in Sonoma. The property was purchased by Count Agoston Haraszthy and a winery constructed in 1857. This venerable property fell into disrepair until it was purchased by Frank Bartholomew in 1943, and for the past decade it has been owned by the Racke family of Germany.

While the Napa Valley has about the same acreage but more wineries, Sonoma County produces more grapes than Napa. Historically a bulk wine producer, the structure of Sonoma wine production has, over the past 20 years, changed to small and medium-sized units that bottle varietal, not generic, wine, of which Chardonnay, Cabernet Sauvignon, Merlot, Sauvignon Blanc, Riesling, Chenin Blanc, Gewurztraminer, and Zinfandel are considered among the finest. While many profess a talent for detecting a Sonoma style of wine, winemaking techniques and styles tend to obscure geographic and climatic influences. Sonoma Chardonnay defies easy generalization-- there are simply too many styles, and no monopoly on a "type." There is a tendency to move away from high alcohol, heavily oaked, ponderous wines; and while more acidic and fresher than those from neighboring Napa, a good deal of them are fruity and well balanced. In recent years sparkling wine production has increased dramatically from fewer than 250,000 cases in 1980 to more than 1.5 million by 1989. Of the twelve largest producers, Korbel, Piper Sonoma, Iron Horse, Gloria Ferrer, Chateau St. Jean, Van der Kamp Champagne Cellars, Rodney Strong Wines, Chateau de Baun, and Adler Fels rank as national leaders in the production of quality sparkling wine. While Chardonnay and Pinot Noir are the two dominant grapes, Gewurztraminer, Riesling, Pinot Blanc, and Chenin Blanc are also used in various proportions in the production of sparkling wine.

The viticultural history of Sonoma has been both long and varied. It contains major elements of American foreign policy, a host of agricultural and viticultural innovations, armed rebellions, and foreign intrigue. While the county was discovered by Sebastian Vizcaino in 1602, it was the further exploration by Francisco de Bodega y Cuadro in 1775 that prepared the way for Spanish settlement along the southern extremities of the sparsely populated county. The first settlers, however, were Russians who established a minor settlement in the extreme northern portion of the county. While this otter hunting community thrived, grapes were first planted in Coleman Valley (originally Rossiya) in 1817 (cuttings were supposedly brought from Peru) on the Pacific coast, but winemaking never developed into a thriving industry. Franciscan fathers were more successful at San Francisco Solano Mission in Sonoma six years later. Founded in 1823 this was the last and northernmost of the 21 Franciscan missions of Alta California, and perhaps the most important. Acting as a propagation hearth (grapes were planted at the mission in 1825), the diffusion of grape culture soon spread eastward to the Napa Valley and beyond. One of the first and most accomplished viticulturists was General Mariano Vallejo, a military Commander of Mexican California, who not only replanted the secularized Sonoma mission's vineyards in 1836, made wine at his 16-acre winery (called Lachryma Montis), but was the first to label wine in California. He was followed by many, of which Maria de Carrillo (who grew grapes and made wine in Santa Rosa), Nicholas Carriger (perhaps the first American settler, who grew grapes in the Valley of the Moon), Cyrus Alexander (who planted grapes in the Alexander Valley in 1843), Jacob Primer Leese, and William McPherson Hill were among the more prominent. By 1863, Sonoma, with 1.1 million grape vines, was second to Los Angeles in grape acreage.

Sonoma Mission, Sonoma. Baxevanis

Winegrowing was enlivened by Count Agoston Haraszthy, commonly referred to as the "Father of the California Wine Industry." Purchasing the Salvador Vallejo vineyard in 1855 and renaming it Buena Vista (Good View), he produced a string of fine wines, and thus began a long and most controversial career in Californian politics and winemaking. Haraszthy's attempts in commercial viticulture were followed by Jacob Gundlach in 1858, and by the late 1850s Isaac De Turk started what is considered the first winery in Cloverdale. While the principal region of grape-growing and winemaking was Sonoma Valley, the search for new vineland began to spread in a northward direction. The first winery in Healdsburg was founded by a Frenchman, George Bloch, in 1872, and by 1880, despite the ravages of phylloxera in the preceding decade, major vineyards were established in the Alexander Valley. In the early 1880s, the Icarians from Switzerland (the Leroux, Dettay, and Vurchers families, in particular) and Andrea Sbarbono, who started Italian Swiss Colony, settled in the extreme northern portion of the county in what is now Asti. In 1887 a winery was built by Captain Everett Wise on what is now the Bellerose Vineyard, and another nearby by the Paxton family. Other late nineteenth century personalities were Captain J.H. Drummond, Charles Kunde, and F. Korbel. By 1889, there were 62 growers and 24 wineries in northern Sonoma, another 40 were found in Geyserville, and a similar number near the town of Sonoma. In 1890 Italian Swiss Colony had 600 planted acres, and county vine acreage increased to 22,000 in 1900 producing more than 5 million gallons of wine. Prohibition years saw the number of wineries decline to 25, while vineland increased by 8,000 acres. Unfortunately, as Prohibition came to an end, grape production declined to less than 16,500 tons in 1933. For the next generation acreage increased by fewer than 70 acres annually, so that on the eve of the wine boom there were but 10,000 acres.

The modern growth period began after World War II when a successful newspaperman, Frank Bartholomew, revived the Buena Vista winery, and a retired United States ambassador, James Zellerbach, established Hanzell Vineyard. In 1955 there were fifteen wineries in the entire county. Sonoma, long known as a bulk producer and second fiddle to the Napa Valley, began to change in the 1960s. As the bulk market shifted from Sonoma to the San Joaquin Valley, it became clear that the future lay in the production of vintage dated, cork finished wines. Soon it became the center for innovation and bold experimentation. Further, a keen insight into microclimates restructured the allocation of grape plantings, vineyard management, and vinification and wine aging methods. One of the very first major departures was the replacement of redwood tanks with stainless steel and oak. As a result, vineland and winery growth has been nothing but spectacular over the past 25 years. Acreage rose from 10,000 in 1959 to 15,000 by 1971, a figure that has since more than doubled. Of the 167 wineries now in operation, all but 30 have been constructed since 1973, significant as there were fewer than 7 in 1950. What assured Sonoma's eventual wine renaissance was a combination of superior grapes, outstanding wineries and winemakers, and massive amounts of capitalization--all of which have raised the image of Sonoma to new heights. Grape growers and winemakers are particularly aggressive in sponsoring a national tasting tour in major cities, operate an efficient public relations office, and the county is the home of one of the largest wine libraries in the nation.

Figure 9.4

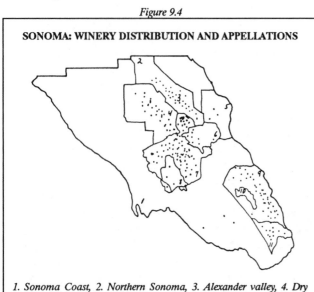

SONOMA: WINERY DISTRIBUTION AND APPELLATIONS

1. Sonoma Coast, 2. Northern Sonoma, 3. Alexander valley, 4. Dry Creek, 5. Knights Valley, 6. Chalk Hill, 7. Russian River, 8. Green Valley, 9. Sonoma Valley, 10. Sonoma Mountain, 11. Carneros Sonoma/Napa.

Urban sprawl, once thought to be a malady of Napa and southern Bay counties, has finally arrived in Sonoma County threatening about 15,000 acres. One of the state's fastest growing counties, the population rose from 300 to 380 thousand during the 1980s. This trend is dangerous as the grape crop, the counties largest in terms of revenues, earns more than $140 million, or more than 40 percent of all agricultural income. The entire wine industry, including tourism, property taxes, and other economic facets, contributes more than $1.5 billion annually to the county's economy. The county produces more than 140,000 tons of wine grapes and 15 million cases of wine annually valued at more than $600 million, the latter figure exceeding the combined imports of France and Italy. Significantly, Sonoma accounts for about 25 percent of all premium wine sold in America.

Climate and Grape Varieties

Sonoma is larger in land area, and, as a consequence, geography and climate present a more complicated picture than that of Napa. Because it lies next to the Pacific Ocean, Sonoma County, with a more pronounced mar-

itime climate, is much cooler than Napa Valley (Sonoma has a much larger percentage of its viticultural acreage located in Regions I and II). Unlike Napa Valley, which has only two sources of cool air (San Pablo Bay and the Petaluma "slot" from Bodega Bay), Sonoma County has a much larger funnel for the same air mass, closer proximity to the Pacific Ocean, and a major break in the Coastal

Figure 9.5

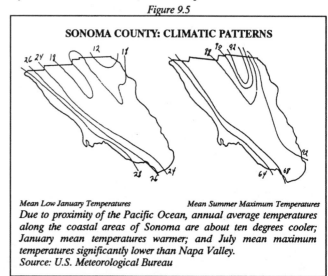

SONOMA COUNTY: CLIMATIC PATTERNS

Mean Low January Temperatures   Mean Summer Maximum Temperatures
Due to proximity of the Pacific Ocean, annual average temperatures along the coastal areas of Sonoma are about ten degrees cooler; January mean temperatures warmer; and July mean maximum temperatures significantly lower than Napa Valley.
Source: U.S. Meteorological Bureau

Range where the Russian River empties into the Pacific. The coastal influence is most apparent in the Russian River Valley region as this is the main entry of Pacific maritime air to central Sonoma County. It moves in early afternoon and by evening reaches Petaluma and Cotati, then spreads north to Santa Rosa and southeast towards southern Sonoma Valley/Carneros. The advantage of this cooler climate is that grapes mature slowly, developing a higher degree of acidity, a lower pH, and better fruit flavor and color. (Sonoma is also the leading county for the production of apples.) The resulting microclimates, based on the degree to which the fog affects daily temperature, are described as either coastal warm or coastal cool. Microclimates abound due to topographic irregularity, proximity to marine influence, and altitude (important because rarely does the fog bank go beyond 1,000 feet in elevation). Invariably, hill and mountain vineyards enjoy more moderating temperatures than valley locations which are subject to extremes of summer fog and heat. Reflecting the above climatic patterns, there is a proclivity now to plant specific grape varieties according to particular microclimatic and soil conditions. Sauvignon Blanc tends to be the first grape to ripen, followed by Chardonnay, Pinot Noir, Chenin Blanc, Riesling, Gewurztraminer, and Cabernet Sauvignon which is nearly always last.

Table 9.4 illustrates the evolution of grape acreage by variety during the period 1979-1990. While white and red grapes are rather evenly divided, six varieties account for 80 percent of the total acreage. The most widely grown variety is Chardonnay (19% of all wine grapes), followed by Cabernet Sauvignon (18%), Zinfandel (14%), Pinot Noir (9%), Sauvignon Blanc (6%), and Merlot (4%). During the 1960s and 1980s, Chardonnay plantings grew from 50 acres in 1964 to more than 9,206 acres by 1988; Cabernet Sauvignon increased from 123 to more than 5,600 acres; and Pinot Noir rose from 145 to nearly 3,000 acres. Of the 11,484 acres in 1958, 4,484 were planted in Zinfandel, 2,035 in Carignane, 1,563 in Golden Chasselas,

Table 9.4

PRINCIPAL GRAPE VARIETY ACREAGE IN SONOMA				
Variety	1979	%	1990	%
Chardonnay	4,034	14.8	11,276	33.8
Sauvignon Blanc			1,627	4.9
Colombard	1,147	4.2	715	1.4
Chenin Blanc	725	2.7	469	
Gewurztraminer	985	3.6	433	
Riesling	1,456	5.3	355	
Pinot Blanc			206	
Semillon			195	
Muscat Blanc			53	
Grey Riesling			42	
Palomino			42	
Symphony			39	
Viognier			13	
Cabernet Sauvignon	4,812	17.7	6,468	19.4
Zinfandel	4,405	16.2	4,130	12.4
Pinot Noir	2,755	10.1	3,130	9.4
Merlot	600	2.2	1,907	5.7
Cabernet Franc			457	
Carignane	1,191	4.4	359	
Petite Sirah	1,155	4.2	318	
Gamay Beaujolais	799	2.9	240	
Napa Gamay	417		221	
Syrah			66	
Alicante Bouschet			55	
Petit Verdot			31	
Grenache			17	
Mourvedre			16	
Other	2,770		449	
Total	27,251	33,321		
Total White		15,643		
Total Red		17,678		

Source: California Agricultural Statistics Service.

Figure 9.6

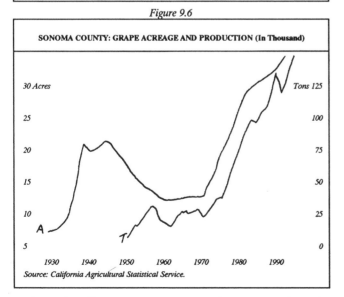

SONOMA COUNTY: GRAPE ACREAGE AND PRODUCTION (In Thousand)

Source: California Agricultural Statistical Service.

and 615 in Alicante Bouschet. For the same period, the most spectacular growth occurred in white grape varieties

(from 6,604 to 15,450 acres), despite the fact that red grape plantings have surpassed white grapes over the past several years. While it is often acknowledged that Napa Valley produces the better Cabernet Sauvignon, Merlot, and Cabernet Franc, the more varied soils and microclimates of Sonoma often produce the better white wines, particularly Chardonnay, Chenin Blanc, Riesling, Sauvignon Blanc, and Gewurztraminer, as well as Pinot Noir (hence, sparkling wines). In fact, Sonoma County Sauvignon Blanc, Pinot Noir, and Chardonnay are the most expensive in California. The underrated Zinfandel, particularly from the Dry Creek area and Sonoma Valley, is considered by many as the finest in the state. Similarly, the reputation of Cabernet Sauvignon has risen to new heights challenging, in the process, the supremacy of Napa Valley in the production of round, full-bodied wines with considerable breadth and elegance, the very best of which are equal or better to any domestic or Bordeaux equivalents.

Approved Viticultural Appellations

Unlike Napa, whose wines have always been identified with the county, Sonoma's wines have shown a proclivity for being identified with smaller grape-growing districts. No other county has a more extensive, well developed number of wine producing delimited *ava's*. In addition to the general county-wide Sonoma *ava*, there are eleven other sub-regions forming the basis of the most elaborate and sophisticated appellation system in the nation. While the Green and Russian River Valleys, and Carneros regions are considered the coolest, the Dry Creek, Alexander, and Knights valleys, the northernmost areas of the county, are the warmest. Yet, while the eleven subregions are geographically distinct, there is considerable diversity in soil type, elevation, and exposure. *Northern Sonoma (1985)* consists almost entirely of the six northernmost *ava's* (Alexander Valley, Green Valley, Knights Valley, Chalk Hill, Russian River Valley, and Dry Creek Valley). It is one of the largest *ava's* in terms of acreage, and, along with the Sonoma Coast *ava*, was created for the purposes of protecting the "estate bottled" designations of a number of wineries. *Sonoma Coast (1987)*, with approximately 480,000 acres, 40 wineries, and more than 11,000 acres of vineland, extends nearly throughout the entire coast and incorporates portions of six other *ava's*.

Alexander Valley (1984), with 6,500 acres of vineland, lies east and north of the Dry Creek Valley (essentially from Healdsburg to Cloverdale) in the center of what was historically a prune, walnut, and grazing region. A narrow valley of about 20 miles in length, it was first settled by Cyrus Alexander, a native of Pennsylvania, in 1842. Although sandwiched by the Mayacamas Mountains to the east and the hilly divide of Dry Creek Valley to the south and west, coastal maritime air does penetrate the valley as morning fog through a gap just north of Healdsburg. The Alexander Valley is considered coastal warm, and planted mainly in Cabernet Sauvignon, its most prestigious and successful grape variety, producing rich, ripe, intensely flavored wines. However, in the slightly cooler area near Healdsburg, Riesling, Gewurztraminer, and Chardonnay are successfully grown, the latter yielding rich, fat, luscious wines that merit considerable attention. Equally important are Sauvignon Blanc and Zinfandel. The deep soils (as much as 20 feet) are loam, gravelly loam, and sandy loam with occasional limestone; the yields are high and the vines very vigorous. Hardly known fifteen years ago, the valley has grown both in size of vine acreage and reputation in recent years. The finest vineyards are invariably located on benchland and hillside, of which the Jimtown Ranch, Belle Terre, and Robert Young, among many others, are considered outstanding. Gauer Ranch, with an excellent exposure and well drained volcanic soil, is the valley's highest and one of the most important vineyards. In 1987, BATF reassigned a 76-acre stretch of vineland bordering with the Chalk Hill *ava* to the Alexander Valley *ava*, and is now considering the addition of another 80-acre parcel along its northern boundary to Mendocino County.

Alexander Valley Vineyards, known for soft, supple wines.

Dry Creek Valley (1983), a two by sixteen mile wide valley with 6,500 acres of vineland, is a superb viticultural region whose vinegrowing history goes back to 1853. Although the Dry Creek region is ideal for the cultivation of Sauvignon Blanc and Zinfandel, it was not until after Prohibition that grapes began to be planted, and it was not until the middle of the 1960s that substantial acreage came under vine cultivation. Nestled between the eastern slope of the coastal mountains and hills above the Russian watershed, it is a hilly region drained by Dry Creek, a tributary of the Russian River that slopes southeast towards Healdsburg. While the northern portion of the *ava* is well protected from fog and the moderating effects of the Pacific Ocean (as a result, it experiences much higher temperatures), the southern area, much closer to the Russian River, is significantly cooler. All excellent for grape-growing, the best soils are:

Dry Creek Valley conglomerate (unique to Sonoma County, heavily mineralized and well drained), Yolo (along the valley floor), and Haire (along the valley margins). Because the wine industry was nurtured by Italian immigrants early in this century (with the taste for robust, full bodied, heavy, and spicy wines), Zinfandel and Petite Sirah dominate among red grape varieties (usually planted on warmer hillsides), and Chardonnay and Sauvignon Blanc (usually planted on the cooler valley floor) among white grapes. Excellent for Zinfandel, the valley is home to several excellent wineries and wines of which Rafanelli, Nalle, Quivira, Dehlinger, Lytton, Mazzocco, Preston, Ravenswood, and others are particularly successful. Sauvignon Blanc, firm in structure (very much like a good Graves) and not overly herbaceous, ripens free of rot, producing a distinct, well balanced wine that is one of the finest in the county. Dry Creek is home to about eighteen wineries.

Knights Valley (1983), named after the first permanent settler, is a relatively new and obscure 36,240-acre (of which 1,500 acres are planted in vines) viticultural region sandwiched between the Alexander and Napa valleys that has generated interest in the production of Merlot, Sauvignon Blanc, and Cabernet Sauvignon. Low yields, low pH, rocky soils, and a mountain climate combine to produce well colored, intensely flavored wines, particularly for Cabernet Sauvignon and Merlot. The *ava* is higher in elevation, surrounded by mountains, and because it is removed from the source of maritime air, it is sunny, hot, and drier than most other Sonoma *ava's*. *Chalk Hill (1983)* is named after the white volcanic ash found in the poor, rocky, and well drained soil of this 3,000-acre appellation (nearly one half of which is planted). Lying higher in elevation (200 to 900 feet), this hilly viticultural region experiences higher temperatures due to the fact that the fog blanket is less intense. The area is mainly planted in white grapes: Chardonnay, Sauvignon Blanc, Riesling, and Chenin Blanc.

Russian River Valley (1983), although the Russian River is shallow and for most of its course scours a narrow valley, south of Healdsburg and between the Chalk Hill and the Green Valley *ava's* it becomes a big, fat, vineyard that contains the single largest concentration of wineries in the county. The Russian River rises out of California's Coast Range and meanders for more than 100 miles through Sonoma County until it veers westward to empty in the Pacific Ocean. It is the largest drainage area in the county and the site of some of the finest vineyards. Because it is one of the first regions to feel the effects of the afternoon fog and the last to see the mid-morning sun, it is cooler than surrounding areas and, consequently, planted in early ripening varieties such as Chardonnay and Pinot Noir, as well as Sauvignon Blanc and Gewurztraminer. However, Zinfandel and Cabernet

Sauvignon do well near Windsor, Santa Rosa, and Forestville. Due to the cooler weather (the valley has an extended two week growing season), the wines are lean, and somewhat restrained in alcohol and flavor. Chardonnay, for example, with higher acid levels and more delicate (not herbaceous) fruit flavors, forms the base for successful sparkling wine production (virtually all Sonoma County sparkling wine is made here and in Carneros). More than half of the 9,000 acres are planted in white grapes.

Sonoma County Green Valley (1983), a small enclave of the Russian River Valley *ava*, lies northwest of Sebastopol in the center of excellent orchard and berry country. Located just 10 miles from the Pacific Ocean, this area is coastal cool (daytime temperatures are 80F-85F while evening temperatures drop to the mid 50F's) and planted mainly in Chardonnay, Pinot Noir, and small quantities of Cabernet Sauvignon. The well drained Goldridge series soils consist of pebble and fractured rock, ideal for good root penetration. Acreage is increasing and now exceeds 1,200. *Sonoma Mountain (1985)*, an enclave of the Sonoma Valley *ava*, encompasses a land area of about 5,000 acres, one-fifth of which is planted in Sauvignon Blanc, Chardonnay, Zinfandel, and Cabernet Sauvignon. It differs from Sonoma Valley because cold air and fog are drained from upland slopes to lower elevations, thus lowering maximum and raising minimum temperatures. The well drained stony soils have attracted considerable attention over the past ten years, and the planted area is expected to grow in the future.

Sonoma Valley (1982), also known as "Valley of the Moon," located in the extreme southeastern portion of the county, is a 8 by 25 mile, crescent-shaped valley sandwiched between the Mayacamas and Sonoma Mountains. Encompassing about 6,300 acres, it is generally regarded as the birthplace of California winemaking because of its early Spanish history. This historic region, first planted in vines in 1824 (Father Jose Altimira planted 1,000 vines next to the mission), is the site of historic Glen Ellen, Jack London's famous Wolfhouse, and one of the nation's oldest wineries--Buena Vista. Sonoma Valley is not a homogeneous geographic unit but a myriad of separate and distinct viticultural areas of plain, hill, and mountain. Ventilated by "four windows," San Pablo Bay in the south, Stage Gulch Canyon in the southwest, Crane Canyon on the west, and Santa Rosa in the northwest, the dry climate varies between Region I and III. The soils (varying from highly thick and productive alluvial material to gravel) are derived from volcanic eruptions, and the mountains encircling the valley are rich in iron oxide and phosphorus, the best of which is called *Manzanita*, a rare soil found in only 2 percent of the total land in Sonoma County. Derived from igneous rock and heavily impregnated with iron oxide, this reddish colored soil produces some of the finest Cabernet Sauvignon and Zinfandel, particularly in Monte Rosso, Carmenet, and Haywood. In the cooler, southern areas Chardonnay, Gewurztraminer, Riesling, and Pinot Noir dominate. Of the 30 different grapes grown, Chardonnay, with nearly 2,000 acres (or 32 percent of the total) is the most commonly planted vine, followed by Pinot Noir (961 acres), Zinfandel (661 acres), Cabernet Sauvignon (600 acres), Gewurztraminer (360 acres), and Riesling (325 acres). These six varietals, with nearly 5,000 acres, account for about 85 percent of the planted area. There are more than 154 growers and at least 24 wineries. Because of the valley's narrow inlet, its floor is ringed by a circle of ridges creating an unusual sun trap--conditions eminently favorable to the production of Cabernet Sauvignon and Zinfandel. The *ava* contains many of the oldest and most prestigious wineries of Sonoma.

CHRONOLOGY: CARNEROS REGION 1836-1985.

1823: Prior to establishment of the Franciscan mission in Sonoma, the area north of San Francisco was largely unsettled.

1836: Mexican land grant is issued in Carneros region entitled "Rancho El Rincon de Los Carneros," named after Spanish word for sheep: Carnero.

1857: Count Agoston Haraszthy established Buena Vista Winery and Vineyards.

1870: First Carneros winery, Winter Winery, is established.

1899: Garetto Winery is established on present site of Chateau Bouchaine.

1930s & 1940s: Andre Tchelistcheff and Louis Martini begin extensive vineyard development in Carneros.

1960: Rene di Rosa purchases old Talcoa Vineyards and Winery Lake is established.

1972: Francis Mahoney founds Carneros Creek Winery and begins production of Carneros Pinot Noir.

1979: Acacia Winery is established and begins production of fine Carneros Pinot Noir and Chardonnay. A. Racke Co. of West Germany, a family owned company founded in 1855, acquires Buena Vista Winery. Clos du Val's "Grand Val Ranch" is planted in Chardonnay and Pinot Noir. Ravenswood Winery is founded and begins production of fine wines.

1980: Chateau Bouchaine is established on 38 acre estate and begins renovation of historic Garetto Winery.

1981: Saintsbury Winery, producer of fine Carneros Pinot Noir and Chardonnay, is founded under the direction of David Graves and Richard Ward.

1982: Perret Vineyards produces first vintage of Chardonnay from 20 acres of Carneros vineyards.

1983: BATF establishes "Carneros" *ava*.

1984: Freixenet Co. of Spain breaks ground for new sparkling wine facility, Gloria Ferrer.

1985: The Carneros Quality Alliance is formed, uniting Carneros grape growers and vintners.

Source: Carneros Quality Alliance.

Los Carneros (1983), a historic outback of both Sonoma and Napa (along with the Guenoc and the Wild Horse *ava's*), is the third *ava* that overlaps Napa County. Sandwiched between the city of Sonoma to the north and the marshlands of San Pueblo Bay to the south, it is a butterfly-shaped area of nearly 37,000 acres, 13,000 of which are currently planted in grapes (representing about 20 percent of the combined vine acreage of both Sonoma and

Napa counties). Carneros means "ram" and was used as a sheep herding region in the early days of Spanish settlement. In the second half of the nineteenth century wheat became important only to be replaced by grapes in the 1880s. George Hussmann, one of the pioneers of California viticulture, recognized the region's grape-growing possibilities and established his headquarters in Carneros. Curiously, despite the present-day predilection to plant Burgundian grape varieties, Carneros at the turn of the century was referred to as "California's Medoc." The combination of phylloxera, indifference, and Prohibition reduced acreage continuously for the next 90 years, so that in 1972 there were but 200 acres, of which 50 were premium. Since then the region has grown like no other in the entire state--on average 400 acres have been planted each year, the value of which has escalated from $900 to more than $60,000 per acre, and because nearly all potential usable acreage is already planted, land prices will continue to increase in the future. The appellation is a veritable hotbed of vineyard acreage transactions with more than 7,400 acres changing hands since 1988. As a consequence, some of the most expensive grapes in the state are to be found in this appellation (the most expensive Pinot Noir and Chardonnay per ton in California).

Grape varieties ideally suited to its combination of microclimate and soils makes this region unusual. Cool bay breezes and fog reduce air temperatures so that vines do not experience high summer afternoon temperatures. Indeed, Los Carneros is not only one of the most foggy, windy, and cold viticultural areas in the state, it has fewer sun hours than the Cote D'Or. In general, winters are 6F to 8F warmer and summers 6F cooler (about 2100 degree days, or Region I) than surrounding inland areas. When compared with Yountville in the Napa Valley, Carneros is 10F-15F cooler in summer, and receives 10 inches less rain (20 inches). While the area is thought to be too cool to adequately mature late ripening Cabernet Sauvignon, it appears to be more suited for early ripening varieties such as Pinot Noir and Chardonnay.

Well drained and ideal to vinegrowing, the dominant soils, Haire/Huichita, not found elsewhere in Sonoma-Napa, are common in hilly, upland areas. They are yellowish in color and alkaline in reaction. By comparison, the low lying, Diablo soils are dark in color, acidic, high in manganese, and imperfectly drained. These soils, a combination of fine alluvium, delta sand, fine gravel, and beach sand with shells, alternate with three other minor but less clayey soils--Cole silt loam, Zamora silt loam, and Yolo loam. In combination, the cool climate, shallow, unyielding soils (less than three tons to the acre), reduced incidence of rot and mildew, and higher vine density per acre produce wines (partly due to higher malic acid content) that are fruity, crisp, well colored, complex, and have a higher flavor intensity than surrounding warmer

areas. The *ava* has recently attained celebrity status with its ability to produce lean Chardonnay, and better balanced Pinot Noir (unlike any other region, except, perhaps, Monterey and Santa Barbara), its two best grape varieties. While Chardonnay is lean and austere, Pinot Noir, critics charge, is a bit too vigorous and the wine overly fruity (some maintain that it is best known for fresh berry, cherry, and spicy flavors and aromas).

Adler Fels, one of the better wineries of Sonoma. Baxevanis

Within the delimited boundaries there are about 60 growers, and sixteen Napa and Sonoma wineries. Two-thirds of the potentially valuable vineland is located in Napa County. The dominant Carneros grapes are Chardonnay (48%) and Pinot Noir (40%), followed by Cabernet Sauvignon (5%), Riesling (2%), and Merlot (2%), the latter, planted in heavy clay soils, is expected to increase in acreage in the coming years as it has recently produced many impressive wines. Although less than 7 percent of the acreage is devoted to Cabernet Sauvignon and Merlot, the quality of fruit, if left to hang on the vine longer than most, will mature more fully, produce a lower yield, and, hence, a far more complex wine than warmer climates in both Sonoma and Napa valleys. The Carneros Alliance (formed in 1985), an association of wineries and growers, has done much in recent years to publicize the virtues of the *ava*, and is attempting through a common bottling to define the style of Carneros Pinot Noir.

The Sonoma wineries are:

Adler Fels (Santa Rosa, 1980), superbly sited, is a 12,000-case winery that makes above-average to excellent, distinctive wines from purchased fruit. Sauvignon Blanc is spicy, full bodied and excellent; sparkling wine is called *Melange a Deux* (a blend of Gewurztraminer and Riesling, and a must for every serious cellar); Gewurztraminer is full bodied, well structured and capable of aging; and Chardonnay (both the reserve and regular bottling) is consistently supple and well flavored. All wines are reliable, well-made, and should be part of every cellar.

Alderbrook Vineyards (Healdsburg, 1982), is a 63-acre, 30,000-case winery that makes rich, well flavored Chardonnay, fruity Sauvignon Blanc, an unusual Semillon, Gewurztraminer, late harvest Sauvignon Blanc, Petite Sirah, and Zinfandel, offering excellent value. The winery has recently been purchased, and several changes are in the making.

Alexander Valley Fruit & Trading Co. (Geyserville, 1984), is an unusual, underrated, 60-acre, 12,000-case firm that makes and distributes expensive gift baskets containing well made, soft Sauvignon Blanc, Chenin Blanc, full bodied Chardonnay, supple Cabernet Sauvignon, Carignane, and zesty Zinfandel (regular and late harvest), offering good value.

Alexander Valley Vineyards (Healdsburg, 1975), is a superb, quality conscious winery of 240 acres producing 47,000 cases of above-average to excellent, intensely flavored Chardonnay, Chenin Blanc, Riesling, Gewurztraminer, Merlot, Cabernet Sauvignon, Pinot Noir, and Zinfandel, offering excellent value. Consistent to a fault, the technically flawless wines may not always exhibit true varietal aroma and flavor, but are always balanced, supple, and eminently drinkable. This property sits on the original land grant by Cyrus Alexander who first came to the valley in 1841. Other label: *Maggie's Farm.*

A. Rafanelli Winery (Healdsburg, 1974), is a 47-acre, 8,000-case winery that makes clean, well structured and full-flavored Zinfandel, and Cabernet Sauvignon.

Armida Winery (Healdsburg, 1990), is a 100-acre, 6,000-case, expanding winery that makes full-bodied, big, well-flavored Chardonnay, Merlot, and Pinot Noir.

Arrowood Vineyards & Winery (Glen Ellen, 1987), is a 4-acre, 20,000-case winery owned by Richard Arrowood, one of the premier winemakers of Sonoma, and long affiliated with Chateau St. Jean. The Chardonnay, though lean, austere, and crisp, is round, full bodied and complex. The Cabernet Sauvignon, rich, ripe, and elegant, contains Merlot, Petit Verdot, and Cabernet Franc. The Merlot is sublime and well-structured. Also made are small quantities of Riesling and Viognier.

Arrowood Vineyards, excellent, handcrafted wines offering good value.
Baxevanis

B.R. Cohn (Glen Ellen, 1984), is a 65-acre, 11,000-case winery that is currently producing stylish, wood aged, and impeccably made Chardonnay and Cabernet Sauvignon under the *Olive Hill Vineyard* label, and Merlot and Cabernet Sauvignon under the *Silver Label Series* label (for non-estate grapes). The hard to find wines belong in every serious cellar.

Balverne Winery & Vineyards (Windsor, 1980), is an aggressive, 250-acre, 25,000-case winery that makes Chardonnay, Gewurztraminer, Sauvignon Blanc, and Cabernet Sauvignon wines with the following vineyard designations: *Pepperwood, Deer Hill, Stone Crest, Oak Creek, Annaberg, Quartz Hill, Stonebridge,* and *Laurel.* The winery has recently reduced its product line, and in the future shall be focusing on Chardonnay, Sauvignon Blanc, and Cabernet Sauvignon. Sonoma-Cutrer has recently purchased a good portion of the property, and the various labels may be discontinued.

Bandiera Winery (Cloverdale, 1937), is a 200-acre (all leased), 150,000-case winery producing moderately priced Chardonnay, Sauvignon Blanc, Cabernet Sauvignon, and Zinfandel, of which the finest are marketed under the *John B. Merritt* label. The original winery, founded in 1937 by Emile Bandiera, was sold to a syndicate, the California Wine Company in 1980.

Barefoot Cellars (Healdsburg, 1986), is a 100,000-case negociant concern that distributes good, reliable Chardonnay, Sauvignon Blanc, and Cabernet Sauvignon.

Barrow Green (Petaluma, 1986), is a 8,000-case brand whose wines are made by La Crema. The three well-made wines--Pinot Noir, Chardonnay, and a Meritage red, are characterized by complexity and restrained fruit, offering good value.

Bellerose Vineyard (Healdsburg, 1979), is an excellent, highly underrated, 45-acre, 8,000-case winery that attempts to capture the elusive qualities of Bordeaux-style (full bodied, complex in flavor and scent, and meant to age) *Reserve Cuvee* Cabernet Sauvignon and Merlot, with Petit Verdot, Cabernet Franc, and Malbec additions. Equally good is a fruity, yet complex, barrel fermented Sauvignon Blanc made with 20% additions of Semillon (one of the finest in the state). The meticulously made estate bottled wines are consistent in quality and should be part of any serious cellar.

Belvedere Winery (Healdsburg, 1979), is a 450-acre, 350,000-case winery that makes quality Alexander Valley and Russian River Chardonnay, and Dry Creek Zinfandel, Cabernet Sauvignon, and Muscat Blanc. Less expensive varietal wines are made under the *Grove Street* label.

Braren Pauli Winery (Petaluma, 1980), is a 140-acre, 9,000-case winery that makes average to above-average Chardonnay, Cabernet Sauvignon, Merlot, and small amounts of Gewurztraminer (sold only at the winery).

Buena Vista Winery & Vineyards (Sonoma, 1857), founded by the legendary Agoston Haraszthy, this 1,360-acre winery is considered the oldest in California. Except for the historic buildings in Sonoma, the heart of this winery is the large 800-acre vineyard in the Carneros section further to the south. The well-made wines, such as the Cabernet Sauvignon Reserve Carneros, Chardonnay, Merlot, Gamay Beaujolais, Zinfandel, Riesling, Gewurztraminer, and Sauvignon Blanc, can be outstanding. The Private Reserve wines are excellent, as is a Pinot Noir under the *Robert Stemmler Vineyard* label. The winery also owns 200 acres in Lake County making outstanding Sauvignon Blanc; the excellent Haywood Winery, and has recently introduced an innovative line of "bistro" wines made from Chardonnay and Symphony, or Semillon. Annual output exceeds 300,000 cases and expanding rapidly. It is envisioned that by 1995 the winery will be shipping 1 million cases, of which half will be exported to Europe. Other label: *Vineyard-Signature Collection.*

Carmenet Vineyard & Winery (Sonoma, 1981), owned by Chalone, this is a 300-acre property (of which 70 acres are planted), state-of-the-art, quality oriented, 30,000-case winery (completely underground) that has been establishment to produce expensive wines capable of competing with the very best from Bordeaux. The Cabernet Sauvignon-based Meritage red, and the barrel fermented and barrel aged white Meritage are both rich, full bodied, complex, opulent, concentrated in flavor and scent, and a must for the serious enophile. The white wines are made from Edna Valley grapes in San Luis Obispo; a small quantity of a surprisingly good wood fermented Napa Valley Colombard (*Cyril Saviez* Vineyard); Chardonnay from *San Giacomo* Vineyard; and Cabernet Franc are also made. The reserve Meritage is outstanding.

Caswell Vineyards (Sebastopol, 1981), is a 12-acre, 4,000-case winery that makes Gewurztraminer, Sauvignon Blanc, Chardonnay, Zinfandel, Petite Sirah, Pinot Noir, and a blend of Cabernet Sauvignon, Malbec, and Merlot called *Claret.* Other label: *Winter Creek,* for fruit and honey wines.

Cecchetti-Sebastiani Cellar (Sonoma, 1985), is a 5,000-case negociant firm that distributes Chardonnay, Cabernet Sauvignon, Merlot, and Pinot Noir.

Chalk Hill Winery (Healdsburg, 1980), formerly Donna Maria Vineyard, is a 250-acre, 60,000-case, underrated winery that makes good, supple, ripe Sauvignon Blanc, Chardonnay, and Cabernet Sauvignon. The late harvest Sauvignon Blanc and Semillon are interesting.

Charis Vineyards (Geyserville, 1981), is a 20-acre, 1,000-case winery that makes excellent, stylish, hand crafted Sauvignon Blanc and Cabernet Sauvignon, both of which offer outstanding value.

Chateau de Baun (Santa Rosa, 1986), is a rapidly expanding, 102-acre, 12,000-case winery that produced, until 1990, nothing but Symphony grape wine. The product of Muscat of Alexandria and Grenache Gris (first developed at UC-Davis), it produces extremely high yields (as much as 10 tons to the acre), and highly fragrant wine. The winery makes three table wines: Chardonnay, Pinot Noir, and Symphony, all of which are full-bodied, well-structured, and above industry standards. Also made are sparkling wines: *Romance* (100% Symphony, *methode champenoise*), and *Rhapsody* (Brut Rose, a blend of Symphony and Pinot Noir). *Finale* (10 to 12% residual sugar), is a superb late harvest 100% Symphony wine. The highly distinctive wines offer remarkable value.

Chateau Diana (Healdsburg, 1979), is a 350,000-case negociant concern that handles Chardonnay, Chenin Blanc, Sauvignon Blanc, Cabernet Sauvignon, Zinfandel, sparkling, peach, and other wines. It also custom bottles for different accounts.

Chateau St. Jean (Kenwood, 1973), is a well regarded, 70-acre (leasing and contracting an additional 2,000 acres), 220,000-case, premium winery known for a wide array of wines. Varietals include Chardonnay, Sauvignon Blanc, Pinot Blanc, Gewurztraminer, Riesling, a Cabernet Sauvignon blend (all are rich, refined, fruity, well balanced and delicate), sparkling wines (including the gold-labeled Brut made mostly from Pinot Noir, a silver-labeled Blanc de Blancs from Chardonnay, and a superb Grand Cuvee), and late harvest, select late harvest, and special select late harvest—all of which are above-average, and often outstanding. Differences in soil and microclimate are preserved by special lot designations. Important vineyards include *Belle Terre, Robert Young, Frank Johnson, St. Jean,* and *La Petite Etoile* (a 44-acre vineyard that the winery owns). While the celebrity of its wines had suffered in the 1980s, quality has improved recently. In Gration (Sonoma County) the winery operates a 30,000-case sparkling wine facility. The winery is now owned by Suntory of Japan.

Chateau St. Jean, home of soft, supple, fruity wines. Baxevanis

Chateau Souverain (Geyserville, 1943), is a 150-acre, 100,000-case winery with an uneven corporate history (briefly owned by the Pillsbury Co.) that has been a division of Wine World since 1986. The winery historically emphasized the production of Green Hungarian, Petite Sirah, and soft, supple Riesling, all of which have been discontinued. Recently, this aggressive and innovative winery has been successful with Chardonnay, Sauvignon Blanc, Merlot, Cabernet Sauvignon, and Zinfandel. The much improved wines are now consistently above-average to excellent, especially the Reserve Chardonnay.

Christopher Creek (Healdsburg, 1974), formerly Sotoyome Winery, is a 10-acre, 3,000-case winery that makes above-average, distinctive Syrah and Petite Sirah, both of which offer excellent value. Other label: *Sotoyome Winery,* currently being phased out of production.

Cline Cellars (Sonoma, 1933), historically Firpo Winery in Oakley, is a 300-acre, 20,000-case winery that makes a Chenin Blanc/Semillon blend, Semillon, Zinfandel, Syrah, Carignane, Cabernet Sauvignon, Mourvedre (this is the oldest and largest acreage in the state), a Cline

Oakley Cuvee (a blend of Mourvedre and Zinfandel), a blend of Cabernet Sauvignon/Mourvedre, and proprietary wines, all of which are well-made, robust, and full-bodied. The winery has recently moved from Oakley in Contra Costa County, purchased land, planted 94 acres, and will emphasize the production of Rhone-type grapes and wines such as Mourvedre, Marsanne, Syrah, Viognier, among others. Sangiovese is also being planted.

Clos du Bois Wines (Geyserville, 1974), is a highly respected, 700-acre (in the Alexander and Dry Creek areas), 325,000-case winery that makes above-average to excellent Sauvignon Blanc, Chardonnay, Cabernet Sauvignon, Merlot, Malbec, Pinot Noir, and Gewurztraminer. It produces a wide range of reliable, blended, estate, reserve, and vineyard designated wines, of which *Flintwood, Calcaire, Briarcrest,* and *Marlstone* (a blend of Cabernet Sauvignon, Merlot, and Cabernet Franc) are all reliable and excellent. Late harvest wines are improving. The winery is owned by The Wine Alliance, a holding firm with a combined output of about 700,000 cases.

Cutler Cellar (Vineburg, 1985), is a 1,500-case label known for expensive, full bodied, well structured, complex, yet finely textured Cabernet Sauvignon from the *Batto Ranch,* the latter, owned by Gundlach Bundschu. Also made is *Satyre,* a red Meritage wine made from Cabernet Sauvignon, Merlot, and Cabernet Franc.

Davis Bynum Winery (Healdsburg, 1965), is an 11-acre, 27,000-case winery best known for Gewurztraminer, Sauvignon Blanc, Chardonnay, Cabernet Sauvignon, Pinot Noir, Zinfandel, Merlot, estate-bottled, and limited release wines. Inconsistent in past years, the wines have recently improved and now offer excellent value.

Dehlinger Winery (Sebastopol, 1975), is a 31-acre, 8,000-case winery that consistently makes above-average to excellent, rich, delicate, wood aged Chardonnay, Zinfandel, Pinot Noir, and Cabernet Sauvignon from hillside-grown grapes. There is also serious experimentation with Cabernet Franc and Petite Sirah.

De Loach Vineyards (Santa Rosa, 1975), is a 278-acre, 90,000-case winery that makes average to excellent, distinctive, fruity, and well flavored Chardonnay, Sauvignon Blanc, Gewurztraminer, Zinfandel (from old vines), Cabernet Sauvignon, Merlot, and Pinot Noir, offering good value.

De Lorimier Winery (Geyserville, 1985), is a 64-acre, 10,000-case, estate winery that makes four proprietary wines: *Spectrum* (a blend of Sauvignon Blanc and Semillon); *Prism* (a blend of four Chardonnay clones); *Mosaic* (a blend of Cabernet Sauvignon, Merlot, and Cabernet Franc); and *Lace* (a late harvest Sauvignon Blanc and/or Semillon), offering good value.

De Natale Vineyards (Healdsburg, 1985), is a 6-acre, 1,000-case winery that makes supple, yet well structured, flavorful Chardonnay, Sauvignon Blanc, Cabernet Sauvignon, and Pinot Noir.

Deux Amis (Windsor, 1987), is a 2,000-case label owned by two outstanding county winemakers who make well-structured but supple, soft, fruity Sauvignon Blanc, Zinfandel, and Cabernet Sauvignon, offering good value.

Diamond Oaks Vineyard (Cloverdale, 1980), is a 250-acre, 30,000-case winery that makes impressive Chardonnay, Sauvignon Blanc, and Cabernet Sauvignon. Other label: *Thomas Knight Signature.*

Domaine Michel Winery (Healdsburg, 1979), is a 50-acre, 19,000-case winery that makes, since 1987, first class wine. Founded by a Swiss banker, it is a meticulously operated and maintained property known for outstanding, well balanced, wood aged and refined Chardonnay and age worthy Cabernet Sauvignon. Major changes are expected as Jacques Schlumberger has assumed controlling interest.

Domaine St. George Winery & Vineyards (Healdsburg, 1934), formerly Cambiaso Winery, is a 30-acre, 350,000-case winery (also buys wines) that makes attractively priced Sauvignon Blanc, Chardonnay, Cabernet Sauvignon, Merlot, Gamay Beaujolais, Zinfandel, and proprietary wines. The firm also markets four reserve wines of which the estate and Dry Creek Cabernet Sauvignon are excellent. The winery is owned by a Thai company. Other label: *Clos St. Nicole* and *Cambiaso Winery.*

Dry Creek Vineyard (Healdsburg, 1972), is a 125-acre, 120,000-case winery that makes estate and non-estate Chardonnay, Sauvignon Blanc, Chenin Blanc, Cabernet Sauvignon, Merlot, and Zinfandel, all of which are appealing. Cabernet Sauvignon and Sauvignon Blanc are currently above-average in quality, but the finest wines are bottled under the reserve and Meritage label designations. Three-quarters of total output is white wine--all crisp, fresh, and well balanced.

Duxoup Wineworks (Healdsburg, 1981), is a meticulous and unusual 2,500-case winery that makes excellent, rich, full bodied, well scented and flavored Zinfandel, Syrah, Charbono, Pinot Noir, and Napa Gamay from old vines, offering outstanding value. The meticulously well-made made wines, consistent to a flaw, deserve prominent cellar space.

E. J. Gallo Winery and Vineyards (Healdsburg, 1885), formerly the Frei Bros. Winery (the oldest operating winery in the Dry Creek area), was purchased in 1975, and it is here that Gallo vinifies between 30 and 40 percent of all Sonoma County grapes. Gallo also owns nearly 2,000 acres (three vineyards: one in the Dry Creek Valley, another in the Alexander Valley, and the latest acquisition is former acreage belonging to the now defunct Italian Swiss Colony Winery in Asti), and 100 acres from the Lyeth winery. The winery makes more than 3 million cases annually. Cabernet Sauvignon is outstanding, and the Zinfandel and Sauvignon Blanc emanating from this facility are also above-average.

Eagle Ridge Winery (Penngrove, 1981), is a 3-acre, 4,000-case winery located on a hill overlooking the Petaluma Valley with a spectacular view of the Sonoma Mountains. The winery specializes in Sauvignon Blanc, and big, powerful Zinfandel. A small quantity of rare Ehrenfelser, Melon, Mourvedre, and a proprietary Rhone-style rose called "Cote de Penngrove," are also made. The meticulously-made wines belong in every serious cellar.

Estancia Alexander Valley Estates (Healdsburg, 1986), is a 240-acre, 140,000-case brand whose vineyards and wine are owned and produced by Franciscan Winery. The winery historically made three value-laden wines: a soft Sauvignon Blanc, a robust Chardonnay, and a fruity Cabernet Sauvignon, but now concentrates only on Cabernet Sauvignon and a Meritage red. About half of total output emanates from Monterey for a good, sound, affordable Chardonnay.

Estate William Baccala Vineyards (Healdsburg, 1986), is a 50,000-case winery that makes well scented and balanced Chardonnay, Sauvignon Blanc, and Merlot. The winery purchases grapes from the 77-acre Stephen Zellerbach estate (the previous owner), and will continue to produce wine (mainly Cabernet Sauvignon and Chardonnay) under the *Stephen Zellerbach* label.

F. Korbel, the largest producer of methode champenoise sparkling wines, offering excellent value. Baxevanis

F. Korbel and Bros. (Guerneville, 1882), with 400-acres and an annual output of 1.3 million cases, this is the largest premium, and oldest *methode Champenoise* producer of fruity, not yeasty, sparkling wines. Output has more than quadrupled over the past eight years, becoming one of the most reliable and consistent sparkling wine producers of Blanc de Noirs, Natural, Brut, Blanc de Blancs, Brut Rose, Sec, and Extra, offering above-average to exceptional value. In addition, the winery also produces brandy, fortified (Sherry and Porto-type wines), and several table wines (Colombard, Sauvignon Blanc, Chardonnay, and Cabernet Sauvignon)--all of which are consistently well made, offering excellent value.

Fallenleaf Vineyard (Sonoma, 1986), is a 25-acre, 4,000-case winery that makes above-average Chardonnay and Sauvignon Blanc.

Ferrari-Carano Winery (Healdsburg, 1981), is a new, stylish, state-of-the-art, 600-acre (divided into ten separate vineyards in Dry Creek,

Alexander Valley, and Carneros), rapidly expanding, 60,000-case winery that makes outstanding, intensely flavored and scented Chardonnay, Sauvignon Blanc (with Semillon), Cabernet Sauvignon (with Petit Verdot, Merlot, Cabernet Franc, and Malbec), Merlot, and late harvest Sauvignon Blanc (labeled *El Dorado Gold*), offering excellent value. The reserve Chardonnay is outstanding. With additional purchased acreage, the winery will, in the future, highlight vineyard designations: Chardonnay from Dell'Oro in the Alexander Valley; Merlot from the Bello Rosso vineyard in the Dry Creek area; Cabernet Sauvignon (as well as other red varieties) from The Mountain vineyard overlapping the Alexander and Knights valleys *ava's*; and Chardonnay from Carneros. The reserve Chardonnay is outstanding. Other vineyards include *La Strada, La Rosa,* and *Tre Terre*. The winery has recently completed "Villa Fiore," a large, red wine aging cellar with a capacity of 1,500 barrels. Other label: *Carano* for Zinfandel, and other varietals and proprietary wines.

The New Wine Aging Cellars of Ferrari-Carano Winery. Courtesy of Ferrari-Carano

Field Stone Winery (Healdsburg, 1976), with 15 acres, is an unusual underground winery producing 10,000 cases of Chardonnay, Sauvignon Blanc, Cabernet Sauvignon, Petite Sirah, and late harvest wines (Riesling and Gewurztraminer).

Fisher Vineyards (Santa Rosa, 1979), is a 75-acre, 12,000-case winery that makes above-average to excellent, stylish, well flavored Chardonnay and Cabernet Sauvignon. *Whitney's Vineyard* Chardonnay is the finest, followed by *Coach Insignia* Chardonnay and Cabernet Sauvignon, all of which exhibit elegance and complexity.

Flax Winery (Healdsburg, 1983), is a 20-acre, 4,500-case property with an emphasis on crisp, fruity, full flavored Chardonnay. Wine quality aside, what attracts the buyer is the unusual label and the fact that it is packaged in a Bordeaux-type bottle.

Foppiano Vineyards (Healdsburg, 1896), one of the oldest wineries in the county, is a 200-acre, 220,000-case winery that makes many wines, of which Sauvignon Blanc, Chardonnay, Petite Sirah, Zinfandel, and Cabernet Sauvignon are particularly good. The finest wines are marketed under the *Fox Mountain* (Cabernet Sauvignon and Chardonnay) and the *Louis J. Foppiano Vineyards* labels (the reserve Cabernet Sauvignon is outstanding). More than 85 percent of production is marketed under the less expensive *Riverside Farm* label. White wines are fruity, medium bodied, and well flavored; the red are full, dark in color, and tannin rich.

Frick Winery (Geyserville, 1976), recently relocated from the Santa Cruz region, this 7-acre, 2,000-case winery makes Petite Sirah, Zinfandel, Cinsault, Cabernet Sauvignon, Syrah, Merlot, and Viognier.

Fulton Valley Cellars (Fulton, 1986), is a 40-acre, 10,000-case winery that makes soft, supple, early maturing Sauvignon Blanc, Chardonnay, Gewurztraminer, Cabernet Sauvignon, and Pinot Noir.

Gan Eden Winery (Sebastopol, 1985), is a 40,000-case winery that makes Chardonnay, Chenin Blanc, Gewurztraminer, Cabernet Sauvignon, and Gamay Beaujolais from purchased grapes. This excellent winery is one of two kosher firms in Sonoma County.

Gary Farrell Wines (Forestville, 1982), is an excellent, 4,000-case label that makes delicate, refined, medium bodied, yet well structured Pinot Noir (*Howard Allen Vineyard*), Sauvignon Blanc (*Laurel Grande Vineyard), Chardonnay (Aquarius Vineyard*), and Zinfandel from purchased grapes. The owner, one of the most talented winemakers in the state, consistently offers outstanding value.

Gauer Estate Vineyard and Winery (Healdsburg, 1987), along with a sister facility (Vinwood Cellars, a 400,000-case, custom crush facility), is a 500-acre winery that makes 10,000 cases of excellent, robust, big and well-structured, estate Chardonnay, Cabernet Sauvignon, and Merlot. Part of a large 5,500-acre ranch, a portion of the property was recently sold to the Chevron Oil Company, thus precipitating many changes. The Vinwood custom facility offers services to more than 30 clients.

Geyser Peak Winery (Geyserville, 1880), with more than 1,150 acres (mainly in the Alexander and Russian River Valley), and an annual output of 450,000 cases, is one of the largest wineries in Sonoma. Historically a bulk producer, the winery changed hands in 1982, and the facilities, philosophy, and wine quality have evolved to a more positive note. The emphasis is now on varietals, mainly Chardonnay, Sauvignon Blanc, Riesling, Gewurztraminer, Chenin Blanc, Cabernet Sauvignon, Pinot Noir, Zinfandel, Merlot, and Petite Sirah. The recently improved wines (especially the *Meritage* white and red, *Chateau Alexandre*, and *Reserve Alexandre*), usually offer good value. The winery purchased 1,000 acres (100 of which are planted) in the Benmore Valley of Lake County. Other labels: *Canyon Road* and *Nervo Winery* (a small separate winery for generic wines on sale at the tasting room only).

Glen Ellen (Glen Ellen, 1980), ranking among the largest wineries in the state, is an aggressive, 85-acre, 3.4 million-case winery that produces varietal, North Coast, estate, and California wine at modest and ulra-premium prices. Although the property dates back to 1868 as a vineyard, the Benziger family purchased the property in 1980, and transformed it into a highly successful, value oriented winery (nearly all wines are marketed under the *Proprietor's Reserve* label, only 6,500 cases shipped in 1982). The wines (Chardonnay, Sauvignon Blanc, Gamay Beaujolais, Cabernet Sauvignon, Zinfandel, Merlot, Grenache, and blended wines) are always fresh, full flavored, and consistently good. Sauvignon Blanc, Semillon, Chardonnay, Pinot Blanc, Muscat Blanc, Cabernet Sauvignon, Zinfandel, and Merlot are marketed under the upscale *Benziger of Glen Ellen* label. A line of unusual and extraordinary wines--Aliatico Blanc de Noir, Cabernet Franc, Trousseau, Petite Sirah, Zinfandel Port, Dolcetto, and late harvest Zinfandel are marketed under the *Imagery Series* label. The Meritage-type wines (labeled *Tribute*) are outstanding. Approximately 80 percent of production is white wine, with Chardonnay alone accounting for 37 percent of total output. All but the estate wines are made by various wineries throughout the state and shipped to Sonoma for blending. This successful winery has recently released its first *methode champenoise* sparkling wine made from Chardonnay.

Gloria Ferrer Champagne Caves (Sonoma, 1986), owned by Freixenet, is a stylish, 175-acre, 65,000-case winery that specializes in the production of sparkling wine (Brut, Vintage Brut, and Carneros Cuvee) from Pinot Noir (more than two-thirds of the *cuvee*) and Chardonnay.

Golden Creek Vineyard (Santa Rosa, 1983), is a 12-acre, 2,000-case, underrated winery that makes above-average to excellent Cabernet Sauvignon, Merlot, and a Cabernet Sauvignon/Merlot blend, offering excellent value.

Grand Cru Vineyards (Glen Ellen, 1970), is a 36-acre, 60,000-case winery that has established a reputation for above-average to excellent, fruity, well balanced, intensely flavored and scented Chenin Blanc, Chardonnay, Sauvignon Blanc, Gewurztraminer, Cabernet Sauvignon, Zinfandel, and late harvest Gewurztraminer from grapes emanating from select vineyards. The Collectors Reserve Cabernet Sauvignon is exceptional. The winery is in the process of being sold with the Bronco Wine Co. recently purchasing the various brands and inventory.

Grape Links/Barefoot Cellars (Healdsburg, 1986), is a 50,000-case negociant firm that distributes Chardonnay, Sauvignon Blanc, and Cabernet Sauvignon under the *California Beau* label.

Gundlach-Bunschu Winery (Vineburg, 1858), reopened in 1973 after decades of inactivity, this historic, 405-acre, 50,000-case winery pro-

duces many wines, of which Riesling, Chardonnay, Gewurztraminer, Cabernet Sauvignon, Cabernet Franc, Zinfandel, Pinot Noir, and Merlot are often excellent. The winery also produces a variety unique to Sonoma--Kleinberger.

H. Coturri and Sons (Glen Ellen, 1979), is a 10-acre, 3,000-case winery that makes flavorful Zinfandel, Cabernet Sauvignon, and Pinot Noir. This is one of several county wineries that makes sulfur-free wines.

Hacienda Wine Cellars (Sonoma, 1973), is a successful and well regarded, 110-acre, 35,000-case winery that sits on a property once owned by Agoston Haraszthy. The expertly made wines, Chardonnay, Chenin Blanc, Cabernet Sauvignon, and Pinot Noir, are known for their moderate alcohol, fragrance, balance, drinkability, and always offering excellent value. The dry Chenin Blanc is one of the finest in the state. The winery also makes small quantities of Porto-type (*Moonlight*) and sweet Riesling wines. A premium proprietary Cabernet Sauvignon-based (with Cabernet Franc and Merlot) is named *Antares*.

Hafner Vineyard (Healdsburg, 1982), is an obscure, 100-acre, 10,000-case winery that only makes barrel fermented, full bodied, complex, elegant Chardonnay and well structured Cabernet Sauvignon. The hard to find wines offer excellent value.

Hanna Winery (Santa Rosa, 1985), is a stylish, expanding, 275-acre, 16,000-case winery best known for rich, spicy, and full bodied Sauvignon Blanc, Chardonnay, and Cabernet Sauvignon (dense and tannin rich), offering good value.

Hanzell Vineyards (Sonoma, 1967), is a 33-acre, 3,500-case winery historically known for estate bottled Chardonnay, Pinot Noir, and Cabernet Sauvignon. The winery, founded by the innovative James Zellerbach, developed a reputation throughout the 1960s and 1970s for high alcohol, complex, but overly oaked wines (he was the first to use French oak barrels in California on a large scale) which commanded the highest prices. The hard to find wines are still expensive, but have been eclipsed in quality by many others in the county.

Haywood Winery (Sonoma, 1980), is a little known, 90-acre, 20,000-case winery that consistently makes excellent to outstanding Chardonnay, Sauvignon Blanc, Riesling, Cabernet Sauvignon, and Zinfandel, offering excellent value. The impeccably made, refined and concentrated, wood aged wines are the product of dry farmed, low yielding vines, and should not be missed. The winery, purchased recently by Buena Vista, is slated for a serious upgrade.

Homewood Winery (Vineburg, 1988), is a 1-acre, 700-case winery known for fruity, well-balanced Chardonnay and Cabernet Sauvignon.

Hop Kiln, an unusual winery that makes first rate wine. Baxevanis

Hop Kiln Winery (Healdsburg, 1975), is a 60-acre, 9,000-case winery known for stylish, well made, full flavored, often complex Riesling, Chardonnay, Petite Sirah, Zinfandel, and Napa Gamay, some of which are made from old vines.

Iron Horse Vineyards (Sebastopol, 1976), is an excellent, 145-acre, 38,000-case winery offering estate produced sparkling (Late Disgorged Brut, Blanc de Blancs, Brut Rose), Chardonnay, Sauvignon Blanc, Pinot Noir, and Cabernet Sauvignon. Although all are fragrant, flavorful, and full bodied, sparkling wines are, by far, the better wines. Recently, the winery has acquired 50 acres for the production of sparkling wine in a partnership with Champagne Laurent-Perrier. Other label: *Tin Pony*.

J. Fritz Winery (Cloverdale, 1979), is a 240-acre, 20,000-case winery that makes well balanced Chardonnay, Sauvignon Blanc, Zinfandel, and Cabernet Sauvignon.

J. Pedroncelli Winery (Geyserville, 1927), is a 120-acre, 125,000-case winery that makes proprietary and varietal wines, of which Chardonnay, Sauvignon Blanc, Riesling, Chenin Blanc, Zinfandel, Pinot Noir, Gamay Beaujolais, Merlot, and Cabernet Sauvignon appear to be above-average in quality. Reserve wines are excellent and offer considerable value.

J. Rochioli Vineyards & Winery (Healdsburg, 1982), is a 100-acre, 5,000-case winery that makes full bodied and well flavored, estate bottled Chardonnay, Sauvignon Blanc, Gewurztraminer, Pinot Noir, Zinfandel, and Cabernet Sauvignon, offering good value. The winery has the reputation of growing the finest Pinot Noir in the area.

Jade Mountain Winery (Cloverdale, 1984), is a 31-acre, 5,000-case ranch located in Cloverdale but crushes in Rutherford. The product mix of earlier years has recently been restructured to emphasize Chardonnay, Syrah, Mourvedre, and white and red Rhone blends.

James Arthur Field (Healdsburg, 1976), is a successful, 50,000-case negociant house that specializes only in 1.5 liter white and red table, and sparkling (Le Champ) wines.

Johnson's Alexander Valley Wines (Healdsburg, 1975), is a 50-acre, 8,000-case winery that makes Chardonnay, Gewurztraminer, Chenin Blanc, Riesling, Pinot Noir, Cabernet Sauvignon, and Zinfandel.

Jordan Sparkling Wine Co. (Healdsburg, 1986), is a 100-acre, 12,000-case sparkling winery that specializes in the production of *methode champenoise* libations marketed under the "J" label. The expensive, full-bodied, yet elegant wines, aged for three years on the lees, are made from Chardonnay and Pinot Noir.

Jordan Vineyards and Winery, known for soft, supple, drinkable Chardonnay and Cabernet Sauvignon. Courtesy of Jordan Vineyards

Jordan Vineyards and Winery (Healdsburg, 1972), is a classy, 276-acre, 80,000-case winery that makes above-average to excellent, soft, supple estate-bottled Chardonnay and Cabernet Sauvignon. The wines, expensive, stylishly made, and expertly merchandised, are quite fashionable and widely distributed despite their non-distinctive character. While never reaching the heights of complexity of the finest producers, the wines, because of their early maturing and soft character, are very appealing and popular.

Joseph Swan Vineyards (Forestville, 1968), is an obscure, 10-acre, 2,000-case winery that makes almost legendary, hard to find, above-average, full bodied, muscular Zinfandel and Pinot Noir. Also made are smaller quantities of Chardonnay and Cabernet Sauvignon. Due to the death of the founder, the winery may alter its winemaking style in the future.

Kenwood Vineyards (Kenwood, 1970), is a 200-acre, 175,000-case winery that makes average to excellent, often concentrated and intensely flavored Chardonnay, Sauvignon Blanc, Chenin Blanc, Riesling, Zinfandel, and Cabernet Sauvignon. The *Artists Series* Cabernet Sauvignon can be outstanding.

Kistler Vineyards (Glen Ellen, 1979), is a 35-acre, 7,000-case winery in the Mayacamas that makes outstanding Chardonnay (*Dutton Ranch, McCrea, Kistler Estate* Vineyards, and *Durrell* Vineyard), Kistler Estate Vineyards Cabernet Sauvignon, and Dutton Ranch and McCrea Pinot Noir. Expertly and consistently made, all wines offer excellent value.

Kunde Estates Winery (Kenwood, 1904), is a 650-acre, 150,000-case winery that makes above-average, round, supple, yet full-bodied Chardonnay, Sauvignon Blanc, Cabernet Sauvignon, Zinfandel, Merlot, Muscat Blanc, Meritage-type, and white and red Rhone-type wines, the latter, labeled *Vallee de la Lune*. The winery was originally founded in 1904 by the same family, closed during W.W. II, and resurrected in 1989.

La Crema Vinera (Sebastopol, 1979), is a 25,000-case winery that makes spicy, well flavored Chardonnay, Sauvignon Blanc, Pinot Noir, and proprietary wines, all of which have shown a marked improvement in recent years. The winery has recently purchased Lost Hills Winery.

Lake Sonoma Winery (Geyserville, 1978), formerly Diablo Vista Winery in Solano County, is a 10-acre, 7,500-case winery that makes robust, full-bodied and round Chardonnay, Sauvignon Blanc, Chenin Blanc, Zinfandel, Cinsault, Merlot, and Cabernet Sauvignon. The Chenin Blanc is fruity and dry; the Chardonnay is big and luscious; the dark, meaty, and rich Cabernet Sauvignon is aged in Nevers oak for 3-1/2 years; and the Zinfandel is meaty and well-structured, offering good value. The winery not only blends Cinsault to Zinfandel, but also makes small quantities of it (unfiltered) as a varietal, an unusual feature for Sonoma. Equal to wine quality is the spectacular view from the tasting room.

Lambert Bridge (Healdsburg, 1975), is a 67-acre, 30,000-case, estate winery known for soft, supple, early maturing but well flavored Chardonnay, Sauvignon Blanc, Chenin Blanc, Cabernet Sauvignon, Merlot, Zinfandel, and late harvest Riesling.

Landmark Vineyards (Kenwood, 1974), is a 85-acre, 18,000-case winery that specializes only in average to above-average Chardonnay. The winery has recently purchased land in Sonoma Valley, and has moved the winery to Kenwood.

Las Montanas Winery (Glen Ellen, 1979), is a tiny, 1,000-case, one woman operation that makes inconsistent, but often big, alcoholic, well structured Zinfandel and Cabernet Sauvignon from organically grown grapes offering excellent value.

Laurel Glen Vineyard (Glen Ellen, 1981), is a 35-acre, 5,000-case winery that specializes in the production of distinctive, firm, well flavored and balanced, often outstanding Cabernet Sauvignon. The vineyards are well positioned 1,000 feet above the valley floor on a hillside containing iron rich volcanic soil. Cabernet Sauvignon from Napa, labeled *Terra Rosa*, is interesting. Other label: *Counterpoint*.

Lyeth Vineyard & Winery (Geyserville, 1981), is a stylish, 90-acre, 25,000-case winery that makes an outstanding, supple, flavorful red wine from a combination of Bordeaux varieties, and an unusual white wine very much in the Graves manner from Sauvignon Blanc, Semillon, and Muscadelle. The red wine, one of the most distinctive in the state, is full bodied, muscular, tannin rich, and complex. First planted in vines in 1973, the property was acquired by Vintech in 1987, a Sonoma County agricultural investment company, and recently purchased by Jean-Claude Boisset, a Burgundian negociant.

Lytton Springs Winery (Healdsburg, 1977), is a 150-acre (50 acres of Zinfandel in the Valley Vista Vineyard near Healdsburg, and 100 acres of Cabernet Sauvignon, Merlot, and Chardonnay in Mendocino), 19,000-case winery that has an established reputation for excellent to outstanding estate private reserve Zinfandel. The non-irrigated vineyard, located on hilly terrain between Dry Creek and Alexander valleys on porous, sandy and gravelly loam soils, produces rich, concentrated, and intensely flavored wines from old, low yielding vines. The winery has recently been acquired by Ridge Vineyards.

M.G. Vallejo Winery (Glen Ellen, 1986), owned by the Glen Ellen Winery, this 400,000-case label is known for moderately priced, soft and appealing Chardonnay, Sauvignon Blanc, Cabernet Sauvignon, Merlot, and Zinfandel, offering good value. Interestingly, the winemaker is Vallejo Haraszthy, a direct descendent of both Count Agoston Haraszthy and General Mariano Guadalupe Vallejo.

MacRostie Winery (Geyserville, 1987), is a 4,500-case label whose wines--distinctive, round, well flavored Chardonnay and Pinot Noir--are made by one of the most accomplished winemakers in the state. A new winery in the Carneros district is in the planning stage.

Manzanita Ridge Winery (Healdsburg, 1989), is a 10,000-case, Chardonnay-only label that makes a good, sound, barrel-fermented libation, offering good value.

Marimar Torres (Sebastopol, Geyserville, 1989), is a developing property of 60 acres (28 in vines) in the Green Valley *ava*. Planted in Chardonnay and Pinot Noir, the proposed winery will be making 15,000 cases of well-structured, lean Chardonnay, and in coming years Pinot Noir with minor infusions of Parellada.

Marietta Cellars (Geyserville, 1979), is a little known, 39-acre, 15,000-case winery that makes robust Zinfandel (regular and reserve), Cabernet Sauvignon, and generic red wines, offering good value.

Marion Wines (Santa Rosa, 1980), is a 40,000-case winery that relocated from Santa Clara. The wine list has been reduced to Chardonnay, Sauvignon Blanc, Cabernet Sauvignon, Zinfandel, and proprietary wines, all of which are well-made and supple, offering good value.

Mark West Vineyards (Forestville, 1976), is a 60-acre, 28,000-case winery that makes good, sound Chardonnay, Riesling, Gewurztraminer (dry and sweet), Pinot Noir, Zinfandel, and sparkling wines.

Martinelli Vineyards (Windsor, 1985), is a 152-acre, 6,000-case winery that makes moderately-priced Chardonnay, Sauvignon Blanc, Gewurztraminer, Muscat Blanc, Zinfandel, and proprietary wines, offering good value.

Martini and Prati (Santa Rosa, 1970), is a 72-acre, 20,000-case winery that markets its finest Chardonnay, Grey Riesling, Cabernet Sauvignon, and Zinfandel under the *Fountain Grove* label. The winery, with a 2.5 million gallon capacity (one of the largest in the county), crushes for others, markets under other labels, and makes fortified and vermouth wines.

Matanzas Creek Winery (Santa Rosa, 1978), is a rapidly expanding, 45-acre, 30,000-case winery that makes excellent to outstanding, full bodied, acidic and robust Chardonnay, Sauvignon Blanc, and Merlot wines, all of which are impeccable. Although the reputation of the winery rests on the production of lightly oaked, crisp, eminently refreshing, round, and consistently good Chardonnay, the Merlot is near perfection.

Mazzocco Vineyards (Healdsburg, 1985), is a 40-acre, 25,000-case winery that makes austere, distinctive Chardonnay (particularly River Lane), Cabernet Sauvignon, Zinfandel, and a Meritage-type red wine. Founded by a Los Angeles physician, the moderately priced wines offer excellent value.

Melim Vineyards (Healdsburg, 1986), is a 70-acre, 5,500-case, estate winery that makes well structured, full flavored Chardonnay, Sauvignon Blanc, and Cabernet Sauvignon, offering excellent value. Other label: *Maacama Creek*.

Mill Creek Vineyards (Healdsburg, 1974), is a 70-acre, 18,500-case winery that produces above-average, estate bottled Sauvignon Blanc, Gewurztraminer, Cabernet Sauvignon, Merlot, and Pinot Noir. This winery was the first to use the name "blush," and owns the trademark to the word as it applies to wine. Other label: *Felta Springs*.

Murphy-Goode Estate Winery (Geyserville, 1985), is a young, aggressive, 315-acre, 35,000-case winery that makes flavorful, above-average Sauvignon Blanc, Chardonnay, Merlot, Cabernet Sauvignon, and late harvest wines, offering excellent value. Other label: *Goode-Ready*.

Nalle Winery (Healdsburg, 1985), is a 4,000-case winery that makes excellent, refined, yet well structured Zinfandel from old, dry farmed vines, offering good value. Without question, this winery is the leader in the production of rich, elegant, age-worthy Zinfandel, a must for every serious cellar.

Nelson Estate Vineyards (Geyserville, 1986), is a 60-acre vineyard that makes 3,000 cases of fruity, well structured, and distinctive Cabernet Franc. While most grapes are sold to other wineries, the Cabernet Franc is the product of 21 acres.

Nunn's Canyon Winery (Glen Ellen, 1989), is a 60-acre, 3,000-case winery that makes supple, moderately-priced Zinfandel, Pinot Noir, and Cabernet Sauvignon.

Optima Wine Cellars (Santa Rosa, 1984), owned by two free-lance winemakers, is a 17,000-case winery that makes an excellent, blended red wine called Optima (Petite Sirah, Merlot, Zinfandel, Cabernet Sauvignon, Cabernet Franc, and others) with restrained oak flavors. Other label: *Fitch Mountain*.

Pastori Winery (Cloverdale, 1914), is a 55-acre, 2,000-case winery that makes Chenin Blanc, Riesling, Cabernet Sauvignon, Zinfandel, Sherrytype, and proprietary wines.

Pat Paulsen Vineyards (Cloverdale, 1970), is a financially troubled, 37-acre, 25,000-case winery that makes variable Sauvignon Blanc, Chardonnay, Muscat Blanc, and Cabernet Sauvignon.

Pellegrini Bros. Wines (Geyserville, 1933), is a 115-acre, 15,000-case winery that makes Chardonnay and Pinot Noir under the *Olivet Lane Estate* label, Cabernet Sauvignon under the *Cloverdale Ranch Pellegrini Family Vineyards* label, and Rhone-type wines under the *Cotes de*

Sonoma label. Other label: *Pellegrini Bros. Wines* for generic wines.

Peter McCoy (Knights Valley, 1984), is a 15-acre, 1,500-case brand that is responsible for excellent, big, firm, well flavored and structured, barrel fermented Chardonnay.

Peter Michael Winery (Knights Valley, 1986), is a 60-acre, 3,000-case winery that makes outstanding Chardonnay, and a full bodied, well structured Cabernet Sauvignon. The *Mon Plaisir* and *Liparita Vineyard* Chardonnay, and *Les Pavots* Cabernet Sauvignon are both excellent. Tiny quantities of Chardonnay fermented with wild yeast is labeled *Indigene*. Small quantities of Sauvignon Blanc are also made.

Piper Sonoma Cellars (Windsor, 1980), owned by Remy Martin, is a fashionable, 170-acre, 125,000-case winery that produces consistently well made, outstanding, firm, yet refined and delicate Brut, Blanc de Noirs, Brut Reserve, and a Tet de Cuvee, all of which rank among the finest in the state, and offer excellent value. The quality of the mousse, and the consistent quality make the wines of this fine winery indispensable for the serious cellar.

Pommeraie Winery (Sebastopol, 1979), is a 1-acre, 2,000-case winery that makes Chardonnay, Muscat Blanc, and Cabernet Sauvignon, offering good value.

Porter Creek Vineyards (Healdsburg, 1982), is a 35-acre, 1,000-case winery that makes fresh, fruity Chardonnay and Pinot Noir, offering good value.

Press Oak Cellars (Sonoma, 1986), is a 21-acre, 750-case vineyard that makes Merlot, Ruby Cabernet, and Zinfandel, the latter, particularly good.

Preston Vineyards & Winery (Healdsburg, 1973), is a 125-acre, 28,000-case winery that produces excellent to outstanding Sauvignon Blanc, Chenin Blanc, Muscat Blanc, Zinfandel, Cabernet Sauvignon, and proprietary wines. Less consistent are Barbera, Gamay Beaujolais, and Syrah blends (Mourvedre, Syrah, Cinsault, Carignane, Grenache, etc.). Recently, the winery has begun production of Viognier, and Marsanne. All the wines are well flavored and scented, delicate, and expertly made offering good value.

Quivira Vineyards (Cloverdale, 1980), named after a legendary northern California kingdom, this 73-acre winery makes 15,000 cases of excellent, moderately priced Sauvignon Blanc, Cabernet Sauvignon, a Grenache blend, and Zinfandel, the latter, dark, refined, and well flavored, ranks as one of the finest in the state.

Quivira Winery, site of soft, elegant Zinfandel. Baxevanis

Rabbit Ridge Vineyards (Healdsburg, 1981), is a 45-acre, 30,000-case winery that makes excellent Chardonnay (barrel fermented, crisp and complex), Sauvignon Blanc, Zinfandel (from old vines and unfined), Cabernet Sauvignon, Cabernet Franc, and a sublime white Meritage called *Mystique*. A Rhone-type wine, made from Syrah, Mourvedre, Grenache, and Carignane, is labeled *Allure*. The expertly made wines, with no acid additions, and a natural low pH, offer exceptional value. The winery also makes wine for two other labels-*Meadow Glen* and *Clairvaux*.

Ravenswood (Sonoma, 1976), is a 40,000-case winery that makes excellent Cabernet Sauvignon, Zinfandel (particularly good are organically farmed Old Hill Ranch, Cooke, and Dickerson Vineyards designations), Merlot (Sangiacomo Vineyard is outstanding), Chardonnay (Sangiacomo), and a proprietary red blend. The *Pickberry Vineyards* Meritage red wine is outstanding, as is the *Gregory* Cabernet Sauvignon. The wines, consistently well made, unfiltered, unfined, dense, well flavored, and distinctive, offer exceptional value.

Richard Michaels Ltd. (Healdsburg, 1987), is a young, aggressive negociant concern of 40,000 cases that markets a line of above-average quality Sauvignon Blanc, Chardonnay, Cabernet Sauvignon, Zinfandel, and blended wines (offering good value) under its own and other labels. The firm is also known as Healdsburg California Cellars.

Richardson Vineyards (Sonoma, 1980), is a 10-acre, 2,500-case winery that makes ripe, round, fruity, yet substantial Pinot Noir, Merlot, Cabernet Sauvignon, and Zinfandel. The expertly and consistently well made wines offer excellent value.

River Road Vineyards (Forestville, 1976), is a 78-acre, 10,000-case winery that makes Chardonnay and Cabernet Sauvignon.

Robert Stemmler Winery (Healdsburg, 1977), is an excellent, 5-acre, 4,000-case winery co-owned by a German-born enologist who makes above-average (but often outstanding) Chardonnay (Dry Creek), Cabernet Sauvignon (Chalk Hill), and late harvest Riesling and Sauvignon Blanc. The non-woody wines, always balanced and supple, offer good value. Other label: *Bel Canto*.

Roche Carneros Estate (Sonoma, 1988), is a 25-acre, 3,500-case winery that is part of a large 2,500-acre ranch. It makes well structured, concentrated, yet lean Chardonnay and Pinot Noir. Other labels: *Tamarix*, for a blush Pinot Noir, and *Le Mirage* for Sauvignon Blanc and Merlot, sold only at the winery.

Rodney Strong Vineyards (Windsor, 1961), formerly Sonoma Vineyards, is a large, 600-acre, 110,000-case winery with a troubled financial history. Recently purchased by Klein Foods of San Francisco, the operation and administration of the winery will surely change. Primary wines made are Chardonnay, Chenin Blanc, Sauvignon Blanc, Gewurztraminer, Riesling (regular and late harvest), Merlot, Pinot Noir, Cabernet Sauvignon, Zinfandel, and sparkling wine. The *Alexander's Crown* Cabernet is an underrated Cabernet Sauvignon-based wine that offers remarkable value. The reserve Cabernet is outstanding. *Windsor Vineyards* (350,000 cases), a mail order label, is partially distributed in New York.

Rose Family Winery (Forestville, 1981), is an excellent, 3,000-case winery that specializes in the production of oak aged Chardonnay and Pinot Noir.

St. Francis Winery (Kenwood, 1971), is a little known, 97-acre, 47,000-case winery that offers above-average estate and non estate bottled Chardonnay, Gewurztraminer, Riesling, Pinot Noir, Cabernet Sauvignon, Merlot, and late harvest Muscat Blanc.

Sausal Winery (Healdsburg, 1973), is a former bulk wine producer that now makes 14,000 cases of Chardonnay, Zinfandel, Cabernet Sauvignon, and Pinot Noir from 125 acres in the Alexander Valley. The Zinfandel reserve and Cabernet Sauvignon are both big, round, ripe, and well flavored, offering excellent value.

Schug Carneros Estate Winery (Sonoma, 1981), formerly Schug Cellars of Napa, is a well-regarded, 40-acre, 7,000-case winery, owned by one of the most competent winemakers in the county, that has recently established a winery in the Carneros region while maintaining the old facility in Napa. It makes above-average to excellent vineyard designated Chardonnay and Pinot Noir, the latter both table and sparkling. The fact that the sparkling wine is red, makes it something more than distinctive.

Sea Ridge Winery (Occidental, 1980), located on a marine ridge just 3 miles from the Pacific Ocean, is a 10-acre, 5,000-case winery that makes crisp, distinctive, and well scented Chardonnay, Sauvignon Blanc, Zinfandel, and Pinot Noir, the best of which are sold with specific vineyard designations.

Sebastiani Vineyards (Sonoma, 1904), with the death of August Sebastiani in 1980, the winery changed direction from a bulk producer to premium varietals. The winery grew rapidly in the 1970s achieving a historic high mark of 4 million cases in 1980, up from 500,000 cases in 1975, dropped to 2.5 million cases in 1985, but has since recovered to 4.8 million cases in 1988. The winery has recently purchased a facility in Woodbridge, near Lodi, to produce generic wines. With this acquisition, output is expected to increase to 8 million cases in the near future, ranking among the top ten wineries in the nation. Under Sam Sebas-

tiani's tenure as president, Sherry-type and sparkling wines were dropped from further production. The winery owns 500 acres, 300 of which are planted in vines. To meet production needs, the winery purchases about one-third of all grapes grown in Sonoma Valley. The original vineyard, adjacent to the winery's binning cellars, was founded in 1825 by Franciscan padres who made altar wines for their mission in Sonoma. The winery makes many generic and varietal wines of which Chardonnay, Zinfandel, Barbera, and Cabernet Sauvignon are all above-average in quality. Most wines are labeled *Sebastiani Vineyards, Vendange, August Sebastiani Proprietor's, Oakbrook, Swan Cellars,* and *Richard Cuneo* (for sparkling wine). Some of the finest wines (60,000 cases) are marketed by the Estates Group division: Cabernet Sauvignon under the *Bell Ranch* and *Cherryblock Vineyard* designations; and Chardonnay under the *Kinneybrook, Niles, Clark Ranch,* and *Wildwood Vineyard* designations.

Seghesio (Healdsburg, 1902), historically a bulk wine producer, this old, family-owned operation has, since 1983, began to bottle under its own label. It is known for full bodied, strongly flavored, old fashioned Chardonnay, Colombard, Cabernet Sauvignon, Zinfandel, Dolcetto, Barbera, and Pinot Noir, offering good value. Today's production, much smaller than formerly, is about 45,000 cases from 400 acres. Other label: *Strata*.

Sellards Winery (Sebastopol, 1980), is a 1-acre, 1,000-case winery that makes Chardonnay, Zinfandel, Cabernet Sauvignon, and late harvest wines.

Simi Winery (Healdsburg, 1890), is a 295-acre, 130,000-case winery that has shown dramatic improvement since it was acquired by Moet-Hennessey in 1981. Wine quality declined in the 1950s and 1960s, and between 1970 and 1976 ownership changed three times. While Sauvignon Blanc, Chardonnay, Semillon, Chenin Blanc, and Cabernet Sauvignon are all excellent, reserve Chardonnay and Cabernet Sauvignon wines are outstanding. Although underrated by many, this is a first class winery that offers excellent value.

Smothers Brothers (Kenwood, 1977), is a label with 35 acres that markets 25,000 cases of Chardonnay and Cabernet Sauvignon. Production and product line have been severely reduced in recent years.

Soda Rock Winery (Healdsburg, 1880), an old bulk wine producer, ceased operations in 1969 and remained idle until it was reopened in 1979. It cultivates 4 acres and makes 4,500 cases of Sauvignon Blanc, Chardonnay, Gewurztraminer, Pinot Noir, Cabernet Sauvignon, Zinfandel, and late harvest Riesling.

Sonoma Creek Winery (Sonoma, 1987), is a 40-acre, 2,900-case winery that makes Chardonnay, Chenin Blanc, Cabernet Sauvignon, Merlot, and Zinfandel, some unfined and unfiltered, but all full-bodied with considerable aging potential, offering good value.

Sonoma-Cutrer Vineyards (Windsor, 1981), is an 800-acre, 90,000-case winery with impeccable credentials for exquisite estate produced Chardonnay, of which *Les Pierres Vineyard* (Carneros), and *Cutrer Vineyard* (Russian River) are excellent to outstanding. The *Founders Reserve* is exceptional. The crisp, fresh, well balanced wines are a function of exacting hand harvesting, careful handling of the harvested grapes, meticulous selection of desirable grapes, and fastidious fermentation.

Stonestreet Winery and Vineyard (Healdsburg, 1990), formerly Stephen Zellerbach Winery, is a 65-acre, 22,000 case winery that makes estate Cabernet Sauvignon, Merlot, and Cabernet Franc, and non-estate Chardonnay, Gewurztraminer, and Pinot Noir. The winery, now owned by Kendall-Jackson, is in the process of expansion.

Taft Street Winery (Forestville, 1982), is an innovative, 20,000-case negociant firm that markets Chardonnay, Sauvignon Blanc, Merlot, and Cabernet Sauvignon.

The Meeker Vineyard (Healdsburg, 1984), is a 60-acre, 4,500-case winery located on steep hillsides overlooking the Dry Creek area. Expertly made, the excellent to outstanding Chardonnay, Zinfandel, and Cabernet Sauvignon are oak aged, well structured, concentrated, and age worthy.

The Merry Vintners (Santa Rosa, 1984), is an 18-acre, 7,500-case winery that makes distinctive, flavorful, barrel and tank fermented Chardonnay from purchased grapes.

Thomas Sellards Winery (Sebastopol, 1980), is a meticulous, 1,500-case winery that makes above-average to excellent, hand crafted Sauvignon Blanc, Chardonnay, Cabernet Sauvignon, Zinfandel, and late harvest

Riesling.

Topolos at Russian River Vineyards (Forestville, 1963), is a 26-acre, 9,000-case, innovative and underrated winery known for big, intensely flavored and scented Zinfandel (in three different styles), Petite Sirah (one of the finest and most expensive in the state), and Alicante Bouschet (one of the very few to be found in California), offering good value.

Toth Cellars (Healdsburg, 1987), is the parent company of J.W. Morris Winery (1975), a 50,000-case winery that produces variable Sauvignon Blanc, Chardonnay, Cabernet Sauvignon, Zinfandel, and Porto-type wines, the latter made from an unusual combination of old Zinfandel, Petite Sirah, and Cabernet Sauvignon vines. The better varietal wines (10,000 cases) are sold under the *Black Mountain Vineyard* label (established in 1983). The source of grapes is an excellent, 115-acre vineyard (30 acres of which are older that 80 years) whose wines are designated by specific names: *Gravel Bar* and *Douglas Hill* Chardonnay, *Laurelwood* Sauvignon Blanc, *Cramer Ridge* Zinfandel, and *Bosun Crest* Petite Sirah, offering excellent value.

Trentadue Winery (Geyserville, 1969), is a 200-acre, 33,000-case winery. Historically known for its inconsistency, it now produces good, sound, often distinctive Chenin Blanc, Merlot, Petite Sirah, Sangiovese, and a rare Carignane. More than one dozen different varieties are grown, including Aleatico.

Unicorn Vineyards and Wine Cellars (Healdsburg, 1988), is a 220,000-case negociant concern that markets a carbonated (8.5% alcohol) wine made from Riesling, Pinot Noir, and Gewurztraminer with a soda pop-type closure under the *Tickler* label.

Valley of the Moon Winery (Glen Ellen, 1951), is a 75-acre, 30,000-case winery owned by the Parducci family. The existing winery, constructed in 1857, and the vineyard have had a long and varied history. While emphasis rests on Semillon, Symphony, Zinfandel, and Cabernet Sauvignon, a good portion of output is proprietary wine.

Van der Kamp Champagne Cellars (Kenwood, 1981), is a 5,000-case winery with an emphasis on three well made, flavorful sparkling wines that should not be missed: Brut (Chardonnay and Pinot Noir, light bodied); English Cuvee (Chardonnay and Pinot Noir, yeasty, full bodied); and Midnight Cuvee (100% Pinot Noir, fresh and tasty).

Viansa (Sonoma, 1986), is the 175-acre, 10,000-case winery that replaced the Sam J. Sebastiani Winery brand. In addition to the three basic wines--Chardonnay, Sauvignon Blanc, and Cabernet Sauvignon, future emphasis will lie on new Italian varieties such as Nebbiolo and Sangiovese Grosso, among others. A blend of Cabernet Franc and Cabernet Sauvignon called *Obsidian*, full bodied and well-flavored, is the winery's entrance into the premium market segment.

Vina Vista Winery (Geyserville, 1971), is an obscure, 2,000-case winery that makes full bodied, well structured, yet flavorful and well balanced Chardonnay, Merlot, and Cabernet Sauvignon.

Weinstock Cellars (Geyserville, 1972), is a 60-acre, 25,000-case, kosher winery that makes Chardonnay, Riesling, Gamay Beaujolais, Cabernet Sauvignon, and Zinfandel.

Wellington Vineyards (Glen Ellen, 1989), is an unusual, 25-acre, 5,500-case winery that makes Chardonnay, Merlot, Cabernet Sauvignon, Zinfandel, Meritage-type, Rhone-type, Alicante Bouschet, and Mission (labeled *Criolla*, a rare table wine) wines.

White Oak Vineyards & Winery (Healdsburg, 1981), is a little known, 12,500-case winery that makes excellent Chardonnay, Sauvignon Blanc, Chenin Blanc, Cabernet Sauvignon, and Zinfandel. The reserve Cabernet Sauvignon and Chardonnay can be outstanding.

Wildcat Wines (Sonoma, 1987), is an obscure, but good, 20-acre, 10,000-case winery that makes Chardonnay, Semillon, Gewurztraminer, Merlot, Gamay Beaujolais, and Pinot Noir.

Wild Hog Winery (Healdsburg, 1985), formerly Federico Winery, is a small, trendy, 2,000-case winery specializing in barrel fermented Chardonnay, superb late harvest Riesling, and small quantities of Pinot Noir, offering excellent value.

William Wheeler Winery (Healdsburg, 1970), is a 30-acre, 20,500-case, mountain winery that makes above-average to excellent, elegant, estate bottled Sauvignon Blanc, Chardonnay, Zinfandel, Cabernet Sauvignon (particularly dense, rich, and flavorful), and proprietary wines. Reserve wines are outstanding. The winery will be releasing an early maturing "Rhone-type" wine (Mourvedre, Carignane, Petite Sirah, Gamay, and Zinfandel) labeled *RS Reserve*. In 1989 Paribas Domaines-USA acquired controlling interest.

Williams-Selyem Winery (Healdsburg, 1981), formerly Hacienda Del Rio, is a 2,500-case winery that specializes in outstanding, full bodied, well structured, supple and elegant Pinot Noir and Zinfandel.

Z Moore Winery (Windsor, 1985), is a 5,000-case winery that specializes in dry, barrel fermented Chardonnay, Gewurztraminer (a rare winery that makes at least three different styles), small quantities of Zinfandel, and an interesting blend of Zinfandel and Petite Sirah named *Legacy*, offering good value. Other label: *Quaff*.

Napa Valley

Superlatives have been associated with Napa Valley wines ever since Robert Louis Stevenson declared them "bottled poetry." Indeed, Napa, the valley and county, is regarded by many as the jewel in the crown of the California wine industry, enjoying a reputation as one of the world's greatest wine regions. Politically delineated by Sonoma County on the west, Lake County on the north, Yolo and Solano counties on the east and south, Napa County, widely considered the cynosure of *Vinus Americanus*, represents the largest concentration of premium grapes, and more wineries per square mile than any other place in California and the nation. The more than 33,000 acres (40 percent more than the celebrated Cote d'Or) found in this narrow valley bounded by the Mayacamas and Atlas ranges attract a tourist flow that is second only to Disneyland.

The name Napa dates back to the baptismal records of Mission Dolores (circa 1795), and again in the dairies of Padre Jose Altimira and Jose Sanchez in 1823. It appears in the names of at least two land grants. Two-thirds of Napa (the name means *grisly bear*, *plenty*, *house*, *near home*, *near mother*, or *motherland*, in Indian) County is essentially hilly and mountainous with several lakes and numerous valleys, the largest and most important of which is Napa. Drained by a small river of the same name, the northwest-southeast valley stretches for 45 miles, and is 25 miles broad in the south tapering in width as one proceeds north.

The county contains about 110,000 inhabitants, of whom half live in the county seat--Napa, and another 15,000 in five other important "wine towns:" Yountville, Oakville, Rutherford, St. Helena, and Calistoga, each of which expresses a peculiar ambience. Calistoga, in the extreme north, is the home of Louis Stevenson, thermal springs, live redwood and petrified forests; St. Helena (founded in 1854) is the center of the wine industry, and the site of several historic wineries; Rutherford and Oakville, two crossroads founded with the completion of the railroad in 1868, are associated with the "Rutherford and Oakville Benches," former river terraces supposedly superior in the production of Cabernet Sauvignon; and Yountville, expressing a late nineteenth century atmosphere, is the site of the first grape plantings. On the north end of Yountville lies the grave of George C. Yount, the first U.S. citizen to be ceded a land grant in the Napa Valley, and the valley's first grape grower and winemaker. Dotted with forested uplands, wild mustard throughout the valley, historic buildings, the largest collection of baronial mansions and wineries, Napa, without question, is not only the center of California's wine aristocracy, but its spiritual center as well. It also produces nearly 10 million cases of wine each year, 6.2 million of which are produced from Napa Valley grapes.

While Napa County is immediately appealing by its small, compact size and historical ambience, its character and lifestyle reflect the rise of a wine aristocracy not too dissimilar from the personalities depicted in the television serial "Falcon Crest." While the remaining North Coast counties exhibit rustic frontier elements, and the vast Central Valley agronomical features total anathema to the courtly Gucci set of Napa, the latter is patrician, polished, and very *degage*. Whereas economic diversity is the norm in all surrounding counties, Napa County lives and breathes wine like no other in California. More than 85 percent of the county's total agricultural value is derived from the grape, and its wines, particularly Chardonnay, Cabernet Sauvignon, Merlot, and Zinfandel, are considered the American standard. As a result, Napa County wines exhibit a certain *cachet*, are readily recognizable, and are relatively effortless to market like no other in the nation.

What makes Napa unique is the presence of a good, friable, well drained volcanic soil and a good predictable climate that is characterized by a long, moderately hot interior (warmest near Calistoga) and a cool region near the south (in Carneros). In the northern part, Cabernet Sauvignon, Merlot, and Zinfandel reach the zenith of perfection; the southern part is planted mainly in Pinot Noir and Chardonnay; and in the higher, cooler elevations, premium Cabernet Sauvignon, Merlot, Zinfandel, and Riesling are found in significant concentrations. Despite a predisposition for high alcohol and pH, red wines are known for an element of refinement, excellent color, and luscious flavors. White wines are somewhat less alcoholic and more variable in quality, but the better Chardonnay, Semillon, and Sauvignon Blanc are full bodied, flavorful and substantial on the palate. The major problem of high alcohol content (which when combined with high pH tends to unbalance and mask the natural fruit of the wine) for both red and white wines has largely been overcome, and the wines, as a consequence, have never been better or more consistent. In this connection, it is estimated that the county, with 5 percent of the state's vine acreage, is responsible for about 45 percent of all premium wine produced in the state.

History

Historically known for tomatoes, prunes and walnuts, grape-growing in Napa County has had three specific historic periods. The first began in 1831 with one George Yount, an indefatigable frontiersman, hunter, and soldier, who converted to Catholicism, became a Mexican citizen, and was given the 11,814-acre Caymus Land Grant where he constructed the first wooden structure. Grapes were first planted by Yount in 1838, and later by several other energetic historic figures. Between 1861 and 1898 Napa underwent a viticultural revolution which founded more than 120 wineries, of which the following were the most important: Charles Krug (1861); Alta (1877); St, Clement (1879); Inglenook (1882); Villa Mt. Eden (1884); Jaeger (1884); Far Niente (1884); Quail Ridge (1885); Beaulieu (1885); Freemark Abbey (1886); Trefethen (1886); Chateau Montelena (1886); Ehlers Lane (1886); The Christian Brothers (1887); Spring Mountain (1889); Flora Springs (1890); Spottswoode (1891); Stag's Leap (1893); Nichelini (1896); and Heitz (1898).

Reflecting the melting pot social climate of the state, Germans, Italians, French, and others came from Old World viticultural areas to tempt history with their winemaking skills. Grapes were planted on valley bottom and bench land, and the growers and winemakers came from Europe by the thousands to begin commercial operations in Napa. By 1895 there were 18,000 acres planted in grapes (10,000 more than in 1860), with more than 50 large commercial and 90 smaller "cottage type" wineries. Although not considered significant at the time, Napa overtook Sonoma, Santa Clara, and Livermore in both the production and celebrity of its wines.

Among the more notable personalities that shaped the fortunes of Napa were: Dr. Edward Bale, planted the first commercial all non-Mission vineyard in 1861; Charles Krug, established the first commercial winery in 1861 which closed during Prohibition, but since 1937 has been operated by the Mondavi family; Jacob Schram, a barber from Germany, established a vineyard in 1862; two German brothers founded Beringer in 1876; Gustave Niebaum, a Finish sea captain, established Inglenook Vineyards in 1879; and George Goodman, built a winery in 1886 (now Trefethen). As important as these early pioneers were in establishing the basic fabric of viticulture, grape-growing and winemaking remained fourth-rate economic activities as a succession of phylloxera, and boom and bust economic conditions reduced vine acreage to 3,000 acres by 1900, only to recover to 7,000 by 1920, rise to 10,000 acres in 1923, and decline again to 7,000 acres by 1932.

Begun after Repeal, the second important historic period was the rise of Christian Brothers, Krug, Martini, Inglenook, Beaulieu, and others, all of which were engaged in the production of wine that was significantly better than innocuous Central Valley blends. More than two dozen pre-Prohibition wineries were reopened, and premium grape varieties began to be planted (there were fewer than 150 acres of Cabernet Sauvignon and only 14 acres of Chardonnay in 1933). Although acreage had remained rather stable during the 1933-1965 period (11,500 acres), the seeds for supremacy had been firmly established. Napa, in fact, was the first viticultural area in 1935 to form a Vintners and Growers Association, and soon after it emerged as the first premium wine producing center of the nation, a circumstance aided by Beringer's introduction of winery tours, a phenomenon that has since grown to a point where the winery accommodates more than 350,000 visitors annually. Winery tourism has since become a major economic activity for the entire valley as reflected by two significant statistics: the total tourist population spends at least $100 million for lodging and food, and $70 million in wine sales. As important as tourism has become, there is increasing concern that the valley is approaching saturation levels with related activities and housing subdivisions, hence restrictive zoning legislation has been introduced.

A combination of rising per capita income in the greater San Francisco metropolitan region, urbanization, and favorable tax incentives, along with many wealthy businessmen, entertainment celebrities, politicians, doctors, lawyers, engineers, playboys, and frustrated ego's begin the third period. The founding of Stony Hill in 1952 marks the beginning of the modern "boutique winery" phenomenon, a base building time period of nearly 20 years when inferior grape varieties were replaced by premium grapes and stainless steel replaced redwood fermenters. Consequently, the past two decades have been a veritable boom period for Napa attracting much attention, as illustrated by the accompanying figures.

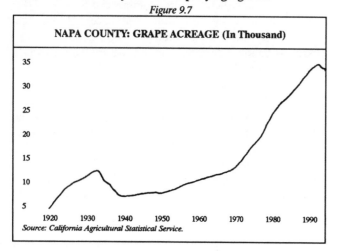

Figure 9.7

NAPA COUNTY: GRAPE ACREAGE (In Thousand)

Source: California Agricultural Statistical Service.

The growth in the number of wineries during the past generation (from 29 to 256) has been nothing but incredible, and despite the "soft" economic climate of the industry over the past six years, the construction of new wineries is likely to continue, though at a slower pace than years past. During this period, although less than 9 per-

cent of the county's 600 square miles are devoted to grape vines, acreage nearly tripled, grape production increased fivefold, and the value of grape output jumped 800 percent. Indeed, the success of the boutique phase may lead to a fourth evolutionary phase called the "foreign period" as evidenced by the insertion of foreign financial involvement both in Napa and Sonoma, as well as other areas in the country. At least six major French Champagne firms have established wineries, and a number of Spanish, Swiss, German, and Italian individuals and firms have also entered the ranks of the Napa aristocracy. The most "notable" of the new arrivals, the Japanese (unusual due to the lack of a historic wine tradition) have acquired at least six Napa wineries. In all, nearly 40 percent of Napa acreage is owned or controlled by non-American interests.

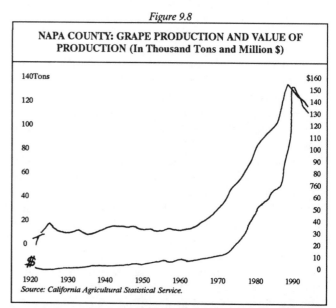

Figure 9.8

NAPA COUNTY: GRAPE PRODUCTION AND VALUE OF PRODUCTION (In Thousand Tons and Million $)

Source: California Agricultural Statistical Service.

Interestingly, Mr. Charles L. Sullivan, the wine historian, reports that in 1890, 49 percent of all wineries were operated by foreigners (there were 43 German winery operators). And Napa Valley was not alone. He reports that there were 23 French winery owners in the Santa Clara Valley, and that 52 percent of all wineries in Alameda County, and 50 percent of all wineries in Santa Cruz County were also owned by non-Americans. Nevertheless, during the 130 years of winemaking history, several wineries have disappeared due to depression, disease, mismanagement, and Prohibition. These "ghost" wineries dot the valley and offer an interesting lesson in the evolution and maturity of the industry. Among the most notable are: the Sciaroni Winery (circa 1880, south of St, Helena, is now a restaurant); Crane-Ramos Sherry Factory (1877, in St. Helena, is now an architects office); the Occidental Wine Cellar (1878, along the Silverado Trail, was a three-story gravity flow winery); and Groezinger Wine Cellars (1870, in Yountville, was one of the largest gravity-flow wineries ever established).

Interestingly, the agricultural history of the county was, until the 1890s, primarily grazing and wheat. The fortunes of the grape and wine market, reflecting economic business cycles, drought, and phylloxera outbreaks, was never certain, and small growers planted prunes and nut trees as a hedge for uncertain times. But with the growth of wine production and consumption since 1960, the poultry segment has largely disappeared, the beef and walnut industries have remained flat, and prunes have declined from a value of $2.5 million in 1950 to nearly zero in 1988. Grape-growing, on the other hand, has risen as sharply as prune production has declined: from a value of $2 million in 1950 to more than $153 million in 1989. Grape tonnage for the same period rose from 24,241 to more than 132,000, and since 1983 grape production has surpassed all other agricultural commodities in value. The value of wine increased from $54 million in 1965 to $578 million in 1986. More significantly, the economic contribution of the wine industry as percent of county total increased from 8.2 percent to 25.7 percent in 1991. The county's reputation rests on the fact that it was the first major premium wine producing region to emerge in California after Prohibition, and although it is warmer, smaller, and contains a narrower range of soils and microclimates than Sonoma, Mendocino and Lake counties, the range of wines made and the quality output are surprisingly high. The county is home to nearly one-third of the state's total number of wineries, 10 percent of all wine grape acreage, 5 percent of the state's wine output, and more than 25 percent of wine value. Of the 256 wineries, perhaps 50 rank among the finest in the nation and the world, particularly in the production of Chardonnay, Sauvignon Blanc, Petit Verdot, Cabernet Sauvignon, Merlot, and Zinfandel. This dedication to excellence is the result of an unusually high concentration of financial, labor, and technical resources. Preeminence is challenged only by Sonoma County and by scattered, newly established vineyards and wineries in the central and southern coastal areas, along with several wineries in the Willamette area and in the Columbia section of Washington.

Still, Napa is about to face a number of serious wine threatening issues in the near future: (1) nearly the entire fertile valley is now planted or subject to urban encroachment as more than 2.5 million tourists visit each year (or about 70,000 a week, most of whom come during the warmest seven months of the year); (2) vineyard expansion in the future can only occur in the more expensive, mountainous areas of the valley (it is estimated that fewer than 10,000 potential vine acres remain); (3) there is increasing competition from Sonoma County, especially in the production of white wines; (4) all of the above, in combination, have helped escalate wine grape land values

from $8,000 an acre in 1970 to an estimated $65,000 an acre in 1990, making Napa the most valuable piece of agricultural real estate in the nation. With a fixed number of vine acres in the county, it is becoming increasingly clear that grape prices will continue to rise as demand intensifies. Given the fact that grape prices have escalated during the past 20 years, and in particular since 1984, the issue of grape acreage is especially troublesome to wineries faced with a dwindling supply of premium grapes.

A portion of the northern section of Napa just south of Calistoga.
Baxevanis

Consequently, wineries have recently scrambled to purchase remaining vineland in Carneros and in hillside locations in order to control their grape sources. The shortage of premium vineland, however, is more limited if one looks at the pattern of present ownership. Approximately seven large wineries own or control about 35 percent of the county's acreage (Robert Mondavi, Beaulieu, Beringer, The Christian Brothers, Charles Krug, and Domaine Chandon, all own more than 1,000 acres each, and produce about 45 percent of all Napa wine), and another 30 own or control another quarter. As wineries today own twice as much vineland as they did in 1979, it is estimated that less than 20 percent of the county's vineland remains in the hands of independent growers. As the number of wineries grew from fewer than forty twenty years ago to more than 200 in 1989, the percentage of vineland owned by wineries has increased proportionally, a movement that is not expected to be reversed in the near future. Rising land costs and grape prices have also forced many growers, who hitherto sold grapes, to establish wineries or labels and sell wine rather than grapes, further reducing the "spot" grape market for wineries with insufficient grape supplies. As wineries come to control premium grape producing sites, they will be better able to control prices, and land poor wineries will find it increasingly difficult to control quality and prices from vintage to vintage. As the reputation of Napa wines increases and demand rises, the competition for wineries to guarantee a supply of quality grapes has risen to the point that a vicious cycle of rising grape prices, wine prices, and ultimately higher land values has been generated beyond reason.

> ### NAPA VALLEY: ONE-ACRE VINEYARD COSTS IN 1883
>
> | | |
> |---|---|
> | Preparing land | $5.00 |
> | 600 Riparia vines | $25.00 |
> | Marking plants | $5.00 |
> | Cultivation--1st year | $10.00 |
> | Cultivation--2nd year | $10.00 |
> | Grafting | $5.00 |
> | Staking and tieing | $10.00 |
> | Cultivation and pruning--3rd year | $20.00 |
> | Cultivation and pruning--4th year | $20.00 |
> | Total | $100.00 |
>
> *Source: Napa Valley Vintners Association, Summer, 1988, Newsletter.*
> Nineteen eighty-nine per acre estimates by the University of California Cooperative Extension are $6,087 for the first year; $7,892 for the second year' $9,555 for the third year; and $11,539 for the fourth year.

There is concern that the valley will lose its identity and charm if winery and non-agricultural developments continue unabated. As a result, there is an active movement to restrict non-agricultural land use patterns. The Napa agricultural preserve and watershed land covers 90 percent of the county. New zones for wineries, called "combining districts" for winery and agricultural uses, are being investigated, and the recently passed Williamson Act stipulates that taxes on agricultural land be based on the income derived from it. Although there would be no outright restriction to new winery construction, new wineries would have to undergo a lengthy review process prior to construction, and "negociant" concerns would definitely be excluded. The latter proposal would require all new wineries to use at least 75 percent Napa grapes (at present, anyone can exploit the name by establishing a makeshift winery using non-Napa grapes), and prohibit negociant firms from having large scale tasting rooms on busy highways. Regulations have also established a 10-acre minimum size for new wineries, and restrict buildings, ponds, and roads to 25 percent of total winery acreage. Moreover, the minimum acreage for a house is 40 acres, and according to new zoning regulations, "agricultural preserve" land must be used for crushing and processing Napa County grapes only. While the litany of additional restrictions continues, the objective of the proposals is to protect agricultural land and to curtail and control tourist volume and patterns of movement. One of the thorniest issues concerns the use of the "mitigating measures" discretion by county planners.

Proponents for unrestricted growth maintain that it is the existing, large wineries that are importing non-Napa Valley grapes/must/wine, and that the new regulations would be ineffective except to keep new people from joining the existing ones. Under grandfather clauses, existing wineries could continue to operate without the above mentioned restrictions, and those wishing to build wineries cite a strong element of bias in favor of the larger wineries (there are about 400 independent grape growers without a winery in the county). Proposed restrictive legislation not withstanding, land speculation, especially in the hilly and mountainous regions flanking the valley and in the Carneros district, is at fever pitch, with prices for planted vineland rising to levels beyond $65,000 the acre.

County planning efforts to restrict development is not limited to the valley, but to the "mountainous" portion of the county as well on the theory that a conservation program is necessary to control erosion, a hazard, it is maintained, caused in part by the grading practices of growers and developers. It is proposed that vineyards on a hill with a slope of 5 to 30 percent would require a county-approved erosion control plan, and anything above 30 percent would require a strict review. Grading on slopes greater than 50 percent would be prohibited.

Another interesting recent development is the subtle but formidable alteration in the geography of wineries and vineland. Historically, wineries and vineyards were located along and west of US 29, but the tendency in recent years is for new wineries to be founded along the Silverado Trail, an old Indian trail along the eastern portion of the valley; in hilly and mountainous areas defining the valley; and in valleys (hitherto unplanted) that are not part of the Napa River drainage area. Of the 219 wineries listed in this book, 155 are located on or along the margins on the valley floor, the rest are sited on upland locations, in interior valleys, and in the newly established Carneros district. Prior to 1952, all but one winery were sited entirely within the valley, and proximate to US 29.

150 YEARS OF NAPA VALLEY GRAPE GROWING

1838: George Yount, the legendary explorer and frontiersman, planted the first vineyard in the Napa Valley on his ranch near what is today the town of Yountville.

1844: Yount's annual production of wine is approximately 200 gallons.

1846: William Wolfskill, a trapper from Tennessee who settled in the Napa Valley, made 2,800 gallons of wine this vintage. Grapes from his vineyards were the first northern California grapes to be sold on the San Francisco market. He also introduced commercial grape-growing and became one of the leading viticulturalists in southern California.

1852: William and Simpson Thompson plant several newly imported wine grape varieties--the first other than Mission grapes in the valley--on their Suscol land grant south of Napa City. They were also the first to introduce irrigation to grape-growing.

1856: The first stone wine cellar in Napa County was built by vintner John Patchett. 1859 is an alternative date.

1857: The first Napa wine transported outside the county's borders was shipped this year. The shipment consisted of 6 casks and 600 bottles.

1859: Sam Brannan, California's first millionaire, founded the city of Calistoga. Joseph Osborne wins recognition for his Oak Knoll vineyard.

1860: Charles Krug crushed grapes with a press, the first used in Napa County. The following year, he founded a winery, and regarded himself as the county's first commercial winemaker.

1863: The Glass Works, California's first glass manufacturing plant, made the first wine bottle in the state on June 16. The San Francisco plant employed 20 glassblowers and 45 other full time workers.

1865: Dr. George Crane's Napa Wines, made from Vinifera cuttings acquired from Agoston Haraszthy, are well received in Europe.

1867: A telegraph line from St. Helena to Calistoga was completed.

1870: Grape culture in California employed more labor than any other branch of farming. In this vintage, Napa Valley's 139 wineries produced 297,000 gallons of wine and 4,000 gallons of brandy.

1870-1880: Wine production doubles, ranking third after Sonoma and Los Angeles counties. In 1881 Napa County became the leading producer of wine in the state.

1875: A case of Napa Valley wine sold for approximately $2.50. The cost of shipping a case of wine overland from San Francisco to Chicago was $4.50.

1876: Founding of Beringer Vineyards.

1879: Founding of Inglenook Winery.

1880-1897: Nearly 80 percent of the viticultural work force was Chinese.

1880: By an act of the state legislature, the University of California, Berkeley, under the auspices of Professor E.W. Hilgard, began research and instruction in viticulture and enology.

1888: The Napa Valley, with an annual production of 5 million gallons (from 14,031 acres of wine grapes, and 140 wine cellars), accounted for more than 25 percent of the state's wine output.

1889: Twenty Napa County wines, out of 34 California wines entered in the World Fair in Paris, win awards. The 2 million gallon Greystone Winery facility is constructed, considered to be at that time the largest in the world. Approximately 140 wineries operating.

1893-1898: 15,000 out of 18,000 vine acres are lost to phylloxera, a major economic loss.

1906: The Great Earthquake hits California. In the Napa Valley more than 100,000 gallons of wine were lost from splintered tanks.

1920: The Volstead Act was passed, and the production, sale, or transportation of alcoholic beverages in the U.S. was prohibited by law. More than 700 California wineries, 120 of them in the Napa Valley, were affected. During the first three years of Prohibition, acreage increased and grape prices rose dramatically from an average of $16 the ton during the two preceding decades to $82 the ton in 1921, and as high as $125 by 1923. Vineland prices rose accordingly from less than $200 the acre to $2,500 in 1923.

1933: Prohibition was repealed and by 1934 there were 380 wineries in California. In the Napa Valley few wineries survived Prohibition, and despite the momentary rise of vine acreage and grape prices in the early 1920s due to the demands of home winemakers, vine acreage and grape prices declined to new low levels with Repeal (below $15 the ton by 1933).

1945: The Napa Valley wine industry was revitalized. More than 6 million gallons of table wine were produced by 47 bonded wineries. Grape prices per ton reached approximately $100.

1956: Helicopters were used for the first time in the Napa Valley to apply sulphur to vineyards.

1960: Twenty five wineries were functioning in the Napa Valley. Of these only 12 made enough wine to sell outside Napa County.

1969: In the Napa Valley winemaking became the principal industry and wine grapes the top valued agricultural crop. Average grape price was $184 the ton.

1976: Napa Valley wines stepped into the international spotlight when a few of them scored very well in a highly publicized blind tasting in Paris which included both California and French wines.

1981: The first Napa Valley Wine Auction was held and $140,000 was raised for two local health facilities. Napa Valley became the first region in California to become an approved viticultural area.

1990: Napa Valley Vintners Association promulgates the Winery Definition Ordinance, designed to protect the region's agricultural identity.

1992: Napa Valley has approximately 34,000 acres and 241 bonded wineries; Napa Valley celebrates the 154th anniversary of the planting of the first vineyard in Napa; mature planted wine grape acreage is sold for $65,000; quality unplanted acreage is sold for $50,000; price of Chardonnay grapes per ton exceeds $1,500. Today, Napa has more wineries than the state did in 1960.

Source: partially taken from The Napa Valley Vintners Association, Summer, 1988, Newsletter.

Climate, Soils and Grapes

Topography and climate are closely related in Napa County. Encircled by hills and mountains on the west, north and east, Napa County is marginally warmer than Sonoma County, its neighbor to the west. Its only opening to maritime influences occurs in the southern portion enabling the entrance of sea breezes, summer fog, and cyclonic storm activity in winter. Local relief and distance from San Pablo Bay spawn the production of distinct microclimatic regions of considerable significance to grape-growing. In general, summer temperatures increase and winter temperatures decrease with distance from San Pablo Bay. The average summer temperature in the Carneros district is 76F, a comforting 16F cooler than Calistoga in the northern portion of Napa Valley. While the highest temperature recorded in the city of Napa is 110F, it was 115F at St, Helena, and 117F in Calistoga. Similarly, the lowest recorded temperature in the city of Napa was 17F, 11F in St. Helena, and 10F in Calistoga.

Winter storm activity approaches Napa from the southwest producing heavier precipitation levels along the western side and northern portion of the valley. Orographic influences are considerable as the city of Napa receives 22 inches of rainfall, Calistoga 36 inches, and Mt. St. Helena 60 inches. Reflecting these north-south and topographic differences, Napa County exhibits six distinct climatic patterns (ranging between Region I and III), and many small individual microclimates in the surrounding uplands: the cool Carneros area; the moderate central region; the warm to hot northern portion; the west-facing mountains and east-facing mountains; and the numerous valleys not drained by the Napa River--all tend to produce rather distinct, and to knowledgeable local winemakers (it is alleged) easily identifiable wines.

Known as Los Carneros, the southern coastal area located adjacent to San Pablo Bay is influenced by maritime air which modifies both summer and winter temperatures. The coolest region in Napa, this low lying, wind-swept, fog-laden region is classified as Region I, and is mainly planted in Chardonnay, Pinot Noir, and, in selected areas, Merlot. Between St. Helena and Yountville, the central portion, with less fog and marine air, is warmer and falls into Region II. Conforming to soil, air drainage, and exposure, planted acreage is mainly in white grapes, with Cabernet and Merlot in selected sites. This central region is most celebrated for the Rutherford Bench, consisting of many notable vineyards (such as Martha's Vineyard), and several well regarded wineries. A former terrace of the Napa River, it has unusually deep, friable soil producing excellent red wines with the characteristic Eucalyptus flavor and aroma. The area has produced an enviable reputation for rather long lived, supple, yet firm, well scented and flavored Cabernet Sauvignon and Merlot.

Barely a mile wide, the valley's extreme northern portion, extending as far as the base of Mt. St. Helena, is a heat trap classified as Region III, and planted in Cabernet Sauvignon and Zinfandel, the two preferred varieties due to uniform hot weather conditions. Since this northern region is so much warmer, it is able to produce excellent red wine from several above-average properties such as Long Vineyards, La Jota, and others. The western hillsides and upper mountainous regions of the Mayacamas are studded with such admirable wineries as: Mayacamas Vineyards, Vose Vineyards, The Hess Collection, and many more. The fourth and fifth climatic zones are the upland areas that ring the valley--Spring Mountain and Mount Veeder on the west, and Howell Mountain, Pritchard Hill and Atlas Peak on the eastern portion of the valley. This area exhibits a climatic pattern of cooler temperatures due to higher elevation, and the absence of a fog layer which lengthens the growing season by several weeks. Due to higher and irregular terrain, air drainage is excellent, minimizing frost (unlike valley bottom sites), while diurnal temperatures are noted for the widest fluctuations. The sixth climatic zone is a collection of minor upland and interior valleys outside the immediate range of the Napa River drainage system, such as Wooden, Browns, Gordon, Foss, Pope, Chiles, and Wild Horse.

Figure 9.9

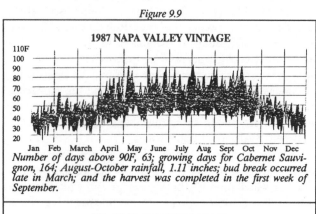

Number of days above 90F, 63; growing days for Cabernet Sauvignon, 164; August-October rainfall, 1.11 inches; bud break occurred late in March; and the harvest was completed in the first week of September.

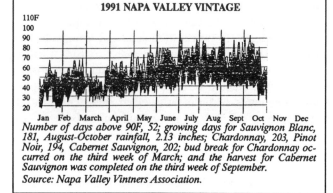

Number of days above 90F, 52; growing days for Sauvignon Blanc, 181, August-October rainfall, 2.13 inches; Chardonnay, 203, Pinot Noir, 194, Cabernet Sauvignon, 202; bud break for Chardonnay occurred on the third week of March; and the harvest for Cabernet Sauvignon was completed on the third week of September.
Source: Napa Valley Vintners Association.

Further to the above 1987 and 1991 vintages, additional climatic variations exist as evidenced by the 1980, 1981, and 1984 vintages--thus dispelling a commonly assumed myth that Napa vintages are pretty much the same every year. While the 1980 growing season began with be-

low normal temperatures, it finished hot and produced highly concentrated Cabernet Sauvignon wines; 1981, hot throughout and one of the earliest harvests on record, produced lighter, less intense, more raisiny wines; the 1984 vintage, even earlier and most unusual due to heavy December precipitation, produced a totally different style of Cabernet Sauvignon. Over the past fourteen years, the harvest season in Napa has varied between 36 to 53 days, stretching from the middle of August in 1984 to the end of November in 1977. Moreover, while the normal sequence of grape ripening is Chardonnay, Sauvignon Blanc, Chenin Blanc, and Cabernet Sauvignon, vintage variations have a tendency to alter this pattern.

Although soils are geologically complex (about two dozen distinct types are recognized), they consist of three major groups for easy analysis: valley bottom, bench (former river bottom), and mountain. Valley bottom soils, poorly drained and rich in organic and mineral matter, produce the highest yields. Benchland soils, adjacent to the valley, are remnants of the receding Napa River. Containing considerable amounts of cobblestone, they are gently sloping and well drained, producing big, concentrated, well colored and flavored/scented wines. These areas, where the more moderate temperatures prolong the growing season, are usually located above the level of temperature inversions, and are subject to late afternoon breezes. Some of the finest Napa wines, however, are made from skeletal, mountain soils located on both sides of the valley, each producing excellent, but totally different wines. These upland soils, in general, have developed under heavier precipitation than have the alluvial and benchland soils. Therefore, forests are more inclined to be present in the upland and mountainous sections, thus making the chemical soil composition different. Depending on location, geologic parent material is highly variegated and consists of volcanic, metamorphic and sedimentary rocks, often in bands of various thickness.

Soils west of the Napa River to the highest elevations of the Mayacamas are derived from dark sedimentary material, usually deep, fertile, and with a high water holding capability. These moist soils support a dense forest of coniferous vegetation, and the vines exhibit exceptional vigor. In comparison to valley bottom sites, vine roots have to fight for moisture in the stony mountainsides, and are sufficiently stressed to develop intense color, scent and flavor. East of the Napa River, the geology of the Vaca Range is the product of recent volcanic activity, and the soils tend to be coarse, low in fertility and water retention. Here, rock outcroppings are common, and the hillsides, sparsely covered with scrub oak, brush and grass, stress the vines thus producing lower yields and less dense leaf canopies. Late maturing varieties, such as Cabernet Sauvignon, Merlot, and Chardonnay, dominate acreage and the grapes possess higher sugar levels and phenolics, lower pH, darker color in red grapes, and greater yellow and green pigmentation in white grapes. All of the foregoing combine to produce well scented, delicate, elegant, and marvelously flavored wines.

Napa County has 33,194 acres of grapes (second only to Sonoma north of San Joaquin), and all except one are planted in wine grapes. While the county has generated a reputation for red wines, it is surprising to note that 16,609 acres, or 53 percent of the planted acreage is in white grapes, and that the county ranks sixth in white wine grapes after Madera, Fresno, Kern, Merced, and Sonoma. The proclivity to produce white grapes is a sharp and recent departure from historic patterns, because as recently as 1966 there were 3,000 more red grape acres than white. White grapes during this period increased from 4,139 acres to 16,609, while red grapes increased from 7,242 to 14,739 acres. This color and variety mix reflects the "second phase" of the planting cycle, and it is expected that the decade of the 1990s will emphasize a larger percentage of Bordeaux-type vines, particularly Petit Verdot, Malbec, and Cabernet Franc.

To The Hon. Board of Supervisors of Napa County.

Gentlemen:

At this time we are able to report the movement of grapes from this county. The shipments for the season totaled 600 carloads. Of this amount 460 carloads went to the eastern markets and 140 went to the bay district. The total tonnage shipped was approximately 8,500 tons. We estimate that 1,500 tons were crushed locally. The total crop production was about one fourth of normal. The money value of the Napa County crop figured on an average price of about $80 per ton was in excess of three quarters of a million dollars. The quality of the grapes was excellent this year. The State Standardization Laws require a sugar content of 17% before shipment and we found only one carload which tested as low as 17%, all other cars went above 20% and the average sugar test was near 23%. Weather conditions were favorable and mold and rot were in evidence to only a slight extent. The high prices have stimulated production and the prospects are good for perhaps a thousand additional acres this coming planting season.

Respectfully,
W.D. Butler,
Commissioner, Court House, Napa
November 1, 1921

Over the past 20 years red grape varieties have exhibited a more stable pattern in relationship to each other and acreage increase than white grapes. Three varieties dominate acreage with 75 percent of total red grape acreage--Cabernet Sauvignon, Pinot Noir, and Zinfandel, which increased by only 3,000 acres, or about half of new Chardonnay acreage. These are followed by Merlot, Petite Sirah, Gamay, Cabernet Franc, and Gamay Beaujolais. It is important to note the stability of Zinfandel as percent of total red grape acreage, the demise of such low quality grapes as Alicante Bouschet, Early Burgundy, Mondeuse, Carignane, Ruby Cabernet, Pinot St. George, etc., and the ascendency of Cabernet Sauvignon, Pinot

Noir, and Merlot. Equally significant is the fact that Napa is the price leader for premium grapes, producing the most expensive Chardonnay, Semillon, Merlot, Cabernet Sauvignon, Petit Verdot, and Cabernet Franc in the state. Although there is a tendency to better match microclimate and soils with specific varieties, few discernable patterns are to be found other than to say that Pinot Noir, Chardonnay, Riesling, and Gewurztraminer are mainly planted in the cool Carneros and upland elevations; Cabernet Sauvignon and Merlot show a concentration around St. Helena, Rutherford, and selected benchland and mountain sites; and Zinfandel, Barbera, Petite Sirah, and Napa Gamay are planted in the hotter, northern Calistoga area.

With 43 percent of total planted acreage, four white grape varieties dominate 90 percent of all white grape acreage. Chardonnay leads the list with 9,639 acres, or 29 percent of the planted area, an increase of more than 8,100 acres during the 1966-1972 period. This is followed by Sauvignon Blanc with an increase of 2,500 acres, and Chenin Blanc with an increase of 1,000 acres. Less than 5 percent of the planted white acreage is composed of Semillon, Colombard, Gewurztraminer, and another dozen minor grape varieties constitute the remaining 5 percent. The second most popular white grape, Sauvignon Blanc, will continue to grow in prominence due to its lower production cost and more versatile character. The hitherto unimportant and underrated Semillon produces round, rich, harmonious, fat wines, and, when expertly made, may in the future produce wines superior to Sauvignon Blanc. Many local experts maintain that despite public unfamiliarity, its acreage is expected to grow beyond 1,000 acres, and may even surpass Chenin Blanc over the next 30 years. Another obscure white variety with promise is Pinot Blanc (currently a hot item in the production of sparkling wine) which has become the second most expensive variety in the county. Also popular is the obscure Viognier. Although difficult to grow (there are fewer than fifteen acres) and pronounce, it has the capacity to produce full bodied, flavorful, complex wine, and appears to do particularly well in Napa County. It is interesting to note the spectacular rise of quality white varietals (such as Chardonnay and Sauvignon Blanc), and the demise of such grapes as Colombard, Burger, Golden Chasselas, Franken Riesling, Sauvignon Vert, Grey Riesling, and Green Hungarian, all within the span of less than 20 years.

While nearly 600 more acres are planted in Chardonnay, it is Cabernet Sauvignon that has an established track record in the Napa Valley, and remains the standard for the rest of the state and nation. Historically made as a 100 percent varietal, the wine is now blended with Merlot and Cabernet Franc to give it more subtleness, finesse, and roundness. It is only a matter of time before Napa Valley winemakers will be producing and adding its ultimate partner--Petit Verdot, the quintessential variety necessary in imparting immeasurable depth, backbone, and essence. The quality of Cabernet Sauvignon varies dramatically with site and exposure: the higher, hilly elevations being far superior to the more fertile valley floor. Over the past fifteen years (with the virtual elimination of open redwood fermenters and/or redwood barrels), Cabernet Sauvignon has evolved from high alcohol, tannin rich, overly oaked monsters to soft, rich, elegant, and refined wines. More than 125 wineries, more than any other county, produce Cabernet Sauvignon. Above-average to outstanding vintages over the past 45 years have been: 1940, 1942, 1946, 1947, 1949, 1951, 1958, 1960, 1964, 1968, 1970, 1974, 1978, 1979, 1980, 1984, 1985, 1986, 1987, 1988, 1990, and 1991. In recent years, the proclivity for Napa Valley Cabernet Sauvignon to escalate in value has prompted several investment schemes to buy quality wine (in outstanding vintages), and cellar it for resale at a handsome profit within a six to ten year period.

Table 9.5

PRINCIPAL WINE GRAPE VARIETIES IN NAPA					
Variety	1966	1972	1979	1990	Percent
Chardonnay	139	1,019	3,717	9,639	29.0
Sauvignon Blanc	293	466		2,873	8.7
Chenin Blanc	175	973	1,997	1,261	3.8
Riesling	299	761	1,444	442	1.3
Semillon	243	212		345	1.0
Pinot Blanc	214		147		
Gewurztraminer	56	216	505	119	
Muscat Blanc		11		79	
Colombard	621	692	487	60	
Grey Riesling	135	275		55	
Sylvaner	52	212			
Viognier				16	
Sauvignon Vert	232	411		14	
Palomino	6	189		12	
Cabernet Sauvignon	682	3,317	5,418	9,131	27.5
Pinot Noir	313	1,445	2,541	2,719	8.2
Merlot	9	239	729	2,148	6.5
Zinfandel	897	832	2,126	1,993	6.0
Napa Gamay	819	838	1,175	357	1.1
Petite Sirah	1,651	1,259	868	452	1.4
Cabernet Franc			636		
Gamay Beaujolais	59	461	489	66	
Petit Verdot			55		
Carignane	731	618	231	36	
Malbec			33		
Syrah			25		
Other			2,720	2,407	
Total	11,739		25,353	33,194	
Total White			8,847	15,876	
Total Red			16,516	18,318	
Source: California Agricultural Statistics Service.					

Eucalyptus aroma and flavor, pronounced in the coolest portions of the valley and particularly in Rutherford Bench vineyards (most notably Heitz, Beaulieu, and Mondavi), make this Cabernet Sauvignon distinctive from the more austere versions in Sonoma. Because the flavor and aroma of Eucalyptus does not appreciably diminish with time, this type of Cabernet Sauvignon is not to everyone's liking. Among white varieties, Chardonnay dominates acreage, monopolizes press releases, and captivates the public's attention. Made in a variety of styles, it has an even greater range in price. At the moment, growers cannot produce enough, winemakers cannot make enough, and consumers cannot drink it fast enough. In the coming years, styles will become more definitive, and due to overplanting prices should stabilize or even decline.

Other red grape varieties with above-average reputations are: Merlot (newer plantings are marred by a grassy and herbaceous flavor, but as the vines mature, this grape variety will be producing excellent wine); Zinfandel (a good deal of the acreage is at least 40 years old producing concentrated, full to medium bodied wine that offers outstanding value); Petite Sirah (excellent value due to the fact that the wine is not currently in fashion); and Petit Verdot, Malbec, and Cabernet Franc (combined acreage is said to be less than 450 acres, but will certainly increase over the next 20 years).

The foregoing has become an appealing and provocative topic of conversation among American wine aficionados, especially in the fascination of comparing the climatic elements between Bordeaux, Burgundy, and coastal California. In this regard, it is important to note that Napa has significantly lower winter temperatures, higher spring temperatures, and a much longer growing season. Most significant, Napa has dramatically lower precipitation patterns in the critical periods of flowering and final grape maturity. In this regard, Napa has one-fifth the rainfall of Burgundy, and one-sixth the rainfall of Bordeaux during August-October. Higher temperatures, a longer growing season, a lower incidence of inclement weather, and lower precipitation during the harvest are substantial and meaningful differences that should not go unnoticed.

In an effort to maintain the Napa Valley in the forefront of the state's viticultural premium industry, The Napa County Resource Conservation District recently purchased a 19-acre, former dairy property in the Carneros region. The goal is to convert the property into an experimental vineyard emphasizing "low input sustainable agriculture," or an attempt to use the absolute minimum of chemicals, physical structures, or special training methods.

Approved Viticultural Areas

Napa County contains eight ava's: *Napa Valley (1983), Howell Mountain (1984), Los Carneros (1983), The Stags Leap District (1989), Wild Horse Valley (1988), Mt. Veeder (1990), Spring Mountain (1992),* and *Atlas Peak (1992).* The first consists of the valley and associated foothills, as well as upland areas not entirely in the drainage of the Napa River. The only area of exclusion within the county of Napa is the area northeast of Putah Creek and Lake Berryessa in which there are neither vineyards nor wineries. The *ava* contains all the county's vineyards and wineries, more than 31,000 acres, four major soil series, and a Region I through III climate. As it contains areas to the east and north of Mt. Veeder, the actual boundaries are not limited by the physical dimensions of the Napa River drainage area. In the final analysis, due to pressure from growers in the northern and eastern outlying areas of Napa County, BATF included every grower in the "Napa Valley" appellation. The *Carneros ava*, an important Region I viticultural area described in the preceding section, lies partly in Napa County, and is planted mostly in Chardonnay and Pinot Noir.

Howell Mountain (1984), an enclave of the Napa Valley *ava*, is forested and too steep and rocky for extensive vineyard development. Out of a total of 14,080 acres, more than 500 are planted in vines, the best of which are Cabernet Sauvignon and Zinfandel. Because it often lies above the valley's fog layer (a primary factor in delimiting *ava* boundaries), it is sunnier and warmer during the summer, and colder in winter. Equally important is the presence of a porous, volcanic (droughty) soil providing excellent root penetration. Significantly, this area (as well as others extending south to the southern portion of the Stags Leap *ava*) contains major outcrops of serpentine rock. When well weathered, this rock produces an excellent soil ideal for the production of outstanding red wine. The *ava* receives 50 percent more rain than valley vineyards, and is rarely threatened by frost. Because of significant climatic, soil, and altitudinal differences, Howell Mountain and other "mountain" regions have generated a reputation for quality grape production and the highest grape prices in the county. Lamborn Family Vineyards, Dunn Vineyards, Summit Lake Vineyards, Woltner Estates, and La Jota are located in this prestigious *ava*.

The *Wild Horse Valley ava*, 5 miles east of the city of Napa, is located on hilly terrain between Napa County, and Solano County's Green Valley *ava*. The delimited area encompasses a topographically irregular valley approximately 5.3 miles long and 1.6 miles wide, contains 3,300 acres, three wineries, and fewer than 200 vine acres. What makes this valley different from others to the west is its proximity to the cooler breezes emanating from Suisun Bay. Containing rocky, significantly different volcanic soils from those found in Napa valleys, and influenced by a persistent wind, Wild Horse Valley is very similar to the Green Valley, and the Suisun Valley *ava's*, approximately 2.5 miles eastward. In all cases, they have a lower annual temperature than the Calistoga region of Napa County. The *ava* takes its name from the fact that wild horses used to roam free in this grass dominated, windy region. The first vineyard (50 acres) was established by one Joseph Vorbe in 1881.

The *Stags Leap District*, lying east of the Napa River and 5 miles north of the city of Napa along the Silverado Trail, is a region dominated by an imposing 1,500-foot basalt bluff, flanked on three sides by hills which open to the southwest. Its topography and exposure create a unique microclimate as the dark volcanic rock absorbs heat during daylight hours causing a marked convection current with the cooling breezes from San Pablo Bay. As a result, some of Stags Leap is markedly hotter earlier in the day and cooler at night than the rest of Stags Leap and the rest of the valley, with the Carneros area an exception. In sharp contrast to the deeper and richer soils located along the low lying areas on both sides of the Napa River, soils consist of bale loam, a coarse medium of low water holding capacity; however on the steeper hillsides is a stony mixture of colluvial volcanic debris derived from the Vaca Range, the latter, particularly good as it is well drained and low yielding.

The area supports 1,500 planted acres (out of 2,700 possible acres) and about seventeen wineries, all of which enjoy a good reputation for the production of quality Cabernet Sauvignon. The latter is known for soft, supple, low tannin libations with delicacy, elegance, and a pronounced cherry flavor (features that have prompted local winemakers to call Stags Leap the "Margaux of California"). In recent years, equally superb Merlot--big, round, dark, fleshy, yet refined and delicate, has also been produced. Cabernet Franc and Petit Verdot are two other grape varieties that will experience an increase in acreage in the coming decades. The controversy with the Stags Leap District *ava* lies not with quality considerations but with the final delineation of boundary lines, and, as a consequence, the appellation petition was delayed for two years. The final ruling places the northern limits as far north as the Yountville Cross Road, thus adding in the process an additional 150 vine acres. Nevertheless, the appellation name means more than most as it includes more than ten excellent to outstanding wineries.

Mt. Veeder is an irregular area (often called "Napa Redwoods") lying at the base of the eastern slopes of the Mayacamas Mountains that has at least 2,000 acres of potential vineland. This *ava* includes all land above the 400-foot elevation contour, and extends from the western hilly region of Oakville to the northern extension of Carneros. The western boundary (highly controversial) of this triangular *ava* is expected to be the Napa-Sonoma county line. The area, though lacking uniformity in geology and climate, is steep and rocky with thin soils ideal for quality grape cultivation. This highland area's exposure to the cooling effects of San Francisco Bay and the Pacific Ocean results in lower temperatures. Combined with Felton series soils (derived from weathered limestone and shale), the result is small-berried grape bunches with intense flavor and scent. There are approximately 1,000 vine acres and five wineries in the *ava*. *Atlas Peak ava*, a small hilly region lying in the southeastern portion of the Valley, includes the mountain of that name as well as the Foss Valley and portions of the Rector and Milliken Canyons. The entire region embraces nearly 12,000 acres, but only 565 vine acres, and one winery. *Spring Mountain*, the latest *ava*, is located within Napa Valley just west of St. Helena, on the eastern slope of the Mayacamas Mountains. The region contains 8,600 acres, 800 of which are planted in vines.

There are thirteen additional candidates for *ava* approval, of which Pope Valley, Chiles Valley, Oak Knoll, Diamond Mountain, Coombsville, St. Helena, Larkmead Bench, Rutherford Bench, Oakville Bench, Rutherford, Oakville, and Calistoga are currently advocating official recognition. Needless to say, all (ranging from vineyard, region, and settlement) are controversial and given to much discussion. *Larkmead Bench* is bounded by Dunweal Lane in the north and Bale Lane in the south, the Silverado Trail on the east and the lower foothills of Spring Mountain. This comparatively small region of poor, rocky, low yielding soils with poor water retention features is known for the production of Cabernet Sauvignon and Merlot grapes exhibiting good fruit and flavor. *Oak Knoll*, lying in a cooler climatic region with a large variety of terrain and soils, has certain sections better suited to the cultivation of white varieties, primarily Chardonnay.

Figure 9.10

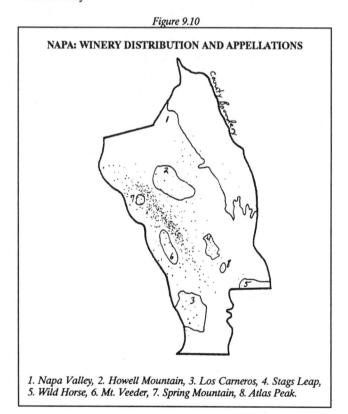

NAPA: WINERY DISTRIBUTION AND APPELLATIONS

1. Napa Valley, 2. Howell Mountain, 3. Los Carneros, 4. Stags Leap, 5. Wild Horse, 6. Mt. Veeder, 7. Spring Mountain, 8. Atlas Peak.

Pope Valley is a beautiful 3 by 8 mile valley trending in a northwest-southeast direction east of Angwin. Drained by Pope Creek, a range of hills divides the valley almost equally. Although grapes have been grown in the valley for more than 100 years, Pope Valley has been better known for its cattle ranches than grapes. Because it is surrounded by higher elevations, there is less fog, more sunlight, higher summer temperatures, and colder winters. Lower real estate costs, delicate and fruity wines, and a more relaxed, rural ambience has created interest in recent years. Vine acreage stands at less than 800 acres, but is expected to increase beyond 2,000 by 1995. Of the three wineries, two are located in an appendage of Pope Valley called Chiles Valley. The small, little known, and highly underrated, 300-acre *Coombsville* area, located in a narrow valley at the foot of the hills east of Napa, is a superb viticultural region. Able to accommodate 4,000 additional grape acres, this viticultural region has generated a reputation for distinctive, well structured, austere Chardonnay with excellent aging potential. The following "valleys" are expected to become future *ava's*: *Conn, Soda, Foss, Capell, Wooden, Gordon, and Congress*.

The most recent controversy concerns the convoluted proposed boundaries of *Rutherford* and *Oakville*, and two enclaves west of the Napa River--*Rutherford Bench* and *Oakville Bench*. Both of these towns, in the very center of prime viticultural land, have long established reputations for grape production, and extend from Zinfandel Lane in the north to Rector Creek in the south, with Skellenger Lane dividing the two *ava's* almost in half. While Oakville and Rutherford are distinct from one another, they both stretch from approximately the 500-foot contour of the Mayacamas on the west to the 600-foot contour line on the eastern hilly regions of the Vaca Range. While few would question apparent legitimacy of "town" *ava's*, very much in the French "commune" manner (as in Margaux and Pauillac, for example), vineland is mainly located on the valley floor (with heavy, wet alluvial soils), and two contrasting hilly regions--one facing east and the other west (both of which have colluvial soil material derived from different rock).

Climatic and soil differences not withstanding, the core of the "ava imbroglio" concerns the western portions of these two proposed *ava's*--commonly referred to as "benches." The proponents maintain that benches have distinctive soils, geology, and "topoclimates" which distinguish them from the larger viticultural areas. Moreover, the two benches, it is maintained, are distinguished from each other, hence the necessity for further delineation. The controversy is fueled by several growers and wineries who maintain that the western portions of both Rutherford and Oakville are gently sloping on benchland west of the Napa River (approximately), and supposedly superior in the production of more distinctive grapes than areas lying east of the river.

On the west are such formidable wineries (with neighboring vineland) as Beaulieu, Beringer, Robert

Mondavi, Inglenook, Far Niente, Grgich Hills, and Niebaum-Coppola Estate--all of which are said to benefit from the Benchland *ava* designation. However, the proposed benchland *ava's* would exclude such notable, and equally formidable wineries as Silver Oak, Groth Vineyards, Girard, and Caymus Vineyards, among others. While the benchland area might exhibit a number of geographical variables, the geographic distinctiveness (or superiority) of the "western benchlands" over the eastern (or among Rutherford and Oakville) has not been scientifically proven. Even more important is the fact that while many wines are excellent to outstanding in quality, they are not superior to other producing regions in Napa County. Furthermore, there is no written evidence of the use of Rutherford and Oakville Bench to describe the viticultural virtues of these two proposed sub-appellations prior to the mid-1970s, a critical issue for the petitioners influencing a favorable BATF ruling. In the absence of geographical distinctiveness and historical evidence on the use of the expression "bench," the proposed communal *ava's* (many in the county maintain that this is the coming pattern) would cause more controversy, and further Balkanize the county with a large number of meaningless *ava's* not based on physical and historical criteria in direct violation of BATF guidelines. Despite their historic acclaim and current efforts to make them separate *ava's*, given the recent successes of other areas within the county, the "Benches" enjoy no monopoly in the production of quality Cabernet Sauvignon. Moreover, less than 40 percent of the "Bench" is planted in Cabernet Sauvignon. One special physical element that may account for its celebrity is the presence of underground springs, a significant element for those vineyards that are dry farmed (an insignificant portion). Twenty above-average quality wineries are located within or on the periphery attest to the area's importance.

Because many geographers maintain that the Napa Valley is a collection of at least 22 separate microclimatic regions, it comes as no surprise to find tremendous pressure to create smaller and smaller sub-appellations. Therefore, with the escalation in wine prices and the establishment of a "Napa Valley nobility," more and more bottle labels highlight the prominence of a specific vineyard to *ava*-type designation. Whatever the merits of this trend, there are at least two dozen vineyards or sub-regions considered important enough to have their own *ava* designation, the most important of which are the Rutherford and Oakville Benches, cited above. Vineyards with an established reputation are: Winery Lake (Pinot Noir, Chardonnay, Merlot); Bosche (Cabernet Sauvignon); Stony Hill (Chardonnay); York Creek (Cabernet Sauvignon, Petite Sirah); Diamond Creek (Cabernet Sauvignon); Martha's Vineyard (Cabernet Sauvignon, perhaps the most celebrated in the Valley and commonly

considered the "benchmark" for all Cabernet Sauvignon); Oak Knoll (Chardonnay); and Eisele (Cabernet Sauvignon), among others. The concern at the moment is the apparent proliferation of sub-appellations into much smaller, overlapping units. It is thought that they will destroy the integrity of the much larger Napa Valley *ava*, and further confuse the public with new names. As a result, a compromise solution has been approved by the California State Legislature making it mandatory after January, 1990 for the Napa Valley *ava* to appear on the label in conjunction with all sub-appellations that are wholly contained in Napa County. The wineries are:

Acacia Winery (Napa, 1979), is a 47-acre, 36,000-case, Carneros winery established for the production of Chardonnay, Pinot Noir, and Cabernet Sauvignon. The winery produces vineyard, proprietary, and appellation labels for each grape variety: for Chardonnay: *Marina*, *Carneros*, and *Vin de Lies*; for Pinot Noir: *Madonna*, *St. Clair*, *Iund*, and *Carneros*. Other label: *Caviste*.

Aetna Springs Wine Ranch (Pope Valley, 1986), is a 26-acre winery (planted in Chardonnay, Cabernet Sauvignon, Merlot, and Shiraz) currently in the development stages.

Alatera Vineyard (Napa, 1977), is an 80-acre, 3,000-case winery that makes Chardonnay, Gewurztraminer, Pinot Noir, Cabernet Sauvignon, and late harvest Riesling, the latter as market conditions dictate.

Alta Vineyard Cellar (Calistoga, 1878), resurrected from inactivity in 1970, is a 2,000-case, mountain winery that makes above-average Chardonnay and Sauvignon Blanc under the Napa Valley and Knights Valley *ava's*.

Altamura Vineyards & Winery (Napa, 1985), is a 70-acre, 2,500-case winery that makes full bodied, complex, estate bottled Chardonnay that should not be missed.

Amizetta Vineyards (St. Helena, 1984), is a 20-acre, 3,000-case winery that makes outstanding, full flavored, flawless Sauvignon Blanc and Cabernet Sauvignon.

Anderson's Conn Valley Vineyards (Napa, 1987), is a 17-acre, 4,700-case winery that makes outstanding, dark, full-bodied, and well-structured Cabernet Sauvignon and minute quantities of Pinot Noir that should not be missed.

Ariel Vineyards (Napa, 1985), recently moved from San Jose, is a rapidly expanding winery that made, until 1989, 100,000 cases of non-alcoholic wine at the J. Lohr Winery. Made by a process known as reverse osmosis (separating water, alcohol, and other wine constituents), the wine has the potential to revolutionize the industry. Production, increasing from fewer than 5,000 cases in 1986 to more than 150,000 in 1990, necessitated the construction of a new winery to accommodate its phenomenal growth. The wines include Riesling, Chardonnay, Zinfandel, Merlot, Brut and Blanc de Noirs sparkling, proprietary blends, and reserve Napa and Sonoma Cabernet Sauvignon and Merlot.

Arroyo Winery (Calistoga, 1984), is a 50-acre, 2,000-case winery that makes Chardonnay, Napa Gamay, Petite Sirah, and Cabernet Sauvignon, the latter, known for staying power.

Artisan Wines (Napa, 1984), is a young, aggressive, 15,000-case, negociant company marketing several different labels: *Michaels* for reserve Cabernet Sauvignon and Chardonnay from the Mt. Veeder area; *Artisan Cellars* for Napa Valley grapes; and *CruVinet*, a label with several California, Napa, and Sonoma *ava* designations.

Atlas Peak Vineyards (Napa, 1986), is a 1,200-acre property (465 acres are already planted with another 330 expected eventually) currently in the development stages. The property and the winery are owned by The Wine Alliance, a division of Allied Lyons. Planted area consists of Chardonnay, Sauvignon Blanc, Sangiovese, and Cabernet Sauvignon, with smaller experimental plots of Cabernet Frank, Petit Verdot, Semillon, Pinot Blanc, Refosco, Nebbiolo, Pinot Noir, Merlot, and Malbec. Production is expected to peak at 110,000 cases. First wines (5,000 cases) include Sangiovese, Cabernet Sauvignon, Chardonnay, and proprietary wines. First Sangiovese release, albeit expensive, is interesting.

Beaulieu Vineyard (Rutherford, 1900), with 800 planted acres and an annual output of 500,000 cases is one of the oldest and largest of the premium North Coast wineries. Beaulieu, French for "a beautiful place," has holdings in Rutherford and Carneros, the former being the original estate of Georges de Latour, the founder. The vineyards, located on the "Rutherford Bench" along the western side of the valley, are composed of thin, well drained volcanic derived soils with a propensity for excellent Cabernet Sauvignon. While the winery makes many wines, it is best known for highly fragrant and intensely flavored reserve Cabernet Sauvignon, Chardonnay, sparkling wine, a sweet Muscat Blanc, and is one of the largest producers of Pinot Noir from Carneros grapes. In addition to blended wines, the winery also makes Riesling, Sauvignon Blanc, other table and fortified wines. This major winery did not close during Prohibition. Beaulieu and Inglenook are owned by Grand Metropolitan, a large English hotel, restaurant, wine and spirits conglomerate, the parent company of Heublein Corporation since 1988. This is also the only winery that has been making a particular, single wine style for two generations from a single vineyard-a very rare phenomenon in California.

Beckstoffer Vineyards (St. Helena, 1985), is an aggressive, highly innovative, and rapidly growing, 1,725-acre vineyard (acreage is located in Mendocino and Napa) that has a moderately priced brand (20,000 cases) of well-made, supple, and fruity Chardonnay, Sauvignon Blanc, and Cabernet Sauvignon, marketed under the *Freemont Creek Wines* label, offering excellent value. The concern is considered the largest, privately held vineyard on the North Coast. The recent acquisition of one of the finest Cabernet Sauvignon vineyards portends a bright future for this outstanding vinegrowing concern.

Beringer Vineyards (St. Helena, 1876), considered the oldest continuously operating winery in the Napa Valley, is a large 6,100-acre (about 1,000 acres in Napa), 3.5 million-case winery (all operations) that has had a varied history over the past 100 years. Owned since 1971 by the Nestle Corporation, it is managed by Wine World Estates, the American division that oversees all wine and food operations. Handicapped by disrepair and inconsistency, the winery has recently upgraded its premium label and improved viticultural practices in several prime vineyards: Knights Valley, Chabot, Home, Gamble Ranch, State Lane, and Hudson Ranch. The winery makes Chardonnay, Sauvignon Blanc, Chenin Blanc, Riesling, Zinfandel, Cabernet Sauvignon, and Cabernet Sauvignon Porto-type wine, all of which are well colored, fruity, robust, and full flavored. The private reserve Chardonnay and Cabernet Sauvignon are particularly good. The expanding winery has recently purchased Chateau Souverain in Sonoma County, Estrella River Vineyards in Paso Robles (now called Meridian), the 308-acre Sisquoc River Ranch Vineyard in Santa Maria, the former vineyard and facility of Italian Swiss Colony in Asti, and is a principal in Maison Deutz Winery in Arroyo Grande. The holding company has also recently purchased more than 1,400 acres in San Luis Obispo County, 194 acres in Lake County, and is expected to acquire additional grape acreage for its existing portfolio of more than 6,000 acres of prime vineland. The aggressive marketing strategy has also targeted 25 percent of all output be exported. It is estimated that more than 300,000 tourists visit this winery each year. C & B Vintage Cellars, the import division of Wine World, distributes more than 500,000 cases annually. Other labels: *Los Hermanos* (700,000 cases), and *Napa Ridge* (this 240,000 case label is a trademark not using Napa Valley grapes).

Bernard Pradel Cellars (Yountville, 1984), is an excellent, 9-acre, 4,000-case winery that makes Chardonnay, Cabernet Sauvignon, and late harvest Sauvignon Blanc, sold mainly at the winery and to restaurants.

Blue Heron Lake Vineyard & Winery (Napa, 1985), located in Wild Horse Valley, is an obscure, underrated, 24-acre, 2,500-case winery known for well structured, crisp Chardonnay, a dry Gewurztraminer and Pinot Noir.

Bouchaine Vineyards (Napa, 1980), is a 31-acre, 20,000-case winery historically known for inconsistent and pricy Chardonnay, Pinot Noir, and Gewurztraminer. In recent years the wines have shown a marked improvement.

Buehler Vineyards (St. Helena, 1978), located north of Lake Hennessey, is a little known but excellent, 60-acre, 35,000-case winery that makes thick, meaty Cabernet Sauvignon, Pinot Blanc, and Zinfandel. Other label: *Bon Marche.*

Burgess Cellars (St. Helena, 1880), located on Howell Mountain, is a 60-acre, well regarded, and consistently good, 30,000-case winery that

makes excellent, bold, well structured Cabernet Sauvignon, Zinfandel, and full bodied, well structured Chardonnay and Chenin Blanc, all of which provide good value. Estate and purchased grapes are mountain grown, and the wines all exhibit balance and true varietal character. Other label: *Bell Canyon.*

CAFARO

Cafaro Cellars (Napa, 1986), is a 1,200-case label that makes excellent to outstanding, full bodied, well structured Cabernet Sauvignon and Merlot by one of the most able winemakers in Napa.

Cain Cellars (St. Helena, 1980), is a 135-acre, 30,000-case, state-of-the-art winery that has quickly established a reputation for excellent, brawny, masculine, wood aged Chardonnay, Sauvignon Blanc (an interesting clone is labeled *Musque*), Cabernet Sauvignon, Merlot, a rare Malbec, and is one of the few wineries that blends all five under the proprietary name of *Cain Cellars Estate Five.* Located high in the Spring Mountain area, quality is improving as the vines mature.

Cakebread Cellars (Rutherford, 1973), is a good, consistent, 46-acre, 40,000-case winery that makes dense, well structured, above-average to excellent Sauvignon Blanc, Chardonnay, and Cabernet Sauvignon, the best of which is the Rutherford Reserve.

Calafia Cellars (St. Helena, 1979), is a small, 2-acre, 4,000-case winery that buys grapes from mountain vineyards in the Mt. Veeder area. The well made Sauvignon Blanc, Cabernet Sauvignon, Zinfandel, and Merlot are all brawny, masculine, spicy wines that age well, offering excellent value. Other label: *Redwood Canyon Cellars* for Gewurztraminer.

California Soleil Vineyards (Yountville, 1982), is an 11-acre vineyard that makes 3,000 cases of Riesling in three different styles. Unusual in its specialization of only Riesling, the wines are distinctive, offering excellent value.

Carneros Creek Winery (Napa, 1972), is a 22-acre, 25,000-case winery that makes above-average to excellent Chardonnay, Cabernet Sauvignon, Pinot Noir, and Merlot, as well as proprietary blends. The Signature Reserve Pinot Noir is outstanding. In 1974 the winery embarked upon an ambitious research project in conjunction with the University of California-Davis to determine which Pinot Noir clone vines would be best suited to the Carneros region. Thus far, 20 clones have been tested to determine yields, cluster and berry size, ripening features, and wine quality. Other label: *Fleur de Carneros.*

Cartledge, Moser & Lawson (St. Helena, 1982), is an aggressive, 65,000-case winery and negociant firm that distributes Chardonnay, Sauvignon Blanc, Cabernet Sauvignon, and Merlot under the *Stratford* label; Chardonnay under the *Cartledge & Browne* label; and Chardonnay and Sauvignon Blanc under the *Cantebury* label. Total output is expected to increase in the future.

Casa Nuestra (St. Helena, 1980), is a 15-acre, 2,000-case winery that specializes in distinctive, well made, and consistently good, barrel fermented, dry, off-dry, and late harvest Chenin Blanc (called Dorado), along with smaller quantities of Cabernet Franc, and a blended proprietary wine called *Tinto.*

Caymus Vineyards (Rutherford, 1971), is a 70-acre, 75,000-case winery with a well established reputation for full bodied Cabernet Sauvignon, Pinot Noir, Cabernet Franc, Zinfandel, and a blended white wine called *Conundrum.* The special selection Cabernet Sauvignon is consistently one of the finest in the state. The late harvest Semillon, and the fresh, fruity Sauvignon Blanc are both good. The winery also bottles California and Chilean wines under the *Liberty School* label.

Chanter Winery (Napa, 1982), is a 14-acre, 1,700-case winery that makes excellent Chardonnay, Cabernet Sauvignon, and Merlot, offering good value.

Chappellet Vineyard (St. Helena, 1968), is a stylish, 150-acre, 25,000-case, well regarded, but often inconsistent winery that makes Chenin Blanc, Chardonnay, Merlot, and Cabernet Sauvignon from hillside vineyards high above Lake Hennessey. Recently planted Sangiovese should yield interesting results in coming years.

Charles F. Shaw Vineyard & Winery (St. Helena, 1978), is a stylish, 36-acre, 40,000-case winery that makes Chardonnay, Sauvignon Blanc, Gamay, and Zinfandel. Other labels: *Bale Mill Cellars* and *Magnolia Ridge*.

Charles Krug Winery (St. Helena, 1861), historically one of the first Napa wineries to distribute nationally in the second half of the 19th century, and a major pioneer in post-Prohibition Napa winemaking, it has had an uneven post-World War II history, and generally not lived up to its potential until recently. This large, 1,200-acre (basically 10 vineyards clustered south of Oakville and Carneros), 1.1 million-case winery has improved its product line, and is now making above-average to excellent wines, especially Chenin Blanc and Cabernet Sauvignon. The *Vintage Selection* Cabernet Sauvignon is excellent. Peter Mondavi, the president of Charles Krug, was a pioneer in cold fermentation in the 1930s, French oak aging, sterile filtration in the 1950s, and is one of the most value conscious winemakers in the valley. Other label: *C.K. Mondavi*, its popular label and largest seller.

Chateau Boswell (St. Helena, 1979), is a well regarded, meticulous, 1-acre, 1,500-case winery with Old World charm specializing in superb, delicate, well flavored, wood aged Chardonnay and Cabernet Sauvignon. The hard to find wines are mainly sold to fine restaurants and at the winery.

Chateau Chevalier Winery (St. Helena, 1884), well situated on Spring Mountain, is a historic, 60-acre, 12,000-case winery that produced Chardonnay, Cabernet Sauvignon, and Pinot Noir. It ceased production in 1985, and a good portion of the vineyard has since been replanted in Cabernet Sauvignon, Cabernet Franc, and Merlot. It will be producing again shortly when the vines mature and all facilities are completely restored.

Chateau Cherve Winery (Yountville, 1979), is a superlative, 4,000-case winery that makes magnificent *ChevReserve* (considered one of the leading wines in the state), Cabernet Sauvignon, Cabernet Franc, Sauvignon Blanc (sublime), and Merlot. Grapes originate from mountain acreage owned by the two partners.

Chateau Montelena Winery (Calistoga, 1882), is a prestigious, quality oriented, 100-acre, 31,000-case winery (restored in 1972) that makes excellent Chardonnay, Riesling, Cabernet Sauvignon, and Zinfandel. Although there were bouts of inconsistency during the 1970s, the wines, in general, are now much improved: fruity, robust, full bodied, big, well structured (the Cabernet Sauvignon, in particular, ages extremely well). After a long period of inactivity, the winery was reopened in 1972. Other label: *Silverado Cellars*.

Chateau Napa Beaucanon (St. Helena, 1987), is a 200-acre (leased and owned), 40,000-case winery owned by a St. Emilion negociant that makes soft, supple Chardonnay, Chenin Blanc, Merlot, and Cabernet Sauvignon under the *Beaucanon Napa Valley* label.

Chateau Potelle (Napa, 1986), is an aggressive, 300-acre, 300,000-case negociant/winery that makes excellent, well-structure, steely Chardonnay, a full bodied, lean, yet complex Cabernet Sauvignon, and a good Sauvignon Blanc. The wines, partially made from purchased grapes, carry many different *ava's*. Other label: *Domaine Potelle*.

Chimney Rock Winery (Napa, 1984), overlooking the Silverado Trail, is a stylish, 75-acre, 17,000-case winery that makes above-average Chardonnay, Sauvignon Blanc and Cabernet Sauvignon. It is also the only winery with a golf course.

Crichton Hall Vineyard (Rutherford, 1985), is a 50-acre, 4,000-case, Chardonnay only winery that makes rich, complex, round, barrel fermented and yeasty wine offering excellent value.

Clos du Val Wine Co. (Napa, 1972), with acreage in both the Stags Leap and Carneros areas, is a 290-acre, 60,000-case, underrated winery that produces stylish, subdued, supple, well made, flavored and scented Chardonnay, Semillon, Pinot Noir, Cabernet Sauvignon, Merlot, and Zinfandel. While Chardonnay is delicate and subdued with an affinity for cream sauces, the Semillon, soft, round, fat, and well balanced, is often the better white wine. Cabernet Sauvignon and Merlot, both expertly made, are delicate, refined, supple, yet capable of aging. Bernard Portet, one of the most gifted of the valley's many winemakers, concen-

trates on elegance and subtlety. All wines, consistent to a fault, should not be missed. Other labels: *Joli Val*, and *Le Clos*.

Clos Pegase Winery (Calistoga, 1986), is a new, stylish, 92-acre, 40,000-case winery that makes well scented, firm and lean Chardonnay, Sauvignon Blanc, Merlot, Cabernet Sauvignon, Cabernet Franc, and proprietary wines under several appellation names. The winery has recently purchased 365 acres in Los Carneros.

Conn Creek Winery (St. Helena, 1974), is a 123-acre, 40,000-case winery that makes excellent, full bodied, crisp Chardonnay, fat Cabernet Sauvignon, and fruity Zinfandel from old vines. Offering considerable value, the consistently faultless wines are big, well structured, flavorful, and capable of extended aging, particularly Cabernet Sauvignon. Clean, functional, and extremely efficient, the winery was recently acquired by Stimson Lane. Other label: *Chateau Maja*.

Cordoniu Napa (Napa, 1988), is a developing, 356-acre (250 of which will be planted in Chardonnay and Pinot Noir), 25,000-case, sparkling wine facility in the Carneros area of Napa with a capacity of 185,000 cases.

Corison Wines (Rutherford, 1987), is a 2,000-case label known for excellent, full-bodied, well-structured Cabernet Sauvignon that belongs in every serious cellar.

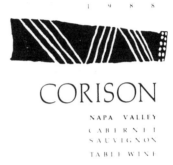

Cosentino Vintners (Yountville, 1982), historically known as Crystal Valley Cellars in Modesto, is a 6-acre, 16,000-case, underrated winery that makes excellent to outstanding Chardonnay, Cabernet Franc, Cabernet Sauvignon, Pinot Noir, and Merlot, the latter particular good. *The Sculptor* (a superb Chardonnay), and *The Poet* (a Meritage-type wine) are both outstanding. The winery also makes small quantities of sparkling, Porto-type, and *Fracesca D'Amore*, a dessert wine made from Sauvignon Blanc and Muscat Alexandria.

Costello Vineyards (Napa, 1982), is a 40-acre, 12,000-case winery that makes Chardonnay and Sauvignon Blanc wines (the former, entirely estate produced, is full bodied and lean), both of which offer good value.

Cuvaison Winery (Calistoga, 1970), is a 400-acre, 60,000-case winery that makes quality Cabernet Sauvignon, Chardonnay (two-thirds of output), Pinot Noir, Zinfandel, and Merlot. The winery, now Swiss owned, has expanded acreage in the Carneros and changed the style of the wines from their historic aggressive, tannin rich, long lived character to a more supple, elegant style, much improved in recent years. Other label: *Calistoga Vineyards*.

D'Anneo Vineyards (Calistoga, 1983), is a 4-acre, 1,000-case label that only makes above-average, spicy Zinfandel.

Dalla Valle Vineyards (Napa, 1986), is a 25-acre, 2,500-case winery that makes interesting, pricy, and hard-to-find blended Cabernet Sauvignon-based wines. After an unsteady beginning, the wines are rapidly being improved by an efficient winemaking team.

Dave Abreau, (St. Helena, 1987), is a 16-acre, 550 case winery that makes excellent Cabernet Sauvignon.

David Arthur Vineyards (St. Helena, 1985), is a 20-acre, 3,000-case label known for excellent, well structured Chardonnay.

DeMoor Winery (Oakville, 1976), founded as Napa Wine Cellars, is a 16,000-case winery recently purchased by a Japanese corporation that makes good, sound, fruity, and moderately priced Chardonnay, Sauvignon Blanc, Chenin Blanc, Cabernet Sauvignon, Zinfandel, and a sweet white wine called "Fie Doux." Reserve wines are interesting, offering good value. Other label: *Napa Cellars*.

Deer Park Winery (Deer Park, 1979), is a little known, 7-acre, 6,000-case winery that makes a fruity Sauvignon Blanc, Chardonnay, spicy

Zinfandel, and Petite Sirah.

Diamond Creek Vineyards (Calistoga, 1968), is a 20-acre, 3,000-case winery that makes excellent, estate produced Cabernet Sauvignon. Acreage is divided into three separate dry-farmed vineyards, each identified by name: *Volcanic Hill* (8 acres, composed of light, grey soil on a steep slope); *Red Rock* (7 acres of terraced, iron rich soil); and *Gravelly Meadows* (5 acres). A rare *Lake* Cabernet Sauvignon is often exceptional. All vines are stressed, give low yields, and the wines, big, muscular, and multi-flavored, are neither fined nor filtered. This is one of the few wineries that specializes in only one grape variety.

Dolce Winery (Oakville, 1989), is a 17-acre, 1,000-case winery that specializes in the production of outstanding botrytized Semillon-Sauvignon Blanc. It is owned by Far Niente.

Domaine Carneros (Napa, 1987), is a new venture by Champagne Taittinger and several American partners who built an imposing sparkling wine facility in the Napa section of Carneros. The vineyard is about 138 acres and the expected output of 80,000 cases is made from a combination of Pinot Noir, Chardonnay, Pinot Meunier, and Pinot Blanc. The wines, full-bodied and refined, are a must for every serious enophile.

Domaine Carneros, an elegant building in the French tradition.
Baxevanis

Domaine Chandon (Yountville, 1973), is a large, 1,950-acre (the winery contracts another 1,400 acres), 595,000-case winery owned by Moet-Hennessey. Highly successful (up from 20,000 cases in 1977), it is known for well made, consistent, but somewhat bland wines, including Blanc de Noirs, Brut, and Reserve, all of which have improved markedly in recent years. It is estimated that this winery produces about 20 percent of the state's total *methode Champenoise* sparkling output. *Etoile*, an elegant, crisp, and lean blend of outstanding cuvees, is superb. Other label: *Shadow Creek*.

Domaine Montreaux (Napa, 1983), is a 21-acre, 10,000-case, sparkling wine facility affiliated with Monticello Cellars. Unlike most California sparkling wine, the wines of this property are often inconsistent, but the finest can be full bodied, robust, distinctive, the product of barrel fermentation, and extended yeast aging. The final blend is composed of 60 percent Pinot Noir and 40 percent Chardonnay, with minor amounts of Pinot Meunier. This facility also houses Ariel Vineyards.

Domaine Napa (St. Helena, 1985), is a 10-acre, 10,000-case winery that makes Sauvignon Blanc, Chardonnay, Cabernet Sauvignon, and Merlot.

Duckhorn Vineyards (St. Helena, 1976), is a 10-acre, 25,000-case winery that makes excellent to outstanding Sauvignon Blanc, Semillon, Merlot, and Cabernet Sauvignon. The superbly crafted wines are consistent, well flavored, capable of aging, and offer excellent value. Merlot (particularly *Three Palm Vineyard*) and Cabernet Sauvignon are both intense and rich; Sauvignon Blanc is crisp, fresh, tart, and one of the finest in the state. Other label: *Decoy*.

Dunn Vineyards (Angwin, 1932), is a superb, 21-acre, 4,000-case,

mountain winery that makes outstanding, full bodied, well structured, meaty, complex Cabernet Sauvignon (under Napa and Howell Mountain *ava's*) offering superb value. The Howell Mountain is particularly good, requiring patience.

Ehlers Lane Winery (St. Helena, 1983), is a 20,000-case winery that makes heavily oaked Cabernet Sauvignon, Sauvignon Blanc, and Chardonnay, the latter, yeasty and round, offers good value. Due to restructuring, the property and wines will surely change in the coming years.

El Molino Winery (St. Helena, 1987), is a 60-acre, 1,000-case winery that traces its history back to 1871; it operated until Prohibition, and was resurrected in 1987. With each passing year this obscure winery has produced improved, rich, opulent Chardonnay and Pinot Noir, both of which exhibit exceptional character and finesse.

Elyse Wine Cellars (St. Helena, 1987), is a 700-case label for excellent Zinfandel marketed under the Rutherford Bench, *Morisoli Ranch* designation, and small quantities of barrel fermented Riesling.

Etude (Oakville, 1982), owned by Tony Soter, one of the finest winemakers in the county, is a 3,000-case winery that specializes in the production of dark, full bodied, well structured, and eminently flavorful Pinot Noir and Cabernet Sauvignon, both of which rank among the finest in the state.

Evensen Vineyards & Winery (Oakville, 1979), is a 6-acre, 700-case winery that specializes in bone-dry, soft Chardonnay, and Alsatian style, fruity, complex Gewurztraminer.

Fairmont Cellars (St. Helena, 1978), is a 7,500-case label for a negociant concern that distributes Chardonnay, Sauvignon Blanc, Cabernet Sauvignon, and sparkling wines.

Far Niente Winery (Oakville, 1885), is an excellent, 120-acre, 30,000-case winery with a reputation for stylish and elegant, but pricy Chardonnay and Cabernet Sauvignon.

Farella-Park Vineyards (Napa, 1985), is a 30-acre, 450-case winery that makes big, but moderately oaked Chardonnay, fresh Sauvignon Blanc and Merlot.

Flora Springs Wine Co. (St. Helena, 1978), is a 375-acre, 25,000-case winery that makes above-average, firm, well structured Sauvignon Blanc (labeled *Soliloquy*), Chardonnay, Cabernet Sauvignon, Merlot, and a Meritage-type wine called *Trilogy*, all of which are well made. The winery and some vineland dating back to the 1880s were owned by Louis Martini until 1978. Other label: *Floreal*.

Folie a Deux Winery (St. Helena, 1981), is a 14-acre, 6,500-case, much improved winery that makes Chardonnay, Chenin Blanc, Cabernet Sauvignon, and sparkling wines. Reputation rests with a full bodied, round, ripe Chardonnay, and a Muscat Blanc.

Forest Hill (Napa, 1987), is a 7-acre, 1,000-case winery that makes a rare and outstanding, well structured Chardonnay. The wine, rich and silky on the palate, offers excellent value despite its high price.

Forman Vineyards (St. Helena, 1984), is a 47-acre, 3,500-case winery owned by one of the finest winemakers in California. It produces absolutely outstanding estate Chardonnay and Cabernet Sauvignon--both of which are restrained in fruit, but refined and complex in substance and structure. Small quantities of Pinot Noir will be made shortly. The vineyards are superbly situated, the winery is modern and efficient, and the wines are handcrafted masterpieces that should not be missed. Other label: *Chateau La Grande Roche*.

Franciscan Vineyards (Rutherford, 1972), is a 1,220-acre, 295,000-case winery with a checkered history hampered by inconsistency under several previous owners. Under the present administration, Chardonnay, Sauvignon Blanc, Zinfandel, Cabernet Sauvignon, and Merlot have recently been improved, offering excellent value. Chardonnay, Sauvignon Blanc, and Cabernet Sauvignon wines, made at Franciscan in Rutherford from grapes grown on the Oakville Estate in Alexander Valley and from newly acquired vineland in Monterey, are sold under the *Estancia* label (all three of which are above-average in quality offering excellent value). The winery has purchased additional land in Monterey. With nearly 1,300 planted acres, it is one of the largest vineyard owners in Sonoma and Napa. The winery also owns Mount Veeder Winery, and the *Estancia* and *Pinnacles* (for Monterey-grown Chardonnay and Pinot Noir) labels, the latter, above-average to outstanding. Chardonnay, late harvest Riesling, Cabernet Sauvignon, Merlot, Zinfandel, and Meritage-type wines are sold under the upscale *Franciscan Oakville Estate* label.

Freemark Abbey Winery (St. Helena, 1967), one of the first "boutique wineries" to emerge in the 1960s, is a 152-acre, 43,000-case winery. The original winery, built in 1886 by Josephine Tychson, closed due to phylloxera in 1894, only to reopen and close again under several other owners. Its most recent restoration was 1967. Quality, consistently high during its formative years (wines were made from the finest grapes owned by several partners, all of which are considered above-average in quality: *Red Barn Ranch, Wood Ranch, Carpy Ranch, Jaeger Vine-yard, Bosche Vineyard,* and *Sycamore Vineyard*), had declined in the late 1970s and early 1980s, but has shown signs of revival. The vineyard designated wines and Edelwein (a botrytized late harvest Riesling) are particularly good.

Frisinger Cellars (Napa, 1987), is a 17-acre, 700-case winery that makes estate bottled Chardonnay.

Frog's Leap Winery (St. Helena, 1981), is a rapidly expanding, 12-acre, 23,000-case winery that makes well balanced Sauvignon Blanc, Chardonnay, Cabernet Sauvignon, and Zinfandel, offering good value.

Girard Winery (Oakville, 1980), is an 80-acre, 15,000-case winery that makes above-average to excellent Chenin Blanc, Sauvignon Blanc, Chardonnay, Semillon, and Cabernet Sauvignon, the latter, dark and tannin rich. Other label: *Stephens.*

Goosecross Cellars (Yountville, 1985), is an 11-acre, 8,000-case winery known only for big, rich, round, and well balanced Chardonnay.

Grace Family Vineyards (St. Helena, 1987), is an immaculate, 2-acre, 1,000-case winery that makes expensive and scarce, rich, complex, well balanced and flavored Cabernet Sauvignon. Until 1987 the grapes were sold to Caymus with the vineyard designated on the label. The wines are a must for the serious cellar.

Green & Red Vineyard (St. Helena, 1972), is an obscure, 16-acre, 3,500-case winery located on a hillside overlooking Chiles Valley. The winery is named after the red, iron rich, and green serpentine soils located as high as 2,000 feet. The distinctive, full bodied, well flavored, and intensely scented Chardonnay and Zinfandel offer excellent value.

Grgich Hills Cellar (Rutherford, 1977), is a partnership between Austin Hills of The Hills Brothers Coffee family, and Miljenko Grgich, son of a Croatian winemaker who studied enology in Zagreb, Yugoslavia before coming to America in 1958. The winery owns 200 acres and produces 60,000 cases of above-average to outstanding, intense, full flavored, and complex Chardonnay, Sauvignon Blanc, Riesling, Cabernet Sauvignon, and Zinfandel. This is a winery that not only makes consistently superb wines, but ranks among the finest in the world.

Groth Vineyard & Winery (Oakville, 1982), although located on the valley floor on well drained, silty clay loam soils, this 165-acre, 30,000-case winery has consistently made excellent to outstanding, full bodied, yet smooth Chardonnay, Sauvignon Blanc, and Cabernet Sauvignon, all offering good value.

Hagafen Winery (Napa, 1979), is a 6,000-case, Carneros kosher winery that makes above-average proprietary, Chardonnay, Riesling, Pinot Noir, Cabernet Franc, and Cabernet Sauvignon, the latter, particularly good.

Hallmark Cellars (St. Helena, 1985), is a 1,100-case label known for distinctive, full bodied, well flavored, wood aged Zinfandel from old vines.

Hans Fahden Winery (Calistoga, 1986), is a 26-acre, 2,500-case Cabernet Sauvignon-only winery offering excellent value.

Hanns Kornell Champagne Cellars (St. Helena, 1952), is a 16-acre, 45,000-case winery known for Riesling/Chenin Blanc-based sparkling

wines. Recently, the markedly improved wines have had larger additions of Chardonnay and Pinot Noir (as in Brut, Blanc de Blancs, and Blanc de Noirs). The firm also makes an interesting off-dry Muscat Alexandria. Recent financial difficulties will redirect winery energies in the years ahead.

Harrison Vineyards (Calistoga, 1989), is an 18-acre, 1,700-case label known for outstanding, full-bodied, multi-dimensional Chardonnay and Cabernet Sauvignon. While the excellent wines are currently being made at a neighboring facility, the owner is in the process of building his own shortly.

HAVENS
RESERVE
1986
MERLOT
CARNEROS
TRUCHARD VINEYARD

MADE AND BOTTLED BY HAVENS WINE CELLARS
RUTHERFORD CA ALC. 13.2% VOL. CONTAINS SULFITES

Havens Wine Cellars (Napa, 1984), is a 3,000-case winery that makes good, sound, multi-faceted Sauvignon Blanc (a late harvest is called *Aurae,* and the single vineyard table wine is called *Clock Vineyard*), Chardonnay, and Merlot, of which the reserve *Carneros Truchard Vineyard* is outstanding.

Heitz Wine Cellars (St. Helena, 1961), one of the oldest and better known of the many premium wineries, is a 150-acre, 40,000-case winery that has an established reputation for magnificently flavored and scented Cabernet Sauvignon that is usually described in superlatives, particularly for those who like the flavor and aroma of eucalyptus. The principal labels (not all of the same quality) are *Martha's Vineyard* (the finest), *Bella Oaks,* and *Napa Valley.* A botrytized Chardonnay is labeled *Alicia.* Other, less celebrated wines include Chardonnay, Grignolino, Zinfandel, Pinot Noir, Angelica, and proprietary wines. The winery has recently purchased 560 acres in the Pope Valley, of which nearly 300 are suitable for grapes.

Inglenook-Napa Valley (Rutherford, 1879), Scottish for "cozy corner," is a 372-acre, 150,000-case winery that makes Chardonnay, Riesling, Gewurztraminer, Chenin Blanc, Sauvignon Blanc, Semillon, Muscat Blanc, Cabernet Sauvignon, Pinot Noir, Charbono, Zinfandel, and Merlot. After a disappointing period during the 1960s and 1970s, the winery embarked on a revitalization program to upgrade production facilities, and is once again making above-average wines, particularly the *Cask Reserve* Chardonnay, Cabernet Sauvignon, and Merlot. Chardonnay and Cabernet Sauvignon from the *Gustave Niebaum, Laird, Mast, Tench,* and *Reference Vineyards* are above-average. *Gravion,* a Semillon/Sauvignon Blanc blend, and *Chevrier,* a blend of Semillon and Sauvignon Blanc from the Herrick Vineyard, are both above-average. The entire operation (along with Beaulieu, The Christian Brothers, and Quail Ridge in the Napa Valley, and Almaden and Navalle in Madera) is part of the Heublein Corporation, now owned by Grand Metropolitan. The combined production from all operations exceeds 8 million cases.

Innisfree Winery (St. Helena, 1982), produced on the same site as the Joseph Phelps Winery, is a 25,000-case facility (treated as a separate winery) that makes Chardonnay and Cabernet Sauvignon.

Inniskillin Napa Vineyards (Rutherford, 1988), is a 23-acre, 30,000-case label owned by Inniskillin Wines of Ontario, Canada that makes Chardonnay and Cabernet Sauvignon under the *Terra* label.

Jack Daniel Society (Napa, 1982), is a partnership between Robin Lail, Marcia Smith, and Christian Moueix. The 90-acre planted site, located on the 124-acre Napanook Vineyard near the southern end of the Rutherford Bench, is the source of grapes destined for the super premium *Dominus Estate* wine made from Cabernet Sauvignon, Merlot, Petit Verdot, Malbec, and Cabernet Franc, all of which are dry-farmed. Not too dissimilar from operations in Opus One, the no-expense spared philosophy has completely renovated the property with new rootstocks, vine clones, and narrow vine spacing. Special pruning methods, ruthless selection, a prohibition on acidification, and no barrel to barrel racking distinguish it from contemporary Napa winemaking methods. Early start-up problems not withstanding, the 6,500-case output is surprisingly full bodied, rich, fleshy, yet firm and complex. Although expensive and inconsistent in quality, this is a wine to watch as it is destined to influence, and perhaps revolutionize Bordeaux-type wine production in the valley.

Jaeger Inglewood Cellar (St. Helena, 1984), is a 30-acre, 3,500-case, estate-produced Merlot only winery. The Jaeger family also has an interest in Rutherford Hill, Freemark Abbey, and other wineries. The mountain vineyard, one of the finest in the county, produces excellent Merlot. The supple, well colored and flavored wines are aged for two years in small Nevers oak, and another two years in the bottle prior to release. This select vineyard is part of a much larger 600-acre estate whose grapes are sold to other wineries. The family owns more than 1,350 additional acres, half of which will be planted in grapes.

Joanna Vineyard (Yountville, 1984), is a 2,500-case winery that makes good, sound, often complex Sauvignon Blanc, Chardonnay, Muscat Blanc, Zinfandel, and Cabernet Sauvignon, offering excellent value.

Johnson Turnbull Vineyards (Oakville, 1979), is an underrated, 21-acre, 10,000-case winery that makes excellent, spicy, well flavored, age-worthy Chardonnay and Cabernet Sauvignon.

Joseph Phelps Vineyards (St. Helena, 1972), is an innovative, 303-acre, 85,000-case winery that makes average to outstanding estate and non-estate wines. The widely diverse vineyards in the Napa Valley produce many wines, of which *Eisele, Backus, and Sangiacomo Vineyards* are outstanding. The *Insignia* designation, modeled after a classic Bordeaux blend, is excellent, as is the late harvest Scheurebe, special select late harvest Riesling, and the botrytis infected Semillon labeled *Delice du Semillon*. Varietal wines under several *ava's* are Riesling, Chardonnay, Sauvignon Blanc, Gewurztraminer, Cabernet Sauvignon, Merlot, Pinot Noir, Syrah, and Zinfandel. Recently, the winery has introduced a new label, *Vin du Mistral*, for a new line of Rhone-type wines, mainly Grenache, Syrah, Viognier, Cinsault, and Mourvedre. The winery also owns acreage through a partnership in Carneros and has just completed construction of a new winery that it shares with the Innisfree Winery.

Judd's Hill Winery (St. Helena, 1989), is an 11-acre, 1,500-case winery that makes above-average to excellent, supple, fruity, yet spicy Cabernet Sauvignon.

Kate's Vineyard (Napa, 1987), is a 4-acre, 1,000-case winery that makes well-structured Chardonnay.

Kent Rasmussen Winery (Napa, 1986), is an outstanding, 10-acre, 7,500-case winery that makes big, expansive, opulent Chardonnay, Pinot Noir, and small quantities of Carmine and Dolcetto, two very unusual red wines. Other label: *Ramsay*.

Klein Vineyards (Napa, 1986), is a 10-acre, 500-case property that makes rich, opulent, Cabernet Sauvignon from acreage in the Santa Cruz Mountains.

Laird Vineyards (Napa, 1980), is a 5,000-case label that makes good, sound Chardonnay and Cabernet Sauvignon, both of which offer good value.

La Jota Vineyard Co. (Angwin, 1889), is a 28-acre, 4,500-case winery that makes excellent to outstanding, big, full-bodied, rich, and well structured Cabernet Sauvignon, Zinfandel, and a rare, delicate, and expensive Viognier.

Lakespring Winery (Napa, 1980), is a 7-acre, 12,000-case winery that makes stylish Sauvignon Blanc, Chenin Blanc, Chardonnay, Merlot, and Cabernet Sauvignon. Although inconsistent in former years, the wines have recently shown considerable improvement.

Lamborn Family Vineyards (Angwin, 1986), is a 9-acre, 1,000-case winery located on Howell Mountain that makes excellent, well flavored, well balanced Zinfandel.

Las Cerezas (Yountville, 1986), is a 5-acre, 800-case label known for zesty and fresh Sauvignon Blanc made in a neighboring winery offering exceptional value.

La Vielle Montagne (St. Helena, 1983), is a 7-acre, 2,000-case winery in the Mayacamas that makes big, rich, dense Cabernet Sauvignon, and mouth filling Riesling.

Limur Winery (Napa, 1988), is a 2-acre, 350-case winery that makes excellent, well structured, full flavored Chardonnay.

Liparita Vineyard (Angwin, 1987), is an 80-acre, 3,000-case label that makes Chardonnay, Cabernet Sauvignon, and Merlot.

Livingston Vineyards (St. Helena, 1984), is a 10-acre, 2,200-case winery that makes well structured, tannin rich, full bodied Cabernet Sauvignon in two styles: the estate, *Moffet Vineyard* Cabernet Sauvignon is blended with other grapes, and the 100% Cabernet Sauvignon *Stanley's Selection* is non-estate. Both are exceptional.

Llords & Elwood Winery (Yountville, 1955), mainly a negociant concern acquired in 1984 by a syndicate, markets more than 100,000 cases of table and fortified wines. Sherry and Porto-type solera facilities are located in Santa Clara, while the Napa Valley facility handles Chardonnay, Riesling, Sauvignon Blanc, Cabernet Sauvignon, Zinfandel, Pinot Noir, and others.

Long Vineyards (St. Helena, 1977), is an 18-acre, 2,500-case winery well situated on the southern portion of Lake Hennessey. It makes excellent, rich, viscous, well structured and expensive Sauvignon Blanc, Riesling, Chardonnay, and Cabernet Sauvignon.

Louis Honig Cellars (Rutherford, 1982), is a 57-acre, 11,000-case winery that makes above-average, well structured, wood aged Sauvignon Blanc, and small quantities of Chardonnay and Cabernet Sauvignon.

Louis Martini Winery (St. Helena, 1933), originally founded in 1922 in Fresno County, the winery opened its doors in the Napa Valley after Prohibition. Today it is a large, 1,800-acre, 250,000-case winery that makes many varietal and proprietary wines. Located in ten separate locations in Sonoma and Napa, acreage doubled since 1960: Monte Rosso (240 acres) in Sonoma, for the production of the finest red wines; Los Vinedos del Rio (172 acres) in Sonoma, mainly for white wine production; La Loma and Las Amigas (340 acres), both in Carneros, planted in Pinot Noir, Chardonnay and others; 146 acres in the Chiles Valley; 10 acres in Pope Valley; and Glen Oak Vineyards (146 acres on a 1,980-acre ranch) on hilly land east of St. Helena mainly for the production of red grapes. In addition, the firm owns more than 500 acres in Lake County, including the Perini Springs Vineyard. The finest vineyard selections include Chardonnay, Sauvignon Blanc, Pinot Noir, Merlot, and Cabernet Sauvignon. Historically a pioneer winery in table wine production (vintage dating, Merlot plantings, and varietal label designations), it is known for red wine production, particularly special selection, reserve, and vineyard designations, of which *Monte Rosso, Las Amigas,* and *Los Vinedos del Rio* are excellent, representing the pick of the crop and the finest cuvees, especially Cabernet Sauvignon and Chardonnay. Also above-average are Sauvignon Blanc, Zinfandel, Gewurztraminer, Barbera, Petite Sirah, and Moscato Amabile, a low alcohol, sweet Muscat Blanc wine. Although the winery over the years had established a reputation for consistency and good value, in recent years wine quality has dramatically improved, the wine line severely reduced (White Zinfandel, Chenin Blanc, and Riesling are no longer made), and there has been an increased output of premium wines. The *Los Ninos* Sonoma Valley, and *Monte Rosso* Cabernet Sauvignon are rich, complex, distinctive, and outstanding in every way. The winery now makes three types of wines: the old white label is the least expensive (under $12), the pink label is the intermediate price level (under $20), and the black label, vineyard designate wines are the most expensive.

Mallard Winery (Napa, 1983), is an expanding, 400-acre, 8,000-case winery specializing in Chardonnay and Pinot Noir. The big, round, hand crafted wines, expertly and consistently well made (released only after extensive barrel aging), offer excellent value.

Manzanita Cellars (St. Helena, 1980), is a 2,500-case winery that makes well aged, big, round Cabernet Sauvignon and Chardonnay.

Mario Perelli-Minetti Winery (St. Helena, 1988), is a 5,000-case winery that makes good, sound Chardonnay and Cabernet Sauvignon.

Markham Vineyards (St. Helena, 1978), is a 222-acre, 80,000-case winery that makes above-average to excellent quality Chardonnay, Sauvignon Blanc, Muscat Blanc, Cabernet Sauvignon, Merlot, and proprietary wines. The wines tend to be richly textured, round, and supple. The winery, acquired in 1987 by Sanraku, Japan's largest winemaker, has recently been expanded. Other label: *Glass Mountain Quarry*, for a moderately-priced "field blend" wine.

Marston Vineyards (St. Helena, 1982), is a 50-acre, 5,000-case winery that makes above-average, full bodied Chardonnay, Cabernet Sauvignon, Zinfandel, and minute quantities of Chenin Blanc, Petite Sirah, and others.

Matera Winery (Calistoga, 1988), is a 15-acre, 1,400-case, estate bottled winery that makes well structured Chardonnay and Pinot Noir.

Mayacamas Vineyards (Napa, 1889), is a superb, 50-acre, 5,400-case winery located high on the Mayacamas producing outstanding Chardonnay, Sauvignon Blanc, Cabernet Sauvignon, Pinot Noir, and Zinfandel (regular and late harvest), all of which are full bodied, well structured, big and powerful. The handcrafted wines, the product of well drained volcanic hillside soils, are consistently good and slow to mature.

Merlion Winery (Napa, 1985), is an aggressive, 17,000-case winery and negociant house that makes Chardonnay, *Sauvrier* (equal amounts of Sauvignon Blanc and Semillon), *Coeur de Melon* (Pinot Blanc), *Chevrier* (100% Semillon), Pinot Noir, and Cabernet Sauvignon, offering considerable value. The winery is unusual in that it does not use stainless steel, preferring instead to ferment and age entirely in wood. Offering good value, the well balanced wines, elegant and supple, are mainly sold to restaurants in northern California. Other label: *Piccolo*.

Merryvale Vineyards (St. Helena, 1983), is a superb, 4,000-case winery responsible for full bodied, firm, complex Cabernet Sauvignon, a Caber-net Sauvignon-based super premium white and red Meritage, Chenin Blanc, Muscat de Frontignan (called *Antigua*), and Chardonnay.

Milat Vineyards (St. Helena, 1986), is a 20-acre, 3,000-case, estate winery that historically grew grapes for sale. First releases of Chenin Blanc, Chardonnay, Zinfandel, and Cabernet Sauvignon exhibit good fruit and firmness, offering good value.

Monticello Cellars (Napa, 1980), is an aggressive, stylish, 250-acre, 25,000-case winery that makes excellent Chardonnay, Gewurztraminer, Sauvignon Blanc, Semillon (labeled *Chevrier Blanc*), Cabernet Sauvignon, Pinot Noir, and Merlot. The state-of-the-art winery and immaculate vineyard combine to produce wines known for their fruit, balance and structure, offering good value. The reserve Chardonnay and Cabernet Sauvignon are outstanding. The owners have interest in many other wineries and vineyards. Other label: *Chateau M.*

Mont St. John Cellars (Napa, 1922), is a 160-acre, 15,000-case winery that makes well structured, robust, full bodied Chardonnay, Sauvignon Blanc, Riesling, Gewurztraminer, Muscat Blanc, Cabernet Sauvignon, Pinot Noir, Petite Sirah, and Zinfandel. A new winery, located in the Carneros portion of Napa County, has replaced the 1922 Oakville site. Other label: *Poppy Hill*.

Moon Vineyards (Napa, 1985), is a 60-acre vineyard located in Carneros that periodically has 2,000 cases of crisp Chardonnay under its own label.

Moss Creek Winery (Napa, 1987), is an interesting, 175-acre, 7,500-case winery that makes Chardonnay, Sauvignon Blanc, Cabernet Sauvignon, and Zinfandel winer.

Mount Veeder Winery (Napa, 1973), is a 28-acre, 10,000-case winery located on Mt. Veeder that makes highly flavorful and well scented Chardonnay (aggressive, complex, austere on the palate, and capable of aging), Zinfandel (late harvest), and Cabernet Sauvignon. Reserve wines are outstanding. Many changes are envisioned as the winery was purchased in 1989 by Franciscan Vineyards.

Mumm Napa Valley (Calistoga, 1984), located on 80 acres along the Silverado Trail, is the new sparkling wine facility of Mumm Champagne of Reims and the Seagram Classics Wine Co. The grapes emanate from 50 separate vineyards, but primarily from Winery Lake Carneros. Product line consists of Brut Prestige, Blanc de Noirs, Vintage Reser-

ve, and Winery Lake, the latter, one of the few vineyard-designated sparkling wines. Initial production, above-average for industry standards, exceeds 135,000 cases with an ultimate goal of 250,000 cases.

Napa Creek Winery (St. Helena, 1980), is a 14,000-case winery that makes good, sound Chardonnay, Gewurztraminer, Riesling, Cabernet Sauvignon, and Merlot, the latter, well-balanced, fruity, and well-structured.

Napa Valley Cooperative Winery (St. Helena, 1934), is a large winery that had made wine for Gallo, but also custom crushes for other firms in addition to its own label--*Bergfeld 1885 Wine Cellars* (100,000 cases). Wines made include: Chenin Blanc, Sauvignon Blanc, Chardonnay, Riesling, Gewurztraminer, Cabernet Sauvignon, Pinot Noir, Zinfandel, Merlot, and proprietary wines. The winery also makes and distributes wines under additional labels, the most important being *J. Wile & Sons*.

Napa Valley Port Cellars Napa, 1984), is a 1,000-case winery that makes Porto-type wine from purchased grapes. The vintage dated Cabernet Sauvignon/Petite Sirah/Zinfandel is aged for four years in wood.

Napa Valley Wine Co. (Napa, 1978), is a 6,000-case winery that makes Chardonnay, Sauvignon Blanc, Cabernet Sauvignon, and Zinfandel, from purchased grapes. Other label: *Don Charles Ross*.

Newlan Vineyards & Winery (Napa, 1981), is a 28-acre, 4,000-case winery that makes supple, well flavored Riesling (dry and late harvest), Chardonnay, Sauvignon Blanc, Semillon, Cabernet Sauvignon, Pinot Noir, and a "field blend" called *Century Selection*.

Newton Vineyard (St. Helena, 1979), is an excellent, 62-acre, 25,000-case winery located on the lower slopes of Spring Mountain that makes extraordinary Chardonnay, Sauvignon Blanc, Merlot, and Cabernet Sauvignon from hillside vineyards. Merlot and Cabernet Sauvignon, in particular, are outstanding, well flavored, balanced, complex, and distinctive, offering excellent value.

Neyers Winery (St. Helena, 1980), is a 15-acre, 7,500-case winery that makes good, complex, distinctive Chardonnay, Cabernet Franc, and Cabernet Sauvignon, offering outstanding value.

Nichelini Winery (St. Helena, 1890), is a 70-acre, 5,000-case winery that makes Chenin Blanc, Petite Sirah, Zinfandel, and Cabernet Sauvignon, offering good value.

Niebaum-Coppola Estate Winery (Rutherford, 1978), is a 125-acre (part of a 1,600-acre estate), 5,000-case winery that makes a super expensive Cabernet Sauvignon-based wine called *Rubicon*--a brawny, masculine, well structured, rich, and powerful wine (from a Meritage blend) that requires at least ten years to mature. The producing acreage is part of the original Gustave Niebaum estate. Recent vintages show a marked improvement in finesse and elegance. The winery is unusual for not releasing its wines for seven years.

Oakford Vineyards (St. Helena, 1987), is an 8-acre, 1,000-case label known for full-bodied, round, well-structured Cabernet Sauvignon.

Opus One Winery (Oakville, 1979), is a 108-acre, 14,000-case, joint venture between Robert Mondavi and Chateau Mouton Rothschild that produces a super premium Meritage wine in part from the *Ballestra Vineyard*. In order to achieve new heights, low yielding rootstocks are used, and vineyard spacing is much narrower increasing the number of vines per acre, thus yielding fewer grapes per vine. The vine canopy is also taller and thinner making it possible for more sunlight to penetrate the grape bunches (in theory, the combined effect is to reduce pH, herbal and vegetative flavors). The style, character, and quality of the wine, made from Cabernet Sauvignon, Cabernet Franc, and Merlot, is still evolving as the first seven vintages are all different. Thus far, it is above-average to excellent but has yet to achieve an exalted status despite its high asking price.

Pahlmeyer Winery (St. Helena, 1985), is a 25-acre, 1,500-case label that makes an excellent, well structured, full bodied, rich Chardonnay and Cabernet Sauvignon, the latter, blended with Cabernet Franc, Merlot, Petit Verdot, and Malbec, should not be missed. The source of the grapes is the excellent *Caldwell Vineyard*.

Peju Province (Rutherford, 1982), is a 30-acre, 5,000-case winery that makes rich, fat, silky, and distinctive Cabernet Sauvignon (*HB Vineyard*), Chardonnay, late harvest Sauvignon Blanc, *Carnival*, a late harvest Colombard, and *Karma*, a proprietary rose wine.

Peter Franus Wine Co. (Napa, 1987), made by an accomplished winemaker, this is a 600-case label (*Franus*) that makes superb, well-flavored, wood-aged, yet elegant Zinfandel from the *Hendry Vineyard* near Mt. Veeder.

Philip Togni Vineyard (St. Helena, 1985), located on Spring Mountain, is a 10-acre, 2,000-case winery that makes long lived, powerful, well structured Cabernet Sauvignon, and a full bodied, fragrant, well balanced Sauvignon Blanc, both of which offer superb value.

Philippe-Lorraine (St. Helena, 1989), is a 3,000-case label owned by a well-known winemaker that makes supple, drinkable and affordable Chardonnay, Merlot, and Cabernet Sauvignon.

Pina Cellars (Rutherford, 1982), is a 22-acre, 2,500-case winery that makes distinctive Chardonnay and Zinfandel.

Pine Ridge (Napa, 1978), is a serious, 164-acre, 70,000-case winery that makes well structured Cabernet Sauvignon, Merlot, Chenin Blanc, and a refined, elegant, complex Chardonnay under many vineyard, reserve, estate, and cuvee designations, offering excellent value. The winery owns vine acreage in the Stags Leap, Oak Knoll, Rutherford Bench, and Diamond Mountain areas. It makes distinctive, age worthy *Andrus Reserve* Cabernet Sauvignon under the Rutherford Bench, Stags Leap, Diamond Mountain, and Howell Mountain designations. With additional land purchases in Carneros, this excellent winery is in the process of expanding operations.

Plam Vineyards & Winery (Napa, 1984), formerly the Hopper Creek Winery, is a 6-acre, 7,500-case property purchased by a Danish-born businessman. The winery makes Sauvignon Blanc, Chardonnay, and Cabernet Sauvignon, all of which are distinctive and often outstanding, offering good value.

Planet of the Grapes Winery (St. Helena, 1981), is a 500-case label whose wines (Chardonnay, Merlot, and Charbono) are mainly found in restaurants.

Pope Valley Winery (Pope Valley, 1897), is a 120-acre, 20,000-case, estate winery that makes Chardonnay, Sauvignon Blanc, Cabernet Sauvignon, and Zinfandel, offering good value.

Prager Winery & Port Works (St. Helena, 1979), is a 4,500-case winery that makes above-average, unfiltered and unfined Chardonnay, Gewurztraminer, Cabernet Sauvignon, Zinfandel, and three Porto-type wines: *Nobel Companion* (from 100 percent Cabernet Sauvignon); *Tawny* (from Pinot Noir); and *Royal Escort* (from Petite Sirah), all of which are unusual due to restrained residual sugar. All wines are distinctive (particularly the Porto-type), offering good value. Port label names will soon be changed as the vineyard sources are budding over to Portuguese varieties. Other label: *La Croix*, grapes from the *Battaglia Vineyard*, sold for charitable purposes.

Quail Ridge Cellars (Napa, 1978), is a 17-acre, 20,000-case winery that makes average to excellent, barrel fermented, full bodied, complex, round and well flavored Chardonnay, Sauvignon Blanc, Cabernet Sauvignon, and Merlot from mountain grown vines. In 1987 it merged with The Christian Brothers winery, and is now part of Heublein. Other label: *Harmonio*.

Raymond Vineyard & Cellars (St. Helena, 1974), is an underrated, quality oriented, 80 acre, 150,000-case winery that makes wine under Napa and California appellation designations. Its reputation rests with flavorful, intense, well rounded, and easily quaffable, yet complex Chardonnay and Cabernet Sauvignon, the latter, one of the finest in

the county. Other wines include Sauvignon Blanc, tiny quantities of Chenin Blanc, and off-dry and semi-sweet Riesling. The winery was acquired by Kirin Breweries in 1988. Other label: *La Belle*.

Revere Vineyard & Winery (Napa, 1985), is an 11-acre, 3,000-case winery located in the Coombsville area that makes big, complex, intense, age worthy, and well structured Chardonnay, offering superb value. The reserve wines are outstanding.

Richard L. Graeser Winery (Calistoga, 1985), is a 10-acre, 2,500-case winery that makes supple, early maturing Chardonnay, Semillon, Cabernet Sauvignon, Cabernet Franc, Merlot, and Meritage-type wines.

Ritchie Creek Vineyards (St. Helena, 1974), is an 8-acre, 1,200-case winery that makes distinctive, well flavored Chardonnay, Cabernet Sauvignon, and a rare Viognier. The vineyard, cited on terraces 2000 feet on Spring Mountain, consistently produces excellent, low yielding fruit that is always made into lean (but often rich), balanced, well structured wines.

Robert Keenan Winery (St. Helena, 1976), is a 45-acre, 12,000-case Spring Mountain winery that makes big, opulent, always well flavored, and often rich and ripe Chardonnay, Cabernet Sauvignon, and Merlot, the latter, full bodied, round, and consistently good.

Robert Mondavi Winery, one of the largest, and always along the cutting edge. Baxevanis

Robert Mondavi Winery (Oakville, 1966), is a highly successful winery that has been in the forefront of several significant enological and marketing innovations. A partnership until 1978 when the Mondavi family bought the Rainer Brewing Company out, it purchased the Woodbridge winery in the Central Valley in 1979 for the production of red, white, and rose table wines, and extensive experimentation of Porto-type wine production from Portuguese grape varieties. However, quality varietal production has remained in the primary Oakville facility, and the neighboring Vichon Winery purchased in the middle 1980s. The winery owns more than 1,600 acres in the Napa Valley and Carneros region, and produces more than 2.5 million cases annually. The two principal Napa vineyards are the 593-acre *To-Kalon* and the 398-acre *Oak-Knoll*. The former, surrounding the winery, is mainly planted in Cabernet Sauvignon, Cabernet Franc, Merlot, Sauvignon Blanc, and Semillon. The smaller Oak-Knoll vineyard, located on higher, cooler ground along the Silverado Trail, is mainly planted in Chardonnay, Pinot Noir, and Riesling. The winery has recently purchased a 500-acre vineyard in the Napa section of Carneros. The winery also buys grapes from 25 different growers in North Coast areas. In addition to blended table wines, the principal varietals are Cabernet Sauvignon, Chardonnay, Pinot Noir, Sauvignon Blanc, Riesling, Chenin Blanc, Merlot, and Muscat Blanc, all of which are average to above-average in quality; the finest cuvees, sold under the reserve label, are often outstanding. The winery also makes two sparkling wines: Napa Valley Brut Reserve (made from Chardonnay and Pinot Noir), and Napa Valley Brut (100% Chardonnay). A popular priced line of wines under the Robert Mondavi name (but with a California *ava*) are made at the Woodbridge facility. Porto-type wines, as yet unreleased, exhibit extraordinary quality and potential, and may prove to be the finest such wines made in the state. Through the purchase of a significant portion of the former Tepusquet Vineyard in Santa Barbara (total acreage holdings in Santa Barbara are approximately 1,500 acres), the Mondavi winery is a major player of quality Chardonnay production. Family members also own the Byron Winery in Santa Barbara.

Robert Pecota Winery (Calistoga, 1978), is a 35-acre, 20,000-case winery that makes consistently rich, meaty, well structured Sauvignon Blanc, Chardonnay, Cabernet Sauvignon, Gamay Beaujolais, Petite Sirah, and a Sweet Muscat Blanc (named *Sweet Andrea*), offering excellent value.

Robert Pepi Winery (Oakville, 1981), is a 70-acre, 19,000-case winery that makes Chardonnay, Semillon, and Cabernet Sauvignon, but the bulk of production is the excellent, fresh, well balanced Sauvignon Blanc. Cabernet Sauvignon from Vine Hill Ranch is big and well structured; Chardonnay is rich, supple, with a delicate fragrance from old vines; and Semillon is succulent, delicate, and fragrant. The winery also makes an interesting Sangiovese Grosso named *Colline di Sassi*. All wines offer excellent value. The winery has experienced considerable success with its trellising system, and for its moderately priced Sauvignon Blanc.

Robert Sinskey Vineyards (Napa, 1986), is a 174-acre, 12,000-case, expanding winery that makes big, lean, round, full bodied, and complex Chardonnay, Pinot Noir, Cabernet Sauvignon, and Merlot. Made by one of the most celebrated winemakers in the valley, the wines belong in every serious cellar. The *RSV Carneros Claret*, a Meritage wine, is outstanding. Other label: *Aries Cuvee Flore*.

Rocking Horse Winery (Napa, 1989), is a 2,000-case label that makes (at a neighboring winery) well-structured, muscular, yet rich Zinfandel and Cabernet Sauvignon.

Rombauer Vineyards (St. Helena, 1980), is a 17-acre, 10,000-case, stylish winery known for well flavored and structured Cabernet Sauvignon, the best of which, marketed as *Le Meilleur du Chai*, is blended with Cabernet Franc and Merlot. Also made and equally expensive is a robust Chardonnay.

Round Hill Winery (St. Helena, 1977), is an aggressive and highly successful, 10-acre winery and negociant firm that grew from 30,000 cases in 1977 to more than 350,000 cases in 1990. The winery makes robust and assertive Sauvignon Blanc, Chardonnay (these two account for about two-thirds of total output), Gewurztraminer, Cabernet Sauvignon, Zinfandel, and Merlot, all offering excellent value. The winery makes "house," "varietal," and "reserve" wines, but most of the wine is bottled for private labels. Other label: *Rutherford Ranch* (for Chardonnay, Sauvignon Blanc, Cabernet Sauvignon, Zinfandel, and Merlot, all of which are barrel aged, unfiltered and unfined).

Rustridge Vineyards & Winery (St. Helena, 1985), located in the Chiles Valley, is a little known, 60-acre, 3,000-case winery (and horse ranch) that makes above-average Riesling (both dry and late harvest), Chardonnay, Sauvignon Blanc, Zinfandel, and Cabernet Sauvignon.

Rutherford Hill Winery (Rutherford, 1976), is a 198-acre, 115,000-case winery historically known for inconsistent, but often spicy and alcoholic Sauvignon Blanc, Gewurztraminer, Chardonnay, Merlot, and Cabernet Sauvignon, all of which exhibit a marked improvement since 1987. Small quantities of Vintage Porto-type wine from Zinfandel is also made. Grapes emanate from vineland (more than 1,000 acres) owned by various partners. Recent organizational and expansionary moves are promising as the winery will emphasize Merlot and Chardonnay production. The *Reserve, Jaeger Vineyards* Chardonnay, and *XVS* wines are excellent. Other label: *Hunter Ashby*.

Rutherford Vintners Winery (Rutherford, 1976), owned by a knowledgeable Alsatian with considerable experience in wine sales, is a 35-acre, 12,000-case winery that makes good, sound, firm Chardonnay, Sauvignon Blanc, Riesling, Muscat of Alexandria, Cabernet Sauvignon, Merlot, and Pinot Noir. Other label: *Chateau Rutherford*.

S. Anderson Vineyard (Yountville, 1979), is a 53-acre, 14,000-case, sparkling wine facility with impeccable credentials for Brut, Blanc de Noirs, and a still Chardonnay, offering excellent value. Chardonnay and Cabernet Sauvignon are also made.

Saddleback Cellars (Oakville, 1983), is a 15-acre, 2,000-case winery that makes excellent, well structured Chardonnay, Cabernet Sauvignon, and Pinot Blanc from old vines, the latter offering good value.

Sage Canyon Winery (Rutherford, 1981), is a small, 1,500-case winery that specializes in crisp and well structured Chardonnay from purchased grapes, offering good value.

St. Andrew's Winery (Napa, 1980), is an 82-acre (nearly all Chardonnay), 20,000-case winery that makes firm, muscular Chardonnay, Sauvignon Blanc, and Cabernet Sauvignon, offering excellent value. As of 1988 it has been acquired by a subsidiary of Clos du Val Winery.

St. Clement Vineyards (St. Helena, 1878), located on Spring Mountain, is a 20-acre, 12,500-case winery (owned by a Japanese Brewery) that makes rich, full Chardonnay, spicy Sauvignon Blanc, and soft, distinctive Cabernet Sauvignon and Merlot. The reserve Chardonnay is outstanding.

St. Michael Winery and Vineyard (Calistoga, 1991), is a 100-acre, 100,000-case, super premium winery currently in its construction and planting stage that will be making Chardonnay, Cabernet Sauvignon, Merlot, and Pinot Noir.

Saintsbury (Napa, 1982), is a 38,000-case, Carneros winery that makes barrel fermented, firm, well structured, age worthy, yet sublime Chardonnay, Pinot Noir, and small quantities of sparkling wine.

Salmon Creek Winery (Napa, 1989), is a 2,000-case label known for a serious, sturdy, full-bodied Chardonnay from the *Bad Dog Vineyard* in Carneros.

San Pietro Vara (Calistoga, 1983), is a 25-acre, 3,000-case, organic winery (the first in the Napa Valley) that makes robust Zinfandel, Cabernet Sauvignon, Merlot, and Charbono.

Schramsberg Vineyards (Calistoga, 1862), one of the oldest and most respected names in sparkling wine, is a 60-acre, 50,000-case winery that makes five different wines: Blanc de Blancs, Blanc de Noirs, Cuvee de Pinot, Cremant Demi-Sec, and Reserve, the latter, the product of the choicest cuvees and extended cellaring, can be outstanding. Although pricy and well known, the wines are often dull and inconsistent. Recently, this winery formed a joint venture, R&S Vineyards, with Remy Martin to produce California Alambic Brandy, and in another partnership in Portugal the firm will produce sparkling wine in the Douro Valley.

Seavey Vineyard (St. Helena, 1990), is 37-acre, 1,500-case winery that makes well-structured, full-bodied Chardonnay and Cabernet Sauvignon.

Sequoia Grove Vineyards (Rutherford, 1980), is a 24-acre, 15,000-case winery that makes Chardonnay and Cabernet Sauvignon, both of which are expertly made, full bodied, distinctive, round, complex, and reliable, offering good value. Chardonnay is crisp and well structured, and the Cabernet Sauvignon, made with other classic Bordeaux varieties, is soft, non-oaky, and multifaceted. Although the reputation rests with Cabernet Sauvignon, both are fruity, smooth, and satisfying, especially estate bottles. The winery purchases most of the fruit, and is expanding acreage through a syndicate in the Carneros district. Also made are minor quantities of Gewurztraminer. Other label: *Allen Family*, available only at the winery.

Shadow Brook Winery (St. Helena, 1984), is a 60-acre, 17,000-case winery that makes fruity, supple Chardonnay and Pinot Noir.

Shafer Vineyards (Napa, 1978), located in the Stags Leap region, is a 148-acre, 22,000-case winery that makes Chardonnay, Cabernet Sauvignon, and Merlot, all of which are the product of dry-farming methods and low yields. The expertly made and intensely flavored wines, particularly the rich and complex Cabernet Hillside Select, are little known, consistent to a fault, age well, and offer good value. The winery's recently purchased 83-acre tract in Carneros will be planted in Chardonnay and Merlot.

Shown & Sons Vineyards (Rutherford, 1979), is a 25-acre, 9,000-case winery that makes big, round, full bodied Zinfandel, Cabernet Sauvignon, and proprietary wines.

Signorello Vineyards (Napa, 1984), is a 100-acre, 5,000-case winery that makes excellent, estate Semillon, Sauvignon Blanc, Chardonnay, Cabernet Sauvignon, and Pinot Noir. Reserve wines are sensational.

Silverado Hill Cellars (Napa, 1979), is a 34-acre, 35,000-case winery that makes stylish and supple Chardonnay, Sauvignon Blanc, and Pinot Noir wines that are mainly available in restaurants and selected retail outlets. Historically known as Pannonia Winery, it was purchased by Louis K. Mihaly in 1984, and sold again in 1988 to the Minami Kyushu Coca-Cola Bottling Co. of Japan, a firm that is also building a Sake facility in Napa.

Silver Oak Wine Cellars (Oakville, 1972), is a quality oriented, 69-acre, 25,000-case winery producing only 100 percent Cabernet Sauvignon that is aged in American oak for three years, and bottle aged for another two years prior to release. Three wines are made: *Alexander Valley*, *Napa Valley*, and *Bonny's Vineyard* Napa Valley. All are big, muscular, robust, multi-flavored monsters that are able of age well into

their second decade. The wines are unusual, atypical of current California fashion, and should not be missed.

Full-bodied, well-structured, big, and age-worthy, the wines of Silver Oak Cellars belong in every serious cellar. Courtesy of Silver Oak Cellars

Silverado Vineyards (Napa, 1981), is an expanding, 340-acre, 75,000-case winery owned by Mrs. Walt Disney and her family that makes fruity, often complex Chardonnay, Sauvignon Blanc, Cabernet Sauvignon, and Merlot, offering excellent value. With the recently purchased vineyard land in the Coombsville area, production is expected to increase beyond 100,000 cases shortly. This is a property to watch.

Skali S.A. (Rutherford, 1982), is an aggressive, 1,500-acre property (650 are planted), 30,000-case winery that makes Chardonnay, Sauvignon Blanc, and Cabernet Sauvignon under the *St. Supery Vineyards & Winery* label. Although the winery is located in the Napa Valley proper, the vineyard represents the largest grape plantings in the Pope Valley.

Sky Vineyards (Napa, 1979), located on Mt. Veeder, is a 20-acre, 2,000-case winery that makes well structured, spicy, distinctive, wood aged, estate Zinfandel.

Smith-Madrone Vineyards (St. Helena, 1971), located on Spring Mountain, is a 40-acre, 6,500-case, underrated winery that makes excellent, strongly scented and flavored Riesling, Chardonnay, and Cabernet Sauvignon from low yielding vines.

Soda Canyon Vineyards (Napa, 1985), is a 12-acre, 3,000-case brand that is known for good, sound, barrel fermented Chardonnay made in two neighboring wineries.

Solari Estate Vineyards (Calistoga, 1984), is a 420-acre, 10,000-case

winery that makes estate-bottled, well flavored Chardonnay, Sauvignon Blanc, Merlot, and Cabernet Sauvignon, offering good value,

Spottswoode Winery (St. Helena, 1982), is a superb, 40-acre, 3,000-case winery that makes full bodied, strapping, unfiltered Cabernet Sauvignon (blended with Cabernet Franc). Sauvignon Blanc, equally good, is less celebrated. Both wines, distinctive and often remarkable, offer excellent value and should not be missed.

Spring Mountain Vineyards (St. Helena, 1968), is a 43-acre, 25,000-case winery with an excellent, but variable reputation for Chardonnay, Sauvignon Blanc, Pinot Noir, and Cabernet Sauvignon. It is expected that substantial changes will be affected as the winery is currently in the process of being sold. Other label: *Falcon Crest*.

Staglin Family Vineyard (Rutherford, 1986), is a 50-acre, 2,000-case vineyard that crushes at a neighboring winery making excellent, well-structured Chardonnay and Cabernet Sauvignon.

Stag's Leap Wine Cellars (Napa, 1972), is a 134-acre, 160,000-case winery that has the ability to make extraordinary Cabernet Sauvignon, Merlot, Chardonnay, Sauvignon Blanc, Petite Sirah, and Riesling. Although there are bouts of inconsistency, the very best wines are well structured, round, rich, fragrant, flavorful, firm, and well balanced. The *Cask 23* Cabernet Sauvignon is a superb, ripe, smooth, multi-layered, refined wine that should not be missed. Other label: *Hawk Crest*, accounts for three quarters of production.

Stags' Leap Winery (Napa, 1972), although lacking the celebrity of its neighbor with a similar name, this is a 100-acre, 30,000-case winery that makes above-average Chardonnay, Chenin Blanc, Petite Sirah, Cabernet Sauvignon, and Merlot. Other label: *Pedregal.*

Star Hill Winery (Napa, 1986), is a serious, 5-acre, 1,500-case winery that makes rich, well-structured Chardonnay and Pinot Noir. The owners also have another small winery, Pacific Star in Mendocino County.

Sterling Vineyards (Calistoga, 1964), is a 1,548-acre (about one-third is leased), 125,000-case winery with a spectacular Greek Aegean motif winery and tasting room located on a knoll in the northern portion of the Napa Valley. A tram ride leads to the winery on top of the knoll which accommodates nearly 200,000 visitors each year. Grapes originate from 14 Napa Valley estate vineyards with good reputations, of which *Winery Lake Vineyard, Three Palms, Diamond Mountain Ranch, Bear Flats & Bothe, Oak Knoll,* and *Rutherford Ranch* are the most important. The winery produces estate and non-estate wines of which the reserve Cabernet Sauvignon, Diamond Ranch Chardonnay and Cabernet Sauvignon, Sauvignon Blanc, and Merlot vary from average to excellent. Part of Joseph E. Seagram & Sons since 1984, the winery is also affiliated with a new sparkling wine facility for Domaine Mumm next to Sterling. The Seagram Classics Wine Company, the holding company, has recently moved operations from San Francisco to Sterling Vineyards, where management will direct all activities for Sterling Vineyards, Mumm Napa Valley, and The Monterey Vineyard.

Steltzner Vineyards (Napa, 1977), located in the Stag's Leap region, contains 49 acres and makes about 5,000 cases of excellent to outstanding Cabernet Sauvignon from old vines. Low yields, well drained soils, and expert vinification combine to produce well structured, distinctive, well flavored and scented wine that ages marvelously.

Stonegate Winery (Calistoga, 1973), is a 35-acre, 22,000-case winery that makes Chardonnay, Sauvignon Blanc, Merlot, and Cabernet Sauvignon. Red grapes are grown on mountainous terrain in the Mayacamas, while white grapes are planted on flat land next to the winery. The wines, inconsistent in the past, have recently improved, and now provide good value. Other label: *Calistoga Cuvee.*

Stony Hill Vineyard (St. Helena, 1952), is a 35-acre, 4,000-case winery that makes outstanding, full bodied, concentrated and highly flavorful Chardonnay, Riesling, and Gewurztraminer. Located in the Mayacamas Mountains, it is one of the first "boutique" wineries that has continued to maintain high standards. Other label: *SHV.*

Storybook Mountain Vineyards (Calistoga, 1883), is a 36-acre (grapes are organically grown), 8,000-case winery that makes excellent Zinfandel, of which Napa Estate Reserve is distinctive, complex and elegant.

Strack Vineyard (Napa, 1985), is a 38-acre, 5,200-case winery that makes soft, affordable Chardonnay.

Straus Vineyards (Calistoga, 1984), is a 10-acre, 4,000-case winery that specializes in fine, delicate, well structured Merlot, and small quantities of Chardonnay.

Streblow Vineyards (St. Helena, 1985), located on Spring Mountain, is a 15-acre, 2,000-case winery that often makes full bodied, round Cabernet Sauvignon and Sauvignon Blanc.

Sullivan Vineyards Winery (Rutherford, 1972), is a 7,000-case winery that makes big, ponderous, dark Cabernet Sauvignon (the finest is labeled *Coeur de Vigne*), Merlot, Zinfandel, and an equally full bodied Chenin Blanc. All wines, laden with extract, are intensely flavored, and well aged in American oak.

Summit Lake Vineyards & Winery (Angwin, 1985), is a 14-acre, 3,400-case, Howell Mountain winery that makes big, well structured Zinfandel, offering good value.

Sunny St. Helena Winery (St. Helena, 1987), originally opened by Cesare Mondavi in 1933 (it was the first winery to be built after Prohibition in the Napa Valley), subsequently used as a storage facility by the Christian Brothers during 1971-1986, and resurrected as a winery by the owners of Merryvale Winery in 1987, is a 32,000-case winery that makes Chardonnay, Sauvignon Blanc, Chenin Blanc, Zinfandel, and Cabernet Sauvignon. The historic facility also houses Merryvale Wines.

Sutter Home Winery (St. Helena, 1946), founded in 1874 by a Swiss German family, was renamed Sutter Home in 1900 when it was sold and operated until it closed during Prohibition. It remained dormant until it was purchased by the present owners in 1946. Today this large winery consists of nearly 4,000 acres (of which 1,200 have recently been acquired in Colusa County for development) fragmented in five different locations producing more than 3.7 million cases. Of the many wines produced--Chardonnay, Chenin Blanc, Sauvignon Blanc, Muscat of Alexandria, Cabernet Sauvignon, and Zinfandel are the most important, but it is the latter, made into sparkling, white and red, that has established the winery's reputation (it is the nation's leading producer of White Zinfandel). The spectacular growth is illustrated by the fact that the winery produced just 2,500 cases in 1975, and more than 3.5 million in 1991. This aggressive winery is also one of the largest producers of Chardonnay-more than 400,000 cases in 1990. Practically all wines are light bodied, well flavored and quaffable. The winery has recently purchased significant acreage in Lake County, and the Montevina Winery in the Sierra Foothills region. The winery has planted 2,000 acres of Zinfandel.

Swanson Vineyards and Winery (Rutherford, 1987), is a 130-acre, 8,000-case, stylish winery that makes full bodied, well flavored Chardonnay (refined and one of the finest in the state), Sauvignon Blanc, Cabernet Sauvignon, and late harvest Semillon.

The Christian Brothers Winery (Napa, 182), is a 1,200-acre, 1.4 million-case winery that simply did not adapt to the changing wine market over the past 20 years. As quality declined sales plummeted 40 percent in the early 1980s, and the product line was substantially reduced by 60 percent to streamline operations. The recently improved wines are divided into four broad groups: premium varietal wines, of which Chardonnay, Sauvignon Blanc, Chenin Blanc, Cabernet Sauvignon, and Zinfandel are considered the finest; premium Napa generic; fortified and brandy (1.3 million cases); and an inexpensive generic line that accounts for 750,000 cases. The winery and vine acreage were sold to Heublein in 1989, and with this acquisition Heublein (which also owns Inglenook, Beaulieu, and Quail Ridge) is with more than 4,400 acres (2,827 of which are leased or controlled) Napa Valley's largest vineland owner.

The Hess Collection Winery (Napa, 1982), is a 295-acre (another 100 to be planted), 40,000-case, Mount Veeder winery that makes excellent Chardonnay and Cabernet Sauvignon (blended with Merlot and Cabernet Franc). The 950-acre estate and winery, owned by a Swiss industrialist, is a serious, impeccably managed and maintained mountain winery with a reputation for supple, technically flawless, well flavored and scented wines offering excellent value. The Reserve Cabernet Sauvignon is outstanding. The wines are made at the historic Mont La Salle Winery built in 1903 and leased from The Christian Brothers Winery. The winery has recently purchased 350 acres in Monterey County near Soledad. Other label: *Hess Select.*

The Hillside Vineyards of The Hess Collection, the wines of which are equally spectacular. Courtesy of The Hess Collection

The Terraces (Rutherford, 1985), is an excellent, 5-acre, 600-case label (wines are made at Caymus) for full bodied, robust, yet multi-dimensional Zinfandel and Cabernet Sauvignon. A 20,000 gallon winery is under construction.

Toad Hall (Rutherford, 1987), is a 12-acre, 500-case winery that makes expensive Meritage-type wines marketed under the *Bodacious* label.

Topaz Wines (St. Helena, 1986), is a 1,200-case label that makes a wine considered to be as good as a first class Sauternes. Made from 60% Sauvignon Blanc and 40% Semillon, this nectar is a product of late harvest grapes. Also made is a muscular, tannin-rich, well-flavored Meritage-type red. Both wines offer good value.

Traulsen Vineyards (Calistoga, 1980), is a 2-acre, 800-case winery that only makes full bodied, flavorful, wood aged Zinfandel.

Trefethen Vineyards (Napa, 1886), one of the oldest and most historic vineyards (known as the *Eshcol Estate*) in the Napa Valley, began a modern sequel to its checkered past when it was purchased, rehabilitated, renamed, and enlarged by its present owners in 1968. It is a large, 604-acre, 95,000-case winery that produces average to excellent estate produced Chardonnay, Riesling, Cabernet Sauvignon, and Pinot Noir. About 40 percent of total production are two proprietary white and red wines named *Eshcol*. While the carefully selected varietal wines are handcrafted, and often rich and delicate, the red wines appear to be more consistent.

Truchard Vineyards (Napa, 1989), is a 175-acre (20 acres are planted), 2,000-case winery that makes Chardonnay, Pinot Noir, Cabernet Sauvignon, and Merlot, and shares output and production with Haven's Wine Cellars.

Tudal Winery (St. Helena, 1979), is a 7-acre, 2,500-case winery that makes subtle, well structured Cabernet Sauvignon very much in the Bordeaux manner that should not be missed.

Tulocay Winery (Napa, 1975), is a 2,500-case winery that makes Chardonnay, Pinot Noir, Cabernet Sauvignon, and Zinfandel.

V. Sattui Winery (St. Helena, 1975), is a highly successful, 65-acre, 135,000-case winery that makes more than twelve different wines, most of which are soft and supple, of which Chardonnay, Sauvignon Blanc, Cabernet Sauvignon, Zinfandel, and two fortified Madeira-type and Muscat Blanc are particularly good. All wines are moderately priced offering good value.

Van Der Heyden Vineyards Winery (Napa, 1984), is a 13-acre, 3,000-case winery that makes well flavored, balanced, yet firm Chardonnay.

Vichon Winery (Oakville, 1980), is a stylish, 60,000-case winery acquired by the Mondavi family in 1985 to produce above-average Chardonnay, Sauvignon Blanc, Semillon, Merlot, and Cabernet Sauvignon, the latter two excellent. The bulk of production is white wine, most of which is made *sur lie*. *Chevrion*, a popular wine, is a blend of equal amounts of Sauvignon Blanc and Semillon. As vines mature and new grower contracts are signed, future offerings will emphasize several regional vineyard designations. Historically, the wines were made lean, tart and crisp, but are now much softer and better balanced. The winery has recently produced an interesting botrytized Semillon.

Villa Helena Winery (St. Helena, 1984), is a 4-acre, 2,000-case winery that makes Chardonnay, Sauvignon Blanc, Pinot Noir, late harvest Zinfandel, and botrytized Semillon and Sauvignon Blanc, the latter, excellent and bottled under the *Dulcinea* proprietary label. Other label: *Greenwood Cellars*.

Villa Mt. Eden (Oakville, 1881), is a reliable, 80-acre, 40,000-case winery known primarily for Chardonnay, Chenin Blanc, Cabernet Sauvignon, Pinot Noir, and Zinfandel. Stimson Lane has acquired the brand, leases production facilities and other vineyards, and maintains long term contracts for estate grapes. The winery has expanded operations by focusing on *Cellar Select*, a moderately-priced line of wines. The reserve wines are plummy and supple.

Villa Zapu (Napa, 1985), is a stylish, 130-acre, 9,000-case label whose Chardonnay and Cabernet Sauvignon wines are made in a neighboring facility. The firm is now in the process of planting grapes, and shall be constructing a winery shortly.

Vincent Arroyo Winery (Calistoga, 1984), is a 50-acre, 2,000-case winery that makes three excellent red wines: Petite Sirah, Cabernet Sauvignon, and Gamay.

Von Strasser Vineyards (Calistoga, 1990), is a 10-acre, 750-case, quality-oriented winery that makes exceptional, well-structured, dense, but supple Cabernet Sauvignon.

Vose Vineyards (Napa, 1970), is a 120-acre, 20,500-case winery located on one of the highest elevations of Mt. Veeder. The expertly made, but underrated and little known wines include Chardonnay, Gewurz-

traminer, Sauvignon Blanc, Cabernet Sauvignon, and Zinfandel, all intensely flavored offering outstanding value. The winery was acquired by Chateau Potelle in 1989.

Wermuth Winery (Calistoga, 1982), is a 10-acre, 3,000-case winery that makes unusual Sauvignon Blanc, Colombard, Gewurztraminer, Napa Gamay, and Cabernet Sauvignon.

Whitehall Lane Winery (St. Helena, 1980), is a stylish, 22-acre, 23,000-case winery that makes full bodied, long lived, tannin rich Cabernet Sauvignon and Merlot, firm Chardonnay, supple Sauvignon Blanc, and well balanced, late harvest Riesling. The winery and vineyard were acquired by a Japanese real estate developer in 1988. Other label: *Fleur d'Helene*.

White Rock Vineyards (Napa, 1986), is a 35-acre, 6,000-case winery with magnificent underground cellars that makes a lean Chardonnay, and a flavorful, complex blend of Cabernet Sauvignon, Merlot, Petit Verdot, and Cabernet Franc, the blends of which are labeled simply as Meritage Claret. The expertly made wines of Blue Heron winery are also made here by an excellent winemaker.

Whitford Cellars (Napa, 1976), is a 38-acre, 2,000-case winery that only makes Chardonnay under the *Haynes Vineyard* designation, offering good value.

William Hill Winery (Napa, 1976), is a 470-acre (out of a total property of 1,642 acres), 100,000-case winery that has established a reputation for exceptional Chardonnay and Cabernet Sauvignon, both made from cool mountain (Mt. Veeder and Atlas Peak, Soda Canyon, and Carneros) vineyards. The owner, totally committed to mountain grown wine grapes, is a successful vineyard speculator as well as a competent winemaker. Cabernet and Chardonnay, divided into" gold" and "silver" labels, are big, well structured, mouth filling, and age extremely well. The winery owns 297 acres of prime Chardonnay acreage in Sonoma for the production of sparkling wine, and also maintains a considerable interest in the Willamette Valley. The winery and name have recently been sold to The Wine Alliance, owners of Clos du Bois, Callaway, and Atlas Peak Vineyards. The former owner will retain most of the acreage as well as interest in Oregon properties.

Winter Creek Winery (Napa, 1984), is an 80-acre, 2,500-case property that makes lean, crisp, refreshing Chardonnay and Sauvignon Blanc, offering excellent value.

Woltner Estates, Ltd. (Angwin, 1985), is a superb, Howell Mountain, 55-acre, 4,000-case winery located on a site first planted by two French vignerons in 1866. Owned by the former owner of Chateau La Mission Haut-Brion, the winery is attempting to produce a super premium Chardonnay. This Chardonnay only winery makes an estate-bottled (Woltner Estates), and three types of expensive, but often inconsistent, barrel fermented, vineyard-designated wines: *St. Thomas, Frederique*, and *Titus*, all under the *Chateau Woltner* label.

ZD Wines (Napa, 1969), is a 3-acre, 30,000-case winery that makes big, distinctive, highly flavored, full bodied, robust, and assertive wines that are aged in red and white American oak. With more than 80 percent of production, Chardonnay (almost always excellent to outstanding) is the most important, followed by Cabernet Sauvignon, Pinot Noir, and late harvest Riesling.

Marin And Solano Counties

Marin County, considered the wealthiest county in the nation, has limited potential as a vinegrowing region because of high taxes and $100,000-an-acre agricultural land values. Grape-growing is almost entirely confined to the Novato region. Lying immediately to the north of San Francisco, it contains just eleven acres (down from nearly 400 acres in 1939) of vineyards and seven wineries:

Brandborg Cellars (Fairfax, 1986), is a 1,500-case winery that makes rich, peppery, full-bodied Zinfandel, Pinot Noir, Charbono, Riesling, and Sauvignon Blanc, mainly from Mendocino and Napa County grapes. **Coastal Wines Ltd.** (Novato, 1982), founded as Vintage Wine Merchants, is a 220,000-case negociant concern marketing under the *Patrick Dore* label. The firm distributes a large line of varietal, sparkling, generic, and fortified wines, of which Cabernet Sauvignon, Chardonnay, Sauvignon Blanc, Zinfandel, and Chenin Blanc are considered the finest. **Kalin Cellars** (Novato, 1977), is a 5,000-case winery that makes above-average to excellent, full bodied, muscular, yet refined Chardonnay, Sauvignon Blanc, Semillon, Cabernet Sauvignon, Pinot Noir, and a sweet blend of Sauvignon Blanc and Semillon called *Cuvee D'Or*. **Pacheco Ranch Winery** (Ignacio, 1979), is a 10-acre, 1,500-case winery that makes flavorful, estate Chardonnay and Cabernet Sauvignon, both of which offer good value. **Ross Valley Winery** (San Anselmo, 1987), is a 500-case winery that makes chewy, serious Zinfandel, Merlot, and Chardonnay. **Sean H. Thackerey Vintner** (Bolinas, 1980), is a superb, low-key, little-known, 2,000-case label that makes exceptional wines: *Aquila* (a blend of Cabernet Sauvignon and Merlot); *Orion* (100% Syrah); *Taurus* (100% Mourvedre); *Sirius* (100% Petite Sirah); and *Pleiades* (a proprietary blend). The wines are full-bodied, often dense, and eminently flavored. **Souzao Cellars** (San Rafael, 1988), is a 1,500-case winery that makes interesting and moderately priced Chardonnay, Pinot Noir, and Zinfandel, the latter two worthy of serious discussion.

Solano County (the state's leading county for sheep and lamb production), located along the eastern border of Napa County, is influenced by the temperate waters of Suisun Bay and the Sacramento River. Framed by these bodies of water and higher mountain land in the north, a good deal of the swamp land in the southern portions has now been reclaimed and used for large agribusiness enterprises. Vineland is confined to the sheltered Green and Suisun valleys, both of which are climatically and geographically similar to Napa. The wines, however, are less celebrated and significantly less expensive. It has two *ava's*: *Solano County Green Valley (1983)*, and *Suisun Valley (1982)*. The former is located in the southwestern portion of Solano County adjacent to Napa and west of Suisun Valley. Sandwiched within the southern end of the Vaca Mountains and the Mount George Range, the one by four-mile valley terminates at the marshlands of Suisun Bay. Significantly foggier than neighboring Suisun Valley, the soils are mainly alluvial and wet as they contain significant accumulations of clay. There are more than 400 acres of planted vines. *Suisun Valley*, approximately 3 x 8 miles wide, lies further inland, hence is sunnier and less foggy than the above. Vine acreage is about twice that of Green Valley, mainly in Zinfandel, Cabernet Sauvignon, and Chardonnay. Soils range from clay and silty loams to sandy loams.

The four wineries are: **Cadenaso Winery** (Suisun, 1906), is a 63-acre, 10,000-case winery that makes Chenin Blanc, Pinot Noir, Cabernet Sauvignon, Zinfandel, and Grenache Noir. **Chateau De Leu Winery** (Suisun, 1981), is an 80-acre, 13,000-case winery that makes Chardonnay, Sauvignon Blanc, Chenin Blanc, Pinot Noir, and Petite Sirah. **West Wind Winery** (Suisun, 1990) is a 76-acre, 3,500-case winery that makes Chardonnay, Gewurztraminer, Sauvignon Blanc, Zinfandel, Merlot, and Cabernet Sauvignon. **Wooden Valley Winery** (Suisun, 1932), is a 236-acre, 30,000-case winery that makes Chardonnay, Sauvignon Blanc, Riesling, Gewurztraminer, Zinfandel, Cabernet Sauvignon, Merlot, and Gamay.

THE WINES OF THE
CENTRAL COAST VITICULTURAL REGION

Between the two largest Pacific Megalopoli is a region of discontinuous coastal ranges, fertile agricultural valleys, grass-covered hills, and oak-studded mountains. The Cen-

tral Coast, from San Francisco in the north to Ventura County in the south, is a 60-mile wide, 300-mile stretch of marine-ventilated hills and valleys that produce a surprising array of wines. This irregular region, united only by geography, consists of eleven counties--San Francisco, Contra Costa, Alameda, San Mateo, Santa Clara, Santa Cruz, San Benito, Monterey, San Luis Obispo, Santa Barbara, and Ventura. It represents some of the state's oldest and newest wineries, one of the nation's largest wineries, and contains the second largest single concentration of wine grapes (as opposed to the mixture of table, raisin, and wine grapes found in the San Joaquin Valley).

Figure 9.11

CENTRAL COAST: WINERY DISTRIBUTION AND APPELLATIONS

1. Oakley, 2. Livermore Valley, 3. San Ysidro, 4. Santa Clara Valley, 5. Santa Cruz Mountains, 6. Chalone, 7. Cienega Valley, 8. Lime Kiln Valley, 9. Mount Harlan, 10. Pacheco pass, 11. San Benito, 12. Arroyo Seco, 13. Carmel Valley, 14. San Lucas, 15. Arroyo Grand Valley, 16. Edna Valley, 17. Paso Robles, 18. Santa Maria Valley, 19. York Mountain, 20. Santa Ynez Valley, 21. Paicines, 22. Monterey.

Another interesting element of the region's viticultural geography is that 90 percent of the vine acreage is less than 25 years old, and nearly all in Monterey, San Luis Obispo, and Santa Barbara counties, a reflection of the post-1960 rush to purchase and plant vines on limestone and/or gravel soil in a cool maritime microclimate. Vine acreage leaped from 5,000 in 1950, to 10,000 in 1970, to 52,000 acres in 1990. The number of wineries, 100 in 1990, represents a fourfold increase since 1970. The attractive elements are not hard to find: less expensive real estate than Sonoma and Napa; a cool climate; excellent pockets of well-drained, essentially, non-volcanic soil; and a new breed of dedicated, innovative winemakers. All of the above have contributed in producing the second most significant premium wine district in the state. Moreover, the Central Coast is the leading center for strawberries, lettuce, cauliflower, broccoli, cut flowers, and carnations. San Luis Obispo is the leading county for the production of cherries, Monterey the leading area for broccoli, artichokes, and cauliflower, and Santa Cruz is the leading county for bush berries.

The Central Coast, with its highly irregular and fragmented Pacific margin and its hilly and mountainous interior, is a mass of intermingled chaparral, coastal scrub, grassland, coniferous forest, broadleaf-evergreen forest, beach strand, and salt marsh. The topographic irregularities produce a myriad of microclimates for the cultivation of a wide spectrum of fine wine grapes, producing an equally large spectrum of distinctive wine styles. The result is that this coastal region has become the state's newest "hot" viticultural area. Lured by environmental, cultural and financial incentives, massive infusions of capital and a steady migration of innovative winemakers have produced majestic wineries, impressive wines, and the largest single contiguous vineyard in the nation. Another unique feature of this region is the high degree of urbanization, and the intricate web of highly specialized agricultural commodities produced in practically every coastal valley. In addition to grapes in Alameda, Monterey, San Luis Obispo, and Santa Barbara, 27 percent of the agricultural economy of Monterey is derived from lettuce, cattle contributes 17 percent of the total agricultural income in San Luis Obispo, and avocados 20 percent in Santa Barbara.

For the sake of convenience, the entire region is divided into three sections: the San Francisco Bay area; the central region of Santa Cruz, San Benito and Monterey; and the southern area of San Luis Obispo, Santa Barbara and Ventura. The first consists of the large San Francisco/Oakland megalopolis, the important Livermore Valley, and the once important Santa Clara Valley. The area immediately to the south includes the eccentric and highly innovative Santa Cruz area, the substantial Monterey County vineyard, and the marginally important county of San Benito. The southern producing region, widely diverse and in a perpetual state of flux, is an area whose wines reflect distinctive soil and climatic variations. Although commercial viticultural features exhibit a widely scattered pattern over these ten counties, detailed examination shows a high concentration of grape-growing in the Livermore, Salinas, Edna, Santa Maria, and Santa Ynez valleys. Represented within the region are eighteen approved viticultural areas, of which the *Central Coast (1985)*, the largest, encompasses the following counties: Monterey, Santa Cruz, Santa Clara, Alameda, San Benito, San Luis Obispo, Sonoma, Napa, Mendocino, Lake, and Marin. (Note the absence of Santa Barbara, and the presence of five counties located north of San Francisco.)

The San Francisco Bay Region

San Francisco, the largest metropolitan area north of Los Angeles, dominates the economic, political, and social life of central California. It is the headquarters of The Wine Institute, the largest number of negociant firms, wine-related publishing, advertising agencies, and the source of financing for all but the smallest viticultural projects. If California is the central focus of America's wine industry, the Greater San Francisco Bay Area is the undisputed enological Mecca. Here the population drinks twice as much wine as the average American.

This area, encompassing the immediate region east, and south of San Francisco, consists of two major viticultural and winemaking regions: the Livermore Valley, mainly for white wine, and the Los Gatos-Gilroy area, mainly for red wine production. This historic, highly diverse region contains many large wineries, and lies within the state's second largest urban region--an area whose insatiable appetite for real estate has already devoured more than three-quarters of vineland, particularly in Santa Clara and Alameda counties. In fact, the San Francisco metropolitan region retains significant financial, commercial, industrial and governmental functions, and its economy is significantly more varied than Los Angeles. It is the haven for major convention and tourist functions, excellent restaurants, superb hotels, unrivaled scenery, and cultural diversity. The entire metropolitan agglomeration of nearly 10 million people represents one of the nation's most sophisticated wine markets. The greater metropolitan region is home to several large holding companies, negociants, and an ever-increasing body of "urban wineries."

Audubon Cellars (Berkeley, 1982), founded as R. Montali Winery, is a 30,000-case, successful winery that makes a complete line of varietals, many of which offer good to exceptional quality. The late harvest Chardonnay is unusual and noteworthy. **Bay Cellars** (Berkeley, 1982), is a 1,500-case winery that makes good, sound Pinot Noir, Chardonnay, Cabernet Sauvignon, Merlot, and blended wines from purchased grapes. **Draper & Esquin** (San Francisco, 1984), is an excellent, 15,000-case retailer for a line of wines (Chardonnay, Cabernet Sauvignon, Sauvignon Blanc, Merlot, Zinfandel) under the *Chestnut Hill* label, all drinkable and consistently good. **Edmunds St. John** (Berkeley, 1985), is an interesting 2,000-case winery with an emphasis on Syrah, Mourvedre, and Grenache Noir from purchased grapes, all of which are distinctive, offering good value. **J.H. Gentili Wines** (Redwood City, 1981) is a 1,000-case winery that makes Chardonnay, Cabernet Sauvignon, and Zinfandel. **Moceri Winery Ltd.** (San Carlos, 1979), is a successful, 55,000-case negociant firm that handles attractively priced Chenin Blanc, Washington Chardonnay, Cabernet Sauvignon, and Sauvignon Blanc. Further south, **Mountain View Vintners** (San Francisco, 1978), is a 125,000-case negociant concern that markets vintaged and non-vintaged Sauvignon Blanc, Chardonnay, Cabernet Sauvignon, Zinfandel, Merlot, Pinot Noir, sparkling, and proprietary wines under many *ava's*. Other label: *Paraiso Springs*, for premium wines. **Rosenblum Cellars** (Emeryville, 1978), is a 17,000-case winery that makes robust and often rich Chardonnay, Sauvignon Blanc, Gewurztraminer, Zinfandel, Cabernet Sauvignon, Petite Sirah, Merlot, Petite Sirah Porto-type, dessert, and sparkling Gewurztraminer under many *ava's* from purchased grapes. This urban, innovative winery, consistently above-average in the production of fine wine, offers good to excellent value. Merlot and Cabernet Sauvignon are often outstanding. **The Grapevine Group** (Oakland, 1987), is an aggressive, 40,000-case marketing company with as many as 15 associated wineries that makes and markets several wines under various labels: *Pour Mon Ami* (California *ava*); *Open Country* (California and American *ava's*, popularly priced for immediate consumption); *Masterpiece Series* (vineyard designated varietals, top of the line wines); and *Christopher James* (a line of non-alcohol wines). **The Wine Group** (San Francisco, 1982), is a holding company for *Franzia, Tribuno, Mogen David, MD 20/20, 20/20 Wine Cooler, Summit Wines, Corbett Canyon Vineyards,* and others. The company, ranking as the fifth largest producer and distributor of wines, operates 2,000 acres of vineland and two large wineries in Ripon, California and Westfield, New York. **Tribaut Devavry** (Hayward, 1984), is a 24,000-case winery that makes Brut, Blanc de Noir, and rose sparkling wines from purchased grapes (Chardonnay and Pinot Noir) under several labels. Although exhibiting bouts of inconsistency, the wines are usually fresh, crisp, tart, austere, and assertive on the palate.

Recently a group of wineries have petitioned BTAF for approval of a new *ava* called *San Francisco Bay*. This appellation would encompass Santa Clara, San Mateo, San Francisco, Contra Costa, and Alameda. This diffused region contains 3,500 acres of vineland, many negociant firms, and about 70 wineries. Historically, grapes emanating from this five-county region (with the sole exception of the Livermore *ava*) were lumped within the Central Coast *ava*. In theory, the growers would enjoy a bigger marketing advantage with the new appellation.

Alameda And Contra Costa

Alameda County is primarily a nursery product, cut flower, and vegetable producing county located along the eastern portion of San Francisco Bay. Grape acreage, a minor entity, is wholly confined to the *Livermore Valley (1982) ava*, a small, flat, rectangular valley (10 by 15 miles) of alluvial origin surrounded by hills on all four sides: the Black Hills on the north, the Pleasanton Hills on the west, the Altamont and Crane Hills on the east, and Rocky Ridge and Cedar Mountain in the south. The valley is very much a funnel with cool maritime air moderating air temperatures (lowering summer and increasing winter temperatures) resulting in a long growing season. It contains twelve wineries and 1,795 acres of vineland, a figure that has remained relatively stable over the past 30 years.

Vineyards in this Region II-III area, located 650 to 800 feet above sea level, are irrigated as annual precipitation is less than fifteen inches. This highly underrated viticultural region, just east of the Oakland Hills, is admirably suited to vinegrowing. It contains excellent, well-drained, gravelly soils (as much as 700 feet deep, and very poor in organic matter), is well ventilated by Bay wind, and appears superb, not only in the production of Sauvignon Blanc and Semillon, but Cabernet Sauvignon and Petite Sirah as well. The marginally longer growing season produces wines that are noticeably fragrant and lower in alcohol than surrounding areas to the south and east.

Two-thirds of acreage is planted in white varieties, of which Grey Riesling, Chardonnay, Sauvignon Blanc, and Semillon dominate. In an effort to counteract urban encroachment, the Livermore wineries have banded together to develop a 6,000-acre tract into an upscale winery resort community. If successful, the idea could be applied to other viticultural areas threatened by suburbanization. In part because of relatively low property values and the dedicated leadership of Wente Winery, it is the only major viticultural region in the Bay area that has successfully resisted urban encroachment.

Referred to as "California's first white wine district," and "America's Sauternes District," Cresta Blanca won a gold medal, the first such award for a California winery in international competition, for Sauvignon Blanc at the Paris Exhibition in 1889. Winegrowing in the Livermore Valley dates back to the middle of the nineteenth century when Robert Livermore established the first commercial vineyard in the 1840s. Grape cultivation, however, took a back seat to grain growing and coal production until, attracted by proximity to the sea and San Francisco, many prominent businessmen, like Julius Smith, the Crellin brothers, Theodore Grier, Carl H. Wente, Charles Wetmore, and James Concannon, developed a number of vineyards and built wineries. Through the efforts of these men, the Livermore Valley is the source of a good deal of the clonal selections for Chardonnay, Cabernet Sauvignon, Semillon, and Sauvignon Blanc.

Vine acreage, which grew from 1,985 in 1869 to 7,083 acres by 1883, became infected with phylloxera, and declined to 3,620 in 1893. The industry recovered slowly, and on the eve of Prohibition the valley contained 26 wineries and nearly 10,000 acres of vineland. Clearly reflecting the painful side effects of Prohibition, vine acreage declined still further to 2,800 acres in the early 1920s, and by 1932 all but two wineries closed their doors. The areas economic recovery was further hampered by the fact that the glamour of post-Repeal Napa bypassed the Livermore Valley. Although acreage is below 2,000, the lowest level in nearly 100 years, there has been a recent resurgence in interest as eight new wineries have begun operations since 1975, and the largest, Wente, has recently expanded.

Another area awaiting *ava* approval is *Sunol Valley*, the only appellation to be planted in white wine varieties only (18 acres). Separated from the Livermore Valley, Sunol contains a cooler microclimate that enables grapes to ripen fully four weeks after the harvest begins in its more famous and larger neighbor, as well as Carneros across the Bay. The soils consist of loamy topsoil resting on top of 300-foot deep gravel. The future appellation contains only one winery-Elliston Vineyards.

The main wineries are:

Cedar Mountain Winery (Livermore, 1990), is a 14-acre, 1,000-case winery that makes good, sound, barrel fermented Chardonnay and Cabernet Sauvignon.

Chouinard Vineyards (Castro Valley, 1985), is a 4-acre, 3,500-case winery that makes Chardonnay, Chenin Blanc, Gewurztraminer, Cabernet Sauvignon, Petite Sirah, late harvest Riesling, and apple wines.

Concannon Vineyards (Livermore, 1883), sold three times within the past ten years, this 176-acre, 100,000-case winery has had a checkered reputation in recent years under various management strategies. The capacity to produce world-class wines is quite good as a large portion of its vine acreage is located on deep quartz gravel. In addition to generic blends at least seven varietals are made, of which the estate bottled Chardonnay, Sauvignon Blanc, Petite Sirah, and Cabernet Sauvignon are the finest. The *Livermore Assemblage*, a blend of Semillon and Sauvignon Blanc, is excellent. The winery has been acquired by the Wente family, and it is envisioned that positive changes will be forthcoming.

Elliston Vineyards (Sunol, 1983), is an expanding, 37-acre, 10,000-case winery known for lean, well-structured Chardonnay, Pinot Gris, Pinot Blanc, Merlot, and Cabernet Sauvignon, all of which are made by a gifted and knowledgeable winemaker. The winery is making plans to plant 34 acres, and has recently purchased Noble Hill Vineyards, a winery of 23 acres.

Fenestra Winery (Livermore, 1980), is a 3,000-case winery that makes Cabernet Sauvignon, Zinfandel, Merlot, Chardonnay, Sauvignon Blanc, and Riesling from purchased grapes.

Ivan Tamas (Livermore, 1984), is an aggressive, 24-acre, 25,000-case, negociant concern that distributes well-made Chardonnay, Sauvignon Blanc, Zinfandel, Cabernet Sauvignon, and a rare Trebbiano, all offering good value. In the future, all but one wine will carry the Livermore *ava* as the firm will move to the old Wetmore Winery in Livermore. The firm also imports Hungarian Pinot Gris.

Livermore Valley Cellars (Livermore, 1978), is a 34-acre, 3,000-case winery known for clean, well-made Colombard, Chardonnay, Grey Riesling, Palomino, and Servant Blanc, the latter only grown on this property.

Murietta's Well (Livermore, 1990), is a 2,000-case winery that makes a red and white Meritage-type wine under the *Vendimia* label, a joint venture of two well-known Livermore vintners.

Retzlaff Winery (Livermore, 1986), is a 14-acre, 2,500-case winery that makes Chardonnay, Grey Riesling, Merlot, and Cabernet Sauvignon.

Stony Ridge Winery (Livermore, 1975), with a checkered history of multiple owners, is a 20,000-case winery known for Chardonnay, Cabernet Sauvignon, Zinfandel, Malvasia Bianca, Riesling, and sparkling wines.

Thomas Coyne Wines (Alameda, 1989), is a 2,500-case label that makes Merlot, Mourvedre, Cabernet Sauvignon, Zinfandel, Petite Sirah, and Sauvignon Blanc, all of which are well structured, rich, well flavored, and moderately priced.

Wente Bros., and Wente Bros. Sparkling Wines (Livermore, 1883), is a 1,985-acre (693 of which are located in the Arroyo Seco region of Monterey), 620,000-case winery that recently expanded in 1981 to include the historic Cresta Blanca facility eight miles from the main winery, and purchased the old Ruby Hill Winery. This fourth generation winery is considered the oldest, continuously operated, family-owned winery in California. It was one of the pioneers of varietal labeling, and one of the first to grow Sauvignon Blanc. It is the largest producer of Grey Riesling in the state. The winery makes several generic blends, a number of estate wines from vineyards in both Livermore and Monterey, and purchases additional grapes from premium vineyards. Chardonnay, Semillon, Cabernet Sauvignon, and sparkling wines are particularly good. All the wines have shown dramatic improvement in recent years, offering excellent value. The primary winery and the Cresta Blanca sparkling facility are immaculate, stylish, and worth a visit. The winery has recently acquired Parrott & Co. (1855), a negociant and distribution concern that makes 80,000+ cases under the *California Dry* and *Coastal Select* labels.

Contra Costa County, one of the original 27 counties, derives its name from Spanish for "opposite coast," and while Alameda County to the south is mainly planted in white grapes, Contra Costa County is red grape country with the highest percentage of red wine grape acreage in the state (mostly Zinfandel, Carignane, and Mourvedre).

Oakley, a future *ava*, and the center of this fledgling industry, is a small region (only 35,000 acres, of which less than 10 percent have agricultural potential) defined by A Street in Antioch on the west, Lone Tree Way and Deer Valley Road on the south, Balfour Road to the east, and by the San Joaquin River on the north. Soils are sandy and deep (as much as 40 feet), and the climate is moderated by relatively strong winds. Until recently the region lacked notoriety (it was known as a source for grapes used in jug blends), but with the escalation of vineyard prices in Napa and Sonoma, and the strong demand for Mourvedre, this region, due to the high quality of its red grapes, is subject to considerable land speculation. Due to the presence of established Mourvedre, Carignane, and Zinfandel vines, the Oakley region is suddenly called the "Rhone Valley of California." Interestingly, one of the largest vineyards (130 acres) belongs to the E.I. DuPont Chemical Company. The entire area contains 919 vine acres (or half of the 1969 total), and one winery: **Conrad Viano Winery** (Martinez, 1946), a 60-acre, 7,500-case winery that makes Cabernet Sauvignon, Chardonnay, Sauvignon Blanc, generics, fortified, and Zinfandel, the latter, well-aged, robust and full-bodied, offers good value.

Santa Clara

Santa Clara, the largest and historically richest of the valleys opening onto the San Francisco Bay region, is cone-shaped and delimited by the high Diablo Range on the east and the Santa Cruz Mountains on the west. The latter, lying obliquely to west-moving maritime air, extracts abundant amounts of precipitation from passing storm activity. The Santa Clara Valley, lying within the rain shadow of the Santa Cruz mountains, receives lower amounts of rainfall as well as considerably more sunshine and high temperatures. The valley, 60 miles in length, is at its widest near the southern terminus of San Francisco Bay, and gradually narrows as one proceeds further south. This well-ventilated valley, with a 300-day growing season and fertile soils, is a Region II viticultural region. Historically known as the "fruit bowl" of America, Santa Clara once ranked as the premier producer of strawberries and prunes, and it continues to rank as the country's leading producer of garlic wine (in Gilroy). Expanding urbanization over the past 40 years has reduced planted agricultural acreage from 115,000 to 35,000 acres, and the total value of agricultural production has declined from $110 million to $60 million for the same period.

In sharp contrast, the population has increased dramatically from less than 300,000 in 1950 to more than 3 million people in 1990 (San Jose, the principal settlement, is the state's fourth largest city). As a consequence, what used to be orchards and grape vines in the northern portion of the valley now houses the nation's leading companies in the production of silicon chips for the computer industry. Reflecting these changes, vineland has declined significantly from a peak of more than 12,000 acres in 1893, to 8,000 acres (and 62 wineries) in 1935, to 961 acres in 1990. Unlike planted acreage in the rest of the state, red grape varieties (principally Cabernet Sauvignon, Zinfandel, Pinot Noir, Carignane, Gamay Beaujolais, and Grenache Noir) dominate acreage.

Historically, the vine growing regions of Santa Clara were divided into three districts: the western slopes (Los Gatos-Saratoga), eastern slopes (the Evergreen area of Mt. Hamilton), and the valley floor (most important grape region is the Morgan Hill-San Martin-Gilroy area). Vine acreage has practically disappeared in the northern portion of the valley, and is now concentrated only in small, discontinuous pockets between the southern suburban terminus of San Jose to San Benito. This is no great loss as the rich, abundantly fertile bottom land was too good to make fine wine. The peripheral areas of the valley, especially near Santa Cruz, contain the better-drained land, and, as a consequence, make far better grape-growing terrain. Despite the highly urbanized profile, the region contains about 26 wineries, nearly all located in the extreme southern portion of the county and along the eastern fringes of the Santa Cruz foothills. Because the Santa Cruz *ava* preceded the Santa Clara, several wineries that are located in Santa Clara County are included in the Santa Cruz appellation. In spite of the recent declines in vine acreage, the county does contain two excellent vineyards--San Ysidro and Mistral.

Although vines were first planted after the founding of Santa Clara Mission and Mission San Jose in 1777, and wine was first made in 1802, the viticultural history of Santa Clara goes back to the mid nineteenth century when many Frenchmen migrated to the Bay Area. One of the first and most successful was Antoine Delmas, the owner of a large and successful nursery who imported Vinifera vines to the area. Another notable personality was Etienne Thee, followed by Charles Lefranc (who established New Almaden Vineyard in 1862), and Pierre Pellier (who is credited with the introduction of Pinot Noir and Colombard in 1854). Santa Clara, therefore, has long claimed to be the oldest wine producing region in northern California. So important was the county in linking the El Camino Real with the central and southern coastal portions of the state, that San Jose was made the first capital, the site of the first American school, and the state's first University. It is suggested that Cabernet Sauvignon as a varietal was produced in 1860, and by 1868 bottle-fermented sparkling wine was also made. The success of Etienne Thee, Charles Lefranc, Pierre Pellier, David Harwood, Pierre Mirassou, Pierre Sainsevain, Henry Naglee, and Paul Masson soon attracted others, and by the middle of the 1880s it is estimated that no fewer than 40 wineries were in production forming one of the largest

wine producing regions in the state. The Santa Clara Viticultural Society was founded by Charles Wetmore in 1881.

With the economic rise of the Bay region after 1950, vine acreage quickly declined by more than 10,000 acres from a 1925 Prohibition-high level. It is interesting to note that the principal grape varieties before 1940--Alicante Bouschet, Zinfandel, Carignane, Petite Sirah, Mission, Grenache Noir, and Mourvedre--all red varieties, have largely remained the same in color except that Cabernet Sauvignon and Zinfandel have replaced Mourvedre and Alicante Bouschet. Of the 459 acres of white grapes, Chardonnay dominates with 223 acres, followed by Pinot Blanc, Sauvignon Blanc, and Semillon. Equally eventful is the fact that the industry has largely remained in the same area--in the southwestern portion of the county, primarily in the Uvas Valley. The latter, "grape" in Spanish, is the site of wild grapes first discovered by Spaniards. For nearly 100 years, southern Santa Clara and a good deal of the Santa Cruz region have exhibited a strong Italian influence in the production of robust, dry red, and a large assortment of sweet wines. Recent history has not been kind to the region as more than 26 wineries have gone out of business or changed hands, a figure that constitutes one-third of the total existing before 1982. The county has one *ava--San Ysidro District (1991)*, a 2,340-acre track that includes about 520 acres of vineland and two wineries. The region located on the southwestern portion of the county has a cool climate and is mainly planted in Chardonnay, Pinot Blanc, Pinot Noir, and Merlot. Historically it was the vineyard that produced Emerald Riesling for Paul Masson. The wineries are:

A. Conrotto Winery (Gilroy, 1926), is a 5-acre, 15,000-case winery that makes robust Cabernet Sauvignon, Chardonnay, and proprietary wines.

Ashly Vineyard (Los Gatos, 1984), is a 1,000-case winery that makes excellent, rich, spicy, yet delicate and refined Chardonnay from the *Sleepy Hollow Vineyard*, and Monterey County grapes. This firm and Jory Winery are jointly owned.

Caporale Winery (Morgan Hill, 1985), is a 10,000-case winery that makes above-average Zinfandel, Chardonnay, Cabernet Sauvignon, and Merlot.

Carrousel Cellars (Gilroy, 1981), is a 2-acre, 1,000-case winery that makes Cabernet Sauvignon, Zinfandel, Chardonnay, and Merlot.

Casa de Fruta (Hollister, 1972), is a 19-acre, 7,000-case winery that makes table, dessert, and berry wines.

1988 CHARDONNAY
SANTA CRUZ MOUNTAINS

Cinnabar

ESTATE BOTTLED

Cinnabar Vineyards & Winery (Saratoga, 1986), is a 24-acre, 4,000-case winery that makes distinctive Cabernet Sauvignon and Chardonnay, both of which offer excellent value.

Emilio Guglielmo Winery (Morgan Hill, 1925), is a 100-acre, 100,000-case winery that makes Chardonnay, Cabernet Sauvignon, Zinfandel, Petite Sirah, Grignolino, Pinot Noir, generic, and fortified wines. Other labels: *Mt. Madonna* for varietals, *Emile's* for generic wines, and *Guglielmo* for reserve and estate premium wines.

Fortino Winery (Gilroy, 1948), is a 65-acre, 25,000-case winery with an emphasis on robust, well-flavored, dry red wines: Petite Sirah, Cabernet Sauvignon, and Charbono, among others.

Gemello Winery (Mountain View, 1934), is a 2,000-case winery with an emphasis on full-bodied, heavy duty Cabernet Sauvignon and Zinfandel. This winery now is owned and operated by Obester Winery in Mendocino County.

Hecker Pass Winery (Gilroy, 1972), is a 14-acre, 6,000-case winery that makes Petite Sirah, Zinfandel, Grenache Noir, Ruby Cabernet, and Carignane.

J. Lohr Winery (San Jose, 1974), is an innovative, rapidly expanding, 1,000-acre, 200,000-case winery that makes fruity, supple Chardonnay, Sauvignon Blanc, Riesling, Chenin Blanc, Cabernet Sauvignon, Zinfandel, and Napa Gamay. Grapes emanate from five vineyards: *Greenfield* and *Cypress* in Monterey, *Carol's* in Napa, *Pheasants Call* in Clarksburg, and Paso Robles, the latter, from a 420-acre vineyard under development. The wines, recently improved in quality, often offer exceptional value. Other label: *Cypress*.

Jory Winery (Los Gatos, 1986), is an excellent, 3,000-case winery that makes well-structured, firm, lean, yet smooth Chardonnay, Pinot Noir, and Merlot from the *San Ysidro* and *La Reina Vineyards*; Oregon Pinot Noir; Mourvedre from Contra Costa County; barrel-fermented Pinot Blanc, and the first vineyard designated sparkling wine (Mistral). Although the expensive wines exhibit considerable variability, they are all polished, handsomely packaged and upscale in distribution.

Kirigin Cellars (Gilroy, 1976), is a 50-acre, 4,500-case winery that makes Riesling, Chardonnay, Gewurztraminer, Chenin Blanc, Zinfandel, Muscat Blanc, Cabernet Sauvignon, sparkling, and cherry wine. Originally built in 1827, the winery sits on a historic site.

Live Oaks Winery (GIlroy, 1912), one of the oldest in the region, is a 3,000-case winery that makes Chenin Blanc, Colombard, Zinfandel, and blended wines.

Mirassou Vineyards (San Jose, 1854), is a fifth generation, grape-growing and winemaking family winery that has shown dramatic growth, from 1,000 cases in 1966 to more than 350,000 cases in 1991. Among the moderately priced wines, Chardonnay, Sauvignon Blanc, Riesling, Gewurztraminer, Chenin Blanc, Zinfandel, Cabernet Sauvignon, Gamay Beaujolais, Petite Sirah, sparkling, and proprietary wines are the finest. The harvest reserve wines (Chardonnay, Sauvignon Blanc, Cabernet Sauvignon, Zinfandel, and Pinot Noir), produced from select lots of the finest grapes, constitute the best that this well-established firm has to offer. All wines (mostly from ungrafted Monterey grapes) are light to medium-bodied, exhibit strong varietal character and fruit, and are consistently well-made offering excellent to exceptional value (this is one of the few wineries that lowered prices in 1989-1990). The winery owns 830 acres, two-thirds of which are planted in white varieties. Other label: *Pastel Winery*, for low-alcohol wines.

Paul Masson Vineyards (Gonzales, 1852), one of the oldest and most venerable of the mid-19th century wineries, is a large, 8 million-case winery. It is essentially a low to mid-priced producer of generic, varietal, light, fortified, and sparkling wines, as well as vermouth and brandy. The winery, suffering from a lack of direction and multiple owners, has recently been purchased by Vintners International, a large holding company that also owns Taylor California Cellars, Great Western Champagnes, Gold Seal, and Taylor, the last three all located in Hammondsport, New York. The historic property in Saratoga has recently been sold. Labels include, *Masson Vineyard* (premium label, Monterey County *ava*, for Chardonnay, Cabernet Sauvignon, Merlot, and Pinot Noir), *Paul Masson Vineyard* (for table, dessert, and sparkling wines), *Deer Valley Vineyards*, *St. Regis* (for non-alcoholic wines), and *Taylor California Cellars*, a multi-million-case label that makes a large assortment of low-priced wines.

Pedrizetti Winery (Morgan Hill, 1913), is a 50,000-case winery that makes Chardonnay, Chenin Blanc, Cabernet Sauvignon, Riesling, Zinfandel, Petite Sirah, Barbera, Gamay Beaujolais, fortified, sparkling, and fruit wines, offering excellent value. Other labels: *Harlequin, Morgan*

Hill Cellars, Crystal Springs, Golden Hills.

Rapazzini Winery (Gilroy, 1962), is a 6,000-case winery that makes a large selection of wines: Garlic, Mead, Muscat Blanc, Riesling, Chardonnay, Sauvignon Blanc, Zinfandel, and Cabernet Sauvignon, among others.

Ronald Lamb Winery (Morgan Hill, 1976), is a 750-case winery that makes above-average Sauvignon Blanc, Chardonnay, Cabernet Sauvignon, and Petite Sirah.

Sarah's Vineyard (Gilroy, 1978), is a 7-acre, 3,000-case winery known for rich, elegant, full-bodied Chardonnay, Riesling, Merlot, a Cabernet Sauvignon/Merlot blend, and sparkling wines. However, the winery's reputation rests with its estate Chardonnay and sparkling wines, two of the most expensive libations in America.

Solis Winery (Gilroy, 1988), is a 15-acre, 7,000-case winery that makes Chardonnay, Riesling, Sauvignon Blanc, Muscat Blanc, Pinot Noir, Merlot, Cabernet Sauvignon, Mourvedre, and proprietary wines.

Summerhill Vineyards (Gilroy, 1917), renamed in 1980 by the new owners, this 5-acre, 30,000-case winery makes Chenin Blanc, Colombard, Emerald Riesling, Cabernet Sauvignon, and Zinfandel.

Sycamore Creek Vineyards (Morgan Hill, 1976), is a 14-acre, 6,000-case winery that makes good Chardonnay, Carignane (often full-bodied and robust), Cabernet Sauvignon, Zinfandel, and Riesling, the latter, made in a late harvest style, can be outstanding.

Thomas Kruse Winery (Gilroy, 1971), is a 1-acre, 4,000-case winery that makes Riesling, Chardonnay, Zinfandel, Cabernet Sauvignon, Pinot Noir, Carignane, sparkling, and proprietary wines.

Troquato Vineyards (Los Gatos, 1985), is a 22-acre, 4,500-case winery that makes moderately priced Chardonnay, Riesling, Chenin Blanc, Muscat Blanc, Cabernet Sauvignon, and Zinfandel.

Villa Paradiso Vineyards (Morgan Hill, 1981), is a 1,500-case winery that makes Zinfandel, Merlot, and Petite Sirah.

San Benito

Immediately to the south of Santa Clara is the less important county of San Benito. Mountainous and sparsely populated, San Benito is sandwiched between the Gabilan Mountains on the west and the Diablo Range on the east. The only appreciable level land is in the northern portion of the county where the Santa Clara Valley extends about 20 miles into San Benito County. In comparison with Santa Clara to the north and Monterey to the west, San Benito is agriculturally poor (total value of agricultural products is less than $40 million), and the planted acreage is mainly devoted to orchards and seed crops. Grape acreage (1,775) is mainly concentrated in the northern portion of the county south of Hollister. Despite its insignificant and declining acreage, the area does have five *ava's* and several quality-oriented wineries.

Although vines were first planted around the immediate confines of San Juan Bautista (San Benito), due to its relative isolation and a more arid climate it has been less celebrated in its viticultural fortunes than Santa Clara. Theophile Vache is given credit for planting the first modern vines south of Hollister in the early 1850s, but considering the lack of good roads and a significant market, acreage did not expand beyond that which was necessary to supply the local population. Acreage expanded under William Palmtag in 1883, and again in the early 1900s in the Cienega and Grass Valley areas. Under the direction of Frederick Bioletti, the El Gavilan Vineyard was formed in 1906, and soon after total county acreage increased to 1,765 during Prohibition, only to drop to 860 acres by 1959. Vineland increased due to the efforts of the W.A. Taylor Company (1943), and Almaden Vineyards in 1956. Despite a momentary rush to bring new land into production in the 1960s, vine acreage is in retreat throughout lowland areas, especially that which is owned by large wineries. While more than 75 percent of the acreage is planted in Chardonnay, Pinot Blanc, Pinot Noir, Gamay Beaujolais, and Cabernet Sauvignon, it is interesting to note that Cabernet Sauvignon and Chardonnay acreage has fallen by half, Pinot Noir and Riesling by three-quarters, and Grenache Noir, Gewurztraminer, Chenin Blanc, and Petite Sirah have nearly disappeared. Although red and white grapes are about equal, the historic reputation rested with red grapes which produce strongly flavored, alcoholic wines, a type of wine that is no longer in demand, hence, one explanation as to the viticultural demise of this region.

San Benito contains five approved viticultural areas. The *Pacheco Pass (1984)*, about 5 miles long and one mile wide, is in a valley with flat to gently sloping terrain north of Hollister. What makes this *ava* different is the presence of well-drained soils and the absence of boron salts, a peculiar condition afflicting the high-perched water tables in lowland areas to the south. It contains about 3,200 acres, of which seventeen are planted in vines, and there is one winery. The transverse *Cienega Valley (1982)*, Spanish for "marsh" or "miry" place, is located at the base of the Gabilan Mountain Range 5 miles south of Hollister, forming a distinct geographic boundary between San Benito and Monterey counties. The entire valley acts as a tunnel for cool, east-flowing air which is reenforced by south-moving air from Monterey Bay toward the San Joaquin Valley. Despite the high incidence of fog, the *ava* is warmer during the summer than the Lime Kiln and Paicines *ava's* slightly to the south. Calera and Cygnet are the two wineries in the appellation.

Lime Kiln Valley (1982), as the name suggests, contains soils composed of dolomite and limestone, an unusual occurrence in California. Although an enclave of the Cienega Valley *ava*, the Lime Kiln region differs sharply by its gravelly loam soils and a climate that is cooler in winter and warmer in summer than surrounding areas. Only a small portion of the 2,300 appellation acres are planted in vines, nearly all belonging to Almaden and the only winery (Enz) in the appellation. *Paicines (1982)*, located southeast of Lime Kiln and 17 miles north of Pinnacles National Monument, is an exposed, windy, nearly denuded region where the surrounding elevations channel cool ocean air, often producing thick fog. To the west are the Cienega Vineyards and the Gabilan Mountains which separate this appellation from San Lucas and King City in neighboring Monterey County. The region gets less rain than neighboring areas, but due to the persistency of wind, it experiences a slightly cooler summer than neighboring areas. Vine acreage, historically owned by Almaden, has recently declined. *San Benito (1987)*, located along the San Benito River 2 miles south of Hollister, completely encompasses the Lime Kiln Valley, Cienega Valley, and the Paicines viticultural areas. It contains approximately 45,000 acres, 2,500 of which are planted in vines, and three wineries. The historic vineyards dating back to the middle of the nineteenth century have largely been abandoned due to boron contamination. The newest appellation, *Mt. Harlan (1991)*, located in a rugged, remote region, contains 7,440 acres, but only 47 planted vine acres, and one major winery.

The county's wineries are: **Calera Wine Co.** (Hollister, 1976), located on limestone-based sites (the name is Spanish for lime kiln) at 2,200 feet in elevation, is a 91-acre, 12,000-case winery with a good reputation for Pinot Noir under the *Selleck, Reed, Jensen*, and *Mills Vineyard* designations. Despite its initial growing pains, the winery, specializing only in Pinot Noir, Chardonnay, and small quantities of Viognier, is often able to produce excellent to outstanding wines. **Cygnet Cellars** (Hollister, 1977), is a 5,000-case winery specializing in big, robust Zinfandel, and smaller quantities of Cabernet Sauvignon, Carignane, Petite Sirah, and Pinot Noir. **Enz Vineyards** (Hollister, 1973), is a 30-acre, 6,500-case winery that makes distinctive, flavorful Pinot St. George, Orange Muscat (both planted in 1895), Zinfandel, and Sauvignon Blanc, all of which are consistently made, offering good value.

Santa Cruz Mountains

The Santa Cruz Mountains region, although principally in Santa Cruz County, overlaps into San Mateo and the western portion of Santa Clara counties. The comparatively small county (220,000 people) lies on the northern portion of Monterey Bay, nearly at the midpoint of the long California coast. Except for the extreme southern portion between Santa Cruz and Watsonville, the bulk of the county is a rugged interior region (nearly two-thirds of the county is covered by mountainous terrain) where redwood forests still dominate the highest elevations. Lacking easy access from north to south, the Santa Cruz region, unlike Santa Clara, never developed into an important link in the El Camino Real network, and remained somewhat backward until demand for good redwood in San Francisco brought loggers and then farmers into the area.

While agricultural acreage has declined from 35,000 to 25,000 acres over the past 30 years, the value of farm production has increased from $40 to $60 million, two-thirds of which are vegetables and nursery crops. Its economic history, reflecting the cool Pacific maritime climate, has shifted from extensive cattle ranching and logging in the nineteenth century, to high value bulbs, strawberries, nursery stock, and brussels sprouts, the latter accounting for more than 90 percent of the nation's production. There are about 350 acres of wine grapes (a figure that doubled since 1980), and the region's 30 wineries (the nation's highest ratio of wineries to vineland) produce 650,000 gallons of wine, or less than 1 percent of the state's total output. Its hilly terrain and rocky soil combine to produce one of the lowest grape yields in the state. The area is unique because it stands, in marked contrast to the bulk, poorly made and eviscerated wines of the large producers of the Central Valley and Monterey, as a premium wine region characterized by a small band of dedicated producers.

Winemaking arrived in the Santa Cruz Mountains during the logging years of 1850-1880, and like many other areas the Mission grape dominated acreage. Although mission friars and the legendary Agoston Haraszthy (the latter, during the years 1854-56) attempted to grow Mission grapes on a commercial scale, commercial wine production began in 1863 when George and John Jarvis planted 270 acres, and produced nearly 13,000 gallons in 1864. In 1875 there were sixteen wineries making more than 40,000 gallons, but a combination of economic depression, over production throughout the state, and poorly made wine depressed prices forcing many producers to close. The industry was revived in the 1880s when new, enthusiastic winemakers like Henry Mel, Dr. John Stewart, Emil Meyer, and others provided new capital and impetus, so that by 1887 there were more than 2,000 acres producing about 150,000 gallons. Although acreage was widely distributed throughout the region, one of the finest producing areas was the Woodside-Portola Valley-Lexington area, widely acclaimed as the Chaine d'Or, or "golden chain."

Although there were repeated cycles of high and low prices until Prohibition, the wine industry continued to grow with the formation of large wineries, such as Santa Cruz Mountain Wine Co., Emmert Rixford, Edgar Preston, John Hooper, Ben Lomond Wine Co., Horstman Vineyard, and other much smaller firms. It is estimated that in 1900 the area was the home to 100 wineries, and as many as 8,000 acres of vineland, nearly all of which were wiped out during Prohibition. The resurrection of the post-Repeal wine industry was slow but steady. Of the six wineries that opened their doors to the public during the first seventeen years after Repeal, the Bargetto family, Chafee Hall, Martin Ray, and D.A. Beauregard were the most prominent. The explosion, however, arrived with the successful formation of Ridge Vineyards in 1959, and David Bruce in 1964. The number of wineries grew from 3 in 1952, to 31 in 1992, of which 24 were founded after 1965. Today the region is a hotbed of many innovative wineries that rank among the finest in the state. Interestingly, nearly all owners are native to the area, and about half do not cultivate vines preferring instead to buy grapes, thus producing a labyrinth of local, regional, state, and even American *ava* names. Of the 132 vine acres in the county (there is an estimated 500 planted throughout the Santa Cruz appellation), Pinot Noir, Cabernet Sauvignon, and Chardonnay dominate. In the cooler regions

Gewurztraminer and Riesling are prominent, and in the warmer, west-facing slopes of Santa Clara County, Syrah, Zinfandel, and other red grapes are more plentiful.

The Santa Cruz Mountain Vintners Association was formed in 1975, and in 1982 the area was delimited by BATF. It should also be noted that the physical demarcation of the Santa Cruz Mountains is a matter of dispute: while it includes portions of Santa Clara and San Mateo counties, the Hecker Pass region in Santa Clara County is usually omitted, as are the foothills near Watsonville. As a consequence, the location of wineries on the border of Santa Cruz, Santa Clara, Monterey, and even San Benito can be confusing. The region contains two *ava's*: *Santa Cruz Mountains (1982)*, and *Ben Lomond (1988)*. The Santa Cruz Mountains *ava*, attaining elevations greater than 3,000 feet (includes all the highland areas of the county), is greatly influenced by the cool Pacific Ocean and orographic air movements producing dense fog and windy conditions. The latter is particularly important because cool, descending air forces warmer air upward, thus lengthening the growing season to 300 days. The best vineyards are located in low Region I areas, with daytime temperatures ranging between 76F-80F, and nighttime temperatures falling to 60F. It is important to note that rainfall, rather heavy on the windward upper margins of the rugged Santa Cruz Mountains, is not conducive to vine cultivation. As a result, most wineries and vineyards are located on the lee side facing the Santa Clara Valley on lower, less wet elevations, or in protected valleys. The soils are identified as Franciscan shale, decomposed granite, and scattered limestone, all of which are unique to coastal California. Historically, the principal area of grape production was along the Santa Cruz-Los Gatos highway, but over the past 20 years, planted acreage has greatly diffused into the hilly regions of the *ava*.

Ben Lomond is a comparatively large, 38,400-acre, hilly region above the 800-foot elevation level that stretches along the Pacific Coast from Santa Cruz to the San Mateo border. An enclave of the much larger Santa Cruz Mountains *ava*, it includes some of the highest elevations, and supports nine important properties. A Scotsman by the name of John Burns established the first vineyard in the 1860s, but the small-scale character of vineyards and wineries never amounted to anything, and disappeared in the twentieth century until the viticultural resurgence of the 1970s. The *ava*, one of the coldest and rainier, faces west towards the Pacific Ocean, and is excellent, due to a long 300-day growing season, for the production of both red and white premium grapes. Generally, white grapes are planted below the 800-foot contour with a predilection for fog, and red grapes above this contour as the marine climate tends to give way to abundant sunshine. The wineries are:

Alghren Vineyard (Boulder Creek, 1976), is a 7-acre, 3,800-case winery known for big, flavorful, well-structured, and rich Chardonnay (*Ventana*, *Buerge*, and *Mayers* vineyards), Semillon (*St. Charles* vineyard), and Cabernet Sauvignon (*Bates* and *Besson Vineyards*).

Aptos Vineyard (Aptos, 1976), with an output of fewer than 700 cases, this winery of four acres makes excellent, round, well-flavored Pinot Noir.

Bargetto's Santa Cruz Winery (Soquel, 1933), is one of the largest and oldest wineries in the region. Long known for fruit and dessert wines, it has now begun to make 40,000 cases of varietal table wines--Gewurztraminer, Chardonnay, Riesling, Sauvignon Blanc, Pinot Noir, Zinfandel, Cabernet Sauvignon, and Nebbiolo, all of which are above-average, offering excellent value. The fruit wine line, one of the finest in the state (marketed under the *Chaucer's* label), is particularly noted for olallieberry, raspberry, plum, apricot, and raspberry wines. Mead, in particular, carries a California *ava* as the honey comes from Tulare, Fresno, and Monterey counties, and is a blend of orange, sage, and alfalfa.

Bonny Doon Vineyard (Bonny Doon, 1983), is a 28-acre, 15,000-case, highly innovative winery with a successful track record for distinctive, high acid, full-bodied, well-flavored Chardonnay, Muscat Blanc, Gewurztraminer, and Semillon (sold as *Vin de Glaciere*, made from frozen grapes), Syrah, superbly blended wines such as *Le Cigare Volant* (a blend of Grenache Noir, Syrah, and Mourvedre), *Old Telegram* (100% Mourvedre), *Clos de Gilroy* (a nouveau Grenache Noir), Claret, *Vin Gris* (Mourvedre and Grenache Noir), fortified fruit and berry wines, and diverse distilled items. In the near future there will be a varietal Viognier, and a Marsanne and Roussanne blend. Other label: *Grahm Crew*.

Byington Winery & Vineyard (Los Gatos, 1988), is an impressive, state-of-the-art, 8-acre, 12,000-case winery that makes big, full-bodied, meaty Chardonnay, Sauvignon Blanc, Pinot Noir, and Cabernet Sauvignon, offering considerable value.

Crescini Wines (Soquel, 1980), is a 1,000-case winery that makes dark, firm, full-bodied Cabernet Sauvignon, Merlot, Cabernet Franc, and Sauvignon Blanc.

CRONIN

1985
santa cruz mountains
Chardonnay
dreyer vineyard

Table Wine produced & bottled by
Cronin Vineyards, Woodside, Calif.

Cronin Vineyards (Woodside, 1980), is a 3-acre, 2,000-case winery that makes well-structured, robust, full-bodied, distinctive Chardonnay and a Cabernet Sauvignon/Merlot blend, both of which offer excellent value.

David Bruce Winery (Los Gatos, 1964), located on a magnificent setting 2,000-feet above sea level, is a 30-acre, 20,000-case winery that makes distinctive Chardonnay, Pinot Noir, Petite Sirah, Cabernet Sauvignon, and sparkling wines, all of which are full-bodied, tannin-rich, intensely flavored/scented, long-aging wines. More powerful in the past, the tendency now is to produce less alcoholic, better balanced, and more refined libations. The owner, a resourceful and innovative winemaker, was one of the first to use whole cluster fermentation, malolactic fermentation, extensive skin contact, and vigorous pressing in the production of his early winemaking endeavors.

Devlin Wine Cellars (Soquel, 1978), is a 7,500-case winery that makes fruity Chardonnay, Sauvignon Blanc, Riesling, Muscat Blanc, Cabernet Sauvignon, Zinfandel, Merlot, and Pinot Noir under a profusion of appellation and vineyard designations.

Hallcrest Vineyards (Felton, 1976), formerly Felton-Empire Vineyards, is an 8-acre, 16,000-case winery that makes above-average quality, light-bodied, but crisp Riesling and Gewurztraminer, Chardonnay, Cabernet Sauvignon (often excellent), Merlot, Barbera, non-alcoholic, and other wines, mainly from purchased grapes. The winery is now owned by the former winemaker of Schumacker Cellars of Davis. Other label: *Organic Wine Works Co.*

Kathryn Kennedy Winery (Saratoga, 1979), is an excellent, 8-acre, 2,000-case winery that only makes big, full-bodied, and distinctive Cabernet Sauvignon from non-irrigated, low-yielding vines.

McHenry Vineyard (Bonny Doon, 1980), is a 4-acre, 500-case winery known for Chardonnay and Pinot Noir.

Mount Eden Vineyards (Saratoga, 1946), is a 36-acre, 2,000-case winery that often makes excellent, refined Cabernet Sauvignon, Chardonnay, and Pinot Noir from old, non-irrigated grapes high in the Santa Cruz Mountains. Other label: *MEV.*

Nicasio Vineyards (Soquel, 1955), is a 1,500-case winery that makes Zinfandel, Cabernet Sauvignon, Chardonnay, Riesling, and sparkling wines.

Noble Hill Vineyards (Felton, 1986), is a 5-acre, 4,000-case, quality oriented winery that makes complex, balanced, crisp Chardonnay, Sauvignon Blanc, and full-bodied Pinot Noir from excellent vineyards under several appellation designations. The winery has recently been acquired by Elliston Winery of Sunol.

Obester Winery (Half Moon Bay, 1977), is a 5,000-case winery known for full-bodied Zinfandel and Cabernet Sauvignon, and lighter Riesling (also late harvest) and Sauvignon Blanc. A sister winery is located in Mendocino County.

P & M Staiger (Boulder Creek, 1973), is a 5-acre, 700-case winery that makes a Cabernet Sauvignon/Merlot blend, and an excellent, oaky, austere Chardonnay.

Page Mill Winery (Los Altos Hills, 1976), is a 2,500-case winery that makes above-average, full-bodied, well-flavored Chardonnay, Sauvignon Blanc, Cabernet Sauvignon, and Zinfandel.

Ridge Vineyards (Cupertino, 1959), located high in the Santa Cruz Mountains, is a superb, 40,000-case winery (mostly red wines) that owns the famous 50-acre *Monte Bello* vineyard. Although the winery makes nearly two dozen different wines, those that have captivated attention are: *York Creek* Petite Sirah, Zinfandel and Cabernet Sauvignon; *Beatty* Zinfandel; *Howell Mountain* Cabernet Sauvignon; *Jimsomare* Cabernet Sauvignon; *Monte Bello* Cabernet Sauvignon and Chardonnay; *Lime Kiln* Zinfandel; *Paso Robles* Zinfandel; and late harvest Zinfandel. Chardonnay is usually austere, tightly knit and requires time to mature. Paul Draper, considered one of the finest winemakers in California, has consistently produced wines with depth, finesse, complexity, and enormous staying power. Despite the obvious success of Cabernet Sauvignon, about 50 to 60 percent of total output is Zinfandel, a major departure from most serious wineries--and a pioneer in the production of classic wines that elevated Zinfandel from obscurity as a jug grape to unparalleled standards. The secret to Draper's success lies in the fact that he demands grapes from superior vineland sites, low yields that are the result of stressed vines, natural yeasts, small cooperage (American, not French oak), traditional winemaking techniques, and minor fining and filtering. The wines, as a consequence, are intensely flavored and scented, and due to prolonged skin contact, complex, alcoholic, deeply colored, expansive on the palate, and known for their aging potential. What makes the Monte Bello Ridge an excellent vineyard is the fact that it is sited on the largest deposit of calcium carbonate along the Coastal Ranges. A former seabed, this chalk mountain, composed from fossilized marine organisms, is reddish in color and mineral-rich, hence, it consistently produces outstanding Cabernet Sauvignon. The winery, founded by four members of the Stanford Research Institute, was sold in 1987 to a Japanese pharmaceutical firm. The firm has recently acquired Lytton Springs Winery.

River Run Vintners (Watsonville, 1978), is a conscientious, 2,500-case winery that makes Chardonnay, Riesling, Cabernet Sauvignon, Zinfandel, and Syrah from purchased grapes.

Roudon-Smith Vineyards (Santa Cruz, 1972), is a conscientious, 5-acre, 10,000-case winery that makes above-average Chardonnay (estate grown), Riesling, Cabernet Sauvignon, Zinfandel, Petite Sirah, Pinot Noir, and proprietary wines from purchased fruit, all of which can often be big, full-bodied, and tannin-rich.

Salamandre Wine Cellars (Aptos, 1985), is an 800-case winery that makes good, tart, intensely-flavored and scented, barrel-fermented Chardonnay, and small quantities of a blended red wine called *Claret*.

Santa Cruz Mountain Vineyard (Santa Cruz Mountains, 1974), is a 15-acre, 5,000-case winery that makes full-bodied, well-structured Chardonnay, Pinot Noir, Merlot, and Cabernet Sauvignon, the latter, often rich, dense, and long-lived (the Bates Ranch is especially good).

Sherrill Cellars (Woodside, 1973), is a 2,500-case winery that makes light-bodied, supple Chardonnay, Sauvignon Blanc, Cabernet Sauvignon, Petite Sirah, and Zinfandel, the latter particularly good.

Silver Mountain Vineyard (Los Gatos, 1979), is a 14-acre, 1,500-case winery that makes lean, well-structured Chardonnay, Zinfandel, and Cabernet Sauvignon..

Soquel Vineyards (Soquel, 1987), is an underrated, 4-acre, 2,000-case winery that makes excellent, full-bodied, well-structured Chardonnay, Pinot Noir, and Cabernet Sauvignon.

Storrs Winery (Santa Cruz, 1988), is a 4,500-case winery that makes above-average Chardonnay, Riesling, Gewurztraminer, Zinfandel, and Petite Sirah.

Sunrise Winery (Cupertino, 1976), is a 40-acre, 2,500-case winery specializing in Chardonnay, Riesling, Pinot Blanc, Cabernet Sauvignon, Pinot Noir, and Zinfandel.

Thomas Fogarty Winery (Portola Valley, 1981), is a 23-acre, 8,000-case winery that makes excellent Chardonnay, Pinot Noir, Cabernet Sauvignon, and Gewurztraminer, the latter particularly good.

Trout Gulch Vineyards (Soquel, 1988), is a new winery founded by a former partner of J. Lohr Winery that makes 1,000 cases of superb Chardonnay and Pinot Noir from 25 acres from a hilly vineyard in the Santa Cruz Mountains.

Walker Wines (Felton, 1979), is a 1,000-case winery that makes Chardonnay, Sauvignon Blanc, Pinot Noir, and Cabernet Sauvignon.

Woodside Vineyards (Woodside, 1960), is an 8-acre, 1,000-case winery that makes Chardonnay, Cabernet Sauvignon, Pinot Noir, and Zinfandel.

Zayante Vineyards (Felton, 1988), is a 10-acre, 500-case winery sitting on the site of an older, turn-of-the-century winery that makes Chardonnay, Zinfandel, Syrah, and Cabernet Sauvignon.

Monterey

Monterey, 120 miles south of San Francisco and one of the largest counties in the state, is a highly diverse area that encompasses the Salinas and Carmel valleys, Big Sur, and Point Lobos. It is home to John Steinbeck, Monterey "Jack Cheese," the stylish and expensive Monterey Peninsula, and the city of Monterey, site of the state's first capital, as well as the ill-fated Mormon country of Deseret. Monterey was first discovered by the explorer Cabrillo in 1542, but named in 1602 by Sebastian Vizcaino. In 1770 Gaspar de Portola established a presidio and Junipero Serra a mission, but despite its central coast location, population and industrial growth have been lacking until recently. While county-wide population numbers were less than 2,000 for 1850, and only 24,146 for 1910, real, sustained growth began with the advent of refrigerated railroads, so that by 1950 the population of 130,000 quickly rose to 361,000 in 1991, nearly all north and west of Salinas in the northern portion of the county.

Agriculturally, the county is dominated by the Salinas Valley (commonly referred to as the "salad bowl"), an immensely productive alluvial valley extending inland nearly 80 miles from the coastal plain with a varying width of 2 to 20 miles. The county has 300,000 acres of agricultural land producing $1 billion of agricultural products,

and ranks as the eighth largest agricultural county in the state. Its fertile, irrigated soils produce two and often three crops annually, mostly broccoli, lettuce, cauliflower and artichokes, and since 1970 large commercial quantities of wine grapes. The valley's incredible productivity is measured by the following: it is responsible for 60 percent of the state's broccoli, 50 percent of its lettuce and cauliflower, and is the nation's leading producer of strawberries and artichokes. Although grapes occupy only 27,000 acres, they are second only to lettuce in total agricultural farm revenue. Regardless of its formidable vine acreage, the county contains fewer than 30 wineries, and it is estimated that about 75 percent of all grapes are vinified into wine outside the county.

Although vineyards were planted at mission sites for sacramental wine production early in the nineteenth century, and wine made at Mission Soledad in the late 1780s, large-scale commercial plantings did not begin until the late 1960s when growers, in an attempt to overcome insufficient rainfall, began to tap the water reserves of the largest underground river in the world--the Salinas River. Even during the Prohibition era when vine acreage increased, Monterey County had fewer than 400 acres, a figure that dropped to 35 acres by 1960. Instead of vines, new refrigerated railroads encouraged the production of truck crops for midwestern and eastern markets. While unrelenting urbanization in the Santa Clara Valley and other Bay counties made grape-growing difficult, several large-scale plantings were undertaken in Monterey County in the late 1960s (Wente, Mirassou, Almaden, and Paul Masson, etc.), thus dramatically raising vine acreage to nearly 2,000 in 1970, and more than 35,000 acres by 1975--all of which were planted in premium varietals. Since then, vineland has declined by 8,000 acres due to sporadic outbreaks of phylloxera and the uprooting of vines originally planted on unsuitable land (a good deal of the Cabernet Sauvignon and nearly all of the Merlot have largely disappeared). Three-quarters of vineland is owned by twelve large growers and farmed in large blocks--a very unusual feature when compared with other coastal valleys. It is estimated that Delicato Winery alone owns about 30 percent of the county's total vine acreage--the San Bernabe Vineyard--considered the largest contiguous vineyard in the free world (about 8,000 acres).

Vine acreage is mainly confined in the Salinas Valley, a broad valley that in the northern portion gets higher in elevation and narrows appreciably as one proceeds southward to San Luis Obispo. It is bounded by the grass-covered Gabilan Range in the east, and the rugged Santa Lucia Range in the west. Most vineyards, located on well-drained soils above 1,000 feet in elevation, are above the frost line. Specific sites are rolling slopes, knolls and alluvial fans. More specifically, vine acreage is highly concentrated between Soledad and Greenfield, and in the much larger and more important southern portion of the county. Soils along the Salinas River and upland areas, derived from granite and alluvial pebble, are sandy, shallow, with little organic matter, and generally known for low yields. Over large stretches, vast "hard pans" necessitate expensive, laborious "ripping" to provide root access to underground water and nutrients.

Climatically, the Salinas Valley, a low Region I to high Region II, is influenced by a composite of dry, cool and windy weather conditions. The latter, the most prominent weather feature of the Salinas Valley, involves the funnelling of cool Pacific air through the valley at speeds between 20-25 mph. This phenomenon, locally known as the "Monterey Mistral," shreds leaves, producing small, scared berries, which means lower yields and late ripening (in an effort to mitigate high wind velocities, many growers have begun to plant corn and sunflowers between rows). The increase in rainfall from south to north and the production of precipitation by orographic means is quite noticeable and a distinct feature of the county's climatic characteristics. Average annual rainfall ranges from less than 14 inches in the southern extremities around San Lucas to 16 inches in Monterey, 21 inches in Watsonville, nearly 60 inches near the higher elevations of Ben Lomond along the western slopes of the Santa Cruz Mountains, and the higher elevations in the central portion of the county often receive 100 inches of rainfall.

Equally important is the fact that temperatures rarely exceed 100F in late afternoon, and the relative humidity is low. A good portion of the Salinas Valley has the coolest, driest, and windiest climate of any coastal viticultural district. Rarely do summer heat waves last for more than three days, and a blanket is required for comfortable night sleep every month of the year. These generalizations not withstanding, Monterey County has developed two distinct grape regions: the northern area, with the lowest rainfall, most wind, and the longest growing season, is primarily a white wine region; while the warmer, southern portion, with much higher elevations, a shorter growing season, higher summer temperatures, and higher yields, contains more red grapes. While the south produces Cabernet Sauvignon, Merlot, Chardonnay, Sauvignon Blanc, and Zinfandel, the northern portion produces above-average to excellent Chardonnay, Riesling, Pinot Noir, Pinot Blanc, and Gewurztraminer, all of which are intensely flavorful, well-balanced, and complex. Throughout the grape-growing regions, there are few dry-farmed vineyards. The climatic pattern causes considerable water stress, and, in the main, raises the pH and potassium level of the wines. Of considerable significance is the fact that the county (along with Santa Barbara) is less susceptible to rain during the harvest season than any other viticultural area in the state.

Interestingly, of the 28,496 acres, nearly 20,000 are

white, dominated by Chardonnay, Chenin Blanc, Riesling, Sauvignon Blanc, Pinot Blanc, and Gewurztraminer. Red grapes, grown mainly in the southern portion, are mainly confined to Cabernet Sauvignon and Zinfandel. The third most widely planted red grape--Pinot Noir, is mainly planted in the cooler, northern district. Among white varieties, Pinot Blanc, a highly underrated grape, is now becoming a serious specialty (Monterey County accounts for 50 percent of all state acreage) for the cooler, northern region. It is becoming an important ingredient in sparkling production, as well as being made as a dry table wine. Chardonnay, the most popular white variety, often marked by delicacy and finesse, rarely exhibits the rich, buttery, lush, thick and overly alcoholic characteristics of Sonoma and Napa. Although there are exceptions, Chenin Blanc, Riesling, and Gewurztraminer are made fruity, fresh, with some residual sugar and never aged in wood (late harvest wines can often be rich, luscious and memorable). On the other hand, Chardonnay, Pinot Blanc, and Sauvignon Blanc are dry, austere on the palate, and often wood aged. Monterey abounds in controversy on the merits of growing Cabernet Sauvignon, primarily because early wines exhibited pronounced vegetal, asparagus, herbaceous, and bell pepper flavors, commonly referred to as the "veggies." Whatever the real or conceived causes, these vegetal flavors have been largely eliminated due to controlled irrigation, better canopy control, and improved virus-free and heat treated rootstock. Equally important, vineyards, improperly planted on rich, irrigated soil, have been uprooted, vine vigor and crop load have been reduced, and vine maturity increased.

Table 9.6

GRAPE ACREAGE IN MONTEREY COUNTY			
Variety	1969	1979	1990	Percent
Chardonnay	173	2,971	6,469	22.7
Chenin Blanc	206	1,639	2,762	9.7
Riesling	69	1,899	2,624	9.2
Sauvignon Blanc	66	798	1,489	5.2
Pinot Blanc	210	670	1,069	3.8
Gewurztraminer	69	568	739	2.6
Colombard	153	378	494	1.7
Semillon	26	307	397	1.4
Malvasia Bianca	167	227		
Muscat Blanc		135	172	
Grey Riesling	25	82	167	
Sylvaner	125	112	138	
Cabernet Sauvignon	451	2,265	3,763	13.2
Zinfandel	20	1,839	1,878	6.6
Pinot Noir	321	1,419	1,616	5.7
Petite Sirah	35	818	780	2.7
Merlot		246	674	2.4
Gamay Beaujolais	197	385	374	1.3
Napa Gamay	60	292	280	1.0
Cabernet Franc	53	137		
Grenache		113	113	
Early Burgundy	116	89		
Other	145	2,229	500	
Total	2,687	17,353	28,496	
Total White	1,343	6,338	18,758	
Total Red	1,344	11,015	9,738	
Source: California Agricultural Statistics Service			

The *Monterey (1984) ava* is distinguished from surrounding areas by the fact that nearly all of it is drained by the Salinas River and its tributaries, but it is not, by any means, homogeneous in terms of soil, altitude or climate. Except for the coastal zone, approximately the entire north-south length of the valley is surrounded by hills and mountains, hence, relatively dry (annual rainfall is less than ten inches) throughout the growing season, and irrigation is necessary from the underground Salinas River. The coastal area just north of Monterey is particularly foggy, Fort Ord recording about 190 days of fog annually. The valley, the longest along the coast and fronting along the cool water of Monterey Bay, acts as a conduit for cool air which keeps summer temperatures low, lengthens the growing season, and prevents harmful spring frosts. What makes all the foregoing interesting is the fact that a good portion of the Salinas Valley and outlying sections have lower temperatures during the months of June through September than Sonoma and Napa (140 miles to the north), thus producing small grape berries with very intense flavors and good acid levels, the latter condition particularly helpful in making sparkling wine. In general, the harvest begins early in September and ends by the middle of October.

The *Carmel Valley (1983) ava* is fast developing into a premium grape-growing region. Its microclimate and soils are sufficiently different from neighboring areas in Salinas and Monterey to prompt BATF to assign a separate *ava* to its 119,200 acres, of which fewer than 300 are planted in grapes. The Carmel Valley, stretching for 25 miles, is distinguished from surrounding areas by a higher elevation, thus allowing a greater incidence of sunshine than the Salinas Valley, and a rainfall pattern that is nearly 15 inches higher than the 10 inches falling in the low lying areas of most of Monterey County. The climate is cool, foggy, and the hilly terrain creates good air drainage. Soils, dry, thin and stony, vary between sandy loam and shaley loam, and the entire valley is fed by underground springs with a high pH. Over the past ten years no fewer than eight vineyards and five wineries have been established. The valley is somewhat poor in agriculture supporting but 6,000 people.

The *Chalone (1982) ava*, a region of 8,640 acres composed of chaparral-type vegetation, deciduous and live oaks, chemise, sage, and buck bush, lies on rolling hills on the west-facing Gabilan Mountain Range overlooking both Monterey and San Benito counties. The vineyards at 1,800 foot elevations are on soils derived mainly of Miocene volcanic and Mesozoic granite rock with some scattered limestone. Precipitation varies between ten inches near the valley to fourteen inches in upland areas. The *ava* is synonymous with the Chalone Vineyard. The *San Lucas (1987) ava*, the southernmost in the county, is a 53 square mile region located between King City and San Ardo in southern Monterey County. A region of allu-

vial fans, and former river terraces, it encompasses nearly 34,000 acres of which nearly 10,000 are planted in grapes. The most common grapes are Cabernet Sauvignon, Chardonnay, Riesling, and Chenin Blanc.

The *Arroyo Seco (1983) ava* is a triangular-shaped area that lies adjacent to Arroyo Seco Creek, a tributary of the Salinas River. Topography and soil distinguish this region from surrounding areas: the entire region slopes for several miles creating good air drainage, while the gravelly soils provide good water drainage and excellent root penetration. Interest in the Arroyo Seco area did not begin until the 1960s when Wente, Paul Masson, Jeckel, and Mirassou began planting vines. This former Spanish land grant, named after the Arroyo Seco Creek, developed rapidly during the 1970s, and by 1983 it was granted *ava* status. It contains nearly 30 square miles, 9,000 acres of vineyards, and exhibits a unique microclimate. Because it is surrounded by hills and mountains, the period of maximum heat stress is reduced to no more than two hours. By early afternoon the cooling sea breezes arrive dropping temperatures rapidly. It is interesting to note that average summer temperatures are so low that Cabernet Sauvignon is often picked in late November, and sometimes as late as the first week of December. The irrigated vineyards receive less than 10 inches of rainfall. Soils are a product of an old geologic river bed that joined the Salinas River south of Greenfield. Geologic faulting created two highly favorable soil conditions known as the Lockwood and Arroyo Seco series. The former consists of soil laced with cobblestones and shale rock, while the latter consists of reddish-brown soil with cobblestone rock, both of which are well-drained. The planted area consists of Chardonnay, Riesling, Sauvignon Blanc, Grey Riesling, Chenin Blanc, Gewurztraminer, Cabernet Sauvignon, and Pinot Noir. The wineries are:

Bernardus (Carmel Valley, 1990), is a 50-acre, 25,000-case winery that makes Chardonnay, Sauvignon Blanc, and Meritage-type wines.

Chalone Vineyard (Soledad, 1960), is a 165-acre, 17,000-case winery located high in the Paicines region of the Gabilan Range. It ranks among the top wineries in the state, particularly for expensive, well-oaked, rich, smooth, yet firm Chenin Blanc, Pinot Blanc, Chardonnay, and Pinot Noir, all of which are well-structured, full-bodied, intensely colored and flavored. Three-quarters of output is white wine, the remainder Pinot Noir. This financially successful winery also owns two other premium wineries: Acacia and Carmenet, is a partner in Edna Valley Vineyards, and currently engaged in the development of a winery in the Columbia Valley. The publicly traded corporation has recently exchanged corporate common stock with Lafite Rothschild. Other label: *Gavilan Vineyards*.

Chateau Julien (Carmel, 1982), located in the Carmel Valley, is a 112,000-case winery that makes Sauvignon Blanc, Semillon, Chardonnay, Riesling, Gewurztraminer, Merlot, Cabernet Sauvignon, and Sherry-type wines. Other label: *Garland Ranch*, for Chardonnay, Cabernet Sauvignon, Zinfandel, and Merlot, the latter imported from Chile. Another label—*Emerald Bay*, is known for Chardonnay, Gewurztraminer, Cabernet Sauvignon, and proprietary wines.

Cypress Ridge Winery (King City, 1989), is a 7,000-acre vineyard with a large non-fermenting facility that crushes a huge quantity of grapes, half of which emanate from the impressive San Bernabe Vineyard. The vineyard and crushing facility are owned by Delicato Winery.

Domaine De Clarck (Carmel, 1989), is a 1,500-case winery that makes above-average to excellent Chardonnay and Pinot Noir, both of which offer excellent value. The reserve wines are outstanding and not to be missed.

Durney Vineyard (Carmel, 1977), part of a 1,200-acre ranch, this 145-acre, 11,000-case winery makes excellent, big, opulent, intensely flavored Chenin Blanc, Riesling, Cabernet Sauvignon, and Gamay Beaujolais, all of which are dry-farmed.

Georis Winery (Carmel, 1988), is a 22-acre, 1,000-case winery that makes spicy, robust, and well-structured Merlot, and a Meritage-type red wine.

Hahn Estates Winery (Soledad, 1990), is a 960-acre, 22,000-case winery that makes Chardonnay, Cabernet Sauvignon, and Merlot.

Jekel Vineyards (Greenfield, 1978), is a 320-acre, 60,000-case, highly successful winery known for robust and intense Cabernet Sauvignon, interesting Cabernet Franc, steely Chardonnay, soft Riesling, fruity Pinot Blanc, and proprietary wines. The winery, acquired in 1989 by Vintech, a holding company for several wineries, has recently been acquired by the Brown-Forman Group.

Joullian Vineyards (Carmel Valley, 1986), is a 40-acre, 7,000-case winery that makes big, opulent Cabernet Sauvignon, Chardonnay, and a Sauvignon Blanc/Semillon blend.

La Reina Winery (Carmel, 1987), is a 15,000-case winery known for crisp, well-made, barrel-fermented Chardonnay, offering good value.

Lockwood Vineyards (San Lucas, 1989), is a 1,600-acre, 40,000-case winery that makes good, sound, Chardonnay, Riesling (three styles), Sauvignon Blanc, Semillon, Pinot Blanc, Muscat Blanc, Semillon, Cabernet Franc, Merlot, Refosco (three styles), and Cabernet Sauvignon, all offering excellent value.

Monterey Peninsula Winery (Sand City, 1974), is a 12,000-case winery known for spicy, big, oaky, tannin-rich, full-bodied Cabernet Sauvignon, Merlot, Barbera (from the *Vineyard View Ranch*), Pinot Noir, Zinfandel, Chardonnay, Pinot Blanc, and sparkling wines (one of the finest as well as the most expensive in the state). The reserve wines are excellent.

Morgan Winery (Salinas, 1982), is an excellent, 22,000-case winery best known for consistently good, supple, fruity, yet well-structured and complex Chardonnay. Recent releases of Sauvignon Blanc, Pinot Noir, and Cabernet Sauvignon have also been impressive.

Paraiso Springs Vineyards (Morgan Hill, 1989), is a 210-acre, 3,000-case excellent winery that makes Pinot Blanc, Chardonnay, Riesling, and Pinot Noir.

Richard Boyer Wines (Soledad, 1985), is an excellent, 1,500-case, Chardonnay label made by the winemaker of a prominent Monterey County winery.

Robert Talbott Vineyards & Winery (Gonzales, 1983), is a 100-acre, 12,000-case winery that makes outstanding, expensive and age worthy Chardonnay that should not be missed. Barrel fermented, the fruity, well-balanced and rich wine lacks the buttery character of most similar libations emanating from Napa and Mendocino counties. Other labels: *Logan* and *Talbott Diamond T Family Estate*.

San Saba Vineyards (Soledad, 1981), is a label for a 70-acre vineyard that produces about 4,000 cases of above-average Cabernet Sauvignon (with a small infusion of Merlot and Cabernet Franc). The vineyard is maintained and the wine made by Smith & Hook Winery.

Sea Cliff Wine Co. (Carmel, 1987), is a 2-acre, 1,000-case winery that makes Chardonnay and Merlot wines under the *Coastanoan Winery* label.

Smith & Hook Winery (Soledad, 1979), is a 1,700-acre, 15,000-case winery that specializes in the production of expertly made, estate-produced, ripe, robust, and masculine Cabernet Sauvignon and complex Merlot. Botrytized Semillon and Riesling are made under the *Gabrielle & Caroline* label. Other label: *Lone Oak Estates*.

The Monterey Vineyard (Gonzales, 1973), is a large, 1,062-acre, 620,000-case winery owned by the Seagram Classics Wine Co. that makes mainly vintage-dated blends and varietal wines: Zinfandel, Pinot Blanc, Pinot Noir, Chardonnay, Cabernet Sauvignon, Chenin Blanc, Riesling, Sauvignon Blanc, Petite Fume (a blend of Sauvignon Blanc and Chenin Blanc), and sparkling wines, all of which have recently shown improvement. The *Limited Release* Chardonnay and Pinot Noir are particularly good.

Ventana Vineyards Winery (Soledad, 1978), is a 300-acre, 40,000-case winery that makes above-average to excellent Pinot Blanc, Sauvignon Blanc, Chenin Blanc, Gewurztraminer, Riesling, Syrah, Pinot Noir, Cabernet Sauvignon, Muscat Blanc, and Chardonnay, the latter, elegant and complex, usually offering outstanding value. Also made is an upscale Cabernet Sauvignon under the *Magnus* label.

Smith & Hook, sited on the lee side of the Coastal Range overlooking the Salinas Valley. Baxevanis

San Luis Obispo, Santa Barbara, And Ventura Counties

Collectively these three counties are a widely dispersed and highly diverse viticultural area that begins north of Paso Robles and continues south to Ventura. The entire region is dominated by north-south Coastal Ranges in San Luis Obispo, and a series of east-west mountain ranges in Santa Barbara and Ventura. Vineyards are mainly confined to the Salinas Valley north and south of Paso Robles, the Estrella River Valley, the Edna Valley, and the Santa Ynez and Santa Maria valleys of Santa Barbara County, all but the first two having an east-west orientation relatively close to the Pacific Ocean. The entire region contains more than 18,000 acres, 5.7 percent of all wine grapes, and accounts for less than 1 percent of the state's total wine output. The three counties have a combined population of 1.5 million inhabitants, little industry, and, hence, a smog-free coastal environment.

Although it boasts a 200 year history of grape-growing and winemaking, this is an area of pioneering winemakers since 70 of the 79 wineries were established after 1970. Due to lower land values, start-up costs are about one-third less than in the Napa Valley, a situation that has not gone unnoticed by young winemakers. As a consequence, the area exhibits a most dynamic atmosphere with constant changes in vineyard ownership, wineries and inevitable name changes. The "newly discovered" Central Coast, therefore, exhibits four important features not generally found in combination in the rest of the state: a high rate of attrition (more than 10 percent of all wineries have gone out of business since 1980); considerable land speculation (one of the state's largest premium grape producers, The Tepusquet Vineyard, has been sold to Robert Mondavi and Kendall-Jackson); rapid growth (vine acreage has leaped from fewer than 700 acres in 1970 to 7,402 in 1978, to 18,400 acres in 1992 making this region one of the fastest wine grape-growing areas in the state); and foreign interest (not only is a significant portion of the small wineries owned by non-Americans, but large corporations such as Santury, Deutz, Chateau Beaucastel-Haas (a proposed 120-acre vineyard and winery located fifteen miles east of San Simeon will be producing red and white wines from Rhone varietals), and Cordoniu have shown a keen interest in this region.

Of the nearly 18,000 acres of vineland in the three counties, more than 11,100 are planted in white grapes, of which Chardonnay (4,838 acres) dominates, followed by Chenin Blanc, Riesling, Sauvignon Blanc, and Gewurztraminer. Two varieties--Gewurztraminer and Riesling, show a sharp clustering in the cooler sections of Santa Barbara County. Of the 5,210 acres of planted red grapes, all, except Pinot Noir and Merlot, tend to be concentrated in the warmer Paso Robles region. The dominant varieties are Cabernet Sauvignon, Zinfandel, Pinot Noir, Merlot, and Gamay Beaujolais.

In the absence of distinct styles of wine made, both red and white wines vary widely in their character based on the various microclimates, each of which imparts a subtle aroma, flavor, and structure peculiarity. For example, Paso Robles, historically known for Zinfandel, now has an established reputation for spicy, but often herbaceous Cabernet Sauvignon. Chardonnay, especially from Santa Ynez, Santa Maria, and the Edna Valley, is full-bodied, firm, low in pH, lean, and often fruity. From Santa Ynez and Santa Maria, Riesling and Gewurztraminer are fruity, well-balanced, and with a pronounced varietal character often lacking from Napa Valley versions.

The main advantage of the Central Coast is a climatic pattern of warm, sunny days and cool evenings that produces high acid grapes balancing high sugar levels. This condition is brought about by the fact that there is a structural break in the Coastal Ranges allowing cool maritime air to enter the coastal valleys of Santa Barbara County, and, to a smaller degree, Paso Robles and Ventura counties. Another important consideration is the presence of highly mineralized, gravelly, phylloxera-free

soils allowing the vines to grow on their own root stock. The blend of high acid and sugar levels, intense fruit and varietal character leads to well-balanced wines. However, because of considerable variations in microclimates and soils, there is controversy concerning grape varieties best suited to the region. While there is widespread support on the virtues of certain white grapes such as Riesling, Muscat Blanc, Chardonnay, Gewurztraminer, and Sauvignon Blanc raised in the cooler regions and gravelly limestone-enriched soils, not all premium red grapes appear to have a particular affinity to the varied microclimates and soils of the region. The main criticism lies in a distinct vegetal aroma, flavor and bitterness in the aftertaste, particularly in Cabernet Sauvignon and Merlot. Among red grapes, Pinot Noir and Zinfandel, when well-tended and handled carefully in the winery, appear to promise the finest future. Sparkling wines, although not produced on a large scale, also appear to be poised for substantial growth. Finally, because of the relative youthfulness of the region, a good deal of experimentation is underway, so the final verdict on the ideal grapes and ultimate wines produced will undoubtedly change in the coming decades. This region shows great potential, and by 2010 the number of wineries is expected to increase from 79 to 165.

San Luis Obispo

Located in the center of the "San-San Gap," San Luis Obispo County, one of the most rapidly growing counties in California, is three times larger than the state of Rhode Island. The element of size is very important here because more than half of the county contains slopes greater than 30 degrees, a condition that tends toward isolation, provincialism, and a myriad of nooks and crannies ideally suited to viticulture. With a population of more than 200,000 people and 8,500 acres of vineland, San Luis Obispo ranks third after Monterey and Santa Barbara counties in vine acreage.

Although best known for San Simeon, Hearst Castle, and the site of the nation's first motel (San Luis Obispo in 1925), the county is a highly diverse area of more than 2 million acres, of which only 62,000 are irrigated. Often referred to as the barley and almond capital of the world, the Carissa Plains region, located in the northeastern portion of the county, is also the largest wheat producing area of California. Viticulturally, vineland has grown from 900 acres in 1970 (almost all Zinfandel, Alicante Bouschet, and Mission) to 8,484 acres in 1990. The establishment of wineries has been equally impressive, mushrooming from 2 to 34 for the same period. Although livestock production provides nearly half of the agricultural wealth of the county, and dry-farmed hay provides an additional 23 percent of agricultural production, the remaining irrigated and dry-farmed orchard and vineyard acreage has shown remarkable growth in the past fifteen years. Despite its recent viticultural successes, it is estimated that more than 80 percent of all grapes in San Luis Obispo and Santa Barbara are processed elsewhere.

San Luis Obispo County, an old winemaking district long forgotten, has become very fashionable since 1970. Vines were first cultivated in 1797 by missionaries at San Miguel Archangel, followed by modern plantings and wineries at York Mountain in 1882, and Rotta Winery in 1890 (the latter winery, in operation until 1987, had been known as Las Tablas Winery). The romance of the area is enhanced by the fact that Ignace Paderewski fell in love with the region, purchased 2,500 acres in 1914 and, for a short time, lived and planted an orchard and Zinfandel vines (half a century later, a good deal of this property became part of the ill-fated Hoffman Mountain Ranch Winery). Today, there is an impatient urgency to purchase suitable vineland on limestone/gravel soils and to be as near as possible to a maritime microclimate, build new wineries, and determine the best possible grape varieties--all of which makes for exciting lifestyles.

Table 9.7

SAN LUIS OBISPO COUNTY: GRAPE ACREAGE			
Variety	1969	1979	1990	Percent
Chardonnay	5	467	2,412	28.4
Sauvignon Blanc		407	702	8.3
Chenin Blanc	12	292	324	3.8
Pinot Blanc		79		
Semillon		17	69	
Riesling		33	26	
Gewurztraminer	0	22		
Muscat Blanc		50	22	
Grey Riesling		20	20	
Colombard	13	77		
Sylvaner	10			
Cabernet Sauvignon	15	839	2,451	28.9
Zinfandel	512	805	1,367	16.1
Merlot		31	201	2.7
Pinot Noir	5	76	180	2.1
Petite Sirah		94	110	1.3
Napa Gamay		63		
Syrah		33	37	
Cabernet Franc	0	31		
Gamay Beaujolais	3	22		
Alicante Bouschet	8	1	10	
Grenache	17	1	6	
Barbera	35	35		
Other	19	1,061	298	
Total	654	4,088	8,484	
Total White	60	1,859	3,844	
Total Red	594	2,229	4,499	
Source: California Agricultural Statistics Service.				

The county has four *ava's: Paso Robles (1983), York Mountain (1983), Edna Valley (1982), and Arroyo Grande Valley (1990). Paso Robles* (the name is derived from El Paso de Robles, or "the Pass of Oaks," given by travelers between the mission of San Miguel and Mission San Luis Obispo), located within San Luis Obispo County, is defined by the Cuesta Grande to the south, the Santa Lucia Range to the west, the Monterey County line to the north, and the Chalame Hills to the east. The area, characterized by rolling hills and valleys with an elevation between 600 and 1,900 feet, is covered by well-drained alluvial and former river terrace deposits. Climatically, the county is influenced by the Santa Lucia Mountains which divide this region into two distinct zones. To the west is the cooler Edna Valley, but on the lee side of the Santa Lucia Range is a drier and hotter climatic pattern better suited for Zinfandel (the best of which is dry-farmed and head pruned) and other red grapes. Classified as Region II, III and IV are the vineyards north and south of Paso Robles, the Estrella River Valley, and the Shandon district.

Rarely receiving the attention that it deserves, this *ava* contains nearly 7,000 acres of vineland, 100 growers, and 22 wineries (with a significant number of wineries as far away as Michigan and Mendocino fermenting grapes in the area and shipping the wine to their respective areas for final blending). Because it is sheltered from oceanic winds, the climate varies from a cool Region II in the west to a very warm Region IV in the east, but because of a pronounced mountain and valley wind, the warm to hot days are tempered by cool evening temperatures, thus maintaining good acid balance in the grapes. Precipitation varies between 10 and 25 inches, the latter figure occurring in the western portion of the *ava*. However, when compared with the Santa Maria and Santa Ynez valleys to the south, average daily temperatures are substantially higher, hence the inclination to plant more red grapes than white. Due to the presence of limestone deposits (along the western slopes of the Salinas River Valley), and calcareous material found at considerable depths in the Estrella River Valley, land speculation and rising land values have escalated in recent years.

The underground Salinas River separates the producing region into two sections: to the east of the city of Paso Robles vines are irrigated, but to the west, the area of most wineries, vineyards are dry farmed, and, as result, have generated a reputation for good Zinfandel (locally known as "big red") and Merlot, both of which are dark, round, well-balanced, and intensely flavored. Along the western portion of the Salinas Valley, mountain limestone soils produce lower yields and more concentrated, full-bodied red wines than the irrigated sections east of the valley. It is, therefore, interesting to note that because of the foregoing there is greater emphasis on red grapes (Zinfandel, Cabernet Sauvignon, Petite Sirah, and Merlot), rather than white, the latter confined to Sauvignon Blanc, Muscat Blanc, Chenin Blanc, and Chardonnay. White wines are generally fruity, alcoholic and substantial on the palate; red wines are deeply colored, spicy, earthy, and full-bodied. In recent years several Italian grapes (Nebbiolo, Aleatico, and Dolcetto) have attracted considerable attention, as have southern French grapes, such as Syrah, Marsanne, Roussanne, and Viognier. While no major Italian winery has entered the viticultural scene, the emergence of Chateau Beaucastel may very well be a harbinger of greater recognition for this *ava*.

York Mountain, located immediately to the west of the *Paso Robles ava*, lies entirely within the confines of a winery of the same name, and is historically important because it is the site of the Ascension Winery founded by Andrew York in 1882. The vineyard receives rather heavy precipitation (45 inches, or twice the amount of neighboring sites), at an altitude of 1,500 feet on the heavily wooded slopes of the Santa Lucia Mountain Range. Oriented along a northwest-southeast axis, *Edna Valley* is an elongated, 35 square mile *ava* that is well defined by the Santa Lucia Mountains on the northeast, a complex of low hills on the southeast, and the San Luis Range on the southwest. What makes it unusual is the presence of sandy clay loam and moderately alkaline calcareous soils, and it commands an unobstructed influence from the cool Pacific Ocean. The climate, therefore, is a frost-free, low Region I and II. Principal grape varieties are Chardonnay, Sauvignon Blanc, and Pinot Noir, all of which are above-average and whose main wine characteristics differ significantly from Sonoma-Napa libations by their restrained fruit, oily texture, and high alcohol. *Arroyo Grande Valley*, the most recent *ava*, is located about 12 miles southeast of the city of San Luis Obispo. Covering an area of approximately 67 square miles, this comparatively small grape-growing region of 450 acres lies northwest of the Santa Maria region, and has three wineries.

The wineries of San Luis Obispo County are:

Abbey d'Or Winery (San Miguel, 1987), is a 85-acre vineyard whose wines (3,000 cases of Chenin Blanc, Chardonnay, Cabernet Sauvignon, and Pinot Noir) are made at a neighboring winery.

Adelaida Cellars (Paso Robles, 1983), is an excellent, 10-acre, 8,000-case label that makes above-average Chardonnay, Zinfandel, Syrah, and Cabernet Sauvignon (blended with Syrah), all of which are distinctive and consistently good.

Arciero. known for acres of roses, antique cars, and soft, supple wines.
Baxevanis

Arciero Winery (Paso Robles, 1984), with a 5-acre rose garden, is an impressive, 517-acre, 125,000-case winery that makes Cabernet Sauvignon, Sauvignon Blanc, Chardonnay, Chenin Blanc, Zinfandel, and Petite Sirah, offering good value.

Baron & Kolb Winery (Paso Robles, 1987), is a 95-acre, 5,000-case winery that makes above-average Chardonnay, Sauvignon Blanc, Cabernet Sauvignon, Zinfandel, and proprietary blends, offering good value.

Belli & Sauret Vineyards (San Miguel, 1982), is an aggressive, 100-acre, 6,000-case winery specializing in Chardonnay, Sauvignon Blanc, and Zinfandel, the latter, ripe, full-bodied, concentrated, and flavorful, the product of non-irrigated vines.

Caparone Winery (Paso Robles, 1979), is a 60-acre, 3,500-case winery that makes full-bodied, distinctive, unfiltered and unfined, hand-crafted red wines only--Zinfandel, Cabernet Sauvignon, Merlot, Nebbiolo, and Brunello.

Castoro Cellars (San Miguel, 1983), recently moved from Atascadero, is an 8,000-case winery that makes Cabernet Sauvignon, Chardonnay, Sauvignon Blanc, Pinot Noir, Zinfandel, sparkling, and Gamay, the latter one of the finest in the state.

Chamisal Vineyard (San Luis Obispo, 1979), is a 60-acre, 5,000-case property that makes excellent, big, ripe, intensely-flavored Chardonnay. This was the first commercial vineyard planted in the Edna Valley.

Clairborne & Churchill Vintners (San Luis Obispo, 1983), is a stylish, 2,500-case winery that makes Alsatian style Riesling, Gewurztraminer, Muscat Blanc, and Edelzwicker (a proprietary blend), all of which are mouth filling and intensely fruity, offering good value.

Cobble Creek Cellars (Paso Robles, 1981), is a 9-acre, 5,000-case winery that makes Zinfandel, Chenin Blanc, Sauvignon Blanc, Chardonnay, Pinot Noir, Merlot, Cabernet Sauvignon, and Petite Sirah, all of which are soft, supple, and early maturing. Until 1988 the winery was known as El Paso de Robles Winery & Vineyard.

Corbett Canyon Vineyards (San Luis Obispo, 1979), founded as Lawrence Winery, it was purchased by Glenmore Distilleries in 1981 (name changed in 1984), and then by The Wine Group in 1988. The largest among the Central Coast region with more than 300,000 cases, it produces several different types of wine: one liter blended and varietal wines under the *Coastal Classic* label; Muscat Blanc, Gewurztraminer, Cabernet Sauvignon, Pinot Noir, Sauvignon Blanc, Chenin Blanc, and Chardonnay under the *Premium* label; Sauvignon Blanc, Zinfandel, Cabernet Sauvignon, and Chardonnay under the *Select and Winemakers Reserve* label. All the wines are clean and expertly made, often offering good value.

Cottonwood Canyon Vineyards (San Luis Obispo, 1989), is an 80-acre, 4,200-case winery that makes rich, opulent Chardonnay and Pinot Noir.

Creston Manor Vineyards & Winery (Creston, 1980), is a 155-acre, 32,000-case winery located at an elevation of 1,700 feet in the La Panz Mountain Range. It makes Sauvignon Blanc, Chardonnay, Cabernet Sauvignon, Zinfandel, and Pinot Noir, all of which are marketed under the *Creston Vineyards* label.

Eberle Winery (Paso Robles, 1984), is a 41-acre, 10,000-case winery that makes oaky, but flavorful and fruity Cabernet Sauvignon, Chardonnay, and Muscat Blanc.

Edna Valley Vineyard (San Luis Obispo, 1980), owned by Chalone and Paragon Vineyards, is a 600-acre, 85,000-case winery that makes above-average Chardonnay (90 percent of output), Pinot Noir, Vin Gris, and small quantities of late harvest Riesling and sparkling wine. The Chardonnay is full-bodied, crisp, steely and characterized by a long, pronounced finish; the Pinot Noir, full on the palate, is often sweet, raisiny, and often overly oaked. The Chalone Wine Group has a 50 percent interest.

Estrella River Winery (Paso Robles, 1977), is a 300-acre, 15,000-case winery that makes fresh, fruity Chardonnay, Muscat Blanc, Sauvignon Blanc, Riesling, Zinfandel, Cabernet Sauvignon, and Syrah. The recently completed winery has also introduced a new label, *Laura's Vineyard*, for Cabernet Sauvignon and Chardonnay.

Farview Farm Vineyard (Templeton, 1979), is a 54-acre, 2,000-case winery that makes estate grown Chardonnay, Merlot, and Zinfandel.

Fratelli Perata (Paso Robles, 1987), is a 25-acre, 1,000-case winery that makes Cabernet Sauvignon, Merlot, Zinfandel, and Nebbiolo.

Haas-Perrine (Paso Robles, 1990), is a 250-acre vineyard currently planted in Roussane, Marsanne, Viognier, Grenache, Syrah, Cournoise, Vaccarese, and Mourvedre. This future vineyard and winery is a joint venture by a prominent wine importer and a major producer of Chateau-Neuf-du-Pape. First crush is expected in 1992, and total production is estimated to mount to 25,000 cases by 1997.

Harmony Cellars (Harmony, 1989), is a 4,000-case winery that makes Chardonnay, Riesling, Muscat Blanc, Cabernet Sauvignon, Pinot Noir, Zinfandel, and proprietary wines.

Hope Farms Winery (Paso Robles, 1990), is a 220-acre, 5,000-case winery that makes Chardonnay, Sauvignon Blanc, Muscat Blanc, Zinfandel, and Cabernet Sauvignon.

Justin Vineyards & Winery (Paso Robles, 1982), is a 70-acre, 5,000-

case, all-estate winery that makes big, classy, elegant, barrel-fermented Chardonnay, Meritage-type wine (labeled *Paso Robles Reserve*), Cabernet Sauvignon, Merlot, and small quantities of Nebbiolo and Orange Muscat.

Le Cuvier (Paso Robles, 1988), is an 1-acre, 1,500-case label that has generated a reputation for full-bodied, well-structured Chardonnay, Syrah, and Cabernet Sauvignon.

Maison Deutz (Arroyo Grande, 1981), is a new, handsome, 800-acre (180 acres planted in vines), sparkling wine-only winery. Located just 4 miles from the Pacific in a Region I climate, it is perhaps the only such wine facility sited on limestone soils. The wines, the product of a wooden basket press, hand riddling and hand disgorgement, are full-bodied, crisp and fruity. Eminently yeasty, they spend a minimum of 18 months *en tirage*, and undergo malolactic fermentation, a sharp departure from traditional California techniques, resulting in an end product that is high in lactic acid, phenols and pH. Production consists of 15,000 cases of Brut Blanc de Blancs, and Blanc de Noir. While Chardonnay and Pinot Noir are the quality grapes, 40 percent of production is with the neutral base of Pinot Blanc. Partially owned by Wine World, this winery is currently making exceptional, rich, lean, tart, full-bodied, complex wines that should not be missed.

Martin Brothers Winery (Paso Robles, 1981), is a 72-acre, 10,000-case winery known for a rare, tart and spicy Nebbiolo, as well as excellent Chardonnay, Zinfandel, Aleatico, Sauvignon Blanc, and Chenin Blanc. This winery is the nation's largest producer of Nebbiolo.

Mastantuono Winery (Templeton, 1977), is a rapidly growing, 65-acre, 15,000-case winery that makes above-averege, quality Zinfandel (big, robust, and full-bodied), Cabernet Sauvignon, Chenin Blanc, Chardonnay, Muscat Blanc, and sparkling wines.

Meridian Vineyards (Paso Robles, 1988), is a 3,900-acre (in both San Luis Obispo and Santa Barbara), 250,000-case property that rests on a hilltop with a superb view. This state-of-the-art winery, placing an emphasis on matching grape varieties with microclimate and soils, makes clean, fresh tasting wines, of which Chardonnay, Cabernet Sauvignon, Syrah, and Pinot Noir are above-average, offering exceptional value. Most of the original 825-acre facility, including the productive assets of the Old Estrella River Winery, are now owned by Wine World Estates that has invested a reported $40 million, and renamed the facility Meridian Vineyards. Most of the grapes will emanate from the newly purchased 2,200-acre *San Antonio Vineyard* (divided into three distinct vineyards) just south of the city of Santa Maria. Wine World Estates owns another 3,550 acres of potential vineland, and one-quarter of all vine acreage in Santa Barbara County.

Mission View Vineyards & Winery (San Miguel, 1984), is a 46-acre, 9,000-case winery that makes Muscat Blanc, Sauvignon Blanc, Chardonnay, Cabernet Sauvignon, and Zinfandel.

Peachy Canyon Winery (Paso Robles, 1988), formerly Tobias Winery, is a 3-acre, 1,000-case winery that makes full-bodied, delicate, polished and refined, unfined and unfiltered Zinfandel.

Pesenti Winery (Templeton, 1934), the oldest family-owned winery in the area, is a 75-acre, 35,000-case firm that makes good, sound and intense Cabernet Sauvignon, Zinfandel, Riesling, Grey Riesling, and proprietary wines.

Piedra Creek Winery (San Luis Obispo, 1984), proudly announces that it is, with an annual production of 300 cases (Chardonnay, Zinfandel, and a proprietary red wine), the smallest winery in the county.

Ross-Keller (Nipomo, 1980), is a 2,000-case winery that makes Zinfandel, Riesling, Pinot Noir, and Chardonnay.

San Luis Obispo Winery (Paso Robles, 1974), is a 55-acre, 10,000-case winery now owned by a group of Japanese investors that will be producing Pinot Noir, Cabernet Sauvignon, and Chardonnay under the *Hidden Mountain Ranch* label.

Saucelito Canyon Vineyard (Arroyo Grande, 1982), is a 17-acre, 2,000-case winery that makes full-bodied, flavorful Zinfandel and Cabernet Sauvignon from non-irrigated vines.

Talley Vineyards (Arroyo Grande, 1986), is a superb, 85-acre, 2,500-case winery that makes big, bold, well-flavored Chardonnay, Sauvignon Blanc, Riesling, Pinot Noir, and Zinfandel, offering good value.

Tobin James (Paso Robles, 1985), is a 3,500-case winery that makes above-average Zinfandel, Pinot Noir, and Chardonnay, offering good value.

Twin Hills Winery (Paso Robles, 1978), is a 40-acre, 15,000-case winery

known for light-bodied, supple, clean, and fresh wines (Sauvignon Blanc, Chardonnay, Chenin Blanc, Zinfandel, and proprietary blends), offering excellent value. Recent reputation rests with Fino and Amontillado Sherry-type wines under the *James J's Private Reserve* label.

Part of the history of York Mountain Winery. Baxevanis

Watson Vineyards (Paso Robles, 1983), is a 10-acre, 3,500-case winery that makes hard to find, estate-bottled Chardonnay, Riesling, Pinot Noir, and Chenin Blanc on land that was once owned by Ignace Paderewski.

Wild Horse Winery & Vineyards (Templeton, 1982), formerly known as Santa Lucia Winery, is an aggressive and highly innovative, 25-acre, 20,000-case winery that makes distinctive, above-average Cabernet Sauvignon, Merlot, Pinot Noir, and Chardonnay, the latter two, austere, dry, crisp, complex, and full-bodied.

York Mountain Winery (Templeton, 1882), historically sitting on land deeded by Ulysses S. Grant, and boasting winemaking attempts by Ignace Paderewski, this winery has an excellent public relations platform. From 5 acres (and purchased grapes), it makes 5,000 cases of Merlot, Pinot Noir, Chardonnay, Zinfandel, Cabernet Sauvignon, sparkling, and Sherry/Port-type wines.

Santa Barbara and Ventura

With more than 10,000 acres of vineland, Santa Barbara is second in importance to Monterey County in grape acreage. Measuring 35 by 55 miles, this compact hilly and mountainous county is dominated by the 6,828-foot Big Pine Mountain, and two rivers that originate within its hilly terrain--the Santa Ynez and Santa Maria--both of which flow westward to the Pacific. The coastline from Point Conception to the Rincon constitutes the only east-west traverse of shoreline from Alaska to Cape Horn. It is this unusual southern exposure, combined with many small microclimates and diverse soils (there are several with considerable shale and sandstone suitable for vinegrowing) that makes Santa Barbara a unique viticultural area characterized by one of the coolest climates in the state. So impressed were the early Spaniards by the physical beauty and climate of Santa Barbara that the coastal fringes were called *La Tierra Adorada*, or the "beloved land." Without question, a good portion of coastal Santa Barbara, commonly referred to as the "California Riviera," and the area between Solvang and Buellton, are above-average in their physical beauty.

In the southernmost quality coastal viticultural areas, grapes were first planted in Santa Barbara by mission fathers early in the nineteenth century only to decline after 1840, and to re-emerge in 1962 with the founding of Santa Barbara Winery, and the planting of a 120-acre vineyard by a San Joaquin vineyardist. Indeed, the growth in vine acreage over the past 20 years has been nothing short of spectacular: from fewer than 450 acres of grapes planted in 1960, and 700 in 1973, the official figure leaped to more than 10,000 acres by 1992, practically all of it in the Santa Maria, Los Alamos, and the Santa Ynez regions. Wine production leaped from zero in 1961 to nearly 400,000 cases in 1992. Because a good deal of the county's available agricultural acreage has been held by a relatively small number of families, the recent excitement of Chardonnay and Pinot Noir increased real estate values to new heights. That the nation's former president and other celebrities reside there has also elevated the social image of the entire region. The fact that more than half of all vineyards changed ownership since 1987 is testimony to the highly fluid character of viticulture in this important Central Coast county, a fitting comment given the fact that grapes have become the fourth largest agricultural crop in Santa Barbara.

Table 9.8

GRAPE ACREAGE IN SANTA BARBARA COUNTY				
Variety	1969	1979	1990	Percent
Chardonnay	0	1,224	5,135	55.1
Riesling	0	905	722	7.7
Chenin Blanc	0	65	503	5.4
Sauvignon Blanc	0	253	443	4.8
Gewurztraminer	0	33	209	2.2
Pinot Blanc	0	29	79	
Muscat Blanc	0	18	22	
Semillon	0	12	22	
Sylvaner	13	13		
Cabernet Sauvignon	0	762	902	9.7
Pinot Noir	0	605	821	8.8
Merlot	0	156	262	2.8
Cabernet Franc	0	2	63	
Syrah	0	0	32	
Gamay Beaujolais	0	46		
Zinfandel	0	41	31	
Other	108	7	76	
Total	121	4,171	9,322	
Total White	19	2,557	7,185	
Total Red	102	1,614	2,137	
Source: California Agricultural Statistics Service.				

What makes this region unusual is that according to the Davis system, the climate varies between low Region I to low Region II due to the east-west orientation of the Coastal Ranges. Unique to the state, the county is bordered on two sides by the Pacific which allows the inland penetration of fog, and the moderating effects of land and sea breezes, and valley and mountain winds. The area is also susceptible to convection fog which occurs during the six summer months, thus making coastal Santa Barbara one of the coolest grape-growing regions in California. Summer days are typically cloud-free, warm until noon, hot between 12 and 6 pm, and then gradually cooling. Three to five times a week, there are periods of fog until late morning. The low humidity and lack of afternoon cloud cover results in large diurnal temperature variations, often as much as 55F. It is felt that this temperature regime accomplishes two things: a wide range of wine varieties can be grown with good to excellent results, and the low night time temperatures produce grapes with high acidity and varietal character, resulting in intense, fruity wines.

Therefore, it is interesting to note that unlike the warmer viticultural regions of San Luis Obispo, more than two-thirds of the planted acreage is devoted to white grapes, mainly Chardonnay, Chenin Blanc, Riesling, Sauvignon Blanc, and Gewurztraminer, all of which are characterized by true varietal flavor, a pungent aroma, and good acid balance. Red grapes are dominated by Pinot Noir, followed by Merlot, and Gamay Beaujolais. Although a recognized Santa Barbara style of wine has yet to be produced, white wine, in particular, differs from North Coast districts by a distinctive fruity flavor and high acid levels (especially true for Riesling and Chardonnay). Red wines, especially Cabernet Sauvignon and Merlot, are also characterized by high fruit flavors and a stemmy, somewhat bitter aftertaste, two features that are not necessarily negative attributes. When all is said and done, the two varieties that gave generated excitement are Chardonnay and Pinot Noir, both of which have acquired an element of celebrity due to their depth of flavor and balance. When subjected to malolactic fermentation and extended lees aging, Chardonnay, in particular, can achieve heights not easily attained in most other areas in the state.

The county contains two *ava's*: *Santa Maria (1981)* and *Santa Ynez (1983)*, both of which are above-average to excellent in both quality of grapes produced and statewide reputation. Currently on the drawing board (with some controversy) is the proposed *Santa Barbara Coast ava*, an ill-defined area designed to accommodate the marketing needs of large North Coast wineries with vineyard interests in the region. It will encompasses the Edna Valley and Arroyo Grande Valley in San Luis Obispo County, and Santa Maria Valley, Santa Ynez Valley, as well as the Los Alamos region in Santa Barbara County. Although the proposed appellation lacks precision, the wineries are interested in the marketing name of Santa Barbara.

The *Santa Maria ava* is a natural funnel-shaped valley located partly in San Luis Obispo, but primarily in Santa Barbara County. The area, approximately eleven miles long by sixteen miles wide, lies between the city of Santa Maria and the town of Sisquoc. While grapes are grown along the valley floor, the best sites are located on west-facing, former river benches 800 feet in elevation, usually on deep sandy loam and clay-loam soils. Having greater access to the ocean, the climate, influenced by prevailing westerly winds, is a cool Region I and II, but because of its interior location, foggy weather is less common. The hilly regions experience considerable diurnal temperature changes, and heavier precipitation than valley locations. Although the bulk of the county's wineries are located in the Santa Ynez *ava*, Santa Maria contains the bulk of the vine acreage, dominated by the large Tepusquet Vineyard. Principal grape varieties are Chardonnay, Riesling, Gewurztraminer, Pinot Noir, Pinot Blanc, Gamay Beaujolais, and Merlot. White wines are known for their crisp acid balance, pronounced aroma and flavor, and the reds (far less important) for their dark color, fullness, and elegance. Because Santa Maria and Santa Ynez, as well as other areas, were former ocean bottoms, the alluvial and colluvial soils are a well-drained mixture of sandstone, shale, silt, clay, limestone, and sand.

HOUTZ VINEYARDS

1986

santa ynez valley

cabernet sauvignon

blanc

The *Santa Ynez ava* is a name given to the mission established in 1804, the town, river, and valley. Located south of Santa Maria, Santa Ynez is a rich playground for large horse ranches, and the entire region has often been described as a "sanctuary spiced with eccentricity." The 285 square mile region contains 29 growers, twelve wineries, and more than 2,000 acres of vineland, half of the pre-Prohibition acreage. The compact, east-west valley is defined by the Purisima Hills and the San Rafael Mountains to the north, and the Santa Ynez Mountains on the south. Located 12 miles east of the Pacific Ocean and 50 miles north of Santa Barbara, Santa Ynez is relatively cool because of the proximity of the foggy coast, hence, it is described as a low Region I and II climatic region. Degree days vary between 1970 and 2880, with summer temperatures increasing as one proceeds in an eastward direction. Precipitation, greater along the westward coastal margins, varies from 20 inches to 14 inches in the protected leeward areas of the interior. The valley, unlike the more elevated Paso Robles area, receives late afternoon sea breezes from two different directions which moderate the high Mediterranean-climatic temperatures, and, hence, is perfectly suited for white grape production. Soils consist of variable mixtures of alluvial sand and loam along the river course, and decomposed shale in upland, hilly areas. Because they are well-drained, highly mineralized, and low in organic matter, they are usually irrigated. The majority of the vineyards are located on up-

land slopes to take advantage of moderating winds, fog, and the absence of frost. Chardonnay, Riesling, Sauvignon Blanc, Merlot, and Cabernet Sauvignon are the important grape varieties. The wineries are:

Au Bon Climat (Los Olivos, 1982), is a 7,000-case winery that makes excellent, distinctive, barrel-fermented Chardonnay, and full-bodied, unfiltered Pinot Noir from purchased grapes. Excellent Cabernet Sauvignon, Merlot, and Chardonnay under the label *Vita Nova* are jointly made with Qupe Winery. Nebbiolo is made under the *Il Podere Dell' Olivos* label.

Austin Cellars (Los Olivos, 1981), is a consistently good, 18-acre, 20,000-case winery that makes distinctive, intensely scented Cabernet Sauvignon, Pinot Noir, two types of Cabernet Franc (20% Merlot, and another with 16% Cabernet Sauvignon), Chardonnay, Riesling, Sauvignon Blanc, Muscat Blanc, and botrytized Sauvignon Blanc and Riesling.

Babcock Vineyards (Lompoc, 1984), is a 40-acre, 7,000-case winery that makes above-average to excellent, barrel-fermented Chardonnay, Sauvignon Blanc, Gewurztraminer, Riesling, and Pinot Noir, all of which are round, full-bodied and complex. The Grand Reserve Chardonnay is a must for the most discriminating cellar.

Ballard Canyon Winery (Solvang, 1978), is a 45-acre, 14,000-case winery that makes Chardonnay, Cabernet Sauvignon, Riesling, Sauvignon Blanc, Muscat Blanc, late harvest and botrytized Cabernet Sauvignon, and proprietary wines, all of which are intensely flavored, fresh, yet rich, offering good value.

Barnwood Vineyards (Old Cuyama, 1985), is a 160-acre, 12,000-case label known for excellent Chardonnay, Sauvignon Blanc, and Cabernet Sauvignon. This is the only winery located in the extreme northeastern portion of the county.

Buttonwood Farm Winery (Solvang, 1989), is a 40-acre, 1,000-case winery that makes good, sound, Sauvignon Blanc, Merlot, and Cabernet Franc.

Byron Vineyard & Winery (Santa Maria, 1984), is a 125-acre, 24,000-case winery that makes Chardonnay, Pinot Noir (both of which account for 85 percent of total output), Sauvignon Blanc, and Cabernet Sauvignon, offering excellent value. This property, recently acquired by the Robert Mondavi Winery, is expected to expand to accommodate the grape production from the Tepusquet Vineyard.

Cambria Winery & Vineyard (Santa Maria, 1988), is a new, 1,200-acre, 45,000-case winery built by the owner of Kendall-Jackson and partners on a portion of the former Tepusquet Vineyard. The state-of-the-art facility makes stylish, full-bodied Chardonnay (in two styles; *Katherine's Vineyard*, and *Reserve*) and Pinot Noir, both of which are above-average for the industry, and a must for the serious cellar.

Carey Cellars (Solvang, 1977), now part of The Firestone Vineyard, is an excellent, 23-acre, 7,000-case winery that makes Sauvignon Blanc, Chardonnay, Cabernet Sauvignon, and Merlot, offering excellent value, particularly the latter two.

Carrari Vineyards (Buellton, 1979), is a 130-acre, 6,000-case vineyard that sells grapes to other wineries, but has wine (above-average Cabernet Sauvignon, Chardonnay, Muscat Blanc, Chenin Blanc, and blended wines) made for distribution under its own label.

Chimere (Santa Maria, 1989), is a 2,000-case label owned by Gary Mosby who produced Tiffany Hill and many other wines. The *Chimere* label is for expertly crafted, barrel fermented Chardonnay, Pinot Blanc, and Pinot Noir from grapes emanating from the MacGregor vineyard in the Edna Valley.

Copehagen Cellars/Stearns Wharf Vintners (Santa Barbara, 1981). These are two expertly managed, highly successful, innovative and consumer-responsive tasting rooms whose wines are made at another winery. Wines consist of Cabernet Sauvignon, Chenin Blanc, Sauvignon Blanc, Riesling, Chardonnay, and Gewurztraminer.

Fess Parker Winery (Los Olivos, 1989), is an expanding, 62-acre, 10,000-case winery that makes Riesling, Chardonnay, Merlot, and Pinot Noir under the *Parker* label.

Foxen Vineyards (Santa Maria, 1987), is a superb, 12-acre, 2,000-case winery that makes distinctive, full-bodied, well-structured Chardonnay, Chenin Blanc, Cabernet Sauvignon, Pinot Noir, and Syrah, primarily from grapes purchased from excellent vineyards. All the wines are barrel-fermented, with low pH, high in alcohol, and have a pronounced finish.

Hitching Post (Buellton, 1984), is an interesting, 300-case label whose wines (Chardonnay and Pinot Noir) are made for a restaurant.

Houtz Vineyards (Los Olivos, 1982), is a 19-acre, 4,000-case winery known for expertly-made and well-aged Chardonnay, Sauvignon Blanc, Chenin Blanc, and Cabernet Sauvignon.

J. Kerr Wines (Santa Maria, 1986), is a 1,000-case winery that makes distinctive and full-bodied Chardonnay, Pinot Noir, and Syrah from county grapes.

Longoria & Son Wine Cellars (Los Olivos, 1982), is a label known for 2,000 cases of above-average Chardonnay and Pinot Noir made by the winemaker of several county wineries.

Mosby Winery and Vineyards (Buellton, 1979), formerly known as Vega Vineyards and Winery, is a 34-acre, 8,500-case winery known for inconsistent Riesling, Chardonnay, Gewurztraminer, and Pinot Noir. Under the ownership of one of the more successful winemakers in the Central Coast, the quality of wine is expected to increase. Other label: *Vega Vineyards and Winery*.

Qupe Wine Cellars (Los Olivos, 1982), is a small, serious winery that makes 7,000 cases of unusual southern Rhone varieties such as Syrah, Marsanne, and experimental Viognier. Also made are Chardonnay and Vin Gris from Pinot Noir. The wines are now made in a winery jointly operated by Au Bon Climat.

Rancho Sisquoc Winery (Santa Maria, 1977), is a 210-acre (part of a 37,000-acre cattle ranch), 5,000-case winery that utilizes only a small portion of its grape production. It produces well-made, hard to find Chardonnay, Sauvignon Blanc, Riesling (dry and late harvest), Sylvaner, Cabernet Sauvignon, Merlot, and late harvest wines. First planted in 1970, this is the second oldest vineyard in the county, and the vineyard with the most extensive Sylvaner acreage.

Sanford Winery (Buellton, 1981), is a 100-acre, 30,000-case, quality-oriented winery with an emphasis on delicate, well-flavored, and complex Pinot Noir, Merlot, Chardonnay, and Sauvignon Blanc.

Sanford & Benedict Vineyards (Lompoc, 1976), is an 110-acre, 8,000-case winery that makes good, sound, well-flavored Pinot Noir, Chardonnay, Cabernet Sauvignon, and Merlot.

Santa Barbara Winery (Santa Barbara, 1962), the oldest active winery in the county, is a good, stylish, 75-acre, 30,000-case winery that makes Zinfandel, Cabernet Sauvignon, Sauvignon Blanc, Riesling, Chenin Blanc, Chardonnay, and Pinot Noir, all of which have a fresh, zesty, yet supple, appealing character, often offering excellent value. The reserve Pinot Noir, Cabernet Sauvignon, Chardonnay, and Sauvignon Blanc are excellent.

Santa Ynez Valley Winery (Santa Ynez, 1969), one of the oldest wineries in the county, is a 110-acre, 12,000-case winery that makes big, yet lean, wood-aged Cabernet Sauvignon, Merlot, a Meritage-type red, Zinfandel, Pinot Noir, Chardonnay, Gewurztraminer, Riesling, Sauvignon Blanc, Semillon, and Pinot Blanc. It also makes 20,000 cases for two other county labels, and a Michigan winery.

The Brander Vineyard (Los Olivos, 1975), is a 40-acre, 10,000-case winery that makes excellent, elegant, complex Chardonnay, Sauvignon Blanc (with small additions of Semillon made in a Graves style), and a delicious blend of equal amounts of Cabernet Franc and Merlot called *Bouchet*. Other label: *St. Carl*.

The Firestone Vineyard (Los Olivos, 1974), is a highly mechanized, state-of-the-art, 265-acre, 85,000-case winery that is part of a 2,300-acre cattle ranch. It was the first bonded commercial winery in the Santa Ynez Valley. The consistently above-average quality, and moderately priced wines include regular and late harvest Riesling, Chardonnay, Gewurztraminer, Cabernet Sauvignon, Merlot, and Pinot Noir. Suntory Spirits and Wine Company is part owner.

The Gainey Vineyard (Santa Ynez, 1984), is a 54-acre, 14,500-case winery that makes above-average Chardonnay, Sauvignon Blanc, Riesling, Merlot, Cabernet Sauvignon, and Pinot Noir. The beautiful, underrated winery and vineyards, part of a large, diversified agribusiness, consistently makes some of the finest wines in the county, often offering excellent value.

Tiffany Hill Vineyards (Santa Maria, 1985), is a 4,000-case label known for good but expensive Chardonnay from grapes emanating from the 800-acre *Paragon Vineyard*.

Zaca Mesa Winery (Los Olivos, 1976), a 1,500-acre property (230 planted in vines) with 60,000 cases, is the second largest winery in Santa Barbara County. The expertly made, above-average to excellent wines include: Sauvignon Blanc, regular and late harvest Riesling, Chardonnay, Cabernet Sauvignon, Syrah, Zinfandel, and Pinot Noir. Also made are reserve Chardonnay, Cabernet Sauvignon, and Pinot Noir, all three of which are excellent. After years of stylistic and marketing problems, the wines have recently been improved offering good value. This property (with partners) has recently purchased the 1,000-acre *Sierra Madre Vineyard*.

Ventura County, a small but heavily populated county located close to Los Angeles, is a major producer of poultry, vegetables, parsley, avocados, oranges, and the state's leading producer of lemons, celery, and cabbage. As one-third of the total land area is privately held and other agricultural activities are prominent, viticultural activities are practically non-existent (the California Statistical Service does not indicate any commercial vine acreage).

The wineries are: **Leeward Winery** (Oxnard, 1979), is a 10,500-case winery known for well-made, clean, distinctive Chardonnay (several different styles), Zinfandel, Pinot Noir, Cabernet Sauvignon, and Merlot. **Old Creek Ranch Winery** (Oakview, 1981), originally built in 1898, is a 5-acre, 1,200-case winery that makes Merlot, Cabernet Sauvignon, Chardonnay, Sauvignon Blanc, Chenin Blanc, and Riesling, the latter particularly good. **Rolling Hills** (Camarillo, 1981), is a 5-acre (in Temecula), 2,000-case winery that makes above-average Chardonnay, Cabernet Sauvignon, Pinot Noir, Merlot, Petite Sirah, and Zinfandel with expert, meticulous care, offering excellent value. **The Daume Winery** (Camarillo, 1982), is a 2,000-case winery that makes average to above-average quality Pinot Noir, Cabernet Sauvignon, Zinfandel, Sauvignon Blanc, and Chardonnay. **The Ojai Vineyard** (Oakview, 1984), is a 5-acre, 1,000-case label whose wines (above-average, peppery Syrah, and an interesting Sauvignon Blanc/Semillon blend) are made in another winery in Santa Maria.

THE SOUTHERN COUNTIES

The South Coast, along with the Sierra Foothills region, is the least important winegrowing district. This area encompasses the counties of Los Angeles, Orange, San Diego, San Bernardino, and Riverside. Containing more than half of the total population, this region is the most urbanized area in the state. With Riverside and San Bernardino as exceptions, it is an area with a declining agricultural base. The value of agricultural production in Los Angeles, Orange, and San Diego declined from $585 million in 1959 to $330 million in 1985, and only in desertic Riverside and San Bernardino has the value of agricultural production increased from $300 to $420 million for the same period. The entire five county region contains 22,492 acres of grapes, of which 14,576 are table, 3,679 wine, and the remaining 4,237 acres used for raisin production. Ninety percent of the total acreage is confined to Riverside County, with the remainder located in San Bernardino. However, while the three Pacific counties of San Diego, Orange, and Los Angeles contain 136 vine acres, they house half of the wineries, a rather surprising figure. With "urban" wineries the only exception, wine production is mainly confined to Temecula and Cucamonga.

Geographically the region is dominated by the Peninsular Ranges, a series of fault lines with many associated coastal and interior valleys that extend from the Traverse Ranges southward to Mexico. Although there are several east-west ranges promoting the easy access of cool maritime air inland, the Peninsular Ranges are more similar to the Sierra Nevadas. An igneous intrusion, the southern California batholith consists principally of granitic rock that is severely faulted producing a highly complex geology. The Los Angeles basin represents the state's largest plain bordering the Pacific Ocean, while the highly dissected range of low mountains comprises most of the area south to Mexico. As the coastal plains with their Mediterranean-type climate are discontinuous and the site of the bulk of urban development, several valleys, such as San Fernando, San Gabriel, and the San Bernardino-Riverside area, became early centers for major agricultural development. It was in these fertile coastal valleys that California agricultural history had its early beginnings, and where the vine, wheat, and olive were first introduced. One reason for the early agricultural successes was the warm, dry summer, and the cool, wet winter. Although located a few miles from the coast, the average diurnal range in temperature for downtown Los Angeles is 20F, while the average annual range in monthly temperature is but 16F. Although temperatures rise beyond 100F each year, it is surprising to note that on average temperatures in Los Angeles rise beyond 90F less than 20 days of the year, or near ideal growing conditions for Mediterranean-type agriculture. East and southeast of Los Angeles is a vast desertic region that experiences the highest temperatures, the lowest humidity, and the smallest annual rainfall. Dry air, meager and unpredictable rainfall, high summer temperatures, and cold desiccating winter winds have produced a denuded landscape and highly mineralized soils. When and where water is available for irrigation, the desert blooms, particularly in the Coachella and Imperial Valleys, and portions of San Bernardino County. The southern counties contain three approved viticultural regions, of which the *South Coast ava (1985)*, located between Los Angeles and the Mexican border (it encompasses portions of Orange, Riverside, and San Diego counties), is the largest. It contains approximately 1,800 square miles, more than 4,000 acres of wine grapes, 26 wineries, engulfs the Temecula and San Pasqual Valley *ava's*, and nearly all quality wine producers.

Southern California exhibits the earliest Spanish viticultural history because Franciscan missionaries first planted the Mission vines in 1778 in San Diego County. Because winemaking was particularly successful in San Juan Capistrano, it quickly diffused to the missions of San Gabriel and San Fernando, but soon languished in obscurity for the next 50 years. After secularization, winemaking and vinegrowing quickly spread to Anaheim and Cu-

camonga, the latter important until the late 1870s. One Joseph Chapman, an adventurer from Missouri, is given credit for planting more than 4,000 vines in Los Angeles during the period 1824-1826. His achievements notwithstanding, the two most important personalities were Jean Louis Vignes and William Wolfskill who organized the industry in the 1830s in what is today downtown Los Angeles. Anaheim was settled by grape-growing German immigrants in 1857; by 1863 Los Angeles had a population of 4,000 and 1 million vines; and until the 1870s southern California--from San Diego to Los Angeles, was the largest wine producing center of the state. Soon after, the thriving wine industry failed because of Pierce's Disease (sometime called Anaheim Disease), with growers switching to oranges, or speculating in real estate.

Figure 9.12

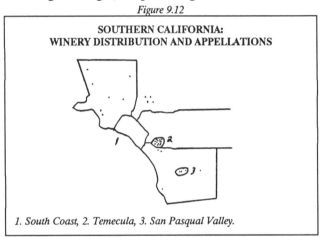

SOUTHERN CALIFORNIA:
WINERY DISTRIBUTION AND APPELLATIONS

1. South Coast, 2. Temecula, 3. San Pasqual Valley.

Due to urbanization and high land costs, winegrape acreage along the three coastal counties has declined steadily from 17,500 acres in 1887 to 126 acres in 1990. Vine acreage in San Bernardino, the county immediately to the east of Los Angeles, declined from 14,270 acres in 1969 to 1,157 by 1990. Riverside, on the other hand, has increased its wine grape acreage from 1,300 to 2,396 acres for the same period. Although there are several climatic constraints, the biggest reason for the decline in wine grape acreage is sustained urbanization. It must be emphasized that while the principal basins within the Los Angeles urban agglomeration constitute an extremely small percentage of the state's total land area, the combination of persistent human migration, the opening of the Panama Canal, petroleum production, the completion of the Southern Pacific and Santa Fe railroads, among many other important factors, created unprecedented urban growth. As a consequence, southern California is not only the single largest population cluster west of New York City, but the largest manufacturing and tertiary center as well. The only exception to this negative condition is the recent rapid development of the Temecula region (the most important quality wine producing region of the southern coast).

The Los Angeles Region

Due to insufficient water, vine acreage in the Los Angeles region remained low during the first 50 years of Spanish settlement. It is estimated that fewer than 50 acres existed in 1818, a figure that doubled by 1830. With the arrival of several energetic French and German immigrants, vine acreage grew to 10,000 by the early 1880s with more than 1 million gallons of wine produced, but with the advent of Pierce's Disease vine acreage quickly dropped to 4,443 acres in 1893. The dominance of Los Angeles, however, was short lived as other producing regions further north began to expand output. While the Los Angeles basin accounted for three quarters of the state's total wine output in 1860, by 1870 it produced only half, and by 1890 it produced but one-tenth of the state total. Soon grapes gave way to oranges and urbanization, the only major wine vineyard remaining until the mid-1970s being Cucamonga, an interior basin east of Los Angeles in San Bernardino County. Today within metropolitan Los Angeles there are seven "urban" wineries and negociants:

Antelope Valley Winery (Lancaster, 1980), formerly McLester Winery, is a 6-acre, 2,500-case winery now relocated in the northern portion of the county that makes Cabernet Sauvignon, Zinfandel, Merlot, and proprietary wines. Other labels: *Rancho Paloma* and *McLester*. **Ballona Creek Winery** (Culver City, 1986), is a small winery and negociant concern under French ownership. **Brown-Forman Corp.** (Los Angeles, 1983), is a 1-million-case winery that bottles 1 million cases in both Los Angeles and Cincinnati, Ohio under the *California Cooler* label. **Donatoni Winery** (Inglewood, 1980), is a 1,400-case winery that makes Cabernet Sauvignon and Chardonnay. **Moraga Vineyards** (Bel Air, 1989), is a 15-acre, 1,300-case label that makes a big, rich, well-structured Meritage-type wine from Cabernet Sauvignon, Merlot, and Cabernet Franc. **Palos Verdes Winery** (Inglewood, 1982), is a 1,500-case winery that makes Chardonnay, Sauvignon Blanc, and Cabernet Sauvignon under many *ava's*. **San Antonio Winery** (Los Angeles, 1917), is the oldest, largest (500,000 cases), and the only winery within the city confines of Los Angeles. Chenin Blanc, Chardonnay, Cabernet Sauvignon, Riesling, Muscat Blanc, and Zinfandel are sold under the *Maddalena Vineyard* label (with Sonoma, Napa, and Central Coast *ava's*), while sparkling, fortified, and proprietary wines are under the *San Antonio* label. The old but reliable and energetic firm owns 200 acres in Sonoma, Napa, and the Central Coast, and 900 acres near Fresno. **Simon Levi Company** (Carson, 1976), is a 300,000-case negociant concern that markets Chardonnay, Sauvignon Blanc, Cabernet Sauvignon, Merlot, Zinfandel, and proprietary wines under the *Stone Creek* (California and Washington *ava's*), and *Valley Ridge* (for Sonoma County wines) labels.

San Bernardino

The second most important grape county, San Bernardino, the largest county in California (larger than Maryland, Connecticut and Hawaii combined), is an immensely productive agricultural region. While it includes such celebrated places as the Mojave Desert, Death Valley, and several other national monuments, it is only the southwestern corner of the county, in the Cucamonga region, that we find it's most productive agricultural area. Located near Los Angeles, it is the state's leading dairy producing region, and ranks third and fourth in grapefruit and chicken production. Not only does the county's population (1 million) reside there, but it is the site of 1,500 (a significant reduction from a high of 20,000 acres in 1945) vine acres and four wineries. In 1919 the county contained more vineyards than either Sonoma or Napa. Unlike grape cultivation in the cooler Temecula region or Riverside County, vine growing in the desertic Cucamonga region is mainly confined to red grapes (more than two-thirds), Grenache Noir, Mourvedre, Zinfandel, and Mission, the latter representing the state's single largest concentration. White grapes are dominated by Palomino and Burger, both of which are used in the production of sweet and vermouth-type wines.

Thomas Vineyards Winery, while no longer operating, the label and sign are still in use. Courtesy of Walter Feller

Although Cucamonga refers to the "land of many waters," or "sandy place," this interior basin is a desertic region with less than 10 inches of precipitation. Located in the extreme southwestern portion of San Bernardino County, it is dominated by the San Gabriel Mountains, Cucamonga Peak, and the Cucamonga-Etiwanda-Ontario-Guasti settlements. Considered a useless desert until one Secondo Guasti realized that a good portion of this desertic basin sat on top of a large water table, he planted one of the largest vineyards in California (4,500 acres, and named it the Italian Vineland Company), and by 1920 more than ten wineries were concentrated in this area, including Captain Garrett, who sold the infamous Vine-Glo during Prohibition. Changes in consumer tastes away from fortified wines and urbanization have reduced acreage from 19,886 in 1960 to less than 3,000 in 1987.

Historically, the area was known for its robust, Italian-style red table wines made principally from Barbera, Zinfandel, Grenache Noir, and Carignane grapes, followed by fortified libations, and small amounts of white wines, the best of which were Muscats. All wines, sold mainly in jugs, were inexpensive, coarse on the palate, poorly made, and never managed to captivate the American taste bud. As a consequence, the principal wineries in the historic Cucamonga interior valley were reduced to four, a decline of more than fifteen from historic high levels after World War II. The four wineries are:

Galleano Winery (Mira Loma, 1933), is a 700-acre, 100,000-case winery with an emphasis on special bottlings, generics, Zinfandel, Pinot Noir, Chardonnay, Chenin Blanc, Riesling, Cabernet Sauvignon, and Petite Sirah. **J. Filippi Vintage Co.** (Mira Loma, 1934), is a 322-acre, 400,000-case winery that makes varietal, generic, sparkling, fruit wines, vermouth, and brandy. It also owns the old, venerable *Thomas Vineyard* label (founded in 1839). **Nabisco** (Etiwanda, 1901), a 300,000-case facility that makes the Regina Brand of cooking wine is now owned by R. J. Reynolds Industries. **Rancho de Philo** (Alta Loma, 1975), is a 2-acre, 200-case winery that only makes 18 year-old, non-fortified (20% alcohol content is raised by the evaporation of wine), viscous, fat, Oloroso, Sherry-type wines from Mission grapes. The smallest winery in southern California is owned by the former owner of Brookside Winery, and his wines should not be missed.

Riverside

Mainly desert, Riverside, 200 miles wide and 50 miles long, is the fourth largest county in the state, of which two-thirds of the land area is owned by the federal government. Like San Bernardino to the north, only the western portion, containing such popular places as Palm Springs and Riverside, is rapidly growing in population. Desertic conditions not withstanding, Riverside is the state's eighth largest agricultural county in terms of value of production, ranking high in dates, grapefruit, cotton, and alfalfa, but fourth in table and fifth in raisin grape production. Of the 20,279 vine acres in 1990, 13,841 were for table, 4,042 for raisin, and 2,396 for wine production, three-quarters of which were planted in white wine grapes, principally Riesling, Sauvignon Blanc, Chardonnay, and Chenin Blanc. Zinfandel, Mission, Grenache Noir, and Cabernet Sauvignon dominate red wine production. While all table and raisin grapes are produced in the Coachella (a primary area for date output) and Palo Verde valleys, nearly all wine grape acreage is found in the cool Temecula region further south.

The Coachella Valley, the northwesterly extension of the Colorado Desert beyond the Salton Sea, resembles the Imperial Valley in climate. The first region in the state to ship large quantities of table grapes to eastern markets, it sits on a huge aquifer that makes possible a thriving winter resort activity, 52 golf courses, and some of the nation's richest farm land. Although Pierce's Disease has recently killed more than 100 vine acres, the disease is considered controllable. Due to the development of double-slip plowing, a means whereby heavy, compacted layered soil consisting of sand and clay creates a perched water table, the Coachella Valley now stands on the forefront of a viticultural resurgence, but not necessarily for wine grapes as the area experiences temperatures of 100F or higher every month from February to October. While it produces less than 10 percent of the state's entire grape output, production represents about 60 percent of America's expensive early season table grapes.

The newest and most important wine vineyard in southern California is the rapidly growing Temecula area (frequently referred to as "Napa Valley south"). Temecula and the surrounding region contain many small to good-sized properties making above-average quality wines. Temecula, an area of rolling hills flanked by snow-capped mountains, takes its name from the Indian word "Teme-ku" for "land where the sun shines through the white mist." Although there is some controversy about the meaning of the word, Temecula appears as a place name as early as 1797, and as a land grant in the early 1800s.

The *Temecula (1986) ava*, lying almost equidistant between Los Angeles and San Diego, is a hilly region where expensive homes, grapefruit, oranges, and grapes coexist. Temecula, a hot and dry region located just 25 miles from the Pacific Ocean, is in the path of major air movement to the Salton Sea Basin in the east, an area that has the lowest barometric pressure in the state. Hot rising air from Palm Springs draws cool Pacific air over the Rainbow Gap towards Temecula, thus lowering temperatures below those of Napa Valley. These breezes carry atmospheric moisture into this rainfall-deficit region (less than half the amount falling in Napa) causing frequent morning mists which lower average daily temperatures through the Rainbow Gap, a v-shaped canyon that faces the Pacific Ocean. The peculiar microclimate is such that ocean air moves briskly from 11 am to sunset almost daily. As a consequence, Temecula lies in a high Region II, low Region III although it is surrounded by Region IV and Region V climatic regions. With minor exceptions, most vineyards are located above the 1,400 foot elevation (surrounding low-lying areas are 25F warmer), and further benefit from cool nights, thus producing grapes with higher acid levels. Nearly the entire region lies on a large plateau surrounded by mountains whose underlying geology forms a huge water storage basin--a major advantage for a water-deficit region (less than 14 inches of rainfall).

Overlooking a small portion of Temecula including the rainbow gap.
Baxevanis

Additional unusual features include high rates of relative humidity enabling botrytis to occur, and although

600 miles south of Sonoma, grapes mature at the same time. The soils are well-drained and composed of degraded, infertile, highly mineralized, granitic material. They are phylloxera and nematode-free, hence vines are planted on their own rootstocks. Yields are low, and the wines at their best are delicate, fruity, and well balanced despite their tendency toward bitterness. The *ava* contains 3,000 acres and is home to eleven wineries, all of which were founded after 1969, and collectively exhibit remarkable market resiliency and financial success. Of the 3,000 planted acres, all but 500 are planted in white grape varieties, mainly Sauvignon Blanc, Chardonnay, Riesling, and Chenin Blanc, in that order, although the latter produces one of the more creditable wines in the state. Cabernet Sauvignon is the leading red, followed by Zinfandel and Merlot, more often than not, all made into blush wine. While red wines have exhibited high pH and rather dull features, recent experimentation with Sangiovese Grosso has proved successful. Another Italian variety exhibiting similar good fortune has been Muscat Blanc. It is expected that a small portion of the *ava* will, in the future, be subdivided into a *Murrieta ava*. The wineries are:

Baily Vineyard & Winery (Temecula, 1986), is a 60-acre, 3,000-case winery that makes Riesling, Chardonnay, Sauvignon Blanc/Semillon, Muscat Blanc, Cabernet Sauvignon, and proprietary wines.

Callaway Vineyard and Winery (Temecula, 1969), with 1,000 acres and an annual output of more than 225,000 cases, is the largest winery in the Temecula region. Although it specializes in white wine production and is meticulous in its detail, equipment, fermentation, and care, the wines are often alcoholic and exhibit bouts of inconsistency. Recent improvements have reduced the product line from nineteen to just Chardonnay, Chenin Blanc, Sauvignon Blanc, Riesling, Muscat Blanc, two late harvest dessert wines--Sweet Nancy (Chenin Blanc) and a late harvest Chardonnay, and sparkling wines. The hitherto all-white winery has recently produced a Cabernet Sauvignon. The winery is owned by The Wine Alliance.

Conglomerate, a well-drained soil in Temecula. Baxevanis

Cilurzo Vineyard & Winery (Temecula, 1978), is an 8-acre, 10,000-case winery that makes well-flavored and scented Chardonnay, Chenin Blanc, Muscat Blanc, Zinfandel, Cabernet Sauvignon, Merlot, a dry and sweet Petite Sirah, and proprietary wines, offering good value.

Clos du Muriel Winery (Temecula, 1989), formerly Britton Cellars, is a 23-acre, 15,000-case winery that makes Chardonnay, Sauvignon Blanc, Muscat Blanc, Zinfandel, Cabernet Sauvignon, Merlot, Cabernet Franc, and red Meritage-type wines.

Filsinger Vineyards & Winery (Temecula, 1980), is a 350-acre, 7,000-case winery that makes Sauvignon Blanc, Chardonnay, Zinfandel, Emerald Riesling, Cabernet Sauvignon, Gewurztraminer, and sparkling wine.

French Valley Vineyards (Murrieta, 1985), is a 5-acre, 3,000-case winery that makes Chardonnay, Sauvignon Blanc, Riesling, Muscat Blanc, Chenin Blanc, Cabernet Sauvignon, and Gamay Beaujolais.

Hart Winery (Temecula, 1980), is an 11-acre, 6,000-case winery that makes soft, fruity Merlot, Riesling, Cabernet Sauvignon, Chardonnay, Sauvignon Blanc, and proprietary wines.

John Culbertson Winery (Temecula, 1981), is an aggressive, 20-acre, 30,000-case winery that makes above-average, full-bodied, austere Brut Rose, Brut, Natural, Blanc de Noir, Cuvee Rouge, Cuvee de Frontignan (refreshing and not overly sweet) sparkling wines, and limited quantities of Sauvignon Blanc, Chardonnay, and Cabernet Sauvignon.

John Piconi Winery (Temecula, 1981), is a 7-acre, 7,500-case winery that makes Sauvignon Blanc, Chardonnay, Chenin Blanc, Riesling, Petite Sirah, Cabernet Sauvignon, and Merlot.

Keysways Winery (Temecula, 1990), is an 8-acre, 3,000-case winery that makes Sauvignon Blanc, Muscat Blanc, Chardonnay, Zinfandel, and Gamay Beaujolais.

Maurice Carrie Winery & Vineyard (Temecula, 1986), is a 110-acre, 30,000-case winery that makes Chenin Blanc, Sauvignon Blanc (one of the better wines in the *ava*), Chardonnay (rich and full-bodied), Zinfandel, Cabernet Sauvignon, Riesling, Muscat Blanc, late harvest Riesling, Merlot, and Pinot Noir proprietary wines, offering excellent value. Recently the winery purchased the 50-acre, 10,000-case Mesa Verde Winery & Vineyard, and will rename it Van Roekel Vineyards sometime in 1992-1993.

Mount Palomar Winery (Temecula, 1975), is a well-managed, 105-acre, 15,000-case winery that makes Riesling, Cabernet Sauvignon, Chardonnay, Sauvignon Blanc, Chenin Blanc, Semillon, Sangiovese Grosso, late harvest Riesling, Porto and Cream-Sherry-type wines, and proprietary wines, offering excellent value. Other label: *Long Valley Vineyards*, the original name of the winery.

Santa Margarita Vineyard & Winery (Temecula, 1985), is a 5-acre, 1,500-case winery that specializes in the production of well-aged, meaty, spicy, and full-bodied Cabernet Sauvignon.

A portion of the stylish, tourist-oriented Culbertson facilities. Baxevanis

San Diego

San Diego County, the site of the first Spanish Mission and theoretically the site of the first vine plantings, enjoyed a more significant viticultural history than now. In 1901 the local county agricultural register recorded 275 acres of table, 4,850 acres of raisin, and 450 acres of wine grapes. While the historic vineyards of El Cajon, Santee,

Witch Creek, Lakeside, Mesa Grande, and Vista have all disappeared, today only Fallbrook, Escondido, and the San Pasqual Valley remain grape producing regions.

South of Temecula, but mainly in the northern outskirts of San Diego, there is one *ava* and six wineries. The *San Pasqual Valley (1981) ava*, located in the Santa Ysabel watershed, nurtured more than 5,000 acres of vineland 30 years ago, a figure that has fallen sharply since then. The narrow, 15-mile long valley with a 9,000-acre agricultural preserve is located 300 to 500 feet above sea level and surrounded on three sides by low mountain ranges. Because it is located 10 miles from the Pacific Ocean, moderating marine influences create a more humid climate, thus distinguishing it from the more desert-like climates further east. Although the appellation size is rather extensive, there is only one winery entirely within its confines, and the fewer than 150 acres are mainly planted in Chenin Blanc, Sauvignon Blanc, Chardonnay, and Muscat Blanc.

The wineries of San Diego County are: **Bernardo Winery** (San Diego, 1889), is a 5-acre, 14,000-case winery that makes Petite Sirah, Golden Chasselas, Grenache Noir, Carignane, Barbera, Cabernet Sauvignon, fortified, and proprietary wines; **Deer Park Escondido** (Escondido, 1990), is a 3-acre, 425-case, Chardonnay-only winery owned by a similarly-named winery in Napa, the latter providing the bulk of the wine for local distribution. **Fallbrook Winery** (Fallbrook, 1978) is a 5-acre, 6,000-case winery owned by the founders of Culbertson Winery in Temecula that makes Chardonnay and Pinot Noir wines. **Ferrara Wine Cellars** (Escondido, 1932), is a 3-acre, 35,000-case winery that specializes in dessert wines (mainly Sherry/Porto-type and Alexandria de Muscat), but also makes Chardonnay, Chenin Blanc, Carignane, Zinfandel, and proprietary wines. **Menghini Winery** (Julian, 1982), is a 5-acre, 3,000-case winery that makes Sauvignon Blanc, Chardonnay, Riesling, Muscat Blanc, Cabernet Sauvignon, Napa Gamay, and Gamay Beaujolais. **Thomas-Jaeger Winery** (Escondido, 1973), formerly San Pasqual Vineyards, is a 40-acre, 25,000-case winery acquired in 1988 by Bill Jaeger and Paul Thomas of Napa Valley. Vineyard acreage is to be expanded, and the production line has been streamlined to Chardonnay, Riesling, Muscat Blanc, Cabernet Sauvignon, and Merlot.

THE CENTRAL VALLEY

Sandwiched between the Coastal Ranges and the Sierra Nevada, the Central Valley, often called the Great Valley, stretches from the foothills of the Klamath Mountains in the north to the Tehachapi Mountains in the south. Extending for 475 miles in a north-south direction (a distance equal to that from New York City to South Carolina), it is 100 miles at its widest, and with 47,500 square miles it is larger than Ohio. This vast structural depression is the largest piece of flat real estate west of the Continental Divide. The valley is drained by two large rivers--the Sacramento and the San Joaquin, both of which meet and form a delta west of Stockton. Ringed by hills and mountains, the entire valley is totally flat, featureless, monotonous, lies below 400 feet, and slopes toward San Francisco Bay, its only outlet to the sea. The entire valley is filled with deep alluvium, in places as much as 2,000 feet thick.

On the north, the Sacramento Valley, narrower, shorter, and higher in elevation, receives between 10 and 20 inches of precipitation, and, as a consequence, it is more verdant than the San Joaquin which receives less than 10 inches. The Sacramento Valley (consisting of Butte, Colusa, Glenn, Shasta, Tehama, Sutter, Sacramento, and Yolo counties) developed a more varied economy, and one less dependent upon viticultural endeavors. Nevertheless, the largest single vineyard (3,500 acres), called "Vina," was developed in the 1880s by Leland Stanford, but ceased operations in the first decade of the twentieth century.

E. & J. Gallo Central Headquarters, Modesto. Baxevanis

With eight important counties, the San Joaquin Valley contains more than half the state's total wine grape acreage and produces more than 75 percent of all wine. The San Joaquin River rises in the Sierra Nevada as do most of its tributaries. Within this vast, fertile region, wine is big business as production and storage facilities of several million gallons are the rule rather than the exception. While the number of wineries is not overly impressive, the six largest wineries account for more than two-thirds of the state's total cooperage capacity. The combined production of Central Valley wineries represents more than three-quarters of all California wine. Not only are the wineries large, and technologically state-of-the-art, but highly efficient in their location to vineyards and the disposition of the grape crop at crush time.

The Central Valley, as defined in this book, consists of sixteen counties: Sacramento, Sutter, Yolo, Glenn, Kern, Colusa, Shasta, Tehama, Butte, Stanislaus, Kings, San Joaquin, Fresno, Madera, Merced, and Tulare. In addition to the stylish capital, Sacramento, the valley contains many growing cities: Redding, Lodi, Modesto, Stockton, Merced, Fresno, and Bakersfield. The rapidly growing population of this entire region is 4 million. It contains 193,810 acres of wine grapes, 78,337 acres of table grapes, 276,347 acres of raisin grapes, 45 wineries, and crushes an excess of 1.8 million tons of wine grapes annually. It is common to describe vineyards in the thousands of acres, and not in the teens as in the case east of the Continental Divide. In terms of wine brands, the Central Valley is home to seven of the nation's ten largest, and if the Central Valley were an independent country, it would rank tenth in vine acreage, and seventh in wine production. It is an area not unlike the Midi of southern France, or Puglia, Italy, a bastion of high yielding vines producing less expensive table and fortified wines, and brandy. Of the nation's 20 leading agricultural counties, 10 are located in the Central Valley, of which Fresno, Tulare, Kern, Merced, and San Joaquin are the most important. The Central Valley also ranks as the national leader in more than 40 agricultural commodities, of which grapes, cattle, milk, poultry, cotton, safflower, rice, watermelons, melons, asparagus, sugar beets, hogs, sorghum, tomatoes, garlic, almonds, peaches, apricots, pistachios, onions, dry beans, walnuts, oranges, plums, figs, olives, nectarines, and honey are the most prominent, all of which grow in an idyllic 250+-day growing season. Needless to say, in terms of geography and agricultural productivity, the Central Valley has no counterpart in North America or the rest of the world.

Delicato Vineyards, Manteca, one of the better large producers in the Central Valley. Baxevanis

The Central Valley is not only the center of California agriculture, but the nerve center of wine, raisin, and table grape production; it is the wine producing capital of the nation responsible for the bulk of standard wine, fortified wine, and total grape acreage. Made possible by the most majestic irrigation complex in the world, it is estimated that more than 40 percent of all vegetables grown in the United States originate in this area. Even in Kern County, the largest oil producing county in California, agriculture is the leading economic activity in terms of total value of product produced. It is here that we find the

largest winery in the world, ten of the twelve largest wineries, and huge agricultural estates like the 188,000-acre Tejon Ranch (with 5,500 vine acres), the Tenneco Corp., and several railroad companies.

Irrigation, as the summers are long, hot, and dry, is much more a practice in the Central Valley than in any other viticultural region except for the Columbia Basin of Washington. Construction of irrigation canals, first from the diversion of water from Sierra Nevada streams (in 1871 with the completion of the San Joaquin and Kings River Canals near Fresno) and later from northern California, greatly facilitated the early establishment of agricultural communities. As soon as irrigation technology became available, growers were able to capitalize on the climatic advantages of the extended growing season. Uppermost is the long period of direct intense sunlight which enables early ripening and a high sugar content. Moreover, hail and summer rain are practically unknown, wind velocities low, and the incidence of humidity-related insects and diseases insignificant. These ideal conditions, in short order, encouraged the cultivation of table and raisin grapes, as well as those for wine. With the introduction of the "Thompson Seedless" the industry managed to produce an almost unbelievable condition of extraordinary no-risk financial investment in grape production. In the 1960s, 39 percent of Thompson Seedless had been used to produce white wine; 10 percent were destined for table use, and the remainder for raisin production. This "three-way" versatility and ability to adapt to a wide array of soils accounted for its early popularity. Four table grapes--Thompson Seedless, Tokay, Emperor, and Malaga, dominate because of their early maturing, attractive appearance, edible features, and ability to withstand shipment and storage. Tokay has important acreage in the northern portion of the San Joaquin Valley; Emperor tolerates excessive heat and attains excellent color in the higher elevations of the middle Joaquin; and Malaga is widely adapted, but does best in the hotter, southernmost regions, along with the Thompson Seedless.

"Warning--here lies the body of M. Theodore Kearny, a visionary who thought he could teach the average farmer, and particularly raisin growers, some of the rudiments of sound business management. For eight years he worked strenuously at the task, and at the end of that time he was no further ahead than at the beginning. The effort killed him."

The above epitaph was found among the papers of Theodore Kearney after his death. Kearney, a noble Englishman, sought, with mixed results, to organize the raisin growers into a cooperative. He built Kearney Farm and a large castle a few miles from Fresno, both of which were bequeathed to the University of California, now forming the present site of the Agricultural Experiment Station.

American settlement, unlike other areas in the state, was slow to spread south of Lodi in the San Joaquin Valley until the second half of the nineteenth century. Not only was land not available due to the large size of existing land grants, but the lack of irrigation water and efficient transportation were formidable obstacles not overcome until the 1870s. This meant that the northern portion of the San Joaquin Valley was developed first, and that grape production in Fresno, Madera, and Kern counties developed much later. As ranching and wheat production proved unprofitable in comparison to intensive fruit and nut cultivation, raisin production, especially around Fresno, grew rapidly so that by 1920 the region produced half the world's total output. Despite the slow growth of American settlement, viticultural experimentation occurred at a comparatively early date. While Charles M. Weber is widely recognized as the first to grow grapes in the San Joaquin Valley in 1850 in his home garden at Stockton, others maintain that Harvey Akers, a native of Arkansas, was the first to do so in 1852. At about the same time George and William West established a nursery and vineyard in Stockton, made wine in 1858, and were the first to grow French Colombard (also called "West's White Prolific") for brandy production. Once irrigation water and transportation accessibility were available, other crops such as tomatoes, cotton, rice, and olives were produced, but it was vine acreage that spread quickly throughout the valley and was to become the important agricultural commodity, especially in the San Joaquin. From 225 acres in 1875, vine acreage leaped to 14,000 in 1890, and continued in an unabated fashion until the early 1980s.

The first recorded winery, Red Mountain, was founded by George Krause in Stanislaus County in 1866 (perhaps 1854), and over the next 70 years he was followed by some of the legendary figures of Central Valley winemaking: George Malter, Francis Eisen, M. Theodore Kearney, Krikor Arakelian, Giuseppe Franzia, Angelo Cribari, John Batista Cella, Antonio Perelli-Minetti, Joseph Di Giorgio, Frank and Paul Garrett, M.F. Tarpey, Harry Hitzl, Benjamin Woodworth, and Alfonse Bisceglia, among many others. The above individuals, along with large cooperatives and national corporations, have been associated with the production of inexpensive jug, fortified, and brandy libations which sold well prior to the mid-1960s wine boom when consumer preference changed to drier varietal wine, particularly white. Consequently, the region responded swiftly to consumer preferences by replacing the less desirable vines with those yielding far better varietal table wine, harvesting earlier, and applying sophisticated winemaking processes for the production of fresh tasting, fruity, dry wines. The industry, in the process, has experienced a significant transformation in the past 20 years: nearly half the wineries have either closed or changed ownership, and while wine production has increased appreciably, the number of wineries has declined from 88 in 1979 to 45 in 1992. Bankruptcies

and corporate takeovers have been so common in recent years that the condition has come to be known as "jug roulette," and practically everyone has restructured their product line to emphasize coolers, sparkling, and varietal wines instead of dessert and generic jug wines (the two historic mainstays of the Central Valley). It is interesting to note that San Joaquin County in 1901 produced 2 million gallons of sweet wine and 1 million gallons of dry table wine. Today, due to improved technology in both the vineyard and winery, the Central Valley is producing the finest and most consistently good *vin ordinaire* in the world. Yet, despite its importance in terms of acreage and production, the Central Valley lacks the romance of the north, central, and south coast wineries. Exhibiting an "industrial look," wineries display a wide array of "warehouse" appearances, are usually unpainted, and located on flat ground behind a chainlink fence next to railroad sidings. The small, hillside "boutique" ambience, so common along coastal California, is nowhere to be found.

The climate, moderately warm at the confluence of the San Joaquin and Sacramento rivers, becomes progressively hotter in a northerly direction toward Red Bluff, and Bakersfield in the extreme southern end. It varies between Region II and V, the former more prevalent along the Sierra Foothills and near the San Francisco Bay region; the latter mainly confined to areas south of Lodi and north of Sacramento near Redding. Summers are hot and dry, and winters, receiving between 5 (in Bakersfield) and 37 inches (in Redding) of precipitation, are moderately warm with frost danger limited to upper elevations and areas prone to temperature inversions. The debilitating nature of high temperature is reflected in Red Bluff and Bakersfield, two climatic stations that experience 100 days per year of +90F temperatures. Sacramento, on the other hand, receives only 70 days of +90F, and Modesto 81 days per year of such high temperatures. The coolest area is the central portion because as the summer season progresses the Central Valley sends huge columns of hot air up and over the Sierra Mountains to the east, siphoning cool, maritime air through the San Francisco Bay, and spreading it over the delta areas of the lower San Joaquin and Sacramento valleys.

This weather pattern is influenced by the three-day weather cycle of the Central Valley. As hot air rises, it pulls cold air from Pacific inland. While Coastal Ranges block air penetration, the large opening at San Francisco allows moist maritime air to penetrate the littoral areas bordering San Francisco Bay. Usually it takes three days to heat up and three days to cool off. The further away you are from San Francisco, the hotter it gets, hence the production of raisins in the extreme southern portions of the San Joaquin Valley. Generally, wine grapes prefer the coolest coastal area, table grapes are intermediate, while raisin grapes are located in the hottest and driest regions of the state. The cool, westerly air lowers air temperature 10F-15F over approximately 200 square miles, hence the production of wine grapes between Lodi and Woodland in Yolo County. This is in sharp contrast to table and raisin grape production south of Modesto, especially the area around Fresno. High summer temperatures and an absence of precipitation (water evaporation exceeds 70 inches) necessitates the irrigation of grape vines and all other crops except wheat. It is a combination of high temperatures, irrigation, and extremely fertile, sandy loam soils that produces the highest yields and sugar levels, and low acid musts in California, a situation also found in more southern counties.

SAN JOAQUIN VALLEY: HARVEST DATES OF GRAPES	
Alicante Bouschet	Sept. 21-Oct. 10; **Sept. 25-Oct. 10.**
Barbera	Sept. 10-Oct. 8; **Sept. 22-Oct. 15.**
Cabernet Sauvignon	**Sept. 16-Oct. 7.**
Carignane	Sept. 16-Oct. 7; **Oct. 1-Oct. 15.**
Carnelian	Sept. 1-Sept. 21; **Sept. 6-Sept. 30.**
Chenin Blanc	Aug. 21-Sept. 16; **Sept. 6-Sept. 22.**
Emerald Riesling	Aug. 16-Sept. 16; **Sept. 1-Sept. 27.**
French Colombard	Sept. 1-Sept. 19; **Sept. 15-Oct. 5.**
Grenache	Sept. 8-Oct. 4; **Sept. 14-Oct. 7.**
Mission	Sept. 24-Oct. 24; **Oct. 1-Oct. 26.**
Muscat of Alexandria	**Sept. 7-Oct. 14.**
Muscat Canelli	Aug. 10-Sept. 30; **Aug. 16-Sept. 12.**
Petite Sirah	Sept. 10-Sept. 30; **Sept. 21-Oct. 14.**
Ruby Cabernet	Sept. 14-Oct. 8; **Sept. 21-Oct. 14.**
Sauvignon Blanc	Aug. 17-Sept. 5; **Aug. 21-Sept. 7.**
Semillon	Aug. 14-Aug. 30; **Aug. 21-Sept. 7.**
Zinfandel	Sept. 3-Sept. 27; **Sept. 14-Sept. 30.**

Note: Light type refers to areas south of Madera; bold type refers to San Joaquin County.
Source: Wine Grape Varieties In The San Joaquin Valley (1980).

Although at first glance the Central Valley looks deceptively similar in its soil composition, there is considerable variability throughout the valley as reflected by the patchwork of agricultural crops grown. While the delta region is characterized by recently deposited alluvium (a good portion of which now lies below sea level), a significant portion of the eastern portion of the valley contains soils that are former terraces characterized by low fertility and the presence of clay pans. Reddish-brown soils dominate in the northern sections of the Sacramento Valley and along the eastern periphery as far south as the San Joaquin River. These soils are mainly loams with varying amounts of clay, silt, and sand. Along the western portion of the San Joaquin Valley, soils are finer textured than on the eastern side, and more alkaline and calcareous. Almost everywhere, the finer grape-growing sites are mainly on sandy and loam soils and in areas of good air movement. Nevertheless, despite the seemingly high intensity land use pattern winegrape expansion is occurring in many new places. One area of growth north of Sacramento is the Dunnigan Hills, an area that has always been grazing land and, until recently, considered worthless for

crop production. Here vineland development is but one-tenth the cost when compared to Napa, and the wines, thus far, have been very impressive. The area is nematode and phylloxera-free, and the cool, clay-dominated soils are excellent for the production of white grapes, something that was discouraged in a Region IV climatic region. The other area of significant growth is the region surrounding the Bay Area.

The Central Valley has four main areas of vine cultivation and winemaking. The first is the lower Sacramento Valley. Although it is the oldest wine producing region in the Central Valley (it is reported that wine was first made in 1842), the widely dispersed region of the Sacramento Valley contains the least acreage, twelve small to medium-sized wineries, and concentrates on making above-average varietal wines from fragrant grape varieties. Despite the lack of contemporary notoriety, the area west and north of Sacramento is important as the site of the first Thompson grape, and in Chico, Governor Leland Stanford established the world's largest winery in the 1880s. While several dozen wineries operated in 1919, Prohibition closed each one by 1920. Today more than half of the vine acreage in the Sacramento Valley, mainly planted in Chenin Blanc, Zinfandel, and Sauvignon Blanc, is concentrated in Sacramento County.

The greater Lodi region is one of the most important quality wine producing regions of the San Joaquin Valley. Dominated by Guild Winery (historically a dessert wine and brandy producer), it is now producing better varietal and sparkling wines, and far smaller quantities of dessert wine. Because of its location, it is one of the coolest areas in the San Joaquin Valley, and the site of the better wine grapes. Straddling two counties, the greater Modesto Region is a major wine grape and wine producer, the latter particularly important in Livingston. Here winemaking and grape-growing is dominated by E. & J. Gallo.

Including Madera, Fresno, Tulare, and Kern counties, the fourth area, scattered between Madera and Bakersfield, is the largest in vine acreage, and the historic sweet wine region of California and the nation. The cloudless, indolent summer months (with intense heat and low humidity), and rich, irrigated soils provide huge, sugar-laden grape yields. This is also the region for generic jug wines, invariably the product of inexpensive, common, and often coarse Alicante Bouschet, Carignane, Zinfandel, Thompson Seedless, and others. It is here that we find one vast sea of raisin, table and wine grapes, and the largest plantings of Thompson Seedless and French Colombard vines. Grapes account for 30 percent of agricultural sales in Madera County, 24 percent in Fresno, 20 percent in Tulare, and 16 percent in Kern. It is in this portion of the Central Valley (from Lodi to Bakersfield), that we find the greatest innovations in viticulture: field crushing, vinification, refrigeration, and storage techniques--all of which make this region the envy of the wine producing world. The viticultural growth of this region is in large part due to the energies of Armenians, a unique ethnic group who first began to arrive in 1874, especially in and around the city of Fresno. Highly adept in fruit growing and trading, early settlers wrote enthusiastic letters to Turkish Armenia, and over the next 50 years more than 100,000 migrated to southern California where they engaged in large scale agricultural pursuits.

Most important, the Central Valley produces the finest, most consistent and least expensive *vin ordinaire*, a wine that has shown steady improvement in quality in recent years. However, important as this region is, the areas with extraordinary viticultural possibilities are the delta, adjacent foothill, and the lower Sacramento regions. During the heat of the summer, this portion of the Central Valley receives a significant amount of cooling from winds blowing through San Pablo and Suisun bays practically every summer afternoon that lower temperatures significantly. This well-known wind is deflected northward, and when combined with well-drained sandy soils offers excellent grape-growing opportunities.

Table 9.9

WINE GRAPE VARIETIES IN THE CENTRAL VALLEY, 1990

Variety	1977	%	1990	%	% CA
Colombard	19,899	17.1	57,005	30.2	96.8
Chenin Blanc	12,661	10.9	23,609	12.5	71.6
Zinfandel	10,484	9.0	19,744	9.9	57.8
Barbera	10,367	8.9	10,557	5.0	98.9
Grenache	10,963	9.4	12,298	7.0	90.1
Carignane	11,641	9.9	10,288	4.9	93.2
Chardonnay	196		7,880	3.9	15.1
Ruby Cabernet	9,250	7.9	6,890	3.7	99.6
Rubired	6,513	5.9	7,132	3.5	99.9
Cabernet Sauvignon	2,041	1.8	6,513	3.5	19.6
Alicante Bouschet	2,261	1.9	1,955	1.8	93.1
Sauvignon Blanc	875		3,114	1.7	23.2
Burger	738		2,204	1.2	95.7
Petite Sirah	2,334	2.0	688		22.4
Emerald Riesling	1,513		1,302		99.9
Palomino	1,360		1,200		80.9
Carnelian	1,266		1,252		100.0
Mission	1,054		770		67.0
Royalty	999		863		100.0
Semillon	867		990		44.4
Salvador	831		734		98.0
Gamay Beaujolais	708		1,424		
Centurian	591		580		100.0
Muscat Blanc	547		741		54.8
Green Hungarian	237		25		
Riesling	223		27		
Other	6,143		10,366		
Total	116,562		188,727		

Source: California Agricultural Statistics Service.

Central Valley wine grape acreage for 1977 and 1990 exhibits four interesting elements: a high degree of vineyard concentration; a high degree of specific grape variety concentration; rapid growth; and a shift from red to white grape production. Despite the occurrence of larger percentage increases in planted acreage over the past fifteen years, 73 percent of total wine grape acreage is found in the counties of Madera, Fresno, San Joaquin, and Kern, another 23 percent in Stanislaus, Merced, and Tulare, and the remaining 5 percent in nine counties, all but one of which are located north of San Joaquin. While all four leading counties have maintained their position as the top wine grape counties in the nation and state, Madera jumped from fourth to first place. The second surprising element is the ability of this historic bulk wine region to increase wine grape acreage from 116,562 acres in 1977 to 188,727 acres in 1990, and to maintain acreage share among the three grape groups. Of the 77,000 new acres, 57,000, or three-quarters, are found in the four leading counties, 16,000 acres, or 20 percent, in the next three counties, and 5 percent in the remaining nine counties. Finally, in response to consumer tastes, the change from red wine grapes to white wine grapes has been most impressive. While red wine grapes grew from 65,678 acres in 1977 to 83,366 acres in 1990, white grape varieties jumped from 41,569 to 105,361 acres.

GENERAL VINE VIGOR RATINGS OF WINE GRAPE VARIETIES, BY THE UNIVERSITY OF CALIFORNIA, DAVIS

When grown on comparable soils in the San Joaquin Valley, wine grape varieties may be grouped according to inherent vigor. The level of vigor may be greatly modified by soil characteristics--texture, depth, and fertility--as well as by cultural practices, such as the pruning/cropping level, irrigation, nitrogen fertilization, and insect and disease control.

On a fertile soil, the following varieties exhibit extreme vigor: Emerald Riesling, Colombard, Grenache Noir, and Sauvignon Blanc. Recommended in-row spacing is 8 feet.

High-vigor varieties are: Carignane, Cabernet Sauvignon, Carnelian, Centurion, Mission, Palomino, Rubired, Ruby Cabernet, Saint Emilion, Thompson Seedless, and Valdepenas. Recommended in-row spacing is 7 or 8 feet.

Moderate-vigor varieties are: Alicante Bouschet, Barbera, Burger, Gamay, Muscat of Alexandria, Muscat Blanc, Petite Sirah, Royalty, Salvador, Semillon, Tinta Madeira, and Zinfandel. Recommended in-row spacing is 6 or 7 feet.

Of the 52,500 new acres planted in white grapes, 37,000, or 71 percent, were in Colombard, a grape widely used in the production of white jug, sparkling, and cooler wines. Another 11,000 acres, or 21 percent, were accounted by Chenin Blanc, and the bulk of the remaining acreage was mainly in Burger, Sauvignon Blanc, and Chardonnay, the last two, superior, but not necessarily comparable in quality to those from cooler growing regions. Changes in red wine grape acreage have been less spectacular but significant for several grape varieties. Zinfandel rose by nearly 9,000 acres, Cabernet Sauvignon by 4,000, Grenache by 1,000, and Rubired by 500. It is also important to note that the Central Valley, particularly the southern portion, is the largest single area for Vinifera hybrids developed especially for the Central Valley. Leading the list is Ruby Cabernet, Rubired, Emerald Riesling, Carnelian, Centurian, Carmine, and others, which, in combination, account for more than 19,000 acres, or 5 percent of the planted wine grape acreage. Nevertheless, the Central Valley has moved somewhat beyond jug wines. Gone is the emphasis on Mission, Carignane, Grenache Noir, Alicante Bouschet, and other less desirable grapes. As a result, the wines are significantly fresher, less subject to oxidation, and dramatically more consistent.

Plagued by uniformly high temperatures, a long growing season, and unusual high yields (8 tons to the acre is considered minimum), the wines of the Central Valley were long known for their low acidity, proclivity to oxidation, coarseness, and astringency. Worse, they were inconsistent in quality, and lacking in varietal scent and flavor. This, in part, because one-third of the crush was (and still is) made from raisin and table grapes, primarily Thompson Seedless. Until the mid-1950s, two-thirds of output was sweet dessert wine, but since then the dessert/table wine ratio has been reversed. Dessert wines declined by 21 million gallons during 1950-1966, and table wine sales increased 34 million gallons to 68 million gallons for the same period. Although the transition from dessert to table wine production was not easy, it, nevertheless, did occur through the aid of new technology. Thompson Seedless now produces acceptable wine without browning, and because table grapes require half as many grapes per gallon as do dessert wines, new table wine plantings have been accommodated easily. As a result, the Central Valley has adjusted nicely over the past 30 years to restructuring table wine acreage.

Irrigated vineyards in the Central Valley: consistency in yield and quality.
Baxevanis

Quality in recent years, particularly for table wines, has improved markedly: white varietals are soft and fragrant, marred only by low acidity and lightness in body; and the reds, less fine, are early maturing, but more reliable than they once were. Partly because of improved vinification and vineyard practices, but also because high acid grapes from coastal counties are used to increase acidity, and heighten color, aroma, and flavor, the very best lack the "hot," harsh taste of years past. In general, quality improves as one progresses from the hotter southern sections of the San Joaquin Valley to the delta region. Cooperage, which doubled during the 1970s, has since

leveled off, and is not expected to vacillate appreciably from the 750 million gallon figure.

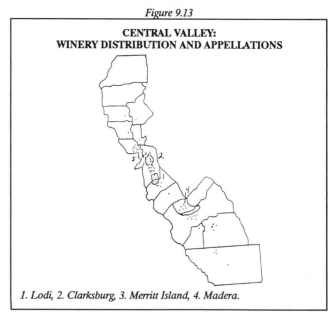

Figure 9.13

CENTRAL VALLEY:
WINERY DISTRIBUTION AND APPELLATIONS

1. Lodi, 2. Clarksburg, 3. Merritt Island, 4. Madera.

There are four *ava's*, all but one located in the central portion of the valley. Named after Napoleon's first spectacular victory in Italy in 1796, *Lodi (1986)*, the largest and most important *ava* in terms of production, vine acreage, and number of wineries, is influenced by two rivers: the Mokelumne and the Consumnes, both of which originate in the Sierra's. Along with the Clarksburg and Merritt Island *ava's*, Lodi is the coolest region in the Central Valley (average summer temperatures are at least 11F cooler). It is responsible for 40 percent of the state's Zinfandel production and nearly all the Flame Tokay grapes used for distillation and table use. Although Flame Tokay was a major historic grape variety in the region, its acreage has declined in recent years and been replaced by better wine grapes such as Chardonnay (nearly 5,000 acres), Colombard and Chenin Blanc (collectively more than 6,000 acres), and 1,400 acres of Sauvignon Blanc. Among red varieties, the Lodi *ava* has the largest amount of Zinfandel in the state (12,723 acres), followed by 3,151 acres of Cabernet Sauvignon. The historic varieties of Grenache Noir, Barbera, and Burger have largely disappeared (3,627 acres of Carignane, however, remain).

Its viticultural history, dating back to the 1860s with the first settlement, became important when wine production began to expand after 1880. Long a center for brandy, dessert wine, and robust red jug wines, the industry, since 1965, has shifted to white table and sparkling wine production. Yet, due to high grape prices in recent years, vine acreage has expanded, particularly for Cabernet Sauvignon, Chardonnay, and Zinfandel, the latter particularly favored by many large North Coast producers for the production of blush wines. Due to underutilized crushing, fermenting, and storage capacity, the area is the center of renewed economic activity. Today, Lodi, with its tree-lined streets, is one of the friendliest small cities in the valley, and the nucleus of a thriving and expanding wine industry.

Clarksburg (1984), located 12 miles south of Sacramento, encompasses 65,000 acres, and because its vineyards are cooled by maritime westerly air masses, it is designated Region II and III. The *ava,* with an established reputation for quality Chenin Blanc and Cabernet Sauvignon, contains 550 acres. The *ava* has, in recent years, attracted much attention for fresh, fruity, well-balanced wines prompting many prestigious Sonoma and Napa wineries to buy grapes from this region. What makes this region unique is the portion of the delimited area that is part of 500,000 acres of former marshland lying below sea level protected by dikes. *Merritt Island (1983),* an enclave within the Clarksburg *ava,* is a small, 5,000-acre, man-made island located in Yolo County. It is part of a number of islands, each several thousand or more acres, surrounded by the meandering channels of the Sacramento, San Joaquin and other tributary rivers. Merritt Island is located just south of Sacramento and forms the first major alluvial fan of the Sacramento delta. The island consists of a fine loam with scattered "peat," or organically rich material. A good deal of the island lies below sea level with vineyards occupying the higher ground of the surrounding levees. The cooling effect brought about by the southwesterly Bay breezes from the Carquinez Straits lowers average summer temperatures by 10F than Sacramento located six miles to the north. Acreage (about 500) is overwhelmingly planted in white grape varieties, particularly Chenin Blanc, a grape variety producing clean, fruity, fresh wines.

AGRICULTURAL ECONOMY OF MADERA COUNTY, 1989

Commodity	Acreage	Production In Tons	Total Value
Almonds	34,323	22,653	$49,837,000
Figs	6,610	7,205	8,034,000
Raisin Grapes	41,603	204,870	80,437,000
Wine Grapes	37,565	334,241	51,701,000
Nectarines	765	6,350	3,321,000
Olives	1,732	7,621	4,649,000
Oranges	3,833	37,602	12,597,000
Peaches	1,368	13,543	7,313,000
Pistachios	15,794	3,317	12,605,000
Plums	1,201	7,146	5,574,000
Walnuts	1,581	2,371	2,241,000
Other Crops			
Total	151,658		$267,456,000

Source: 1989 Madera County Agricultural Report.

The *Madera (1985) ava* is a large 600 square mile region containing nearly 83,000 vine acres. It is located between the Chowchilla River on the north and the San Joaquin on the south, but also includes portions of Madera and Fresno counties, and six wineries. Although predominantly a raisin producing region, wine grape acreage, historically red (Carignane, Barbera, Grenache Noir, Rubired, and Ruby Cabernet), has recently shifted to white grapes, mainly Colombard and Chenin Blanc, and Portuguese red grape varieties for the production of Porto-type wines. Vines were first planted in the 1870s, and by 1880 Italian Swiss Colony, one of the largest wineries in the state, was founded. Today the *ava* contains several large wineries and two smaller firms specializing in sweet fortified wines. Within the county, grapes are the dominant agricultural commodity in terms of cash receipts--more than $45 million. The six wineries employ more people than any other manufacturing industry. It is also interesting to note that the elevation of the county varies from a low of 180 to a high of 13,150 feet.

The wineries are:

Anderson Wine Cellars (Exeter, 1980), is a 20-acre, 2,000-case winery that makes Colombard, Ruby Cabernet, Zinfandel, Chardonnay, and Chenin Blanc.

A. Nonini Winery (Fresno, 1936), is a 200-acre, 50,000-case winery that makes generic and varietal wines, of which Grenache Noir, Barbera, and Zinfandel enjoy a wide following in the Fresno area.

ASV Wines (Delano, 1981), is a 2.7 million-case winery that makes generic and varietal wines, vermouth, brandy, and concentrate. It also operates the San Martin winery in Monterey County.

Bella Napoli Winery (Manteca, 1934), is a 60-acre, 55,000-case winery that makes generic wines under the *Vine Flow, Family Vineyard,* and *A la Sante* labels.

Belle Creek Ranch (Paradise, 1983), located in Butte County, is a 15-acre, 1,000-case, organic winery that makes Cabernet Sauvignon, Zinfandel, Chardonnay, and blended wines.

Bisceglia Bros. Wine Co. (Madera, 1880), is a 1.2 million-case, bulk winery owned by the Canandaigua Wine Co. of New York that makes brandy, table and fortified wines, grape juice, and concentrate.

Blackwell Wine Co. (Lost Hills, 1975), is a 3,300-acre vineyard that periodically makes generic and varietal wines.

Bogle Vineyards (Clarksburg, 1979), is a 650-acre, 45,000-case winery that makes good, sound, flavorful Chardonnay, Sauvignon Blanc, Petite Sirah, Zinfandel, Cabernet Sauvignon, and Merlot.

Borra's Cellar (Lodi, 1975), is a 45-acre, 1,500-case winery that makes distinctive, robust Barbera and Sauvignon Blanc. The white Barbara is a tasty, interesting wine that offers considerable value.

Cache Cellars (Davis, 1978), is a 6,500-case winery that makes Sauvignon Blanc, Chardonnay, Cabernet Sauvignon, and Pinot Noir.

Cache Creek Winery (Woodland, 1985), is an interesting, 5-acre, 1,300-case winery that makes Symphony, Zinfandel, Carnelian, and Carmine.

California Cellar Masters (Lodi, 1974), is a 25,000-case winery that makes generic, varietal, fortified, sparkling, and flavored wines under the *Coloma Cellars, Mother Lode,* and *Gold Mine* labels.

California Fruit Products Company (Fresno, 1900), owned by the Canandaigua Wine Company of New York, is a 7 million-case winery that makes brandy, generic wines, concentrate, and grape juice.

Chico Cellars (Chico, 1989), is 2-acre, 1,000-case winery that makes Zinfandel and Cabernet Sauvignon.

Delicato Vineyards (Manteca, 1935), is an underrated, 8,400-acre, 2 million-case winery that makes a complete line of generic, varietal, sparkling, fortified, and fruit wines. One of the better and more consistent of the large Central Valley producers, this winery offers excellent value. It boasts a new facility in Monterey County where it controls more than 28 percent of the county's total vine acreage. The winery also has an additional 4,000 acres suitable for planting. Other label: *Settler's Creek.*

E. & J. Gallo Winery (Modesto, 1933), with 9,000 acres and a total output of more than 95 million cases and sales exceeding $1 billion, is the largest winery in the world. Two brothers, Ernest and Julio Gallo, have created the largest, most efficient, state-of-the-art, quality conscious, economy-of-scale winery in the world. Meticulous attention to detail, patience, large-scale and long-term planning, accurate market research, and consistency of product are legendary hallmarks. Not only has Gallo been a major training ground for many winemakers and executives, but its firm grip on hard work and a sense of scientific dedication has dispelled wine folklore and encouraged scientific methodology. In addition to Central Valley grapes, the winery is the market for approximately 18 percent of Napa Valley, 32 percent of Sonoma-Mendocino, and 21 percent of Central Coast grape harvests. State-wide, Gallo purchases roughly 30 percent of all grapes. The winery's own 5,400 acres (3,200 acres in Livingston along benchlands of the Merced River and Modesto, and 2,200 acres combined in the Dry Creek and Russian River areas of Sonoma) produce but 5 percent of its requirements. While made in Healdsburg, Livingston, and Fresno, the wine is aged, blended, and bottled in a huge, 250-acre facility in Modesto. This incredible complex contains administrative offices, the largest bottle factory in the country, and a 37-acre warehouse with a storage capacity of more than 330 million gallons. The firm acquired the Andy Frei Winery in Sonoma County in 1977.

Gallo has pioneered a number of major enological and viticultural practices, and is the preeminent leader in wine marketing. Historically, Gallo was strictly a bulk producer of generic red, white, fortified, specialty, and brandy products. In the late 1970s, sensing a change in consumer behavior, the company shifted emphasis to the production of varietal, and, more recently, vintage dated Chardonnay, Sauvignon Blanc, Zinfandel, and Cabernet Sauvignon. Although more than one-third of the wine grape crush is composed of Thompson Seedless and Colombard, the Gallo winery is the largest market for premium grapes. The winery owns eight of the nation's top 20 brands, including the number one cooler, Bartles & Jaymes. It produces 30 percent of the wine consumed in the nation, and 40 percent of all the wine made in California. Gallo sells more wine than the next five competitors combined. Annually, it ships more than 18 million cases of generic wine, 17 million cases of Carlo Rossi, and 6 million cases of Andre sparkling wine. The rapidly growing varietal wines account for less than 3.5 million cases. All wines are intensely flavored and scented, consistently well made, and offer good to excellent value. With nearly 50 percent of total production, Gallo is also the nation's largest brandy distiller, followed by Christian Brothers (20%), and Korbel (8%). Faced with declining sales of jug wines and coolers, the firm is currently emphasizing and expanding its line of vintage-dated varietal wines (cork-finished wines now comprise 37 percent of total output). It would be an understatement to say that E. & J. Gallo makes more good wine than anyone else in the world. Furthermore, the winery, beginning with the 1990 vintage, will be marketing super-premium Cabernet Sauvignon and Chardonnay.

East Side Winery (Lodi, 1934), is a 125-member cooperative that makes 700,000 cases of table, dessert and fortified wines, vermouth, and brandy (excellent) under the *Oak Ridge Vineyards*, and *Royal Host Cellars* labels.

Ficklin Vineyard (Madera, 1948), is an unusual winery because it produces just 10,500 cases of Porto-type wine. It is the oldest of the small, dessert wine producers, and the first American winery to make Porto-type wine from four Portuguese grape varieties grown in family-owned vineyards (50 acres).

Fransinetti Winery (Sacramento, 1897), is a 25,000-case winery that makes Chardonnay, Sauvignon Blanc, Riesling, Cabernet Sauvignon, Merlot, Zinfandel, dessert, and proprietary wines.

Gibson Wine Co. (Elk Grove, 1934), is a 6,000-acre, 1 million-case cooperative that makes generic, varietal, fruit, berry, fortified wines, and vermouth under several different labels: *Silverstone Cellars, Ramano, Farley's, Gibson Vineyards, Gibson's Fruit & Berry Wines.*

Giumarra Vineyards (Edison, 1946), is a 10,000-acre (mostly table grapes), 1.5 million-case winery that began bottling under its own label in 1974 (200,000 cases). In addition to custom crushing and bottling for other wineries, it makes generic and the following varietals: Chenin Blanc, Colombard, Riesling, Cabernet Sauvignon, Zinfandel, Chardonnay, and Gewurztraminer.

Golden State Vintners (Cutler and Fresno, 1936), known as California Growers Winery until 1988, is an 8,000-acre, 12 million-case winery that sells grapes, custom-crushes, makes brandy, vermouth, table (Chenin Blanc, Zinfandel, Chardonnay, Cabernet Sauvignon, and Colombard are the most important), generic, and sparkling wines under many la-

bels, of which *Le Blanc* is the most important.

Guild Wineries (Lodi, 1948), the nation's largest grower-owned cooperative (500 members), makes more than 3.5 million cases, and is the nation's third largest wine company in terms of storage (more than 60 million gallons). Guild maintains 5 wineries, 12 major brands, makes a complete line of blended wines with generic names, several vintage and non-vintage varietals, fortified, sparkling, coolers, brandy, and distilled products. It owns the popular *Cribari, Cresta Blanca,* and *Cook's* brands. The latter, Cook's Champagne Cellars (second largest sparkling wine brand that makes Spumante and standard sparkling wines), is a rapidly expanding, low price sparkling wine of more than 1.6 million cases. A new label, *Cook's Captain's Reserve California,* will concentrate on a new line of Chardonnay, White Zinfandel, Merlot, and Cabernet Sauvignon. An upscale sparkling wine—*Chase-Limogere* is interesting. In addition, Guild sells grape juice, grape concentrate, and non-alcoholic wines. The winery has recently been acquired by the Canandaigua Winery of New York.

Harbor Winery (West Sacramento, 1972), is a 1,000-case winery that makes above-average Cabernet Sauvignon, Zinfandel, Chardonnay, and an unusual dessert wine from Mission grapes (labeled *Mission Del Sol*). Hand-crafted and distinctive, the wines, made by a University of California-Davis professor, are from purchased grapes.

Heck Cellars (Di Giorgio, 1986), is a winery with multiple owners over the past 30 years. Recently acquired by Korbel Champagne Cellars, the facility, with a capacity of 8 million cases, will make brandy and custom crush.

Heritage Cellars (Fresno, 1985), is a 12,000-case winery (historically the Old Master Winery) that makes Colombard, Chardonnay, Sauvignon Blanc, Riesling, Cabernet Sauvignon, Zinfandel, Mourvedre, and generic wines.

Heublein (Madera, 1852), with an output of 15 million cases (all divisions) is the nation's third largest winery, and one of the oldest in California. It makes a bewildering number of bulk, vintage-dated, varietal, fortified, sparkling, and distilled products. Quality and production have stumbled during the past 20 years (particularly Almaden), but it is assumed that Hueblein (a subsidiary of Grand Metropolitan), who recently purchased and moved operations to Madera, will make necessary improvements. The premium varietal line is marketed under the *Charles Lefranc* label, while the sub-premium line is labeled *Inglenook Navalle*. Production, dramatically increased from 2.6 million cases in 1970, has recently fallen, reflecting the general national weakness in the jug wine market. The historic facility in San Jose is now closed, but the facility in Paicines in San Benito County is still producing bulk wines. The company owns 800 acres in Paicines, San Benito County. An interesting sparkling wine, *Le Domaine*, made in Madera, offers good value. Other labels: *Jacare, Hartley,* and *T.J. Swann.*

J.F.J. Bronco Winery (Ceres, 1973), is a 10,000-acre, 6 million-case winery that makes wine and buys excess wine inventories, then blends, matures, and bottles a complete line of mostly generic wines. The winery has recently purchased the *Domaine Laurier* label (Sonoma). Other labels: *CC Vineyard Wines, J.F.J Winery.*

Las Vinas Winery (Lodi, 1986), is a 900-acre vineyard that makes 15,000 cases of Chardonnay, barrel fermented Chenin Blanc, Cabernet Sauvignon (the *Peltier Vineyard* is excellent), Zinfandel, dry and late harvest Symphony, and proprietary wines, offering good value.

Le Montpelier Winery (Waterford, 1987), is a 320-acre, 2,000-case winery (with a near goal for 100,000 cases) owned by members of the Mondavi and Franzia families. The vintage-dated Chardonnay, White Zinfandel, and Cabernet Sauvignon are made in the Mondavi facility in Woodbridge under the *Waterford Hills* label. Vineyards are located in eastern Stanislaus County against the Sierra Nevada Foothills. First releases of the moderately-priced wines are above-average.

Matson Vineyards (Redding, 1984), is a 3-acre, 500-case winery that makes proprietary white, rose, and red wines.

Moresco Vineyards (Stockton, 1987), is an 158-acre, 100,000-case winery that makes Chardonnay, Sauvignon Blanc, Riesling, Chenin Blanc, Carignane, Cabernet Sauvignon, Petite Sirah, Zinfandel, and generic wines. Other labels: *Moresco Cellars, Little John's Creek.*

Nicholas G. Verry (Parlier, 1933), is a 25,000-case winery that makes Greek Retzina (one of two in the state) from a variety of white grapes, and engages in custom crushing for others.

Orleans Hill Vinicultural Association (Woodland, 1980), is a 76-acre,

7,000-case winery that makes smooth, yet firm Sauvignon Blanc, a woody, well-flavored Chardonnay, and Cajun Red, a unique, spicy, well-flavored wine made from Petite Sirah and Cabernet Sauvignon meant to compliment Cajun cuisine.

Papagni Vineyards (Madera, 1973), used to be a 2,500-acre, 750,000-case winery that made table and sparkling wines, brandy and vermouth before it was sold in 1988. Long engaged in grape-growing, the family first bonded their winery in 1973 mainly for the production of bulk wines. Historically, the wines, based on Alicante Bouschet and other similar varieties, were full-bodied, robust, well-colored, and well-flavored. The wines, dramatically improved during the 1978-1988 period, consisted of interesting versions of Barbera, sparkling Chenin Blanc, Chardonnay, Zinfandel, and Alicante Bouschet, the latter made from vines planted by Demetrio Papagni in the 1920s. Wine will continue to be made in the same facility and grapes from existing vineyards, but under leasing agreements.

Paradise Vintners (Paradise, 1982), is a 6-acre, 25,000-case winery that makes more types of wine than any other winery in the nation (40).

Philips Farms (Lodi, 1984), is a 130-acre, 2,500-case winery (part of a much larger farm operation) that makes generic, Chardonnay, Cabernet Sauvignon, Colombard, Carignane, and Symphony.

R. & J. Cook Winery (Clarksburg, 1978), a 700-acre, 65,000-case winery, is the first major enterprise in the delta region of Yolo County. In addition to proprietary red, white, and blush blends, the principal varietals are Chardonnay, Sauvignon Blanc, Orange Muscat, Chenin Blanc, Petite Sirah, Merlot, and Cabernet Sauvignon.

R. H. Phillips Vineyards (Woodland, 1984), is an innovative, 450-acre, 160,000-case winery located in the Dunnigan Hills of Yolo County. Grapes are picked at night, and the winery has an established reputation for soft, well-balanced Semillon, Sauvignon Blanc, Chardonnay, Chenin Blanc, Cabernet Sauvignon, and Syrah, offering excellent value. It is estimated that by 1993, when the vines begin bearing commercial quantities of grapes, this winery will be the largest producer of Syrah in the state. Other label: *Chateau St. Nicholas* in association with the John Wesley Wine Company.

Robert Mondavi Winery (Woodbridge, 1979), is a 100-acre, 2 million-case winery that makes Cabernet Sauvignon, Sauvignon Blanc, White Zinfandel, generic white and red, and Porto-type wines. Beginning with the 1976 harvest, when Porto-type wine was made from Zinfandel and Tinta Madera from selected vineyard plots, it has become the center of a major California breakthrough in the production of genuine Portuguese Porto-type wines. With the purchase of the Woodbridge winery in 1979, other varieties (Cabernet Sauvignon, Petite Sirah, Carnelian, and Barbera) were added to the blend. By 1984, encouraged by the character of the vines and the quality of wines, it was decided that authentic Portuguese varieties, such as Avaralho, Bastardo, Souzao, Touriga, and Tinta Cao, would form the core of an expanding and serious effort to make Portuguese-style Porto in the Central Valley. Individual and blended wines, tasted in the summer of 1986, proved to be absolutely magnificent beyond belief. Not only were the wines better than any hitherto-made in this country, but equal or better to authentic imported versions. Long a leader in merchandising varietal wines, the Robert Mondavi Winery is at the very threshold of a significant coupe in American enology. The primary activity, however, of this facility is to act as a warehouse and distribution center for other Mondavi wines, and to make White Zinfandel, red, rose, and white table wines.

Quady Winery (Madera, 1975), is a 15,000-case winery specializing in dessert wines from purchased grapes. Primarily a Zinfandel Porto-type establishment, the recently improved wines are now made with larger infusions of Portuguese Porto varieties such as Tinta Cao, Tinta Amarella, Alvaralho, and Bastardo. Port of the Vintage is the less expensive, early maturing wine, while Vintage Port contains superior grapes and is intended for longer aging. The desire to recreate the legendary Ports of Portugal has met with limited success, Two other, recently introduced wines are *Essencia* (an Orange Muscat), and *Elysium* (made from the Black Muscat), both of which are excellent. Also made are small quantities of low alcohol Orange Muscat.

Satiety (Davis, 1977), is a 29-acre, 3,000-case winery that makes good, sound red, white, and rose blended wines, offering good value.

Sebastiani Vineyards (Lodi, 1988), is a generic and bulk wine facility with a capacity of 6 million cases.

Sonora Winery & Port Works (Sonora, 1986), is an unusual, 1-acre,

1,200-case label that specializes in the production of excellent Porto-type wine (labeled *Vintage Port St. Amant Vineyard*) from Tinta Cao, Touriga, Alvaralho, Souzao, and Bastardo grapes. The grapes, grown in Amador County, are crushed at another facility. Also made are minute quantities of Zinfandel, Sauvignon Blanc, and Chardonnay. A new winery will be built in Stockton shortly.

Tejon Marketing Co. (Lebec, 1975), is a 5,500-acre, 2,500-case winery that makes generic wines.

The Beverage Source (Sanger, 1987), is a 1.3 million case crush facility owned by Erly Industries.

The Lucas Winery and Vineyards (Lodi, 1978), is a 30-acre, 1,000-case winery that makes just one wine--Zinfandel--from 65-year old vines. Also made is a 100% barrel fermented White Zinfandel. The hard to find, well-made wines, supple, flowery and well-scented, offer remarkable value.

The Wine Group (Ripon, 1987), is a holding company for Franzia, Tribuno, Mogen David, Summit Wines, Willow Glen, Corbett Canyon Vineyards, and others. The company, ranking among the six largest wineries in the nation (it produces more than 10 million cases), operates 2,000 acres of vineland and two large wineries (Ripon, California, and Westfield, New York). It makes complete lines of inexpensive generic, varietal, sparkling wines, vermouth, and coolers.

Tremont Vineyards (Davis, 1982), is a 3-acre, 2,000-case winery that makes unusual wine from UC-Davis-developed vines: Centurion, Symphony, Carnelian, Flora, and Carmine. The owner is the son of Harold Olmo, the famed geneticist.

Verdugo Vineyards (Acampo, 1934), is a 5-acre, 300,000-case winery, now owned by La Crema Winery of Sonoma, that makes Zinfandel, Cabernet Sauvignon, Sauvignon Blanc, Riesling, Chardonnay, flavored, and Porto-type wines under the *Lost Hills, Barengo,* and *Dudenhoefer* labels.

Vie-Del Co. (Fresno, 1946), is a 4 million-case, bulk winery that also makes grape concentrate and brandy, all of which are marketed under customer labels.

Villa Bianchi Winery (Kerman, 1974), is a 580-acre, 1.5 million-case winery that makes generic, varietal, and cooler wines. Approximately 60,000 cases of varietal wine (Chardonnay, Zinfandel, and Cabernet Sauvignon) are made. Other labels: *Villa Sorrento, Bianchi,* and *Villa Bianchi.*

Winters Winery (Winters, 1980), is a 7-acre, 2,000-case winery that makes muscular Petite Sirah, Sauvignon Blanc, Zinfandel, and Pinot Noir. Other labels: *Putah Creek Gold, Storm Cellars, Putah Creek Red.*

Woodbridge Vineyard Assn. (Lodi, 1905), in a reorganization phase, is a 700,000-case cooperative.

THE SIERRA FOOTHILLS

The Sierra Nevada, the highest range of mountains in the state, stretch for 430 miles, are 80 miles wide, and nearly 15,000 feet high. Named *una gran sierra nevada,* or "the great snowy inland mountains" by the Spanish, the backbone of this large geological province, a huge mass of igneous rock, heavily eroded, forested, and with significant local relief, is one of the most definitive elements of California. Not only are the Sierra Nevada's one of the longest single mountain ranges in the world, but they harbor Sequoias more than 20 stories high and pines older than the pyramids. It is no wonder that the famed naturalist, John Muir, said that "God always seems to be doing his best here."

Facing the Central Valley, the Sierra Foothills, the historically famous "mother lode" region which attracted thousands in the middle of the nineteenth century, consist of Amador, El Dorado, Calaveras, Yuba, Mariposa, Placer, Nevada, and Tuolomne counties, an area of recent and serious viticultural interest. All eight counties have similar geographic, economic and cultural histories: small populations; an absence of large cities; an agricultural economy based on animal products (more than half of agricultural income is based on cattle); the preponderance of government-owned land; and a climate that ranges from near desert near the Central Valley to alpine at elevations beyond 7,000 feet. These mountains have long been considered impediments to travel, major recreational treasures, and fantastic collectors and reservoirs of water.

Frontier justice restored for the tourist in "Old Hangtown," now known as Placerville. Baxevanis

Located 25 miles east of Sacramento, the Sierra Foothills is an area of hills and high mountains, walnuts, ranching, spectacular scenery, and although the historic sites of Placerville, Sutter Creek, Camino, and Coloma (it was here that James Marshall discovered gold in 1848) belie a mineral-rich frontier, the important agricultural interest over the past 20 years is grape vines, and, in particular, Zinfandel and Sauvignon Blanc. This rapidly growing viticultural area contains 4,500 acres of vineland and produces more than 300,000 gallons of wine, or less than 1 percent of the state's total output. While the industry is widely diffused within the eight counties, the Fiddletown-Shenandoah Valley has the largest single concentration,

with Fairplay and the Columbia areas being two ancillary, but rapidly developing areas.

Winemaking arrived in the Sierras with gold miners in 1849, and the first winery--D'Agostini--dates back to 1856 (it was considered the third oldest in the state until it ceased operations in 1988). The industry received a special impetus when in 1855 the state legislature passed a law which exempted from taxation all newly planted grape vines for four years. As a result, vine acreage grew from 30 acres to more than 120 in three years, and over the next 35 years, acreage in the Sierra Foothill region rose beyond 10,000. While the Sierra Foothills boasted more wineries than Sonoma and Napa combined in 1870 (Calaveras County ranked as the fourth largest winemaking county in 1860, and the second largest in the early 1890s; El Dorado had 100 wineries in 1900), economic conditions worsened as gold prospecting came to an abrupt halt, and the subsequent combination of phylloxera, depopulation and Prohibition shut the wineries until the 1960s. Although Prohibition reduced acreage (from 5,000 acres in 1920 to 200 in 1934), many Sierra growers managed to maintain vineyards by raising grapes for the Italian and Basque market, the latter extending as far as Montana.

Table 9.10

WINE GRAPE VARIETIES IN THE SIERRA FOOTHILLS, 1990					
Variety	1969	1974	%	1990	%
Sauvignon Blanc		54		422	14.1
Chardonnay		8		221	7.4
Chenin Blanc		40		77	
Riesling	2	13		44	
Colombard		51		29	
Semillon				24	
Muscat Blanc		7		20	
Zinfandel	428	1,032	48.1	1,413	47.1
Cabernet Sauvignon	38	87		314	10.5
Barbera		58		177	5.9
Petite Sirah	1	29		52	
Carignane		22		38	
Cabernet Franc		34		16	
Merlot		48		9	
Mourvedre		135	6.3	2	
Grenache		12		1	
Mission	91	104	4.9		
Alicante Bouschet		13			
Ruby Cabernet		162	7.6		
Other	96	235		140	
Total	656	2,144		2,999	
Source: California Agricultural Statistics Service					

Today there are 46 wineries, nearly all of which were established after 1973. Most of them are, by California standards, small, family-owned, and undercapitalized. The eight-county region, along the well-travelled US 80, is in the center of the legendary "gold country," and with close proximity to Yosemite National Park presents unusual opportunities for a major tourist-induced wine revival. In fact, it is an unusual combination of topography, history, accessibility, and low real estate values that is responsible for the viticultural rebirth of this region. The area is studded with dozens of historical towns (Murphys, Coloma, Placerville, Garden Valley, Kelsey, Chili Bar, Diamond

Springs, Fairplay, Columbia [in 1853, the second most populous city], Strawberry, Pollock Pines, Camino, among others), and probably more museums per square mile than any other region in the state. Frontier and Spanish folklore have also created an ambience quite conducive to tourist attractions and second home construction (Calaveras, for example, is derived from Spanish for skulls, and for places having human skeletons). It is estimated that the region has more than 350 abandoned mining towns.

Figure 9.14

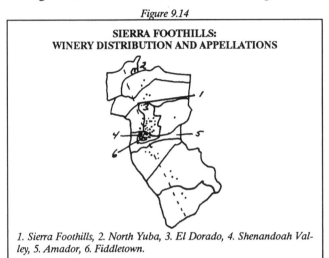

SIERRA FOOTHILLS: WINERY DISTRIBUTION AND APPELLATIONS

1. Sierra Foothills, 2. North Yuba, 3. El Dorado, 4. Shenandoah Valley, 5. Amador, 6. Fiddletown.

What makes the Sierra Foothill region unique is the hilly terrain, the fragmented nature of the vineyard sites, the relative isolation of the region (the installation of electrical service to Shenandoah occurred after W.W. II), the 1,000 to 3,400 foot high elevations of most vineyard sites (the highest vineyards in the state), the granite-based (colluvial and alluvial) soils, and the small scale character of wineries. The region is a series of long, gently sloping ridges with deep river canyons dividing them. The early spring season is cooler and bud break is later than most coastal counties.

Generally, elevations under 1,200 feet are considered Region IV; between 1,200 and 2,000 feet, and nearly all the Shenandoah Valley, Region III; between 2,000 and 3,300 feet, Region II (Placerville); and at elevations above 3,400 feet broadleaf deciduous vegetation gives way to more conifers and practically no commercial vineyards. Lying along the lower portions of the Sierra's, the area between 1,000 and 3,400 feet is a narrow, but discontinuous belt of land "above the fog and below the snow," an important reference to the fact that this viticulturally valuable land is usually above the fog of the Central Valley and below the heavy snows and colder temperatures of the High Sierra. Most vineyards are located on ridges and, hence, are frost-free (severe frosts occur once every ten years). Even for many stations at 5,000 feet in elevation, the record low temperature is above 5F. Indeed, nowhere else in California does elevation affect vineyard

climates so intensely. Nevertheless, the entire region lacks the glamor of Napa and Sonoma, and the small, undercapitalized wineries are widely scattered, creating a rustic frontier ambience with considerable potential for future growth. The region is important for the production of hydroelectric potential, irrigation water, mineral exploitation, and is proximate to Yosemite National Park, the nation's most highly developed park.

Historically, the reputation of the Sierra Foothills rested entirely on Zinfandel and Sauvignon Blanc. The former (accounting for 50 percent of the planted acreage) is known as distinctive, robust, and, for its variety, a rich flavor of spice. In these parts, Zinfandel, when made in a full-bodied style, has a briary flavor, can be alcoholic, well-balanced, and when it is the product of old vines, a memorable experience. Given to market pressures, 70 percent of Zinfandel from the Sierra Foothill region, which was made into "white wine" throughout a good portion of the 1980s, has now been reversed in favor of red wine; but, unlike the legendary alcoholic wines of yesteryear, the new versions are fruitier and significantly more supple. The Sauvignon Blanc is softer, more supple and early maturing than those from North Coast counties, and significantly better balanced and more flavorful than that emanating from the Central Valley. The value of grapes per ton is consistently at least twice that of the Central Valley.

Overlooking a portion of the Shenandoah ava. Baxevanis

Other grapes grown and becoming increasingly important are Chardonnay, Merlot, Petite Sirah, Riesling, and Muscat Blanc. Merlot, in particular, makes excellent, full-bodied, well-structured wines; Charbono also makes good wine and acreage is increasing; sweet wines, particularly from Muscat Blanc, also offer good possibilities; and cool variety grapes, such as Pinot Noir, Riesling, Gewurztraminer, and others, have a bright future on high elevations. The versatile Sierra region, because of the large range in climatic patterns, has the potential to produce nearly every grape variety grown elsewhere in California.

It is interesting to note that, due to cool weather, grape acids are high enough to discourage acidification of the wine, a radical departure from other wine producing regions. The wines, as a consequence, are unfamiliar, but well-balanced and fragrant, and more robust than those from the Central Valley. Quality wines have been produced from several physically diverse vineyards, such as Eschen, Grandpere, and Esola, all of which are planted in old Zinfandel vines. The viticultural issue, however, is not closed. Recent empirical successes with specific varieties at varying elevations have added a new dimension to the potential of this area.

For a small region, the Sierra Foothills contain six *ava's*: *Fiddletown (1983)*, *California Shenandoah Valley (1983)*, *North Yuba (1985)*, *Amador, El Dorado (1983)*, and *Sierra Foothills (1987)*. Of the six, the single most important producing region is the California *Shenandoah Valley*, an 18 square mile triangular area, east and south of Plymouth that historically attracted gold prospectors, but has recently developed an excellent reputation for exceptional Zinfandel, known for high sugar levels, well-balanced acid levels, and lush flavors. Being partial to the flavor of Zinfandel, the early Italian and Yugoslav settlers planted 3,000 acres by the mid-1800s. Studded with oak, walnut and pine trees, the *ava* today contains half the wineries of the Sierra's. A misnomer, this *ava* is a collection of small valleys and forested, rounded hills lying between the forks of Dry Creek and the Cosumnes that were historically settled by people from the Shenandoah Valley of Virginia. Valley floors are located between 1,200 and 1,800 feet above sea level, and although classified as Region III, summer temperatures vary between 85F and 95F during the day, but fall to 55F-65F at night. Freezing rarely occurs, and cool, maritime air flows during the ripening stage reducing temperatures sufficiently to maintain high acid levels. The desired soil, the Shenandoah-Sierra series, a decomposed, red granite *Terra Rosa* whose depth varies from inches to more than ten feet, is highly permeable and facilitates excellent root development (the volcanic Supra-Iron Mountain soil is also excellent). The appellation contains more than 2,000 acres of vines, 1,400 of which are Zinfandel and 400 in Sauvignon Blanc. Most Zinfandel vineyards are dry-farmed producing intense, rich, complex, and well-favored wines that have an amazing sweet aftertaste due to a high glycerine content.

The largest *ava*, *Sierra Foothills*, is a 4,200 square mile region that includes 4,500 acres of vineland, 150 growers, and all wineries in the eight county "foothill belt" area only. Vineland not included are portions of the Central Valley below 500 feet, and elevations beyond 3,500 feet. Nevertheless, this *ava* is large, stretching for 170 miles from Yuba to Mariposa, and its width varies between 5 and 35 miles. It totally surrounds and encom-

passes all other Sierra Foothill *ava's*. This large region is drained by more than eight rivers, of which the Yuba, Bear, American, Cosumnes, Mokelumne, Calaveras, Stanislaus, Tuolumne, and Merced are the most important. Although the "foothills" are defined as the intermediate area between the High Sierras and the Central Valley, they are by no means homogeneous in terms of topography and soils, the latter highly variable as they are weathered from igneous, sedimentary, metamorphic, and volcanic rocks. Its most unusual physical feature is a highly variable climate strongly influenced by topography and aspect. Increased elevation leads to greater temperature extremes with considerable fluctuations between diurnal lows and highs. As temperature decreases with increasing altitude, summer nights are much cooler in sharp contrast to the Mediterranean and semi-desertic climates to the west. Precipitation, similar to the Mediterranean climate, occurs mainly in the three winter months, the total amount directly dependent upon altitude. Frost is a troublesome occurrence, particularly in low-lying, protected valleys that are subject to temperature inversions.

The *Fiddletown ava* differs from the Shenandoah *ava*, of which it is an enclave, in terms of a higher elevation, cooler night time temperatures, and more rainfall. In fact, the *ava*, between 1,500 and 2,000 feet in elevation, receives between 30 and 40 inches of precipitation, and is surrounded by rugged, colder terrain. The unirrigated, sandy loam soils (phylloxera-free) produce low yields, higher acid levels, and concentrated, well flavored wines, considered the finest in the Sierra's. The name is derived from a group of Missourians who brought their fiddles while they panned for gold. There is also a Fiddle Creek, a Fiddler Canyon, and a Fiddler Creek. The *El Dorado ava*--a 720-acre region, has rich viticultural traditions (in 1890 there were more wineries here than in Sonoma-Napa combined). This hilly, highly fragmented region is delimited in part by the North and Middle Fork of the American River, the Rubicon River, and the South Fork of the Cosumnes River. In recent years there has been a keen interest in the planting and grafting of Syrah, Mourvedre, Cinsault, and Grenache. The *ava* contains eleven wineries, and 32 growers.

Amador, the most prestigious of the eight counties, is named after Jose Maria Amador, son of one of the wealthiest land owners of northern California. Despite its proximity to Sacramento it is one of the most rural wine producing counties in the state (the 2,700 residents still lack a traffic light). Despite its historic association with Zinfandel, viticultural growth has been recent: vine acreage grew from fewer than 400 in 1950, to 800 in 1977, to nearly 1,900 in 1990. The county ranks twentieth in size in terms of wine output, but seventh in the production of Zinfandel, its most prestigious grape variety. All grapes, in fact, account for 42 percent of the county's total agricultural value. Amador County contains 18 of the 40 wineries sited in the Sierra Foothill region, two of which are the oldest in the entire foothill region.

What makes Amador County different from all other Sierra Foothill counties is its long growing season, precipitation patterns, and excellent soils (mainly decomposed granite). Precipitation varies between 30 and 36 inches, with most vineyards dry-farmed. As a result, Amador County Zinfandel exhibits an intense, ripe, fruity fragrance and flavor, and matures and softens much sooner than wines originating in other areas. However, when made in a high alcohol style, with extended skin maceration, dark in color, high in tannin, and with extended wood aging, Zinfandel can be one of the longest-lived red wines in the state. In order to protect the name, Amador County wineries have an embossed bottle with the Amador logo that is granted to any wine approved by a tasting review board. This is the first time an American wine region has established a mechanism designed to guarantee quality. Wineries outside the county can use the bottle if they use at least 95 percent Amador wine in the final bottling.

The *North Yuba (1985) ava*, the smallest and north-ernmost of the Sierra Foothills *ava's*, is a 35 square mile region with 500 vine acres and one winery. The region is framed by a 1,000-2,000 foot contour, and although similar in topography and soils as areas further south, this appellation experiences somewhat elevated precipitation levels. After a maximum of 1,000 vine acres in 1930 and five wineries, acreage and wine production dropped to zero after Prohibition until the late 1950s. The name is derived from the Spanish word, *uva*, for grape. The wineries are:

Amador Foothill Winery (Plymouth, 1980), is a 20-acre, 10,000-case winery that makes supple, soft Sauvignon Blanc and Zinfandel, offering good value.

Argonaut Winery (Ione, 1975), is a 3,000-case winery that makes Sauvignon Blanc, Syrah, Zinfandel, and Barbera.

Baldinelli Vineyards (Plymouth, 1979), is an 81-acre, 20,500-case winery that makes well-structured Sauvignon Blanc, Zinfandel, and Cabernet Sauvignon from very old vines.

Black Sheep Vintners (Murphys, 1987), formerly Chispa Cellars, is a 1,000-case winery that makes Sauvignon Blanc, Muscat Blanc, Cabernet Sauvignon, and Zinfandel.

Boeger Winery (Placerville, 1972), is a 50-acre, 12,000-case winery that makes full-bodied, sturdy, well flavored, lean Semillon, Chenin Blanc, Sauvignon Blanc, Chardonnay, Riesling, Cabernet Sauvignon, Zinfandel, Barbera, and Merlot, the latter quite interesting. In addition to proprietary wines, the winery also makes special select private reserve wines which bear the designation *George Babbin Vintage*. Recently, the winery has begun grafting and planting Sangiovese, Nebbiolo, Syrah, Grenache, and other similar grapes. On the National Register of Historic Places, the original winery, built in 1872, serves as a tasting room.

Butterfly Creek Winery (Mariposa, 1987), is an excellent, 20-acre, 3,000-case winery known for distinctive, full-bodied Pinot Blanc, Cabernet Sauvignon, and Merlot, offering good value.

Charles Spinetta Winery (Plymouth, 1988), is a 49-acre, 5,000-case label that markets Zinfandel, Chenin Blanc, and Cabernet Sauvignon.

Chatom Vineyards (San Andreas, 1985), this 65-acre, quality oriented vineyard and winery sells most of its grapes, but does make 4,000 cases of Chardonnay, Sauvignon Blanc, Zinfandel, Cabernet Sauvignon, and Merlot.

Clockspring Vineyards (Plymouth, 1982), is a 350-acre (the largest vineyard in the Sierras), 7,500-case label that makes Sauvignon Blanc and Zinfandel. Other label: *Pigeon Creek Wines*.

Domaine de la Terre Rouge (Fiddletown, 1985), is a 4-acre, 2,500-case winery that makes interesting, stylish, red Rhone-type wines (primarily from Syrah, Grenache Noir, Cinsault, and Mourvedre), and a dry *Vin Gris* from Zinfandel.

El Dorado Vineyards (Camino, 1976), is a 20-acre, 3,000-case winery that specializes in Chardonnay, Cabernet Sauvignon, Merlot, and proprietary wines.

Fiddle Farm Winery (Ione, 1988), is a developing, 3-acre winery that makes Sauvignon Blanc, Chenin Blanc, and Zinfandel.

Fitzpatrick Winery (Fairplay, 1980), is an unusual, organic, 40-acre, 3,000-case winery that specializes in red wines, all of which are above-average to excellent, the best of which are designated by vineyard names. Located on hilly terrain, the winery makes wine under both the El Dorado and Shenandoah Valley *ava's*. It is currently expanding Zinfandel output, and planting red Rhone and north Italian red varieties.

Gerwer Winery (Fairplay, 1981), is an 11-acre, 3,500-case winery that makes Chardonnay, Sauvignon Blanc, Semillon, Petite Sirah, Ruby Cabernet, and Cabernet Sauvignon.

Gold Hill Vineyard (Coloma, 1985), is a 35-acre, 3,000-case winery that makes Chardonnay, Chenin Blanc, Riesling, Cabernet Sauvignon, and a Meritage-type red wine.

Granite Springs Winery (Somerset, 1981), is a 23-acre, 12,000-case winery that makes above-average, tannin-rich Zinfandel, as well as fruity Chenin Blanc, Chardonnay, Cabernet Sauvignon, Sauvignon Blanc, Petite Sirah, Porto-type wines, and proprietary wines, offering good value.

Greenstone Winery (Ione, 1980), is a 32-acre, 10,000-case winery that makes Colombard, Sauvignon Blanc, Cabernet Sauvignon, and Zinfandel.

Indian Rock Vineyard (Murphys, 1984), is an interesting, rapidly growing 20-acre, 15,000-case winery that makes Chardonnay, Merlot, Cabernet Sauvignon, and Charbono.

Indian Springs Vineyards (Penn Valley, 1987), is an 118-acre, 3,000-case winery that makes Chardonnay, Sauvignon Blanc, Semillon, Merlot, and Cabernet Sauvignon.

Jackson Valley Vineyards (Ione, 1990), is an excellent, 50-acre, 12,000-case winery that makes Chardonnay, Chenin Blanc, Zinfandel, Porto-type (from Portuguese varieties), and unusual sweet and dry proprietary wines.

Karly Wines (Plymouth, 1979), is a 18-acre, 8,000-case winery that makes excellent to outstanding Sauvignon Blanc, Chardonnay, and Zinfandel, offering good value.

Kautz Vineyards (Murphys, 1989), is a 10,000-case winery that makes Chardonnay, Symphony, Cabernet Sauvignon, and Merlot. Other labels: *John Kautz Vineyards, Angels Creek*.

Kenworthy Vineyards (Plymouth, 1978), is a 8-acre, 1,000-case winery that makes well structured Chardonnay, Zinfandel, and Cabernet Sauvignon.

Latcham Vineyards (Mt. Aukum, 1980), is a 26-acre, 3,000-case winery that makes Chardonnay, Sauvignon Blanc, Chenin Blanc, Cabernet Sauvignon, Cabernet Franc, Zinfandel, and proprietary wines.

Latrobe Vineyards (Shingle Springs, 1985), is a 10-acre, 2,000-case label that only makes Sauvignon Blanc.

Lava Cap Winery (Placerville, 1986), is a 30-acre, 5,000-case winery that makes intense, flavorful, well-structured Chardonnay, Sauvignon Blanc, Cabernet Sauvignon, and Zinfandel, offering excellent value.

Madrona Vineyards (Camino, 1980), is a 35-acre, 10,000-case winery that makes full-bodied, rich Gewurztraminer, Chardonnay, dry and late harvest Riesling, Cabernet Sauvignon, Merlot, Cabernet Franc, and dry and late harvest Zinfandel from 3,000 foot-high vineyards, one of the highest in the state. Other label: *Crystal Range*.

Milliaire Winery (Murphys, 1986), is a 1,000-case winery that makes intense, powerful Chardonnay, Orange Muscat, Sauvignon Blanc, Cabernet Sauvignon, Merlot, and Zinfandel (dry and late harvest).

Montevina Wines (Plymouth, 1973), is a 313-acre (135 of which are planted in vines), 50,000-case winery that makes Semillon (dry and late harvest), Chardonnay, Sauvignon Blanc, Zinfandel, Cabernet Sauvignon, and Barbera. With the acquisition by Sutter Home Winery, the wines have improved markedly. One major modification in historic practice is the planting of Italian varieties, principally Sangiovese Grosso, Brunello, Nebbiolo, Barbera, Aleatico, and Refosco.

Nevada City Winery (Nevada City, 1980), is an aggressive, quality-conscious, 8,000-case winery that makes Chenin Blanc, Gewurztraminer, Riesling, Chardonnay, Sauvignon Blanc, Zinfandel, Petite Sirah, Charbono, and sparkling wines.

Radanovich Vineyards & Winery (Mariposa, 1986), is a 17-acre, 3,000-case winery that makes well-flavored and scented Sauvignon Blanc and Zinfandel, the latter particularly rich and flavorful due to the addition of Merlot and Cabernet Franc.

Renaissance Vineyard & Winery (Renaissance, 1978), with 365 acres and an annual output of 25,000 cases (mainly excellent Sauvignon Blanc, Riesling, and Cabernet Sauvignon), is the largest winery in Yuba County. Well-aged for what is an incredible amount of time, both white wines exhibit a deep golden color, multiple layers of flavor, and all wines, aged in German oak, are distinctive and complex, offering good value. The winery, owned by the non-denominational Fellowship of Friends Church, sits on property replete with a community dining hall, a town hall, a cluster of shops, and formal gardens. Moderately priced, the wines of this immaculate property should not be missed. They belong in every serious cellar.

Santino Winery (Plymouth, 1979), is a highly successful, innovative, 30,000-case winery that makes Orange Muscat, Sauvignon Blanc, late harvest Riesling, Barbera, Zinfandel (dry, white, late harvest, TBA, and ice wine), and Porto-type wines (the 1987 was made from Souzao, Touriga, Alvarelhao, Tinta Cao, Barbera, Zinfandel, Syrah, and Cabernet Sauvignon grapes). Made in several styles and colors, Zinfandel, comprising 90 percent of total output, is particularly good as it is made

from 120-year old vines (from the *Grandpere Vineyard*, considered the oldest in the state). Zinfandel from *Eschen Vineyards, Dry Berry Select White,* and *Lisa Marie* (a Porto-type wine) are all excellent. *Satyricon*, a blend of 43 percent Syrah, 45 percent Grenache, and 12 percent Mourvedre, is interesting.

Shenandoah Vineyards (Plymouth, 1977), is an aggressive and highly successful, 54-acre, 50,000-case winery. It makes several styles of Zinfandel, Cabernet Sauvignon, Sauvignon Blanc, Porto-type wine, and an assortment of sweet Riesling, and Black and Orange Muscat, the latter two outstanding. Considerably improved in recent years, all wines offer excellent value, and should not be missed. This innovative winery, with 16 different grape varieties, six different trellising techniques, and six different rootstocks, is a mini-viticultural experiment station.

Sierra Vista Winery (Placerville, 1977), located 2,900 feet above sea level, this 30-acre, 8,000-case winery makes robust, fruity, well-scented Chardonnay, Sauvignon Blanc, Syrah, Cabernet Sauvignon, Zinfandel, and proprietary blends.

Silver Family Vineyard (Mariposa, 1989), is an 8-acre, 1,000-case winery that makes big, dense Merlot, Cabernet Sauvignon, Zinfandel, and Meritage-types wines.

Smith Vineyard (Grass Valley, 1987), is an interesting, organic vineyard of 12 acres that makes 2,000 cases of supple, flavorful Chardonnay, Chenin Blanc, and Cabernet Sauvignon.

Sobon Estate Winery (Plymouth, 1856), after many years of inactivity, is the new name for the D'Agostini Winery, one of the most important viticultural historical landmarks established in 1856 (the third oldest in the state) that still contains a small plot of original Zinfandel vines, and the only winery in the Sierra Foothill country to survive Prohibition. Some maintain the thought that this was the sight of the first Zinfandel plantings in the state. Owned by neighboring Shenandoah Vineyards, this 113-acre winery will only be making 5,000-cases of superb, premium, well-structured Cabernet Sauvignon, Zinfandel, Sauvignon Blanc, and, in the future, Rhone-type wine. Currently one of the top properties in the region, this is a property to watch.

Stevenot Winery (Murphys, 1978), is a 26-acre, 60,000-case winery that makes Sauvignon Blanc, Chardonnay, Chenin Blanc, Muscat Blanc, Zinfandel, Merlot, and Cabernet Sauvignon. The reserve wines from *Chatom Ranch* and *Clockspring Vineyards*, and late harvest Zinfandel are particularly noteworthy. Owned by a family that literally pioneered in the region in 1850, it is the only winery that still mines gold on its property.

Stoneridge (Sutter Creek, 1975), is a 4-acre, 1,000-case winery that makes full-bodied, robust Zinfandel and Ruby Cabernet.

Story Vineyard (Plymouth, 1973), is a 40-acre, 5,000-case winery that makes supple Chenin Blanc, and robust, spicy, well-flavored, complex Zinfandel.

TKC Vineyards (Plymouth, 1981), makes 2,000 cases of big, fruity Zinfandel, late harvest Riesling, and an unusual blend of Gewurztraminer and Sauvignon Blanc called *Pokerville White*.

Truckee River Winery (Truckee, 1989), is an unusual, 1,000-case winery that makes Chardonnay, Sauvignon Blanc, and Pinot Noir. Sited near the Donner Pass at 5,900 feet in elevation, it is the highest winery in the state. However, it purchases all its grapes as it is too cold to grow grapes at this altitude.

Virginiatown Winery (Newcastle, 1984), is a 4-acre, 2,500-case winery that makes Chardonnay, Sauvignon Blanc, Chenin Blanc, Cabernet Sauvignon, Charbono, and Barbera.

Windwalker Winery (Somerset, 1986), formerly L.W. Richards Winery, is an 8-acre, 1,500-case winery that makes excellent Chardonnay, Chenin Blanc, Zinfandel, Cabernet Sauvignon, and Merlot.

Winterbrook Vineyards (Ione, 1980), is a 90-acre, 74,000-case, much improved winery under new ownership. It produces well-structured, full-bodied Chenin Blanc, Sauvignon Blanc, Chardonnay, Zinfandel, and Porto-type wine (made from the Souzao grape).

Wolterbeek-Westwood Winery (Shingle Springs, 1984), is an 8-acre, 5,000-case winery that makes barrel fermented Chardonnay, Cabernet Sauvignon, Pinot Noir, and Charbono under the *Westwood Winery* label, and Sauvignon Blanc under the *Wolterbeek Winery* label.

Yankee Hill Winery (Columbia, 1970), is a 3,000-case winery that makes fruit, sparkling, proprietary, and several varietals, all of which are sweet.

Yuba Foothills Vineyards & Winery (Sicard Flat, 1984), is an 8-acre,

1,000-case label that markets Muscat Blanc and Petite Sirah.

OTHER STATES

Nevada
Pahrump Valley Vineyards (Pahrump, 1990), with 6-acres, and a total output of 5,000-cases, this is the states first winery making Symphony, a Riesling/Colombard blend, Cabernet Sauvignon, and proprietary wines. As the nation's 41st state to house a bonded grape winery, there is no doubt that it will become a tourist attraction, but whether it will be the first to have slot machines is another issue.

Hawaii
Located on the island of Maui is the nation's westernmost and south-ernmost grape winery--**Tedeschi Vineyard**. Founded in 1974, this 23-acre winery, planted in Carnelian grapes 2,000-feet high on one of the world's largest dormant volcano's, makes 25,000 cases of table, sparkling, but primarily pineapple wines. Along with Florida and a few minor Gulf Coast wineries, it is the only winery with a vineyard sited in an area without winter dormancy.

Utah
Arches Vineyards (Moab, 1989), is a 40-acre, 4,000-case winery that makes Chenin Blanc, Riesling, Gewurztraminer, Semillon, Chardonnay, and Zinfandel.
Summum (Salt lake City, 1980), is a non-commercial winery operated by a religious order that makes 1,000 cases of sacramental wine.

Schramsberg's Underground Caves Carved Into The Hillside. Courtesy of Schramsberg Vineyards Company

BIBLIOGRAPHY

Abel, Dominick, *Guide To The Wines Of The United States*. New York, Cornerstone Library, 1979.

Adams, Leon, *The Wines of America*. New York, McGraw-Hill, 1990.

John Adlum, *A Memoir On The Cultivation Of The Vine In America, And The Best Mode Of Making Wine*. Washington, Davis and Force, 1823.

Allen, J. Fisk., *A Practical Treatise On The Culture And Treatment Of The Grape Vine*. New York, C.M. Saxton & Company, 1856.

Bailey, L.H., *The Species Of Grapes Peculiar To North America*. Ithaca, New York, 1934. Number four on the series *Gentes Herbarum*, Occasional Papers on the kinds of Plants, Vol. III., no date.

Baldwin, John L., *Climates Of The United States*. Washington, D.C., U.S. Department of Commerce, 1973.

Bioletti, F.T., *Grape Culture In California; Improved Methods Of Wine Making*. Berkeley, California Agricultural Experiment Station, Bulletin No. 197, 1908.

Blout, J.S., *Brief Economic History Of The California Winegrowing Industry*. San Francisco, The Wine Institute, 1943.

Buchanan, Robert, *A Treatise On Grape Culture In Vineyards, In The Vicinity Of Cincinnati, By A Member Of The Cincinnati Horticultural Society*. Cincinnati, Wright, Ferris and Co., 1850.

Buchanan, Robert, *Culture Of The Grape And Wine-Making*. Cincinnati, Moore & Anderson, 1854.

Carosso, V., *The California Wine Industry*. Berkeley, University of California Press, 1951.

Chazanof, William, *Welch's Grape Juice; From Corporation To Co-operative*. Syracuse, New York, Syracuse University press, 1977.

Chirich, Nancy, *Life With Wine*. Oakland, Ed-It, 1984.

Clark, Corbet, *American Wines of the Northwest*. New York, William Morrow and Company, 1989.

Conway, James, *Napa; The Story of An American Eden*. Boston, Houghton Mifflin Company, 1990.

De Blij, Harm Jan, *Wine, A Geographic Appreciation*. Totowa, New Jersey, Rowman & Allanheld, 1983.

De Treville-Lawrence, R. (ed.), *Jefferson And Wine; Model Of Moderation*. The Plains, Virginia, The Vinifera Wine Growers Association, 1989.

Dobson, Betty, *Fruit Of The Vine: 200 Years Of Winemaking In California*. San Francisco, Lexicos, 1988.

Dufour, John James, *The American Vine-Dresser's Guide, Being A Treatise On The Cultivation Of The Vine, And The Process Of Wine Making; Adapted To The Soil And Climate Of The United States*. Cincinnati, S.J. Browne, 1826.

English, Sara Jane, *The Wines of Texas; A Guide And A History*. Austin, Texas, Eakin Press, 1990.

Feldman, Herman., *Prohibition: It's Economic And Industrial Aspects*. New York, D. Appleton and Company, 1927.

Fuller, Andrew S., *The Grape Culturist: A Treatise On The Cultivation Of The Native Grape*. New York, Orange Judd & Co., 1867.

Garrett, Paul, *Wine As An American Industry*. Privately printed, Pioneer American Wine Growers, no date.

Giordano, Frank, *Texas Wines & Wineries*. Austin, Texas, Texas Monthly Press, 1984.

Hedrick, U.P., *The Grapes Of New York; Report Of The New York Agricultural Experiment Station For The Year 1907*. Albany, New York, J.B. Lyon Company, State Printers, 1908. State of New York, Department of Agriculture, Fifteenth Annual Report, Vol. 3, Part II.

Hedrick, U.P., *Manual Of American Grape-Growing*. New York, The Macmillan Company, 1919.

Heintz, William F., *Wine Country; A History of Napa Valley, The Early Years: 1838-1920*. Santa Barbara, Capra Press, 1990.

Holden, Ronald and Glenda, *Northwest Wine Country*. Seattle, Holden Pacific, 1989.

Husman, George., *American Grape Growing And Wine Making*. New York, Orange Judd Company, 1883.

Jackson, David., and Danny Schuster, *The Production Of Grapes & Wine In Cool Climates*. Wellington, Butterworths, 1987.

Jacob, Harry Ernst, *Grape Growing In California*. Berkeley, California Agricultural Extension Service, College of Agriculture, University of California, Circular No. 116, 1947.

Kasimatis, A.N., and others. *Wine Grape Varieties In The San Joaquin Valley*. Davis, University of California, 1980.

Kasimatis, A.N., and others. *Wine Grape Varieties In The North Coast Counties Of California*. Davis, University of California, 1981.

Krosch, Penelope, "Grape Research in Minnesota." *Agricultural History*, 1988, Vol. 62, No. 2, pp. 258-269.

Laube, James, *California's Great Chardonnays; The Wine Spectator's Ultimate Guide For Consumers, Collectors and Investors*. San Francisco, Wine Spectator Press, 1990.

Laube, James, *California's Great Cabernets; The Wine Spectator's Ultimate Guide For Consumers, Collectors and Investors*. San Francisco, Wine Spectator Press, 1989.

Leggett, Herbert B., *Early History Of Wine Production In California*. San Francisco, The Wine Institute, 1941. Unpublished manuscript.

Lolli, Georgio, Emidio Serianni, Grace M. Golder, and Pierpaolo Luzzatto-Fegiz, *Alcohol In Italian Culture; Food And Wine In Relation To Sobriety Among Italians And Italian Americans*. Glencoe, Illinois, The Free Press, 1958.

McMurtree, William, *Report Upon Statistics Of Grape Culture And Wine Production In The United States For 1880*. Washington, D.C., Department of Agriculture Special Report No. 36, 1881.

Moore, Bernard, *Wines Of North America*. London, Winchmoore Publishing Series, 1983.

Mu(e)nch, Frederick, *School For American Grape Culture: Brief But Thorough And Practical Guide To The Laying Out Of Vineyards, The Treatment Of Vines, And The Production Of Wine In North America*. St. Louis, Conrad Witter, 1865.

Meredith, Ted Jordan, *Northwest Wine; Winegrowing Alchemy Along The Pacific Ring Of Fire*. Kirkland, Washington, Nexus Press, 1990.

Meyer, Justin, *Plain Talk About Fine Wine*. Santa Barbara, Capra Press, 1989.

Millner, Cork, *Vintage Valley; The Wineries of Santa Barbara County*. Santa Barbara, McNally & Loftin, 1983.

Morton, Lucie T., *Winegrowing In Eastern America; An Illustrated Guide To Viniculture East Of The Rockies*. Ithaca, Cornell University Press, 1985.

Munson, T.V., *Foundations Of American Grape Culture*. Denison, Texas, T.V. Munson & Son, 1903. Also published by Orange Judd Company, New York, 1909.

New York. Task Force On Critical Problems, *Tending The Vineyards; Renewed Growth For New York's Grape/Wine Industry*. Albany, New York State Senate, 1984.

Nickelsburg, Janet., *California's Climates*. New York, Coward-McCann, 1964.

Olken, C., et. al., *The Connoisseurs' Handbook of California Wines*. New York, Alfred A. Knopf, 1980.

Oregon. Agricultural Experiment Station, *The Grape In Oregon, Part I, Western Oregon*. Bulletin No. 66. Corvallis, Oregon Agricultural College Printing Office, 1901.

Oregon Winegrowers' Association, *Oregon Winegrape Grower's Guide*. Portland, The Oregon Winegrowers' Association, 1992.

Peninou, Ernest P., and Sidney S. Greenleaf, *A Directory Of California Wine Growers And Wine Makers In 1860*. Berkeley, Tamalpais Press, 1967.

Prince, William, *Treatise On The Vine; Embracing Its History From The Earliest Ages To The Present Day*. New York, T & J Swords, 1830.

Rafinesque, C.S., *American Manual Of The Grape Vines And The Art Of Making Wine*. Philadelphia, by the author, 1830.

Ray, Cyril, *Robert Mondavi Of The Napa Valley*. London, Heinemann/Peter Davis, 1984.

Rittich, Virgil J., Eugene A. Rittich., *European Grape Growing In Cooler Districts Where Winter Protection Is Necessary*. Minneapolis, Burgess, 1941,

Rosenberg, Norman, and Blaine Blad, and Shashi Verna, *Microclimate: The Biological Environment*. New York, John Wiley & Sons, 1983.

Scheef, Robert F., *Vintage Missouri; A Guide To Missouri Wineries*. St. Louis, The Patrice Press, 1991.

Schoenman, Theodore, *The Father Of California Wine, Agoston Haraszthy*. Santa Barbara, Capra Press, 1979.

Schoonmaker Frank, and Tom Marvel, *American Wines*. New York,

Duell, Sloan and Pearce, 1941.

Shear, S. W. (ed.), *Grape Industry Statistics As Of November 1951*. Berkeley, University of California, College of Agriculture, 1951. Unpublished.

Sifritt, Susan K., *The Ohio Wine And Wine Grape Industries*. Kent, Ohio, Kent State University, unpublished dissertation, 1976.

Slade, Daniel Denison, *The Evolution Of Horticulture In New England*. New York, G.P. Putnam's Sons, 1895.

Smith, Robert E., *The California Grape-Growing Industry*. Unpublished doctoral dissertation, Department of Economics, University of California at Los Angeles, 1962.

Smith, Wallace, *Garden Of The Sun; A History Of The San Joaquin Valley-1772-1939*. Los Angeles, Lymanhouse, 1939.

Sorensen, Lorin, *Beringer; A Napa Valley Legend*. St. Helena, California, Silverado Publishing Company, 1989.

State Fruit Experiment Station, *Cold Hardiness Of Grapes; A Guide For Missouri Growers*. Mountain Grove, Southwest Missouri State University, College of Health and Applied Sciences, Bulletin, 41, 1984.

Sullivan, Charles L., *Like Modern Edens; Winegrowing In Santa Clara Valley And Santa Cruz Mountains 1798-1981*. Cupertino, California, California History Center, 1982.

Thompson, Bob, *Webster's Wine Tours: California, Oregon, And Washington*. New York, Prentice Hall and Simon & Schuster, 1987.

Thompson, Bob, *Notes On A California Cellarbook; Reflections On Memorable Wines*. New York, Beech Tree Books/William Morrow, 1988.

Topolos, Michael, and Betty Dopson, *California Wineries; Napa Valley*. Napa, Vintage Image Book, 1975.

University of California; College of Agriculture, Agricultural Experiment Station, *Report Of The Viticultural Work During The Seasons 1887-89*. Sacramento, A.J. Johnston, Superintendent State Printing, 1892.

University of California; College of Agriculture, Agricultural Experiment Station, *Report Of The Viticultural Work During The Seasons 1887-93*. Sacramento, A.J. Johnston, Superintendent State Printing, 1896.

United States Department of Agriculture, *Report of the Commission on Agriculture For the Year 1868*. Washington, D.C., Government Printing Office, 1869.

United States Department of Agriculture, *Report of the Commission on Agriculture For The Year 1902*. Washington, D.C., Government Printing Office, 1903.

Villa Maior. *Manual de Viticultura Practica*. Coimbra, Imprensa da Universidade, 1875.

Wagner, P.M., *Grapes Into Wine*. New York, Knopf, 1976.

Wine Institute and J. Walter Thompson Company, *1946 Wine Consumer Survey*. San Francisco, Wine Advisory Board, 1946.

Winkler, A.J., James A. Cook, W.M. Kliewer, and Lloyd A. Lider. *General Viticulture*. Berkeley, University of California Press, 1974.

Young, Alan, *Chardonnay; Your International Guide*. Napa, International Wine Academy, 1991.

Columbia Crest Vineyards, Columbia Plateau ava. Courtesy of Columbia Crest

INDEX